Rick S

ITALY

2017

CONTENTS

Italy

Luzern · Lake Luzern
★ Bern
Murten · Fribourg · Spiez · Interlaken
Lausanne · Montreux · Gimmelwald
Lake Geneva · BERNER OBERLAND
Saas Fee · Domo-dossola
Matterhorn · Zermatt
Chamonix · AIGUILLE DU MIDI · Breuil-Cervinia
Mont Blanc · Courmayeur · Stresa
Pré-St Didier · Aosta · Lago di Orta
Modane
Turin
Briançon · PIEDMONT · Asti · Alba · Barolo
Cuneo
Colle di Tonda Pass
FRANCE · Finale · Alassio
Ventimiglia
Nice · Villefranche · Antibes · MONACO
Cannes
St-Tropez

LIECH. · Vaduz
Brenner Pass · Vipiteno
REIFENSTEIN CASTLE
SWITZERLAND
Merano · Castelrotto
St. Moritz · Samedan · Bolzano · ALPE DI SIUSI
Pontresina · Glurns
BERNINA EXPRESS · TRENTINO ALTO ADIGE
GLACIER EXPRESS · TICINO
Locarno · Lago di Como
Lugano · Menaggio · Varenna · Trento
Lago Maggiore · Lago di Lugano · Bellagio · Riva
Chiasso · Como · Lecco · Lago d'Iseo · Lago di Garda
Bergamo · Sirmione · Verona
Malpensa · Monza · Orio al Serio · Brescia · Desenzano · Vicenza
Milan · Linate · Catullo
LOMBARDY · Mantua
Po · Cremona · Adige
Piacenza
Parma · Modena
EMILIA · Reggio · Bologna
Santa Margherita Ligure · ROMAGNA
Sestri Levante · ITALY
Genoa · Levanto · APUAN ALPS
Camogli · Monterosso · Vernazza
Savona · CINQUE TERRE · La Spezia · Carrara
Portofino · Pistoia · Amerigo Vespucci
Porto Venere · Viareggio · Lucca · Florence
LIGURIA · Pisa · Arno · CHIANTI
Ligurian Sea · Livorno · Galileo · San Gimignano · TUSCANY
Volterra · Siena
Capraia · Montalcino
COTE D'AZUR · VIA AURELIA
Porto-ferraro · Piombino
Elba · Grosseto
Monte Argentario
To Marseille, France
L'Ile Rousse · Bastia
CORSICA (France)
See Tuscany & Umbria detail map
Ajaccio
Tyrrenhian
Propriano
Bonifacio · Maddalena
Mediterranean Sea · S.Teresa · EMERALD COAST
Asinara · Olbia
Porto Torres · Olbia
Sassari · SARDINIA (Italy)
GROTTO OF NEPTUNE

50 kilometers
50 miles

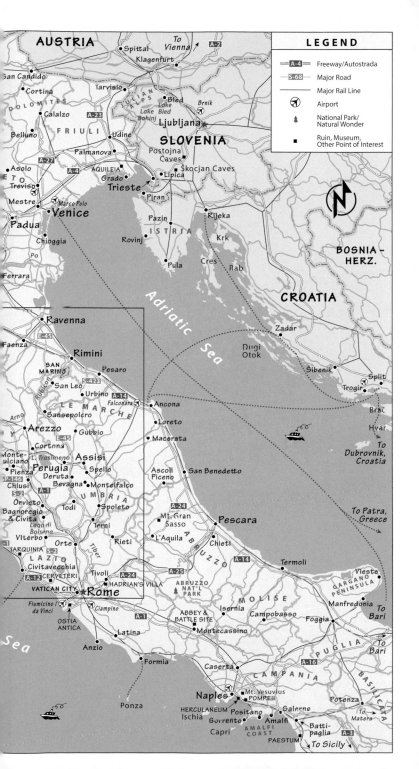

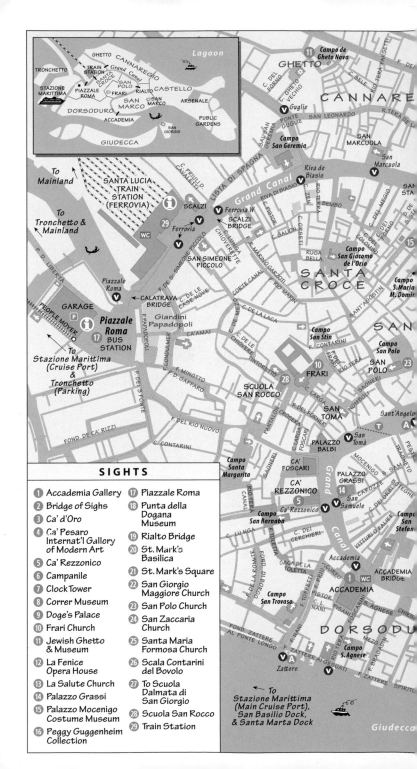

SIGHTS

1. Accademia Gallery
2. Bridge of Sighs
3. Ca' d'Oro
4. Ca' Pesaro Internat'l Gallery of Modern Art
5. Ca' Rezzonico
6. Campanile
7. Clock Tower
8. Correr Museum
9. Doge's Palace
10. Frari Church
11. Jewish Ghetto & Museum
12. La Fenice Opera House
13. La Salute Church
14. Palazzo Grassi
15. Palazzo Mocenigo Costume Museum
16. Peggy Guggenheim Collection
17. Piazzale Roma
18. Punta della Dogana Museum
19. Rialto Bridge
20. St. Mark's Basilica
21. St. Mark's Square
22. San Giorgio Maggiore Church
23. San Polo Church
24. San Zaccaria Church
25. Santa Maria Formosa Church
26. Scala Contarini del Bovolo
27. To Scuola Dalmata di San Giorgio
28. Scuola San Rocco
29. Train Station

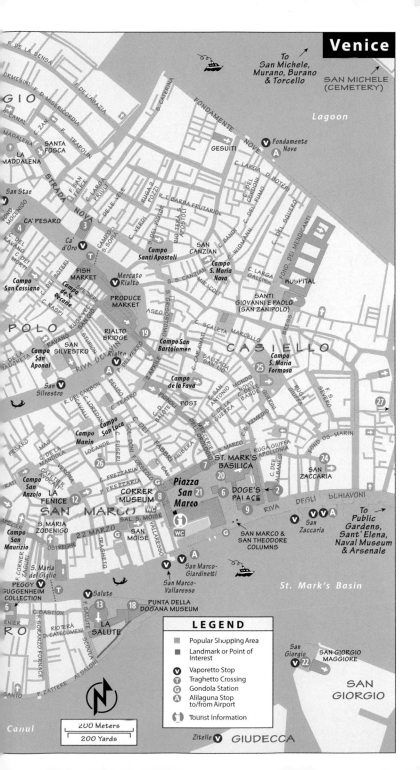

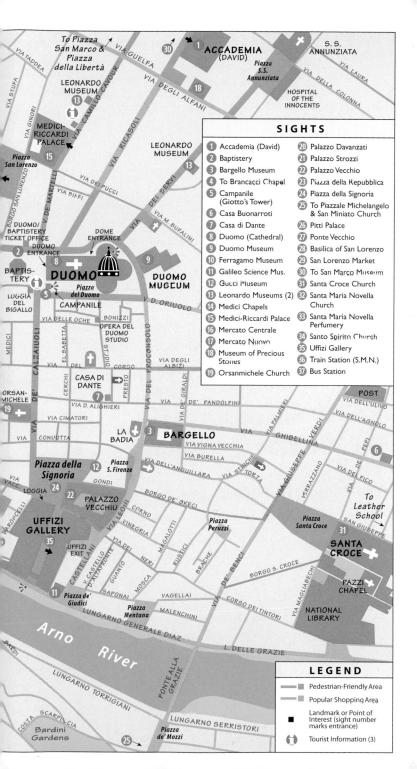

SIGHTS

1	Accademia (David)	20	Palazzo Davanzati
2	Baptistery	21	Palazzo Strozzi
3	Bargello Museum	22	Palazzo Vecchio
4	To Brancacci Chapel	23	Piazza della Repubblica
5	Campanile (Giotto's Tower)	24	Piazza della Signoria
6	Casa Buonarroti	25	To Piazzale Michelangelo & San Miniato Church
7	Casa di Dante	26	Pitti Palace
8	Duomo (Cathedral)	27	Ponte Vecchio
9	Duomo Museum	28	Basilica of San Lorenzo
10	Ferragamo Museum	29	San Lorenzo Market
11	Galileo Science Mus.	30	To San Marco Museum
12	Gucci Museum	31	Santa Croce Church
13	Leonardo Museums (2)	32	Santa Maria Novella Church
14	Medici Chapels	33	Santa Maria Novella Perfumery
15	Medici-Riccardi Palace	34	Santo Spirito Church
16	Mercato Centrale	35	Uffizi Gallery
17	Mercato Nuovo	36	Train Station (S.M.N.)
18	Museum of Precious Stones	37	Bus Station
19	Orsanmichele Church		

LEGEND

- ▬ Pedestrian-Friendly Area
- ▬ Popular Shopping Area
- ■ Landmark or Point of Interest (sight number marks entrance)
- ✛ Tourist Information (3)

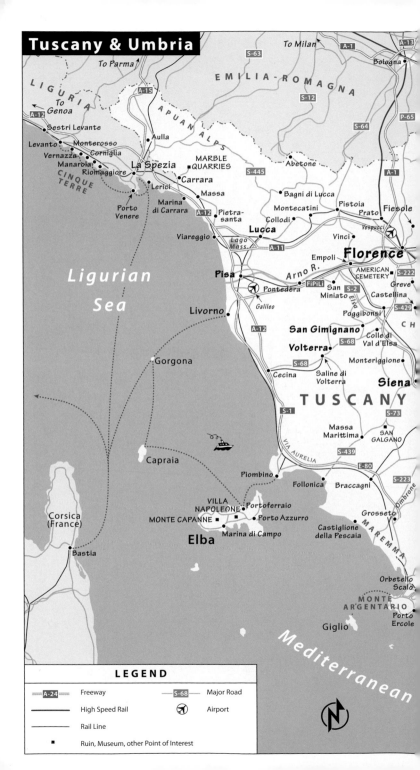

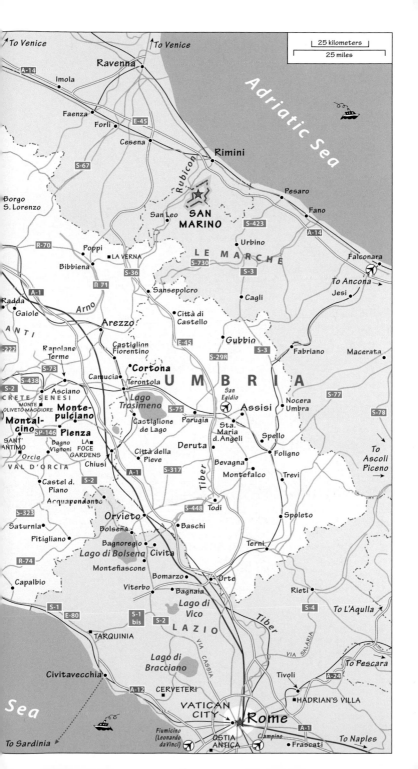

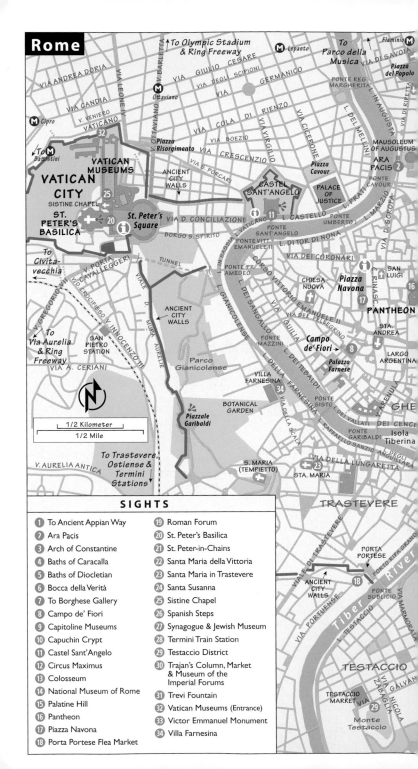

Rome

↑ To Olympic Stadium & Ring Freeway
To Parco della Musica
Ⓜ Lepanto
Ⓜ Flaminio
VIA DI SAVOIA
Piazza del Popolo

VIA ANDREA DORIA
VIA GIULIO CESARE
VIA DEGLI SCIPIONI
VIA GERMANICO
VIA BARLETTA
VIA LEONE IV
PONTE REG MARGHERITA
L. IN AUGUSTA
L. DEI MELLINI
VIA DI RIPETTA

VIA CANDIA
V. VENIERO
VIA VATICANO
Ottaviano
VIA COLA DI RIENZO
VIA CICERONE
VIA CRESCENZIO
MAUSOLEUM OF AUGUSTUS
ARA PACIS ②

Ⓜ Cipro
Ⓜ Battistini
To Ⓜ
32
Piazza Risorgimento
VIA BOEZIO
VIA B. PORCARI
VIA VIRGILIO
VIA CRESCENZIO
Piazza Cavour
PONTE CAVOUR

VATICAN MUSEUMS
VATICAN CITY
ANCIENT CITY WALLS
CASTEL SANT'ANGELO
PALACE OF JUSTICE

25
SISTINE CHAPEL
ST. PETER'S BASILICA
20
St. Peter's Square
VIA D. CONCILIAZIONE
ⓘ 11
L. CASTELLO
PONTE UMBERTO I
L. PRATI
L. MARZIO
L. DI SCOFRO

To Civita-vecchia
BORGO S. SPIRITO
PONTE SANT'ANGELO
PONTE VITT. EMANUELE II
L. DI TOR DI NONA
VIA DEI CORONARI
ⓘ SAN LUIGI
16

V. GREGORIO VII
V. DI PORTA CAVALLEGGERI
V. CROCIFISSO
TUNNEL
VIALE D. MURA AURELIE
PONTE PR. AMEDEO
CORSO VITTORIO EMANUELE II
CHIESA NUOVA
Piazza Navona
17
PANTHEON
STA. ANDREA

To Via Aurelia & Ring Freeway
SAN PIETRO STATION
V. INNOCENZO III
ANCIENT CITY WALLS
VIA DEI PELLEGRINO
VIA GIULIA
Campo de' Fiori → 8
LARGO ARGENTINA

VIA A. CERIANI
Parco Gianicolense
VILLA FARNESINA
34
BOTANICAL GARDEN
Palazzo Farnese
PONTE MAZZINI
VIA DELLA FARNESINA
PONTE SISTO
L. DEI VALLATI
DEI CENCI
GHE

Ⓝ
1/2 Kilometer
1/2 Mile
Piazzale Garibaldi
VIA DELLA SCALA
L. RAFFAELLO SANZIO
PONTE GARIBALDI
Isola Tiberina
L. DEGLI ANGUILLARA

V. AURELIA ANTICA
To Trastevere, Ostiense & Termini Stations
S. MARIA (TEMPIETTO)
STA. MARIA
23
VIA DELLA LUNGARETTA

VIA PORTUENSE
TRASTEVERE
VIA D. TRASTEVERE
PORTA PORTESE
PORTO FSPA GRANDE

SIGHTS

❶ To Ancient Appian Way	⓵⑨ Roman Forum
❼ Ara Pacis	⓶⓪ St. Peter's Basilica
❸ Arch of Constantine	㉑ St. Peter-in-Chains
❹ Baths of Caracalla	㉒ Santa Maria della Vittoria
❺ Baths of Diocletian	㉓ Santa Maria in Trastevere
❻ Bocca della Verità	㉔ Santa Susanna
❼ To Borghese Gallery	㉕ Sistine Chapel
❽ Campo de' Fiori	㉖ Spanish Steps
❾ Capitoline Museums	㉗ Synagogue & Jewish Museum
❿ Capuchin Crypt	㉘ Termini Train Station
⓫ Castel Sant'Angelo	㉙ Testaccio District
⓬ Circus Maximus	㉚ Trajan's Column, Market & Museum of the Imperial Forums
⓭ Colosseum	
⓮ National Museum of Rome	㉛ Trevi Fountain
⓯ Palatine Hill	㉜ Vatican Museums (Entrance)
⓰ Pantheon	㉝ Victor Emmanuel Monument
⓱ Piazza Navona	㉞ Villa Farnesina
⓲ Porta Portese Flea Market	

PONTE SUBLICIO
Tiber River
L. TESTACCIO
VIA MARMORATA
TESTACCIO
TESTACCIO MARKET
Monte Testaccio
VIA NICOLA ZABAGLIA
VIA GALVANI
29

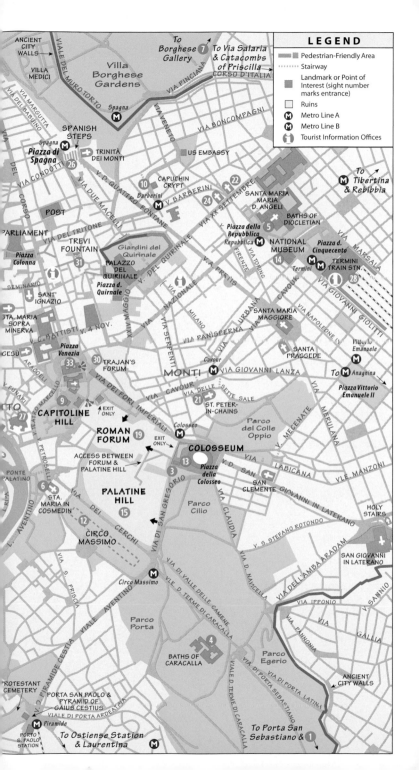

Italy

Italia

Bell'Italia! Italy has Europe's richest, craziest culture. If you take Italy on its own terms, you'll experience a cultural keelhauling that actually feels good.

Some people, often with considerable effort, manage to hate this country. Italy bubbles with emotion, corruption, stray hairs, inflation, traffic jams, strikes, rallies, holidays, crowded squalor, and irate ranters shaking their fists at each other one minute and walking arm-in-arm the next. Have a talk with yourself before you cross the border. Promise yourself to relax and accept it all as a package deal.

After all, Italy is the cradle of European civilization— established by the Roman Empire and carried on by the Roman Catholic Church. As you explore Italy, you'll stand face-to-face with some of the world's most iconic images from this 2,000-year history: the Colosseum of Ancient Rome, the medieval Leaning Tower of Pisa, Michelangelo's *David* and Botticelli's *Venus,* the playful Baroque exuberance of the Trevi Fountain...and the Italian city that preserves this legacy in a state of elegant decay: Venice.

Beyond these famous sights, though, Italy offers Europe's richest culture. Traditions still live within a country that is vibrant and fully modern. Go with an eye open to both the Italy of the past and of the present.

Italy is diverse, encompassing German-flavored Alps; Mediterranean beaches; sunbaked Sicily; romantic hill towns; the urban jungle of Naples; the business center of Milan; and the art-drenched cities of Venice, Florence, and Rome. The country is reasonably small and laced with freeways and train lines, so you're never more than a day's journey from any of these places. Each of Italy's 20 regions

has its own distinct character, whether it's scenic Tuscany, busy Lombardy, chaotic Campania, or the place where it all mixes together—Lazio, home of the capital, Rome.

Many travelers discover that there are two Italys: The North is industrial, aggressive, and "time is money" in its outlook. The weather is temperate, and the people are more like Northern Europeans. The South is hot and sunny, crowded, poor, relaxed, farm-oriented, and traditional. Families here are very close-knit and usually live in the same house for many generations. Loyalties are to family, city, region, soccer team, and country—in that order.

Economically, Italy has had its problems, but somehow things have always worked out. Today, Italy is the world's eighth-largest industrial power, and the fourth-largest in Europe. Ferraris, Fiats, Maseratis, and Lamborghinis are world-renowned (though they're not really major exports). Tourism is big business—Italy is considered the world's fifth-most-visited tourist destination.

Cronyism, which complicates my work, is an integral part of the economy. Much of Italy's business is hidden in a large "black market" unreported to government officials. Labor unions are strong, strikes are frequent, and the country today is faced with pressure to compete globally.

While most Italians are nominally Catholic, the true dominant religion is life: motor scooters, soccer, fashion, girl-watching, boy-watching, good coffee, good wine, and *il dolce far niente* (the sweetness of doing nothing). The Italian character shows itself on the streets, in the maniacal yet skilled drivers and the classy dressers who star in the ritual evening stroll, or *passeggiata.*

Italians are more social and communal than most other Europeans. In small towns, everyone knows everyone. People get out of their apartments to socialize on the main square. Young women walk hand in hand, and young teenagers shove or punch each other playfully or hang all over each other.

Because they're so outgoing and their language is so fun, Italians are a pleasure to communicate with. Be melodramatic and talk with your hands. Hear the melody; get into the flow. Italians want to connect, and they try harder than any other Europeans. Play with them. Even in nontouristy towns, where English is rare and Italian is the norm, showing a little warmth lets you hop right over the language barrier. If a local starts chattering at you in Italian, don't resist. Go with it. You may find you understand more than you'd expect.

Like most Europeans (and Americans), Italians enjoy watching TV (game shows, sitcoms, etc.), going to movies (American films are almost always dubbed, not subtitled), and listening to their homegrown pop music. Though Italy

Italy Almanac

Official Name: Repubblica Italiana (Italian Republic); Italia for short.

Population: 61 million, composed almost entirely of indigenous Italians who speak Italian (German and French are spoken in some Alpine regions) and are nominally Roman Catholic (80 percent).

Latitude and Longitude: 43°N and 12°E (similar to Oregon and Maine).

Area: 116,000 square miles, including the islands of Sicily, Sardinia, and others.

Geography: Italy is shaped like a boot, 850 miles long and 150 miles wide, jutting into the central Mediterranean. (By comparison, Florida is 500 miles long.) The terrain is generally mountainous or hilly, with the Alps in the north and a north-south "spine" of the Apennine Mountains. The highest point is Mont Blanc (15,771 feet), on the border with France. Outside the Alps, the highest point on the peninsula is Corno Grande (9,554 feet). Italy has 5,000 miles of coastline. Major rivers include the Po (the longest at 400 miles), Arno, Adige, and Tiber. Italy has three active volcanoes: Vesuvius, Etna, and Stromboli.

Regions: Italy is divided into 20 regions (including Tuscany, Umbria, Veneto, and Lazio). Locally, there are some 8,200 "communes," each with a community council and mayor.

Major Cities: Rome (the capital, 2.7 million), Milan (1.3 million), and Naples (1 million).

Economy: The Gross Domestic Product is $2.1 trillion; the GDP per capita is $29,800. About 74 percent of the economy consists of service jobs (especially tourism), 24 percent is industry (textiles, chemicals), and 2 percent is agriculture (fruit, vegetables, olives, wine, plus fishing). There are 12,500 miles of train lines (mostly government-run) and 4,300 miles of expressway (autostrada).

Government: Italy is a republic, with three branches of government. The chief executive is Prime Minister Matteo Renzi. The bicameral legislature is elected by (mostly) direct voting. Since World War II, the fragmented country has had 63 national governments.

Flag: Three vertical bands of green, white, and red.

Italian Inventions: Opera, cologne, thermometer, barometer, pizza, wireless telegraph, espresso machine, typewriter, batteries, nitroglycerin, yo-yos...and the ice-cream cone.

Museums: 3,800.

Average "Gio": The average Italian is 44 years old, has 1.4 kids, and will live to the ripe old age of 82 (1 in 5 Italians is older than 65). Every day, he or she consumes two servings of pasta, a half-pound of bread, and two glasses of wine. Despite Italian cuisine, Gio isn't fat—only 23 percent of Italians are considered obese.

is the birthplace of opera and much classical music, it's not much more "cultured" today than America is.

Italian food, however, is a cut above. If America's specialty is fast food, Italy's is slow food: locally grown ingredients, in season, bought daily, prepared with love, and enjoyed in social circumstances with friends and family. Even in modern cities, big supermarkets are rare. Instead, people buy their bread from the baker and their meats from the butcher, enjoying a chance to catch up on gossip with the shopkeeper. Italians buy foods in season, celebrating the arrival of fresh artichokes in the spring and porcini mushrooms in the fall.

The three-hour meal is common. For many Italians, dinner is the evening's entertainment. They eat in courses, lingering over each one. A typical meal might start with an antipasto plate of cold cuts and veggies. Next comes the pasta *(primo)*, then the meat dish *(secondo)*, then a salad. No meal is complete without dessert (Italian gelato is considered the best ice cream in the world), accompanied by coffee or a digestif.

Wine complements each course. Italy is the world's number-one wine producer (just ahead of France). It'd be a shame to visit Italy without sampling the specialties from each region, whether it's the famous Chianti from central Italy, a white Soave from the Veneto, Bardolinos from the North, or a Lacryma Christi from the South.

Italian "bars" are not taverns, but cafés…and social watering holes. In the morning, they serve coffee, orange juice, and croissants to workers on the go. At lunch, it's sandwiches *(panini)* and mini-pizzas for university students. In the afternoon, housewives might drop in for an ice-cream bar. At night, men and women enjoy a glass of wine and watch TV while the kids play a video game in the corner.

Besides food, travelers enjoy sampling Italy's other wares. While no longer a cheap country, Italy is still a hit with shoppers. Find glassware in Venice; gold, silver, leather, and prints in Florence; and high fashion in Rome and Milan.

Italians are obsessed with sports—though not American sports. Italian sports idols are soccer players (Francesco Totti, Antonio Cassano), skiers (Giorgio Rocca), and cyclists (Paolo Savoldelli). Motor racing—Formula 1/Grand Prix—is huge. And since many Italians grow up zipping through narrow streets on small Vespas, it's little wonder that motorcycle racing (*moto,* led by Valentino Rossi) is a major sport here. A favorite participant sport is bocce, played casually at parks throughout Italy. The players take turns tossing small metal balls on a dirt court, aiming at a small wooden ball.

Italy's undisputed number-one sport is soccer (called *il calcio*). Soccer fans *(tifosi)* are passionate. Star players are paid millions and treated like movie stars.

Little kids everywhere grow up pretending to score the winning goal just like them. On big game nights, bars are packed with men crowded around TV sets. After a loss, they drown their sorrows. After a victory, fans celebrate by driving through the city streets honking horns and waving team flags. Many Italians place their national, regional, and personal pride on the backs of their athletes. It's a cliché that remains true: In a Europe at peace, the soccer field is the battleground.

But even as Europe evolves, Italy remains a mix of old and new. Appreciate the extreme changes Italian society has gone through in just half a century: the "economic miracle" of the 1950s and 1960s, a wave of domestic terrorism (from the left and the right) in the 1970s and 1980s, stronger integration in the European Union in the 1990s, and the current economic downturn. Italian politics are a reckless pendulum that swings between right- and left-wing extremes. It seems that nobody holds office for very long, but it's always possible to bounce back.

Italy, home of the Vatican, is mostly Catholic...but not particularly devout. Most people would never think of renouncing their faith, but they don't attend church regularly. They baptize their kids at the local church (there's one every few blocks), but they hold modern opinions on social issues, often in conflict with strict Catholic dogma. Italy is

now the land of legalized abortion, the lowest birth rate in Europe, nudity on TV, socialist politics, and a society whose common language is decidedly secular.

For Italians, it's very important to exhibit a positive public persona—a concept called *la bella figura.* While some Americans don't think twice about going to the supermarket in sweats, Italians dress well any time they leave the house—and they'd rather miss their bus than get all sweaty and mussed-up rushing to catch it. An elderly woman will do her hair and carefully put on makeup for her monthly doctor's appointment, and no matter how hot it gets, Italian men wear long pants—never shorts (except at the beach). At a restaurant, few Italians would ask for tap water or request a "doggy bag" for uneaten food—which, to them, comes off as cheap. This thinking is partly a holdover from the very lean postwar years, when Italians were self-conscious about their poverty and wanted to put their best foot forward.

Some traditions thrive. Italian families and communities are more close-knit than many others in the modern world. Many Italians, especially in rural

regions and small towns, still follow the traditional siesta schedule (called *reposo* in Italy). At about 13:00, shops close and people go home for a three-hour break to have lunch, socialize with friends and family, and run errands. (While a few old-timers take a short nap in front of the TV, most Italians are quite busy during this time.) And on festival days, locals still dress up in medieval garb to paddle gondolas (Venice), race horses (Siena), battle over a bridge (Pisa), or play rugby or soccer (Florence). But these days, the traditional ways are carried on by choice. Italians are wary of the dangers of a fast-paced global lifestyle. Their history is long, and they're secure in their place in the world.

Accept Italy as Italy. Zero in on the fine points. Don't dwell on the problems. Savor your cappuccino, dangle your feet over a canal (if it smells, breathe through your mouth), and imagine what it was like centuries ago. Ramble through the rabble and rubble of Rome and mentally resurrect those ancient stones. Look into the famous sculpted eyes of Michelangelo's *David* and understand Renaissance Man's assertion of himself. Sit silently on a hilltop rooftop. Get chummy with the winds of the past. Write a poem over a glass of local wine in a sun-splashed, wave-dashed Riviera village. If you fall off your moral horse, call it a cultural experience. Italy is for romantics.

INTRODUCTION

This book will help you make the most of your trip. It breaks Italy into its top destinations—offering a balanced, comfortable mix of exciting cities and cozy towns, from brutal but *bella* Rome to *tranquillo*, traffic-free Riviera villages. It covers the predictable biggies and stirs in a healthy dose of "Back Door" intimacy. Along with marveling at Michelangelo's masterpieces, you'll enjoy a snack of bruschetta prepared by a village boy. I've been selective, including only the most exciting sights and experiences. For example, after visiting many hill towns, I recommend just my favorites.

You'll get all the specifics and opinions necessary to wring the maximum value out of your limited time and money. If you plan a month or less in Italy, and you have a normal appetite for information, this book is all you need. If you're a travel-info fiend like me, you'll find that this book sorts through all the superlatives and provides a handy rack upon which to hang your supplemental information.

Italy is my favorite European country. Experiencing its culture, people, and natural wonders economically and hassle-free has been my goal for three decades of traveling, tour guiding, and writing. With this book, I pass on to you the lessons I've learned, updated for 2017.

The best of Italy is, of course, only my opinion. But after spending half my adult life researching Europe, I've developed a sixth sense for what travelers enjoy.

ABOUT THIS BOOK

Rick Steves Italy 2017 is a personal tour guide in your pocket. This book is organized by destinations. Each is a minivacation on its own, filled with exciting sights, strollable neighborhoods, afford-

INTRODUCTION

Map Legend

⅃ Viewpoint	⊙ Airport	🍦 Gelato
✦ Entrance	ⓣ Taxi Stand	▬ Pedestrian Zone
❶ Tourist Info	ⓑ Bus Stop	----- Railway
WC Restroom	℗ Parking	.... Ferry/Boat Route
✡ Synagogue	)(Mtn. Pass	—🇹— Tram
⛪ Church	⬡ Park	▪▪▪▪▪▪▪ Stairs
Ⓥ Vaporetto Dock	▪ Statue/Point of Interest	· · · · Walk/Tour Route
Ⓣ Traghetto (Venice)		
Ⓖ Gondola Station	🏰 Castle	------ Trail
Ⓐ Alilaguna Stop		

able places to stay, and memorable places to eat. For destinations covered in this book, you'll find these sections:

Planning Your Time suggests a schedule for how to best use your limited time.

Orientation has specifics on public transportation, helpful hints, local tour options, easy-to-read maps, and tourist information.

Sights describes the top attractions and includes their cost and hours. Major sights have self-guided tours.

Self-Guided Walks take you through interesting neighborhoods, pointing out sights and fun stops.

Sleeping describes my favorite hotels, from good-value deals to cushy splurges.

Eating serves up a buffet of options, from inexpensive cafés to fancy restaurants.

Connections outlines your options for traveling to destinations by train, bus, and plane. When describing car-friendly regions, I've included route tips for drivers.

The **Italian History** chapter gives you a helpful overview of Italy's history, art, and architecture.

The **Practicalities** chapter near the end of this book is a traveler's tool kit, with my best advice about money, sightseeing, sleeping, eating, staying connected, and transportation (trains, buses, boats, driving, and flights).

The **appendix** has the nuts-and-bolts: useful phone numbers and websites, a holiday and festival list, recommended books and films, a climate chart, a handy packing checklist, and Italian survival phrases.

Throughout this book, you'll find money- and time-saving tips for sightseeing, transportation, and more. Some businesses—especially hotels and walking tour companies—offer special discounts to my readers, indicated in their listings.

Browse through this book, choose your favorite destinations,

Key to This Book

Updates

This book is updated every year—but things change. As soon as you pin down Italy, it wiggles. For the latest, visit www. ricksteves.com/update.

Abbreviations and Times

I use the following symbols and abbreviations in this book: Sights are rated:

▲▲▲ Don't miss
▲▲ Try hard to see
▲ Worthwhile if you can make it
No rating Worth knowing about

Tourist information offices are abbreviated as **TI,** and bathrooms are **WCs.** Accommodations are categorized with a **Sleep Code** (described on page 80); eateries are classified with a **Restaurant Price Code** (page 97). To indicate discounts for my readers, I include **RS%** in the listings.

Like Europe, this book uses the **24-hour clock.** It's the same through 12:00 noon, then keeps going: 13:00, 14:00, and so on. For anything over 12, subtract 12 and add p.m. (14:00 is 2:00 p.m.).

When giving **opening times,** I include both peak season and off-season hours if they differ. So, if a museum is listed as "May-Oct daily 9:00-16:00," it should be open from 9 a.m. until 4 p.m. from the first day of May until the last day of October (but expect exceptions).

A ∩ symbol indicates that a free, downloadable self-guided Rick Steves **audio tour** is available.

For **transit** or **tour departures,** I first list the frequency, then the duration. So a train connection listed as "2/hour, 1.5 hours" departs twice each hour, and the journey lasts an hour and a half.

and link them up. Then have a great trip! Traveling like a temporary local, you'll get the absolute most out of every mile, minute, and dollar. As you visit places I know and love, I'm happy that you'll be meeting some of my favorite Italian people.

Planning

This section will help you get started planning your trip—with advice on trip costs, when to go, and what you should know before you take off.

TRAVEL SMART

Many people travel through Italy thinking it's a chaotic mess. They feel that any attempt at efficient travel is futile. This is dead

INTRODUCTION

Top Destinations in Italy

DOLOMITES

THE LAKES

TOWNS NEAR VENICE

MILAN

VENICE

RIVIERA TOWNS

CINQUE TERRE

FLORENCE

PISA & LUCCA

SIENA

VOLTERRA & SAN GIMIGNANO

HEART OF TUSCANY

ASSISI

ORVIETO & CIVITA

ROME

NAPLES

POMPEII

AMALFI COAST & PAESTUM

SORRENTO & CAPRI

100 Kilometers

100 Miles

wrong—and expensive. Italy, which seems as orderly as spilled spaghetti, actually functions quite well. Only those who understand this and travel smart can enjoy Italy on a budget.

This book can save you lots of time and money. But to have an "A" trip, you need to be an "A" student. Read it all before your trip, noting holidays, specific advice on sights, and days when sights are closed. A smart trip is a puzzle—a fun, doable, and worthwhile challenge.

Make your itinerary a mix of intense and relaxed stretches. To maximize rootedness, minimize one-night stands. It's worth taking a long drive after dinner (or a train ride with a dinner picnic) to get settled in a town for two nights. Hotels are more likely to give a better price to someone staying more than one night. Every trip—and every traveler—needs slack time (laundry, picnics, people-watching, and so on). Pace yourself. Assume you will return.

Reread this book as you travel, and visit local tourist infor-

Please Tear Up This Book!

There's no point in hauling around a big chapter on Rome for a day in Assisi. That's why I've designed this book to be ripped apart. Before your trip, attack this book with a utility knife to create an army of pocket-sized mini-guidebooks—one for each area you visit.

I love the ritual of trimming down the size of guidebooks I'll be using: Fold the pages back until you break the spine, neatly slice apart the sections you want with a box cutter or utility knife, then pull them out with the gummy edge intact. If you want, finish each one off with clear, heavy-duty packing tape to smooth and reinforce the spine, and/or use a heavy-duty stapler along the edge to prevent the first and last pages from coming loose.

To make things even easier, I've created a line of laminated covers with slide-on binders. With every stop, you can make a ritual of swapping out the last chapter with the new one. (For more on these binders, see www.ricksteves.com.)

As you travel, throw out the chapters you're done with (or, much better, give them to a needy fellow traveler). While you may be tempted to keep this book intact as a souvenir of your travels, you'll appreciate even more the footloose freedom of traveling light. Rip it up!

mation offices (abbreviated as TI in this book). Upon arrival in a new town, lay the groundwork for a smooth departure; confirm the train, bus, or road you'll take when you leave.

Even with the best-planned itinerary, you'll need to be flexible. Update your plans as you travel. Get online or call ahead to learn the latest on sights (special events, tour schedules, and so on), book tickets and tours, make reservations, reconfirm hotels, and research transportation connections.

Enjoy the friendliness of the Italian people. Connect with the culture. Set up your own quest for the best piazza, bell tower, or gelato. Slow down and be open to unexpected experiences. Ask questions—most locals are eager to point you in their idea of the right direction. Keep a notepad in your pocket for confirming prices, noting directions, and organizing your thoughts. Wear your money belt, learn the currency, and figure out how to estimate prices in dollars. Those who expect to travel smart, do.

Italy's Best Three-Week Trip (by Train and Bus)

Day	Plan	Sleep in
1	Arrive in Milan	Milan
2	Milan to Lake Como	Varenna
3	Lake Como	Varenna
4	To Dolomites via Verona	Bolzano/Castelrotto
5	Dolomites	Bolzano/Castelrotto
6	To Venice	Venice
7	Venice	Venice
8	To Cinque Terre	Vernazza
9	Cinque Terre	Vernazza
10	Pisa, then to Florence	Florence
11	Florence	Florence
12	Florence, late to Siena	Siena
13	Siena	Siena
14	To Assisi (by bus)	Assisi
15	To Orvieto and Civita	Orvieto
16	To Sorrento	Sorrento
17	Naples and Pompeii	Sorrento
18	Capri or Amalfi Coast	Sorrento
19	Morning to Rome	Rome
20	Rome	Rome
21	Rome	Rome
22	Fly home	

With limited time: Skip the Dolomites.

To modify for drivers: The big sights of Italy (Rome, Florence, Venice, Sorrento/Naples/Capri/Amalfi, and Cinque Terre) are inconvenient by car and easy by public transportation. Those wanting to drive will find a car most helpful for the hill towns of Tus-

TRIP COSTS

Six components make up your trip costs: airfare to Europe, transportation in Europe, room and board, sightseeing and entertainment, shopping and miscellany, and gelato.

Airfare to Europe: A basic round-trip flight from the US to Milan or Rome can cost, on average, about $1,000-2,000 total, depending on where you fly from and when (cheaper in winter). Smaller budget airlines provide bargain service from several European capitals to many cities in Italy. If your trip covers a wide area, consider saving time and money in Europe by flying into one city and out of another—for instance, into Milan and out of Rome. Overall, Kayak.com is the best place to start searching for flights on a combination of mainstream and budget carriers.

Transportation in Europe: For a three-week whirlwind trip

Italy's Best Three-Week Trip

(LAKES)
VARENNA

CASTELROTTO
(DOLOMITES)

MILAN

VERONA

VENICE

100 Kilometers

100 Miles

RAVENNA

CINQUE
TERRE

FLORENCE

PISA

*Ligurian
Sea*

SIENA

ASSISI

*Adriatic
Sea*

CIVITA · ORVIETO

ROME ⊛

*Tyrrhenian
Sea*

NAPLES ·

· POMPEII

SORRENTO

· PAESTUM

Mediterranean Sea

AMALFI
COAST

● Overnights
· Other Stops

cany and Umbria and for the Dolomites. I'd start by touring most
of the country by train, then use a car to explore a region or two
(even if it means backtracking a few extra hours by train or car).

of my recommended destinations by public transportation, allow
$550 per person for buses and second-class trains ($750 for first-
class trains). If you plan to rent a car, allow at least $230 per week,
not including tolls, gas, and supplemental insurance. If you'll be
using the car for three weeks or more, look into leasing, which can
save you money on insurance and taxes for trips of this length. Car
rentals and leases are cheapest if arranged from the US. Rail passes
normally must be purchased outside of Europe, but aren't necessarily your best option—you may save money by simply buying tickets as you go. Don't hesitate to consider flying—a short flight can
be cheaper than taking the train (check www.skyscanner.com for
intra-European flights). For more on these topics, see "Transportation" in Practicalities.

Room and Board: You can manage comfortably in Ita'

INTRODUCTION

2017 on $125 a day per person for room and board (more in big cities). This allows $5 for breakfast, $15 for lunch, $25 for dinner, and $80 for lodging (based on two people splitting the cost of a $160 double room). Students and tightwads can enjoy Italy for as little as $65 a day ($35 for a bed, $30 for meals and snacks).

Sightseeing and Entertainment: In big cities, figure about $12-22 per major sight (museums, Colosseum), $5-8 for minor ones (climbing church towers), and $30 for splurge experiences (such as walking tours and concerts). An overall average of $35 a day works for most people. Don't skimp here. After all, this category is the driving force behind your trip—you came to sightsee, enjoy, and experience Italy.

Shopping and Miscellany: Figure $2 per postcard (including postage) and $3 per coffee, soft drink, or gelato. Shopping can vary in cost from nearly nothing to a small fortune. Good budget travelers find that this category has little to do with assembling a trip full of lifelong memories.

SIGHTSEEING PRIORITIES

So much to see, so little time. How to choose? Depending on the length of your trip, and taking geographic proximity into account, here are my recommended priorities:

4 days:	Rome, Florence
6 days, add:	Venice
8 days:	slow down
10 days, add:	Cinque Terre
12 days, add:	Siena
14 days, add:	Sorrento, Naples, Pompeii, Amalfi Coast
17 days, add:	Milan, Lake Como, Varenna
21 days, add:	Padua, Volterra, Orvieto, or slow down

This includes nearly everything on the "Italy's Best Three-Week Trip" map on the previous page. If you don't have time to see it all, prioritize according to your interests. The "Italy at a Glance" sidebar on page 10 can help you decide where to go.

WHEN TO GO

Italy's best travel months (also its busiest and most expensive) are May, June, September, and October. These months combine the convenience of peak season with pleasant weather.

The most grueling thing about travel in Italy—particularly in the south—is the summer heat in July and August, when temperatures hit the high 80s and 90s. Most midrange hotels come with air-conditioning—important in the summer—but it's usually available only from June through September.

Peak season (roughly May-Oct in the north and May-June and Sept-Oct in the south) offers the longest hours and the most exciting slate of activities—but terrible crowds. During peak times, many resort-area hotels maximize business by requiring that guests take half-pension, which means buying a meal per day (usually dinner) in their restaurants. August, the month when many Italians take their summer vacations, isn't as bad as many make it out to be, but big cities tend to be quiet (with discounted hotel prices), and beach and mountain resorts are jammed (with higher hotel prices). Note that Italians generally wear shorts only at beach resort towns. If you want to blend in, wear lightweight long (or Capri) pants in Italy, even in summer, except at the beach.

Between November and April, you can usually expect pleasant weather, and you'll miss most of the sweat and stress of the tourist season. Off-season, expect shorter hours, more lunchtime breaks, and fewer activities. However, spring and fall can be cool, and many hotels—thanks to a national interest in conserving energy—aren't allowed to turn on their heat until winter. In the winter, it often drops to the 40s in Milan and the 50s in Rome (see the climate chart in the appendix).

KNOW BEFORE YOU GO

Check this list of things to arrange while you're still at home.

You need a **passport**—but no visa or shots—to travel in Italy. You may be denied entry into certain European countries if your passport is due to expire within six months of your ticketed date of return. Get it renewed if you'll be cutting it close. It can take up to six weeks to get or renew a passport (for more on passports and requirements for Italy, see www.travel.state.gov). Pack a photocopy of your passport in your luggage in case the original is lost or stolen.

Book rooms well in advance if you'll be traveling during peak season (spring and fall) and any major holidays (see page 1178).

Call your **debit- and credit-card companies** to let them know the countries you'll be visiting, to ask about fees, to request your PIN if you don't already know it, and more. See page 1116 for details.

Do your homework if you're considering **travel insurance.** Compare the cost of the insurance to the cost of your potential loss. Also, check whether your existing insurance (health, homeowners, or renters) covers you and your possessions overseas. For more tips, see www.ricksteves.com/insurance.

If you're taking an **overnight train** and need a couchette *(cuccetta)* or sleeper—and you must leave on a certain day—consider booking it in advance through a US agent (such as www.ricksteves.com/rail), even though it may cost more than buying it in Italy. Other Italian trains, such as high-speed ES trains, require a seat reservation, but it's usually possible to make these arrangements in

Italy at a Glance

These attractions are listed (as in this book) roughly from north to south.

▲▲▲Venice Romantic island city, powerful in medieval times; famous for St. Mark's Basilica, the Grand Canal, and singing gondoliers.

▲Near Venice Several interesting towns: Padua (with Giotto's gloriously frescoed Scrovegni Chapel), Verona (Roman amphitheater plus Romeo and Juliet sights), and Ravenna (top Byzantine mosaics).

▲The Dolomites Italy's rugged rooftop with a Germanic flair, featuring Bolzano (home of Ötzi the Iceman), Castelrotto (charming village), and Alpe di Siusi (alpine meadows laced with lifts and hiking trails).

▲The Lakes Two relaxing lakes, each with low-key resort towns and a mountainous backdrop: Lake Como, with quaint Varenna and upscale Bellagio; and Lake Maggiore, with straightforward Stresa, manicured islands, and elegant villas.

▲▲Milan Powerhouse city of commerce and fashion, with the prestigious La Scala opera house, Leonardo's *Last Supper,* and three airports.

▲▲▲The Cinque Terre Five idyllic Riviera hamlets along a rugged coastline (and part of a national park), connected by scenic hiking trails and dotted with beaches.

Riviera Towns More Italian Riviera fun, including the northern beach towns of Levanto, Sestri Levante, the larger Santa Margherita Ligure, and gem-like Portofino; and to the south, resorty Porto Venere and workaday La Spezia (transportation hub).

▲▲▲Florence The cradle of the Renaissance, with the world-class Uffizi Gallery, Brunelleschi's dome-topped Duomo, Michelangelo's *David,* and Italy's best gelato.

▲Pisa and Lucca Two classic towns: Pisa, with its famous Leaning Tower and surrounding Field of Miracles, and Lucca, with a charming walled old center.

▲▲▲**Siena** Florence's smaller and (some say) more appealing rival, with its grand Il Campo square and striking striped cathedral.

▲**Volterra and San Gimignano** Two hill towns in north Tuscany: vibrant, refreshing Volterra and multi-towered, touristy San Gimignano.

▲▲**Heart of Tuscany** Picturesque, wine-soaked villages of Italy's heartland, including mellow Montepulciano, Renaissance Pienza, and Brunello-fueled Montalcino.

▲▲**Assisi** St. Francis' hometown, perched on a hillside, with a divinely Giotto-decorated basilica.

▲▲**Orvieto and Civita** More hill-town adventures, featuring Orvieto's classic views and ornate cathedral, plus the adorable pocket-sized village of Civita di Bagnoregio.

▲▲▲**Rome** Italy's capital, the Eternal City, studded with Roman remnants (Forum, Colosseum, Pantheon), romantic floodlit-fountain squares, and the Vatican—home to one of Italy's top museums and the Sistine Chapel.

▲▲**Naples** Gritty, in-love-with-life port city featuring vibrant street life and a top archaeological museum.

▲**Pompeii and Nearby** Famous ruins of the ancient towns of Pompeii and Herculaneum, stopped in their tracks by the eruption of Mount Vesuvius.

▲**Sorrento and Capri** The seaside resort port of Sorrento, and a short cruise away, the jet-set island getaway of Capri, with its Blue Grotto.

▲**Amalfi Coast and Paestum** String of seafront villages—including hilly Positano and workaday Amalfi—tied together by a scenic mountainous coastal road. Farther south is Paestum, with its well-preserved ancient Greek temples.

🎧 Rick Steves Audio Europe 🎧

My free **Rick Steves Audio Europe app** is a great tool for enjoying Europe. This app makes it easy to download my audio tours of top attractions, plus hours of travel interviews, all organized into destination-specific playlists.

My self-guided **audio tours** of major sights and neighborhoods are free, user-friendly, fun, and informative. In this book, these audio tours include major sights and neighborhoods in Venice, Florence, Assisi, and Rome. Sights covered by my audio tours are marked with this symbol: 🎧. These audio tours are hard to beat: Nobody will stand you up, your eyes are free to appreciate the sights, you can take the tour exactly when you like, and the price is right.

The Rick Steves Audio Europe app also offers a far-reaching library of insightful **travel interviews** from my public radio show with experts from around the globe—including many of the places in this book.

This app and all of its content are entirely free. (And new content is added about twice a year.) You can download Rick Steves Audio Europe via Apple's App Store, Google Play, or the Amazon Appstore. For more information, see www.ricksteves.com/audioeurope.

Italy just a few days ahead. (For more on train travel, see Practicalities.)

If you're planning on **renting a car** in Italy, bring your driver's license and an International Driving Permit (see page 1168). Driving is prohibited in some city centers; if you drive in restricted areas marked with signage and monitored by cameras, you can be fined (see page 1200).

While you can stroll right in at plenty of sights, the famous ones come with long lines. These lines are often avoidable if you follow the strategies in this book, often by **buying tickets or making reservations in advance.** Book as soon as you know when you'll be in town for **Florence**'s Uffizi Gallery (Renaissance paintings) and Accademia (Michelangelo's *David*)—or buy a Firenze Card when you arrive in Florence (see page 468). For **Milan,** reserve several months in advance for Leonardo's *Last Supper* (see page 290); for **Padua,** book at least two days in advance for Giotto's Scrovegni Chapel (see page 130); and for **Rome,** book several days to a week ahead for the Borghese Gallery (Bernini sculptures; see page 879). Reservations let you skip the ticket line at Rome's Vatican Museums (see page 869), as do the Roma Pass or advance tickets for the Colosseum (see page 831) and Forum (see page 836).

How Was Your Trip?

Were your travels fun, smooth, and meaningful? You can share tips, concerns, and discoveries at www.ricksteves.com/feedback. I value your feedback. Thanks in advance.

If you plan to hire a **local guide,** reserve ahead by email. Popular guides can get booked up.

If you're bringing a **mobile device,** consider signing up for an international plan for cheaper calls, texts, and data (see page 1151). Download any apps you might want to use on the road, such as translators, maps, transit schedules, and **Rick Steves Audio Europe** (see sidebar).

Check for recent updates to this book at www.ricksteves.com/update.

If you're planning some Riviera **beach** time (such as in the Cinque Terre), be aware that many Italian beaches are pebbly or rocky rather than sandy. In addition to your swimsuit, you may want to pack (or buy in Europe) a pair of water shoes for wading.

Traveling as a Temporary Local

We travel all the way to Italy to enjoy differences—to become temporary locals. You'll experience frustrations. Certain truths that we find "God-given" or "self-evident," such as cold beer, ice in drinks, bottomless cups of coffee, "the customer is king," and bigger being better, are suddenly not so true. One of the benefits of travel is the eye-opening realization that there are logical, civil, and even better alternatives. A willingness to go local ensures that you'll enjoy a full dose of Italian hospitality. And with an eagerness to go local, you'll have even more fun.

Europeans generally like Americans. But if there is a negative aspect to Italians' image of Americans, it's that we are loud, wasteful, ethnocentric, too informal (which can seem disrespectful), and a bit naive. Think about the rationale behind "crazy" Italian decisions. For instance, many hoteliers turn off the heat in spring and don't turn on the air-conditioning until summer. The point is to conserve energy, and it's mandated by the Italian government. You could complain about being cold or hot...or bring a sweater in winter, and in summer, be prepared to sweat a little like everyone else.

While Italians, flabbergasted by our Yankee excesses, say in disbelief, *"Mi sono cadute le braccia!"* ("I throw my arms down!"), they nearly always afford us individual travelers all the warmth we deserve.

Judging from all the happy feedback I receive from travelers who have used this book, it's safe to assume you'll enjoy a great, affordable vacation—with the finesse of an independent, experienced traveler.

Thanks, and *buon viaggio!*

Rick Steves

Back Door Travel Philosophy

From *Rick Steves Europe Through the Back Door*

Travel is intensified living—maximum thrills per minute and one of the last great sources of legal adventure. Travel is freedom. It's recess, and we need it.

Experiencing the real Europe requires catching it by surprise, going casual..."through the Back Door."

Affording travel is a matter of priorities. (Make do with the old car.) You can eat and sleep—simply, safely, and enjoyably—anywhere in Europe for $100 a day plus transportation costs. In many ways, spending more money only builds a thicker wall between you and what you traveled so far to see. Europe is a cultural carnival, and time after time, you'll find that its best acts are free and the best seats are the cheap ones.

A tight budget forces you to travel close to the ground, meeting and communicating with the people. Never sacrifice sleep, nutrition, safety, or cleanliness to save money. Simply enjoy the local-style alternatives to expensive hotels and restaurants.

Connecting with people carbonates your experience. Extroverts have more fun. If your trip is low on magic moments, kick yourself and make things happen. If you don't enjoy a place, maybe you don't know enough about it. Seek the truth. Recognize tourist traps. Give a culture the benefit of your open mind. See things as different, but not better or worse. Any culture has plenty to share. When an opportunity presents itself, make it a habit to say "yes."

Of course, travel, like the world, is a series of hills and valleys. Be fanatically positive and militantly optimistic. If something's not to your liking, change your liking.

Travel can make you a happier American, as well as a citizen of the world. Our Earth is home to seven billion equally precious people. It's humbling to travel and find that other people don't have the "American Dream"—they have their own dreams. Europeans like us, but with all due respect, they wouldn't trade passports.

Thoughtful travel engages us with the world. It reminds us what is truly important. By broadening perspectives, travel teaches new ways to measure quality of life.

Globetrotting destroys ethnocentricity, helping us understand and appreciate other cultures. Rather than fear the diversity on this planet, celebrate it. Among your most prized souvenirs will be the strands of different cultures you choose to knit into your own character. The world is a cultural yarn shop, and Back Door travelers are weaving the ultimate tapestry. Join in!

VENICE

Venezia

Soak all day in this puddle of elegant decay. Venice is Europe's best-preserved big city. This car-free urban wonderland of a hundred islands—laced together by 400 bridges and 2,000 alleys—survives on the artificial respirator of tourism.

Born in a lagoon 1,500 years ago as a refuge from barbarians, Venice is overloaded with tourists and is slowly sinking (not because of the tourists). In the Middle Ages, the Venetians became Europe's clever middlemen for East-West trade and created a great trading empire. By smuggling in the bones of St. Mark (San Marco) in A.D. 828, Venice gained religious importance as well. With the discovery of America and new trading routes to the Orient, Venetian power ebbed. But as Venice fell, her appetite for decadence grew. Through the 17th and 18th centuries, Venice partied on the wealth accumulated through earlier centuries as a trading power.

Today, Venice is home to 55,000 people in its old city, down from about twice that number just three decades ago. While there are about 270,000 people in greater Venice (counting the mainland, not counting tourists), the old town has a small-town feel, and locals seem to know everyone.

Venice is expensive for residents as well as tourists because everything must be shipped in and hand-trucked to its final destination. I find that the best way to enjoy Venice is to succumb to its charms, accept that prices are higher than on the mainland, and blow through a little money. It's a unique place that's worth paying a premium to fully experience.

Escape the Rialto-San Marco tourist zone and savor the town early and late, without the hordes of vacationers day-tripping in from cruise ships and nearby beach resorts. A 10-minute walk from the madness puts you in an idyllic Venice that few tourists see.

PLANNING YOUR TIME

Venice is worth at least a day on even the speediest tour. Hyper-efficient train travelers take the night train in and/or out. Sleep in the old center to experience Venice at its best: early and late. For a one-day visit, cruise the Grand Canal, do the major sights on St. Mark's Square (the square itself, Doge's Palace, and St. Mark's Basilica), enjoy the action at the Rialto Bridge and Rialto Market, see the Frari Church for art, and wander the back streets of the Dorsoduro district to the Accademia Bridge and back to St. Mark's Square. Enjoy an evening gondola ride and then a drink with the orchestras on St. Mark's Square. Venice's greatest sight is the city itself. While doable in a day, Venice is worth two. It's a medieval cookie jar, and nobody's looking. Make time to simply wander.

Orientation to Venice

The inland city of Venice is shaped like a fish. Its major thorough-fares are canals. The Grand Canal winds through the middle of the fish, starting at the mouth where all the people and food enter, passing under the Rialto Bridge, and ending at St. Mark's Square (Piazza San Marco). Park your 21st-century perspective at the mouth and let Venice swallow you whole.

VENICE: A VERBAL MAP

Venice is a car-less kaleidoscope of people, bridges, and odorless canals. It's made up of more than a hundred small islands—but for simplicity, I refer to the whole shebang as "the island."

Venice has six districts (*sestieri*, shown on map on next page): **San Marco** (from St. Mark's Square to the Accademia Bridge),

Castello (the area east of St. Mark's Square), **Dorsoduro** (the "belly" of the fish, on the far side the Accademia Bridge), **Cannaregio** (between the train station and the Rialto Bridge), **San Polo** (west of the Rialto Bridge), and **Santa Croce** (the "eye" of the fish, across the canal from the train station).

The easiest way to navigate is by landmarks. Many street corners have a sign pointing you to *(per)* the nearest major landmark, such as San Marco, Accademia, Rialto, and Ferrovia (train station). Obedient visitors stick to the main thoroughfares as directed by these signs... and miss the charm of back-street Venice.

VENICE

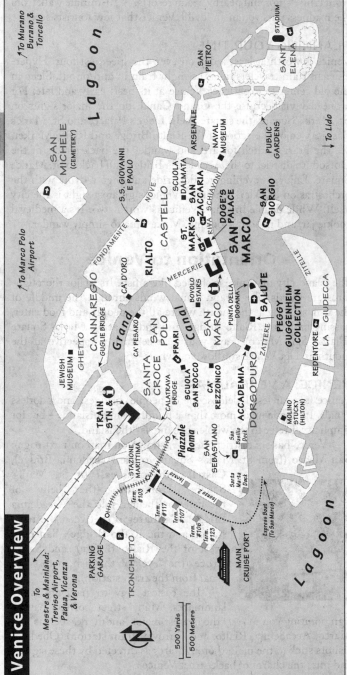

Venice Overview

To
Mestre & Mainland:
Treviso Airport,
Padua, Vicenza
& Verona

To Murano &
Burano &
Torcello

To Marco Polo
Airport

Lagoon

SAN
MICHELE
(CEMETERY)

SAN
PIETRO

SANT'
ELENA

STADIUM

To Lido

PUBLIC
GARDENS

NAVAL
MUSEUM

ARSENALE

SCUOLA
DALMATA

SAN
ZACCARIA

S.S. GIOVANNI
E PAOLO

NOVE

FONDAMENTE

CASTELLO

ST.
MARK'S

RIVA SCHIAVONI

DOGE'S
PALACE

SAN
MARCO

SAN
GIORGIO

RIALTO

CA' D'ORO

CANNAREGIO

MERCERIE

BOVOLO
STAIRS

SAN
MARCO

PUNTA DELLA
DOGANA

SALUTE

PEGGY
GUGGENHEIM
COLLECTION

ZITELLE

Grand

Canal

GUGLIE BRIDGE

JEWISH
MUSEUM

GHETTO

SANTA
CROCE

SAN
PESARO

SAN
POLO

FRARI

SCUOLA
SAN ROCCO

CALATRAVA
BRIDGE

CA'
REZZONICO

ACCADEMIA

ZATTERE

DORSODURO

LA GIUDECCA

REDENTORE

MOLINO
STUCKY
(HILTON)

TRAIN
STN. &

STAZIONE
MARITTIMA

Piazzale
Roma

SAN
SEBASTIANO

San Basilio
Dock

Santa
Marta
Dock

Term.
#103

Term.
#117

Term.
#107

Term.
#106
Term.
#125

Isonzo 1

Isonzo 2

Express Boat
(To San Marco)

MAIN
CRUISE PORT

PARKING
GARAGE

P

TRONCHETTO

Lagoon

Lagoon

500 Yards

500 Meters

Beyond the city's core lie several other islands, including San Giorgio (with great views of Venice), Giudecca (more views), San Michele (old cemetery), Murano (famous for glass), Burano (lace-making), Torcello (old church), and the skinny Lido (with Venice's beach).

TOURIST INFORMATION

With this chapter, a free city map from your hotel, and the events schedule on the TI's website, there's little need to make an in-person visit to a TI in Venice. That's fortunate, because though the city's TIs try to help, they are understaffed and don't have many free printed materials to hand out. If you need to check or confirm something, try phoning the TI information line at 041-2424 or visit www.turismovenezia.it; this website can be more helpful than the actual TI office. Other useful websites are www.veneziaunica. it (vaporetto and event schedules), www.venicexplorer.net (detailed maps), www.aguestinvenice.com (sights and events), www. veniceforvisitors.com (general travel advice), www.venicelink. com (public and private transportation tickets), and www. museicivicivenezziani.it (city-run museums in Venice).

If you must visit a TI, you'll find four convenient branches: **St. Mark's Square** (in the far-left corner with your back to the basilica, open 9:00-19:00); **airport** (daily 9:00-20:00); **bus station** (inside the huge white Autorimessa Comunale parking garage, daily 8:30-14:00); and **train station** (white kiosk in front of the station near the vaporetto stop, daily 9:00-16:00).

Be wary of the travel agencies or special information services that masquerade as TIs but serve fancy hotels and tour companies. They're in the business of selling things you don't need.

Maps: Of all places, Venice demands a good map. Hotels give away freebies (similar in quality to the small color one at the front of this book). TIs and vaporetto ticket booths sell decent €3 maps—but you can find a wider range at bookshops, newsstands, and postcard stands. The cheap maps are pretty bad, but if you spend €5, you'll get a map that shows all the tiny alleys. Investing in a good map can be the best €5 you'll spend in Venice.

Also consider a mapping **app** for your smartphone, which uses GPS to pinpoint your location—extremely useful if you get lost in twisty back streets. To avoid data-roaming charges, look for an offline map that can be downloaded in its entirety before your trip. The **City Maps 2Go** and **Google Maps** apps have good maps, including Venice, that are searchable even when you're not online—as long as you download them in advance.

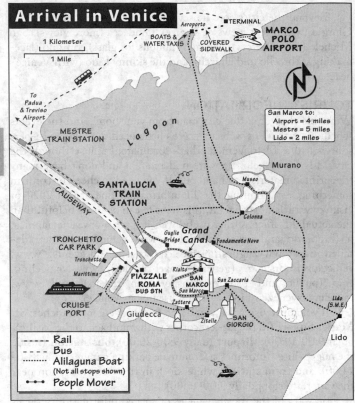

Arrival in Venice

1 Kilometer
1 Mile

To Padua & Treviso Airport

MARCO POLO AIRPORT

TERMINAL

Aeroporto

BOATS & WATER TAXIS

COVERED SIDEWALK

MESTRE TRAIN STATION

Lagoon

San Marco to:
Airport = 4 miles
Mestre = 5 miles
Lido = 2 miles

Murano

Museo

SANTA LUCIA TRAIN STATION

Colonna

CAUSEWAY

Guglie Bridge

Grand Canal

Fondamente Nove

TRONCHETTO CAR PARK

Tronchetto

Rialto

San Zaccaria

Marittima

PIAZZALE ROMA BUS STN

SAN MARCO
San Marco

CRUISE PORT

Zattere

Lido (S.M.E.)

Giudecca

Zitelle

SAN GIORGIO

Lido

---- Rail
- - - Bus
········· Alilaguna Boat
(Not all stops shown)
•—•—• People Mover

ARRIVAL IN VENICE

A two-mile-long causeway (with highway and train lines) connects Venice to the mainland. Mestre, the sprawling mainland section of Venice, has fewer crowds, cheaper hotels, and plenty of inexpensive parking lots, but zero charm. Don't stop in Mestre unless you're changing trains, parking your car, or sleeping there.

By Train

All trains to "Venice" stop at Venezia Mestre (on the mainland). Most continue on to **Santa Lucia Station** (a.k.a. Venezia S.L.) on the island of Venice itself. If your train happens to terminate at Mestre, you'll need to buy a €1.25 Mestre-Santa Lucia ticket and validate it before hopping any nonexpress, regional train (with an R or RV prefix) for the ride across the causeway to Venice (6/hour, 10 minutes).

Santa Lucia train station plops you right into the old town on the Grand Canal, an easy vaporetto ride or fascinating 45-minute walk to St. Mark's Square. You'll find the **TI** in a white kiosk out front, next to the vaporetto dock.

The station has a **baggage check** (€6/5 hours, €17/24 hours, daily 6:00-23:00, no lockers; along track 1). Pay **WCs** are at track 1 and in the back of the big bar/cafeteria area inside the station.

Before heading into town, confirm your departure plan (use the ticket machines or study the *partenze*/departures posters on walls). The banks of user-friendly ticket machines are handy (but cover Italian destinations only). They take euros and credit cards, display schedules, and issue tickets. Some ticket machines are only for Trenitalia trains (toll tel. 892-021, www.trenitalia.it); the red machines are for the high-speed Italo service (tel. 06-0708, www.italotreno.it).

If you need international tickets or live help, head to the ticket windows in the corner, near track 14 (Trenitalia open 6:00-21:00; Italo open 8:15-20:10). Or you could take care of these tasks online or at a downtown travel agency (ticket fee, see page 26).

Getting from the Train Station to Central Venice: It's best by **vaporetto.** Walk straight out of the station to the canal, where you'll see five vaporetto docks, each serving different boats. Electronic signboards show which boats are leaving when and from which dock. From left to right, it's dock A, bridge, and docks B, C, D, and E: Dock A (circular-route boats #4.1 and #5.1), Dock B (circular-route boats #4.2 and #5.2), Dock C (fast boat #2, wrong direction), Dock D (fast boat #2 to Rialto and San Marco), and Dock E (slow boat #1, making every stop down the Grand Canal all the way to San Marco). Buy a €7.50 ticket before you board, and even though you're an expert now, confirm that your boat is going to your stop as you hop on. For details on vaporetto tickets and passes, see page 27.

A **water taxi** from the train station to central Venice costs about €60-70 (the taxi dock is straight ahead).

By Bus

Venice's "bus station" is actually an open-air parking lot called Piazzale Roma. The square itself is a jumble of different operators, platforms, and crosswalks over busy lanes of traffic. But bus stops are well-signed. The ticket windows for ACTV (including #5 to Marco Polo Airport) are in a building between the bridge and vaporetto stop. The ATVO ticket office (express buses to Marco Polo and Treviso airports and to Padua) is at #497g in the big, white building, on the right side of the square as you face away from the canal (office open daily 7:30-22:30).

Piazzale Roma also has two big parking garages and the People Mover monorail (€1.50, links to the cruise port and then the parking-lot island of Tronchetto). A baggage-storage office is next to the monorail at #497m (€7/24 hours, daily 6:00-21:00).

If you arrive here, find the vaporetto docks (just left of the modern bridge) and take #1 or the faster #2 down the Grand Canal to reach the Rialto, Accademia, or San Marco (St. Mark's Square) stops. Electronic boards direct you to the dock you want. Before buying a single-ride vaporetto ticket, consider getting a transit pass (see page 27). If your hotel is near here or near the train station, you can get there on foot.

By Car

The freeway (monitored by speed cameras) dead-ends after crossing the causeway to Venice. At the end of the road you have two parking-garage choices: Tronchetto or Piazzale Roma. As you drive into the city, signboards with green and red lights indicate which lots are full. (You can also park in Mestre, on the mainland, but this is less convenient.)

Parking at Tronchetto: This big garage is a bit farther out, but it's a bit cheaper and well-connected by vaporetto (€3-5/hour, €21/24 hours, tel. 041-520-7555, www.veniceparking.it).

From the garage, cross the street to the brick building and go right to the vaporetto dock (not well-signed, look for *ACTV*). At the dock, catch vaporetto #2 in one of two directions: via the Grand Canal (more scenic, stops at Rialto, 40 minutes to San Marco), or via Giudecca (around the city, faster, no Rialto stop, 30 minutes to San Marco).

Don't be waylaid by aggressive water taxi boatmen. They charge €100 to take you where the vaporetto will for far less. Also avoid the travel agencies masquerading as TIs; deal only with the ticket booth at the vaporetto dock or the VèneziaUnica public transport office. If you're going to buy a local transport pass, do it now.

If you're staying near the bus or train station, you can take the €1.50 **People Mover** monorail, which brings you from Tronchetto to the bus station at Piazzale Roma. From there, it's a five-minute walk across the Calatrava Bridge to the train station (buy tickets with cash or credit card from machine, 3-minute trip).

Parking at Piazzale Roma: The two garages here are more convenient but a bit more expensive and likelier to be full. Both garages face the busy Piazzale Roma, where the road ends. The big white building on your right is the **Autorimessa Comunale** city garage (€26/24 hours, TI office in payment lobby open daily 8:30-14:00, tel. 041-272-7211, www.avmspa.it). In a back corner of the square is the private **Garage San Marco** (€30/24 hours, tel. 041-523-2213, www.garagesanmarco.it). At either of these, you'll have to give up your keys. Near the Garage San Marco, avoid the Parcheggio Sant'Andrea, which charges obscene rates.

Parking in Mestre: The **Parcheggio Stazione** garage across from the train station in Mestre (on the mainland) makes sense only if you have light bags and are staying within walking distance of Santa Lucia Station (€2.50/hour, €14/day, www.sabait.it).

By Plane or Cruise Ship

For information on Venice's airport and cruise ship terminal, see the end of this chapter.

HELPFUL HINTS

Exchange Rate: €1 = about $1.10

Country Calling Code: 39 (see page 1154 for dialing instructions)

Theft Alert: The dark, late-night streets of Venice are generally safe. Even so, pickpockets (often elegantly dressed) work the crowded main streets, docks, and vaporetti. Your biggest risk of pickpockets is inside St. Mark's Basilica, near the Accademia or Rialto bridges (especially if you're preoccupied with snapping photos), or on a tightly packed vaporetto.

A handy polizia station is on the right side of St. Mark's Square as you face the basilica (at #63, near Caffè Florian). To call the police, dial 113. The Venice TI handles complaints—which must be submitted in writing—about local crooks, including gondoliers, restaurants, and hotel rip-offs (fax 041-523-0399, complaint.apt@turismovenezia.it).

It's illegal for street vendors to sell knockoff handbags, and it's also illegal for you to buy them; both you and the vendor can get big fines.

Medical Help: Venice's Santi Giovanni e Paolo hospital (tel. 118) is a 10-minute walk from both the Rialto and San Marco neighborhoods, located behind the big church of the same name on Fondamenta dei Mendicanti (toward Fondamente Nove). You can take vaporetto #4.1 from San Zaccaria, or #5.2 from the train station or Piazzale Roma, to the Ospedale stop. Also, a first-aid station staffed by English-speaking doctors is on St. Mark's Square (at #63—same address as *polizia* station, daily 8:00-20:00), on the right-hand side as you face the basilica.

Sightseeing Tips: The city is inundated with cruise-ship passengers and tours from mainland hotels daily from 10:00 to about 16:00. Major sights are busiest in the late morning, it's a delightful time to explore the back lanes. The sights that have crowd problems get even more packed when it rains.

To avoid the worst of the crowds at **St. Mark's Basilica,** go early or late, or reserve a time online. You can usually bypass the line if you have a large bag to check (see page 53).

At the **Doge's Palace,** purchase your ticket at the never-crowded Correr Museum across St. Mark's Square. You can also visit later in the day.

For the **Campanile,** ascend first thing in the morning or go late (it's open until 21:00 July-Sept), or skip it entirely if you're going to the similar San Giorgio Maggiore bell tower.

Picnics: Picnicking is illegal anywhere on St. Mark's Square, and offenders can be fined. The only place nearby for a legal picnic is in Giardinetti Reali, the small bench-filled park along the waterfront west of the Piazzetta near St. Mark's Square. Elsewhere in Venice, picnicking is no problem.

Dress Modestly: When visiting St. Mark's Basilica or other major churches, men, women, and even children must cover their shoulders and knees. Remove hats when entering a church.

Public Toilets: Handy public pay WCs are near major landmarks, including: St. Mark's Square (behind the Correr Museum and at the waterfront park, Giardinetti Reali), Rialto, and the Accademia Bridge. Use free toilets whenever you can—any museum you're visiting, or any café you're eating in. A cup of coffee at the counter of a nice bar and a trip to the WC is cheaper than the cost of using a pay WC.

Best Views: A slow vaporetto ride down the Grand Canal—ideally very early or just before sunset—is a shutterbug's delight (try to sit in the front seats, available on some older boats). On St. Mark's Square, enjoy views from the soaring Campanile or the balcony of St. Mark's Basilica (both require admission). The Rialto and Accademia bridges provide free, expansive views of the Grand Canal, along with a cooling breeze. Or get off the main island for a view of the Venetian skyline: Ascend San Giorgio Maggiore's bell tower, or venture to Giudecca Island to visit the swanky bar of the Molino Stucky Hilton Hotel (the free-to-"customers" shuttle boat leaves from near the San Zaccaria-B vaporetto dock).

Water: I carry a water bottle to refill at public fountains. Venetians pride themselves on having pure, safe, and tasty tap water piped in from the foothills of the Alps. You can actually see the mountains from Venice's bell towers on crisp, clear winter days.

Pigeon Poop: If your head is bombed by a pigeon, resist the initial response to wipe it off immediately—it'll just smear into your hair. Wait until it dries, and it should flake off cleanly. But if the poop splatters on your clothes, wipe it off immediately to avoid a stain.

SERVICES

Wi-Fi: Almost all hotels have Wi-Fi, many have a computer that guests can use, and most provide these services for free.

Useful App: ∩ For free audio versions of my Grand Canal Cruise and tours of St. Mark's Square, St. Mark's Basilica, and Frari Church, get the **Rick Steves Audio Europe** app (see page 12).

Post Office: The main post office is a little south of the Rialto Bridge on Marzaria San Salvador, part of the main shopping drag running toward San Marco (Mon-Fri 8:30-19:00, Sat 8:30-12:30, closed Sun). You'll find branch offices with shorter hours (generally mornings only) around town, including a handy one right behind St. Mark's Square (near the TI).

Bookstores: In keeping with its literary heritage, Venice has classy and inviting bookstores. The small **Libreria Studium,** a block

behind St. Mark's Basilica, has a carefully chosen selection of new English books, including my guidebooks (daily 9:00-19:30, on Calle de la Canonica at #337—see map on page 51, tel. 041-522-2382).

Used-bookstore lovers shouldn't miss the funky **Acqua Alta** ("high water") bookstore, whose quirky owner Luigi has prepared for the next flood by displaying his wares in a selection of vessels, including bathtubs and a gondola. Look for the "book stairs" in his back garden (daily 9:00-20:00, large and classically disorganized selection includes prints of Venice, just beyond Campo Santa Maria Formosa on Lunga Santa Maria Formosa, Castello 5176, see map on page 87, tel. 041-296-0841).

For a solid selection of used books in English, visit **Marco Polo,** on Calle del Teatro o de l'Opera, close to the St. Mark's side of the Rialto Bridge, just past the Coin department store and behind the church (daily 9:30-19:30, Cannaregio 5886a—see map on page 87, tel. 041-522-6343).

Baggage Storage: The train station has a pay **baggage check** (daily 6:00-23:00, no lockers; along track 1).

Laundry: Venice has two coin-operated launderettes. **Orange Self-Service Lavanderia** is across the Grand Canal from the train station (€15/load, daily 7:30-22:30, on Ramo de le Chioverete, Santa Croce 665b—see map on page 94, mobile 346-972-5446). The other, called **Effe Erre,** is off Campo Santa Maria Formosa (about €12/load, daily 6:30-23:00, on Ruga Giuffa, Castello 4826—see map on page 82, mobile 349-058-3881, Massimo).

To save time and spend about the same amount, take your

laundry to the full-service **Lavanderia Gabriella,** a few streets north of St. Mark's Square (€15/load includes wash, dry, and fold; drop off Mon-Fri 8:00-12:30, closed Sat-Sun; pick up 2 hours later or next working day, on Rio Terà de le Colonne, San Marco 985—see map on page 82, tel. 041-522-1758, Elisabetta).

Travel Agencies: You can avoid a time-consuming trip to Venice's crowded train station by booking online or using a downtown travel agency. **Oltrex Travel** is handy (one bridge past the Bridge of Sighs, just across from the San Zaccaria vaporetto stop—see map on page 51, daily 9:00-13:00 & 14:00-17:30; tel. 041-476-1926, Luca and Beatrice).

Agenzie 365 is in the main lobby of the train station, where you can buy vaporetto and train tickets (about an 8 percent surcharge on train tickets, daily 8:00-19:30; tel. 041-275-9412).

English Church Services: San Zulian Church offers a Mass in English (generally May-Sept Mon-Fri at 9:30 and Sun at 11:30, Oct-April Sun at 10:30, 2 blocks toward Rialto off St. Mark's Square, tel. 041-523-5383). **St. George's Anglican Church** welcomes all to its English-language Eucharist (Sun at 10:30, located on Campo San Zio in Dorsoduro, midway between Accademia and Peggy Guggenheim Collection, www.stgeorgesvenice.com).

GETTING AROUND VENICE
On Foot

The city's "streets" are narrow pedestrian walkways connecting its docks, squares, bridges, and courtyards. To navigate, look for signs on street corners pointing you to *(per)* the nearest major landmark. The first landmarks you'll get to know are San Marco (St. Mark's Square), Rialto (the bridge), Accademia (another bridge), Ferrovia ("railroad," meaning the train station), and Piazzale Roma (the bus station). Determine whether your destination is in the direction of a major signposted landmark, then follow the signs through the maze.

As you get more comfortable with the city, dare to disobey these signs, avoid the posted routes, and make your own discoveries. While 80 percent of Venice is, in fact, not touristy, 80 percent of the tourists never notice. Escape the crowds and explore on foot. Walk and walk to the far reaches of the town. Don't worry about getting lost—in fact, get as lost as possible. Keep reminding yourself, "I'm on an island, and I can't get off." When it comes time to find your way, just follow the arrows on building corners or simply ask a local, *"Dov'è San Marco?"* ("Where is St. Mark's?") People in the tourist business (that's most Venetians) speak some English.

If they don't, listen politely, watch where their hands point, say *"Grazie,"* and head off in that direction. If you're lost, refer to your map, your smartphone app, or pop into a hotel and ask for their business card—it probably comes with a map and a prominent "You are here."

Every building in Venice has a house number. The numbers relate to the district (each with about 6,000 address numbers), not the street. Therefore, if you need to find a specific address, it helps to know its district, street, house number, and nearby landmarks.

Some helpful street terminology: *Campo* means square, a *campiello* is a small square, *calle* (pronounced "KAH-lay" with an "L" sound) means "street," and a *ponte* is a bridge. A *fondamenta* is the embankment along a canal or the lagoon. A *rio terà* is a street that was once a canal and has been filled in. A *sotoportego* is a covered passageway. *Salizzada* literally means a paved area (usually a wide street). The abbreviations S. and S.S. mean "saint" and "saints" respectively. Don't get hung up on the exact spelling of street and square names, which may sometimes appear in Venetian dialect (which uses *de la, novo,* and *vechio*) and other times in standard Italian (which uses *della, nuovo,* and *vecchio*).

By Vaporetto

Venice's public transit system, run by a company called ACTV, is a fleet of motorized bus-boats called *vaporetti.* They work like city buses except that they never get a flat, the stops are docks, and if you jump off between stops, you might drown. For the same prices, you can purchase tickets and passes at docks and from ACTV affiliate VèneziaUnica (ACTV-tel. 041-2424, www.actv.it; VèneziaUnica—www. veneziaunica.it).

Tickets and Passes

Individual Vaporetto Tickets: A single ticket costs €7.50. Kids age 6 and up pay the same fare as an adult (kids under 6 travel free). Tickets are good for 75 minutes; you can hop on and off at stops and change boats during that time. Your ticket (a plastic card embedded with a chip) is refillable—don't toss it after the first use. You can put more money on it at the automated kiosks and avoid waiting in line at the ticket window. The fare is reduced to €5 for a few one-stop runs *(corsa semplice)* that are hard to do by foot, including

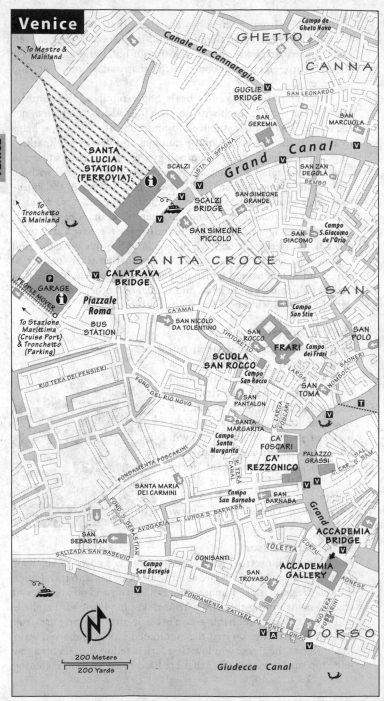

Venice

GHETTO

Campo de
Gheto Nova

CANNA

Canale de Cannaregio

To Mestre &
Mainland

GUGLIE
BRIDGE

SAN LEONARDO

SAN
GEREMIA

SAN
MARCUOLA

Grand Canal

SANTA
LUCIA
STATION
(FERROVIA)

SCALZI

LISTA DI SPAGNA

SAN ZAN
DEGOLA

To
Tronchetto
& Mainland

SCALZI
BRIDGE

SAN SIMEONE
GRANDE

BEMBO

SAN SIMEONE
PICCOLO

SAN
GIACOMO

Campo
S.Giacomo
de l'Orio

SANTA CROCE

P   GARAGE

CALATRAVA
BRIDGE

PEOPLE MOVER

SAN

To Stazione
Marittima
(Cruise Port)
& Tronchetto
(Parking)

Piazzale
Roma

BUS
STATION

CA'AMAI

SAN NICOLO
DA TOLENTINO

Campo
San Stin

SAN
POLO

TINTORETTO

SAN
ROCCO

FRARI

Campo
dei Frari

SCUOLA
SAN ROCCO

Campo
San Rocco

LARGA

SAN
TOMA

SAONERI

RIO TERA DEI PENSIERI

FOND. DEL RIO NOVO

SAN
PANTALON

NOMBOLI

SANTA
MARGARITA

C. LARGA
FOSCARI

CA'
FOSCARI

Campo
Santa
Margarita

PALAZZO
GRASSI

CA'
REZZONICO

T

FONDAMENTA FOSCARINI

SANTA MARIA
DEI CARMINI

R. TERA
CANAL

Campo
San Barnaba

SAN
BARNABA

Grand

SAN
SEBASTIAN

FOND. S. SEBASTIAN

C. LUNGA S. BARNABA

CORFU

ACCADEMIA
BRIDGE

SALIZADA SAN BASEGIO

TOLETTA

ACCADEMIA
GALLERY

Campo
San Basegio

OGNISANTI

SAN
TROVASO

AGNESE

RIO TERA
FOSCARINI

FONDAMENTA ZATTERE AL PONTE LONGO

DORSO

N

200 Meters

200 Yards

Giudecca Canal

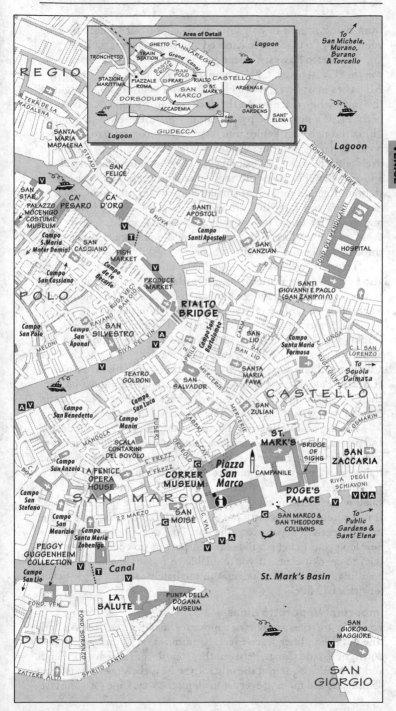

from San Zaccaria to San Giorgio Maggiore. It's smart to keep your receipt (in case you're checked and your ticket is faulty).

Vaporetto Passes: You can buy a pass for unlimited use of *vaporetti:* €20/24 hours, €30/48 hours, €40/72 hours, €60/7-day pass. All passes must be validated each time you board by touching it to the small white machine on the dock. Because single tickets cost a hefty €7.50 a pop, these passes can pay for themselves in a hurry. Think through your Venice itinerary before you step up to the ticket booth to pay for your first vaporetto trip. The 48-hour pass pays for itself with five rides (for example: to your hotel on your arrival, on a Grand Canal joyride, into the lagoon and back, and to the train station). Keep in mind that smaller and/or outlying stops, such as Sant'Elena and Biennale, are unstaffed—another good reason to buy a pass. It's fun to be able to hop on and off spontaneously, and avoid long ticket lines. On the other hand, many tourists just walk through Venice and rarely use a boat.

Travelers ages 14-29 can get a 72-hour pass for €22 if they also buy a **Rolling Venice** discount card for €6 (see page 50). Those settling in for a much longer stay can ride like a local by buying the Vènezia Unica card (details at www.veneziaunica.com).

Passes are also valid on some of ACTV's mainland buses, including bus #2 to Mestre (but not the #5 to the airport nor the airport buses run by ATVO, a separate company). Pass holders get a discounted fare for all ACTV buses that originate or terminate at Marco Polo Airport (€6 one-way, €12 round-trip, must be purchased at the same time as the pass; otherwise, the airport shuttle costs €8 one-way, €15 round-trip).

Buying and Validating Tickets and Passes: Purchase tickets and passes from the automated machines at most stops, from ticket windows (at larger stops), or from the VèneziaUnica offices at the train station, bus station, and Tronchetto parking lot.

Before you board, validate your ticket by holding it up to the small white machine on the dock until you hear a pinging sound. If you purchase a vaporetto pass, you need to touch the pass to the machine each time you board the boat. The machine readout shows how long your ticket is valid—and inspectors do come by now and then to check tickets. If you're unable to purchase a ticket before boarding, seek out the conductor immediately to buy a single ticket (or risk a €50 fine).

Important Vaporetto Lines

For most travelers, only two vaporetto lines matter: **line #1** and **line #2.** These lines leave every 10 minutes or so and go up and down the Grand Canal, between the "mouth" of the fish at one end and St. Mark's Square at the other. Line #1 is the slow boat, taking 45 minutes and making every stop along the way. Line #2 is the fast boat that zips down the Grand Canal in 25 minutes, stopping only at Tronchetto (parking lot), Piazzale Roma (bus station), Ferrovia (train station), Rialto Bridge, San Tomà (Frari Church), San Samuele (opposite Ca' Rezzonico), Accademia Bridge, and San Marco (west end of St. Mark's Square, end of the line).

Sorting out the different directions of travel can be confusing. Some boats run on circular routes, in one direction only (for example, lines #5.1 and #5.2, plus the non-Murano sections of lines #4.1 and #4.2). Line #2 runs in both directions and is almost, but not quite, a full loop. The #2 boat leaving from the San Marco stop goes in one direction (up the Grand Canal), while from the San Zaccaria stop—just a five-minute walk away—it goes in the opposite direction (around the tail of the "fish"). Make sure you use the correct stop to avoid taking the long way around to your destination.

To clear up any confusion, ask a ticket-seller or conductor for help (sometimes they're stationed on the dock to help confused tourists). Get a copy of the most current ACTV map and timetable (in English and Italian, theoretically free at ticket booths but usually unavailable—can be downloaded from www.actv.it). System maps are posted at stops, but it's smart to print out your own copy of the map from the ACTV website before your trip.

Boarding and Riding

Many stops have two boarding platforms, and large stops—such as San Marco, San Zaccaria, Rialto, Ferrovia (train station), and Piazzale Roma—have multiple platforms. At these larger stops, helpful electronic boards display which boats are coming next, and when, and from which platform they leave; each platform is assigned a letter (clearly marked above the gangway). At smaller stops without electronic displays, signs on each platform

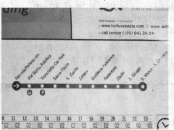

show the vaporetto lines that stop there and the direction they are headed. As you board, confirm your destination by looking for an electronic sign on the boat or just asking the conductor.

You may notice some *vaporetti* sporting a *corsa bis* sign, indicating that it's running a shortened or altered route, and that riders may have to hop off partway (at Rialto, for example) and wait for the next boat. If you see a *corsa bis* sign, before boarding ask the conductor whether the boat is going to your desired destination (e.g., simply ask "San Marco?").

Handy *Vaporetti* from San Zaccaria, near St. Mark's Square

Several *vaporetti* leave from the San Zaccaria docks, located 150 yards east of St. Mark's Square. There are four San Zaccaria docks spaced about 70 yards apart, with six different berths, lettered A to F. Check the big electronic board (next to the C/D dock), which indicates the departure time, line number, destination, and berth letter of upcoming *vaporetti*. Once you've figured out which boat you want, go to that letter berth and hop on.

Line #1: This vaporetto goes up the Grand Canal, making all the stops, including San Marco, Rialto, Ferrovia (train station), and Piazzale Roma (but it does not go as far as Tronchetto). In the other direction, it goes from San Zaccaria to Arsenale and Giardini before ending on the Lido.

Line #2: This vaporetto zips over to San Giorgio Maggiore, the island church across from St. Mark's Square (5 minutes, €5 ride). From there, it continues on to stops on the island of Giudecca, the parking lot at Tronchetto, and then down the Grand Canal. Note: You cannot ride the #2 up the Grand Canal (for example, to Rialto or the train station) directly from this stop—you'll need to walk five minutes along the waterfront, past St. Mark's Square, to the San Marco-Giardinetti dock and hop the #2 from there.

Line #4.1: This boat goes to San Michele and Murano (45 minutes).

Line #7: This is the summertime express boat to Murano (25 minutes).

Molino Stucky Shuttle Boat: This takes even non-guests to the Hilton Hotel, with its popular view bar (20-minute ride, 3/hour, from its own dock near the San Zaccaria-B dock).

Lines #5.1 and **#5.2:** These are the *circulare* (cheer-koo-LAH-ray), making a loop around the perimeter of the island, with a stop at the Lido—perfect if you just like riding boats. Line #5.1 goes coun-

Crowd-Beating Tips

For fun, take my self-guided Grand Canal Cruise. But be warned: Grand Canal *vaporetti* in particular can be absolutely jam-packed, especially during the tourist rush hour (during mornings heading in from Piazzale Roma, and in evenings heading out to Piazzale Roma). Riding at night, with nearly empty boats and chandelier-lit palace interiors viewable from the Grand Canal, can be a highlight of your Venetian experience.

By Traghetto

Only four bridges cross the Grand Canal, but *traghetti* (shuttle gondolas) ferry locals and in-the-know tourists

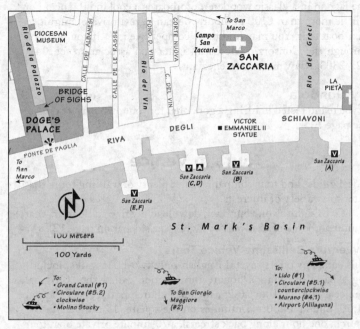

VENICE

terclockwise, and #5.2 goes clockwise. Both run less frequently in the evenings.

Alilaguna Shuttle Boat: This runs to and from the airport, stopping here as well.

across the Grand Canal at three additional locations (marked on the color map of Venice at the front of this book). Just step in, hand the gondolier €2, and enjoy the ride—standing or sitting. Some *traghetti* are seasonal, some stop running as early as 12:30, and all stop by 18:00. *Traghetti* are not covered by any transit pass.

By Water Taxi

Venetian taxis, like speedboat limos, hang out at busy points along the Grand Canal. Prices are regulated: €15 for pickup, then €2 per minute; €5 per person for more than four passengers (boats can carry around 10 people); and €10 between 22:00 and 6:00. If you have more bags than passengers, the extra ones cost €3 apiece. (For information on taking the water taxi to/from the airport, see page 116.) Despite regulation, prices can be soft; negotiate and settle on the price or rate before stepping in. For travelers with lots of luggage or small groups who can split the cost, taxi boat rides can be a worthwhile and time-saving convenience—and skipping across the lagoon in a classic wooden motorboat is a cool indulgence. For a little more than €100 an hour, you can have a private, unguided taxi-boat tour. You may find more competitive rates if you prebook through the Consorzio Motoscafi water taxi association tel. 041-522-2303, www.motoscafivenezia.it).

By Gondola

If you're interested in hiring a gondolier for your own private cruise, see page 73.

Tours in Venice

Local guides and tour companies offer plenty of walking tours that cater to a variety of interests.

🎧 To sightsee on your own, download my free audio tours that illuminate some of Venice's top sights (see sidebar on page 12).

Avventure Bellissime Venice Tours

This company offers several English-only two-hour walks, including a basic St. Mark's Square introduction called the "Original Venice Walking Tour" (€25, includes church entry, most days at 11:00, Sun at 14:00; 45 minutes on the square, 15 minutes in the church, one hour along back streets), a 70-minute private boat tour of the Grand Canal (€48, daily at 16:00, 8 people maximum), a "Hidden Venice" tour (€25, in summer 3/week at 11:30), and mainland excursions (details at www.tours-italy.com, tel. 041-970-499, info@tours-italy.com). For a 10 percent Rick Steves discount, contact them ahead of time for a promo code.

Alessandro's Classic Venice Bars Tour and Backstreets Tour

Debonair Alessandro Schezzini is a connoisseur of Venetian *bacari*—classic old bars serving wine and traditional *cicchetti* snacks. He organizes two-hour Venetian bar tours (€35/person, most nights at 18:00) that include sampling *cicchetti* with wines at three *bacari*. (If you think of this tour as a light dinner with a local friend, it's a particularly good value.) He also runs a relaxed, 1.5-hour Backstreets Tour that gets you beyond the clichés and into offbeat Venice (€20/person, most nights at 16:30).

Both tours depart almost daily in season when six or more sign up. Meet 50 yards north of the Rialto Bridge under the big clock on Campo San Giacomo. (Book via email, alessandro@schezzini.it, or by phone, mobile 335-530-9024; www.schezzini.it.)

VENICE

Artviva Tours

This company offers several tours, including general intro-to-Venice tours, themed tours (Grand Canal, Venice Walk, Doge's Palace, Gondola Tour), or a private "Learn to Be a Gondolier" tour (for details, see www.italy.artviva.com). They offer a 10 percent Rick Steves discount (www.artviva.com/ricksteves, username "ricksteves" and password "reader").

Venicescapes

Michael Broderick's private, themed tours of Venice are intellectually demanding and beyond the attention span of most mortal tourists. But travelers with a keen interest and a desire to learn find him passionate and engaging. Your time with Michael is like a rolling, graduate-level lecture (see his website for various 4- to 6-hour itineraries, 2 people-$280-310 or the euro equivalent, $60/person after that, admissions and transport extra, tel. 041-850-5742, mobile 349-479-7406, www.venicescapes.org, info@venicescapes.org).

Local Guides

Plenty of licensed, trained guides are available. If you organize a small group from your hotel at breakfast to split the cost (figure on €75/hour with a 2-hour minimum), the fee becomes more reasonable. I've enjoyed working with the following guides:

Walks Inside Venice is enthusiastic about teaching (€270/3 hours per group of up to 6; Roberta: mobile 347-253-0560; Sara: mobile 335-522-9714; www.walksinsidevenice.com, info@walksinsidevenice.com). They also do side-trips to outlying destinations, and offer regularly scheduled small-group, English-only walking tours (€62.50, Mon-Sat at 14:30, 2.5 hours). Ask about Rick Steves discounts.

Corine Govi and **Elisabetta Morelli,** who run **2Guides-4Venice,** are informative and reliable (Corine, mobile 347-966-8346, corine_g@libero.it; Elisabetta, tel. 041-526-7816, mobile 328-753-5220, bettamorelli@inwind.it, www.2guides4venice.com).

Venice with a Guide, a co-op of 10 good guides, offers a range of tours (€150 for a 2-hour tour; for more, go to www.venicewithaguide.com).

Tour Leader Venice, a.k.a. **Treviso Car Service,** specializes in getting you outside of Venice by car or minivan—to countryside villas, wine-and-cheese tastings, and the Dolomites—but

VENICE

Venice at a Glance

▲▲▲**St. Mark's Square** Venice's grand main square. **Hours:** Always open. See page 50.

▲▲▲**St. Mark's Basilica Cathedral** with mosaics, saint's bones, treasury, museum, and viewpoint of square. **Hours:** Mon-Sat 9:45-17:00, Sun 14:00-17:00 (until 16:00 Nov-Easter). See page 53.

▲▲▲**Doge's Palace** Art-splashed palace of former rulers, with prison accessible through Bridge of Sighs. **Hours:** Daily 8:30-19:00, Nov-March until 17:30. See page 59.

▲▲▲**Rialto Bridge** Distinctive bridge spanning the Grand Canal, with a market nearby. **Hours:** Bridge—always open; market—souvenir stalls open daily, produce market closed Sun, fish market closed Sun-Mon. See page 68.

▲▲**Correr Museum** Venetian history and art. **Hours:** Daily April-Oct 10:00-19:00, Nov-March until 17:00. See page 63.

▲▲**Accademia** Venice's top art museum. **Hours:** Mon 8:15-14:00, Tue-Sun until 19:15. See page 65.

▲▲**Peggy Guggenheim Collection** Popular display of 20th-century art. **Hours:** Wed-Mon 10:00-18:00, closed Tue. See page 67.

▲▲**Frari Church** Franciscan church featuring Renaissance masters. **Hours:** Mon-Sat 9:00-18:00, Sun 13:00-18:00. See page 68.

▲▲**Scuola San Rocco** "Tintoretto's Sistine Chapel." **Hours:** Daily 9:30-17:30. See page 70.

▲**Campanile** Dramatic bell tower on St. Mark's Square with elevator to the top. **Hours:** Daily Easter-June and Oct 9:00-19:00, July-Sept until 21:00; Nov-Easter 9:30-15:45. See page 64.

▲**Bridge of Sighs** Famous enclosed bridge, part of Doge's Palace, near St. Mark's Square. **Hours:** Always viewable. See page 64.

▲**La Salute Church** Striking church dedicated to the Virgin Mary. **Hours:** Daily 9:00-12:00 & 15:00-17:30. See page 67.

▲**Ca' Rezzonico** Posh Grand Canal palazzo with 18th-century Venetian art. **Hours:** Wed-Mon 10:00-18:00, Nov-March until 17:00, closed Tue year-round. See page 67.

▲**Punta della Dogana** Museum of contemporary art. **Hours:** Wed-Mon 10:00-19:00, closed Tue. See page 67.

Church of San Zaccaria Final resting place of St. Zechariah, plus a Bellini altarpiece and an eerie crypt. **Hours:** Mon-Sat 10:00-12:00 & 16:00-18:00, Sun 16:00-18:00. See page 65.

Church of San Polo Has works by Tintoretto, Veronese, and Tiepolo. **Hours:** Mon-Sat 10:00-17:00, closed Sun. See page 70.

Nearby Islands
▲**San Giorgio Maggiore** Island facing St. Mark's Square, featuring church with Palladio architecture, Tintoretto paintings, and fine views back on Venice. **Hours:** Daily 7:00-19:00, Nov-March closes at dusk. See page 65.

San Michele Cemetery island on the lagoon. **Hours:** Daily 7:30-18:00, Oct-March until 16:30. See page 71.

▲**Murano** Island famous for glass factories and glassmaking museum. **Hours:** Glass Museum open daily 10:00-18:00, Nov-March until 17:00. See page 71.

▲▲**Burano** Sleepy island known for lacemaking and lace museum. **Hours:** Museum open Tue-Sun 10:00-18:00, Nov-March until 17:00, closed Mon year-round. See page 72.

▲**Torcello** Near-deserted island with old church, bell tower, and museum. **Hours:** Church open daily March-Oct 10:30-18:00, Nov-Feb 10:00-17:00, museum closed Mon. See page 72.

▲**Lido** Family-friendly beach. See page 73.

VENICE

also offers guided walks in Venice (mobile 348-900-0700 or 333-411-2840; www.trevisocarservice.com, tvcarservice@gmail.com; for Venice tours also see www.tourleadervenice.com, info@tourleadervenice.com; Igor, Andrea, and Marta). They also provide transfer services to Venice's airport and cruise terminal (see page 116).

Tour Packages for Students

Andy Steves (Rick's son) runs **Weekend Student Adventures** (WSA Europe), offering 3-day and 10-day budget travel packages across Europe including accommodations, skip-the-line sightseeing, and unique local experiences. Locally guided and DIY unguided options are available for student and budget travelers in 12 of Europe's most popular cities, including Venice (guided trips from €199, see www.wsaeurope.com for details).

Grand Canal Cruise

Take a joyride and introduce yourself to Venice by boat, an experience worth ▲▲▲. Cruise the Canal Grande all the way to St. Mark's Square, starting at the train station (Ferrovia) or the bus station (Piazzale Roma, where you're more likely to find an empty seat). Consider topping it off with my self-guided tour of St. Mark's Basilica (see page 53). If it's your first trip down the Grand Canal, you might want to stow this book and just take it all in—Venice is a barrage on the senses that hardly needs narration. But these notes give the cruise a little meaning and help orient you to this great city.

This tour is designed to be done on the slow boat #1. The express boat #2 travels the same route, but it skips many stops. To help you enjoy the visual parade of canal wonders, I've organized this tour by boat stop. I'll point out both what you can see from the current stop, and what to look forward to as you cruise to the next stop.

You can break up the tour by hopping on and off at various sights—but remember, a single-fare vaporetto ticket is good for just 75 minutes (passes let you hop on and off all day).

Length of This Tour: Allow 45 minutes. With limited time, take the 25-minute express vaporetto #2. Or do only half the trip—choose either Ferrovia-to-Rialto or Rialto-to-San Marco. Early and late in the day, the vaporetto #2 terminates at Rialto; you'll have to get off and switch to #1 to do the whole tour.

Tours: ⋒ Download my free Grand Canal Cruise audio tour.

Where to Sit: Some *vaporetti* have seats in the bow (in front of the captain's bridge), the perfect vantage point for spotting sights left, right, and forward. Otherwise, your options include sitting inside (and viewing the passing sights through windows); standing in the open middle deck (where you can move from side to side when the boat's not crowded—especially easy after dark); or sitting outside in the back (where you'll miss the wonderful forward views). For views, the left side has a slight edge, with more sights and the best light late in the day.

OVERVIEW

The Grand Canal is Venice's "Main Street." At more than two miles long, nearly 150 feet wide, and nearly 15 feet deep, it's the city's largest canal, lined with its most impressive palaces. It's the remnant of a river that once spilled from the mainland into the Adriatic. The sediment it carried formed barrier islands that cut Venice off from the sea, forming a lagoon.

Venice was built on the marshy islands of the former delta, sitting on wood pilings driven nearly 15 feet into the clay (alder was the preferred wood). About

25 miles of canals drain the city, dumping like streams into the Grand Canal. Technically, Venice has only three canals: Grand, Giudecca, and Cannaregio. The 45 small waterways that dump into the Grand Canal are referred to as rivers (e.g., Rio Novo).

Venice is a city of palaces, dating from the days when the city was the world's richest. The most lavish palaces formed a grand architectural cancan along the Grand Canal. Once frescoed in reds and blues, with black-and-white borders and gold-leaf trim, they made Venice a city of dazzling color. This cruise is the only way to truly appreciate the palaces, approaching them at water level, where their main entrances were located. Today, strict laws prohibit any changes in these buildings, so while landowners gnash their teeth, we can enjoy Europe's best-preserved medieval/Renaissance city—slowly rotting. Many of the grand buildings are now vacant. Others harbor chandeliered elegance above mossy, empty (often flooded) ground floors.

◉ SELF-GUIDED CRUISE

This tour starts at the Ferrovia vaporetto stop (at Santa Lucia train station). If you want to board upstream at the less-crowded Piazzale Roma, it's a five-minute walk over the Calatrava Bridge from the Ferrovia stop. At Piazzale Roma, check the electronic boards to see which dock the next #1 or #2 is leaving from, hop on board

Grand Canal

VENICE

To Jewish Ghetto

STRADA

GUGLIE BRIDGE

Candle de Camaregio

SAN MARCUOLA

PALAZZO CORRER CONTARINI

SAN GEREMIA

PALAZZO GRITTI

CASINO

PALAZZO VENDRAMIN CALERGI

LISTA DI SPAGNA

PALAZZO FLANGINI

Canal

TURKISH EXCHANGE

SCALZI

SANTA LUCIA TRAIN STATION (FERROVIA)

PALAZZO CALBO CROTTA

Grand

PALAZZO GIOVANELLI

PALAZZO MARCELLO

SAN ZAN DEGOLA

PALAZZO CA'TRON

PAL. GRITTI

PALAZZO DONA BALBI

SCALZI BRIDGE

SAN SIMEONE PICCOLO

SANTA CROCE

CALATRAVA BRIDGE

SAN

PIAZZALE ROMA & PEOPLE MOVER TO STAZIONE MARITTIMA & TRONCHETTO

FRARI

PALAZZO CAPPELLO-LAYARD

Vaporetto Stops

① Ferrovia
② Riva de Biasio
③ San Marcuola
④ San Stae
⑤ Ca' d'Oro
⑥ Rialto Mercato
⑦ Rialto
⑧ San Silvestro
⑨ Sant'Angelo
⑩ San Tomà
⑪ Ca' Rezzonico
⑫ Accademia
⑬ Santa Maria del Giglio
⑭ Salute
⑮ San Marco – Giardinetti
⑯ San Marco – San Zaccaria

SAN TOMÀ

PALAZZO GIUSTINIANI

PALAZZO BARBARIGO

PALAZZO BALBI

FIRE STATION

CA' FOSCARI

PALAZZO GIUSTINIAN

CA' REZZONICO

PALAZZO MOCENIGO

PALAZZO VECCHIA

PALAZZO MORO LIN

PALAZZO GRASSI

PALAZZO MALIPIERO-CAPPELLO

PALAZZO LOREDAN

PALAZZO FALIER

PALAZZO GIUSTINIAN LOLIN

PALAZZO CONTARINI DEGLI SCRIGNI

PALAZZO QUERINI

ACCADEMIA BRIDGE & GALLERY

PALAZZO BARBARO

PALAZZO BARBARIGO

FONDAMENTA ZATTERE AL PONTE LONGO

DORSODURO

Giudecca Canal

To Zattere

to get your pick of seats, and start reading the tour when your vaporetto reaches Ferrovia.

❶ Ferrovia: This site has been the gateway into Venice since 1860, when the first train station was built. The **Santa Lucia station,** one of the few modern build-

ings in town, was built in 1954. The "F.S." logo above the entry stands for "Ferrovie dello Stato," the Italian state railway system. Consider that before the causeway was built in the mid-1800s, Venice was an island with no road or train access and no water system. With the causeway the city got a train line, an aqueduct, and a highway.

More than 20,000 people a day commute in from the mainland, making this the busiest part of Venice during rush hour. The **Calatrava Bridge,** spanning the Grand Canal between the train station and Piazzale Roma upstream, was built in 2008 to alleviate some of the congestion.

❷ Riva de Biasio: Venice's main thoroughfare is busy with all kinds of **boats:** taxis, police boats, garbage boats, ambulances, construction cranes, and even brown-and-white UPS boats. Somehow they all manage to share the canal in relative peace.

About 25 yards past the Riva de Biasio stop, look left down the broad **Cannaregio Canal** to see what was the **Jewish Ghetto.** The twin, pale-pink, six-story "skyscrapers"—the tallest buildings you'll see at this end of the canal—are reminders of how densely populated the world's original ghetto was. Set aside as the local Jewish quarter in 1516, this area became extremely crowded. This urban island developed into one of the most closely knit business and cultural quarters of all the Jewish communities in Italy, and gave us our word "ghetto" (from *geto,* the copper foundry located here).

❸ San Marcuola: At this stop, facing a tiny square just ahead, stands the unfinished Church of San Marcuola, one of only five churches fronting the Grand Canal.

Centuries ago, this canal was a commercial drag of expensive real estate in high demand by wealthy merchants. About 20 yards ahead on the right (across the Grand Canal) stands the stately gray **Turkish Exchange** (Fondaco dei Turchi), one of the oldest houses in Venice. Its horseshoe arches and roofline of triangles and dingle balls are reminders of its Byzantine heritage. Turkish traders

in turbans docked here, unloaded their goods into the warehouse on the bottom story, then went upstairs for a home-style meal and a place to sleep. Venice in the 1500s was very cosmopolitan, welcoming every religion and ethnicity, so long as they carried cash. (Today the building contains the city's Museum of Natural History—and Venice's only dinosaur skeleton.)

Just 100 yards ahead on the left (the tallest building with the red canopy), Venice's **Casinò** is housed in the palace where German composer Richard *(The Ring)* Wagner died in 1883. See his distinct, strong-jawed profile in the white plaque on the brick wall. In the 1700s, Venice was Europe's Vegas, with casinos and prostitutes everywhere. *Casinòs* ("little houses" in Venetian dialect) have long provided Italians with a handy escape from daily life. Today they're run by the state to keep Mafia influence at bay. Notice the fancy front porch, rolling out the red carpet for high rollers arriving by taxi or hotel boat. Across the canal, the plain brick 15th-century building was a granary. Now it's a grade school.

❹ San Stae: The San Stae Church sports a delightful Baroque facade. Opposite the San Stae stop is a little canal opening—on the second building to the right of that opening, look for the peeling plaster that once made up **frescoes** (you can barely distinguish the scant remains of little angels on the lower floors). Imagine the facades of the Grand Canal at their finest. Most of them would have been covered in frescoes by the best artists of the day. As colorful as the city is today, it's still only a faded, sepia-toned remnant of a long-gone era, a time of lavishly decorated, brilliantly colored palaces.

Just ahead (on the right, with blue posts) is the ornate white facade of **Ca' Pesaro,** which houses the International Gallery of Modern Art. *"Ca'"* is short for *casa* (house).

In this city of masks, notice how the rich marble facades along the Grand Canal mask what are generally just simple, no-nonsense brick buildings. Most merchants enjoyed showing off. However, being smart businessmen, they only decorated the sides of the buildings that would be seen and appreciated. But look back as you pass Ca' Pesaro. It's the only building you'll see with a fine side facade. Ahead (about 100 yards on the left) is Ca' d'Oro, with its glorious triple-decker medieval arcade (just before the next stop).

❺ Ca' d'Oro: The lacy Ca' d'Oro (House of Gold) is the best example of Venetian Gothic architecture on the canal. Although a simple brick construction, its facade is one of the city's finest. Its three

stories offer different variations on balcony design, topped with a spiny white roofline. Venetian Gothic mixes traditional Gothic (pointed arches and round medallions stamped with a four-leaf clover) with Byzantine styles (tall, narrow arches atop thin columns), filled in with Islamic frills. Like all the palaces, this was originally painted and gilded to make it even more glorious than it is now. Today the Ca' d'Oro is an art gallery.

Look at the Venetian chorus line of palaces in front of the boat. On the right is the arcade of the covered **fish market,** with the open-air **produce market** just beyond. It bustles in the morning but is quiet the rest of the day. This is a great scene to wander through—even though European Union hygiene standards have made it cleaner but less colorful than it once was.

Find the ***traghetto*** gondola ferrying shoppers—standing like Washington crossing the Delaware—back and forth. While once much more numerable, today only three *traghetto* crossings survive along the Grand Canal, each one marked by a classy low-key green-and-black sign. Piloting a *traghetto* isn't the normal day job of these gondoliers. As a public service, all gondoliers are obliged to row a *traghetto* a few days a month. Make a point to use them. At

€2 a ride, *traghetti* offer the cheapest gondola rides in Venice (but at this price, don't expect them to sing to you).

❻ Rialto Mercato: This stop serves the busy market. The long, official-looking building at the stop is the Venice courthouse. Directly ahead (on the left), is the former **German Exchange** (Fondaco dei Tedeschi, a trading center for German merchants in the 16th century). It was the central post office and is slated to be a modern shopping center. Rising above it is the tip of the Campanile (bell tower), crowned by its golden angel weathervane at St. Mark's Square, where this tour will end.

You'll cruise by some trendy and beautifully situated wine bars on the right, but look ahead as you round the corner and see the impressive Rialto Bridge come into view.

A major landmark of Venice, the **Rialto Bridge** is lined with shops and tourists. Constructed in 1588, it's the third bridge built on this spot. Until the 1850s, this was the only bridge crossing

the Grand Canal. With a span of 160 feet and foundations stretching 650 feet on either side, the Rialto was an impressive engineering feat in its day. Earlier bridges here could open to let big ships in, but not this one. By the time it was completed in the 16th century, Venetian trading power was ebbing. After that, much of the Grand Canal was closed to shipping and became a canal of palaces.

When gondoliers pass under the fat arch of the Rialto Bridge, they take full advantage of its acoustics: *"Volare, oh, oh..."*

❼ **Rialto:** A separate town in the early days of Venice, Rialto has always been the commercial district, while San Marco was the religious and governmental center. Today, a winding street called the Mercerie connects the two, providing travelers with human traffic jams and a mesmerizing gauntlet of shopping temptations. This is one of the only stretches of the historic Grand Canal with landings upon which you can walk. Boats unloaded the city's basic necessities here: oil, wine, charcoal, iron. Today, the quay is lined with tourist-trap restaurants.

Venice's sleek, black, graceful **gondolas** are a symbol of the city (for more on gondolas, see page 73). With about 500 gondoliers joyriding amid the churning *vaporetti,* there's a lot of congestion on the Grand Canal. Pay attention—this is where most of the gondola and vaporetto accidents take place. While the Rialto is the highlight of many gondola rides, gondoliers understandably prefer the quieter small canals. Watch your vaporetto driver curse the better-paid gondoliers.

Ahead 100 yards on the left, two gray-colored **palaces** stand side by side (City Hall and the mayor's office). Their horseshoe-shaped, arched windows are similar and their stories are the same height, lining up to create the effect of one long balcony.

❽ **San Silvestro:** We now enter a long stretch of important **merchants' palaces,** each with proud and different facades. Because ships couldn't navigate beyond the Rialto Bridge, the biggest palaces—with the major shipping needs—line this last stretch of the navigable Grand Canal.

Palaces like these were multi-functional: ground floor for the warehouse, offices and showrooms upstairs, and living quarters above, on the "noble floors" (with big windows to allow in maximum light). Servants lived and worked on the very top floors (with the smallest windows). For fire-safety reasons, kitchens were also located on the top floors. Peek into the noble floors to catch a glimpse of their still-glorious chandeliers of Murano glass.

The **Palazzo Grimani** (across from the San Silvestro dock)

VENICE

sports a heavy white Roman-style facade—a reminder that the Grimani family included a cardinal and had strong Roman connections.

The **Palazzo Papadopoli,** with the two obelisks on its roof (50 yards beyond the San Silvestro stop on the right, with the blue posts), is the very fancy Aman Hotel where George Clooney was married in 2014.

❾ Sant'Angelo: Notice how many buildings have a foundation of waterproof white stone *(pietra d'Istria)* upon which the bricks sit high and dry. Many canal-level floors are abandoned as the rising water level takes its toll.

The **posts**—historically painted gaily with the equivalent of family coats of arms—don't rot underwater. But the wood at the waterline, where it's exposed to oxygen, does. On the smallest canals, little "no motorboats" signs indicate that these canals are for gondolas only (no motorized craft, 5 kph speed limit, no wake).

❿ San Tomà: Fifty yards ahead, on the right side (with twin obelisks on the rooftop) stands **Palazzo Balbi,** the palace of an early-17th-century captain general of the sea. This palace, like so many in the city, flies three flags: Italy (green-white-red), the European Union (blue with ring of stars), and Venice (a lion on a field of red and gold). Today it houses the administrative headquarters of the regional government.

Just past the admiral's palace, look immediately to the right, down a side canal. On the right side of that canal, before the bridge, see the traffic light and the **fire station** (the 1930s Mussolini-era building with four arches hiding fireboats parked and ready to go).

The impressive **Ca' Foscari,** with a classic Venetian facade (on the corner, across from the fire station), dominates the bend in the canal. This is the main building of the University of Venice, which has about 25,000 students. Notice the elegant lamp on the corner—needed in the old days to light this intersection.

The grand, heavy, white **Ca' Rezzonico,** just before the stop of the same name, houses the Museum of 18th-Century Venice (described on page 67). Across the canal is the cleaner and leaner **Palazzo Grassi,** the last major palace built on the canal, erected in the late

1700s. It was purchased by a French tycoon and now displays part of Punta della Dogana's contemporary art collection.

⓫ **Ca' Rezzonico:** Up ahead, the Accademia Bridge leads over the Grand Canal to the **Accademia Gallery** (right side), filled with the best Venetian paintings (described on page 66). There was no bridge here until 1854, when a cast-iron one was built. It was replaced with this wooden bridge in 1933. While meant to be temporary, it still stands today, nearly a century later.

⓬ **Accademia:** From here, look through the graceful bridge and way ahead to enjoy a classic view of **La Salute Church,** topped by a crown-shaped dome supported by scrolls (described on page 67). This Church of St. Mary of Good Health was built to ask God to deliver Venetians from the devastating plague of 1630 (which had killed about a third of the city's population).

The low, white building among greenery (100 yards ahead, on the right, between the Accademia Bridge and the church) is the **Peggy Guggenheim Collection.** The American heiress "retired" here, sprucing up a palace that had been abandoned in midconstruction. Peggy willed the city her fine collection of modern art (described on page 67).

Two doors past the Guggenheim, Palazzo Dario has a great

set of characteristic **funnel-shaped chimneys.** These forced embers through a loop-the-loop channel until they were dead—required in the days when stone palaces were surrounded by humble wooden buildings, and a live spark could make a merchant's workforce homeless. Three doors later is the **Salviati building,** which once served as a glassworks. Its fine Art Nouveau mosaic, done in the early 20th century, features Venice as a queen being appreciated by the big shots of society.

⓭ **Santa Maria del Giglio:** Back on the left stands the fancy Gritti Palace hotel. Hemingway and Woody Allen both stayed here (but not together).

Take a deep whiff of Venice. What's all this nonsense about stinky canals? All I smell is my shirt. By the way, how's your captain? Smooth dockings?

❶ **Salute:** The huge La Salute Church towers overhead as if squirted from a can of Catholic Reddi-wip.

As the Grand Canal opens up into the lagoon, the last building on the right with the golden ball is the 17th-century **Customs House,** which now houses the Punta della Dogana contemporary art museum (see page 67). Its two bronze Atlases hold a statue of Fortune riding the ball. Arriving ships stopped here to pay their tolls.

❶ **San Marco:** Up ahead on the left, the green pointed tip of the Campanile marks **St. Mark's Square,** the political and religious center of Venice... and the final destination of this tour. You could get off at the San Marco stop and go straight to St. Mark's Square (and you'll have to if you're on vaporetto #2, which terminates here). But I'm staying on the #1 boat for one more stop, just past St. Mark's Square (it's a quick walk back).

Survey the lagoon. Opposite St. Mark's Square, across the water, the ghostly white church with the pointy bell tower is San Giorgio Maggiore, with great views of Venice (see page 65). Next to it is the residential island Giudecca, stretching from close to San Giorgio Maggiore past the Venice youth hostel (with a nice view, directly across) to the Hilton Hotel (good nighttime view, far right end of island).

Still on board? If you are, as we leave the San Marco stop look left and prepare for a drive-by view of St. Mark's Square. First comes the bold white facade of the old mint (in front of the bell tower) marked by a tiny cupola yet as sturdy as Fort Knox, where Venice's golden ducat, the "dollar" of the Venetian Republic, was made. Next door is the library, its facade just three windows wide. Then comes the city's ceremonial front door: twin columns topped by St. Theodore and the winged lion of St. Mark, who've welcomed visitors since the 15th century. Between the columns, catch a glimpse of two giant figures atop the **Clock Tower**—they've been whacking their clappers every hour since 1499. The domes of **St. Mark's Basilica** are soon eclipsed by the lacy facade of the **Doge's Palace.** Next you'll see many gondolas with their green breakwater buoys, the **Bridge of Sighs** (leading from the palace to the prison—

check out the maximum-security bars), and finally the grand harborside promenade—the **Riva.**

Follow the Riva with your eye, past elegant hotels to the green area in the distance. This is the largest of Venice's few **parks,** which hosts the annual Biennale festival (see page 75). Much farther in the distance is the **Lido,** the island with Venice's beach. Its sand and casinos are tempting, though given its car traffic, it lacks the medieval charm of Venice.

 ⑯ San Zaccaria: OK, you're at your last stop. Quick—muscle your way off this boat! (If you don't, you'll eventually end up at the Lido.)

At San Zaccaria, you're right in the thick of the action. A number of other *vaporetti* depart from here (see page 32). Otherwise, it's a short walk back along the Riva to St. Mark's Square. Ahoy!

Sights in Venice

Venice's city museums offer youth and senior discounts to Americans and other non-EU citizens. When you see a 🎧 in a listing, it means the sight is covered in a free audio tour (via my Rick Steves Audio Europe app—see page 12).

SIGHTSEEING PASSES FOR VENICE

Venice offers a dizzying array of combo-tickets and sightseeing passes. For most people, the best choice is the Museum Pass, which covers entry into the Doge's Palace, Correr Museum, and more. Note that seven of the most visit-worthy sights in town (the Accademia, Peggy Guggenheim Collection, Scuola San Rocco, Campanile, and the three sights within St. Mark's Basilica that charge admission) are not covered by any pass.

All of the passes described below are sold at the TI (except for the combo-ticket), and most are also available at participating sights.

Combo-Ticket: A €19 combo-ticket covers both the Doge's Palace and the Correr Museum. To bypass the long ticket-buying line at the Doge's Palace, buy your combo-ticket at the never-crowded Correr Museum (or online). These two sights are also covered by the Museum Pass and Venice Card.

Museum Pass: Busy sightseers may prefer this more expensive pass, which covers these city-run museums: the Doge's Palace; Correr Museum; Ca' Rezzonico (Museum of 18th-Century Venice); Palazzo Mocenigo Costume Museum; Casa Goldoni (home of the Italian playwright); Ca' Pesaro (modern art); Museum of Natural History in the Santa Croce district; the Glass Museum on the island of Murano; and the Lace Museum on the island of

VENICE

Burano. At €24, this pass is the best value if you plan to see the Doge's Palace/Correr Museum and even just one of the other covered museums. You can buy it at any of the participating museums or via their websites.

Chorus Pass: This pass gives church lovers admission to 18 of Venice's churches and their art (generally €3 each) for €12 (www.chorusvenezia.org). The Frari church is included, but not St. Mark's. The typical tourist is unlikely to see more than two of these.

Venice Card: This pass (also called a "city pass") combines the 11 city-run museums and the 16 churches covered by the Chorus Pass, plus a few minor discounts, for €40. A cheaper variation, San Marco Pack, is more selective: It covers the Correr Museum, Doge's Palace, and your choice of any three churches for €28. But it's hard to make either of these passes pay off (valid for 7 days, www.veneziaunica.com).

Rolling Venice: This youth pass offers discounts at dozens of sights and shops, but its best deal is for transit. If you're under 30 and want to buy a 72-hour transit pass, it'll cost you just €22—rather than €40—with the Rolling Venice pass (€6 pass for ages 14-29, sold at TIs, vaporetto ticket offices, and VèneziaUnica shops; for more info see www.veneziaunica.it and search for "Rolling Venice").

Transportation Passes: Venice sells transit-only passes that cover *vaporetti* and mainland buses. For a rundown on these, see "Getting Around Venice," earlier.

SAN MARCO DISTRICT
▲▲▲St. Mark's Square (Piazza San Marco)

This grand square is surrounded by splashy, historic buildings and sights: St. Mark's Basilica, the Doge's Palace, the Campanile bell tower, and the Correr Museum. The square is filled with music, lovers, pigeons, and tourists by day, and is your private rendezvous with the Venetian past late at night, when Europe's most magnificent dance floor is *the* romantic place to be.

∩ For a detailed explanation of St. Mark's Square, download my free audio tour.

Visiting the Square: St. Mark's Basilica dominates the square with its Eastern-style onion domes and glowing mosaics. Mark Twain said it looked like "a vast warty bug taking a meditative walk." (I say it looks like tiara-wearing ladybugs copulating.) To the right of the basilica is its 325-foot-tall Campanile. Behind the Campanile, you can catch a glimpse of the pale-pink Doge's Palace. Lining the square are the former government offices *(procuratie)* that managed the treasury of St. Mark's, back when the church and state were one, and administered the Venetian empire's

St. Mark's Square

Eateries & Entertainment

1. Caffè Florian
2. Gran Caffè Quadri
3. Gran Caffè Lavena
4. Gran Caffè Chioggia
5. Eden Bar
6. Caffè Aurora

Other

7. Galleria San Marco Glassblowing
8. Il Merletto Lace Shop
9. Libreria Studium Bookstore
10. Oltrex Travel

vast network of trading outposts, which stretched all the way to Turkey.

With your back to the church, survey one of Europe's great urban spaces, and the only square in Venice to merit the title "Piazza." Nearly two football fields long, it's surrounded by the offices of the republic. On the right are the "old offices" (16th-century Renaissance). At left are the "new offices" (17th-century High Renaissance). Napoleon called the piazza "the most beautiful drawing room in Europe," and added to the intimacy by building the final wing, opposite the basilica, that encloses the square.

The arcade ringing the square, formerly lined with dozens of fine cafés, still provides an elegant promenade—complete with drapery that is dropped when necessary to provide relief from the sun.

Imagine this square full of water. That happens every so often at very high tides *(acqua alta)*, a reminder that Venice and the sea are intertwined. (Now that one is sinking and the other is rising, they are more intertwined than ever.)

Watch out for pigeon speckle. Venetians don't like pigeons, but they do like seagulls—because they eat pigeons. In 2008, Venice outlawed the feeding of pigeons. But tourists—eager for a pigeon-clad photo op—haven't gotten that message.

The original **Campanile** (cam-pah-NEE-lay, bell tower) was an observation tower and a marvel of medieval and Renaissance architecture until 1902, when it toppled into the center of the piazza. It was rebuilt 10 years later; an elevator takes you to the top (see page 64 for more about the Campanile).

For a slow and pricey evening thrill, invest €15 or so (including any cover charge for the music) for a drink at one of the elegant cafés with the dueling orchestras (see "Cafés on St. Mark's Square," page 60). For an unmatched experience that offers the best people-watching, it's worth the splurge.

The **Clock Tower** (Torre dell'Orologio), built during the Renaissance in 1496, marks the entry to the main shopping drag,

called the Mercerie (or "Marzarie," in Venetian dialect), which connects St. Mark's Square with the Rialto Bridge. From the piazza, you can see the bronze men (Moors) swing their huge clappers at the top of each hour. In the 17th century, one of them knocked an unsuspecting worker off the top and to his death—probably the first-ever killing by a robot. The tower sports one of the world's first "digital" clocks (with dramatic flips every five minutes).

You can go inside the Clock Tower with a prebooked guided tour that takes you close to the clock's innards and out to a terrace with good views over the square and city rooftops (€12 combo-ticket includes Correr Museum—where the tour starts—but not Doge's Palace; €7 for the tour if you already have a Museum Pass or Correr/Doge's Palace combo-ticket; tours in English Mon-Wed at 10:00 and 11:00, Thu-Sun at 14:00 and 15:00; no kids under age 6). While reservations are required for the Clock Tower tour, you have a decent chance of being able to "reserve" on the spot—try dropping by the Correr Museum for same-day (or day-before) tickets. To ensure a spot in advance, reserve by calling 848-082-000, or book online at http://torreorologio.visitmuve.it.

The small square between the basilica and the water is the **Pi-azzetta.** This "Little Square" is framed by the Doge's Palace on the left, the library on the right, and the waterfront of the lagoon. The pale-pink **Doge's Palace** is the epitome of the style known as Venetian Gothic. Columns support traditional, pointed Gothic arches, but with a Venetian flair—they're curved to a point, ornamented with a trefoil (three-leaf clover), and topped with a round medallion of a quatrefoil (four-leaf clover). The pattern is found on buildings all over Venice and on the formerly Venetian-controlled Croatian coast, but nowhere else in the world (except Las Vegas).

Where the basilica meets the Doge's Palace is the traditional entrance to the palace, decorated with four small Roman statues—the **Tetrarchs.** No one knows for sure who they are, but I like the legend that says they're the scared leaders of a divided Rome during its fall, holding their swords and each other as all hell breaks loose around them.

The two large 12th-century **columns** near the water were looted from Constantinople. Mark's winged lion sits on top of one. The lion's body (nearly 15 feet long) predates the wings and is more than 2,000 years old. The other column holds St. Theodore (battling a crocodile), the former patron saint who was replaced by Mark. In the distance, on an island across the lagoon, is one of the grandest views in the city, of the **Church of San Giorgio Maggiore.** With its four tall columns as the entryway, the church, designed by the late-Renaissance architect Andrea Palladio, influenced the appearance of future government and bank buildings around the world.

▲▲▲St. Mark's Basilica (Basilica di San Marco)

Built in the 11th century to replace an earlier church, this basilica's distinctly Eastern-style architecture underlines Venice's connec-

tion with Byzantium (which protected it from the ambition of Charlemagne and his Holy Roman Empire). It's decorated with booty from returning sea captains—a kind of architectural Venetian trophy chest. The interior glows mysteriously with gold mosaics and colored marble. Since about A.D. 830, the saint's bones have been housed on this site.

Cost and Hours: Basilica entry is free, except if you pay €2 for an online reservation that lets you skip the line. Three interior sights charge admission (see next). Church open Mon-Sat 9:45-17:00, Sun 14:00-17:00 (Sun until 16:00 Nov-Easter), interior

VENICE

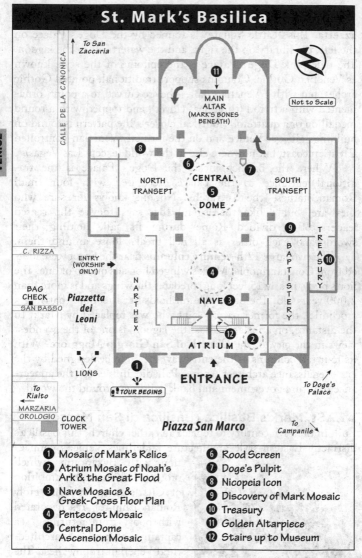

St. Mark's Basilica

Not to Scale

To San Zaccaria

CALLE DE LA CANONICA

11 MAIN ALTAR (MARK'S BONES BENEATH)

8

6 CENTRAL **5** DOME

7

NORTH TRANSEPT

SOUTH TRANSEPT

9

C. RIZZA

ENTRY (WORSHIP ONLY)

BAG CHECK
SAN BASSO

Piazzetta dei Leoni

N A R T H E X

4

NAVE **3**

B A P T I S T E R Y

T R E A S U R Y

10

To Rialto

MARZARIA OROLOGIO

LIONS

1

2

12

ATRIUM

ENTRANCE

CLOCK TOWER

📱 TOUR BEGINS

Piazza San Marco

To Doge's Palace

To Campanile

1 Mosaic of Mark's Relics
2 Atrium Mosaic of Noah's Ark & the Great Flood
3 Nave Mosaics & Greek-Cross Floor Plan
4 Pentecost Mosaic
5 Central Dome Ascension Mosaic
6 Rood Screen
7 Doge's Pulpit
8 Nicopeia Icon
9 Discovery of Mark Mosaic
10 Treasury
11 Golden Altarpiece
12 Stairs up to Museum

brilliantly lit daily 11:30-12:30, museum open daily 9:45-16:45, including on Sunday mornings when the church itself is closed; if considering a Sunday visit, note that the museum has a balcony that provides a fine view down to the church's interior. The treasury and the Golden Altarpiece are both open Easter-Oct Mon-Sat 9:45-17:00, Sun 14:00-17:00; Nov-Easter Mon-Sat 9:45-16:00, Sun 14:00-16:00; St. Mark's Square, vaporetto: San Marco or San Zaccaria. Tel. 041-270-8311, www.basilicasanmarco.it.

Three separate exhibits within the church charge admission: the **Treasury** (€3, includes audioguide), **Golden Altarpiece** (€2), and **San Marco Museum** (€5). The San Marco Museum has the original bronze horses (copies of these overlook the square), a balcony offering a remarkable view over St. Mark's Square, and various works related to the church.

Dress Code: Modest dress (no bare knees or bare shoulders) is strictly enforced for men, women, and even kids. Shorts are OK if they cover the knees.

Bag Check (and Skipping the Line): Small purses and shoulder bags are usually allowed inside, but larger bags and backpacks are not. Check them for free for up to one hour at the nearby church called Ateneo San Basso, 30 yards to the left of the basilica, down narrow Calle San Basso (see map on facing page; daily 9:30-17:00). Note that you generally can't check small bags that would be allowed inside. Those with a bag to check usually get to skip the line, as do their companions (meaning about one or two others—keep it within reason; this is at the guard's discretion). Leave your bag at Ateneo San Basso and pick up your claim tag. Take your tag to the basilica's tourist entrance. Keep to the left of the railing where the line forms and show your tag to the gatekeeper. He'll generally let you in, ahead of the line.

Theft Alert: St. Mark's Basilica is the most notorious place in Venice for pickpocketing—inside, it's always a crowded jostle.

Tours: Free, hour-long English tours (heavy on the mosaics' religious symbolism) are offered many days at 11:30 (meet in atrium, schedule varies, see schedule board just inside entrance).

∩ Download my free St. Mark's Basilica audio tour.

◐ Self-Guided Tour

Start outside in the square, far enough back to take in the whole facade. It's a riot of domes, columns, and statues, completely unlike the towering Gothic churches of northern Europe or the heavy Baroque of much of the rest of Italy. Inside is a decor of mosaics, colored marbles, and oriental treasures that's rarely seen elsewhere. The Christian symbolism is unfamiliar to Western eyes, done in the style of Byzantine icons and even Islamic designs. Older than most of Europe's churches, St. Mark's feels like a remnant of a lost world.

The church is encrusted with materials looted from buildings throughout the Venetian empire. Their prize booty was the four bronze horses that adorn the balcony, stolen from Constantinople during the Fourth Crusade (these are copies); the atrium you're about to enter was added on to the church as their pedestal. Later, it was decorated with a mishmash of plundered columns. The architectural style of St. Mark's has been called "Early Ransack."

Is Venice Sinking?

Venice has battled rising water levels since the fifth century. But today, the water seems to be winning. Several factors, both natural and man-made, cause Venice to flood about 100 times a year—usually from October until late winter—a phenomenon called the *acqua alta.*

On my last trip I asked a Venetian how much the city is sinking. He said, "Less than the sea is rising." Venice sits atop sediments deposited at the ancient mouth of the Po River, which are still compacting and settling. Early industrial projects, such as offshore piers and the railroad bridge to the mainland, affected the sea floor and tidal cycles in ways that made the city more vulnerable to flooding. Twentieth-century industry worsened things by pumping massive amounts of groundwater out of the aquifer beneath the lagoon for nearly 50 years before the government stopped the practice in the 1970s. In the last century, Venice has sunk by about nine inches.

Meanwhile, the waters around Venice are rising, a phenomenon that's especially apparent in winter. The highest so far was in November of 1966, when a huge storm (the same one that famously flooded Florence) raised Venice's water level to more than six feet above the norm. The notorious *acqua alta* happens when an unusually high tide combines with strong sirocco winds and a storm. Although tides are minuscule in the Mediterranean, the narrow, shallow Adriatic Sea has about a three-foot tidal range. When a storm—an area of low pressure—travels over a body of water, it pulls the surface of the water up into a dome. As strong sirocco winds from Africa blow storms north up the Adriatic, they push this high water ahead of the front, causing a surging storm tide. Add to that the worldwide sea-level rise that's resulted from recent climate change (melting ice caps, thermal expansion of the water, more frequent and more powerful storms) and it makes a high sea that much higher.

If the *acqua alta* appears during your visit, you'll see the first

Now zero in on the details.

❶ Exterior—Mosaic of Mark's Relics: The **mosaic over the far left door** shows two men (in the center, with crooked staffs) bearing a coffin with the body of St. Mark. Eight centuries after Mark's death, his holy body was in Muslim-occupied Alexandria, Egypt. In A.D. 829, two visiting Venetian merchants "rescued" the body from the "infidels" and spirited it away to Venice.

puddles in the center of paved squares, pooling around the limestone grates at the square's lowest point. These grates cover cisterns that long held Venice's only source of drinking water. That's right: Surrounded by the lagoon and beset by constant flooding, this city had no natural source of fresh water. For centuries, resi-

dents carried water from the mainland with much effort and risk. In the ninth century, they devised a way to collect rainwater by using paved, cleverly sloped squares as catchment systems, with limestone filters covering underground clay tubs. Venice's population grew markedly once citizens were able to access fresh water by simply dropping buckets down into these "wells."

Several thousand cisterns provided the city with drinking water up until 1884, when an aqueduct was built (paralleling the railroad bridge) to bring in water from nearby mountains. Now the wells are capped, the clay tubs are rotted out, and rain drains from squares into the lagoon—or up from it, as the case may be.

So, what is Venice doing about the flooding? After the 1966 flood, officials knew something had to be done, but it took about four decades to come up with a solution. In 2003, a consortium of engineering firms began construction on the MOSE Project. Named for the acronym of its Italian name, *Modulo Sperimentale Elettromeccanico*, it's also a nod to Moses and his (albeit temporary) mastery over the sea.

Underwater "mobile" gates are being installed on the floor of the sea at the three inlets where the open sea enters Venice's lagoon. When the seawater rises above a certain level, air will be pumped into the gates, causing them to rise and shut out the Adriatic. The first gates are already installed and on the verge of becoming operational. But, in good Italian fashion, greedy government officials were unable to resist the opportunity for personal enrichment and a corruption scandal has stranded the entire project for the foreseeable future.

• *Enter the atrium of the basilica, and look up and to the right into an archway decorated with fine mosaics.*

❷ **Atrium—Mosaic of Noah's Ark and the Great Flood:** In the scene to the right of the entry door, Noah and sons are sawing logs to build a boat. Below that are three scenes of Noah putting all species of animals into the ark, two by two. Across the arch, the flood hits in full force, drowning the wicked. Noah sends out a dove twice to see whether there's any dry land where he can dock.

He finds it, leaves the Ark with a gorgeous rainbow overhead, and offers a sacrifice of thanks to God.

• *Climb seven steps, pass through the doorway, and enter the nave. Just inside the door, step to the far left, stop, let your eyes adjust, and survey the church.*

❸ The Nave—Mosaics and Greek-Cross Floor Plan: These golden mosaics are in the Byzantine style, though many were designed by artists from the Italian Renaissance and later. The often-overlooked lower walls are covered with green-, yellow-, purple-, and rose-colored marble slabs, cut to expose the grain, and laid out in geometric patterns. Even the floor is mosaic, with mostly geometrical designs. It rolls like the sea. Venice is sinking and shifting, creating these cresting waves of stone. The

church is laid out with four equal arms, topped with domes, radiating out from the center to form a Greek cross (+).

• *Find the chandelier near the entrance doorway (in the shape of a Greek cross cathedral space station), and run your eyes up the support chain to the dome above.*

❹ Pentecost Mosaic: In a golden heaven, the dove of the Holy Spirit shoots out a pinwheel of spiritual lasers, igniting tongues of fire on the heads of the 12 apostles below, giving them the ability to speak other languages without a Rick Steves phrase book. You'd think they'd be amazed, but their expressions are as solemn as...icons. One of the oldest mosaics in the church (c. 1125), it has distinct "Byzantine" features: a gold background and apostles with halos, solemn faces, almond eyes, delicate blessing hands, and rumpled robes, all facing forward.

• *Shuffle along with the crowds up to the central dome.*

❺ Central Dome—Ascension Mosaic: Gape upward to the very heart of the church. Christ—having lived his miraculous life and having been crucified for man's sins—ascends into the starry sky on a rainbow. In Byzantine churches, the window-lit dome represented heaven, while the dark church below represented earth—a microcosm of the hierarchical universe.

Under the Ascension Dome: Look around at the church's furniture and imagine a service here. The **❻ rood screen,** (like the iconostasis in a Greek church) topped with 14 saints, separates the congregation from the high altar, heightening the "mystery" of the Mass. The **❼ pulpit** on the right was reserved for the doge, who led prayers and made important announcements.

North Transept: In the north transept (left of the altar), today's Venetians pray to a painted wooden icon of Mary and Baby Jesus known as ❽ **Nicopeia,** or Our Lady of Victory (it's a small painting crusted over with a big stone canopy). In its day, this was the ultimate trophy—the actual icon, used to protect the Byzantine army in war, looted by the Crusaders.

• *In the south transept (right of main altar), find the dim mosaic high up on the three-windowed wall above the entrance to the treasury.*

❾ **Discovery of Mark Mosaic:** This mosaic isn't a biblical scene; it depicts the miraculous event that capped the construction of the present church. (It's high up and hard to read.)

It's 1094, the church is nearly complete (see the domes shown in cutaway fashion), and it's time to reinter Mark's bones under the new altar. There's just one problem: During the decades of construction, locals forgot where they'd stored his body!

So (on the left), all of Venice gathers inside the church to bow down and pray for help finding the bones. The doge (from the Latin *dux,* meaning leader) leads them. Soon after (on the right), the patriarch (far right) is inspired to look inside a hollow column where he finds the relics. Everyone turns and applauds, including the womenfolk, who stream in from the upper-floor galleries. The relics were soon placed under the altar in a ceremony that inaugurated the current structure.

Additional Sights: The ❿ **Treasury** (Tesoro) and ⓫ **Golden Altarpiece** (Pala d'Oro) give you the easiest way outside of Istanbul or Ravenna to see the glories of the Byzantine Empire. Venetian crusaders looted the Christian city of Constantinople and brought home piles of lavish loot (perhaps the lowest point in Christian history until the advent of TV evangelism). Much of this plunder is stored in the Treasury of San Marco. As you view these treasures, remember that most were made in about A.D. 500, while Western Europe was stuck in the Dark Ages. Beneath the high altar lies the body of St. Mark ("Marce") and the Golden Altarpiece, made of 250 blue-backed enamels with religious scenes, all set in a gold frame and studded with 15 hefty rubies, 300 emeralds, 1,500 pearls, and assorted sapphires, amethysts, and topaz (c. 1100).

In the ⓬ **San Marco Museum** (Museo di San Marco) upstairs you can see an up-close mosaic exhibition, a fine view of the church interior, a view of the square from the balcony with bronze horses, and (inside, in their own room) the original horses. The staircase up to the museum is in the atrium, near the basilica's main entrance, marked by a sign that says *Loggia dei Cavalli, Museo.*

▲▲▲Doge's Palace (Palazzo Ducale)

The seat of the Venetian government and home of its ruling duke, or doge, this was the most powerful half-acre in Europe for 400 years. The Doge's Palace was built to show off the power

Cafés on St. Mark's Square

In Venice's heyday, it was said that the freedoms a gentleman could experience here went far beyond what any true gentleman would actually care to indulge in. But one extravagance all could enjoy was the ritual of publicly consuming coffee: showing off with an affordable luxury, doing something trendy, while sharing the ideas of the Enlightenment.

Exotic coffee was made to order for the fancy café scene. Traders introduced coffee, called the "wine of Islam," from the Middle East (the plant is native to Ethiopia). The first coffeehouses opened in the 17th century, and by 1750 there were dozens of cafés lining Piazza San Marco and 200 operating in Venice.

Today, several fine old cafés survive and still line the square. Those with live music feature similar food, prices, and a three- to five-piece combo playing a selection of classical and pop hits, from Brahms to "Bésame Mucho."

You can wander around the square listening to the different orchestras, or take a seat at a café and settle in. At any café with live music, it's perfectly acceptable to nurse a cappuccino for an hour—you're paying for the music with the cover charge. And remember, you can sip your coffee at the bar at a nearly normal price—even with the orchestra playing just outside.

For locations of the following cafés, see the map on page 51.

Caffè Florian (on the right as you face the church) is the most famous Venetian café and was one of the first places in Eu-

and wealth of the Republic. The doge lived with his family on the first floor up, near the halls of power. From his once-lavish (now sparse) quarters, you'll follow the one-way tour through the public rooms of the top floor, finishing with the Bridge of Sighs and the prison. The place is wallpapered with masterpieces by Veronese and Tintoretto.

Cost and Hours: €19 combo-ticket includes Correr Museum, also covered by Museum Pass—see page 49, daily 8:30-19:00, Nov-March until 17:30, last entry one hour before closing, café, photos allowed without flash, next to St. Mark's Basilica, just off St. Mark's Square, va-

rope to serve coffee (daily 9:00-24:00, shorter hours in winter, www.caffeflorian.com). It was originally named "Triumphant Venice" (Venezia Triomfante). But under French occupation, in the early 19th century, that politically incorrect name was changed. If you sit outside and get just an espresso—your cheapest option— expect to pay €12.50: €6.50 for the coffee and a €6 cover charge when the orchestra is playing (which is most of the day).

The Florian has been a popular spot for a discreet rendez- vous in Venice since 1720. Each room has a historic or artistic theme. For example the "Room of the Illustrious Men" features portraits of great Venetians from Marco Polo to Titian. The out- side tables are the main action, but do walk inside through the richly decorated, old-time rooms where Casanova, Lord Byron, Charles Dickens, and Woody Allen have all paid too much for a drink. The café's orchestra—the most serious on the square— plays daily from 10:00 to 24:00. Each hour comes with a musical theme (operetta, Latin, Romantic, jazz, Venetian, and so on—you can ask for the program).

Gran Caffè Quadri, opposite the Florian and established in 1780, has another illustrious roster of famous clientele.

Gran Caffè Lavena, near the Clock Tower, is less storied—al- though it dates from 1750 and counts composer Richard Wagner as a former regular. Drop in to check out its dazzling but politi- cally incorrect chandelier.

Gran Caffè Chioggia, on the Piazzetta facing the Doge's Pal- ace, charges no cover and has one or two musicians playing—usu- ally a pianist (€7 cocktails, music from 10:30 to 23:00—jazz after 21:00).

Eden Bar and **Caffè Aurora** are less expensive and don't have live music.

poretto stops: San Marco or San Zaccaria, tel. 041-271-5911, http:// palazzoducale.visitmuve.it.

Avoiding Lines: If the line is long at the Doge's Palace, buy your combo-ticket at the Correr Museum across the square; then go straight to the Doge's Palace turnstile, skirting along to the right of the long ticket-buying line and entering at the "prepaid tickets" entrance. Or, you can buy your ticket online—at least 48 hours in advance—for an extra €0.50 on the museum website.

Tours: The audioguide tour is dry but informative (€5, or €8 for two people, need ID for deposit). For a 1.25-hour live guided tour, consider the Secret Itineraries Tour, which takes you into palace rooms otherwise not open to the public (€20, includes Doge's Palace admission but not Correr Museum admission; €14 with combo-ticket; three English-language tours each morning). Though the tour skips the palace's main hall, you're welcome to

VENICE

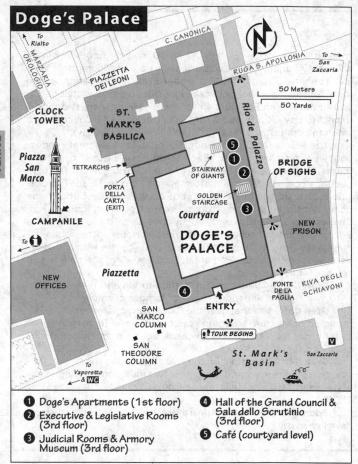

Doge's Palace

1 Doge's Apartments (1st floor)
2 Executive & Legislative Rooms (3rd floor)
3 Judicial Rooms & Armory Museum (3rd floor)
4 Hall of the Grand Council & Sala dello Scrutinio (3rd floor)
5 Café (courtyard level)

visit the hall afterward on your own. Reserve ahead for this tour in peak season—it can fill up as much as a month in advance. Book online (http://palazzoducale.visitmuve.it), or reserve by phone (tel. 848-082-000, from the US dial 011-39-041-4273-0892), or you can try just showing up at the info desk. Avoid the Doge's Hidden Treasures Tour—it reveals little that would be considered a "treasure" and is a waste of €20.

Visiting the Doge's Palace: You'll see the restored facades from the **courtyard.** Notice a grand staircase (with nearly naked Moses and Paul Newman at the top). Even the most powerful visitors climbed this to meet the doge. This was the beginning of an architectural power trip.

In the **Senate Hall,** the 120 senators met, debated, and passed laws. Tintoretto's large *Triumph of Venice* on the ceiling (central painting, best viewed from the top) is an allegory of the city in all her glory. Lady Venice is up in heaven with the Greek gods, while barbaric lesser nations swirl up to give her gifts and tribute.

The **Armory**—a dazzling display originally assembled to intimidate potential adversaries—shows remnants of the military might that the empire employed to keep the East-West trade lines open (and the local economy booming).

The giant **Hall of the Grand Council** (175 feet by 80 feet, capacity 2,600) is where the entire nobility met to elect the senate and doge. It took a room this size to contain the grandeur of the Most Serene Republic. Ringing the top of the room are portraits of the first 76 doges (in chronological order). The one at the far end that's blacked out (in the left corner) is the notorious Doge Marin Falier, who opposed the will of the Grand Council in 1355. He was tried for treason, beheaded, and airbrushed from history.

On the wall over the doge's throne is Tintoretto's monsterpiece, *Paradise,* the largest oil painting in the world. Christ and Mary are surrounded by a heavenly host of 500 saints. The painting leaves you feeling that you get to heaven not by being a good Christian, but by being a good Venetian.

Cross the covered **Bridge of Sighs** over the canal to the **prisons.** Circle the cells. Notice the carvings made by prisoners—from olden days up until 1930—on some of the stone windowsills of the cells, especially in the far corner of the building.

Cross back over the Bridge of Sighs, pausing to look through the marble-trellised windows at all of the tourists.

More Sights on the Square
▲▲Correr Museum (Museo Correr)

This uncrowded museum gives you a good overview of Venetian history and art. The doge memorabilia, armor, banners, statues (by Canova), and paintings (by the Bellini family and others) re-create the festive days of the Venetian Republic. And it's all accompanied—throughout the museum—by English descriptions and views of St. Mark's Square. But the Correr Museum has one more thing to offer, and that's a quiet refuge—an elegant Neoclassical space—in which to rise above St. Mark's Square when the piazza is too hot, too rainy, or too overrun with tourists.

Cost and Hours: €19 combo-ticket also includes the Doge's Palace; daily April-Oct 10:00-19:00, Nov-March 10:00-17:00, last entry one hour before closing; bag check free and mandatory for bags bigger than a large purse, elegant café, enter at far end of square directly opposite basilica, tel. 041-240-5211, http://corre visitmuve.it.

Avoid long lines at the crowded Doge's Palace by buyir combo-ticket at the Correr Museum. For €12 you can see rer Museum and tour the Clock Tower on St. Mark's Square, but this ticket doesn't include the Doge's Palace (and the €19 combo-ticket mentioned above doesn't include the Clock Tower). For more on reserving a Clock Tower tour, see page 52.

▲Campanile (Campanile di San Marco)

This dramatic bell tower replaced a short-er tower, part of the original fortress that guarded the entry of the Grand Canal. That tower crumbled into a pile of bricks in 1902, a thousand years after it was built. Ride the elevator 325 feet to the top of the bell tower for the best view in Venice (especially at sunset). For an ear-shattering experience, be on top when the bells ring. The golden archangel Gabriel at the top always faces into the wind. Beat the crowds and enjoy the crisp morning air at 9:00 or the cool evening breeze at 18:00. Go inside to buy tickets; the kiosk in front only rents €4 audiogu-ides and is operated by a private company.

Cost and Hours: €8, daily Easter-June and Oct 9:00-19:00, July-Sept 9:00-21:00, Nov-Easter 9:30-15:45, may close during thunderstorms, tel. 041-522-4064, www.basilicasanmarco.it.

Behind St. Mark's Basilica
▲Bridge of Sighs

This much-photographed bridge connects the Doge's Palace with the prison. Travelers popularized this bridge in the Romantic 19th century. Supposedly, a condemned man would be led over this bridge on his way to the prison, take one last look at the glory of Venice, and sigh. Though overhyped, the Bridge of Sighs is undeniably tingle-worthy—especially after dark, when the crowds have dispersed and it's just you and floodlit Venice. During the middle of the day, however, being immersed in the pandemonium of global tourism (and selfie sticks) can be a fascinating experience in itself.

Getting There: The Bridge of Sighs is ..d the corner from the Doge's Palace. ..ward the waterfront, turn left along the water, and look up ..l on your left. You can walk across the bridge (from the ..ng the Doge's Palace.

Church of San Zaccaria

This historic church is home to a sometimes-waterlogged crypt, a Bellini altarpiece, a Tintoretto painting, and the final resting place of St. Zechariah, the father of John the Baptist.

Cost and Hours: Free, €1.50 to enter crypt, €0.50 coin to light up Bellini's altarpiece, Mon-Sat 10:00-12:00 & 16:00-18:00, Sun 16:00-18:00 only, two canals behind St. Mark's Basilica.

ACROSS THE LAGOON FROM ST. MARK'S SQUARE

▲San Giorgio Maggiore

This is the dreamy church-topped island you can see from the waterfront by St. Mark's Square. The striking church, designed by Palladio, features art by Tintoretto

and stunning views from its bell tower of Venice and the lagoon. And even if you're not interested in any of the above, it's worth a trip just to escape from tourist-mobbed St. Mark's Square.

Cost and Hours: Free entry to church; daily 7:00-19:00, Nov-March closes at dusk. The bell tower costs €6 and is accessible by elevator (runs until 15 minutes before the church closes but is not accessible Sun during services).

Getting There: To reach the island from St. Mark's Square, take the one-stop, three-minute ride on vaporetto #2 from San Zaccaria (6/hour, €5 special vaporetto ticket, direction: Tronchetto).

DORSODURO DISTRICT

▲▲Accademia (Galleria dell'Accademia)

Venice's top art museum, packed with highlights of the Venetian Renaissance, features paintings by the Bellini family, Titian, Tintoretto, Veronese, Tiepolo, Giorgione, Canaletto, and Testosterone. It's just over the wooden Accademia Bridge from the San Marco action.

Cost and Hours: €15, Mon 8:15-14:00, Tue-Sun 8:15-19:15, last entry one hour before closing, dull audioguide-€6, no flash photos allowed. At Accademia Bridge, vaporetto: Accademia, tel. 041-522-2247, www.gallerieaccademia.org.

Avoiding Lines: Just 360 people are allowed into the gallery at one time, so you may have to wait. It's most crowded on Tue mornings and whenever it rains; it's least crowded Wed, Thu, and Sun mornings (before 10:00) and late afternoons (after 17:00). Wh it's possible to book tickets in advance (€1.50/ticket surcharg ther book online at www.gallerieaccademia.org or call 041-520-0345), it's generally not necessary if you avoid the busiest times.

Renovation: This museum seems to be in a constant state of disarray. A major expansion and renovation has been dragging on for years. Paintings come and go, and the actual locations of the pieces are hard to pin down. Still, the museum contains sumptuous art—the best in Venice. Be flexible: You'll probably just end up wandering around and matching descriptions to blockbuster paintings when you find them. If you don't find a particular piece, check Room 23, which seems to be their catchall holding pen for displaced art.

Visiting the Accademia: The Accademia is the greatest museum anywhere for Venetian Renaissance art and a good overview of painters whose works you'll see all over town. Venetian art is underrated and, I think, misunderstood. It's nowhere near as famous today as the work of the florescent Florentines, but—with historical slices of Venice, ravishing nudes, and very human Madonnas—it's livelier, more colorful, and simply more fun. The Venetian love of luxury shines through in this collection, which starts in the Middle Ages and runs to the 1700s. Look for grand canvases of colorful, spacious settings, peopled with happy locals in extravagant clothes having a great time.

Medieval highlights include elaborate altarpieces and golden-haloed Madonnas, all painted at a time when realism, depth of field, and emotion were considered beside the point. Medieval Venetians, with their close ties to the East, borrowed techniques such as gold-leafing, frontal poses, and "iconic" faces from the religious icons of Byzantium (modern-day Istanbul).

Among early masterpieces of the Renaissance are Mantegna's studly *St. George.* As the Renaissance reaches its heights, so do the paintings, such as Titian's magnificent *Presentation of the Virgin.* It's a religious scene, yes, but it's really just an excuse to display secular splendor (Titian was the most famous painter of his day—perhaps even more famous than Michelangelo). Veronese's sumptuous *Feast in the House of Levi* also has an ostensibly religious theme (in

VENICE

the middle, find Jesus eating his final meal)—but it's outdone by the luxury and optimism of Renaissance Venice. Life was a good thing and beauty was to be enjoyed. (Veronese was hauled before the Inquisition for painting such a bawdy Last Supper...so he fine-tuned the title.)

End your tour in the largest room in the museum, Room 23, whose inner court generally holds the finest works—including masterpieces by Giovanni Bellini (such as his *Madonna degli Albe-retti*) and Giorgione (such as *The Tempest*).

▲▲Peggy Guggenheim Collection

The popular museum of far-out art, housed in the American heir-ess' former retirement palazzo, offers one of Europe's best reviews of the art of the first half of the 20th century. Stroll through styles represented by artists whom Peggy knew personally—Cubism (Picasso, Braque), Surrealism (Dalí, Ernst), Futurism (Boccioni), American Abstract Expressionism (Pollock), and a sprinkling of Klee, Calder, and Chagall.

Cost and Hours: €15, usually includes temporary exhibits, Wed-Mon 10:00-18:00, closed Tue, audioguide-€7, pricey café, a 5-minute walk from the Accademia Bridge, vaporetto: Accademia or Salute, tel. 041-240-5411, www.guggenheim-venice.it.

▲La Salute Church (Santa Maria della Salute)

This impressive church with a crown-shaped dome was built and dedicated to the Virgin Mary by grateful survivors of the 1630 plague.

Cost and Hours: Free entry to church, €3 to enter the Sac-risty; daily 9:00-12:00 & 15:00-17:30. It's a 10-minute walk from the Accademia Bridge; the Salute vaporetto stop is at its doorstep, tel. 041-274-3928, www.seminariovenezia.it.

▲Ca' Rezzonico (Museum of 18th-Century Venice)

This Grand Canal palazzo offers the most insightful look at the life of Venice's rich and famous in the 1700s. Wander under ceilings by Tiepolo, among furnishings from that most decadent century, enjoying views of the canal and paintings by Guardi, Canaletto, and Longhi.

Cost and Hours: €10, Wed-Mon 10:00-18:00, Nov-March until 17:00, closed Tue year-round; audioguide-€5 or €6/2 people; ticket office closes one hour before museum, no flash photography, café, at Ca' Rezzonico vaporetto stop, tel. 041-241-0100, http://carezzonico.visitmuve.it.

▲Punta della Dogana

This museum of contemporary art, opened in 2009, makes the Dorsoduro a major destination for art lovers. Housed in the former Customs House at the end of the Grand Canal, it features cutti

VENICE

VENICE

edge 21st-century art in spacious rooms. This isn't Picasso and Matisse, or even Pollock and Warhol—those guys are ancient history. But if you're into the likes of Jeff Koons, Cy Twombly, Rachel Whiteread, and a host of newer artists, the museum is world class. The displays change completely about every year, drawn from the museum's large collection—so large it also fills Palazzo Grassi, farther up the Grand Canal.

Cost and Hours: €15 for one locale, €20 for both; Wed-Mon 10:00-19:00, closed Tue, last entry one hour before closing; audioguide sometimes available, small café, tel. 199-112-112 within Italy, 041-200-1057 from abroad, www.palazzograssi.it.

Getting There: Punta della Dogana is near La Salute Church (vaporetto: Salute). Palazzo Grassi is a bit upstream, on the east side of the Grand Canal (vaporetto #2: San Samuele).

SAN POLO DISTRICT
▲▲▲Rialto Bridge

One of the world's most famous bridges, this distinctive and dra-

matic stone structure crosses the Grand Canal with a single confident span. The arcades along the top of the bridge help reinforce the structure...and offer some enjoyable shopping diversions, as does the **market** surrounding the bridge (produce market closed Sun, fish market closed Sun-Mon).

▲▲Frari Church
(Basilica di Santa Maria Gloriosa dei Frari)

My favorite art experience in Venice is seeing art in the setting for which it was designed—as it is at the Frari Church. The Franciscan "Church of the Brothers" and the art that decorates it are warmed by the spirit of St. Francis. It features the work of three great Renaissance masters: Donatello, Giovanni Bellini, and Titian—each showing worshippers the glory of God in human terms.

Cost and Hours: €3, Mon-Sat 9:00-18:00, Sun 13:00-18:00, audioguide-€2, no flash photos allowed, modest dress recommended, on Campo dei Frari, near San Tomà vaporetto and *traghetto* stops, tel. 041-272-8618, www.basilicadeifrari.it.

A Dying City?

Venice's population (55,000 in the historic city) is half what it was just 30 years ago, and people are leaving at a rate of a thousand a year. Of those who stay, 25 percent are 65 or older.

Sad, yes, but imagine raising a family here: Apartments are small, high up, and expensive. Humidity and occasional flooding make basic maintenance a pain. Home-improvement projects require navigating miles of red tape, and you must follow regulations intended to preserve the historical ambience. Everything is expensive because it has to be shipped in from the mainland. You can easily get glass and tourist trinkets, but it's hard to find groceries or get your shoes fixed. Running basic errands involves lots of walking and stairs—imagine crossing over arched bridges while pushing a child in a stroller and carrying a day's worth of groceries.

With millions of visitors a year (150,000 a day at peak times), on any given day Venetians are likely outnumbered by tourists. Despite government efforts to subsidize rents and build cheap housing, the city is losing its residents. The economy itself is thriving, thanks to tourist dollars and rich foreigners buying second homes. But the culture is dying.

Greedy residents could sink Venice long before the sea swallows it up. Locals happily rent apartments to tourists a few times a month rather than affordably to local families, and shopkeepers sell trinkets to tourists before pots and pans to the local population. Even the most hopeful city planners worry that in a few decades Venice will not be a city at all, but a museum, a cultural theme park, a decaying Disneyland for adults.

Tours: You can rent an audioguide for €2, or 🎧 download my free Frari Church audio tour.

Visiting the Frari Church: In **Donatello's wood statue of St. John the Baptist** (just to the right of the high altar), the prophet of the desert—dressed in animal skins and nearly starving from his diet of bugs 'n' honey—announces the coming of the Messiah. Donatello was a Florentine working at the dawn of the Renaissance.

Bellini's *Madonna and Child with Saints and Angels* painting (in the sacristy farther to the right) came later, done by a Venetian in a more Venetian style—soft focus without Donatello's harsh realism. While Renaissance humanism demanded Madonnas and saints that were accessible and human, Bellini places them in a physical setting so beautiful that it creates its own mood of serene holiness. The genius of Bellini, perhaps the greatest Venetian painter, is obvious in the pristine clarity, rich colors (notice Mary's clothing), believable depth, and reassuring calm of this three-paneled altarpiece.

Finally, glowing red and gold like a stained-glass window over the high altar, **Titian's** *Assumption of the Virgin* sets the tone of exuberant beauty found in the otherwise sparse church. Titian the Venetian—a student of Bellini—painted steadily for 60 years...you'll see a lot of his art. As stunned apostles look up past the swirl of arms and legs, the complex composition of this painting draws you right to the radiant face of the once-dying, now-triumphant Mary as she joins God in heaven.

Feel comfortable to discreetly freeload off passing tours. For many, these three pieces of art make a visit to the Accademia Gallery unnecessary (or they may whet your appetite for more). Before leaving, check out the Neoclassical pyramid-shaped Canova monument flanking the nave just inside the main entrance and (opposite that) the grandiose tomb of Titian. Compare the carved marble *Assumption* behind Titian's tombstone portrait with the painted original above the high altar.

▲▲Scuola San Rocco

Sometimes called "Tintoretto's Sistine Chapel," this lavish meeting hall (next to the Frari Church) has some 50 large, colorful Tintoretto paintings plastered to the walls and ceilings. The best paintings are upstairs, especially the *Crucifixion* in the smaller room. View the neck-breaking splendor with the mirrors available in the Grand Hall.

Cost and Hours: €10, daily 9:30-17:30, no flash photography, tel. 041-523-4864, www.scuolagrandesanrocco.it.

▲Church of San Polo

This nearby church, which pales in comparison to the two sights just listed, is only worth a visit for art lovers. One of Venice's oldest churches (from the ninth century), San Polo features works by Tintoretto, Veronese, and Tiepolo and son.

Cost and Hours: €3, Mon-Sat 10:00-17:00, closed Sun.

VENICE'S LAGOON

The island of Venice sits in a lagoon—a calm section of the Adriatic protected from wind and waves by the natural breakwater of the Lido. Beyond the church-topped island of San Giorgio Maggiore (directly in front of St. Mark's Square—see page 65), four interesting islands hide out in the lagoon: San Michele, Murano, Burano, and Torcello. A fifth island has the beach—the Lido—a nice outing for a beach break on a sunny day.

Lagoon Tour

These four islands make a good, varied, and long day trip that you can do on your own (see "Getting There" directions, later).

San Michele (a.k.a. Cimitero) is the cemetery island—the final resting place of Venetians and a few foreign VIPs, from poet Ezra Pound to composer Igor Stravinsky. The stopover is easy, since boats come every 10 minutes. If you even half-enjoy wandering through old cemeteries, you'll dig this one—it's full of flowers, trees, scurrying lizards, and birdsong, and has an intriguing chapel (cemetery open daily 7:30-18:00, Oct-March until 16:30; reception to the left as you enter, free WC to the right, no picnicking).

Murano (worth ▲) is famous for its glassmaking. From the Colonna vaporetto stop, skip the glass shops in front of you, walk to the right, and wander up the street along the canal, **Fondamenta dei Vetrai** (Glassmakers' Embankment). The Faro district of Murano, on the other side of the canal, is packed with factories *(fabriche)* and their furnaces *(fornaci)*. You'll pass dozens of **glass shops** along the canal. Window-shopping here can be as much fun as buying—the personality, style, and prices of wares vary wildly from place to place. Early along this promenade, at #47, is the venerable **Venini** shop, with glass that's a cut above much of what else is on offer here, and with an interior showing off the ultimate in modern Venetian glass design (Mon-Sat 9:30-18:00, closed Sun).

Murano's **Glass Museum** (Museo Vetrario) traces the history of this delicate art, with the very best examples of 500 years of Venetian glassmaking on display (€10, daily 10:00-18:00, Nov-March until 17:00, tel. 041-739-586, http://museovetro.visitmuve.it).

Burano, known for its lacemaking and countless lace shops (and worth ▲▲), offers a delightful pastel village alternative to big, bustling Venice. The tight **main drag** is packed with tourists and lined with shops, some of which sell Burano's locally produced white wine. Wander to the far end of the island and the mood shifts. A grassy area, with benches and a waterside promenade,

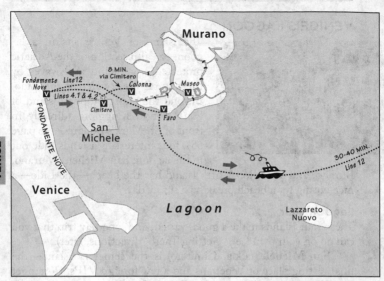

makes for a pretty picnic spot. Continuing all the way around the church and its leaning bell tower brings you into a peaceful yet intensely colorful, small-town world.

Burano's **Lace Museum** (Museo del Merletto di Burano) shows the island's lace heritage (€5, Tue-Sun 10:00-18:00, Nov-March until 17:00, closed Mon year-round, tel. 041-730-034, http://museomerletto.visitmuve.it).

Torcello (worth ▲) is the birthplace of Venice, where some of the first mainland refugees settled, escaping the barbarian hordes. Yet today, it's the least-developed island (pop. 20) in the most natural state, marshy and shrub-covered. There's little for tourists to see except the Santa Maria Assunta Church, the oldest in Venice, which still sports some impressive mosaics, a climbable bell tower, and a modest museum of Roman sculpture and medieval sculpture and manuscripts (10-minute walk from the dock, €12 combo-ticket covers museum, church, and bell tower; €9 combo-ticket covers church and bell tower; combo-tickets include audioguide; museum only—€3; church and bell tower—€5 each; church open daily 10:30-18:00, Nov-Feb until 17:00, museum and campanile close 30 minutes earlier, museum closed Mon year-round; museum tel. 041-730-761, church/bell tower tel. 041-730-119).

Getting There: You can travel to any of the four islands by vaporetto. Because single vaporetto tickets (€7.50) are only valid for 75 minutes, getting a vaporetto pass for this lagoon excursion makes more sense (see page 27 for more on vaporetto tickets). *Vaporetti* can be very crowded; if you want a seat for the longer rides, show up at the boat dock a bit early to get in line.

For a route that takes you to all four islands, start at the **Fon-**

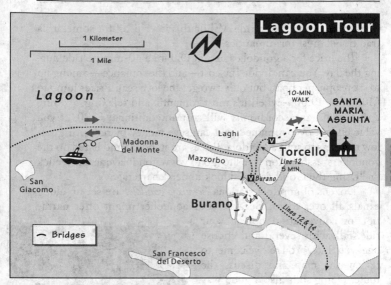

damente Nove vaporetto stop on the north shore of Venice (the "back" of the fish). Lines #4.1 and #4.2 converge here before heading out to Murano. Catch either one (every 10 minutes); you'll first cross to San Michele (whose stop is called Cimitero) in six minutes, then continue another three minutes to Murano-Colonna. Stroll through Murano, then leave that island from a different stop: Murano-Faro, where you can board vaporetto #12 for the 30- to 40-minute trip to Burano. From Burano, you can side-trip to Torcello on vaporetto #12 (5-minute trip each way, make sure it stops at Torcello). To make a quick return to Venice from Burano, hop vaporetto #12 (some of these boats skip Torcello), which returns you to Fondamente Nove (45 minutes).

▲Lido Beach

Venice's nearest beach is the Lido, across the lagoon on an island connected to the mainland (which means car traffic). The sandy beach is pleasant, family-friendly, and good for swimming. You can rent an umbrella, buy beach gear at the shop, get food at the self-service café, or have a drink at the bar. Everything is affordable and in the same building (vaporetto: Lido S.M.E., walk 10 minutes on Gran Viale S. Maria Elisabetta to beach entry).

Experiences in Venice

GONDOLA RIDES

Riding a gondola is simple, expensive, and one of the great experiences in Europe. Gondoliers hanging out all over town are eager to have you hop in for a ride. While this is a rip-off for some, it's a traditional must for romantics.

The price for a gondola starts at €80 for a 40-minute ride during the day. You can divide the cost—and the romance—among up to six people per boat, but only two get the love seat. Prices jump to €100 after 19:00—when it's most romantic and relaxing. Adding a singer and an accordionist will cost an additional €120. If you value budget over romance, you can save money by recruiting fellow travelers to split a gondola. Prices are standard and listed on the gondoliers' association website (go to www.gondolavenezia.it, click on "Using the Gondola," and look under "charterage").

Dozens of gondola stations *(servizio gondole)* are set up along canals all over town. Because your gondolier might offer narration or conversation during your ride, talk with several and choose one you like. You're welcome to review the map and discuss the route. Doing so is also a good way to see if you enjoy the gondolier's personality and language skills. Establish the price, route, and duration of the trip before boarding, enjoy your ride, and pay only when

you're finished. While prices are pretty firm, you might find them softer during the day. Most gondoliers honor the official prices, but a few might try to scam you out of some extra euros, particularly by insisting on a tip. (While not required or even expected, if your gondolier does the full 40 minutes and entertains you en route, a 5-10 percent tip is appreciated; if he's surly or rushes through the trip, skip it.)

If you've hired musicians and want to hear a Venetian song *(un canto Veneziano)*, try requesting *"Venezia La Luna e Tu."* Asking to hear *"O Sole Mio"* (which comes from Naples) is like asking a Chicago lounge singer to sing "Swanee River."

Glide through nighttime Venice with your head on someone's shoulder. Follow the moon as it sails past otherwise unseen buildings. Silhouettes gaze down from bridges while window glitter spills onto the black water. You're anonymous in the city of masks, as the rhythmic thrust of your striped-shirted gondolier turns old crows into songbirds. This is extremely relaxing (and, I think, worth the extra cost to experience at night). Suggestion: Put the camera down and make it a point for you and your partner to enjoy a threesome with Venice. Women, beware...while gondoliers can be extremely charming, locals say that anyone who falls for one of these Venetian Romeos "has slices of ham over her eyes."

For cheap gondola thrills during the day, stick to the €2 one-minute ferry ride on a Grand Canal *traghetto*. At night, *vaporetti* are nearly empty, and it's a great time to cruise the Grand Canal on the slow boat #1. Or hang out on a bridge along the gondola route and wave at romantics.

FESTIVALS

Venice's most famous festival is **Carnevale,** the celebration Americans call Mardi Gras (Feb 11-28 in 2017; www.carnevale.venezia. it). It's most festive on weekends, and can be particularly quiet during the first week. Carnevale, which means "farewell to meat," originated centuries ago as a wild two-month-long party leading up to the austerity of Lent. In Carnevale's heyday—the 1600s and 1700s—you could do pretty much anything with anybody from any social class if you were wearing a mask. These days it's a tamer 18-day celebration, culminating in a huge dance lit with fireworks on St. Mark's Square. Sporting masks and costumes, Venetians from kids to businessmen join in the fun. Drawing the biggest crowds of the year, Carnevale has nearly been a victim of its own success, driving away many Venetians (who skip out on the craziness to go skiing in the Dolomites).

Every year, the city hosts the **Venice Biennale International Art Exhibition,** a world-class contemporary fair, alternating between art in odd years and architecture in even years. The exhibition spreads over the Arsenale and Giardini park. When the Biennale focuses on visual art, representatives from 70 nations offer the latest in contemporary art forms: video, computer art, performance art, and digital photography, along with painting and sculpture (take vaporetto #1 or #2 to Giardini-Biennale; for details and an events calendar, see www.labiennale.org). The actual exhibition usually runs from June through November, but other events loosely connected with the Biennale—film, dance, theater—are held throughout the year (starting as early as February) in various venues on the island.

Other typically Venetian festival days filling the city's hotels with visitors and its canals with decked-out boats are **Feast of the Ascension Day** (May 25 in 2017), **Feast and Regatta of the Redeemer** (Festa del Redentore) on the third weekend in July (with spectacular fireworks show Sat night), and the **Historical Regatta** (old-time boats and pageantry, first Sat and Sun in Sept). **Vogalonga** is a colorful regatta that attracts more than 1,500 human-powered watercraft; teams of often-costumed participants follow a 20-mile course through the canals and lagoon (late May-early June, www.vogalonga.it). Smaller regattas include the **Murano Regatta** (early July) and the **Burano Regatta** (mid-Sept).

Venice's patron saint, **St. Mark,** is commemorated every April 25. Venetian men celebrate the day by presenting roses to the women in their lives (mothers, wives, and lovers).

Every November 21 is the **Feast of Our Lady of Good Health.** On this local "Thanksgiving," a bridge is built over the Grand Canal so that the city can pile into La Salute Church and remember how Venice survived the gruesome plague of 1630. On this day, Venetians eat smoked lamb from Dalmatia (which was the cargo of the first ship admitted when the plague lifted).

Shopping in Venice

Shoppers like Murano glass (described earlier), Burano lace (fun lace umbrellas for little girls), Carnevale masks (fine shops and artisans all over town), art reproduc-tions (posters, postcards, and books), prints of Venetian scenes, traditional stationery (pens and marbled paper products of all kinds), calendars with Venetian scenes, silk ties, scarves, and plenty of goofy knickknacks (Ti-tian mousepads, gondolier T-shirts, and little plastic gondola condom holders).

In touristy areas, shops are typically open from 9:00 to 19:30 (sometimes with a break from about 13:00 until 15:00 or 16:00), and more stores are open on Sunday here than in the rest of the country. If you're buying a substantial amount from nearly any shop, bargain—it's accepted and almost expected. Offer less and offer to pay cash; merchants are very conscious of the bite taken by credit-card companies.

Venice is particularly known for "needle lace," with intricate flowers, leaves, and curling stems, which was used for cuffs, gowns, and frilly collars. The **Il Merletto** shop just off St. Mark's Square sells pieces crafted by students of the Scuola dei Merletti, the local lace-making school in Burano (exit the square near the northwest corner through Sotoportego del Cavaletto, then across the little bridge to the right, daily 10:00-17:00, San Marco 95, tel. 041-520-8406).

Popular Venetian glass is available in many forms: vases, tea sets, decanters, glasses, jewelry, lamps, mod sculptures (such as solid-glass aquariums), and on and on. Shops will ship it home for you, but you're likely to pay as much or more for the shipping as you are for the item(s), and you may have to pay duty on larger purchases. Make sure the shop insures their merchandise *(assicurazione)*, or you're out of luck if it breaks. If your item arrives broken and it has been insured, take a photo of the pieces, send it to the shop, and they'll replace it for free.

Some visitors feel that because they're in Venice, they ought to grab the opportunity to buy glass. Remember that you can buy fine glass back home, too (Venice stopped forbidding its glassblowers from leaving the republic a few centuries ago)—and under less time pressure.

Also be aware that much of the cheap glass you'll see in Venice is imported (a sore point for local vendors dealing in the more expensive, locally produced stuff). Genuine Venetian glass comes with the Murano seal.

If you'd like to watch a quick glassblowing demonstration, try **Galleria San Marco,** a tour-group staple just off St. Mark's Square, which offers great demos every few minutes. They typically let individual travelers flashing this book sneak in with tour groups until 16:00 to see the show (and sales pitch). If you buy anything, show this book and they'll take 20 percent off the listed price. The gallery is in an alley that runs behind the north side of the square; walk through the passageway between #140 and #141, then look for #181a—see map on page 51, on your left and go up to the second floor (daily 8:30-18:00, on Calle del Cappello Nero, San Marco 181a, tel. 041-271-8671, info@galleriasanmarco.it, manager Aldo Dinon).

If you're serious about glass, visit the island of **Murano,** its glass museum, and many shops (described earlier, under "Venice's Lagoon"). You'll find greater variety on Murano, but prices are usually the same as in Venice.

Nightlife in Venice

You must experience Venice after dark. The city is quiet at night, as tour groups stay in the cheaper hotels of Mestre on the mainland, and the masses of day-trippers return to their beach resorts and cruise ships. Gondolas cost more, but are worth the extra expense (see page 73).

Venice has a busy schedule of events, church concerts, festivals, and entertainment. Check at the TI or the TI's website (www.turismovenezia.it) for listings. The free monthly *Un Ospite di Venezia* lists all the latest happenings in English (free at fancy hotels, or check www.aguestinvenice.com).

Baroque Concerts

Venice is a city of the powdered-wig Baroque era. For about €25, you can take your pick of traditional Vivaldi concerts in churches throughout town. Homegrown Vivaldi is as ubiquitous here as Strauss is in Vienna and Mozart is in Salzburg. In fact, you'll find frilly young Vivaldis hawking concert tickets on many corners. Most shows start at 20:30 and generally last 1.5 hours. You'll see posters in hotels all over town (hotels sell tickets at face-value).

Tickets for Baroque concerts in Venice can usually be bought the same day as the concert, so don't bother with websites that sell tickets with a surcharge. The general rule of thumb: Musicians in wigs and tights offer better spectacle; musicians in black-and-white suits are better performers.

The **Interpreti Veneziani orchestra,** considered the best group in town, generally performs 1.5-hour concerts nightly at 21:00 inside the sumptuous San Vidal Church (€28, church ticket booth open daily 9:30-21:00, north end of Accademia Bridge, tel. 041-277-0561, www.interpretiveneziani.com).

Other Performances

Venice's most famous theaters are **La Fenice** (grand old opera house, box office tel. 041-2424, www.teatrolafenice.it), **Teatro Goldoni** (mostly Italian live theater), and **Teatro Fondamenta Nuove** (theater, music, and dance).

Musica a Palazzo is a unique evening of opera at a Venetian palace on the Grand Canal. You'll spend about 45 delightful minutes in each of three sumptuous rooms (about 2.25 hours total) as eight musicians (usually four instruments and four singers) perform. They generally present three different operas on successive nights—enthusiasts can experience more than one. With these kinds of surroundings, under Tiepolo frescoes, you'll be glad you dressed up. As there are only 70 seats, you must book by phone or online in advance (€75, nightly at 20:30, Palazzo Barbarigo Minotto, Fondamenta Duodo o Barbarigo, vaporetto: Santa Maria del Giglio, San Marco 2504, mobile 340-971-7272, www. musicapalazzo.com).

Venezia is advertised as "the show that tells the great stories of Venice" and "simply the best show in town." I found the performance to be slow-moving and a bit cheesy, and the venue disappointing (€39, nightly March-Oct at 20:00, Nov-Feb at 19:00; 80 minutes, just off St. Mark's Square on Campo San Gallo, San Marco 1097, tel. 041-241-2002, www.teatrosangallo.net).

St. Mark's Square

For tourists, St. Mark's Square is the highlight, with lantern light and live music echoing from the cafés. Just being here after dark is a thrill, as **dueling café orchestras** entertain. The ultimate Venetian music scene is at the venerable Caffè Florian. But Gran Caffè Chioggia (facing the Doge's Palace) doesn't charge extra for music and has good jazz nightly (see sidebar on page 60). Every night, enthusiastic musicians play the same songs, creating the same irresistible magic. Hang out for free behind the tables (allowing you to move easily on to the next orchestra when the musicians take a break), or spring for a seat and enjoy a fun and gorgeously set concert. If you sit a while, it can be about €13-22 well spent (for a drink and the cover charge for music). Dancing on the square is free—and encouraged.

Several venerable cafés and bars on the square serve expensive drinks outside but cheap drinks inside at the bar. The scene in a bar like **Gran Caffè Lavena** (in spite of its politically incorrect chandelier) can be great. The touristy **Bar Americano** is lively until late (under the Clock Tower). You'll hear people talking about the famous **Harry's American Bar,** which sells overpriced food and American cocktails to dressy tourists near the San Marco-Vallaresso vaporetto stop. But it's a rip-off...and the last place Hemingway would drink today. It's far cheaper to get a drink at any of the hole-in-the-wall bars just off St. Mark's Square; you can get a bottle of beer or even prosecco-to-go in a plastic cup.

Wherever you end up, streetlamp halos, live music, floodlit history, and a ceiling of stars make St. Mark's magic at midnight. You're not a tourist, you're a living part of a soft Venetian night...an alley cat with money. In the misty light, the moon has a golden hue. Shine with the old lanterns on the gondola piers, where the sloppy lagoon splashes at the Doge's Palace...reminiscing.

Sleeping in Venice

I've listed rooms in four areas: St. Mark's bustle, the Rialto action, the quiet Dorsoduro area behind the Accademia art museum, and near the train station.

Book your accommodations well in advance if you'll be traveling during peak season (April-June and Sept-Oct) or if your trip coincides with a major holiday or festival (see page 1178).

Hotels in Venice can be tricky to locate. Use the maps and directions in this chapter and you'll be fine. If necessary, ask locals for help when you get close. Hotel websites are particularly valuable for Venice because they often include detailed directions (including maps that you can print out) that will help you get to your rooms with a minimum of wrong turns in this navigationally challenging city. The website Venicexplorer.net allows you to search using a hotel's address number and district (I've included these in my listings; click "Venice Civic Number" to open the search window);

Sleep Code

Hotels are classified based on the average price of a standard double room with breakfast in high season.

$$$$	**Splurge:** Most rooms over €170
$$$	**Pricier:** €130-170
$$	**Moderate:** €90-130
$	**Budget:** €50-90
¢	**Backpacker:** Under €50
RS%	**Rick Steves discount**

Unless otherwise noted, credit cards are accepted, hotel staff speak basic English, and free Wi-Fi is available. Comparison-shop by checking prices at several hotels (on each hotel's own website, on a booking site, or by email). For the best deal, *book directly with the hotel.* Ask for a discount if paying in cash; if the listing includes **RS%**, request a Rick Steves discount.

it's better than other map websites, including Google Maps, which choke on Venetian addresses. Remember that Venice has six districts: San Marco, Castello, Cannaregio, San Polo, Santa Croce, and Dorsoduro.

NEAR ST. MARK'S SQUARE

To get here from the train station or Piazzale Roma bus station, ride the slow vaporetto #1 to San Zaccaria or the fast #2 (which also leaves from Tronchetto parking lot) to San Marco. Consider using your ride to follow my tour of the Grand Canal (see Grand Canal Cruise, page 38); to make sure you arrive via the Grand Canal, confirm that your boat goes *"via Rialto."*

East of St. Mark's Square

Located near the Bridge of Sighs, just off the Riva degli Schiavoni waterfront promenade, these places rub drainpipes with Venice's most palatial five-star hotels.

$$$$ Hotel Campiello, lacy and bright, was once part of a 19th-century convent. Ideally located 50 yards off the waterfront on a tiny square, its 16 rooms offer a tranquil, friendly refuge for travelers who appreciate comfort and professional service (RS%, air-con, elevator, just steps from the San Zaccaria vaporetto stop, Castello 4647; tel. 041-520-5764, www.hcampiello.it, campiello@hcampiello.it; family-run for four generations, currently by Thomas, Nicoletta, and Monica). They also rent three modern family apartments, under rustic timbers just steps away.

$$$$ Hotel Fontana, two bridges behind St. Mark's Square, ￼pleasant family-run place with 15 sparse but classic-feeling ￼overlooking a lively square (two rooms with terraces, family rooms, air-con, elevator, Wi-Fi in common areas, on Campo San Provolo at Castello 4701, tel. 041-522-0533, www.hotelfontana.it, info@hotelfontana.it, cousins Diego and Gabriele).

$$$$ Hotel la Residenza is a grand old palace facing a peaceful square. It has 16 small rooms on three levels (with no elevator) and a huge, luxurious lounge that comes with a piano and a stingy breakfast. This is a good value for romantics—you'll feel like you're in the Doge's Palace after hours (some view rooms, air-con, Wi-Fi in most rooms, on Campo Bandiera e Moro at Castello 3608, tel. 041-528-5315, www.venicelaresidenza.com, info@venicelaresidenza.com, Giovanni).

$$$$ Locanda al Leon, which feels a little like a medieval tower house, is conscientiously run and rents 12 rooms just off Campo Santi Filippo e Giacomo (RS%, some view rooms, family rooms, air-con, 2 apartments with kitchens, Campo Santi Filippo e Giacomo, Castello 4270, tel. 041-277-0393, www.hotelalleon.com, leon@hotelalleon.com, Giuliano and Marcella). Their annex down the street, **B&B Marcella,** has three newer, classy, and spacious rooms for the same rates (check in at main hotel).

$$$ Albergo Doni, situated along a quiet canal, is dark and quiet. This time-warp—with creaky floors and 13 well-worn, once-classy rooms—is run by friendly Tessa and her two brothers, Barnaba and an Italian stallion named Nikos (cheaper rooms with shared bath, family rooms, ceiling fans, a few rooms have air-con, Wi-Fi in common areas, on Fondamenta del Vin at Castello 4656, tel. 041-522-4267, www.albergodoni.it, albergodoni@hotmail.it). The hotel also has three nice overflow apartments at the same prices (but without breakfast).

¢ Casa per Ferie Santa Maria della Pietà is a wonderful facility renting 53 beds in 15 rooms just a block off the Riva, with a fabulous lagoon-view roof terrace that could rival those at the most luxurious hotels in town. Institutional, with generous public spaces and dorm-style comfort, there are no sinks, toilets, or showers in any of its rooms, but there's plenty of plumbing down the hall (cash only, 2-night minimum on weekends in peak season, only twin beds, private rooms available, air-con, 100 yards from San Zaccaria-Pietà vaporetto dock, down Calle de la Pietà from La Pietà Church at Castello 3701, take elevator to third floor, tel. 041-244-3639, www.bedandvenice.it, info@bedandvenice.it).

North of St. Mark's Square

$$$ Hotel Orion rents 21 simple, welcoming rooms in the center of the action. Steep stairs (there's no elevator) take you from the touristy street into a peaceful world high above (RS%—use code "RSTEVES," air-con, 2 minutes inland from St. Mark's Square,

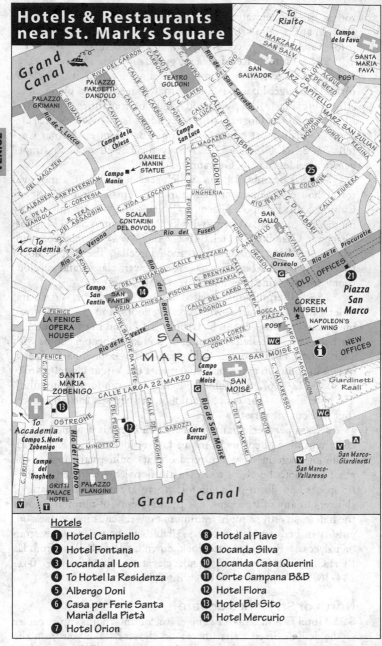

Hotels & Restaurants near St. Mark's Square

Hotels

1. Hotel Campiello
2. Hotel Fontana
3. Locanda al Leon
4. To Hotel la Residenza
5. Albergo Doni
6. Casa per Ferie Santa Maria della Pietà
7. Hotel Orion
8. Hotel al Piave
9. Locanda Silva
10. Locanda Casa Querini
11. Corte Campana B&B
12. Hotel Flora
13. Hotel Bel Sito
14. Hotel Mercurio

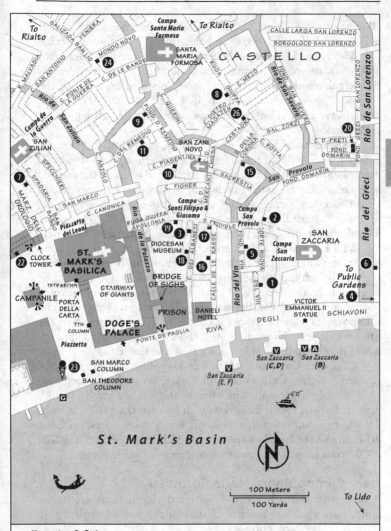

Eateries & Other

15 Ristorante Antica Sacrestia
16 Birreria Forst Café
17 Bar Verde
18 Ristorante alla Basilica
19 Ristorante Cinese Capitol

20 Ponte dei Greci Canalside Eateries
21 Gran Caffè Quadri (Bistro)
22 Gran Caffè Lavena (Gelato)
23 Todaro Gelato
24 Co-op Supermarket
25 Lavanderia Gabriella
26 Lavanderia Effe Erre

10 steps toward St. Mark's from San Zulian Church at Calle Spadaria 700a, tel. 041-522-3053, www.hotelorion.it, info@hotelorion.it).

$$$ Hotel al Piave, with 28 rooms above a bright, tight lobby and breakfast room, is comfortable and cheery, and you'll enjoy the neighborhood (RS%, family rooms, lots of narrow stairs, air-con, on Ruga Giuffa at Castello 4838, tel. 041-528-5174, www.hotelalpiave.com, info@hotelalpiave.com; Mirella, Paolo, Ilaria, and Federico).

$$$ Locanda Silva is a big, scruffy, but beautifully located hotel with a functional 1960s feel and a peaceful terrace. It rents 23 decent, old-school rooms that are particularly worth considering if you're willing to share a bathroom to save some money (RS%, closed Dec-Jan, family rooms, air-con, lots of stairs, on Fondamenta del Remedio at Castello 4423, tel. 041-522-7643, www.locandasilva.it, info@locandasilva.it; Sandra, Katia, and Massimo).

$$$ Locanda Casa Querini rents six bright, high-ceilinged rooms on a quiet square tucked away behind St. Mark's. You can enjoy your breakfast or a sunny happy-hour picnic sitting at their tables right on the sleepy little square (RS%, family rooms, in-room fridges, air-con, halfway between San Zaccaria vaporetto stop and Campo Santa Maria Formosa at Castello 4388 on Campo San Zaninovo/Giovanni Novo, tel. 041-241-1294, www.locandaquerini.com, info@locandaquerini.com; Patrizia and Caterina).

$$ Corte Campana B&B, run by enthusiastic and helpful Riccardo and his Californian wife Grace, rents three quiet, spacious, characteristic rooms in a homey flat just behind St. Mark's Square. For one room, the private bath is down the hall (cash only, 2-night minimum, family rooms, air-con, slow elevator, on Calle del Remedio at Castello 4410, tel. 041-523-3603, mobile 389-272-6500, www.cortecampana.com, info@cortecampana.com).

Near Campo Santa Maria Formosa

A bit farther north of the options listed above, these are in the quiet, somewhat less touristy Castello area, beyond the inviting Campo Santa Maria Formosa.

$$$ Locanda la Corte is perfumed with elegance without being snooty. Its 14 attractive, high-ceilinged, wood-beamed rooms—Venetian-style, done in earthy pastels—circle a small, sun-drenched courtyard and a ground-level restaurant (RS%, family rooms, air-con, on Calle Bressana at Castello 6317, tel. 041-241-1300, www.locandalacorte.it, info@locandalacorte.it, Marco and Oscar the dog).

$$ Alloggi Barbaria, a good budget choice, rents eight simple, characterless rooms on one floor around a bright but institutional-feeling common area. Beyond Campo San Zanipolo/Santi Giovanni e Paolo, it's a fair walk from the action, but in a pleasant residential neighborhood. The Ospedale vaporetto stop is two minutes away on foot, with no steps (RS%, limited breakfast of bread and jam, air-con in summer, Wi-Fi in common areas, on Calle de le Capucine at Castello 6573, tel. 041-522-2750, www. alloggibarbaria.it, info@alloggibarbaria.it, well-traveled Fausto). You can reach the Ospedale stop on vaporetto #5.2 from the train or bus stations, or (on request) via the Alilaguna blue line from the airport.

West of St. Mark's Square

These more expensive hotels are solid choices in a more elegant neighborhood.

$$$$ Hotel Flora sits buried in a sea of fancy designer boutiques and elegant hotels almost on the Grand Canal. It's formal, with uniformed staff and grand public spaces, yet the 40 rooms have a homey warmth and the garden oasis is a sanctuary for well-heeled, foot-weary guests (RS%, air-con, elevator, family apartment, on Calle Bergamaschi at San Marco 2283a, tel. 041-520-5844, www.hotelflora.it, info@hotelflora.it).

$$$$ Hotel Bel Sito offers pleasing Old World character, 34 smallish rooms, generous public spaces, a peaceful courtyard, and a picturesque location—facing a church on a small square between St. Mark's Square and the Accademia (some view rooms, air-con, elevator; near Santa Maria del Giglio vaporetto stop—line #1, on Campo Santa Maria Zobenigo/del Giglio at San Marco 2517, tel. 041-522-3365, www.hotelbelsitovenezia.it, info@hotelbelsitovenezia.it, graceful Rossella).

$$$$ Hotel Mercurio, a lesser value a block in front of La Fenice Opera House, offers 29 peaceful, comfortable rooms (some view rooms, family rooms, air-con, lots of stairs, on Calle del Fruttariol at San Marco 1848, tel. 041-522-0947, www.hotelmercurio.com, info@hotelmercurio.com; Monica, Vittorio, Marco, Piereangelo, and Giacomo).

NEAR THE RIALTO BRIDGE

These places are on opposite sides of the Grand Canal, within a short walk of the Rialto Bridge. Express vaporetto #2 brings you to the Rialto quickly from the train station, the Piazzale Roma bus station, and the parking-lot island of Tronchetto, but you'll need to take the "local" vaporetto #1 to reach the minor stops closer to the last two listings. To locate the following hotels, see the map on page 87.

$$$$ Hotel al Ponte Antico is exquisite, professional, and small. With nine plush rooms, a velvety royal living/breakfast room, and its own dock for water taxi arrivals, it's perfect for a romantic anniversary. Because its wonderful terrace overlooks the

VENICE

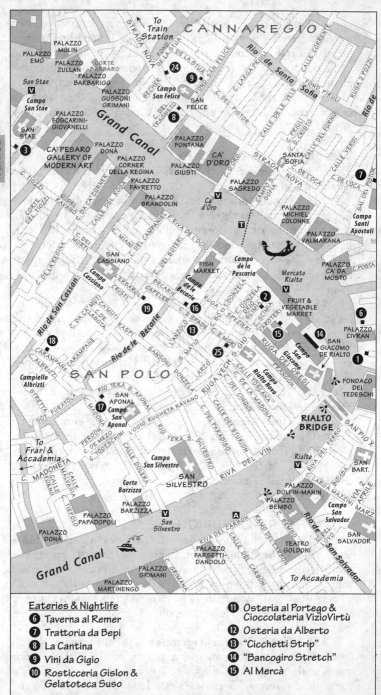

Hotels & Restaurants near the Rialto Bridge

VENICE

Hotels
1. Hotel al Ponte Antico
2. Pensione Guerrato
3. Hotel al Ponte Mocenigo
4. Locanda la Corte
5. To Alloggi Barbaria

16. Ristorante Vini da Pinto
17. Osteria al Ponte Storto
18. Trattoria Antiche Carampane
19. Ostaria al Garanghelo
20. Osteria alle Testiere
21. Osteria al Mascaron

22. Peter Pan Kebabs & Pizza
23. La Boutique del Gelato
24. Supermarkets (2)
25. Alimentari (Deli)

Grand Canal, Rialto Bridge, and market action, its rooms without a canal view may be a better value (air-con, 100 yards from Rialto Bridge at Cannaregio 5768, use Rialto vaporetto stop, tel. 041-241-1944, www.alponteantico.com, info@alponteantico.com, Matteo makes you feel like royalty).

$$$ **Pensione Guerrato,** right above the colorful Rialto produce market and just two minutes from the Rialto Bridge, is run by friendly, creative, and hardworking Roberto and Piero. Their 800-year-old building—with 22 spacious, charming rooms—is simple, airy, and wonderfully characteristic (RS%, cheaper rooms with shared bath, family rooms, air-con, on Calle drio la Scimia at San Polo 240a, take vaporetto #1 to Rialto Mercato stop to save walk over bridge, tel. 041-528-5927, www.hotelguerrato.com, info@hotelguerrato.com, Monica and Rosanna). My tour groups book this place for 60 nights each year. Sorry. The Guerrato also rents family apartments in the old center (great for groups of 4-8) for around €60 per person.

$$$ **Hotel al Ponte Mocenigo** is off the beaten path—a 10-minute walk northwest of the Rialto Bridge—but it's a great value. This 16th-century Venetian palazzo has a garden terrace and 10 comfy, beautifully appointed, and tranquil rooms (air-con, Santa Croce 2063, tel. 041-524-4797, www.alpontemocenigo.com, info@alpontemocenigo.com, Sandro and Valter). Take vaporetto #1 to the San Stae stop, head inland along the right side of the church, and take the first left down tiny Calle della Campanile.

NEAR THE ACCADEMIA BRIDGE

As you step over the Accademia Bridge, the commotion of touristy Venice is replaced by a sleepy village laced with canals. This quiet area, next to the best painting gallery in town, is a 15-minute walk from the Rialto or St. Mark's Square. The fast vaporetto #2 to the Accademia stop is the typical way to get here from the train station, Piazzale Roma bus station, Tronchetto parking lot, or St. Mark's Square (early and late, #2 terminates at the Rialto stop, where you change to #1). For hotels near the Zattere stop, vaporetto #5.1 (or the Alilaguna speedboat from the airport) are good options.

To locate the following hotels, see the map on page 91.

South of the Accademia Bridge, in Dorsoduro

$$$$ **Pensione Accademia** fills the 17th-century Villa Maravege like a Bellini painting. Its 27 comfortable, elegant rooms gild the lily. You'll feel aristocratic gliding through its grand public spaces and lounging in its wistful, breezy gardens (family rooms, must pay first night in advance, air-con, no elevator but most rooms on ground floor or one floor up, on Fondamenta Bollani at Dorso-

duro 1058, tel. 041-521-0188, www.pensioneaccademia.it, info@pensioneaccademia.it).

$$$$ Hotel la Calcina, the home of English writer John Ruskin in 1876, maintains a 19th-century formality. It comes with three-star comforts in a professional yet intimate package. Its 26 nautical-feeling rooms are squeaky clean, with nice wood furniture, hardwood floors, and a peaceful waterside setting facing Giudecca Island (some view rooms, air-con, no elevator and lots of stairs, rooftop terrace, buffet breakfast outdoors in good weather on platform over lagoon, near Zattere vaporetto stop at south end of Rio de San Vio at Dorsoduro 780, tel. 041-520-6466, www.lacalcina.com, info@lacalcina.com).

$$$$ Hotel Belle Arti, with a stiff, serious staff, lacks personality but has a grand entry, an inviting garden terrace, and 67 heavily decorated rooms (air-con, elevator, 100 yards behind Accademia art museum on Rio Terà A. Foscarini at Dorsoduro 912a, tel. 041-522-6230, www.hotelbellearti.com, info@hotelbellearti.com).

$$$$ Casa Rezzonico, a tranquil getaway far from the crowds, rents seven inviting, nicely appointed rooms with a grassy private garden terrace. All the rooms overlook either the canal or the garden (RS%, family rooms, air-con, near Ca' Rezzonico vaporetto stop—line #1, a few blocks past Campo San Barnaba on Fondamenta Gherardini at Dorsoduro 2813, tel. 041-277-0653, www.casarezzonico.it, info@casarezzonico.it, brothers Matteo and Mattia).

$$$$ Hotel Galleria has nine tight, old-fashioned, velvety rooms, most with views of the Grand Canal. Some rooms are quite narrow. It's run with a family feel by Luciano and Stefano (cheaper rooms with detached private bath, breakfast in room, ceiling fans, free minibar, 30 yards from Accademia art museum, next to recommended Foscarini pizzeria at Dorsoduro 878a, tel. 041-523-2489, www.hotelgalleria.it, info@hotelgalleria.it).

$$$ Don Orione Religious Guest House is a big cultural center dedicated to the work of a local man who became a saint in modern times. With 80 rooms filling an old monastery, it feels cookie-cutter-institutional (like a modern retreat center), but is also classy, clean, peaceful, and strictly run. It's beautifully located, comfortable, and a good value supporting a fine cause: Profits go to mission work in the developing world (family rooms, groups welcome, air-con, elevator, on Rio Terà A. Foscarini, Dorsoduro 909a, tel. 041-522-4077, www.donorione-venezia.it, info@donorione-venezia.it). From the Zattere vaporetto stop, turn right, then turn left. It's just after the church at #909a.

$$$ Ca' San Trovaso rents six newly renovated rooms in a little three-floor, formerly residential building. The location is peace-

VENICE

VENICE

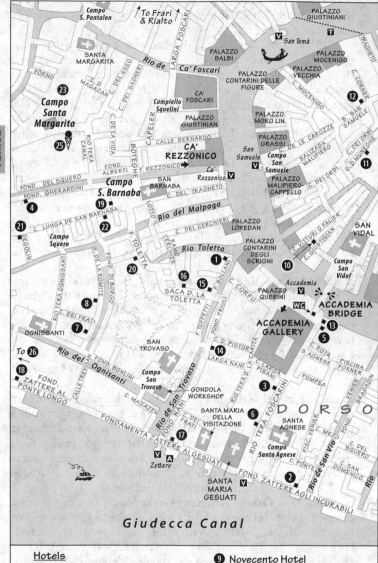

Giudecca Canal

<u>Hotels</u>
1 Pensione Accademia
2 Hotel la Calcina
3 Hotel Belle Arti
4 Casa Rezzonico
5 Hotel Galleria
6 Don Orione Religious Guest House
7 Ca' San Trovaso
8 Casa di Sara
9 Novecento Hotel
10 Foresteria Levi
11 Istituto Ciliota
12 Hotel San Samuele

<u>Eateries & Nightlife</u>
13 Bar Foscarini
14 Enoteca Cantine del Vino Già Schiavi

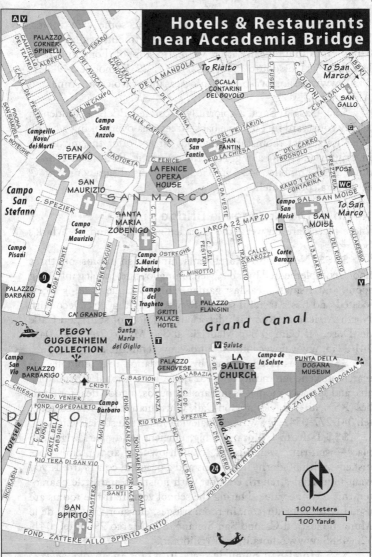

Hotels & Restaurants near Accademia Bridge

VENICE

15 Bar al Maraveje
16 Al Vecio Marangon
17 Terrazza del Casin dei Nobili
18 Oke Pizzeria
19 Ristoteca Oniga
20 Osteria Enoteca Ai Artisti
21 Pizzeria al Proteta
22 Enoteca e Trattoria la Bitta

23 Campo Santa Margarita Eateries & Nightlife
24 Ristorante Lineadombra
25 Il Doge Gelateria
26 Supermarket

ful, on a small, out-of-the-way canal (RS%, some view rooms, breakfast in your room, tiny roof terrace, apartments available with 3-night minimum, near Zattere vaporetto stop, off Fondamenta de le Romite at Dorsoduro 1350, tel. 041-241-2215, mobile 349-125-3890, www.casantrovaso.com, info@casantrovaso.com, Anna and Alessandra).

$$$ Casa di Sara, a colorfully decorated B&B, is hidden in a leafy courtyard in a humble back-street area overlooking a canal. Their four quiet rooms and tiny roof terrace offer the maximum in privacy (air-con, along Fondamenta de le Romite at Dorsoduro 1330, mobile 342-596-3563, www.casadisara.com, info@casadisara.com, Aniello).

North of the Accademia Bridge

These places are between the Accademia Bridge and St. Mark's Square.

$$$$ Novecento Hotel rents nine plush rooms on three floors, complemented by a big, welcoming lounge, an elegant living room, and a small breakfast garden. This boutique hotel is nicely located and has a tasteful sense of style, mingling Art Deco with North African and Turkish decor (air-con, lots of stairs, on Calle del Dose, off Campo San Maurizio at San Marco 2683, tel. 041-241-3765, www.novecento.biz, info@novecento.biz).

$$$$ Foresteria Levi, run by a foundation that promotes research on Venetian music, offers 32 quiet, institutional yet comfortable and spacious rooms—some are loft quads, a good deal for families (RS%, air-con, elevator, on Calle Giustinian at San Marco 2893, tel. 041-277-0542, www.foresterialevi.it, info@foresterialevi.it).

$$$ Istituto Ciliota is a big, efficient, and sparkling-clean place—well-run, well-located, church-owned, and plainly furnished—with 30 dorm-like rooms and a peaceful courtyard. If you want industrial-strength comfort with no stress and little character, this is a fine value. During the school year, half the rooms are used by students (air-con, in-room fridges, elevator, on Calle de le Muneghe just off Campo San Stefano, San Marco 2976, tel. 041-520-4888, www.ciliota.it, info@ciliota.it).

$$$ Hotel San Samuele rents 10 rooms in an old *palazzo* near Campo San Stefano. It's in a great locale, and the rooms with shared bath can be a good deal (no breakfast, fans, some stairs, on Salizada San Samuele at San Marco 3358, tel. 041-520-5165, www.hotelsansamuele.com, info@hotelsansamuele.com, Judith).

NEAR THE TRAIN STATION

I don't recommend the train station area. It's crawling with noisy, disoriented tourists with too much baggage and people whose life's calling is to scam visitors out of their money. It's so easy just to hop on a vaporetto upon arrival and sleep in the Venice of your dreams. Still, some like to park their bags near the station, and if so, these places stand out. The farther you get from the station, the more pleasant the surroundings.

Close to the Station

These hotels are very close to the station, but each is down a side street, away from the throngs along the main drag.

$$$$ Hotel Abbazia fills a former abbey with both history and class. The refectory makes a grand living room for guests, a garden fills the old courtyard, and the halls leading to 50 rooms are monkishly wide (RS%, air-con, no elevator but plenty of stairs, fun-loving staff, 2 blocks from the station on the very quiet Calle Priuli dei Cavaletti, Cannaregio 68, tel. 041-717-333, www.abbaziahotel. com, info@abbaziahotel.com).

$$ Hotel S. Lucia, 150 yards from the train station, is oddly modern and sterile, with bright and spacious rooms and tight showers. Its 13 rooms are simple and clean. Guests enjoy their sunny garden area out front (cheaper rooms with shared bath, air-con, closed Nov-Feb, on Calle de la Misericordia at Cannaregio 358, tel. 041-715-180, www.hotelslucia.com, info@hotelslucia.com, Gianni, Alessandra, and their son, Lorenzo).

$ Hotel Rossi, sitting quietly at the end of a dead-end street off the main Lista di Spagna, rents 17 tired, well-worn rooms that are cheap in every sense—the budget-minded will find it tolerable for a night or two, but consider yourself forewarned (cheaper rooms with shared bath, air-con, lots of stairs, on Calle de le Procuratie, Cannaregio 262, tel. 041-715-164, www.hotelrossi.ve.it, info@ hotelrossi.ve.it).

Across the Bridge from the Train Station

These two places are in a quieter area on the other side of the Grand Canal from the train station—you'll have to haul your bags across a big bridge. Both are also convenient to the bus station at Piazzale Roma.

$$$ Albergo Marin is loosely run, with 20 nice but sloppily kept rooms. It's close enough to the station to be convenient, but far enough to be quiet, sane, and residential (cheaper rooms with shared bath, air-con, on Ramo de le Chioverete at Santa Croce 670b, tel. 041-718-022, www.albergomarin.it, info@albergomarin. it, brothers Giacomo and Filippo).

$$ Hotel Ai Tolentini is a pleasant couple of hundred yards from the Piazzale Roma bus station—just far enough to make you feel like you're actually in Venice. The seven rooms are on two floors, up narrow stairs above a restaurant that can be noisy (no

Hotels near the Train Station

1. Hotel Abbazia
2. Hotel S. Lucia
3. Hotel Rossi
4. Albergo Marin & Launderette
5. Hotel Ai Tolentini
6. Locanda Ca' San Marcuola
7. Locanda Herion
8. Hotel Henry
9. Antica Birraria la Corte (Restaurant)

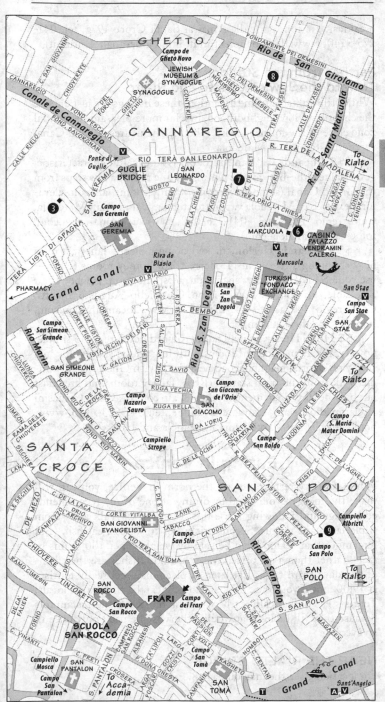

GHETTO

Rio de San Girolamo

FONDAMENTE DEI ORMESINI

Campo de Gheto Novo

JEWISH MUSEUM & SYNAGOGUE

8

SYNAGOGUE

GHETTO VECHIO

FOND. PESCARIA

Canale de Cannaregio

CANNAREGIO

FOND. SAVORGNAN

R. TERA DE LA MADALENA

Ponte di Guglie

V

RIO TERA SAN LEONARDO

GUGLIE BRIDGE

SAN LEONARDO

7

R. de Santa Marcuola

To Rialto

3

Campo San Geremia

SAN GEREMIA

SAN MARCUOLA

6

CASINO PALAZZO VENDRAMIN CALERGI

TERA LISTA DI SPAGNA

Riva de Biasio

V

San Marcuola

PHARMACY

Grand Canal

RIVA DI BIASIO

Campo San Zan Degola

TURKISH "FONDACO" EXCHANGE

San Stae

Campo San Simeon Grande

Rio Marin

RIO d. S. Zan Degola

Campo San Stae

SAN STAE

Campo San Simeone Grande

To Rialto

RUGA VECHIA

Campo San Giacomo de l'Orio

Campo S. Maria Mater Domini

Campo Nazario Sauro

RUGA BELLA

SAN GIACOMO

DA L'ORIO

Campiello Strope

Campo San Boldo

SANTA CROCE

SAN POLO

SAN GIOVANNI EVANGELISTA

CORTE VITALBA

Campiello Albrizti

9

Campo San Stin

Rio de San Polo

Campo San Polo

SAN POLO

To Rialto

SAN ROCCO

FRARI

Campo dei Frari

SCUOLA SAN ROCCO

Campo San Rocco

SAN PANTALON

Campo San Tomà

SAN TOMÀ

Grand Canal

Campiello Mosca

Campo San Pantalon

To Accademia

Sant'Angelo

T

A V

breakfast, air-con, on Calle Amai at Santa Croce 197g, tel. 041-275-9140, www.albergoaitolentini.it, info@albergoaitolentini.it).

Farther from the Station, Toward the Jewish Ghetto and Rialto

While still walkable from the station, these listings are just outside the chaotic station neighborhood, in a far more pleasant residential zone close to the former Jewish Ghetto. The nearest Grand Canal vaporetto stop is San Marcuola.

$$$ Locanda Ca' San Marcuola is a peaceful, characteristic, good-value oldie-but-goodie renting 14 fine rooms a few steps from the Grand Canal (some view rooms, family rooms, air-con, elevator, next to San Marcuola vaporetto stop on Campo San Marcuola, Cannaregio 1763, tel. 041-716-048, www.casanmarcuola.com, info@casanmarcuola.com).

$$$ Locanda Herion, tucked down a sleepy lane just off a busy shopping street, rents 13 beige-tiled, homey rooms (RS%—use code STEVES, a few shared terraces, one room is wheelchair accessible, air-con, pay Wi-Fi, on Campiello Augusto Picutti, Cannaregio 1697a, tel. 041-275-9426, www.locandaherion.com, info@locandaherion.com).

$$ Hotel Henry, a small family-owned hotel, rents 15 simple, flowery, nicely maintained rooms with few public spaces. It's in a sleepy residential neighborhood near the Jewish Ghetto, a 10-minute walk from the train station (RS%, family rooms, no breakfast but bars nearby, apartments available, air-con, on Calle Ormesini at Campiello Briani, Cannaregio 1506e, tel. 041-523-6675, www.hotelhenry.it, info@hotelhenry.it, Manola and Henry).

Eating in Venice

While touristy restaurants are the norm in Venice, you can still make the most of your meal by dining at one of my recommended listings and following these tips. First trick: Walk away from triple-language menus. Second trick: For freshness, eat fish. (But remember that seafood can be sold by weight—per 100 grams or *etto*—rather than a set price.) Many seafood dishes are the catch-of-the-day. Third trick: Eat later. A place may feel really touristy at 19:00, but if you come back at 21:00, it can be filled with locals. Tourists eat barbarically early, which is fine with the restaurants because they fill tables that would otherwise be used only once in an evening.

NEAR THE RIALTO BRIDGE

For locations, see the map on page 87.

Restaurant Price Code

I've assigned each eatery a price category, based on the average cost of a typical main course (pasta or *secondi*). Drinks, desserts, and splurge items (steak and seafood) can raise the price considerably.

$$$$	**Splurge:** Most main courses over €20
$$$	**Pricier:** €15-20
$$	**Moderate:** €10-15
$	**Budget:** Under €10

In Italy, pizza by the slice and other takeaway food is **$**; a basic trattoria or sit-down pizzeria is **$$**; a casual but more upscale restaurant is **$$$**; and a swanky splurge is **$$$$**.

North of the Bridge

These restaurants and wine bars are located near or beyond Campo Santi Apostoli, on or near the Strada Nova, the main drag going from Rialto toward the train station.

$$$ Taverna al Remer is a creative place with its own private square overlooking the Grand Canal (across from the Rialto Market). Its restaurant seating is deep in an old, candle-lit warehouse, and its happy-hour "yard" offers a chance to sit on their private pier and enjoy the Grand Canal and Rialto Bridge action (free buffet accompanying drinks, Thu-Tue 17:30-19:00). They also offer a good lunch buffet (€20 plus drink, Mon-Tue & Thu-Fri 12:00-15:00) and have live jazz after 21:00 (closed Wed, Cannaregio 5701, tel. 041-522-8789). From Campo San Bartolomeo, head north (behind the statue) and cross one bridge. Then, just past the pink church (San Giovanni Crisostomo), about 10 yards before the next bridge, venture down the tiny dark lane on the left.

$$$ Trattoria da Bepi, bright and alpine-paneled, feels like a classic, where Loris carries on his mother's passion for good, traditional Venetian cuisine. Ask for the seasonal specialties: The seafood appetizer plate and crab dishes are excellent. There's good seating inside and out. If you trust Loris, you'll walk away with a wonderful dining memory (Fri-Wed 12:00-14:30 & 19:00-22:00, closed Thu, reservations recommended, half a block off Campo Santi Apostoli on Salizada Pistor, Cannaregio 4550, tel. 041-528-5031, www.anticatrattoriadabepi.it).

$$$ La Cantina is an elegant *enoteca*, both rustic and sophisticated—you won't find a menu here. Rather than cook (there's no kitchen), they serve wonderful gourmet cold plates of meat, cheese, and fish. Though short on smiles and expensive (meat-and-cheese plates-€18/person, seafood plates-€35/person), you'll enjoy the best ingredients paired with fine wines. You can sit inside and watch the preparation scene or enjoy the parade of passersby from great seats right on the Strada Nova (Mon-Sat 11:00-22:00, closed Sun, facing Campo San Felice on Strada Nova near Ca' d'Oro, Cannaregio 3689, tel. 041-522-8258).

$$$$ Vini da Gigio, a more expensive option, has a traditional Venetian menu and a classy but unsnooty setting that's a pleasant mix of traditional and contemporary (Wed-Sun 12:00-14:30 & 19:00-22:30, closed Mon-Tue, 4 blocks from Ca' d'Oro vaporetto stop on Fondamenta San Felice, behind the church on Campo San Felice, Cannaregio 3628a, tel. 041-528-5140, www.vinidagigio.com).

East of the Rialto Bridge

The next few places hide away in the twisty lanes between the Rialto Bridge and Campo Santa Maria Formosa. Osteria da Alberto is a tad farther north of the others, in Cannaregio.

$ Rosticceria Gislon is a cheap—if confusing—self-service diner. This throwback budget eatery—kind of an Italian Mel's Diner—has a surly staff: Don't take it personally. Notice that the different counters serve up different types of food—pastas, *secondi*, fried goodies, and so on. You can get it to go, grab one of the few tiny tables, or munch at the bar—but I'd skip their upper-floor restaurant option (great fried *mozzarella al prosciutto*, fruit salad, cheap glasses of wine, prices listed on wall behind counter, no cover and no service charge, daily 9:00-21:30, San Marco 5424, tel. 041-522-3569). To find it, imagine the statue on Campo San Bartolomeo walks backward 20 yards, turns left, and goes under a passageway. Follow him.

$$ Osteria al Portego is a small and popular neighborhood eatery near Campo San Lio. Carlo serves good meals, bargain-priced house wine, and excellent €1-3 *cicchetti*—best enjoyed early, around 18:00. The *cicchetti* here can make a great meal, but consider sitting down for a dinner from their menu. From 12:00-14:30 & 17:30-21:30, their six tables are reserved for those ordering from the menu; the *cicchetti* are picked over by 21:00. Reserve ahead if you want a table (daily 11:30-15:00 & 17:30-22:00, on Calle de la Malvasia, Castello 6015, tel. 041-522-9038, www.osteriaalportego.it, Federica). From Rosticceria Gislon (listed above), continue over a bridge to Campo San Lio, turn left, and follow Calle Carminati straight 50 yards over another bridge.

$$ Osteria da Alberto, up near Campo Santa Maria Novo, is one of my standbys. They offer up excellent daily specials: seafood dishes, pastas, and a good house wine in a woody and characteristic interior (although it's set along a canal, you can't see it from the dining area). It's smart to reserve at night—I'd request a table in front (daily 12:00-15:00 & 18:30-22:30; on Calle Larga Giacinto Gallina, midway between Campo Santi Apostoli and

Campo San Zanipolo/Santi Giovanni e Paolo, and next to Ponte de la Panada bridge, Cannaregio 5401; tel. 041-523-8153, www.osteriadaalberto.it, run by Graziano and Giovanni).

Rialto Market Area

The north end of the Rialto Bridge is a great area for menu browsing, bar-hopping, drinks, and snacks; it also has fine sit-down restaurants. As with market neighborhoods anywhere, you'll find lots of hard-working holes-in-the-wall with a line on the freshest of ingredients and catering to local shoppers needing a quick, affordable, and tasty bite. This area is very crowded by day, nearly empty early in the evening, and packed with young Venetian clubbers later.

My listings below include a stretch of dark and rustic pubs serving *cicchetti* (Venetian tapas), a strip of trendy places fronting the Grand Canal, a few little places on the market, and a couple of "normal" restaurants serving solid pasta, pizza, and *secondi*. All but the last two eateries are within 200 yards of the market and each other.

The *Cicchetti* Strip: Four Venetian Tapas Bars

Cicchetti bars specialize in finger foods and appetizers that combine to make a speedy and tasty meal. The selection and ambience are best on workdays—Monday through Saturday for lunch or early dinner (see "The Stand-Up Progressive Venetian Pub-Crawl Dinner," on page 104). An *ombra* ("shadow") is a small glass of wine often offered with *cicchetti*.

The 100-yard-long stretch starting two blocks inland from the Rialto Market (along Sotoportego dei Do Mori and Calle de le Do Spade) is beloved among Venetian *cicchetti* enthusiasts for its delightful bar munchies, good wine by the glass, and fun stand-up conviviality. These four **$** places serve food all day, but the spread is best at around noon (generally open daily 12:00-15:00 & 18:00-20:00 or 21:00; two of the places I list are closed Sun). Each place offers a fine bar-and-stools scene, and a couple can be treated like a restaurant—order from their rustic menu and grab a table. Scout these places in advance (listed in the order you'll reach them, if coming from the Rialto Bridge) to help decide which ambience is right for the experience you have in mind. Then pick one, dig in, and drink up.

At each place, look for the list of snacks and wine by the glass at the bar or on the wall. When you're ready for dessert, try dipping a Burano biscuit in a glass of strawberry-flavored *fragolino* or another sweet dessert wine. Most bars are closed 15:00-18:00 and offer glasses of house wine for under €1, better wine for around €2.50, and *cicchetti* for €1.50-2.

VENICE

Venetian Cuisine

Even more so than the rest of Italy, Venetian cuisine relies heavily on fish, shellfish, risotto, and polenta. Along with the usual pizza-and-pasta fare, here are some typical foods you'll encounter. For more on Italian food, including *salumi* and cheeses, see page 1140.

Sandwiches
Panini: Sandwiches made with rustic bread, filled with meat, vegetables, and cheese, served cold or toasted *(riscaldato)*.
Piadini: Flatbread or wrap-like sandwiches.
Tramezzini: Sandwiches served cold and stuffed with filling (like egg, tuna, or shrimp), mixed with mayonnaise.

Antipasti (Appetizers)
Cicchetti: Finger-food appetizers sold in some pubs
Antipasto di mare: Marinated mix of fish and shellfish served chilled.
Asiago cheese: A regional specialty, this cow's-milk cheese is either *mezzano* (young/creamy) or *stravecchio* (aged/pungent).
Sarde in saor: Sardines marinated with onions.

Risi (Rice), Pasta, and Polenta
Bigoli in salsa: Long, fat, whole-wheat noodle in anchovy sauce.
Pasta alla buzzara: Pasta in a rich seafood-tomato sauce, generally with shrimp.
Pasta al pomodoro: Pasta in a simple tomato sauce.
Pasta al vongole: Pasta with clams.
Pasta e fagioli: Bean-and-pasta soup.
Polenta: Thick cornmeal porridge served soft or cut into firm slabs and grilled.
Risi e bisi: Rice and peas.
Risotto: Short-grain rice simmered in broth and flavored with seafood, meat, or veggies. *Risotto nero* is made with squid and its ink.

Frutti di Mare (Seafood)
Venetian fish are generally smaller than American salmon and trout (think sardines and anchovies). The weirder the seafood (eel, octopus, frogfish), the more local it is.
Baccalà: Atlantic salt cod that's rehydrated and served with polenta; or chopped up and mixed with mayonnaise as a topping for *cicchetti* (appetizers), called *baccalà mantecato.*
Branzino: Sea bass, grilled and served whole.
Calamari: Squid, oftencut into rings and deep-fried or marinated.
Cozze: Mussels, often steamed in an herb broth with tomato.
Gamberi: Shrimp: *gamberetti* are small, and *gamberoni* are large.
Moleche col pien: Fried soft-shell crabs.
Orata: Sea bream (usually farmed).
Pesce fritto misto: Deep-fried seafood (often calamari and prawns).
Pesce spada: Swordfish.

Rombo: Turbot, a flatfish similar to flounder.

Rospo: Frogfish, a small marine fish.

Salmone: Salmon (typically farm-raised).

Seppia: Cuttlefish, a squid-like creature. *Seppia al nero* is the squid served in its own ink, often over spaghetti. It's sweet and tender when grilled (*grigliata* or *alla griglia*).

Sogliola: Sole, served poached or oven-roasted.

Vitello di mare: "Sea veal," like swordfish—firm, mild, and grilled.

Vongole: Clams, often steamed with fresh herbs and wine, or served as *spaghetti alle vongole*.

Zuppa di pesce: Seafood stew.

Dolci (Desserts)

Rather than order dessert in a restaurant, I like to stroll with a cup or cone of gelato from one of Venice's popular *gelaterie*. Cookies are also popular. The numerous varieties are due perhaps to Venice's position in trade (spices) and love of celebrations. Many treats were created for feast days and religious holidays.

Bisse: Seahorse-shaped cookies

Bussola: Ring-shaped cookies made for Easter.

Croccante: Toasted almond confection, similar to peanut brittle.

Fritole: Tiny doughnuts associated with Carnevale (Mardi Gras).

Pinza: Rustic cornmeal and wheat-flour cake filled with dried fruit; made for Epiphany, January 6.

Tiramisù: Spongy ladyfingers soaked in coffee and Marsala, layered with mascarpone cheese and bitter chocolate.

Cocktails and Local Wines

Amarone: Rich and intense red, made from dried Valpolicella grapes that yield a wine high in alcohol—often around 15 percent.

Bardolino: Beaujolais-like wine made from Valpolicella grapes.

Bellini: Cocktail of Prosecco and white-peach puree (invented at the pricey Harry's American Bar near St. Mark's Square).

Fragolino: A sweet, slightly fizzy dessert wine made from a strawberry-flavored grape.

Prosecco: Sparkling white wine. Connoisseurs say the best hails from Valdobbiadene.

Recioto: Sweet dessert wine made with dried, aged Valpolicella grapes.

Sgroppino: Traditional after-dinner drink of squeezed lemon juice, lemon gelato, and vodka.

Soave: Crisp, dry white wine, great with seafood. "Soave Classico" designates a higher quality.

Spritz: White wine, soda, and ice mixed with Campari (bitter) or Aperol (sweeter).

Tiziano: Grape juice and Prosecco.

Valpolicella: Light, dry, fruity red wine, often served as the *vino della casa* (house wine)

Bar all'Arco, a bustling one-room joint, is particularly enjoyable for its tiny open-face sandwiches (closed Sun, San Polo 436; Francesco, Anna, Matteo).

Cantina Do Mori has been famous with locals (since 1462) and savvy travelers (since 1982) as a convivial place for fine wine. They serve a forest of little edibles on toothpicks and *francobolli* (a spicy selection of 20 tiny, mayo-soaked sandwiches nicknamed "stamps"). Go here to be abused in a fine atmosphere—the frowns are part of the shtick (closed Sun, can be shoulder-to-shoulder, San Polo 430).

Osteria ai Storti, with a cool photo of the market in 1909, is more of a sit-down place (tables inside and on street). It's run by Alessandro, who speaks English and enjoys helping educate travelers, and his sister Baby—pronounced "Bobby" (daily, around corner from Cantina Do Mori on Calle San Matio—follow signs, San Polo 819).

Cantina Do Spade is expertly run by Francesco, who clearly lists the *cicchetti* and wines of the day (also good for sit-down meals, 30 yards down Calle de le Do Spade from Osteria ai Storti at San Polo 860, tel. 041-521-0583).

The Bancogiro Stretch: Five Places Overlooking the Grand Canal

Just past the Rialto Bridge, between Campo San Giacomo and the Grand Canal, this strip of five popular places in a recently renovated old building has some of the best canalside seating in Venice. I call this the "Bancogiro Stretch" (the restaurants front a former banking building called Bancogiro).

Each place has a unique character and formula. Unless otherwise noted, all are open daily and serve drinks, *cicchetti*, and inventive, somewhat pricey sit-down meals. While you can get a drink anytime, dinner is typically served only after 19:00 or 19:30. During meals, they charge more and limit table seating to those ordering full lunches or dinners; but between mealtimes you can enjoy a drink or a snack at fine prices. After dinner hours, the Bancogiro Stretch—especially in the surrounding alleys that house low-rent bars—becomes a youthful and trendy nightspot. Before or after dinner, this strip is one of the best places in town for a *spritz*.

Here's the rundown (in the order you'll reach them from the Rialto Bridge): **$$$ Bar Naranzaria** serves Italian dishes with a few Japanese options. **$$ Caffè Vergnano** is your cheapest option—especially during mealtimes (vegan dishes and a busy microwave oven). **$$$ Osteria al Pescador** has a friendly staff and serves local specialties. **$$$ Bar Ristorante Bancogiro** has the best reputation for dinner, a passion for the best cheese, and good *cicchetti* options at the bar (nice €17 cheese plate, closed Mon, tel.

041-523-2061, www.osteriabancogiro.it). The more modern **$$ Bar Ancòra** seems to be most popular with the local bar crowd, with a live piano player crooning lounge music during busy times (*cicchetti* at the bar).

Other Good Eateries near the Rialto Market

$ Al Mercà ("At the Market"), a few steps away and off the canal, is a lively little nook with a happy crowd, where law-office workers have lunch and young locals gather in the evening for drinks and little snacks. The price list is clear, and the youthful crowd seems to enjoy connecting with curious tourists (stand at bar or in square—there are no tables and no interior, Mon-Sat 10:00-14:30 & 18:00-21:00, closed Sun, on Campo Cesare Battisti, San Polo 213).

$$ Ristorante Vini da Pinto is a tourist-friendly eatery facing the fish market, with a large menu and relaxing outdoor seating. Owner George visits the market each morning to select the day's best catch. Enjoy the fixed-price, three-course seafood meal for €17, including a pasta, seafood sampler plate, veggies, and dessert. Grander versions cost €20-25. Rick Steves readers receive a welcoming prosecco and a farewell *limoncello* and homemade cookie (daily 11:00-23:00, Campo de le Becarie, San Polo 367a, tel. 041-522-4599).

$$ Osteria al Ponte Storto, a little family-run place on a quiet canalside corner a block off the main drag, is worth seeking out for its good-value main dishes, daily specials, and peaceful location (Tue-Sun 12:00-15:00 & 19:00-21:45, closed Mon, down Calle Bianca from San Aponal church, San Polo 1278, tel. 041-528-2144).

Between the Rialto Bridge and Frari Church

$$$$ Trattoria Antiche Carampane is a dressy, family-run place with an open kitchen and a local following. They have a passion for fish (and make a point: no pizza) and serve traditional Venetian dishes with a fresh twist that change with the season. It's small—there's just 30 seats with six tables on the street (closed Sun-Mon, reservations necessary, Rio Tera delle Carampane, San Polo 1911, tel. 041-524-0165, www.antichecarampane.com, Francesco).

$$ Ostaria al Garanghelo is a happy little eatery with an inviting menu, a love for fresh fish, and an old but shiny ambience. They have a few seats on the street—good for people-watching—and offer a seafood tasting platter and vegetarian dishes (daily, Calle dei Boteri, San Polo 1570, tel. 041-721-721).

$$ Antica Birraria la Corte is an everyday eatery on the delightful Campo San Polo. Popular for its pizza, calzones, and wonderful selection of hearty salads, it fills the far side of this cozy, family-filled square. Although the interior is sprawling and mod-

The Stand-Up Progressive Venetian Pub-Crawl Dinner

My favorite Venetian dinner is a pub crawl (*giro d'ombra*)—a tradition unique to Venice, where no cars means easy crawling. (*Giro* means stroll, and *ombra*—slang for a glass of wine—means shade, from the old days when a portable wine bar scooted with the shadow of the Campanile bell tower across St. Mark's Square.)

Venice's residential back streets hide plenty of characteristic bars (*bacari*), with countless trays of interesting toothpick munchies (*cicchetti*) and blackboards listing the wines that are uncorked and served by the glass. This is a great way to mingle and have fun with the Venetians. Bars don't stay open very late, and the *cicchetti* selection is best early, so start your evening by 18:00. Most bars are closed on Sunday. For a stress-free pub crawl, consider taking a tour with the charming Alessandro Schezzini (see page 34).

Cicchetti bars have a social stand-up zone and a cozy gaggle of tables where you can generally sit down with your *cicchetti* or order from a simple menu. In some of the more popular places, the crowds happily spill out into the street. Food generally costs the same price whether you stand or sit.

I've listed plenty of pubs in walking order for a quick or extended crawl. If you've crawled enough, most of these bars make a fine one-stop, sit-down dinner.

ern, it's a joy to eat on the square, where metal tables teeter on the cobbles, the wind plays with the paper mats, and children run free (daily 12:00-15:00 & 18:00-23:30, on Campo San Polo at #2168—see map on page 94, tel. 041-275-0570).

NEAR ST. MARK'S SQUARE

While my first listing is a serious restaurant, the other places listed here are cheap-and-cheery options convenient to your sightseeing. For locations, see the map on page 82.

$$$$ Ristorante Antica Sacrestia is a classic restaurant where the owner, Pino, takes a hands-on approach to greeting guests. His staff serves creative fixed-price meals (€35, €55, or €80), a humdrum *menù del giorno,* and wonderful pizzas. (Be warned: These meals seem designed to overwhelm you with too much food. There's no wine by the glass. Order carefully. Pizza is your only budget escape.) You can also order à la carte; their €22 antipasto spread looks like a lagoon aquarium spread out on a plate. My

While you can order a plate, Venetians prefer going one-by-one...sipping their wine and trying this...then give me one of those...and so on. Try deep-fried mozzarella cheese, gorgonzola, calamari, artichoke hearts, and anything ugly on a toothpick. *Crostini* (small toasted bread with a topping) are popular, as are marinated seafood, olives, and prosciutto with melon. Meat and fish (*pesce;* PESH-ay) munchies can be expensive; veggies (*verdure*) are cheap, at about €3 for a meal-sized plate. In many places, there's a set price per food item (e.g., €1.50). To get a plate of assorted appetizers for €8 (or more, depending on how hungry you are), ask for *"Un piatto classico di cicchetti misti da €8"* (oon pee-AH-toh KLAH-see-koh dee cheh-KET-tee MEE-stee dah OH-toh eh-OO-roh). Bread sticks (*grissini*) are free for the asking.

Bar-hopping Venetians enjoy an *aperitivo*, a before-dinner drink. Boldly order a Bellini, a *spritz con Aperol*, or a prosecco, and draw approving looks from the natives.

Drink the house wines. A small glass of house red or white wine (*ombra rosso* or *ombra bianco*) or a small beer (*birrino*) costs about €1. The house keg wine is cheap—€1 per glass, about €4 per liter. *Vin bon*, Venetian for fine wine, may run you from €2 to €6 per little glass. There are usually several fine wines uncorked and available by the glass. A good last drink is *fragolino*, the local sweet wine—*bianco* or *rosso*. It often comes with a little cookie (*biscotto*) for dipping.

readers are welcome to a free *sgroppino* (lemon vodka after-dinner drink) upon request (Tue-Sun 11:30-15:00 & 18:00-23:00, closed Mon, behind San Zaninovo/Giovanni Novo Church on Calle Corona, Castello 4463, tel. 041-523-0749, www.anticasacrestia.it).

"Sandwich Row": On Calle de le Rasse, just steps away from the tourist intensity at St. Mark's Square, is a handy strip I call "Sandwich Row." Lined with sandwich bars, it's the closest place to St. Mark's to get a decent sandwich at an affordable price with a place to sit down (most places open daily 7:00-24:00, €1 extra to sit; from the Bridge of Sighs, head down the Riva and take the second lane on the left). I particularly like **$ Birreria Forst,** a pleasantly unpretentious café that serves busy local workers a selection of meaty €3 sandwiches with tasty sauce on wheat bread or made-to-order sandwiches (daily 9:30-23:00, air-con, rustic wood tables, Castello 4540, tel. 041-523-0557, Romina), and **$ Bar Verde,** a more modern sandwich bar with clear and good pricing plus fun people-watching views from its corner tables (also splittable salads, fresh pastries, at the end of Calle de le Rasse facing Campo Santi Filippo e Giacomo, Castello 4526).

$$ Ristorante alla Basilica, just one street behind St. Mark's Basilica, is a church-run, indoor, institutional-feeling place that serves a solid €16 fixed-price lunch, often amid noisy school groups. It's not self-serve—you'll be seated and can choose a pasta, a *secondi*, and a vegetable side dish off the menu. Don't expect high cuisine or ingratiating service—but it's efficient and filling (Wed-Mon 12:00-15:00, closed Tue, air-con, Calle dei Albanesi, Castello 4255, tel. 041-522-0524).

$ Ristorante Cinese Capitol, around the corner from the listings above, provides a break from Italian. It serves inexpensive but tasty Chinese standards to eat in or take out (daily 11:00-15:30 & 17:30-23:00, on Campo S.S. Filippo e Giacomo, Castello 4294, tel. 041-522-5331).

Picnicking: Though you can't picnic on St. Mark's Square, you can legally take your snacks to the nearby Giardinetti Reali, the small park along the waterfront west of the Piazzetta.

NORTH OF ST. MARK'S SQUARE, NEAR CAMPO SANTA MARIA FORMOSA

For a (marginally) less touristy scene, walk a few blocks north to the inviting Campo Santa Maria Formosa. For locations, see the map on page 87.

$$$$ Osteria alle Testiere is my top dining splurge in Venice. Hugely respected, Luca and his staff are dedicated to quality, serving up creative, artfully presented market-fresh seafood (there's no meat on the menu), homemade pastas, and fine wine in what the chef calls a "Venetian Nouvelle" style. With only 22 seats, it's tight and homey, with the focus on food and service. They have daily specials, 10 wines by the glass, and one agenda: a great dining experience. This is a good spot to let loose and trust your host. They're open for lunch (12:00-15:00), and reservations are a must well in advance for their two dinner seatings: 19:00 and 21:30 (plan on spending €50 for dinner, closed Sun-Mon, on Calle del Mondo Novo, just off Campo Santa Maria Formosa, Castello 5801, tel. 041-522-7220, www.osterialletestiere.it).

$$$ Osteria al Mascaron is a rustic little bar-turned-restaurant where I've gone for years to watch Gigi, Momi, and their food-loving band of ruffians dish up rustic-yet-sumptuous pastas with steamy seafood to salivating foodies. The €16 *antipasto misto* plate—have fun pointing—and two glasses of wine make a terrific light meal (Mon-Sat 11:00-15:00 & 17:30-23:00, closed Sun, reservations smart Fri-Sat, Wi-Fi; on Calle Lunga Santa Maria Formosa, a block past Campo Santa Maria Formosa, Castello 5225; tel. 041-522-5995, www.osteriamascaron.it). While they advertise pastas only for two, you are welcome to have a half-order for half-price—still plenty big.

Fast and Cheap Eats: The veggie stand on Campo Santa Maria Formosa is a fixture. For *döner kebabs* and pizza to go, head down Calle Lunga Santa Maria Formosa to **$ Peter Pan** at #6249 (daily 12:00-23:00, Castello).

DORSODURO

All of these recommendations are within a 10-minute walk of the Accademia Bridge (for locations, see the map on page 91). Dorsoduro is great for restaurants and well worth the walk from the more touristy Rialto and San Marco areas. The first listings, near the Accademia, are best for lunch. The places in Zattere overlook the Giudecca Canal. Best for dinner are the four restaurants near Campo San Barnaba. Last are a handful of pizzerias and *cicchetti* bars on Campo Santa Margarita. My top Dorsoduro listing, **Ristorante Lineadombra,** is described later in "Splurging on a Water (or Otherwise Great) View."

Near the Accademia Bridge

$$ Bar Foscarini, next to the Accademia Bridge and Galleria, offers decent pizzas and *panini* in a memorable Grand Canal-view setting. The food is forgettable and drinks are pricey. But you're paying a premium for this premium location. On each visit to Venice, I grab a pizza lunch here while I ponder the Grand Canal bustle. They also serve breakfast (daily 8:00-23:00, until 20:30 Nov-April, on Rio Terà A. Foscarini, Dorsoduro 878c, tel. 041-522-7281, Paolo and Simone).

$ Enoteca Cantine del Vino Già Schiavi, with a wonderfully characteristic *cicchetti*-bar ambience, is much loved for its €1.20 *cic-*

chetti, €4 sandwiches (order from list on board), and €1-2 glasses of wine. You're welcome to enjoy your wine and finger food at the bar or out on the sidewalk. This is primarily a wine shop with great prices for bottles to go—and plastic glasses for picnickers (Mon-Sat 8:30-20:30, closed Sun, 100 yards from Accademia art museum on San Trovaso canal; facing the Accademia, take a right and then a forced left at the canal to the second bridge—it's at Dorsoduro 992, tel. 041-523-0034).

$ Bar al Maraveje is handy for a sandwich, with quiet, comfy tables just minutes from the Accademia. They serve a range of fresh sandwiches, from less expensive *topolini* (four-bite sandwiches) and *tramezzini* (crustless sandwich triangles) to heartier ciabatta sandwiches (daily, 100 yards west of the Accademia, just over a bridge on Calle de la Toletta, Dorsoduro 1185, tel. 041-523-5768).

$ **Al Vecio Marangon** glows like a dream come true on its corner tucked away from the frenzy of Venice, about 100 yards west of the Accademia. This stylishly rustic bar serves *cicchetti*-style dishes and pastas within its tight and picturesque interior or at a line of outdoor tables. Consider their splittable *piatto di cicchetti misti*, a sampler of sardines, octopus, codfish, and seafood salad. As they take no reservations, arrive early or be prepared to wait (daily 12:00-23:00, on Calle de la Toletta, Dorsoduro 1210, tel. 041-525-5768).

Zattere

$$$ **Terrazza del Casin dei Nobili** takes full advantage of the warm, romantic evening sun. They serve regional specialties at tolerable prices. The breezy and beautiful seaside seating comes with the rumble of *vaporetti* from the nearby stop. The interior is bright and hip (daily 12:00-24:00; from Zattere vaporetto stop, turn left to Dorsoduro 924; tel. 041-520-6895).

$ **Oke Pizzeria** is playful, with casual tables on the embankment and a sprawling pizza-parlor interior. It's a hit with young Venetians for its fun atmosphere (daily 11:30-15:30 & 18:30-23:00, a couple of hundred yards from the Zattere vaporetto stop, Dorsoduro 1414, tel. 041-520-6601).

On or near Campo San Barnaba

This small square is a delight—especially in the evening. As these places are within a few steps of each other—and the energy and atmosphere can vary—I like to survey the options before choosing (although reservations may be necessary to dine later in the evening).

$$$ **Ristoteca Oniga** is all about fresh fish and other sea creatures, with a chic-and-shipshape interior, great tables on the square, and the enthusiastic direction of Raffaele. The menu is accessible and always includes a good vegetarian dish (daily 12:00-14:30 & 19:00-22:30, except closed Tue in winter, reservations smart, Campo San Barnaba, Dorsoduro 2852, tel. 041-522-4410, www.oniga.it).

$$$ **Osteria Enoteca Ai Artisti** serves well-presented quality dishes, with seating within its tight little wine-snob interior or at a few petite, romantic canalside tables. They serve good wines by the glass. When reserving, make sure they know your preference—a table on the canal or inside (Mon-Sat 12:30-15:00 & 19:00-21:00, closed Sun, Fondamenta de la Toletta, Dorsoduro 1169a, tel. 041-523-8944, www.enotecaartisti.com, Vicenzo).

$$ **Pizzeria al Profeta** is a casual place popular for great pizza

and steak. Its sprawling interior seems to stoke conviviality, as does its leafy garden out back (Wed-Mon 12:00-14:30 & 19:00-23:30, closed Tue; from Campo San Barnaba, a long walk down Calle Lunga San Barnaba to #2671, tel. 041-523-7466).

$$$ Enoteca e Trattoria la Bitta is dark and woody, with a soft-jazz bistro feel, tight seating, and a small, forgettable back patio. They serve beautifully presented, traditional Venetian food with—proudly—no fish. Their helpful wait staff and small, hand-written daily menu are focused on local ingredients (including rabbit) and a "slow food" ethic. As it has an avid following, they do two dinner seatings (19:00 and 21:00) and require reservations (dinner only, Mon-Sat 18:30-23:00, closed Sun, cash only, just off Campo San Barnaba on Calle Lunga San Barnaba, Dorsoduro 2753a, tel. 041-523-0531, Debora and Marcellino).

On Campo Santa Margarita

For a fresh, youthful, and neighborhood vibe away from the tourist crowds and cutesy Venice, hike out to Campo Santa Margarita, where you'll find a multigenerational slice-of-life scene by day and a trendy college-bar scene after dark. The square is ringed by bakeries, pubs, pizzerias, and fruit stands offering options for everything from picnics to finer dining. If slumming, a picnic or takeout pizza on this square (with fine benches and trees) is great. The area gets a little sketchy late at night.

$$ Osteria Do Torri is a family affair delightfully situated with tables overlooking the square. Loretta and Paolo offer wines, little Venetian plates, love, and passion (closed Mon, tel. 041-522-0686).

$$ Osteria alla Bifora is a former butcher shop, serving lots of polenta and classic dishes in their candle-lit woody interior and tables on the square. For rustic *cicchetti* plates ranging from sardines, anchovies, and cod to platters of fine salamis and cheeses, this is a good choice (daily, tel. 041-523-6119, Franco and Mirella).

$$ Pier Dickens Ristorante-Pizzeria, with good tables on the square, serves a huge selection of pizzas as well as three-course fixed-price meals (daily, tel. 041-241-1979).

Various **hole-in-the-wall** *cicchetti* **bars** (on the square and just off it) serve drinks and tapas plates to local eaters with a contagious love of life.

SPLURGING ON A WATER OR OTHERWISE GREAT VIEW

Overlooking the Giudecca Canal: $$$$ Ristorante Lineadombra, immediately behind La Salute Church, is peacefully situated on the Giudecca Canal, with commanding lagoon views from their big floating terrace and a spacious, modern, and dressy interior. This

VENICE

Romantic Canalside Settings

Of course, if you want a meal with a canal view, it generally comes with lower quality and/or a higher price. But if you're determined to take home a canalside memory, these places (many described elsewhere in this chapter) can be great.

Near the Rialto Bridge: The five places I call the "Bancogiro Stretch" offer wonderful canalside dining and a great place to enjoy a drink and/or a snack between meals or after dinner (see page 102).

Rialto Bridge Tourist Traps: Venetians are embarrassed by the lousy food and aggressive "service" at the string of joints dominating the best romantic, Grand Canal-fringing real estate in town. Still, if you want to linger over dinner with a view of the most famous bridge and the songs of gondoliers oaring by (and don't mind eating with other tourists), this can be enjoyable. Don't trust the waiter's recommendations for special meals. The budget ideal would be to get a simple pizza or pasta and a drink for €15, and savor the ambience without getting ripped off. But few restaurants will allow you to get off that easy. To avoid a dispute over the bill, ask if there's a minimum charge before you sit down (most places have one).

Near the Accademia: Next to the Accademia Bridge, **Bar Foscarini** offers decent pizzas overlooking the canal with no cover or service charge (see page 107).

Ponte dei Greci, East of St. Mark's Square: Two delightful canals meet at the Ponte dei Greci. Restaurants have gobbled

is a gourmet treat, with gorgeously presented dishes that are local and modern at the same time. Each dish is a memory, and even though plates are pricey (€20 appetizers and pastas, €30 *secondi*), you are welcome to share. The appetizers especially are big and are happily served on two smaller plates. Reserve ahead and choose seating inside or on their terrace. Service is friendly yet professional (daily 12:00-15:00 & 19:00-22:00, closed Tue off-season, a short walk behind La Salute Church, directly across the island from the Salute vaporetto stop, Dorsoduro 19, tel. 041-241-1881, www. ristorantelineadombra.com).

On Fondamente Nove, with a Lagoon View: $$$$ Ristorante Algiubagiò is a good place to eat as you look over the northern lagoon. You could combine a meal here with a trip to Murano or Burano. The name joins the names of the four owners— Alberto, Giulio, Barbara, and Giovanna—who strive to impress up every inch of canalside real estate to feed tourists forgettable food—and great memories. Three cheap pizzerias are busy along Canal San Provolo. For nicer fare, two pricier restaurants on Fondamenta San Lorenzo (**Ristorante alla Conchiglia** and **Trattoria da Giorgio ai Greci**) are lit up like Christmas trees after dark. With gondolas gliding by, you can't argue with the setting.

Overlooking the Giudecca Canal: Located in Zattere—on the Venice side of the wide Giudecca Canal—**Terrazza del Casin dei Nobili** is particularly nice just before sunset (vaporetto: Zattere, see page 108). For a cheaper perch on the same canal, consider **Oke Pizzoria,** described on page 108. **I Figli delle Stelle Ristorante,** on the island of Giudecca, is a classy restaurant offering romantic canalside seating and a wonderful experience (vaporetto: Zitello, see below). **Ristorante Lineadombra,** with a terrace on the Giudecca Canal, serves gourmet dishes to a dressy crowd (see page 109).

On Fondamente Nove with a View of the Open Lagoon: Try **Ristorante Algiubagiò** for a good opportunity to eat well while overlooking the north lagoon (see page 110).

On Burano: Trattoria al Gatto Nero sits on a tranquil canal under a tilting bell tower in the pastel townscape of Burano. If you're touring the lagoon and want to enjoy Burano without the crowds, go late and consider a dinner here.

visitors with quality, creative Venetian cuisine made with the best ingredients. Reserve a waterside table or sit in their classy cantina dining room (daily 12:00-15:00 & 19:00-22:30, between the two sets of vaporetto docks on Fondamente Nove, Cannaregio 5039, tel. 041-523-6084, www.algiubagio.net).

On Giudecca Island, with a View of St. Mark's Square: $$$ I Figli delle Stelle Ristorante offers a delightful dining experience with an excuse to ride the boat from St. Mark's Square across to the island of Giudecca. Simone and his staff artfully serve Venetian classics with a dash of Rome and Puglia and a passion for fish and lamb. While they have inside seating, the reason to venture here is to sit canalside with fine views of Venice across the broad Giudecca Canal and all the water traffic. Reserve ahead to specify "first line" seating along the water, "second line" seating a few steps away, or a table inside (Wed-Mon 12:30-14:30 & 19:00-23:00, closed Tue, 50 yards from Zitelle vaporetto dock—from San Marco, ride line #4.2 or #2, Giudecca 70, tel. 041-523-0004, www.ifiglidellestelle.it).

On St. Mark's Square: $$$$ Gran Caffè Quadri is the place to go if you want to eat fancy on Piazza San Marco. Upstairs is their Michelin-star restaurant, but this bistro, also dressy and a bit pretentious, shares the same kitchen, with a more traditional and accessible menu, and prices that won't ruin your appetite. While its 15 tables are all inside, the orchestra is just out the window (daily for lunch and dinner, reservations smart, San Marco 121, tel. 041-522-2105).

PICNICS AND SWEETS
Picnicking

You're legally forbidden from picnicking anywhere on or near St. Mark's Square except for Giardinetti Reali, the waterfront park near the San Marco vaporetto docks. Though it's legal to eat outdoors elsewhere around town, you may be besieged by pigeons who are, in turn, besieged by aggressive seagulls.

Venice has one main produce market and several convenient supermarkets:

Outdoor Market near the Rialto Bridge: The **fruit and vegetable market** that sprawls for a few blocks to the north of the Rialto Bridge is a fun place to assemble a picnic (best Mon-Sat 8:00-13:00, liveliest in the morning, closed Sun). The adjacent **fish market** is wonderfully slimy (closed Sun-Mon). Side lanes in this area are speckled with fine hole-in-the-wall munchie bars, bakeries, and cheese shops. The Rialto Mercato vaporetto stop is convenient to both.

Neighborhood Deli near the Rialto Market: This tiny *alimentari* just down the street from the market sells a flavorful concoction of cheese, Kalamata olives, sun-dried tomatoes, olive oil, and hot peppers that they call *intruglio*. It goes great with a fresh roll. It's at Sotoportego dei do Mori, at the end of my favorite strip of *cicchetti* bars (Mon-Sat 9:00-20:00, Sun 11:00-19:00, San Polo 414; see map on page 87).

Produce Stands: Many larger squares have a produce stand. To find the one nearest St. Mark's Square, face St. Mark's Basilica, then walk along its left side, heading east down Calle de la Canonica. Cross the bridge and turn left at Campo Santi Filippo e Giacomo. There are also stands on Campo Santa Maria Formosa and Campo Santa Margarita.

Supermarket near St. Mark's Square: A handy **Co-op** supermarket is between St. Mark's and Campo Santa Maria Formosa, on the corner of Salizada San Lio and Calle del Mondo Novo at Castello 5817. It has a deli counter and a great selection of picnic supplies, including packaged salads for €3 and fresh sandwiches (daily 8:30-20:30).

Other Supermarkets: The largest supermarket in town is the **Co-op** at Piazzale Roma, next to the vaporetto stop at Santa Croce 504 (daily 8:30-20:00). It's an easy walk from the train station, as is the **Conad** supermarket on Campo San Felice (daily 8:00-23:30, along the Strada Nova between the train station and Rialto area, Cannaregio 3660). Another **Conad** supermarket is convenient for those staying in Dorsoduro: It's at #1492, as far west as possible on the Zattere embankment, by the San Basilio vaporetto stop and the cruise-ship docks (daily 8:00-23:00). And just beyond the Rialto vaporetto stop is another handy **Co-op** (facing the Grand Canal on Riva del Carbon).

Good Gelato and Chocolate Spots

You'll find good *gelaterie* in every Venetian neighborhood, typically offering one-scoop cones for about €1.50 (plus €1 per extra scoop). Look for the words *artigianale* or *produzione propria*, which indicates that a shop makes its own gelato. All of these are open long hours daily. Here are a few to consider:

St. Mark's Side of the Rialto Bridge: An expensive gourmet gelato shop, **Gelatoteca Suso,** serves delectable flavors in bowls you can eat (next to recommended Rosticceria Gislon on Calle de la Bissa, San Marco 5453).

St. Mark's Square: Several of the cafés have gelato counters in summer. Try **Gran Caffè Lavena** at #134, or **Todaro** (on the corner of the Piazzetta at #5, near the water and just under the column topped by St. Theodore slaying a crocodile).

On Campo Santa Margarita and Campiello San Tomà: Il Doge has Sicilian-style *granita*—slushy ice flavored with fresh fruit—as well as regular flavors.

Near Campo Santa Maria Formosa: On Salizada San Lio is the popular **La Boutique del Gelato** (next to Hotel Bruno). And nearby is a hit with chocolate lovers: **Cioccolateria VizioVirtù** (Vice and Virtue). Across from the recommended Osteria al Portego, it's a modern lab of deliciousness with fine gelato as a bonus (10:00-19:30, closed Mon, Castello 5988, tel. 041-275-0149).

Venice Connections

BY TRAIN

From Venice by Train to: Padua (2/hour, 25-50 minutes), **Vicenza** (2/hour, 45-75 minutes), **Verona** (2/hour, 1.5-2.5 hours), **Ravenna** (roughly hourly, 3 hours, transfer in Ferrara or Bologna), **Florence** (hourly, 2 hours, often crowded so make reservations), **Bolzano/ Dolomites** (to Bolzano about hourly, 3 hours, transfer in Verona;

catch bus from Bolzano into mountains), **Milan** (2/hour, most direct on high-speed ES trains, 2.5 hours), **Cinque Terre/Monterosso** (5/day, 6 hours, change in Milan), **Rome** (roughly hourly, 3.5 hours, overnight possible), **Naples** (almost hourly, 5.5 hours, some change in Bologna or Rome), **Brindisi** (5/day, 9 hours, change in Rome or Bologna). These departures are operated by Trenitalia; Italo offers additional high-speed connections to major Italian cities including **Bologna, Florence,** and **Rome** (see page 1157).

International Destinations: Interlaken (4/day, 6-6.5 hours with 2 changes), **Munich** (1/day direct, 6.5 hours, more with change in Verona; reservable only at ticket windows or via www.bahn.com), **Innsbruck** (1/day direct, 5 hours, more with change in Verona; reservable only at ticket windows or via www.bahn.com), **Salzburg** (4/day, 6-7 hours with change in Villach), **Paris** (2/day direct, 11 hours; 1 direct night train, 14.5 hours, reserve up to 4 months in advance, no rail passes accepted, www.thello.com); **Geneva** (1/day direct, 7 hours). Travelers to **Ljubljana** and **Vienna** can take an Austrian Railways bus (1-2/day in the morning) to Villach in Austria, and continue from there by direct train (bus leaves from Tronchetto and Mestre railway station; buy tickets from windows in train station). To **Ljubljana,** there's also a direct DRD bus from Mestre (1/day, 3.25 hours, www.drd.si) and a private shuttle service (www.goopti.com). To **Vienna,** you can also take a direct evening train (1/day, 8 hours) or night train (1/day, 11 hours).

BY PLANE

Marco Polo is Venice's main airport. Some budget flights, including Ryanair, use the smaller airport in the nearby city of Treviso.

Marco Polo Airport

Venice's small, modern airport is on the mainland shore of the lagoon, six miles north of the city (airport code: VCE). There's one sleek terminal, with a TI (daily 9:00-20:00), car rental agencies, ATMs, a bank, and a few shops and eateries. For flight information, call 041-260-9260, visit www.veniceairport.com, or ask your hotel.

Getting Between the Airport and Venice

You can get between the airport and central Venice in any of four ways: by Alilaguna boat, water taxi, airport bus, or land taxi.

Type	Speed	Cost	Notes
Alilaguna boat	Slow	Moderate	No transfer
Water taxi	Fast	Expensive	No transfer
Airport bus to Piazzale Roma	Medium	Cheap	Transfer to vaporetto
Land taxi to Piazzale Roma	Medium	Moderate	Transfer to vaporetto

The Alilaguna boats reach most of this chapter's recommended hotels very simply, with no changes. Hotels near the train station, however, are better served by the bus to Piazzale Roma.

Both Alilaguna boats and water taxis leave from the airport's boat dock, an eight-minute walk from the terminal. Exit the arrivals hall and turn left, following signs along a covered sidewalk.

When flying out of Venice, allow yourself plenty of time to get to the airport. Water transport can be slow—just getting there can take up to two hours. Alilaguna boats are small and can fill up. In an emergency, you can always hop in a water taxi and get to the airport in 30 minutes.

Alilaguna Airport Boats

These boats make the scenic journey across the lagoon, shuttling passengers between the airport and the island of Venice (€15, €27 round-trip, €1 surcharge if bought on boat, discount if bought online, includes 1 suitcase and 1 piece of hand luggage, additional bags-€3 each, roughly 2/hour, 1-1.5-hour trip depending on destination). Alilaguna boats are not covered by city transit passes, but they do use the same docks and ticket windows as the regular *vaporetti*. You can buy Alilaguna tickets online at www.alilaguna.it or www.venicelink.com.

There are three key Alilaguna lines for reaching St. Mark's Square. From the airport, the **blue line** *(linea blu)* heads first to Fondamente Nove (40 minutes), then loops around to San Zaccaria and San Marco (about 1.5 hours) before continuing on to Zattere and the cruise terminal (almost 2 hours). The **orange line** *(linea arancio)* runs down the Grand Canal, reaching Guglie (handy for Cannaregio hotels, 45 minutes), Rialto (1 hour), and San Marco (1.25 hours). In high season, the **red line** *(linea rossa)* runs to St. Mark's in just over an hour. It circumnavigates Murano and then runs parallel to the blue line, ending at Giudecca Zitelle. For a full schedule, visit the TI, see the website (www.alilaguna.it), call 041-240-1701, ask your hotelier, or scan the schedules posted at the docks.

From the Airport to Venice: You can buy Alilaguna tickets at the airport's TI, the ticket desk in the terminal, and at the ticket booth at the dock. Any ticket seller can tell you which line to catch to get to your destination. Blue- and orange-line boats from the airport run roughly twice an hour; red goes once an hour (blue line from 6:15, orange line from 7:45, red line from 9:40; blue and orange lines run until about midnight, red line makes its last run at 18:40).

From Venice to the Airport: Ask your hotelier which dock and which line is best. Blue-line boats start leaving Venice as early as 3:50 in the morning. Scope out the dock and buy your ticket in advance to avoid last-minute stress.

Water Taxis

Luxury taxi speedboats zip directly between the airport and the closest dock to your hotel, getting you within steps of your final destination in about 30 minutes. The official price is €110 for up to four people; add €10 for every extra person (10-passenger limit). You may get a higher quote—politely talk it down. A taxi can be a smart investment for small groups and those with an early departure.

From the airport, arrange your ride at the water-taxi desk or with the boat captains at the dock. From Venice, book your taxi trip the day before your departure, either through your hotel or directly with the Consorzio Motoscafi water taxi association (tel. 041-522-2303, www.motoscafivenezia.it).

Airport Shuttle Buses

Buses between the airport and Venice are fast, frequent, and cheap. They drop you at Venice's bus station, at the square called Piazzale Roma. From there, you can catch a vaporetto down the Grand Canal—convenient for hotels near the Rialto Bridge and St. Mark's Square. If you're staying near the train station, you can walk from Piazzale Roma to your hotel.

Two bus companies serve this route: ACTV and ATVO. ATVO buses take 20 minutes and go nonstop. ACTV buses make a few stops en route and take slightly longer (30 minutes), but you get a discount if you buy a Venice vaporetto pass at the same time (see page 30). The service is equally good (either bus: €8 one-way, €15 round-trip, runs about 5:00-24:00, 2/hour, drops to 1/hour early and late, check schedules at www.atvo.it or www.actv.it).

From the Airport to Venice: Buses leave from just outside the arrivals terminal. Buy tickets from the TI, the ticket desk in the terminal, the kiosk near baggage claim, or ticket machines. ATVO tickets are not valid on ACTV buses and vice versa. Double-check the destination; you want Piazzale Roma. If taking ACTV, you want bus #5.

From Venice to the Airport: At Piazzale Roma, buy your ticket from the ACTV windows (in the building by the bridge) or the ATVO office (at #497g) before heading out to the platforms. The newsstand in the center of the lot also sells tickets.

Land Taxi or Private Minivan

It takes about 20 minutes to drive from the airport to Piazzale Roma or the cruise port. A **land taxi** can do the trip for about €50. To reserve a private minivan, contact **Treviso Car Service** (minivan-€55, seats up to 8; car-€50, seats up to 3; mobile 338-204-4390 or 333-411-2840, www.trevisocarservice.com).

Treviso Airport

Several budget airlines, such as Ryanair and Wizz Air, use Treviso Airport, 12 miles northwest of Venice (airport code: TSF, tel. 042-231-5111, www.trevisoairport.it). The fastest option into Venice (Tronchetto parking lot) is on the **Barzi express bus,** which does the trip in just 40 minutes (€12, buy tickets on board, every 1-2 hours, www.barziservice.com). From Tronchetto, hop on a vaporetto, or take the People Mover monorail to Piazzale Roma for €1.50. **ATVO buses** are a bit more frequent and drop you right at Piazzale Roma (saving you the People Mover ride), but take nearly twice as long (€12 one-way, €22 round-trip, about 2/hour, 70 minutes, www.atvo.it; buy tickets at the ATVO desk in the airport and stamp them on the bus). **Treviso Car Service** offers minivan service to Piazzale Roma (minivan-€75, seats up to 8; car-€65, seats up to 3; for contact info, see listing above).

BY CRUISE SHIP

Most cruise ships dock at Venice's Stazione Marittima, at the west end of town. From the cruise port, the most direct way to reach St. Mark's Square is to take the Alilaguna **express boat** (2/hour in each direction, 30 minutes, www.alilaguna.it). Another option is to take the **People Mover** monorail from the port to Piazzale Roma, then hop on a **vaporetto.** It's about a five-minute walk to the People Mover, then a three-minute ride to Piazzale Roma, where you'll find a stop for *vaporetti* to St. Mark's Square (45 minutes on boat #1, 25 minutes on boat #2).

Other options for getting to the center from the cruise port include **walking** (about an hour to St. Mark's Square) or an expensive **water taxi** ride (at least €70-80).

For more details, see my *Rick Steves Mediterranean Cruise Ports* guidebook.

NEAR VENICE

Padua • Vicenza • Verona

Venice is just one of many towns in the Italian region of Veneto (VEN-eh-toh), but few visitors venture off the lagoon. That's a shame, as there's much to see within a very short hop of Venice. The trip from Venice westward to Milan is a route strewn with temptations: the Dolomites peaks, Italy's famous lakes, and—closer to Venice—the important and worthwhile towns of Padua, Vicenza, and Verona.

If you can't make it to all three, pick the one that interests you. Art lovers will want to head to **Padua** to see Giotto's celebrated Scrovegni Chapel. History buffs should see **Verona**'s impressive Roman ruins. Verona is also the pick for star-crossed lovers retracing Romeo and Juliet's steps. Architecture fans could consider a quick stop in Palladio-designed **Vicenza,** located about halfway between Padua and Verona.

If you're Padua-bound, remember that you need to reserve ahead to see the Scrovegni Chapel. Don't bother visiting Vicenza on a Monday, when many of the top sights are closed; in Verona, several sights don't open until 13:30 on Mondays.

Spending a day at one of these towns as a side-trip from Venice or town-hopping between Venice and Milan is exciting and efficient. Padua, Verona, and Vicenza are on the same train line. Connected by at least two trains per hour, they're easy to visit.

Train travelers find that the "fast regional" trains (marked with an RV prefix on schedules and ticket machines) offer the best mixture of speed, convenience, and savings. Frecce express trains cost three to four times as much—and though rail-pass holders don't have to pay the fare, they do have to commit to a time and pay to reserve a seat. Regional trains don't require (or even accept)

Towns near Venice

VENETO

To Bolzano & Innsbruck (Austria)

To Milan

To Udine

Treviso

To Trieste

Vicenza

Verona

Marco Polo

Catullo

Mestre

Venice

Padua

Lido

ITALY

Lagoon

Adriatic Sea

Rovigo

Chioggia

15 Kilometers

15 Miles

To Florence

To Ravenna (via Ferrara) & Florence

seat reservations. The regular regional trains (R prefix) offer the same savings as the RV ones but are much slower, especially on the longer journey to Verona.

Padua

This inexpensive, easily appreciated city is a fine destination on its own and a convenient base for day trips all around the region. Nicknamed "The brain of Veneto," Padua (*Padova* in Italian) is home to

the prestigious university (founded in 1222) that hosted Galileo, Copernicus, Dante, and Petrarch. Pilgrims know Padua as the home of the Basilica of St. Anthony, where the reverent assemble to touch his tomb and ogle his remarkably intact lower jaw and tongue. And lovers of early Renaissance art come here to make a pilgrimage of their own: to gaze at the remarkable frescoes by Giotto in the Scrovegni Chapel. But despite the fact that Padua's museums and churches hold their own in Italy's artistic big league, its hotels are reasonably priced, and the city doesn't feel touristy. Padua's old town center is elegantly arcaded, filled with students, and sprinkled with surprises, including some of Italy's most inviting squares for lingering over an *aperitivo* as the sun slowly dips low in the sky.

From Padua, architecture fans can ride by train (15-25 minutes) to Vicenza and its celebrated Palladian buildings (see page 148).

PLANNING YOUR TIME: PADUA IN SIX HOURS

Day-trippers can do a quick but enjoyable blitz of Padua—including a visit to the Scrovegni Chapel—in six hours. Trains from Venice are cheap, take 25-50 minutes, and run frequently. Once in Padua, everything is a 10-minute walk or a quick tram ride apart.

To see Giotto's Scrovegni Chapel, you need to make a reservation; your entry time will dictate the order of your sightseeing (see "Reservations" on page 132). When planning your day, also consider these factors: The station has a reliable baggage check desk; the open-air markets are vibrant in the morning; student life is best at the university late in the day; and the Basilica of St. Anthony is open all day, but the reliquary chapel closes midday, from 12:45 to 14:30.

Ideally, I'd do it this way: 9:00—market action and sightseeing in town center, 11:00—Basilica of St. Anthony, 13:00—lunch, 15:00—Scrovegni Chapel tour.

Orientation to Padua

Padua's main tourist sights lie on a north-south axis through the heart of the city, from the train station to Scrovegni Chapel to the market squares (the center of town) to the Basilica of St. Anthony. It's roughly a 10-minute walk between each of these sights, or about 30 minutes from end to end. Padua's wonderful, single tram line makes lacing things together quick and easy (see "Getting Around Padua," later).

TOURIST INFORMATION

Padua has two TIs: in the **center** (in the alley behind Caffè Pedrocchi at Vicolo Cappellatto Pedrocchi 9, Mon-Sat 9:00-19:00, closed Sun) and at the **train station** (Mon-Sat 9:00-19:00, Sun 10:00-16:00, tel. 049-201-0080, www.turismopadova.it).

At either TI, pick up the seasonal *Padova Today* entertainment listing (with a list of sights in the back). The TI's free I-PADova audio tour is creative and works well; you can download it to your smartphone or tablet from their website and follow any of the five routes in town (www.discoverpadova.com, search for "audio guide"; smart to print out audio-tour map ahead of time).

The **Padova Card** includes entry to all my recommended sights—except the university's Anatomy Theater and the Oratory of St. George—plus unlimited tram rides and free parking near Prato della Valle (€16/48 hours, €21/72 hours, buy at either TI, the Scrovegni Chapel, or online at www.padovacard.it). The card will likely pay off if you're doing at least two of these three things: seeing the Scrovegni Chapel, parking a car, or staying overnight (giving you time to sightsee the next day).

While the Padova Card covers the Scrovegni Chapel, you

still need to make a reservation in advance to enter the chapel (€1 extra reservation fee). If you go through the chapel website (www. cappelladegliscrovegni.it), you can buy the card and make a chapel reservation at the same time. Collect your prepurchased cards from either TI or at the chapel.

ARRIVAL IN PADUA

By Train: The efficient station is a user-friendly shopping mall with whatever you may need (Despar supermarket open Mon-Sat 7:00-21:00, Sun 10:00-21:00). Along track 1 are pay WCs and baggage storage (daily 6:30-18:00, bring photo ID).

To get downtown, simply hop on Padua's handy **tram** (see "Getting Around Padua," later). Purchase your ticket (€1.30, or €3.80 day pass) from shops inside the station or in the low brown rectangular booth in front of the station, which has both machines and a staffed window. Leaving the station, the tram stop is 100 yards to the right at the foot of the bridge. A **taxi** into town (a good option after dark) costs about €8-10.

By Bus: The bus station is 100 yards east of the train station. Buses arrive here from Venice's Piazzale Roma and Marco Polo Airport.

HELPFUL HINTS

Exchange Rate: €1 = about $1.10

Country Calling Code: 39 (see page 1154 for dialing instructions)

Pronunciation: You say Padua (PAD-joo-wah), they say Padova (PAH-doh-vah). The city's top sight, Scrovegni Chapel, is pronounced skroh-VEHN-yee.

Wi-Fi: There's public Wi-Fi at both TIs and on the square in front of Café Pedrocchi (network name: Padova WiFi). The central TI has a guest computer (free for 15 minutes).

Bookstore: Feltrinelli, with books in English, is one block from the main university building (Mon-Sat 9:00-19:45, Sun 10:00-13:00 & 15:30-20:00, Via San Francesco 7, tel. 199-151-173).

Launderette: Lavami is central, tiny, and modern. Two of the three washers are supersized and cost more (€5-8/wash, €1.50/12 minutes to dry, daily 7:00-21:30, Via Marsala 22 near intersection with Via dell'Arco, tel. 049-876-4532).

Travel Agency: Leonardi Viaggi-Turismo, only a block from the train station, offers ticketing services for trains, planes, and boats for a small fee (Mon-Fri 9:00-19:00, Sat 9:00-13:00, closed Sun, up the main drag, Corso del Popolo 14, tel. 049-650-455, www.leonardiviaggi.com).

Local Guide: Charming **Cristina Pernechele** is a great teacher (€110/half-day, mobile 338-495-5453, cristina@pernechele.eu).

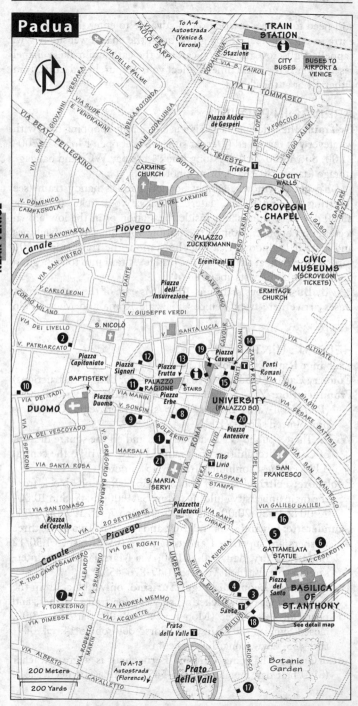

Padua

To A-4
Autostrada
(Venice &
Verona)

VIA FRA PAOLO SARPI

TRAIN STATION

Stazione

CITY BUSES

BUSES TO AIRPORT & VENICE

VIA DELLE PALME

VIA B. CAIROLI

VIA CODALUNGA

VEDDARA

VIA SAN GIOVANNI

VIA SUOR E. VENDRAMINI

VIALE CODALUNGA

VIA DELLA ROTONDA

VIA N. TOMMASEO

VIA BEATO PELLEGRINO

VIA SAN PIETRO

VIA GIOTTO

VIA TRIESTE

V. DEL POPOLO

V. FOSCOLO

V. DIEGO VALERI

V. GABBARE GOZZI

Piazza Alcide de Gasperi

Trieste **T**

OLD CITY WALLS

CARMINE CHURCH

VIA DEL CARMINE

CORSO GARIBALDI

SCROVEGNI CHAPEL

V. GASO.

V. DOMENICO CAMPAGNOLA

VIA DEI SAVONAROLA

Piovego

Canale

PALAZZO ZUCKERMANN

CIVIC MUSEUMS (SCROVEGNI TICKETS)

V. CARLO LEONI

Eremitani **T**

ERMITAGE CHURCH

CORSO MILANO

VIA DANTE

Piazza dell' Insurrezione

V. SAN FERMO

V. GIUSEPPE VERDI

VIA ALTINATE

VIA DEI LIVELLO

S. NICOLÒ

SANTA LUCIA

CAVOUR

V. PATRIARCATO

2

VIA ZABARELLA

14

Piazza Cavour

CONTI ROMANI

Piazza Capitaniato

12

Piazza Signori

13

Piazza Frutta

19

Ponti Romani Rovia

BAPTISTERY

11

PALAZZO RAGIONE

STAIRS

15

SAN BIAGIO

10

Piazza Duomo

V. MANIN

Piazza Erbe

8

UNIVERSITY (PALAZZO BO)

VIA CESARE BATTISTI

DUOMO

V. SONCIN

9

20

VIA DEI TADI

VIA DEI VESCOVADO

SOLFERINO

Piazza Antenore

V. SPERONI

VIA SANTA ROSA

MARSALA

1

RIVIERA TITO LIVIO

Tito Livio **T**

V. GASPARA STAMPA

SAN FRANCESCO

VIA SAN FRANCESCO

V. S. GREGORIO BARBARIGO

21

S. MARIA SERVI

VIA ROMA

VIA SAN TOMASO

20 SETTEMBRE

Piazza del Castello

Piazzetta Palatucci

VIA SANTA CHIARA

VIA GALILEO GALILEI

16

Canale

Piovego

VIA DEI ROGATI

VIA UMBERTO

RIVIERA RUZANTE

VIA RUDENA

GATTAMELATA STATUE

V. CESAROTTI

6

R. TISO CAMPOSAMPIERO

VIA A. ALEARDO

VIA SEMINARIO

VIA ANDREA MEMMO

Piazza del Santo

BASILICA OF ST. ANTHONY

See detail map

7

V. TORRESINO

4

3

VIA DIMESSE

VIA ACQUETTE

Santo **T**

18

VIA BELLUDI

VIA ALBERTO

VIA ROBERTO MARIN

Prato della Valle **T**

V. BRIOSCO

Botanic Garden

To A-13 Autostrada (Florence)

CAVALLETTO

Prato della Valle

17

200 Meters

200 Yards

N

NEAR VENICE

Padua Key

1. Hotel Majestic Toscanelli
2. Albergo Verdi
3. Hotel Belludi 37
4. Hotel Al Fagiano
5. Hotel Al Santo & Antica Trattoria dei Paccagnella
6. Hotel/Rist. Casa del Pellegrino
7. Ostello Città di Padova
8. Osteria dei Fabbri
9. Osteria L'Anfora
10. Enoteca dei Tadi
11. Rist. Dante alle Piazze
12. La Lanterna Ristorante
13. Bar dei Osei
14. Brek Cafeteria
15. PAM Supermarket & Brek
16. Pizzeria Pago Pago
17. Zairo Rist./Pizzeria
18. Pollodoro la Gastronomica
19. Caffè Pedrocchi
20. Feltrinelli Bookstore
21. Launderette

GETTING AROUND PADUA

Ignore the city buses; pretend there is only the **tram** and rely on it. There's just one line, which efficiently and without stress connects everything you care about. Buy tickets from tobacco shops, newsstands, or the booth on the square in front of the train station and validate them on board; there are also ticket machines at some stops, but they sell only single tickets and don't give change (€1.30 single ticket good for 1.25 hours, €3.80 *biglietto giornaliero* good for one calendar day; departs every 8 minutes during the day Mon-Sat, every 20 minutes evenings and Sun). The rubber-wheeled trams run on a single rail.

Before boarding, note the tram direction on posted schedules and above the front window (Pontevigodarzere is northbound, Capolinea Sud is southbound). Stops that matter to tourists include Stazione FS (train and bus stations), Eremitani (Scrovegni Chapel), Ponti Romani (old town center, market squares, university), Tito Livio (ghetto, old town center, Hotel Majestic Toscanelli), Santo (Basilica of St. Anthony and neighborhood hotels), and Prato della Valle (hostel).

Padua's **hop-on, hop-off tour buses** are not worth the time or money.

Sights in Padua

IN THE CENTER

Padua's two main sights (Basilica of St. Anthony and Scrovegni Chapel) are, respectively, at the southern and northern reaches of downtown. But its atmospheric, cobbled core—with bustling markets, vibrant student life, and inviting sun-and-café-speckled piazzas—is its own ▲▲▲ attraction. You could simply stroll the area aimlessly or seek out some of the following spots.

▲▲Market Squares

The stately Palazzo della Ragione (described later) provides a dramatic backdrop for Padua's almost exotic-feeling produce market that fills the surrounding squares—

Piazza delle Erbe and **Piazza della Frutta**—each morning and all day Saturday (Mon-Fri roughly 8:00-13:00, Sat 8:00-19:00 but a bit quieter in the afternoon, closed Sun). Second only to the produce market in Italy's gastronomic capital of Bologna, this market has been renowned for centuries as having the freshest and greatest selection of herbs, fruits, and vegetables. The presentation is an art in itself. As you wander, appreciate the local passion for good food: Residents can tell the month by the seasonal selections, and merchants share recipe tips with shoppers. You'll notice quite a few Sri Lankans working here (Italy took in many refugees from Sri Lanka's civil war).

Don't miss the **indoor market** zone on the ground floor of the Palazzo della Ragione. Wandering through this H-shaped arcade—where you'll find various butchers, *salumerie* (delicatessens), cheese shops, bakeries, and fishmongers at work—is a sensuous experience. For centuries, this was a market for luxury items (furs, fine fabrics, silver, and gold—notice the imposing iron gates used to lock it up each evening). Then, the devastating loss to the French in 1797 marked the end of good times, and with no market for luxury items, the arcade was used to sell perishables—meat and cheese—out of the sun.

Students gather in the squares after the markets have closed, spilling out of colorful bars and cafés, drinks in hand (see sidebar on page 126). Pizza by the slice is dirt-cheap. For pointers on a recommended local sandwich stand, **Bar dei Osei,** and a neighboring seafood-snack stand, see page 147. Just a few steps away from these is a classic old pharmacy that dates to 1841: The licorice-perfumed **Ai Due Cantini d'Oro,** which stocks retail items like it did before World War II, sells odd foods and specialty items for every dietary need (Tue 16:00-19:30, Wed-Sun 9:00-13:00 & 16:00-19:30, closed Mon, Piazza della Frutta 46, tel. 049-875-0623).

Piazza dei Signori, just a block away, is a busy clothing market in the morning and the most popular gathering place in the evening for students out for a drink. The circa-1400 clock decorates the former palace of the ruling family. The aggressive lion with unfurled wings on the column was a reminder of the Venetian determination to assert its control. Today that lion can be seen as representing the Veneto region's independence from Rome: Italy's North (Veneto and Lombardy) is tired of subsidizing the South. Grumbling about this issue continues to stir talk of splitting the country.

Palazzo della Ragione

Looming over Padua's two big central market squares (Piazza delle Erbe and Piazza della Frutta), this grand 13th-century palazzo—commonly called *il Salone* (the great hall)—once held the medieval law courts. Its first floor consists of a huge hall—265 feet by 90 feet—that was at one time adorned with frescoes by Giotto. A fire in 1412 destroyed those paintings, and the palazzo was redecorated with the 15th-century art you

see today: a series of 333 frescoes depicting the signs of the zodiac, labors of the month, symbols representing characteristics of people born under each sign, and, finally, figures of saints to legitimize the power of the courts in the eyes of the Church.

The hall is topped with a hull-shaped roof, which helps to support the structure without the use of columns—quite an architectural feat in its day, considering the building's dimensions. The biggest thing in the hall is the giant, very anatomically correct horse. Its prominent placement represents the pride locals feel for the Veneto's own highly respected breed of horse. (After the bronze ones in St. Mark's Basilica, these are the favorite horses in the region.) The curious black stone in the corner opposite the big wooden horse is the "Stone of Shame," which was the seat of debtors being punished during the Middle Ages. It was introduced as a compassionate alternative to prison by St. Anthony in 1230. Instead of being executed or doing prison time, debtors sat upon this stone, surrendered their possessions, and denounced themselves publicly before being exiled from the city. The computer kiosks provide excellent information with entertaining videos.

Cost and Hours: €4, more during special exhibitions; Tue-Sun 9:00-19:00, Nov-Jan until 18:00, closed Mon year-round; enter through the east end of Piazza delle Erbe and go up the long staircase, Ponti Romani tram stop, tel. 049-820-5006. The WCs are through the glass doors at the opposite end of the hall from the wooden horse.

Drinking a *Spritz* with the Student Crowd

Each early evening, before dinner, students enliven Padua by enjoying a convivial drink in their favorite places. Piazza dei Signori is trendier, with people of all ages, while the scene on Piazza della Erbe is more bohemian and alternative. Or you could sit in front of the university, nurse your drink, and watch the graduates get roasted with their crazy gangs of friends.

The drink of choice is a *spritz,* an aperitif generally made with Campari (a red liqueur infused with bitter herbs), white wine, and sparkling water, and garnished with a blood-orange wedge. Traditionally, men opt for the heavier and bitterer Campari *spritz,* while women prefer a sweeter and lighter *spritz* made with Aperol (an orange-flavored liqueur with less alcohol content).

Grab a table and be part of the scene. This is a classic opportunity to enjoy a real discussion with smart, English-speaking students who see tourists not as pests, but as interesting people from far away. For an instant conversation starter, ask about the current political situation in Italy, the right-wing party's policy on immigrants, or the cultural differences between Italy's North and South.

Caffè Pedrocchi

The white-columned, Neoclassical Pedrocchi building is much more than just a café on the ground floor. A complex of meeting rooms and entertainment venues, it stirs the Italian soul (or the patriotic Italian soul, at least). Built in 1831 during the period of Austrian rule, Caffè Pedrocchi was inaugurated for the fourth Italian Congress of Scientists, which convened during the mid-19th century to stir up nationalistic fervor as Italy struggled to become a united nation. As a symbol of patriotic hope, it was the target (no surprise) of a student uprising plot in 1848.

Each of the café's three dining rooms is decorated and furnished in a different color (denoted by the hue of velvet on the chairs): red, white, or green—representing the colors of the Italian flag. In the outer, unheated Sala Verde (Green Room), people are welcome to sit and relax without ordering anything or having to pay. This is where Italian gentlemen read their newspapers and gather with friends to chat about the old days. In the Sala Rossa (Red Room), the clock over the bar is flanked by marble reliefs of morning and night, signaling that it was once open 24 hours a day (in the 19th century). In the rooms on either side, the maps of the hemispheres with south up top reflect the anti-conventional spirit of the place. In the Sala Bianca (White Room), where one of the revolutionaries in that ill-fated 1848 uprising was killed, you can still see a bullet hole in the wall (framed in tarnished silver).

The menu offers teahouse fare, including sandwiches and ice-cream sundaes, a variety of breakfast combos, and the writer Stendhal's beloved *zabaglione,* a creamy custard made with *marsala* wine. A shiny new bar in the center of the building has a praline and ice-cream counter and serves sandwiches at outdoor tables. Remember that in Italy, you can order a basic coffee standing up at the bar of any place, no matter how fancy, and pay the same low, government-regulated price.

Cost and Hours: Café interior free, daily 8:00-23:00, two entrances across from Via VIII Febbraio 14 and 20 near Ponti Romani tram stop, tel. 049-878-1231, www.caffepedrocchi.it.

Visiting the Café's Piano Nobile: To see the café's even more elaborate upstairs, you can pay to enter this "noble floor" of the Pedrocchi building (€4, Tue-Sun 9:30-12:30 & 15:30-18:00, closed Mon; to find entrance, head outside to Piazza Cavour, face café, and go through the door on the right; tel. 049-878-1231). The rooms are all in different styles, such as Greek, Etruscan, or Egyptian. These rooms were intended to evoke memories of the glory of past epochs, which a united Italy had hopes of reliving.

The Piano Nobile also hosts the small **Museum of the Risorgimento,** which traces Padua's role in Italian history, from the downfall of the Venetian Republic (1797) to the founding of the Republic of Italy (1948). Exhibits include uniforms, medals, weaponry, old artillery, fascist propaganda posters, and a 30-minute propagandistic video (in Italian, but mostly fascinating footage without narration). The video, played on demand, is a "Luce" production (meaning a Mussolini production) and features great scenes of the town in the 1930s, including clips of Il Duce's visit and later WWII bombardments. The war and propaganda posters in the last room are haunting. An old woman pleads to those who question the fascist-driven war effort: "Don't betray my son." Another declares, "The Germans are truly our friends." And another asks, "And you...what are *you* doing?"

University of Padua

The main building of this prestigious university, known as Palazzo Bò, is adjacent to Caffè Pedrocchi. Founded in 1222, it's one of the first, greatest, and most progressive universities in Europe. Back when the Church controlled university curricula, a group of professors and students broke free from the University of Bologna to create this liberal school, which would be independent of Catholic constraints and accessible to people of other faiths.

A haven for free thought, the university attracted intellectuals from all over Europe, including the great astronomer Copernicus, who realized here that the universe didn't revolve around him. And Galileo—notorious for disagreeing with the Church's views on science—called his 18 years on the faculty here the best of his life.

Access to Palazzo Bò is via a mostly underwhelming 45-minute guided tour, but the gawking public can get a peek at a few of its exterior courtyards (see below). The most exciting part of the tour is Europe's first great **Anatomy Theater** (from 1594). Despite the Church's strict ban on autopsies, more than 300 students would pack this theater to watch professors dissect human cadavers (the bodies of criminals from another town). This had to be done in a "don't ask, don't tell" kind of way, because the Roman Catholic Church only started allowing the teaching of anatomy through dissection in the late 1800s.

Cost and Hours: Grounds—free; Palazzo Bò tour—€5, March-Oct Mon-Sat generally three tours a day, no tours on Sun, reduced schedule Nov-Feb; Ponti Romani tram stop, 049-827-3047, www.unipd.it/en/guidedtours).

Confirm tour times and availability on website or by calling or stopping by the ticket desk (opens 15 minutes before each tour, through a door off the fascist-era courtyard, described next). School groups often book the entire visit. Tours are in Italian and another language (depending on the composition of the group). The tiny bar by the ticket desk is fun for a cheap drink and to see photos of university life.

Visiting the University Courtyards on Your Own: On weekdays and Saturday mornings, you can poke into two of the university's **courtyards** (when closed, just peer through the gate). Find the entrance at Via VIII Febbraio 7, under the "Gymnasium" inscription (30 yards from Caffè Pedrocchi, facing City Hall). You'll pop into a 16th-century courtyard, the school's historic core. It's littered with the coats of arms

Graduation Antics in Padua

With 60,000 students, Padua's university always seems to be hosting graduation ceremonies. There's a constant trickle of happy grads and their friends and families celebrating the big event.

During the school year, every 20 minutes or so, a student steps into a formal room (upstairs, above the university courtyard) to officially meet with the leading professors of his or her faculty. When they're finished, the students are given a green laurel wreath. They pose for ceremonial group photos and family snapshots. It's a sweet scene. Then, craziness takes over.

The new graduates replace their somber clothing with raunchy outfits, as gangs of friends gather around them on Via VIII Febbraio, the street in front of the university. The roast begins. The gang rolls out a giant butcher-paper poster with a generally obscene caricature of the student and a litany of *This Is Your Life* photos and stories. The new grad, subject to various embarrassing pranks, reads the funny statements out loud. The poster is then taped to the university wall for all to see. (Find the plastic panels to the right of the main entry, facing Via VIII Febbraio. Graduation posters are allowed to stay there for 24 hours. The panels are emptied each morning, but by nighttime a new set of posters is affixed to the plastic shields.)

During the roast, the friends sing the catchy but obscene local university anthem, reminding their newly esteemed friend not to get too huffy: *Dottore, dottore, dottore del buso del cul. Vaffancul, vaffancul* (loosely translated: "Doctor, doctor. You're just a doctor of the a-hole...go f-off, go f-off"). After you've heard this song (with its fanfare and oom-pah-pah catchiness) and have seen all the good-natured fun, you can't stop singing it.

The crazy show is usually staged late in the afternoon. Outdoor café tables afford great seats to enjoy the spectacle.

of important faculty and leaders of the university over the ages. Classrooms, which open onto the square, are still used. Today, students gather here, surrounded by memories of illustrious alumni, including the first woman in the world to receive a university degree (in 1678).

A passageway leads from here to an adjacent second courtyard, dating from the fascist era (c. 1938). The relief celebrates heroic students in World War I. Off this courtyard, notice the richly decorated stairway, frescoed fascist-style in the 1930s with themes celebrating art, science, and the pursuit of knowledge.

▲Baptistery

Located next to Padua's skippable Duomo, this richly frescoed little building was once the private chapel of Padua's ruling family, the Carraresi. In the 1370s, they hired a local artist, Giusto de' Menabuoi, to do a little interior redecoration. Later, in 1405, Venice conquered Padua and deposed the Carraresi; the building was turned into a baptistery, but the decorations survived.

Cost and Hours: €3, daily 10:00-18:00, on Piazza Duomo.

Visiting the Baptistery: The Baptistery's frescoes, like those in St. Mark's Basilica in Venice, show Byzantine influence. Almighty Christ, the Pantocrator, is in majesty on top, while approachable Mary and the multitude of saints provide the devout with access to God. Find the world as it was known in the 14th century (the disk below Mary's feet). It kicks off a cycle of scenes illustrating Creation (clockwise from the creation of Adam). The four evangelists (Matthew, Mark, Luke, and John) with their books and symbols fill the corners. A vivid Crucifixion scene faces a gorgeous Annunciation. And the altar niche features a dim, blue-toned, literal Apocalypse from the book of Revelation.

While the Baptistery was created 70 years after Giotto, it feels older. Because de' Menabuoi was working for a private family, he needed to be politically correct and not threaten or offend the family's allies—especially the Church. While still mind-blowing, the Baptistery's art seems relatively conservative compared to Giotto's Scrovegni Chapel. Giotto, supported by the powerful Scrovegni family and the Franciscans, could get away with being more progressive and bold.

▲▲▲Scrovegni Chapel and Civic Museums

Wallpapered with Giotto's beautifully preserved cycle of nearly 40 frescoes, the glorious, renovated Scrovegni Chapel holds scenes depicting the lives of Jesus and Mary. You must make reservations in advance to see the chapel. Scrovegni Chapel tickets also cover the Civic Museums, featuring the worthwhile Pinacoteca and Multimedia Room, as well as the skippable Archaeological Museum and the little-visited Palazzo Zuckermann.

Cost: €13 ticket covers the Scrovegni Chapel and Civic Museums. It's €10 for just the museums.

Giotto di Bondone (c. 1267-1337)

Although details of his life are extremely sketchy, we know that the 12-year-old shepherd Giotto was discovered painting pictures of his father's sheep on rock slabs. He grew to become the wealthiest and most famous painter of his day. His achievement is especially remarkable because painters at that time weren't considered anything more than craftsmen—and weren't expected to be innovators.

After making a name for himself by painting frescoes of the life of St. Francis in Assisi, the Florentine tackled the Scrovegni Chapel (c. 1303-1305). At age 35, he was at the height of his powers. His scenes were more realistic and human than anything that had been done for a thousand years. Giotto didn't learn technique by dissecting corpses or studying the mathematics of 3-D perspective; he had innate talent. And his personality shines through in the humanity of his art.

The Scrovegni frescoes break ground by introducing nature—rocks, trees, animals—as a backdrop for religious scenes. Giotto's people, with their voluminous, deeply creased robes, are as sturdy and massive as Greek statues, throwbacks to the Byzantine icon art of the Middle Ages. But these figures exude stage presence. Their gestures are simple but expressive: A head tilted down says dejection, an arm flung out indicates grief, clasped hands indicate hope. Giotto created his figures not just by drawing outlines and filling them in with single colors; he filled the outlines in with subtle patchworks of lighter and darker shades, and in doing so pioneered modern modeling techniques. Giotto's storytelling style is straightforward, and anyone with knowledge of the episodes of Jesus' life can read the chapel like a comic book.

The Scrovegni represents a turning point in European art and culture—away from scenes of heaven and toward a more down-to-earth, human-centered view.

NEAR VENICE

Hours: The **chapel** is open daily 9:00-19:00; tel. 049-201-0020, www.cappelladegliscrovegni.it. The **Multimedia Room** has the same hours, as do the **Pinacoteca** and **Archaeological Museum,** except they are closed Mon; **Palazzo Zuckermann** is open Tue-Sun 10:00-19:00, closed Mon; museums tel. 049-820-4551, palazzo tel. 049-820-5664.

Chapel Entry Times: To protect the paintings from excess humidity, only 25 people are allowed in the chapel at a time. Every

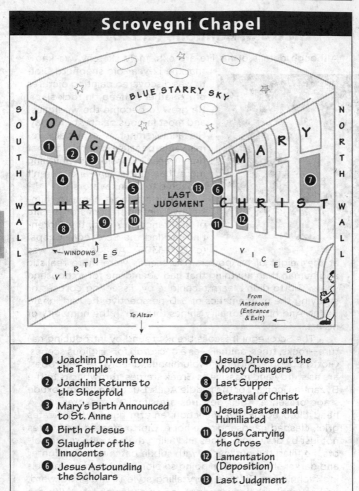

Scrovegni Chapel

1. Joachim Driven from the Temple
2. Joachim Returns to the Sheepfold
3. Mary's Birth Announced to St. Anne
4. Birth of Jesus
5. Slaughter of the Innocents
6. Jesus Astounding the Scholars
7. Jesus Drives out the Money Changers
8. Last Supper
9. Betrayal of Christ
10. Jesus Beaten and Humiliated
11. Jesus Carrying the Cross
12. Lamentation (Deposition)
13. Last Judgment

15 minutes (on the quarter-hour), a new group is admitted for a 15-minute video presentation in an anteroom, followed by 15 minutes in the chapel itself. In the evening, visitors can pay €12 (plus €1 reservation fee) to stay inside for a double period (40 minutes)—reservation must be made by phone.

Reservations: Prepaid reservations are required. It's wise to reserve at least two days in advance and easiest to do online at www.cappelladegliscrovegni.it. (If you'll be staying overnight in Padua or parking a car, consider paying the €3 extra for a Padova Card—described on page 120.) You can also reserve by phone (tel. 049-201-0020).

Without a reservation, it's sometimes possible to buy a same-day ticket (especially for single visitors), but don't count on it. Drop by the ticket office and see if anything is available (you might see a Post-it note stuck to the desk indicating the next available entry time). Tickets for daytime visits are generally released at 9:00; showing up early will increase your chances of getting a slot (likely for later in the day). You can't book next-day reservations in person—only online or by phone. You might also see local tour guides, who have to book blocks of tickets, trying to unload unneeded tickets.

Helpful Hint: If you packed binoculars, bring them along for a better—and more comfortable—view of the uppermost frescoes. No photos are allowed.

Getting There: From the train station, it's a 10- to 15-minute walk, or a quick, two-stop tram ride to the Eremitani stop.

Getting In: To reach the chapel, enter through the Eremitani building, where you'll find the museums, ticket office, and a free but mandatory bag check. Though you're instructed to pick up your tickets at the ticket office at least one hour before your visit, in practice, I've found that 30 minutes is enough to weather any commotion at the desk. Present your confirmation number at the ticket desk, verify your time, pick up your ticket, and check any bags or purses.

While waiting for your reserved time, blitz the Pinacoteca and Multimedia Room (described later). Read the chapel description before you enter, since you'll only have a short time in the chapel itself.

The chapel is well-signed: From the ticket office, go outside and walk 100 yards down the path, passing some ruins of Roman Padua (described later). Be at the chapel doors at least five minutes before your scheduled visit. The doors are automatic, and if you're even a minute late, you'll forfeit your visit and have to rebook and repay to enter.

At your appointed time, you first enter an anteroom to watch a very instructive 15-minute video (with English subtitles) and to establish humidity levels before continuing into the chapel. Although you have only a short visit inside the chapel, it is divine. You're inside a Giotto time capsule, looking back at an artist ahead of his time.

Scrovegni Chapel (Cappella degli Scrovegni)

Painted by Giotto and his assistants from 1303 to 1305 and considered by many to be the first piece of modern art, this work makes it clear: Europe was breaking out of the Middle Ages. A sign of the Renaissance to come, Giotto placed real people in real scenes, expressing real human emotions. These frescoes were radical for their 3-D nature, lively colors, light sources, emotion, and humanism.

The chapel was built out of guilt for white-collar crimes. Reginaldo degli Scrovegni charged sky-high interest rates at a time when the Church forbade the practice. He even caught the attention of Dante, who placed him in one of the levels of hell in his *Inferno*. When Reginaldo died, the Church denied him a Christian burial. His son Enrico tried to buy forgiveness for his father's sins by building this superb chapel. After seeing Giotto's frescoes for the Franciscan monks of St. Anthony, Enrico knew he'd found the right artist to decorate the interior (and, he hoped, to save his father's soul). The Scrovegni residence once stood next to the chapel, but it was torn down in 1824.

Giotto's Frescoes

Giotto painted the entire chapel in 200 working days over two years, but you'll get only 15 minutes to see it.

As you enter the long, narrow chapel, look straight to the far end—the rear wall is covered with Giotto's big *Last Judgment*. Christ in a bubble is flanked by crowds of saints and by scenes of heaven and hell. This is the final, climactic scene of the story told in the chapel's 38 panels—the three-generation history of Jesus, his mother Mary, and Mary's parents.

The story begins with Jesus' grandparents, on the long south wall (with the windows) in the upper-left corner. ❶ In the first frame, a priest scolds the man who will be Mary's father (Joachim, with the halo) and kicks him out of the temple for the sin of being childless. ❷ In the next panel to the right, Joachim returns dejectedly to his sheep farm. ❸ Meanwhile (next panel), his wife is in the bedroom, hearing the miraculous news that their prayers have been answered—she'll give birth to Mary, the mother of Jesus.

From this humble start, the story of Mary and Jesus spirals clockwise around the chapel, from top to bottom. The top row (both south and north walls) covers Mary's birth and life.

Jesus enters the picture in the middle row of the south (windowed) wall. ❹ The first frame shows his birth in a shedlike manger. In the next frame, the Magi arrive and kneel to kiss his little

toes. Then the child is presented in the tiny temple. Fearing danger, the family gets on a horse and flees to Egypt. ❺ Meanwhile, back home, all the baby boys are slaughtered in an attempt to prevent the coming of the Messiah *(Slaughter of the Innocents)*.

Spinning clockwise to the opposite (north) wall, you see

(in a badly damaged fresco) ❻ the child Jesus astounding scholars with his wisdom. Next, Jesus is baptized by John the Baptist. His first miracle, at a wedding, is turning jars of water into wine. Next, he raises a mummy-like Lazarus from the dead. Riding a donkey, he enters Jerusalem triumphantly. ❼ In the temple, he drives out the wicked money changers.

Turning again to the south wall (bottom row), we see scenes from Jesus' final days. ❽ In the first frame, he and his followers gather at a table for a Last Supper. Next, Jesus kneels humbly to wash their feet. ❾ He is betrayed with a kiss and arrested. Jesus is tried. ❿ Then he is beaten and humiliated.

⓫ Finally (north wall, bottom row), he is forced to carry his own cross, crucified, and prepared for burial, while his followers

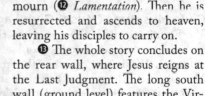

mourn (⓬ *Lamentation*). Then he is resurrected and ascends to heaven, leaving his disciples to carry on.

⓭ The whole story concludes on the rear wall, where Jesus reigns at the Last Judgment. The long south wall (ground level) features the Virtues that lead to heaven, while the north wall has the (always more interesting) Vices. And all this unfolds beneath the blue, starry sky overhead on the ceiling.

Some panels deserve a closer look:

Joachim Returns to the Sheepfold (south wall, upper left, second panel): Though difficult to appreciate from ground level, this oft-reproduced scene is groundbreaking. Giotto—a former shepherd himself—uses nature as a stage, setting the scene in front of a backdrop of real-life mountains and adding down-home details like Joachim's jumping dog, frozen in midair.

Betrayal of Christ, a.k.a. *Il Bacio*, "The Kiss" (south wall, bottom row, center panel): Amid the crowded chaos of Jesus' arrest, Giotto skillfully creates a focus upon the central action, where Judas ensnares Jesus in his yellow robe (the color symbolizing envy), establishes meaningful eye contact, and kisses him.

Lamentation, a.k.a. *Deposition* (north wall, bottom row, middle): Jesus has been crucified, and his followers weep and wail over the lifeless body. John the Evangelist spreads his arms wide and shrieks, his cries echoed by anguished angels above. Each face is a study in grief. Giotto emphasizes these saints' human vulnerability.

Last Judgment (big west wall): Christ in the center is a glorious vision, but the real action is in hell (lower right). Satan is a Minotaur-headed ogre munching on sinners. Around him, demons give sinners their just desserts in a scene right out of Dante...who

NEAR VENICE

was Giotto's friend and fellow Florentine. Front and center is Enrico Scrovegni, in a violet robe (the color symbolizing penitence), donating the chapel to the Church in exchange for forgiveness of his father's sins.

Before the guard scoots you out, take a look at the actual altar. Though Enrico's father's tomb is lost, Enrico Scrovegni himself is in the tomb at the altar. The three statues are by Giovanni Pisano—Mary (in the center) supports Baby Jesus on her hip with a perfectly natural, maternal, S-shape. She's flanked by anonymous deacons.

Nearby: Between the museum and the chapel are the scant remains of **Roman Padua.** The remnants are from the wall of an arena and also include nicely fitting pipes that once channeled water so that the arena could be flooded for special spectacles.

Civic Museums (Musei Civici agli Eremitani)

The Eremitani, the building next to the Scrovegni Chapel, was once an Augustinian hermit's monastery and now houses several museums. While you can skip the ground-floor Archaeological Museum (with Roman and Etruscan artifacts and no English descriptions), the Pinacoteca and the Multimedia Room are worth visiting. Another part of the museum, Palazzo Zuckermann, is across the street.

Pinacoteca

The museum's highlight is upstairs, in the Pinacoteca (picture gallery). The collection has 13th- to 18th-century paintings by Titian, Tintoretto, Giorgione, Tiepolo, Veronese, Bellini, Canova, Guariento, and other Veneto artists. But I'd make a beeline for the room with the Giotto crucifix (upstairs and to the right, through the upper gallery). Ask for *"La Croce di Giotto?"* (lah KROH-cheh dee JOH-toh?)

The remarkable crucifix, painted by Giotto on wood, originally hung in the Scrovegni Chapel between the Scrovegni family's private zone and the public's worshipping zone. If you actually sit on the floor and look up, the body really pops. The adjacent "God as Jesus" piece *(L'Eterno)* was the only painting in the otherwise frescoed chapel. (The original hangs here for conservation purposes; its copy is the only nonoriginal art in the chapel.) Studying these two masterpieces affirms Giotto's greatness.

Behind the crucifix room is a collection of 14th- and 15th-century art. While the works here are exquisite—and came well after Giotto—they're clearly not as modern.

Multimedia Room

Dedicated to taking a closer look at the Scrovegni Chapel, this small but interesting exhibit is downstairs. To head straight from the museum entrance to the Multimedia Room, use the entrance to the right of the main entry, step into the courtyard, make a sharp right, go through the glass doors at the end of the corridor, and head down the stairs.

Rows of computer screens offer a virtual Scrovegni Chapel visit and provide cultural insights into daily life in the Middle Ages. There are explanations of the individual panels, Giotto's fresco technique, close-ups of the art, and a description of the restoration. You'll also see a life-size re-creation of the house of Mary's mother, St. Anne, as depicted in Giotto's fresco. A 12-minute video (English headphones available) tells the history of the chapel and is similar—but not identical—to the one that precedes your chapel visit. For me, it's worth just taking some time to enjoy a second video that features a mesmerizing, slow montage of close-ups of the Giotto frescoes.

Palazzo Zuckermann

This overlooked wing of the Civic Museum is just across a busy street. Its first two floors offer a commotion of applied and decorative arts—clothes, furniture, and ceramics—from the Venetian Republic (1600s-1700s). On the top floor, the Bottacin collection takes you to the 19th century with coins and delightful (but noname) pre-Impressionist paintings.

▲▲▲Basilica of St. Anthony

Friar Anthony of Padua, "Christ's perfect follower and a tireless preacher of the Gospel," is buried here. Construction of this

impressive Romanesque/Gothic church (with its Byzantine-style domes) started immediately after St. Anthony's death in 1231. As a mark of his universal appeal and importance in the medieval Church, he was sainted within a year of his death. Speedy. And for nearly 800 years, his remains and this glorious church have attracted pilgrims to Padua.

Cost and Hours: The **basilica** is free and open daily 6:20-19:45 (Nov-March Mon-Fri closes at 18:45). The various sights within the basilica have slightly different hours: The important **Chapel of the Reliquaries** (free) keeps the basilica's hours but closes for lunch (12:45-14:30). Other, less important sights include a **museum** (€2.50, Tue-Fri 9:00-13:00, Sat-Sun 9:00-13:00 & 14:00-18:00, closed Mon), a **multimedia exhibit** (free, daily 9:00-12:30 & 14:00-17:30), and the **Oratory of St. George** and **Scuola**

del Santo (€3 apiece or €5 together, 9:00-12:30 & 14:30-18:00, Nov-March closes at 17:00). The nearest tram stop is Santo.

Dress Code: A modest dress code is enforced.

Information: Look for the information desk at the southern entrance to the cloisters (near the basilica entry), where you can pick up a free pamphlet on the saint's life and the basilica; make a donation in the Chapel of the Reliquaries to get a more detailed booklet. Tel. 049-822-5652, www.basilicadelsanto.org.

Church Services: The church hosts six separate Masses each morning (the last at 11:00), as well as at 17:00 and 18:00 in summer and on Sunday year-round, plus additional Sunday services at 12:15, 16:00, and 19:00.

Visitor Services: WCs and a picnic area are inside the cloisters.

◯ Self-Guided Tour
Basilica

Before heading inside, take a look at the basilica's red-brick facade. St. Anthony looks down and blesses all. He holds a book, a symbol of all the knowledge he had accumulated as a quiet monk before starting his preaching career.

A golden angel—the weathervane atop the spire—points her trumpet into the wind. (While you can never really be sure with angels, locals say they know it's a woman because she always tells the truth.)

Guarding the church is Donatello's life-size equestrian statue of the Venetian mercenary general, Gattamelata. Though it looks like a thousand other man-on-a-horse statues, it was a landmark in Italy's budding Renaissance—the first life-size, secular, equestrian statue cast from bronze in a thousand years.

The church is technically outside Italy. When you pass the banisters that mark its property line, you're passing into Vatican territory.

• *Enter the basilica.*

Interior: Grab a pew in the center of the nave and let your eyes adjust. Sit and appreciate the space. Gaze past the crowds and through the incense haze to Donatello's glorious crucifix rising from the altar, and realize that this is one of the most important pilgrimage sites in Christendom.

Along with the crucifix, Donatello's bronze statues—Mary with Padua's six favorite saints—grace the high altar. Late in his career, the great Florentine sculptor spent more than a decade in Padua (1444-1455), creating the altar and Gattamelata.

• *Head to the left side of the nave to find the gleaming marble masterpiece that is the focus of the visiting pilgrims—the tomb of St. Anthony.*

St. Anthony's Tomb: Pilgrims file slowly through this side

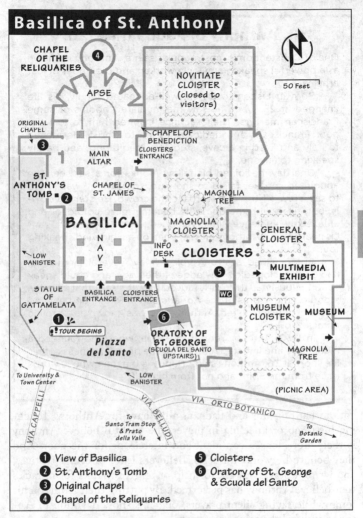

Basilica of St. Anthony

- CHAPEL OF THE RELIQUARIES
- **4**
- APSE
- ORIGINAL CHAPEL
- **3**
- MAIN ALTAR
- ST. ANTHONY'S TOMB
- **2**
- CHAPEL OF ST. JAMES
- **BASILICA**
- N A V E
- LOW BANISTER
- STATUE OF GATTAMELATA
- BASILICA ENTRANCE
- **1** TOUR BEGINS
- *Piazza del Santo*
- To University & Town Center
- LOW BANISTER

- NOVITIATE CLOISTER (closed to visitors)
- 50 Feet
- CHAPEL OF BENEDICTION
- CLOISTERS ENTRANCE
- MAGNOLIA TREE
- MAGNOLIA CLOISTER
- GENERAL CLOISTER
- INFO DESK
- **CLOISTERS**
- **5**
- MULTIMEDIA EXHIBIT
- CLOISTERS ENTRANCE
- WC
- **6**
- ORATORY OF ST. GEORGE (SCUOLA DEL SANTO UPSTAIRS)
- MUSEUM CLOISTER
- **MUSEUM**
- MAGNOLIA TREE
- (PICNIC AREA)

- NEAR VENICE

- VIA CAPPELLI
- VIA BELLUDI
- VIA ORTO BOTANICO
- To Santo Tram Stop & Prato della Valle
- To Botanic Garden

- **1** View of Basilica
- **2** St. Anthony's Tomb
- **3** Original Chapel
- **4** Chapel of the Reliquaries
- **5** Cloisters
- **6** Oratory of St. George & Scuola del Santo

chapel around the tomb, so focused on the saint that they hardly notice the nine fine marble reliefs. (While the long queue looks intimidating, these folks are just waiting their turn to touch the tomb; you can easily skirt around the side of this group for a closer look at each panel.) These Renaissance masterpieces were carved during the 16th century and show scenes and miracles from the life of the saint. As you enjoy each scene, notice the Renaissance mastery of realism and 3-D perspective and the intricate frames, which celebrate life with a burst of exuberance. Note also the vivid faces with their powerful emotions.

Stand in the corner for a moment, observing the passionate de-

St. Anthony of Padua (1195-1231)

One of Christendom's most popular saints, Anthony is known as a powerful speaker, a miracle worker, and the finder of lost articles.

Born in Lisbon to a rich, well-educated family, his life changed at 25, when he saw the mutilated bodies of some Franciscan martyrs. Their sacrifice inspired him to join the poor Franciscans and dedicate his life to Christ. He moved to Italy and lived in a cave, studying, meditating, and barely speaking to anyone.

One day, he joined his fellow monks for a service. The appointed speaker failed to show up, so Anthony was asked to say a few off-the-cuff words to the crowd. He started slowly, but, filled with the Spirit, he became more confident and amazed the audience with his eloquence. Up in Assisi, St. Francis heard about Anthony and sent him on a whirlwind speaking tour.

Anthony had a strong voice, knew several languages, had an encyclopedic knowledge of theology, and could speak spontaneously as the Spirit moved him. It's said that he even stood on the shores of the Adriatic Sea in Rimini and enticed a school of fish to listen. Anthony also was known as a prolific miracle worker.

In 1230, Anthony retired to Padua, where he founded a monastery and initiated reforms for the poor. An illness cut his life short at 36. Anthony said, "Happy is the man whose words issue from the Spirit and not from himself!"

votion that pilgrims and Paduans alike have for Anthony. Touching his tomb or kneeling in prayer, the faithful believe Anthony is their protector—a confidant and intercessor for the poor. And they believe he works miracles. Believers leave offerings, votives, and written prayers to ask for help or to give thanks for miracles they believe Anthony has performed. By putting their hands on his tomb while saying silent prayers, pilgrims show devotion to Anthony and feel the saint's presence.

Popular Anthony is the patron saint of dozens of things: travelers, amputees, donkeys, pregnant women, infertile women, and flight attendants. Most pilgrims ask for his help in his role as the "finder of things"—from lost car keys to a life companion. You'll see dozens of photos posted on his tomb in prayer or as thanks, including many of fervently wished-for newborns.

Before leaving, pause to appreciate how the entire chapel is an integrated artistic wonder.

• *Leave the chapel and step into the oldest part of the church. This is the...*

Original Chapel: This is where Anthony was first buried in 1231. To the left of the altar, note the fine (and impressively realistic for the 14th century) view of medieval Padua, with this church outside the wall (finished by 1300 and looking like it does today). Below the cityscape, in a circa-1380 fresco, Anthony on his cloud promises he'll watch over Padua.

As you exit this chapel, you'll notice many tombs nearby. People wanted to be buried near a saint. If you could afford it, this was about the best piece of real estate a dead person could want. (The practice was ended with Napoleonic reforms in 1806.)

• *Continue your circuit of the church by going behind the altar into the apse, to the Chapel of the Reliquaries. (At busy times, you may have to line up and trudge slowly up the stairs past the reliquaries.)*

Chapel of the Reliquaries

The most prized relic is in the glass case at center stage—Anthony's tongue. When Anthony's remains were exhumed 32 years after his death (in 1263), his body had decayed to dust, but his tongue was found miraculously unspoiled and red in color. How appropriate for the great preacher who, full of the Spirit, couldn't stop talking about God.

Entering the chapel, join the parade of pilgrims working their way clockwise around the chapel and up the stairs. First, on the left, look for the red, triangular vestment in which Anthony's body was wrapped. Next is his rough-hewn wood coffin. Then, up the stairs, is his pillow—a comfy rock (chest level in first glass case). The center display case contains (top to bottom) the saint's lower jaw with all his teeth impressively intact *(il mento,* located about 8 feet high), his uncorrupted tongue *(lingua,* at about eye level), and, finally, his vocal chords *(apparato vocale,* at about waist level) discovered intact when his remains were examined in 1981. In the last display case, a fragment of the True Cross *(la croce)* is held in a precious cross-shaped reliquary. Finally, descend the stairs and pass St. Anthony's holy, and holey, tunic *(tonaca)*.

Above the relics, decorating the cornice, is the *Glorification of St. Anthony*. In this Baroque fantasy—made in 1691 of carved marble and stucco—a cloud of angels and giddy *putti* tumble to the left and right in jubilation as they play their Baroque-era musical instruments to celebrate Anthony's arrival in heaven.

• *Leaving this relic chapel, continue circling the apse. You'll come to the* **Chapel of Benediction.** *Here, under a powerful modern fresco of the Crucifixion (by Pietro Annigoni, who died in 1982), a priest is waiting to bless anyone who cares to be blessed.*

Next, past the sacristy (where you can peek in at priests preparing for Mass), is a door leading to the cloisters. But before heading out, walk just beyond this passage to the...

Chapel of St. James

Exactly opposite the tomb of St. Anthony, this chapel features an exquisite 14th-century fresco by Altichiero da Zevio. Study the vivid commotion around the Crucifixion, clearly inspired by Giotto (this was created 70 years after the Scrovegni Chapel). The faces are real—right off the streets of 14th-century Padua.

• *Next, head out into the cloisters. From the right side of the nave as you face the altar, follow signs to* chiostro; *from outside, find signs on the right side of the church.*

Cloisters

The main cloister is dominated by an exceptionally bushy magnolia tree, planted in 1810 (the magnolia tree was exotic for Europe when it was imported from America in 1760). Also in the cloister are the graves of the most illustrious Paduans, such as Gabriel Fallopius, the scientist who gave his name to his discovery, the Fallopian tube. When Napoleon decreed that graves should be moved out of cities, this once grave-covered courtyard was cleared of tombstones. But the bodies were  left in the ground, perhaps contributing to the magnolia tree's fecundity. Today the tree remains an explosion of life.

Of the four cloisters here, you can wander in three. In one, picnic tables invite pilgrims and tourists to enjoy meals (it's covered and suitable even when rainy, also has WCs).

The **multimedia exhibit** on the life of St. Anthony is kitschy, as pilgrimage multimedia exhibits tend to be (30 minutes, free, you move three times as you use headphones to listen to the story of each tableau).

At the far end, a fascinating little **museum** is filled with votives and folk art recounting miracles attributed to Anthony. The abbreviation *PGR* that you'll see on many votives stands for *per grazia ricevuta*—for answered prayers.

Oratory of St. George and Scuola del Santo

The small but sumptuous **Oratory of St. George** faces the little square in front of the basilica. The oratory ("ora" means prayer) is not actually a church, though it's certainly a fine place to pray—it's filled with vivid, circa-1370 frescoes showing scenes not of Anthony but from the life of St. Catherine. Because many lovers credit St. Anthony with finding them their partners—and this is the closest place to St. Anthony where you can be married—it's popular for weddings. While you can see it all from the door, paying the entry fee lets you sit and enjoy this peaceful spot.

Next door and upstairs (buy ticket and get info sheet in the oratory) is the skippable **Scuola del Santo** (a.k.a. La Scoletta), the former meeting hall of the Confraternity of Anthony, with frescoes and paintings by various artists—including some by Titian.

NEAR THE BASILICA
Prato della Valle

The square is 150 yards southwest of the basilica (down Via Luca Belludi). Once a Roman theater and later Anthony's preaching

grounds, this square claims to be the largest in Italy. It's a pleasant, 400-yard-long, oval-shaped piazza with fountains, walkways, dozens of statues of Padua's eminent citizens, and grass. It's also a lively **market** scene (though smaller than those previously listed): fruit and vegetables (Mon-Fri 8:00-13:00), clothing, shoes, and household goods (Sat 8:00-19:00), and antiques (third Sun 8:00-19:00). This place is often busy with special events and festivals. Ask at the TI or your hotel if anything's going on at Prato della Valle.

Botanic Garden (Orto Botanico)

Green thumbs appreciate this nearly five-acre botanical garden, which contains the university's vast collection of rare plants. Founded in 1545 to cultivate medicinal plants, it's the world's oldest academic botanical garden still in its original location. A visitors center—in a little cottage to the right of the garden's entrance—houses models of the garden's layout and computer terminals that describe the history and composition of the garden.

Cost and Hours: €10; daily 9:00-19:00, closes earlier off-season; last entry one hour before closing; entrance 150 yards south of Basilica of St. Anthony—with your back to the facade, take a hard left; Santo tram stop, tel. 049-201-0222, www.ortobotanicopd.it.

Sleeping in Padua

Rooms in Padua's hotels are more spacious and a better value than those in Venice. I've listed two hotels in the center and a group of accommodations near the basilica. All are reachable from the station by tram; only Albergo Verdi is more than a five-minute walk from the nearest tram stop.

NEAR VENICE

> # Sleep Code
>
> Hotels are classified based on the average price of a standard double room with breakfast in high season.
>
> | | |
> |---|---|
> | **$$$$** | **Splurge:** Most rooms over €170 |
> | **$$$** | **Pricier:** €130-170 |
> | **$$** | **Moderate:** €90-130 |
> | **$** | **Budget:** €50-90 |
> | **¢** | **Backpacker:** Under €50 |
> | **RS%** | **Rick Steves discount** |
>
> Unless otherwise noted, credit cards are accepted, hotel staff speak basic English, and free Wi-Fi is available. Comparison-shop by checking prices at several hotels (on each hotel's own website, on a booking site, or by email). For the best deal, *book directly with the hotel.* Ask for a discount if paying in cash; if the listing includes **RS%,** request a Rick Steves discount.

IN THE CENTER

$$ Hotel Majestic Toscanelli, an old-fashioned, borderline-gaudy, family-run, 34-room hotel, owns a perfectly convenient location right in the town center—buried in the characteristic ghetto with wonderful cobbled ambience. At night, this area is popular with noisy students; request a quiet room on the back side (RS%, spacious attic "loft" rooms with kitchenettes and low beams, air-con, elevator, pay parking, Via dell'Arco 2, Tito Livio tram stop, tel. 049-663-244, www.toscanelli.com, majestic@toscanelli.com, Mario Morosi and family). From the tram stop, follow the passageway next to #26, then jog left down Via Marsala and turn right on Via dell'Arco.

$$ Albergo Verdi, an Ikea-mod little place, is crammed into an old building on a small back street beyond Piazza dei Signori. While public spaces are tight, the 14 rooms are comfortable (air-con, tiny elevator, Via Dondi dall'Orologio 7, Ponti Romani tram stop, tel. 049-836-4163, www.albergoverdipadova.it, info@albergoverdipadova.it). From Piazza dei Signori, walk through the arch under the clock tower and go to the far end of Piazza del Capitaniato; the hotel is on the side street to your right.

NEAR THE BASILICA OF ST. ANTHONY

Santo is the nearest tram stop for the following hotels. Use the Prato della Valle tram stop for the hostel.

$$$ Hotel Belludi 37 is a slick, stylish, almost pretentious place renting 16 modern rooms shoehorned into an old building. The decor is dark, woody, and fresh (RS%, some rooms with basilica view, air-con, lots of stairs with no elevator, apartments available nearby, a block from the Santo tram stop at Via Beato Luca Belludi 37, tel. 049-665-633, www.belludi37.it, info@belludi37.it).

$$ Hotel Al Fagiano feels like an art gallery with crazy, sexy, modern art everywhere. The hotel is all about the union of a man and a woman (quite romantic). They rent 37 bright and cheery rooms, each uniquely decorated with Rossella Fagiano's canvases (RS%, air-con, elevator, pay parking, 50 yards from the Santo tram stop at Via Locatelli 45, tel. 049-875-0073, www.alfagiano.com, info@alfagiano.com; Anita, artist Rossella, and husband Amato).

$ Hotel Al Santo, run with charm by Valentina and Antonio, offers 15 spacious rooms with all the comforts on two floors above their restaurant, a few steps from the basilica. Given the warm welcome and pleasant location, it's a fine value (family rooms, double-paned windows, quieter rooms off street, some rooms with basilica views, air-con, elevator, pay parking, Via del Santo 147, tel. 049-875-2131, www.alsanto.it, alsanto@alsanto.it).

$ Hotel Casa del Pellegrino, with 148 spotless, cheap, bare rooms and straight pricing, is owned by the friars of St. Anthony. It's home to the pilgrims who come to pay homage to the saint in the basilica next door. Any visitor to Padua is welcome, making it popular with professors and students. Some rooms with basilica views also come with more noise—both from the street and, starting at 6:00 in the morning, the church bells—while others are in *dipendenza,* the hotel's modern wing (cheaper rooms with shared bath, family rooms, ask for a room off the street, breakfast extra, air-con, elevator, pay parking, Via Melchiorre Cesarotti 21, tel. 049-823-9711, www.casadelpellegrino.com, info@casadelpellegrino.com).

Hostel: ¢ Ostello Città di Padova, near Prato della Valle, is well-run and has 90 beds (private rooms available, includes breakfast, reception open 7:30-9:30 & 15:30-23:00, 23:30 curfew unless you get a key, Via Aleardo Aleardi 30, Prato de Valle tram stop, tel. 049-875-2219, www.ostellopadova.it, ostellopadova@gmail.com). From the tram stop, exit the square ahead of you to the right and make an immediate left down Via Memmo; after the church, continue straight one block on Via Torresini and turn right on Via Aleardi.

Eating In Padua

The university population means cheap, good food abounds. My recommended restaurants are all centrally located in the historic core. You'd think there would be fine dining on the charming market squares, but on the piazzas it's a takeout-pizza and casual-bar scene (dominated by students after dark). La Lanterna, at the neighboring Piazza dei Signori, is the best on-square option—but they only offer functional Italian classics. The dreamily atmospher-

Restaurant Price Code

I've assigned each eatery a price category, based on the average cost of a typical main course (pasta or *secondi*). Drinks, desserts, and splurge items (steak and seafood) can raise the price considerably.

$$$$ **Splurge:** Most main courses over €20
$$$ **Pricier:** €15-20
$$ **Moderate:** €10-15
$ **Budget:** Under €10

In Italy, pizza by the slice and other takeout food is **$;** a basic trattoria or sit-down pizzeria is **$$;** a casual but more upscale restaurant is **$$$;** and a swanky splurge is **$$$$.**

ic ghetto neighborhood (just two blocks off the market squares) thrives after dark with trendy bars and a lively student *spritz* scene.

DINING NEAR THE CENTER

$$ Osteria dei Fabbri, with shared rustic tables, offers a good mix of class and accessibility, quality, and price. The dining room is spacious, and the dishes are traditional Venetian and Paduan. Ask to peek into their back courtyard, where you can see the door of an old synagogue (daily 12:30-14:30 & 19:00-22:30, but closed Sun for dinner, Via dei Fabbri 13, on a side street on south side of Piazza Erbe, tel. 049-650-336).

$$ Osteria L'Anfora is a classic place serving classic dishes in an informal, fun-loving space. Don't be put off by the woody, ruffian decor, the squat toilet, and the fact that it's a popular hangout for a premeal drink. They take food seriously and serve it at good prices, and the energy and commotion add to a great dining experience (meals served Mon-Sat 12:30-15:00 & 19:30-22:30, bar open 9:00-24:00, closed Sun, reservations smart for dinner, Via dei Soncin 13, tel. 049-656-629).

$ Enoteca dei Tadi is a small, quirky place with seven tables filling a cozy back room behind a convivial little bar (avoid their basement). Roberto and Anna serve traditional Paduan dishes and have earned a local following for their small but tasty menu. The selection is driven by what's fresh and in season, and they offer good wines by the glass (Tue-Sun 18:30-24:00, closed Mon, Via dei Tadi 16, tel. 049-836-4099, mobile 338-408-3434).

$$$ Ristorante Dante alle Piazze is a respected fixture in town for its dressy white-tablecloth dining. They are passionate about their meat and fish dishes. Reservations are smart at night (Wed-Sat and Mon 12:00-14:30 & 18:15-22:00, Sun 12:00-14:30, closed Tue, Via Daniele Manin 8, tel. 049-836-0973, www.dadanteallepiazze.com).

CHEAP EATS NEAR THE CENTER

Affordable Meals on Piazza dei Signori: $$ La Lanterna has a forgettable interior and a predictable menu of pizzas, pastas, and *secondi*. But its prime location on Piazza dei Signori provides a rare-in-Padua chance to sit in a grand square under the stars, surrounded by great architecture (reservations recommended). Its pizzas are a local favorite—takeaway available (Fri-Wed 12:00-15:00 & 18:00-24:00, closed Thu, Piazza dei Signori 39, tel. 049-660-770, www.lalanternapadova.it).

Light Meals on Piazza della Frutta: $ Bar dei Osei, on Piazza della Frutta, is a very simple sandwich bar with some of the best outdoor seats in town. While Paduans love their delicate *tramezzini*—white-bread sandwiches with crusts cut off, I'd choose their *porchetta*—savory roasted pork sandwiches. You'll find a two-foot-long mother lode waiting on the counter for you; tell friendly Marco how big a slice you'd like. Wines are listed on the board (Mon-Sat 7:00-21:00, closed Sun, Piazza della Frutta 1, tel. 049-875-9606). In the evenings, just a few feet away, a **snack stand** selling all kinds of fresh, hot, and ready-to-eat seafood appetizers sets up between 17:00 and 20:30 (daily except Sun). Belly up to the bar with your drink and try whatever Massimiliano's serving.

Fast Food: $ Brek, with one entrance next to the Ponti Romani tram stop and another tucked into a corner of Piazza Cavour at #20, is an easy self-service chain *ristorante* with healthy and affordable choices. It's big, bright, practical, and family-friendly (daily 11:30-15:00 & 18:30-22:00, tel. 049-875-3788). **$ Brek Foccacceria** (part of the same chain), across from Caffè Pedrocchi and next door to the PAM supermarket, is a café selling big sandwiches and slices of pizza that you can eat at outdoor tables. During happy hour (18:30-21:00), you can buy a drink and pay €1.50 more to fill a plate at their *antipasti* buffet, which can easily turn into a light dinner (open daily 9:00-21:00, Piazzetta della Garzeria 6, tel. 049-876-1651).

Groceries: Stock up on picnic items at the outdoor markets, or visit the **PAM supermarket,** in the tiny *piazzetta* east of Caffè Pedrocchi (Mon-Sat 8:00-21:00, Sun 9:00-20:00, Piazzetta Garzeria 3).

NEAR THE BASILICA OF ST. ANTHONY

$$ Antica Trattoria dei Paccagnella, the most serious restaurant near the basilica, serves up nicely presented, seasonal local dishes with modern flair and an impressive attention to ingredients. The place has friendly service, modern art on the walls, and no pretense. It's thoughtfully run by two brothers, Raffaele and Cesare, who happily explain why they are so excited about local hens (Mon

19:00-22:00, Tue-Sun 12:00-14:00 & 19:00-22:00 except closed Sun in summer, Via del Santo 113, tel. 049-875-0549).

$ Pizzeria Pago Pago dishes up wood-fired Neapolitan pizzas (a local favorite) and daily specials depending on what's in season. Get there early for dinner or wait (Wed-Mon 12:00-14:00 & 19:00-24:00, closed Tue; 2 blocks from Basilica of St. Anthony, up Via del Santo and right onto Via Galileo Galilei to #59; tel. 049-665-558, Gaetano and Modesto).

$ Casa del Pellegrino Ristorante caters to St. Anthony pilgrims with simple, basic, and hearty meals, served in a cheery dining room just north of the basilica (good €15 fixed-price meal, kid-friendly, Tue-Sun 12:00-14:00 & 19:00-21:00, closed Mon, Via Cesarotti 21, tel. 049-876-0715).

$ Zairo is a huge indoor/outdoor *ristorante*/pizzeria with reasonable prices, delicious homemade pastas, Veneto specialties, snappy service, and a local clientele. As it's next to the vast and inviting Prato della Valle square/park, consider combining dinner here with a relaxing stroll through the park (Tue-Sun 11:30-15:30 & 18:30-late, closed Mon, east side of Prato della Valle at #51, tel. 049-663-803).

$ Pollodoro la Gastronomica, my pick of the takeout delis near the basilica, sells roast chicken, pastas, pizza, and veggies. They'll also make sandwiches (Wed-Sat and Mon 9:00-14:00 & 17:00-20:00, Sun 8:30-14:00, closed Tue, 100 yards from basilica at Via Belludi 34, tel. 049-663-718). You can picnic at the nearby cloisters of the basilica.

Padua Connections

From Padua by Train on Trenitalia to: Venice (2/hour, 25-50 minutes), **Vicenza** (at least 2/hour, fewer on weekends, 15-25 minutes), **Milan** (1-2/hour, 2-3 hours), **Verona** (2/hour, 40-80 minutes). When taking the train to Venice, Vicenza, or Verona, buy a ticket on a regional train (R or RV). The Trenitalia Frecce or Italo express trains cost much more and get you there only marginally faster (especially when compared to a Trenitalia RV train).

By Bus to: Venice's Marco Polo Airport (65 minutes, €8.50 from ticket windows, €10 on board, hourly at :25 past the hour from 6:25 to 21:25, leaves from platform 11 at Padua's bus station, next to the train station; recheck times at www.fsbusitalia.it). If flying into the airport, take this bus to get directly to Padua (buy tickets at windows in arrivals hall or at airport TI). It's also possible—but not recommended—to connect the airport and Padua **by bus and train**—from the airport ride ACTV bus #15 (2/hour, 30 minutes, www.actv.it) to Venice's Mestre train station and take a train from there (4-5/hour, 15 minutes).

By Minibus to Airports: An Air Service minibus runs from Padua to **Marco Polo Airport** (€32/person) or **Treviso Airport** (€41/person, reservations required, tel. 049-870-4425, www.airservicepadova.it).

Vicenza

To many architects, Vicenza (vih-CHEHN-zah) is a pilgrimage site. Entire streets look like the back of a nickel. This is the city of Andrea Palladio (1508-1580), the 16th-century Renaissance architect who defined the Palladian style that is now so influential in countless British country homes. But as grandiose as Vicenza's Palladian facades may feel, there is little marble here because the city lacked the wealth to build with much more than painted wood and plaster.

If you're an architecture buff, Vicenza merits a quick day trip on any day but Monday, when major sights are closed. If you're packing light, it's an easy stop, located on the same train line as Padua, Verona, and Venice. However, because you can't store bags at the train station, it's not worth stopping here if you have lots of luggage (though in a pinch, the TI may be willing to store bags for you while you walk around town).

Tourist Information: The TI is next to the Olympic Theater at Piazza Matteotti 12 (daily 9:00-13:30 & 14:00-17:30, tel. 0444-320-854, www.visitvicenza.org). Ask for the free brochure on Palladio's buildings. Architecture fans appreciate the booklet titled *Vicenza and the Villas of Andrea Palladio*.

Arrival in Vicenza: From the **train station,** I'd head straight for the most distant sight, the Olympic Theater (with a TI next door) and then see other sights on the way back. Go straight out the train station's front door, and use the crosswalk on the right side of the roundabout. From here, it's a five-minute walk straight ahead up wide Viale Roma to the PAM supermarket at the bottom of Corso Palladio; turn right through the gate, and then it's a good 10 minutes more down the Corso to the Olympic Theater (a taxi costs €8). **Drivers** can park in one of the cheap parking lots (Parcheggio Bassano and Parcheggio Cricoli) and catch a free shuttle bus to the center.

Sights in Vicenza

Helpful bilingual signs in front of Palladio's buildings explain their history. Arrows around town point you to his major works.

All the sights mentioned (except the villas outside town) are

Vicenza

covered by the **Museum Card** combo-ticket (€15, €18 family pass, good for 3 days, sold at Olympic Theater and Palazzo Leoni Montanari Galleries).

▲▲Olympic Theater (Teatro Olimpico)

Palladio's last work, one of his greatest, shouldn't be missed. This indoor theater is a wood-and-stucco festival of classical columns,

statues, and an oh-wow stage bursting with perspective tricks. When you step back outside, take another look at the town's main drag—named after Palladio. It's the same main street you saw on the stage of his theater.

Cost and Hours: €12.50, also covered by Museum Card; Tue-Sun 9:00-17:00, closed Mon, very occasionally closed when theater is in use, audioguide available, entrance to left of TI at Piazza Matteotti 11, info tel. 0444-222-800, tickets tel. 044-496-4380, www.teatrolimpicovicenza.it.

▲Church of Santa Corona (Chiesa di Santa Corona)

A block away from the Olympic Theater, this "Church of the Holy Crown" was built in the 13th century to house a thorn from the Crown of Thorns, given to the Bishop of Vicenza by the French

King Louis IX. The church has two artistic highlights: Paolo Veronese's *Adoration of the Magi* (1573) and Giovanni Bellini's fine *Baptism of Christ* (c. 1502).

Cost and Hours: Free, Tue-Sun 9:00-12:00 & 15:00-18:00, closed Mon, Contrà Santa Corona 2, tel. 0444-323-644.

Archaeological and Natural History Museum (Museo Naturalistico Archeologico)

Located next door to the Church of Santa Corona, this museum's ground floor features Roman antiquities (mosaics, statues, and artifacts excavated from Rome's Baths of Caracalla, plus swords) and a barbarian warrior skeleton complete with sword and helmet. Prehistoric scraps are upstairs. Look for English description sheets near exhibit entryways throughout.

Cost and Hours: €3.50, covered by Museum Card, Tue-Sun 9:00-17:00, closed Mon, Contrà Santa Corona 4, tel. 0444-222-815, www.museicivicivicenza.it.

Palazzo Leoni Montanari Galleries (Gallerie di Palazzo Leoni Montanari)

Across the street from the Church of Santa Corona, this small museum is a palatial riot of Baroque, with cherub-cluttered ceilings jumbled like a preschool in heaven. A quick stroll shows off Venetian paintings and a floor of Russian icons.

Cost and Hours: €8.50, Tue-Sun 10:00-18:00, closed Mon, Contrà Santa Corona 25, tel. 800-578-875, www.palazzomontanari.com.

Piazza dei Signori

Vicenza's main square has been the center of town ever since it was the site of the ancient Roman forum. The commanding **Basilica Palladiana,** with its 270-foot-tall, 13th-century tower, dominates the square. This was once the meeting place for local big shots. It was young Palladio's proposal to redo Vicenza's dilapidated Gothic palace of justice in the Neo-Greek style that established him as the city's favorite architect. The rest of Palladio's career was a one-man construction boom. The basilica hosts special exhibitions that sometimes involve a fee, but you can often pop in for a free look.

Villas on the Outskirts of Vicenza

Vicenza is surrounded by dreamy Venetian villas. Venice's commercial empire receded in the 1500s when trade began to pick up along the Atlantic seaboard and dwindle in the Mediterranean. Venice redirected its economic agenda to agribusiness, which led to the construction of lavish country villas, such as **Villa la Rotonda,** the inspiration for Thomas Jefferson's Monticello (www.villalarotonda. it), and **Villa Valmarana ai Nani** (www.villavalmarana.com). Located southeast of the town center, both houses are furnished with period pieces (closed Mon). Pick up the free brochure on Palladio's villas from the TI if you plan to visit.

Vicenza Connections

From Vicenza by Train to: Venice (2/hour, 45-75 minutes), **Padua** (at least 2/hour, fewer on weekends, 15-25 minutes), **Verona** (2/hour, 30-60 minutes), **Milan** (1-2/hour, 2 hours). You'll save money by taking the slow R or the faster RV trains instead of the speedy Freccia or *ES* trains.

Verona

Romeo and Juliet made Verona a household word. Alas, a visit here has nothing to do with those two star-crossed lovers. You can pay

to visit the house that falsely claims to be Juliet's (with an almost believable balcony and a courtyard swarming with tour groups), join in the tradition of rubbing the breast of Juliet's statue to help find a lover (or to pick up the sweat of someone who can't), and even make a pilgrimage to what isn't "La Tomba di Giulietta."

Fiction aside, Verona has been an important crossroads for 2,000 years and is, therefore, packed with genuine history. R&J fans will take some solace in the fact that two real feuding families, the Montecchi and the Cappellos, were the models for Shakespeare's Montagues and Capulets. And, if R&J had existed and were alive today, they would still recognize much of their "hometown."

Verona's main attractions are its wealth of Roman ruins; the remnants of its 13th- and 14th-century political and cultural boom brought about by its leading family, the Scaligeri; its 21st-century, pedestrian-only ambience; and its world-class opera festival, held each summer. After Venice's festival of tourism, the Veneto region's second city is a cool and welcome sip of pure Italy, where dumpsters are painted by schoolchildren as class projects and public spaces are primarily the domain of locals, not tourists. If you like Italy but don't need blockbuster sights, this town is a joy.

Orientation to Verona

Verona's old town fills an easy-to-defend bend in the River Adige. The vibrant and enjoyable core of Verona lies along Via Mazzini between Piazza Brà (pronounced "bra") and Piazza Erbe, Verona's market square since Roman times. Each evening the two main streets from Piazza Brà to Piazza Erbe, Via Mazzini and Corso Porta Borsari, are enlivened by a wonderful *passeggiata*...bustling with a slow and elegant parade of strollers. For a good day trip to Verona, take my self-guided walk, beginning with a visit to the Roman Arena.

TOURIST INFORMATION

Verona's helpful TI is just off **Piazza Brà**—from the square, head to the big yellow building with columns and cross the street to Via degli Alpini 9 (Mon-Sat 10:00-13:00 & 14:00-18:00, Sun 10:00-15:00, shorter hours and closed Sun off-season, tel. 045-806-8680, www.tourism.verona.it). If you're staying the night, ask the TI about concerts. The monthly entertainment guide, *Carnet Verona*, sold at newsstands, is in Italian only (€2).

Sightseeing Passes: The **Verona Card** covers city transportation and entry to all recommended Verona sights except the ArenaMuseOpera (though you can get a discount there with the card). The card can save day-trippers intent on blitzing the city almost a third off their sightseeing costs (€18/24 hours, €22/48 hours, sold at TI and at participating sights, www.tourism.verona.it).

The €6 **Church Card,** sold at four churches that require admission (San Zeno, Duomo, Sant'Anastasia, and San Fermo, normally €2.50 each), pays off if you visit three (www.chieseverona.it).

Walking Tours: The TI organizes 75-minute tours in English (March-Oct Sat-Sun at 11:30, €10/person). Tours meet inside the Piazza Brà TI and stroll all the way through the old town (confirm schedule, no reservation necessary).

ARRIVAL IN VERONA

By Train: Verona's main train station is called Verona Porta Nuova. In the main hall, you'll find pay WCs and a baggage-check office (daily 8:00-20:00). Buses and taxis are immediately outside.

Avoid the boring 15-minute walk from the station to Piazza Brà. **Buses** are cheap, easy, and leave every few minutes. Buy a ticket from the tobacco shop inside the station (€1.30/90 minutes, €4 day pass valid until midnight), or buy one on board using coin-op machines for €0.70 more. Leaving the station, angle right across the street to the bus stalls, find platform A, and hop on a bus: #11, #12, and #13 run Monday-Saturday before 20:00; #90, #92, #93, and #98 run after 20:00 and all day Sunday; and #51 and #52 run daily, even after 20:00. If in doubt, confirm that your bus is headed to the city center by asking, *"Per il centro?"* (pehr eel CHEN-troh). Validate your ticket by stamping it in the machine on the bus.

Drivers don't announce stops, but you'll know Piazza Brà because of the mass exodus and the can't-miss-it Roman Arena (bus stops in front of big, yellow, Neoclassical building). The TI is just a few steps beyond the bus stop, against the medieval wall. You can catch return buses to the station (same numbers) from the stop on the piazza side of the street, or from another bus stop on Piazza Brà, near the WCs.

Taxis pick up only at taxi stands (at Piazza Brà, Piazza Erbe, and the train station) and cost about €8-10 for the quick ride between the train station and the center of town (€2 more on Sundays and after 22:00, €1/big bag).

If you're in downtown Verona and need train tickets or reservations, drop by Welcome Travel (see "Helpful Hints," later).

By Car: The old town center (where nearly all my recommended hotels are located) is closed to traffic. Your hotel can get you permission to drive in—ask when you book. Otherwise your license plate will be photographed, and a €100 ticket might be waiting in the mail when you get home.

Drivers will find reasonably priced parking in well-marked lots and garages just outside the center. The underground **Cittadella garage,** at Piazza Cittadella (a block off Piazza Brà, behind the TI), is huge, convenient, and easy to find (€2/hour, €16/24 hours). The **Città di Nimes/Parking Stazione** lot is near the wall, a five-minute walk from the train station (€1.50/hour, €7/day). **Street parking** is limited to two hours and costs €1/hour (spaces marked with blue lines, buy ticket at a tobacco shop or ticket machine, place ticket on dashboard; some hotels can give you a free street-parking permit—ask).

By Plane: Efficient buses connect Verona's airport (known as Catullo or Verona-Villafranca, 12 miles southwest of the city, airport code: VRN, tel. 045-809-5666, www.aeroportoverona.it) with its train station (€6, buy tickets on board or at tobacco shop, daily about 5:15-23:00, 3/hour, 15 minutes, bus stop is by front door of train station, to the right).

HELPFUL HINTS

Sightseeing Schedules: Most sights (except churches) are closed on Monday mornings and typically open at 13:30.

Opera: From mid-June through early September, Verona's opera festival brings the city to life, with 15,000 music fans filling the Roman Arena for almost nightly performances. The city is packed and festive—restaurants have prescheduled seatings for dinner, and hotels jack up their prices (cheap upper-level seats-€29, day-of-show tickets often available). You can book tickets at the TI (extra charge if paying by credit card) or through the official box office (buy online at www.arena.it or call 045-800-5151; box office open Mon-Fri 9:00-12:00 & 15:15-17:45, Sat 9:00-12:00, closed Sun; during opera season, open daily 10:00-17:45, or until 21:00 on performance days; Via Dietro Anfiteatro 6b). If you're not here for the festival, you can still explore the arena and/or visit Verona's opera-focused ArenaMuseOpera museum.

Travel Agency: If you need train tickets or reservations, stop by **Welcome Travel** (small fee added to tickets but saves a trip to the station, Mon-Fri 9:00-19:00, Sat 9:30-12:30 & 15:00-18:00, closed Sun, Corso Porta Nuova 11, tel. 049-806-0111).

Private Guides: Three excellent and enthusiastic Verona guides enjoy giving private tours of the town and region tailored to your interests—villas, wine tasting, and so on (€120-125/2 hours, €260/5 hours). They are **Marina Menegoi** (mobile 328-958-1108, www.marinamenegoi.com, mmenegoi@gmail.com), **Valeria Biasi** (€32 for small-group tour, €130 for 2.5-hour private tour, mobile 348-903-4238, www.aguideinverona.com or www.veronatours.com, valcria@aguideinverona.com), and **Franklin Baumgarten** (mobile 347-566-6765, franklin_baumgarten@web.de).

Verona Walk

This walk covers the essential sights in the town core, starting at Piazza Brà and ending at the cathedral. Allow two hours (including the tower climb and dawdling).

❶ Piazza Brà

If you're wondering about the name, it comes from the local dialect and means "big open space." A generation ago this piazza was

noisy with cars. Now it's open and people-friendly—it's become the community family room and natural festival grounds.

Grab a bench near the central **fountain** called "The Alps." This was a gift from Verona's sister city Munich, which is just over the mountains to the north. You'll see in the middle of the fountain the symbols of the two cities separated by the Alps, carved out of pink marble from this region. In general, Verona has a bit of an alpine feel; historically it was the place where people rested and prepared before crossing the mountains, and to this day it's the place where the main west-east, Milan-Venice train line meets the north-south line up to Bolzano, the Dolomites, and Austria.

The ancient **arena** looming over the piazza is a reminder that the city's history goes back to Roman times. On this walk, we'll meander across what was the ancient city, from the arena on this side to the theater across the river.

With the fall of Rome in the fifth century, Verona became a favored capital of barbarian kings. In the Middle Ages, noble families had to choose sides in the civil struggles between emperors (Ghibellines) and popes (Guelphs). During this time (1200s), the town bristled with several hundred San Gimignano-type towers, built by different families to symbolize their power. When the Scaligeri family rose to power here in the 14th century, they established stability on their terms and made the other noble families lop off their proud towers—only the Scaligeri were allowed to keep theirs. To add insult to injury, the Scaligeri paved the city's roads with bricks from the other families' toppled towers. But interfamily feuds made it impossible for the Scaligeri to maintain a stable government, and in 1405 the town essentially gave itself to Venice, which ruled Verona until Napoleon stopped by in 1796. During the 19th century, a tug-of-war between France and Austria actually divided the city for a time, with the river marking the border of each country's domain. Eventually Verona, like Venice, fell into Austrian hands.

Reminders of Austrian rule remain: The huge yellow Neoclassical **city hall** facing Piazza Brà (look for the flags) was built by the Austrians to serve as their 19th-century military headquarters. Their former arsenal stands just across the river, and an Austrian fortress caps the hill looking over the city. But the big **equestrian statue** is of Italy's first king, Victor Emmanuel II, celebrating Italian independence and unity, which was won in the 1860s. The **statue of a modern soldier** striking a *David* pose, with a machine gun instead of a sling over his shoulder, honors Verona's war dead.

Apart from all its history, Piazza Brà is about strolling—the evening *passeggiata* is a national sport in Italy. The broad, shiny sidewalk (named "Liston" after a Venetian promenade; note the fine Venetian-style marble pavement slabs) was built by 17th-century Venetians, who made it big and wide so that promenading socialites could see and be seen in all their finery.

❷ Roman Arena

The Romans built this stadium outside their town walls, just as

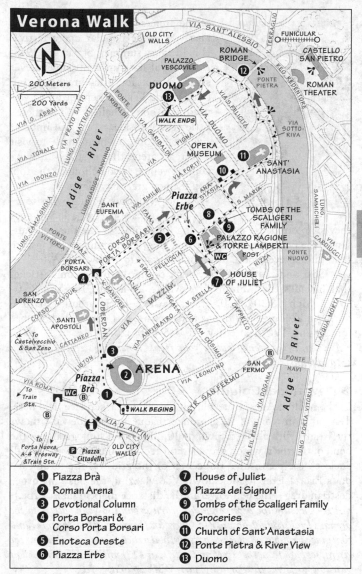

Verona Walk

- OLD CITY WALLS
- VIA SANT'ALESSIO
- FUNICULAR
- V. TERRAGLIO
- CASTELLO SAN PIETRO
- PALAZZO VESCOVILE
- ROMAN BRIDGE
- PONTE PIETRA
- REG. REDENTORE
- ROMAN THEATER
- DUOMO ⓭
- VIA S. FELICIA
- VIA DUOMO
- VIA SOTTO RIVA
- WALK ENDS
- PONTE GARIBALDI
- VIA PRATO SANTO
- LUNG. G. MATTEOTTI
- LUNGADIGE PANVINO
- Adige River
- VIA GARIBALDI
- PIGNA
- OPERA MUSEUM ⓫
- ⓬
- SANT' ANASTASIA
- ⓾
- VIA G. ABBA
- VIA TONALE
- VIA ISONZO
- SANT EUFEMIA
- VIA EMILEI
- VIA FAMA
- CORSO PORTA BORSARI
- Piazza Erbe
- VIA ANA-STASIA
- S. MARIA
- LUNG. SAMMICHELI
- VIA CAMPAGNOLA
- PONTE VITTORIA
- DIAZ
- PORTA BORSARI ❹
- ❺
- ❻
- ❽
- ❾
- TOMBS OF THE SCALIGERI FAMILY
- PALAZZO RAGIONE & TORRE LAMBERTI
- POST
- WC
- VIA CARDUCCI
- PONTE NUOVO
- SAN LORENZO
- CORSO CAVOUR
- SANTI APOSTOLI
- CASTELLO
- 4 SPADE
- V. CANTORE
- V. OBERDAN
- CASALDI
- PELLICCIAI
- VIA NIZZA
- HOUSE OF JULIET ❼
- To Castelvecchio & San Zeno
- CATTANEO
- VIA ANFITEATRO
- MAZZINI
- SCALA
- V. STELLA
- VIA SAN COSIMO
- VIA CAPPELLO
- ❸
- LISTON
- ❷ ARENA
- VIA LEONCINO
- SAN FERMO
- PONTE NAVI
- Adige River
- Piazza Brà
- ❶
- WALK BEGINS
- VIA D. ALPINI
- STR. SAN FERMO
- VIA DOGANA
- VIA PORTA VITTORIA
- L'ACQUA MORTA
- VIA ROMA
- To Train Stn.
- WC
- To Porta Nuova, A-4 Freeway & Train Stn.
- P
- Piazza Cittadella
- OLD CITY WALLS
- VIA FIL PEINI
- 200 Meters
- 200 Yards
- NEAR VENICE

❶ Piazza Brà
❷ Roman Arena
❸ Devotional Column
❹ Porta Borsari & Corso Porta Borsari
❺ Enoteca Oreste
❻ Piazza Erbe
❼ House of Juliet
❽ Piazza dei Signori
❾ Tombs of the Scaligeri Family
❿ Groceries
⓫ Church of Sant'Anastasia
⓬ Ponte Pietra & River View
⓭ Duomo

modern stadiums are usually located outside downtown districts. With 72 aisles, this elliptical, 466-by-400-foot amphitheater is the third largest in Italy (and it was originally 50 percent taller). Most of the stone you see is original. Dating from the first century A.D., it looks great in its pink marble. Over the centuries, crowds of up to 25,000 spectators have cheered Roman gladiator battles, medieval executions, rock concerts, and modern plays, all taking advantage

of the arena's famous acoustics. This is also where the popular opera festival is held every summer. Started in 1913, the festival has run continuously ever since, except for brief breaks during both World Wars, when the arena was used as a bomb shelter. While there's little to see inside except the impressive stonework, it's memorable to visit a Roman arena that is still a thriving concert venue. If you climb to the top, you'll enjoy great city views.

The gladiators posing with tourists out front are part of a local gang; they're notorious for overcharging for photos. While they're a nuisance, the police say it's better that they're scamming a living here than finding even more disreputable ways to get by.

Cost and Hours: €7.50, don't bother with the combo-ticket that includes the unimpressive Maffei Museum, Tue-Sun 8:30-19:30, Mon 13:30-19:30, closes earlier—likely around 16:00—during mid-June-early Sept opera season, last entry one hour before closing, WC near entry, tel. 045-800-3204.

• *As you exit the arena, look to your right. Where the street splits you'll see a column.*

❸ Devotional Column

In the Middle Ages, this column blessed a marketplace held here. Ten yards in front of it, a bronze plaque in the sidewalk shows the Roman city plan—a town of 20,000 placed strategically in the bend of the river, which provided protection on three sides. A wall enclosed the peninsula. The center of the grid was the forum, today's Piazza Erbe. (Look down Via Mazzini, the busy main pedestrian drag—the bell tower in the distance marks Piazza Erbe.)

• *After viewing the bronze plaque, turn around so your back is to the arena. Head straight down Via Oberdan (bearing left at the fork) and continue a couple of blocks (passing a derelict fascist-era theater, the Astra, set back from the street on the left, at #13) until you see an ancient gate to your right, the Porta Borsari. Walk up to it.*

❹ Porta Borsari and Corso Porta Borsari

You're standing before the main entrance to Roman Verona; back then, this gate functioned as a tollbooth (*borsari* means purse, referring to the collection of tolls here). Below the spiral, fluted columns (which parents nickname *"tortiglioni"*—a pasta kids can relate to), carved into the rock, is a tribute to the emperor who restored this gate. Outside the adjacent Caffè Rialto, the stone on the curb is

from a tomb: In Roman times, the roads outside the walls were lined with tombstones, because burials were not allowed within the town itself. Turn around, look down Corso Cavour, and imagine it in Roman times, leading away from the city gate and lined with tombs. Step into the café. A glass panel in the floor shows the original Roman foundations and pavement stones.

Back outside, cross under the Roman gate and head into the ancient city. Walk down Corso Porta Borsari, the Roman main drag, toward what was the forum. As you walk, make it a scavenger hunt. You'll discover bits of the town's illustrious past—(chips of Roman columns, medieval reliefs, fine old facades, fossils in marble)—as well as signs of its elegant present (fancy shops and well-turned-out pedestrians). On the right, you'll pass the recommended Osteria del Bugiardo, a popular wine bar and a good place to take a break and hang out with Verona's young and trendy.

• *Between Corso Porta Borsari 13 and 15, detour right down Vicolo San Marco in Foro, following the* Pozzo dell'Amore *sign. Twenty yards ahead on your right, you'll find...*

❺ Enoteca Oreste

This funky wine-and-grappa bar is still run by owner Oreste like a 1970s, old-style *enoteca*. Browse and sample and clown around with Oreste. This historic *enoteca* was once the private chapel of the archbishop of Verona. Traces of the past hide between the bottles—ask Oreste to tell you the story (light food, Vicolo San Marco in Foro 7, tel. 045-803-4369).

• *Return to Corso Porta Borsari and continue one block until you hit a big square.*

❻ Piazza Erbe

This bustling market square is a photographer's delight. Its pastel buildings corral the fountains, pigeons, and people who have congregated here since Roman times, when this was a forum. Notice the Venetian lion hovering above the square atop a column, reminding locals of the conquest of 1405. Wander into the market, to the fountain in the middle. A fountain has bubbled here for 2,000 years. The original Roman statue lost its head and arms. After a sculptor added a new head and arms, the statue became Verona's Madonna. She holds a small banner that reads, roughly, "The city of Verona deserves respect and justice." During medieval times, the stone canopy in the center of the square (past the fountain) held the scales where merchants measured the weight of goods they bought and sold, such as silk and wool.

If you were standing here in the Middle Ages, you would have been surrounded by proud noble family towers. Medieval nobles showed off with towers. Renaissance nobles showed off with finely painted facades on their palaces. Find remnants of the 16th-century days when Verona was nicknamed "the painted city."

Locals like to start their evening with an *aperitivo* here. Each bar caters to a different market segment. Survey the scene and, if or when the time is right, choose the terrace that suits you and join in the ritual. It's simple: Grab a spot, adjust your seat for the best view, and order a *spritz* to drink (€4 with a plate of olives and chips).

• *At the far end of Piazza Erbe is a market column featuring St. Zeno, the patron of Verona, who looks at the crazy crowds flushing into the city's silly claim to touristic fame: the House of Juliet (100 yards down Via Cappello to #23, on the left—just follow the crowds). Side-trip there now (but watch your wallet—it's a pickpocket's haven).*

❼ House of Juliet

The tiny, admittedly romantic courtyard is a spectacle: Tourists from all over the world pose on the balcony, while those hoping for love wait their turn to polish Juliet's bronze breast. Residents marvel that each year, about 1,600 Japanese tour groups break their Venice-Milan ride for an hour-long stop in Verona just to see this courtyard (free, gates open roughly 8:30-19:30 or longer). It's fun to stand in the corner and observe the scene, knowing that all this commotion was started by a clever tour guide in the early 1970s as a way to attract visitors to Verona.

The courtyard walls have long been filled with amorous graf-

fiti. The latest trend is to affix a paper note to the gates or walls with chewing gum. The wall of padlocks is another gimmick, enabling lovers to blow money in an attempt to prove that their hearts are thoroughly locked up. (The shop that sells the locks also sells pens to write on them.) The red mailbox is for love letters to Juliet. There's actually a Juliet Club that reviews these—and all the letters mailed from around the world to "Juliet, Verona, Italy." Each year, the club awards the author of the sweetest letter a free vacation to Verona.

Even those who milk their living out of this sight freely admit, "While no documentation has been discovered to prove the truth of the legend, no documentation has disproved it either." The "museum," which displays art inspired by the love story, plus costumes and the bed from Franco Zeffirelli's film *Romeo and Juliet,* is certainly not worth the €6 entry fee.

Was there ever a real Juliet Capulet? You just walked down Via Cappello, the street of the cap makers. Above the courtyard entry (looking out) is a coat of arms featuring a hat—representing a family that made hats and which would be named, logically, Capulet.

The public's interest in a fictional Romeo and Juliet—or at least Juliet—is a sign that there's a hunger for a Juliet in our world. Observing the mobs clamoring to polish her breast or blow kisses from her bogus balcony, I try to appreciate what she means to people, and to psychoanalyze what she provides to those who come to Verona specifically for this: the message that love will prevail. In love, you can lose, and still be a winner. Juliet is brave, tragic, honest, outspoken, timeless, and passionate. She's a mover and a shaker, a dreamer and a fighter. In a way, this is a pagan temple where the spirit of Juliet gives people something to believe in...or maybe it's just a bunch of baloney appreciated by a simple-minded crowd.

• *Return to Piazza Erbe. From the middle of the piazza, head right on Via della Costa. Walk down Via della Costa, into the big square.*

❽ Piazza dei Signori

Literally the "Lords' Square," this is Verona's sitting room, quieter and more harmonious than Piazza Erbe. The buildings—which span five centuries—define the square and are all linked by arches. From one arch dangles a whale's rib. It was likely a souvenir brought home by a traveling merchant from a trip to the Orient, reminding the townspeople that there was a big world out there. The long portico on the left is inspired by a building in Florence: Brunelleschi's Hospital of the Innocents, considered the first Renaissance building.

Locals call the square Piazza Dante for the statue of the Italian poet **Dante Alighieri** that dominates it. Dante—always pensive, never smiling—seems to wonder why the tourists choose Juliet over him. Dante was expelled from Florence when that city sided with the pope (who didn't appreciate Dante's writing) and banished its

Sidebar: NEAR VENICE

greatest poet. Verona and its ruling Scaligeri family, however, were at odds with the pope (siding instead with the Holy Roman Emperor), and granted Dante asylum.

With the whale's rib behind you, you're facing the brick, crenellated, 14th-century Scaligeri residence. Behind Dante is the yellowish, 15th-century Venetian Renaissance-style Portico of the Counsel. At Dante's two o'clock is the 12th-century Romanesque Palazzo della Ragione.

Looking back the way you came, follow the white *toilette* signs into the courtyard of the **Palazzo della Ragione**. The impressive stairway is the only surviving Renaissance staircase in Verona. Within the palazzo you can visit the Gallery of Modern Art (skippable) and climb the 13th-century **Torre dei Lamberti** for a grand city view. The elevator saves you 243 steps—but you'll still need to walk up 46 more to get to the tower's first viewing platform. It's not worth continuing up 79 more spiral stairs to the second viewing platform (€8 ticket covers tower and Gallery of Modern Art, €4 for just the gallery, no individual tower tickets sold, Mon-Fri 10:00-18:00, Sat-Sun 11:00-19:00, ticket office next to staircase, tel. 045-800-1903, www.palazzodellaragioneverona.it).

• *Exit the courtyard the way you entered and turn right, continuing downhill. Within a block, you'll find the...*

❾ Tombs of the Scaligeri Family

These exotic and very Gothic 14th-century tombs, with their fine, original, wrought-iron protective cages, evoke the age when one family ruled Verona. The Scaligeri were to Verona what the Medici family was to Florence. These were powerful people. They changed the law so that they could be buried within the town. They forbade the presence of any noble family's towers but their own. And, by building tombs atop pillars, they arranged to be looked up to, even in death.

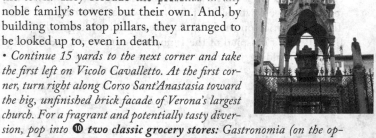

• *Continue 15 yards to the next corner and take the first left on Vicolo Cavalletto. At the first corner, turn right along Corso Sant'Anastasia toward the big, unfinished brick facade of Verona's largest church. For a fragrant and potentially tasty diversion, pop into* ❿ **two classic grocery stores:** *Gastronomia (on the opposite corner at the start of the street, at #33, closed Sun afternoon) and Albertini, located on your left in the next block. Gastronomia can rustle up tasty sandwiches.*

⓫ Church of Sant'Anastasia

This church was built from the late 13th century through the 15th century. Although the facade was never finished (the builders ran

out of steam), the interior was—and still is—brilliant. Step inside to see the delightful way this region's medieval churches were painted. Note the grimacing hunchbacks holding basins of holy water on their backs (near main entrance at base of columns). And don't miss Pisanello's fresco of *St. George and the Princess of Trebizond* (1438; at the tip of the arch, high above chapel to right of altar). Once colorful, it has oxidized over time to its current monochrome state. For a closer look at

its wonderful detail, check out the images on the computer terminal below the fresco. Ask for the English brochure, which describes the story of the church.

Cost and Hours: €2.50; Mon-Sat 9:00-18:00, Sun 13:00-18:00; Nov-Feb Mon-Sat 10:00-13:00 & 13:30-17:00, Sun 13:00-17:00; www.chieseverona.it.

• *Leaving the church, make two lefts, and walk along the right side of the church to Via Sottoriva. To the right, the Sottoriva arcade was once busy with colorful wine bars and osterie, some of which still exist (see "Eating in Verona," later). But for now, head to the left on Via Sottoriva. In a block, you'll reach a small riverfront area with stone benches that usually have a few modern-day Romeos and Juliets gazing at each other rather than at the view. Belly up to the river view.*

⓬ Ponte Pietra and River View

The white stones of the Ponte Pietra footbridge are from the original Roman bridge that stood here. After the bridge was bombed

in World War II, the Veronese fished the marble chunks out of the river to rebuild it. From here, you can see across the river to the Roman Theater, built into the hillside behind the green hedge (see page 167). Way above the theater (behind the cypress trees) is the fortress, Castello San Pietro.

The wide spot in the river here was called the "Millers' Widening," where boats stopped and unloaded grain to be milled. Water wheels once lined the river and powered medieval Verona, employing technology imported from the Holy Land by 10th-century Crusaders.

Continue up the river toward the bridge. Keep an eye out for the recommended **Gelateria Ponte Pietra,** at #13, where Mirko,

Mariam, and Stefano dish out fine gelato. Walk to the high point on the bridge and enjoy the view.

• *From the bridge, look back 200 yards at the tall white spire...that's where you're heading. Walk back off the bridge, then turn right, keeping an eye on the left for the steeple of the...*

⓭ Duomo

Started in the 12th century, this church was built over a period of several hundred years. Before entering, note the fine Romanesque carvings on its facade.

Cost and Hours: €2.50; Mon-Sat 10:00-17:00, Sun 13:30-17:00, shorter hours off-season.

Visiting the Church: Step inside, pick up the leaflet that explains the church's highlights, and head to the back-left corner of the church. In the last chapel on the left is Titian's 16th-century *Assumption of the Virgin.* Mary calmly rides a cloud—direction up—to the shock and bewilderment of the crowd below. Notice a handful of tombs embedded in the walls about 15 feet above floor level—an unusual feature. (Generally, tombs are found in the floor of the church or in crypts below.)

Now head up the aisle to the last door on the left (left of high altar), where you'll find the **ruins** of an older church. These are the 10th-century foundations of the Church of St. Elena, turned intriguingly into a modern-day chapel featuring exposed fourth-century mosaic floors from the Roman church that originally stood here.

From there, pass through the little open-air courtyard into the adjacent **baptistery,** with its clean Romanesque lines, hanging 14th-century crucifix, and fine marble font. Try to identify the eight biblical scenes carved on its panels before referring to my answers. (Answers, starting with the panel just to the right of center and working counterclockwise: Annunciation; first Christmas, with animals licking Baby Jesus and giving him a barnyard welcome; announcement to shepherds of Jesus' birth, with their flock stacked on one side; Epiphany, with the Three Kings giving their gifts to Baby Jesus; Herod commanding that all male infants be killed; Slaughter of the Innocents; flight to Egypt; and finally, facing the entry door, John the Baptist baptizing Christ.)

Finally, after leaving the church, circle around its left side (as you face the main facade) to find the peaceful Romanesque **cloister** *(chiostro),* with mosaics from a fifth-century Christian church exposed below the walk.

Sights in Verona

IN THE TOWN CENTER
▲▲Evening *Passeggiata*

For me, the highlight of Verona is the *passeggiata* (stroll)—especially in the evening. Make a big circle from Piazza Brà through the old town on Via Mazzini (one of Europe's many "first" pedestrian-only streets) to the colorful Piazza Erbe, and then back down Corso Porta Borsari to Piazza Brà. This is a small town, where people know each other, and they're all out on parade. Like peacocks, the young and nubile spread their wings. The classy shop windows are integral to the *passeggiata* as, for many of the ladies, shopping is a sport. Their never-finished wardrobes are considered a work in progress, and this is when they gather ideas. If you're going to complement your stroll with a stop in a café or bar, the best plan is to enjoy a *spritz* drink—not on Piazza Brà, but on Piazza Erbe (the oldest and most elegant bars are on the end farthest from Juliet's balcony).

ArenaMuseOpera (AMO)

This slick museum, which opened in 2013 to celebrate the 100th anniversary of the city's renowned opera festival, fills the old Palazzo Forti in the sleepy streets at the northern edge of downtown. The underwhelming permanent exhibit, swaddled in red velvet, uses a few scant artifacts, sparse descriptions, and a handful of interactive touchscreens to trace the creation of an opera from words *(libretto)* to score *(partitura)* to staging (*rappresentazione*, including designers' sketches, along with actual sets and costumes from some of the performances that have graced the arena's stage). Opera lovers may enjoy this museum—particularly if it's hosting any interesting special exhibits (these can be excellent).

Cost and Hours: €8, more with special exhibits, Tue-Sun 10:30-18:30, closed Mon, closed Nov-March except by request, Via Massalongo 7, tel. 045-803-0461, www.arenamuseopera.com.

WEST OF PIAZZA BRÀ AND THE ARENA
▲Castelvecchio

Verona's powerful Scaligeri family built this castle (1343-1356) as both a residence and a fortress. The castle has two parts: the family palace and the quarters for their private army (separated, for the nervous family's security, by a fortified wall and an internal moat). Today, it houses the city's art gallery, with an extensive, enjoyable collection of sculpture and paintings.

Cost and Hours: €6, Tue-Sun 8:30-19:30, Mon 13:30-19.30, last entry 45 minutes before closing, Corso Castelvecchio 2, tel. 045-806-2611, see map on page 169 for location. Info sheets are available throughout, but the €4 audioguide (€6/2 people) is still worthwhile.

Visiting the Castle: Religious statues were Verona's medieval forte, while paintings were the city's Renaissance forte. From the entrance, you'll head right toward the **statues,** once brightly painted. Cross to the next wing and head upstairs to walk through two floors that trace the evolution of **painting** from the 13th through the 17th century, including minor works by many major masters (such as Bellini, Mantegna, and Veronese). You'll also pass by a small armory collection.

En route, watch for the chance to roam the **ramparts** with fine views of the city, river, and Ponte Scaligero (described below). Kids (and kids at heart) enjoy scrambling across the delightfully crenellated parapets. Verona was an independent city-state from 1176 to 1387. Then came a long period of subjugation under other powers which, in more modern times, included the Austrians. From the ramparts you can see remnants of Austrian rule: the arsenal across the river and the castle atop the distant hill.

Nearby: Next to Castelvecchio, the picturesque red-brick bridge called **Ponte Scaligero**—fortified and crenellated, as if a continuation of the castle—is free, open to the public, and fun to stroll across. Destroyed by the Germans in World War II, it was rebuilt in the 1950s using many of its original bricks, which were dredged out of the river. Today it's understandably a favorite for wedding-day photos.

▲Basilica of San Zeno Maggiore

This church, outside the old center, is dedicated to the patron saint of Verona, whose remains are buried in the crypt under the main altar. In addition to being a fine example of Italian Romanesque, the basilica features Mantegna's *San Zeno Triptych* (1456-1459) with its marvelous perspective, peaceful double-columned cloisters, and a set of 48 paneled 11th-century bronze doors nicknamed "the poor man's Bible." Pretend you're an illiterate medieval peasant and do some reading. Facing the altar, on the walls of the right-side aisle, you can see frescoes painted on top of other frescoes and graffiti dating from the 1300s. These were done by people who fled into the church in times of war or flooding and scratched prayers into the walls. Druidic-looking runes are actually decorated letters typical of the Gothic period, like those in illuminated manuscripts.

Cost and Hours: €2.50, Mon-Sat 8:30-18:00, Sun 12:00-18:00; Nov-Feb Mon-Sat 10:00-13:00 & 13:30-17:00, Sun 12:00-17:00; located on Piazza San Zeno, a 15-minute walk upriver beyond Castelvecchio, www.chieseverona.it.

ACROSS THE ROMAN BRIDGE, NORTH OF THE CENTER

Roman Theater (Teatro Romano)

Dating from about the time of Christ, this ancient theater was discovered in the 19th century and restored. Admission includes

the Roman Museum, located high in the building above the theater (reach it via elevator—start at the stage and walk up the middle set of stairs, then continue straight on the path through the bushes).

The museum displays a model of the theater, a small chapel, and Roman artifacts, including mosaic

floors, busts and other statuary, clay and bronze votive figures, and architectural fragments. There's not much to see. Unless you've never seen a Roman ruin, I'd skip it.

Cost and Hours: €4.50—only €1 if museum is closed for restoration, Tue-Sun 8:30-19:30, Mon 13:30-19:30, last entry one hour before closing, theater located across the river near Ponte Pietra footbridge, tel. 045-800-0360. From mid-June through August, the theater stages Shakespeare plays—only a little more difficult to understand in Italian than in Elizabethan English.

Giusti Garden (Giardino Giusti)

You'll see this picturesque Renaissance garden capping the steep hilltop just across the Roman Bridge at the northern edge of the city. It's a little oasis with manicured box hedges, towering cypress trees, and a city view from the top of its hill. For most people, however, it's not worth the hike, time, or money.

Cost and Hours: €7, daily 9:30-20:00, Oct-March 9:00-19:00, across the river, beyond Ponte Nuovo.

Sleeping in Verona

($$$$ = Splurge, $$$ = Pricier, $$ = Moderate, $ = Budget)
Hotel prices soar (at least €20-30 more per night) from mid-June through early September (opera season), in early April (during the Vinitaly wine festival—see "The Wines of Verona" sidebar, later), and during big trade fairs or major holidays. Unless your goal is opera, consider coming before mid-June or after early September. Prices are lowest from November to March.

NEAR PIAZZA ERBE

$$$ Hotel Aurora, at the corner of Piazza Erbe and Via Pelliciai, has friendly family management, attention to detail, a welcoming terrace with wonderful piazza views, and 18 fresh, modern rooms (family rooms, elevator, air-con, Piazzetta XIV Novembre 2, tel. 045-594-717, www.hotelaurora.biz, info@hotelaurora.biz, Rita). Coming from the train station, you can hop off at Piazza Brà, cross the square, and walk 10 minutes up the main pedestrian street; or, for a slightly shorter walk, stay on the bus two stops longer until the San Fermo stop (from here, walk away from the river, following signs for *Piazza Erbe*).

$ Protezione della Giovane, run by an association that houses poor women, also rents rooms and dorm beds to female tourists (and their children, up to age 12 for boys). Buried deep in the old town and up several flights of stairs, this place offers 20 cheap beds in a clean, institutional, and peaceful setting (women only, dorm bed-€22, private rooms available, no breakfast, 23:00 curfew, reception open 9:00-20:00, Wi-Fi in common areas, self-service coin-op washing machine but no dryer, Via Pigna 7, tel. 045-596-880, www.protezionedellagiovane.it, info@protezionedellagiovane.it).

NEAR PIAZZA BRÀ

You'll find several options in the quiet streets just off Piazza Brà, within 200 yards of the bus stop. From the square, white or yellow signs point you to the hotels. Most of these are big, fairly impersonal business-class places; the Torcolo is more homey and friendly. Albergo Arena is a little farther out, near Castelvecchio (10-minute walk to Piazza Brà).

$$$$ Hotel Giulietta e Romeo is on a quiet side street just 50 yards behind the Roman Arena. It's stylish and well-managed; 10 of its 37 sexy, ultra-modern rooms have balconies (air-con, elevator, free loaner bikes, fitness room, pay parking in garage or ask for free street parking permit, Vicolo Tre Marchetti 3, tel. 045-800-3554, www.hotelgr.it, info@hotelgr.it).

$$$ Hotel Colomba d'Oro is a sprawling, stately, elegant place renting 51 spacious rooms with Baroque flourishes. It has

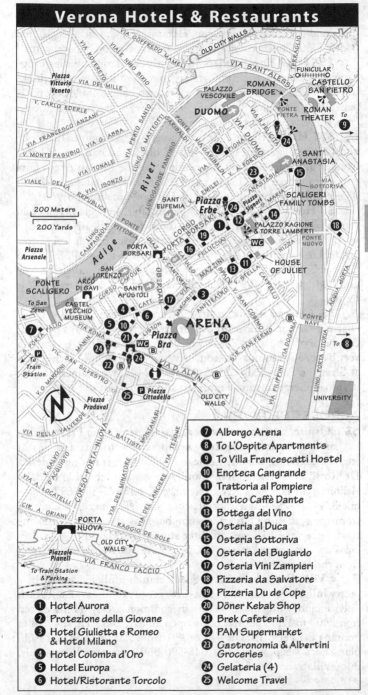

Verona Hotels & Restaurants

NEAR VENICE

1 Hotel Aurora
2 Protezione della Giovane
3 Hotel Giulietta e Romeo & Hotel Milano
4 Hotel Colomba d'Oro
5 Hotel Europa
6 Hotel/Ristorante Torcolo

7 Albergo Arena
8 To L'Ospite Apartments
9 To Villa Francescatti Hostel
10 Enoteca Cangrande
11 Trattoria al Pompiere
12 Antico Caffè Dante
13 Bottega del Vino
14 Osteria al Duca
15 Osteria Sottoriva
16 Osteria del Bugiardo
17 Osteria Vini Zampieri
18 Pizzeria da Salvatore
19 Pizzeria Du de Cope
20 Döner Kebab Shop
21 Brek Cafeteria
22 PAM Supermarket
23 Gastronomia & Albertini Groceries
24 Gelateria (4)
25 Welcome Travel

generous public spaces, including a serene garden, and overlooks a quiet and central street (air-con, elevator, Via C. Cattaneo 10, tel. 045-595-300, www.colombahotel.com, info@colombahotel.com).

$$$ Hotel Europa offers 46 slightly dated rooms with springtime colors and classic comfort. Try to request a balcony overlooking the *piazzetta* below (air-con, elevator, a couple of blocks off Piazza Brà at Via Roma 8, tel. 045-594-744, www.veronahoteleuropa.com, info@veronahoteleuropa.com).

$$$ Hotel Milano is an arty hotel with 57 rooms. The lobby and fancier rooms are tricked out in black and chrome. It has a wonderful terrace and hot tub overlooking the Roman Arena (air-con, elevator, pay parking in garage, Vicolo Tre Marchetti 11, tel. 045-596-011, www.hotelmilano-vr.it, info@hotelmilano-vr.it).

$$ Hotel Torcolo offers 19 comfortable, lovingly maintained rooms with Grandma's furnishings (breakfast extra, air-con, fridge in room, elevator, pay parking in garage; from Piazza Brà promenade, head down the alley to the right of #16 and walk to Vicolo Listone 3; tel. 045-800-7512, www.hoteltorcolo.it, hoteltorcolo@virgilio.it, well-run by Silvia, Diana, Riccardo, and helpful Caterina).

$$ Albergo Arena, a little dreary but with no-frills 1960s charm, is a good value for those on a budget. Located in a peaceful courtyard off a busy street a few blocks from Piazza Brà, it offers 15 very basic, quiet rooms (air-con, elevator, just west of Castelvecchio at Stradone Porta Palio 2, tel. 045-803-2440, www.albergoarena.it, info@albergoarena.it, Francesco and Elena).

ACROSS THE RIVER

$$ L'Ospite, a 10-minute walk across the river from Piazza Erbe, has six cozy, immaculate, fully equipped apartments and lots of stairs. The rooms, warmly managed by English-speaking Federica De Rossi, sleep two to four (family rooms, no reception or daily cleaning, air-con, Via XX Settembre 3, tel. 045-803-6994, mobile 329-426-2524, www.lospite.com, info@lospite.com). Coming from the station by bus (ride same buses as those headed downtown—see page 153), get off three stops past Piazza Brà, just after crossing the bridge, at the XX Settembre stop (across the street from the apartments).

¢ Villa Francescatti is a good, church-affiliated hostel in a pretty hillside setting (dorm bed–€18, private rooms available, cash only, includes breakfast, Wi-Fi in common areas, rooms closed from 9:00 to 17:00 but reception open all day, 24:00 curfew; Salita Fontana del Ferro 15, bus #73 or #91 from station to Piazza Isolo plus short steep walk, tel. 045-590-360, www.ostelloverona.it, info@villafrancescatti.it).

Eating in Verona

(\$\$\$\$ = Splurge, \$\$\$ = Pricier, \$\$ = Moderate, \$ = Budget)
Every restaurant listed here is within a 10-minute walk of the others. They're mostly small and intimate and found along side streets. It's tempting to grab a table next to the *passeggiata* action along Piazza Brà, but you'll be sacrificing service, value, and quality for your view of the floodlit Roman Arena and Verona on parade (perhaps a fair trade-off). Except for Brek Cafeteria, restaurants on the piazza tend to charge a cover and service fee, making even pizza a pricey choice.

FINE DINING

\$\$\$\$ Enoteca Cangrande is enthusiastically run by Giuliano and Corrina, who enjoy turning people on to great, well-matched food and wine. You can sit on a quiet street or in a plush little dining area inside. Their star offering is a €40 set menu, a festival of *antipasti* treats, an imaginative pasta, a meat or fish course, and dessert. They also offer a light à la carte menu at lunch (daily 12:00-22:30, closed Tue off-season; a block off Piazza Brà at Via Dietro Liston 19D—if the equestrian statue jogged slightly right, he'd head straight here; tel. 045-595-022, www.ristorantecangrande.it).

\$\$\$ Trattoria al Pompiere, which has a commitment to regional traditions, is bigger, with formal waiters weaving among its tight tables and walls plastered with photos of big shots from the area. This bustling place is a favorite of local foodies. Marco and his gang serve gourmet meats and cheeses as *antipasti* from their larger-than-life back counter, ideal for a mixed plate to complement the huge selection of fine wines. Reservations are wise (Mon-Sat 12:40-14:00 & 19:40-22:30, closed Sun, chivalry lives—ladies' menus come without prices; halfway between Piazza Erbe and Juliet's courtyard—head down narrow side street next to Via Cappello 8 to Vicolo Regina d'Ungheria 5; tel. 045-803-0537, www.alpompiere.com).

\$\$\$ Antico Caffè Dante is a high-end place with a 19th-century pedigree and elegant service on the coziest and classiest square in town. You can enjoy a memorable meal of classic Veneto cuisine either at romantic tables on the square or inside. While it's not cheap, if you want to dress up and enjoy a slow, romantic, memorable meal, this can be a good value (Mon-Sat 12:30-14:30 & 19:30-22:30—but closed Mon in summer, Sun 12:00-14:30, Piazza dei Signori 2, tel. 045-800-0083, www.caffedante.it).

\$\$\$ Bottega del Vino is pricey, venerable, and a bit pretentious. Under a high ceiling and walls of wine bottles, brisk, black-vested waiters match traditional dishes (polenta, duck, game) with glasses of fine wine. Choose from 40 open bottles. The waitstaff,

The Wines of Verona

Wine connoisseurs love the high-quality wines of the Verona area. The hills to the east are covered with grapes to make Soave; to the north is Valpolicella country; and Bardolino comes from vineyards to the west.

Valpolicella grapes, which are used to make the fruity, red Valpolicella table wine (found everywhere), are also the basis for full-bodied red Amarone and the sweet dessert wine Recioto. To produce Amarone, grapes are partially dried (*passito*) before fermentation, then aged for a minimum of four years in oak casks, resulting in a rich, velvety, full-bodied red. Recioto, which in local dialect means "ears," uses only the grapes from the top of the cluster (so they sort of look like the "ears" of the cluster's "head"). Because these grapes get the most sun, they mature the fastest and have the highest concentration of sugar. Before pressing, the grapes are dried for months until all moisture has gone out; the wine is then aged for one to three years.

Bardolino, from the vineyards near Lake Garda, is a light, fruity wine, like a French Beaujolais. It's a perfect picnic wine.

Soave, which might be Italy's best-known white wine, goes well with seafood and risotto dishes. While Soave can vary widely in quality, the best are called "Soave Classico" and come from the heart of the region, near the Soave Castle. Soave is sometimes aged in oak casks, giving it a mellow, rounded flavor.

Sample these and many others at the numerous *enoteche* (wine-tasting bars) or at any restaurant around town. In early April, Verona hosts Vinitaly, the most important international convention of domestic and international wines. Vintners vie for prestigious awards for the past year's vintage. Tourists are welcome to attend at the end of the week and are shuttled to the convention hall from Piazza Brà. Hotels book up months in advance. Check with the TI and www.vinitaly.com for details.

If you're visiting the area in the fall, consider a day trip to nearby Monteforte d'Alpone, east of Verona. The town hosts a fun, raucous wine festival in September—ask at the TI for more information on this and other regional wine festivals.

ambience, and food have deep roots in local culture. I like their front room best. Reservations are smart for dinner (good daily specials, daily 12:00-23:00—kitchen closed 14:30-19:00, bar open later, off Via Mazzini at Via Scudo di Francia 3, tel. 045-800-4535, www.bottegavini.it).

MODERATE RESTAURANTS

$$ Osteria al Duca is a fun, family-run place with a lively atmosphere and good traditional dishes. Locals line up for its affordable, two-course, €18 fixed-price meal with lots of choices. I much prefer their ground floor (*piano terra*—worth requesting). Reservations are advised (Mon-Sat 12:00-14:30 & 18:30-22:30, closed Sun, half-block east of Scaligeri family tombs at Via Arche Scaligere 2, tel. 045-594-474, www.osteriaalduca.it, Alessandro or Daniela).

$$ Ristorante Torcolo is a family restaurant, with mom (Paola) running the kitchen, and father and son (Roberto and Luca) serving the meals. While it feels a bit dressy, it lacks pretense. They serve all the classics, including a €35 fixed-price meal featuring traditional Verona dishes, and have an accessible menu and extensive wine list. Eat in their dining hall or on the tiny courtyard outside (Tue-Sun 12:30-14:30 & 19:00-22:30, closed Mon, just behind the Piazza Brà scene on a quiet street, Via Carlo Cattaneo 11, tel. 045-803-3730).

EATING IN OSTERIE (OLD BARS)

Wandering around the old town, you'll see plenty of Verona's thriving little watering holes. While these characteristic old bars focus more on wine than on food, most serve memorable, characteristic, and affordable plates. Menus are simple and rustic—sometimes just bar munchies and the daily pasta. Service is relaxed and the clientele is young and local. For drinks it's mostly wine or water—fine wines are served by the glass, with bottles open and prices listed on blackboards. (I saw one sign suggesting that patrons "don't drive too much to drink.")

I've listed three places below: a classic antique *osteria* with more of a menu; a trendy, more modern place in the old center; and a small one-man show just off Piazza Brà, where you're most likely to make a new friend.

$$ Osteria Sottoriva survives from an era when Verona's river served as the town thoroughfare, and business deals could be made over a glass of wine at rustic riverside eateries. Located in a fine old covered arcade (the portico of Via Sottoriva), Sottoriva offers simple soups and pastas, with both cozy indoor and outdoor seating (daily 11:00-15:00 & 18:00-22:30—but open all day long in summer, closed Wed in winter, behind the Church of Sant'Anastasia at Via Sottoriva 9, tel. 045-801-4323). Don't confuse this with the nearby Ostregheteria Sottoriva 23.

$$ Osteria del Bugiardo is jammed with a hip, young crowd that spills out into the pedestrian-filled Corso Porta Borsari. They have a buffet of little sandwiches, can whip up a plate of top-quality cheeses, and serve a good pasta-of-the-day. They showcase their own Buglioni wines and are proud to tell you more about them (daily 11:00-24:00, Corso Porta Borsari 17a, tel. 045-591-869).

$$ Osteria Vini Zampieri, with a tiny bar and five tables, keeps a tradition of stoking conviviality with good wine since 1937. Its young and energetic manager, Leo, is passionate about organic

NEAR VENICE

wines, slow food, and his own home-brewed beer. As the drinks are their priority, they don't serve much food—just some bar munchies and a nice *antipasti* plate—but at lunchtime, Leo can whip up a simple pasta to complement your wine (Tue-Sun 11:00-14:00 & 17:00-late, Mon 17:00-late, a few steps off Piazza Brà and next to Via Mazzini at Via Alberto Mario 23, tel. 045-597-053). You're welcome to play foosball downstairs on what Italians call the *calcio balilla* ("the little boy soldiers of Mussolini").

PIZZA, CHEAP EATS, AND SWEETS

$ **Pizzeria da Salvatore,** Verona's first pizzeria, opened in 1961, when pizza was considered a foreign food...from Naples. They serve the best pizza in town, and a visit here offers a nice excuse to stroll across the river into a part of town with no tourists. It's family-friendly, not fancy or romantic, and you'll squeeze into a tight row of tiny tables, rubbing elbows with your neighbors. While it's not quite Naples, it's justifiably popular—come early, or plan to leave your name on the list and wait awhile (Tue-Sat 12:30-14:30 & 19:00-23:00, Sun 19:00-23:00 only, closed Mon, no reservations, across Ponte Nuovo to Piazza San Tomaso 6, tel. 045-803-0366).

$$ **Pizzeria Du de Cope** is a colorful, high-energy, informal place (with paper placemats) that buzzes with smartly attired young waiters and locals who keep coming back for the pizza (daily 12:00-14:30 & 19:00-23:00, flamboyant desserts, families welcome, no reservations, at Galleria Pelliciai 10, tel. 045-595-562).

$ *Döner kebab* shops all over town serve hearty, cheap kebabs to munch on from a stool or to take out (most open daily roughly noon-midnight). *Piadine* (pita-bread) kebabs are worth the €4, and the super-sized kebabs can fill a couple on a very tight budget for a total of €7. The best kebabs, according to local assessments, are behind the Roman Arena at Via Leoncino 44. There's another good place on the other side of Piazza Brà, near Hotel Europa, at Via Teatro Filarmonico 6b. The benches in the center of Piazza Brà are handy for a scenic place to munch your cheap meal.

$ **Brek Cafeteria,** a well-run and modern chain right on Piazza Brà, offers a cheap and easy self-serve option inside. Or, if you want to sit out on the square, you can order off the pricier menu—and enjoy a view that's worth paying a little extra for (daily 11:30-15:00 & 18:30-22:00, longer hours for outdoor seating during summer, facing equestrian statue at Piazza Brà 20).

Groceries: PAM supermarket is just outside the historic gate on Piazza Brà (Mon-Sat 8:00-21:00, Sun 9:00-20:00, exit Piazza Brà through the gate and take the first right to Via dei Mutilati 3). Near the Church of Sant'Anastasia are two classic grocery stores, **Gastronomia** and **Albertini** (described on page 162).

A Mobile Feast Through Verona

Verona is a great town to sample the *aperitivo* ritual. All over town, locals enjoy a refreshing *spritz,* ideally on Piazza Erbe between 18:00 and 20:00. Choose a nice perch, and then, for about €4, you'll get the drink of your choice and a few nibbles (olives and/or potato chips) and a chance to feel very local as you enjoy the *passeggiata* scene.

Consider this for a fun sampling of many dimensions of the Verona eating and socializing scene: Start with an *aperitivo* on **Piazza Erbe** (the most refined bars are the farthest from Juliet's balcony), then walk across Ponte Nuovo to **Pizzeria da Salvatore** and enjoy the town's best pizza. If you have to wait for a table, have another *spritz* at the neighboring bar. Then stroll along the river to **Osteria Sottoriva,** and enjoy a little sampling of bar food with a glass of Amarone (wine to meditate with) under the old arcade. Finish by meandering through the old center back to Piazza Brà for a gelato at **Gelateria Savoia.** *Buon appetito!*

Gelato: The venerable **Gelateria Savoia** has been in business since 1939. It's in an arcade just off Piazza Brà, marked by a crowd licking their distinctive *semi-freddo*—a specialty of bitter-almond amaretto, cream, and cookie (open long hours daily, just off Piazza Brà at Via Roma 1b). On the other side of town, near Ponte Pietra and the Duomo, is **Gelateria Ponte Pietra** (open late most nights in summer, Via Ponte di Pietra 13). **Gelato Pretto,** a pricey gourmet *gelateria,* has two prime locations—right on Piazza Erbe (at #40) and near Piazza Brà (on Porta Nuova, just past the main arch).

Verona Connections

You have three options for getting train tickets in the Verona station: the standard station ticket office (with slow-moving lines, daily 6:00-21:00), a bank of modern machines (good English descriptions, cash and credit cards accepted), and the Deutsche Bahn ticket office (20 yards from baggage check office in the tunnel, offering tickets at the same cost as the station office but with German efficiency and no lines, Mon-Sat 8:00-18:00, closed Sun).

Every hour, at least two trains connect Verona with Venice, Padua, and Vicenza. Choose one of the cheaper regional trains (R or RV) instead of the faster Frecce express train, which gets you there slightly sooner but costs much more.

From Verona by Train to: Venice (2/hour, 1.5-2.5 hours), **Padua** (2/hour, 40-80 minutes), **Vicenza** (2/hour, 30-60 minutes),

Florence (*Firenze,* about hourly, 1.5 hours direct or 2.5 hours with transfer in Bologna), **Bologna** (hourly, 1.5 hours), **Milan** (2/hour, 1.5-2 hours), **Rome** (at least hourly, 4-5 hours, often with transfer in Bologna, also 1 direct night train, 6.5 hours), and **Bolzano** (about hourly, 2-2.5 hours, avoid "fast" trains that take the same amount of time but cost much more).

THE DOLOMITES

Dolomiti

Italy's dramatic rocky rooftop, the Dolomites, offers some of the best mountain thrills in Europe. The city of Bolzano—blending Austrian tidiness with an Italian love for life—is the gateway to the Dolomites. And the village of Castelrotto is a good home base for your exploration of Alpe di Siusi (Seiser Alm), Europe's largest alpine meadow. Dolomite, a sedimentary rock similar to limestone, gives these mountains their distinctive shape and color. The bold, light-gray cliffs and spires flecked with snow, above green, flower-speckled meadows and beneath a blue sky, offer a powerful and memorable mountain experience.

A hard-fought history has left the region bicultural, with an emphasis on the German. In the mountains and closer to the border, most locals speak German first, and some wish they were still part of Austria. In the Middle Ages, as part of the Holy Roman Empire, the region faced north. Later, it was firmly in the Austrian Habsburg realm. By losing World War I, Austria's South Tirol became Italy's Alto Adige. Mussolini did what he could to Italianize the region, including giving each town an Italian name and building a severely fascist-style new town in Bolzano. But even as recently as the 1990s, secessionist groups agitated violently for more autonomy—with some success (see sidebar on page 180).

The government has wooed locals with economic breaks, which have made this one of Italy's richest areas (as local prices attest), and today all signs and literature in the province of Alto Adige/Südtirol are in both languages. Some include a third language, Ladin—an ancient Romance language still spoken in a few traditional areas. (I have listed both the Italian and German, so the

The Dolomites

AUSTRIA

ITALY
Rome
200 Miles

To Innsbruck
BRENNER PASS

Vipiteno/
Sterzing

REIFENSTEIN
CASTLE

A-22

S-49

ITALY

Brunico/
Bruneck

To Lienz &
Salzburg

Fortezza

S-508

KLOSTER
NEUSTIFT

Ponte
Gardena/
Waldbruck

"CHIUSA/
KLAUSEN"
EXIT

Bressanone/
Brixen

TRENTINO-
ALTO ADIGE

Dobbiaco/
Toblach

Tre
Cime

S-51

Castelrotto/
Kastelruth

Val Gardena

Oberbozen

Ortisei

PASSO
SELLA

PASSO
GARDENA

Cortina
d'Ampezzo

Lago
Misurina

Bolzano/
Bozen

"SÜD"
EXIT

"NORD"
EXIT

Compatsch

Seis/
Siusi

Langkofel

Sella

Corvara

See detail map

S-48

PASSO
FALZAREGO

S-241

ALPE DI SIUSI /
SEISER ALM

Vigo

Canazei

PASSO
PORDOI

PASSO
CAMPOLONGO

Pieve di
Cadore

Marmolada

Alleghe

S-48

A-22

Cavalese

10 Kilometers

S-203

S-51

To Trento
& Verona

10 Miles

To
Belluno

To
Venice

confusion caused by this guidebook will match that experienced in your travels.)

The Dolomites are well developed, and the region's most famous destinations suffer from après-ski fever. But in spite of all the glamorous resorts and busy construction cranes, the regional color survives in a warm, blue-aproned, ruddy-faced, felt-hat-with-feathers way. There's yogurt and yodeling for breakfast. Culturally, as much as geographically, the area is reminiscent of Austria. In fact, the Austrian region of Tirol is named for a village that is now part of Italy.

Bolzano

Willkommen to the Italian Tirol! If Bolzano ("Bozen" in German) weren't so sunny, you could be in Innsbruck. This enjoyable old city is the most convenient gateway to the Dolomites, especially if you're relying on public transportation. It's just the place to take a Tirolean stroll.

Bolzano feels like a happy castaway between the Germanic and Italian worlds. The people are warm and friendly, but organized. One person greets you in Italian, the next in German. But everyone can agree the city has a special verve, with lively shopping arcades, a food-and-flower market more bustling than anything you'll find north of the border in Austria, and a tidy main square with a backdrop of colorful churches and wooded foothills.

The town has only one museum worth entering, but it's world class, offering the chance to see Ötzi the Iceman—a 3,500-year-old Tirolean found frozen on a mountaintop—in the (shriveled, leathery) flesh. Beyond that, Bolzano is made for strolling, relaxing, and hiking in the nearby hills—and works well as a home base for venturing deeper into the mountains (though Castelrotto is closer to the high-mountain lifts).

Orientation to Bolzano

Virtually everything I mention in Bolzano (pop. 100,000) is in the compact and strollable old town, which radiates out from the main square, Piazza Walther/Waltherplatz. Those curious about fascist architecture can head 10 minutes west of the center to see Mussolini's "New Bolzano" development. And many enticing hikes into the foothills that cradle Bolzano begin from your hotel's doorstep.

DOLOMITES

TOURIST INFORMATION

Bolzano's TI, just down the street from the train station, is helpful (Mon-Fri 9:00-19:00, Sat 9:30-18:00, closes 12:30-14:00 Nov-March and in slow times, closed Sun year-round—except may open Sun July-Aug 9:30-13:30, Via Alto Adige/Südtiroler Strasse 60, www.bolzano-bozen.it).

Discount Card: Consider buying the **Museummobil Card,** which covers most museums in the South Tirol (including the archaeology museum, with its famous Iceman), plus trains, buses, the Funivia del Renon/Rittner Seilbahn cable car, and more (€30/3 days, available at local TIs and the train station baggage storage office, www.mobilcard.info). It'll pay for itself only if you're very busy (for example, if you visit the Iceman, ride the Renon cable car, and take the bus round-trip from Bolzano to Castelrotto). The **Mobilcard** is a transit-only version that covers trains, buses, and lifts (€15/1 day, €23/3 days, sold at TIs and transit offices, www.mobilcard.info).

Walking Tours: The TI offers a guided town walking tour in English on Saturdays in season (€6, March-Oct at 11:00, departs from TI).

Ich bin ein Italiener

With the exception of Bolzano, where Italian has become the primary language, you'll hear mostly German in Dolomite villages. Overall, seven in ten Italians living in the South Tirol speak German as their mother tongue. Many are fair-skinned and blue-eyed and prefer dumplings and strudel to pasta and gelato. Most have a working knowledge of Italian, but they watch German-language TV, read newspapers *auf Deutsch,* listen to jaunty oompah music, and live in Tirolean-looking villages.

At the end of World War I, the region was ceded by Austria (loser) to Italy (winner). Mussolini suppressed the Germanic cultural elements as part of his propaganda campaign to praise all things Italian. Many German speakers hoped that Hitler would "liberate" them from Italy, but Hitler's close alliance with Mussolini prevented that from happening. Instead, in June of 1939, residents were given six months to make a hard choice: Move north to the Fatherland and become German citizens, or stay in their homeland *(Heimat)* under Italian rule. The vast majority (212,000, or 85 percent) decided to leave, but with the outbreak of World War II, only 75,000 actually moved.

After the war, German speakers were again disappointed when the Allies refused to grant them autonomy or the chance to become Austrian citizens. Instead, the victors decided to stick with the prewar arrangement. The region rebuilt and the two linguistic groups patched things up, but for the remainder of the 20th century, German speakers were continually outvoted by the Italian-speaking majority in the regional government (comprising two provinces, Italian-speaking Trentino and German-speaking Alto Adige/Südtirol).

German speakers lobbied the national government for more control on the provincial (not regional) level, even turning to demonstrations and violence. Over the years, Rome has slowly and grudgingly granted increased local control. The country's 2001 constitution gave Alto Adige/Südtirol a large measure of autonomy—similar to Sicily and Sardinia—though it's still officially tied to Trentino. Roads, water, electricity, communications, and schools are all under local control, including the Free University of Bozen-Bolzano, founded in 1998.

A good way to sum it all up: In many ways the people of the Dolomites feel a closer bond with their Austrian ancestors than with their countrymen to the south. But when Italy plays Austria in a big soccer match, who do locals root for? Italy.

ARRIVAL IN BOLZANO

By Train: There are two train stations for Bolzano—you want just *Bolzano,* not *Bolzano Süd.* Free WCs are in the underground passage by track 1, and luggage storage is nearby (see "Helpful Hints," next). To reach the **TI,** exit the station, turn left, and walk two blocks. To get **downtown,** jog left up the tree-lined Viale della Stazione/Bahnhofsallee, and walk past the bus station (on your left) two blocks to Piazza Walther/Waltherplatz and the start of my self-guided walk.

By Car: Be careful driving in Bolzano—keep an eye out for ZTL zones (marked with a red circle), where you'll be automatically ticketed. The most convenient parking lot for a short visit is the P3 garage, right under the main square (€2.50/hour, cheaper overnight; to find it, make your way to the train station, then drive up Viale della Stazione/Bahnhofsallee, watching for the *P3/Piazza Walther* entrance on your right). For longer stays or to save a few euros, try P8 (Parking Centro/Mitte), just south of the ring road and west of the train station—about a 10-minute walk from the main square (€1.50/hour, cheaper overnight, enter from Via Josef Mayr Nusser).

HELPFUL HINTS

Exchange Rate: €1 = about $1.10

Country Calling Code: 39 (see page 1154 for dialing instructions)

Sleepy Sundays: This small, culturally conservative city is really dead on Sunday (young locals add, "and during the rest of the week, too").

Markets: Piazza Erbe/Obstplatz hosts an ancient and still-thriving open-air produce market (Mon-Sat all day, closed Sun). Wash your produce in the handy drinking fountain in the middle of the market. Another market (offering more variety, not just food) runs Saturday mornings on Piazza della Vittoria.

Baggage Storage: You can store bags at **Base Camp Dolomites,** at the train station by track 1 (daily 8:30-18:30, tel. 0471-971-733, Matteo and Lukas).

Laundry: Ecomatic is at Via Rosmini/Rosministrasse 39, southwest of the South Tirol Museum of Archaeology (€5/wash, €4/dry, daily 7:00-22:30, doors lock automatically at closing time, mobile 347-220-2323).

Bike Rental: The city has a well-developed bike-trail system and cheap, city-subsidized rental bikes (€2/6 hours, €5/6-24 hours, €10 refundable deposit, ID required, Mon-Sat 7:30-19:50, closed Sun and Nov-March, just off Piazza Walther/Waltherplatz on the road to the station, tel. 0471-997-578).

DOLOMITES

Bolzano

To Maretsch & Runkelstein Castles

CORSO DELLA LIBERTA
To Petrarcha Park
17

Piazza della Vittoria

VICTORY MONUMENT

SOUTH TIROL MUSEUM OF ARCHAEOLOGY (ÖTZI THE ICEMAN)

VIA DEI VANGA

VIA ROGGIA

15

VIA MUSEO

PONTE TALVERA

Talvera River

NEW BOLZANO

VIA PETER MAYR

VIALE VENEZIA

VIA SAN QUIRINO

MUSEO CIVICO

VIA CASSA DI RISPARMIO

EUROPA GALLERY

VIA LEONARDO DA VINCI

WALK ENDS

18

Piazza delle Erbe

12
10   VIA
13

Piazza Sernesi

VIA DELLA MOSTRA

FREE UNIVERSITY OF BOLZANO

VIA ROSMINI

19

VIA OSPEDALE

6

Piazza Domenicani

VIA D.

POST

DOMINICAN CHURCH

VIA CAPPUCCINI

CHIESA DEI CAPPUCCINI

Bike Path

Isarco/Eisack

① Parkhotel Laurin
② Hotel Greif
③ Stadt Hotel Città
④ Hotel Figl
⑤ Hotel Feichter
⑥ Kolpinghaus Bozen
⑦ Youth Hostel Bolzano
⑧ Weisses Rössl Restaurant
⑨ Ca' de Bezzi/Gasthaus Batzenhäusl
⑩ Hopfen & Co. Restaurant

⑪ Paulaner Stuben
⑫ Humus Restaurant
⑬ Enoteca Il Baccaro
⑭ Dai Carretai Bar
⑮ Drago D'Oro Chinese
⑯ Gul Indian
⑰ To Officina del Gelo Avalon (Gelato)
⑱ DeSpar Supermarkets (3)
⑲ Launderette
⑳ Bike Rental

For a higher-quality mountain bike or electric bike, try Base Camp Dolomites at the station (described earlier under "Baggage Storage").

Bolzano Walk

This brief self-guided walk will help you get your bearings in central Bolzano.

• *Start the walk in...*

Piazza Walther/Waltherplatz: The statue in the center honors the square's namesake, Walther von der Vogelweide, a 12th-century politically incorrect German poet who courageously stood up to the pope in favor of the Holy Roman (German) Emperor. Walther's spunk against a far bigger power represents the Germanic pride of this region. The statue is made of marble quarried in the village of Laas, north of

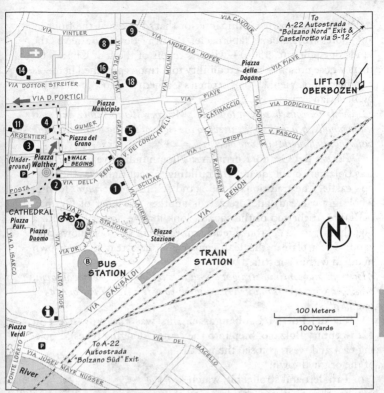

Bolzano. (The US chose this same marble for the 86,000 crosses and Stars of David needed to mark the WWII dead buried at Normandy and other battlefields across Europe.

When not hosting Bolzano's Christmas market, flower market (May Day), or Speck Fest (a spring ham festival), Piazza Walther/Waltherplatz is simply the town's living room. And locals care about it. It was the site of Italy's first McDonald's, which, in the early 1990s, became the first McDonald's to be shut down by locals protesting American fast food. Today the square is home to trendy cafés such as Café Walther, where (outside of meal times) you're welcome to nurse a "Venetian" *spritz* or a pricier cocktail as long as you like.

• *Cross the street to the big church.*

The Cathedral: The cathedral's glazed-tile roof is typical of the Germanic world—a reminder from the sixth century until 1919, when Italy said *benvenuti* to the Südtirol, German was the region's official language. The church was flattened in World War II (a common consequence of being located near a train station in 20th-century Europe).

Walk around to the right, to the Romanesque Lion's Gate (at the far end), and step inside. The place feels Teutonic, rather than

Italian, with a mostly Gothic interior that's broken at the front by an impressive Baroque tabernacle. Partway down the nave, the sandstone pulpit (c. 1500)—with its reliefs of the four Church fathers whose presence gave credibility to sermons preached here—is reminiscent of Vienna's St. Stephen's Cathedral. Most of the art is by Bavarian artists.

• *Leaving the church, return to Piazza Walther/Waltherplatz and cross it diagonally, heading up the street to the right of the big Sparkasse bank building. Follow this for one block, to...*

Piazza del Grano/Kornplatz: Nine hundred years ago, this was Bolzano's main square. The building to your right was the bishop's castle. The traditional food stand selling *Vollkornbrot* (dense, whole-grain bread) and pretzels is another reminder of German heritage. At the top of the square, look for the flower bed with a big, chunky rock. A bronze relief embedded in the rock shows Bolzano's street plan in the 12th century: a one-street arcaded town huddled within a fortified wall.

• *Jog right and continue straight ahead into the original medieval town, passing a* wurstel *(frankfurter) stand on your left. You'll pop out in the middle of...*

Via dei Portici/Laubengasse: This was the only street in 12th-century Bolzano. Step into the center (dodging bikes). Looking east and west, you see the width of the original town.

Turn left and stroll a bit, watching on the right for the frescoed, pointed arches of the old City Hall—the street's only Gothic building. Notice that the other buildings, with uniform round arches, are all basically the same: Each had a storm cellar, cows out back, a ground-level shop, and living quarters upstairs. Bay windows were designed for maximum light—just right for clerks keeping track of accounts and for women doing their weaving. The arcades *(Lauben)*, typical of Tirol, sheltered merchants and their goods from both snow and sun. Narrow side passages lead to neighboring streets.

A bit farther along on the left, the only balcony marks the street's lone Baroque building—once the mercantile center (with a fine worth-a-look courtyard), now a skippable museum.

• *Continue to the end of the street, where you'll find a bustling market.*

Piazza Erbe/Obstplatz: This square hosts an open-air produce market, liveliest in the morning (closed Sun). The historic market fountain gives Bolzano its only hint of the sea—a 17th-century statue of Neptune. Stroll around and see what's in season. All of the breads, strudel, and hams *schmecken sehr gut.*

• *From the market, Via Museo/Museumstrasse (called Butcher Street until the 19th century, when a museum opened) leads straight ahead to Frozen Fritz.*

Sights in Bolzano

▲▲▲South Tirol Museum of Archaeology (Museo Archeologico dell'Alto Adige/Südtiroler Archäologiemuseum)

This excellent museum, which illuminates the prehistory of the region, boasts a unique attraction: the actual corpse of Ötzi the Iceman, who spent more than five millennia stuck in a glacier. With Ötzi as the centerpiece, the museum takes you on an intriguing journey through time, recounting the evolution of humanity—from the Paleolithic era to the Roman period and finally to the Middle Ages—in vivid detail. The interactive exhibit offers informative displays and models, and video demonstrations of Ötzi's extraction and his personal effects. Everything's well described in English (skip the €4 audioguide).

Cost and Hours: €9, €37.50 guided tour for up to 15 people (must reserve ahead), Tue-Sun 10:00-18:00, closed Mon except July-Aug and Dec, near the river at Via Museo/Museumstrasse 43, tel. 0471-320-100, www.iceman.it.

Crowd-Beating Tips: Capacity is limited, and ticket lines can be long. It's busiest on rainy days in July and August. To skip the line, it's smart to buy tickets online (same price as at site, must purchase at least one day in advance, exchangeable if your schedule changes). Show your emailed receipt or confirmation code for admission.

Background: Ötzi's frozen body was discovered high in the mountains on the Italian/Austrian border by a German couple in

1991. Police initially believed the corpse was a lost hiker, and Ötzi was chopped roughly out of the glacier, damaging his left side. But upon discovering his pre-Bronze Age hatchet, officials realized what they had found: a 5,300-year-old, nearly perfectly preserved man with clothing and gear in excellent condition for his age. Austria and Italy squabbled briefly over who would get him, but surveys showed that he was located 100 yards inside Italian territory. Tooth enamel studies have now shown that he did grow up on the Italian side. An Austrian journalist dubbed him Ötzi, after the Ötztal valley, where he was discovered.

Visiting the Museum: The permanent exhibit is smartly displayed on three floors (plus temporary exhibits on the top floor). First you'll learn about Ötzi's discovery, excavation, and preservation. Upstairs, you'll walk through displays of his incredibly well-preserved and fascinating clothing and gear, including a finely stitched two-color coat, his goathide loincloth, a fancy hat, shoes, a well-crafted hatchet, 14 arrows, a longbow, a dagger, and shreds of his rucksack (which held fire-making gadgets and a tree fungus used as a primitive antibiotic). And finally, you'll peek into a heavily fortified room to see Ötzi himself—still kept carefully frozen.

One floor up, exhibits focus on the Copper Age. The discovery of Ötzi helped researchers realize that the use of copper occurred in this region more than a millennium earlier than previously thought. There's also a complete medical workup of Ötzi, including an interactive flatscreen where you can zoom in on different parts of his body to see the layers of skin, muscle, and bone. And you'll learn how researchers have used modern forensic science techniques to better understand who Ötzi was and how he died. (Think of it as a very, very, very cold case.)

From all of this, scientists have formed a complete picture of the Iceman: In his mid-40s at the time of his death, Ötzi was 5 feet, 3 inches tall, with brown hair and brown eyes. He weighed about 110 pounds, was lactose-intolerant, ate too much animal fat, and likely had trouble with his knees. And they've even determined the cause of death: an arrowhead buried in Ötzi's left shoulder. At the end of the exhibit, you'll see an eerily lifelike reconstruction of how Ötzi may have looked when he was alive.

Dominican Church (Chiesa dei Domenicani/ Dominikanerkirche)

Art lovers can drop by this otherwise stark and sterile 13th-century church to see its Chapel of St. John (San Giovanni/St. Johannes; chapel is through the archway and on the right), frescoed in the 14th century by the Giotto School.

Cost and Hours: Free, €0.50 coin lights dim interior, Mon-Sat 7:00-19:00, Sun 12:00-18:00, on Piazza Domenicani, two blocks west of Piazza Walther/Waltherplatz.

Lift to Oberbozen and Renon/Ritten

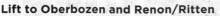

The **Funivia del Renon/Rittner Seilbahn** cable car whisks you over the hills from Bolzano to the touristy resort village of Oberbozen on the high plateau of Renon/Ritten, where Sigmund Freud and his wife once celebrated their wedding anniversary. The reasonably priced, 12-minute ride itself is the main attraction, offering views of the town, surrounding mountains, made-for-yodeling farmsteads, and 18-wheelers downshifting along the expressway from Austria. While the cable car is fun, it's no replacement for a trip to Castelrotto and Alpe di Siusi.

Cost and Hours: €10 round-trip, departures year-round Mon-Sat 6:30-22:45, Sun 7:10-22:45; leaves every 4 minutes, or every 12 minutes after 21:00; closes for maintenance for a week in March and Nov; for info call regional transport hotline at tel. 840-000-471 or visit www.sii.bz.it.

Getting There: The cable car's valley station is a five-block walk east from the Bolzano train station along Via Renon/Rittner Strasse or from Piazza Municipio/Rathausplatz in the old center.

At the Top: Oberbozen (elevation 4,000 feet) is mostly a collection of resort hotels. From Oberbozen, a narrow-gauge train makes the 16-minute trip to **Klobenstein,** a larger and slightly less touristy village at 3,800 feet (€3.50 one-way, €6 round trip, €15 round-trip for both cable car and train, daily departures every 30 minutes—reduced to hourly early and late). The local TI has branches in both villages (www.ritten.com). In Oberbozen, the TI is in the train station building, just steps from the lift station (Mon-Fri 9:00-12:30 & 15:00-18:00, Sat 9:00-12:30, closed Sun in summer, shorter hours off-season, tel. 0471-345-245). The Klobenstein TI is a five-minute walk from the train station (Mon-Fri 8:30-18:00, Sat 8:30-12:00, closed Sun, tel. 0471-356-100).

The lift station and TIs have brochures suggesting short walks. More interesting than Oberbozen itself (though not a must-see) are the nearby **"earth pyramids"**—Bryce Canyon-like pinnacles that rise out of the ridge, created by eroding glacial debris dumped at the end of the last ice age. Some of these are visible from the Oberbozen cable car, but are challenging to hike to; an easier-to-reach area is a 15-minute walk from Klobenstein. Another walk is the **Freudpromenade,** a fairly level, 1.5-hour stroll between Oberbozen and Klobenstein (you can take the train back).

New Bolzano (Nuova Bolzano)

Just across the river from the Museum of Archaeology, the fascist-style **Victory Monument** (Monumento alla Vittoria) glistens in white Zandobbio marble. It marks the beginning of the "new" city built by the fascist government in the 1920s, in an effort to Italian-ize the otherwise Germanic-looking city. Indeed, you won't hear much German spoken in the shops and bars along the colonnaded Corso della Libertà—it feels a world away from the old town. A visit to New Bolzano comes with a delightful stroll over the river and the inviting, parklike Talvera promenade (described later).

In the basement of the arch-like structure, you'll find a small but informative exhibit about the history of the monument itself, the Italianization of South Tirol, and the effort of the local people to keep their language, culture, and traditions alive. History and architecture buffs will appreciate a quick stop here (monument al-ways viewable, exhibit free and open April-Sept Tue-Sun 11:00-13:00 & 14:00-17:00, Thu 15:00-21:00, shorter hours off-season, closed Mon year-round, good information in English, tel. 324-581-0101, www.monumentoallavittoria.com).

The grand plans for this part of the city were never fully re-alized. But several blocks of buildings were constructed in a re-petitive Modernist design, following the idea of imperial monu-mentalism trumpeting the dawn of a new era in Italy. Most of the structures were intended to house state institutions and highly desirable apartments for state employees. (A few blocks south on Piazza Tribunale, you can still find the somewhat faded image of Mussolini waving from one of the buildings.)

While visiting this neighborhood, consider a stop at **Officina del Gelo Avalon,** a gourmet, organic gelato shop tucked away in an unassuming corner of Corso della Libertà. Try the pistachio or one of the half-dozen kinds of chocolate (Wed-Mon 13:00-22:00, closed Tue and in winter, Corso della Libertà 44, tel. 0471-260-434).

Runkelstein Castle (Castel Roncolo/Schloss Runkelstein)

This 13th-century "illustrated manor" perches above the river just north of downtown. Inside is an impressively large collection of secular medieval frescoes, with scenes from the everyday lives of knights and ladies. To get here, walk the promenade along the Talvera River (30 minutes from downtown; see "Bolzano Walks," next).

Cost and Hours: €8, Tue-Sun 10:00-18:00, closed Mon, 1.5 miles north of Ponte Talvera on Kaiser-Franz-Josef Weg, tel. 0471-329-808, www.runkelstein.info.

Bolzano Walks

Pick up the clearly marked map at the TI for scenic, accessible strolls that provide a different perspective on the region. One pop-ular option is the easy, shaded **Talvera promenade** just west of the Museum of Archaeology, following the river embankment north. This route has great people-watching in the summer, with views of vineyards and Maretsch Castle (Castello Mareccio/Burg Maretsch) to the right. In about 30 minutes, you'll reach the Bridge of St. Antonio, where you can cross and follow the river for another 15 minutes to the impressive **Runkelstein Castle** (described previously).

To extend your hike, go back to the Bridge of St. Antonio and head up the hill about 45 minutes for the **St. Oswald** walk. This route takes you to the church of Santa Magdalena (with its 14th-century frescoes), offering great views back to the city.

Sleeping in Bolzano

All of the places listed here are in the city center, within walking distance of the train and bus stations. Bolzano has no real high or low season. Most hotels have the same rates all year, but they're most likely to make deals in March and November.

$$$$ Parkhotel Laurin is a fancy Old World hotel near the train station, with 100 tastefully decorated rooms, marble bathrooms, a chic dining room and terrace, a swimming pool, an extensive and luxurious garden, and attentive staff. Frescoes throughout the grand lobby and atmospheric bar depict the legend of King Laurin (air-con, nonsmoking rooms, elevator, fitness room, pay parking, Via Laurin/Laurinstrasse 4, tel. 0471-311-000, www. laurin.it, info@laurin.it).

$$$$ Hotel Greif, a luxury boutique hotel, is right on Piazza Walther/Waltherplatz. Each of the 33 individually designed rooms makes you feel like you're in a modern-art installation (its website gives a room-by-room tour). It's not exactly "cozy," but it is striking, and a stay here comes with one of my favorite breakfasts in Italy (family rooms, nonsmoking, air-con, elevator, pay parking at P3/Parking Walther under main square—enter hotel directly from level 1 of the garage, Via della Rena/Raingasse 28, tel. 0471-318-000, www.greif.it, info@greif.it).

$$$ Stadt Hotel Città, a venerable old hotel with 99 modern, straightforward rooms, is ideally situated on Piazza Walther/Waltherplatz. The hotel's café spills out onto the piazza, offering a prime spot for people-watching (family rooms, air-con, elevator, pay parking at P3/Parking Walther under main square—enter hotel directly from level 1 of the garage, Piazza Walther/Waltherplatz 21, tel. 0471-975-221, www.hotelcitta.info, info@hotelcitta. info, Francesco and Hannelore, and their kids Fabio and Sandra). This place is an especially good value if you plan to spend an afternoon in their free-for-guests Wellness Center (generally open mid-Sept-June Mon-Sat 16:00-21:30, closed Sun and in summer; Turkish bath, whirlpool, Finnish sauna, biosauna, massage by appointment)—a fine way to unwind.

DOLOMITES

DOLOMITES

Sleep Code

Hotels are classified based on the average price of a standard double room with breakfast in high season.

$$$$	**Splurge:** Most rooms over €170
$$$	**Pricier:** €130-170
$$	**Moderate:** €90-130
$	**Budget:** €50-90
¢	**Backpacker:** Under €50
RS%	**Rick Steves discount**

Unless otherwise noted, credit cards are accepted, hotel staff speak basic English, and free Wi-Fi is available. Comparison-shop by checking prices at several hotels (on each hotel's own website, on a booking site, or by email). For the best deal, *book directly with the hotel.* Ask for a discount if paying in cash; if the listing includes **RS%**, request a Rick Steves discount.

$$ Hotel Figl, warmly run by Anton and Helga Mayr, has 23 comfy, bright, good-value rooms. It's situated over a popular-with-locals café on a pedestrian square located a block from Piazza Walther/Waltherplatz (breakfast extra, air-con, elevator, nonsmoking, pay parking at P3/Parking Walther under main square—take the escalator to the square and walk a couple of minutes, Piazza del Grano/Kornplatz 9, tel. 0471-978-412, www.figl.net, info@figl.net, include a backup phone number if you email).

$$ Hotel Feichter is an inexpensive, well-kept, family-run place with simple but sufficient amenities in a great location. Some of the 34 rooms share a communal terrace overlooking the rooftops of Bolzano. Papà Walter, Mamma Hedwig, Hannes, Irene, and Wolfi Feichter have run this homey hotel since 1969 (family rooms, pay parking, fans, ground-floor café serves lunches Mon-Fri 11:30-14:00; from station, walk up Via Laurin/Laurinstrasse, which becomes Via Grappoli/Weintraubengasse—hotel is on the right at #15; tel. 0471-978-768, www.hotelfeichter.it, info@hotelfeichter.it).

$$ Kolpinghaus Bozen, modern, clean, and church-run, has 34 rooms with two twin beds (placed head to toe) and 71 air-conditioned single rooms with all the comforts. Though institutional, it's a great deal...and makes me feel thankful (elevator, pay laundry, pay parking, 4 blocks from Piazza Walther/Waltherplatz near Piazza Domenicani at Largo A. Kolping/Adolph-Kolping-Strasse 3, tel. 0471-308-400, www.kolpingbozen.it, info@kolpingbozen.it). The line of people in front of the building at lunchtime consists mainly of office workers waiting for the cafeteria to open (generally Mon-Fri 11:45-14:00, Sat 12:00-13:30, closed Sun).

¢ Youth Hostel Bolzano is the most comfortable and inviting hostel that I've seen in Italy. It has 17 four-bed rooms (each with two bunk beds and a full bathroom; fifth bed possible) and 10 delightful singles with bath. The bright, clean, modern rooms make it feel like a dorm in a fancy university. With no age limit, easy online reservations, and family discounts, this is a utopian hostel (elevator, pay laundry, 9:00 checkout, 100 yards to the right as you leave the train station at Via Renon/Rittner Strasse 23; tel. 0471-300-865, www.ostello.bz, bolzano@ostello.bz).

Eating in Bolzano

All of my recommendations are in the center of the old town. Prices are consistent (you can generally get a good plate of meat and veggies for €10). While nearly every local-style place serves a mix of Germanic/Tirolean and Italian fare, I favor eating Tirolean here in Bozen. Many restaurants have no cover charge but put a basket of bread on the table; as in Austria, if you eat the bread, you'll be charged a small amount. Bolzano's restaurants tend to stay open all day, but at a few places the kitchen closes in the afternoon with only snacks available.

$$ Weisses Rössl ("White Horse") offers affordable, mostly Tirolean food with meat, fish, and fine vegetarian options. Located in a traditional woody setting, it's good for dining indoors among savvy locals (Mon-Fri 11:00-24:00, Sat 10:00-15:00, closed Sun, 2 blocks north of Piazza Municipio at Via Bottai/Bindergasse 6, tel. 0471-973-267).

$$ Ca' de Bezzi/Gasthaus Batzenhäusl is historic. It's Bolzano's oldest inn, with two Teutonic-feeling upper floors; by contrast, the patio and back room are refreshingly modern and untouristy. They make their own breads and pastas and serve traditional Tirolean fare—stick-to-your-ribs grub (daily 12:00-15:00 & 18:00-24:00, one of the rare places open on Sun, Via Andreas Hofer/Andreas-Hofer-Strasse 30, tel. 0471-050-950).

$$ Hopfen and Company fills an 800-year-old house with happy eaters, drinkers, and the beer lover's favorite aroma: hops *(Hopfen)*. A tavern since the 1600s, it's a stylish, fresh microbrewery today. This high-energy, boisterous place is packed with locals who come for its homemade beer, delicious Tirolean food, and reasonable prices (great salads, limited menu outside of mealtimes, daily 9:30-24:00, Piazza Erbe/Obstplatz 17, tel. 0471-300-788).

$$ Paulaner Stuben is a restaurant-pizzeria-*Bierstube* serving good food (more Italian than German) and a favorite Bavarian beer. It has good outside seating and a take-me-to-Germany interior (Mon-Sat 11:00-22:30, closed Sun, Via Argentieri/Silbergasse 16—or use back entrance at Via dei Portici/Laubengasse 51, tel. 0471-980-407).

DOLOMITES

Restaurant Price Code

I've assigned each eatery a price category, based on the average cost of a typical main course (pasta or *secondi*). Drinks, desserts, and splurge items (steak and seafood) can raise the price considerably.

$$$$	**Splurge:** Most main courses over €20
$$$	**Pricier:** €15-20
$$	**Moderate:** €10-15
$	**Budget:** Under €10

In Italy, pizza by the slice and other takeaway food is **$**; a basic trattoria or sit-down pizzeria is **$$**; a casual but more upscale restaurant is **$$$**; and a swanky splurge is **$$$$**.

$$ Humus is a trendy eatery packed with locals enjoying a hearty mix of Italian and Middle Eastern dishes. With an emphasis on organic food, this place feels fresh, lively, and inviting (Mon-Sat 8:00-22:00, closed Sun, Silbergasse/Via Argentieri 16D, tel. 0471-971-961).

Drinks and Light Food: $ Enoteca Il Baccaro, a nondescript hole-in-the-wall wine bar, is an intriguing spot for a glass of wine and bar snacks amid locals. Wines available by the glass are listed on the blackboard (Mon-Fri 8:00-14:00 & 17:00-21:00, Sat 8:00-14:00, closed Sun, located a half-block east of Hopfen and Company on a hidden alley off Via Argentieri/Silbergasse 17, look for *vino* or *wein* sign next to fountain on south side of street and enter courtyard, tel. 0471-971-421). **$ Dai Carretai** is a popular *cicchetti* bar where locals meet after work over a glass of wine—the crowd spills out onto the street. Browse the array of toothpick snacks at the counter, or order a bruschetta from the menu (also serves hot lunches, Mon-Fri 7:00-14:00 & 16:30-21:00, Sat 7:00-14:00, closed Sun, Via Dr. Streiter/Dr.-Streiter-Gasse 20b, tel. 0471-970-558).

International Food: $ Drago D'Oro is a good and affordable Chinese restaurant in the old town (Mon 11:30-15:00, Tue-Sun 11:30-15:00 & 18:00-23:00, Via Roggia/Rauschertorgasse 7a, tel. 0471-977-621). **$$ Gul** has Indian-Pakistani standards (Mon-Sat 12:00-14:30 & 18:00-23:00, closed Sun, at Via Dr. Streiter/Dr.-Streiter-Gasse 2, tel. 0471-970-518). Both are takeout-friendly, as are several small pizzerias in the same area.

Picnics: Assemble the ingredients at the **Piazza Erbe/Obstplatz** market and dine in the park along the Talvera River (the green area with benches past the museum). Or visit one of the three **DeSpar supermarkets:** The largest is at the end of the Galleria Greif arcade (enter arcade from Piazza Walther/Waltherplatz by Hotel Greif and walk to far end—the supermarket is downstairs;

Tirolean Cuisine

During your visit to the Dolomites, take a break from Italian-style pizzas and pastas to sample some of the region's traditional cuisine...with a distinctly Austrian flavor. For simplicity, I've generally listed Italian names here, though local menus are in both Italian and German (and usually also English).

Wurst and sauerkraut are the Tirolean clichés. More adventurous eaters seek out *speck,* a raw (prosciutto-style) ham smoked for five months then thinly sliced and served as an antipasto or in sandwiches. *Canederli*—large dumplings with bits of *speck,* liver, spinach, or cheese—are often served in broth, or with butter and cheese. (Never cut a dumpling with a knife—it'll destroy the chef.) Pastas aren't an integral part of the local cuisine, but you will see *mezzelune*—half-moon-shaped ravioli.

The stars of Tirolean cuisine are the hearty meat dishes—which, unlike traditional Italian main courses, are nearly always served with side dishes of doughy dumplings or vegetables and potatoes. Try *stinco di maiale* (roasted pork shank, usually garnished with potatoes) and *crauti rossi* (a sweetish sauerkraut made from red cabbage). *Carrè affumicato* is pork shank that is first smoked, then boiled. *Selvaggina,* or wild game, comes in the form of *capriolo* (fawn), *cervo* (venison), or *camoscio* (chamois/antelope). Game is eaten smoked and thinly sliced in *antipasti;* in meat sauce *(ragù)* with fresh pasta or as ravioli stuffing; or in entrées, as tender chunks grilled or roasted in a rich sauce *(spezzatino).*

For dessert, strudel is everywhere, filled with the harvest from this region's renowned apple orchards. Cakes and pies are loaded with other locally grown fruits, raisins, and nuts. *Kaiserschmarrn* is an interesting alternative: a tall, eggy crêpe prepared with raisins and topped with powdered sugar and red currant jam.

Bier (birra) is king in the Alto Adige (the best-known brand, Forst, is brewed in nearby Merano), but the wines of the area are well-matched to the local fare. *Magdalener* is a light, dry red made from Schiava grapes. *Lagrein scuro* is a full-bodied red, dry and fruity, similar to a cabernet sauvignon or merlot. *Gewürztraminer* is a dry white wine with a spicy fruit flavor. For something stronger, try grappa made from Williams pears (and served with a wedge of fresh pear), or *grappa nocino*—a darker, sweeter brew similar to Jägermeister. *Guten Appetit und Prost!*

Mon-Sat 8:30-19:30, closed Sun). Smaller branches are on Piazza Erbe/Obstplatz and at Via Bottai/Bindergasse 29 (both open Mon-Sat 8:30-19:30, closed Sun).

Bolzano Connections

Most trains from Bolzano are operated by Trenitalia (departures marked *R, RV,* or *AV* on schedules; ticket windows open daily 6:00-21:00, www.trenitalia.com). But many long-distance trains on the Innsbruck-Bolzano-Verona line are run by the German (or Austrian) railways—DB/ÖBB for short (trains marked *Eurocity, EC,* or *Trenord;* the DB *Reisebüro* ticket office is open Mon-Fri 8:00-19:00, Sat 8:00-14:50, closed Sun, www.oebb.at). Because the German and Italian systems don't cooperate very well, it's best to book tickets through the company that's running your specific departure. Trenitalia ticket machines usually won't sell tickets for German-run trains.

From Bolzano by Train to: Milan (about hourly, 3.5-4 hours, change in Verona), **Verona** (about hourly, 2-2.5 hours, take the regional/"R" trains—avoid fast trains that take same time for double the cost), **Venice** (about hourly, 3-3.5 hours, change in Verona), **Florence** (every 1-2 hours, 3.5-5 hours, change in Verona and/or Bologna), **Innsbruck** (1-2/hour, 2-2.5 hours, some regional connections change in Brennero), **Munich** (called "Monaco" in Italy, 5/day direct, 4 hours).

By Bus: Bus #170 connects Bolzano with the **cable car to Compatsch** (putting you at the gateway to all the Alpe di Siusi hikes in about an hour) and the town of **Castelrotto** (direction: Castelrotto, 2/hour Mon-Sat, hourly on Sun, last departure Mon-Sat at 20:10, Sun at 19:10, free schedule at bus station, €4 each way, buy tickets from driver, toll tel. 840-000-471, www.sii.bz.it).

The bus leaves from Bolzano's bus station (one block west of train station) and then winds high into the mountains. For Alpe di Suisi, ask the driver to let you off near the cable-car station (Seiser Alm Bahn/Cabinovia Alpe di Siusi, 40 minutes from Bolzano), then ascend to Compatsch (for more on Alpe di Siusi, see page 207). Otherwise, stay on the bus another 10 minutes to be dropped in the center of Castelrotto.

Castelrotto

Castelrotto (altitude: 3,475 feet) is the ideal home base for a day of hiking at Alpe di Siusi/Seiser Alm. Relax on the traffic-free main square, surrounded by a mountain backdrop and a thousand years of history, with an oversized (and hyperactive) bell tower above

you. You'll feel almost lost in another world. (Stay two nights.) Easy bus and cable-car connections bring you up to the trails at Alpe di Siusi and down to Bolzano.

With a population of around 2,000, Castelrotto is a combination of real town, ski resort, and administrative center for surrounding villages. Tourism has become increasingly important here; locals remind visitors that farming—which occupied most of the population in the 1960s—is minimal nowadays. Castelrotto's good lodging and services help make your stay trouble-free. Though I've used the town's Italian name, life here goes on almost entirely in German, and locals call their town Kastelruth. (Fewer than 5 percent of Castelrotto's residents are native Italian speakers.)

PLANNING YOUR TIME

One night in Castelrotto will give you a feel for South Tirol's alpine culture. But it's best to stay at least two nights, so as to have an entire day to hike. Plan an early start up to Compatsch, the gateway to the high Alpe di Siusi meadow. Tenderfeet stroll and ride the lifts from there. For serious mountain thrills, do an all-day hike. And for an unforgettable memory, spend a night in a mountain hut. Always check the latest transportation timetables before you set out.

Hiking season is mid-June through mid-October. The region is particularly crowded, booming, and blooming from mid-July through mid-September (but once you're out on the trails, you'll leave the crowds behind). It's packed with Italian vacationers in August. Spring is usually dead, with lifts shut down, huts closed, and the most exciting trails still under snow. Many hotels and restaurants close in April and November. By mid-May, most businesses reopen, some lifts start running (check dates at www.seiseralm. it), and—if you luck into good weather—a few rewarding hikes are already possible. Ski season (Dec-Easter) is busiest—and most expensive—of all.

DOLOMITES

Orientation to Castelrotto

TOURIST INFORMATION

The helpful TI is on the main square at Piazza Kraus 2 (Mon-Sat 8:30-12:00 & 15:00-18:00, closed afternoons April and Nov, closed Sun except June-Aug 10:00-12:00, tel. 0471-706-333, www.seiseralm.it). If you plan to hike, pick up the TI's free *Living the Dolomites* pictorial hiking map, which includes estimated walking times and trail numbers. For longer hikes, 1:25,000 maps are about €5.

Transit Deals: If you're sleeping anywhere in the Castelrotto/Alpe di Siusi area (but not in Bolzano), ask your hotel for a free **Alpe di Siusi Live Card.** It covers local buses between Castelrotto and places like Bolzano and the base of the Alpe di Siusi cable car. It doesn't cover anything above the cable car base (at Seis/Siusi). You'll only get the card if you ask...so ask.

The TI sells a **Combi-Card,** which covers some cable cars and buses; if you're making a few trips up to (and around) Alpe di Siusi, this will likely pay for itself (€39/any 3 days in a 7-day validity period, €52/7 days).

HELPFUL HINTS

Annual Events: The Oswald-von-Wolkenstein Riding Tournament, held the first or second weekend of June, features medieval-style equestrian tournament games, followed by a feast. The town also holds religious processions with locals dressed in traditional costumes, usually on the Sunday after Corpus Christi (June 18 in 2017); on the feast day of the village protectors, Sts. Peter and Paul (June 29—often celebrated on the nearest Sunday instead); and on the local Thanksgiving (first Sun in Oct). In mid-October, the town is packed for the Kastelruther Spatzenfest, a concert weekend for the local musical heartthrobs, the Kastelruther Spatzen.

Spring and Fall Closures: The periods between ski season and hiking season (April-mid-May and Nov) are quiet, with lifts closed for maintenance and most hotels and restaurants shut down (this is when locals take their own vacations).

Sightseeing Schedule: Shops in Castelrotto close from 12:00 to 15:00—a good time for a long lunch, a hike in the hills...or a siesta. In summer, there's usually a free band concert on Thursday evenings and a small farmers' market on the square on Friday mornings.

Wi-Fi: A free hotspot is available in the main square (network name: Wi-Free). Most recommended accommodations also have Wi-Fi.

Launderette: There's none in the area.

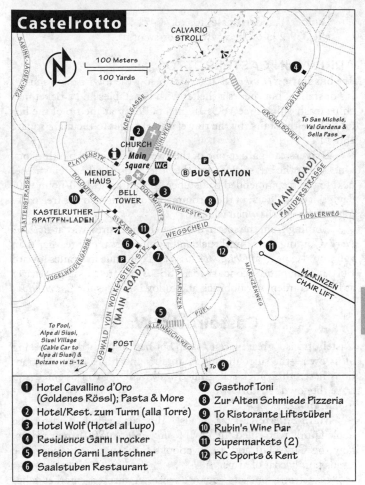

Castelrotto

CALVARIO STROLL

100 Meters
100 Yards

CHURCH
Main Square
WC
MENDEL HAUS
BELL TOWER
KASTELRUTHER SPATZEN-LADEN

BUS STATION

To San Michele,
Val Gardena &
Sella Pass

WEGSCHEID
(MAIN ROAD)
PANIDERSTRASSE
TIOSLERWEG

MARINZEN CHAIR LIFT

To Pool,
Alpe di Siusi,
Siusi Village
(Cable Car to
Alpe di Siusi) &
Bolzano via 9-12

POST

To 9

DOLOMITES

1 Hotel Cavallino d'Oro
  (Goldenes Rössl); Pasta & More
2 Hotel/Rest. zum Turm (alla Torre)
3 Hotel Wolf (Hotel al Lupo)
4 Residence Garni Trocker
5 Pension Garni Lantschner
6 Saalstuben Restaurant

7 Gasthof Toni
8 Zur Alten Schmiede Pizzeria
9 To Ristorante Liftstüberl
10 Rubin's Wine Bar
11 Supermarkets (2)
12 RC Sports & Rent

Recreation: A heated outdoor **swimming pool** with alpine views and nearby tennis courts is in the hamlet of Telfen, between Castelrotto and Seis/Siusi (mid-May-mid-Sept 9:00-21:00, tel. 0471-705-090). You can **rent a horse** at Unter-Lanzinerhof in Telfen (tel. 339-868-6868, www.reiterhof-oberlanzin.com, Karin speaks some English). For more excitement, tandem **paragliding** flights—you and the pilot—depart from Alpe di Siusi and land either there or in Castelrotto (tel. 335-603-6400, www.tandem-paragliding.com, Ruben and Kurt). You can rent **skis and snowboards** at both the bottom and top stations of the Alpe di Siusi lift, or at RC Sports and Rent in Castelrotto (Nov-Easter, near the Marinzen lift at Via

Panider/Paniderstrasse 10, tel. 0471-711-079, Robert—mobile 339-293-9725, www.rc-sportsrent.it).

ARRIVAL IN CASTELROTTO

The **bus station** *(Bushof)* is 100 yards below the town's main square. It's unstaffed, but there's a shelter with timetables and a ticket machine (cash only). Free WCs are in a building at the tip of the bus loop. Take the stairs (by the tiny elevator) to get to the main square and TI.

Drivers can park in one of the two underground parking lots: One is near the bus station, and the other is on Wolkensteinstrasse, next to the recommended Saalstuben Restaurant (€1.70/hour, €10/day, cash only). Each of the recommended hotels also has free parking (ask for details when you book).

Coming from the south, drivers exit the expressway at *Bolzano Nord.* Coming from Innsbruck and points north, exit (earlier than you would expect) at *Chiusa/Klausen* and continue five miles toward Bolzano along the secondary road (SS-12) before crossing the river at Ponte Gardena/Waidbruck and following signs for *Castelrotto*.

Castelrotto Walk

Castelrotto is a great place to sleep but has only a little sightseeing of its own—the surrounding mountains and hikes are the attractions here. This quick self-guided walk will get you oriented and trace the town's history.

• *Start in the...*

Main Square (Piazza Kraus): This square is named for the noble family who ruled the town from 1550 to 1800. Their palace, now the City Hall and TI, overlooks the square and sports the Kraus family coat of arms.

Castelrotto puts its square to use. A farmers' market takes place here on Friday mornings in the summer (June-Oct), and a clothing market fills the square most Thursday mornings. Before and after Sunday Mass, the square is crowded with villagers and farmers (who fill the church) dressed in traditional clothing. The main Mass (Sat at 20:00 and Sun at 10:00) is in German. In July and August, when Italian tourists visit, another Mass takes place in Italian (at 11:30).

• *A landmark in the square is the...*

Bell Tower: At 250 feet, the freestanding bell tower dominates the town. It was once attached to a church, which burned down in 1753. While the bell tower was quickly rebuilt, the gutted church was torn down, and the church you see today was constructed farther back, enlarging the square.

When you feel the pride that the locals have in their tower—which symbolizes their town—you'll better understand why Italy has been called "the land of a thousand bell towers." The bells of Castelrotto, which are a big part of the town experience, ring on the hour from 6:00 until 22:00. While sleepy tourists wonder why they clang so very early in the morning, locals who grew up with the chimes find them comforting. The beloved bells mark the hours, summon people to work and to Mass, announce festivals, and warn when storms threaten. In the days when people used to believe that thunder was the devil approaching, the bells called everyone to pray. (Townspeople thought the bells' sound cleared the clouds.) Bells ring big at 7:00, noon, and 19:00. The biggest of the eight bells (7,500 pounds) peals only on special days. When the bells ring at 15:00 on Friday, this commemorates Christ's sacrifice at the supposed hour of his death—a little bit of Good Friday every Friday. The colorful poles in front of the church (yellow-and-white for the Vatican, red-and-white for Tirol) fly flags on festival days. The towering May Pole, a Bavarian tradition, was a gift from Castelrotto's sister city in Bavaria.

• *Also on the square is the...*

Church: Before entering, notice the plaque on the exterior. This commemorative inscription honors the tiny community's WWI dead—*Fraktion Dorf* means from the village itself, and the other sections list soldiers from the surrounding hamlets. Stepping into the church, you're surrounded by harmonious art from about 1850. The church is dedicated to Sts. Peter and Paul, and the paintings that flank the high altar show how each was martyred (crucifixion and beheading). The pews (and smart matching confessionals) are carved of walnut wood.

• *Back outside, belly up to the...*

Fountain: Opposite the church, Castelrotto's fountain dates from 1884. St. Florian, the protector against fires, keeps an eye on it today as he did when villagers (and their horses) first came here for a drink of water.

• *With your back to the church and the fountain on your left, walk a half-block down the lane to see the finely frescoed...*

Mendel Haus: This house, with its traditional facade, contains a wood-carving shop. Its frescoes (from 1886) include many symbolic figures, as well as an emblem of a carpenter above the door—a relic from

DOLOMITES

the days when images, rather than address numbers, identified the house. Notice St. Florian again; this time, he's pouring water on a small painting of this very house engulfed in flames. Inside Mendel Haus are fine carvings, a reminder that this region—especially nearby Val Gardena—is famous for its woodwork. You'll also see many witches, folk figures that date back to when this area was the Salem of this corner of Europe. Women who didn't fit society's mold—including midwives, healers, and redheads—were sometimes burned as witches.

• *Continue downhill to the left of Mendel Haus, then before the underpass, climb the stairs on your right. At the top of the stairs, turn left on Dolomitenstrasse. In 50 yards, on the left at #21, is a shop dedicated to Castelrotto's big hometown heroes.*

Kastelruther Spatzen-Laden: The ABBA of the Alps, the folk-singing group Kastelruther Spatzen (literally "sparrows") is a gang of local boys who put Castelrotto on the map in the 1980s. They have a huge following here and throughout the German-speaking world. Though he's now in his 50s, the lead singer, Norbert Rier, is a Germanic heartthrob on par with Tom Jones. You'll see his face on ads all over town—in the recommended Saalstuben Restaurant, suggesting what to order for dessert, or in the Co-op supermarket, reminding you to drink lots of Tirolean milk. The group's feel-good folk-pop style—an alpine version of German *Schlager* music—is popular with the kind of conservative, working-class Germans who like to vacation in the South Tirol. (Younger, more progressive Germans cringe at this stuff, with its nationalistic overtones.) At a big festival in Castelrotto on the second weekend in October, the band puts on a hometown concert, filling this place with fans from as far away as the Alsace, Switzerland, and the Netherlands. They also hold an open-air concert here in June and a Christmas concert.

Browse the store, which is part souvenir shop and part insignia and apparel outlet. Downstairs is a sprawling, folksy museum slathered with gifts, awards, and gold records. The group has won 13 Echo Awards..."more than Robbie Williams." Watch the continuously playing video (€2 museum, entry refunded if you spend €5 in the shop, Mon-Sat 9:00-12:00 & 14:00-18:00, closed Sun).

• *Leaving the shop, cross the street for a...*

Fine Mountain View of the Schlern: This bold limestone peak—so typical of the Dolomites—is a symbol of the Südtirol. Witches are said to live there, and many locals climb it yearly (it's actually an easy—if long—walk up the back side).

Look left—the street points to a ridge in the distance. That's Puflatsch (a high meadow with a popular trail called the Trail of the Witches—described on page 214).

• *Continue up the hill 50 yards, cross left at the crosswalk, pass the little*

The Dramatic Dolomites

The Dolomites have been called the most beautiful mountains on earth, and certainly they are among the most dramatic. They differ from the rest of the Alps because of their dominant rock type, dolomite, which forms sheer vertical walls of white, gray, and pink that rise abruptly from green valleys and meadows. Many parts of the mountains (including Alpe di Siusi) have been turned into regional or national parks, where development is restricted. Still, rail lines, roads, and innumerable lifts make this group of mountains very accessible.

Once dubbed the "Pale Mountains" or the "Venetian Alps," this mountain range was named after French mineralogist Dolomieu, who in the late 1700s first described the rock type responsible for the region's light-colored bluffs and peaks. These sedimentary rocks (similar to limestone) were formed in warm tropical seas during the Triassic Period (about 250 million years ago). The marine sediments, along with the fossilized remains of coral reefs and other animals, were buried, hardened, and later scooped upward along with the rest of the Alps by the tectonic-plate action of Africa slowly smashing into Europe. Today, marine fossils are found atop the region's highest peaks, including the skyscraping, nearly 11,000-feet-high Marmolada.

During World War I, the front line between the Italian and Austro-Hungarian forces ran through these mountains, and many paths were cut into the range for military use. Today mountaineers can still follow networks of metal rungs, cables, and ladders (called *via ferrata*). One famous wartime trail is the "Strada delle Gallerie," near Rovereto, which passes through 52 tunnels *(gallerie)*. A paradise for hikers and climbers in summer, the Dolomites are even better known as a popular skiing destination. The 1956 Olympics in Cortina d'Ampezzo put the region on the map. A popular winter activity for intrepid skiers is the "Sella Ronda"—circling the Sella massif using a system of lifts and 28 miles of ski runs.

Whether you experience the Dolomites with your hand on a walking stick, a ski pole, or an *aperitivo* while mountain-gazing from a café, it's easy to enjoy this spectacular region.

DOLOMITES

parking lot square, and find two stones marking the top of a cobbled pedestrian lane that leads downhill back into town. Look up at the top of the bell tower. Ahead stands the elegant...

Hotel Wolf Facade: This was painted by the same artist who did the Mendel Haus. St. Florian is still pouring water on burning houses and locals are busy enjoying the local wine.

As you head left, uphill back to the town square, enjoy windows filled with traditional Südtirol formal wear—delightful dirndls. You'll pass an old hotel which, by the looks of its street sign, must be called The Golden Horse (*Cavallino d'Oro* or *Goldenes Rössl*). Ahead of you is the inviting sound of a refreshing drink from the town fountain.

• *Our walk is over. Ahead (through a white arch just left of the TI) are two big pictorial maps showing the region in summer and in ski season, as well as a modern café with ice cream and a nice terrace under a tree. The arch to the right of the TI leads up to Calvario (Calvary Hill) for a fine little loop walk, described next.*

Sights in Castelrotto

Calvario Stroll

For an easy stroll to Castelrotto's finest postcard views—the giant bell tower with a dramatic alpine backdrop—take a 15-minute mini hike around the town's hill, Calvario (Calvary). Originally, this was the site of the ancient Roman fortress, and later the fortified home of the medieval lord. One lane circles the hill while another spirals to the top past seven little chapels, each depicting a scene from Christ's Passion and culminating in the Crucifixion. Facing the TI, take the

road under the arch to the right, and then follow signs to *Kofelrunde* (to go around the hill) or *Kalvarienberg* (to get directly to the top). The light is best late in the day, and the stroll is also great after dark—romantically lit and under the stars. (The lead singer of Kastelruther Spatzen enjoyed his first kiss right here.) For a longer walk back into town, take the Friedensweg (Peace Trail) from the top of the hill. This 30-minute forest walk is decorated with peace-themed artwork by local elementary students.

Marinzen Lift

The little Marinzen chairlift trundles you up above town in two-person seats to the Marinzenhütte café (at 4,875 feet), which has a playground and animal park for kids (open when the cable car runs). The views from the top are nothing special, but several hikes leave from here—and as you ride back down, you'll enjoy pleasant panoramas over Castelrotto. (Alternatively, it's a scenic one-hour hike back down.) While the chairlift doesn't compare with going up to Alpe di  Siusi, it's still a nice activity. Catch it right in town, up the lane behind the Co-op/Konsum-Market.

Cost and Hours: €7.50 one-way up, €6.50 one-way down, €10.50 round-trip, daily mid-May-mid-Oct 9:00-17:00, a slow-and-scenic 22 minutes each way, closed off-season and rainy mornings, tel. 0471-707-160, www.marinzen.com.

NEAR CASTELROTTO
Pflegerhof Herb Farm

On a narrow country road a little outside the nearby town of Seis/Siusi, you'll find an organic farm that grows dozens of varieties of herbs. Walk among the scent-filled, fully labeled beds and browse the wide variety of herbal products in the shop. To reach the farm from Castelrotto, drive through Seis/Siusi, pass the turnoff for the cable car on your left, and after about a half-mile turn right following *St. Oswald* and *Pflegerhof* signs.

Cost and Hours: Free, Mon-Sat 10:00-18:00, Sept-March until 17:00, closed Sun year-round, St. Oswald 24, tel. 0471-706-771, www.pflegerhof.com.

Nightlife in and near Castelrotto

The recommended **Zur Alten Schmiede Pizzeria** in Castelrotto is a fun spot that's open late. **Rubin's,** next door to the Hotel Schgaguler in Castelrotto (tel. 0471-712-502), and **Sasso's,** on Schlernstrasse in the nearby town of Seis/Siusi (tel. 0471-708-068), are trendy wine bars. A popular hangout for the younger crowd in Seis/Siusi is **Santners** (the only disco club in the area). It's at the Seiser Alm Bahn cable-car station (tel. 0471-727-913). If you're here on the weekend, the "Nightliner" shuttle bus can bring you home in the wee hours (Fri-Sat roughly hourly 20:40-2:40, schedules at www.silbernagl.it; €2.50/ride, €4/all-night pass).

Sleeping in and near Castelrotto

($$$$ = Splurge, $$$ = Pricier, $$ = Moderate, $ = Budget)
Castelrotto has the largest selection of accommodations and is the only truly convenient option for those traveling in this region by

DOLOMITES

public transport. If you've come to hike at Alpe di Siusi, you could also stay in one of the hotels there (in or around Compatsch)—I've listed two less expensive options—or even in a mountain hut. Dozens of farmhouses in the area also offer accommodations, usually practical only if you have a car. (There's a full list on the TI website.) Some are working farms; others have been converted to tourist accommodations. I've listed a few that are willing to accept guests for one or two nights (the typical American stay). German and Italian tourists—who make up the bulk of the area's business—are more likely to stay for a week and to rent apartments with a kitchen but with no breakfast or daily cleaning service—which can save a great deal of money, especially for families.

Rates skyrocket during July, August, and around Christmas. Accommodations often close in November and from April to mid-May. I've categorized these accommodations based on the price of a double room in June or September; you may pay higher in the peak of peak season (typically in August).

If sleeping in this area, you're entitled to an **Alpe di Siusi Live Card**—a free pass for many local buses (described earlier, under "Tourist Information"). Be sure to ask your hotelier for one.

IN CASTELROTTO VILLAGE

These listings are within 300 yards of the bus station. The first three are in the traffic-free area of the old town; hotel guests are allowed to drive in to park. All have free parking.

$$$ Hotel Cavallino d'Oro (in German, **Goldenes Rössl**), right on the main square, is plush and welcoming, with the best Tirolean character in town. Run by helpful Stefan and Susanne, the entire place is dappled with artistic, woodsy touches—painted doors, carved wood, and canopy beds in many rooms—and historical photos. If you love antiques by candlelight, this nearly 700-year-old hotel is the place for you (elevator, free self-service laundry, open all year, Piazza Kraus 1, tel. 0471-706-337, www.cavallino.it, info@cavallino.it). Stefan converted his wine cellar into a Roman steam bath and Finnish sauna (free for guests, great after a hike, can book an hour for exclusive use)—complete with heated tile seats, massage rooms, a solarium for tanning, and tropical plants.

$$ Hotel zum Turm (in Italian, **Albergo alla Torre**) is comfortable, cozy, and warmly run by Gabi and Günther. The 15 rooms are woody and modern. If you're staying at least three nights, the €12 per person half-board option is a great value (family rooms, elevator, free passes for Marinzen chairlift, closed April and Nov, Kofelgasse 8, tel. 0471-706-349, www.zumturm.com, info@zumturm.com). From Castelrotto's main square, walk (or drive) through the upper of the two archways.

$$ Hotel Wolf (in Italian, **al Lupo**) is pure Tirolean, with all the comforts in 23 neat-as-a-pin rooms, most with balconies (elevator, coin-op laundry, closed April-late May and Nov-mid-Dec, a block below main square at Wolkensteinstrasse 5, tel. 0471-706-332, www.hotelwolf.it, info@hotelwolf.it, Malknecht family).

$ **Residence Garni Trocker** is run by the Moser family, who rent 11 great rooms in a place that's bomb-shelter solid yet warm-wood cozy. While the family is shy and less welcoming than others listed here, their compound is beautifully laid out—with a café-bar (a popular, often-smoky local hangout), garden, sauna, steam bath, roof deck with Jacuzzi, and coin-op laundry (family rooms, apartments available, elevator, closed Nov, Fostlweg 3, tel. 0471-705-200, www.residencetrocker.com, garni@residencetrocker.com, Stefan). If arriving on Sunday (the family's day off), be sure to let them know in advance what time you'll arrive.

$ **Pension Garni Lantschner** is family-run and a good budget value. Its 10 rooms—on the two upper floors of a large traditional house—are a little smaller, simpler, and older than at my other listings, but all are comfortable and have balconies with views (Kleinmichlweg 8, tel. 0471-706-025, www.garni-lantschner.com, info@garni-lantschner.com).

FARM STAYS NEAR CASTELROTTO

Dozens of working farms around Castelrotto take in visitors, mostly in apartments with a kitchen and a minimum stay of five to seven nights (the TI has a complete list). A few farms also accept guests for short stays—even one night—and serve breakfast. Expect rustic doubles with bath for about €60. Staying in these places is practical only if you have a car. Consider the following: $ **Goldrainerhof** (a 10-minute uphill trudge from Castelrotto, Tioslerweg 10, tel. 0471-706-100, www.goldrainerhof.com); $ **Tonderhof** (a fruit farm in a dramatic hillside setting along the road down to Waidbruck/Ponte Gardena, Tisens 25, tel. 0741-706-733, www.tonderhof.com) and their neighbor, the $ **Schiedhof** (Tisens 23, mobile 345-583-7278, www.schiedhof.it); and $ **Formsunhof** (along the road up to Alpe di Siusi, before the checkpoint, St. Valentin 12, tel. 0471-706-015, www.formsunhof.com).

IN ALPE DI SIUSI/SEISER ALM, NEAR THE HIKING TRAILS

There are more than two dozen hotels in Alpe di Siusi, most in Compatsch (where the cable car from Seis/Siusi arrives) but some farther into the park. Most are quite expensive, four- and five-star affairs, with doubles costing around €200 in July and August. The two hotels listed here cost less—because Compatsch and the park entrance are a 10- to 15-minute uphill walk away. These are only practical for drivers. Half-board is wise here, as there's nowhere else to eat dinner (except other hotels). Serious hikers should consider staying at the park's high-altitude mountain huts (mentioned under "Hiking in Alpe di Siusi," later).

$$ Hotel Seelaus, with 25 rooms, is a friendly, mellow, family-run, creekside place with an Austrian feel (family rooms, hearty €15 dinners, free wellness area with sauna, hydro-massage, and minipool, Wi-Fi in common areas only, closed mid-April-mid-May and mid-Oct-early Dec, Compatschweg 8, tel. 0471-727-954, www.hotelseelaus.it, info@hotelseelaus.it, Roberto). Roberto offers free rides from the bus or cable-car station, and affordable transfers to/from Bolzano—arrange in advance.

$$ Hotel Schmung is along the road and has fine, recently renovated rooms. During the day, the Seiser Alm Bahn cable cars float through the air just outside the front balconies (dinner available, free sauna, closed April-May and Nov-mid-Dec, Compatsch 12, tel. 0471-727-943, www.schmung.com, info@schmung.com).

Eating in Castelrotto

($$$$ = Splurge, $$$ = Pricier, $$ = Moderate, $ = Budget)
$$$ Saalstuben Restaurant serves a selection of hearty and tasty Austrian-Italian dishes indoors or on their terrace, including big salads, vegetarian plates, lots of grilled meats, and Tyrolean classics. Their dessert specialty is *Kaiserschmarrn,* a favorite of Austrian Emperor Franz Josef. This eggy pancake with jam is plenty big for two (dressy indoors, Fri-Wed 11:30-14:00 & 17:30-21:00, closed Thu, Wolkensteinstrasse 12, tel. 0471-707-394, www.saalstuben. com).

$$$ Hotel zum Turm tries hard to up the culinary bar in town, focusing on locally sourced ingredients and serving good, meaty fare, including venison. You can sit in the humdrum breakfast room, the cozy and very traditional *Stube,* or out on the back terrace (salad bar, Thu-Tue 12:00-14:00 & 18:00-20:45, closed Wed, closed April-mid-May and Nov, tel. 0471-706-349, www. zumturm.com).

$$ Gasthof Toni, along the main road at the town's main intersection, pleases hungry locals with huge €15 two-course meals served at both lunch and dinner (pick one pasta and one meat course, includes side salad). It's cozy inside but the outdoor tables are just off a noisy street. They also have good pizza (Mon-Sat 12:00-14:00 & 17:00-21:00, pizza until 23:00, closed Sun, Wolkensteinstrasse 15, tel. 0471-706-306).

$$ Zur Alten Schmiede Pizzeria is a great place to enjoy an evening drinking Forst, the local beer, and playing darts. They offer a wide range of nothing-fancy grub—pizzas, pastas, meaty dishes, and *wurst* meals (Tue-Sun 12:00-14:00 & 17:30-21:00, pizza until

23:00, closed Mon, outdoor seating, near bus station entrance at Paniderstrasse 7, tel. 0471-707-390).

$ Pasta & More, right on the main square, is where Martin dishes up lasagna, vegetable strudel, pastas, and other simple meals—either packed to go or served at a few indoor tables or a couple delightful tables on the square (Mon-Sat 9:00-14:00 & 17:00-19:00, closed Sun, Piazza Kraus 5, tel. 0471-711-085).

Ristorante Liftstüberl is a good bet if you'd like to eat in nature rather than in town. It's a charming local favorite offering good traditional dishes with a classic woody interior and picnic benches with mountain views. Find it in a meadow about a half-mile hike south of town (closed Sun, Via Marinzen 35, tel. 0471-706-804).

Picnics: Castelrotto has several supermarkets. **Eurospar** is the handiest, at the town's main intersection, and has the longest hours (Mon-Sat 8:00-19:30, closed Sun, on Wolkensteinstrasse). The **Co-op/Konsum-Market** has the best selection of locally produced food, and a hardware section where you can pick up a bell for your cow—no joke (Mon-Sat 7:30-12:30 & 15:00-19:00, closed Sun, Paniderstrasse 24).

Castelrotto Connections

From Castelrotto by Bus to: Bolzano (#170, 2/hour Mon-Sat, hourly Sun, 50 minutes, last departure around 19:00; if you're connecting to a train in Bolzano, hop off at the train station—otherwise stay on for the bus station, which is slightly closer to the main square). From Bolzano, you can easily connect to **Verona, Venice, Innsbruck, Munich,** and beyond. Get bus schedules at the TI, toll tel. 840-000-471, or check www.sii.bz.it or www.silbernagl.it. For connections to **Alpe di Siusi/Seiser Alm,** see "Getting There," later.

Alpe di Siusi

This grassy mountain plateau above the village of Seis/Siusi (the next over from Castelrotto) is the largest high meadow—and summer pastureland—in the Alps. It's a premier hiking and skiing area, and also home to hundreds of cows every summer. Undulating rather than flat, broken by rushing streams, and dappled with shapely evergreens, what makes Alpe di Siusi (Seiser Alm in German) really spectacular are the views of the surrounding Dolomite peaks. Well-kept huts, trails, and lifts make hiking here a joy. It's family-friendly, with lots of playgrounds. Being here on a sunny summer day comes with the ambience of a day at the beach.

The cows munching away in this vast pasture all summer after a winter huddled in Castelrotto produce two million gallons of milk annually, much of which is sent to Bolzano to make cheese. After tourism, dairy is the leading industry here.

To enjoy Alpe di Siusi, you'll need a full day and decent weather. Arrive in Compatsch (the main entry point) as early as you can, then hike (or bike) as much as you please. Plan a picnic, or lunch at a high mountain hut, and aim to wrap up the day in midafternoon—many upper lifts close at 17:00, and thunderclouds tend to gather even on days that start out sunny.

The hiking season runs roughly from mid-June through mid-October (though if the weather's good, you can hit some of the trails as early as mid-May). The trails are pretty dead in April, early May, and November. For a fragrant festival of wildflowers suited to growing at 6,000 feet, come in June.

With additional time, you can explore more of the park or overnight in one of the mountain huts as a base for more remote and challenging hikes. You're more than a mile high here, so take it easy and give yourself frequent breaks to catch your breath.

Get to know the park's mountains by sight. The jagged peaks called **Langkofel** (Sasso Lungo, "Long Stone") and **Plattkofel** (Sasso Piatto, "Flat Stone") together form an "M" at the far end of Alpe di Siusi—providing a storybook Dolomite backdrop. The dark, eerie saddle between them fires the imagination. To the right, and closer to Compatsch, the long, flat ridge called the **Schlern** (Sciliar in Italian) ends in spooky crags that boldly stare into the summer haze. The Schlern, looking like a devilish *Winged Victory*, gave ancient peoples enough willies to spawn legends of supernatural forces. The Schlern witch, today's tourist-brochure mascot, was the cause of many a broom-riding medieval townswoman's fiery death.

Compatsch provides great views of the Schlern, but only a peek-a-boo glimpse of Langkofel and Plattkofel. For better views, gain some altitude on a lift, or hop the bus (or hike) toward **Saltria,** at the far end of Alpe di Suisi. (Because Saltria sits down in a valley, the views are even better from the road just above it, near the hut called Rauchhütte.)

GETTING THERE

By Car: The winding, six-mile road up to Compatsch starts between Castelrotto and Seis/Siusi (at San Valentino). To keep the meadow serene, it's closed to cars during the day (9:00-17:00), unless you're staying in one of the hotels in the park. (The road is unblocked, but you'll likely be stopped by roving traffic monitors—be ready to show your hotel reservation confirmation.) But if you're an early riser, there's no reason not to drive up if you can arrive at the checkpoint before 9:00. (You can drive back down at any time.) Compatsch has a huge parking lot (€16/day—the same price as one round-trip cable-car ticket, so groups of at least two save by driving).

From Bolzano or Castlerotto to the Seiser Alm Bahn Cable Car at Seis/Siusi: Regular buses from Bolzano and Castlerotto link to the bottom of the cable car that whisks visitors from Seis/Siusi to Alpe di Siusi (described next). Buses #3 and #4 run from Castelrotto (4/hour July-Aug in morning and afternoon peak times, otherwise 2/hour, 10 minutes, €1.50, use machine, if no machine pay driver). These buses stop directly at the cable-car station. Some buses, including #170 from Bolzano (see page 194), stop at the turnoff just below the cable-car station—a steep five-minute hike up.

By Cable Car from Seis/Siusi: A cable car (the Seiser Alm Bahn; in Italian, Cabinovia Alpe di Siusi) runs hikers and skiers up to Compatsch from just outside Seis/Siusi (mid-May-early Nov daily 8:00-19:00, closed most of Nov and mid-April-mid-May, runs continuously during open hours, 15-minute ride to the top, €10.50 one-way, €16 round-trip, tel. 0471-704-270, www.seiseralmbahn. it). You can reach the valley station either by car (free outdoor parking; garage parking-€3/day) or by bus (see above). The lower cable-car station is a slick mini shopping mall, with lots of outdoor outfitters and a tempting local-products store.

By Bus from Castelrotto: "Express" bus #10 runs from Castelrotto all the way to Compatsch. This is practical but costs the same as the more dramatic and memorable—and environmentally friendly—cable car (8 buses/day mid-June-mid-Oct, 20 minutes, fewer mid-May-mid-June and late Oct, www.silbernagl.it). Note that the Siusi Live Card does not cover buses that go above Seis/Suisi.

GETTING AROUND ALPE DI SIUSI

Shuttle Buses: The plateau is essentially car-free, except for guests staying at a few hotels inside the park. The #11 shuttle bus takes visitors to and from key points along the tiny road between Compatsch—the gateway to Alpe di Siusi—and Saltria, at the foot of the postcard-dramatic Sasso peaks and the base of the Florian lift (2-3/hour mid-June-mid-Oct, fewer mid-May-mid-June and in late Oct, runs about 8:40-18:40—check local schedules, 15 minutes from Compatsch to Saltria, €2, buy ticket at vending machines

Alpe di Siusi

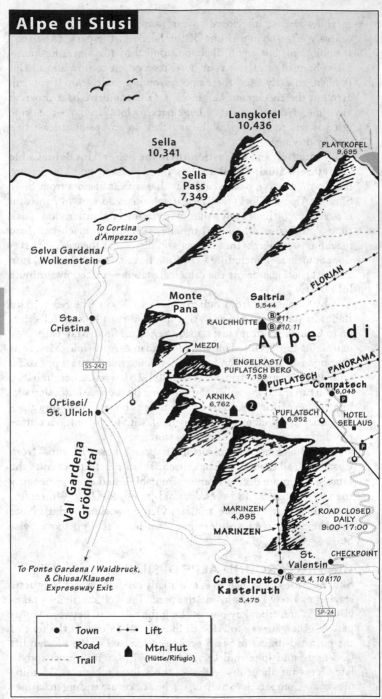

DOLOMITES

Langkofel
10,436

Sella
10,341

PLATTKOFEL
9,695

Sella Pass
7,349

To Cortina
d'Ampezzo

⑤

Selva Gardena/
Wolkenstein

FLORIAN

Monte
Pana

Saltria
5,544

Ⓑ #11

RAUCHHÜTTE   Ⓑ #10, 11

Sta.
Cristina

MEZDI

A l p e   d i

ENGELRAST/
PUFLATSCH BERG
7,139

PANORAMA

SS-242

ARNIKA
6,762

①

PUFLATSCH

Compatsch
6,048

P

Ortisei/
St. Ulrich

②

PUFLATSCH
6,952

HOTEL
SEELAUS

P

MARINZEN
4,895

ROAD CLOSED
DAILY
9:00-17:00

MARINZEN

CHECKPOINT

To Ponte Gardena / Waidbruck,
& Chiusa/Klausen
Expressway Exit

St.
Valentin

Castelrotto/
Kastelruth
3,475

Ⓑ #3, 4, 10 &170

SP-24

●	Town	←•→	Lift
	Road	▲	Mtn. Hut
- - -	Trail		(Hütte/Rifugio)

Val Gardena Grödnertal

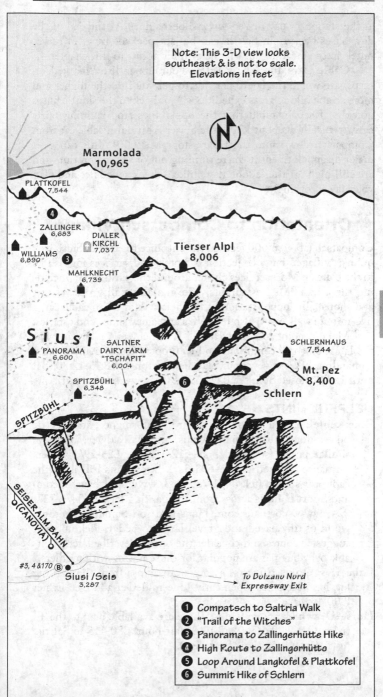

Note: This 3-D view looks southeast & is not to scale. Elevations in feet

Marmolada
10,965

PLATTKOFEL
7,544

4

ZALLINGER
6,683

DIALER
KIRCHL
7,037

Tierser Alpl
8,006

WILLIAMS
6,890

3

MAHLKNECHT
6,739

S i u s i

PANORAMA
6,600

SALTNER
DAIRY FARM
"TSCHAPIT"
6,004

SCHLERNHAUS
7,544

Mt. Pez
8,400

SPITZBÜHL
6,348

6

Schlern

SPITZBÜHL

SEISER ALM BAHN
(CANOVIA)

#3, 4 &170 **B**

Siusi/Seis
3,287

To Bolzano Nord
Expressway Exit

1 Compatsch to Saltria Walk
2 "Trail of the Witches"
3 Panorama to Zallingerhütte Hike
4 High Route to Zallingerhütte
5 Loop Around Langkofel & Plattkofel
6 Summit Hike of Schlern

DOLOMITES

at the station or pay driver, www.silbernagl.it). At the end of the day, buses back from Saltria can be jam-packed. Bus #14 serves hotels in the meadow but isn't helpful for points in this chapter.

Cable Cars and Chair Lifts: Four upper lifts (marked on maps) are worth the €6-10 per ride to get you into the higher and more scenic hiking areas expeditiously (or back to the shuttle buses quickly). Keep in mind that the upper lifts stop running fairly early (typically at about 17:00; the Seiser Alm Bahn cable car from Compatsch down into the valley stops at 19:00). This can be a major disappointment if you're running out of steam and time and are still high up after a long day's hike. Check schedules and plan your day accordingly.

Orientation to Compatsch Village

Compatsch (about 6,000 feet), at the entrance to Alpe di Siusi, isn't quite a "village," but a collection of hotels and services for visitors to the plateau. Most services cluster around the parking lot (including the TI, ATMs, restaurants, bike rental, small grocery store, and shops). The upper station of the Seiser Alm Bahn cable car, a five-minute walk away, also has WCs and a few shops and eateries.

Make a point to stop by the **TI,** which sells maps and has the latest on snow conditions and trail openings. If considering a demanding hike, review your plan here (Mon-Fri 8:15-12:30, Sat until 12:00, closed Sun, tel. 0471-727-904, www.seiseralm.it).

HELPFUL HINTS

Bike Rental: Two shops offer standard, performance, and electric bikes, along with helmets, maps, and trail advice, and have similar prices (standard bike-€12/1 hour, €25-29/day; performance or electric bike-€43/day). **Sporthaus Fill** is by the cable-car station (tel. 0471-729-063, www.sporthausfill.com) and **Sport Hans** is across from the parking lot (tel. 0471-727-824, www.sporthans.com, Hans and son Samuel). There's a world of tiny paved and gravel lanes to pedal. Pick up their suggested routes and consider the ones I describe later. Rentable baby buggies are popular for those hiking with toddlers.

Groceries: Onkel Eugen's, a tiny store across from the parking lot, has necessities (open early-June-mid-Oct and Dec-Easter 8:00-16:00).

Horse-Drawn Carriage Rides: These are available next to the TI (May-Oct 9:00-16:00, €30-40/half-hour, €80-115 to Saltria, price depends on size of carriage).

Hiking in Alpe di Siusi

Easy meadow walks abound in Alpe di Siusi, giving novice hikers classic Dolomite views from baby-stroller trails. Experienced hik-

ers should consider the tougher, more exciting treks. Before attempting a hike, call or stop by the TI to confirm lift schedules and check your understanding of the time and skills required. As always, when hiking in the mountains, assume weather can change quickly, and pack accordingly. Meadow walks, for flower lovers and strollers, are

pretty—for advanced hikers, they're pretty boring. Chairlifts are springboards for more dramatic and demanding hikes. Upper lifts generally close at 17:00.

Trails are very well marked, and the brightly painted numbers are keyed into local maps. Signs also display the next mountain hut along the trail, which serve as helpful navigational landmarks. (When asked for directions, most locals will know the trail by the huts it connects rather than its number.) For simple hikes, you can basically string together three or four names off the free pictorial map. For anything more serious, invest in a good 1:25,000 map from the TI (about €5). Huts (*Hütte* in German, *rifugi* in Italian) offer food and, often, beds. The Alpe di Siusi website (www.seiseralm.it) has more information (click on "Summer Active," then "Hiking," then "Hiking Trails").

Shoulder-Season Strategies: The Seiser Alm Bahn cable car up to Compatsch starts running in late May, but upper lifts begin operating a few weeks later; there's a similar gap at the end of the season (mid-Oct-early Nov). But even during these shoulder seasons, Alpe di Siusi can still be worth visiting (and busy with hikers) in good weather. Many of the hikes listed here are doable without a lift—but only if you're willing to hike to the trailhead (most realistic for the "Trail of the Witches"). Get local advice about snow levels and which hikes are possible. The simplest option is to hike trail #30 or ride bus #11 along the valley floor between Compatsch and Saltria, enjoying the views along the way.

Hiking Club: If you're headed up into the mountains, the Alpenverein Südtirol, a local hiking club, provides good, free trail maps for the whole region on its website (www.trekking.suedtirol.info).

WALKS AND HIKES FROM COMPATSCH

I've listed these hikes roughly in order of difficulty, from easiest to hardest.

Easy Hikes
Along the Main Road to Saltria

Bus #11 connects Compatsch to Saltria (at the far end of Alpe di Siusi, tucked under Langkofel and Plattkofel) in about 15 minutes—zipping past some impressive scenery en route. For a very easy, mostly level walk, follow this same route by foot, in about 50 minutes (using trail #30, which parallels the route). The last stretch—into Saltria—is steeply downhill and has less impressive views; consider going only as far as **Rauchhütte** (a charming old hut serving good food, spectacular views, closed Wed), located where the road starts to switchback down. Bus #11 stops at various points along this route (including Rauchhütte and Ritschhütte)—making it easy to do as much or as little of this by foot as you like. (Saltria is not a good destination in itself. It's a steep walk below Rauchhütte and has hotels, trail heads, and a bus stop, but no shops.)

The "Trail of the Witches"

This two-hour loop trail—past the legendary stone "witches' benches" *(Hexenbänke)*—is popular with first-time visitors and can be crowded in peak season. You'll enjoy ever-changing views as you get a handy 360-degree panorama of the peaks and valleys that ring Alpe di Siusi. It's mostly downhill all the way around, with a few brief uphill stretches.

First, ride the €6 cable car from Compatsch up to Puflatsch Berg (6,952 feet). A two-minute walk above the lift, an engraved map at the Engelrast ("Angel's Rest") observation point identifies the surrounding mountains. The counterclockwise hike follows *PU/Puflatsch* signs around the rim of the Puflatsch plateau. First you'll have Langkofel and Plattkofel on your right. Eventually you'll hit a little cross overlooking the valley village of St. Ulrich (far below in Val Gardena), then hook left and trace the dramatic rim of the valley. Soon tiny Castelrotto pops into view, you'll pass Arnikahütte (with a café), and finally you'll head back toward the Schlern. Near the end of the loop, you can either hike steeply back up to the Engelrast/Puflatsch Berg cable-car station, or—better and easier—keep going downhill all the way into Compatsch, with fine valley views the entire time.

Note: If you're here when the upper lifts aren't running (or even in the early evening, assuming you're staying in Compatsch or have a car for returning to the valley after the main lift stops running), this is your most realistic and rewarding option. But be ready for a very steep 30-minute uphill hike to the Puflatsch Berg cable-car station to begin the hike.

Moderate Hikes
Panorama to Zallingerhütte

This walk on well-marked trails is a great introduction to Alpe di Siusi. While it starts and ends at about the same altitude, it includes plenty of ups and downs. It comes with fine vistas, changes of scenery (meadows, woods, and high valleys), fun stops along the way, and lifts up and down on each end. Though signs rate it at three hours without stops, allow five or six hours (including the lift from Compatsch, lift down to Saltria, and bus back to Compatsch) so you'll have time to dawdle, yodel, and eat.

Start by riding the €6 lift from Compatsch to Panorama (6,600 feet). From Panorama, follow trail #2 across the meadow to the paved road and then join trail #7. You'll pass the rustic Edl-weishütte (snacks only), and the Almrosenhütte (hot food); after about 1.5 hours total you'll reach the Mahlknechthütte (6,739 feet, hot food). From here, you'll cross two streams (one on stepping stones, another by bridge). After the bridge, you can take an uphill scenic detour off trail #7 (20 minutes) to climb briefly to the highest point of the walk, a small wooden church (Dialer Kirchl, 7,037 feet) that makes a good picnic spot. Continuing on trail #7, you'll go gently downhill through woods for another hour and a quarter to Zallingerhütte (6,683 feet). From here it's a 10-minute climb to Williamshütte (6,890 feet, full restaurant), where you catch the €10 Florian lift to Saltria and the shuttle-bus stop (return to Compatsch on bus #11).

For shorter versions, you can ride either lift up, stroll around, and hike or ride the lift back down.

Note: Local hikers often skip the Compatsch-Panorama lift, as you need to hike five minutes down from Compatsch just to catch it, and it's only a brisk 20-30 minute climb from Compatsch to the top of the Panorama lift.

High Route to Zallingerhütte

For a more thrilling, demanding version of the previous hike—longer by two hours—branch off at the wooden church (Dialer Kirchl) following trail #4B and then the high #4 ridge trail, with commanding views both left and right, to Plattkofelhütte (7,544 feet). Then descend steeply to Zallingerhütte and Williamshütte (6,890 feet). No special experience or gear is needed for this trail, and it richly rewards those who take it.

Consider these tips: The hut on the ridge serves excellent lunches (Schutzhaus Plattkofelhütte/Rifugio Sasso Piatto, tel. 0462-601-721). You could do an abbreviated version of this hike by side-tripping from the wooden church a half-hour to the ridge for the view, then returning to trail #7 to continue the lower walk to Zallingerhütte. Serious hikers can hike a steep and satisfying hour from the Plattkofelhütte to the peak of Plattkofel/Sasso Piatto.

Loop Around Langkofel and Plattkofel

Another dramatic but medium-difficulty hike is the 10-mile, six-hour circular walk around the dramatic Langkofel and Plattkofel peaks, partly on what's called the Friedrich August (Federico Augusto) trail. The trail can be narrow (vertigo-inducing) and has sections of loose rocks; good shoes are essential, as is a proper map. Get details and advice from the TI before you start. To reach this trail, ride the bus from Compatsch to Saltria, take the €10 Florian chairlift to Williamshütte, and walk 10 minutes to the Zallinger-hütte (one of several possible starting points). On the far side, at Sellajoch Haus, you can ride a lift high up to the ¢ Toni-Demetz-Hütte (8,790 feet, food and simple beds, www.tonidemetz.it) and back down again. (A path from this hut actually crosses the saddle between the Langkofel and Plattkofel, but it's often icy and impassable without technical equipment—even in summer.)

Consider overnighting at the 15-room **$$$ Zallingerhütte** before this walk—you're actually allowed to drive to the hut if staying there (dorms and private rooms, tel. 0471-727-947, www. zallinger.com, info@zallinger.com).

Challenging Hikes
Summit Hike of Schlern

For a serious 12-mile (six-hour) hike—with a possible overnight in a traditional mountain refuge (generally open mid-June-Sept)—consider hiking to the summit of Schlern (Sciliar). This route is popular with hardy hikers; some call it the best hike in the region.

Start at the €6 Spitzbühl chairlift, a 20-minute walk below Compatsch (5,659 feet, free parking, Castelrotto-Compatsch bus stops here), which brings you up to 6,348 feet. Trail #5 takes you through a high meadow, down to the Saltner dairy farm (6,004 feet—you want the Saltner dairy farm at Tschapit, not the one near Zallingerhütte), across a stream, and steeply up the Schlern mountain. About three hours into your hike, you'll meet trail #1 and

walk across the rocky tabletop plateau of Schlern to the **Schlern-haus** mountain "hut," really a simple restaurant and 120-bed hostel

(7,544 feet, called Rifugio Bolzano in Italian). From this dramatic setting, you can enjoy a meal and get a great view of the Rosengarten range. Hike 20 more minutes up the nearby peak (Monte Pez, 8,400 feet), where you'll find a lofty meadow, cows in the summer, and the region's ultimate 360-degree alpine panorama. Unless you're staying overnight, hike back the way you came.

Overnight Option: To do the Schlern summit hike as an overnight, either sleep at the ¢ **Schlernhaus** (bunks and private rooms, cash only, open early June-mid-Oct, no hot water, summer-only tel. 0471-612-024, off-season tel. 0471-724-094, can reserve by email before hut opens in June, www.schlernhaus.it, info@schlernhaus.it) or walk two hours farther along the Schlern to the hut at ¢ **Tierser Alpl,** at 8,006 feet (bunks and private rooms, open late May-late Oct, tel. 0471-727-958 or 0471-707-460, mobile 333-654-6865, www.tierseralpl.com, info@tierseralpl.com). From Tierser Alpl, you can descend to Saltria or Compatsch by any of several different scenic routes.

Trail Running

The Running Park Seiser Alm includes 46 miles of signed running trails in the meadow. Year after year, the clean air and high mountain altitude attract many international runners/masochists. During a one-day, scenic half-marathon on the first Sunday of July, they invite the public to run with them...or at least try. Contact the Compatsch TI for trail info and maps, or go to www.seiseralm.it and click on "Summer Active," then "Running."

Biking in Alpe di Siusi

Bikes are easy to rent (including electric ones—see "Helpful Hints," earlier), welcome on many lifts for free or a small fee, and permitted on many of the trails and lanes in Alpe di Siusi. The Compatsch TI has a good information flier that lists the best routes. You can also go to www.seiseralm.it, then click on "Summer Active," then "Mountain Bike," then "Mountain Bike Trails." Get local advice to confirm difficulty levels and your plan before starting any ride; the TI hands out helpful bike-route cards. Those with a bike don't need to worry about lifts shutting down at 17:00 (but remember that the Seiser Alm Bahn cable car down from Compatsch closes at 19:00).

For a fairly easy, 2.5-hour ride that gives you the same scenic thrills as the **"Panorama to Zallingerhütte"** hike recommended above, try this: Start from Compatsch (6,048 feet), bike or ride the lift to Panorama (6,600 feet), and take road #7, which runs generally uphill to Goldknopf and then follows a series of hills and dips to Mahlknechthütte (6,739 feet). Then take road #8 downhill to

Saltria (5,544 feet) and back to Compatsch (6,048 feet). About 60 percent is paved and 40 percent is gravel lanes.

More Sights in the Dolomites

▲▲Mountain Drive from Venice to Bolzano

Between Venice and Bolzano, most drivers just take the expressway through Verona. But going across the mountains gives you the definitive Dolomite experience. You'll take the Venice-Belluno autostrada, then this route: Belluno-Cortina-Pordoi Pass-Val di Fassa-Bolzano (about 125 miles). If you aren't traveling in summer, check road conditions before you depart (call 0471-200-198, in Italian or German only).

▲▲Short Dolomite Loop Drive

You could spend a day from Bolzano or Castelrotto driving a loop over the scenic Sella Pass (Sellajoch, Passo di Sella)—it's about 70 miles on windy roads, so allow four hours. Going clockwise, you drive first through a long valley, the Grödner Tal/Val Gardena, which is famous for its skiing and hiking resorts, traditional Ladin culture (notice the trilingual road signs), and wood-carvers (the wood-carving company ANRI is from the town of St. Cristina).

You'll pass through the large town of St. Ulrich (with the base station of a different cable car up to Alpe di Siusi—used for more challenging hikes). Within an hour, you'll reach Sella Pass (7,349 feet). After a series of tight hairpin turns a half-mile or so over the pass, you'll see some benches and cars. Pull over and watch the rock climbers. Over the pass is the town of Canazei, with nice ambience and altitude (4,642 feet). From Canazei, lifts (mid-June-late Sept daily 8:30-12:30 & 13:45-17:20) take you to Col dei Rossi Belvedere, where you can hike the Bindelweg trail past Rifugio Belvedere along an easy but breathtaking ridge to Rifugio Viel del Pan (check with the Canazei TI for lift info: tel. 0462-609-500, www.fassa.com). This three-hour round-trip hike has views of the highest mountain in the Dolomites—the Marmolada—and the Dolomighty Sella range. Leaving Canazei, you can either follow very twisty roads (via St. Zyprian and Tiers) back to Castelrotto, or take the easier and slightly faster route via Welschnofen and Birchabruck back to Bolzano and the main valley highway.

DOLOMITES

Brixen (Bressanone)

This charming small city (pop. 20,000), on the highway between Bolzano and Innsbruck, is a worthwhile pit stop (park at garage P2 and take the pedestrian underpass into the old town; the main square is a 5-minute stroll away). With an illustrious history of powerful bishops—and a sleepy present—Brixen feels like a charming, mini Bolzano with a bit more Germanic character. It has a sprawling, traffic-free old town; a big main square with two stately churches (connected by a fine cloister); arcaded shopping streets; and plenty of al fresco cafés and restaurants. Explore the lanes beyond the main square to find a beautiful waterside walking and biking path.

Near Brixen: More impressive than any sight in Brixen itself, the **Kloster Neustift** (Abbazia di Novacella) just two miles north—is an Augustinian monastery complex that's open to the public. The centerpiece is a basilica with the region's most glorious Bavarian-style Baroque interior—slathered with decadent white and pink stucco, frilly curlicues, twisty columns, and pudgy winged babies everywhere. While a quick stroll through the grounds and a look at the church interior is plenty satisfying, you can also take a guided tour or try the monk-made wines in the *enoteca* (tel. 0472-836-189, www.kloster-neustift.it).

DOLOMITES

▲Reifenstein Castle (Castel Tasso)

Reifenstein Castle, with one of my favorite castle interiors in Europe, is just off the highway at the town of Sterzing/Vipiteno. While

easy for drivers, it's not worth the trouble for those without wheels—it's unique and interesting but only open for a few non-English tours a day. The castle is privately owned and has not been developed for tourism (no gift shop, no café). Its layout and decor have changed little since the 15th century, when it passed into the hands of the Teutonic Knights. Since 1813, a branch of the noble Thurn and Taxis family has owned the castle. The current heads of the family (an elderly brother and sister) live in Innsbruck, and have chosen to keep the castle just as it was when they spent summer vacations here in the 1940s as children. On your tour, you'll see most of the building, including bedrooms with original wall paneling and decorations, a real dungeon, wooden boxes knights slept in, and a medieval kitchen with a roof that is black with centuries of soot.

Cost and Hours: €7, open early April-Oct; tours Sun-Fri at 10:30, 14:00, and 15:00, late July-early Sept also at 16:00, closed

Sat; show up punctually at these times at drawbridge, ideally call ahead to confirm tour, minimum of four people needed for tour to run—but if fewer people show up you can pay the extra admission prices, mobile 339-264-3752 (call between 8:00-10:30, 11:30-14:00, or 17:00-20:00), visit www.sterzing.com, click "Culture," and then "Castles." Frau Steiner, the castle guide and caretaker, can do one-hour private tours in English by appointment for a reasonable price.

Getting There: By car, the castle is about 45 minutes from Bolzano, Castelrotto, and Innsbruck. Exit the Innsbruck-Bolzano expressway at Sterzing/Vipiteno (just on the Italian side of the Brenner Pass and Austrian/Italian border), and carefully follow brown *Reifenstein* signs. Park at the base of the castle's rock and hike up the castle drive (10 minutes). Of the two castles here, Reifenstein is the one to the west of the expressway.

▲Glurns

Between the Dolomites and Lake Como, the scenic high road (SS-38, via Meran and Bormio) is only a half-hour slower than the expressway through Verona. On the way, you can eat lunch or spend the night in the amazing little town of Glurns (Glorenza in Italian, 45 minutes west of touristy Meran, www.glurns.eu). Glurns still lives within its square wall on the Adige River, with a church bell tower that has a thing about ringing, typical Tirolean arcaded streets, and real farms rather than tourist boutiques. The arcades' short arches seem to cause the locals, whose families go back eons, to take on a Quasimodo-like posture. Far off most tourists' itinerary, the only disappointing thing about Glurns is that the center isn't traffic-free. There are several small hotels in the town, but I'd stay in a private home (such as **$ Family Hofer,** 4 rooms, discount for 4 nights or longer, cash only, 100 yards from town square, near church, just outside wall on river, Etschdammweg 1, tel. 0473-831-597, www.hofer.bz.it, privatzimmer.hofer@rolmail.net).

THE LAKES

Commune with nature where Italy is joined to the Alps, in the lovely Italian lakes district. In this land of lakes, the million-euro question is: Which one? For the best mix of accessibility, scenery, and offbeatness, the village of Varenna on Lake Como is my top choice, while Lake Maggiore is a suitable backup. In either place, you'll get a complete dose of Italian-lakes wonder and aristocratic-old-days romance.

You could spend a busy day side-tripping from Milan (about one hour away by train) to either lake, do some island- and villa-hopping, and be home in time for dinner. But the lakes are an ideal place to slow down and take a break from your busy vacation. Settle in here, and bustling Milan doesn't even exist. Now it's your turn to be *chiuso per restauro* (closed for restoration). If relaxation's not on your agenda, the lakes shouldn't be either.

Lake Como

Lake Como (Lago di Como)—lined with elegant 19th-century villas, crowned by snowcapped mountains, and busy with ferries, hydrofoils, and slow, passenger-only boats—is a good place to take a break from the intensity and turnstile culture of central Italy. It seems like half the travelers you'll meet have tossed their itineraries into the lake and are actually relaxing.

Lake Como is Milan's quick getaway, and the sleepy mid-lake village of Varenna is the handiest base of operations. With good connections to other mid-lake towns (and Milan), Varenna is my

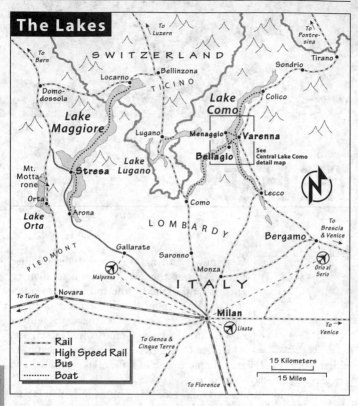

The Lakes

Rail
High Speed Rail
Bus
Boat

15 Kilometers
15 Miles

LAKES

favorite place to stay on the lake. While Varenna has a village vibe, beautiful Bellagio has earned its ritzy allure and feels a bit more like a real city, making it a good alternative.

The hazy, lazy lake's only serious industry is tourism. Every day, hundreds of lakeside residents commute to work in Lugano, just across the border in Switzerland. The lake's isolation and flat economy have left it pretty much the way the 19th-century Romantic poets described it: heaven on earth.

PLANNING YOUR TIME

Even though there are no essential activities, plan for at least two nights so you'll have an uninterrupted day to see how slow you can get your pulse. Spend some time exploring your home-base town, take my self-guided ferry tour to take in the scenery (with visits to the lake's two main villas), and hop off the boat to poke around the town you're not staying in. With additional time, visit more lakeside villas or go for a hike.

Lake Como is also workable as a day trip from Milan. Take a morning train to Varenna, ride the boat to Lenno (and tour Villa

Balbianello), then take a boat to Villa Carlotta to tour the gardens. From there, head either to Bellagio or back to Varenna to linger and explore (or, with more time and energy, see a little of both) before taking the train back to Milan from Varenna. Start early to pack everything in; otherwise, you'll have to be more selective (with time to see just one of the villas).

GETTING TO LAKE COMO

By Train via Varenna: From any destination covered in this book, you'll reach Lake Como via Milan. The quickest, easiest, and cheapest way to get from Milan to any mid-lake town is to take the train to Varenna. From Varenna you can hop on a boat to Bellagio.

At Milan's central train station (Milano Centrale), catch a train heading for Sondrio or Tirano—sometimes the departure board also says "Lecco/Tirano." (Tirano is often confused with Torino...wrong city.) All Sondrio-bound trains stop in Varenna, as noted in the fine print on the *partenze* (departures) schedule posted at Milan's train station. Trains leave Milan nearly hourly at :20 past the hour, with a few gaps when a train doesn't leave for two hours (confirm times at station or online at www.trenitalia.com). Get a second-class ticket, since most of these trains don't have first-class cars (rail passes accepted). If you plan to head back to Milan on the train, you might as well also buy a return ticket. Stamp your ticket in the yellow box or risk a €50 fine. If you run into a problem or need to validate your rail pass at Milan's train station, find the helpful Trenitalia office on the ground floor.

Leaving Milan, sit on the left for maximum lake-view beauty. Get off at Varenna-Esino-Perledo. (Even though train schedules list just Varenna or Varenna-Esino, Varenna-Esino-Perledo is what you'll see at the platform.) The long trains that serve Varenna's tiny station stop only briefly—be ready to hop out. The single platform is very narrow, and your car may actually stop before or after the platform. Look out the window. If even part of the train is at the station, you'll need to get out and walk. Tips: Board midtrain to land next to a platform. Leave from the door through which you entered, since you know it's working. If necessary, pull hard on the red handle (or push the button) to open the door.

By Boat via Como: For a less convenient, much slower, but more scenic trip, you can get to Varenna or Bellagio from Milan via the town of Como. Trains take you from Milan to Como (2/hour, 30-60 minutes). From the station in Como, it's a 10-minute walk to the dock, where you catch either the speedy hydrofoil or the leisurely *battello* (slow boat—great for enjoying the scenery) for the ride up the lake to Bellagio or Varenna. Boats leave Como about hourly (*battello:* €11.60, 2.5 hours, last departure about 15:20; hydrofoil: €16.20, 1 hour, last departure about 19:20, fewer on Sun).

Boat Schedule Literacy

Types of Boats
Traghetto or *autotraghetto*: Car and passenger ferry
Aliscafo or *servizio rapido*: Hydrofoil (pricier, faster, enclosed, and less scenic)
Battello ship: Slow passenger-only boat going all the way to Como
Battello navetta: Shuttle serving mid-lake only

Schedule Terms
Feriali: Monday-Saturday
Festivi: Sundays and holidays
Partenze da...: Departing from...

By Plane via Milan's Airports: Take the Malpensa Express train from Malpensa Airport, the Airport Bus Express from Linate Airport, or any of the buses from Bergamo's Orio al Serio Airport to Milano Centrale train station (see page 312 or 314), and then transfer to a Varenna-bound train.

By Taxi: Taxis between Varenna and Milan or its airports won't save money over the train, even for groups, but can be worth it for the convenience. **Marco Barili** (and his wife Nelly) don't add surcharges for baggage or early/late departures (€150 to central Milan or Linate Airport for up to 4 people/€200 for 5-8 people in a minibus, €160/€220 to Malpensa Airport, €130/€180 to Orio al Serio Airport, tel. 0341-815-061, taxi.varenna@tiscali.it).

GETTING AROUND LAKE COMO

By Boat: Boats go about every 30 minutes between Varenna and Bellagio (€4.60/hop, 15-20 minutes, daily approximately 7:00-22:30). If you're staying in one of these towns, you'll probably limit your cruising to this scenic mid-lake area. Express boats cost a little more and save only a couple of minutes per leg. Because boats are frequent and the schedule is hard to read, I just show up, buy a ticket for the next boat, and wait. Always ask which slip

(pontile) your boat will leave from—it's not posted, and Bellagio has several docks (boat info: toll-free tel. 800-551-801 or tel. 031-579-211, www.navigazionelaghi.it). On sunny days, long lines can form at ticket booths; don't dillydally, and consider buying your tickets in advance at a quieter time. The one-day €15 mid-lake pass makes

sense only if you take four or more rides—unlikely (pass does not cover fast hydrofoils).

If you're making more complex plans, pick up a free **boat schedule** and ask for help to decipher it. It's a good idea to ask your hotelier to help review your possible connections before you set out so you can pace your day smartly. You'll find the schedule at travel agencies, hotels, and boat docks. Confusingly, the schedule requires you to scan four different timetables to know all the departures; for key terms, see the sidebar.

By Car: With scarce parking, traffic jams, and expensive car ferries, this is no place to drive. While it's possible to drive around the lake, the road is narrow, congested, and lined with privacy-seeking walls, hedges, and tall fences. Parking in Bellagio is more difficult than in Varenna. If you do have a car, park it in Varenna, and use the boat to get around (for parking tips in Varenna, see page 227).

While you can rent cars in Bellagio, for most travelers, it's best to take the train to Milan and pick up a car there, either at the central train station or at one of Milan's three airports.

Varenna

This well-manicured village of 800 people offers the best of all lake worlds. Easily accessible by train, on the less-driven side of the

lake, Varenna has a romantic promenade, a tiny harbor, steep and narrow stepped lanes, and some scenic sights (a ruined castle and two villas). It's just the right place to savor a lakeside cappuccino or *aperitivo*. There's wonderfully little to do here, and it's very quiet at night...unless you're here during one of the hundred or so annual American wedding parties. The

passerella (lakeside promenade, well-lit and inviting after dark) is adorned with caryatid lovers pressing silently against each other in the shadows. Varenna is a popular destination with my readers and European vacationers—book well in advance for visits in summer (May-Oct). From November to mid-March, Varenna practically shuts down; hotels close for the winter, and restaurants and shops reduce their hours.

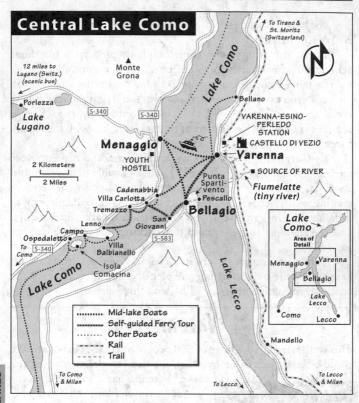

Central Lake Como

To Tirano &
St. Moritz
(Switzerland)

Lake Como

12 miles to
Lugano (Switz.)
(scenic bus)

Monte
Grona

Porlezza

Lake
Lugano

Bellano

S-340

S-340

VARENNA-ESINO-
PERLEDO
STATION

CASTELLO DI VEZIO

Menaggio

Varenna

YOUTH
HOSTEL

SOURCE OF RIVER

2 Kilometers

Punta
Sparti-
vento

Fiumelatte
(tiny river)

2 Miles

Cadenabbia
Villa Carlotta

Pescallo

Tremezzo

San
Giovanni

Bellagio

Lenno

Campo

Lake
Como

Ospedaletto

Villa
Balbianello

S-583

Area of
Detail

To
Como

S-340

Isola
Comacina

Menaggio

Varenna

Bellagio

Lake Como

Lake Lecco

Lake
Lecco

Como

Lecco

.... Mid-lake Boats

Self-guided Ferry Tour

Other Boats

Rail

Trail

Mandello

To Como
& Milan

To Lecco

To Lecco
& Milan

Orientation to Varenna

TOURIST INFORMATION

The TI is near the **main square** (June-Sept daily 10:00-13:00 &
15:00-18:30; April-May and Oct Tue-Sat 10:00-12:30 & 14:30-
18:00, Sun 10:00-12:30, closed Mon; weekends only Nov-March;
just past the bank at Via IV Novembre 7, tel. 0341-830-367, www.
varennaturismo.com). The Tivano travel agency, located in the
train station, also operates as a TI (see "Helpful Hints"). At either
TI (or your hotel), pick up the latest edition of the *Varenna Tourist
Info* booklet.

ARRIVAL IN VARENNA

Varenna is small, and pretty much everything is within a 15-min-
ute walk.

By Train: From Varenna's train station, you can **walk** along
the marked pedestrian lane down to the main road. If you're heading for the ferry to Bellagio, go straight; otherwise, turn left along
the main road and keep rolling into town (a 10- to 15-minute walk

from the station; watch for traffic where the sidewalk ends). If you have a bag with wheels, avoid using the lakeside promenade, which ends in stairs and cobbles.

A **taxi** from the station costs about €10. Reliable Marco Barili (or his wife Nelly) can meet you at the train station if you know your exact arrival time. Look for a flashing sign with your name on it (tel. 0341-815-061, taxi.varenna@tiscali.it).

By Boat: The boat dock is close to the train station and a 10-minute stroll north of the main square and old town.

By Car: Avoid on-street parking in Varenna; the few spots are mostly reserved for residents. The easiest (though most expensive) option for parking is the spiffy multilevel lot at the south end of town, across from the entrance to Villa Monastero (€2/hour 6:00-22:00, otherwise €1/hour, €20/24 hours).

At the train station, it's free to park overnight, but you'll have to pay from 9:00 to 20:00 daily in summer months (June-Aug) and on Saturdays, Sundays, and holidays in high season (€1.20/hour, free to park Mon-Fri Sept-May, feed coins into meter in center of lot and put ticket on dashboard; €10 day pass available from I Viaggi del Tivano travel agency or Café III Binario at the station).

HELPFUL HINTS

Exchange Rate: €1 = about $1.10

Country Calling Code: 39 (see page 1154 for dialing instructions)

Travel Agency: Varenna's travel agency, **I Viaggi del Tivano,** is conveniently located in the train station. In addition to acting as a TI, they book planes, trains, and automobiles (Mon-Fri 9:00-13:00 & 14:30-18:30, Sat-Sun 9:00-16:00, Oct-April Sat until 13:00 and closed Sun; good place to pick up boat schedules, no service charge for regional train tickets, €5 booking fee for long-distance train tickets, tel. 0341-814-009, www.tivanotours.com, info@tivanotours.com, helpful Cristina and Eleonora). They also offer half-day and daylong bus and boat tours of the region, including Switzerland (April-Sept only, book tours by noon the day before).

Train Tickets: The train station doesn't have ticket windows, but you can buy tickets at the **I Viaggi del Tivano** travel agency there (see above). Don't cut it too close, in case there's a line. You can also buy tickets at the **Barilott** bar/tobacco shop downtown, which is also a lively place to buy a *panino* and/or a glass of wine and use the Wi-Fi (May-Sept daily 7:00-20:00, closed Sun off-season, Via IV Novembre 6, tel. 0341-815-045, Claudia and Fabrizio).

Money: One bank is near Varenna's main square; another is located inland from the boat dock. Both have ATMs (see the Varenna map on page 228).

LAKES

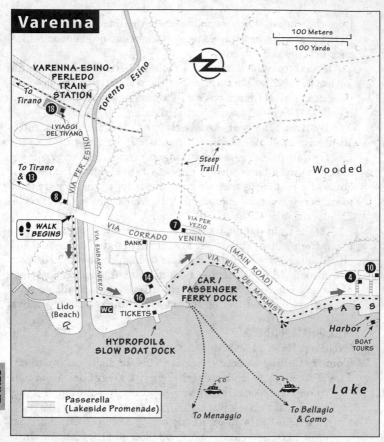

Post Office: It's at the bottom corner of the main square (Tue and Thu-Fri 8:30-13:45, Sat 8:20-12:45).

Laundry: Lavanderia Pensa Barbara can wash and dry your laundry within 24 hours (priced by weight, figure around €15-18/load, no self-service, closed Sun, Via Venini 31, tel. 0341-830-478). A self-service machine is tucked in the back of the little **"Il Bottaio"** shopping mall facing the harbor (€1 entry voucher covers WC or can be used toward food or drinks at nearby Nilus Bar, wash-€3.50, dry-€1.50/10 minutes, daily 8:00-24:00).

Varenna Walk

Since you came here to relax, this short self-guided walk gives you just the town basics.

• *Begin by standing in the little piazza next to the...*

Bridge Just Below Train Station: This main bridge spans the

Map legend:

1 Hotel du Lac
2 Villa Cipressi & Ristorante la Contrada
3 Hotel Royal Victoria
4 Albergo Milano, Casa Rossa & Ristorante la Vista
5 To Hotel Eremo Gaudio
6 Albergo/Ristorante del Sole
7 Hotel Montecodeno
8 Albergo Beretta
9 Ristorante il Cavatappi
10 Osteria Quatro Pass
11 Varenna Monamour
12 Nilus Bar & Bar Il Molo
13 To Ristorante il Caminetto & Cooking Course
14 Pub l'Orso
15 Vecchia Varenna
16 Hotel/Ristorante Olivedo
17 Gelateria Riva
18 Café III Binario
19 Grocery Stores (2)
20 Laundry
21 Barilott Bar (Train Tickets)
22 Villa Monastero Entrance

LAKES

tiny Esino River, which divides two communities: Perledo (which sprawls up the hill—notice the church spire high above) and the old fishing town of Varenna (huddled around its harbor). The train station, called Varenna-Esino-Perledo, gives due respect to both, as well as the village of Esino, eight miles higher in the hills.

Go down the tree-lined promenade on the right (north) side of the river. You'll run into the entrance to the town's public beach— the *lido* (small fee to enter)—and then cross the cute pedestrian bridge to the small square, which hosts a market on Wednesdays.

The yellow inn facing the ferry dock, Hotel Olivedo, has greeted ferry travelers since the 19th century and is named for the olive groves you can see growing halfway up the hill. Natives claim this is the farthest north that olives grow in Europe.

• *Across from Hotel Olivedo is Varenna's*

Ferry Landing: Since the coming of the train in 1892, this has been the main link to Milan and the world for the "mid-lake" communities of Bellagio, Menaggio (described later), and Varenna.

From this viewpoint, you can almost see how Lake Como is shaped like a man. The head is the north end (to the right, up by the Swiss Alps). Varenna is the left hip (to the east). Menaggio, across the lake, is the right hip (to the west). And Bellagio (hiding behind the smaller wooded hill to your left) is the crotch—or, more poetically, Punta Spartivento ("Point that Divides the Wind"). In a more colorful description, a traditional poem says, "Lake Como is a man, with Colico the head, Lecco and Como the feet, and Bellagio the testicles." (In the regional dialect, this rhymes—ask a native to say it for you.)

The farthest ridges high above the right hip mark the border of Switzerland. This region's longtime poverty shaped the local character (much like the Great Depression shaped the outlook of a generation of Americans). Many still remember that the Varenna side of the lake was the poorest, because those on the Menaggio side controlled the lucrative cigarette-smuggling business over the Swiss border. Today, the entire region is thriving—thanks to tourism.

• *Walk past the ferry dock and the small playground to Varenna's elevated shoreline walk, called the...*

Passerella: A generation ago, Varenna built this elegant lakeside promenade, which connects the ferry dock with the old town center. Strolling this lane, you'll come to the tiny, two-dinghy, concrete breakwater of a villa. Lake Como is lined with swanky 19th-century villas; their front doors face the lake to welcome visitors arriving by boat. At this point, the modern *passerella* cuts between this villa's water gate and its private harbor. Just around the bend,  enjoy a good Varenna town view. These buildings are stringently protected by preservation laws; you can't even change the color of your villa's paint.

Just over the hump (which allows boats into a covered moorage), look back and up at another typical old villa—with a private *passerella*, a lovely veil of wisteria, and a prime lakeview terrace. Many of these villas are owned by the region's "impoverished nobility." Bred and raised not to work, eventually they were unable to pay for the upkeep of their sprawling houses. Some of these villas have now been bought by the region's nouveau riche.

• *At the community harbor, walk to the end of the pier for a town overview, then continue under the old-time arcades toward the multihued homes facing the harbor.*

Varenna Harborfront: There are no streets in the old town—just the characteristic stepped lanes called *contrade*. Varenna was

originally a fishing community. Even today, old-timers enjoy Lake Como's counterpart to Norwegian lutefisk: *missoltino*, air-dried and salted lake "sardines."

Imagine the harbor 200 years ago—busy with coopers fitting chestnut and oak staves into barrels, stoneworkers carving the black marble that was quarried just above town, and fishermen dragging boats onto the sloping beach. The little stone harbor dates from about 1600. Today, the fishing boats are just for recreation, and residents gather here with their kids to relax by the lake.

At the south end of the harbor (in front of the recommended Bar Il Molo), belly up to the banister of the terrace for a colorful town view. Another traditional ditty goes, "If you love Lake Como, you know Bellagio is the pearl...but Varenna is the diamond."

• *Continue straight, leaving the harbor. A lane curves around Hotel du Lac (its fine lakeside terrace welcomes even nonguests for a drink), finishing with an unexpected hill. Finally you'll reach the tiny pebbly town beach below. From here, climb the stairs and go through the yellow arch to the square called...*

Piazza San Giorgio: Several churches face Varenna's town square. The main church (Chiesa di San Giorgio) dates from the 13th century. Romantic Varenna is an understandably popular spot for weddings—rice often litters the church's front yard. Stepping inside, you'll find a few humble but centuries-old bits of carving and frescoes. The black floor and chapels are made from the local marble.

Just past the church and the municipal building is the TI and the Ornithology and Natural Science Museum, with a small collection of stuffed birds and other wildlife (small entry fee, same hours as TI).

The Hotel Royal Victoria, also on the main square, recalls the 1839 visit of Queen Victoria, who registered herself as the Countess of Clare in an attempt to remain anonymous.

The trees in the square are planted to make a V for Varenna. The street plan survives from Roman times, when gutters flowed down to the lake. The little church on the lake side of the square is the baptistery. Dating from the ninth century, it's one of the oldest churches on the lake, but is rarely open for visits.

Our walk is over. Facing the church, you can head right to visit the gardens or to take a demanding hike up to the castle (both described next, under "Sights and Activities in Varenna"). You can

LAKES

go left to get to the train station or ferry dock—or for a less-demanding but still steep hike to the castle. Head back downhill to enjoy the beach (take either of the lanes flanking the Hotel Royal Victoria down to the water).

Sights and Activities in Varenna

▲Hike to Vezio Castle (Castello di Vezio)

A steep and stony trail leads to Varenna's ruined hilltop castle, located in the peaceful, traffic-free, one-chapel hamlet of Vezio. Take the small road, Via per Vezio (about 100 feet south of—and to the right of—Hotel Montecodeno), and figure on a 20-minute walk one-way. Arriving in Vezio, follow *castello* signs. You'll reach a bar (with drinks, light food, and WCs) that serves as the castle's ticket desk. Once inside the grounds, the views are the main attraction: Follow the little loop trail on the lake side of the castle for vistas down on Varenna's rooftops and the adjacent lakefront community of Pino. The castle itself is barren—a courtyard protecting an empty tower, where you can cross a drawbridge and climb 62 rickety wooden steps to earn 360 degrees of Lake Como panoramas.

Cost and Hours: €4, April-Sept Mon-Fri 10:00-18:00, Sat-Sun 10:00-19:00, July-Aug stays open one hour later, March and Oct closes one hour earlier, closed Nov-Feb and in bad weather, mobile 333-448-5975, www.castellodivezio.it, Nicola.

Falconry Shows: The castle hosts low-key falconry shows, usually around 15:30—but check the website or call in the morning for times.

Hiking Back Down: You can hike back the way you came or make a loop by continuing down to the east end of Varenna, on a steeper, narrower, less-manicured trail. From the castle gate, turn right and follow signs for *Varenna Scabium* and *Sentiero del Viandante*. You'll wander past some backyards and some scenic tennis courts, then start to gradually descend, popping out at the parking garage for the Hotel Eremo Gaudio. From here, head down to the right to walk back into Varenna, passing the entrances for both Villa Monastero and Villa Cipressi (described next) on your way to the main square.

Gardens

Two separate manicured lakeside gardens sit next door to each other just a short distance from the main square. First are the small but lush terraces of **Villa Cipressi**; just beyond are the more open grounds of **Villa Monastero**, which also admits visitors into the former residence of the De Marchi family, now a museum

filled with overly ornate furnishings from the late 1800s. It's the handiest look inside one of the old villas that line the lakeshore, but the lack of information makes the place feel sterile. While the villas and gardens elsewhere on the lake are more magnificent (see "More Sights on Lake Como," later), these are a sufficient substitute if you're staying around Varenna.

Cost and Hours: Villa Cipressi—€4, May-Nov daily 8:00-20:00, closed Dec-April, www.hotelvillacipressi.it; Villa Monastero—gardens—€5, gardens and museum—€8; gardens open March-Oct daily 9:30-19:00, closed Nov-Feb; museum open March-Oct Fri-Sun 9:30-19:00, closed Mon-Thu—except open daily in Aug, closed Nov-Feb; bar in garden serves snacks, tel. 0341-295-450, www.villamonastero.eu.

Nearby: The **Sala De Marchi,** across the street from the Villa Monastero entrance, hosts a different exhibition each month through the summer. Ask at the TI or check the posters to see what's on.

Swimming
There are three spots to swim in Varenna: the free little beach behind the Hotel Royal Victoria off Piazza San Giorgio, the central lakefront area by Nilus Bar, and the *lido.* The *lido* is by far the best-equipped for swimmers. Just north of the boat dock, it's essentially a wide concrete slab with sand and a swimming area off an old boat ramp. It has showers, bathrooms, a restaurant, a bar, and lounge chairs and umbrellas for rent (€2 entry, tel. 0341-815-3700). Swimming by the boat dock is strictly forbidden for safety reasons.

Boat Tours
Taxi Boat Varenna organizes hour-long central lake tours (€30/person), plus a 2.5-hour version that adds a stop at Villa Balbianello (€55/person, includes one-hour guided villa tour). They also offer 50-minute romantic private tours (€150/couple). Ask Luca about his special 2.5-hour "Tour George." Book directly on the website (April-Oct only, mobile 349-229-0953, www.taxiboatvarenna.com, info@taxiboatvarenna.com). A similar company works out of Bellagio.

Hiking
The town of **Fiumelatte,** about a half-mile south of Varenna, was named for its "milky river." Promoted as the shortest river in Italy (at 800 feet), it runs—like most of the area's tourist industry—only from April through September (though even then it may be dry, depending on the weather). The *La Sorgente del Fiumelatte* brochure, available at Varenna's TI, lays out a walk from Varenna to the Fiumelatte, then to the castle, and back. It's a 30-minute hike to the source *(sorgente)* of the river (at Varenna's monastery, take the

LAKES

high road, drop into the tranquil and evocative cemetery, and climb steps to the wooded trail leading to the peaceful and refreshing cave from which the river spouts).

For a longer hike in the opposite direction with lake views, ask the TI about the **Wayfarers' Path** (hike one-way up the lake, about 2-2.5 hours, not quite as steep as Fiumelatte hike). You can return by train or boat from Bellano (check schedule before you go).

Cooking Course

Chef Moreno of the recommended Ristorante il Caminetto picks you up in Varenna, zips you up the mountain to his restaurant (experience Italian driving!), and then teaches you some basics of Italian cooking. Learn how to handcraft fresh pasta or prep regional specialties. Classes last about three hours, plus time to *mangiare*. People love the experience and find Moreno a charming teacher and host (€60 includes trip, lesson, recipes, and lunch complete with wine, cookies, and coffee; Mon, Tue, Thu, and Fri; 10:00 pickup from Varenna landing, return by 16:00, reservations mandatory, tel. 0341-815-127, www.ilcaminettoonline.com, info@ilcaminettoonline.com).

Sleeping in Varenna

Reservations are tight in August, snug May through October, and wide open most of the rest of the year. Many places close in winter. High-season prices are listed here; prices get soft off-season.

$$$$ Hotel du Lac, filling a refined and modernized 19th-century villa, is the finest hotel in town. From its exclusive private perch on the point, it offers a quiet lakefront breakfast terrace; genteel public spaces; a friendly, professional staff; and 16 delightful rooms—all but three with lake views (air-con, some rooms with elevator access, pay parking, Via del Prestino 11, tel. 0341-830-238, www.albergodulac.com, info@albergodulac.com).

$$$$ Villa Cipressi is a sprawling, centuries-old lakeside mansion with 33 warmly outfitted, modern rooms. Its elegant but understated public spaces are often busy with wedding parties. Rooms without views face the street and can be noisy. The villa sits in a huge, quiet, terraced garden that nonguests pay to see (RS%, some view rooms, all rooms have air-con or ceiling fans, elevator, garden access, Via IV Novembre 18, tel. 0341-830-113, www.hotelvillacipressi.it, info@hotelvillacipressi.it, Davide Dellera).

$$$$ Hotel Royal Victoria, a central splurge facing the main square, has a classic, grand-hotel lobby, an inviting terrace with a swimming pool just above the lake, and 43 richly furnished rooms with modern amenities (RS%, some lake view rooms, air-con, el-

Sleep Code

Hotels are classified based on the average price of a standard double room with breakfast in high season.

$$$$	**Splurge:**	Most rooms over €170
$$$	**Pricier:**	€130-170
$$	**Moderate:**	€90-130
$	**Budget:**	€50-90
¢	**Backpacker:**	Under €50
RS%	Rick Steves discount	

Unless otherwise noted, credit cards are accepted, hotel staff speak basic English, and free Wi-Fi is available. Comparison-shop by checking prices at several hotels (on each hotel's own website, on a booking site, or by email). For the best deal, *book directly with the hotel*. Ask for a discount if paying in cash; if the listing includes **RS%,** request a Rick Steves discount.

evator, pay Wi-Fi, pay parking, Piazza San Giorgio 2, tel. 0341-815-111, www.royalvictoria.com, info@royalvictoria.com).

$$$ Albergo Milano, located right in the old town, is graciously run by Egidio and his Swiss wife, Bettina. Fusing the best of Italy with the best of Switzerland, this well-run, romantic hotel has eight comfortable rooms with extravagant views, balconies, or big terraces (ceiling fans, no elevator; from the station, take main road to town and turn right at steep alley where sidewalk and guardrail break; Via XX Settembre 35, tel. 0341-830-298, www. varenna.net, hotelmilano@varenna.net). This place whispers *luna di miele*—honeymoon (see website for honeymoon deal). Nearby is **$$$ Casa Rossa,** an annex with five comfortable rooms and one apartment that works well for families (breakfast served at main hotel, nonview rooms are more budget-friendly). Their recommended Ristorante la Vista is worth considering for dinner.

$$$ Hotel Eremo Gaudio stands out with a commanding lake view high above Varenna. Once an orphanage, it became a hermitage run by the Catholic Church, and then—since 2000—a peaceful hotel with awe-inspiring view balconies and a breakfast terrace. Thirteen bright, plain-but-comfy rooms climb up the main building, and 14 less dramatic but equally comfortable rooms huddle below at the foot of the funicular (all rooms have lake views, air-con in summer; from the station, it's a steep walk up hills and steps—taking a taxi is recommended; 8-minute walk from Varenna's main square at Via Roma 25, tel. 0341-815-301, www. hoteleremogaudiovarenna.it, eremogaudio@yahoo.it).

$$$ Albergo del Sole rents eight simple, comfortable rooms (with partial-lake or piazza views) above a restaurant right on the town square, which can be lively at night. Run by fun-loving Enzo

LAKES

and Francesco (family rooms, open all year, fans, hardwood floors, shiny bathrooms, elevator, Piazza San Giorgio 17, tel. 0341-815-218, www.albergodelsolevarenna.it, albergo.sole@virgilio.it).

$$ Hotel Montecodeno, with 11 decent rooms and no views, is a functional concrete box along the main road. It's a five-minute walk from the train station and ferries (RS%, air-con, no elevator, attached restaurant, Via della Croce 2, tel. 0341-830-123, mobile 340-356-7688, www.hotelmontecodeno.com, info@ hotelmontecodeno.com, Marco Bartesaghi).

$ Albergo Beretta, on the main road a block below the station, has 10 small, basic rooms, several with balconies (and street noise). Second-floor rooms are quietest. This good-value option, above a coffee shop that doubles as the reception, feels dated and lacks lakeside glamour (elevator, Wi-Fi in common areas, limited free parking—reserve ahead, Via per Esino 1, tel. 0341-830-132, hotelberetta@iol.it, Renato Brambilla).

Eating in Varenna

Lavarello, a lake whitefish, is popular on menus. For something more adventurous, consider *missoltino,* which are salted little fish often served with pasta or local-style polenta (buckwheat is mixed in with the corn). As with Varenna's hotels, many of these restaurants close off-season (generally November through February or March).

DINING WITH A LAKE VIEW

$$$$ Ristorante la Vista, at Albergo Milano, feels like a private hotel restaurant but also welcomes nonguests. On a balmy evening, their terrace overlooking the town and the lake is hard to beat. Egidio (or Egi—pronounced "edgy") and his staff give traditional cuisine a creative twist, and his selection is great for foodies with discerning tastes. While you can order à la carte, I'd go with his €40 three-course fixed-price dinner (Mon and Wed-Sat 19:00-22:00, closed Sun except June-Aug, closed Tue year-round; reservations required, Via XX Settembre 35, tel. 0341-830-298, www. varenna.net).

$$$$ Ristorante la Contrada, with its terrace-side location, is run by the Villa Cipressi and takes advantage of the villa's elegant garden, trickling fountain, and lake view. Indoor seating glows with a warm and romantic air, and the garden is a delight on warm summer evenings. Fresh daily specialties and professional service make this a worthwhile splurge. However, weddings can crowd the place and distract from the service (daily 12:15-14:30 & 19:15-22:00, may close for weddings, Via IV Novembre 22, tel. 0341-830-113, www.hotelvillacipressi.it).

Restaurant Price Code

I've assigned each eatery a price category, based on the average cost of a typical main course (pasta or *secondi*). Drinks, desserts, and splurge items (steak and seafood) can raise the price considerably.

$$$$	**Splurge:**	Most main courses over €20
$$$	**Pricier:**	€15-20
$$	**Moderate:**	€10-15
$	**Budget:**	Under €10

In Italy, pizza by the slice and other takeaway food is **$**; a basic trattoria or sit-down pizzeria is **$$**; a casual but more upscale restaurant is **$$$**; and a swanky splurge is **$$$$**.

DINING WITHOUT A LAKE VIEW

$$$ Ristorante il Cavatappi, a classy little place on a quiet lane just off the town square, has only seven tables, so the cook-and-waiter team can connect personally with diners (Thu-Sun 12:00-14:00 & 18:30-21:00, Mon-Wed 12:00-14:00 only, closed Oct-March, reservations recommended for dinner, Via XX Settembre 10, tel. 0341-815-349, www.cavatappivarenna.it).

$$$ Osteria Quatro Pass is a welcoming bistro known for its homemade pasta, lake fish, and meat. It offers 18 candlelit tables under picturesque vaults, plus sidewalk seating. Its fun energy lets you know that it's a popular spot (daily 12:00-14:00 & 18:30-22:00, closed Wed in winter, Via XX Settembre 20, tel. 0341-815-091; Lilly serves while her son Giuseppe cooks).

$$$ Varenna Monamour's split-level interior, done up with stone and beams, feels sleek but casual. Their menu has a nouvelle cuisine flair, and they pride themselves on specializing in seafood—not lake fish (May-Sept daily 12:00-14:30 & 18:30-23:30, shorter hours and closed Tue off-season, Contrada Scoscesa 7, tel. 0341-814-016, www.varennamonamour.it).

EATING SIMPLY ON THE WATER

Along the waterfront in Varenna's old section are two simple eateries, both with great lakefront seating and relaxed (read: slow) service. Either of these is ideal for lingering over affordable (but forgettable) food in a stunning setting.

$$ Nilus Bar, with a young waitstaff, serves crêpes, pizzas, big mixed salads, hot sandwiches, soup of the day, a few pastas, and cocktails (Wed-Mon 12:00-22:30, closed Tue, bar open longer, tel. 0341-815-228, Fulvia and Giovanni).

$$ Bar Il Molo, next door, is good for a casual meal on the harbor or a gelato with a view (daily 11:00-24:00, free Wi-Fi, tel. 0341-830-070). They also have a room full of gifty edibles for sale.

LAKES

EATING SIMPLY WITHOUT A LAKE VIEW

$$$ Ristorante del Sole, facing the town square, serves respectable, well-priced meals and Neapolitan-style pizzas. This family-friendly restaurant provides a fun atmosphere, a cozy, walled-in garden in back, and tables on the square. Try their delicious and hearty *pizzocchere,* a handmade buckwheat pasta with melted cheese, potatoes, and greens (daily 11:00-16:00 & 18:30-late, closed Tue Nov-Feb, free Wi-Fi, Piazza San Giorgio 17, tel. 0341-815-218, www.albergodelsolevarenna.it; Francesco and Enzo).

High Above Town: **$$$ Ristorante il Caminetto** is a homey, backwoods mountain trattoria in Gittana, a tiny town in the hills above Varenna. Getting there entails a curvy 10-minute drive—they'll pick you up for free in Piazza San Giorgio, deliver you to the restaurant, and then dish up classic fare at small-town prices. Moreno, Rossella, and daughter Francesca take pride in their specialties, including grilled meats and risotto with porcini mushrooms and berries. This is a good place to set a price and trust your host to bring whatever's best (€28 three-course fixed-price meal, open Thu-Tue 19:30-21:30, Sat-Sun also 12:30-14:30, closed Wed, reservations mandatory to confirm pickup from Varenna, Viale Progresso 4, tel. 0341-815-127, mobile 347-331-2238, www.ilcaminettoonline.com).

OTHER EATERIES

$$ Pub l'Orso is the hot spot in town for wine or beer and a light meal. Oozing character, it's behind Hotel Olivedo in a renovated shed that used to be a joiner's workshop (closed Mon). The venerable **$$$ Vecchia Varenna** is the only classy restaurant actually on the harbor (old place with new management). And at **$$$ Hotel Olivedo,** a grand old hotel facing the ferry dock, you can eat in a classic dining hall.

Pizza: $ Ristorante del Sole is known among locals for quality, well-priced pizza. Across the piazza, **Victoria Grill** (at the recommended Hotel Royal Victoria) offers slightly higher-priced pizza that you can enjoy on-site or as takeaway.

Gelato: At **Gelateria Riva,** overlooking the water, get a cup or cone to go, then grab a pillowy seat on the bulkhead. Duilio is the only guy in town who prepares his gelato fresh every day. Try his *nocciola* (hazelnut) before making your choice. Ask the day before if you want to watch the gelato being made (daily 10:30-19:00, open later June-Sept).

Picnics: Varenna's two little grocery stores have all you need for a tasty balcony or breakwater picnic. The *salumeria* on the main square is best for meats, cheese, and bread; try their homemade salami (Tue-Sat 8:30-12:30 & 16:00-19:30, Sun-Mon 8:30-12:30 only, Via IV Novembre 2). The store just north of the main square by the pharmacy stocks fresh fruits, veggies, and a few essentials (June-Sept Tue-Sat 7:30-19:00, Sun-Mon until 12:30; Oct-May daily 7:30-12:30 plus Tue-Sat 16:00-19:30, Via Venini 6).

At the Train Station: $ Café III Binario adds charm and class, offering fresh salads, homemade pizza, sandwiches, pasta, pastries, and even breakfast for those with early departures. Enjoy your food on their terrace or take it to go (Mon-Sat 6:00-22:00, Sun from 7:00, closes earlier off-season).

Varenna Connections

BY TRAIN

Before leaving Varenna, buy your tickets from the I Viaggi del Tivano travel agency in the station. (Or, to avoid lines and stress at the station, buy tickets in advance in the town center at the Barilott bar/tobacco shop just off the main square.) Stamp your ticket in the yellow machine at the station before boarding. If the office is closed and you can't buy tickets, win the sympathy of the conductor and buy your ticket as soon as you get on board for a small additional fee. (Find him before he finds you—or you'll face a €50 fine.)

Varenna to Milan: Trains from Varenna to Milano Centrale take about an hour and leave at :37 past most hours (with a few two-hour gaps; confirm schedule at the station or online at www.trenitalia.com). Additional connections require a change in Lecco and an extra 30 minutes.

Varenna to Stresa (on Lake Maggiore): You'll have to take the train back to Milano Centrale, then connect from there to Stresa (3-4 hours).

Varenna to St. Moritz (Switzerland): Take the train from Varenna to Tirano (1 hour), where you'll have a layover before boarding the scenic Bernina Express train to St. Moritz (another 2.5 hours, 3 connections/day in summer, 1/day late Oct-early May, www.rhb.ch). A quicker, more frequent, but less scenic route is to take the train to Chiavenna (changing in Colico), then transfer to the bus, which takes you over the Maloja Pass to St. Moritz (5-6/day, 3.5 hours total). For times and tickets, stop by the I Viaggi del Tivano travel agency (see "Helpful Hints," earlier). Don't forget your passport for trips into Switzerland.

Bellagio

The self-proclaimed "Pearl of the Lake" is a classy combination of tidiness and Old World elegance. If you don't mind that "tramp in a palace" feeling, it's a fine place to shop for ties and umbrellas while surrounding yourself with the more adventurous posh travelers. Heavy curtains between the harborfront arcades create welcome shade and keep visitors and their poodles from sweating. Thriving yet still cute, Bellagio is a much more substantial town than Varenna. And as much as I'd like to disdain a town that gave its name to a Las Vegas casino, I gotta admit—Bellagio is pretty nice.

Orientation to Bellagio

TOURIST INFORMATION

The TI is at the passenger boat and hydrofoil dock (Mon-Sat 9:00-12:30 & 13:30-17:30, Sun 10:30-12:30 & 14:30-17:30, shorter hours Nov-March, tel. 031-950-204, www.bellagiolakecomo.com). The TI has free brochures for three well-crafted walking tours, varying from one to three hours, all of which explore the city and environs. They also sell a hiking map that shows four different hikes with a range of difficulty and duration.

ARRIVAL IN BELLAGIO

Bellagio is best reached by boat from Varenna or Como.

By Boat: Bellagio has two sets of docks a couple of hundred yards apart. (When you depart, be sure you're at the right dock—ask when you buy your ticket.) For more details on boat schedules, see "Getting Around Lake Como," page 224).

By Car: Parking is difficult, but you can try for a spot near the lake, in the parking lot at the ferry dock, or at the top of town adjacent to San Giacomo Church. Spaces marked with white lines are always free, yellow lines are for residents only, and blue lines are pay-to-park (use pay-and-display machines—€1.50/hour from 8:00-20:00, free overnight).

HELPFUL HINTS

Market: There's a lakeside market every third Wednesday of the month.

Laundry: La Lavandera is handy. Don't be discouraged if it looks closed; the lights come on automatically when you enter (wash-€4, dry-€4.50, detergent-€1, coins only, change machine, daily 24 hours, Salita Carlo Grandi 21, tel. 339-410-6852).

Sights and Activities in Bellagio

Villa Serbelloni Park

If you need a destination, you can visit this park (accessible only with guided tour), which overlooks the town. The villa itself, owned by the Rockefeller Foundation, is not open to the public.

Cost and Hours: €9, required tour mid-March-Oct Tue-Sun at 11:00 and 15:30; no tours Mon, Nov-mid-March, or when rainy; 1.5 hours, first two-thirds of walk is uphill, show up at the little tour office in the medieval tower on Piazza della Chiesa 15 minutes before tour time to buy tickets, confirm time at office, tel. 031-951-555.

Strolling

Explore the steep-stepped lanes rising from the harborfront. While Johnnie Walker and jewelry sell best at lake level, the natives shop up the hill. Piazza della Chiesa, near the top of town, has a worth-a-look church (with a golden altarpiece under glitter-ing mosaics; pick up the Eng-lish handout that describes its art).

North of Town: The de facto capital of the mid-lake re-gion, Bellagio is located where the two legs of the lake split off to the south. For an easy break in a park with a great view, wander right on out to the crotch. Mean-der behind the rich and famous Hotel Villa Serbelloni, and walk 10 minutes up a concrete alley to **Punta Spartivento** ("Point that Divides the Wind"). You'll pop out to find a Renoir atmosphere complete with an inviting bar-restaurant (see "Eating in Bellagio," later), a tiny harbor, and a chance to sit on a park bench and gaze north past Menaggio, Varenna, and the end of the lake to the Swiss Alps.

South of Town: For another stroll, head south from the car-ferry dock down the tree-shaded promenade. Ten minutes later, you'll pass the town's concrete swimming area and then the pleas-ant **Villa Melzi Gardens.** This lakeside expanse of exotic plants, flowers, trees, and Neoclassical sculpture was assembled by the vice president of Napoleon's Italian Republic in the early 19th century. Although a bit pricey and not as elaborate as some of the lake's finer gardens, it has a pleasant, tree-shaded promenade for a lakefront stroll. At the entrance, pick up the map identifying both sculptures and plants (€6.50, April-Oct daily 9:30-18:30, closed Nov-March, mobile 339-457-3838, www.giardinidivillamelzi.it).

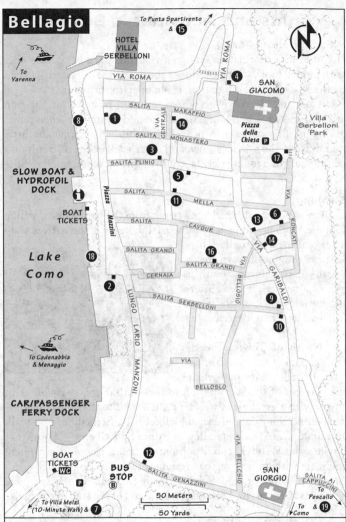

Bellagio

1. Hotel Florence
2. Hotel/Rist./Snack Bar Metropole
3. Hotel Centrale
4. Albergo Europa
5. Il Borgo Apartments
6. Bellagio B&B Apartments
7. To Giardini di Villa Melzini Apartments
8. The Florence Ristorante
9. Trattoria San Giacomo
10. Bilacus Ristorante & Aperitivo Et Al
11. Rist. Terrazza Barchetta
12. Enoteca Cava Turacciolo
13. Gelateria del Borgo
14. Groceries (2)
15. To La Punta Ristorante
16. Launderette
17. Villa Serbelloni Park Tickets
18. Bellagio Water-Limousines Lake Tours
19. To Bellagio Water Sports (Kayak Tours)

About 15 minutes beyond the far end of the garden, you'll reach San Giovanni, with a pebbly public beach (no showers).

Boating and Water Sports

With a small stand at the boat docks, **Bellagio Water Limousines** (run by Australian Jennine and Italian Luca) offers tours and private service in their luxurious and powerful boat. Their basic 2.5-hour tour, guided by Luca, includes a fun hour at mid-lake, with a float-by of Richard Branson's villa, as well as a stop at Villa del Balbianello, where you'll take an English tour (€55, 10 percent discount if you reserve directly and bring this book, price includes entry and tour of villa, generally runs April-Oct Tue and Thu-Sun at 13:30 and also often at 11:00, different tours Mon and Wed, check blackboard for day's offerings or call mobile 338-524-4914, www.bellagiowaterlimousines.com, bellagiowaterlimousines@gmail.com).

At **Bellagio Water Sports,** friendly Michele offers kayaking tours within a 10-minute walk of the town center. His popular two-hour tour (€35) covers the Bellagio coast, while his three-hour tour (€45) includes a stop at Villa Melzi. He also rents kayaks for those willing to go solo. Book in advance or call ahead to be sure he is there (no tours Sun, weather-dependent late March and Oct, closed Nov-mid-March, located on Pescallo Bay near Hotel La Pergola at Via Sfondrati 1, mobile 340-394-9375, www.bellagiowatersports.com, info@bellagiowatersports.com).

Sleeping in Bellagio

($$$$ = Splurge, $$$ = Pricier, $$ = Moderate, $ = Budget)

This is a "boom or bust" lake resort, with high-season prices (those listed here) straight through from May to September, plus a brief shoulder season (with discounted prices) in April and from October to November. Bellagio closes down almost completely from December to February and is only half-open in March.

$$$$ Hotel Florence has a prime lakefront setting in the center of town. The 160-year-old, family-run place features 30 rooms, hardwood floors, bold earth tones with splashes of bright colors, and a rich touch of Old World elegance (some rooms with view and balcony, air-con, elevator, Piazza Mazzini 46, tel. 031-950-342, www.hotelflorencebellagio.it, info@hotelflorencebellagio.it, run by the Austrian Ketzlar family).

$$$ Hotel Metropole, dominating Bellagio's waterfront between the ferry docks, is a grand old place with plush public spaces. Its modern rooms have all the comforts and classic flair. All of its 42 rooms have lake views, either side or full (air-con, elevator, stunning roof terrace, Piazza Mazzini 1, tel. 031-950-409, www. albergometropole.it, info@albergometropole.it).

$$$ Hotel Centrale, managed with pride and care by Giacomo Borelli, warmly welcomes its guests into a true-blue family operation: Signore Borelli's two sons help out, his mama painted the art, and grandpa crafted much of the Art Deco-era furniture. The 17 bright, comfortable but dated rooms lack views, but the public spaces are generous (air-con, elevator, free calls to North America from reception, Salita Plinio 7, tel. 031-951-940, www.hc-bellagio. com, info@hc-bellagio.com).

$$ Albergo Europa, run with low energy, is in a concrete annex behind a restaurant, away from the waterfront. Its nine basic rooms are harmlessly behind the times but get the job done (no elevator, free parking, Via Roma 21, tel. 031-950-471, www. hoteleuropabellagio.it, info@hoteleuropabellagio.it, Marchesi family).

$$ Il Borgo Apartments offers seven efficient, modern units in the old center. Equipped with kitchenettes, these are a great deal for families or small groups. Easygoing Flavio is available for check-in daily 11:00-14:00, or by appointment (RS%, cash preferred, no breakfast, air-con, elevator, Salita Plinio 4, tel. 031-952-497, mobile 338-193-5559, www.borgoresidence.it, info@borgoresidence.it).

$ Bellagio B&B Apartments rents three units at the top of town, up the street from the *gelateria* (kitchens but no breakfast, Salita Cavour 37, tel. 031-951-680, www.bellagiobedandbreakfast. com, info@bellagiobedandbreakfast.com). Owner Giulio also has five large apartments a 15-minute walk from Bellagio (toward Como, www.bellagioronchi.com).

South of Town: About a 15-minute walk south of Bellagio, **$$ Giardini di Villa Melzi Apartments** features three modern doubles and three studios with kitchenettes in the little harbor of Loppia. A free pass allows guests to take a shortcut to Bellagio through the Villa Melzi Gardens (cash only, no breakfast, free parking, Via Melzi d'Eril 23, at the southern entrance to the gardens, tel. 339-221-4394, www.facebook.com/bellagiowelcome, appbellagio@gmail.com or info@bellagiowelcome.com, Ornella).

Eating in Bellagio

ON THE LAKEFRONT
($$$$ = Splurge, $$$ = Pricier, $$ = Moderate, $ = Budget)
The restaurants in these two recommended hotels offer wonderful lakeside tables and, considering the setting, acceptable prices.

Hotel Metropole's **$$$ Terrazzo Ristorante,** while a mediocre food value, has a full menu and is a relaxing delight with good service. **$$ Hotel Metropole Snack Bar,** next to the restaurant, with good service in a great location, has simple pastas and sandwiches and fine salads (both open long hours daily, restaurant closes for midafternoon break, Piazza Mazzini 1, tel. 031-950-409).

$$$ The Florence is nicely situated under a trellis of flowers across from the Florence Hotel, away from the ferry fumes. This is a lovely perch for a drink or dinner (also simpler lunch menu of salads and lighter fare, April-Sept daily 12:00-14:30 & 19:00-22:00, bar open all day, tel. 031-950-342).

IN THE OLD TOWN, WITHOUT LAKE VIEWS

$$ Trattoria San Giacomo is a high-energy place with traditional cuisine, such as *riso e filetto di pesce* (rice and perch fillet in butter and sage). It has seasonal specials and inviting €25 fixed-price meals (choose meat or fish) based on regional specialties. It offers fun seating on a steep, cobbled lane or tight seating inside (Mon and Wed-Thu 12:00-14:30 & 19:00-21:30, Fri-Sun open later midday and evenings, closed Tue, Salita Serbelloni 45, tel. 031-950-329, www.trattoriabellagio.it, Aurelio).

Across the street and sharing the same owner, **$$ Bilacus Ristorante** has a brighter, more open dining room, a fine garden terrace, an emphasis on wine (including some top-quality vintages by the glass), and a menu with a bit more variety beyond local specials (Tue-Sun 11:30-15:00 & 18:30-22:00, closed Mon, Salita Serbelloni 32, tel. 031-950-480, www.bilacusbellagio.it).

$$$ Ristorante Terrazza Barchetta, set on a terrace with no lake view and bedecked with summery colors, puts a creative twist on regional favorites such as lake fish. Don't confuse it with the street-level bar-trattoria—head up the stairs to the second floor. Reservations are recommended (daily 12:00-23:00, Salita Mella 13, tel. 031-951-389, www.ristorantebarchetta.com).

OTHER OPTIONS

Wine Tasting: Step into the vaulted stone cellar of the funky **$$$ Enoteca Cava Turacciolo** to taste three regional wines with a sampling of cheeses, meats, and breads (€19 for Rick Steves readers, April-Oct Thu-Tue 10:30-24:00, shorter hours Nov-Dec and March, closed Wed and Jan-Feb, Salita Genazzini 3, tel. 031-950-975, www.cavaturacciolo.it, Norberto and Rosy). **$$$ Aperitivo Et Al,** slick and jazzy, is a trendier wine bar; it also offers mixed *salumi* and *formaggi* plates, big fresh salads, and light lunches. There's a great selection of wines by the glass (daily 11:30-24:00, closed Mon off-season, Wi-Fi, Salita Serbelloni 34, tel. 031-951-523).

Gelato: Residents agree that you won't find the best *gelate-*

ria in town among the sundaes served on the waterfront. Instead, climb to the top of town to **Gelateria del Borgo** (late March-Oct daily 10:00-20:00, longer hours July-Aug, Via Garibaldi 46, tel. 031-950-755, Stefania and Gianfranco).

Picnics: You'll find benches at the park, along the waterfront in town, and lining the promenade south of town. Two little groceries can make sandwiches and also sell a few prepared foods: the fancier **Butti Macelleria e Salumeria,** on the upper street near the *gelateria* (Tue-Sat 8:00-13:00 & 16:00-19:00, Sun 8:00-13:00, closed Mon, Via Garibaldi 42, tel. 031-950-333); and the simpler **Gastronomia Antichi Sapori,** on a cross street below the church (Tue-Fri 8:30-13:00 & 15:30-19:00, Sat-Sun 8:30-18:00, closed Mon, Via Centrale 3, tel. 031-950-431).

Punta Spartivento: This dramatic natural park, a 10-minute walk north of town (see "Strolling," page 241), is a great place for either a picnic or a meal at the family-run **$$ La Punta Ristorante**—try the fish; it was swimming in the lake this morning (March-Oct daily 11:00-22:00, tel. 031-951-888, www.ristorantelapunta.it).

More Sights on Lake Como

For the best one-day look at Lake Como, take my self-guided ferry tour to get your bearings, and hop off at the towns and villas of your choice. The two main villas worth considering (both described after the tour) are Villa Carlotta—with a sterile, museum-like interior and gorgeous, sprawling gardens—and Villa del Balbianello, a bit harder to reach but with a more striking setting, gardens that are more architectural than botanical, and a fascinating tour of the lived-in interior. If you have time, visit both—they're complementary. In this section, I also describe two other lake towns: Menaggio and Como, plus how to side-trip to Lugano in Switzerland.

▲▲Self-Guided Ferry Tour

The best simple day out is to take the *battello navetta* (mid-lake ferry) on its entire 50-minute Varenna-Bellagio-Villa Carlotta-

Tremezzo-Lenno route (generally departs Varenna at :23 past each hour, confirm times locally; for more information, see page 224). On the return trip, hop off at any sights that interest you: Lenno (to see Villa del Balbianello), Villa Carlotta, and/or Bellagio. This commentary describes what you'll see along the way, leaving from Varenna, though it's doable from Bellagio too.

Leaving Varenna: Looking back at Varenna from the lake, you'll see Vezio Castle rising above the town, with new Varenna on the left (bigger buildings and modern ferry dock), and old Varenna on the right (tighter, more colorful buildings). The big development

high on the hillside is an ugly example of cronyism (without the mayor involved, this would never have happened). Under the castle is a grove of olives— reputedly the northernmost ones grown in Italy. Because the lake is protected from the north wind, exotic flowers grow well in the lake's many fine gardens.

To the right of Varenna's castle are the town cemetery, a lift up to Hotel Eremo Gaudio (a former hermitage), and a spurt of water gushing out of the mountain just above lake level. This is the tiny Fiumelatte, Italy's shortest river.

• *On your way across to Bellagio, take a look around.*

Mid-Lake: The Swiss Alps rise to the north. Directly across the lake from Varenna is Menaggio, and just over the ridge from there are Lugano and the "Swiss Riviera." The winds alternate between north and south. In preindustrial times, traders harnessed the wind to sail up and down the lake. Notice the V-shaped, fjord-like terrain. Lake Como is glacier-cut. And, at more than 1,200 feet deep, it's Europe's deepest lake. You'll cruise past the Punta Spartivento, the bulbous point that literally "splits the wind," and where the two "legs" of the lake join (Lake Lecco is on the left/east, and Lake Como on the right).

• *Before long, you'll be...*

Approaching Bellagio: Survey the park at Punta Spartiven-to—it's a pleasant walk from town. Bellagio has three times the

number of hotel rooms as Varenna, as you can see upon approach. The town, with its strip of swanky hotels, is bookended by Villa Serbelloni (five stars) on the left, dominating the lakefront, and the sprawling Grand Hotel Bretagne (four stars) on the right. In the 19th century, aristocratic Russians hung out in the Serbelloni, and well-heeled English chose the Bretagne. These days, the Serbelloni is the second-most-luxurious hotel on the lake after Villa d'Este, while Bretagne is mired in a long renovation project.

• *Leaving Bellagio, about half the boats make a stop at* **San Giovanni,** *a small, nondescript lakefront community just down the shore from Bellagio. Whether your boat stops here or not, soon you'll head across the lake for a stop at...*

Villa Carlotta: Because of lake taxes and high maintenance costs, owners of once-elite villas have been forced to turn them into hotels or to open their doors to the paying public. Since 1927, this has been an example of the latter. One of the finest properties on the lake, Villa Carlotta has some good Neoclassical sculpture (including works by Canova) and one of the lake's lushest gardens (see listing below).

• *The shortest hop on this route (you could walk it in less than 10 minutes) takes you along to the town of...*

Tremezzo: As you leave the dock at Villa Carlotta, notice the Grand Hotel Tremezzo, with its striking Liberty-Style (Art Nouveau) facade and swimming pool floating on the lake. Above the town is a villa built in the 19th-century Romantic Age to resemble a medieval castle (next to the stub of a real one).

After the Tremezzo stop—and just before the Tremezzo church—you'll see a public park with a fountain and balustrade. When the road separated this land from its villa, its owners gave it to the community. Here the lake is dotted by a string of old villas with elegant landings and gated boathouses. Built in the days before motors, they are now too small for most modern lake boats.

Lenno: This pleasant resort town—with a long, arcing bay sheltering lots of little docks, and a generously shaded promenade—is the boat's last stop.

It's decision time: If you want to see the recommended **Villa del Balbianello,** hop off here and skip ahead to facing page. Return boats depart hourly; check the schedule before you set off. If you'd prefer to sail back to **Villa Carlotta, Bellagio,** or **Varenna,** you can probably stay put—this is the end of the line, so the boat's going to turn around and head back that way (but for some departures, you may be evicted and need to wait for the next boat).

▲Villa Carlotta

For gardens and flowers (its forte), this is the best of Lake Como's famed villas—especially in spring, when the many flowers are in bloom. For gardeners, it's worth ▲▲▲. I see the lakes as a break from Italy's art, but if you need a culture fix, Villa Carlotta also offers an elegant Neoclas-

sical interior with a sculpture gallery, including works by Antonio Canova.

Cost and Hours: €9 includes villa/museum and gardens, daily April-mid-Oct 9:00-19:30, last ticket sold at 18:00, museum closes at 18:30, shorter hours last 2 weeks of March and mid-Oct-mid-Nov, closed mid-Nov-mid-March, tel. 034-440-405, www.villacarlotta.it.

Getting There: Villa Carlotta, at the southern end of the town of Tremezzo, has its own ferry dock (served by the *battello* passenger ferries). It's also less than a 10-minute walk from the Tremezzo and Cadenabbia docks (each served by a variety of boats). In a pinch, you can also use bus #C10 to zip along the lakefront to Lenno, near Villa del Balbianello (1-2/hour, buy ticket on bus, bus stop to the right as you exit Villa Carlotta).

Visiting the Villa: When buying your ticket, pick up the map that identifies the rooms in the house and the major plant groups in the gardens.

From the entrance, hike up the grand staircase and enter the **villa** itself. The main floor is filled with Neoclassical sculpture, including Antonio Canova's *Maddalena Penitente* and *Palamede* and works by his students (look for the impressive replica of Canova's famous *Love and Psyche Reclining*). There are also pieces by the great Danish sculptor Bertel Thorvaldsen. On the next floor up are generally well-presented special exhibits, and on the top floor are painstakingly appointed period rooms with elegant Empire Style furniture.

Then explore the main attraction, the **gardens,** which sprawl in both directions from the villa. To the south (toward Tremezzo) is the classical Old Garden. To the north, things get more interesting: pretty camellias, luscious azaleas, a maze of rhododendrons, a bamboo garden, and the gasp-worthy Valley of the Ferns—a lush jungle gorge with a river coursing through it.

▲▲Villa del Balbianello

The dreamiest villa on the lake perches on a romantic promontory near Lenno, overlooking Lake Como and facing Bellagio. Built

at the end of the 18th century on the remains of an old Franciscan church, today the villa reflects the exotic vision of its last owner, explorer and mountaineer Guido Monzino, who died in 1988—leaving his villa and everything in it to the state. It's well worth paying extra to tour the interior to get to know Monzino, who led the first Italian expedition to climb Mount Everest in 1973. But the real masterpiece here is

LAKES

the terraced garden and elegant loggia, where the land fits the architecture and landscaping in a lovely way. This is a favorite choice for movie directors when they need a far-out villa to feature; this is where James Bond recovered from a particularly bruising experience in *Casino Royale,* and where Anakin first kissed Padmé (and later married her) in *Star Wars: Episode II—Attack of the Clones.*

Cost and Hours: Garden only—€8, garden with villa tour—€17, Thu-Sun and Tue 10:00-18:00, closed Mon and Wed and mid-Nov-mid-March, last entry to garden 45 minutes before closing, tel. 034-456-110, www.visitfai.it/villadelbalbianello.

Tours: The only way inside the villa is with an English tour. Limited to 15 people per tour, these depart at least hourly (more frequently with demand); the first tour is usually at 11:15 and the last at 16:30.

Getting There: It's at the end of a hilly point next to the town of Lenno. From the Lenno ferry dock, turn left and stroll around to the far end of the harbor (about 5 minutes). Here, you can either pay for a **speedboat shuttle** (€5.50 one-way, €7.50 round-trip, mobile 333-410-3854) or carry on by foot. If you choose to **walk,** continue past the boat dock and through the gate marked *Via del Balbianello,* where two options are clearly signposted in kilometers: a 20-minute, 1-kilometer (half-mile) hike (including some up and down), or a more challenging 45-minute, 2.5-kilometer (about 1 mile) huff over the top.

Visiting the Villa: Your visit includes two parts: the villa and the gardens.

Poke around the **gardens** while waiting for your villa tour to begin. On the Bellagio-facing side, you'll find a tranquil terrace with sweeping lake views. Along the path, notice the circular stone shed.  Originally used for refrigeration (they used ice from the mountains to keep things cool), today this shed houses the tomb of Guido Monzino. On the opposite side of the point, you'll find a terrace in front of the original Franciscan church (now a gift shop selling overpriced drinks). A WC is nearby, and just down the steps is the dock for the speed boat return to Lenno.

The 50-minute tour of the **villa** is as fascinating as its larger-than-life former owner. You'll tour the loggia (with a library and a study), then spend the rest of the time seeing 18 of the main building's 25 rooms. While finely decorated, these feel cozy, lived-in, and not too extravagant. Each one gives you a bit more insight into Monzino, from his personal living quarters, to his extensive collection of prehistoric artifacts from around the world, to the top-floor museum of his expeditions, with memorabilia from his North Pole and Mount Everest adventures. You'll see secret passages, learn why his furniture came with handles, and find out what's hiding behind the faux bookcase.

Menaggio

Menaggio—the third of the "big three" mid-lake towns (along with Varenna and Bellagio)—has more urban bulk than its neigh-

bors, but visitors are charmed by its lovely lakefront park. Since many find Lake Como too dirty for swimming, consider spending time in Menaggio's fine public pool (look for the *lido*). This is the starting point for a few hikes. (Just a few decades ago, cigarette smugglers used these trails at night to sneak back into Italy from Switzerland with their tax-free booty.) The TI has information about mountain biking and catching the bus to trailheads on nearby Mount Grona. Ask for the free *Walking in the Province of Como* booklet, with information on 18 different walks detailing historical, artistic, and natural features (**TI** on Piazza Garibaldi, tel. 0344-32-924, www.menaggio.com, infomcnaggio@tiscali.it).

Sleeping in Menaggio: ¢ La Primula Youth Hostel is a classic, old-school hostel, offering sailing lessons, Italian-language courses, cooking classes, kayak and bike rentals, and a great location on the lake, a two-minute walk from the ferry dock (Via IV Novembre 106, tel. 0344-32356, www.lakecomohostel.com, info@lakecomohostel.com).

Menaggio Connections: In addition to being connected to Varenna and Bellagio by all the regular boats, bus #C10 connects Menaggio to **Como town** in about an hour (1-2/hour): Menaggio is also a springboard for visiting Switzerland. Public bus #C12 departs about every hour or two from Piazza Roma for **Lugano** (around €10 round-trip, 1 hour, buy tickets at bus stop on Via Calvi). In summer, the yellow Palm Express bus runs once daily to **St. Moritz** (3.5 hours; off-season runs only weekends; reservations are required, www.postbus.ch)—remember to bring your passport.

Como Town

On the southwest tip of the lake, Como has a good, traffic-free old town, an interesting Gothic/Renaissance cathedral, a cable car up to a mountaintop viewpoint, and a pleasant lakefront with a promenade (**TI** at Piazza Cavour 17, tel. 031-269-712, www.lakecomo.it). It's an easy 10-minute walk from the boat dock to the train station (trains to Milan depart about twice per hour, 30-60 minutes).

For details on the two types of boats that connect Como to Bellagio and Varenna—the slow 2.5-hour ferry and the speedy 1-hour hydrofoil—see page 224.

All-Day Lugano Side-Trip

From Varenna or Bellagio, you can make a loop that lets you nip into Switzerland to see the elegant lake resort of Lugano, pass through the town of Como, and cruise a good part of Lake Como. Here's a good day plan (times are approximate—confirm schedules locally): about 9:30—ferry to Menaggio (15 minutes from Varenna); 10:30—bus to Lugano (1 hour, bring your passport); 11:30—explore Lugano; 16:00—train to Como (45 minutes); 17:00/18:00/19:00—fast hydrofoil from Como to Varenna (1 hour). For more information on Lugano, see www.ricksteves.com/lugano.

Lake Maggiore

Lake Maggiore is ringed by mountains, snowcapped in spring and fall, and lined with resort towns such as Stresa. Although Lake Maggiore lacks the cozy charm of Lake Como, a visit here may be worth the trouble for two islands, both with exotic gardens and lovely villas built by the Borromeo family.

The Borromeos—through many generations since 1630—lovingly turned their islands into magical retreats, with elaborate villas and fragrant gardens. Isola Bella has a palace and terraced garden; Isola Madre has a villa and sprawling English-style (more casual) garden. A third island, Isola Superiore (a.k.a. Isola Pescatori), is simply small, serene, and residential. The Borromeos, who made their money from trade and banking, enjoyed the arts—from paintings (hung in lavish abundance throughout the palace and villa) to plays (performed in an open-air theater on Isola Bella) and marionette shows (you'll see the puppets that once performed here). Although it's a characterless resort, the town of Stresa is a handy departure point for exploring Lake Maggiore's exotic garden islands.

Tourists flock here in May and June, when flowers are in bloom, and in September. Concerts held in scenic settings draw music lovers, particularly during the summer Stresa Festival (get details from Stresa TI). For fewer crowds, visit in April, July, August (when Italians prefer the Mediterranean beaches), or October. In winter, the snow-covered mountains (with resorts a 1.5-hour drive away) attract skiers.

PLANNING YOUR TIME

This region is best visited on a sunny day, when the mountains are clear, the lake is calm, and the heat of the sun brings out the scent of the blossoms. The two top islands for sightseeing are Isola Bella and Isola Madre (if tight on time, focus on Isola Bella). Isola Superiore has no sights, but is a peaceful place for lunch. You can stay the night in Stresa, but a day trip is sufficient for most.

Day Trip from Milan: Catch the one-hour, early train from Milan to the town of Stresa (usually at 8:25, which may require reservations, and likely also at 9:29—but check times carefully, as there's often a midmorning gap until 11:25). Upon arrival in Stresa, walk 10 minutes downhill to the boat dock, and catch a boat to Isola Madre. Work your way back to Isola Superiore for a lazy lunch, and then go on to Isola Bella for the afternoon, before returning to Stresa and back to Milan (trains leave about hourly—jot down your departure options on arrival in Stresa).

GETTING AROUND LAKE MAGGIORE

Boats link the islands and Stresa, running about twice hourly. Allow roughly 10 minutes between stops. Since short round-trip hops can add up fast (€6.80 for Isola Bella, €7.80 for Isola Superiore, €10 for Isola Madre, €12.40 for Villa Taranto), it's usually best to buy a **free circulation ticket,** which allows you to get off and on at intermediate stops between your departure and arrival ports (for instance, €13.80 includes Bella and Superiore, €16.90 covers all the islands, and €20.70 includes the islands and Villa Taranto).

Boats run daily April through September. The map on page 255 shows most of the route: Stresa, Carciano/Lido (at the base of the cable car—but most boats skip this stop), Isola Bella, Isola Superiore, Baveno (lakeside town), Isola Madre, Pallanza, and Villa Taranto. This route is part of a longer one. To follow the boat schedule (free, available at boat docks and the TI), look at the Arona-Locarno timetable for trips from Stresa to the islands, and the Locarno-Arona timetable for the return trip to Stresa. Off-season, the boats cover a shorter route (public boat info: toll-free tel. 800-551-801, www.navigazionelaghi.it).

Buy boat tickets directly from the dock ticket booth under the gallery to the left of the TI. On the promenade to the boat dock, don't be fooled by the private taxi-boat drivers, most dressed in sailor outfits—they'll try to talk you into paying way too much for private tours on their smaller boats.

LAKES

Sights on Lake Maggiore

Don't linger in Stresa—it's just a functional springboard. The main attractions are the islands and gardens.

STRESA

The town of Stresa—which means "thin stretch"—was named for the original strip of fishermen's huts that lined the shore. Today, grand old hotels run along that same shore.

Arrival in Stresa and Orientation: At the train station, ask for a free city map at the newsstand (to the far right of the tracks as you exit the train). To get downtown, exit right from the station and take your first left (on Viale Duchessa di Genova). This takes you straight down to the lake (once you're there, the boat dock is about four blocks to your right; ask for boat schedule at ticket window). The helpful **TI** is located to the right of the ticket window at the boat dock (March-Oct daily 10:00-12:30 & 15:00-18:30, off-season closed Sat afternoon and all day Sun, Piazza Marconi 16, tel. 0323-31308, www.stresaturismo.it). Taxis charge a fixed rate of €11 for even the shortest ride in town.

Visiting Stresa: The **old town**—basically a traffic-free touristy shopping mall—is just a few blocks deep, stretching inland from the main boat dock. Stresa's stately 19th-century lakeside hotels date back to the days when this town was on the Grand Tour circuit.

In any Romantic Age resort like Stresa, hotels had names designed to appeal to Victorian aristocrats...like Regina Palace (rather than Palazzo), Astoria, Bristol, and Victoria.

The **Grand Hotel des Iles Borromees** was the first (built in 1862). In 1918, 19-year-old Ernest Hemingway—wounded in Slovenia as an ambulance driver for the Italian Red Cross—was taken to Stresa's Grand Hotel des Iles Borromees, which served, like its regal neighbors, as an infirmary during World War I. Hemingway returned to the same hotel in 1948, stayed in the same room (#205, now called the "Hemingway suite"—you can stay there for a couple of thousand dollars a night), and signed the guest book as "an old client." Another "old client" was Winston Churchill, who honeymooned here.

A fine waterfront promenade leads past the venerable old hotels to the Lido, with the Carciano boat dock and the **Stresa-Alpino-Mottarone cable car.** This cable car takes you up—in two stages and a 20-minute ride—to the top of Mount Mottarone (€19 round-trip to the top, €11.50 one-way, daily 9:30-17:30 in summer, shorter hours in winter, 2-3/hour, bar midway up, tel. 0323-30295, www.stresa-mottarone.it). From the top (about 5,000 feet), you get great panoramic views of neighboring peaks and, by taking a short

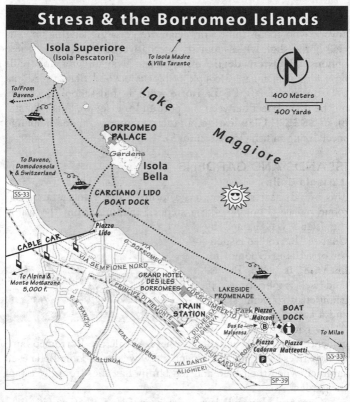

Stresa & the Borromeo Islands

Isola Superiore
(Isola Pescatori)

To Isola Madre
& Villa Taranto

To/From
Baveno

Lake

Maggiore

**BORROMEO
PALACE**

Gardens

To Baveno,
Domodossola
& Switzerland

Isola
Bella

SS-33

**CARCIANO / LIDO
BOAT DOCK**

Piazza
Lido

CABLE CAR

VIA
G. BORROMEO

VIA SEMPIONE NORD

To Alpina &
Monte Mottarone
5,000 f.

V. K. SANZIO

VIALE SIEMENS

V. SELVALUNGA

PRINCIPE DI PIEMONTE

**GRAND HOTEL
DES ILES
BORROMEES**

CORSO UMBERTO

DUCHESSA
DI GENOVA

**TRAIN
STATION**

VIA DANTE
ALIGHIERI

VIA GIOSUE CARDUCCI

LAKESIDE
PROMENADE

Park

Piazza
Marconi

Bus to
Malpensa

Piazza
Cadorna

**BOAT
DOCK**

To Milan

Piazza
Matteotti

SS-33

SP-39

400 Meters

400 Yards

LAKES

hike, a bird's-eye view of the small, neighboring Lake Orta (described later).

Halfway up the cable-car line are the **Alpine Gardens,** which come with fine lake views and picnic spots, but these gardens can't compare with what you'll see on the islands. To visit the gardens, get off at the midway Alpino stop and walk 10 minutes (turn left as you leave; €4, April-Oct daily 9:30-18:00, closed Nov-March). If you plan to hike down, pick up the *Trekking* map from the TI and allow four hours from the top of Mount Mottarone, or two hours from the Alpine Gardens (mountain biking also possible—ask at TI).

Sleeping in Stresa: Because Stresa's town generally lacks appeal, I'd day-trip from Milan. But if you'd like to stay, here are some options: **$$$ Hotel Milan Speranza Au Lac** is a big, group-oriented hotel facing the boat dock (www.milansperanza.it); **$$ Hotel Saini Meublè** is a small, homey, affordable choice in the old town center (www.hotelsaini.it); and **$$ Hotel Moderno** is a midsize, midrange option in the old town (www.hms.it).

Eating in Stresa: The main square, **Piazza Cadorna,** is one big tourist trap, yet it does have a certain charm. (At night, it seems anyone who claims to be a musician can get a gig singing for diners.) For a (slightly) less touristy alternative, seek out one of these options: **$$ Osteria degli Amici,** tucked away under a vine trellis on a forgotten square a couple of blocks beyond Piazza Cadorna (Via Bolongaro 33); **$$ La Botte,** with an old-school diner vibe on the main street between the port and the square (Via Mazzini 6); or **$$$$ Il Clandestino,** a fancier, romantic, modern splurge specializing in fish (Via Rosmini 5).

ISLANDS AND GARDENS
▲▲Isola Bella
This island, nearest Stresa, has a formal garden and a fancy Baroque palace. Looking like a stepped pyramid from the water, the island was named by Charles Borromeo (sponsor of Milan's Duomo) for his wife, Isabella. The island itself is touristy, with a gauntlet of souvenir stands and a corral of restaurants. A few back streets provide

evidence that people actually live here. While the Borromeo family now lives in Milan, they spend a few weeks on Isola Bella each summer (when their blue-and-red family flag flies from the top of the garden).

Cost and Hours: Palace and garden-€15, €20.50 combo-ticket includes the villa at Isola Madre, daily 9:00-18:00, shorter hours for palace's picture gallery, closed late-Oct-late-March, no photos in villa, tel. 0323-30556, www.isoleborromee.it.

Tours: A fine €3 audioguide describes the palace, which also has posted English descriptions. A €1.50 booklet explains the gardens.

Services: A WC is located halfway through your visit, where you leave the villa and enter the gardens.

Eating: Several restaurants cluster between the boat docks and the villa. Picnicking is not allowed in the garden, but you can picnic in the pebbly park at the point of the island, beyond the villa (free and open to the public).

Visiting the Island: There are two docks on this island, one for each direction. It's a short walk from the boat to the hulking villa (turn left from the dock; on the way, you'll pass a public WC). Once inside, your visit is a one-way tour, starting with the palace and finishing with the garden. (There's no way to see the garden without the palace.)

In the lavishly decorated Baroque **palace,** stairs lead up under stucco crests of Italy's top families (balls signify the Medici, bees mean the Barberini, and a unicorn symbolizes the Borromeos' motto: Humility). You'll loop through the picture gallery, containing 130 beautifully restored 16th-century paintings from the Borromeo family's private collection, hung wall to ceiling in several cramped rooms. Then you'll get a peek at the canopied bed chambers and ogle the ornate throne room. Continue through the dining room, with a portrait of the first Borromeo, and into a richly stuccoed grand hall, with an 80-foot-high dome and featuring an 18th-century model of the villa, including a grand water entry that never materialized.

Next comes the music room, the site of the 1935 Stresa Conference, in which Mussolini met with British and French diplomats in a united attempt to scare Germany out of starting World War II. Look for a copy of the treaty with Mussolini's signature on the wall next to the exit. Unfortunately, the "Stresa Front" soon fizzled when Mussolini attacked Ethiopia and joined forces with Hitler.

Napoleon's bedroom comes with an engraving that depicts his 1797 visit (Napoleon is on a bench with his wife and sister enjoying festivities in his honor). Continue through several more opulent halls, many of which display souvenirs and gifts that the Borromeo family picked up over the generations.

Downstairs, many of the famous Borromeo marionettes are on display. (A larger collection is on Isola Madre.) The 18th-century, multiroom grotto, decorated from ceiling to floor with shell motifs and black-and-white stones, still serves its original function of providing a cool refuge from Italy's heat. The dreamy marble statues are by Gaetano Monti, a student of Antonio Canova. Climbing out of the basement, look up at the unique, cantilevered, spiral stairs; they're from a 16th-century fortress that predates this building.

Pass through the mirrored corridor and follow the route through more rooms until you come to the ornate hall of 16th-century Flemish tapestries. This leads to the finale of this island visit: the beautiful **garden,** complete with Chinese white peacocks, which give it an exotic splash. (Before continuing to the garden, consider heading up the stairs near the WC to stroll through Elisa's Greenhouse, named for Napoleon's sister and home to tropical plants.)

From the palace, head straight up the stairs into the main part of the garden. Baroque—which is exactly what you see here—is all about controlling nature. The centerpiece is a pyramid-shaped outdoor grotto, crowned by the Borromeo family unicorn. Up the stairs and behind this fanciful structure is a vast terrace with views over the lower gardens and Stresa. Back downstairs, follow the signs (hidden in the bushes) to the café and bookshop, which anchor the far points of the island, to see the terraces behind the "pyramid." Finally, follow *exit* signs to pop out a side gate at the top of a twisty, stepped lane back through town to the boat docks.

▲Isola Superiore (Pescatori)

This sleepy island—home to 35 families—is the smallest and most residential of the three. It has a few good fish restaurants, ample pizza-by-the-slice take-out joints, picnic benches, views, and, blissfully, nothing much to do—all under arbors of wisteria. Simply stroll the narrow, cobbled lanes, or relax at the long, skinny, pebbly park/beach at the tip of the island. A delight for photographers and painters, the island is never really crowded, except at lunchtime.

▲Isola Madre

Don't come to this island unless you intend to tour the sight, because that's all there is: an interesting furnished villa and a lovely garden filled with exotic birds and plants.

Cost and Hours: Villa and garden-€12, €20.50 combo-ticket includes Isola Bella, daily 9:00-18:00, closed late-Oct-late-March, no photos in villa, tel. 0323-31261, www.isoleborromee.it.

Information: The villa has a few sparse English descriptions. Garden lovers can invest a few euros in a booklet about the plantings.

Services: A WC is next to the chapel. You'll also find a café/bookshop (selling basic sandwiches) just outside the villa. While eating is best on Isola Superiore, Isola Madre has one real restaurant, **La Piratera Ristorante Bar,** which owns a big, beautiful terrace over the lake. You'll run into this immediately after leaving the villa/garden complex (€24 fixed-price tourist meal, daily 8:00-18:00, sit-down meals 12:00-15:30, simple sandwiches and slices of pizza to go anytime, picnic at rocky beach a minute's walk from restaurant, just to your right as you exit the gardens, tel. 0323-31171).

Visiting the Island: Visiting is a one-way affair. From the boat dock, walk up the stairs to the ticket desk for the villa. Then, once through the gate, take the level path to the right to loop around the gardens and end at the villa (*ingresso al giardino* signs). Or, if you're in a rush, take the stairs to the left instead to go straight to the villa.

First you'll circle all the way around the **gardens.** Eight gardeners (with the help of water continually pumped from the lake) keep this English-style garden paradise lush. It's a joy, even for those bored by flowers and foliage. You'll see trees from around the world, and an exotic bird menagerie with golden and silver pheasants and Chinese peacocks. (You'll see and hear them roaming wild; also look for the bird cages partway up the main staircase to the villa, on the left.)

In front of the villa, a once-magnificent **Himalayan cypress tree** paints your world a streaky green. The 150-year-old tree, knocked down by a tornado in 2006 but successfully saved, is an attraction in its own right, with steel guy-wires now anchoring it firmly in place.

The 16th-century **villa** is the first of the Borromeo palaces. A century older than the Isola Bella villa, it's dark, somber, and dates from the Renaissance. The clever angled hinges keep the doors from flapping in the lake breeze. The family's huge collection of dolls, marionettes, and exquisite 17th-century marionette theater sets—painted by a La Scala opera set designer—fills several rooms. A corner room is painted to take you into an 18th-century Venetian Rococo sitting room under a floral greenhouse.

Some of the garden's best flowers are in view immediately after leaving the villa. Walk down the stairs to the terrace in front of the chapel, with WCs tucked around the left side. Stairs lead directly down to the boat dock from here. Or you can loop past the villa to exit at the far end, just above La Piratera restaurant. From there, you can walk through the shop to reach a terrace path that leads you back to the boat dock.

Villa Taranto Botanical Gardens

Garden lovers will enjoy this large landscaped park, located on the mainland across the lake from Stresa. Although it's the most sprawling garden in the area, and enjoyable for a stroll in a park, it's a bit underwhelming. The gardens are a Scotsman's labor of love. Starting in the 1930s, Neil McEacharn created this garden of delights—bringing in thousands of plants from all over the world—and here he stays, in the small mausoleum. The park's highlight is a terraced garden with a series of cascading pools. Villa Taranto is directly across the street from the boat dock.

Cost and Hours: €10, daily mid-March-Sept 8:30-18:30, Oct 9:00-16:00, closed Nov-mid-March, tel. 0323-404-555, www.villataranto.it.

Getting There: It's two stops (about 15 minutes) past Isola Madre. On the way, you'll pass a scenic promontory speckled with villas. Note that only about half of the lake boats stop here, which means an hour between return departures—check schedules carefully.

DAY TRIP FROM STRESA
▲Lake Orta

Just on the other side of Mount Mottarone is the small lake of Orta. The lake's main town, Orta San Giulio, has a beautiful lakeside piazza ringed by picturesque build-ings. The piazza faces the lake with a view of Isola San Giulio. Taxi boats (€4 round-trip) make the five-minute trip throughout the day. The island is worth a look for the Church of San Giulio and the circular "path of si-lence," which takes about 10 minutes. In peak season, Orta is anything but

silent, but off-season or early or late in the day, this place is full of peace and magic (TI on Via Panoramica next to the parking lot downhill from the train station, tel. 0322-905-163).

Getting There: The train ride from Stresa to Orta-Miasino (a short walk from the lakeside piazza) takes 1.5-2 hours and requires a change or two (5/day). Public buses from Stresa's Piazza Marconi to Orta depart from near the TI (around €9 round-trip, about 1 hour, 2-3/day mid-June–mid-Sept, confirm schedule at TI or at www.safduemila.com).

MILAN

Milano

For every church in Rome, there's a bank in Milan. Italy's second city and the capital of the Lombardy region, Milan is a hardworking, fashion-conscious, time-is-money city of 1.3 million. It's a melting pot of people and history. Milan's industriousness may come from the Teutonic blood of its original inhabitants, the Lombards, or from its years under Austrian rule. Milan is Italy's fashion, industrial, banking, TV, publishing, and convention capital. The economic success of postwar Italy can be attributed, in part, to this city of publicists and pasta power-lunches.

As if to make up for its rough, noisy big-city-ness, the Milanesi people are works of art. Milan is an international fashion capital with a refined taste. Window displays are gorgeous, cigarettes are chic, and even the cheese comes gift-wrapped. Yet thankfully, Milan is no more expensive for tourists than other Italian cities.

Three hundred years before Christ, the Romans called this place Mediolanum, or "the place in the middle." By the fourth century A.D., it was the capital of the western half of the Roman Empire. Emperor Constantine issued the Edict of Milan from here, legalizing Christianity. After some barbarian darkness, medieval Milan became a successful mercantile city, eventually rising to regional prominence under the Visconti and Sforza families. By the time of the Renaissance, it was nicknamed "the New Athens," and was enough of a cultural center for Leonardo da Vinci to call it home. Then came 400 years of foreign domination (Spain, Austria, France, more Austria). Milan was a center of the 1848 revolution against Austria and helped lead Italy to unification in 1870.

Mussolini left a heavy fascist touch on the architecture here (such as the central train station). His excesses also led to the

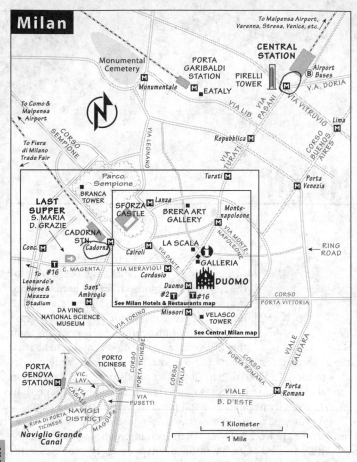

Milan

To Malpensa Airport,
Varenna, Stresa, Venice, etc.

CENTRAL STATION

Monumental Cemetery

PORTA GARIBALDI STATION

Monumentale

EATALY

PIRELLI TOWER

Airport Buses

V.A. DORIA

To Como & Malpensa Airport

CORSO SEMPIONE

VIA LEGNANO

VIA LIB.

VIA PASANI

VIA VITRUVIO

Lima

To Fiera di Milano Trade Fair

VIA TURATI

Repubblica

CORSO BUENOS AIRES

Parco Sempione

Turati

Porta Venezia

BRANCA TOWER

LAST SUPPER
S. MARIA D. GRAZIE

SFORZA CASTLE

Lanza

BRERA ART GALLERY

Monte-napoleone

VIA MONTE NAPOLEONE

RING ROAD

CADORNA STN

Cadorna

LA SCALA

Conc.

Cairoli

VIA DANTE

GALLERIA

To #16

C. MAGENTA

VIA MERAVIGLI

Cordusio

DUOMO

Sant' Ambrogio

To Leonardo's Horse & Meazza Stadium

Duomo

#2

#16

CORSO PORTA VITTORIA

DA VINCI NATIONAL SCIENCE MUSEUM

See Milan Hotels & Restaurants map

Missori

VELASCO TOWER

VIA TORINO

See Central Milan map

PORTA GENOVA STATION

PORTO TICINESE

CORSO PORTA TICINESE

PORTA TICINESE

VIC. LAV.

VIA CASALE

CORSO ITALIA

CORSO PORTA ROMANA

VIALE CALDARA

VIA FUSETTI

VIALE B. D'ESTE

Porta Romana

RIPA DI PORTA TICINESE

NAVIGLI DISTRICT

MAGOLFA

Naviglio Grande Canal

1 Kilometer

1 Mile

WWII bombing of Milan. But the city rose again. The 1959 Pirelli Tower (the skinny skyscraper in front of the station) was a trendsetter in its day. Today, Milan is people-friendly, with a great transit system and inviting pedestrian zones.

Many tourists come to Italy for the past. But Milan is today's Italy. While it's not big on the tourist circuit, the city has plenty to see. And seeing Milan is not difficult: People-watchers and pigeon feeders could spend their entire visit never losing sight of the Duomo.

For pleasant excursions from the city, consider visiting Lake Como or Lake Maggiore—both are about an hour from Milan by train (see the previous chapter).

PLANNING YOUR TIME

OK, it's a big, intense city, so you may not want to linger. Milan can't compare with Rome and Florence when it comes to art, but the city does have several unique and noteworthy sights: the Duomo and the Galleria Vittorio Emanuele II arcade, La Scala Opera House, Michelangelo's last pietà sculpture in Sforza Castle, and Leonardo's *Last Supper*.

With two nights and a full day, you can gain an appreciation for the town and see the major sights. On a short visit, I'd focus on

the center. Tour the Duomo, hit any art you like (reserve ahead if you want to see *The Last Supper*), browse elegant shops and the Galleria Vittorio Emanuele II, and try to see an opera. To maximize your time in Milan, use the Metro to get around.

For those with a round-trip flight into Milan: The city is a cold plunge into the Italian deep end, so save it for the end of your trip and start your journey softly by going first to Lake Como (one-hour ride to Varenna) or the Cinque Terre (3 hours to Monterosso). Then spend the last night or two of your trip in Milan before flying home.

Monday is a terrible sightseeing day, since many museums are closed (including *The Last Supper*). August is oppressively hot and muggy, and locals who can vacate at this time do, leaving the city quiet. Those visiting in August find that the nightlife is sleepy, and many shops and restaurants are closed.

A Three-Hour Tour: If you're just changing trains at Milan's Centrale station (as, sooner or later, you probably will), consider catching a later train and taking this blitz tour: Check your bag at the station, ride the subway to the Duomo, peruse the square, explore the cathedral's rooftop and interior, drop into the Duomo Museum, have a scenic coffee in the Galleria Vittorio Emanuele II, spin on the floor mosaic of the bull for good luck, maybe see a museum or two (most are within a 10-minute walk of the main square), and return by subway to the station. Art fans could make time for *The Last Supper* (if they've made reservations) and/or the Michelangelo *pietà* in Sforza Castle (no reservations necessary).

Orientation to Milan

My coverage focuses on the old center. Most sights and hotels listed are within a 15-minute walk of the cathedral (Duomo), which is a straight eight-minute Metro ride from the Centrale train station.

Rome vs. Milan: A Classic Squabble

In Italy, the North and South bicker about each other, hurling barbs, quips, and generalizations. All the classic North/South traits can be applied to Milan (the business capital) and Rome (the government and religious capital). Italians like to say that people come to Milan to sin, and they go to Rome to ask for forgiveness.

The Milanesi say the Romans are lazy. Government jobs in Rome come with short hours—made even shorter by multiple coffee breaks, three-hour lunches, chats with colleagues, and phone calls to friends and relatives. Milanesi contend that "Roma *ladrona*" (Rome, the big thief) is a parasite that lives off the taxes of people up North. There's still a strong Milan-based movement promoting secession from the South.

Romans, meanwhile, dismiss the Milanesi as uptight workaholics with nothing else to live for—gray like their foggy city. Romans do admit that in Milan, job opportunities are better and based on merit. And the Milanesi grudgingly concede the Romans have a gift for enjoying life.

While Rome is more of a family city, Milan is the place for

TOURIST INFORMATION

Milan's TI, at the La Scala end of the Galleria Vittorio Emanuele II, isn't worth a special trip (Mon-Fri 9:00-19:00, Sat 9:00-18:00, Sun 10:00-18:00, Metro: Duomo, tel. 02-884-5555, www.turismo.milano.it).

ARRIVAL IN MILAN

By Train: Visitors disembark at one of three major train stations: Milano Centrale, Porta Garibaldi, or Cadorna. Most Trenitalia trains, as well as airport buses and some airport trains, stop at Milano Centrale. Porta Garibaldi receives trains from France, some Trenitalia trains, and Italo trains from elsewhere in Italy. And Cadorna is the main terminus for trains from Malpensa Airport.

At Milano Centrale: The huge, sternly decorated, fascist-built (in 1931) central train station is a sight in itself. Recently cleaned, the halls feel more monumental than ever. Notice how the art makes you feel small—it emphasizes that a powerful state is a good thing. In the front lobby, heroic people celebrate "modern" trans-

high-powered singles on the career fast-track. Milanese yuppies mix with each other...not the city's longtime residents. Milan is seen as wary of foreigners and inward-looking, and Rome as fun-loving, tolerant, and friendly. In Milan, bureaucracy (like social services) works logically and efficiently, while in Rome, accomplishing even small chores can be exasperating. Everything in Rome—from finding a babysitter to buying a car—is done through friends.

Milanesi find Romans vulgar. The Roman dialect is considered one of the coarsest in the country. Much as they try, Milanesi just can't say "Damn your dead relatives" quite as effectively as the Romans. Still, Milanesi enjoy Roman comedians and love to imitate the accent.

The Milanesi feel that Rome is dirty and Roman traffic nerve-wracking. But despite the craziness, Rome maintains a genuine village feel. People share family news with their neighborhood grocer. Milan lacks people-friendly piazzas, and entertainment comes at a high price. But in Rome, *la dolce vita* is as close as the nearest square, and a full moon is enjoyed by all.

portation (circa-1930 ships, trains, and cars) opposite reliefs depicting old-fashioned sailboats and horse carts.

Moving walkways link the station's three main levels: platforms on top, shops on a small mezzanine, and most services at ground level (pay WCs and ATMs are abundant). For baggage check *(deposito bagagli),* taxis, or buses to the airports, head toward the ground-level exit marked *Piazza Luigi di Savoia.* Outside the station's front entrance, under the atrium, are car-rental offices for Avis, Budget, and Maggiore, as well as a post office-run ATM. You'll also find escalators down to the Metro and a fourth basement level with a few shops. (You can also enter the Metro from inside the station—just follow signs.)

"Centrale" is a misnomer—the Duomo is a 35-minute walk away. But it's a straight shot on the Metro (8 minutes). Buy a €1.50 ticket at a kiosk or from the machines, follow signs for yellow line 3 (direction: San Donato), go four stops to the Duomo stop, surface, and you'll be facing the cathedral.

To **buy train tickets,** follow blue signs to *Bigletti* and use the Trenitalia machines for most domestic trips (Trenord machines

MILAN

by track 3 sell commuter-rail tickets for Malpensa Airport). For international tickets or complicated questions, join the line at the Trenitalia ticket office on the ground floor. Another alternative is the Agenzie 365 travel agency, a private company selling tickets at several offices in the station (7 percent markup can be a reasonable price to skip the Trenitalia ticket lines, but not if the agency's outlets have lines of their own).

At Milano Cadorna: You're most likely to use this commuter station if you take the Malpensa Express airport train, which uses track 1. The Cadorna Metro station—with a direct connection to the Duomo on Metro red line 1—is directly out front.

At Milano Porta Garibaldi: Italo trains, with high-speed service to Florence, Rome, and Naples, use Porta Garibaldi Station, north of the city center (see map on page 268), as do some Trenitalia trains and the high-speed TGV from Paris. Porta Garibaldi is on Metro green line 2, two stops from Milano Centrale.

By Car: Leonardo never drove in Milan. Smart guy. Driving here is bad enough to make the €30/day fee for a downtown garage a blessing. If you're driving in Italy, do Milan (and Lake Como) before or after you rent your car, not while you've got it. If you must have a car, use the safe, affordable, well-marked park-and-ride lots at suburban Metro stations such as Cascina Gobba. These are shown on the official Metro map, and full details are at www.atm.it (select English, then "Car Parks," then "Parking Lots").

By Plane: See "Milan Connections" at the end of this chapter.

HELPFUL HINTS

Exchange Rate: €1 = about $1.10

Country Calling Code: 39 (see page 1154 for dialing instructions)

Theft Alert: Be on guard. Milan's thieves target tourists, especially at the Centrale train station, getting in and out of the subway, and around the Duomo. They can be dressed as tourists, businessmen, or beggars, or they can be gangs of too-young-to-arrest children. Watch out for ragged people carrying newspaper and cardboard—they'll thrust these at you as a distraction while they pick your pocket. If you're ripped off and plan to file an insurance claim, fill out a report with the police (main police station, "Questura," Via Fatebenefratelli 11, Metro: Turati, open daily 24 hours, tel. 02-62261).

Sightseeing Pass: The three-day Milano Tourist Museum Card covers a dozen city museums, including Sforza Castle, Museo del Novecento, the Archaeological Museum, and Risorgimento Museum (€12, purchase at participating museums, www.comune.milano.it).

Medical Help: There are two medical clinics with emergency care facilities (both closed Sat-Sun): the **International Health**

Center in Galleria Strasburgo (between Via Durini and Corso Europa, at #3, third floor, Metro: San Babila, tel. 02-7634-0720, www.ihc.it) and the **American International Medical Center** at Via Mercalli 11 (Metro: Missori or Crocetta, call for appointment, tel. 02-5831-9808, www.aimclinic.it).

Bookstores: The handiest major bookstore is **La Feltrinelli,** under the Galleria Vittorio Emanuele II (daily, tel. 02-8699-6903). The **American Bookstore** is at Via Manfredo Camperio 16, near Sforza Castle (closed Sun, Metro: Cairoli, tel. 02-878-920).

Laundry: Self-service laundry is hard to find in Milan. **Allwash,** at Via Savona 2, just off Via Zugna, is the closest launderette to the center. Take tram #14 (direction: Cim. Maggiore-Lorenteggio) to Piazzale Cantore, or go by Metro to Porta Genova and walk 5-10 minutes (daily 8:00-22:00, English instructions, tel. 800-030-653, www.allwash.it).

Soccer: For a dose of Europe's soccer mania (which many believe provides a necessary testosterone vent to keep Europe out of a third big war), catch a match while you're here. A.C. Milan and Inter Milan are the ferociously competitive home teams (www.acmilan.com or www.inter.it, bring your passport to the game for security checks). Both teams play in the 85,000-seat Meazza Stadium (a.k.a. San Siro) most Sunday afternoons from September to June (ride the Metro purple line 5 to San Siro Stadio).

GETTING AROUND MILAN

By Public Transit: It's a pleasure to use Milan's great public transit system, called ATM ("ATM Point" info desk in Duomo Metro station, www.atm.it). The clean, spacious, fast, and easy **Metro** zips you nearly anywhere you may want to go, and trams and city buses fill in the gaps. The handiest Metro line for a quick visit is the yellow line 3, which connects Centrale station to the Duomo. The other lines are red (1), green (2), and purple (5). A new line 4 will eventually connect San Babila and Linate Airport...but this is Italy, so no one knows for sure when that might be. The Metro shuts down about half past midnight, but many trams continue until 1:00 or even 2:00.

A **single ticket,** valid for 90 minutes, can be used for one ride, including transfers, on all forms of transport (€1.50; sold at newsstands, tobacco shops, shops with *ATM* sticker in window, and at machines in subway stations). Other ticket options include a *carnet* (€13.80 for 10 rides—it's one magnetic ticket that can be validated 10 times); a **24-hour pass** (€4.50, worthwhile if you take at least four rides); and a **48-hour pass** (€8.25, pays off with six rides).

MILAN

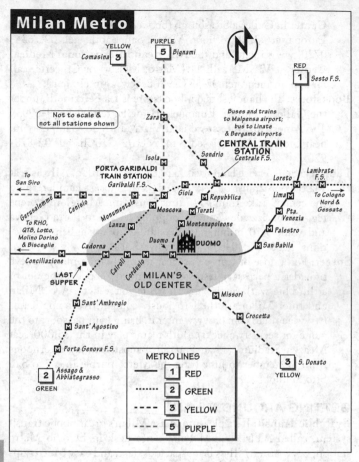

Milan Metro

YELLOW
Comasina **3**

PURPLE
5 Bignami

RED
1 Sesto F.S.

Not to scale &
not all stations shown

Zara Ⓜ

Buses and trains
to Malpensa airport;
bus to Linate
& Bergamo airports
**CENTRAL TRAIN
STATION**
Centrale F.S.

Isola Ⓜ

Sondrio Ⓜ

Lambrate
F.S.

Loreto

To San Siro

**PORTA GARIBALDI
TRAIN STATION**
Garibaldi F.S.

Gerusalemme   Cenisio   Ⓜ   Gioia Ⓜ   Repubblica

Lima Ⓜ

To Cologno
Nord &
Gessate

To RHO,
QT8, Lotto,
Molino Dorino
& Bisceglie

Monumentale   Moscova Ⓜ   Turati Ⓜ

Lanza Ⓜ   Montenapoleone Ⓜ

Pta.
Venezia Ⓜ

Palestro Ⓜ

Cadorna Ⓜ   Duomo Ⓜ **DUOMO**

Conciliazione   Cairoli   Cordusio

San Babila Ⓜ

**LAST
SUPPER**

**MILAN'S
OLD CENTER**

Missori Ⓜ

Ⓜ Sant'Ambrogio

Crocetta Ⓜ

Ⓜ Sant'Agostino

Ⓜ Porta Genova F.S.

2 Assago &
Abbiategrasso
GREEN

METRO LINES

—— **1** RED	
···· **2** GREEN	
– – **3** YELLOW	
–·– **5** PURPLE	

3 S. Donato
YELLOW

Tickets must be run through the machines at Metro turnstiles and at the front and rear of trams—including each time you transfer.

By Taxi: Small groups go cheap and fast by taxi (drop charge–€3.30, €1.10/kilometer; €5.40 drop charge on Sun and holidays, €6.50 from 21:00 to 6:00 in the morning). It can be easier to walk to a taxi stand than to flag down a cab. Handy stands are at Piazza del Duomo and in front of Sforza Castle (tel. 02-8585 or 02-6969).

By Bike: Milan's public bike system, **BikeMi,** lets you set up a temporary subscription (€9/week or €4.50/day) online or at an "ATM Point" public transit info office (a handy one is in the Duomo Metro station). You'll receive a user code and password, allowing you to pick up a bike at any BikeMi station (generally located near Metro stations). Enter your code and password on the keypad, grab the assigned bike, and you're on your way (first 30 minutes free, then €0.50/30 minutes up to 2 hours, after that €2/hour, www.bikemi.com). Download the BikeMi app to see available bikes and parking spots.

Tours in Milan

Local Guides

Lorenza Scorti is a hardworking young guide who knows her city's history and how to teach it (€160/3 hours, €320/6 hours, same price for individuals or groups, evenings OK, mobile 347-735-1346, lorenza.scorti@libero.it). **Sara Cerri** is another good licensed local guide who enjoys passing on her knowledge (€195/3 hours, then €50/hour, mobile 380-433-3019, www.walkingtourmilan.it, walkingtourmilan@gmail.com). **Ludovic Charles Goudin** is energetic and has a passion for teaching art (€180/3 hours, mobile 331-289-3464, ludovicgoudin@yahoo.it).

Walking and Bus Tours with *The Last Supper*

If your visit to Milan is fast approaching and you can't get a reservation for *The Last Supper,* consider joining a walking or bus tour that includes a guided visit to Leonardo's masterpiece. These €60-75 tours (usually three hours) also take you to top sights such as the Duomo, Galleria Vittorio Emanuele II, La Scala Opera House, and Sforza Castle. Ideally book at least a week in advance, but it's worth a try at the last minute, too.

For the best experience, I'd book a walking tour with **Veditalia** (www.veditalia.com) or **City Wonders** (www.citywonders.com). Both have good guides and solid reputations. The bus-and-walking tours are less satisfying, but you can try **Autostradale** ("Look Mi" tour, offices in passage at far end of Piazza del Duomo and in front of Sforza Castle, tel. 02-8058-1354, www.autostradaleviaggi.it) or **Zani Viaggi** (office disguised as a "tourist information" point, corner of Foro Buonaparte and Via Cusani at #18, near Sforza Castle, tel. 02-867-131, www.zaniviaggi.com).

Hop-On, Hop-Off Option: Zani Viaggi also operates **CitySightseeing Milano** hop-on, hop-off buses (look for the red buses—easiest at Duomo and La Scala, €22/all day, €25/48 hours, buy on board, recorded commentary, www.milano.city-sightseeing.it). With a bus ticket, you can pay an additional €33 for a *Last Supper* reservation—exorbitant but worth considering for the wealthy and the desperate (April-Oct only).

MILAN

Milan at a Glance

▲▲**Duomo** Milan's showpiece cathedral, with an amazing roof you can walk on. **Hours:** Church—daily.8:00-19:00, last entry at 18:00; rooftop terraces—daily 9:00-19:00, last ascent at 18:00. See page 272.

▲▲**Galleria Vittorio Emanuele II** Glass-domed arcade on the main square, perfect for window shopping and people-watching. **Hours:** Always open. See page 281.

▲▲**La Scala Opera House and Museum** The world's most prestigious opera house. **Hours:** Museum daily 9:00-12:30 & 13:30-17:30. See page 284.

▲▲**Basilica di Sant'Ambrogio** Historic, art-packed church dating to early Roman times. **Hours:** Mon-Sat 10:00-12:30 & 14:30-18:30, Sun 15:00-17:00. See page 288.

▲▲*The Last Supper* Leonardo da Vinci's masterpiece, displayed in the Church of Santa Maria delle Grazie (viewable only with a reservation). **Hours:** Tue-Sun 8:15-18:45 (last entry), closed Mon. See page 290.

▲**Duomo Museum** Church art and original sculptures from Milan's cathedral. **Hours:** Thu-Tue 10:00-18:00, closed Wed. See page 278.

▲**Piazza del Duomo** Milan's main square, full of energy, history, and pickpockets. **Hours:** Always open. See page 280.

▲**Museo del Novecento** Milan's 20th-century art collection, housed in the fascist-era City Hall. **Hours:** Mon 14:30-19:30; Tue-Wed, Fri, and Sun 9:30-19:30; Thu and Sat 9:30-22:30. See page 282.

▲**Piazza dei Mercanti** The evocative medieval heart of the city. **Hours:** Always open. See page 282.

▲**Gallerie d'Italia** Three adjacent palaces filled with 19th- and 20th-century Italian art. **Hours:** Tue-Sun 9:30-19:30, Thu until 22:30, closed Mon. See page 285.

▲**Pinacoteca Ambrosiana** Oldest museum in Milan, with works by Raphael, Leonardo, Botticelli, Titian, and Caravaggio. **Hours:** Tue-Sun 10:00-18:00, closed Mon. See page 286.

▲**Church of San Maurizio** The "Sistine Chapel of Lombardy," gorgeously frescoed by Bernardino Luini, a follower of Leonardo. **Hours:** Tue-Sun 9:30-19:30, closed Mon. See page 287.

▲**Leonardo da Vinci National Science and Technology Museum** Leonardo's designs illustrated in wooden models, plus a vast collection of historical and technological bric-a-brac and machines. **Hours:** Tue-Fri 9:30-17:00, Sat-Sun 9:30-18:30, closed Mon. See page 290.

▲**Brera Art Gallery** World-class collection of Italian paintings (13th-20th century), including Raphael, Caravaggio, Gentile da Fabriano, Piero della Francesca, Mantegna, and the Bellini brothers. **Hours:** Tue-Sun 8:30-19:15, closed Mon. See page 293.

▲**Sforza Castle** Milan's castle, whose highlight is an unfinished Michelangelo pietà. **Hours:** Tue-Sun 9:00-17:30, closed Mon. See page 294.

▲**Via Dante** Human traffic frolics to lilting accordions on one of Europe's longest pedestrian-only boulevards. **Hours:** Always open. See page 297.

▲**Naviglio Grande** Milan's old canal port—once a working-class zone, now an atmospheric nightspot for dinner or drinks. **Hours:** Always open. See page 298.

▲**Monumental Cemetery** Evocative final resting spot with tombs showcasing expressive art styles from 1870 to 1930. **Hours:** Tue-Sun 8:00-18:00, closed Mon. See page 299.

Risorgimento Museum Italy's rocky road to unification on one floor. **Hours:** Tue-Sun 9:00-13:00 & 14:00-17:30, closed Mon. See page 294.

Poldi Pezzoli Museum Italian paintings (15th-18th century), weaponry, and decorative arts. **Hours:** Wed-Mon 10:00-18:00, closed Tue. See page 294.

Bagatti Valsecchi Museum 19th-century Italian Renaissance furnishings. **Hours:** Tue-Sun 13:00-17:45, closed Mon. See page 294.

Leonardo's Horse Gargantuan equestrian monument built from Leonardo's designs. **Hours:** Always viewable. See page 298.

MILAN

Sights in Milan

▲▲DUOMO (CATHEDRAL)

The city's centerpiece is the fourth-largest church in Europe (after the Vatican's, London's, and Sevilla's). At 525 by 300 feet, the place  is immense, with more than two thousand statues inside (and another thousand outside) and 52 one-hundred-foot-tall, sequoia-size pillars representing the weeks of the year and the liturgical calendar. If you do two laps, you've done your daily walk. It was built to hold 40,000 worshippers, the entire population of Milan when construction began. A visit here has three parts: the church interior; the adjacent Duomo Museum; and an elevator ride (or long climb) up to the rooftop for a stroll through its forest of jagged spires.

Cost: Duomo and Duomo Museum—€2, includes skippable San Gottardo Church; rooftop terraces—€13 by elevator, €8 via stairs. To visit the Archaeological Area under the church, you'll need to purchase a separate €6 ticket or combo-ticket (€11-15); check website for details.

Hours: Duomo and Archaeological Area—daily 8:00-19:00, last entry at 18:00; Duomo Museum and San Gottardo Church—Thu-Tue 10:00-18:00, closed Wed, last entry at 17:00; rooftop terraces—daily 9:00-19:00, last ascent at 18:00.

Buying Tickets: Ticket booths are located on the north, east, and south sides of the cathedral (daily 8:00-18:00; seasonal north booth has shorter hours), as well as at the Duomo Museum (closed Wed). The booth directly behind the east end of the church is generally uncrowded because it's the farthest from the Duomo entrance—but it's closest to the terrace elevator and also hosts the **Duomo Info Point** office (Mon-Sat 9:30-17:30, Sun 11:00-15:00).

Information: Church tel. 02-7202-2656, museum tel. 02-860-358, www.duomomilano.it.

Dress Code: Modest dress is required to visit the church. Don't wear shorts or anything sleeveless—even children.

Tours: A €6 audioguide for the church is available at a kiosk inside the main door of the church (no rentals Sun, 1.5 hours).

Background

Back when Europe was fragmented into countless tiny kingdoms and dukedoms, the dukes of Milan wanted to impress their counterparts in Germany and France. Their goal was to earn Milan recognition and respect from both the Vatican and the kings and princes of northern Europe by building a massive, richly ornamented cathedral. Even after Renaissance-style domes had come into vogue elsewhere in Italy, conservative Milan stuck with the Gothic style. The dukes thought northerners would relate better to Gothic, and they loaded the cathedral with pointed arches and spires. For good measure, the cathedral was built not from ordinary stone, but from marble, top to bottom. Pink Candoglia marble was rafted in from a quarry about 60 miles away, across Lake Maggiore and down a canal to a port at the cathedral. Construction lasted from 1386 to 1810, with final touches added as late as 1965. In 2014, archaeologists probing for ancient Roman ruins beneath the Duomo discovered the remains of what might be a temple to the goddess Minerva.

❂ Self-Guided Tour
Begin by looping around the Duomo's exterior, then head inside to enjoy its remarkable bulk, fine stained-glass windows, and Baroque altar.

Exterior
Walk around the entire church exterior and notice the statues, made between the 14th and 20th centuries by sculptors from all over Europe. There are hundreds of them—each different and quite creative. Look at the statues on the tips of the many spires...they seem so relaxed, like they're just hanging out, waiting for their big day. Functioning as drain spouts, the 96 fanciful gargoyle monsters are especially imaginative.

As you stand outside at the back of the church (near the Duomo Info Point), imagine the glory of this first wall. These were the earliest stones, laid at the end of the 14th century. The sun-in-rose window was the proud symbol of the city's leading Visconti family; it's flanked by the angel telling Mary she's going to bear the Messiah. And to your right is a shrine to the leading religion of the 21st century: soccer. The Football Team store is filled with colorful vestments and relics of local soccer saints.

Continue circling the cathedral. Back at the front, enjoy the statues enlivening the facade. The lower ones—full of energy and movement—are early Baroque, from about 1600. Of the five doors, the center one is biggest. Made in 1907 in the Liberty Style (Italian Art Nouveau), it features the Joy and Sorrow of the Virgin Mary. Sad scenes are on the left, joyful ones on the right, and on top is the coronation of Mary in heaven by Jesus, with all the saints and angels looking on. Step up close and study the fine reliefs.

MILAN

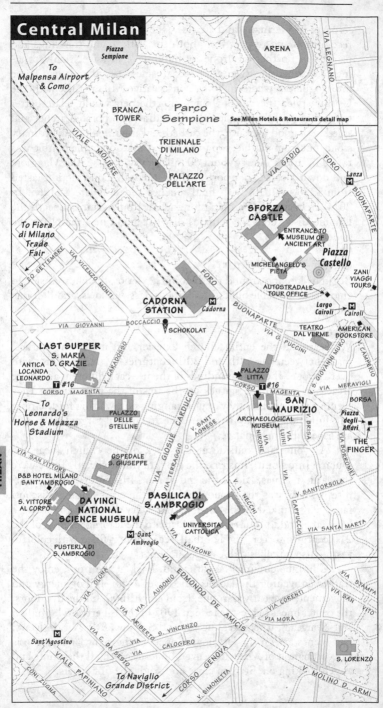

Central Milan

MILAN

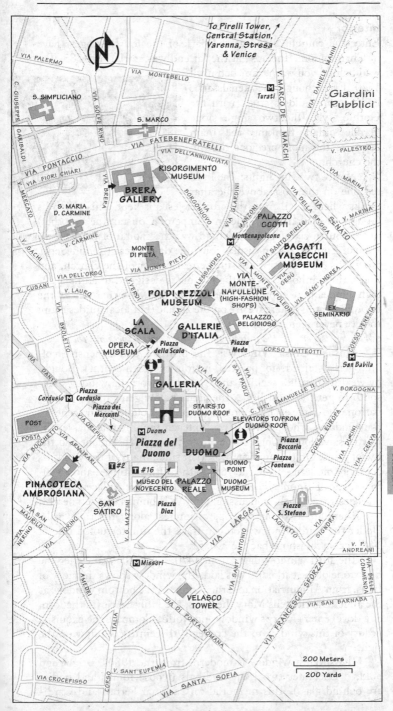

Interior

Enter the church. Stand at the back of the fourth-longest nave in Christendom. The apse at the far end was started in 1385. The wall behind you wasn't finished until 1520. Even though the Renaissance had begun, builders stuck with the Gothic style. The two single-stone marble pillars flanking the main door are the most precious ones in the church.

Notice two tiny lights: The little red one on the cross above the altar marks where a nail from the cross of Jesus is kept. This relic was brought to Milan by St. Helen (Emperor Constantine's mother) in the fourth century, when Milan was the capital of the western Roman Empire. It's on display for three days a year (in mid-Sept). Now look high to the right, in the rear corner of the church, and find a tiny pinhole of white light. This is designed to shine a 10-inch sunbeam at noon onto the bronze line that runs across the floor, indicating where we are on the zodiac (but local guides claim they've never seen it work).

• *Wander deeper into the church, up the right aisle. Check out the...*

Stained-Glass Windows: The brilliant and expensive colored glass (stained, not painted) is from the 15th century. Bought by wealthy families seeking the Church's favor, the windows face south to get the most light. The altars below generally honor the patron who made each window possible. Pick out familiar scenes in the windows, whose purpose was to teach the illiterate masses the way to salvation through stories from the Old Testament and the life of Jesus. On the opposite wall (left side), many of the windows are more modern—from the 16th to the 20th century—and are either made of dimmer, cheaper painted glass or are replacements for ones destroyed by the concussion of WWII bombs that fell nearby.

There are a couple of stops of interest along the right aisle. Under the third window, you can trace the uninterrupted rule of 144 local archbishops back to A.D. 51.

The fifth window dates from 1470, "just" 85 years after the first stone of the cathedral was laid. The window shows the story of Jesus, from Annunciation to Crucifixion. In the bottom window, as the angel Gabriel tells Mary the news, the Holy Spirit (in the form of a dove) enters Mary's window and world. Compare the exquisite beauty of this window to the cruder 19th-century window on the right.

The seventh window is modern, from the 1980s. Bright and bold, it celebrates two local cardinals (whose tombs and bodies are behind glass). This memorial to Cardinal Ferrari and Cardinal Schuster, who heroically helped the Milanese out of their post-WWII blues, is a reminder that this great church is more than a tourist attraction—it's a living part of Milan.

• *Now face the...*

Main Altar: While the church is Gothic, the area around the altar is Baroque—a dramatic stage-like setting in the style of the Vatican in the 1570s (a Roman-Catholic statement to counter the mostly Gothic Protestant churches of the north). Napoleon crowned himself King of Italy under this dome in 1805. Now look to the rear, up at the ceiling, and see the fancy "carving" (between the ribs)—nope, that's painted. It looks expensive, but paint is more affordable than carved stone.

• *In the south (right) transept, find the bald statue lit by the open door.*

St. Bartolomeo Statue: This is a grotesque 16th-century statue of St. Bartolomeo, an apostle and first-century martyr skinned alive by the Romans. Examine the details (face, hands, feet) of the poor guy wearing his own skin like a robe. Carved by a student of Leonardo da Vinci, this is a study in human anatomy learned by dissection, forbidden by the Church at the time.

• *As you walk around the interior, look down at the fine 16th-century inlaid-marble...*

Floor: The pieces around the altar are original. You can tell that the black marble (quarried from Lake Como) is harder because it looks and feels less worn than the other colors (white from Lake Maggiore, pink from Verona).

• *Walk toward the altar, then bear right around the corner 30 steps. You'll see a door marked* Scurolo di S. Carlo. *This leads down to the...*

Crypt of St. Charles Borromeo: Steps lead under the altar to the tombs of St. Charles Borromeo (1538-1584, the economic power behind the church) and his family. You can still see Charles' withered body in the glass case. Charles was bishop of Milan, and the second most important hometown saint after St. Ambrose. Tarnished silver reliefs around the ceiling show scenes from Charles' life.

• *Now continue around the apse, looking up at the...*

Windows: The apse is lit by three huge windows, all 19th-century painted copies. The originals, destroyed in Napoleonic times, were made of precious stained glass.

• *Circling around to the far side, head all the way up the aisle. Before you leave, directly to the right of the main door, notice the entrance and stairs down, marked* Archaeological Area. *This takes you down to the...*

Paleo-Christian Baptistery of San Giovanni: This church stood here long before the present one. Milan was an important center of early Christianity. In Roman times, Mediolanum's streets were 10 feet below today's level. You'll see the scant remains of an eight-sided baptistery (where Sts. Augustine and Ambrose were baptized) and a little church. Back then, since you couldn't enter the church until you were baptized (which didn't happen until age 18), churches had a little "holy zone" just outside for the unbaptized. This included a baptistery like this one.

More Duomo Sights
▲▲Duomo Rooftop

Strolling between the frilly spires of the cathedral rooftop is the most memorable part of a Duomo visit. You can climb the stairs

or take the elevator (for specifics, see "Cost," earlier). Both entrances are around the left side of the church: the stairs are in front of the transept, and the elevator is behind it. (Even those taking the elevator will have to climb some stairs.)

Once up there, you'll do a one-way loop around the rooftop, wandering through a fancy forest of spires with great views of the city, the square, and—on clear days—the crisp and jagged Alps to the north. And, 330 feet above everything, La Madonnina overlooks it all. This 15-foot-tall gilded Virgin Mary is a symbol of the city.

▲Duomo Museum (Museo del Duomo)

This museum, across from the Duomo in the Palazzo Reale, helps fill in the rest of the story of Milan's cathedral, and lets you see its original art and treasures up close (your Duomo ticket includes museum admission; see "Cost," earlier). The collection lacks description (in any language) and is virtually meaningless without an audioguide (€5). It's worth a walk-through if you have an interest in old church art.

Visiting the Museum: Just after the ticket taker, notice (on the wall to your right) the original **inlaid-marble floor** of the Duomo. The black (from Lake Como) marble is harder. Go ahead, wear down the white a little more.

Now follow the one-way route. Among the early treasures of the cathedral is a 900-year-old, Byzantine-style **crucifix.** Made of copper gilded with real gold and nailed onto wood, it was part of the tomb of the archbishop of Milan. A copy is in today's cathedral.

You'll pass a big, wooden model of the church (we'll get a better look at this later, on the way out). Then you'll step through a long room with paintings, chalices, glass monstrances, and lifelike reliquary busts of Sts. Charles, Sebastian, and Thecla.

MILAN

Look for the big statue of **St. George.** Although this is a copy, the 600-year-old original is among the cathedral's oldest statues and once stood on the front (and first constructed) spire of the Duomo. Some think this is the face of Duke Visconti—the man who started the cathedral. The museum is filled with statues and spires like this, carved of *marmo di Candoglia*—marble from Candoglia. The duke's family gave the entire Candoglia quarry (near Stresa) to the church for all the marble it would ever need.

You'll pop into a long room filled with more statues. On your left, gaze—as did pilgrims 500 years ago—into the eyes of **God the Father.** Made of wood, wrapped in copper, and gilded, this giant head covered the keystone connecting the tallest arches directly above the high altar of the Duomo.

Continue into a narrow room lined with grotesque **gargoyles.** When attached to the cathedral, they served two purposes: to scare away evil spirits and to spew rainwater away from the building.

Twist through several more rooms of statues big and small. In one long, brick-walled hall, watch on the left for **St. Paul the Hermit,** who got close to God by living in the desert. While wearing only a simple robe, he's filled with inner richness. The intent is for pilgrims to commune with him and feel at peace (but I couldn't stop thinking of the Cowardly Lion—"Put 'em up! Put 'em up!").

A few steps beyond Paul, look for the 15th-century dandy with the rolled-up contract in his hand. That's Visconti's descendant, Galeazzo Sforza, and if it weren't for him, the church facade might still be brick as bare as the walls of this room. The contract he holds makes it official—the church now owns the marble quarry (and it makes money on it to this day).

In the next room, study the brilliantly gilded and dynamic statue of *God the Father* (1554). Also keep an eye out for a sumptuous Flanders-style **tapestry,** woven of silk, silver, and gold. Half a millennium ago, this hung from the high altar. In true Flemish style, it weaves vivid details of everyday life into the theology. It tells the story of the Crucifixion by showing three scenes at once. Note the exquisite detail, down to the tears on Mary's cheeks.

Next you'll step through a stunning room with 360 degrees of gorgeous **stained glass** from the 12th to 15th century, telling the easily recognizable stories of the Creation, the Tower of Babel, and David and Goliath. Take a close look at details that used to be too far above the cathedral floor to be seen clearly.

Farther on, you'll reach a display of **terra-cotta panels** juxtaposed with large **monochrome paintings** (1628) by Giovanni Battista Crespi. After Crespi finished the paintings, they were translated into terra-cotta, and finally sculpted in marble to decorate the doorways of the cathedral. Study Crespi's *Creation of Eve (Creazione di Eva)* and its terra-cotta twin. This served as the model

MILAN

for the marble statue that still stands above the center door on the church's west portal (1643). You'll pass a few more of these scenes, then hook into a room with the original, stone-carved, swirling *Dancing Angels*, which decorated the ceiling over the door.

After passing several big tapestries, and a huge warehouse where statues are stacked on shelves stretching up to the ceiling, you'll reach the *Frame of the Madonnina* (1773). Standing like a Picasso is the original iron frame for the statue of the Virgin Mary that still crowns the cathedral's tallest spire. In 1967, a steel replacement was made for the 33 pieces of gilded copper bolted to the frame. The carved-wood face of Mary (in the corner) is the original mold for Mary's cathedral-crowning copper face.

Soon you'll get a better look at that **wooden model** of the Duomo. This was the actual model—necessary in that precomputer age—used in the 16th century by the architects and engineers to build the church. This version of the facade wasn't actually built; other rejected facades line the walls.

On your way out, you'll pass models for the Duomo's doors. And stepping outside, as your eyes adjust to the sunlight, you'll see the grand church itself—looking so glorious thanks to the many centuries of hard work you've just learned about.

AROUND THE DUOMO
▲Piazza del Duomo

Milan's main square is a classic European scene and a popular local gathering point. Professionals scurry, fashion-conscious kids loiter,

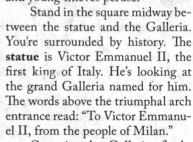

and young thieves peruse.

Stand in the square midway between the statue and the Galleria. You're surrounded by history. The **statue** is Victor Emmanuel II, the first king of Italy. He's looking at the grand Galleria named for him. The words above the triumphal arch entrance read: "To Victor Emmanuel II, from the people of Milan."

Opposite the Galleria, flanking Via Marconi, are the twin fascist buildings of the Arengario Palace, which houses the **Museo del Novecento** (described later). Mussolini made grandiose speeches from their balconies. Study the buildings' relief panels, which tell—with fascist melodrama—the history of Milan.

To the left of these buildings is the historic ducal palace, **Palazzo Reale.** This building, now housing the Duomo Museum (described earlier) and temporary art exhibits, was redone in the Neoclassical style by Empress Maria Theresa in the late 1700s, when Milan was ruled by the Austrian Habsburgs.

Behind the Victor Emmanuel II statue (opposite the cathedral, about a block beyond the square), hiding in a small courtyard, is **Piazza dei Mercanti,** the center of medieval Milan (described later).

▲▲Galleria Vittorio Emanuele II

This breathtaking four-story glass-domed arcade, next to Piazza del Duomo, is a symbol of Milan. The iron-and-glass structure

(built during the age of Eiffel and the heady days of Italian unification) showcased a new, modern era. It was the first building in town to have electric lighting, and from its inception it's been an elegant and popular meeting place. (Sadly, its designer, Giuseppe Mengoni, died the day before the gallery opened.) Here you can turn an expensive cup of coffee into a good value by enjoying some of Europe's best people-watching.

The venerable **Bar Camparino** (at the Galleria's Piazza del Duomo entry), with a friendly staff and a period interior, is the former haunt of famous opera composer Giuseppe Verdi and conductor Arturo Toscanini, who used to stop by after their performances at La Scala. It's a fine place to enjoy a drink and people-watch (€3.50 for an espresso is a great deal to take a seat, relax and enjoy the view, or pay €1.10 at the bar just to experience the scene). The café is named after the Campari family (its first owners), originators of the famous red Campari bitter (Tue-Sun 7:30-20:00, closed Mon and Aug, tel. 02-8646-4435).

Wander around the Galleria. Its art celebrates the establishment of Italy as an independent country. Around the central dome, patriotic mosaics symbolize the four major continents (sorry, Australia). The mosaic floor is also patriotic. The white cross in the center represents the king. The she-wolf with Romulus and Remus (on the south side—facing Rome) honors the city that, since 1870, has been the national capital. On the west side (facing Torino, the provisional capital of Italy

from 1861 to 1865), you'll find that city's symbol: a *torino* (little bull). For good luck, locals step on his irresistible little testicles. Two local girls explained to me that it works better if you spin—two times, and it must be clockwise. Find the poor little bull and observe for a few minutes...it's a cute scene. With so much spinning, the mosaic is replaced every few years.

Luxury shops have had outlets here from the beginning. Along with Gucci, Louis Vuitton, and Prada, you'll find Borsalino (at the end near Piazza della Scala), which has been selling hats here since the gallery opened in 1877.

If you cut through the Galleria to the other side, you'll pop out at Piazza della Scala, with its famous opera house and the Gallerie d'Italia (all described later).

▲Museo del Novecento

Milan's 20th-century art fills the two buildings of the Arengario Palace, Mussolini's fascist-era City Hall. In the beautifully laid-out museum, you'll work your way up the escalators and through the last century, one decade at a time. Each section is well described, and the capper is a fine panoramic view over Piazza del Duomo through grand fascist-era arches.

Cost and Hours: €5, free from two hours before closing; Mon 14:30-19:30; Tue-Wed, Fri, and Sun 9:30-19:30; Thu and Sat 9:30-22:30; last entry one hour before closing, audioguide-€5, facing Piazza del Duomo at Via Marconi 1, tel. 02-8844-4072, www.museodelnovecento.org.

Visiting the Museum: As you spiral up the big ramp, the first painting you'll see, partway up, is Giuseppe Pellizza da Volpedo's *The Fourth Estate* (1901). It celebrates the humanistic, socialist spirit that came with the arrival of the 20th century, and prepares you for the spirit of the collection. The first rooms feature small pieces by big international names (Picasso, Braque, Matisse), but the stars of the show are Italian avant-garde artists such as Umberto Boccioni, a seminal Futurist whose abstract paintings and sculptures convey the dynamism of the modern age. From here, watch art styles evolve, from anything-goes modernism, to a lull of pretty landscapes between the world wars, to the rigid rise of fascist art. Other highlights include sculptures from the 1930s by Arturo Martini and Fausto Melotti. Finally, you'll arrive nearly at the present day, with abstraction, contemporary installations, and kinetic (moving) art, as well as a special exhibit on Marino Marini, an influential mid-20th-century sculptor.

▲Piazza dei Mercanti

This small square, the center of political power in 13th-century Milan, hides one block off Piazza del Duomo (directly opposite the cathedral). A strangely peaceful place today, it offers a fine smat-

tering of historic architecture that escaped the bombs of World War II.

The arcaded, red-brick building that dominates the square was the City Hall (Palazzo della Ragione); its arcades once housed the market hall. Overlooking the wellhead in the middle of the square is a balcony with a coats of arms—this is where new laws were announced. Eventually two big families—Visconti and Sforza—took power, Medici-style, in Milan; the snake is their symbol. Running the show in Renaissance times, these dynasties shaped much of the city we see today, including the Duomo and the fortress. In 1454, the Sforza family made peace with Venice while enjoying a friendship with the Medici in Florence (who taught them how to become successful bankers). This ushered in a time of stability and peace, when the region's major city-states were run by banking families, and money was freed up for the Renaissance generation to make art, not war.

This square also held the Palace of Justice (the 16th-century courthouse with the clock tower), the market (not food, but crafts: leather, gold, and iron goods), the bank, the city's first university, and its prison. All the elements of a great city were right here on the "Square of the Merchants."

ON PIAZZA DELLA SCALA

To reach these sights, cut through the Galleria Vittorio Emanuele II from Piazza del Duomo.

Piazza della Scala

This smart little traffic-free square, between the Galleria and the opera house, is dominated by a statue of Leonardo da Vinci. The statue (from 1870) is a reminder that Leonardo spent his best 20 years in Milan, where he found well-paid, steady work. He was the brainy darling of the Sforza family (who dominated Milan as the Medici family dominated Florence). Under the great Renaissance genius stand four of his greatest "Leonardeschi." (He apprenticed a sizable group of followers.) The reliefs show his various contributions as a painter, architect, and engineer. Leonardo, wearing his hydro-engineer hat, reengineered Milan's canal system, complete with locks. (Until the 1920s, Milan was one of Italy's major ports, with canals connecting the city to the Po River and Lake Maggiore. For more on this footnote of Milan's history, read about the Naviglio Grande on page 298.)

The statue of Leonardo is looking at a plain but famous Neoclassical building, arguably the world's most prestigious opera house (described next).

▲▲La Scala Opera House and Museum

Milan's famous Teatro alla Scala opened in 1778 with an opera by Antonio Salieri (Mozart's wannabe rival). Today, opera buffs can get a glimpse of the theater and tour the adjacent museum's extensive collection.

Cost and Hours: Museum-€7, daily 9:00-12:30 & 13:30-17:30, Piazza della Scala, tel. 02-8879-7473, www.teatroallascala.org.

Museum: The collection features Verdi's top hat, Rossini's eyeglasses, Toscanini's baton, Fettuccini's pesto, original scores, diorama stage sets, busts, portraits, and death masks of great composers and musicians. Upstairs are several tidy rooms of a music library, often displaying costumes. The main reason to visit is the opportunity (on most days) to peek into the actual theater. The stage is as big as the seating area on the ground floor. (You can see the towering stage box from Piazza della Scala across the street.) A recent five-year renovation corrected acoustical problems caused by WWII bombing and subsequent reconstruction. The royal box is just below your vantage point, in the center rear. Don't overlook the massive chandelier made of Bohemian crystal.

Events in the Opera House: The show goes on at the world-famous La Scala Opera House, which also hosts ballet and classical concerts. There are performances in every month except August, and show time usually is at 20:00 (for information, check online or call Scala Infotel Service, daily 9:00-18:00, tel. 02-7200-3744). On the opening night of an opera, a dress code is enforced for men (suit and tie).

Advance Booking: Seats sell out quickly. Online tickets go on sale two months before performances (www.teatroallascala.org). You can also book through an automated phone system: Call 02-860-775 and press 2 for English. Tickets are also sold at an office beneath Piazza del Duomo (daily 12:00-18:00, use stairs down in front of the Duomo and follow *ATM Point* signs). The "evening box office" *(Biglietteria Serale)* at the opera house itself—see below—opens two hours before show time.

Same-Day Tickets: On performance days, 140 sky-high, restricted-view, peanut-gallery tickets are offered at a low price (generally less than €15) at the box office (located down the left side of the theater toward the back on Via Filodrammatici, and marked with *Biglietteria Serale* sign). It's a bit complicated: You have to show up with an official ID (a driver's license or passport) at 13:00 to put your name on a list (one ticket per person), then return at 17:00 for the roll call. You must be present when your name is called to receive a voucher, which you'll then show at the window to purchase your ticket. (Matinees and symphonic concerts follow a different timetable; check the website.) Finally, one hour before show time, the box office sells any remaining tickets at a 25 percent discount.

▲Gallerie d'Italia

This museum fills three adjacent buildings on Piazza della Scala with the amazing art collections of a bank that once occupied part

of this space. The bank building's architecture is early 20th-century, Tiffany-like Historicism, with a hint of Art Nouveau; it's connected to two impressive palazzos that boast the nicest Neoclassical interiors I've seen in Milan. They are filled with exquisite work by 19th- and 20th-century Italian painters.

Cost and Hours: €5, more during special exhibitions, includes audioguide, Tue-Sun 9:30-19:30, Thu until 22:30, closed Mon, last entry 1 hour before closing, across from La Scala Opera House at Piazza della Scala 6, toll-free tel. 800-167-619, www.gallerieditalia.com.

Visiting the Museum: Enter through the bank building facing Piazza della Scala and take the red-velvet stairs to the basement to pick up an audioguide (also downstairs is a bag check, WCs, and the original bank vault, which now stores racks and racks of paintings not on display).

Back upstairs, head into the main atrium of the bank, and consider the special exhibits displayed there. Then, to tackle the permanent art collection in chronological order, head to the far end of the complex and work your way back (follow signs for *Palazzo Anguissola Antona Traversi* and *Palazzo Brentani*). You'll go through the café back into the Neoclassical palaces, where you'll trace the one-way route through the "Da Canova a Boccioni" exhibit, including marble reliefs by the Neoclassical sculptor Antonio Canova and Romantic paintings by Francesco Hayez. Upstairs, you'll see dramatic and thrilling scenes from the unification of Italy, as well as beautiful landscapes and cityscapes, especially of Milan. (An entire room is devoted to depictions of the now-trendy Naviglio Grande canal area in its workaday prime.)

On your way back to the bank building and the rest of the exhibit, take a moment to poke around the courtyard to find the *officina di restituzioni alle gallerie*—a lab where you can watch art restorers at work. Rejoining the permanent exhibit, you'll see paintings from the late-19th and early-20th centuries: Romantic landscapes; hyperrealistic, time-travel scenes of folk life; and Impressionism.

Finally you'll catch up to the art of the late-20th century, tucked between old bank teller windows.

WEST OF THE DUOMO

These sights are listed roughly in the order you'll reach them, as you travel west from Piazza del Duomo. The first one is just a few short blocks from the cathedral, while the last is just over a mile away.

▲Pinacoteca Ambrosiana

This oldest museum in Milan was inaugurated in 1618 to house Cardinal Federico Borromeo's painting collection. It began as a teaching academy, which explains its many replicas of famous works of art. Highlights include original paintings by Botticelli, Caravaggio, and Titian—and, most important, a huge-scale sketch by Raphael (may be under restoration when you visit) and a rare oil painting by Leonardo da Vinci.

Cost and Hours: €15, Tue-Sun 10:00-18:00, closed Mon, last entry at 17:00, audioguide-€3, near Piazza del Duomo at Piazza Pio XI 2, Metro: Duomo or Cordusio, tel. 02-806-921, www.ambrosiana.eu.

Visiting the Museum: Pick up the English-language map locating the rooms and major works I highlight below, and rent the audioguide (covers both permanent and special exhibits). Then head upstairs to begin your visit.

Raphael's Cartoon (Room 5): Filling an entire wall, this drawing served as an outline for Raphael's famous *School of Athens* fresco at the Vatican Museums. (A cartoon—*cartone* in Italian—is a full-size sketch that's used to transfer a design to another surface.) While the Vatican's much-adored fresco is attributed entirely to Raphael, it was painted mostly by his students. But this *cartone* was wholly sketched by the hand of Raphael. To transfer the fresco design to the wall, his assistants riddled this cartoon with pinpricks along the outlines of the figures, stuck it to the wall of the pope's study, and then applied a colored powder. When they removed the *cartone*, the figures' shapes were marked on the wall, and completing the fresco was a lot like filling in a coloring book. Also in this room, look for Caravaggio's naturalistic *Basket of Fruit*.

Jan Brueghel (Room 7): As Cardinal Borromeo was a friend of Jan Brueghel, this entire room is filled with delightful works by the artist and other Flemish masters. Study the wonderful detail in Brueghel's *Allegory of Fire* and *Allegory of Water*. The Flemish paintings are extremely detailed—many are painted on copper to heighten the effect—and offer an insight into the psyche of the age. If the cardinal were asked why he enjoyed paintings that celebrated the secular life, he'd likely say, "Secular themes are God's book of nature."

Leonardo Hall (Room 24): During his productive Milan years, Leonardo painted *Portrait of a Musician*—as delicate, mysterious, and thought-provoking as the *Mona Lisa*. (This is the only one of his canvases that remains in Milan.) The large fresco filling the far wall—with Christ receiving the crown of thorns—is by Bernardino Luini, one of Leonardo's disciples. But I find the big replica painting of *The Last Supper* most interesting. When the cardinal realized that Leonardo's marvelous frescoed original was fading, he commissioned Andrea Bianchi to create a careful copy to be displayed here for posterity. Today, this copy gives a rare chance to appreciate the original colorful richness of the now-faded masterpiece.

Piazza degli Affari and a Towering Middle Finger

This square and monument mark the center of Milan's financial district. The bold fascist buildings in the neighborhood were built in the 1930s under Mussolini. Italy's major stock exchange, the Borsa, faces the square. Stand in the center and appreciate the modern take on ancient aesthetics (you're standing atop the city's ancient Roman theater). Find the stern statues representing various labors and occupations and celebrating the nobility of workers—typical whistle-while-you-work fascist themes. Then notice the equally bold modern statue in the center. After a 2009 contest to find the most appropriate sculpture to grace the financial district, this was the winner. With Italy's crippling financial problems, a sentiment similar to the one that powered the Occupy Movement in the US rumbles in this society as well. Here we see how "the 99 percent" feel when they stand before symbols of corporate power in Italy. (Notice how the finger is oriented—it's the 1 percent, and not the 99 percent, that's flipping the bird.) The 36-foot-tall, Carrara marble digit was made by Maurizio Cattelan, the most famous—or, at least, most controversial—Italian sculptor of our age. *L.O.V.E.*, as the statue is titled, was temporary at first. But locals liked it, and, by popular demand, it's now permanent.

▲Church of San Maurizio
(San Maurizio al Monastero Maggiore)

This church, part of a ninth-century convent built into a surviving bit of Milan's ancient Roman wall, dates from around 1500.

Despite its simple facade, it's a hit with art lovers for its amazing cycle of Bernardino Luini frescoes. Stepping into this church is like stepping into the Sistine Chapel of Lombardy.

Cost and Hours: Free, Tue-Sun 9:30-19:30, closed Mon, Corso Magenta 15 at the Monastero Maggiore, Metro: Cadorna or Cairoli, tel. 02-8645-0011.

Visiting the Church: Bernardino Luini (1480-1532), a follower of Leonardo, was also inspired by his contemporaries Michelangelo and Raphael. Sit in a pew and take in the art, which has the movement and force of Michelangelo and the grace and calm beauty of Leonardo.

Maurizio, the patron saint of this church, was a third-century Roman soldier who persecuted Christians, then converted, and eventually worked to stop those same persecutions. He's the guy standing on the pedestal in the upper right, wearing a bright yellow cape. The nobleman who paid for the art is to the left of the altar, kneeling and cloaked in black and white. His daughter, who joined the convent here and was treated as a queen (as nuns with noble connections were), is to the right. And all around are martyrs—identified by their palm fronds.

The adjacent **Hall of Nuns** (Coro delle Monache), a walled-off area behind the altar, is where cloistered sisters could worship apart from the general congregation. Fine Luini frescoes appear above and around the wooden crucifix. The Annunciation scene at the corners of the arch features a cute Baby Jesus zooming down from heaven (see Mary, on the right, ready to catch him). The organ dates from 1554, and the venue, with its fine acoustics, is popular for concerts with period instruments. Explore the pictorial Bible that lines the walls behind the wooden seats of the choir. Luini's landscapes were groundbreaking in the 16th century. Leonardo incorporated landscapes into his paintings, but Luini was among the first to make landscape the main subject of the painting.

Nearby: You'll exit the Hall of Nuns into the lobby of the adjacent **Archaeological Museum,** where you can pay €5 to see part of the ancient city wall and a third-century Roman tower.

▲▲Basilica di Sant'Ambrogio

One of Milan's top religious, artistic, and historic sights, this church was first built on top of an early Christian martyr's cem-

etery by St. Ambrose around A.D. 380, when Milan had become the capital of the fading (and Christian) western Roman Empire.

Cost and Hours: Free, Mon-Sat 10:00-12:30 & 14:30-18:30, Sun 15:00-17:00, Piazza Sant'Ambrogio 15, Metro: Sant'Ambrogio, tel. 02-8645-0895, www.basilicasantambrogio.it.

Visiting the Church: Ambrose was a local bishop and one of the great fathers of the early Church. Besides his writings, he's remembered for converting and baptizing St. Augustine of Hippo, who himself became another great Church father. The original fourth-century church was later (in the 12th century) rebuilt in the Romanesque style you see today.

As you step "inside" from the street, you emerge into an arcaded **atrium**—standard in many churches back when people weren't allowed to actually enter the church until they were baptized. The unbaptized waited here during Mass. The courtyard is textbook Romanesque, with playful capitals engraved with fanciful animals. Inset into the wall (right side, above the pagan sarcophagi) are stone markers of Christian tombs—a reminder that this church, like St. Peter's at the Vatican, is built upon an ancient Roman cemetery.

From the atrium, marvel at the elegant 12th-century **facade,** or west portal. It's typical Lombard medieval style. The local bishop would bless crowds from its upper loggia. As two different monastic communities shared the church and were divided in their theology, there were also two different bell towers.

Step into the **nave** and grab a pew. The mosaic in the apse features Jesus Pantocrator (creator of all) in the company of Milanese saints. Around you are pillars with Romanesque capitals and surviving fragments of the 12th-century frescoes that once covered the church.

The 12th-century **pulpit** sits atop a Christian sarcophagus dating from the year 400. Study its late Roman and early Christian iconography—on the side facing the altar, Apollo on his chariot morphs into Jesus on a chariot. You can see the moment when Jesus gave the Old Testament (the first five books, anyway) to his apostles.

The precious, ninth-century golden **altar** has four ancient porphyry columns under an elegant Romanesque 12th-century canopy. The entire ensemble was taken to the Vatican during World War II to avoid destruction. That was smart—the apse took a direct hit in 1943. A 13th-century mosaic was destroyed; today we see a reconstruction.

Step into the **crypt,** under the altar, to see the skeletal bodies of three people: Ambrose (in the middle, highest) and two earlier Christian martyrs whose tombs he visited before building the church.

Nearby: For a little bonus after visiting the church, consider this: The **Benedictine monastery** next to the church is now Cattolica University. With its stately colonnaded courtyards designed by Renaissance architect Donato Bramante, it's a nice place to study. It's fun to poke around and imagine being a student here.

MILAN

▲Leonardo da Vinci National Science and Technology Museum (Museo Nazionale della Scienza e Tecnica "Leonardo da Vinci")

The spirit of Leonardo lives here. Most tourists focus on the hall of Leonardo—the core of the museum—where wooden models illustrate his designs. But the rest of this immense collection of industrial cleverness is fascinating in its own right. There are exhibits on space exploration, mining, and radio and television (with some original Marconi radios); old musical instruments, computers, and telephones; chunks of the first transatlantic cable; and interactive science workshops. Out back are several more buildings containing antique locomotives and a 150-foot-long submarine from 1957. Ask for an English museum map from the ticket desk—you'll need it. On weekends, this museum is very popular with families, so come early or be prepared to wait in line.

Cost and Hours: €10, Tue-Fri 9:30-17:00, Sat-Sun until 18:30, closed Mon, Via San Vittore 21, Metro: Sant'Ambrogio; tel. 02-485-551, www.museoscienza.org.

▲▲Leonardo da Vinci's *The Last Supper* (*L'Ultima Cena/Cenacolo Vinciano*)

Decorating the former dining hall *(cenacolo)* of the Church of Santa Maria delle Grazie, this remarkable, exactingly crafted fresco by Leonardo da Vinci is one of the ultimate masterpieces of the Renaissance. Reservations are mandatory and must be booked several months in advance if you want to get in (see reservation options below).

Cost and Hours: €12, includes €2 reservation fee (9:30 and 15:30 visits cost €3.50 extra and include English tour). Open Tue-Sun 8:15-18:45 (last entry), closed Mon. Show up 20 minutes before your scheduled entry time. When an attendant calls your time, get up and move into the next room.

Reservations: Mandatory timed-entry reservations can be made either online or by phone (through an outfit called Vivaticket). Reservations for each calendar month go on sale about three months ahead; for example, bookings for July open in early April. Spots are snapped up quickly, so plan ahead.

To book **online,** go to www.vivaticket.it, then choose "Cenacolo Vinciano." A calendar will show available time slots for the coming months.

If you book by **phone,** you'll have a greater selection of days and time slots to choose from, since the website doesn't reflect cancellations. Note that you can't reserve same-day tickets (tel. 02-9280-0360, from the US dial 011-39-02-9280-0360, office open Mon-Sat 8:00-18:30, closed Sun; the number is often busy— once you get through, select 2 for an English-speaking operator).

Tour Option: If you can't get a reservation, you can book a more expensive (€60-75) walking or bus tour that includes a guided visit to *The Last Supper.* These should be reserved at least one week ahead (for details, see "Tours in Milan," earlier).

Last-Minute Tickets: A few scattered same-day spots may be available due to cancellations. It's a low-percentage play, but you can try just showing up and asking at the desk—even if the *sold out* sign is posted (ideally when the office opens at 8:00, more likely on weekdays). You may get lucky—but don't count on it.

Audioguide: Consider the fine €3.50 audioguide. Its spiel fills every second of the time you're in the room—so try to start listening just before you enter (ideally in the waiting room while studying the reproduction of *The Last Supper*).

Getting There: The Church of Santa Maria della Grazie is a 10-minute walk from either Metro: Cadorna or Conciliazione. Or take tram #16 from the Duomo (direction: San Siro or Piazzale Segesta), which drops you off in front of the church.

Photography: No photos are allowed.

Background: Milan's leading family, the Sforzas, hired Leonardo to decorate the dining hall of the Dominican monastery that adjoins the church (the Dominican order traditionally placed a Last Supper on one end of their refectories, and a Crucifixion at the other). Leonardo worked on the project from about 1492 until 1498. This gift was essentially a bribe to the monks so that the Sforzas could place their family tomb in the church. Ultimately, the French drove the Sforzas out of Milan, they were never buried here, and the Dominicans got a great fresco for nothing.

Deterioration began within six years of *The Last Supper*'s completion because Leonardo painted on the wall in layers, as he would on a canvas, instead of applying pigment to wet plaster in the usual fresco technique. The church was bombed in World War II, but— miraculously, it seems—the wall holding *The Last Supper* remained

MILAN

standing. A 21-year restoration project (completed in 1999) peeled away 500 years of touch-ups, leaving Leonardo's masterpiece faint but vibrant.

Visiting *The Last Supper:* To minimize damage from humidity, only 30 tourists are allowed in, every 15 minutes for exactly 15 minutes. While you wait, read the history of the masterpiece. As your appointed time nears, you'll be herded between several rooms to dehumidify, while doors close behind you and open up slowly in front of you.

And then the last door opens, you take a step, you look right, and...there it is. In a big, vacant, whitewashed room, you'll see faded pastels and not a crisp edge. The feet under the table look like negatives. But the composition is dreamy—Leonardo captures the psychological drama as the Lord says, "One of you will betray me," and the apostles huddle in stressed-out groups of three, wondering, "Lord, is it I?" Some are scandalized. Others want more information. Simon (on the far right) gestures as if to ask a question that has no answer. In this agitated atmosphere, only Judas (fourth from left and the only one with his face in shadow)—clutching his 30 pieces of silver and looking pretty guilty—is not shocked.

The circle meant life and harmony to Leonardo. Deep into a study of how life emanates in circles—like ripples on a pool hit by a pebble—Leonardo positioned the 13 characters in a semicircle. Jesus is in the center, from whence the spiritual force of God emanates, or ripples out.

The room depicted in the painting seems like an architectural extension of the church. The disciples form an apse, with Jesus as the altar—in keeping with the Eucharist. Jesus anticipates his sacrifice, his face sad, all-knowing, and accepting. His feet even foreshadow his death by crucifixion. Had the door, which was cut out in 1652, not been added, you'd see how Leonardo placed Jesus' feet atop each other, ready for the nail.

The perspective is mathematically correct, with Jesus' head as the vanishing point where the converging sight lines meet. In fact, restorers found a tiny nail hole in Jesus' left eye, which anchored the strings Leonardo used to establish these lines. The table is cheated out to show the meal. Notice the exquisite lighting. The walls are lined with tapestries (as they would have been), and the one on the right is brighter in order to fit the actual lighting in the refectory (which has windows on the left). With the extremely natural effect of the light and the drama of the faces, Leonardo created a masterpiece.

NORTH OF THE DUOMO
▲Brera Art Gallery (Pinacoteca di Brera)

Milan's top collection of Italian paintings (13th-20th century) is world-class, but it can't top Rome's or Florence's. Established in 1809 to house Napoleon's looted art, it fills the first floor above a prestigious art college. You'll dodge scruffy starving artists here... and wonder if there's a 21st-century Leonardo in your midst.

Cost and Hours: €10, more during special exhibits, free first Sun of month, open Tue-Sun 8:30-19:15, closed Mon, last entry 45 minutes before closing, audioguide-€5 (useful as English information is limited, ID required), free lockers, no flash photos, Via Brera 28, Metro: Lanza or Montenapoleone, tel. 02-722-631, www.brera.beniculturali.it.

Visiting the Museum: Enter the grand courtyard of a former monastery, where you'll be greeted by the nude *Napoleon with Tinkerbell* (by Antonio Canova).

Climb the stairway (following signs to *Pinacoteca*), buy your ticket, and pick up an English map of the museum's masterpieces, some of which I've highlighted below. You'll follow a clockwise, chronological route through the huge collection.

In **Rooms IV-VI,** examine the altar paintings by late-Gothic master Gentile da Fabriano, hinting at the realism of the coming Renaissance (check out the lifelike flowers and realistic, bright gold paint—he used real gold powder). In the darkened section at the far end of **Room VII,** don't miss Andrea Mantegna's tour-de-force, *The Dead Christ.* It's a textbook example of feet-first foreshortening.

Next, to experience the peak of 16th-century Venetian painting, check out the color-rich canvases by the great masters Tintoretto and Veronese in **Room IX.**

Stop by the glass-enclosed restoration lab in **Room XVIII** to watch various conservation projects in progress.

Here in **Rooms XXII-XXIX,** you can see how Carlo Crivelli, a contemporary of Leonardo, employed Renaissance technique while clinging to the mystique of the Gothic Age (that's why I like him so much). In the next few rooms, don't miss Raphael's *Wedding of the Madonna* (Room XXIV), Piero della Francesca's *Madonna and Child with Saints* (also Room XXIV), and the gritty-yet-intimate realism of Caravaggio's *Supper at Emmaus* (Room XXIX).

Next, in **Rooms XXXI-XXXV,** you'll see Dutch and Flemish masters, including a big Rubens (Room XXXI) and a small Rembrandt (Room XXXIII). Room XXXV displays several of Canaletto's picture-postcards of Venetian cityscapes. This is ahead-of-

MILAN

its-time Impressionism—there's not a single line in these works, just strategically placed daubs of paint.

Finally, in **Room XXXVII,** you'll greet the modern age with Giuseppe Pellizza da Volpedo's rousing *Human Flow,* a study for his famous *Fourth Estate* (exhibited at the Museo del Novocento; see page 282). Also in this room, spice things up with Francesco Hayez's hot and heavy *The Kiss (Il Bacio).*

Risorgimento Museum

With a quick 30-minute swing through this quiet one-floor museum, you'll get an idea of the interesting story of Italy's rocky road to unity: from Napoleon (1796) to the victory in Rome (1870). You'll see paintings, uniforms, monuments, a city model, and other artifacts. But limited English makes this best left to people already familiar with this important period of Italian history.

Cost and Hours: €5, free entry after 16:30 (Tue after 14:00), open Tue-Sun 9:00-13:00 & 14:00-17:30, closed Mon, just around the block from Brera Art Gallery at Via Borgonuovo 23, Metro: Montenapoleone, tel. 02-8846-4176, www.museodelrisorgimento.mi.it.

Poldi Pezzoli Museum

This classy house of art features Italian paintings of the 15th through 18th century, old weaponry, and lots of interesting decorative arts, such as a roomful of old sundials and compasses. It's all on view in a sumptuous 19th-century residence.

Cost and Hours: €10, Wed-Mon 10:00-18:00, closed Tue, last entry one hour before closing, audioguide-€1, Via Manzoni 12, Metro: Montenapoleone, tel. 02-794-889, www.museopoldipezzoli.it.

Bagatti Valsecchi Museum

This unique 19th-century collection of Italian Renaissance furnishings was assembled by two aristocratic brothers who spent a wad turning their home into a Renaissance mansion.

Cost and Hours: €9 includes audioguide, €6 on Wed; open Tue-Sun 13:00-17:45, closed Mon; Via Gesù 5, Metro: Montenapoleone, tel. 02-7600-6132, www.museobagattivalsecchi.org.

SFORZA CASTLE AND NEARBY
▲Sforza Castle (Castello Sforzesco)

The castle of Milan tells the story of the city in brick. Today it features a vast courtyard, a sprawling museum (with a few worthwhile highlights and Leonardo da Vinci connections), and—most important—a chance to see Michelangelo's final, unfinished *pietà.*

Cost and Hours: €5, free entry after 16:30 (Tue after 14:00); open Tue-Sun 9:00-17:30, closed Mon; WCs and free/mandatory lockers downstairs from ticket counter, Metro: Cairoli or Lanza, tel. 02-8846-3700, www.milanocastello.it.

Background: Built in the late 1300s as a military fortress, Sforza Castle guarded the gate to the city wall and defended Milan from enemies "within and without." It was beefed up by the Sforza duke in 1450 in anticipation of a Venetian attack. Later, the Sforza family made it their residence, building their Renaissance palace into the fortress. It was even home to their in-house genius, Leonardo. (When he applied for a position with the Sforza family, he did so as a military engineer and contributed to the design of the ramparts.) During the time of foreign rule (16th-19th century), it was a barracks for occupying Spanish, French, and Austrian soldiers. Today it houses an array of museums, but I'd concentrate on the Michelangelo *pietà* and the Museum of Ancient Art.

➋ Self-Guided Tour: This tour begins outside the fortress, then focuses on the highlights inside.

The Fortress: The **gate** facing the city center stands above a ditch that was once filled with water. A relief celebrates Umberto I, the second king of Italy. Above that, a statue of St. Ambrose, the patron of Milan (and a local bishop in the fourth century), oversees the action. Notice the diagram facing the gate that shows how the city was encircled first by a crude medieval wall, and then by a state-of-the-art 16th-century wall—of which this castle was a key element. It's apparent from the enormity of these walls that Milan was a strategic prize. Today, the walls are gone, giving the city two circular boulevards.

This immense brick fortress—exhausting at first sight—can only be described as heavy. Its three huge courtyards originally functioned as military parade grounds, but today host concerts and welcome the public. (The holes in the walls were for scaffolding.)

• *As you enter the main courtyard, look to your left to see the restored hospital building that houses the...*

Museo Pietà Rondanini (Michelangelo): This is a rare opportunity to enjoy a Michelangelo statue with relatively few crowds. Michelangelo died while still working on this piece, his fourth pietà—a representation of a dead Christ with a sorrowful Virgin Mary. While unfinished and seemingly a mishmash of corrections and reworks, it's a thought-provoking work by a genius at nearly 90 years old, who knows he's fast approaching the end of his life. The symbolism is of life and of death: Jesus returning to his mother, as two bodies seem to become one.

MILAN

Michelangelo's more famous pietà at the Vatican (carved when he was in his 20s) features a beautiful, young, and astonished Mary. Here, Mary is older and wiser. Perhaps Mary is now better able to accept death as part of life...as is Michelangelo. The pietà at the Vatican is simple and clear, showing two different people: the mother holding her dead son. Contemplating the *Pietà Rondanini*, you wonder who's supporting whom. It's confused and complex, each figure seeming to both need and support the other.

This unfinished statue shows the genius of Michelangelo midway through a major rework—Christ's head is cut out of Mary's right shoulder, and an earlier arm is still just hanging there. Above Mary's right ear, you can see the remains of a previous face (eye, brow, and hairline).

And there's a certain power to this rawness. Walk around the back to see the strain in Mary's back (and Michelangelo's rough chisel work) as she struggles to support her son. The sculpture's elongated form hints at the Mannerist style that would follow.

Facing the pietà is a bronze, life-size head, based on a death mask made at the artist's passing in 1564. Imagine him working on his pietà—still vibrant and seeking.

• *From the pietà, go over the little drawbridge in the back wall—directly across from where you entered the complex. Here you'll find the entrance to the...*

Museum of Ancient Art (Museo d'Arte Antica): This sprawling collection fills the old Sforza family palace with interesting medieval armor, furniture, early Lombard art, and much more.

In the first room, among ancient sarcophagi (with early Christian themes), stands a fine 14th-century **equestrian statue**—a memorial to Bernabò Visconti. Of the four virtues, he selected only two (strength and justice) to stand beside his anatomically correct horse, opting out of love and patience.

Farther along, the room of **tapestries** is dominated by a big embroidery of St. Ambrose defeating the heretical Arians. While that was a fourth-century struggle, 12 centuries later, he was summoned back in spirit to deal with Protestants, in the form of Archbishop Borromeo. As a Counter-Reformation leader, with St. Peter's Basilica behind him, Ambrose stands tall and strong in defense of the Roman Church. The room is lined by 16th-century Flemish tapestries, which were easy to pack up quickly as the nobility traveled. These were typical of those used to warm chilly stone palaces.

Next, you'll come to the **Sala Alberata** ("tree-lined room;"

MILAN

may be closed for restoration when you visit). The Visconti family grew rich making silk in the Lake Como area. While plastered over for centuries, this room was restored around 1900. Not much sparkle survives, but you can appreciate the intricate canopy woven with branches and rope in complicated knots—the work of Leonardo himself, in 1498. The tiny Leonardo-esque painting of Madonna and Child is by Francesco Napoletano, a pupil of Leonardo. The painting's structure, anatomy, and subtle modeling of the color with no harsh lines *(sfumato)* are all characteristic of Leonardo. In the upper right, notice the castle, as it looked in 1495.

From here, you'll pass through rooms filled with weapons and armor from the 16th and 17th centuries.

• *At this point, you're free to go. But if you have a larger-than-average attention span, follow signs upstairs to the Decorative Arts Museum, then the Painting Gallery (Pinacoteca), and finally the Musical Instruments Museum. When you're done, consider popping out the back door of the fortress and taking a break in the lush Sempione Park (described next).*

Parco Sempione

This is Milan's equivalent of Central Park. With its circa-1900 English-style gardens, free Liberty-Style aquarium, views of the triumphal arch, and sprawling family-friendly grounds, this park is particularly popular on weekends.

A five-minute walk through the park, on the left, is the erector-set **Branca Tower** (Torre Branca), built for an exposition in the 1930s. For an inexpensive, commanding city view, you can ride an elevator as high as the Mary that crowns the Duomo (best in daylight, erratic hours—call or confirm at TI before making a special trip, Metro: Cadorna, tel. 02-331-4120).

Next to the tower is the excellent **Triennale di Milano,** a design museum with changing exhibits that celebrate one of this city's fortes (www.triennale.org).

At the far end of the park is the monumental **Arco della Pace.** Originally an arch of triumph, it comes with Nike, goddess of victory, commanding a six-horse chariot. It was built facing Paris to welcome Napoleon's rule and to celebrate the ideals of the French Revolution, destined to lift Italy into the modern age. When the locals learned Napoleon was just another megalomaniac, they turned the horses around, their tails facing France.

▲Via Dante

This grand pedestrian boulevard and popular shopping street leads from Sforza Castle toward the town center and the Duomo. Via Dante was carved out of a medieval tangle of streets to celebrate Italian unification (c. 1870) and make Milan a worthy metropolis. Consequently, all the facades lining it are relatively new. Enjoy

MILAN

strolling this beautiful people zone, where you'll hear the whir of bikes and the lilting melodies of accordion players instead of traffic noise. Photo exhibits are frequently displayed up and down the street. In front of Sforza Castle, a commanding statue of Giuseppe Garibaldi, a hero of the unification movement, looks down one of Europe's longest pedestrian zones. From here you can walk to the Duomo and beyond (about 1.5 miles), appreciating Italian design both in shop windows and on smartly clothed Milanese.

AWAY FROM THE CENTER
▲Naviglio Grande (Canal District)

Milan, although far from any major lake or river, has a sizable port, literally called the "Big Canal." Since 1170, boats have been able to sail from Milan to the Mediter-ranean via the Ticino River (which flows into the Po River on its way to the Adriatic Sea). Five hundred years ago, Leonardo helped design a modern lock system. During the booming Industrial Age in the 19th century—and especially with the flurry of construction after Italian unification—ships used the canals to bring in the marble and stone needed to make Milan the great city it is today. In fact, one canal (filled in during the 1930s) let barges unload stone right at the building site of the great cathedral. In the 1950s, landlocked Milan was the seventh-biggest port in Italy, as its canals aided in rebuilding the bombed-out city. Today, disused train tracks parallel the canal, old warehouse buildings recall the area's working-class heritage, and former workers' tenements—once squalid and undesirable— are being renovated. The once-rough area now dubbed Milan's "Little Venice" is trendy, traffic-free, pricey, and thriving with inviting bars and eateries. Come here for dinner or a late-afternoon drink (for recommendations, see "Eating in Milan," later).

Getting There: Ride the Metro (or tram #2) to Porta Genova, exit following signs to Via Casale, and walk the length of Via Casale one block directly to the canal. Most bars and restaurants are to the left, on both sides of the canal.

Leonardo's Horse

The largest equestrian monument in the world is a modern reconstruction of a model created in 1482 by Leonardo da Vinci for the Sforza family. The clay prototype was destroyed in 1499 by invading French forces, who used it for target practice. In 1982, American Renaissance-art collector Charles Dent decided to build the 15-ton, 24-foot-long statue from Leonardo's design, planning to present it to the Italians in homage to Leonardo's genius. Unfortunately, Dent died before the project could be completed. In 1997, American sculptor Nina Akamu created a new clay model that became the template for the final statue; it was unveiled in 1999.

Getting There: The statue (free to view) is at a horse racetrack on the western outskirts of town—ride Metro purple line 5 to San Siro Ippodromo.

▲Monumental Cemetery (Il Cimitero Monumentale)

Europe's most artistic and dreamy cemetery experience, this grand place was built just after unification to provide a suitable final rest-

ing spot for the city's "famous and well-deserving men." Any cemetery can be evocative, but this one—with its super-emotional portrayals of the deceased and their heavenly escorts (in art styles c. 1870-1930)—is in a class by itself. It's a vast garden art-gallery of proud busts and grim reapers, heartbroken angels and weeping widows, too-young soldiers and countless old smiles, frozen on yellowed black-and-white photos.

Cost and Hours: Free, Tue-Sun 8:00-18:00, closed Mon, pick up map at the entrance gate, ride Metro purple line 5 to Monumentale, tel. 02-8846-5600.

Shopping in Milan

HIGH FASHION IN THE QUADRILATERAL

For world-class window shopping, visit the Quadrilateral, an elegant high-fashion shopping area around Via Montenapoleone, northeast of La Scala. This was the original Beverly Hills of Milan. In the 1920s, the top fashion shops moved in, and today it remains *the* place for designer labels. Most shops close Sunday and for much of August. On Mondays, stores open only after 16:00. In this land where fur is still prized, the people-watching is as entertaining as the window shopping. Notice also the exclusive penthouse apartments with roof gardens high above the scene. Via Montenapoleone and the pedestrianized Via della Spiga are the best streets.

Whether you're gawking or shopping, here's the best route:

MILAN

From La Scala, walk up Via Manzoni to the Metro stop at Monte-napoleone, browse down Via Montenapoleone, and cut left on Via Santo Spirito (lined with grand aristocratic palazzos—peek into the courtyard at #7). Across the street, step into the elegant court-yard at #10 to check out the café sitters and their poodles. Con-tinue to the end of Via Santo Spirito, then turn right to window shop down traffic-free Via della Spiga. After a few short blocks, turn right on Via Sant'Andrea and then left, back onto Monte-napoleone, which leads you through a final gauntlet of temptations to Corso Giacomo Matteotti, near the Piazza San Babila. Then (for less-expensive shopping thrills), walk back to the Duomo down the pedestrian-only Corso Vittorio Emanuele II.

NEAR THE DUOMO

For a (slightly) more reasonably priced shopping excursion, step into **La Rinascente**—one of Europe's classic department stores. (As you face the front of the Duomo, it's around the left side.) Sim-ply riding the escalator up and up gives a fun overview of Italian design and marketing. The seventh floor is a top-end food circus with recommended restaurants, terrace views of the Duomo, and a public WC. The store's name translates roughly as "the place reborn" and fits its history. In an earlier life, this was a fine Art Nouveau-style building—until it burned down in 1918. Rebuilt, it was bombed in World War II and rebuilt once again (Mon-Thu 9:30-21:00, Fri-Sat 9:30-22:00, Sun 10:00-21:00, has a VAT re-fund office, faces north side of the Duomo on Piazza del Duomo).

Heading away from the Duomo, stroll between the arcades on the Corso Vittorio Emanuele II, surrounded by clothing stores and other tempting material pleasures. At Via Passarella, detour to the right to check out **Excelsior,** a bold high-end concept store. Moving walkways take you from level to colorful level with puls-ing music and electronic art installations. If you're looking for the perfect €1,000 shirt, you've come to the right place. Otherwise, hit **Eat's Food Market,** a stylish deli in the basement, and pick up a tasty high-design salad to go (daily 9:00-22:00, Galleria del Corso 4, two long blocks behind the Duomo, tel. 027-630-7301).

Double back to the Corso Vittorio Emanuele II to continue shopping all the way to the San Babila Metro station (and the ritzy Quadrilatero area described earlier).

Nightlife in Milan

For evening action, check out the artsy Brera area in the old center, with several swanky sidewalk cafés to choose from and lots of bars that stay open late. Home to the local art university, this district has a sophisticated, lively people-watching scene. Another great neighborhood for nightlife, especially for a younger scene, is Naviglio Grande (the canal district), Milan's formerly bohemian, now gentrified "Little Venice" (described earlier; Metro: Porta Genova; tram #2).

There are always concerts and live music playing in the city at various clubs and concert halls. Specifics change quickly, so it's best to rely on the entertainment information in periodicals from the TI.

Sleeping in Milan

My recommended hotels are all within a few minutes' walk of a Metro station. With Milan's fine subway system, you can get anywhere in town in a flash.

Hotel prices in Milan rise and fall with the convention schedule. In March, April, September, and October, the city can be completely jammed by conventions, and hotel prices go sky-high; it's best to avoid the city entirely at these times if you can (for the convention schedule, see www.fieramilano.it). My rankings are based on regular prices, not the much-higher convention rates.

Summer is usually wide-open, with soft or discounted prices, though many hotels close in August for vacation. Hotels cater more to business travelers than to tourists, so prices and availability are a little better on Fridays and Saturdays.

There are only a few small, family-style hotels left in the center, and the good ones charge top dollar for their location. To save money, consider searching online for a deal at a basic chain hotel (such as Ibis) near a Metro stop.

NEAR THE DUOMO

The Duomo area is thick with people-watching, reasonably priced eateries, and the major sightseeing attractions, but hotel prices are high.

$$$$ Hotel Spadari boasts a modern, Art Deco-inspired lobby designed by the Milanese artist Giò Pomodoro ("Joe Tomato" in English). The 40 rooms have billowing drapes, big paintings, and designer doors. It's next to the recommended Peck Gourmet Deli, and two blocks from the Duomo (RS%, air-con, elevator, Via Spadari 11, tel. 02-7200-2371, www.spadarihotel.com, reservation@spadarihotel.com).

$$$$ Hotel Gran Duca di York, three blocks from the Duomo, is on a stark street of banks and public buildings. Public areas are comfortable and spacious, and the 33 rooms are modern and bright (RS%, air-con, elevator, near Metro stops: Cordusio or Duomo, Via Moneta 1, tel. 02-874-863, www.ducadiyork.com, info@ducadiyork.com).

MILAN

Sleep Code

Hotels are classified based on the average price of a standard double room with breakfast in high season.

$$$$	**Splurge:** Most rooms over €170
$$$	**Pricier:** €130-170
$$	**Moderate:** €90-130
$	**Budget:** €50-90
¢	**Backpacker:** Under €50
RS%	Rick Steves discount

Unless otherwise noted, credit cards are accepted, hotel staff speak basic English, and free Wi-Fi is available. Comparison-shop by checking prices at several hotels (on each hotel's own website, on a booking site, or by email). For the best deal, *book directly with the hotel*. Ask for a discount if paying in cash; if the listing includes **RS%**, request a Rick Steves discount.

BETWEEN LA SCALA AND SFORZA CASTLE

These slightly less central places are close to the Via Dante and Via Brera shopping and restaurant scenes.

$$$$ Antica Locanda dei Mercanti offers 15 rooms in an 18th-century palazzo. While each room has its own personality (some have kitchens, others have spacious terraces), all have a fresh-flower vibe that embraces old and new—a nice change for business-like Milan (RS%—use code "RSMILANO", air-con, elevator, Via San Tomaso 6, reception on first floor, Metro: Cairoli or Cordusio, tel. 02-805-4080, www.locanda.it, locanda@locanda.it, Alex and Eri).

$$$ Hotel Star rents 30 rooms, most of which are spacious, modernized, and feature animal murals. Fourth-floor rooms are somewhat dated and gaudy; interior rooms are quieter (air-con, elevator, usually closed for 2 weeks in mid-Aug, Via dei Bossi 5, Metro: Cordusio, tel. 02-801-501, www.hotelstar.it, hotelstar@hotelstar.it, cheeky Vittoria).

$$$ London Hotel is a faded, old-school hotel with a living room-like lobby and 29 basic rooms with tiny bathrooms. It's overpriced for what you get, but in a fine location (cheaper rooms with shared bath, breakfast extra—better to grab something on Via Dante, air-con, elevator, Via Rovello 3, Metro: Cairoli, tel. 02-7202-0166, www.hotellondonmilano.com, info@hotellondonmilano.com, sisters Tanya and Licia).

NEAR *THE LAST SUPPER*

These two hotels are farther from the action in a sleepy, mostly residential zone, but the prices are lower. For locations (about a

15-minute walk or quick tram or Metro ride west of the Duomo), see the map on page 274.

$$$ Antica Locanda Leonardo, just down the street from *The Last Supper,* has a romantic, Old World vibe and antique furnishings. Each of its 16 uniquely decorated rooms face either a courtyard (cheaper, some street noise) or a tranquil garden (RS%, some rooms with garden balcony, air-con, elevator, Corso Magenta 78, tel. 02-48014197, www.anticalocandaleonardo.com, info@ anticalocandaleonardo.com). From the Duomo area, you can ride tram #16 or take the Metro to either Cadorna or Conciliazione and walk five minutes.

$$ B&B Hotel Milano Sant'Ambrogio, part of a chain of budget hotels, has 75 efficient, cookie-cutter rooms. They come with some tram noise (request a quieter one) but are worth considering if you can get a deal (breakfast extra, air-con, elevator, Via degli Olivetani 4, Metro: S. Ambrogio, tel. 02-4810-1089, www. hotelbb.com, mi.santambrogio@hotelbb.com). It's on a side street near the Leonardo da Vinci Science Museum, about a five-minute walk from either *The Last Supper* or Basilica Sant'Ambrogio.

NEAR MILANO CENTRALE TRAIN STATION

The train station neighborhood is more practical than characteristic. Its hotels are utilitarian business-class places with prices that bounce all over depending upon the convention schedule; most of the year, many have rooms in the €100-125 range. You'll find more shady characters than shady trees in the parks, and lots of ethnic restaurants and massage parlors as you head away from the immediate vicinity of the station. But it's convenient to trains, the Metro, and airport shuttles, and if you hit it outside of convention times, the prices are hard to beat.

On Via Napo Torriani: This street, a five-minute walk in front of the station, is lined with midrange hotels (exit the station, head straight across the square, then veer left onto Via Napo Torriani). **$$ Hotel Berna** feels like a classic European hotel, with an old-school lobby, uniformed bellhops, and 116 faded rooms with some nice upgrades (Via Napo Torriani 18, tel. 02-677-311, www. hotelberna.com). **$$ Hotel Garda** is cheaper and less welcoming, with 55 rooms (RS%—email first to get a promo code, then book on their website; breakfast extra, Via Napo Torriani 21, tel. 02-6698-2626, www.hotelgardamilan.com).

Hostel: ¢ Ostello Bello Grande has converted what was a business-class hotel into a well-priced hostel with hipster flair. Worth considering even if you're not a hosteler, it comes with an inviting rooftop terrace and a shared kitchen (private rooms available, includes breakfast and *aperitivo* happy-hour snacks, air-con, elevator, laundry, Via Lepetit 33, tel. 02-670-5921, www.ostellobello.

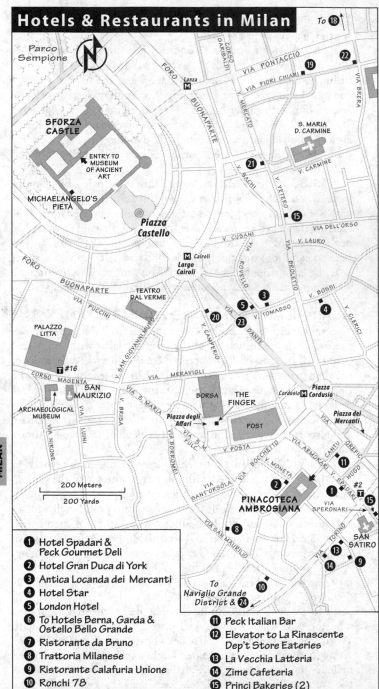

Hotels & Restaurants in Milan

To 18

Parco Sempione

N

SFORZA CASTLE

ENTRY TO MUSEUM OF ANCIENT ART

MICHAELANGELO'S PIETÀ

Piazza Castello

PALAZZO LITTA

SAN MAURIZIO

ARCHAEOLOGICAL MUSEUM

TEATRO DAL VERME

BORSA

THE FINGER

POST

Piazza degli Affari

Piazza Cordusio

Piazza dei Mercanti

PINACOTECA AMBROSIANA

SAN SATIRO

To Naviglio Grande District & 24

200 Meters

200 Yards

MILAN

1 Hotel Spadari &
   Peck Gourmet Deli
2 Hotel Gran Duca di York
3 Antica Locanda dei Mercanti
4 Hotel Star
5 London Hotel
6 To Hotels Berna, Garda &
   Ostello Bello Grande
7 Ristorante da Bruno
8 Trattoria Milanese
9 Ristorante Calafuria Unione
10 Ronchi 78

11 Peck Italian Bar
12 Elevator to La Rinascente
   Dep't Store Eateries
13 La Vecchia Latteria
14 Zime Cafeteria
15 Princi Bakeries (2)

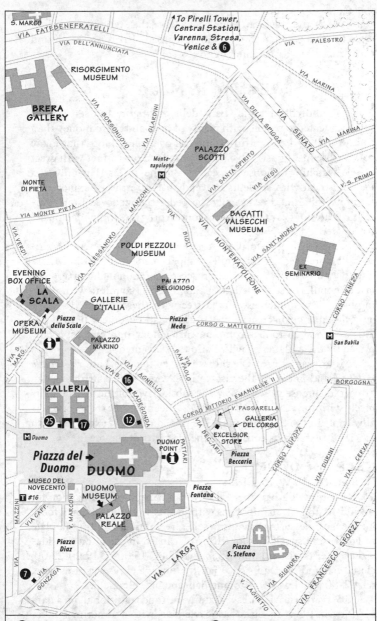

To Pirelli Tower, Central Station, Varenna, Stresa, Venice & 6

MILAN

16 Luini Panzerotti & Cioccolati Italiani
17 Il Mercato del Duomo
18 To Eataly
19 Via Fiori Chiari Eateries
20 Antica Osteria Milanese
21 Convivium Ristorante and Pizza
22 Bar Brera & Via Brera Eateries
23 Via Dante Eateries
24 To Naviglio Grande Eateries
25 Bar Camparino

com). With the tracks to your back, leave the station to the left, cross the taxi stand, and then cross the road. The hostel is around the corner from Ristorante Giglio Rosso.

Eating in Milan

Milan's hundreds of trendy bars, delis, *rosticcerie*, and self-service cafeterias cater to people with plenty of taste and more money than time. You'll find delightful eateries all over town (note that many places close in August). To eat mediocre food on a street with great people-watching, choose an eatery on the pedestrian-only Via Dante. To eat with students in trendy little trattorias, explore the Brera neighborhood (especially the pedestrianized Via Fiori Chiari). To eat well near the Duomo, consider the recommended places listed later.

Some locals like to precede lunch or dinner with an *aperitivo*—a before-meal drink (while Campari made its debut in Milan, a simple glass of *vino bianco* or prosecco, the Italian champagne, is just as popular). At about 17:00, bars fill their counters with inviting baskets of munchies, served free with these drinks. If you're either likable or discreet, a cheap drink can become a light meal. This *aperitivo* custom is common throughout Italy but especially prized by the Milanesi—who claim they invented it.

Milan's signature dishes (often served together) are *risotto alla milanese* and *ossobuco*. The risotto is flavored with saffron, which gives it its intense yellow color. The subtle flavor of the saffron pairs nicely with the veal shanks of *ossobuco* (meaning "marrow" or, literally, "hole in the bone" shank). The prized marrow, extracted with special little forks, is considered the best part of the meal.

NEAR THE DUOMO
Restaurants with Class

$$ Ristorante da Bruno serves Tuscan cuisine with a passion for fresh fish. This place impresses with its dressy waiters, hearty food, inexpensive desserts, and a fine self-serve antipasto buffet (a plate full of Tuscan specialties for €10). You can eat inside or on the sidewalk under fascist columns (Sun-Fri 12:00-15:00 & 19:00-23:00, closed Sat and Aug, air-con, Via M. Gonzaga 6, reservations wise, tel. 02-804-364, www.ristorantedabruno.biz, Graziella).

$$ Trattoria Milanese is family-run and traditional, on a dark back street. It has an enthusiastic clientele, with a sometimes-lukewarm staff—the restaurant didn't even bother to get a phone until 1988. Expect a Milanese ambience. Eat early for a less-crowded atmosphere (Mon-Sat 12:00-15:00 & 19:00-23:30, closed Sun and mid-July-Aug, evening reservations recommended, air-con, Via Santa Marta 11, near Pinacoteca Ambrosiana, tel. 02-8645-1991).

Restaurant Price Code

I've assigned each eatery a price category, based on the average cost of a typical main course (pasta or *secondi*). Drinks, desserts, and splurge items (steak and seafood) can raise the price considerably.

$$$$	**Splurge:**	Most main courses over €20
$$$	**Pricier:**	€15-20
$$	**Moderate:**	€10-15
$	**Budget:**	Under €10

In Italy, pizza by the slice and other takeout food is **$**; a basic trattoria or sit-down pizzeria is **$$**; a casual but more upscale restaurant is **$$$**; and a swanky splurge is **$$$$**.

$$ Ristorante Calafuria Unione is a thriving Milanese-style eatery that attracts a sizable lunch crowd for its pizza and local dishes. It feels like a well-loved diner (Mon-Sat 12:00-15:00 & 19:00-24:00, closed Sun, air-con, a few blocks south of Piazza del Duomo at Via dell'Unione 8, Metro: Missori, tel. 02-866-103).

$$$ Ronchi 78, a Milan institution for a century, is tight and atmospheric. The main dining room is cozy, while downstairs, more seating sprawls through vaulted cellars. Come here for traditional Milanese cuisine—and, if you're eating late like the Italians do, stay for the nightly "guitarroche" live music (cheaper at lunch, closed Sun, Via San Maurilio 7, tel. 02-867-295, www.ronchi78.it).

$$ Peck Italian Bar is a hit with the sophisticated office crowd, which mobs the place at lunch for its fast, excellent meals with im-peck-able service. It's owned by the same people who run the recommended high-end Peck Gourmet Deli (listed later), so be prepared to spend—getting to hang out and be part of the scene makes it worth the money. Any time you find yourself among such a quality-conscious group of Milanesi, you know you're getting good food (Mon-Fri 7:30-22:00, Sat 9:00-22:00, closed Sun, Via Cantù 3, tel. 02-869-3017, www.peck.it).

Dining with a Duomo View

The seventh floor of La Rinascente department store, alongside the Duomo, has an upscale food court. Three of its many eateries share a sunny outdoor terrace with views of the cathedral's rooftop: **$$$ Obicà** is a swanky "mozzarella bar" (part of a chain), offering this heavenly cheese in all its various forms—cow's milk, buffalo, and smoked—in salads, on pizzas, or on splittable €23 antipasto sampler plates, accompanied by *salumi*, tapenades, and vegetables (there are dishes without mozzarella, too). **$$$ Ristorante Maio** has pricey full-meal service. And **$$$ Il Bar,** living-room cozy with cushy divans and low coffee tables, serves light meals (salads, pasta), coffee, desserts, and cocktails (all three open daily until 24:00; after store hours, use the elevator on Via S. Radegonda to enter).

Cheaper Eats and Takeout near the Duomo

$$ **La Vecchia Latteria,** with a 50-year history, is a bright hole-in-the-wall that serves a good vegetarian lunch. This busy joint—with tight seating in front and behind the kitchen—serves soup, salads, pastas, and imaginative veggie entrées at affordable prices. Their star offering is *il misto forno*, a delicious assortment of soufflés, quiches, and roasted and sautéed veggies (Mon-Sat 12:00-16:00, closed Sun, just off Via Torino at Via dell'Unione 6, a few blocks southwest of the Duomo, Metro: Missori, tel. 02-874-401).

$$ **Zime** cafeteria, in a basement a short walk from the Duomo, is popular with office workers at lunch. Though windowless and a bit noisy, it's inexpensive, authentic, tastefully decorated, and air-conditioned. Decide on one of the set-price combos listed on the wall, and then choose from the dishes on offer (Mon-Fri 9:00-15:00, closed Sat-Sun, free Wi-Fi; enter the gallery at Via Torino 23, then go downstairs; tel. 02-9163-8484).

$ **Princi** bakery is mobbed with locals vying for focaccia, olive breadsticks, and luscious pastries. Notice the stacked-wood-oven action in the back. For most pastry items (like the brioche), pay the cashier first; for items sold by weight (such as pizza and cake), get it weighed before you pay. Consider a pasta lunch (12:00-15:00 only) for €6 per plate (open Mon-Sat 7:00-20:00, Sun 9:00-19:30; off Via Torino, a block southwest of Piazza del Duomo at Via Speronari 6; tel. 02-874-797). Another Princi bakery, more like a café, is near Sforza Castle and is listed later.

Peck Gourmet Deli is an aristocratic deli with a pricey gourmet grocery, *rosticceria*, and pastry/gelato shop on the main level; a fancy restaurant upstairs; and an expensive *enoteca* wine cellar in the basement. Even if all you can afford is the aroma, peek in. Check out the classic circa-1930 salami slicers and the gourmet assembly line in the kitchen in the back. The *rosticceria* serves delectable fancy food to go for a superb picnic dinner. It's sold by weight; order by the *etto*—100-gram unit, 250 grams equals about a half-pound (Mon 15:30-20:30, Tue-Fri 9:30-20:30, Sat 9:00-20:00, Sun 10:00-17:00, Via Spadari 9, tel. 02-802-3161).

$ **Luini Panzerotti,** a local institution, is a bakery that serves up €3-5 piping-hot mini calzones *(panzerotti)* stuffed with mozzarella, tomatoes, ham, or whatever you like (Mon 10:00-15:00, Tue-Sat 10:00-20:00, closed Sun and Aug, Via S. Radegonda 16, tel. 02-8646-1917). From the back of the Duomo, head north and look for the lines out front. Order from the menus posted on the wall behind the cash registers. Traditionally, Milanesi munch their hot little meals on nearby Piazza San Fedele. Don't overlook the *dolci* half of the menu. Across the street is another local hit, **Cioccolati Italiani,** for chocoholics in search of a treat.

Upscale Food Halls
Throughout Europe, gourmet food halls are taking over formerly underutilized spaces. The same is true in Milan. Across from the Duomo, next to Galleria Vittorio Emanuele II, **Il Mercato del Duomo** has conquered several floors above La Feltrinelli bookstore. Budget options abound with a pasta bar, focaccia/sandwich section, "street food," and a *cafféteria*. Lighter fare is at their salad and *salumi* bar. For a fancy drink, head to the champagne bar or the Aperol terrace. And for a splurge, go to the top-restaurant Spazio Milano, run by three-star Michelin chef Niko Romito's cooking school (daily 11:00-22:00, Piazza del Duomo 1, tel. 02-8633-1924, www.ilmercatodelduomo.it).

Similarly, **Eataly** (also in Rome, Florence, and New York) has turned the former Teatro Smeraldo into a gourmet megastore. It's overwhelming but oddly enchanting, with its overpriced Italian market goods and restaurants with all the major food groups—pasta, meats, vegetables, chocolate, and, of course, gelato (daily 10:00-24:00, Piazza XXV Aprile 10, Metro: Moscova, tel. 02-4949-7301, www.eataly.net).

EATING NEAR VIA BRERA AND VIA DANTE
These restaurants are near the Cairoli and Lanza Metro stations and are convenient to Sforza Castle and nearby recommended hotels. The Brera neighborhood, surrounding the Church of St. Carmine, is laced with narrow, inviting pedestrian streets. Make an evening of your visit by having an *aperitivo* with snacks at recommended Bar Brera or any other bar—most serve munchies with drinks from 17:00 until 21:00. Afterward, stroll along restaurant row on Via Fiori Chiari and Via Brera, or duck into the semicircular lane of Via Madonnina to survey the sidewalk cafés as you pass fortune tellers, artists, and knockoff handbag vendors. To locate these eateries, see the map on page 304.

$$ Antica Osteria Milanese is a hardworking family place with a smart local following and spacious, stylish seating. They serve good-quality, typical Milanese favorites (Mon-Sat 12:15-14:30 & 19:30-23:00, closed Sun, Via Camperio 12, tel. 02-861-367, Alessandro).

$$$ Convivium Ristorante and Pizza is popular for its extensive wine list, clever dishes (especially beef and fish), and conviviality. It's trendy but classy (daily 12:00-14:30 & 19:00-24:00, facing Santa Maria del Carmine church at Via Ponte Vetero 21, tel. 02-8646-3708, Claudio and Nicola).

$ Princi bakery's branch on Via Ponte Vetero works the same as the one on Via Speronari (listed earlier), only it's more like a restaurant, with seating both inside and on the street. While the bakery and café are open all day, their meal counter (with €6 plates) serves only from 12:00 to 15:00 (Mon-Sat 7:00-20:00, Sun from 9:00, Via Ponte Vetero 10, tel. 02-7201-6067).

$ Bar Brera serves inexpensive sandwiches, pastas, and salads to throngs of art students and has a lively *aperitivo* happy hour (drinks and a buffet of hearty snacks starts at 18:00; open daily 7:00-late, Via Brera 23, tel. 02-877-091).

Fancy Via Dante Bars and Cafés: Thriving and central, Via Dante is lined with hardworking eateries where you can join locals for a lively lunch. Or just swing by for a morning *caffè*, watching the parade of Milanesi heading to work.

IN NAVIGLIO GRANDE (CANAL DISTRICT)

Consider ending your day at the former port of Milan. The Naviglio Grande district bustles with memorable and affordable bars and restaurants and a great people scene. In addition to endless *aperitivo* spreads and traditional trattorias, there are some more creative choices, too: Greek fare, artisanal microbrews, and "Brazilian sushi."

Getting There: Ride the Metro or tram #2 to Porta Genova and walk down Via Casale, which dead-ends a block away at the canal. Walk halfway across the metal bridge and survey the scene. The street you just walked has plenty of cheap options. Most of the action—and all of my other recommendations—are to the left, on or near the canal. Do a reconnaissance stroll before settling in somewhere: Walk down the left bank of the canal to the bridge with cars, then go back on the other side.

Here are a few good options to consider, listed in the order you'll pass them.

$$$$ Ristorante Brellin is the top romantic splurge, with a dressy crowd and fine food. The menu is international while clinging to a bit of tradition (daily 12:30-15:00 & 19:00-24:00; kitchen closes at 23:00; located where a small lane, Vicolo dei Lavandai, branches off from the canal; tel. 02-5810-1351, www.brellin.it).

$ Pizzeria Tradizionale, at the far end of the walk after you cross the bridge, is a local favorite (Thu-Tue 12:00-14:30 & 19:00-24:00, Wed 19:00-24:00, at the far end of canal walk, Ripa di Porta Ticinese 7, tel. 02-839-5133).

$$ Cucina Fusetti is a charming little place a few doors off the canal, serving pan-Mediterranean cuisine, including *bacalao*—salt cod (Mon-Sat 19:00-23:00, closed Sun; near the curved bridge with the zigzag design, go away from canal on Via Argelati to Via M. Fusetti 1; mobile 340-861-2676).

$ **Pizzeria Spaghetteria La Magolfa,** down a side street, feels like a neighborhood hangout, offering good, cheap salads, pastas, and pizzas. You can sit inside, on a veranda, or at a table on the street. For less than €20, two people could split a hearty pizza and a good bottle of wine (Mon-Sat 11:00-16:00 & 18:00-24:00, Sun 18:00-24:00, go a long block past Cucina Fusetti to end of street, Via Magolfa 15, tel. 02-832-1696.

On your way back to the Metro or tram, stop by **Orso Bianco** for "artisanal" gelato. Their *nocciola*—or hazelnut—is *buonissimo* (Via Casale 7, on your right as you walk back to the Metro, tel. 02-97386848).

Milan Connections

BY TRAIN

From Milano Centrale by Train to: Venice (2/hour, most direct on high-speed ES trains, 2.5 hours), **Florence** (hourly, 2 hours), **Genoa** (hourly, 2 hours), **Rome** (2-3/hour, 3-3.5 hours), **Brindisi** (4 direct/day, 2 night trains, 9-15 hours), **Cinque Terre/La Spezia** (hourly, 3 hours direct or with change in Genoa; trains from La Spezia to the villages go nearly hourly), **Cinque Terre/Monterosso al Mare** (8/day direct, otherwise hourly with change in Genoa, 3 hours), **Varenna** on Lake Como (1 hour; small line direct to Lecco/Sondrio/Tirano leaves at :20 past most hours—confirm these times), **Stresa** on Lake Maggiore (about hourly; 50-minute fast train may require reservations, while 1.5-hour train doesn't), **Como** (2/hour, 30-60 minutes, boats go from Como to Varenna until about 19:00), **Naples** (direct trains hourly, 5 hours, more with change in Rome, overnight possible); see www.trenitalia.com for details.

From Milano Porta Garibaldi by High-Speed Train: Italo offers additional high-speed connections (some direct) to **Florence** (10/day, 2 hours), **Rome** (16/day, 3-3.5 hours), and **Naples** (12/day, 4.5-5 hours). While Italo is often cheaper (particularly if you book long in advance), it doesn't accept rail passes, and you'll have to change stations in Milan if you're connecting to or from anywhere else (for details on Italo, see page 1157 or visit www.italotreno.it).

International Destinations: Basel, with connections to Frankfurt (3/day, 4 hours), **Geneva** (4/day, 4 hours), **Lugano** (almost hourly, 1 hour), **Munich** (night train weekdays only, 9 hours), **Nice** (6/day, change in Ventimiglia, 5 hours), **Paris** (3/day from Milano Porta Garibaldi, 7 hours; daily night train from Milano Centrale, 11 hours), **Vienna** (night train on weekdays only, 11 hours), **Zürich** (4/day, 3 hours).

Train Connections from Milan

BY PLANE

To get flight information for Malpensa or Linate airports or the phone number of your airline, call 02-74851 or 02-232-323 and wait for English options, or check www.sea-aeroportimilano.it.

Note: While the train works best for Malpensa, if you want to take a shuttle bus to any of Milan's airports, just go to Milano Centrale station and walk out the door marked *Piazza Luigi di Savoia*. There, you'll find little sales kiosks aggressively selling tickets for all your options.

Malpensa Airport

Most international flights land at Terminal 1 of the manageable Malpensa Airport (airport code: MXP), 28 miles northwest of Milan. Low-cost EU flights use Terminal 2 (buses connect the two). Both have ATMs and exchange offices. Terminal 1 has a pharmacy, eateries, and a hotel-reservation service disguised as a TI. When you leave the baggage-carousel area, go right to reach services and exit (tel. 02-5858-0080).

Trains from Malpensa to Milan: The Malpensa Express train is usually the most sensible (not covered by rail passes, tel. 800-500-005, www.malpensaexpress.it). Trains leave from an underground station at Terminal 2; buy your ticket from a kiosk in the

MILAN

arrivals hall or from Trenord ticket machines in the baggage claim hall (credit cards accepted). A big electronic board shows the next departure times. There are two lines: Malpensa-Milano Cadorna and Malpensa-Milano Centrale. For either, the ride costs €12 one-way. Validate your ticket in the little machines, and double-check to make sure your train is going to the destination you want.

If you are headed downtown or to most other points in the city, take the **Cadorna** line, which is quicker, runs more often and later, and drops you at a convenient downtown Metro station (2/hour, 35 minutes; usually departs airport at :28 and :58 past the hour, generally departs Cadorna at :27 and :57 past the hour, last train from airport leaves 1:03 in the morning, first train from Cadorna leaves 4:27).

If you are heading to the area around Milano Centrale train station, or connecting by train to other destinations, take the **Centrale** line (2/hour, 50 minutes, usually departs airport at :05 and :35 past the hour and Milano Centrale at :25 and :55 past the hour, last train from airport leaves 22:43, first train from Milano Centrale leaves 5:25).

If you're **leaving Milan** to go *to* the airport, purchase your ticket before you board, either from the green Trenord ticket machines or, at Cadorna Station, from the staffed ticket windows. At Milano Centrale, trains leave from tracks 2 and 3; ticket machines are at the end of track 3, which is hidden behind track 4 and poorly signed. Cadorna is a little easier to deal with; trains usually depart from track 1.

By Shuttle Bus: Two bus companies run between Malpensa Airport and Milano Centrale train station, offering virtually identical, competing services. They each charge about €10 for the one-hour trip (buy ticket from driver) and depart from the same places: in front of Terminal 2 (outside exit 4) and from Piazza Luigi di Savoia (on the east side of Milan's central train station—with your back to the tracks, exit to the left). They also pick up and drop off at Terminal 1, which, if your flight docks there, makes the bus an option rather than taking the train. Buses leave about every 20 minutes, every day, from very early until just after midnight (Malpensa Shuttle tel. 02-5858-3185, www.malpensashuttle.it; Autostradale tel. 02-3391-0794, www.autostradale.it).

By Taxi: Taxis into Milan cost a fixed rate of €90; avoid hustlers in airport halls (catch taxis outside exit 6). Considering how far the city is from the airport and how good the train and bus services are, Milan is the last place I'd take an airport taxi.

Linate Airport

Most European flights land at Linate (airport code: LIN), five miles east of Milan. The airport has a bank with an ATM (just

MILAN

past customs) and a hotel-finding service disguised as a TI (daily 7:30-23:30, tel. 02-7020-0443). Eventually the Metro's new line 4 will link Linate with the city. For now, you can get to downtown Milan by bus or taxi.

By Bus: Public bus #73 connects Linate in about 20 minutes to the San Babila Metro station (ride one stop to the Duomo on red line 1 or walk 10 minutes; covered by €1.50 public transit ticket, which is valid for connecting to Metro, departs every 10 minutes, less frequently evenings and Sun).

If you're *leaving* Milan to go to the airport, follow underground signs at San Babila Metro station to bus #73 and airport. From the exit, cross the street. With Teatro Nuovo on your right, walk 100 yards to the bus stop.

Private companies also run shuttles to Milano Centrale train station (handy only if you're catching a train; €5, 2/hour, 35 minutes, www.airportbusexpress.it).

By Taxi: Taxis from Linate to the Duomo cost about €25.

Bergamo (Orio al Serio) Airport

Some budget airlines, such as Ryanair and Wizz Air, use Bergamo Airport—about 30 miles from Milan—as their Milan hub (airport code: BGY, tel. 035-326-323, www.sacbo.it). At least three bus companies ply the route between the east side of Milano Centrale train station (Piazza Luigi di Savoia) and Orio al Serio (€5, about 5/hour, 1 hour): Autostradale (www.airportbusexpress.it), Terravision (www.terravision.eu), and the Orio Shuttle (www.orioshuttle.com).

THE CINQUE TERRE

Riomaggiore • Manarola • Corniglia • Vernazza • Monterosso al Mare

Along a beautifully isolated six-mile stretch of the most seductive corner of the Italian Riviera lies the Cinque Terre (CHINK-weh TAY-reh)—five *(cinque)* small towns gently and steadily carving a good life out of difficult terrain.

Each village fills a ravine with a lazy hive of human activity. Calloused locals and sunburned travelers enjoy the area's unique mix of Italian culture and nature. With a traffic-free charm—a happy result of their natural isolation—these towns are the rugged alternative to the glitzy Riviera resorts nearby (covered in the next chapter). There's not a Fiat or museum in sight—just sun, sea, sand (well, pebbles), wine, and pure, unadulterated Italy. Choose a home base according to just how cut off you'd like to be from the outer world.

Enjoy the villages, swimming, hiking, boat rides, and evening romance of one of God's great gifts to tourism. While the Cinque Terre is now discovered and can be miserably jam-packed, I've never seen happier, more relaxed tourists.

This chunk of coast was first described as "the five lands" in medieval times. In those days, this land was watched over by castles. Tiny communities grew up in their protective shadows, ready to run inside at the first hint of a pirate raid. Marauding pirates from North Africa were a persistent problem until about 1400. Many locals were kidnapped and ransomed or sold into slavery, and those who remained built fires on flat-roofed watchtowers to relay warnings—alerting the entire coast to imminent attacks. The last major raid was in 1545.

As the threat of pirates faded, the villages prospered, catching fish and cultivating grapes. Churches were enlarged with a grow-

The Cinque Terre

To A-12 Autostrada
(Carrodano Exit)

To A-12 Autostrada
(Brugnato Exit)

To
Genoa
A-12

SP-566

SP-1

To
La Spezia
& Pisa

To
Sestri Levante,
Santa Margherita,
Genoa & Bonassola

2 Kilometers

2 Miles

Beverino

Pignone

SP-370

Levanto

To New Town
(Fegina)

To Monterosso's
Old Town

SP-38

Pian di
Barca

SP-1

SP-1

SP-63

These roads may be closed.
Inquire locally.

To
La Spezia
& A-12

Monterosso
al Mare

5

SANDY
BEACH

4

Vernazza

Corniglia

3   SP-51

Punta
Mesco

Ligurian

CORNIGLIA STATION

Volastra

Manarola

2

VIA DELL'AMORE ♥

VIA
LITORANEA

To
La Spezia
& A-12

Sea

1

Riomaggiore

SP-370

To Porto Venere

ing population. But until the advent of tourism in this generation, the towns remained isolated. Even today, traditions survive, and each of the five villages comes with a distinct dialect and proud heritage.

In this chapter, I first cover general tips for your visit to the Cinque Terre, then describe the five towns in order from south to north—from Riomaggiore to Monterosso. Since I still get the names of the towns mixed up, I think of them by number: #1 Riomaggiore (a workaday town), #2 Manarola (mellow and picturesque), #3 Corniglia (the hill town), #4 Vernazza (the region's cover girl—the most touristy and dramatic), and #5 Monterosso al Mare (the closest thing to a beach resort).

PLANNING YOUR TIME

The ideal stay is two or three full days; my recommended minimum stay is two nights and a completely uninterrupted day. Speed demons arrive in the morning, check their bags in La Spezia, ride a train to their starting point, take the five-hour hike through all five towns (depending on which trails are open), laze away the afternoon on the beach or rock of their choice, and zoom away on a high-speed evening train to somewhere back in the real world. But be warned: The Cinque Terre has a strange way of messing up your momentum. (The evidence is the number of Americans who have fallen in love with the region and/or one of its residents...and are still here.) Frankly, staying fewer than two nights is a mistake that you'll likely regret.

The towns are just a few minutes apart by train or boat. There's no checklist of sights or experiences—just hiking trails, the towns themselves, and your fondest vacation desires. Study this chapter in advance and piece together your best day, mixing hiking, swimming, trains, and a boat ride.

The vast majority of visitors to the Cinque Terre are day-trippers. Between 10:00 and 15:00—especially on weekends—masses of gawkers unload from boats, tour buses, and cruise ships, inundating the villages and changing the feel of the region. So make a point to get the most out of the cool, relaxed, and quiet hours early in the day and in the evening.

Market days perk up the Cinque Terre and nearby towns from around 8:00 to 13:00 on Tuesday in Vernazza, Wednesday in Levanto, Thursday in Monterosso, Friday in La Spezia and Santa Margherita Ligure, and Saturday in Sestri Levante. (Levanto, Sestri Levante, La Spezia, and Santa Margherita Ligure are covered in the next chapter.)

The winter is really dead—most hotels and some restaurants close from January to March. The long Easter weekend (April 14-17 in 2017), May, June, and September are the peak of the peak—and the toughest times to find rooms. July and August are hotter and generally a bit less crowded. In spring, the Cinque Terre can feel inundated with day-tripping Italian families and school groups (who can't afford to sleep in this expensive area).

Orientation to the Cinque Terre

TOURIST AND PARK INFORMATION

Each town's train station has a Cinque Terre National Marine Park information office, which generally also serves as a gift shop and an all-purpose town TI. They can usually answer basic questions about trails (including closures), shuttle bus schedules, and so on. For more information on the region, see www.cinqueterre.it.

ARRIVAL IN THE CINQUE TERRE

By Train: Most big, fast trains from elsewhere in Italy speed right past the Cinque Terre. (There are some exceptions: A few IC trains connect Monterosso to Milan or Pisa.)

Unless you're coming from a nearby town, you'll have to

CINQUE TERRE

The Cinque Terre at a Glance

The Cinque Terre

▲**Riomaggiore (Town #1)** The biggest and most workaday of the five villages. See page 341.

▲▲**Manarola (Town #2)** Low-key, hiking-focused waterfront village wrapped in vineyards and dotted with a picturesque mix of shops and cliff-climbing houses. See page 352.

▲**Corniglia (Town #3)** Quiet hilltop village known for its cooler temperatures (it's the only one of the five villages set above the water), fewer tourists, and tradition of fine wines. See page 361.

▲▲▲**Vernazza (Town #4)** The region's gem, crowned with a ruined castle above and a lively waterfront cradling a natural harbor below. See page 366.

▲▲**Monterosso al Mare (Town #5)** Resorty, flat, and spread out, with a charming old town, a modern new town, and the Cinque Terre's best beaches, swimming, and nightlife. See page 388.

Near the Cinque Terre

The best of the Riviera towns north and south of the Cinque Terre make for fun, easy side-trips—and some are workable home bases. For more on Levanto, Sestri Levante, Santa Margherita Ligure, and Portofino (to the north), and Porto Venere (to the south), see the next chapter.

change trains at least once to reach Manarola, Corniglia, or Vernazza. Generally, if you're coming from the north, you'll change trains at Sestri Levante, Levanto, or Genoa's Piazza Principe station. If you're coming from the south or east, you'll probably switch trains at La Spezia's Centrale station (not La Spezia Migliarina).

For details on riding the train between Cinque Terre towns, see "Getting Around the Cinque Terre," later; for information on arrival in each town, see the "Arrival" section for each village. For outbound trains, see "Cinque Terre Connections" on page 341.

By Car: Given the narrow roads and lack of parking, I wouldn't bring a car to the Cinque Terre. If your plans require it, however, here are some basic tips: Stay in a hotel that includes parking, use public transportation or hike between towns, and—for the easiest day-trip parking—go to Monterosso, Riomaggiore, or Manarola. Don't drive to Vernazza: The roads are in poor condition and parking is scarce.

Milan to the Cinque Terre (130 miles): Drivers speed south on the A-7 autostrada from Milan, skirt Genoa, and drive a little bit of Italy's curviest and narrowest freeways (A-12) toward La Spezia (about 3 hours). Another option is to take the slightly straighter A-1 via the city of Parma, followed by A-15 to La Spezia (2.5 hours).

To reach **Monterosso** from A-12 (about 30 minutes from the autostrada), take the Carrodano-Levanto exit (see page 316 for the route into town). As of this printing, you can't reach Monterosso from La Spezia via the other Cinque Terre towns; you'll have to loop up to the SP-1/SP-38 highway.

For **Vernazza, Riomaggiore, Corniglia,** or **Manarola,** leave the freeway at La Spezia and follow the road that parallels the coast (with access to each town). The drive down to Vernazza is narrow and scary; it's better to park in Levanto or La Spezia and ride the train in. A secondary road connects Vernazza and Monterosso, but it's not recommended. For a map of the greater Italian Riviera region, see page 316.

Within the Cinque Terre: On busy weekends, holidays, and in summer, both Vernazza and Monterosso fill up, and police at the top of town will deny entry to cars without a hotel reservation. It's smart to have your hotel confirmation in hand.

Parking Tips: For parking, see the "By Car" sections in each village. Riomaggiore, Manarola, and Monterosso each have parking lots and a shuttle bus to get you into town. Blue signs post valid hours for pay parking (use cash), which usually don't charge from 24:00 to 8:00 (but read the signs or ask locals to be sure).

If you plan to park in any of the Cinque Terre towns, try to arrive between 9:00 and 11:00, when overnight visitors are usually departing. Or you can park your car in Levanto or La Spezia (see the next chapter), then take the train into the town of your choice. Parking anywhere in the Cinque Terre is truly a mess in July and August.

HELPFUL HINTS FOR THE CINQUE TERRE

Exchange Rate: €1 = about $1.10

Country Calling Code: 39 (see page 1154 for dialing instructions)

Pickpocket Alert: At peak times, the Cinque Terre can be notoriously crowded, and pickpockets aggressively and expertly work the most congested areas. Be on guard, especially in train stations, on train platforms, and on the trains themselves during any crush of people. Keep your things zipped up and buttoned down.

Money: Banks and ATMs are plentiful throughout the region.

Wi-Fi: All Cinque Terre train stations offer free Wi-Fi with a

Events in the Cinque Terre in 2017

For more festival information and to confirm dates, check www.cinqueterre.it and www.turismoinliguria.it. The food festivals in particular are subject to change.

April 2	Sciacchetrail trail race (see page 337)
April 16-17	Easter Sunday and Monday
April 25	Italian Liberation Day (avoid this day, as locals literally shut down the trails)
May 1	Labor Day (local holiday packs the place with day-trippers)
Mid-May	Monterosso: Lemon Festival (third Sat)
Mid-June	Monterosso: Anchovy Festival (third Sat)
June 18	Monterosso and Vernazza: Feast of Corpus Domini (procession on carpet of flowers)
June 24	Riomaggiore and Monterosso: Feast day of St. John the Baptist (procession and fireworks, floating candles on the sea; big fire on Monterosso's old town beach the day before)
June 29	Corniglia: Feast day of Sts. Peter and Paul
July 20	Vernazza: Feast day of patron St. Margaret, with fireworks
Early Aug	Vernazza: Feast of Nostra Signora di Reggio (hike up to Reggio Sanctuary for food and church procession; first Sun)
Aug 10	Manarola: Feast day of patron St. Lawrence
Aug 15	Feast of the Assumption (Ferragosto)
Sept 8	Monterosso: Feast of Madonna di Fegina (luminarias and procession up to hilltop sanctuary)
Mid-Sept	Monterosso: Anchovies and Olive Oil Festival (third Sat)

Cinque Terre park card (see page 325). Many cafés and bars offer free Wi-Fi if you buy something.

Baggage Storage: You can pay to store bags at or near the train stations in Riomaggiore, Vernazza, and Monterosso (all covered in this chapter), as well as in La Spezia (see the next chapter).

Services: Every train station has a free WC, but it's smart to bring your own toilet paper.

Taxi: Cinqueterre Taxi covers all five towns (mobile 334-776-1946 or 347-652-0837, www.cinqueterretaxi.com). The pricey **5 Terre Transfer** service can come in handy if you need to connect the five towns or beyond (Luciana mobile 339-130-1183; Marzio mobile 340-356-5268).

Booking Agency: Cinque Terre Riviera, professionally run by Miriana, books vacation rentals in the Cinque Terre towns and La Spezia—including some exclusive properties (ask about discounts for properties they manage). They also sell tickets for Vernazza's summer opera and can arrange transportation, cooking classes, and weddings (office in Vernazza at Via Roma 24, tel. 0187-812-123, mobile 340-794-7358, www.cinqueterreriviera.com, info@cinqueterreriviera.com).

Local Guides: Andrea Bordigoni is both knowledgeable and a delight (€125/half-day, €210/day, mobile 393-133-9409, bordigo@inwind.it). Other local guides are **Marco Brizzi** (mobile 328-694-2847, www.hi-ke.com, marco_brizzi@yahoo.it) and **Paola Tommarchi** (paolatomma@alice.it).

Tours and Activities: Arbaspàa, which has an office in Manarola, can arrange Cinque Terre experiences such as vineyard wine tastings, cooking classes (6-person minimum), fishing trips with local sailors, paragliding, rock climbing, and more (see website for options and book in advance, tel. 0187-920-783, www.arbaspaa.com; their Explora shop in Manarola is at Via Discovolo 204).

Tour Packages for Students: Andy Steves (Rick's son) runs Weekend Student Adventures (WSA Europe), offering travel packages across Europe, including a "DIY Detour" tour of the Cinque Terre; see www.wsaeurope.com for details.

Nightlife: There's not much in this sleepy region, though Monterosso and Riomaggiore are your best bets for lively bars after-hours (see pages 387 and 341). My favorite Cinque Terre evenings are spent at Vernazza's summer opera series (see page 379).

Useful Blogs: Cinqueterreinsider.com, written by a resident American expat, is filled with well-researched, up-to-the-minute practicalities for visitors to this always-in-flux region. Another good, all-purpose site, run by caring locals, is **Visit Vernazza** (www.visitvernazza.org). Anna Merulla runs the **BeautifuLiguria** blog, where she shares cultural and offbeat insights into the region and organizes excursions and tours (www.beautifuliguria.com).

GETTING AROUND THE CINQUE TERRE

Within the Cinque Terre, you can connect towns in three ways: by train, boat, or foot. **Trains** are the cheapest, fastest, and most frequent option. But don't get stuck in a train rut: In calm weather, **boats** connect the towns nearly as frequently—and with much better scenery. (If you're in a rush, take whichever form of transport is leaving first.) And **hiking** lets you enjoy more pasta. When it's open, the Via dell'Amore trail between Riomaggiore and Manarola takes just a few minutes—making the train not worth the wait.

(For details on hiking, see "Experiences in the Cinque Terre," later in this chapter.)

By Train

By train, the five towns are just a few minutes apart.

Tickets: A train ride of any length between Cinque Terre towns costs a hefty €4 during peak times—whether you're hopping one town or four. (It's half-price after about 19:00 and before 8:30.) There may also be an all-day ticket (likely €10). You can buy tickets at station windows or Cinque Terre park desks, but to save time in line, use the self-service machines. These have English instructions, provide schedule information, and accept US credit cards (and often also cash).

Be sure to validate your ticket before you board by stamping it in the green-and-white machines located on train platforms and in station passages. Conductors here are notorious for levying stiff fines on tourists riding with an unstamped ticket. You can buy several tickets at once and use them as you like, validating as you go. If you have a Eurail Pass, don't spend one of your valuable travel days on the cheap Cinque Terre.

Schedules: In peak season, trains generally run about twice hourly in each direction, connecting all five towns. (There can be troublesome gaps after about 19:00—check the schedule in advance.) Since the train is the Cinque Terre's lifeline, shops, hotels, and restaurants often post the current schedule, and many hand out copies. Study the key carefully to know which departures are only for weekdays, Sundays, and so on. The most foolproof option is to stop by the station and check the real-time TV monitors to see the next departure time.

Important: Any train stopping at Vernazza, Corniglia, or Manarola is going to all of the towns. Trains from Levanto, Monterosso, Riomaggiore, or La Spezia sometimes skip lesser stations, so confirm that the train will stop at the town you need.

At the Platform: Monitors posted in each station clearly show departure times for the next trains in each direction (and, if they're late—*in ritardo*—how many minutes behind they are; *SOPP* means "cancelled"). On the monitors, northbound trains are marked for *(per)* Levanto, Genova, or Sestri Levante; southbound trains are marked for La Spezia. To be sure you get on the right train, it helps to know your train's number and final destination. Northbound trains use the tracks closest to the water; southbound trains use the tracks on the mountain side.

Assuming you're on vacation, accept the unpredictability of Cinque Terre trains. They're often late—unless you are, too, in which case they're on time. Relax while you wait. Buy an ice cream or cup of coffee at a station bar, and scout the platform you need in advance. This is especially easy in Monterosso, with its fine café-with-a-view on track #1 (northbound), and in Vernazza, where you can hang out at the Blue Marlin Bar with a prepaid drink and dash when the train pulls in.

Getting Off: Know your stop. As the train leaves the town just before your destination, go to the door and get ready to slip out before the mobs flood in. A word to the wise for novice tourists, who often miss their stop: The stations are small and the trains are long, so (especially in Vernazza) you might have to get off deep in a tunnel. Also, the doors don't open automatically—you may have to open the handle of the door yourself (push the green button, twist the black handle, or lift up the red one).

By Boat

From Easter through October, a daily boat service connects Monterosso, Vernazza, Manarola, Riomaggiore, Porto Venere, and beyond. Though they can be very crowded, these boats provide a scenic way to get from town to town. I see the tour boats as a syringe, injecting each town with a boost of euros. The towns are addicted, and they shoot up hourly through the summer.

In peaceful weather, boats can be more reliable than trains. But because the boats nose in and tourists have to gingerly disembark onto little more than a plank, even just a small chop can cancel some or all of the stops.

Tickets: The ticket price depends on the length of the boat ride (€5 for a short hop, and up to €15 for a five-town, one-way ticket with stops). An all-day Cinque Terre pass costs €22; another all-day boat pass for €30 extends to Porto Venere; for an extra €5, you can add a 40-minute scenic ride around three small islands (2/day). Buy tickets at the little stands at each town's harbor (tel. 0187-818-440).

Schedules: Boat schedules are posted at docks, harbor bars, Cinque Terre park offices, and hotels (www.navigazionegolfodeipoeti.it). Boats depart Monterosso about hourly (10:30-18:00), stopping at the Cinque Terre towns (except Corniglia) and ending up an hour

Crowd-Beating Tips in the Cinque Terre

Italy's undiscovered slice of traffic-free Riviera has been discovered, frustrating both locals and conscientious visitors. The most dramatic influx is created by groups—whether day-tripping tours or mobs of cruise-ship sightseers. Avoid the worst of the logjams by following these tips:

Time your visit carefully. The busiest months are May, June, and September; July and August are slightly less crowded. Shoulder season—April and October—can be ideal, with fewer crowds and cooler temperatures for hiking (but can be too cold to swim). Good-weather holiday weekends (Easter, Italian Liberation Day on April 25) and school breaks can bring peak-season crowds.

Make the most of your time early and late. Cruisers and day-trippers start pouring into the Cinque Terre around 10:00 and typically head out by 18:00. Those midday hours are the time to hit the beach, discover a back-street bar to nurse a glass of *sciacchetrà,* or find a hike away from the main trails. At midday, the main coastal trail is a hot human traffic jam. Starting a hike at 8:00 or 16:00 makes a world of difference.

Escape to less crowded trails, towns, and activities. There are plenty of hikes beyond the busy coastal trail where you'll scarcely see another tourist. Or, on very crowded days, simply leave the Cinque Terre altogether. If you want to hit the beach but Monterosso is a human parking lot, hop the train a few minutes to Levanto, rent a bike, and pedal on a level path to the delightful beach at Bonassola (described on page 410). Or, stick around the Cinque Terre but find something fun to do away from the crowds—such as a wine tasting or a massage.

Sleep in the Cinque Terre—not nearby. Levanto and La Spezia are close and well-connected by train, making them popular home bases. But it's easier to enjoy the Cinque Terre early and late if you're actually sleeping here. I'd rather skip town during the day and come back when it's quiet and cool—even if I pay a premium for accommodations.

Be careful on train platforms. The Cinque Terre's trains and platforms can be a perfect storm of crowds. At peak times, be cautious, and always stay well behind the yellow line. Spread out to less crowded areas to wait.

Hire your own boat. Regularly scheduled, high-capacity boats are a good, scenic alternative to trains. But if the boats are jammed, why not hire your own boat to zip you to the next town? Captains hang out at each town's harbor, offering one-way transfers to any other town or hour-long cruises (for details, see page 325).

later in Porto Venere. Boats making the return run from Porto Venere to Monterosso go from about 8:45 until 17:00.

Private Boats: If the trains, boats, and trails are jammed—or if you just feel like a scenic splurge—hire a captain to ferry you between towns. For example, at the harbor in Vernazza, you can pay €30-50 to hop to any other Cinque Terre town. If you split the cost among a few fellow travelers, it can be quite affordable. Or you can hire a captain for a full tour of the region (figure €150/1 hour). Look for captains offering their services at the harbors in Monterosso, Vernazza, Riomaggiore, and Manarola (see also specific listings in Monterosso and Vernazza sections).

By Shuttle Bus

ATC shuttle buses (which locals call *pulmino*) connect each Cinque Terre town with its closest parking lot and various points in the hills (but they don't connect the five towns to each other). The one you're most likely to use runs between Corniglia's train station and its hilltop town center. Most rides cost €1.50 (€2.50 from driver), and are free with a Cinque Terre park card (see "Hiking the Cinque Terre," below). Buy tickets and ask about bus schedules at park info offices or TIs (or check times posted at bus stops). But be aware that shuttle schedules change constantly: Confirm the details before planning your day around the bus. Note that shuttles may not run during mid-afternoon lunch breaks (about 12:30-15:00). As you board, it's smart to tell the driver where you want to go. Departures often coordinate with train arrival times.

Some shuttles go beyond the parking lots and high into the hills—often terminating at the town's sanctuary church. To soak in the scenery, you can ride up and hike down, or just cruise both ways (30-45 minutes round-trip, covered by one ticket).

Experiences in the Cinque Terre

HIKING THE CINQUE TERRE

All five towns are connected by good trails, marked with red-and-white paint, white arrows, and some signs (*sentiero* means trail). Most visitors stick to the main coastal trail that links the villages, but hardy hikers can sidestep the crowds by venturing onto one of the region's many alternate routes (see descriptions later).

Cinque Terre Park Cards: Visitors hiking on the mainline

coastal trails must buy a park pass (good for one or two days, with an option covering trains). Passes can be purchased at train stations, TIs, and trailheads, and are valid until midnight on the expiration date (and include free Wi-Fi at train stations). Write your name on your card or risk a fine. Those under 18 or over 70 get a discount, as do families of four or more (see www.parconazionale5terre.it). The configuration and pricing of these cards is often in flux—the following details may change.

The **Cinque Terre Trekking Card** costs €7.50 for one day of hiking or €14.50 for two days (covers trails and ATC shuttle buses, but not trains).

The **Cinque Terre Treno Multi-Service Card** covers what the Trekking Card does, plus local trains connecting all Cinque Terre towns, plus Levanto and La Spezia (€16/1 day, €29/2 days, validate card at train station by punching it in the machine). To break even with this card, you'd have to hike and take two train trips every day.

Trail Closures: Trails can be closed in bad weather or due to landslides. Before planning your hiking day, confirm whether any trail segments are closed. Official closures are noted on the national park website (www.parconazionale5terre.it) and are posted at the park-information desks in each town's train station. Some trails are really closed because they are impassable, while a few are technically "closed" (for political reasons) but still perfectly hikable (at your own risk). Ask locals or fellow hikers for the latest on which trails are actually passable, but err on the side of caution.

Shuttle Buses: The ATC shuttle buses (see page 378) can make the going easier, connecting coastal villages to higher-up trailheads. Wherever shuttles will save steps, I've mentioned them in the hike description.

Hiking Conditions: Other than the wide, easy Riomaggiore-Manarola segment, the main coastal trail is generally narrow, steep, rocky, and comes with lots of challenging steps. Don't overestimate your hiking abilities. I get many emails from readers who say the trail was tougher than they'd expected. The rocks and metal grates can be slippery in the rain (I'd avoid the very steep Monterosso-Vernazza stretch if it's wet). Don't venture up on these rocky cliffs without sun protection (and/or a hat), water, and proper shoes. (Locals roll their eyes at the many tourists who wear flip-flops on the trails.) Bug spray can also be useful. And keep in mind that going down can be more challenging (vertigo, shaky knees) than going up. Pace yourself. While the main coastal trail is strenuous, it's doable for any fit hiker...and worth the sweat.

When to Go: The coastal trail can be extremely crowded (and very hot) at midday. For the best light, coolest temperatures, and fewest crowds, start your hike early or late. Before setting out for

The Cinque Terre National Park: Peaks and Valleys

Founded in 1999, the Cinque Terre National Marine Park was intended to get everyone thinking creatively about how to improve the area for the good of nature, the local communities, and its many visitors. The park designation has brought plenty of good things: money (in the form of trail fees), regulations to protect wildlife, park-sponsored information centers at each train station, shuttle buses to distant trailheads, and improved walkways, trails, beaches, breakwaters, and docks.

But, perhaps predictably, the system has been corrupted by power and money. A charismatic past park president made great inroads before his cronyism forced him from office in disgrace. Frequent landslides cut off trails—the main reason many people come here—and repairs are excruciatingly slow. Local grassroots movements have arguably done more to preserve the Cinque Terre than has the park, even with its substantial budget. The current park president, a retired sea admiral, is determined to make the park work. But given this region's old-fashioned ways and history of bureaucratic failure, no one is counting on it.

With all of this in mind, don't be surprised if park details given here (including entrance fees, shuttle buses, information desks, and so on) have changed by the time you visit. In addition, park authorities—who struggle with the ever-increasing crowds—have considered requiring visitors to prebook a limited number of tickets to use the trails, or even to enter the towns. While this seems unlikely, ask locals or check the park website for the latest.

an evening hike, find out when the sun will set, and leave yourself plenty of time to arrive at your destination before then; there's no lighting on the trails.

Navigation: Maps aren't necessary for the basic coastal hikes. But for the more challenging routes that leave the crowds behind, pick up a good hiking map (about €5, sold everywhere). The national park recently renumbered its trails (using three digits), but many locals still think in terms of the old trail numbers (one digit). I've listed both.

Guided Hikes and Excursions: Your park ticket includes guided hikes and other local excursions (such as town walking tours), which take place several times each month. Even if you don't have a park ticket valid that day, these events are still cheap—usually around €2.50. Look for schedules locally, or email visiteguidate@ati5terre.it for details. (These are also listed at www.visitvernazza.org.)

Give a Hoot: To leave the park cleaner than you found it,

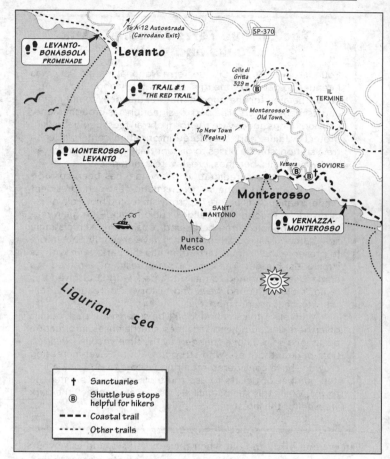

bring a plastic bag *(sacchetto di plastica)* and pick up a little trail trash along the way. It would be great if American visitors—who get so much joy out of this region—were known for this good deed. Note that while the trails themselves are part of the national park, the property to either side is private (no nibbling on veggies or grapes from the vines).

The Main Coastal Trail

The seven-mile coastal trail (officially trail "SVA," a.k.a. "the Blue Trail" or #592) is the ultimate Cinque Terre experience. Unfortunately, big chunks of it are often closed. The stretch between Manarola and Corniglia sits under unstable slopes, and is likely to be closed indefinitely. And the trail from Manarola to Riomaggiore (the famed Via dell'Amore) has been closed off and on for years (hopes are high that soon—possibly in 2017—it will reopen permanently).

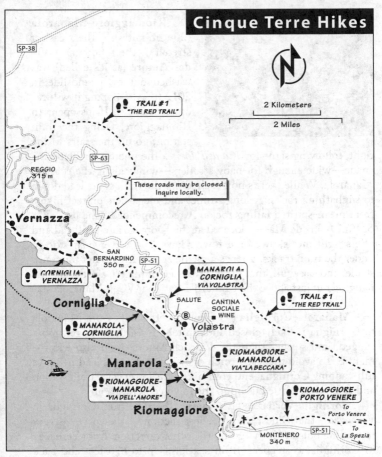

Cinque Terre Hikes

SP-38

TRAIL #1
"THE RED TRAIL"

2 Kilometers

2 Miles

SP-63

REGGIO
315 m

These roads may be closed.
Inquire locally.

Vernazza

SAN
BERNARDINO
350 m

SP-51

MANAROLA-
CORNIGLIA
VIA VOLASTRA

CORNIGLIA-
VERNAZZA

TRAIL #1
"THE RED TRAIL"

Corniglia

SALUTE

CANTINA
SOCIALE
WINE

MANAROLA-
CORNIGLIA

(B)

Volastra

Manarola

RIOMAGGIORE-
MANAROLA
VIA "LA BECCARA"

RIOMAGGIORE-
MANAROLA
"VIA DELL'AMORE"

Riomaggiore

RIOMAGGIORE-
PORTO VENERE

To
Porto Venere

SP-51

To
La Spezia

MONTENERO
340 m

The sections of the main coastal trail, most likely to be open during your visit, are also the most challenging (and crowded): Corniglia to Vernazza, and Vernazza to Monterosso. Check locally for updates, as trail conditions often change. Remember that hikers need to pay a fee to use the main coastal trail (see "Cinque Terre Park Cards," earlier).

If open, the entire seven-mile coastal hike can be done by fit hikers in about four hours, but allow five or six for dawdling. Germans (with their task-oriented *Alpenstock* walking sticks) are notorious for rushing too fast through the region. Take it slow...smell the cactus flowers and herbs, notice the scurrying lizards, listen to birds singing in the olive groves, and enjoy vistas on all sides.

If sections of the coastal trail are closed, you can fill in the gaps by train or, far more scenically, by boat. Or choose one of the more challenging trails described later (under "Alternates to the Main Coastal Trail").

Riomaggiore-Manarola (20 minutes): The easiest stretch, the popular **Via dell'Amore** (as it's called) was washed out by a landslide in 2012 (they're hoping it will reopen in 2017). If it's open: In Riomaggiore, facing the train station, go up the stairs to the right, following signs for *Via dell'Amore*. The photo-worthy promenade—wide enough for baby strollers—winds along the coast to Manarola. While there's no beach along the trail, stairs lead down to sunbathing rocks. A long tunnel and mega-nets protect hikers from mean-spirited falling rocks. A recommended wine bar—Bar & Vini A Piè de Mà—is located at the Riomaggiore trailhead and offers light meals, awesome town views, and clever boat storage under the train tracks. There's a picnic zone with a water fountain, shade, and a seagull, that must have been human in a previous life, hanging out just above the Manarola station (WC at Manarola station).

Manarola-Corniglia (45 minutes): The walk from Manarola to Corniglia is likely closed indefinitely. It's a little longer, more rugged, and steeper than the Via dell'Amore—and also less romantic. To avoid the last stretch of switchback stairs leading up to hill-capping Corniglia, end your hike at its lower-level train station and catch the shuttle bus up to the town center (2/hour).

Corniglia-Vernazza (1.5 hours): The hike from Corniglia to Vernazza—the wildest and greenest section of the coast—is very rewarding but very hilly (going the other direction, from Vernazza to Corniglia, is steeper—from sea level up to 690 feet and back down again). From the Corniglia train station and beach, zigzag up to the town (via the steep stairs, the longer road, or the shuttle bus). Keep going through vineyards toward Vernazza. After about 10 minutes, you'll see a faded sign to Guvano beach, far beneath you (the region's nude beach). The scenic trail continues through lots of fragrant and flowery vegetation into Vernazza. If you need a break before reaching Vernazza, stop at Bar la Torre, with a strip of amazingly scenic and delightfully shady tables perched high above the town.

Vernazza-Monterosso (1.5 hours): The trail from Vernazza to Monterosso is a scenic up-and-down-a-lot trek and the most challenging of the bunch. (Start in Monterosso if you want to tackle the toughest section, with many steep stairs, while you're fresh.) Trails are narrow, steep, and crumbly in spots, with a lot of steps but easy to follow. The views just out of Vernazza, looking back at the town, are spectacular. From there you'll gradually ascend up to 550 feet,

Via dell'Amore

The Cinque Terre towns were extremely isolated until the last century. Villagers rarely married anyone from outside their town. After the blasting of a second train line in the 1920s, a trail was built between Riomaggiore and Manarola. (The gunpowder warehouses built on each end, safely away from the townspeople, house cute little bars today.)

This new lane changed the social dynamics between the two towns and made life much more fun, especially for courting couples. Happy with the trail, the villagers asked that it be improved as a permanent connection between neighbors. After World War II, the trail became established as a lovers' meeting point for boys and girls from the two towns. (After one extended closure in 1949, the trail was reopened just in time for a Christmas marriage.) A journalist who noticed all the amorous graffiti along the path coined the trail's now-established name, Via dell'Amore: "Pathway of Love."

If the trail is open when you visit, you'll see padlocks locked to wires, cables, and fences. Closing a padlock with your lover at a lovey-dovey spot—often a bridge—is a common ritual in Italy. (The hardware store next to Bar Centrale in Riomaggiore sells these locks—some come with the park logo.) Some tourists are put off by the graffiti that lines the trail. But it's all part of the history of the Cinque Terre's little lovers' lane.

Major construction work has made the trail safer. Notice how the brick-lined arcades match the train tunnel below. Rock climbers from the north ("Dolomite spiders") were imported to help with the treacherous construction work. As you hike, look up and notice the massive steel netting bolted to the cliffside. Look down at the boulders that fell before the nets were added, and up at the boulders that have been caught...and be thankful for those Dolomite spiders.

Continuing the romance theme, benches along the way are named for lovers from Greek mythology. Many agave plants sport carved love notes—etched by amorous couples who likely don't know that the plant flowers once, and then dies.

passing some scenic waterfalls populated by croaking frogs. You'll find a few scenically positioned picnic tables located about midway along the trail. As you approach Monterosso, you'll descend steeply through vineyards—on very deep, knee-testing stairs—and eventually follow a rivulet to the sea. The last stretch into Monterosso is along a pleasant, paved pathway clinging to the cliff. You'll pop out right at Monterosso's refreshing old town beach.

Scenic Jogs: Very hardy, sure-footed joggers enjoy running between Monterosso and Vernazza (1.5 hours round-trip) or Vernazza and Corniglia (about an hour round-trip).

Alternates to the Main Coastal Trail

If the primary trails outlined above are closed—or you want a less crowded or more demanding alternative—consider these options.

Manarola-Corniglia via Volastra (2.5 hours): In the likely event that the Manarola-Corniglia trail is closed (but rewarding even if it isn't), consider the challenging hike from Manarola up to the village of Volastra, then north through high-altitude vineyard terraces, and steeply down through a forest to Corniglia (about four miles total). You can shave the two steepest miles off this route by riding the shuttle bus for 15 minutes from Manarola up to Volastra (about hourly).

If you prefer to hike to Volastra, you have two options. The national park's official route (trail #6/#506) cuts up through the valley, with less scenery. Locals have cleared a more scenic alternate route that begins with the vineyard hike on my self-guided walk for Manarola (page 353). Partway along this walk, where you reach the wooden religious scenes scampering up the hillside, take a sharp right and walk uphill, following signs for *Panoramico Volastra (Corniglia)*. While steeper than the official route, this trail follows the ridge at the top of the vineyard, with wonderful sea views.

Tiny Volastra, perched between Manarola and Corniglia, hosts lots of Germans and Italians in the summer. Just below town, in the hamlet of Groppo, is the Cantina Sociale, a cooperative winery. When you're ready to head for Corniglia, make your way to the village church (where the shuttle bus drops off) and look for *Corniglia* signs. From the front door of the church, directly across the piazza, find the trailhead (marked by an iron cross) for trail #6d/#586 to Case Pianca.

Here begins one of the finest hikes in the region, tight-roping

Cinque Terre Hikes

Each of these hikes—as well as listings of short town hikes and variations—are described in the "Hiking the Cinque Terre" section. Hikes can be done in either direction.

Main Coastal Trail

▲▲▲**Riomaggiore-Manarola** (Via dell'Amore): Easy, short, romantic stroll just above the water on a well-tended, level path; likely closed through 2017 (and possibly longer)—inquire locally.

▲**Manarola-Corniglia:** Scenic, moderately easy path just above the train tracks and coastline, but typically closed due to landslide threat.

▲▲▲**Corniglia-Vernazza:** Most scenic and rewarding stretch of the main coastal trail, with fine views, significant elevation changes, and moderately challenging stretches on uneven stone steps.

▲▲**Vernazza-Monterosso:** Challenging but dramatic trail, including long stretches of steep steps above Monterosso.

Extending the Coastal Trail to the North

▲**Monterosso-Levanto:** Logical northward continuation of the main coastal trail, over Punta Mesco; a notch more challenging than the rest of the coastal trail.

▲**Levanto-Bonassola Promenade:** Level rails-to-trails path that cuts through the mountains (largely through tunnels) to connect Levanto to the sleepy beach town of Bonassola; fine by foot but even better by bike.

Moderate and Challenging Alternates to the Coastal Trail

▲▲**Manarola-Corniglia via Volastra:** Demanding but gorgeous hike through vineyards high over the coast; made much easier if you take the shuttle bus from Manarola to Volastra.

▲**Riomaggiore-Manarola via "La Beccara":** Brief but challenging trail traversing mostly stone steps.

▲**Riomaggiore-Porto Venere:** Very demanding, all-day trek high into the hills, ending at picturesque Porto Venere.

▲▲**Trail #1** ("The Red Trail"): Remote, cliff-capping trail high above the main coastal trail and the sanctuary trails—best for well-equipped, hardy hikers.

▲▲▲**Sciacchetrail:** A 29-mile trail connecting all five towns and beyond, site of a competitive trail race each spring. This route is the ultimate trek for very experienced hikers.

along narrow trails tucked between vineyard terraces, with spectacular bird's-eye views over the entire Cinque Terre. You'll cut up and down the terraces a bit—just keep following the red-and-white markings and arrows. After passing a little village (and following signs through someone's seaview backyard), the trail enters a forest and begins its sharp, rocky descent into Corniglia. (To skip the descent, backtrack to Volastra and return by shuttle bus to Manarola.) High above Corniglia, you'll reach a fork, where you turn left to proceed downhill on trail #7a/#587 to Corniglia.

Riomaggiore-Manarola via "La Beccara" (1.5 hours): If the Via dell'Amore is closed, you may be tempted to take this alternate route (on trail #531) up and over the mountain between these two towns. But be warned: It's essentially stairs all the way up, then all the way down—"shorter," but more intense and dizzying than other parts of the coastal trail. Fit hikers with proper footwear can handle it.

Other Cinque Terre Trails

Besides the main coastal trail, the national park maintains a free, far more extensive network of trails higher in the hills. Particularly

with the overcrowding epidemic along the main route, these much quieter trails are great for breaking out of the coastal rut. For pointers, ask at a TI or park office. Serious hikers find it worth a trip to Manarola to get advice from Christine and Nicola at Cinque Terre Trekking (see page 358). There are also plenty of user-friendly, shorter rambles that originate in each of the towns.

I've outlined your options—from easy to challenging—below. The Cinque Terre Park Card is not required for the following hikes.

Easy Hikes

Some of the best Cinque Terre hikes require a brief (if steep) jaunt from the villages into the hills. Try one of these to earn great views.

From **Vernazza**, a 10-minute uphill hike in either direction takes you to stunning vistas back over the town. You can also hike up to Vernazza's hilltop cemetery for yet another angle down on town. For details, see "Hikes from Vernazza" on page 376.

Manarola offers one of the most rewarding easy hikes in the region: a stroll through vineyards with great town and sea views (follow the "Manarola Vineyard Walk" portion of my self-guided Manarola Walk; see page 356).

In **Monterosso,** hike up to the cemetery over town ("Part 2" of my self-guided Monterosso Walk; see page 391).

In **Riomaggiore,** the beginning of my self-guided walk (page 343) offers a gentle hike from the station to the top of town; for views over the other side of town, you can hike up to the town's playground (*parco giochi,* see page 346).

Take the train to **Levanto,** then stroll (or better yet, bike) the easy, level, rails-to-trails promenade to the beach town of Bonassola (see page 410). This is an especially good plan for skipping out on the Cinque crowds.

Moderate Hikes

For a more substantial hike, consider these. They're roughly equivalent in difficulty to the Corniglia-Vernazza and Vernazza-Monterosso hikes on the coastal trail—but much, much quieter.

Sanctuary Trails (La Strada dei Santuari): Each of the five towns has its own sanctuary, with a chapel or church dedicated to the Virgin Mary, hovering in the hills a mile or two above town, and accessible by a long, steep hike. Villagers feel deeply connected to these spiritual retreats, where they remember lost relatives and feel part of a timeless community. A network of "sanctuary trails" crisscrosses the hills above the main coastal route. There's no single path, but with a good map you can link the trails up. In most towns, the local shuttle bus can take you from the town center to the sanctuary— simply ride up and hike down, or start your hike between towns from the top.

Each *santuario* is named for a different "Our Lady." For navigational purposes, it helps to know their names: Above **Riomaggiore** is Madonna di Montenero; above **Manarola,** in Volastra, is Madonna della Salute; above **Corniglia,** in San Bernardino, is Madonna delle Grazie; above **Vernazza** is Madonna di Reggio; and above **Monterosso** is Madonna di Soviore.

My favorite sanctuary hike is the one from **Vernazza to Reggio** (see "Hikes from Vernazza" on page 376). Another, longer hike connects the sanctuaries of **Monterosso** and **Vernazza.** From Monterosso, first hike (trail #9/#509) or, much easier, take the shuttle bus up to Monterosso's Soviore sanctuary. From there, follow mostly level trail #1/#591 to Termine, then #8b/#582 down to Reggio (above Vernazza), then #8/#508 very steeply down into Vernazza. Plan on 2.5 hours (if you take the shuttle bus).

Monterosso-Levanto (3 hours): This lovely, rugged-and-wild hike on the coastal trail (SVA) will take you all the way into Levanto. It's no joke: Bring lots of water and wear good shoes.

Starting from Monterosso, look for signs for the coastal trail at the west end of the new town, and head steeply up. You'll hike up and over Punta Mesco, the bluff that separates the two towns. The

Cinque Terre Winds

As in many communities whose livelihoods are tied to the sea, locals have names for the different types of winds. *Scirocco* is a warm, southeasterly wind that blows in clouds from North Africa; sometimes it even carries sand from the Sahara. It causes a condition called *macaia*—sticky, heavy, wet, still, and overcast weather that puts everyone in a rotten mood. Conversely, the *tramontana* is a cool, clear, refreshing, northerly breeze that comes "across the mountains," bringing sunny weather and calm seas. The *libeccio* wind, from the southwest (and named for Libya), means "sun but big waves." The *maestrale* is a stiff northwesterly wind that generally comes with sunny weather (and isn't as intense as France's notorious mistral). And *gregale* is a strong, cold, northeasterly wind from Russia that produces chilly drizzle and sometimes snow in the mountains.

first stretch, out of Monterosso, is almost entirely big steps; the rest is mostly a gradual up-and-down.

For a short scenic detour, not far out of Monterosso look for trail #1/#591. This brief jog leads to the ruined chapel of Sant'Antonio.

To begin the hike in Levanto, see page 409.

Monterosso-Levanto Alternatives: You can enjoy an even **higher hike** by skipping the steepest stretch and riding one of Monterosso's shuttle buses to Colle di Gritta (at Hotel Monterosso Alto). From there, follow trail #1/#591 along the ridge and down to Colle di Bagari, where several trails intersect. You can follow trail #571c from here or go a little lower to #571—both head down to trail SVA and Levanto. Or, to make your **hike a loop** that returns directly to Monterosso, continue from Colle di Bagari along trail #1/#591 to trail SVA, and drop steeply into Monterosso.

Challenging Hikes

These hikes are best left to experienced hikers who are in great shape, comfortable navigating on their own, and outfitted with real hiking boots, poles, a phone in case of emergency, plenty of water, and detailed maps. Before attempting any of these hikes, equip yourself with detailed local advice.

Riomaggiore-Porto Venere: This challenging trek takes about five hours one-way. You'll hike from Riomaggiore up on trail #3/#593 (a continuation of the coastal trail SVA) to the sanctuary at Montenero, then up to Colle del Telegrafo; and then all the way down to Porto Venere on trail #1/AV5T. Partway along, the town of Campiglia has a little bar/restaurant (and buses to La Spezia).

Trail #1 ("The Red Trail," AV5T, or #591): Above the coastal trails, and even higher than the sanctuary trails, is the 22-mile trail #1 connecting Porto Venere to Levanto—and offering sky-high views over the Cinque Terre seafront. Marked on maps as "AV5T"—*alta via* ("high route") *5 Terre*—it's cool, uncrowded, and at the top of the world.

Sciacchetrail: This high-mountain, 29-mile route (elevation gain 8,500 feet) is designed for the annual Sciacchetrail trail-running race, which takes place before Easter. But for more casual hikers, the route is split into three shorter segments, to be done at your own pace. The name is a pun on the local dessert wine, *sciacchetrà:* The route leads to wineries where you can mix local vintages into your day of hiking. For details, see new.sciacchetrail.com, or stop by Cinque Terre Trekking in Manarola.

SWIMMING AND KAYAKING IN THE CINQUE TERRE

Every town in the Cinque Terre has a beach—or, at least, a rocky place to swim. Monterosso has the biggest and sandiest beach, with umbrellas and beach-use fees (but any stretch of beach without umbrellas is free). Vernazza's main beach is tiny—better for sunning than swimming; the newer, flood-created beach there is another option. Manarola and Riomaggiore have the worst beaches (no sand), but Manarola offers the best deep-water swimming. Corniglia has no beach to speak of but does have sunning rocks. Levanto, just a few minutes' train ride past Monterosso and covered in the next chapter, has big and broad beaches, with even better ones an easy bike ride away, in Bonassola (see page 410).

Wear your walking shoes and pack your swim gear. Several beaches have showers. Don't tote your white hotel towels; most hotels will provide beach towels (sometimes for a fee). Underwater sightseeing is full of fish—goggles are sold in local shops. Sea urchins can be a problem if you walk on the rocks, and sometimes jellyfish wash up on the pebbles, so water shoes are essential.

You can rent kayaks or boats in Riomaggiore and Monterosso (see town listings in this chapter). While experienced boaters have a blast here, if you're not comfortable navigating a tippy kayak, the Cinque Terre is probably not the place to start.

Sleeping in the Cinque Terre

Vernazza, the spindly and salty essence of the Cinque Terre, is my top choice for a home base. But if you think too many people have my book, you'll get fewer crowds and better value for your money in other towns. Monterosso is a good choice for sun-worshipping softies, those who prefer the ease of a real hotel, and the younger crowd (more nightlife). Hermits, anarchists, wine lovers, and mountain goats like Corniglia. Serious hikers and sophisticated

Cruise Ship Travelers Not Welcome in the Cinque Terre

In the past few years, cruise lines have discovered the Cinque Terre. Ships stop in La Spezia, Genoa, or even Livorno, and offer guided excursions to the five towns. While cruisers have the right to enjoy every corner of the beautiful Mediterranean, to me it just makes no sense for cruise lines to dump literally thousands of travelers on a place like the Cinque Terre, which doesn't have the infrastructure for huge crowds.

When the cruise ships are in, Cinque Terre trains and plat-

forms are dangerously over-crowded, the trails become almost impassable, and the towns' tiny main lanes are clogged human traffic jams. Sure, those cruise travelers can cross the Cinque Terre off their "bucket list." But nobody arriving with a cruise ship horde can really experience the Cinque Terre. Locals don't like cruise tourists, and that feeling grows stronger every year. It's just a very bad scene.

Please, visit on your own. Don't try to experience the villages and fragile trails of the Cinque Terre as part of a cruise ship mob. (Do a cruise excursion to Pisa and Lucca instead—they can handle the crowds. If you must have a seaside experience, consider Porto Venere, or ride the train up to Sestri Levante or Santa Margherita Ligure—all covered in the next chapter.) I love cruising. And I love the Cinque Terre. But in my *Rick Steves Mediterranean Cruise Ports* guidebook I barely mention the Cinque Terre. They just don't mix.

Europeans choose charming but not overrun Manarola, which has a good range of professional-feeling small accommodations, but fewer dining or evening options. Riomaggiore—bigger than Vernazza and less resorty than Monterosso—has the cheapest beds and rivals Monterosso for nightlife, but it's gritty, and its hoteliers can be flaky.

While the Cinque Terre is too rugged for the mobs that ravage the Spanish and French coasts, it's popular with Italians, Germans, French, and in-the-know Americans. Accommodations charge more and are packed on holidays (including Easter); in May, June, and September; and on Fridays and Saturdays all summer. (With climate change, sweltering August is no longer considered peak season on this stretch of the Riviera.) During these busy periods, it's essential to reserve in advance.

Private Rooms for Rent *(Affittacamere):* Many accommodations in the Cinque Terre (especially in Vernazza) are *affittacamere*, or private rooms for rent. These range from simple bedrooms with shared baths, to fancy bedrooms with private baths to comfortable apartments (often with small kitchens), where you get the key and come and go as you like, rarely seeing your landlord. Plan on paying cash. If you must cancel an *affittacamere* reservation, do it as early as possible—since people renting rooms usually don't take deposits, they lose money if you don't show up.

Outside of peak times, you can land a double room on any day just by arriving in town (ideally by noon) and asking around at bars and restaurants. Most locals know someone who rents rooms. Many travelers enjoy the opportunity to shop around a bit and get the best price by bargaining.

Amenities: Breakfast is not included at most *affittacamere* and other simple accommodations. (Locals take breakfast about as seriously as flossing.) The basic, very Italian choice is simply to drop by a neighborhood bar for a cappuccino and a *cornetto* (croissant) or a piece of focaccia (I've listed your options in each town). Some pricier places include breakfast, but this often consists of a few paltry items (yogurt, instant coffee, packaged croissants) in a minifridge in your room.

While air-conditioning is essential in the summer elsewhere in Italy, in the breezy Cinque Terre you can generally manage fine without it. Expect thin walls (pack earplugs).

Eating in the Cinque Terre

Hanging out at a seaview restaurant while sampling local specialties could become one of your favorite memories.

The key staple here is anchovies (*acciughe;* ah-CHOO-gay)—ideally served the day they're caught. There's nothing cool about being an anchovy virgin. If you've always hated anchovies (the harsh, cured-in-salt American kind), try them fresh here. They are prepared in a dizzying variety of ways: marinated, salted, drenched in lemon juice, butterflied and deep-fried (sometimes with a delicious garlic/vinegar sauce called *giada*), and so on. *Tegame alla vernazzana* is the most typical main course in Vernazza: a layered, casserole-like dish of whole anchovies, potatoes, tomatoes, white wine, oil, and herbs.

Other seafood is common, of course. You'll often see *muscoli ripieni* (stuffed mussels). And, while antipasto means cheese and salami in Tuscany, here you'll get *antipasti frutti di mare* (or simply *antipasti misti*): a plate of mixed "fruits of the sea." Many restaurants are particularly proud of their *frutti di mare*—it's how they show off—and it's a fine way to start a meal. For two diners, splitting one of these and a pasta dish can be plenty.

This region is the birthplace of pesto. Basil, which loves the temperate Ligurian climate, is ground with cheese (half parmigiano and half pecorino), garlic, olive oil, and pine nuts, and then poured over pasta. You'll see it on gnocchi or, better yet, on pasta designed specifically for pesto to cling to: *trenette* (the long, flat Ligurian noodle ruffled on one side) or *trofie* (short, dense, toothsome twists made of flour with a bit of potato). Many also like pesto lasagna, always made with white sauce, never red. If you become addicted, small jars of pesto are sold in local grocery stores and gift shops.

Pansotti are ravioli with ricotta and a mixture of greens, often served with a walnut sauce *(salsa di noci)*...delightful and filling.

Focaccia—pillowy, flat, salty, olive-oily bread—also originates here in Liguria. Locals say the best focaccia is made between the Cinque Terre and Genoa. The baker roughs up the dough with finger holes, sprinkles it with salt water, then bakes it. Focaccia comes plain or with onions, sage, or olive bits, and is a local favorite for a snack on the beach. Bakeries sell it in rounds or slices by weight (a portion is about 100 grams, or *un etto*).

Farinata, a humble flatbread snack sold at pizza and focaccia places, is made from chickpea flour, water, oil, and pepper and baked on a copper tray in a wood-burning stove. It's dense, filling, and less flavorful than other local cuisine.

The region also loves its locally grown lemons, though to my mind, Liguria is a distant second to Sorrento and the Amalfi Coast in terms of Italian lemon production.

Vino delle Cinque Terre, while not one of Italy's top wines, flows cheap and easy throughout the region. It's white— crisp, refreshing, and great with seafood. Local wines are typically blends, predominantly using the bosco grape (found only here).

For a sweet dessert wine, *sciacchetrà* (shah-keh-TRAH) is worth the splurge (€4 per small glass, often served with dunkable cookies). You could order the fun dessert *torta della nonna* ("grandmother's cake") and dunk chunks of it into your glass. Aged *sciacchetrà* finishes dry and costs more (up to €12/glass). While 10 kilos of grapes yield 7 liters of local wine, *sciacchetrà* is made from near-raisins, and 10 kilos of grapes make only 1.5 liters of the wine. The word means "push and pull"—push in lots of grapes, pull out the best wine. If your room is up a lot of steps, be warned: *sciacchetrà* is 18 percent alcohol, while regular wine is only 11 percent.

Cinque Terre Connections

The five towns of the Cinque Terre are on a milk-run line (described earlier, under "Getting Around the Cinque Terre—By Train"), with trains coming through about every 30 minutes in peak season (and connecting with La Spezia and Levanto). For points beyond the Cinque Terre (for example, Milan or Pisa), you'll usually have to change in La Spezia, Monterosso, Levanto, or Sestri Levante (local train info tel. 0187-817-458, www.trenitalia.com).

From La Spezia Centrale by Train to: Rome (8/day direct, more with transfers in Pisa, 3-4.5 hours; an evening train—departing around 20:00—gives you a complete day in the region while still getting you to Rome that night), **Pisa** (about hourly, 1 hour), **Florence** (5/day direct, 2.5 hours, otherwise nearly hourly with change in Pisa), **Milan** (about hourly, 3 hours direct or with change in Genoa), **Venice** (about hourly, 5-6 hours, 1-3 changes).

From Monterosso by Train to: Venice (5/day, 6 hours, change in Milan), **Milan** (8/day direct, otherwise hourly with change in Genoa, 3 hours), **Genoa** (hourly, 1.5 hours), **Turin** (8/day, 3-4 hours), **Pisa** (hourly, 1-1.5 hours), **Sestri Levante** (hourly, 30 minutes, most trains to Genoa stop here), **La Spezia** (2-3/hour, 15-30 minutes), **Levanto** (2-3/hour, 4 minutes), **Santa Margherita Ligure** (at least hourly, 45 minutes), **Rome** (hourly, 4.5 hours, change in La Spezia). For destinations in **France,** change trains in Genoa.

Riomaggiore (Town #1)

The most substantial town of the group, Riomaggiore is a disappointment from the train station. But just walk through the tunnel next to the tracks, and you'll discover a more real and laid-back town than its more touristy neighbors. The main drag, while traffic-free, feels more urban than "village," and surrounding the harbor is a fascinating tangle of pastel homes leaning on each other like  drunken sailors. Despite Riomaggiore's workaday soul, the views back on its harbor from the breakwater—especially at sunset—are some of the region's prettiest.

Orientation to Riomaggiore

TOURIST INFORMATION

Tourist information is skimpy here. There are two "TIs" at the train station—one is actually the train ticket window, and the other is a shop for the national park (both open daily 8:00-20:00, shorter hours off-season)—but both can be too busy to be helpful. If you're in a pinch for tourist information, try asking Amy and Francesco at Riomaggiore Reservations (see "Sleeping in Riomaggiore," later); or Ivo and Alberto at the recommended Bar Centrale.

ARRIVAL IN RIOMAGGIORE

By Train: Riomaggiore's train station is separated from the town center by a steep hill. To get to the center, take the pedestrian tunnel that begins by the big mural (and parallels the rail tunnel). You'll exit at the bottom of Via Colombo; most recommended accommodations are a short hike up this steep artery.

If you're staying near the top of town, you can catch the sporadic shuttle bus at the bottom of Via Colombo and ride it partway up, or pay €1 to ride the elevator up from the pedestrian tunnel (if it's running—often closed for repairs). For a scenic route into town (for those not carrying luggage), see my "Riomaggiore Walk," later.

By Car: Day-trippers park at one of two pay-and-display lots above town (€3.50/hour, €23/day). If staying overnight, your hotel may have parking. Otherwise, Riomaggiore allows overnighters to drive into the town center long enough to drop off or pick up bags, but only during designated times (confirm with your hotelier). It may be easier to park at La Spezia's train station and ride the train in (see the next chapter).

HELPFUL HINTS

Bag Storage and Delivery: You can check your bag at the casually run *deposito bagagli* office, which is straight ahead as you exit the station (€3/bag, daily 8:30-19:00, closed in winter). If you're staying in town and want help hauling your bags, **Roberto** will do it for €5 per bag. He can also deliver your bags to other towns so they're waiting for you at the other end of a hike (call ahead to arrange, mobile 329-896-6219).

Services: There's a WC near the Co-op grocery on Via Colombo, and another under the tunnel where the street dead-ends.

Laundry: A self-service launderette is on the main street (daily in summer 8:30-20:00, shorter hours off-season, Via Colombo 107).

CINQUE TERRE

Riomaggiore Walk

Here's a partly uphill but easy self-guided loop walk that takes the long way around from the station into town. You'll enjoy some fine views before strolling down the main street to the harbor.

• *Start at the train station. (If you arrive by boat, cross beneath the tracks and take a left, then hike through the tunnel along the tracks to reach the station.) You'll see some...*

Faded Murals: These beautiful murals, with subjects modeled after real-life Riomaggiorians, glorify the nameless workers who

constructed the nearly 300 million cubic feet of mortarless, dry-stone walls that run throughout the Cinque Terre. These walls give the region its characteristic *muri a secco* terracing for vineyards and olive groves. Unfortunately, the murals, created by Argentinean artist Silvio Benedetto, were painted on wood panels—and are starting to chip away.

Looking left, notice the stairs climbing up just past the station building. These lead to the trail to Manarola, the **Via dell'Amore** (described on page 330).

• *Facing the mural, turn left, then go right up the wide street just before the station café. Head up this street for about 100 yards, and watch for the stairs leading through the garden on your right to the upper switchback. Then, once on high ground, turn right (back toward the sea). Soon you'll pass the top of the concrete elevator tower and, a bit farther, arrive at a fine viewpoint.*

Top o' the Town: Here you're treated to spectacular sea views. When you're ready to move on, hook left around the bluff; rounding the bend, ignore the steps marked *marina seacoast* (which lead to the harbor) and continue another five minutes along level ground to the church (follow *salita castello* signs). You'll go by the city hall, with murals celebrating the heroic grape-pickers and fishermen of the region (also by Silvio Benedetto), then pass the town preschool.

• *Before reaching the church, pause at the big terrace to enjoy the...*

Town View: The major river of this region once ran through this valley, as implied by the name Riomaggiore (local dialect for "river" and "major"). As in the other Cinque Terre towns, the main street covers its *rio maggiore*, which carved the canyon now filled by the town's pastel high-rises. The romantic arched bridges that once connected the two sides have been replaced by a practical modern road.

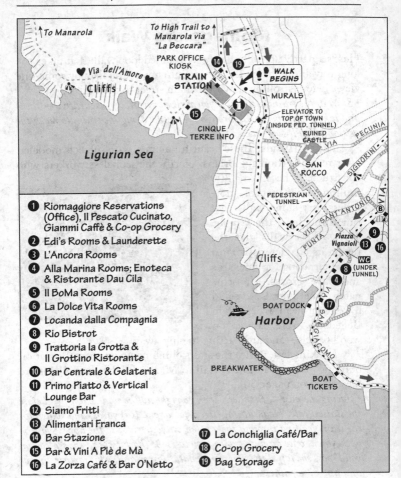

1 Riomaggiore Reservations (Office), Il Pescato Cucinato, Giammi Caffè & Co-op Grocery

2 Edi's Rooms & Launderette

3 L'Ancora Rooms

4 Alla Marina Rooms; Enoteca & Ristorante Dau Cila

5 Il BoMa Rooms

6 La Dolce Vita Rooms

7 Locanda dalla Compagnia

8 Rio Bistrot

9 Trattoria la Grotta & Il Grottino Ristorante

10 Bar Centrale & Gelateria

11 Primo Piatto & Vertical Lounge Bar

12 Siamo Fritti

13 Alimentari Franca

14 Bar Stazione

15 Bar & Vini A Piè de Mà

16 La Zorza Café & Bar O'Netto

17 La Conchiglia Café/Bar

18 Co-op Grocery

19 Bag Storage

Notice the lack of ugly aerial antennae. In the 1980s, every residence got cable. Now, the TV tower on the hilltop behind the church steeple brings the modern world into each home. The church was rebuilt in 1870, but was first established in 1340. It's dedicated to St. John the Baptist, the patron saint of Genoa, the maritime republic that once dominated the region.

• *Continue straight past the church and along the narrow lane, watching on the right for wide stairs leading down to Riomaggiore's main street...*

Via Colombo: Start downhill. Recent deregulation has led to an explosion in creative new businesses lining this street. First you'll pass (on the right, at #62) a handy pizzeria/*focacceria*, facing the Co-op grocery store across the street (at #55). Below that is a delicious fresh pasta takeaway place (Primo Piatto, at #72—handy for a picnic lunch or dinner). Farther along, the big covered terrace

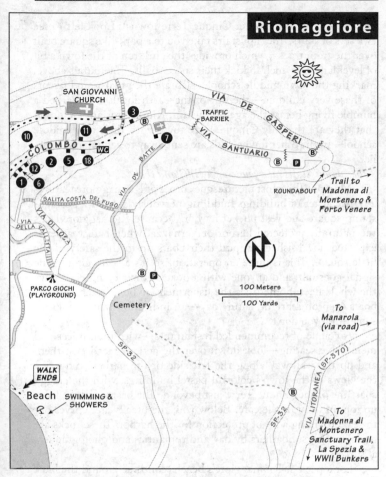

Riomaggiore

SAN GIOVANNI CHURCH

VIA DE GASPERI

TRAFFIC BARRIER

VIA SANTUARIO

3

B

7

COLOMBO

10   11

WC

12   2   5   18

1   6

VIA DE BATTE

ROUNDABOUT

Trail to
Madonna di
Montenero &
Porto Venere

B   P

B

SALITA COSTA DEL FUSO

VIA DI LOCA

VIA DELLA PALETTA

N

100 Meters
100 Yards

PARCO GIOCHI
(PLAYGROUND)

B   P

Cemetery

To
Manarola
(via road)

SP-32

VIA LITORANEA (SP-370)

WALK ENDS

Beach   SWIMMING & SHOWERS

B

SP-32

To
Madonna di
Montenero
Sanctuary Trail,
La Spezia &
WWII Bunkers

on the right belongs to the recommended Bar Centrale, the town's most popular hangout for international visitors (at #144).

As you round the bend to the left, notice the old-timey pharmacy just above (on the right). On your left, at #199, peek into the Il Pescato Cucinato shop, where Laura fries up her husband Edoardo's fresh catch; grab a paper cone of deep-fried seafood as a snack. Where the road bends sharply right, notice the bench on your left (just before La Zorza Café)—the hangout for the town's old-timers, who keep a running commentary on the steady flow of people. Straight ahead, you can already see where this street will dead-end. The last shop on the left, Alimentari Franca (at #251), is a well-stocked grocery where you can gather the makings for a perfect picnic out on the harbor or along the Via dell'Amore.

Where Via Colombo dead-ends, look right to see the tunnel leading back to the station (and the Via dell'Amore to Manarola, and eventually to the other Cinque Terre towns). Look left to see two sets of stairs. The "up" stairs take you to a park-like square built over the train tracks, which provides the children of the town a bit of level land on which to kick their soccer balls. The murals above, marking the town middle school, celebrate the great-grandparents of these very children—the salt-of-the-earth locals who earned a humble living before the age of tourism. Riomaggorians are proud that they are the only Cinque Terre town with their own middle school—in the other towns, kids are sent away to school much earlier.

• *The "down" stairs take you to a pay WC and the...*

   Marina: This most picturesque corner of Riomaggiore features a tight cluster of buildings huddling nervously around a postage-stamp square and vest-pocket harbor. Because Riomaggiore lacks the naturally protected harbor of Vernazza, when bad weather is expected, local fishermen pull their boats up to the safety of the little square. This is quite an operation, so it's a team effort—the signal goes out, and anyone with a boat of their own helps move the whole fleet. Sometimes the fishermen are busy beaching their boats even on a bright, sunny day—an indication that they know something you don't.

   A couple of recommended restaurants—with high prices and memorable seating—look down over the action. Head past them and up the walkway along the left side of the harbor, and enjoy the views of the town's colorful pastel buildings, with the craggy coastline of the Cinque Terre just beyond. The best views are from up top, in front of the café. Below you, the breakwater curves out to sea, providing a bit of protection for the harbor. These rocks are popular with sunbathers by day and romantics and photographers at sunset.

   For a peek at Riomaggiore's beach, continue around the bluff on this trail toward the Punta di Montenero, the cape that defines the southern end of the Cinque Terre. As you walk you'll pass the rugged boat landing and eventually run into Riomaggiore's uncomfortably rocky but still inviting beach *(spiaggia)*. Ponder how Europeans manage to look relaxed when lounging on football-sized "pebbles."

Experiences in Riomaggiore

Hikes from Riomaggiore

For an **easy walk** along the lip of the one-time river ravine, take Via di Loca, which veers off the main drag at the top of town (directly across from the stairs at the upper end of Via Colombo—described earlier, in my self-guided walk). This leads in just a few minutes to the town playground *(parco giochi)*, benches, neighborhood pea patches, and pleasant views over town (especially at sunset). There's also a steep staircase from here up to the town cemetery; from there, an even steeper trail runs all the way up to the sanctuary described next (though the trail outlined next is easier).

A **scenic trail** rises from Riomaggiore to the 14th-century **Madonna di Montenero sanctuary,** high above the town (about one hour, take the main road inland until you see signs; or ride the shuttle bus 12 minutes from the town center to the sanctuary trail, then walk uphill another 15 minutes; great picnic spot up top).

For details on the **Via dell'Amore** trail from Riomaggiore to Manarola, plus more ambitious **hikes from Riomaggiore** throughout the region—including the five-hour trail to **Porto Venere,** and the steep 1.5-hour **"La Beccara" hike** over the bluff to Manarola— see "Hiking the Cinque Terre" on page 325.

Beach

Riomaggiore's rugged and tiny "beach" is rocky, but it's clean and peaceful. It's just around the bluff from the harbor, past the boat landing—to find it, see the end of my self-guided walk, above. There's a shower here in the summer, and another closer to town by the boat landing—where many enjoy sunning on and jumping from the rocks.

Kayaks and Water Sports

The town has a diving center (scuba, snorkeling, kayaks; office down the stairs and under the tracks on Via San Giacomo, daily May-Sept 9:00-18:00, open in good weather only—likely weekends only in shoulder season, tel. 0187-920-011, www.5terrediving.it).

Nightlife in Riomaggiore

With a youthful spirit and lively evening bustle, Riomaggiore may have the Cinque Terre's most appealing nightlife. Stroll the main drag, scope out these listings (serving €6-8 cocktails), and find the one that appeals. Several of these places have full menus if you are looking to eat; see the map on page 354 for locations.

Bar Centrale, run by sociable Ivo, Alberto, and the gang, offers "nightlife" any time of day—it's a magnet for tourists (and a few young locals, too). Ivo, who lived in the Bay Area, fills his bar with San Franciscan rock and a fun-loving vibe; it feels a little like the village's living room (great mojitos, daily 7:30-late, free Wi-Fi with drink, Via Colombo 144).

Enoteca & Ristorante Dau Cila is a mellow little hideaway with a jazz-and-Brazilian-lounge ambience. Located down at the minuscule harbor, it's cool for cocktails and open nightly until midnight (snacks and meals, fine wine by the glass; Via San Giacomo 65).

Bar & Vini A Piè de Mà, at the Via dell'Amore trailhead, has piles of charm, frequent music, and stays open until midnight June through September.

More Bars and Cafés: Near the bottom of Via Colombo, facing each other, are the hip **La Zorza Café** (appealing to international tourists with thumping music and freestyle bartender) and the classier **Bar O'Netto** (geared more for locals, with a mellower vibe and nice outdoor seating). Higher up on Via Colombo (at #76), **Vertical Lounge Bar** has a lively and loose ambience, light food, and a fine people-watching perch near the top of the promenade zone. And at sunset, you can't beat **La Conchiglia**—the simple café/bar on the bluff overlooking the harbor—a perfect location for watching the sun disappear into the Ligurian Sea and the lights of Monterosso twinkling on the horizon.

Twilight Hike: The marvelous (currently closed) **Via dell'Amore** trail, lit only with subtle ground lighting so that you can see the stars, welcomes romantics after dark. When open, the trail is free after the ticket booth closes (typically around 19:00).

Sleeping in Riomaggiore

Given the relatively lousy value of most Riomaggiore hotels, I recommend staying in one of the town's many private rooms for rent. Remember, very few private rooms include breakfast; for ideas, see "Breakfast" on page 351.

ROOM-BOOKING SERVICES

Several room-booking agencies—with relatively predictable office hours, English-speaking staff, and email addresses—line up within a few yards of each other on the Via Colombo. Each manages a corral of local rooms for rent; the quality and specific amenities can vary wildly, so get a complete picture of the room before you commit. These offices sometimes close unexpectedly, so it's smart to settle up the day before you leave in case they're closed when you need to depart. Expect lots of stairs—ask how many when you book.

$ Riomaggiore Reservations, run with care and smooth communication by American expat Amy and her Italian husband, Francesco, offers six rooms and six apartments (RS%, cash only, reception open daily 9:00-13:00 & 14:00-17:00 in season, some rooms have air-con, Via Colombo 181, tel. 0187-760-575, www.riomaggiorereservations.com, info@riomaggiorereservations.com).

$ Edi's Rooms manages four double rooms and 12 apartments. You pay extra for views (family rooms, office open daily in summer 8:30-20:00, in winter 10:30-12:30 & 14:30-18:00, some

Sleep Code

Hotels are classified based on the average price of a standard double room with breakfast in high season.

$$$$	**Splurge:** Most rooms over €170
$$$	**Pricier:** €130-170
$$	**Moderate:** €90-130
$	**Budget:** €50-90
¢	**Backpacker:** Under €50
RS%	Rick Steves discount

Unless otherwise noted, credit cards are accepted, hotel staff speak basic English, and free Wi-Fi is available. Comparison-shop by checking prices at several hotels (on each hotel's own website, on a booking site, or by email). For the best deal, *book directly with the hotel.* Ask for a discount if paying in cash; if the listing includes **RS%**, request a Rick Steves discount.

rooms with air-con, closed Jan-Feb, reception at Via Colombo 111, tel. 0187-760-842, www.appartamenticinqueterre.net, edivesigna@iol.it). They also rent three hotelesque but pricey rooms of their own, called **$$ L'Ancora** (air-con, no breakfast, www. lancoracinqueterre.com).

ROOMS FOR RENT *(AFFITTACAMERE)*

Another option is to book directly with someone who rents just a few rooms of their own.

$$ Alla Marina is Riomaggiore's best value, with five rooms and an apartment at the top of one of the very tall, skinny buildings that rise up from the harbor. The furnishings are a stylish combination of modern and nautical, and friendly brothers Sandro and Andrea take pride in running a tight ship (RS%, one cheaper nonview room, breakfast served in-room, snacks, air-con, free minibar, pay parking, Via San Giacomo 61—ask about the easier back-door entrance, mobile 328-013-4077, www.allamarina.com, info@allamarina.com). They also rent a few rooms in other parts of town.

$$ Il BoMa—named for the owners, American Maddy and her Italian husband, Bombetta—has three pricey but well-appointed rooms right along the main drag. They also rent three nearby apartments (includes in-room breakfast with freshly baked brioche, one cheaper room has private bathroom down the hall and fans, others have air-con, up three flights at Via Colombo 99, tel. 0187-920-395, mobile 320-0748826, www.ilboma.com, info@ilboma.it).

$ La Dolce Vita offers six modern, good-value rooms on the main drag, plus two apartments elsewhere in town (some with air-con, no breakfast, open daily 9:30-19:30—if they're closed, they're full; Via Colombo 167, tel. 0187-762-283, agonatal@libero.it, helpful Giacomo and Simone).

$ Locanda dalla Compagnia, loosely run by Alessandro, rents five rooms at the top of town, just 300 yards below the parking lot and tucked behind a little church. All rooms—decent but rather dim and dated—are on the same tranquil ground floor and share a lounge (air-con, mini-fridge, no views, reception closes at 19:00, Via del Santuario 239, tel. 0187-760-050, www.dallacompa.com, lacomp@libero.it).

Eating in Riomaggiore

For even more options, see "Nightlife in Riomaggiore," earlier.

ON THE HARBOR
Harborfront dining comes with slightly higher prices but glorious views. These two eateries share the same owner; the first one's menu is more traditional Italian, while the second is a bit more modern.

$$$$ Enoteca & Ristorante Dau Cila (pronounced "dow CHEE-lah") is decked out like a black-and-white movie set in a centuries-old boat shed with extra tables outside on a rustic deck over dinghies. Try their antipasto specialty of several seafood appetizers and listen to the waves lapping at the harbor below (cheaper lunch menu with salads and *bruschette,* daily 12:00-24:00, closed Feb, Via San Giacomo 65, tel. 0187-760-032, Luca).

$$$$ Rio Bistrot, small and intimate at the top of the harbor, tries to jazz up its Ligurian cuisine with international influences. You can order à la carte from the short but well-designed menu, but they tend to push their €37 tasting menu (simpler and cheaper lunch menu, daily 12:00-16:00 & 18:00-22:00, Via San Giacomo 46, tel. 0187-920-616).

ON THE MAIN STREET, VIA COLOMBO
$$ Trattoria la Grotta, right in the town center (with no view), has a passion for anchovies and mussels. You'll enjoy reliably good food and friendly service surrounded by historical photos and wonderful stonework in a dramatic, dressy, cave-like setting. Vanessa is warm and helpful, while her mother, Isa, is busy cooking (daily 12:00-14:30 & 17:30-22:30, closed Wed in winter, Via Colombo 247, tel. 0187-920-187). Next door and run by the same family, **$$$ Il Grottino Ristorante** is slightly more upscale, with a similar approach and decor but a somewhat different menu (same hours but closed Wed in winter, tel. 0187-920-938).

$$ Bar Centrale, the popular bar and expat hangout listed earlier under "Nightlife in Riomaggiore," has a menu of Italian

Restaurant Price Code

I've assigned each eatery a price category, based on the average cost of a typical main course (pasta or *secondi*). Drinks, desserts, and splurge items (steak and seafood) can raise the price considerably.

$$$$ **Splurge:** Most main courses over €20
$$$ **Pricier:** €15-20
$$ **Moderate:** €10-15
$ **Budget:** Under €10

In Italy, pizza by the slice and other takeout food is **$**; a basic trattoria or sit-down pizzeria is **$$**; a casual but more upscale restaurant is **$$$**; and a swanky splurge is **$$$$**.

specialties (pasta dishes, anchovies) and a few American comfort food standbys (hamburgers). They also have their own *gelateria* on site (open long hours daily).

Light Meals: Various handy carry-out eateries along the main drag offer good lunches or snacks. Choose a bench on Via Colombo, or head out to the breakwater for a scenic munch. **$ Primo Piatto,** at the top of town, offers takeaway handmade pastas and sauces, cooked to order on the spot. It's cheap and delicious (Wed-Mon 10:30-19:30 or later, closed Tue, Via Colombo 72, tel. 0187-920-038). For deep-fried seafood in a paper cone, I prefer **$ Il Pescato Cucinato,** where Edoardo fishes and his wife, Laura, fries (chalkboard out front explains what's fresh, daily 11:20-20:30, near the bottom of Via Colombo at #199, mobile 339-262-4815). A few doors away, **$ Siamo Fritti** also has fried fish (daily 10:00-21:00, Via Colombo 161, mobile 347-826-1729, Andrea and Isabella).

Picnics: Groceries and delis lining Via Colombo sell food to go for a picnic at the harbor or beach. The two **Co-op** grocery stores have the best prices. For a more appealing selection and good service, head to the handy **Alimentari Franca,** at the very bottom of the main street, right by the train-station tunnel and stairs to the marina/beach (daily 8:00-12:45 & 15:30-19:30, Via Colombo 251).

Breakfast: Most of my recommended accommodations don't serve breakfast—and those that do often simply leave a coffee kettle and some basic continental breakfast fixings in your room. For eggs or a good croissant-and-espresso fix, drop by **Bar Centrale** (described earlier); **Giammi Caffè,** with outdoor tables on the main drag (daily 7:00-24:00, Via Colombo 189, mobile 331-608-3512); or **Bar Stazione,** at the train station.

NEAR THE TRAIN STATION AND VIA DELL'AMORE

$$ Bar & Vini A Piè de Mà, at the trailhead on the Manarola end of town, is good for a scenic light bite or quiet drink at night. The downstairs bar, with great outdoor seating, is self-service: Head into the bar to place your order, then bring it out to your preferred perch (daily 10:00-20:00, June-Sept until 24:00, closed Mon-Tue off-season, free Wi-Fi, tel. 0187-921-037). Enjoy a meal on its dramatically situated terrace for an indelible Cinque Terre memory. In the summer they open a restaurant with table service upstairs—but I prefer the cheaper, simpler terrace.

Manarola (Town #2)

Mellow Manarola fills a ravine, bookended by its wild little harbor to the west and a diminutive hilltop church square inland to the east. Manarola is exceptional for being unexceptional: While Vernazza is prettier, Monterosso glitzier, Riomaggiore bigger, and Corniglia more rustic, each of those towns is also sorely lacking in other regards. Manarola hits a fine balance, giving it the "just right" combination of Cinque Terre qualities. Perhaps that's why it's a favorite among savvy Europeans seeking a relatively untrampled home base. The tour-

isty zone squeezed between the cement-encased train tracks and the harbor can be stressfully congested, but head just a few steps uphill and you can breathe again. Popular with hikers, it may be the Cinque Terre's steepest town—but the higher you go, the less crowded it gets, culminating in the essentially tourist-free residential zone that clings to the ridge.

Manarola, whose hillsides are blanketed with vineyards, also provides the easiest access to the Cinque Terre's remarkable dry-stone terraces. The trail ringing the town's cemetery peninsula, adjacent to the main harbor, provides some of the most strikingly beautiful town views anywhere in the region (best light late in the day). For a look at all the facets of this delightful town, follow my gentle self-guided stroll from the waterfront to the church, through the vineyards, and down to the harborside park.

Orientation to Manarola

TOURIST INFORMATION
The TI/national park information office is in the train station (likely daily 8:00-19:30, shorter hours off-season).

ARRIVAL IN MANAROLA

By Train: From the station, to reach Manarola's elevated square, you'll walk through a 200-yard-long tunnel that's lined with interesting photos. (During WWII air raids, these tunnels provided refuge and a safe place for rattled villagers to sleep.) To reach the busy harbor—with touristy restaurants, boat dock, and the start of my self-guided walk—cross the piazza, then go down the other side. To reach the town, hilltop church, and vineyard strolls, turn right.

The ATC **shuttle bus** runs from near the post office (halfway up Manarola's main street), stopping first at the parking lots above town, and then going all the way up to Volastra (about 2/hour except for afternoon breaks).

By Car: Unless you're sleeping here, you're not allowed to drive into Manarola. Park your car in one of the two lots just before town (€2/hour), then walk down the road to the church; from there, it's an easy downhill walk to the main piazza, train-station tunnel (and trailhead for the Via dell'Amore to Riomaggiore), and harbor (the start of my self-guided walk)—or you can wait for the shuttle bus. If you're sleeping here, ask your hotelier for parking advice.

Manarola Walk

From the harbor, this 45-minute self-guided circular walk shows you the town and surrounding vineyards and ends at a fantastic viewpoint, perfect for a picnic.

• *Start down at the waterfront. Belly up to the wooden banister overlooking the rocky harbor, between the two restaurants.*

The Harbor: Manarola is tiny and picturesque, a tumble of buildings bunny-hopping down its ravine to the fun-loving waterfront. The breakwater—which attempts to make this jagged harbor a bit less dangerous—was built just over a decade ago. Notice how the I-beam crane launches the boats (which must be pulled ashore when bad weather is expected to avoid being smashed or swept away).

Facing the water, look up to the right, at the hillside Punta Bonfiglio cemetery and park. The trail running around the base of the point—where this walk ends—offers magnificent views back on this part of town.

The town's swimming hole is just below you. Manarola has no sand, but offers the best deep-water swimming in the area. The first "beach" has a shower, ladder, and

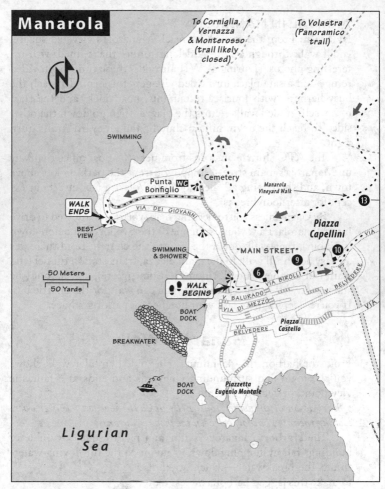

wonderful rocks. The second has tougher access and no shower, but feels more remote and pristine (follow the paved path toward Corniglia, just around the point). For many, the tricky access makes this "beach" dangerous.

• *Go inland up the town's main drag—you'll climb a steep ramp to reach Manarola's "new" square, which covers the train tracks.*

Piazza Capellini: Built in 2004, this square is an all-around great idea, giving the town a safe, fun zone for kids. Locals living near the tracks also enjoy a little less train noise. Check out the mosaic in the middle of the square, which depicts the varieties of local fish in colorful enamel. The recommended Ristorante di Aristide has an inviting terrace right on the square.

• *Go down the stairs at the upper end of the square. On your right, notice*

To Volastra
(car, shuttle bus)

To Volastra
(Official
trail)

P

P

VIA LITORANEA

SP-370

TUNNEL

To **8**

Manarola
Vineyard Walk
Entrance

7

5

14

4

VIA DISCOVOLO

BELL
TOWER

SAN LORENZO
CHURCH

POST

B

15

11

1

ORATORY

DISCOVOLO

B

Piazza
Papa Innocenzo IV

12

2

ROLLANDI

RESIDENTIAL
ZONE

3

PEDESTRIAN TUNNEL

TRAIN STATION

Via dell'Amore ♥
Trail

To Riomaggiore

1	La Torretta Rooms
2	B&B Da Baranin
3	Aria di Mare Rooms
4	Ostello 5-Terre
5	Albergo Ca' d'Andrean
6	Marina Piccola Rooms & Restaurant
7	Da Paulin Rooms
8	To Hotel il Saraceno
9	Trattoria il Porticciolo
10	Ristorante di Aristide
11	Via Discovolo Eateries
12	Trattoria dal Billy
13	Grocery
14	Cinque Terre Trekking
15	Shuttle Bus to Parking Lot & Volastra

the tunnel that leads to Manarola's train station (and the Via dell'Amore trailhead). But for now, head up...

Via Discovolo: Manarola's sleepy main street twists up through town, lined by modest shops and filled with pooped hikers. About 100 yards up, just before the road bends sharply right, watch (on the right) for a waterwheel. This recalls the origin of the town's name—local dialect for "big wheel" (one of many possible derivations). Mills like this once powered the local olive oil industry. As you continue up (all the way to the church), you'll still hear the rushing waters of Manarola's stream. Like the streams in Riomaggiore, Monterosso, and Vernazza, Manarola's rivulet was covered over by a modern sewage system after World War II. Before that time, romantic bridges arched over its ravine. You can peek below the concrete street in several places to see the stream surging below your feet.

Across the street from the waterwheel and a bit farther up, notice the **Cinque Terre Trekking** shop on your left, which outfits hikers with both information and gear (see page 358 for details).

• *Keep switchbacking up until you come to the square at the...*

Top of Manarola: The square is faced by a church, an oratory—now a religious and community meeting place—and a bell tower, which served as a watchtower when pirates raided the town (the cupola was added once the attacks ceased). Behind the church is Manarola's well-run youth hostel, originally the church's schoolhouse. To the right of the oratory, a stepped lane leads to Manarola's sizable tourist-free residential zone.

Check out the **church.** According to the white marble plaque in its facade, the Parish Church of St. Lawrence (San Lorenzo) dates from "MCCCXXXVIII" (1338). Step inside to see two altarpiece paintings from the unnamed Master of the Cinque Terre, the only painter of any note from this region (left wall and above main altar). While the style is Gothic, the work dates from the late 15th century, long after Florence had entered the Renaissance. Note the humble painted stone ceiling, which replaced the wooden original in the 1800s. It features Lawrence, patron saint of the Cinque Terre, with his grill, the symbol of his martyrdom (he was roasted on it).

• *With the bell tower on your left, head about 20 yards back down the main street below the church and find a wooden railing. It marks the start of a delightful stroll around the high side of town, and back to the seafront. This is the beginning of the...*

Manarola Vineyard Walk: Don't miss this experience. Simply follow the wooden railing, enjoying lemon groves and wild red valerian (used for insomnia since the days of the Romans). Along the path, which is primarily flat, you'll get a close-up look at the region's famous dry-stone walls and finely crafted vineyards (with dried-heather thatches to protect the grapes from southwest winds). Smell the rosemary. Study the structure of the town, and pick out the scant remains of an old fort. Notice the S-shape of the main road—once a riverbed—that flows through town. The town's roofs are traditionally made of locally quarried slate and held down by rocks during windstorms.

Halfway along the lip of the ravine, a path marked *Panoramico Volastra (Corniglia)* leads steeply up into the vineyards on the right. This path passes a variety of simple wooden religious scenes, the work of local resident Mario Andreoli. Before his father died, Mario promised him he'd replace the old cross on the family's vineyard. Mario has been adding figures ever since. On religious holidays, everything's lit up: the Nativity, the Last Supper, the Cruci-fixion, the Resurrection, and more. Some of the scenes are left up year-round. (You can see more of his figures across the ravine, in a little open patch between buildings.)

High above, a recent fire burned off the tree cover, revealing ancient terraces that line the terrain like a topographic map. This path also marks the start of the scenic route to Volastra, on the hilltop above, and eventually to Corniglia (this challenging route is described on page 332).

• *Continue on the level trail around the base of the hill. Soon the harbor comes into view. Keep looping around the hill for even better views of town. Once you're facing the sea (after passing the cemetery peninsula below you), the trail takes a sharp left and heads down toward the water on concrete steps. Once on the lower path, continue back across the vine-yards toward the harbor. When you're almost back to town, you'll see the entrance (on your right) to...*

The Cemetery: Ever since Napoleon—who was king of Italy in the early 1800s—decreed that cemeteries were health risks, Cinque Terre's burial spots have been located outside the towns. The result: The dearly departed generally get first-class sea views. Each cemetery—with evocative yellowed photos and finely carved Carrara marble memorial reliefs—is worth a visit (Manarola's is the most easily accessible).

In cemeteries like these, there's a hierarchy of four places to park your mortal remains: a graveyard, a spacious death condo *(lo-culo)*, a mini bone-niche *(ossario)*, or the communal ossuary. Be-cause of the tight space, a time limit is assigned to the first three options (although many older tombs are grandfathered in). Bones go into the ossuary in the middle of the chapel floor after about a generation. Traditionally, locals make weekly visits to loved ones here, often bringing flowers. The rolling stepladder makes access to top-floor *loculi* easy.

• *The Manarola cemetery is on...*

Punta Bonfiglio: This point offers some of the most com-manding views of the entire region. To find the best vantage point, take the stairs just below the cemetery (through the green gate), then walk farther out toward the water through a park (playground, drinking water, WC, and picnic benches). Your Manarola finale is the bench at the tip of the point. Pause and take in the view. The easiest way back to town is to take the stairs at the end of the point, which join the main walking path—offering more spectacu-lar town views on the way back to the harbor, where we started.

CINQUE TERRE

Experiences in Manarola

Hikes from Manarola

From Manarola, the coastal trail leads to **Corniglia** in one direction, and to **Riomaggiore** (on the easy and romantic Via dell'Amore) in the other. But in recent years both trails have been closed on and off due to landslides; check the latest before you head out. If—as is often the case—the main Corniglia trail is closed, consider taking the **high route to Corniglia via Volastra** (much easier if you ride the shuttle bus, rather than hike, up to Volastra). For details, see "Hiking the Cinque Terre" on page 325.

For something less challenging, one of my favorite easy hikes in the region is to head up into the **vineyards above Manarola,** then drop down into the town cemetery. This route is outlined in my self-guided "Manarola Walk" (see page 353).

Hiking Gear and Tips: Cinque Terre Trekking, near the top of the main street (halfway up to the church), is a wonderful resource for hikers. Christine and Nicola are generous with hiking advice, and fill their cramped little shop with all the hiking gear you may need: boots, clothes, walking sticks, maps, and more. If you're serious about hiking, stop in here to confirm your plans and to gear up (daily 9:00-13:00 & 14:00-20:00, shorter hours off-season, Via Discovolo 136, tel. 0187-920-715, www.cinqueterretrekking.com).

Boat Rides

To get to the dock and the boats that connect Manarola with the other Cinque Terre towns, find the steps to the left of the harbor view—they lead down to the ticket kiosk. Continue around the left side of the cliff (as you're facing the water) to catch the boats.

Sleeping in Manarola

($$$$ = Splurge, $$$ = Pricier, $$ = Moderate, $ = Budget)

Manarola has some of the most appealing, well-run accommodations in the region (rivaling Monterosso's). Like the others, it also has plenty of private rooms; ask in bars and restaurants. If you need breakfast, the recommended Café Aristide is your best choice. Otherwise grab a coffee and croissant in a bar.

To transfer luggage from the station to your accommodations, call ahead and arrange with Roberto, based in Monterosso (€15 for all your bags, mobile 329-896-6219).

IN THE RESIDENTIAL ZONE ABOVE THE CHURCH

This area is a 10-minute, steeply uphill hike from the train station—just huff up the main drag to the church. All of these are within a five-minute walk from there.

$$$$ La Torretta offers 12 trendy, upscale rooms (most with private deck) that cater to a demanding clientele. Probably the most elegant retreat in the region, this peaceful refuge has all the comforts for those happy to pay, including a communal hot tub with a view. Guests enjoy a complimentary snack and glass of prosecco on arrival, wine tastings, an ample breakfast buffet, and minibars. Each chic room is distinct (top-end family suite, book several months in advance, closed Dec-March; on request, they'll pick you up at the station tunnel in a golf cart; on Piazza della Chiesa beside the bell tower at Vico Volto 20, tel. 0187-920-327, www.torrettas. com, torretta@cdh.it).

$$ B&B Da Baranin, with seven good rooms and three apartments, is a bit too pricey but has sleek modern style (family rooms, air-con, Via Aldo Rollandi 29, tel. 0187-920-595, www. baranin.com, info@baranin.com, Sara).

$ Aria di Mare Rooms rents four sunny, tidy, well-equipped rooms and an apartment a few steps beyond Trattoria dal Billy at the very top of town. While it's a steep hike up (high above the tourists), this is an excellent value. Three rooms have spacious terraces with knockout views and lounge chairs (RS%, includes breakfast snacks in room, air-con, upstairs on the left at Via Aldo Rollandi 137, mobile 349-058-4155, www.ariadimare.info, info@ ariadimare.info, Maurizio, ask at Billy's if no one's home).

¢ Ostello 5-Terre, Manarola's modern hostel, occupies the former parochial school above the church square and offers 48 beds and a huge roof terrace. This is not a party hostel—it's a calm and peaceful place where quiet is greatly appreciated. They rent dorm rooms as doubles with separated beds. Reserve well in advance (not co-ed except for couples and families, all ages, breakfast extra, office closed 13:00-16:00—except maybe in summer, check-in until 20:00, Via B. Riccobaldi 21, tel. 0187-920-039, mobile 346-532-8078, www.hostel5terre.com, ostello5terre@gmail.com).

ON THE MAIN STREET

These options line up along the main street, between the harbor and the church. While in a less atmospheric area than the ones near the church, they're closer to the station—and therefore a bit handier for those packing heavy.

$$$ Albergo Ca' d'Andrean is quiet, comfortable, and chic. It has 10 big, sunny, industrial-mod rooms (with lots of tile and concrete). Public spaces artfully display family artifacts, and the cool garden oasis comes complete with lemon trees. If you don't mind stairs, consider one of their pricier top-floor rooms, with great views from their terraces (breakfast extra, air-con, up the hill at Via Discovolo 101, tel. 0187-920-040, www.cadandrean.it, info@cadandrean.it, Simone and Nicola).

$$$ Marina Piccola, a lesser value, offers 12 stylish rooms on the water (some with sea views). It's expensive and impersonal, but it's handy to the harbor area (air-con, Via Birolli 120, tel. 0187-920-770, www.hotelmarinapiccola.com, info@hotelmarinapiccola.com).

$$ At **Da Paulin,** charming Donatella and Eraldo (the town's retired policeman) rent three surprisingly modern, fresh, well-equipped, air-conditioned, hotelesque rooms with a large and inviting common living room. They also rent three apartments (fans, no air-con). This fine value is at the bend in the main street, a five-minute hike above the train tracks (no breakfast, Via Discovolo 126, mobile 334-389-4764, www.dapaulin.it, prenotazioni@dapaulin.it).

HIGH ABOVE MANAROLA, IN VOLASTRA

$$ Hotel il Saraceno, with seven spacious, modern, functional rooms, is a deal for drivers. Located above Manarola in the tiny town of Volastra (chock-full of vacationing Germans and Italians in summer), it's serene, clean, and right by the shuttle bus to Manarola (free parking, tel. 0187-760-081, www.thesaraceno.com, hotel@thesaraceno.com, friendly Antonella).

Eating in Manarola

($$$$ = Splurge, $$$ = Pricier, $$ = Moderate, $ = Budget)
Restaurant options are limited in Manarola, but you have at least two excellent options (Billy's and Aristide). I've listed these from lowest to highest, in terms of both quality and elevation.

The vast majority of the town's (decidedly touristy) restaurants are concentrated between Piazza Capellini and the harbor. They are mostly interchangeable, but the Scorza family works hard at **$$ Trattoria il Porticciolo** (Thu-Tue 12:00-21:30, closed Wed, Via Birolli 92, tel. 0187-920-083). At the harborfront itself, **$$$ Marina Piccola** is famous for great views, lousy service, and price-gouging naive tourists (closed Mon).

$$ Ristorante di Aristide, right on Piazza Capellini, is run by three generations of hardworking women and offers a trendy atmosphere and a pleasant outdoor setting, with a view of budding soccer stars rather than harborfront glitz (Fri-Wed 12:00-22:30). Down the stairs, at the bottom of the main street, their **$ café** has indoor and streetside seating, a simpler menu, and breakfast options (omelets, pizzas, sandwiches, salads; open Fri-Wed from 8:00, food served until restaurant opens for dinner; both closed Thu and Jan-Feb, Via Discovolo 290, tel. 0187-920-000, charming Elena, Mamma Monica, and Nonna Grazia).

Via Discovolo, the main street climbing up through town from Piazza Capellini to the church, is lined with simpler places, including a popular *gelateria* and some small grocery stores where you can browse for a picnic. This strip—and the short street between the elevated square and the harbor—also has several focaccia, pizza-by-the-slice, and fried-goodies carryout shops that are fine for a quick lunch.

Up at the residential zone above the church, dining options are sparse, but the place that's here is a good one: **$$$ Trattoria dal Billy**. Many find it's worth the climb for Edoardo and chef Enrico's homemade black pasta with seafood and squid ink, green pasta with artichokes, and homemade desserts. Their *antipasto misto di mare* comes with a dazzling array of seafood treats—each one perfectly executed. Billy's outdoor terraces offer commanding views over Manarola, while across the street an elegant, glassy dining room is carved into the rock. Either setting is perfect for a romantic candlelight meal. Dinner reservations are a must (Fri-Wed 12:00-15:00 & 18:00-22:00, closed Thu, Via Aldo Rollandi 122, tel. 0187-920-628, www.trattoriabilly.com).

Corniglia (Town #3)

If you think of the Cinque Terre as the Beatles, Corniglia is Ringo. This tiny, sleepy town—the only one of the five not directly on the

water—owns a mellow main square. According to a (likely fanciful) local legend, the town was originally settled by a Roman farmer who named it for his mother, Cornelia (how Corniglia is pronounced). Its ancient residents produced a wine so widely exported that—some say—vases have been found at Pompeii stamped with the town name. Regardless of the veracity of the legends, wine remains Corniglia's lifeblood today. Follow the pungent smell of ripe grapes into an alley cellar and get a local to let you dip a straw into a keg.

Less visited than the other Cinque Terre towns, Corniglia has fewer tourists, cooler temperatures, a few restaurants, a windy overlook on its promontory, and plenty of private rooms for rent (ask at any bar or shop, no cheaper than other towns).

Hilltop Corniglia has rocky sea access below its train station (toward Manarola). The beach here has all been washed away—but look for signs that say *al mare* or *Marina*, where a trail leads from the town center steeply down to sunning rocks (with a shower). Corniglia's infamous Guvano beach (a bit along the coast toward

CINQUE TERRE

Vernazza) is now essentially closed down. Created in 1893 by a landslide that cost the village a third of its farmland—and notorious throughout Italy as a nude beach—Guvano was accessed via an unused train tunnel and attracted visitors with an appetite for drug use. Now the tunnel is closed, and the national park wants people to keep their clothes on.

Thankfully, hill-capping Corniglia comes with a hardworking little shuttle bus with a reliable schedule posted both at the station and in the town. If leaving by train, review the shuttle schedule and time your visit to catch the bus down to conveniently arrive at the station in time for your departure. Because of the long, steep hike between the town and its train station, and Corniglia's lack of a boat dock, it's a less convenient home base for town-hopping.

Orientation to Corniglia

TOURIST INFORMATION

A TI/park information office is at the train station (likely daily 8:00-20:00, shorter hours off-season).

ARRIVAL IN CORNIGLIA

By Train: From the station far below town, a footpath zigzags up 385 steps (and nearly that many switchbacks) to the town in about 20 minutes. If you'd rather not walk, take the tiny shuttle bus—generally timed to meet arriving trains—which connects the station with Corniglia's main square, the start of my self-guided walk (1-2/hour).

By Car: Only residents can park on the main road between the recommended Villa Cecio and the point where the steep switchback staircase meets the road. Beyond that area, parking is €2/hour (up to €10/day). All parking areas are within an easy and fairly level walk of the town center.

Corniglia Walk

We'll explore this tiny town—population 240—and end at a scenic viewpoint. This self-guided walk might take up to 30 minutes...but only if you let yourself browse and lick a gelato cone.

• *Begin near the shuttle bus stop located at a...*

Town Square: The gateway to this community is "Ciappà" square, with an ATM, old wine press, and bus stop. The Cinque Terre's designation as a national park sparked a revitalization of the town. Corniglia's young generation is more likely now to stay put, rather than migrate into big cities the way locals did in the past.

• *Look for the arrow pointing to the* centro. *Stroll along Via Fieschi, the*

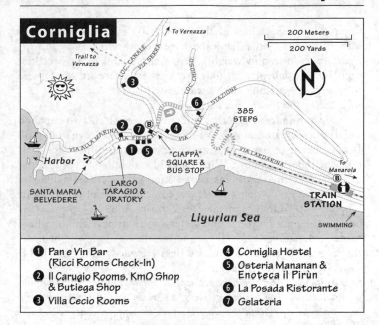

Corniglia

To Vernazza

Trail to Vernazza

LOC. CANALE

VIA SERRA

LOC. CHIOSO

VIA ALLA STAZIONE

200 Meters
200 Yards

N

385 STEPS

VIA ALLA MARINA

VIA FIESCHI

VIA LARDARINA

To Manarola

Harbor

"CIAPPÀ" SQUARE & BUS STOP

SANTA MARIA BELVEDERE

LARGO TARAGIO & ORATORY

Ligurian Sea

TRAIN STATION

SWIMMING

1 Pan e Vin Bar
   (Ricci Rooms Check-In)
2 Il Carugio Rooms, KmO Shop
   & Butiega Shop
3 Villa Cecio Rooms
4 Corniglia Hostel
5 Osteria Mananan &
   Enoteca il Pirùn
6 La Posada Ristorante
7 Gelateria

spine of Corniglia. In the fall, the smell of grapes (on their way to becom-
ing wine) wafts from busy cellars. Along this main street, you'll see...

Corniglia's Enticing Shops: As you enter Via Fieschi, a trio
of neighboring, fiercely competitive *gelaterias* jockey for your business. Don't settle for second-best: My favorite is the last one you
come to (at #74, on the right), **Alberto's Gelateria.** Before ordering, get a free taste of Alberto's *miele di Corniglia,* made from local
honey; he's also proud of his basil flavor, and his lemon slush *(granita)* takes pucker to new heights.

Farther along, on the left, **Enoteca il Pirùn**—named for a
type of oddly shaped old-fashioned wine pitcher designed to aer-
ate the wine and give the alcohol more kick as you squirt it into
your mouth—is located in a cool cantina at Via Fieschi 115. Sample
some local wines (small tastes generally free, €3/glass). If you order
wine to drink from the *pirùn,* Mario will give you a bib. While this
is a practical matter (rookies are known to dribble), it also makes a
nice souvenir.

A bit farther along are two interesting shops—particularly for
picnic shoppers. On the left, at #151, Franco's shop **Km0** ("kilometer zero") focuses on locally sourced wines and beers from the
Cinque Terre, and meats and cheeses from within a few miles of
here (panini, smoothies; daily 10:00-21:00, closed Tue off-season).
They've even reclaimed some farmland on the adjacent hill (visible
from just outside the shop) to grow their own produce.

Across the street, at the **Butiega** shop (#142), Vincenzo sells organic local specialties (daily 8:00-19:30). For picnickers, they offer €3 made-to-order ham-and-cheese sandwiches and a fun *antipasti misti* (priced by weight). Veronica prepares local specialties such as pesto daily in the shop's tiny kitchen. There are good places to picnic farther along on this walk.

• *Following Via Fieschi, you'll end up at the...*

Main Square: On Largo Taragio, tables from two bars and a trattoria spill around a WWI memorial and the town's old well. It once piped in natural spring water from the hillside to locals living without plumbing. What looks like a church is the Oratory of Santa Caterina. (An oratory is a kind of a spiritual clubhouse for a service group doing social work in the name of the Catholic Church—see "Oratory of the Dead" on page 394.) Up the stairs behind the oratory, you'll find a clearing that local children have made into a soccer field. The stone benches and viewpoint make this a peaceful place for a picnic (less crowded than the end-of-town viewpoint, described next).

• *Opposite the oratory, notice how steps lead steeply down (in 5 minutes) on Via alla Marina to sunning rocks, a shower, and a small deck (with a treacherous entry into the water). From the square, continue up Via Fieschi to the...*

End-of-Town Viewpoint: The Santa Maria Belvedere, named for a church that once stood here, marks the scenic end of Corniglia. This is a super picnic spot. From here, look high to the west (right), where the village and sanctuary of San Bernardino straddle a ridge (a good starting point for a hike; accessible by shuttle bus from Monterosso or a long uphill hike from Vernazza). Below is the tortuous harbor, where locals hoist their boats onto the cruel rocks.

Experiences in Corniglia

Hikes from Corniglia

From Corniglia, you can hike on the coastal trail to **Vernazza** or—when it's open—to **Manarola**. If the Manarola trail is closed, or even if it isn't, consider the challenging but very rewarding "high road" to **Manarola via Volastra.** For details on these options, see "Hiking the Cinque Terre" on page 325.

Sleeping in Corniglia

($$$$ = Splurge, $$$ = Pricier, $$ = Moderate, $ = Budget)
Corniglia is riddled with humble places that charge too much (given its harborless location) and whose hosts have a limited ability to converse with tourists—so it's almost never full.

$ Cristiana Ricci communicates well and is reliable, renting three small, clean, and peaceful rooms—one with a terrace and sweeping view—just inland from the bus stop (family rooms, check in at the Pan e Vin bar at Via Fieschi 123, mobile 338-937-6547, cri_affittacamere@virgilio.it). She also rents three big, modern apartments.

$ Il Carugio has nine modern, fresh, sunny rooms right in the center of the village, most with sea views. The communal rooftop terrace offers a commanding view of the coast (air-con, no breakfast but small self-service kitchen, free parking, free self-serve laundry, tel. 0187-812-293, mobile 335-175-7946 or 339-228-3803, www.ilcarugiodicorniglia.com, info@ilcarugiodicorniglia.com, Lidia). They also have a two-bedroom apartment facing the main square.

$ Villa Cecio (pronounced "chay-choh") feels like an abandoned hotel. They offer eight well-worn rooms on the outskirts of town, with saggy beds and little character. Some rooms have great views, and three have terraces—worth requesting when you check in. All rooms share a big rooftop view terrace (breakfast extra, four rooms have air-con, on main road 200 yards toward Vernazza at Via Serra 58, tel. 0187-812-043, mobile 366-285-1178, www.cecio5terre.com, info@cecio5terre.com, Giacinto). They also rent eight similar rooms in an annex on the square where the bus stops.

¢ Corniglia Hostel, the town's former schoolhouse, rents 24 beds in a pastel-yellow municipal building up some steps from the square where the bus stops (find the entrance at the back of the building). The playground in front is often busy with happy kids. Despite its strict and institutional atmosphere, the hostel's prices, central location, and bright, clean rooms ensure its popularity. Its hotelesque double rooms are open to anyone (breakfast extra, office open 7:00-13:00 & 15:00-1:30 in the morning, dorms closed 10:30-15:00, private rooms closed 13:00-15:00, 1:30 curfew, air-con, self-serve laundry, Via alla Stazione 3, tel. 0187-812-559, www.ostellocorniglia.com, ostellocorniglia@gmail.com, Andrea, Alessandro, and Elisabetta).

Eating in Corniglia

Corniglia has few restaurants. The typical array of pizzerias, *focacerie,* and *alimentari* (grocery stores) line the narrow main drag. I've highlighted a few places for a quick bite on my self-guided walk. For a full, sit-down meal, consider one of these options.

$$ Osteria Mananan—between the Ciappà bus stop and the main square at Via Fieschi 117—serves what many consider the best food in town in its small, stony, elegant interior (Tue-Sun 12:30-14:30 & 19:30-22:00, closed Mon, no outdoor seating, tel. 0187-821-166).

$$ Enoteca il Pirùn, next door on Via Fieschi, has a small restaurant above the wine bar, where Mario serves typical local dishes (daily 12:00-16:00 & 19:30-23:30, tel. 0187-812-315).

$$ La Posada Ristorante offers dinner in a garden under trees, overlooking the Ligurian Sea. To get here, stroll out of town to the top of the stairs that lead down to the station (daily 12:00-16:00 & 19:00-23:00, tel. 0187-821-174, mobile 338-232-5734).

Vernazza (Town #4)

With the closest thing to a natural harbor—overseen by a ruined castle, a stout stone church, and a Crayola-colored canyon of fisherfolk homes—Vernazza is the jewel of the Cinque Terre. Only the regular noisy slurping up of the train by the mountain reminds you of the modern world.

The action is at the harbor, where you'll find outdoor eateries ringing a humble piazza, a restaurant hanging on the edge of the castle, and a breakwater with a promenade, corralled by a natural amphitheater of terraced hills. In the summer, the beach becomes a soccer field, with teams fielded by local bars and restaurants providing late-night entertainment. In the dark, locals fish off the promontory, using glowing bobbers that shine in the waves.

Proud of their Vernazzan heritage, the town's 500 residents like to brag: "Vernazza is locally owned. Portofino has sold out." Fearing the change it would bring, keep-Vernazza-small proponents stopped the construction of a major road into the town and region. Families are tight and go back centuries; you'll notice certain surnames (such as Basso and Moggia) everywhere. In the winter, the population shrinks, as many people return to their more comfortable big-city apartments to spend the money they reaped during the tourist season.

Leisure time is devoted to taking part in the *passeggiata*—strolling lazily together up and down the main street. Sit on a bench and study the passersby doing their *vasche* (laps). Explore the characteristic alleys, called *carugi*. Learn—and live—the phrase "*la vita pigra di Vernazza*" (the lazy life of Vernazza).

CINQUE TERRE

Orientation to Vernazza

TOURIST INFORMATION

At the train station, you can get answers to basic questions at the gift shop (daily 8:00-20:00, closed in winter) or the ticket desk/park office (likely daily 8:00-20:00, shorter hours off-season, tel. 0187-812-533). Public WCs are just behind. Locals run their own helpful tourist board/website, called Visit Vernazza (www.visitvernazza.org).

ARRIVAL IN VERNAZZA

By Train: Vernazza's train station is only about three train cars long, but the trains themselves are much longer—so most of the cars come to a stop in a long, dark tunnel. Get out anyway, and walk through the tunnel to the station. From there the main street flows through town right to the harbor. If you're sleeping here, many locals who rent rooms will meet you at the station and walk you to your place (call first to tell them which train you're on).

By Car: Roads to Vernazza are in terrible shape, and parking is strictly limited. The best advice: Don't drive to Vernazza. If you're coming from the north, park in Levanto. If arriving from the south, park your car in La Spezia. From those towns, hop on the train.

If you must drive, get precise advice from your hotelier about which roads are open, how to drive in, and where to park. Yellow lines mark parking spots for residents only.

HELPFUL HINTS

Tuesday Morning Market: Vernazza's skimpy business community is augmented Tuesday mornings (8:00-13:00), when a meager gang of cars and trucks pulls into town for a tailgate market. Eros is often among the vendors; his family has sold flowers here for years (and he's also an amazing opera singer).

Baggage Storage: You can leave your bags at the train-station gift shop (€1/hour, €10/day, daily 8:00-20:00, closed in winter). Friendly Francesco and his staff will happily haul your luggage between the train station and your accommodations (€3/piece).

Laundry: A small self-serve launderette is at the top of town next to the post office (€5/wash, €5/dry, daily 7:00-23:00). There's also a full-service laundry in nearby Monterosso, which offers an efficient "drop off and pick up later" service (see page 390).

Massage: Kate Allen offers a super-relaxing fusion of aromatic/Swedish/holistic massage and reflexology in her little studio in the center across from the pharmacy (€60/hour, tel. 0187-812-537, mobile 333-568-4653, www.vernazzamassage5terre.com).

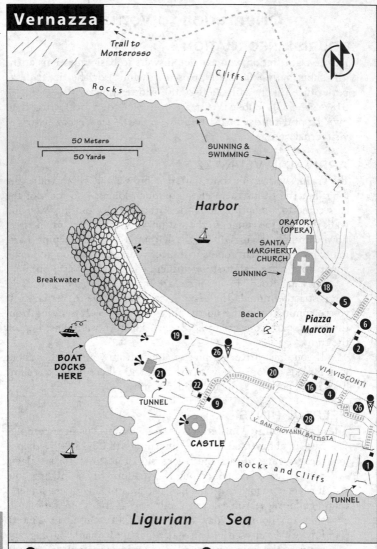

Vernazza

Trail to Monterosso

Cliffs

Rocks

50 Meters
50 Yards

SUNNING & SWIMMING

Harbor

ORATORY (OPERA)

SANTA MARGHERITA CHURCH

SUNNING →

Breakwater

18

5

Beach

Piazza Marconi

6

BOAT DOCKS HERE

19

2

26

VIA VISCONTI

TUNNEL

21

20

22

16

4

9

26

CASTLE

28

V. SAN GIOVANNI BATTISTA

Rocks and Cliffs

1

TUNNEL

Ligurian Sea

CINQUE TERRE

1. La Malà & La Marina Rooms (call first)
2. Francamaria Reception & Albergo Barbara Rooms
3. Vernazza Rooms Reception & Blue Marlin Bar
4. Rosa Vitali Rooms
5. Martina Callo Rooms, Capitano Rooms Reception & Trattoria del Capitano
6. Nicolina Rooms Reception & Ristorante Pizzeria Vulnetia
7. Rooms Francesca Reception (Enoteca Sciacchetrà)
8. Ivo's Camere Reception (Pizzeria Fratelli Basso)
9. Monica Lercari Rooms
10. Eva's Rooms & Trattoria da Sandro
11. Rooms Elisabetta (call first)
12. Giuliano Basso Rooms
13. Camere Fontana Vecchia

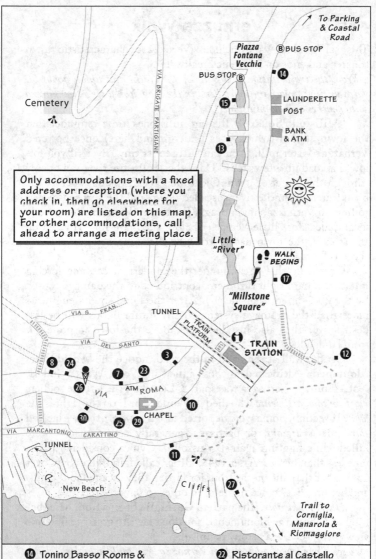

Only accommodations with a fixed address or reception (where you check in, then go elsewhere for your room) are listed on this map. For other accommodations, call ahead to arrange a meeting place.

To Parking & Coastal Road

Piazza Fontana Vecchia

BUS STOP Ⓑ

BUS STOP Ⓑ

⑭

LAUNDERETTE

POST

BANK & ATM

⑮

⑬

Cemetery

Little "River"

WALK BEGINS

⑰

"Millstone Square"

VIA S. FRAN.

TUNNEL

TRAIN PLATFORM

TRAIN STATION

VIA DEL SANTO

⑧ ㉔ ③

⑫

⑦ ㉓

VIA ㉖ ATM ROMA

CHAPEL ⑩

㉚ ㉕ ㉙

VIA MARCANTONIO CARATTINO

TUNNEL

⑪

New Beach

Cliffs

㉗

Trail to Corniglia, Manarola & Riomaggiore

CINQUE TERRE

⑭ Tonino Basso Rooms & Il Pirata delle Cinque Terre Café

⑮ La Rosa dei Venti (call first)

⑯ Gianni Franzi Reception/Ristorante

⑰ Pensione Sorriso

⑱ Ananasso Bar

⑲ Pizzeria Baia Saracena

⑳ Gambero Rosso Ristorante

㉑ Ristorante Belforte

㉒ Ristorante al Castello

㉓ Antica Osteria il Baretto

㉔ Forno Bakery

㉕ Lunch Box

㉖ Gelaterias (3)

㉗ Bar la Torre

㉘ Vernazza Wine Experience

㉙ Vineria Santa Marta

㉚ Cinque Terre Riviera Agency (Opera Tickets)

Vernazza Walk

This self-guided walk includes Vernazza's characteristic town squares and ends on its scenic breakwater.

• *From the train station, walk under the tracks and uphill about 30 yards until you reach the sharp bend in the road. You'll see a tiny piazza with benches and big millstones.*

"**Millstone Square**": The big millstones are a reminder that the town stream (which goes underground here) once powered Vernazza's water mill. (You can still see its tiny "river" if you follow this road up a few steps.) Until the 1950s, the river ran openly through the center of town. Old-timers recall the days before the breakwater, when the river cascaded down and the surf sent waves rolling up Vernazza's main drag. (The name "Vernazza" is actually local dialect for "little Venice"—before the main road covered up the stream, the town had a string of charming bridges, evoking those in Venice.)

Corralling this stream under the modern street, and forcing it to take a hard right turn here, contributed to the damage caused by the 2011 flood (see sidebar). After the flood, Swiss engineers redesigned the drainage system, so any future floods will be less destructive. They also installed nets above the town to protect it from landslides.

On the wall at the bend in the road, notice the **World Wars Monument**—dedicated to those killed in World Wars I and II. Not a family in Vernazza was spared. Listed on the left are soldiers *morti in combattimento* who died in World War I; on the right is the WWII section. Some were deported to *Germania;* others—labeled *Part* (for *partigiani,* or partisans, generally communists)—were killed while fighting against Mussolini. Cynics considered partisans less than heroes. After 1943, Hitler called up Italian boys over 15. Rather than die on the front for Hitler, they escaped to the hills and became "resistance fighters" in order to remain free.

Hikers take note: The **path to Corniglia** begins from here (behind and above the monument). You don't have to go far to find fine views over Vernazza's stony peninsula.

• *To see a more workaday part of Vernazza, you could wander a couple of minutes uphill from here, for a look at the...*

Top of Town: First you'll pass (on the left, at #7, with big brown garage doors and a *croce verde Vernazza* sign) the ambulance barn, where a group of volunteers is always on call for a dash to the hospital, 40 minutes away in La Spezia. Farther up, you'll come to a functional strip of modern apartment blocks facing the river. In this practical zone—the only place in town that allows cars—are a bank, the post office, a launderette, and the tourist hub bar/café called Il Pirata delle Cinque Terre. The parking lot fills a square

The Cinque Terre Flood and Recovery

On October 25, 2011, after a very dry summer, a freak rainstorm hit the Cinque Terre. Within four hours, 22 inches of rain fell. Flash floods rushed down the hillsides. The water quickly drained in Riomaggiore, Manarola, and Corniglia. But parts of old Monterosso and Vernazza were devastated, buried under 10 feet of mud and left without water, electricity, or phone connections.

The destruction occurred mostly along former ravines, where, historically, streams ran through the towns. In the last century, the ravines were covered with roads, and the streams channeled into underground canals. Like congested arteries, the drainage canals couldn't handle the raging flow. Water pressure caused streets to explode upward. Medieval wells in basements became geysers. Rivers of raging mud carrying rocks, trees, furniture, and even cars and buses rampaged down the main streets, burying shops and restaurants. Four villagers lost their lives. (For a sense of the devastation, search "Cinque Terre 2011 flood" on YouTube.)

The people of the Cinque Terre were taught a tough lesson. It's their beautiful land that brings the tourists. But as farmers became hoteliers and restauranteurs, the fragile landscape was neglected. With centuries-old dry-stone terracing crumbling and vineyards left unplanted (the far-reaching root systems of vines help combat erosion), the unprotected land was washed down into the towns by the violent weather.

Today, you'll find the Cinque Terre is back to normal. You may not even realize that in the affected areas of Vernazza and Monterosso, everything is brand-new: stoves, tables, chairs, plates, walls lined with bottles of wine, and so on, all had to be replaced from scratch. Strolling through these towns today, keep in mind everything these people have been through—and appreciate the resilience of the human spirit.

CINQUE TERRE

called Fontana Vecchia, named for an "old fountain" that's so old, it's long gone. Shuttle buses run from here to hamlets and sanctuaries in the hills above.

Looming over this neighborhood is a terraced hill capped by the town cemetery (a steep 20-minute hike) and, an hour's climb beyond that, the town's sanctuary; for details on these hikes, see "Hikes from Vernazza" on page 376.

• *Whether or not you head up to the top of town, the next leg of our walk follows...*

Vernazza's "Main Street": Just before the tracks, the town provides limited space for advertising for political parties. The walls under the tracks serve as a sort of community information center. The bulletin board on the right lists local volunteers and when they are on call to drive the ambulance.

The second set of train tracks (nearer the harbor) was recently renovated to lessen disruptive noise (locals say it made no difference). At the base of the stairs a handy monitor displays up-to-the-minute schedules for arriving and departing trains (including any running late—*ritardo*).

On the left, just past the tracks, a giant poster shows photos of the 2011 flood *(alluvione)* and the shops it devastated. "The 25th of October" is a day that will live forever in this town's lore. Vernazza is built around one street—basically a lid over the stream in its ravine. On that fateful day, the surrounding hills acted like a funnel, directing flash-flood waters right through the middle of town. As you stroll from here to the harbor, imagine this street buried under 13 feet of mud. Every shop, restaurant, and hotel on the main drag had to be rewired, replumbed, and re-equipped.

You're now strolling through Vernazza's "commercial center": souvenir shops, wine shops, the Blue Marlin Bar (Vernazza's top nightspot), and so on. The small stone chapel with iron grillwork over the window (on the left) is the tiny Chapel of Santa Marta, where Mass is celebrated on special Sundays. Farther down, you'll walk by a *gelateria,* bakery, pharmacy, grocery, and another *gelateria.* There are plenty of fun and cheap food-to-go options here. While it's easy to get distracted by all the tourists, try to see through them to notice locals going about their business.

• *On the left, in front of the second* gelateria, *a stone arch was blasted away by the 2011 flood. Scamper through the hole in the rock to reach Vernazza's shrinking...*

"New Beach": This is where the town's stream used to hit the sea back in the 1970s. Older locals remember frolicking on

a beach here when they were kids, but the constant, churning surf eventually eroded it all the way back to the cliff. When the 2011 flood hit, it blew out the passageway and deposited landslide material here from the hills above. In the flood's aftermath, Vernazza's main drag and harbor were filled with mud and silt. Workers used the debris to fill in even more of this beach. But as time goes on, the forces of nature are once again taking it away.

• *Back on the main drag, continue downhill to the...*

Harbor Square (Piazza Marconi) and Breakwater: Vernazza, with the Cinque Terre's only natural harbor, was established as the sole place boats could pick up the fine local wine. The two-foot-high square stone at the foot of the stairs (on the left) is marked *Sasso del Sego* (stone of tallow). Workers crushed animal flesh and fat in its basin to make tallow, which drained out from the tiny hole below. The tallow was then used to waterproof boats or wine barrels. Stonework is the soul of the region. Take some time to appreciate the impressive stonework of the restaurant interiors facing the harbor.

On the far side (behind Ristorante Pizzeria Vulnetia), peek into the tiny street with its commotion of arches. Vernazza's most characteristic side streets *(carugi)* lead up from here. The narrow stairs mark the beginning of the trail that leads up, up, up to the quintessential view of Vernazza—and, eventually, on to Monterosso.

Following the 2011 flood, Vernazza attracted worldwide sympathy—including that of prominent architect Richard Rogers (who designed London's Millennium Dome and, with Renzo Piano, Paris' Pompidou Center). Having enjoyed many relaxing vacations in Vernazza, Rogers wanted to give something back. He helped redesign the spine of the town, from this piazza, all along the main street, to the parking lot at the top of town (basically the route of this walk). His plans are helping to reshape Vernazza—making it more up-to-date, but keeping its traditional soul.

Vernazza's harborfront **church** sits on a tiny piazza, decorated with a river-rock mosaic. This popular hangout spot is where Vernazza's old ladies soak up the last bit of sun, and kids enjoy a patch of level ball field. The church is unusual for its east-facing entryway, rather than the more typical western orientation. With relative peace and prosperity in the 16th century, the townspeople doubled the church in size, overtaking a little piazza that once faced the west facade.

From the square, use the "new" entry and climb the steps, noticing how high above the sea line the church must sit to stay dry. Inside, the lighter pillars in the back mark the 16th-century extension. Three historic portable crosses hanging on the walls are carried through town during religious processions. These are replicas of crosses that (locals like to believe) Vernazzan ships once carried on crusades to the Holy Land. The town priest, Don Giovanni, is popular—he stopped the church bells from ringing through the night (light sleepers rejoiced).

• *Finish your town tour seated out on the breakwater (perhaps with a glass of local white wine or something more interesting from a nearby bar—borrow the glass, they don't mind). Face the town, and see...*

The Harbor: In a moderate storm, you'd be soaked, as waves routinely crash over the *molo* (breakwater, built in 1972). Waves can rearrange the huge rocks—depositing them from the breakwater onto the piazza and its benches. Freak waves have even washed away tourists squinting excitedly into their cameras. (I've seen it happen.) In 2007, an American woman was swept away and killed by a rogue wave. Enjoy the waterfront piazza—carefully.

The train line (to your left) was constructed in 1874 to tie together a newly united Italy, linking Turin and Genoa with Rome. A second line (hidden in a tunnel at this point) was built in the 1920s. The yellow building alongside the tracks was Vernazza's first train station. Along the wall behind the tracks, you can see the four bricked-up alcoves where people once waited for trains. Notice the wonderful concrete sunbathing strip (and place for late-night privacy) laid below the tracks along the rocks.

Vernazza's fishing fleet is down to just a few boats with net spools, but Vernazzans are still more likely to own a boat than a car. Boats are moored on buoys, except in winter or when the red storm flag indicates bad seas (see the pole at the start of the breakwater). At these times, the boats are pulled up onto the square—which is usually reserved for restaurant tables. In the 1970s, tiny Vernazza had one of Italy's top water polo teams, and the harbor was their "pool." Later, when the league required a real pool, Vernazza dropped out.

The Castle (Castello Doria): On the far right, the castle, which is now a grassy park with great views (and nothing but stones), still

guards the town (€1.50, not covered by Cinque Terre park card, daily 9:30-20:00, summer until 21:00, closed Nov-March; from harbor, take stairs by Trattoria Gianni and follow *Ristorante al Castello* signs, tower is a few steps beyond). This was the town's watchtower back in pirate days, and a Nazi lookout in World War II. The castle tower looks new because it was rebuilt after the British bombed it, chasing out the Germans.

The squat tower on the water, Ristorante Belforte, is a great spot for a glass of wine or a meal. From the breakwater, you could follow the rope to the restaurant and pop inside, past an actual submarine door. A photo of a major storm showing the entire tower under a wave (not uncommon in the winter) hangs near the bar.

The Town: Before the 12th century, pirates made the coast uninhabitable, so the first Vernazzans lived in the hills above (near the Reggio sanctuary). The town itself—and its towers, fortified walls, and hillside terracing—are mostly from the 12th through 15th century, when Vernazza was allied with the Republic of Genoa.

Vernazza has two halves. *Sciuiu* (Vernazzan dialect for "flowery") is the sunny side on the left, and *luvegu* (dank) is the shady side on the right. Houses below the castle were connected by an interior arcade—ideal for fleeing attacks.

The "Ligurian pastel" colors of the buildings are regulated by the regional government's commissioner of good taste. The square before you is locally famous for some of the area's finest restaurants. The big red central house—on the site where Genoan warships were built in the 12th century—used to be a guardhouse.

In the Middle Ages, there was no beach or square. The water went right up to the buildings, where boats would tie up, Venetian-style. Imagine what Vernazza looked like in those days, when it was the biggest and richest of the Cinque Terre towns. Buildings had a water gate (facing today's square) and a front door on the higher inland side. There was no pastel plaster—just fine stonework (traces of which survive above the Trattoria del Capitano). Apart from the added plaster, the general shape and size of the town has changed little in five centuries. Survey the windows and notice inhabitants quietly gazing back.

While the town has 1,500 residents in summer, only 500 stay here through the winter. Vernazza has accommodations for about 500 tourists.

Above the Town: The small, round tower above the red guardhouse—another part of the city fortifications—reminds us of the town's importance in the Middle Ages. Back then, Genoa's enemies (rival maritime republics, especially Pisa) were Vernazza's enemies. Bar la Torre, just above and beyond the tower, welcomes hikers who are finishing, starting, or simply contemplating the Corniglia-Vernazza hike, with great town views. That tower recalls a time when the entire town was fortified by a stone wall.

Vineyards fill the mountainside beyond the town. Notice the many terraces. Someone—probably after too much of that local wine—calculated that the roughly 3,000 miles of dry-stone walls built to terrace the region's vineyards have the same amount of stonework as the Great Wall of China.

For six centuries, the economy was based on wine and olive oil. Then came the 1980s—and the tourists. Locals turned to tourism to make a living, and stopped tending the land. Many vineyards were abandoned, and the terraces fell into disrepair. But it's the stonework of the terracing in the surrounding hills that helps prevent flooding—a lesson learned in the worst possible way in 2011.

Although many locals still maintain their tiny plots and proudly serve their family wines, the patchwork of local vineyards is atomized and complex because of inheritance traditions. Historically, families divided their land among their children. Parents wanted each child to get some good land. Because some lots were "kissed by the sun" while others were shady, the lots were split into increasingly tiny, unviable, and eventually abandoned pieces.

A single steel train line winds up the gully behind the tower. It is for the vintner's *trenino*, the tiny service train. Play "Where's *trenino*?" and see if you can find two trains. The vineyards once stretched as high as you can see, but since fewer people sweat in the fields these days, the most distant terraces have gone wild again.

The Church, School, and City Hall: Vernazza's Ligurian Gothic church, built with black stones quarried from Punta Mesco (the distant point behind you), dates from 1318. Note the gray stone that marks the church's 16th-century expansion. The gray-and-red house above the spire is the local elementary school (about 25 children attend). Older students go to the "big city," La Spezia. The red building on the hill to the right of the schoolhouse, a former monastery, is the city hall. Vernazza and Corniglia function as one community. Through most of the 1990s, the local government was Communist. In 1999, residents elected a coalition of many parties working to rise above ideologies and simply make Vernazza a better place. That practical notion of government continues here today.

Finally, on the top of the hill, with the best view of all, is the town cemetery. It's only fair that hardworking Vernazzans—who spend their lives climbing up and down and up and down and up and down the hillsides that hem in their little town—are rewarded with a world-class view from their eternal resting place.

Experiences in Vernazza

Hikes from Vernazza

For a full rundown of more ambitious hikes around Vernazza—including the main coastal trail—see page 328. Here are some easier alternatives close to town.

From Vernazza, you can hike in either direction for classic photo ops. Both hikes are steeply, but briefly, uphill (about 10 minutes to the best views and park ticket checkpoints).

For the best light, follow the trail **toward Corniglia** in the morning; you'll twist up through vineyards to earn great views down over the stony back side of Vernazza's peninsula, with its round castle tower poking up and a Monterosso backdrop. The best views are from just before the national park ticket checkpoint. If you need a rewarding rest up here, Bar la Torre offers drinks with a grand view.

The trail **toward Monterosso** has the best light in the evening. From the harbor, you'll hike up through the steep and narrow *carugi* alleys before popping out on the trail above town. Follow this around the bluff, enjoying better and better views of Vernazza's tidy pastel harbor. The views are fine before the ticket booth, but even better after—if you don't want to buy a national park ticket, you can hike up here in the evening, after the park officially closes.

Another good option is to hike up to Vernazza's sweet little **cemetery.** Find the steep lane from the ravine at the top of town (mentioned on my "Vernazza Walk," earlier). From here, it's a 20-minute hike to the top. You'll find a peaceful world of lovingly tended family graves enjoying stunning views over the Cinque Terre. Imagine the entire village sadly trudging up here during funerals. The cemetery is peaceful and evocative at sunset, when the fading light touches each crypt.

For something more ambitious, you can continue higher past the cemetery (about one steep hour) to the town's sanctuary, **Madonna di Reggio.** From town, head straight up the ridge on trail #8/#508, passing Stations of the Cross, to the sanctuary. Locals who enjoy a sturdy hike favor this scenic, quiet trail. For a much easier Reggio experience, you can ride the shuttle bus up here (departs from top of town, near post office), then hike down.

Beaches

The harbor's sandy cove has sunning rocks and showers by the breakwater. There's also a ladder on the breakwater for deep-water access. The sunbathing lane directly under the church has a shower. And, while it's getting smaller and rockier each year, Vernazza's "new beach" can be accessed through a hole halfway along the town's main drag.

Boat Rides

In addition to the regularly scheduled big boats that depart from Vernazza's harbor (see page 323), hiring your own boat can be handy for intertown transport. It's also a great way to escape the crowds and get a different angle on Cinque Terre splendor. From Vernazza, figure around €30 one-way to Monterosso, €40 to Manarola, or €50 to Riomaggiore (for up to six passengers in an outboard; a comfier 10-person boat costs more). Or hire a boat for a one-hour sightseeing cruise of the entire Cinque Terre (about €150); one popular stop is the tiny *acqua pendente* (waterfall) cove between Vernazza and Monterosso, which locals call their *laguna blu*.

At Vernazza's breakwater you'll find **Nord Est,** run by Vincenzo (with help from Cesare), the best-established option (mobile 338-700-0436, info@nordest-vernazza.com). **Vernazza Water Taxi,** run by Pietro, is another choice (mobile 338-911-3869, info@vernazzawatertaxi.it).

Shuttle Bus Joyride

For a cheap and scenic joyride, with a chance to chat about the region with friendly, English-speaking Mirco, Pietro, or Graziella, ride the ATC shuttle bus from the top of town (in front of the post office) to the sanctuaries and hamlets high in the hills—including the Reggio sanctuary (see "Hikes from Vernazza," earlier) or the San Bernadino sanctuary above Corniglia—and back again (generally about 5/day, times are unpredictable—ask at train station TI or get schedule from bus driver).

Sustainable Tourism Activities

Save Vernazza, which began as a flood relief organization in 2011, has evolved into an all-purpose Vernazza advocacy group, with an emphasis on sustainable tourism. If you enjoy the Cinque Terre and would like to give something back, contact them to participate in a project designed to protect and promote Vernazza. Their "voluntourism" activities, scheduled regularly through the high season, include rebuilding terrace walls and harvesting grapes (reservations required, lunch and wine provided, generally 2/week late May-Oct 8:30-13:30, see website for schedule, www.savevernazza.com, workwithus@savevernazza.com, mobile 349-357-3572, Michelle and Ruth).

Wine Tasting

Vernazza Wine Experience hides out like a resort for jet-setters at the top of town just under the castle. Run by Alessandro, a sommelier, it's romantic, with mellow music, and a hardwood, ship-deck ambience. He enjoys explaining wines and the €15 small plates matched with them (like his meat-and-cheese plate served on a slab of olive tree). You'll pay €15 for three very different wines. He also has a €15 dessert wine/cheese/cookie deal. While the bill can add up, the quality is excellent and the view is unforgettable (daily 17:00-21:00, cash only, hike from harborfront and turn left before castle, Via S. Giovanni Battista 31, tel. 331-343-3801).

　　Vineria Santa Marta is simpler and mellower, with less scenery and pretense. This wine shop/tasting bar is run by brothers Wolfgang and Michael, who share their love of wine on a stone terrace along the main drag. A basic tasting of three local wines plus light snacks is €9 per person (also serves salads and *bruschette,* daily 9:30-20:30, above the little chapel on Via Roma, tel. 0187-882-1084).

A Little Taste of Opera

During little Vernazza's summer opera series, a big-name maestro from Lucca brings talented singers to town twice weekly to show off before an appreciative audience. Performances fill the small oratory tucked behind the town's big church (find the steps up and around, next to Ananasso Bar), which was beautifully restored for just this purpose. Performances begin at 19:00 and last just over an hour—strategically timed to squeeze between a late-afternoon *aperitivo* on the harbor and a 20:30 dinner reservation (€13 in advance, €15 at the door, April-Oct Wed and Fri at 19:00 but confirm times locally, book tickets at Cinque Terre Riviera office at #24 on the main street—see map on page 368, tel. 0187-812-123, info@cinqueterreriviera.com).

Nightlife in Vernazza

Vernazza's nightlife centers on the bars on its waterfront piazza, which is the place to "see and be seen." Vernazza's younger restaurant workers work hard throughout the tourist season, but they let loose after-hours and enjoy connecting with international visitors in the town's few nightspots (which must all close by midnight). For a more genteel option, consider an opera performance or a wine tasting (both described in the previous section). Or in the cool, calm evening, sit on Vernazza's breakwater with a glass of wine and watch the phosphorescence in the waves.

The **Blue Marlin Bar** dominates the late-night scene with a mix of locals and tourists, home-cooked food until 23:00, good drinks, and occasional piano jam sessions. If you're young and hip, this is *the* place to hang out. If you play piano, you're welcome to contribute to the scene. **Ananasso Bar** offers early-evening happy-hour fun and cocktails *(aperitivi)* that both locals and visitors enjoy. Its harborfront tables get the last sunshine of the day. For more on these bars, see their listings under "Eating in Vernazza," later.

Really Late: A little cave on the beach just under the church lends itself to fun in the wee hours, when everything else is closed.

Sleeping in Vernazza

(**$$$$** = Splurge, **$$$** = Pricier, **$$** = Moderate, **$** = Budget)
Vernazza lacks any real hotels, and almost all of my listings are *affittacamere* (private rooms for rent). I favor hosts who rent multiple rooms and have a proven track record of good communication (they speak just enough English, have email, and are reliable). But in many ways, the real Vernazza gems are stray single rooms with owners who have no interest in taking advance reservations. If you have the guts to just show up without a reservation and ask around,

you may score a great deal. But—especially in busy times—it's safer to book ahead.

Most places accept only cash, promise free Wi-Fi (often spotty), and don't include breakfast (for suggestions, see "Eating in Vernazza," later). Some have killer views; some come with lots of stairs. Expect noise at night: Trains tearing through, church bells (after 7:00 and before 22:00), crashing waves, cars in the upper town. Come to think of it, just pack earplugs.

While a few places have all their beds in one building, most have rooms scattered over town. Better-organized outfits have an informal "reception desk" (sometimes at a restaurant or other business) where you can check in. But many places have no reception at all. (On the Vernazza map, I've marked only places that have a fixed address or reception office; if I say "reception," you'll check in there, then continue on to your actual room.)

Because this can be confusing, I strongly recommend that you communicate your arrival time (by phone or email) and get clear instructions on where to meet the owner and pick up the keys. They'll usually offer to meet you at the train station—but only if they know when you're coming.

ROOMS FOR RENT (AFFITTACAMERE)
Scattered Through the Town Center

Remember that the **Cinque Terre Riviera** agency, based in Vernazza and described on page 320, rents rooms here and throughout the region. Unless otherwise noted, none of these include breakfast.

$$$ La Malà is Vernazza's jet-setter pad. Four crisp, pristine white rooms boast fancy-hotel-type extras and a common seaview terrace. It's a climb—way up to the top of town—but they'll carry your bags to and from the station. Book early—this place fills up quickly (includes breakfast at a bar, family rooms, air-con, mobile 334-287-5718, www.lamala.it, info@lamala.it, charming Giamba and his mama, Armanda). They also rent the simpler **$ "Armanda's Room"** nearby—a great value, since you get Giamba's attention to detail and amenities without paying for a big view (includes simple breakfast, air-con).

$$ La Marina Rooms is run by hardworking Christian, who speaks English and happily meets guests at the station to carry bags. There are five well-tended (if slightly dated) units, most high above the main street: One single works as a (very) tight double, and three doubles share a fine oceanview terrace; they also have two **$$$** apartments—one with terrace and sea views, and the other on the harborfront square (mobile 338-476-7472, www.lamarinarooms.com, mapcri@yahoo.it).

$$ Emanuela Colombo has two rooms—one spacious and classy on the harbor square, the other a *molto* chic split-level apartment located on a quiet side street (sleeps up to four; Emanuela often works at the Bottega dell'Arte on the main street, tel. 339-834-2486, www.vacanzemanuela.it, manucap64@libero.it).

$$ Francamaria and her husband Andrea rent 10 sharp, comfortable, and creatively renovated rooms—all detailed on her website. Their reception desk is on the harbor square (on the ground floor at Piazza Marconi 30), but the rooms they manage are all over town (family rooms, some with air-con, spotty Wi-Fi, tel. 0187-812-002, mobile 328-711-9728, www.francamaria.com, info@francamaria.com).

$$ Vernazza Rooms, run by Daria Bianchi, Chiara, and Davide, rents 11 rooms: Four are above the Blue Marlin Bar looking down on the main street, and seven are a steep climb higher up, just under the city hall (big family apartments, ring bell at Via Roma 41—next to Blue Marlin Bar, a few with air-con and others with fans, limited English, mobile 338-581-4688 or 338-413-8696, www.vernazzarooms.com, info@vernazzarooms.com).

$$ Rosa Vitali rents two four-person apartments across from the pharmacy overlooking the main street (and beyond the train noise). One has a terrace and fridge (top floor); the other has windows and a full kitchen (family rooms, ring bell at Via Visconti 10—just before the tobacco shop near Piazza Marconi, tel. 0187-821-181, mobile 340-267-5009, www.rosacamere.it, rosa.vitali@libero.it).

$$ Maria Capellini rents two simple, clean rooms that face each other across the harbor; one is at ground level with a view, the other looks over a skinny street (family rooms, fans, mobile 338-436-3411, www.mariacapellini.com, mariacapellini@hotmail.it, kindly Maria and Giacomo).

$$ Martina Callo's four old-fashioned, spartan rooms overlook the harbor square; they're up plenty of steps near the silent-at-night church tower. While the rooms are simple, guests pay for and appreciate the views (family rooms, cheaper nonview room, air-con, ring bell at Piazza Marconi 26, tel. 0187-812-365, mobile 329-435-5344, www.roomartina.it, roomartina@roomartina.it).

$$ Nicolina Rooms consists of seven units in three different buildings. Two cheaper rooms are in the center over the pharmacy, up a few steep steps; another, pricier studio with a terrace is on a twisty lane above the harbor; and four more rooms are in a building beyond the church, with great views and church bells (all include breakfast, Piazza Marconi 29—check in at Pizzeria Vulnetia, tel. 0187-821-193, mobile 333-842-6879, www.camerenicolina.it, camerenicolina.info@cdh.it).

$ Rooms Francesca's two tidy rooms and one apartment hide out in the steep streets just below city hall (family rooms, check in at Enoteca Sciacchetrà at Via Roma 19, tel. 0187-821-

CINQUE TERRE

112, www.5terre-vernazza.it, moggia.franco@libero.it; Francesca, Franco, and Sabine).

$ **Ivo's Camere** rents two tight but well-appointed rooms several flights of stairs above the main street (air-con, Via Roma 6, reception at Pizzeria Fratelli Basso—Via Roma 1, rooms across the street, mobile 333-477-5521, www.ivocamere.com, post@ivocamere.com).

$ **Albergo Barbara** rents nine basic-but-tidy, affordable top-floor rooms overlooking the square. Only a few rooms have real views; most have small windows and small views. It's run by English-speaking Giuseppe and his no-nonsense Swiss wife, Patricia (cheaper rooms with shared bathroom are a good value, more for views, closed Dec-Feb, reserve online with credit card but pay cash, Piazza Marconi 30, tel. 0187-812-398, mobile 338-793-3261, www.albergobarbara.it, info@albergobarbara.it).

$ **Memo Rooms** rents three clean and spacious rooms overlooking the main street, in what feels like a miniature hotel. Enrica will meet you if you call upon arrival (Via Roma 15, try Enrica's mobile first at 338-285-2385, otherwise tel. 0187-812-360, www.memorooms.com, info@memorooms.com).

$ **Monica Lercari** rents several rooms with modern comforts, perched at the top of town (more for seaview terrace, includes breakfast, air-con, tel. 0187-812-296, mobile 320-025-4515, alcastellovernazza@yahoo.it). Monica and her husband, Massimo, run the Ristorante al Castello, in the old castle tower overlooking town.

More Options: $ Capitano Rooms (3 rooms several flights of stairs above main drag, fans; ask for Julia, Paolo, or Barbara at Trattoria del Capitano restaurant on main square at Piazza Marconi 21; tel. 0187-812-201, www.tavernavernazza.com, info@tavernavernazza.com); **$$ Eva's Rooms** (3 rooms on main street, air-con, train noise, meet at boutique at Via Roma 68, tel. 334-798-6500, www.evasrooms.it, evasrooms@yahoo.it); **$$ Rooms Elisabetta** (3 tight, recently renovated, casually run rooms at the tip-top of town with Vernazza's ultimate 360-degree roof terrace—come here for the views; family rooms, fans, partway up Corniglia path at Via Carattino 62, mobile 347-451-1834, www.elisabettacarro.it, carroelisabetta@hotmail.com, Elisabetta); and **$$ Manuela Moggia** (family rooms, more for room with kitchen or view, some behind train station at Via Gavino 22, tel. 0187-812-397, mobile 333-413-6374, www.manuela-vernazza.com, info@manuela-vernazza.com).

In the Inland Part of Town

Above the Train Station: $$ Giuliano Basso's four carefully crafted, well-appointed rooms form a cozy little compound on the green hillside just above town, straddling a ravine among orange trees. Giuliano—the town's last stone-layer—proudly built the place himself (2 rooms have air-con, more train noise than others; follow the main road up above the station, take the ramp up toward Corniglia just before Pensione Sorriso, follow the path, and watch for a sharp left turn toward the US and California flags; mobile 333-341-4792, www.cdh.it/giuliano, giuliano@cdh.it).

In the Ravine at the Top of Town: These practical options are a five-minute, gentle uphill stroll behind the train station. While this functional zone is less atmospheric and feels less central, it does provide easier access (with fewer steep stairs). There's no train or church-bell noise—the constant soundtrack is Vernazza's gurgling river—but there can be traffic noise. Il Pirata delle Cinque Terre is the neighborhood hub (offering breakfast, tourist bonding, and Wi-Fi; see page 384), and Vernazza's launderette is right next door.

$$ Camere Fontana Vecchia, run by Annamaria, is the best choice here, with eight bright and cheery rooms overlooking the ravine and its rushing river (cheaper room with shared bath, more for terrace, Via Gavino 15, tel. 0187-821-130, mobile 333-454-9371, www.cinqueterrecamere.com, m.annamaria@libero.it). **$$ Tonino Basso** has four overpriced but colorful rooms in a drab, elevator-equipped, modern apartment block (air-con, Via Gavino 34, mobile 339-761-1651, www.toninobasso.com, Alessandra).

$ La Rosa dei Venti ("The Compass Rose"), run by Giuliana Basso, houses three airy, good-value rooms in her childhood home, on the third floor of an apartment building (call to arrange meeting time, air-con, Via Gavino 19, mobile 333-762-4679, www.larosadeiventi-vernazza.it, info@larosadeiventi-vernazza.it).

GUESTHOUSES (PENSIONES)

These guesthouses (pensiones) have many rooms and something resembling a reception desk, but still, I'd consider them a last resort. They're overpriced and lack the thoughtful touches of a Vernazzan who oversees just a couple of private rooms.

$$$ Gianni Franzi, a busy restaurant on the harbor square, rents 25 small rooms scattered across three buildings one hundred tight, winding stairs above the harbor square. Some rooms (including a few cheaper ones with shared bathrooms) are funky and decorated à la shipwreck, with tiny balconies and grand sea views; the comfy, newer rooms lack views. All rooms have access to a super-scenic cliff-hanging guests' garden (where breakfast is served mid-April-mid-Oct). Steely Marisa requires check-in before 16:00 or a phone call to explain when you're coming. Emanuele, Simona, Caterina, and the staff speak a little English (RS%, closed Jan-Feb, Piazza Marconi 1, tel. 0187-812-228, tel. 0187-821-003,

mobile 393-9008-155, www.giannifranzi.it, info@giannifranzi.it).
Pick up your keys at Gianni Franzi restaurant on the harbor square
(on Wed, when the restaurant is closed, call ahead to make other
arrangements).

$$$ Pensione Sorriso rents 13 decent but overpriced rooms
just up the road from the train station (cheaper rooms with shared
bath and no air-con, breakfast extra, train noise, closed Nov-
March, Via Gavino 4, tel. 0187-812-224, www.pensionesorriso.
com, info@pensionesorriso.com, Francesca and Aldo).

Eating in Vernazza

($$$$ = Splurge, $$$ = Pricier, $$ = Moderate, $ = Budget)

BREAKFAST

If you're seeking a real breakfast, you have five basic options: Blue
Marlin and Capitano for their extensive menus; Il Pirata for sugary
stuff and a lively welcome; Ananasso for coffee and a sweet roll on
the harborfront; or any bakery for picnic goodies.

$$ Blue Marlin Bar (midtown, just below the train station)
serves a good array of clearly priced à la carte breakfast items in-
cluding eggs and bacon (8:30-11:30)—figure around €10 total with
a *caffè lungo*. It's run by Massimo and Carmen with the capable
assistance of Jeff, an American who now lives in Vernazza. If you're
awaiting a train any time of day, the Blue Marlin's outdoor seat-
ing—within view of the tracks—beats the platform (Thu-Tue 7:00-
24:00, closed Wed).

$$ Trattoria del Capitano offers outdoor seating on the harbor, as well as cozy spots inside the restaurant. You can order single
items (€6 egg dishes including focaccia and small salad) or opt for
the €12 full-and-filling breakfast (Wed-Mon from 8:00, closed
Tue except in Aug).

$ Il Pirata delle Cinque Terre is located in the workaday zone
at the parking lot at the top of town. The fun, playful service of
the dynamic duo Gianluca and Massimo (hardworking Sicilian
twins, a.k.a. the Cannoli brothers) makes up for the lack of a view.
Massimo is a likeable loudmouth, while Gianluca is a pastry artist.
Their sweet pastry breakfasts include an array of treats like *panze-*
rotto (with ricotta, cinnamon, and vanilla) and hot cheese and pesto
bruschetta. They proudly serve no bacon and eggs (since "this is
Italy"). While the atmosphere of the place feels more like suburban
Milan, it has a curious charisma among its customers (daily 6:30-
24:00, Via Gavino 36, tel. 0187-812-047).

$$ Ananasso Bar has a youthful energy and great location
with little tables right on the harbor. They offer toasted *panini*, pas-
tries, and designer cappuccino. You can eat a bit cheaper at the bar

(you're welcome to picnic on the nearby bench or seawall rocks with a Mediterranean view) or enjoy the best-situated tables in town (Fri-Wed 8:00-late, closed Thu).

Picnic Breakfast: Drop by one of Vernazza's many little bakeries, focaccia shops, or grocery stores to assemble a breakfast to eat on the breakwater. Top it off with a coffee in a nearby bar.

LUNCH AND DINNER

Vernazza's restaurants take pride in their cooking. Wander around at about 20:00 and compare the ambience, but don't wait too late to eat—many kitchens close at 22:00. If you dine in Vernazza but are staying in another town, be sure to check train schedules before sitting down to eat, as evening trains run less frequently and with gaps in the schedule. To get an outdoor table on summer weekends, reserve ahead. Expect to spend around €10-14 for pastas, €15-22 for *secondi*, and €2-3 for a cover charge. Harborside restaurants and bars are easygoing. You're welcome to grab a cup of coffee or glass of wine and disappear somewhere on the breakwater, returning your glass when you're done. For details on the local cuisine, see "Eating in the Cinque Terre," on page 339.

Harborside

$$$ Gianni Franzi is an old standby for well-prepared seafood and pastas. Emanuele, Alessandro, and their crew provide steady, reliable, and friendly service. The outdoor seating is partially tucked under an arcade, while the indoor setting is big, open, and classy (check their *menù cucina tipica Vernazza*, Thu-Tue 12:00-15:00 & 19:00-22:00, closed Wed except in Aug, tel. 0187-812-228).

$$$ Trattoria del Capitano feels unpretentious and serves a short menu of straightforward local dishes, including *spaghetti allo scoglio*—pasta entangled with various types of seafood, and *grigliata mista*—a mix of seasonal Mediterranean fish (Wed-Mon 12:00-22:00, closed Tue and Dec-Jan, tel. 0187-812-201, hardworking Paolo and Barbara speak English).

$$$ Ristorante Pizzeria Vulnetia has a nautical, jovial atmosphere. Like the others listed here, it serves regional specialties; but unlike the others, it also dishes up affordable pizzas—making this a good choice for a group with differing tastes, those on a budget, and families (Tue-Sun 12:00-22:00, closed Mon, Piazza Marconi 29, tel. 0187-821-193, Giuliano and Tullio).

$$ Pizzeria Baia Saracena ("Saracen Bay") is the budget option on the harbor, serving forgettable pizza and pastas out on the breakwater. Eat here not for high cuisine, but for a memorable atmosphere at reasonable prices (Sat-Thu 10:30-22:00, closed Fri, tel. 0187-812-113, Luca).

$$$$ Gambero Rosso rounds out the options on the harbor.

It's the priciest place on the square, but—ever since it was sold to a big-city restaurateur who runs it from afar—the quality can be hit-or-miss. Still, it has a fine interior and great outdoor tables (Fri-Wed 12:00-15:00 & 19:00-21:30, closed Thu and Dec-Feb, Piazza Marconi 7, tel. 0187-812-265).

Above the Harbor, by the Castle

$$$$ Ristorante Belforte serves a fine blend of traditional and creative cuisine, including a hearty *zuppa Michela* (€30/person for a boatload of seafood, 2-person minimum), fishy *spaghetti alla Bruno*, *trofie al pesto* (hand-rolled noodles with pesto), and classic *antipasto misto di pesce* (€20/person for 5 plates; 2-person minimum). From the breakwater, follow either set of stairs that lead up from the harbor. You'll find a web of tables embedded in four levels of the old castle. For the ultimate seaside perch, call and reserve one of the tables on the *terrazza con vista* (view terrace); for a really special meal, request the "lovers' table" on its own little terrace. Most of Belforte's seating is outdoors—if the weather's bad, the interior can get crowded (Wed-Mon 12:00-15:00 & 19:00-22:00, closed Tue and Nov-March, tel. 0187-812-222, Michela).

$$$ Ristorante al Castello is run by gracious and English-speaking Monica, her husband Massimo, and their sometimes-gruff staff. Hike high above town to just below the castle for commanding views. Reserve one of the dozen romantic cliff-side seaview tables for two—some of the tables snake around the castle, where you'll feel like you're eating all alone with the Mediterranean. Monica offers a free *sciacchetrà* or *limoncello* with biscotti with this book by request (Thu–Tue 12:00–15:00 & 19:00–22:00, closed Wed and Nov–April, tel. 0187-812-296).

On or near the Main Street

Several of Vernazza's inland eateries manage to compete without the harbor ambience but with slightly cheaper prices.

$$ Trattoria da Sandro, on the main drag, mixes quality Genovese and Ligurian cuisine with friendly service and can be a peaceful alternative to the harborside scene. The family proudly maintains its cultural traditions and dishes up award-winning stuffed mussels (Wed-Mon 12:00-15:00 & 18:30-22:00, closed Tue, Via Roma 62, tel. 0187-812-223, Argentina and Alessandro).

$$ Antica Osteria il Baretto is another solid bet for homey, reasonably priced traditional cuisine, run by Simone and Jenny. As it's off the harbor and less glitzy than the others, it's favored by locals who prefer less noisy English while they eat great homemade fare. Sitting deep in their interior can be a peaceful escape (Tue-Sun 12:00-22:00, closed Mon, indoor and outdoor seating in summer, Via Roma 31, tel. 0187-812-381).

Other Eating Options

$$ Blue Marlin Bar (on the main street and described under "Breakfast," earlier) busts out of the Vernazzan-cuisine rut with a short, creative menu of more casual dishes (pizzas, pastas, and *secondi*). It's a good choice if you want to just grab some reliable food rather than dine. Locals enjoy a meal here when they don't feel like cooking at home (closed Wed).

$$ Il Pirata delle Cinque Terre, an endearing tourist trap, is best for breakfast but also attracts many travelers for lunch and dinner. Come here not for the cuisine or the ambience, but for a memorable evening with the Cannoli twins, who entertain while they serve. The menu (pastas and salads, no *secondi*) is aimed squarely at American tourists' taste buds (lunch daily from 12:00, dinner from 18:00, good Sicilian slushies, at the top of town; see complete listing under "Breakfast," earlier).

Pizzerias, Sandwiches, and Groceries: Vernazza's mainstreet eateries offer a fine range of quick meals. Two **pizzerias** mostly do takeout, but they'll let you sit and eat for the same cheap price. One has tables on the street, and the other, called Ercole, hides a tiny terrace and a few tables out back. **Forno Bakery** has good focaccia and veggie tarts (at #5), and several bars sell sandwiches and pizza by the slice. **Pino's grocery store** also makes inexpensive sandwiches to order (generally Mon-Sat 8:00-13:00 & 17:00-19:30, closed Sun). **Lunch Box** is a notch above, with panini, salads, and fresh fruit juices. If it's not too busy, they invite you to assemble your own salad (or juice) from a long list of ingredients (daily 8:00-21:00, shorter hours off-season, Via Roma 34, tel. 338-908-2841, Stefano).

Gelato: The town has three *gelaterias:* **Gelateria Vernazza,** near the top of the main street, takes its gelato seriously, occasionally flirting with creative ingredients (soy) and flavors (*riso*—rice, and ricotta and fig). **Gelateria Amore Mio** (midtown) used to be Gelateria Stalin, founded in 1968 by a pastry chef with that unfortunate name; now it's run by his niece Sonia and nephew Francesco, with great people-watching tables but the least exciting gelato in town. And out on the harbor, the aptly named **Gelateria Il Porticciolo** ("Marina") is arguably the best; they use fresh ingredients to create intense flavors (try their *cannella*—cinnamon, or *nocciola*—hazelnut).

Monterosso al Mare (Town #5)

This is a resort with a few cars and lots of hotels, rentable beach umbrellas, crowds, and a little more late-night action than the neighboring towns. Monterosso al Mare—the only Cinque Terre town with some flat land—has two parts: A new town (called Fegina) with a parking lot, train station, and TI; and an old town (Centro Storico), which cradles Old World charm in its small, crooked lanes. In the old town, you'll find hole-in-the-wall  shops, rustic pastel townscapes, and a new generation of creative small-businesspeople eager to keep their visitors happy.

A handy pedestrian tunnel connects the old with the new. But for a nicer walk, take a small detour around the point. It offers a close-up view of two sights: a 16th-century lookout tower, built after the last serious pirate raid in 1545; and a Nazi "pillbox," a small, low concrete bunker where gunners peeked out the narrow slits. (During World War II, nearby La Spezia was an important Axis naval base, and Monterosso was bombed while the Germans were here.)

Strolling the waterfront promenade, you can pick out each of the Cinque Terre towns decorating the coast. After dark, they sparkle. Monterosso is the most enjoyable of the five for backpackers (or the young-at-heart) wanting to connect with others looking for a little evening action. Even so, Monterosso is not a full-blown Portofino-style resort—and locals appreciate quiet, sensitive guests.

Orientation to Monterosso

TOURIST INFORMATION

The TI Proloco is next to the train station (mid-April-mid-Oct daily 9:00-18:30, shorter hours off-season, baggage storage, exit station and go left a few doors, tel. 0187-817-506, www.prolocomonterosso.it). For national park tickets and information, head upstairs within the station to the ticket office near platform 1 (likely daily 8:00-20:00, shorter hours off-season).

ARRIVAL IN MONTEROSSO

By Train: Train travelers arrive in the new town. To get to the old town, turn left from the station, follow the seafront promenade, then duck through the tunnel just before the point—it's a scenic, flat 10-minute stroll. To reach most recommended hotels in the new town, turn right from the station.

Notice the bar at track 1, which overlooks both the tracks and the beach. This is a handy place (serving salads, sandwiches, drinks) to hang out while waiting for a train to pull in. As many trains run late, this can turn a frustration into a blessing.

ATC **shuttle buses** run along the waterfront between the old town (Piazza Garibaldi, just beyond the tunnel), the train station, and the parking lot at the end of Via Fegina (*Campo Sportivo* stop). The bus saves you a 10-minute schlep with your bags but only goes once an hour (see page 325 for details). A few of these shuttles go farther into the hills—making hikes easier (see "Hikes from Monterosso" on page 395).

Taxis usually wait outside the train station—but you may have to call (€7 from station to old town, mobile 335-616-5842, 335-616-5845, or 335-628-0933).

By Car: Monterosso is 30 minutes off the freeway (exit: Carrodano-Levanto). Note that about three miles above Monterosso, there's an intersection where you must choose either *Monterosso Centro Storico* (old part of town—Via Roma parking lot with only a few spots, and the new Loreto garage) or *Monterosso Fegina* (new town and beachfront parking). Know where you want to go, because you can't drive directly from the new town to the old center (which is closed to cars without special permits).

Most drivers should choose the *Fegina* fork. Parking is easy (except July-Aug and summer weekends) in the huge beachfront guarded lot in the new town (€18/24 hours). If instead you head to the old town, you'll find the Loreto parking garage on Via Roma, a 10-minute downhill walk to the main square (€1.70/hour, €18/24 hours). For the cheapest Monterosso rates, park along the blue lines (€1/hour up to €10/day, a few minutes farther uphill from the Loreto garage).

See "Arrival in the Cinque Terre" on page 317 for directions from Milan and tips on driving in the Cinque Terre.

HELPFUL HINTS

Medical Help: The town's bike-riding, leather bag-toting, English-speaking physician is **Dr. Vitone** (simple visit-€50-100, less for poor students, mobile 338-853-0949, vitonee@yahoo.it).

Thursday Morning Market: Every Thursday morning (8:00-13:00), trucks pull into the old town and fill the public area by the beach with temporary stalls where locals get items not otherwise available in this small town.

Baggage Storage: The **TI** next to the station will store bags (€6/

CINQUE TERRE

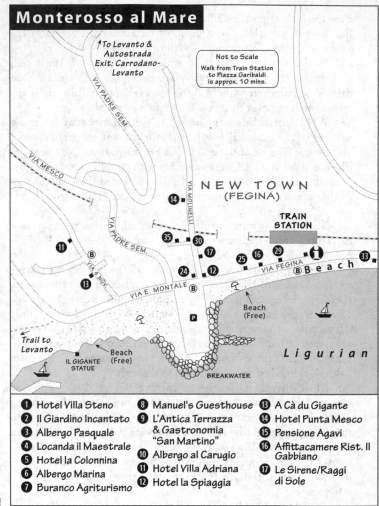

Monterosso al Mare

↑To Levanto &
Autostrada
Exit: Carrodano-
Levanto

Not to Scale
Walk from Train Station
to Piazza Garibaldi
is approx. 10 mins.

VIA PADRE SEM.

VIA MESCO

VIA PADRE SEM.

NEW TOWN
(FEGINA)

VIA MOLINELLI

TRAIN
STATION

⓮

㉟ ㉚

⓫

Ⓑ

⓱

VIA 4 NOV.

㉕ ⓰ ㉙

Ⓘ ㉝

⓭

㉔

⓬

VIA FEGINA Ⓑ B e a c h

VIA E. MONTALE Ⓑ

Beach
(Free)

P

L i g u r i a n

Trail to
Levanto

Beach
(Free)

IL GIGANTE
STATUE

BREAKWATER

❶ Hotel Villa Steno
❷ Il Giardino Incantato
❸ Albergo Pasquale
❹ Locanda il Maestrale
❺ Hotel la Colonnina
❻ Albergo Marina
❼ Buranco Agriturismo
❽ Manuel's Guesthouse
❾ L'Antica Terrazza
   & Gastronomia
   "San Martino"
❿ Albergo al Carugio
⓫ Hotel Villa Adriana
⓬ Hotel la Spiaggia
⓭ A Cà du Gigante
⓮ Hotel Punta Mesco
⓯ Pensione Agavi
⓰ Affittacamere Rist. Il
   Gabbiano
⓱ Le Sirene/Raggi
   di Sole

day—but confirm closing time). **Wash and Dry Lavarapido,** two blocks from the station, provides a €5 bag-check service (see next).

Laundry: For full-service, same-day laundry in the new town, try **Wash and Dry Lavarapido.** They'll pick up at your hotel or you can drop it at their shop. The owners speak little English, so ask your hotelier to arrange the details (€13/load, daily 8:00-19:00, Via Molinelli 17, mobile 339-484-0940, Lucia and Ivano). Or head to the **Luètu Lavanderia** in the old town, uphill on Via Roma, across from the post office (€4/wash, daily 8:00-20:00, may be open later in summer, tel. 328-286-1908).

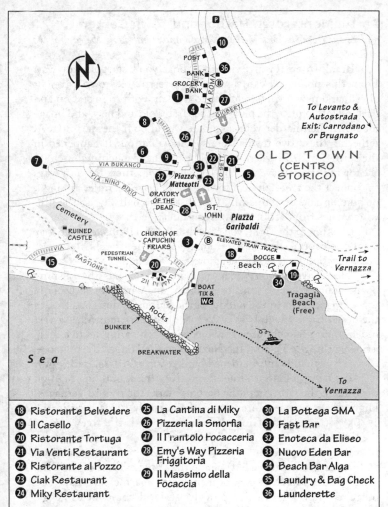

18 Ristorante Belvedere	25 La Cantina di Miky
19 Il Casello	26 Pizzeria la Smorfia
20 Ristorante Tortuga	27 Il Frantolo Focacceria
21 Via Venti Restaurant	28 Emy's Way Pizzeria Friggitoria
22 Ristorante al Pozzo	29 Il Massimo della Focaccia
23 Ciak Restaurant	
24 Miky Restaurant	

30 La Bottega SMA
31 Fast Bar
32 Enoteca da Eliseo
33 Nuovo Eden Bar
34 Beach Bar Alga
35 Laundry & Bag Check
36 Launderette

CINQUE TERRE

Massage: Giorgio Moggia, the local physiotherapist, gives good massages at your hotel or in his studio (€70/hour, tel. 339-314-6127, giomogg@tin.it).

Monterosso Walk

This self-guided walk will introduce you to Monterosso, beginning in the old town with an easy and lazy sweep of the sights as seen from the breakwater. Part 1, focusing on the mostly level town center, takes about 30 minutes; for Part 2, summiting the adjacent hill, allow another hour or so.

Part 1: Monterosso Harbor and Town Center

• *Hike out from the dock in the old town and stand along the edge of the concrete...*

Breakwater: If you're visiting by boat, you'll start here anyway. From this point you can survey Monterosso's old town (straight ahead) and new town (stretching to the left, with train station and parking lot). Notice the bluff that separates old and new, and imagine how much harder your commute would be if the narrow road tethering these two towns were somehow cut off. It happened in the spring of 2013, when the wall below the Capuchin church (at the top of the hill) gave way in a landslide. For a time, the only ways to connect the two halves of town were to drive six miles around... or hike up and over this hill. (The little fort halfway up the hill, which dates from 1550, is now a private home.)

Looking to the right, you can actually see all *cinque* of the *terre* from one spot: Vernazza, Corniglia (above the shore), Manarola, and a few buildings of Riomaggiore beyond that.

These days, the harbor hosts more paddleboats than fishing boats. Sand erosion is a major problem. The partial breakwater (a row of giant rocks in the middle of the harbor) is designed to save the beach from washing away. While old-timers remember a vast beach, their grandchildren truck in sand each spring to give tourists something to lie on. (The Nazis liked the Cinque Terre, too—find two of their bomb-hardened bunkers, near left and far right.)

The fancy four-star Hotel Porto Roca (pink building high on the hill, on the far right of the harbor) marks the trail to Vernazza. High above, you see an example of the costly roads built in the 1980s to connect the Cinque Terre towns with the freeway over the hills.

The two prominent capes (Punta di Montenero to the right, and Punta Mesco to the left) define the Cinque Terre region. The closer Punta Mesco is part of a protected marine sanctuary and home to a rare seagrass that provides an ideal home for fish eggs. Buoys keep fishing boats away. The cape was once a quarry, providing employment to locals who chipped out the stones used to build the local towns (the greenish stones making up part of the breakwater are from there).

On the far end of the new town, marking the best free beach around, you can just see the statue named *Il Gigante* (hard to spot because it blends in with the gray rock). It's 45 feet tall and once held a trident. While it looks as if it were hewn from the rocky cliff, it's actually made of reinforced concrete and dates from the beginning of the 20th century, when it supported a dancing terrace for a *fin de siècle* villa. A violent storm left the giant holding nothing but memories of Monterosso's glamorous age.

Looking back up at the beach, notice the openings of two big drains. Monterosso sustained serious damage in the 2011 flood, but quickly rebuilt. These drains are the outlet for a newly reen-gineered network of drainage canals that run beneath the main street through the old town. If you listen carefully as you explore, you may hear the gurgle of carefully routed runoff flowing from the surrounding hills into the sea.

• *From the breakwater, walk toward the old town and under the train tracks. Then venture right into the square and find the statue of a dandy holding what looks like a box cutter (near the big playground).*

Piazza Garibaldi: The statue honors Giuseppe Garibaldi, the dashing firebrand revolutionary who, in the 1860s, helped unite the people of Italy into a modern nation. Facing Garibaldi, with your back to the sea, you'll see (from right to left) the orange city hall (with the European Union flag beside the Italian one) and a big home and recreation center for poor and homeless elderly. You'll also see A Ca' du Sciensa restaurant (with historic town photos inside and upstairs; you're welcome to pop in for a look).

After the October 2011 flood, it was on this square that the National Guard set up an emergency tent, used for staging deliver-ies and community meals. The local civil protection unit is now named for 40-year-old volunteer Sandro Usai, Monterosso's one casualty. Sandro was last seen heroically trying to open up a grate to increase canal drainage (his body washed ashore a week later). Sandro posthumously received the highest civilian award the Ital-ian government gives.

Just under the bell tower (with your back to the sea, it's on your left), a set of covered arcades facing the sea is where the old-timers hang out (they see all and know all). The crenellated bell tower marks the church.

• *Go to church.*

Church of St. John the Baptist (Chiesa di San Giovanni Bat-tista): First, walk alongside the church (past the arcade). Near the second side door, find the high-water mark *(altezza massima)* from an October 1966 flood—which also famously devastated Florence. Nearby, a second (higher) plaque commemorates the crippling 2011 flood.

Now hook left, around the church—which is where you'll find its black-and-white-striped main façade. With white marble from Carrara and green marble from Punta Mesco, the church is typical of this region's Romanesque style. Note the lacy, stone rose window above the entrance. It's as delicate as crochet work, with 18 slender mullions (the petals of the rose). The marble stripes get narrower the higher they go, creating the illusion that the church is taller than it really is.

Step inside for more Ligurian Gothic: original marble columns and capitals with pointed arches to match. The octagonal baptismal font (in the back of the church) was carved from Carrara marble in 1359. Imagine the job getting that from the quarries to here. In the chapel to the right of the high altar, look for the wooden statue of St. Anthony, carved about 1400, which once graced a church that stood atop Punta Mesco. The church itself dates from 1307—see the proud inscription on the left-middle column: "MilloCCCVII."

• *Leaving the church, immediately turn left and go to church again.*

Oratory of the Dead (Oratorio dei Neri): During the Counter-Reformation, the Catholic Church offset the rising influence of the Lutherans by creating brotherhoods of good works. These religious Rotary clubs were called "confraternities." Monterosso had two, nicknamed White and Black. This building is the oratory of the Black group, whose mission—as the macabre decor filling the interior indicates—was to arrange for funerals and take care of widows, orphans, the shipwrecked, and the souls of those who ignore the request for a €1 donation. It dates from the 16th century, and membership has passed from father to son for generations. Notice the fine, carved choir stalls (c. 1700), just inside the door, and the haunted-house chandeliers. Look up at the ceiling to find the symbol of the confraternity: a skull-and-crossbones and an hourglass...death awaits us all.

• *On that cheery note, if you're in a lazy mood, you can discreetly split off from our walking tour now to enjoy strolling, shopping, gelato-licking, a day at the beach...or all of the above. But if you're up for a hike, continue with me on Part 2. As you face out to sea, look to the right and imagine the views from the top of that hill. Now...go see them.*

Part 2: Capuchin Church and Hilltop Cemetery

• *Return to the beach and find the brick steps that lead up to the hill-capping church (between the train tracks and the pedestrian tunnel, and passing in front of Albergo Pasquale). Approaching the bend in the path, watch for the stairs leading steeply and sharply to the right. This lane (Salita dei Cappuccini) is nicknamed* Zii di Frati, *or...*

Switchbacks of the Friars: Follow the yellow brick road (OK, it's orange...but I couldn't help singing as I skipped skyward). Pause at the terrace above the seaside castle at a statue of St. Francis and a wolf taking in a grand view. Enjoy another opportunity to see all five of the Cinque Terre towns. From here, backtrack 20 yards and continue uphill.

• *When you reach a gate marked* Convento e Chiesa Cappuccini, *you have arrived at the...*

Church of the Capuchin Friars: The former monastery is now manned by a single caretaker friar. Before stepping inside, notice the church's striped Romanesque facade. It's all fake. Tap it—no marble, just cheap 18th-century stucco. Go inside and sit in the rear pew. The high altarpiece painting of St. Francis can be rolled up on special days to reveal a statue of Mary standing behind it. Look at the statue of St. Anthony to the right and smile (you're on convent camera). Wave at the security camera—they're nervous about the precious painting to your left.

This fine painting of the **Crucifixion** is attributed to Anthony van Dyck, the 17th-century Flemish master who lived and worked for years in nearby Genoa (though art historians suspect that, at best, it was painted by someone in the artist's workshop). When Jesus died, the earth went dark. Notice the eclipsed sun in the painting, just to the right of the cross. Do the electric candles work? Pick one up, pray for peace, and plug it in. (Leave €0.50, or unplug it and put it back.)

• *Leave and turn left through another gate to hike 100 yards uphill to the cemetery filling the ruined castle at the top of the hill. Reaching the cemetery's gate, look back and enjoy the view over the town.*

Cemetery in the Ruined Castle: In the Dark Ages, the village huddled within this castle. Slowly it expanded. Notice the town view from here—no sea. You're looking at the oldest part of Monterosso, tucked behind the hill, out of view of 13th-century pirates.

Respectfully explore the cemetery. Ponder the black-and-white photos of grandparents past. Read the headstones: *Q.R.P.* is *Qui Riposa in Pace* (a.k.a. R.I.P.). Rich families had their own little tomb buildings. That this is still a place treasured by the living is demonstrated by the abundance of fresh flowers.

Climb to the very summit—the castle's keep, or place of last refuge. Priests are buried in a line of graves closest to the sea, but facing inland, toward the town's holy sanctuary high on the hillside (above the road, with its triangular steeple peeking above the trees). Each Cinque Terre town has a lofty sanctuary, dedicated to Mary and dear to the village hearts.

• *Your tour is over—any trail leads you back into town.*

Experiences in Monterosso

Hikes from Monterosso

For a relatively easy in-town hike, "Part 2" of my self-guided Monterosso Walk (above) takes you on a rewarding climb up to the **hilltop cemetery** in the middle of town.

Several more ambitious hikes begin in Monterosso, including the path to **Vernazza** on the main coastal trail, and—in the opposite direction—the path over the Punta Mesco bluff to **Levanto.** For more on these and other routes, see "Hiking the Cinque Terre" on page 325.

You can readily use Monterosso's **shuttle buses** (see "Arrival in Monterosso") to make challenging hikes a little easier. If hiking to Vernazza, skip the many steep stairs at the start of the trail by riding to Vettora. Or, if you're tackling the tough hike to Levanto, ride up to Colle di Gritta—making most of the rest of the hike downhill (details on page 336). Locals know all the options—and the shuttle bus schedules—so ask around. But be aware that only one or two departures a day head into the high country (and only in summer).

Beaches

Monterosso's **new town** has easily the Cinque Terre's best—and most crowded—beach (immediately in front of the train station). Most of the beach is technically private, where you'll pay €20-25 to rent two chairs and an umbrella for the day (a worthwhile investment if you're lingering; prices get very soft in the afternoon). Light lunches are served by beach cafés to sunbathers at their lounge chairs. Various outfits along here rent kayaks and stand-up paddeboards (look for signs at the west end of the beach—near the parking lot—or ask around).

If there are no umbrellas on a stretch of beach, it's public, so you can spread out a towel anywhere. There's a free beach at the far-west end, near the Gigante statue; others are marked on the map on page 390.

The **old town** also has its own, predominantly private beach (rent umbrellas, chairs, kayaks, and paddleboats at the Beach Bar Alga, which is also a scenic spot for a drink). Tucked just beyond the private beach—under Il Casello restaurant at the east end of town—is the free public beach called Tragagià, which is gravelly and generally less crowded. The bocce ball court (next to Il Casello) is busy with the old boys enjoying their favorite pastime.

Wine Tasting

Buranco Agriturismo offers visits to their vineyard and cantina (reserve two days ahead). You'll taste some of their wines plus a grappa and a *limoncino,* along with home-cooked food (€20-30/person with snacks, English may be limited, follow Via Buranco uphill to path, 10 minutes above town, tel. 0187-817-677, www.burancocinqueterre.it). They also rent apartments; see "Sleeping in Monterosso," later.

For more places to sample the local wine, see "Nightlife in Monterosso," next.

Boat Rides

In addition to the regularly scheduled big boats (see page 323), you can hire your own captain for transfers to other towns or for a full nautical tour. For example, **Stefano** has two six-person boats: the *Matilde* and the *Babaah* (about €100/hour, one hour is enough for a quick spin, two hours includes time for swimming stops; longer trips to Porto Venere and offshore islands possible; mobile 333-821-2007, www.matildenavigazione.com, info@ matildenavigazione.com).

Nightlife in Monterosso

Although I've listed these establishments for their nightlife, they work any time of day for a drink and spot to relax (especially the beach bars).

Enoteca da Eliseo, my favorite wine bar in town, comes with operatic ambience. Eliseo and his wife, Mary, love music and wine. Taste by the glass *(bicchiere),* or select a fine bottle from their shop shelf and enjoy it and the village action from their cozy tables Eliseo stocks more than a hundred varieties of grappa (Wed-Mon 14:00-23:30, closed Tue, Piazza Matteotti 3, a block inland behind church, tel. 0187-817-308).

Fast Bar, the best bar in town for young travelers and night owls, is located on Via Roma in the old town. Customers mix travel tales with big, cold beers, and the crowd (and the rock 'n' roll) gets noisier as the night rolls on. Come here to watch Italian or American sporting events on TV all day (cheap *panini, piandine,* salads, and other light meals usually served until midnight, open Fri-Wed 9:30-late, closed Thu except in peak season; Alex, Francesco, and Stefano).

La Cantina di Miky, in the new town just beyond the train station, is a trendy bar-restaurant with an extensive cocktail and grappa menu; they sometimes host live music. The seating is in three zones: overlooking the beach, in the garden, or in the cellar. Try the fun "five villages" wine tasting with local meats and cheeses (€15/person for just wine, €20/person with food). This is the best place in town for top-end Italian microbrews (Thu-Tue until late, closed Wed, Via Fegina 90, tel. 0187-802-525).

Beach Bars: On a balmy evening, enjoy a memorable drink with a view of swimmers, sunbathers, and the languid Ligurian Sea. In the new town, try **Nuovo Eden Bar,** overlooking the beach by the big rock (€6 cocktails, drinks come with a light snack, good ice cream, open long hours daily but closed Mon off-season). In the old town, **Beach Bar Alga** has an island ambience (daily until 20:00).

Sleeping in Monterosso

($$$$ = Splurge, $$$ = Pricier, $$ = Moderate, $ = Budget)
Monterosso, the most beach-resorty of the five Cinque Terre towns, offers maximum comfort and ease. The TI Proloco just outside the train station can give you a list of rooms for rent. Rooms in Mon-

terosso are a better value than similar rooms in crowded Vernazza, and the proprietors seem more genuine and welcoming. To locate the hotels, see the map on page 390.

IN THE OLD TOWN

$$$$ Hotel Villa Steno is lovingly managed and features great view balconies, panoramic gardens and a roof terrace with sun beds, air-conditioning, and the friendly help of Matteo and his wife, Carla. Of their 16 rooms, 14 have view balconies (RS%, family rooms, hearty buffet breakfast, elevator, laundry service, ask about pay parking when you reserve, hike up to the panoramic terrace, Via Roma 109, tel. 0187-817-028 or 0187-818-336, www. villasteno.com, steno@pasini.com). It's a 15-minute climb (or €8 taxi ride) from the train station to the top of the old town. Readers get a free Cinque Terre info packet and a glass of local wine when they check in—ask for it.

$$$$ Il Giardino Incantato ("The Enchanted Garden") is a charming and comfortable four-room B&B with impressive attention to detail in a tastefully renovated 16th-century Ligurian home in the heart of the old town. It's run by kind and eager-to-please Fausto and Mariapia and their gregarious staff. Sip their homemade *limoncino* upon check-in, and have breakfast under lemon trees in a delightful hidden garden, which is illuminated with candles in the evening (RS%, air-con, free minibar and tea and coffee service, laundry service, Via Mazzini 18, tel. 0187-818-315, mobile 333-264-9252, www.ilgiardinoincantato.net, giardino_incantato@ libero.it).

$$$$ Albergo Pasquale is a modern, comfortable place with 15 seaview rooms, run by the same family as the Hotel Villa Steno (listed earlier). Located right on the harbor, it's just a few steps from the beach, boat dock, and tunnel entrance to the new town. While there is some train noise, the soundtrack is mostly a lullaby of waves. It has an elevator and offers easier access than most (RS%, family room, same welcome drink as Villa Steno, air-con, laundry service, Via Fegina 8, tel. 0187-817-550 or 0187-817-477, www.hotelpasquale.it, pasquale@pasini.com, Felicita and Marco).

$$$ Locanda il Maestrale rents six small, stylish rooms in a sophisticated and peaceful little inn. Although renovated with all the modern comforts, it retains centuries-old character under frescoed ceilings. Its peaceful sun terrace overlooking the old town and Via Roma action is a delight. Guests enjoy free drinks and snacks each afternoon (RS%, air-con, Via Roma 37, tel. 0187-817-013, mobile 338-4530-531, www.locandamaestrale.net, maestrale@ monterossonet.com, Stefania).

$$$ Hotel la Colonnina has 21 big rooms (some older, some stylishly up-to-date), generous and meticulously cared-for public spaces, a cozy garden, and an inviting shared seaview terrace with sun beds. It's buried in the town's fragrant and sleepy back streets (family rooms, many rooms with private terraces, cash preferred, air-con, fridges, elevator, a block inland from the main square at Via Zuecca 6, tel. 0187-817-439, www.lacolonninacinqueterre.it, info@lacolonninacinqueterre.it, Cristina).

$$$ Albergo Marina, creatively run by enthusiastic husband-and-wife team Marina and Eraldo, has 23 pleasant rooms and a garden with lemon trees. With a free and filling buffet featuring local specialties each afternoon, they offer a fine value (RS%, family rooms, elevator, air-con, free kayak and snorkel equipment, Via Buranco 40, tel. 0187-817-613, www.hotelmarina5terre.com, marina@hotelmarina5terre.com).

$$$ Buranco Agriturismo, a 10-minute hike above the old town, has wonderful gardens and views over the vine-covered valley. Its primary business is wine and olive-oil production, but they offer three apartments. It's a rare opportunity to stay in a farmhouse but still be able to get to town on foot (air-con, €10 taxi from station, tel 0187-817-677, mobile 349-434-8046, www.burancocinqueterre.it, info@buranco.it, informally run by Loredana, Mary, and Giulietta).

$$$ Manuel's Guesthouse, perched high above the town among terraces, is a garden getaway run by Lorenzo and his father, Giovanni (and named for their uncle/brother, a disheveled artist who prefers to set up his easels down below these days). They have six big, bright rooms and a grand view. After climbing the killer stairs from the town center, their killer terrace is hard to leave—especially after a few drinks (cash only, air-con, up about 100 steps behind church—you can ask Lorenzo to carry your bags up the hill, Via San Martino 39, mobile 333-439-0809, www.manuelsguesthouse.com, manuelsguesthouse@libero.it).

$$ L'Antica Terrazza rents five classy rooms right in town. With a pretty terrace overlooking the pedestrian street and minimal stairs, Raffaella and John offer a good deal (RS%, cheaper room with private bath down the hall, air-con, Vicolo San Martino 1, mobile 380-138-0082 or 347-132-6213, www.anticaterrazza.com, post@anticaterrazza.com).

$ Albergo al Carugio is a practical nine-room place in a big apartment-style building at the top of the old town. It's quiet, comfy, and a fine value for those on a budget (RS%, no breakfast, air-con—but only during the daytime June-Sept, Via Roma 100, tel. 0187-817-453, www.alcarugio.it, info@alcarugio.it, conscientiously run by Andrea).

IN THE NEW TOWN

$$$$ Hotel Villa Adriana is a big, contemporary, bright hotel on a church-owned estate set in a peaceful garden with a pool, free parking, and a no-stress style. They rent 54 rooms—some with terraces and/or sea views—ask for one when you reserve, but no guarantees (family rooms, air-con, elevator, free loaner bikes, affordable dinners, Via IV Novembre 23, tel. 0187-818-109, www.villaadriana.info, info@villaadriana.info).

$$$$ Hotel la Spiaggia is a venerable old 19-room place facing the beach. Half the rooms come with sea views (cash only, air-con, elevator, free parking—reserve in advance, Via Lungomare 96, tel. 0187-817-567, www.laspiaggiahotel.com, hotellaspiaggia@libero.it, Maria and her dad, Andrea).

$$$ A Cà du Gigante, despite its name, is a tiny yet chic refuge with nine rooms. About 100 yards from the beach (and surrounded by blocky apartments and big hotels on a modern street), the interior is tastefully done with upscale comfort in mind (RS%, air-con, limited free parking, Via IV Novembre 11, tel. 0187-817-401, www.ilgigantecinqueterre.it, gigante@ilgigantecinqueterre.it, Claudia).

$$$ Hotel Punta Mesco is a tidy, well-run little haven renting 17 quiet, casual rooms at a good price. While none have views, 10 rooms have small terraces (RS%, family room, air-con, parking, Via Molinelli 35, tel. 0187-817-495, www.hotelpuntamesco.it, info@hotelpuntamesco.it; Roberto, Diego, and Manuel).

$$$ Pensione Agavi has 10 spartan, bright, overpriced rooms along the waterfront promenade. I'd skip it—unless you can score one of the rooms with a grand view over the beach (cheaper rooms with shared bath, breakfast extra, cash only, refrigerators, turn left out of station to Fegina 30, tel. 0187-817-171, www.hotelagavi.com, info@hotelagavi.com, Hillary).

$$ Affittacamere Ristorante il Gabbiano, a touristy restaurant right on the beach, rents five basic, dated, but affordable rooms upstairs. Three rooms face the sea, with small balconies; two overlook a little garden at the back. The Gabbiano family restaurant serves as your reception (family rooms, cash only, air-con, Via Fegina 84, tel. 0187-817-578, www.affittacamereristoranteilgabbiano.com, affittacamereilgabbiano@live.it).

$ Le Sirene/Raggi di Sole, with nine simple rooms in two humble buildings, is a decent budget choice in this pricey town. It's run from a hole-in-the-wall reception desk a block from the station, just off the water. I'd request the Le Sirene building, which has smaller bathrooms but no train noise, and is a bit more spacious and airy than Raggi di Sole (RS%, family rooms, fans, Via Molinelli 10, mobile 331-788-1088, www.sirenerooms.com, sirenerooms@gmail.com, Ermanna).

Eating in Monterosso

($$$$ = Splurge, $$$ = Pricier, $$ = Moderate, $ = Budget)

WITH A SEA VIEW

$$ Ristorante Belvedere, big and sprawling, is *the* place for a good-value meal indoors or outdoors on the harborfront. Their €48 *anfora belvedere*—mixed seafood stew dumped dramatically at the table from a pottery amphora into your bowl—is huge, and can easily be split among up to four diners. Their *misto mare* plate (2-person minimum, €15/person), a fishy treat, nearly makes an entire meal. Mussel fans will enjoy the *tagliolini della casa*. It's energetically run by Federico and Roberto (Wed-Mon 12:00-14:30 & 18:00-22:00, closed Tue except Aug, on the harbor in the old town, tel. 0187-817-033).

$$ Il Casello is the only place for a fun meal on a terrace overlooking the old town beach. With outdoor tables on a rocky outcrop, it's a pleasant spot for a salad, pasta, or *secondo* (daily April-Oct 12:00-22:00, closed Nov-March, mobile 333-492-7629, Bacco).

$$$ Ristorante Tortuga is the top option in Monterosso for seaview elegance, with gorgeous outdoor seating high on a bluff and a lovely white-tablecloth-and-candles interior. The food doesn't quite live up to the fuss, and the service is uneven, but the setting is memorable. Drop by to choose and reserve a table for later (Tue-Sun 12:00-15:00 & 18:00-21:30, closed Mon; at the tip of the point between the old and new towns—just outside the tunnel at the new town end, or climb up the ramp in front of the old town's Albergo Pasquale; tel. 0187-800-065, mobile 333-240-7956, Silvia and Giamba).

IN THE OLD TOWN

$$$ Via Venti is a quiet little trattoria, hidden in an alley deep in the heart of the old town, where Papa Ettore and co-chef Ilaria create imaginative seafood dishes using the day's catch and freshly made pasta. Ilaria's husband Michele serves up delicate and savory gnocchi with crab, tender ravioli stuffed with fresh fish, and pear-and-pecorino pasta. The outdoor tables are on a lane as nondescript as the humdrum interior—but you're here for the food (Fri-Wed 12:00-14:30 & 18:30-22:30, closed Thu, Via XX Settembre 32, tel. 0187-818-347).

$ Gastronomia "San Martino," warmly and passionately run by Moreno, is tiny, humble, and almost without ambience. But this excellent-value place serves surprisingly affordable, quality dishes. Eat (from plastic plates) at one of the few tables—inside or out on a pleasant street—or find a driftwood log for a takeaway seafront feast (Tue-Sun 12:00-15:00 & 18:00-22:00, closed Mon, next to recommended L'Antica Terrazza hotel at Vicolo San Martino 2, mobile 346-109-7338).

$$$ Ristorante al Pozzo is a favorite among locals. It's family-run, with good old-fashioned quality, as Gino (with his long white beard) cooks, and his engaging English-speaking son, Manuel, serves. They have one of the best wine lists in town, serve only homemade pasta, and are known for their raw fish and wonderful seafood *antipasti misti* (Fri-Wed 12:00-15:00 & 18:30-22:30, closed Thu, Via Roma 24, tel. 0187-817-575).

$$$ Ciak, high-energy and tightly packed, is a local institution with reliably good food, higher prices, and (sometimes) a bit of an attitude. It's known for its huge, sizzling terra-cotta crock for two crammed with the day's catch and accompanied by risotto or spaghetti, or served swimming in a soup *(zuppa)*. Other popular choices are fish ravioli with shrimp sauce and the seafood *antipasto Lampara*. Stroll a couple of paces past the outdoor tables up Via Roma to see what Signore Ciak (who wears his Popeye cap in the kitchen) has on the stove. Reservations are smart in summer (Thu-Tue 12:00-15:00 & 18:00-22:30, closed Wed, Piazza Don Minzoni 6, tel. 0187-817-014, www.ristoranteciak.net).

IN THE NEW TOWN

Even if you're not sleeping in the new town, consider venturing over for dinner at one of these options; as a bonus, the walk is mostly along a scenic and lively beachfront promenade.

$$$$ Miky is packed with well-dressed locals who know their seafood and want to eat it in a classy environment. For elegantly presented, top-quality food that celebrates local ingredients and traditions, this is my Cinque Terre favorite. It's a proud family operation: Miky (dad), Simonetta (mom), charming Sara (daughter, who greets guests), and the attentive but easygoing waitstaff all work hard. Try their "pizza pasta"—finished in a bowl topped with a thin pizza crust, then flambéed at your table. Many of the wines on their fine list are available by the glass if you ask. If I were ever to require a dessert, it would be their mixed sampler plate, *dolce misto*—plenty for two (Wed-Mon 12:00-15:00 & 19:00-23:00, closed Tue, reservations wise in summer, in the new town 100 yards from train station at Via Fegina 104, tel. 0187-817-608, www.ristorantemiky.it).

$$$ La Cantina di Miky, a few doors down (toward the station), serves artfully crafted Ligurian specialties that follow in Miky's family tradition of quality. Run by son Manuel—and Christine from New Jersey—it's more youthful and informal, and the setting is unpretentious (sit downstairs, in the garden, or overlooking the sea). The €20 anchovy tasting plate is an education in the many ways to prepare this local specialty (creative desserts, large selection of Italian microbrews, Thu-Tue 12:00-24:00, closed Wed, Via Fegina 90, tel. 0187-802-525). This place doubles as a cocktail bar in the evenings.

LIGHT MEALS, TAKEOUT FOOD, AND BREAKFAST

In the Old Town: Lots of shops and bakeries sell pizza and focaccia to eat in or take out for an easy picnic on the beach or trail. **$ Pizzeria la Smorfia**—a local favorite—cooks up good pizza; the large can feed three (Fri-Wed 11:00-24:00, closed Thu, Via Vittorio Emanuele 73, tel. 0187-818-395). At **$ Il Frantoio,** Simone makes tasty pizza and focaccia (Fri-Wed 9:00-14:00 & 16:30-20:00, closed Thu, just off Via Roma at Via Gioberti 1). **$ Emy's Way Pizzeria Friggitoria** offers thick-crust pizzas—whole and by the slice—and deep-fried seafood in to-go cones (daily 11:00-20:00, later in summer, along the skinny street next to the church, Emiliano).

In the New Town, near the Station: For a quick bite right at the train station (or on the beach), consider **$ Il Massimo della Focaccia** for quiche-like tortes, sandwiches, focaccia pizzas, and desserts. With benches just in front, this is a good bet for a light meal with a sea view (Thu-Tue 9:00-19:00, closed Wed except June-Aug, Via Fegina 50 at the station). **La Bottega SMA** is a smart minimart with fresh produce, *antipasti,* deli items, and other picnic fare. They'll even make you a sandwich: Select a bread and filling, and pay by weight (daily 8:00-13:00 & 16:30-19:30—until 13:00 on Sun, shorter hours off-season, near Lavarapido at Vittoria Gianni 21).

Breakfast: Most hotels here include breakfast in the room rate. But if you're looking, **Fast Bar** has an American-style breakfast for €10, or cheaper à la carte (see listing under "Nightlife in Monterosso," earlier).

CINQUE TERRE

RIVIERA TOWNS

Levanto • Sestri Levante • Santa Margherita Ligure •
Portofino • La Spezia • Carrara • Porto Venere

The Cinque Terre is tops, but there's much more to the Italian Riviera. To the north is a trio of beach towns: Levanto, the northern gateway to the Cinque Terre; Sestri Levante, stunningly situated on a narrow peninsula flanked by two beaches; and Santa Margherita Ligure, a thriving small city with an active waterfront and easy connections to yacht-happy Portofino. At the other end of the Cinque Terre is the region's southern gateway, gritty La Spezia, as well as the picturesque resort of Porto Venere.

The best of these towns—the high-end yin to the Cinque Terre's ramshackle yang—can be user-friendly home bases for day trips along the Riviera coast. But they are also worth visiting in their own right. After exploring the villages and trails of the Cinque Terre, coming here feels like a return to civilization—for reasons both good (modern amenities and an agreeable urban bustle) and bad (traffic and greedy big-resort pricing).

HOME-BASING ON THE ITALIAN RIVIERA

Levanto, Sestri Levante, and Santa Margherita Ligure are practical home bases for drivers wanting to park at their hotel and side-trip to the Cinque Terre by train, or for those who want modern hotels with all the predictable resort amenities. (They're also worth a look if you're finding the Cinque Terre towns booked up.) **Levanto—**

Riviera Towns at a Glance

North of the Cinque Terre

Levanto Surfers' hangout with a long beach, functional center, and speedy train connections to the Cinque Terre; also the gateway to ▲**Bonassola,** a sleepy and scenic "Back Door" beach village. See page 406.

▲**Sestri Levante** Charming town on a peninsula flanked by two picturesque beaches. See page 415.

▲▲**Santa Margherita Ligure** Easygoing old-school resort town with an enjoyable urban bustle, a handful of sights, and close proximity to Portofino. See page 419.

▲**Portofino** Glitzy yacht-harbor resort with grand scenery and easy connections (by boat, bus, or foot) from Santa Margherita Ligure. See page 429.

South of the Cinque Terre

La Spezia Beachless transportation hub with the region's nitty-gritty essentials. See page 435.

▲▲**Porto Venere** Enchanting seafront village perfect for a scenic side-trip by boat from the Cinque Terre. See page 438.

just minutes beyond Monterosso by train—is particularly handy. **Sestri Levante** is a bit farther and less well-served by trains, but still workable. **Santa Margherita Ligure** is the most distant and requires a transfer on most connections to the Cinque Terre, but the town compensates by being the most appealing—and it gives you easy access to posh Portofino.

If you do home-base here, keep in mind that you'll be competing with other day-trippers for space on prime midday trains. Turn this problem into an advantage: On especially busy days, enjoy your home-base town during the day, then head into the Cinque Terre villages in the late afternoon for untrampled charm, a romantic dinner, and a late train back.

Hotels in these towns aren't necessarily cheaper than the Cinque Terre—but they are more likely to have space. High season is July and August; prices go down in April-June and September-October, and are soft the rest of the year. Some hotels close off-season. Especially in peak season, some hotels want you to take half-pension (lunch or dinner).

Getting Around: Public transportation is the best way to get around this region, which is well connected by train and/or boat.

Riviera Towns

To Nice & Milan

A-12

Genoa

SP-1

Rapallo

FREEWAY AUTOSTRADA

Camogli
San Fruttuoso

Portofino

See Portofino Area detail map

Santa Margherita Ligure

Sestri Levante

SP-1

A-12

A-31

To Parma & Milan

SP-566

Framura • Bonassola

Levanto

Monterosso

SP-1

La Spezia

To Carrara & Pisa

Ligurian Sea

Vernazza

Corniglia

Manarola

Riomaggiore

Lerici

Gulf of Poets

10 Kilometers

10 Miles

CINQUE TERRE

See detail map in Cinque Terre chapter

Porto Venere

Palmaria

North of the Cinque Terre

When most people imagine the "Italian Riviera," they're thinking of the shimmering resort towns north of the Cinque Terre. Big, stately, Old World hotels loom over crowded pebble beaches with rentable umbrellas. Fastidiously landscaped parks and promenades are jammed with more Italian visitors than American tourists. These towns are perfect for day-tripping—or even an overnight.

Levanto

Graced with a long, sandy beach, Levanto (LEH-vahn-toh) is packed in summer and popular with surfers. The rest of the year, it's just a small, sleepy town. It has a fraction of the charm of the Cinque Terre, but it enjoys fewer crowds, more varied dining options, and quick connections to the Cinque Terre (4 minutes to Monterosso by train, continuing to the rest of the Cinque Terre villages on the same line). This beach town isn't the "real" Cinque Terre, but it can be a perfectly workable home base. (It has a high number of family rooms and affordable, large apartments with kitchenettes.) From Levanto, you can hop a train or boat to the Cinque Terre towns and beyond; take the no-wimps-allowed hike to Monterosso (3 hours); or bike or stroll on a delightful, level path to the nearby, uncrowded beach town of Bonassola.

Orientation to Levanto

Levanto (pop. 5,600) is dominated by an uninspiring new town, a regular grid street plan of five-story apartment buildings that stretches from the train station down to the broad, curving beach. The sleepy, twisty old town (bisected by a modern street) is tucked up against the adjacent hill.

TOURIST INFORMATION

There's a Cinque Terre National Park info center at the train station. The helpful TI is on Piazza Cavour (daily 9:00-13:00 & 15:00-18:00 except closed Sun afternoon, shorter hours off-season, tel. 0187-808-125, www.comune.levanto.sp.it). In peak season, the TI leads a weekly walking tour in English of Levanto's medieval architecture (cheap or free, tips expected, 2 hours, once a week at 18:00 from Piazza Cavour, get details and sign up at TI).

ARRIVAL IN LEVANTO

By Train: From the train station (no bag storage), head through the parking lot and down the stairs, turn right, and cross the bridge onto Corso Roma—the main drag. The beach is straight ahead, and most of my recommended hotels, restaurants, and the TI are in the grid of streets to your left. You can walk from the station to most places listed in this chapter in about 10 minutes.

By Car: If your hotel doesn't offer parking—or if you're not sleeping here—you have three good alternatives. The lots surrounding the **train station** are affordable and handy for hopping a train to the Cinque Terre towns (€1.20/hour, €10.80/day). For longer stays, park in the **free lot** a few blocks north of the station (across the river from the hospital on the way into town—first left after the hospital, cross the bridge and immediately turn left). If you're heading for the beach, the parking lot there is handy but expensive (€1.80/hour, €18/day).

HELPFUL HINTS

Exchange Rate: €1 = about $1.10
Country Calling Code: 39 (see page 1154 for dialing instructions)
Markets: Levanto's modern covered *mercato,* which sells produce and fish, is on Via del Mercato, between the train station and the beach (Mon-Sat 8:00-13:00, closed Sun). On Wednesday morning, an **open-air market** with clothes, shoes, and housewares fills the street in front of the *mercato.*

Laundry: A **self-service launderette** stuffed with snack and drink vending machines is at Piazza Staglieno 38, facing an inviting park (open 24 hours daily, mobile 338-701-6341). Another self-service place, **Speedy Wash,** is at Via Garibaldi 32 (daily 8:00-22:00, mobile 338-701-6341).

Bike Rental: Relatively flat Levanto, with light traffic, is a great bike town—and the ride to nearby Bonassola is easy and delightful. **Cicli Raso North Shore** rents bikes (€10-20/day depending on type of bike, daily 9:30-12:30 & 15:30-19:00, closed Sun Nov-April, Via Garibaldi 63, tel. 0187-802-511, www.cicliraso.com). The **Sensafreni Bike Shop** is convenient to the beach boardwalk (€3/hour, €5/half-day, €15/all day, Mon-Sat 9:30-12:30 & 16:00-19:30, closed Sun, Piazza del Popolo 1, tel. 0187-807-128).

Electric Bike Tours: Ebikein offers a variety of guided tours on electric bikes—giving you a helpful boost on the hills. Options range from a 2.5-hour loop around town (€39) to an ambitious 4-hour pedal up to some of the sanctuaries over Cinque Terre towns (€55, also pricey rentals, www.ebikein.com, mobile 334-190-0496).

Sports Rentals: Rosa dei Venti rents kayaks, canoes, surfboards, and windsurfing equipment right on the beach (Marco's mobile 329-451-1981 or 335-608-9277, www.levantorosadeiventi.it).

Sights in Levanto

Beach

Levanto's beach hides below a parking lot and promenade that's elevated above the sand—look for underpasses or stairs along its length. There are pretty boardwalks up on the elevated promenade and down along the beachfront. As you face the harbor, the boat dock is to your far left, and the diving center is to your far right (rental boats available at either place in summer). You can also rent a kayak or canoe just below the east end of the Piazza Mazzini parking lot.

During the summer, three parts of the beach are free: both sides of the boat dock, and near Piazza Mazzini. The rest of the beach is broken up into private sections that charge admission. You can always stroll along the beach, even through the private sections—just don't sit down. Off-season, roughly October through May, the entire beach is free, and you can lay your towel anywhere you like.

Old Town

The old town clusters around Piazza del Popolo. Until a few decades ago, the town's open-air market was held at the 13th-century

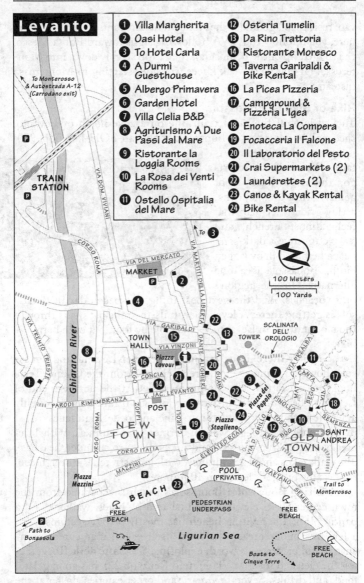

Levanto

1. Villa Margherita
2. Oasi Hotel
3. To Hotel Carla
4. A Durmì Guesthouse
5. Albergo Primavera
6. Garden Hotel
7. Villa Clelia B&B
8. Agriturismo A Due Passi dal Mare
9. Ristorante la Loggia Rooms
10. La Rosa dei Venti Rooms
11. Ostello Ospitalia del Mare
12. Osteria Tumelin
13. Da Rino Trattoria
14. Ristorante Moresco
15. Taverna Garibaldi & Bike Rental
16. La Picea Pizzeria
17. Campground & Pizzeria L'Igea
18. Enoteca La Compera
19. Focacceria il Falcone
20. Il Laboratorio del Pesto
21. Crai Supermarkets (2)
22. Launderettes (2)
23. Canoe & Kayak Rental
24. Bike Rental

loggia (covered set of archways) in the square. Explore the back streets.

Hike to Monterosso

This strenuous, three-hour hike is described in more detail on page 330. To begin in Levanto, start at the old town's Piazza del Popolo, and head uphill to the striped church, Chiesa di Sant'Andrea. From the church courtyard, follow the sign to the *castello* (a private residence), go under the stone arch, and continue uphill. From here, you'll follow trail SVA (following signs toward Punta Mesco, the rugged tip of the peninsula), then drop steeply down into Monterosso. (If you have weak knees, consider starting in Monterosso instead.)

Hike or Bike to Bonassola

Tucked just off the main train line on a cove north of Levanto, the small beach resort of Bonassola (boh-nah-SOH-lah, pop. 950) is a peaceful little eddy. As far as Riviera beach resorts go, this is a Back Door gem. With a low-key vibe, a tidy grid street plan that feels almost French, and a picturesque dark-sand beach hemmed in by jagged bluffs, Bonassola is a fine alternative to the region's other beaches. And the next best thing to a beach day in Bonassola is getting there: A level, easy, rails-to-trails path cuts through the mountain from Levanto—enjoyable by foot, but even better by bike.

Getting There: Local **trains** run between Levanto and Bonassola (hourly, 3 minutes—requires a change from the Cinque Terre line). But I'd rather take the **promenade.** At the northern end of Levanto's beachfront road/parking lot, you'll find a level, roughly 1.5-mile path neatly divided into bike and pedestrian lanes. Most of the route is through well-lit former train tunnels, with brief breaks overlooking the sea (and hikes down to secluded beaches). The walk takes about 25 minutes, with long stretches through cool tunnels; by bike, it's less than 10 minutes.

Visiting Bonassola: Bonassola's beach is separated from the town center by its elevated road (shared by bikes, walkers, and a parking lot). The inviting **beach** has mostly private sections, with a few free public areas. The town itself—with manicured promenades and piazzas—is worth exploring. **$$ Caffè delle Rose,** facing the elevated road (at Via Fratelli Rezzano 22), has good gelato, food, and drinks. Several *foccacerie* and other eateries cluster at the far end of town.

For a scenic **walk/hike,** head to the far (north) end of the beach, where a promenade snakes along the base of the rocky cliff (with rocky perches for sunbathing and swimming). For higher views, find the stairs near the flagpole, and follow the steps up on the right side of the yellow church. Popping out at the top, turn left along the scenic, private road as it curls around the top of the bay, with great views back on the town and beach; the path ends at the blocky little Madonnina della Punta chapel.

Bonassola to Framura (Best for Bikers): From Bonassola, the promenade continues another 1.5 miles to the town of **Framura**—a settlement made up of five hamlets scattered across a hillside. Because this part of the route is almost entirely through tunnels, it's boring for walkers—but quick for bikers. You'll pop out overlooking Framura's rocky little harbor, behind its train station (no direct access—don't count on taking your bike back on the train). Hike down to the harbor, or up to the village—or simply enjoy the views, then turn around and pedal back to Bonassola and Levanto.

Sleeping in Levanto

$$$ Villa Margherita is across the river and a bit uphill (about a 10-minute walk from the town center or train station), but the shady gardens, 11 characteristic colorfully tiled rooms, and tranquility are worth the walk (family rooms, air-con, elevator one flight up from street level, free parking, Via Trento e Trieste 31, tel. 0187-807-212, mobile 328-842-6934, www.villamargherita.net, info@villamargherita.net).

$$$ Oasi Hotel, well-run by Silvia, has 14 rooms in a cozy small hotel behind the market hall. Some rooms have balconies, others have direct access to the garden, and a few have neither—request your choice when you reserve (air-con, elevator, parking extra, Via Ferraro, tel. 0187-807-356, www.oasihotel.eu, info@oasihotel.eu).

$$$ Hotel Carla sits in a humdrum residential zone, about 10 minutes from the beach and the station. Its 30 rooms come with surprising style—most have balconies, and all are decorated in soothing, neutral colors (family rooms, air-con, elevator, Via Martiri della Libertà 28, tel. 0187-808-275, www.carlahotel.com, info@carlahotel.com).

$$ A Durmì is a happy little guesthouse owned by lovely Graziella, Gianni, and their two daughters, Elisa and Chiara. Their sunny patios, green leafy gardens, six immaculate beach bungalow-type rooms, and five sunlit apartments make a welcoming place to stay (breakfast extra, family rooms, air-con, bar, pay parking, Via D. Viviani 12, tel. 0187-800-823, mobile 349-105-6016, www.adurmi.it, info@adurmi.it).

$$ Albergo Primavera is family-run, with 17 colorful rooms—10 with balconies (but no views)—just a half-block from the beach (family rooms, request a quiet room off the street, includes hearty breakfast buffet, air-con, pay parking, free loaner bikes, Via Cairoli 5, tel. 0187-808-023, www.primaverahotel.com,

Sleep Code

Hotels are classified based on the average price of a standard double room with breakfast in high season.

$$$$	**Splurge:**	Most rooms over €170
$$$	**Pricier:**	€130-170
$$	**Moderate:**	€90-130
$	**Budget:**	€50-90
¢	**Backpacker:**	Under €50
RS%	Rick Steves discount	

Unless otherwise noted, credit cards are accepted, hotel staff speak basic English, and free Wi-Fi is available. Comparison-shop by checking prices at several hotels (on each hotel's own website, on a booking site, or by email). For the best deal, *book directly with the hotel.* Ask for a discount if paying in cash; if the listing includes **RS%,** request a Rick Steves discount.

info@primaverahotel.com; friendly Carlo, cheerful Daniela, and daughters Giuditta and Gloria).

$$ Garden Hotel offers 17 functional, modern rooms (all with balconies but no views) on the first floor of an apartment building. While it's a lesser value, you're paying for proximity to the beach—it's just across the street (more expensive fifth-floor rooms have sea views and terrace, closed Nov-mid-March, air-con, elevator for fifth floor only, free parking but not on-site, loaner bikes, Corso Italia 6, tel. 0187-808-173, www.nuovogarden.com, info@nuovogarden.com, Davide and Damiano).

$$ Villa Clelia B&B offers five dark, air-con rooms (named for the winds—*scirocco, maestrale,* and so on) with minifridges and terraces. The rooms, on an exterior corridor, surround a garden courtyard just a short walk up from the sea (minimal in-room breakfast, free parking; with loggia on your left, it's straight ahead at Piazza da Passano 1; tel. 0187-808-195, mobile 329-379-4859, www.villaclelia.it, info@villaclelia.it). They also have seven central apartments that economically sleep up to five.

$ Agriturismo A Due Passi dal Mare is an in-town oasis, just a five-minute walk from the beach or the train station. Friendly Francesca and husband Maurizio rent four crisp, quiet rooms—with sizable bathrooms—in the 1920s home built by her grandfather; their back garden is open to guests (free on-site parking, closed Jan-Feb, right on the main drag at Corso Roma 37, tel. 0187-809-177, mobile 338-960-1537, www.a2passidalmare.com, info@a2passidalmare.com).

$ Ristorante la Loggia has eight cozy and older—yet cheap—rooms perched above the old loggia on Piazza del Popolo (cash only, request balcony, quieter rooms in back, two basic side-by-side apartments great for families of 4-8, lots of stairs, air-con, free parking, reception open 9:00-23:00, Piazza del Popolo 7, tel. 0187-808-107, mobile 335-641-7701, www.loggialevanto.com, Nerina does not speak English).

$$ La Rosa dei Venti is an *affittacamere* just a couple of blocks from the beach, in the old town. Enthusiastic Rosanna and her son Marco rent five old-fashioned, overpriced rooms with dark hardwood floors, comfy rugs, and glittery seashore decor (air-con, free parking, across from Piazza del Popolo, Via della Compera, tel. 0187-808-165, Marco's mobile 328-742-8268, www.larosadeiventilevanto.com, info@larosadeiventilevanto.com).

Hostel: ¢ Ostello Ospitalia del Mare, a budget gem, is run by the city tourist association. It has 70 basic beds, airy rooms, an elevator, and a terrace in a well-renovated medieval palazzo a few steps from the old town (dorms with private bath and private rooms, includes breakfast, self-service laundry, no curfew, no lockout; office open daily April-Oct 8:00-12:30 & 16:00-19:30, until 23:00 weekend nights; may close Nov-March, Via San Nicolò 1, tel. 0187-802-562, www.ospitaliadelmare.it, info@ospitaliadelmare.it).

Eating in Levanto

$$$ Osteria Tumelin, a local favorite, has a dressy, sophisticated ambience in its elegant dining room, a casual covered terrace out front, and a wide selection of fresh seafood. Reservations are smart on weekends or to dine outside. Check out the aquarium containing giant lobster and moray eels in the first dining room on the right (daily 12:00-14:30 & 19:00-22:30, closed Thu Oct-May, Via D. Grillo 32, across the square from the loggia, tel. 0187-808-379, www.tumelin.it).

$$ Da Rino, a small trattoria on a quiet pedestrian lane, dishes up reasonably priced fresh seafood and homemade Ligurian specialties prepared with care. Consider the grilled *totani* (squid), *pansotti con salsa di noci* (ravioli with walnut sauce), and *trofie al pesto* (local pasta with pesto sauce). Dine indoors or at one of the outdoor tables. On busy nights, they open up a second dining room across the street. Sommelier Anna will help you choose a good wine (Wed-Mon 19:00-22:00, closed Tue, Via Garibaldi 10, tel. 0187-813-475).

$$ Ristorante la Loggia, next to the old loggia, makes fine food, including appealing daily fish specials. Choose between the homey, wood-paneled dining room or the little terrace overlooking the square (daily 12:30-14:00 & 19:00-22:00, closed Nov-Feb, Piazza del Popolo 7, tel. 0187-808-107).

$$$ Ristorante Moresco serves large portions of pasta and

Restaurant Price Code

I've assigned each eatery a price category, based on the average cost of a typical main course (pasta or *secondi*). Drinks, desserts, and splurge items (steak and seafood) can raise the price considerably.

$$$$ **Splurge:** Most main courses over €20
$$$ **Pricier:** €15-20
$$ **Moderate:** €10-15
$ **Budget:** Under €10

In Italy, pizza by the slice and other takeout food is $; a basic trattoria or sit-down pizzeria is $$; a casual but more upscale restaurant is $$$; and a swanky splurge is $$$$.

---

seafood at reasonable prices in a vaulted, candlelit room decorated with Moorish-style frescoes. The best value is their €25 four-course tasting menu (drinks extra, 2-person minimum, daily 12:00-14:00 & 19:00-21:00, reservations appreciated, Via Jacopo 24, tel. 0187-807-253, busy Roberto and Francesca).

$$ Taverna Garibaldi is a good-value, cozy place on the most characteristic street in Levanto, serving focaccia with various toppings, made-to-order *farinata* (savory chickpea crêpe), over 30 types of pizza, and salads (Fri-Wed 19:00-22:00, closed Thu, Via Garibaldi 57, tel. 0187-808-098).

$$ La Picea serves up prizewinning wood-fired pizzas to go, or dine at one of their few small tables (Wed-Sun 19:00-24:00 or until they use up their pizza dough, closed Mon-Tue, just off Piazza Cavour at Via della Concia 18, tel. 0187-802-063).

$$ Pizzeria L'Igea is tucked just inside the Campeggio Acquadolce campground, 50 yards past the hostel. It's a favorite among locals who know you don't have to be a camper to enjoy freshly made, budget-conscious pizza. Their specialty is *gattafin*, deep-fried herb-stuffed ravioli (daily 12:00-14:30 & 18:45-22:30, takeaway available, Via Guido Semenza 5, tel. 0187-807-293).

$ Enoteca La Compera offers a quiet respite on a hidden courtyard across the way from the campground. It's casual and friendly, serving a wide variety of panini that you can buy to-go, as well as plenty of wine, including affordable tastings, or *degustazione* (March-Oct daily 10:00-20:00, follow the red-brick road—under the stone arch—to Piazza della Compera 3, mobile 334-712-8517).

Picnics or Bites on the Go: *Focaccerie, rosticcerie,* and delis with takeout pasta abound on Via Dante Alighieri. **$ Focacceria il Falcone** has a great selection of focaccia with different toppings (daily 9:30-22:00, shorter hours off-season, Via Cairoli 19, tel. 0187-807-370). For more picnic options, try the *mercato* (mornings except Sun; see "Helpful Hints," page 407). It's fun to grab a crusty loaf of bread, then pair it with a pot of freshly made Genovese pesto (and other gifty edibles) from **$ Il Laboratorio del Pesto** (daily, Via Dante 14, tel. 0187-807-441). There are two **Crai supermarkets:** One is just off Piazza Cavour at Via del Municipio 5 (daily 8:00-13:00 & 16:30-20:00); the other is nearby on Piazza Staglieno (similar hours; for a shaded setting, lay out your spread on a bench in the grassy park at this piazza). Another fine picnic spot is Piazza Cristoforo Colombo, located east of the swimming pool, with benches and sea views.

Levanto Connections

From Levanto: To get to the Cinque Terre, you can take the **train** (2-3/hour, 4 minutes to Monterosso). A slower, more scenic option is the **boat**, which stops at every Cinque Terre town—except Corniglia—before heading to Porto Venere (April-Sept 2/day at 10:00 and 14:00, price depends on distance—for example, €9 one-way to Vernazza—or get a €32 all-day hop-on, hop-off ticket; only one return boat daily from Porto Venere—departs at about 17:00; get latest boat schedule and price sheet at TI or boat dock, tel. 0187-732-987 or 0187-818-440, www.navigazionegolfodeipoeti.it).

Sestri Levante

This peninsular town is squeezed as skinny as a hot dog between its two beaches. The pedestrian-friendly Corso Colombo, which runs down the middle of the peninsula, is lined with shops that sell takeaway pizza, pastries, and beach paraphernalia.

Hans Christian Andersen enjoyed his visit here in the mid-1800s, writing, "What a fabulous evening I spent in Sestri Levante!" One of the bays—Baia delle Favole—is named in his honor (*favole* means "fairy tale"). The small mermaid curled on the edge of the fountain behind the TI is another nod to the beloved Danish storyteller.

Orientation to Sestri Levante

Sestri Levante (pop. 18,000) is dominated by its big, dull modern town (in front of the train station). But don't be discouraged—the old town peninsula, a 10-minute walk away, has charm to spare.

Arrival in Sestri Levante: From the train station (no baggage storage), head straight out and across the piazza to go down Via Roma. When you reach the park, turn left and look for the TI (in a freestanding kiosk). Nearby, Corso Colombo heads along an enjoyable pedestrian zone to the old town peninsula and beaches.

Tourist Information: It's at Piazza Sant'Antonio 10 (June-Sept daily 10:00-14:00 & 15:00-18:00, shorter hours off-season and closed Mon mornings and all day Sun, tel. 0185-457-011). They can tell you about the local bike sharing program and direct you to the trail (south of town) for a 1.5-hour hike (each way) to the scenic Punta Manara promontory.

Market Day: It's on Saturday at Piazza Aldo Moro (8:00-13:00). Local producers of olive oil, cheese, jam, and honey set up on the first and third Saturdays of each month on Via Asilo Maria Teresa (where Via XXV Aprile and Corso Columbo meet).

Laundry: A self-service launderette is in the urban zone southeast of the train station (daily 8:30-20:30, Via Costantino Raffo 8, mobile 389-101-1454).

Sights in Sestri Levante

Stroll the Town

From the TI, take Corso Colombo (to the left of Bermuda Bar, eventually turns into Via XXV Aprile, then Via alla Penisola), which runs up the peninsula. Follow this street—lively with shops, eateries, and delightful pastel facades—for about five minutes. Just before you get to Piazza Matteotti with the large white church at the end, turn off for either beach (free Silenzio beach is on your left). Or continue on the street to the left of the church and head uphill. You'll pass a scenic amphitheater, then the evocative arches of a ruined chapel (bombed during World War II and left as a memorial). A few minutes farther on, past a stony Romanesque church, the road winds to the right to the Grand Hotel dei Castelli. The rocky, forested bluff at the end of the town's peninsula is actually the huge private backyard of this fancy hotel.

Beaches

These are named after the bays *(baie)* that they border. The less scenic, bigger beach, **Baia delle Favole,** is divided up much of the year (May-Sept) into sections that you must pay to enter. Fees, up to €30 per day in August, generally include chairs, umbrellas, and fewer crowds. There are several small free sections: at the ends and in the middle (look for *libere* signs, and ask *"Gratis?"* to make sure that it's free). For less expensive sections of beach (where you can rent a chair for about €8-10), ask for *spiaggia libera attrezzata* (spee-AH-jah LEE-behr-ah ah-treh-ZAHT-tah). The usual beach-town activities are clustered along this *baia:* boat rentals, sailing lessons, and bocce courts.

The town's other beach, **Baia del Silenzio,** is picturesque, narrow, virtually all free, and jam-packed, providing a good chance to see Italian families at play. There isn't much more to do here than unroll a beach towel and join in. Because of the bay's small size

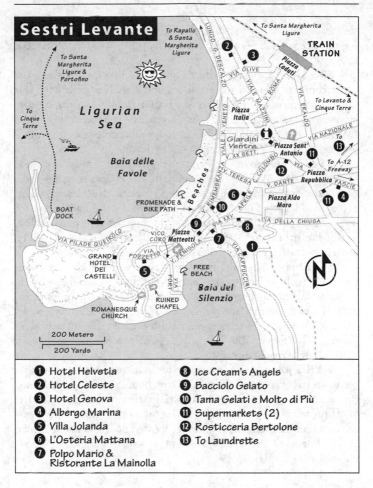

Sestri Levante

To Rapallo & Santa Margherita Ligure

To Santa Margherita Ligure

TRAIN STATION

To Santa Margherita Ligure & Portofino

To Cinque Terre

Ligurian Sea

Baia delle Favole

Beaches

BOAT DOCK

PROMENADE & BIKE PATH

To Levanto & Cinque Terre

To A-12 Freeway

Piazza Italia

Giardini Ventre

Piazza Sant' Antonio

Piazza Repubblica

Piazza Aldo Moro

VIA DELLA CHIUSA

VIA PILADE QUEIROLO

VICO CORO

Piazza Matteotti

VIA POZZETTO

GRAND HOTEL DEI CASTELLI

ROMANESQUE CHURCH

RUINED CHAPEL

FREE BEACH

Baia del Silenzio

200 Meters

200 Yards

1. Hotel Helvetia
2. Hotel Celeste
3. Hotel Genova
4. Albergo Marina
5. Villa Jolanda
6. L'Osteria Mattana
7. Polpo Mario & Ristorante La Mainolla
8. Ice Cream's Angels
9. Bacciolo Gelato
10. Tama Gelati e Molto di Più
11. Supermarkets (2)
12. Rosticceria Bertolone
13. To Laundrette

and the currents, the water gets warmer here than at **Baia delle Favole.** At the far end of Baia del Silenzio (under Hotel Helvetia) is **$$** Citto Beach bar, which offers front-row seats with bay views (summer until very late, spring and fall until sunset, sandwiches and salads at lunchtime only, Gilberto).

Sleeping in Sestri Levante

($$$$ = Splurge, $$$ = Pricier, $$ = Moderate, $ = Budget)
$$$$ Hotel Helvetia, overlooking Baia del Silenzio, feels posh and romantic, with 21 plush rooms, a large sun terrace with a heated, cliff-hanging swimming pool, and a peaceful garden atmosphere. This is a big splurge—with doubles north of €300 in peak season—but it sure is enticing (family rooms, air-con, elevator,

RIVIERA TOWNS

shuttle to off-site pay parking, closed Nov-March, Via Cappuccini 43, tel. 0185-41175, www.hotelhelvetia.it, helvetia@hotelhelvetia. it, Alex).

$$$ Hotel Celeste, a dream for beach lovers, rests along the waterfront. Its 41 rooms are modern and crisp. It's pricey for this range, but you're paying for the sea breeze (family rooms, air-con, elevator, attached beachside bar/breakfast terrace, Lungomare Descalzo 14, tel. 0185-485-005, www.hotelceleste.com, info@ hotelceleste.com, Franco).

$$ Hotel Genova, well-run by the Bertoni family, is a ship-shape hotel with 19 shiny-clean, modern, and cheery rooms—three with sea view, sunny lounge, rooftop sundeck, free loaner bikes, and a good location just two blocks from Baia delle Favole (ask for quieter room in back, family rooms, air-con, elevator, pay parking, Viale Mazzini 126, tel. 0185-41057, www.hotelgenovasestrilevante. com, info@hotelgenovasestrilevante.com, Stefano).

$$ Albergo Marina's friendly Magda and her brother Santo rent 23 peaceful, clean, good-value rooms done in sea-foam green. Though the hotel is located on a busy boulevard in the more urban part of town, rooms face a quiet back courtyard (family rooms, air-con, elevator, free self-service laundry, pool table, closed Nov-Easter, Via Fasce 100, tel. 0185-41527, www.marinahotel.it, marinahotel@marinahotel.it).

$ Villa Jolanda is a homey, bare-bones *pensione* on the hilly old town streets beyond the pedestrian zone. It has 17 dated rooms (five with little balconies and territorial views) and a garden court-yard/sun terrace—perfect for families on a budget...and the own-er's cats (family rooms, free parking, located near Baia del Silenzio at Via Pozzetto 15, tel. 0185-41354, www.villajolanda.it, info@ villajolanda.it, Mario).

Eating in Sestri Levante

($$$$ = Splurge, $$$ = Pricier, $$ = Moderate, $ = Budget)
Everything listed is on classic Via XXV Aprile, which also abounds with *focaccerie*, takeout pizza by the slice, and little grocery shops. Assemble a picnic or try one of the places below.

At **$$ L'Osteria Mattana,** where everyone shares long tables in two dining rooms (the second one is past the wood oven and brazier), you can mix with locals while enjoying traditional cuisine, listed on chalkboard menus (Mon-Fri 19:30-22:30, Sat-Sun 12:30-14:30 & 19:30-22:30, no dinner served Mon Nov-April, cash only; follow Corso Colombo from TI as it turns into Via XXV Aprile, restaurant on right at #34; tel. 0185-457-633, Marco).

$$$ Polpo Mario is classier, with a fun people-watching location on the main drag (Tue-Sun 12:15-15:00 & 19:00-23:00, closed Mon, Via XXV Aprile 163, tel. 0185-480-203).

$$ Ristorante La Mainolla offers pizzas, big salads, focaccia sandwiches, and reasonably priced pastas near Baia del Silenzio (daily 12:00-16:00 & 19:00-22:00, Via XXV Aprile 187, mobile 338-157-0877, tel. 0185-42792).

Gelato: There's no shortage of good gelato options. Tourists flock to **Ice Cream's Angels** at the intersection of Via XXV Aprile and Via della Chiusa. Riccardo and Elena artfully load up your cone and top it with a dollop of Nutella chocolate-hazelnut cream (open daily until late in summer). **Bacciolo** enjoys a similar popularity (closed Thu, Via XXV Aprile 51, on the right just before the church). **Tama Gelati e Molto di Più** makes their gelato with fresh ingredients daily (near the beach at Baia delle Favole, Viale Rimembranza 34).

Supermarket: You can stock up on picnic supplies at two **Carrefour Express** branches on Piazza della Repubblica, at #1 (Mon-Sat 8:00-13:00 & 15:30-19:30, closed Sun) and #28 (daily 8:00-24:00).

Deli: For a takeout meal, head to **$ Rosticceria Bertolone** for roasted anything—beef, pork, chicken, or vegetables. Assemble an entire meal from their deli and ask them to heat it for you (Mon-Sat 7:30-13:00 & 16:00-19:30, open Sun mornings in summer but otherwise closed Sun, Via Fascie Vincenzo 12, tel. 0185-487-098).

Sestri Levante Connections

By **train,** Sestri Levante is just 30 minutes from Monterosso (hourly connections with Monterosso; nearly hourly with other Cinque Terre towns, requiring a change in Levanto or Monterosso) and 30 minutes from Santa Margherita Ligure (2/hour).

Boats depart to the Cinque Terre, Porto Venere, Santa Margherita Ligure, Portofino, and San Fruttuoso from the dock *(molo)* on the peninsula (Easter-Oct, tel. 0185-284-670, www.traghettiportofino.it).

Santa Margherita Ligure

If you need the Riviera of movie stars, park your yacht at Portofino. Or you can settle down with more elbow room in nearby and more personable Santa Margherita Ligure (pop. 10,200, one hour by train from the Cinque Terre). While Portofino's velour allure is tarnished by a nonstop traffic jam in peak season, Santa Margherita tumbles easily downhill from its train station. The town has a fun Old World resort character and a breezy harborfront with a beach promenade. With its nice big-city vitality, it feels bustling and lived-in, even off-season.

On a quick day trip from Milan or the Cinque Terre, walk the beach promenade and see the small old town of Santa Margherita Ligure before catching the bus or boat to Portofino to discover what all the fuss is about. With more time, Santa Margherita makes a fine overnight stop or home base for hiking the Portofino peninsula or a foray into the Cinque Terre.

Orientation to Santa Margherita Ligure

TOURIST INFORMATION

The TI is as central as can be (at the harborside of the city traffic hub, Piazza Veneto). The ATP bus office is next door, and bus #82 to Portofino stops at the curb in front (April-Sept daily 9:30-13:00 & 16:30-19:00, shorter hours off-season, tel. 0185-287-485, www. smlturismo.it).

ARRIVAL IN SANTA MARGHERITA LIGURE

By Train: The station is a pleasant, low-stress scene. The bar/café (facing track 1) stores bags (€2.50/day) and sells bus, train, and sightseeing-boat tickets. Enjoy its crazy clocks while you sip an espresso awaiting your train.

To get from the station to the city center, take the stairs marked *Mare* (sea) down to the harbor; or turn right and head more gently down Via Roma, which leads to the town center, TI, start of my town walk, and recommended hotels (about 10 minutes away on foot). Bus #82 to Portofino stops a few steps below the station (2/hour, €3 from station bar/café, €5 from driver).

By Car: Ask your hotel about parking (some have free spots). Otherwise, try a private lot (about €15/half-day, €20/24 hours) such as **Autopark,** next to the post office (Via Roma 38, tel. 0185-287-818). An hourly parking lot is by the harbor, in front of the fish market (pay-and-display, €2.50/hour). Parking is generally free where there are white lines; blue lines mean you pay.

HELPFUL HINTS

Laundry: Close to Piazza Mazzini is **Bolle Blu** (daily 7:00-22:30, Via Roccatagliata 39, mobile 335-642-7203).

Bike Rental: GM Rent is at Via XXV Aprile 11 (also rents scooters and Smart Cars, daily 10:00-13:00 & 16:30-20:00, mobile 329-406-6274, www.gmrent.it, Francesco).

Taxi: Taxis wait outside the train station and charge €15 for a ride to anywhere in town, €25 to Paraggi beach, and €35 to Portofino (tel. 0185-286-508).

Driver: Helpful taxi driver **Alessandro,** who has five cars and two minivans, offers airport transfers to Genoa, Milan, Florence, and Nice. He is also available for local excursions, including all-day trips to the Cinque Terre (mobile 338-860-2349, www.alessandrotaxi.com, alessandrotaxi@yahoo.it).

Local Guide: Roberta De Beni is good (€100/half-day, €165/day, mobile 349-530-4778, diodebe@inwind.it).

Santa Margherita Ligure Walk

Get your bearings and cover the basics of Santa Margherita Ligure with this little self-guided walk.

• *Start at the square facing the exuberant Baroque facade of the Basilica of Santa Margherita.*

Piazza Caprera: Each day this square hosts a few farmers selling their produce. On the corner of Via Cavour, just next to the basilica, visit **Seghezzo,** a venerable grocer where locals know they'll find whatever they need (described later, under "Eating in Santa Margherita Ligure").

• *Now take a side trip right up the* "via principale" *(main drag) of the city, Via Palestro/Via Cavour. You'll go two blocks up to Piazza Mazzini and back.*

"Via Principale": The main "street" here is really two parallel streets divided by very tall and skinny buildings. We'll start by taking Via Cavour (on the left, by Seghezzo grocery) and come back on Via Palestro. As you walk, study the characteristic, Art Nouveau house-painting from the turn of the last century. Before 1900, people distinguished their buildings with pastel paint and distinctive door and window frames. Then they decided to get fancy and paint entire exteriors with false balconies, weapons, saints, beautiful women, and 3-D Gothic effects.

Strolling up Via Cavour, look through the skinny shops on the right, which also front Via Palestro. Where the two streets merge is the recommended Angolo 48 restaurant (you might reserve a table for dinner as you pass by).

Continue strolling to the big square, Piazza Mazzini, then do a U-turn to return on Via Palestro toward the big church. At #34 (on the left), you'll pass a traditional *panificio* (bakery) where you can say, *"Vorrei un etto di focaccia"* to treat yourself to about a quarter-pound of the region's famed bread (a hearty snack for two). Just beyond, on the right at #13, **Fruttivendolo "Milanese"** sells a

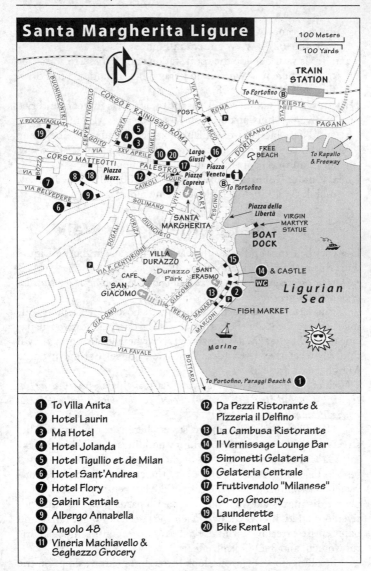

Santa Margherita Ligure

100 Meters
100 Yards

- ① To Villa Anita
- ② Hotel Laurin
- ③ Ma Hotel
- ④ Hotel Jolanda
- ⑤ Hotel Tigullio et de Milan
- ⑥ Hotel Sant'Andrea
- ⑦ Hotel Flory
- ⑧ Sabini Rentals
- ⑨ Albergo Annabella
- ⑩ Angolo 48
- ⑪ Vineria Machiavello & Seghezzo Grocery
- ⑫ Da Pezzi Ristorante & Pizzeria il Delfino
- ⑬ La Cambusa Ristorante
- ⑭ Il Vernissage Lounge Bar
- ⑮ Simonetti Gelateria
- ⑯ Gelateria Centrale
- ⑰ Fruttivendolo "Milanese"
- ⑱ Co-op Grocery
- ⑲ Launderette
- ⑳ Bike Rental

staggering variety of tempting produce and glass-jarred delicacies. In general, the family and community feel all along here is a joy.

• *See you back at the church.*

Basilica of Santa Margherita: The town's main church is textbook Italian Baroque (free, daily 7:30-12:00 & 15:00-18:30). Its 18th-century facade hides a 17th-century interior slathered with art and dripping with chandeliers. The altar is typical of 17th-century Ligurian altars—shaped like a boat, with lots of shelf space for candles, flowers, and relics. Its centerpiece is a much-venerated statue of Our Lady of the Rose. She's adorned this altar since 1756 and is credited with lots of miracles.

Baroque is theater...and this altar is stagecraft. After the Vatican II decrees of the 1960s, priests began to face their flocks instead of the old altars. For this reason, all over the Catholic world, modern tables serving as post-Vatican II altars stand in front of earlier altars, like the one here, that are no longer the center of attention during Mass.

Wander the church and its chapels, noticing the inlaid-marble floors and sparkling glass chandeliers. As you marvel at the richness, remember that the region's aristocrats amassed wealth from trade from the 11th to the 15th century. When Constantinople fell to the Turks in 1453, free trade in the Mediterranean stopped, and Genovese traders became bankers—making even more money. A popular saying of the day was, "Silver is born in America, lives in Spain, and dies in Genoa." Bankers here served Spain's 17th-century royalty and aristocracy, and the accrued wealth paid for a Golden Age of art.

• *Walk straight in front of the church a block to busy Largo Antonio Giusti. Next to the cinema (across the street), a penguin marks a recommended gelateria. Head right to Piazza Veneto, with its busy roundabout and little park on the harbor. In the park facing the roundabout stands the TI, ATP bus office, and a bus #82 stop for Portofino. Use the crosswalks to negotiate the busy intersection and reach the promenade.*

Beachfront Promenade: Stroll to the left along Corso Doria. The sidewalk is wider than the street, an indication that for more than 100 years this has been the place to promenade under century-old pastel facades. You'll pass the grand old **Lido Palace Hotel** with its view balconies overlooking a crowded beach scene.

• *Turn around and go back to Piazza Veneto. Continue walking the other direction along the water toward the little castle.*

You'll pass a rack of metal panels limiting political advertising for each party (great idea, wouldn't you say?). Next comes a Christopher Columbus statue. He was born "Cristoforo Colombo" in 1451 in Genoa, near here—although some claim he was Spanish or Portuguese—and first sailed on Genovese boats along this Ligurian coast. Next comes a statue of King Victor Emmanuel II, always ready to brandish his sword and create Italy.

• *Before arriving at the castle, head out the little pier with the white statue facing out to sea.*

View from the Pier: From here, standing with "Santa Margherita Virgin Martyr," you can take in all of Santa Margherita Ligure—from the villas dotting the hills, to the castle built in the 16th century to defend against pirates, to the exclusive hotels.

Tourist boats to Portofino, the Cinque Terre, and beyond depart from this pier.

• *Continue along the waterfront on Corso Marconi.*

Harbor and Fish Market: Notice the trendy, recommended Il Vernissage Lounge Bar with tables up at the base of the castle. Continuing around the corner from the castle (closed to visitors), walk along the harbor. The region's largest fishing fleet—20 boats—ties up here. The fishing industry survives, drag-netting octopus, shrimp, and miscellaneous "blue fish." (Anchovies are no longer fished from here but from nearby Sestri Levante). The fish market (Mercato del Pesca, across the street, inside the rust-colored building with arches and columns) wiggles weekdays from about 16:00 until 20:00 or so—depending on who's catching what and when. It's a cool scene as fishermen take bins of freshly caught fish directly to waiting customers.

• *Climb the narrow brick stairs just to the right of the fish market to a delightful little square. Find the characteristic, black-and-white pebble mosaic and relax on the benches to enjoy harbor views. Facing the square is the little...*

Oratory of Sant'Erasmo: Named for St. Erasmus, the protector of sailors, this church is actually an "oratory," where a brotherhood of faithful men who did anonymous good deeds congregated and worshipped. While rarely open, do check. The interior is decorated with ships and paintings of storms that the local seafarers survived—thanks to St. Erasmus. The huge crosses standing in the nave are carried through town on special religious holidays.

• *Your walk is over. For a little extra exercise and to see a delightful park, climb the long stairs from here up to the Church of San Giacomo (with an interior similar to the Basilica of Santa Margherita) and Durazzo Park (described next).*

Sights in Santa Margherita Ligure

Durazzo Park (Parco di Villa Durazzo)
This park is a delight, with a breezy café, a carefully coiffed Italian garden, and an intentionally wild "English garden" below (free, daily 9:00-19:00, until 20:00 July-Aug, closes earlier off-season, WC near café). The Italian garden is famous for its varied collection of palm trees and an extensive collection of camellias. It's OK to feed the large turtles in the central pond (they like bits of fish or meat). The park is dominated by **Villa Durazzo;** it's not worth touring but hosts concerts—mostly in summer.

Beaches
The handiest free Santa Margherita beaches are just below the train station toward the boat dock. But the best beaches are on the south side of town. Among these, I like **"Giò e Rino Beach"** (just

Rise of a Resort: The History of Santa Margherita Ligure

This town, like the entire region (from the border of France to La Spezia), was once ruled by the Republic of Genoa. In the 16th

century, when Arab pirates from North Africa plagued the entire coastal area, Genoa built castles in the towns and look-out towers in the neighboring hills.

At the time, Santa Margherita was actually two bickering towns—each with its own bay. In 1800, Napoleon came along, took over the Republic of Genoa, and turned the rival towns into one city—naming it Porto Napoleone. When Napoleon fell in 1815, the town stayed united and took the name of the patron saint of its leading church, Santa Margherita.

In 1850, residents set to work creating a Riviera resort. They imported palm trees from North Africa and paved a fine beach promenade. Santa Margherita (and the surrounding area) was studded with fancy villas built by the aristocracy of Genoa. English, Russian, and German aristocrats discovered the town in the 19th century. Mass tourism only hit in the last generation. Even with the increased crowds, the town decided to stay chic and kept huge developments out. Its neighbor, Rapallo, chose the extreme opposite—giving the Italian language a new word for uncontrolled growth ruining a once-cute town: *rapallizzazione*.

before Covo di Nord Est)—not too expensive, with fun, creative management and a young crowd. Also nice is the beach on the south side of **Hotel Miramare,** which offers a more relaxing sun-worshipping experience. Both beaches have free entry and rentable chairs and umbrellas. They're a 20-minute walk from downtown, or take the bus from either the train station or Piazza Veneto (bus tickets-€1.80, €2.80 from driver).

Paraggi beach, which is halfway to Portofino (with an easy bus connection—see "Portofino," later in this chapter, and the map on page 430), is better than any Santa Margherita beach, but it's pricey (as much as €50/day in July and August). One Paraggi beach operator, Bosetti, offers a more reasonable rate (€30/day, includes umbrella, lounge chair, and towel). In high season, the Paraggi beach may be all booked up by big shots from Portofino, which has no beach—only rocks. Off-season, the entire beach is all yours and free of charge. A skinny patch of sand smack-dab in the middle of Paraggi beach is free year-round.

▲▲Portofino Side-Trip

One of the most beautiful and famous little Mediterranean resorts—Portofino—is just a couple miles down the coast and is so easy to visit from Santa Margherita that it can be considered a sight (details on page 429).

Sleeping in Santa Margherita Ligure

($$$$ = Splurge, $$$ = Pricier, $$ = Moderate, $ = Budget)

$$$$ Villa Anita is an elegant-yet-homey family hotel run by Daniela and her son, Sandro. They rent 12 tidy rooms—nearly all with terraces and all with new, high-tech bathrooms—overlooking a peaceful residential neighborhood a five-minute uphill walk from the seaside boulevard. The in-house chef offers a varying menu of Ligurian specialties (dinner extra—not available Mon, family rooms, playground, small gym, small heated pool and sauna, aircon, free parking, closed in winter, Viale Minerva 25, tel. 0185-286-543, www.hotelvillaanita.com, info@hotelvillaanita.com).

$$$$ Hotel Laurin offers slick, modern, air-conditioned, pricey American-style lodgings fixated on harborfront views. All 44 rooms face the sea, most have terraces, and a small pool and gym are on the sundeck. Enrico and staff are helpful (RS%, double-paned windows, elevator, air-con, limited pay parking—request when you reserve, just past the castle, Corso Marconi 3, tel. 0185-289-971, www.laurinhotel.it, info@laurinhotel.it).

$$$ Ma Hotel is a charming, crystal-chandelier-classy boutique hotel with a fresh, modern flair. Although it sits along a busy street, its 11 stylish and spacious rooms are set at the back of the building (air-con, patio, free minibar, loaner bikes, Via XXV Aprile 18, tel. 0185-280-224, www.mahotel.it, info@mahotel.it).

$$$ Pastine Hotels: This small chain of well-run hotels combines solid service, sumptuous public spaces, and older rooms. The two main branches are around the corner from each other, an easy walk from the station: **Hotel Jolanda** has 50 rooms, lavish public spaces, and regal colors, but many rooms come with street noise and are getting a bit long in the tooth (RS%, air-con, elevator, free use of small weight room, wet and dry saunas, free loaner bikes, Via Luisito Costa 6, tel. 0185-287-512, www.hoteljolanda.it, info@hoteljolanda.it); **Hotel Tigullio et de Milan** is smaller and tidier, with updated rooms (the superior rooms are especially nice and worth a few extra euros) and a rooftop sun terrace with a bar and hot tub in the summer (RS%, air-con, elevator, a few free parking spots, free loaner bikes, Via Rainusso 3, tel. 0185-287-455, www.

hoteltigullio.eu, info@hoteltigullio.eu). The newest branch, the boutique-y **Hotel Sant'Andrea,** has 12 rooms near Piazza Mazzini (RS%, air-con, elevator, free parking, Via Belvedere 10, mobile 366-661-8616, www.hotelsantandrea.net, info@hotelsantandrea.net).

$$ Hotel Flory, spanning two buildings surrounded by flowers and greenery, is an old-school, basic hotel with 16 dated rooms and thin walls. It's run enthusiastically by Florinda (who wants to practice her English with you) and Enrico, whose three kids make this a family-friendly place (family rooms, some rooms have balconies, cheaper rooms with private bath down the hall, small public patio, fans, no elevator, rooftop terrace, free loaner bikes, laundry service, pay parking, Via Bozzo 3, tel. 0185-286-435, www.hotelflory.it, hotelflory@hotelflory.it).

$$ Sabini Rentals, in a dull residential zone, offers three straightforward rooms and one apartment with a tiny corner kitchen (RS%, family rooms, 2-night minimum, cash only, Via Belvedere 31, mobile 338-902-7582, www.sabinirentals.com, info@sabinirentals.com, Cristina and Giancarlo).

$ Albergo Annabella is an old-style budget throwback, with nine basic rooms. The **$$** rooms with bathrooms and air-conditioning are overpriced, but the **$** rooms with shared bath and fans are a solid budget option (family rooms, no breakfast, Via Costasecca 10, mobile 380-328-0542, tesibruno@gmail.com, Annabella speaks limited English).

Eating in Santa Margherita Ligure

IN THE CITY CENTER

$$$ Angolo 48, run by savvy Elisa and Valentina, serves beautifully presented and reasonably priced Genovese and Ligurian dishes. At this cool-without-the-pretense locale, reservations are important; there's great seating both on the square and inside. Try their handmade *pansotti* in walnut sauce (lunch served Wed and Sat-Sun 12:00-13:45, dinner nightly 18:30-22:00, Via Palestro 48, tel. 0185-286-650).

$$ Vineria Machiavello feels more urban Tuscan than seaside Ligurian. This well-stocked *enoteca* (wine shop) offers tastings and full bottles, but also serves a short and enticing menu of well-priced dishes at a few humble tables tucked between the wine racks. The menu, which goes beyond seafood and pesto, is a nice break from the Riviera rut (Wed-Mon 10:00-14:00 & 17:30-24:00, closed Tue, in the heart of the pedestrian zone at Via Cavour 17, tel. 0185-286-122).

$$ Da Pezzi, with a cheap cafeteria-style atmosphere, is packed with locals at midday and at night. They're munching *fari-*

nata (crêpes made from chickpeas, available Oct-May 18:00-20:00) standing at the bar, or enjoying pesto and fresh fish in the dining room. Consider the deli counter with its Genovese picnic ingredients (Sun-Fri 10:00-14:00 & 17:00-21:00, table service after 12:00 and 18:00, closed Sat, Via Cavour 21, tel. 0185-285-303, Giancarlo and Giobatta).

ON THE WATERFRONT

All along the harbor side of Via Tommaso Bottaro, south of the marina, you'll find restaurants, pizzerias, and bars serving food with a nautical view. These places are a notch above.

$$$ La Cambusa, perched above the fish market, is popular for its seafood. While the food is forgettable, the view from its harborside terrace is not. In cooler weather, the terrace is covered and heated. Diners receive a free glass of *sciacchetrà* (dessert wine) and biscotti with this book (daily 12:00-15:00 & 19:00-24:00 except closed Thu Oct-June, Via Tommaso Bottaro 1, tel. 0185-287-410, www.ristorantelacambusa.net).

At **$$ Il Vernissage Lounge Bar,** you can nurse your €8 drink with a million-dollar view. There are 20 wines by the glass, plus cocktails and spritzes, which always come with a nice plate of finger food (March-Oct daily 18:00-late, Sun from 11:00, Salita al Castello 8, mobile 349-220-5846, Sandro).

BUDGET OPTIONS

$$ Pizzeria il Delfino serves thin, big, wood-fired pizzas. It's a rustic and fun local scene with a few quiet tables outside and tight inside seating under nautical bric-a-brac (daily 12:00-15:00 & 18:00-23:00 except closed Tue dinner, Via Cavour 29, tel. 0185-286-488).

Gelato: The best *gelateria* I found in town—with chocolate-truffle *tartufato*—is **Simonetti** (under the castle at Piazza Martiri della Libertà 48). **Gelateria Centrale,** just off Piazza Veneto near the cinema, serves up their specialty—*pinguino* (penguin), a cone with your choice of gelato dipped in chocolate (Largo Antonio Giusti 14).

Groceries: Classy **Seghezzo** is great for a meal to go—ask them to *riscaldare* (heat up) their white *lasagne al pesto* or dish up their special *carpaccio di polpo*—thinly sliced octopus (daily June-Aug 7:30-13:00 & 15:30-20:00, closed Wed Sept-May, right of the church on Via Cavour, tel. 0185-287-172). The **Co-op** grocery, off Piazza Mazzini at Corso Giacomo Matteotti 9, is cheaper and less romantic (daily 8:15-13:00 & 15:30-19:30 except closed Sun afternoons). Either is a good place to stock up on well-priced Ligurian olive oil, pasta, and pesto.

Santa Margherita Ligure Connections

From Santa Margherita Ligure by Train: To reach the **Cinque Terre** towns (beyond Monterosso), you'll usually have to change in Sestri Levante, Levanto, or Monterosso (around 1.5 hours total). Other connections: **Sestri Levante** (2/hour, 30 minutes), **Monterosso** (hourly, 45 minutes), **La Spezia** (hourly, 1-1.5 hours), **Pisa** (1-2/hour, 2 hours, most with transfer, less frequent InterCity/IC goes direct), **Milan** (about hourly, 2.5 hours, more with transfer in Genoa), **Ventimiglia**/French border (4/day, 4 hours; or hourly with change in Genoa), **Venice** (at least hourly, 6 hours with changes). For **Florence,** transfer in Pisa (8/day, 4 hours). See "Getting Around the Cinque Terre—By Train" on page 322 for details.

By Boat to the Cinque Terre: Tour boats make various trips to Vernazza, Porto Venere, and other ports about daily for around €20. Pick up a schedule of departures and excursion options from the TI, visit the ticket shack on the dock, call tel. 0185-284-670, or check online at www.traghettiportofino.it.

Portofino

Santa Margherita Ligure, with its aristocratic architecture, hints at old money. But nearby Portofino (pop. 500)—with its sleek jewelry

shops, art galleries, and haute couture boutiques filling a humble village shell—has the sheen of new money. It's the kind of place where the sailing masts are taller than the houses and church steeples. But the *piccolo* harbor, classic Italian ar-
chitecture, and wooded peninsula turn glitzy Portofino into an appealing package. It makes a fun and easy day trip from Santa Margherita Ligure.

Planning Your Time: My favorite Portofino plan is to visit in the late afternoon. Leave Santa Margherita on the bus at about 16:30, get off at Paraggi beach, and hike about 30 minutes over the bluff into Portofino. Explore: Splurge for a drink on the harborfront, or get a takeout fruity sundae (*paciugo;* pah-CHOO-goh) and sit by the water. Then return by bus to Santa Margherita for dinner (confirm late departures). If you plan to do some hiking around Portofino, come earlier in the day.

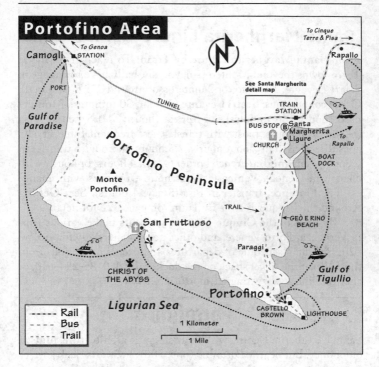

GETTING TO PORTOFINO

Portofino makes an easy day trip from Santa Margherita by bus, boat, bike, or foot. For a fun combination, go one way by boat, and the other via bus and on foot from Paraggi.

By Bus: Catch bus #82 from Santa Margherita's train station or at bus stops along the harbor (main stop in front of TI, €3 one-way or €4 from driver, €5 round-trip, 2/hour—hourly on Sun, 15 minutes, goes to Paraggi beach and then to Portofino). Buy tickets at the train station bar; at Piazza Veneto's green bus kiosk or the nearby green ticket machine (next to the TI); or at any newsstand, tobacco shop, or shop that displays a *Biglietti Bus* sign. If you're at the Piazza Veneto kiosk, grab a bus schedule to plan your return (last bus around 23:00, earlier on Sun).

By Boat and Bus: If you've arrived in Portofino by boat but are bussing back, follow the narrow lanes up from the harbor to find Piazza Martiri della Libertà and the bus stop (ticket machine on right; tobacco store on left also sells tickets).

By Taxi: A taxi from Santa Margherita will cost around €35 to Portofino or €25 to Paraggi beach. (Taxi stands in Santa Margherita are at the train station and down by the water on Via Pescino, not far from the TI.)

By Boat: The boat makes the 15-minute trip with more class and scenery, and without the traffic jams (€6.50 one-way, €9.50 round-trip; hourly departures April-Oct daily 10:15-16:15, fewer off-season; dock is a 2-minute walk from Piazza Veneto off Piazza Martiri della Libertà, tel. 0185-284-670, www.traghettiportofino.it).

By Bike: The 25-minute bike ride from Santa Margherita to Portofino is doable for cautious cyclists. While there are no steep hills to struggle up, the road is narrow, with many blind corners. Many of my recommended hotels provide free loaner bikes (though they may not be in the best condition); you can also rent your own wheels (see page 420).

On Foot: To hike the entire distance from Santa Margherita Ligure to Portofino, you have two options: You can follow the sidewalk along (and sometimes hanging over) the sea (1 hour, 2.5 miles)—although traffic can be noisy, and in places, the footpath disappears. Or, if you're hardy and ambitious, you can take a quieter two-hour hike by leaving Santa Margherita at Via Maragliano, then follow the Ligurian-symbol trail markers (keep a close eye out for red-and-white stripes). This hike takes you high into the hills. Keep left after Cappelletta delle Gave. Several blocks past a castle, you'll drop down into the Paraggi beach, where you'll take the Portofino trail the rest of the way.

Bus-and-Hike Option: For a shorter—but very rewarding—30-minute hike into Portofino, ride bus #82 from Santa Margherita only as far as the small but ritzy Paraggi beach. (Ask on board where to get off—watch for an inland bay with green water and a sandy beach.) At the far end of the beach, cross the street, climb the steps, and follow the hilly, paved trail marked *Pedonale per Portofino* high above the road. There's a fair amount of up and down, but it's all well-paved and scenic. After Paraggi, you'll curl around another bay—with the famously top-end Hotel Splendido hovering on the hill above—before snaking your way to Portofino. You'll enter Portofino at a yellow-and-gray-striped church labeled *Divo Martino*—which I figure means "the divine Martin" and has something to do with Dean Martin giving us all "Volare" (which I couldn't get out of my head for the rest of the day).

It's easy to **reverse the bus-and-hike option,** going from Portofino to Santa Margherita: Find the *Pedonale per Paraggi* trail near the Divo Martino church, hike over to the beach, and find the bus #82 stop right where you pop out at the bay. This option is recommended only when things are relatively quiet—on busy days, return buses fill up in Portofino and won't stop in Paraggi.

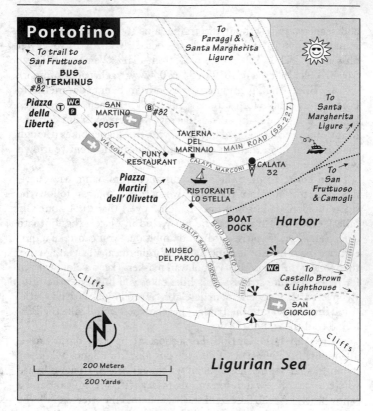

Portofino

To Paraggi &
Santa Margherita
Ligure

To trail to
San Fruttuoso

BUS
Ⓑ TERMINUS
#82

Piazza
della
Libertà
Ⓣ WC P
🅿 POST
SAN
MARTINO
Ⓑ #82

To
Santa
Margherita
Ligure

TAVERNA
DEL
MARINAIO
MAIN ROAD (SS-227)

VIA ROMA
PUNY ◆
RESTAURANT
CALATA MARCONI
CALATA
32

Piazza
Martiri
dell' Olivetta
RISTORANTE
LO STELLA

To
San
Fruttuoso
& Camogli

BOAT
DOCK
Harbor

SALITA SAN GIORGIO
MOLO UMBERTO I
MUSEO
DEL PARCO

WC
To
Castello Brown
& Lighthouse

Cliffs

SAN
GIORGIO

Cliffs

200 Meters
200 Yards

Ligurian Sea

Sights in Portofino

▲▲Self-Guided Visual Tour from the Harbor

Stand or sit on the angled boat launch where Piazza Martiri dell'Olivetta meets the harbor (or nurse an overpriced cocktail at the nearby café tables), and get oriented to Portofino.

Scanning the humble houses around the harbor, notice the painted-on details—as in Santa Margherita Ligure. You may also see laundry hanging out to dry—a jarring reminder that, while Ferragamo and Prada may reside on street level, actual villagers still live upstairs.

Now look out to the well-protected natural harbor—which has held substantial strategic value ever since the Romans first founded a town here. Since then, it has been appreciated by everyone from Napoleon to the Nazis.

A new flock of fans arrived in the 1950s, when *National Geographic* did a beautiful exposé on the idyllic port. Locals claim that's when the Hollywood elite took note. Liz Taylor and Richard Burton came here annually (as did Liz Taylor and Eddie Fisher).

During one famous party, Rex Harrison dropped his Oscar into the bay (it was recovered). Ava Gardner came down from her villa each evening for a drink—sporting her famous fur coat. Greta Garbo loved to swim naked in the harbor, not knowing (or caring) that half the town was watching. Truman Capote also called Portofino home. But VIPs were also here a century earlier. Friedrich Nietzsche famously wrote about philosophizing with the mythical prophet Zarathustra on the path between Portofino and Santa Margherita.

Today, the celebrity cachet lives on. When you tell locals you're going to Portofino, they say, "Maybe you'll see George Clooney!" Count the yachts and the tall-masted sailboats, and imagine who might be on them.

Now scan the panorama on the hillside in front of you. On the left is the **Castello Brown,** an actual medieval castle built by the Genovese in the 16th century to protect this strategic harbor. It later became a private mansion, and today is a museum featuring lush gardens, sweeping viewpoints, and special exhibits about Portofino and its history (€5, daily June-Aug 10:00-19:00, April-May and Sept-Oct until 18:00, shorter hours off-season, tel. 0185-267-101, www.castellobrown.com).

Panning right, you'll see the **Church of San Giorgio,** with its popular viewpoint terrace looking down over the port and out over the open ocean. This is an easy option for a hike with rewarding views. Boats back to Portofino, or on to the San Fruttuoso Abbey, depart from the harborfront below this church. The Museo del Parco (described next) is also along this embankment.

Now look back toward town. A tidy grid of narrow cobbled streets angles gently uphill to the modern part of town, around Piazza Martiri della Libertà (where you'll find the bus stop back to Santa Margherita Ligure). These streets—where budget takeaway eateries and grocery stores are mixed in with swanky shops—are a good place to hunt for picnic fixings. Up on the right is the striped church of San Martino, marking the well-manicured, rewarding 30-minute trail to Paraggi beach.

Museo del Parco

For an artsy break, walk around the harbor to the right, where you can stroll around a park littered with 148 contemporary sculptures by mostly Italian artists, including a few top names (€5, June-Sept Wed-Mon 10:00-13:30 & 15:00-20:00; closed Tue, off-season, and in bad weather; mobile 337-333-737).

Hikes

The **Parco di Portofino** can provide detailed information on the many hiking trails that crisscross Portofino's regional parklands (tel. 0185 289-479, www.parcoportofino.it). Here are a few options easily accessible from Portofino itself:

Lighthouse Hike: A paved stone path winds up and down to the lighthouse *(faro)* at the scenic point beyond the Church of San Giorgio. Take the stairs on the right just after Museo del Parco, and keep going past the church. Hedges block views until the end, when you'll be rewarded with the open sea—and a lounge/bar (open May-Sept, 25-minute walk). Consider popping into the medieval Castello Brown on the way up or down (described earlier).

Paraggi Beach Hike: You can stroll the hilly pedestrian promenade through the trees from Portofino to Paraggi beach, and, if you're lucky, see a wild boar en route (30 minutes, path starts to the right of striped Divo Martino church just above the harborfront piazza, and ends at ritzy Paraggi beach, where bus #82 stops on its way back to Santa Margherita Ligure).

San Fruttuoso Abbey Hike: Another option is to hike out to San Fruttuoso Abbey and the nearby underwater Christ statue—see next.

NEAR PORTOFINO
San Fruttuoso Abbey (Abbazia di San Fruttuoso)
This 11th-century abbey is accessible only by foot or boat. But the abbey itself isn't the main attraction. The more intriguing draw is

60 feet underwater, offshore from the abbey, in a specially protected marine area: the statue *Christ of the Abyss (Cristo degli Abissi)*. A boat will take you out to a spot above the statue, where you can look down to just barely see the arms of Jesus—outstretched, reaching upward. Some people bring goggles and dive in for a better view. The statue was placed there in 1954 for the divine protection of the region's divers (€6, trips depart from San Fruttuoso July-Aug Sat at 15:30, some Mon and Wed sailings—check schedule at www.sopraesottoilmare.net or ask at the Santa Margherita Ligure TI).

Cost and Hours: Abbey entry-€5; June-mid-Sept daily 10:00-17:45; shorter hours off-season and closed Mon in winter; last entry 45 minutes before closing, tel. 0185-772-703, http://eng.fondoambiente.it

Getting There by Boat: The same boats that link Santa Margherita Ligure and Portofino continue on to the San Fruttuoso Abbey (schedule at www.traghettiportofino.it). From Easter through September, a different company's boats continue north from the abbey to Camogli (train station), Recco, and Punta Chiappa (€5-8 one-way, can return to Santa Margherita by train from Camogli or buy round-trip boat tickets, tel. 0185-772-091, schedule at www.golfoparadiso.it). For details inquire at the TI in Santa Margherita.

Getting There by Foot: The trail from Portofino to the abbey is steep at the beginning and end (about 2.5 hours—pick up the trailhead at the inland-most point of town, past Piazza Martiri della Libertà and the *carabinieri* station). You can also hike all the way there from Santa Margherita in about 4.5 hours via Portofino.

Eating in Portofino

Portofino offers all kinds of harborside dining, but the quality often doesn't match the high prices. I'd rather dine in Santa Margherita Ligure. But if you do eat in Portofino, **$$$ Ristorante lo Stella,** just a few steps from the boat dock, has well-prepared dishes, friendly servers, and portholes in the bathrooms. **$$$ Taverna del Marinaio,** across the harbor, has a prime location (soaking up the last of the day's sun), tables under arcades, and a small, cozy/classy interior. And **$$$$ Puny,** at the top of the harborfront square, is a famous splurge (reserve ahead, www.tavernadelmarinaio.com).

If you're on a **budget,** you'll find a variety of *foccacerie,* pizzerias, and grocery stores hiding out in the tiny grid of streets just up from the water. For dessert, opposite the boat dock, little **Calata 32** is well-regarded for its gelato.

South of the Cinque Terre

The area south of the Cinque Terre is known to most travelers for the transit-hub nothing-special town of La Spezia, with its excellent train connections. But nearby is a little gem—the resort town of Porto Venere.

La Spezia

While just a quick train ride south of the fanciful Cinque Terre (20-30 minutes), the working city of La Spezia (pop. 94,000) feels like "reality Italy." Primarily a transit point connecting to the Cinque Terre, lovely Porto Venere, or to Pisa, Lucca, and other Tuscan towns, La Spezia is slim on sights and has no beaches. In

La Spezia

400 Meters
400 Yards

To Il Gelsomino

To Cinque Terre & Genoa

TRAIN STATION
CINQUE TERRE
PARK OFFICE & ⓘ

RAIL TUNNEL

To Pisa

SPALLANZANI TUNNEL

Piazza Brin

Piazza S. Bon.

MUSEO AMADEO LIA

PIAZZA D'ARMI

To Porto Venere & Cinque Terre

Piazza Cavour

POST

To Santa María del Mare Monastery & A12 Autostrada

Lagora Canal

Piazza Chiodo

VIALE ITALIA WATERFRONT PROMENADE

NAVAL MUSEUM

Boats to Lerici, Porto Venere & Cinque Terre (April-Oct)

❶ Hotel Firenze e Continentale
❷ Mary Hotel
❸ Casa Danè
❹ L'Arca di Noè B&B
❺ Covered Market
❻ Launderette
❼ Piazza d'Armi (Free Parking)
❽ Porto Venere Bus Stop

recent years, La Spezia has become the entry point for big cruise ships that funnel groups into the Cinque Terre.

Arrival in La Spezia: The **La Spezia Centrale train station** has various services lined up along track 1: At the Cinque Terre end are pay WCs and luggage storage (€3/day, 8:00-22:00—if nobody's there ring the bell); and in the middle of the platform are an often-closed city TI and a Cinque Terre National Park information point (where you can buy park tickets—including the Cinque Terre Treno Multi-Service Card that includes both trains and trails; daily 7:30-19:30, off-season 9:00-17:30, tel. 0187-743-500, www.parconazionale5terre.it). Don't use the La Spezia Migliarina station, where some trains terminate, which is more remote.

If arriving by **car,** the easiest parking is under the train station, at the slick and modern Park Centro Stazione (enter from Via Fiume, €18/day, www.mobpark.eu/it/. Free parking is at Piazza d'Armi, a 20-minute walk or short bus ride from the station (entrance at Via XV Giugno 1918).

Visiting La Spezia: If you find yourself with time to kill here, exit the station, turn left, and walk a long downhill block to the roundabout at Piazza Saint Bon, which marks the start of a pleasant pedestrian zone on **Via del Prione;** following this to the gardens along the harbor makes a pleasant stroll. Along the way, you'll pass the nearly deserted **Museo Amedeo Lia,** which displays Italian paintings from the 13th to 18th century, including minor works by Venetian masters Titian, Tintoretto, and Canaletto (tel. 0187-731-100, http://museolia.spezianet.it).

Sights near La Spezia: Without a doubt, the most appealing things to see and do here are outside of town. **Porto Venere,** a gorgeous Cinque Terre-esque town overlooking a beautiful bay, is a 30-minute bus ride away (see next section). **Carrara,** with the world's most famous marble quarries, is just east of La Spezia (and an easy on-the-way stop if you're driving from Pisa). Michelangelo himself traveled to these valleys to pick out the marble that he worked into his masterpieces. The Marble Museum (Museo Civico del Marmo) in Carrara traces the story of marble-cutting here from pre-Roman times until today (Viale XX Settembre 85, tel. 0585-845-746). For a guided visit, Sara Paolini is excellent (€80/half-day tour, will meet you at Carrara freeway exit or pick up from La Spezia train station, mobile 373-711-6695, sarapaolini@hotmail.com).

Sleeping in and near La Spezia: Stay in the Cinque Terre if you can. But if you're in a bind, these accommodations are within a 10-minute walk of the station and include breakfast: **$$$$ Hotel Firenze e Continentale** is your grand, Old World splurge (68 rooms, RS%, air-con, elevator, pay parking garage, Via Paleocapa 7, tel. 0187-713-200 or 0187-713-210, www.hotelfirenzecontinentale. it, info@hotelfirenzecontinentale.it). **$$ Mary Hotel,** directly across from the train station, has 48 basic, old-school rooms (air-con, elevator, Via Fiume 177, tel. 0187-743-254, www.hotelmary.it, info@hotelmary.it, friendly Luca).

For *affittacamere* rooms for rent, consider the stylish **$ Casa Danè** (10 chic rooms with comfy linens and orange trees outside the door, plus 20 more rooms inside the station building itself, some rooms overlook the tracks but the windows are good, family rooms, air-con, Via Paleocapa 4, mobile 347-351-3239, www. casadane.it, reception@casadane.it, Paolo), or the homey **$ L'Arca di Noè B&B** (three bright, artsy, affordable rooms—two with bathroom inside the room, the other with private bath down the hall; air-con, communal kitchen, Via Fiume 39, mobile 320-485-2434, montialessandra@email.it, Alessandra). **$ Il Gelsomino,** best for drivers, is a homey and tranquil, three-room B&B in the hills above La Spezia overlooking the Gulf of Poets (family rooms, reconfirm arrival time in advance, Via dei Viseggi 9, tel. 0187-704-201, www.ilgelsomino.biz, ilgelsomino@inwind.it, gracious Carla and Walter Massi).

A handy self-service **launderette** is just below the train station (daily 8:30-20:30, Via Fuime 95).

Eating in La Spezia: If you're stuck in town and need a meal, turn left from the train station and head one block down the angled Via Paleocapa Pietro to the pleasant Piazza Saint Bon. From here, traffic-free Via Fiume leads to a pedestrian zone with several eateries.

La Spezia Connections: Trains leave about twice hourly for the **Cinque Terre towns** (direction: Levanto). A few express trains (headed to Genoa or Milano) stop only at Monterosso. Other connections include **Carrara** (2/hour, 25 minutes), **Pisa** (about hourly, 1-1.5 hours), **Florence** (5/day direct, 2.5 hours, otherwise nearly hourly with change in Pisa), **Rome** (8/day direct, more with transfers in Pisa, 3-4.5 hours), **Milan** (about hourly, 3 hours direct or with change in Genoa), **Venice** (about hourly, 5-6 hours, 1-3 changes).

It's also possible to go by **boat** to the Cinque Terre, Porto Venere, and outer islands from the La Spezia dock (www.navigazionegolfodeipoeti.it).

City **buses to Porto Venere** generally depart from Viale Garibaldi; the bus stop is about a 10-minute walk from the station—see map on page 436 for location (bus #P, 2/hour, 30 minutes, €2.50 each way; bus #11 also makes this trip, but only mid-June–mid-Sept and sporadically off-season; buy tickets at TI, tobacco shops or newsstands).

Porto Venere

The perfect antidote to gritty La Spezia hides just around the bay: the enchanting resort of Porto Venere (POR-toh VEH-neh-reh). Comparably scenic to the Cinque Terre towns—but with a bit of glitz—this village clings to a rocky, fortress-crowned promontory. A rainbow of tall-but-skinny pastel facades rises up from an inviting harborfront promenade.

Porto Venere is light on sights, but it's easy to reach by boat from the Cinque Terre, and fun to explore: The higher you go, the

better the views. Rather than the open sea, Porto Venere faces the beautiful Gulf of La Spezia—more romantically known as the Gulf of Poets—where Lord Byron was said to have gone for a hardy swim despite rough seas and local warnings to the contrary. (He survived...

at least, for a little while longer.) Scanning the bay, you'll see the outskirts of muscular La Spezia, the often-snow-covered peaks of the Apuan Alps, the resort town of Lerici, and—across a narrow strait—the rugged island of Palmaria.

Getting There: Porto Venere is an easy day trip from the Cinque Terre towns by **boat** (mid-June-Oct, 4/day, 1 hour from Monterosso, €16 one-way, €25 day pass includes hopping on and off, www.navigazionegolfodeipoeti.it). You can also cruise between Porto Venere and Santa Margherita Ligure, with stops in Vernazza and Sestri Levante, using another boat line (www.traghettiportofino.it)—see page 429. The scenic **bus** ride between La Spezia and Porto Venere curls around the Gulf of Poets (see facing page). **Parking** is challenging. In peak season, shuttle buses connect the parking lot just outside Porto Venere to the harborside square. Otherwise, test your luck with the pay spots on the seaside.

Visiting Porto Venere: The **TI** fills an old guard tower at the top of the main square (Piazza Bastreri 7, tel. 0187-790-691, www.prolocoportovenere.it). The town is essentially two streets deep: the harborfront promenade and, a block uphill, the main street (Via Capellini). A complete loop around Porto Venere includes both of these streets and a moderately steep hike up to the town's two main churches and fortress for the views. You can see everything in just a few hours; add more time for lunch or lingering.

Along the **harborfront,** seafood restaurants enjoy a Technicolor backdrop, and local boat captains try to talk you into a 40-minute excursion around the bay. But the real town lives on **Via Capellini** (just through the big arch from the TI—or hike up any of the narrow stepped lanes from the harbor). Skinny and shaded, Via Capellini has a mix of restaurants, focaccia-and-pizza takeaway stands, boutiques selling gourmet gifty edibles and gaudy beachwear, and a few local shops.

At the west end of the promenade and Via Capellini, the town comes to a point at the late 13th-century **Church of San Pietro,** with Gothic features and a black-and-white-striped interior typical of this region. Climb the stairs to the roof terrace for fine views in both directions (including the "Grotta Byron" sea cave).

More viewpoints line the walk from here up the stairs to the town's other big church, **San Lorenzo.** With a dark and brooding Romanesque interior, this church—like much of Porto Venere—was built by the Genovese to establish a strategic foothold at the entrance to the bay in the 12th century.

From in front of the church, more steps lead up to the town's fortress, **Castello Doria.** A hulking but empty shell, it's not worth the money to go inside, but a hike up to the terrace out front is rewarded with striking panoramas.

From the castle, head back into town; to make this walk a loop, bear left to follow the very steeply stepped lane that runs just inside the crenellated wall back down to the TI.

Hardy **hikers** enjoy the five-hour (or more) hike to Riomaggiore, the nearest Cinque Terre town. Get details on this (and other hikes) at the TI; for more on hiking the Cinque Terre, see page 325.

Eating in Porto Venere: On the harbor, next to colorful bobbing boats, take your pick of views and menus (seafood/pizza) for a meal in a memorable setting. For better values and more variety, stroll one block inland to Via Capellini. For a sit-down meal along here, try **$$ Portivene (Un Mare di Sipori),** serving local dishes with modern flair at reasonable prices (reservations smart, closed Mon, at #94, tel. 0187-792-722). Better yet, browse the fun selection of takeaway shops (selling pizza slices, bruschetta, focaccia, and top-notch deli items) to put together a picnic to enjoy by the port. **$ Anciùa** (at #40) assembles fresh panini to order with interesting ingredients; they also have fresh fried anchovies and other Ligurian street food.

RIVIERA TOWNS

FLORENCE

Firenze

Florence, the home of the Renaissance and birthplace of our modern world, has the best Renaissance art in Europe. In a single day, you could look Michelangelo's *David* in the eyes, fall under the seductive sway of Botticelli's *Birth of Venus,* and climb the modern world's first dome, which still dominates the skyline.

Get your bearings with a Renaissance walk. Florentine art goes beyond paintings and statues—enjoy the food, fashion, and street markets. You can lick Italy's best gelato while enjoying some of Europe's best people-watching.

PLANNING YOUR TIME

Florence deserves at least one well-organized day: See the Accademia *(David),* tour the Uffizi Gallery (Renaissance art), visit the Duomo Museum (great bronze work) or underrated Bargello (best statues), and do my Renaissance Walk (see page 459; to avoid heat and crowds, do this walk in the morning or late afternoon). Art lovers will want to chisel out another day for the many other Florentine cultural treasures. Shoppers and ice-cream lovers may need to do the same.

Skipping Lines at Major Sights: This day plan assumes that you'll use my strategies to avoid wasting hours in line for the big attractions—especially the Uffizi Gallery and Accademia. These sights nearly always have long ticket-buying lines, especially in peak season (April-Oct) and on holiday weekends. Crowds thin out on off-season weekdays. (Note that both of these major sights are closed on Monday.) You have two surefire options for skipping lines: Buy a **Firenze Card** or **make reservations** (both described

FLORENCE

Florence Overview

MERCATO CENTRALE
SAN LORENZO
CAVOUR
RICASOLI
ACCADEMIA (DAVID)
S.M.N. TRAIN STN.
CERRETANI
DUOMO
DUOMO MUSEUM
SANTA MARIA NOVELLA
Piazza della Repubblica
VIA DE' CALZAIUOLI
RITZY SHOPPING ZONE
Piazza della Signoria
PALAZZO VECCHIO
AREA OF ANCIENT ROMAN TOWN →
UFFIZI
SANTA CROCE
PONTE VECCHIO
LUNGARNO
BRANCACCI CHAPEL
OLTRARNO
Arno River
SANTO SPIRITO
PITTI PALACE
GUICCIARDINI
Boboli Gardens
To San Miniato & Piazzale Michelangelo
Not to Scale

on pages 468 and 470). Another place where you're likely to encounter lines are the Duomo sights, especially for climbing to the top of the dome. These sights don't take reservations, but you can skip the line at the dome with a Firenze Card—or try visiting at a time when it's less crowded.

The Firenze Card makes things easy—just show up and flash your card—but it's expensive (€72). Because the card is valid for three days, it's not a good value if you're in town for just one or two days—buy one only if you want to pay a premium to skip lines or avoid making reservations. For a three-day visit with lots of sightseeing, the Firenze Card can be a great value.

Closures: In general, Sundays and Mondays are not ideal for sightseeing, as many places are either closed or have shorter hours. Sights may also have shorter hours off-season.

Free Sundays: On the first Sunday of the month all state museums are free. While that's good news for more overlooked sights, free admission makes both the Accademia and the Uffizi impossibly crowded. I'd skip those sights on that day.

Siena: Connoisseurs of smaller towns should consider taking the bus to Siena for a day or evening trip (1.5 hours one-way, confirm when last bus returns; see the Siena chapter). Siena is magic after dark.

FLORENCE

Orientation to Florence

The best of Florence lies on the north bank of the Arno River. The main historical sights cluster around the venerable dome of the cathedral (Duomo). Everything is within a 20-minute walk of the train station, cathedral, or Ponte Vecchio (Old Bridge). The less famous but more characteristic Oltrarno area (south bank) is just over the bridge.

Though small, Florence is intense. Prepare for scorching summer heat, crowded narrow lanes and sidewalks, slick pickpockets, few WCs, steep prices, and long lines. Easy tourist money has corrupted some locals, making them greedy and dishonest (check your bill carefully)

FLORENCE: A VERBAL MAP

Florence (pop. 380,000) is remarkably compact and easy to navigate. Here's a neighborhood-by-neighborhood rundown:

Historic Core: The Duomo—with its iconic, towering dome—is the visual and geographical center of Florence; all other sights radiate out from here. The Duomo sits at the northeast corner of the oblong, grid-planned old town (immediately apparent on any map, and dating from Roman times). At the southeast corner is Piazza della Signoria—marked by the tower of the Palazzo Vecchio (city hall) and adjacent Uffizi Gallery, with the Galileo Science Museum tucked just behind it. These two main landmarks are connected by the wide, pedestrianized, heavily tourist-trod Via de' Calzaiuoli, which bisects the old Roman town. To the west is a glitzy shopping zone (between Piazza della Repubblica and the river), and to the east is a characteristic web of narrow lanes. This central axis—Duomo to Piazza della Signoria by way of Via de' Calzaiuoli—is the spine for Florentine sightseeing and the route of my self-guided Renaissance Walk.

Accademia/San Lorenzo (North of the Duomo): Via Cavour runs north from the Duomo, past the Medici-Riccardi Palace and through a nondescript urban zone. For the sightseer, the eastern part of this zone is dominated by the Accademia, with Michelangelo's *David;* nearby are the Museum of San Marco and the quintessentially Renaissance Piazza S.S. Annunziata. The western part clusters around the Basilica of San Lorenzo, with its Medici Chapels, and (a block north) Mercato Centrale, with the vendor stalls of San Lorenzo Market. The streets immediately surrounding Mercato Centrale (especially the pedestrianized Via Faenza) are tourist-central: They teem with midrange and budget hotels, and trattorias catering exclusively to out-of-towners, creating a touristy area that's convenient, but one that insulates you from a more authentic slice of Florence.

FLORENCE

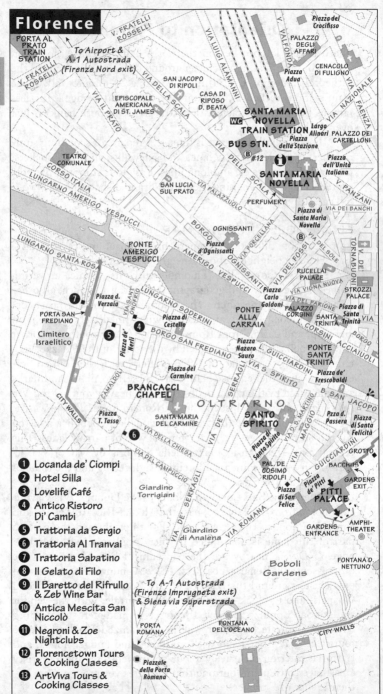

Florence

PORTA AL PRATO TRAIN STATION

To Airport & A-1 Autostrada (Firenze Nord exit)

V. FRATELLI ROSSELLI

V. FRATELLI ROSSELLI

V. IL PRATO

VIA DELLA SCALA

SAN JACOPO DI RIPOLI

CASA DI RIPOSO D. BEATA

V. LUIGI ALAMANNI

V. VALFONDA

Piazza del Crocifisso

PALAZZO DEGLI AFFARI

CENACOLO DI FULIGNO

V. NAZIONALE

Piazza Adua

EPISCOPALE AMERICANA DI ST. JAMES

CORSO ITALIA

TEATRO COMUNALE

SANTA MARIA NOVELLA TRAIN STATION

WC

BUS STN.

B #12

i

SANTA MARIA NOVELLA

Largo Alipari

Piazza della Stazione

PALAZZO DEI CARTELLONI

Piazza dell'Unità Italiana

VIA FAENZA

V. PANZANI

LUNGARNO AMERIGO VESPUCCI

SAN LUCIA SUL PRATO

VIA DELLA SCALA

VIA PALAZZUOLO

PERFUMERY

Piazza di Santa Maria Novella

VIA DEI BANCHI

PONTE AMERIGO VESPUCCI

LUNGARNO SANTA ROSA

OGNISSANTI

L. AMERIGO VESPUCCI

Piazza d'Ognissanti

BORGO OGNISSANTI

VIA PORCELLANA

B

VIA DEL SOLE

RUCELLAI PALACE

VIA DEL FOSSI

VIA DELLA VIGNA NUOVA

V. DEI TORNABUONI

STROZZI PALACE

PIAZZA d. Verzaia

LUNGARNO SODERINI

VIA SANT'ONOFRIO

Piazza di Cestella

Piazza de' Nerli

BORGO SAN FREDIANO

Piazza Carlo Goldoni

PONTE ALLA CARRAIA

VIA DEL PARIONE

PALAZZO CORSINI

L. CORSINI

Piazza di Santa Trinità

SANTA TRINITÀ

PONTE SANTA TRINITÀ

BORGO

ACCIAIUOLI

7

PORTA SAN FREDIANO

Cimitero Israelitico

CITY WALLS

V. CAMALDOLI

5

4

Piazza Nazaro Sauro

L. GUICCIARDINI

VIA S. SPIRITO

Piazza de' Frescobaldi

B. SAN JACOPO

Piazza del Carmine

BRANCACCI CHAPEL

OLTRARNO

SANTA MARIA DEL CARMINE

VIA DE' SERRAGLI

SANTO SPIRITO

VIA DE'S. MARTINO

V. D. S. MARTINO

Pzza d. Passera

Piazza di Santa Felicità

GROTTO

BACCHUS

Piazza T. Tasso

6

VIA DELLA CHIESA

VIA DEL CAMPUCCIO

Piazza di Santo Spirito

VIA MAGGIO

V. D. GUICCIARDINI

PAL. DE COSIMO RIDOLFI

Piazza de' Pitti

PITTI PALACE

GARDENS EXIT

GARDENS ENTRANCE

AMPHI-THEATER

Giardino Torrigiani

VIA DE' SERRAGLI

VIA ROMANA

Giardino di Analena

Piazza di San Felice

FONTANA D. NETTUNO

Boboli Gardens

To A-1 Autostrada (Firenze Impruneta exit) & Siena via Superstrada

PORTA ROMANA

FONTANA DELL'OCEANO

CITY WALLS

Piazzale della Porta Romana

1	Locanda de' Ciompi
2	Hotel Silla
3	Lovelife Café
4	Antico Ristoro Di' Cambi
5	Trattoria da Sergio
6	Trattoria Al Tranvai
7	Trattoria Sabatino
8	Il Gelato di Filo
9	Il Baretto del Rifrullo & Zeb Wine Bar
10	Antica Mescita San Niccolò
11	Negroni & Zoe Nightclubs
12	Florencetown Tours & Cooking Classes
13	ArtViva Tours & Cooking Classes

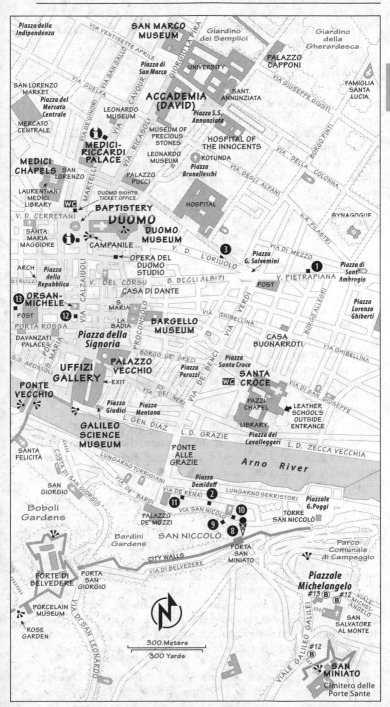

Train Station/Santa Maria Novella (West of the Duomo): Northwest of the historic core, things get a bit more urban and dreary. This area, dominated by the train station and Church of Santa Maria Novella, specializes in inexpensive hotels and characteristic eateries. Closer to the river (especially around Palazzo Strozzi) is a posh shopping zone, with a more affordable mix of shops lining Via del Parione and Borgo Ognissanti.

Santa Croce (East of the Duomo): Tourists make the 10-minute trek from Piazza della Signoria east to Piazza Santa Croce, facing this neighborhood's main landmark, the Church of Santa Croce. Along the way—effectively across the street from the old town—is the Bargello, filling a former police station with some of Florence's best sculptures. The area stretching north and west from Santa Croce is increasingly authentic and workaday (especially along Via Pietrapiana and Borgo la Croce), offering an insightful glimpse at untouristy Florence.

Oltrarno (South of the River): Literally the "Other Side of the Arno River," this neighborhood opens up just across Ponte Vecchio from the main tourist zone. While the streets immediately around that bridge are jammed and tacky, two or three blocks away are pockets of Florence from a time before tourism. Many artisans still have workshops here, and open their doors to passing visitors. The Oltrarno is roughly divided in half by the giant Pitti Palace and surrounding gardens (Boboli and Bardini). To the west of the palace are Piazza di Santo Spirito (with its namesake church) and—a bit farther out—the Church of Santa Maria del Carmine, with its lavishly frescoed Brancacci Chapel. To the east of Pitti and the gardens, perched high on the hill, is the magnificent-view Church of San Miniato; just below that sits Piazzale Michelangelo (with Florence's most popular viewpoint), and tucked below and between there and the river is the funky little San Niccolò neighborhood, with its lively bars and eateries.

TOURIST INFORMATION

The city TI has three branches. The crowded main branch is across the square from the **train station** (Mon-Sat 9:00-19:00, Sun 9:00-14:00; with your back to tracks, exit the station—it's 100 yards away, near corner of church at Piazza della Stazione 4; tel. 055-212-245, www.firenzeturismo.it). Upstairs, drop by the easy-to-miss "Experience Florence" visitors center, with big touch screens to help you virtually explore the city and plan an itinerary, and a well-produced 3-D movie about the city, offering evocative slices of Florentine life and lingering images of the big landmarks (free, 13 minutes, English subtitles).

The smaller branch is centrally located at **Piazza del Duomo,** at the west corner of Via de' Calzaiuoli (inside the Loggia; Mon-

Sat 9:00-19:00, Sun 9:00-14:00, tel. 055-288-496). They also have a branch at the **airport.**

A separate TI, which covers both the city and the greater province of Florence, can be less crowded and more helpful. It's a couple of blocks **north of the Duomo,** just past Medici-Riccardi Palace (Mon-Fri 9:00-13:00, closed Sat-Sun, at Via Cavour 1 red, tel. 055-290-832).

The TIs sell the **Firenze Card,** an expensive but handy sight-seeing pass that allows you to skip the lines at top museums (see page 468).

Publications: At any TI, you'll find free, handy resources in English. Pick up a city map and information sheet with the latest opening hours; or search for "Monuments and Museums" on their website. For information on goings-on around town, pick up the monthly *Florence & Tuscany News,* and check *The Florentine* news-paper, which has great articles with cultural insights (in English, published monthly and updated online every other Thu at www.theflorentine.net), along with the similar *Florence Is You* (www.florenceisyou.com).

ARRIVAL IN FLORENCE
By Train

Florence's main train station is called **Santa Maria Novella** (*Firenze S.M.N.* on schedules and signs). The city also has two subur-ban train stations: **Firenze Rifredi** and **Firenze Campo di Marte.** Note that some trains don't stop at the main station—before board-ing, confirm that you're heading for S.M.N., or you may overshoot the city. (If this happens, don't panic; the other stations are a short taxi ride from the center.)

For general information on train travel in Italy—including ticket-buying options—see page 1159. As at any busy train station, be on guard: Don't trust "porters" who want to help you find your train or carry your bags (they're not official), and politely decline offers of help using the ticket machines by anyone other than uni-formed staff.

To orient yourself to Santa Maria Novella station, stand with your back to the tracks. Look left to see the green cross of a 24-hour pharmacy *(farmacia)* and the exit to the taxi queue. Baggage storage *(deposito bagagli)* is also to the left, halfway down track 16 (long hours daily, passport required). Fast-food outlets and a bank are also along track 16. Directly ahead of you is the main hall *(salone biglietti),* where you can buy train and bus tickets. Pay WCs are to the right, near the head of track 5.

To reach the **TI,** walk away from the tracks and exit the sta-tion; it's straight across the square, 100 yards away, by the stone church.

Buying Tickets: For travel within Italy, there's no reason to stand in line at a window. Take advantage of the self-service ticket *(biglietto)* machines that display schedules, issue tickets, and even make reservations for rail-pass holders. Some take only credit cards; others take cards and cash. Using them is easy—just tap "English."

There are two train companies: Trenitalia, with most connections (toll tel. 892-021, www.trenitalia.it), and Italo, with some high-speed routes between larger cities (no rail passes accepted, sometimes cheaper than Trenitalia, tel. 06-0708, www.italotreno. it). Both companies have bright-red machines, so be sure you use the right one.

For most international tickets, you'll need to either go to a Trenitalia ticket window (in the main hall) or a travel agency (ask at your hotel for the nearest one).

For Trenitalia information, use window #18 or #19 (take a number). For Italo tickets and information, use window #10 or #11, or visit their main office, opposite track 5, near the exit. Also near track 5, you'll find the Trenitalia Frecciaclub (first-class lounge).

To buy ATAF city bus tickets, stop at windows #8-9 in the main hall—and ask for a transit map while you're there (TIs do not have them).

Eating: **$ VyTA,** across from track 13, has good sandwiches, snacks, and pastries. Modern and refined **$$ Reale** serves drinks, salads, and other goodies and offers perhaps the best seats in the station (daily 8:00-24:00, 100 yards down track 16, just beyond baggage storage, tel. 055-264-5114). A food court is near track 16. The handiest supermarket is the classy **Sapori & Dintorni Conad,** across the busy street toward the Duomo (daily until 21:00, Largo Alinari 6).

Services: **Feltrinelli** has English language books and magazines and a café (across from track 14) while a modern **shopping gallery** with clothing stores and another café is down the escalator, across from tracks 11-12.

Getting to the Duomo and City Center: The Duomo and town center are to your left (with your back to the tracks). Out the doorway to the left, you'll find city buses and the taxi stand. **Taxis** cost about €6-8 to the Duomo, and the line moves fast, except on holidays. To **walk** into town (10-15 minutes), exit the station straight ahead (with your back to the tracks), through the main hall and head straight across the square outside (toward the Church of Santa Maria Novella). On the far side of the square, keep left and head down the main Via dei Panzani, which leads directly to the Duomo.

By Bus
BusItalia Station is 100 yards west of the train station on Via Santa

Caterina da Siena. Exit the station through the main door, and turn left along the busy street toward the brick dome. Downtown Florence is straight ahead and a bit to the right.

By Car

The autostrada has several exits for Florence. Get off at the Nord, Scandicci, Impruneta (formerly Certosa), or Sud exits and follow signs toward—but not into—the *Centro*.

Don't even attempt driving into the city center (instead, park on the outskirts—described later—and take a bus, tram, or taxi in). Florence has a traffic-reduction system that's complicated and confusing even to locals. Every car passing into the "limited traffic zone" (*Zona Traffico Limitato*, or *ZTL*) is photographed; those who haven't jumped through bureaucratic hoops to get a permit can expect a €100 ticket in the mail (and an "administrative" fee from the rental company). If you get lost and cross the line several times...you get several fines. Since this is Italy, it can take as long as a year for your ticket to show up. If you have a reservation at a hotel within the ZTL area—and it has parking—ask in advance if they can get you permission to enter town.

Another potentially expensive mistake drivers make in Florence is using the lanes designated for buses only (usually marked with yellow stripes). Driving in these lanes can also result in a ticket in the mail. Pay careful attention to signs.

Car Rental: If you're picking up a rental car upon departure, don't struggle with driving in the center. Taxi with your luggage to the car-rental office, and head out from there.

Parking in Florence: The city center is ringed with big, efficient parking lots (signposted with a big *P*). From these, you can ride into the center (via taxi, bus, or possibly tram). Check www.firenzeparcheggi.it for details on parking lots, availability, and prices. From the freeway, follow the signs to *Centro*, then *Stadio*, then *P*.

I usually head for Parcheggio del Parterre, just beyond Piazza della Libertà (€2/hour, €20/day, €70/week, open 24 hours daily, tel. 055-500-1994, 600 spots, automated, pay with cash or credit card, never fills up completely). To get into town, find the taxi stand at the elevator exit, or ride one of the minibuses that connect major parking lots with the city center (see www.ataf.net for routes).

Parcheggio Sansovino, a convenient lot for drivers coming from the south, is on the Oltrarno side of the river, right at a tram stop. Park, then ride four quick stops to Santa Maria Novella Station (€1/hour, €12/day, open 24 hours daily, Via Sansovino 53—from A-1 take the Firenze Scandicci exit, tel. 055-363-362, www.scaf.fi.it).

You can park for free along any suburban curb that feels safe;

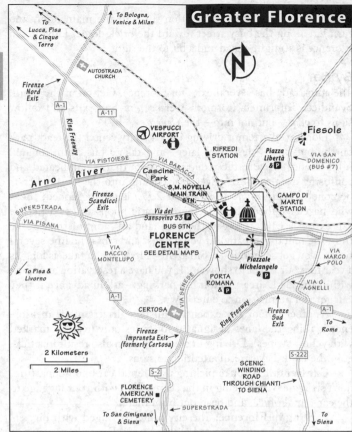

Greater Florence

pick a place near a bus stop and bus into the city center. Check for signs that indicate parking restrictions—for example, a circle with a slash through it and "*giovedi dispari,* 0,00-06,00" means "don't park on Thursdays between midnight and six in the morning."

There's talk of closing the free parking lot at Piazzale Michelangelo (see page 497), but if it's open, don't park where the buses drop off passengers; park on the side of the piazza farthest from the view. To get from Piazzale Michelangelo to the center of town, take bus #13.

By Plane

Amerigo Vespucci Airport, also called Peretola Airport, is about five miles northwest of the city (open 4:00-24:30, no overnighting allowed, TI, airport code: FLR, tel. 055-306-1830, www. aeroporto.firenze.it).

Shuttle buses (to the far right as you exit the arrivals hall) connect the airport with Florence's train and bus stations (2/hour, 30 minutes, runs 5:00-23:30, €6 one-way—buy ticket on board and validate immediately). If you're changing to a different intercity bus in Florence (for instance, one bound for Siena), stay on the bus through the first stop (at the train station); it will continue on to the bus station nearby. Allow about €25 and 30 minutes for a taxi.

Car Rental: The airport's rental-car offices share one big parking lot that's a three-minute drive away. Streets around the airport (which is tucked behind a big elevated highway) are a dizzying maze, making it tricky to find the place to drop off your car. One option is to drive to the airport, wait for the shuttle bus to show up, then follow that bus to the lot.

By Cruise Ship
For details on arriving at Florence's port, Livorno, see page 533.

HELPFUL HINTS
Exchange Rate: €1 = about $1.10

Country Calling Code: 39 (see page 1154 for dialing instructions)

Theft Alert: Florence has hardworking thief gangs who hang out near the train station, the station's underpass (especially where the tunnel surfaces), and at major sights. American tourists are considered easy targets. Some thieves even dress like tourists to fool you. Logically, any crowded bus likely holds at least one thief. Also beware of the "slow count": Cashiers may count change back with odd pauses in hopes you'll gather up the money early and say *"Grazie."*

Medical Help: To reach a doctor who speaks English, call **Medical Service Firenze** (tel. 055-475-411, www.medicalservice.firenze.it); the phone is answered 24/7. You can have a doctor come to your hotel within an hour of your call, or go to the clinic when the doctor's in (Mon-Fri 11:00-12:00, 13:00-15:00 & 17:00-18:00, Sat 11:00-12:00 & 13:00-15:00, closed Sun, no appointment necessary, Via Roma 4, between the Duomo and Piazza della Repubblica).

Dr. Stephen Kerr is an English doctor specializing in helping sick tourists (drop-in clinic open Mon-Fri 15:00-17:00, other times by appointment, Piazza Mercato Nuovo 1, between Piazza della Repubblica and Ponte Vecchio, tel. 055-288-055, mobile 335-836-1682, www.dr-kerr.com). The TI has a list of other English-speaking doctors.

There are 24-hour **pharmacies** at the train station and on Borgo San Lorenzo (near the Baptistery).

Museum Strategies: If you want to see a lot of museums, the pricey Firenze Card—which saves you from having to wait in line or make reservations for the Uffizi and Accademia—can be a worthwhile investment (see page 468).

Visiting Churches: Modest dress is required in some churches, including the Duomo, Santa Maria Novella, Santa Croce, Santa Maria del Carmine/Brancacci Chapel, and the Medici Chapels (see page 481 for details). Be respectful of worshippers and the paintings; don't use a flash. Many churches, though not the biggies we mention, close from 12:00 or 12:30 until 15:00 or 16:00.

Chill Out: Schedule several breaks into your sightseeing when you can sit, pause, cool off, and refresh yourself with a sandwich, gelato, or coffee. Carry a water bottle to refill at Florence's twist-the-handle public fountains (near the Duomo dome entrance, around the corner from the "Piglet" at Mercato Nuovo, or in front of the Pitti Palace). Try the *fontanello* (dispenser of free cold water, *gassata* or *naturale*) on Piazza della Signoria, behind the statue of Neptune (on the left side of the Palazzo Vecchio).

Addresses: Florence has a ridiculously confusing system for street addresses, with "red" numbers for businesses and "black" numbers for residences; in print, addresses are indicated with "r" (as in Via Cavour 2r) or "n" (for black—*nero,* as in Via Cavour 25n). Red and black numbers are interspersed together on the same street; each set goes in roughly consecutive order, but their numbers bear no connection with each other. I'm lazy and don't concern myself with the distinction (if one number's wrong, I look nearby for the other) and easily find my way around.

Pedestrian Safety: Once nightmarish for pedestrians, the city is increasingly delightful on foot, though even in traffic-free zones nearly silent hybrid taxis nudge their way through crowds with a persistent bccp-beep-beep.

Wi-Fi: Virtually all Florence hotels have Wi-Fi free for guests, and many cafés and restaurants will tell you their password if you buy something. The city has a free Wi-Fi hotspot network that covers all the main squares in town (network name is "Firenze WiFi"—click on *"Accedi";* good for two hours).

Useful App: ∩ For free audio versions of my Florence Renaissance Walk, and tours of the Uffizi, Accademia, Bargello, and Museum of San Marco, get the **Rick Steves Audio Europe** app (for details, see page 12).

Bookstores: For a good selection of brand-name guidebooks (including mine), try these: **Paperback Exchange** has the widest selection of English books, new and used (Mon-Fri 9:00-19:30, Sat 10:30-19:30, closed Sun and a couple of weeks in Aug, just south of the Duomo on Via delle Oche 4 red, tel. 055-293-

460). **RED** (stands for "Read, Eat, Dream"), a flagship store for the Feltrinelli chain (the Italian Barnes & Noble) with a café and restaurant inside, has a small selection of English books (daily 9:30-23:00, on Piazza della Repubblica).

WCs: Public restrooms are scarce. Use them when you can, in any café or museum you patronize. Pay public WCs are typically €1. Convenient locations include one at the Baptistery ticket office (near the Duomo), just down the street from Piazza Santa Croce (at Borgo Santa Croce 29 red), up near Piazzale Michelangelo, and inside the train station (near track 5).

Laundry: The **Wash & Dry Lavarapido** chain offers long hours and efficient, self-service launderettes at several locations (about €8 for wash and dry, change machine but bring plenty of coins just in case, generally daily 7:30-23:00). These locations are close to recommended hotels: Via dei Servi 105 red (near *David*), Via del Sole 29 red and Via della Scala 52 red (between train station and river), Via Ghibellina 143 red (Palazzo Vecchio), and Via dei Serragli 87 red (Oltrarno neighborhood). For more options, ask your hotelier or the TI.

Bike Rental: The **city of Florence** rents bikes cheaply at the train station (€2/hour, €5/5 hours, €10/day, mobile 346-883-7821; information at any TI). **Florence by Bike** rents two-wheelers of all sizes (€3/hour, €9/5 hours, includes bike lock and helmet; Mon-Fri 9:00-13:00 & 15:30-19:30, Sat 9:00-19:00, Sun 9:00-17:00, closed Sun Nov-March; a 15-minute walk north of the Duomo at Via San Zanobi 54 red, tel. 055-488-992, www.florencebybike.it).

Travel Agencies: Convenient travel agencies in the town center are **Intertravel Viaggi** (also a DHL package mailing office, Mon-Fri 9:00-18:30, Sat 9:30-12:30, closed Sun, centrally located south of Piazza della Repubblica at Via de Lamberti 39 red, tel. 055-280-706) and **Turishav Travel** (Mon-Fri 9:30-18:00, closed Sat-Sun, Via dei Servi 23 red, a block off the Duomo, tel. 055-292-237).

GETTING AROUND FLORENCE

I organize my sightseeing geographically and do it all on foot. I think of Florence as a Renaissance treadmill—it requires a lot of walking. You likely won't need public transit, except maybe to head up to Piazzale Michelangelo and San Miniato Church for the view.

By Bus

The city's full-size buses don't cover the old center well (the whole area around the Duomo is off-limits to motorized traffic). Pick up a map of transit routes at the ATAF windows at the train station; you'll also find routes online (www.ataf.net) and on the app "ATAF

Florence at a Glance

▲▲▲**Accademia** Michelangelo's *David* and powerful (unfinished) *Prisoners.* Reserve ahead or get a Firenze Card. **Hours:** Tue-Sun 8:15-18:50, closed Mon. See page 477.

▲▲▲**Uffizi Gallery** Greatest collection of Italian paintings anywhere. Reserve well in advance or get a Firenze Card. **Hours:** Tue-Sun 8:15-18:35, closed Mon. See page 486.

▲▲▲**Bargello** Underappreciated sculpture museum (Michelangelo, Donatello, Medici treasures). **Hours:** Tue-Sat 8:15-17:00, until 13:50 if no special exhibits; also open second and fourth Mon and first, third, and fifth Sun of each month. See page 492.

▲▲▲**Duomo Museum** Freshly renovated cathedral museum with the finest in Florentine sculpture. **Hours:** Daily 9:00-22:00, April and Nov until 21:00, Dec-March until 19:00, closed first Tue of every month. See page 474.

▲▲**Duomo** Gothic cathedral with colorful facade and the first dome built since ancient Roman times. **Hours:** Mon-Fri 10:00-17:00 (Thu until 16:00 May and Oct, until 16:30 Nov-April), Sat 10:00-16:45, Sun 13:30-16:45. See page 472.

▲▲**Museum of San Marco** Best collection anywhere of artwork by the early Renaissance master Fra Angelico. **Hours:** Tue-Fri 8:15-13:50, Sat 8:15-16:50; also open 8:15-13:50 on first, third, and fifth Mon and 8:15-16:50 on second and fourth Sun of each month. See page 479.

▲▲**Medici Chapels** Tombs of Florence's great ruling family, designed and carved by Michelangelo. **Hours:** Tue-Sat 8:15-16:50, Nov-March until 13:50; also open second and fourth Mon and first, third, and fifth Sun of each month. See page 480.

▲▲**Palazzo Vecchio** Fortified palace, once the home of the Medici family, wallpapered with history. **Hours:** Museum and excavations open Fri-Wed 9:00-23:00 (Oct-March until 19:00), Thu 9:00-14:00 year-round; tower keeps similar but shorter hours. See page 491.

▲▲**Galileo Science Museum** Fascinating old clocks, telescopes, maps, and three of Galileo's fingers. **Hours:** Wed-Mon 9:30-18:00, Tue until 13:00. See page 491.

▲▲**Santa Croce Church** Precious art, tombs of famous Florentines, and Brunelleschi's Pazzi Chapel in 14th-century church. **Hours:** Mon-Sat 9:30-17:30, Sun 14:00-17:30. See page 493.

▲▲**Church of Santa Maria Novella** Thirteenth-century Dominican church with Masaccio's famous 3-D painting. **Hours:** Mon-Thu 9:00-19:00 (Oct-March until 17:30), Fri 11:00-19:00 (Oct-March until 17:30), Sat 9:00-17:30 (July-Aug until 18:30), Sun 13:00-17:30 (July-Aug 12:00-18:30). See page 494.

▲▲**Pitti Palace** Several museums in lavish palace plus sprawling Boboli and Bardini Gardens. **Hours:** Palatine Gallery, Royal Apartments, and Gallery of Modern Art open Tue-Sun 8:15-18:50, closed Mon; gardens and other galleries open daily June-Aug 8:15-19:30, April-May and Sept until 18:30, March and Oct until 17:30, Nov-Feb until 16:30, closed first and last Mon of each month. See page 495.

▲▲**Brancacci Chapel** Works of Masaccio, early Renaissance master who reinvented perspective. **Hours:** Mon and Wed-Sat 10:00-17:00, Sun 13:00-17:00, closed Tue. Reservations required, though often available on the spot. See page 496.

▲▲**San Miniato Church** Sumptuous Renaissance chapel and sacristy showing scenes of St. Benedict. **Hours:** Daily 9:30-20:00, mid-Oct-Easter 9:30-13:00 & 15:30-19:00. See page 497.

▲**Climbing the Duomo's Dome** Grand view into the cathedral and, after 463 steps, a glorious city vista. **Hours:** Mon-Fri 8:30-19:00, Sat until 17:40, Sun 13:00-16:40. See page 472.

▲**Campanile** Bell tower with views similar to Duomo's, 50 fewer steps, and shorter lines. **Hours:** Daily 8:15-19:30. See page 473.

▲**Baptistery** Bronze doors fit to be the gates of paradise. **Hours:** Doors always viewable; interior open Mon-Fri 8:15-10:15 & 11:15-19:00, Sat 8:15-19:00, Sun 8:15-14:00. See page 473.

▲**Piazza S.S. Annunziata** Lovely square epitomizing Renaissance harmony, with Brunelleschi's Hospital of the Innocents, considered the first Renaissance building. **Hours:** Always open. See page 478.

▲**Medici-Riccardi Palace** Lorenzo the Magnificent's home, with fine art, frescoed ceilings, and Gozzoli's lovely Chapel of the Magi. **Hours:** Thu-Tue 8:30-19:00, closed Wed. See page 481.

▲**Ponte Vecchio** Famous bridge lined with gold and silver shops. **Hours:** Bridge always open. See page 491.

▲**Piazzale Michelangelo** Hilltop square with stunning view of Duomo and Florence, with San Miniato Church just uphill. **Hours:** Always open. See page 497.

2.0" (free from Apple's App Store and Google Play). Of the many bus lines, I find these to be of most value for seeing outlying sights:

Bus **#12** goes from the train station, over the Carraia bridge to Porta Romana, then up to San Miniato Church and Piazzale Michelangelo. Bus #13 makes the return trip down the hill.

The train station and Piazza San Marco are two major hubs near the city center; to get between these two, either walk (about 15 minutes) or take bus #1, #6, #14, #17, or #23.

Fun little **minibuses** (many of them electric—*elettrico*) wind through the tangled old center of town and up and down the river—just €1.20 gets you a 1.5-hour joyride. These buses, which run every 10 minutes from 7:00 to 21:00 (less frequent on Sun), are popular with sore-footed sightseers and eccentric local seniors. The minibuses also connect many major parking lots with the historic center (buy tickets from machines at lots).

Bus **#C1** stops behind the Palazzo Vecchio and Piazza Santa Croce, then heads north, passing near San Marco and the Accademia before ending up at Piazza Libertà. On its southbound route, this bus also stops near the train station and the Basilica of San Lorenzo.

Bus **#C2** twists through the congested old center from the train station, passing near Piazza della Repubblica and Piazza della Signoria to Piazza Beccaria.

Bus **#C3** goes up and down the Arno River, with stops near Piazza Santa Croce, Ponte Vecchio, the Carraia bridge to the Oltrarno (including the Pitti Palace), and beyond.

Bus **#D** goes from the train station to Ponte Vecchio, cruises through the Oltrarno (passing the Pitti Palace), and finishes in the San Niccolò neighborhood at Ponte San Niccolò.

Buying Bus Tickets: Buy bus tickets at tobacco shops *(tabacchi)*, newsstands, or the ATAF ticket windows inside the train station (€1.20/90 minutes, €4.70/4 tickets, €5/24 hours, €12/3 days, €18/week, day passes aren't always available in tobacco shops, tel. 800-424-500, www.ataf.net). Be sure to validate your ticket in the machine on board. You can sometimes buy a ticket on board, but you'll pay more (€2; must have exact change), and you still need to validate it in the machine. Follow general bus etiquette: Board at front or rear doors, exit out the center.

By Taxi

The minimum cost for a taxi ride is €5 (€8.30 after 22:00, €7 on Sundays); rides in the center of town should be charged as tariff #1. A taxi ride from the train station to the Duomo costs about €8. Taxi fares and supplements (e.g., €2 extra if you call a cab rather than hail one) are clearly explained on signs in each taxi. Look for an official, regulated cab (white; marked with *Taxi/Comune di Fi-*

renze, red fleur-de-lis, and one of the official phone numbers: 4390 or 4242). Before getting in a cab at a stand or on the street, ask for an approximate cost (*"Più o meno, quanto costa?"* pew oh MEH-noh, KWAHN-toh KOH-stah). If you can't get a straight answer or the price is outrageous, wait for the next one. It can be hard to find a cab on the street; to call one, dial 055-4390 or 055-4242 (or ask your waiter or hotelier to call for you).

Tours in Florence

Tour companies big and small offer plenty of excursions that go out to smaller towns in the Tuscan countryside (the most popular day trips: Siena, San Gimignano, Pisa, and into Chianti country for wine-tasting). Florence city tours are readily available, but for most people, the city is really best on foot.

🎧 To sightsee on your own, download my free audio tours that illuminate some of Florence's top sights and neighborhoods (see sidebar on page 12 for details).

For extra insight with a personal touch, consider the tour companies and individual Florentine guides listed here. Hardworking and creative, they offer a worthwhile array of organized sightseeing activities. Study their websites for details. If you're taking a city tour, remember that individuals save money with a scheduled public tour (such as those offered daily by Florencetown or Artviva). If you're traveling as a family or small group, however, you're likely to save money by booking a private guide (since rates are hourly for any size of group).

Walking (and Biking) Tours

While I've outlined the general offerings for each company, check their websites or brochures for other tour options and to confirm times and prices. Several of the below companies—as well as some dedicated culinary schools—offer food tours and cooking classes, sometimes including a shopping trip to pick up ingredients at a local market. This can be fun, memorable, educational, efficient (combining a meal with a "sightseeing" experience)...and delicious.

Florencetown

This company runs English-language tours on foot or by bike. They offer student rates (10 percent discount) to anyone with this book, with an additional 10 percent off for second tours (if booking online, enter code "RICKSTEVES"). Their most popular offerings: "Walk and Talk Florence" (basic stops including the Oltrarno, €25, 2.5 hours) and "I Bike Florence" (15-stop blitz of town's top sights, €29, 2.5 hours on one-speed bike, helmets optional; in bad weather it goes as a walking tour). Their office is at Via de Lamberti 1 (facing Orsanmichele Church); they also have a "Tourist Point" kiosk on Piazza della Repubblica, under the arches at the corner with Via Pellicceria (also offers cooking classes, tel. 055-281-103, www.florencetown.com).

Artviva

Artviva offers an intriguing variety of tours (guided by native English speakers, 18 people maximum). Popular choices include their overview tours (€29 "Original Florence" 3-hour town walk; €99 "Florence in One Glorious Day" combines town walk and tours of the Uffizi and Accademia, over 6 hours total). They also have stand-alone Uffizi and Accademia tours, cooking classes, minibus tours around Tuscany and to the Cinque Terre, and more. They offer a 10 percent discount at www.artviva.com/ricksteves (username "ricksteves," password "reader"). Their office is above Odeon Cinema near Piazza della Repubblica (Mon-Sat 8:00-18:00, Sun 8:30-13:30, Via de' Sassetti 1, second floor, tel. 055-264-5033, www.artviva.com).

Walks Inside Florence

Two art historians—Paola Barubiani and Marzia Valbonesi—and their partners provide quality guided tours. They offer a daily 2.5-hour introductory tour (€55/person, 8 people maximum; includes *David*—Accademia entry fee not included) and three-hour private tours (€190, €60/hour for more time, price is a discounted Rick Steves rate and for groups of up to 6 people). Among their tour options are an insightful shopping tour that features select artisans, a guided evening walk, and cruise excursions from the port of Livorno (Paola's mobile 335-526-6496, www.walksinsideflorence.com, paola@walksinsideflorence.it).

Florentia

Top notch private walking tours—geared for thoughtful, well-heeled travelers with longer-than-average attention spans—are led by one of six Florentine scholars. The tours range from introductory city walks and museum visits to in-depth thematic walks, such as the Oltrarno, Jewish Florence, and family-oriented tours (tours-€275 and up, includes planning assistance by email, www.florentia.org, info@florentia.org).

Context Florence

This scholarly group of graduate students and professors leads "walking seminars," such as a 3.5-hour study of Michelangelo's work and influence (€85/person, plus museum admission) and a two-hour evening orientation stroll (€70/person). I enjoyed the fascinating three-hour fresco workshop (€80/person plus materials, take home a fresco you make yourself). See their website for other innovative offerings: Medici walk, family tours, and more (tel. 06-

9672-7371, US tel. 800-691-6036, www.contexttravel.com, info@
contexttravel.com).

Local Guides for Private Tours

Alessandra Marchetti, a Florentine who has lived in the US, gives
private walking tours of Florence and driving tours of Tuscany
(€60-75/hour, mobile 347-386-9839, www.tuscanydriverguide.
com, alessandramarchettitours@gmail.com).

Paola Migliorini and her partners offer museum tours, city
walking tours, private cooking classes, wine tours, and Tuscan excursions by van—you can tailor tours as you like (€60/hour without
car, €70/hour in a van for up to 8 passengers, mobile 347-657-2611,
www.florencetour.com, info@florencetour.com). They also do excursions from the cruise port of Livorno (€580 for up to 4 people,
€680 for up to 6, €780 for up to 8, includes a driver/tour guide).

Elena Fulceri, specializing in art, history, and secret corners, is a delightful and engaging guide. She organizes heartfelt,
tailor-made private tours, has good Oltrarno artisan connections,
and enjoys family tours (€60/hour, tel. 347-942-2054, www.
florencewithflair.com, info@florencewithflair.com).

Tour Packages for Students

Andy Steves (Rick's son) runs Weekend Student Adventures
(WSA Europe), offering 3-day and 10-day budget travel packages
across Europe including accommodations, skip-the-line sightseeing, and unique local experiences. Locally guided and DIY unguided options are available for student and budget travelers in 12
of Europe's most popular cities, including Florence (guided trips
from €199, see www.wsaeurope.com for details).

Renaissance Walk

As great and rich as this city is, it's easily covered on foot. This
walk gives you an overview of Florence's top sights. We'll start with
the soaring church dome that stands as the proud symbol of the
Renaissance spirit. Just opposite, you'll find the Baptistery doors
that opened the Renaissance. Finally, we'll reach Florence's political center, dotted with monuments of that proud time. For more
details on many of the sights on this walk, see the individual listings under "Sights in Florence," later in this chapter.

Length of This Walk: Allow two hours, including visits to the
interiors of the Baptistery and Orsanmichele Church (but not the
other sights mentioned).

Tours: ∩ Download my free Renaissance Walk audio tour.

Services: Pay WCs are at the ticket office opposite the Baptistery. You can refill your water bottle at public twist-the-handle

fountains at the Duomo (left side, by the dome entrance), the Palazzo Vecchio (behind the Neptune fountain), and on Ponte Vecchio.

BACKGROUND

During the Dark Ages, it was especially obvious to the people of Italy—sitting on the rubble of Rome—that there had to be a brighter age on the horizon. The long-awaited rebirth, or Renaissance, began in Florence for good reason. Wealthy because of its cloth industry, trade, and banking; powered by a fierce city-state pride (locals would pee into the Arno with gusto, knowing rival city-state Pisa was downstream); and fertile with more than its share of artistic genius (imagine guys like Michelangelo and Leonardo attending the same high school)—Florence was a natural home for this cultural explosion.

The Renaissance—the "rebirth" of Greek and Roman culture that swept across Europe—started around 1400 and lasted about 150 years. In politics, the Renaissance meant democracy; in science, a renewed interest in exploring nature. The general mood was optimistic and "humanistic," with a confidence in the power of the individual. Renaissance art was a return to the realism and balance of Greek and Roman sculpture and architecture. Domes and round arches replaced Gothic spires and pointed arches. The Duomo kicked off the architectural Renaissance in Florence.

◑ SELF-GUIDED WALK

• *The Duomo, the cathedral with the distinctive red dome, is the center of Florence and the orientation point for this walk. If you ever get lost, home's the dome.*

The dome of the Duomo is best viewed just to the right of the facade, from the corner of the pedestrian-only Via de' Calzaiuoli. Stand near the kiosk.

The Duomo and Its Dome

The dome of Florence's cathedral—visible from all over the city—inspired Florentines to do great things. (Most recently, it inspired the city to make the area around the cathedral delightfully traffic-free.) The big church itself (called the Duomo) is Gothic, built in the Middle Ages by architects who left it unfinished.

Think of the confidence of the age: The Duomo was built with a big hole in its roof, just waiting for a grand dome to cover it. They could envision it—but the technology needed to create such a dome had yet to be invented. *Non c'è problema.* The Florentines knew that someone would soon be able to handle the challenge. In the 1400s, the architect Filippo Brunelleschi was called on to finish the job. Brunelleschi capped the church Roman-style—with a tall, self-

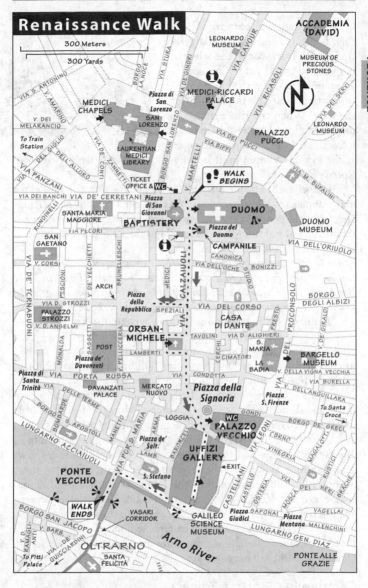

supporting dome as grand as the ancient Pantheon's (which he had studied).

He used a dome within a dome. What you see is the outer shell, covered in terra-cotta tile. The inner dome is thicker and provides much of the structural support. The grand white skeletal ribs connect at the top, supporting each other in a way similar to a pointed arch. Hidden between them are interlocking bricks, laid in a herringbone pattern. Rather than being stacked horizontally, like traditional brickwork, the alternating vertical bricks act as "bookends." The dome grew upward like an igloo, supporting itself as it proceeded from the base. When the ribs reached the top, Brunelleschi arched them in and fixed them in place with the cupola  at the top. His dome, built in only 14 years, was the largest since Rome's Pantheon.

Brunelleschi's dome was the wonder of the age, the model for many domes to follow, from St. Peter's to the US Capitol. Michelangelo, setting out to construct the dome of St. Peter's, drew inspiration from the dome of Florence. He said, "I'll make its sister... bigger, but not more beautiful."

• *Step to the front of the church, into the zone between the Duomo and the Baptistery that local tour guides call the "Piazza of Paradise." The Baptistery is the octagonal building facing the church, showing off its recently cleaned two-tone original stone facade from the 11th century.*

The church's **facade** looks old, but is actually Neo-Gothic—only from 1870. For several centuries it was unfinished—bare brick awaiting its decorative stone cover. The facade was rushed to completion (about 600 years after building began in 1296) to celebrate Italian unity, here in the city that for a few years served as the young country's capital. Its "retro" look captures the feel of the original medieval facade, with green, white, and pink marble sheets that cover the brick construction; Gothic (pointed) arches; and three horizontal stories decorated with mosaics and statues. The facade is ridiculed by some as too ornate, while others' jaws drop in admiration when they see it for the first (or fiftieth) time. Scanning up the central axis of the facade, it's clear: The Duomo is all about the Virgin Mary, to whom it's dedicated. The cavernous interior feels bare after being cleaned out during the Neoclassical age and by the terrible flood of 1966. (For more about the dome climbing and the Duomo interior, see page 472.)

Campanile (Giotto's Tower)

The bell tower (to the right of the cathedral's front) offers an easier, less crowded, and faster climb than the Duomo's dome. Though the unobstructed views from the Duomo are better, the bell tower does offer a bird's-eye view of the dome (see page 473 for information about climbing the tower). Giotto, like any good Renaissance genius (even though he was pre-Renaissance), wore several artistic hats. He's considered the father of modern painting, as well as being the architect of this 270-foot-tall bell tower for the Duomo, built two centuries before the age of Michelangelo. (For details on climbing the tower, see page 473).

• *Turn around to admire the Baptistery and its famous doors. If you decide to go inside, get a ticket at the office across the piazza (Firenze Card holders need to get a ticket at the ticket office). If you just want to look at the exterior doors, there's no charge.*

Baptistery and Ghiberti's Bronze Doors

The Baptistery's bronze doors bring us out of the Middle Ages and into the Renaissance. (These are copies; the originals are in the

Duomo Museum and described in greater detail on page 475.) Some say the Renaissance began precisely in the year 1401, when Florence staged a competition to find the best artist to design the Baptistery's **north doors** (around to the right, where tourists go in). A 24-year-old Lorenzo Ghiberti won easily, beating out a 24-year-old Filippo Brunelleschi, sparking a decades-long rivalry. After Ghiberti completed the first set of doors, he was commissioned to create the **east doors** (facing the cathedral). Ghiberti's bronze panels for these doors added a whole new dimension to art—depth. Michelangelo

said these doors were fit to be the "Gates of Paradise." Here we see how the Renaissance masters merged art and science. Realism was in, and Renaissance artists used math, illusion, and dissection to create it. Ghiberti spent 27 years (1425-1452) working on these panels. That's him in the center of the door frame, atop the second row of panels—the head on the left with the shiny male-pattern baldness.

The Baptistery **interior** features a fine example of pre-Renaissance mosaic art (1200s-1300s) in the Byzantine style (see listing on page 130).

• *Now head south, down the busy pedestrian-only street that runs from here toward the Arno River.*

Via de' Calzaiuoli The former "street of the stocking makers" (pronounced kahlts-ay-WOH-lee) has long been the main axis of the city, and was part of the ancient Roman grid plan that became Florence. In medieval times, this street connected the religious center (where we are now) with the political center (where we're heading), a five-minute walk away. In recent years this historic core has been transformed into a pleasant place to stroll, people-watch, window-shop, lick the drips on your gelato cone, and wonder why American cities can't become more pedestrian-friendly.

• *Continue down Via de' Calzaiuoli. Two blocks down from the Baptistery, look right on Via degli Speziali to see a triumphal arch that marks Piazza della Repubblica. Side-trip one block (and from out of the Renaissance and into the 19th century) to see this square.*

Piazza della Repubblica

This large square sits on the site of the original Roman Forum. The square's lone column—nicknamed the "belly button of Florence"—once marked the intersection of the two main roads (Via Corso and Via Roma). Look at any map of Florence today, and you'll see the ghost of Rome in its streets: a grid-plan city center surrounded by what was the Roman wall.

The square was the site of the Jewish quarter in the 1500s; in 1571, Cosimo I had it walled in and made into a ghetto. In the 1860s, the city was spiffed up for its stint as the capital of the newly united nation of Italy—the Jewish ghetto was razed, and the city walls were taken down to make grand European-style boulevards and open up this imposing, modern forum surrounded by stately circa-1890 buildings. (For more on this square, see page 485.)

• *Return to the main street and continue walking toward the river. A block farther, at the intersection with Via Orsanmichele, is the...*

Orsanmichele Church

Originally, this was an open loggia (covered porch) with a huge grain warehouse upstairs. The arches of the loggia were artfully filled in (14th century), and the building gained a new purpose—as a church. The 14 niches in the exterior walls feature replicas of the remarkable-in-their-day statues paid for by the city's rising middle class of merchants and their 21 guilds. Florence in 1400 was a republic, a government working for the interests not of a king, but of these guilds, which commissioned statues as PR gestures.

The interior has a glorious Gothic tabernacle (1359), a painted wooden panel that depicts *Madonna delle Grazie* (1346), and a museum displaying most of the original statues from the niches (for more on the interior, see page 484).

Head up Via Orsanmichele (to the right of the church) and circle the church exterior counterclockwise to enjoy the statues. In the third niche is **Nanni di Banco's** *Quattro Santi Coronati* (c. 1415-1417). These four early Christians were sculptors martyred by the Roman emperor Diocletian because they refused to sculpt pagan gods. They seem to be contemplating the consequences of the fatal decision they're about to make.

While Banco's saints are deep in the church's niche, the next statue, just to the right, feels ready to step out. **Donatello's** *St.*

George is alert, perched on the edge of his niche, scanning the horizon for dragons and announcing the new age with its new outlook. His knitted brow shows there's a drama unfolding. Sure, he's anxious, but he's also self-assured. Comparing this Renaissance-style *St. George* to *Quattro Santi Coronati*, you can psychoanalyze the heady changes underway. This is humanism. (This statue is a copy of the c. 1417 original, which is now in the Bargello.)

The back side of the church is decorated by three statues worth a look: *St. Matthew*, *St. Stephen*, and *St. Eligius*. *St. Matthew*, patron of bankers, and *St. Stephen*, patron of wool merchants (both by Ghiberti), are a reminder that banking and textiles were mainstays of the Florentine economy. Nanni di Banco's *St. Eligius*, patron of metalworkers, shows workers shoeing a horse.

Around the corner, the first niche you come to features **Donatello's *St. Mark*** (1411-1413). The evangelist cradles his gospel in his strong, veined hand and gazes out, resting his weight on the right leg while bending the left. Though subtle, St. Mark's twisting *contrapposto* pose was the first seen since antiquity. Eighty years after young Donatello carved this statue, a teenage Michelangelo Buonarroti stood here and marveled at it.

• *Continue down the mall 50 more yards, to the huge and historic square...*

Piazza della Signoria

What a view! The main civic center of Florence is dominated by the Palazzo Vecchio, the Uffizi Gallery, and the marble greatness of old Florence littering the cobbles. Piazza della Signoria, with the feel of an open-air museum of statuary, still vibrates with the echoes of the city's past—executions, riots, and great celebrations. There's even Roman history: Look for the **chart** showing the ancient city (on a freestanding display to your right as you enter the square, in front of Chanel). Today, it's a tourist's world with pigeons, selfie sticks, horse buggies, and tired spouses. If it would make your tired hubby or weary wife come to life, stop in at the recommended but expensive **Rivoire** café to

enjoy its fine desserts, pudding-thick hot chocolate, and the best view seats in town (see page 519).

Before you towers the **Palazzo Vecchio,** the "old palace" and palatial Town Hall of the Medici—a fortress designed to contain riches and survive the many riots that went with local politics. The windows are just beyond the reach of angry stones, and the tower was a handy lookout post. Justice was doled out sternly on this square. Until 1873, Michelangelo's *David* stood where you see the replica today. The original was damaged in a 1527 riot (when a bench thrown from a palace window knocked its left arm off), but it remained here for several centuries, before being moved indoors for protection.

Step past the fake *David* through the front door into the Palazzo Vecchio's courtyard (free). This palace was Florence's symbol of civic power. You're surrounded by art for art's sake—a cherub frivolously marks the courtyard's center, and ornate stuccoes and frescoes decorate the walls and columns. Such luxury represented a big change 500 years ago. (For more on the Palazzo and climbing its tower, see page 491.)

• *Back outside, check out the statue-filled...*

Loggia dei Lanzi (a.k.a. Loggia della Signoria)

The loggia, once a forum for public debate, was perfect for a city that prided itself on its democratic traditions. But later, when the Medici figured that good art was more desirable than free speech, it was turned into an outdoor sculpture gallery. Notice the squirming Florentine themes—conquest, domination, rape, and decapitation. The statues lining the back are Roman originals brought back to Florence by a Medici when his villa in Rome was sold. Two statues in the front deserve a closer look: Giambologna's *The Rape of the Sabine Women* (c. 1583)—with its pulse-quickening rhythm of muscles—from the restless Mannerist period, which followed the stately and confident Renaissance, and Benvenuto Cellini's **Perseus** (1545-1553), the loggia's most noteworthy piece, showing the Greek hero who decapitated the snake-headed Medusa.

• *Cross the square to Bartolomeo Ammanati's big **fountain of Neptune** that Florentines (including Michelangelo) consider a huge waste of marble. The guy on the horse, to the left, is Cosimo I, the post-Renaissance Medici who commissioned the Uffizi.*

Find the round bronze plaque on the ground 10 steps in front of the fountain.

Savonarola Plaque

The Medici family was briefly thrown from power by an austere and charismatic monk named Savonarola, who made Florence a constitutional republic. He organized huge rallies lit by roaring bonfires here on the square where he preached. While children sang hymns, the devout brought their rich "vanities" (such as paintings, musical instruments, and playing cards) and threw them into the flames.

Encouraged by the pope, the Florentines fought back and arrested Savonarola. For two days, they tortured him, trying unsuccessfully to persuade him to see their side of things. Finally, on the very spot where Savonarola's followers had built bonfires of vanities, the monk was burned. The bronze plaque, engraved in Italian *("Qui dove...")*, reads, "Here, Girolamo Savonarola and his Dominican brothers were hanged and burned" in the year "MCCCCXC-VIII" (1498), ending his theocracy. Soon after, the Medici returned to power and the Renaissance picked up where it left off.

• *Stay cool, we have 200 yards to go. Follow the gaze of the fake David into the courtyard of the two-tone horseshoe-shaped building.*

Uffizi Courtyard

The top floor of this building, known as the *uffizi* (offices) during Medici days, is filled with the greatest collection of Florentine painting anywhere. It's one of Europe's top four or five art galleries. (For an overview of the can't-miss-it-art you'll find inside, see page 486).

The courtyard, filled with souvenir stalls and hustling young artists, is watched over by 19th-century statues of the great figures of the Renaissance: artists (Michelangelo, Giotto, Donatello, and Leonardo), philosophers (Niccolò Machiavelli), scientists (Galileo), writers (Dante), poets (Petrarch), cartographers (Amerigo Vespucci), and the great patron of so much Renaissance thinking, Lorenzo "the Magnificent" de' Medici. After hours, talented street musicians take advantage of the space's superior acoustics.

• *Exiting at the far end of the courtyard, pause at the Arno River, overlooking...*

Ponte Vecchio

Before you is Ponte Vecchio (Old Bridge), which has spanned this narrowest part of the Arno since Roman times (for more about the bridge, see page 491). To get into the exclusive little park below (on the north bank), you'll need to join the Florence rowing club.

• *Hike to the center of the bridge.*

A fine bust of the great goldsmith Cellini graces the central point of the bridge. This statue is a reminder that, in the 1500s, the Medici booted out the bridge's butchers and tanners and installed the gold- and silversmiths who still tempt visitors to this day.

During World War II, the Nazi occupiers were ordered to blow up Ponte Vecchio. An art-loving German consul intervened and saved the bridge. The buildings at either end were destroyed, leaving the bridge impassable but intact. Look up to notice the protected and elevated passageway that led the Medici from the Palazzo Vecchio through the Uffizi, across Ponte Vecchio, and up to the immense Pitti Palace, four blocks beyond the bridge.

• *After this introduction to Florence's medieval roots and Renaissance greats, several of the finest museums in Europe await your discovery—or perhaps it's time for a nice espresso or gelato. Enjoy.*

Sights in Florence

A 🎧 in a listing means the sight is covered in a free audio tour (via my Rick Steves Audio Europe app—see page 12).

SIGHTSEEING STRATEGIES

Florence's two most popular sights (the Uffizi Gallery and the Accademia with *David*) have notorious lines all year long. Smart travelers save hours by buying tickets with a reserved entry time online, or purchasing a Firenze Card, which lets you skip the line.

Overview: The **Firenze Card** (€72/person) is the easiest way to avoid lines at multiple sights. (And it's the *only* way to skip the often-long lines to ascend the Duomo's dome.) Getting the card makes the most sense from April through October, when crowds are worst. You'll have to sightsee like mad for the full three-day validity period just to break even.

On a shorter visit (1-2 days), or if you won't be entering too many sights, you can save money and still avoid the lines by skipping the Firenze Card and instead making **reservations** for the Accademia and Uffizi.

A €15 **combo-ticket** covers Duomo-related sights: the Baptistery, dome, Campanile, Duomo Museum, and Santa Reparata (the church crypt, inside the Duomo). You should only get the combo-ticket if you don't have a Firenze Card (which covers the same sights).

Firenze Card

This three-day sightseeing pass gives you admission to many of Florence's sights, including the Uffizi Gallery and Accademia. Just as important, it lets you skip the ticket-buying lines without making reservations. With the card, you simply go to the entrance at a covered sight (look for the Firenze Card logo), show the card, and they let you in (though there still

FLORENCE

may be delays at popular sights with bottleneck entryways or capacity limits). At some sights, you must first present your card at the ticket booth or information desk to get a physical ticket before proceeding to the entrance.

Cost and Coverage: The Firenze Card costs €72 and is valid for 72 hours from when you validate it at your first museum (e.g., Tue at 15:00 until Fri at 15:00). Validate your card only when you're ready to tackle the covered sights on three consecutive days. Make sure the sights you want to visit will be open (many sights are closed Sun or Mon). The Firenze Card covers the regular admission price as well as any special-exhibit surcharges, and is good for one visit per sight.

What's Included: To figure out if the card is a good deal for you, tally up the entry fees for what you want to see.
- Uffizi Gallery (€12.50, or €8 if no special exhibits, plus €4 fee if reserved ahead)
- Accademia (same as Uffizi)
- Palazzo Vecchio (€10 apiece for museum or tower, €18 for combo-ticket that includes museum, tower, and excavations)
- Bargello (€8, or €4 if no special exhibits)
- Medici Chapels (€8, or €4 if no special exhibits)
- Museum of San Marco (€4)
- Duomo sights: Baptistery, Campanile, dome climb, Santa Reparata crypt (inside the Duomo), and Duomo Museum (€15)
- Pitti Palace sights: Palatine Gallery and Royal Apartments (€13, or €8.50 if no special exhibits)
- Santa Croce Church (€8)
- Basilica of San Lorenzo (€5)

If you enter all of the above sights within three days—an ambitious plan—the Firenze Card will pay for itself. For a complete list of included sights, see www.firenzecard.it.

Buying the Firenze Card: You can buy the card at some TIs (across from train station, at Via Cavour 1 red, facing the Campanile, and at the airport). Several participating sights also sell them: the Uffizi Gallery's door #2 (enter to the left of the ticket-buying line), the back entrance of the Church of Santa Maria Novella, the Bargello, the Palazzo Vecchio, Brancacci Chapel, the Pitti Palace, and Palazzo Strozzi. Lines are shortest at Palazzo Strozzi, the Via Cavour TI (credit cards only), the Bargello, and Santa Maria Novella (facing the train station, at Piazza della Stazione 4); if you're doing the Uffizi first, door #2 is relatively quick. Don't bother buying the card online, as you have to go to one of these desks to swap the voucher for the actual pass.

The Fine Print: The Firenze Card is not shareable, and there are no family or senior discounts for Americans or Canadians.

Children under 18 are allowed free into any state museum in Italy, and into any municipal museum in Florence. However, at the Uffizi and Accademia, to skip the lines with their Firenze Card-holding parents, children still must (technically) pay the €4 "reservation fee" (which can be paid on the spot—no need to reserve ahead). However, in practice, enforcement of this policy seems to vary. Don't confuse this card with the Firenze PASSport.

Advance Reservations (Without the Firenze Card)

If you don't get a Firenze Card, it's smart to make reservations at the often-crowded Accademia and Uffizi Gallery. Some other Florence sights—including the Bargello, Medici Chapels, and the Pitti Palace—offer reservations, but they are unnecessary. The Brancacci Chapel officially requires a reservation, but it's usually possible to get it on the spot.

Accademia and Uffizi Reservations

Get reservations for these two top sights as soon as you know when you'll be in town. Without a reservation at the Accademia and Uffizi, you can usually enter without significant lines from November through March after 16:00. But from April through October and on weekends, it can be crowded even late in the day. Any time of year, I'd reserve a spot. Note that reservations are not possible on the first Sunday of the month, when the museums are free and very busy.

There are several ways to make a reservation:

Online: You can book and pay for your Accademia or Uffizi visit via the city's official site (€4/ticket reservation fee, www. firenzemusei.it—click on "B-ticket"). You'll receive an order confirmation email, which is followed shortly by a voucher email. Bring your voucher to the ticket desk to swap for an actual ticket.

Pricey middleman sites—such as www.uffizi.com and www. tickitaly.com—are reliable and more user-friendly than the official site, but their booking fees run about €10 per ticket. (When ordering from these broker sites, don't confuse Florence's Accademia with Venice's gallery of the same name.)

By Phone: From a US phone, dial 011-39-055-294-883, or from an Italian phone call 055-294-883 (€4/ticket reservation fee; booking office open Mon-Fri 8:30-18:30, Sat 8:30-12:30, closed Sun). When you get through, an English-speaking operator walks you through the process—a few minutes later you say *grazie,* having secured an entry time and a confirmation number. You'll present your confirmation number at the museum and pay for your ticket. You pay only for the tickets you pick up (e.g., if you reserved two tickets but only use one, you'll pay for just one ticket).

Through Your Hotel: Some hoteliers are willing to book

museum reservations for their guests (ask when you reserve your room); some offer this as a service, while others charge a small booking fee.

Private Tour: Various tour companies—including the ones listed on page 457—offer tours that include a reserved museum admission.

Last-Minute Strategies: If you arrive without a reservation, call the reservation number (see "By Phone," earlier), ask your hotelier for help, or head to a booking window, either at Orsanmichele Church (daily 9:00-16:00, closed Sun off-season, along Via de' Calzaiuoli) or at the My Accademia Libreria bookstore across from the Accademia's exit (Tue-Sun 8:15-17:30, closed Mon, Via Ricasoli 105 red). It's also possible to go to the Uffizi's official ticket office (use door #2 and skirt to the left of the long ticket-buying line), and ask if they have any short-notice reservations available. Any of these options will cost you the €4 reservation fee. Because the museums are closed on Mondays, the hardest day to snare a last-minute, same-day reservation is Tuesday— get an early start. As a last resort, remember that even if you're in town for just a few hours and neglected to get reservations, if you're determined to see the Uffizi and *David* at the Accademia you can always buy a Firenze Card just for the line-skipping privileges.

THE DUOMO AND NEARBY SIGHTS

While the Duomo itself is free to enter, several associated sights are covered by a single €15 **combo-ticket,** valid for 48 hours: the Baptistery, dome, Campanile, Duomo Museum, and Santa Reparata crypt (enter from inside the Duomo). The main ticket office faces the Baptistery entrance (at #7 on the square) and has a staffed counter (credit cards or cash) as well as self-service machines (credit cards only, requires PIN); there's another office at the Duomo Museum. You can buy cash-only tickets at the Santa Reparata crypt or at the Campanile. Advance tickets are available online (www.museumflorence.com).

All of these sights are also covered by the Firenze Card (see page 468), which lets you skip the often-long lines for climbing the dome. But before entering any of the Duomo sights, you must present your Firenze Card at the ticket office opposite the Baptistery to obtain a free combo-ticket.

Tours: Themed tours (€30 each, price includes combo-ticket) include a Duomo visit and access to the north terrace of the church (daily at 10:30), an opportunity to watch contemporary stonemasons at work in the same workshop where Michelangelo carved *David* (Mon, Wed, and Fri at 12:00), and an up-close look at the mosaics of the Baptistery (Mon, Wed, and Fri at 16:30). To book a spot, call 055-230-2885, email info@operaduomo.firenze.it, or stop by the main ticket office.

🎧 The Duomo, dome, Campanile, and Baptistery are also covered on my free Renaissance Walk audio tour.

▲▲Duomo (Cattedrale di Santa Maria del Fiore)

Florence's Gothic cathedral has the third-longest nave in Christendom. The church's noisy Neo-Gothic facade (from the 1870s) is covered with pink, green, and white Tuscan marble. The cathedral's claim to artistic fame is Brunelleschi's magnificent dome—the first Renaissance dome and the model for domes to follow. While viewing it from the outside is well worth ▲▲, and described earlier on my Renaissance Walk, the massive but empty-feeling interior is lucky to rate ▲—it doesn't justify the massive crowds that line up to get inside. Much of the church's great art is housed in the Duomo Museum behind the church.

Cost and Hours: Free; Mon-Fri 10:00-17:00 (Thu until 16:00 May and Oct, until 16:30 Nov-April), Sat 10:00-16:45, Sun 13:30-16:45, opening times sometimes change due to religious functions, audioguide—€5, modest dress code enforced, tel. 055-230-2885, www.museumflorence.com.

▲Climbing the Duomo's Dome

For a grand view into the cathedral from the base of the dome, a chance to see Brunelleschi's "dome-within-a-dome" construction,

and a glorious Florence view from the top, climb 463 steps up the dome. While you're waiting in line—as you likely will unless you have a Firenze Card—spend a few minutes studying the precious Donatello sculpture above the recently restored side entrance door, called the Porta della Mandorla ("Almond Door"): Madonna and Bambino are carried by angels in an almond-shaped frame, above the delicately carved door frame and Annunciation mosaics by Nanni di Banco. If you look up from here you'll see an empty pedestal atop the transept. Michelangelo's *David* was originally destined to adorn one of these. The claustrophobic one-way route takes you up narrow staircases and walkways to the top.

Cost and Hours: €15 combo-ticket covers all Duomo sights, covered by Firenze Card, Mon-Fri 8:30-19:00, Sat 8:30-17:40, Sun 13:00-16:40, last entry 40 minutes before closing, crowds may subside a bit at lunchtime (13:00-14:30) or near the end of the day, enter from outside church on north side. Because it's slippery, the dome is closed during rain.

▲Campanile (Giotto's Tower)

The 270-foot bell tower has 50-some fewer steps than the Duomo's dome (but that's still 414 steps—no elevator); offers a faster, relatively less-crowded climb (with typically shorter lines); and has a view of that magnificent dome to boot. On the way up, there are several intermediate levels where you can catch your breath and enjoy ever-higher views. The stairs narrow as you go up, creating a mosh-pit bottleneck near the very top—but the views are worth the hassle. While the various viewpoints are enclosed by cage-like bars, the gaps are big enough to let you snap great photos.

Cost and Hours: €15 ticket covers all Duomo sights, covered by Firenze Card, daily 8:15-19:30, last entry 40 minutes before closing.

▲Baptistery

Michelangelo said the bronze doors of this octagonal building were fit to be the gates of paradise. Check out the gleaming copies of Lorenzo Ghiberti's bronze doors facing the Duomo (the originals are in the Duomo Museum). Making a breakthrough in perspective, Ghiberti used mathematical laws to create the illusion of receding distance on a basically flat surface. The doors on the north side of the building (around to the right) were designed by Ghiberti when he was young; he'd won the honor and opportunity by beating Brunelleschi in a competition (the rivals' original entries are in the Bargello). Inside, sit and savor the medieval mosaic ceiling, where it's always Judgment Day and Jesus is giving the ultimate thumbs-up and thumbs-down.

Cost and Hours: €15 ticket covers all Duomo sights, covered by Firenze Card, interior open Mon-Fri 8:15-10:15 & 11:15-19:00, Sat 8:15-19:00, Sun 8:15-14:00. The (facsimile) bronze doors are on the exterior, so they are always "open" and viewable.

Visiting the Baptistery's Interior: Workers from St. Mark's in Venice came here to make the remarkable ceiling mosaics (of Venetian glass) in the late 1200s.

The Last Judgment on the ceiling gives us a glimpse of the medieval worldview. Life was a preparation for the afterlife, when you would be judged and saved, or judged and damned—with no in-between. Christ, peaceful and reassuring, blessed those at his right hand with heaven (thumbs up) and sent those on his left to hell (the ultimate thumbs-down), to be tortured by demons and gnashed between the teeth of monsters.

The rest of the ceiling mosaics tell the history of the world, from Adam and Eve (over the north/entrance doors, top row) to Noah and the Flood (over south doors, top row), to the life of Christ (second row, all around) to the life, ministry, and eventual beheading of John the Baptist (bottom row, all around)—all bathed in the golden glow of pre-Renaissance heaven.

▲▲▲Duomo Museum (Museo dell'Opera del Duomo)

The cathedral museum, recently reopened after a major renovation, is marvelous: Brunelleschi's dome, Ghiberti's bronze doors, and

Donatello's statues. These creations define the 1400s (the Quattrocento) in Florence, when the city blossomed and classical arts were reborn. Copies of the doors and statues now decorate the exteriors of the cathedral, Baptistery, and Campanile, while the original sculptured masterpieces of the complex are now restored and thoughtfully displayed here. The museum also has two powerful statues by Florence's powerhouse sculptors—Donatello's *Mary Magdalene* and Michelangelo's *Pietà* (intended as his sculptural epitaph).

Cost and Hours: €15 combo-ticket covers all Duomo sights, valid 48 hours, covered by Firenze Card; daily 9:00-22:00, April and Nov until 21:00, Dec-March until 19:00, closed first Tue of every month, last entry one hour before closing; one of the few museums in Florence always open on Mon; behind the church at Via del Proconsolo 9, tel. 055-282-226, www.museumflorence.com.

Visiting the Museum: Start in Room 6, the big Sala del Paradiso (Hall of Paradise), which dominates the museum. This room re-creates the facades of the Duomo and the Baptistery, which were a showcase of the greatest art of Florence from roughly 1300 to 1600. The original statues, doors, and reliefs face each other as they once did on the buildings they were designed for. (They were moved to the museum to better preserve them; copies now adorn the buildings.)

Facing the facade of the church, as they did in the Middle Ages, are the famous **bronze doors** of the Baptistery. The Renaissance began in 1401 with a citywide competition to build new doors for the Baptistery. Lorenzo Ghiberti (c. 1378-1455) won the job and built the doors for the north side of the building. Everyone

FLORENCE

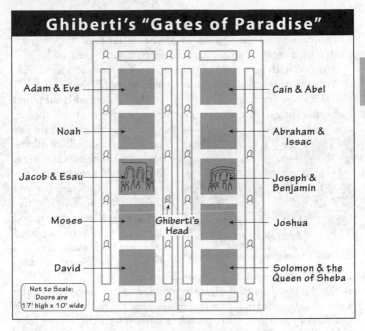

Ghiberti's "Gates of Paradise"

Adam & Eve

Noah

Jacob & Esau

Moses — Ghiberti's Head

David

Cain & Abel

Abraham & Issac

Joseph & Benjamin

Joshua

Solomon & the Queen of Sheba

Not to Scale: Doors are 17' high x 10' wide

loved them, so he was then hired to make another set of doors for the east entrance, facing the Duomo. These bronze "Gates of Paradise" revolutionized the way Renaissance people saw the world around them. Each panel is bronze with a layer of gold on top. They tell several stories in one frame using perspective and realism as never before.

Moving from left to right and top to bottom, here are the Old Testament stories depicted in the 10 original panels:

Adam and Eve: God creates Adam, Eve, the snake, the apple, and original sin, then expels the humans.

Cain and Abel: Cain and Abel tend sheep, till the soil, and make a sacrifice, then Cain kills Abel and talks to God.

Noah: Noah and sons emerge from the ark (shown as a pyramid) after the flood, then Noah makes a sacrifice and gets drunk.

Abraham and Isaac: An angel prevents the sacrifice of Isaac.

Jacob and Esau: Isaac's son Jacob buys and deceives his way into the birthright of his elder brother, Esau.

Joseph and Benjamin: After his brothers sell him into slavery in Egypt, Joseph recognizes them when they visit and frames Benjamin as a thief.

Moses: Onlookers exult as Moses receives the Tablets of the Law from God.

Joshua: Joshua leads the chosen people into the Promised Land and in celebration as the walls of Jericho fall.

FLORENCE

David: The young hero conquers the giant Goliath.

Solomon and the Queen of Sheba: After traveling to Jerusalem with a great retinue and many gifts, a queen meets a king.

Armed with new rules of perspective, Ghiberti rendered reality with a mathematical precision revolutionary for the time.

The space created by the arches in the **Jacob and Esau panel** is as interesting as the scenes themselves. At the center is the so-

called vanishing point on the distant horizon, where all the arches and floor tiles converge. Those closest to us, at the bottom of the panel, are big and clearly defined. Distant figures are smaller, fuzzier, and higher up. Ghiberti has placed us as part of this casual crowd of holy people—some with their backs to us—milling around an arcade.

In the **Joseph and Benjamin panel,** notice how, with just the depth of a thumbnail, Ghiberti creates a temple in the round that's inhabited by workers. This round temple wowed the Florentines. Suddenly the world acquired a whole new dimension—depth.

The receding arches stretch into infinity in the **Solomon and the Queen of Sheba panel,** giving the airy feeling that we can see forever.

Also on the ground floor are rooms dedicated to the museum's most famous and evocative statues. Donatello's *Mary Magdalene* (*Maddalena*, c. 1455), carved from white poplar and originally painted with realistic colors, is a Renaissance work of intense devotion. The aging Michelangelo (1475-1564) designed his own tomb, with a *Pietà* (1547-1555) as the centerpiece. Three mourners tend the broken body of the crucified Christ. We see Mary, his mother; Mary Magdalene (on the left); and Nicodemus, the converted Pharisee, whose face is that of Michelangelo himself.

Upstairs, the first floor displays original **statues and panels** from the bell tower's third story, where copies stand today, two marble **choir lofts** (*cantorie;* by Lucca della Robbia and Donatello) that once sat above the sacristy doors of the Duomo, an exquisite half-ton **silver altar** honoring John the Baptist that once stood in the Baptistery, and **Brunelleschi's model** of the dome.

SIGHTS NORTH OF THE DUOMO
▲▲▲Accademia (Galleria dell'Accademia)

This museum houses Michelangelo's *David,* the consummate Renaissance statue of the buff, biblical shepherd boy ready to take on the giant. When you look into the eyes of this magnificent sculpture, you're looking into the eyes of Renaissance Man.

Cost and Hours: €12.50 (or €8 if there's no special exhibit), additional €4 for recommended reservation, free and crowded on first Sun of the month, covered by Firenze Card; Tue-Sun 8:15-18:50, closed Mon; audioguide €6, Via Ricasoli 60, reservation tel. 055-294-883, www.galleriaaccademiafirenze.beniculturali.it. To avoid long lines in peak season, get the Firenze Card or make reservations (see pages 469 and 470).

∩ Download my free Accademia audio tour.

Visiting the Museum: In 1501, Michelangelo Buonarroti, a 26-year-old Florentine, was commissioned to carve a large-scale work. The figure comes from a Bible story. The Israelites are surrounded by barbarian warriors, who are led by a brutish giant named Goliath. When the giant challenges the Israelites to send out someone to fight him, a young shepherd boy steps forward. Armed only with a sling, David defeats the giant. This 17-foot-tall symbol of divine victory over evil represents a new century and a whole new Renaissance outlook. This is the age of Columbus and classicism, Galileo and Gutenberg, Luther and Leonardo—of Florence and the Renaissance.

Michelangelo was given a block of marble that other sculptors had rejected as too tall, shallow, and flawed to be of any value. But Michelangelo picked up his hammer and chisel, knocked a knot off what became *David*'s heart, and started to work.

The statue captures David as he's sizing up his enemy. He stands relaxed but alert, leaning on one leg in a classical pose known as *contrapposto.* In his powerful right hand, he fondles the handle of the sling, ready to fling a stone at the giant. His gaze is steady—searching with intense concentration, but also with extreme confidence. Michelangelo has caught the precise moment when David is saying to himself, "I can take this guy."

While some think that he's already slain the giant, the current director of the Accademia believes, as I do, that Michelangelo has portrayed David facing the giant. (Unlike most depictions of

David after the kill, this sculpture does not show the giant's severed head.)

David is a symbol of Renaissance optimism. He's no brute. He's a civilized, thinking individual who can grapple with and overcome problems. He needs no armor, only his God-given physical strength and wits. Look at his right hand, with the raised veins and strong, relaxed fingers—many complained that it was too big and overdeveloped. But this is the hand of a man with the strength of God on his side. No mere boy could slay the giant. But David, powered by God, could...and did.

Originally, *David* was meant to stand on the roofline of the Duomo, but was placed more prominently at the entrance of Palazzo Vecchio (where a copy stands today). In the 19th century, *David* was moved indoors for his own protection, and stands under a wonderful Renaissance-style dome designed just for him.

Nearby are some of the master's other works, including his powerful (unfinished) *Prisoners, St. Matthew,* and a *Pietà* (possibly by one of his disciples). Florentine Michelangelo Buonarroti, who would work tirelessly through the night, believed that the sculptor was a tool of God, responsible only for chipping away at the stone until the intended sculpture emerged. Beyond the magic marble are some mildly interesting pre-Renaissance and Renaissance paintings, including a couple of lighter-than-air Botticellis, the plaster model of Giambologna's *Rape of the Sabine Women,* and a musical instrument collection with an early piano.

▲Piazza S.S. Annunziata

The most Renaissance square in Florence is tucked just a block behind the Accademia. It's like an urban cloister from the 15th century, with three fine buildings—a convent church, a hospital, and an orphanage—ringing a fine equestrian statue of Ferdinand, a Medici grand duke. Stand in the center and slowly spin, imagining being here in 1500 as you survey the only Renaissance square in Florence, with the towering Duomo down the street.

Filippo Brunelleschi's **Hospital of the Innocents** (Ospedale degli Innocenti), built in the 1420s, is considered the first Renaissance building. Its graceful arches and columns, with each set of columns forming a square, embody the quintessence of Renaissance harmony and typified the new aesthetic of calm balance and symmetry. It's ornamented with terra-cotta medallions by Luca della Robbia—each showing a different way to wrap an infant (meant to help babies grow straight, and practiced in Italy until about a century ago). Terra-cotta—made of glazed and painted clay—was a combination of painting and sculpture, but cheaper than either. For three generations the Della Robbia family guarded the secret recipe and made their name by bringing affordable art to Florence.

With its mission to care for the least among society (parentless or unwanted children), this hospital was also an important symbol of the increasingly humanistic and humanitarian outlook of Renaissance Florence. For four centuries (until 1875), orphans would be left at the "wheel of the innocents" (the small, barred window at the far left of the porch). Today the building houses a **museum** (Museo degli Innocenti), telling the story of the babies left here, and serving as UNICEF's local headquarters.

I love sleeping on this square (at the recommended Hotel Loggiato dei Serviti) and picnicking here during the day (with the riffraff, who remind me of the persistent gap—today as in Medici times—between those who appreciate fine art and those just looking for some cheap wine).

The 15th-century **Santissima Annunziata church** (with its Bill and Melinda Gates-type patronage attribution to the Pucci brothers: Alexander and Roberto) is also worth a peek. The welcoming cloister has early 16th-century frescoes by Andrea del Sarto, and the church's interior is slathered in Baroque—rare in Florence.

▲▲Museum of San Marco (Museo di San Marco)

Located one block north of the Accademia, this 15th-century monastery houses the greatest collection anywhere of frescoes and paintings by the early Renaissance master Fra Angelico. The ground floor features the monk's paintings, along with some works by Fra Bartolomeo.

Upstairs are 43 cells decorated by Fra Angelico and his assistants. While the monk/painter was trained in the medieval religious style, he also learned and adopted Renaissance techniques and sensibilities, producing works that blended Christian symbols and Renaissance realism. Don't miss the cell of Savonarola, the charismatic monk who rode in from the Christian right, threw out the Medici, turned Florence into a theocracy, sponsored "bonfires of the vanities" (burning books, paintings, and so on), and was finally burned himself when Florence decided to change channels.

Cost and Hours: €4, free and crowded on first Sun of the month, covered by Firenze Card, Tue-Fri 8:15-13:50, Sat 8:15-16:50; also open 8:15-13:50 on first, third, and fifth Mon and 8:15-16:50 on second and fourth Sun of each month; on Piazza San Marco, tel. 055-238-8608.

Basilica of San Lorenzo

The Basilica of San Lorenzo—on the site of the first Christian church in Florence—was built outside the Roman walls and con-

secrated in A.D. 393, then rebuilt in the early 1400s. That's when Filippo Brunelleschi was hired to replace a Romanesque church that stood here. Brunelleschi designed the building, and Donatello worked on the bronze pulpits inside (among other things). Adjacent to the church is a cloister where you can visit the crypt (with the tombs of Cosimo the Elder, and his friend Donatello) and the Laurentian Medici Library, designed by Michelangelo. (The famed Medici Chapels, with Michelangelo's tomb sculptures, are part of the church complex but have a separate ticket; see next listing.)

Cost and Hours: €5 for the church and crypt, buy ticket just inside cloister to the left of the facade, €7.50 combo-ticket also covers the library, covered by Firenze Card; church and crypt open Mon-Sat 10:00-17:30, Sun 13:30-17:30, closed Sun Nov-Feb; library open Mon, Wed, and Fri 8:00-14:00, Tue and Thu 8:00-17:30, closed Sat-Sun; Piazza di San Lorenzo, tel. 055-214-042, www.operamedicealaurenziana.it.

▲▲Medici Chapels (Cappelle Medicee)

The burial site of the ruling Medici family in the Basilica of San Lorenzo includes the dusky crypt; the big, domed Chapel of Princes; and the magnificent New Sacristy, featuring architecture, tombs, and statues almost entirely by Michelangelo. The Medici made their money in textiles

and banking, and patronized a dream team of Renaissance artists that put Florence on the cultural map. Michelangelo, who spent his teen years living with the Medici, was commissioned to create the family's final tribute.

Cost and Hours: €8 (or €4 if no special exhibits), free and crowded on first Sun of the month, covered by Firenze Card; Tue-Sat 8:15-16:50, Nov-March until 13:50; also open second and fourth Mon and first, third, and fifth Sun of each month; audioguide-€6, modest dress required, tel. 055-238-8602.

▲San Lorenzo Market

Florence's vast open-air market sprawls in the streets ringing Mercato Centrale, between the Duomo and the train station (daily 9:00-19:00, closed Mon in winter). More popular with tourists than locals, it's a hodgepodge of vendors selling T-shirts, scarves, cheap souvenirs, and leather goods of varying quality. Many of the leather stalls are run by Iranians selling South American leather that was tailored in Italy. At stalls or shops, prices are soft don't be shy about bargaining.

▲Mercato Centrale (Central Market)

Florence's giant iron-and-glass-covered central market, a wonderland of picturesque produce, is fun to explore. While the nearby San Lorenzo Market—with its garment and souvenir stalls in the streets—feels only a step up from a haphazard flea market, Mercato Centrale retains a Florentine elegance, particularly now that the upper level has been completely renovated and turned into an upscale food court. Wander around.

Downstairs, you'll see parts of the cow (and bull) you'd never dream of eating (no, that's not a turkey neck), enjoy free samples, watch pasta being made, and have your pick of plenty of fun eateries sloshing out cheap and tasty pasta to locals (Mon-Fri 7:00-14:00, Sat 7:00-17:00, closed Sun).

Upstairs, the meticulously restored glass roof and steel rafters soar over a sleek and modern food court, serving up a bounty of Tuscan cuisine (daily 10:00-24:00). For eating ideas downstairs, upstairs, and around the market, see "Eating in Florence," later.

▲Medici-Riccardi Palace (Palazzo Medici-Riccardi)

Lorenzo the Magnificent's home is worth a look for its art. The tiny Chapel of the Magi contains colorful Renaissance gems such as the *Procession of the Magi* frescoes by Benozzo Gozzoli. The former

FLORENCE

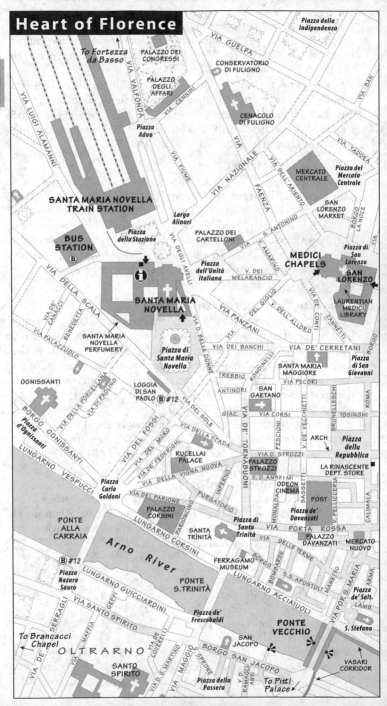

Heart of Florence

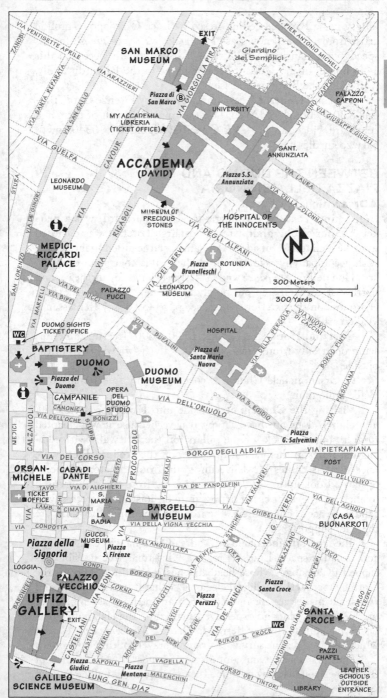

library has a Baroque ceiling fresco by Luca Giordano, a prolific artist from Naples known as "Fast Luke" *(Luca fa presto)* for his speedy workmanship. While the Medici originally occupied this 1444 house, in the 1700s it became home to the Riccardi family, who added the Baroque flourishes.

Cost and Hours: €7, cash only, covered by Firenze Card, Thu-Tue 8:30-19:00, closed Wed, ticket entrance is north of the gated courtyard, videoguide-€4, Via Cavour 3, tel. 055-276-0340, www.palazzo-medici.it.

BETWEEN THE DUOMO AND PIAZZA DELLA SIGNORIA
▲Orsanmichele Church

In the ninth century, this loggia (covered courtyard) was a market used for selling grain (stored upstairs). Later, it was enclosed to make a church. Outside are dynamic, statue-filled niches, some with accompanying symbols from the guilds that sponsored the art. Donatello's *St. Mark* and *St. George* (on the northeast and northwest corners) step out boldly in the new Renaissance style. (For more on the exterior statues, see page 459 of my Renaissance Walk, earlier.)

Cost and Hours: Free, daily 10:00-17:00, free upstairs museum open only Mon, niche sculptures always viewable from the outside.

♪ Orsanmichele Church is covered on my free Renaissance Walk audio tour.

Visiting the Church: Step inside into Florence, circa 1350. The church does not have a typical nave because it was adapted from a granary. Look for the pillars (on the left wall) with rectangular **holes** in them about three feet off the ground. These were once used as chutes for delivering grain from the storage rooms upstairs. Look up to see the **rings** hanging from the ceiling, used to anchor pulleys for either lifting grain or hoisting platforms with candles to act as chandeliers. The iron bars spanning the vaults are there for support.

The fanciful **tabernacle** by Andrea Orcagna was designed exactly for this space: Like the biggest Christmas tree possible, it's capped by an angel whose head touches the ceiling. Take in the Gothic tabernacle's medieval elegance. What it lacks in depth and realism it makes up for in color, with an intricate assemblage of marble, glass, gold, and expensive lapis lazuli. The elaborate tabernacle was built to display Bernardo Daddi's *Madonna delle Grazie,* which received plague survivors' grateful prayers of thanks—*grazie.*

Upstairs is a free museum displaying most of the originals of the statues you just saw outside. They represent virtually every big name in pre-Michelangelo Florentine sculpture: Donatello, Ghiberti, Brunelleschi, Giambologna, and more.

Evening Concerts: You can give the *Madonna delle Grazie* a special thanks if you're in town when the church is hosting an evening concert (sometimes held in museum, tickets sold on day of concert from door facing Via de' Calzaiuoli; also books Uffizi and Accademia tickets, ticket window open daily 9:00-16:00, closed Sun off-season).

▲Mercato Nuovo (a.k.a. the Straw Market)

This market loggia is how Orsanmichele looked before it became a church. Originally a silk and straw market, Mercato Nuovo still functions as a rustic yet touristy market (at the intersection of Via Calimala and Via Porta Rossa; daily 9:00-18:30). Prices are soft, but San Lorenzo Market (listed earlier) is much better for haggling. Notice the circled X in the center, marking the spot where people landed after being hoisted up to the top and dropped as punishment for bankruptcy (easiest to find when the market is closed and the vendors disappear). You'll also find *Il Porcellino* (a statue of a wild boar nicknamed "The Piglet"), which people rub and give coins to ensure their return to Florence. This new copy, while only a few years old, already has a polished snout. At the back corner, a wagon sells tripe (cow innards) sandwiches—a local favorite.

▲Piazza della Repubblica

Located on the site of the original Roman Forum, this square holds all that survives of Roman Florence: a single column nicknamed the "belly button of Florence." In the 1500s, this historical square served as the center of the city's Jewish quarter (which became a ghetto after Cosimo I walled it up in 1571). The city razed the ghetto and the city walls in the 1860s to make way for Florence's transformation into the grand capital of the newly united nation of Italy. This square was to be its centerpiece, and the triumphal arch is inscribed accordingly: "The squalor of the ancient city is given a new life."

▲Palazzo Davanzati

This five-story, late-medieval tower house offers a rare look at a noble dwelling built in the 14th century. The ground-floor

loggia and first floor are always open to visitors; to see the remaining floors (more living quarters and the kitchen), you must make a timed-entry reservation with an escort (usually at 10:00, 11:00, and 12:00; call ahead to be sure there's space or ask when you arrive). Like other buildings of the age, the exterior is festooned with 14th-century horse-tethering rings made from iron, torch holders, and poles upon which to hang laundry and fly flags. Inside, though the furnishings are pretty sparse, you'll see richly painted walls, a long chute that functioned as a well, plenty of fireplaces, a lace display, and even an indoor "outhouse." You can borrow English descriptions in each room.

Cost and Hours: €6, covered by Firenze Card, Tue-Sat 8:15-13:50; also open first, third, and fifth Sun and second and fourth Mon of each month; Via Porta Rossa 13, tel. 055-238-8610.

ON AND NEAR PIAZZA DELLA SIGNORIA
▲▲▲Uffizi Gallery

This greatest collection of Italian paintings anywhere features works by Giotto, Leonardo, Raphael, Caravaggio, Titian, and Michelangelo, and a roomful of Botticellis, including the *Birth of Venus*. Start with Giotto's early stabs at Renaissance-style realism, then move on through the 3-D experimentation of the early 1400s to the real thing rendered by the likes of Botticelli and Leonardo. Finish off with Michelangelo and Titian. Because only 600 visitors are allowed inside the building at any one time, there's generally a very long wait. The good news: no Vatican-style mob scenes inside. The museum is nowhere near as big as it is great. Few tourists spend more than two hours inside.

Cost and Hours: €12.50 (or €8 if there's no special exhibit), extra €4 for recommended reservation, free and crowded on first Sun of the month, covered by Firenze Card; Tue-Sun 8:15-18:35, closed Mon, last entry 45 minutes before closing; audioguide-€6, reservation tel. 055-294-883, www.uffizi.beniculturali.it. To avoid the long ticket lines, get a Firenze Card (see page 468) or make reservations (see page 470).

Getting In: There are several entrances; which one you use depends on whether you have a Firenze Card, a reservation, or neither.

Firenze Card holders enter at door #1 (labeled *Reservation Entrance*), close to the Palazzo Vecchio. Get in the line for individuals, not groups.

People **buying a ticket on the spot** line up with everyone else

FLORENCE

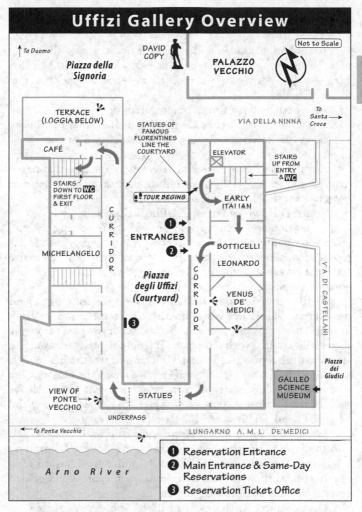

Uffizi Gallery Overview

To Duomo

Piazza della Signoria

DAVID COPY

PALAZZO VECCHIO

Not to Scale

TERRACE (LOGGIA BELOW)

STATUES OF FAMOUS FLORENTINES LINE THE COURTYARD

VIA DELLA NINNA

To Santa Croce

CAFÉ

ELEVATOR

STAIRS UP FROM ENTRY & **WC**

STAIRS DOWN TO **WC** FIRST FLOOR & EXIT

TOUR BEGINS

EARLY ITALIAN

MICHELANGELO

❶ ➤

ENTRANCES

❷ ➤

BOTTICELLI

LEONARDO

Piazza degli Uffizi (Courtyard)

CORRIDOR

CORRIDOR

VENUS DE' MEDICI

V·A DI CASTELLANI

❸

Piazza dei Giudici

VIEW OF PONTE VECCHIO

STATUES

GALILEO SCIENCE MUSEUM

UNDERPASS

To Ponte Vecchio

LUNGARNO A. M. L. DE'MEDICI

Arno River

❶ Reservation Entrance

❷ Main Entrance & Same-Day Reservations

❸ Reservation Ticket Office

at door #2, marked *Main Entrance*. (The wait can be hours long—an estimated wait time is posted.)

To **buy a Firenze Card,** or to see if there are any same-day reservations available (€4 extra, but could save you time), enter door #2 to the left of the same-day ticket-buying line (marked *Booking Service and Today* or *Advance Sale*). Don't be shy—and don't get into the long ticket-buying line. The left side of the doorway is kept open for same-day reservation buyers.

If you've **already made a reservation** and need to pick up your ticket, go to door #3 (labeled *Reservation Ticket Office,* across the courtyard from doors #1 and #2, closer to the river). Tickets are available for pickup 10 minutes before your appointed time. If you booked online and have already paid, you'll exchange your voucher for a ticket. If you (or your hotelier) booked by phone, give them your confirmation number and pay for the ticket. Then walk briskly past the looooong ticket-buying line—pondering the IQ of this gang—to door #1. Get in the right queue—one is for groups, one for individuals.

At especially busy times, be prepared for a wait even if you have a reservation or Firenze Card in hand. There may be a queue to pick up your reservation at door #3 and another 30-minute wait to enter at door #1.

Just after the doors are metal detectors and X-ray machines—remember to leave pocketknives and corkscrews at your hotel, and expect a slow shuffle through security.

Tours: 🎧 Download my free Uffizi Gallery audio tour.

Expansion and Renovation: The gallery is nearing the end of a major, multiyear overhaul. Pieces frequently move, and new rooms open, allowing the museum to display more of its extensive collection. If you can't find a work, ask a guard, *"Scusi, dov'è...?"* and point to the picture in the book.

Visiting the Museum: The Uffizi is U-shaped, running around the courtyard. This left wing contains Florentine paintings from medieval to Renaissance times. At the far end, you pass through a short hallway filled with sculpture. The right wing (which you can see across the courtyard) has later Florentine art (the big names, including Michelangelo) and a café terrace facing the Duomo. The visit continues downstairs with many more rooms of art, showing how the Florentine Renaissance spread to Rome (Raphael) and Venice (Titian), and inspired the Baroque (Caravaggio).

Medieval (1200-1400): Paintings by **Duccio, Cimabue,** and **Giotto** show the slow process of learning to paint a 3-D world on a 2-D surface, moving from the flat Byzantine style toward realism. In each work, Mary and Baby Jesus sit on a throne in a golden never-never land symbolizing heaven.

Duccio's piece is the most medieval and two-dimensional. The large throne in Cimabue's work creates an illusion of depth. In his *Madonna and Child with Angels,* Giotto creates a revolutionary three-dimensionality—he creates a space and fills it. The throne has angels in front, prophets behind, and a canopy over the top, clearly defining its three dimensions. The steps up to it create an extension of our world. And Mary is monumental, like a Roman statue, with knees and breasts that stick out at us. Giotto offers a taste of the Renaissance a century before it began.

Early Renaissance (mid-1400s): Piero della Francesca's *Federico da Montefeltro and Battista Sforza* heralds the era of humanism and the new centrality of ordinary people in art, warts and all. In medieval times, only saints and angels were worthy of being painted. In the humanistic Renaissance, however, even nonreligious folk like this husband and wife had their features preserved for posterity.

Fra Filippo Lippi's radiantly beautiful Madonnas are light years away from the generic Marys of the medieval era. We don't need the wispy halo over her head to tell us she's holy—she radiates sweetness and light from her divine face. Heavenly beauty is expressed by a physically beautiful woman.

Renaissance (1450-1500): Florence in 1450 was in a Firenz-y of activity. There was a can-do spirit of optimism in the air, led by prosperous merchants and bankers and a strong middle class. Lorenzo de' Medici, head of the powerful Medici family, epitomized this new humanistic spirit. He gathered Florence's best and brightest around him for evening wine and discussions of great ideas. One of this circle was the painter Botticelli.

The Botticelli room is filled with masterpieces and classical fleshiness. Botticelli's *Spring* is the Renaissance in its first bloom, its "springtime" of innocence. Madonna is out, Venus is in. This is a return to the pre-Christian pagan world of classical Greece, where things of the flesh are not sinful. Botticelli emphasizes pristine beauty over gritty realism. The lines of the bodies have pleasing, S-like curves. The faces are idealized but have real human features. There's a look of thoughtfulness and even melancholy in the faces—as though everyone knows that the innocence of spring will not last forever.

Birth of Venus is a masterpiece of Western art. This is the purest expression of Renaissance beauty. Venus' naked body is not sensual,

but innocent. Botticelli thought that physical beauty was a way of appreciating God.

In *Slander,* the classical architectural setting is classic Brunelleschi, but look what's taking place beneath those stately arches. These aren't proud Renaissance men and women but a ragtag, medieval-looking bunch, a Court of Thieves in an abandoned hall of justice. Botticelli got caught up in the teachings of Savonarola. He burned some of his own paintings and changed his artistic tune. The first flowering of the Renaissance was over.

Classical Sculpture: If the Renaissance was the foundation of the modern world, the foundation of the Renaissance was classical

FLORENCE

sculpture. Sculptors, painters, and poets alike turned for inspiration to these ancient Greek and Roman works as the epitome of balance, 3-D perspective, human anatomy, and beauty.

In the Tribune Room, the highlight is the *Venus de' Medici,* a Roman copy of the lost original by the great Greek sculptor Praxiteles. Balanced, harmonious, and serene, the statue embodies the attributes of Greece's "Golden Age," when balance was admired in every aspect of life.

Perhaps more than any other work of art, this statue *(Venere dei Medici)* has been the epitome of both ideal beauty and sexuality. In the 18th and 19th centuries, sex was "dirty," so the sex drive of cultured aristocrats was channeled into a love of pure beauty. Wealthy sons and daughters of Europe's aristocrats made the pilgrimage to the Uffizi to complete their classical education...where they swooned in ecstasy before the cold beauty of this goddess of love.

The sculpture hall has more 2,000-year-old copies of 2,500-year-old Greek originals...and the best view in Florence of the Arno River and Ponte Vecchio through the window, offering the sort of pleasure Renaissance painters wanted you to get from their paintings.

High Renaissance (1500-1550): Don't miss Michelangelo's *Holy Family,* the only surviving completed easel painting by the greatest sculptor in history (in the Michelangelo Room). Michelangelo was a Florentine—in fact, he was like an adopted son of the Medici, who recognized his talent—but much of his greatest work was done in Rome as part of the pope's face-lift of the city. We can see here some of the techniques he used on the Sistine Chapel ceiling—monumental figures; dramatic angles (looking up Mary's nose); accentuated, rippling muscles; and bright, clashing colors. These elements added a dramatic tension that was lacking in the graceful work of Leonardo and Botticelli.

After a break to enjoy Duomo views from the café terrace, head downstairs to find Raphael's *Madonna of the Goldfinch,* with Mary and the Baby Jesus brought down from heaven into the real world of trees, water, and sky (Room 66); and Titian's voluptuous *Venus of Urbino* (Room 83).

More Art on the Lower Floor: On your way out, you'll see temporary exhibitions and works by foreign painters. It's worth pausing in Room 90, with works by Caravaggio.

Nearby: The statue-filled Uffizi court-

FLORENCE

yard and Loggia dei Lanzi are covered in the "Renaissance Walk," earlier.

▲▲Palazzo Vecchio

This castle-like fortress with the 300-foot spire dominates Florence's main square. In Renaissance times, it was the Town Hall, where citizens pioneered the once-radical notion of self-rule. Its official name—Palazzo della Signoria—refers to the elected members of the city council. In 1540, the tyrant Cosimo I made the building his personal palace, redecorating the interior in lavish style. Today the building functions once again as the Town Hall.

Entry to the ground-floor courtyard is free, so even if you don't go upstairs to the museum, you can step inside and feel the essence of the Medici. There's also a fine little exhibit of scenes from old Florence. Paying customers can see Cosimo's (fairly) lavish royal apartments, decorated with (fairly) top-notch paintings and statues by Michelangelo and Donatello. The highlight is the Grand Hall (Salone dei Cinquecento), a 13,000-square-foot hall lined with huge frescoes and interesting statues.

Cost and Hours: Courtyard-free, museum-€10, tower climb-€10 (418 steps), museum plus tower-€14, excavations-€4, combo-ticket for all three sights-€18, covered by Firenze Card (first pick up ticket at ground-floor information desk before entering museum). Museum and excavations open Fri-Wed 9:00-23:00 (Oct-March until 19:00), Thu 9:00-14:00 year-round; tower has similar but shorter hours (last entry one hour before closing); last tickets for all sights sold one hour before closing; videoguide-€5, English tours available, Piazza della Signoria, tel. 055-276-8224, www.musefirenze.it.

▲Ponte Vecchio

Florence's most famous bridge has long been lined with shops. Originally these were butcher shops that used the river as a handy disposal system. Then, when the powerful and princely Medici built a passageway (the Vasari Corridor) over the bridge, the stinky meat market was replaced by the more elegant gold and silver shops that remain here to this day. A statue of Benvenuto Cellini, the master goldsmith of the Renaissance, stands in the center, ignored by the flood of tacky tourism.

Ponte Vecchio is also covered on the Renaissance Walk, earlier, and my ∩ free Renaissance Walk audio tour.

▲▲Galileo Science Museum
(Museo Galilei e Istituto di Storia della Scienza)

When we think of the Florentine Renaissance, we think of visual arts: painting, mosaics, architecture, and sculpture. But when the visual arts declined in the 1600s (abused and co-opted by politi-

FLORENCE

cal powers), music and science flourished in Florence. The first opera was written here. And Florence hosted many scientific breakthroughs, as you'll see in this fascinating collection of Renaissance and later clocks, telescopes, maps, and ingenious gadgets. Trace the technical innovations as modern science emerges from 1000 to 1900. Some of the most talked about bottles in Florence are the ones here that contain Galileo's fingers. Exhibits include various tools for gauging the world, from a compass and thermometer to Galileo's telescopes. Other displays delve into clocks, pumps, medicine, and chemistry. It's friendly, comfortably cool, never crowded, and just a block east of the Uffizi on the Arno River.

Cost and Hours: €9, €22 family ticket, covered by Firenze Card, Wed-Mon 9:30-18:00, Tue 9:30-13:00, guided tours available, Piazza dei Giudici 1, tel. 055-265-311, www.museogalileo.it.

EAST OF PIAZZA DELLA SIGNORIA
▲▲▲Bargello (Museo Nazionale del Bargello)
This underappreciated sculpture museum is in a former police station-turned-prison that looks like a mini-Palazzo Vecchio. The Re-

naissance began with sculpture—the great Florentine painters were "sculptors with brushes." You can see the birth of this revolution of 3-D in the Bargello (bar-JEL-oh), which boasts the best collection of Florentine sculpture. It's a small, uncrowded museum and a pleasant break from the intensity of the rest of Florence.

Highlights include Donatello's very influential, painfully beautiful *David* (the first male nude to be sculpted in a thousand years), multiple works by Michelangelo, and rooms of Medici treasures. Moody Donatello, who embraced realism with his lifelike statues, set the personal and artistic style for many Renaissance artists to follow. The best pieces are in the ground-floor room at the foot of the outdoor staircase (with fine works by Michelangelo, Cellini, and Giambologna) and in the "Donatello room" directly above (including his two different *David*s, plus Ghiberti and

Brunelleschi's revolutionary dueling door panels and yet another *David* by Verrocchio).

Cost and Hours: €8 (or €4 if no special exhibits), cash only, free and crowded on first Sun of the month, covered by Firenze Card; Tue-Sat 8:15-17:00—or until 13:50 if no special exhibits; also open these times on the second and fourth Mon and the first, third, and fifth Sun of each month, last entry 45 minutes before closing; reservations possible but unnecessary, Via del Proconsolo 4, tel. 055-238-8606.

▲▲Santa Croce Church

This 14th-century Franciscan church, decorated with centuries of precious art, holds the tombs of great Florentines. The loud 19th-

century Victorian Gothic facade faces a huge square ringed with tempting shops and littered with tired tourists. Escape into the church and admire its sheer height and spaciousness.

Cost and Hours: €8, covered by Firenze Card, Mon-Sat 9:30-17:30, Sun 14:00-17:30, multimedia guide-€6 (€8/2 people), modest dress required, 10-minute walk east of the Palazzo Vecchio along Borgo de' Greci, tel. 055-246-6105, www.santacroceopera.it. The **leather school,** at the back of the church, is free and sells church tickets—handy when the church has a long line (daily 10:00-18:00, closed Sun Nov-March, has own entry behind church plus an entry within the church, www.scuoladelcuoio.com).

Visiting the Church: On the left wall (as you face the altar) is the tomb of **Galileo Galilei** (1564-1642), the Pisan who lived his last years under house arrest near Florence. His crime? Defying the Church by saying that the earth revolved around the sun. His heretical remains were only allowed in the church long after his death.

Directly opposite (on the right wall) is the tomb of **Michelangelo Buonarroti** (1475-1564). Santa Croce was Michelangelo's childhood church, as he grew up a block west of here. Farther up the nave is the tomb of **Niccolò Machiavelli** (1469-1527), a champion of democratic Florence and author of *The Prince,* a how-to manual on hardball politics—which later Medici rulers found instructive.

The first chapel to the right of the main altar features the famous *Death of St. Francis* fresco by Giotto. With simple but eloquent gestures, Francis' brothers bid him a sad farewell. In the hallway near the bookstore, notice the photos of the devastating flood of 1966. Beyond that is the leather school (free entry).

Exit between the Rossini and Machiavelli tombs into the delightful cloister (open-air courtyard). On the left, enter Brunelleschi's Pazzi Chapel, which captures the Renaissance in miniature.

▲Casa Buonarroti (Michelangelo's House)

On property once owned by Michelangelo, this house was built after the artist's death by his grandnephew, who turned it into a little museum honoring his famous relative. The highlights—his less-than-monumental first sculptures and some early sketches—are not must-sees in art-heavy Florence, but are appreciated by Michelangelovers.

Cost and Hours: €6.50, covered by Firenze Card, Wed-Mon 10:00-17:00, closed Tue, Via Ghibellina 70, tel. 055-241-752, www.casabuonarroti.it.

NEAR THE TRAIN STATION

▲▲Church of Santa Maria Novella

This 13th-century Dominican church is rich in art. Along with crucifixes by Giotto and Brunelleschi, it contains the textbook example of the early Renaissance mastery of perspective: *The Trinity* by Masaccio. The exquisite chapels trace art in Florence from medieval times to early Baroque. The outside of the church features a dash of Romanesque (horizontal stripes), Gothic (pointed arches), Renaissance (geometric shapes), and Baroque (scrolls). Step in and look down the 330-foot nave for a 14th-century optical illusion.

Next to the church are the cloisters and the **museum,** located in the old Dominican convent of Santa Maria Novella. The museum's highlight is the breathtaking Spanish Chapel, with walls covered by a series of frescoes by Andrea di Bonaiuto.

Cost and Hours: Church and museum-€5, covered by Firenze Card; Mon-Thu 9:00-19:00 (Oct-March until 17:30), Fri 11:00-19:00 (Oct-March until 17:30), Sat 9:00-17:30 (July-Aug until 18:30), Sun 13:00-17:30 (July-Aug 12:00-18:30), last entry 45 minutes before closing; multimedia guide-€3, modest dress required, main entrance on Piazza Santa Maria Novella, tel. 055-219-257, www.chiesasantamarianovella.it.

SIGHTS IN THE OLTRARNO
(SOUTH OF THE ARNO RIVER)
▲▲Pitti Palace

The imposing Pitti Palace, several blocks southwest of Ponte Vecchio, offers many reasons for a visit: the palace itself, with its imposing exterior and lavish interior; the second-best collection of paintings in town; the statue-dotted Boboli Gardens; and a host of secondary museums. Do yourself a favor and stay focused on the highlights: Stick to the Palatine Gallery, which has the painting collection, plus the sumptuous rooms of the Royal Apartments. The paintings pick up where the Uffizi leaves off, at the High Re-

naissance. Lovers of Raphael's Madonnas and Titian's portraits will find some of the world's best of each at the Pitti Palace. If it's a nice day, take a stroll in the Boboli Gardens, a rare and inviting patch of extensive green space within old Florence.

Cost and Hours: The Palatine Gallery, Royal Apartments, and Gallery of Modern Art are covered by **ticket #1**—€13 (€8.50 if no special exhibits)—and are open Tue-Sun 8:15-18:50, closed Mon, last entry 45 minutes before closing. The Boboli and Bardini Gardens, Costume Gallery, Argenti/Silverworks Museum (the Medici treasures), and Porcelain Museum are covered by **ticket #2**—€10 (€7 if no special exhibits)—and are open daily June-Aug 8:15-19:30, April-May and Sept 8:15-18:30, March and Oct 8:15-17:30, Nov-Feb 8:15-16:30, closed first and last Mon of each month, last entry one hour before closing. All palace sights are covered by the Firenze Card. The place is free and crowded on the first Sun of the month. The €8 audioguide (€13/2 people) explains the sprawling palace. Tel. 055-238-8614, www.uffizi.beniculturali.it.

Visiting the Museum: In the **Palatine Gallery** you'll walk through one palatial room after another, walls sagging with masterpieces by 16th- and 17th-century masters, including Rubens, Titian, and Rembrandt. The Pitti's Raphael collection is the second-biggest anywhere—the Vatican beats it by one. Use the information folders in each room to help find the featured paintings.

The collection is all on one floor. To see the highlights, walk straight down the spine through a dozen or so rooms. Before you exit, consider a visit to the Royal Apartments. These 14 rooms (of which only a few are open at any one time) are where the Pitti's rulers lived in the 18th and 19th centuries. Each room features a different color and time period. Here, you get a real feel for the splendor of the dukes' world.

The rest of Pitti Palace is skippable, unless the various sights match your interests: the **Gallery of Modern Art** (second floor; Romantic, Neoclassical, and Impressionist works by 19th- and 20th-century Tuscan painters), **Argenti/Silverworks Museum** (ground and mezzanine floors; Medici treasures from jeweled crucifixes to gilded ostrich eggs), **Costume Gallery, Porcelain Museum,** and **Boboli and Bardini gardens** (behind the palace; enter from Pitti Palace courtyard—be prepared to climb uphill).

▲▲Brancacci Chapel

For the best look at works by Masaccio (one of the early Renaissance pioneers of perspective in painting), see his restored frescoes here.

Instead of medieval religious symbols, Masaccio's paintings feature simple, strong human figures with facial expressions that reflect their emotions. The accompanying works of Masolino and Filippino Lippi provide illuminating contrasts.

Your ticket includes a 20-minute film (English subtitles) on the chapel, the frescoes, and Renaissance Florence; find it in the room next to the bookstore. The film's computer animation brings the paintings to 3-D life—they appear to move—while narration describes the events depicted in the panels. The film takes liberties with the art, but it's visually interesting and your best way to see the frescoes close up.

Cost and Hours: €6, cash only, covered by Firenze Card; free and easy reservations required if you don't have a Firenze Card (see next); Mon and Wed-Sat 10:00-17:00, Sun 13:00-17:00, closed Tue, last entry 45 minutes before closing; free 20-minute film, videoguide-€3, knees and shoulders must be covered, in Church of Santa Maria del Carmine on Piazza del Carmine, reservations tel. 055-276-8224, ticket desk tel. 055-284-361, http://museicivicifiorentini.comune.fi.it.

Reservations: Although reservations are required, on weekdays and any day off-season, it's often possible to walk right in, especially if you come before 15:30. To reserve in advance, call the chapel a day ahead (tel. 055-276-8224, English spoken, call center open Mon-Sat 9:30-13:00 & 14:00-17:00, Sun 9:30-12:30). You can also try via email—info@muse.comune.fi.it.

FLORENCE

▲Piazzale Michelangelo

Overlooking the city from across the river (look for the huge bronze statue of *David*), this square has a superb view of Florence

and the stunning dome of the Duomo. It's worth the 25-minute hike, taxi, or bus ride.

An inviting café (open seasonally) with great views is just below the overlook. The best photos are taken from the street immediately below the overlook (go around to the right and down a few steps). Off the west side of the piazza is a somewhat hidden terrace, an excellent place to retreat from the mobs. After dark, the square is packed with school kids licking ice cream and each other. About 200 yards beyond all the tour groups and teenagers is the stark, beautiful, crowd-free, Romanesque San Miniato Church (next listing). A WC is located just off the road, halfway between the two sights.

Getting There (and Back): It makes sense to take a taxi or ride the bus up and then enjoy the easy downhill walk back into town. Bus #12 takes you up (departs from train station, near Piazza di Santa Maria Novella, and just over the Ponte alla Carraia bridge on Oltrarno side of river—see map on page 482 for bus stops; takes 20-30 minutes, longer in bad traffic).

The hike down is quick and enjoyable (or take bus #13 back down). Find the steps between the two bars on the San Miniato Church side of the parking lot (Via San Salvatore al Monte). At the first landing (marked #3), peek into the rose garden (Giardino delle Rose). After a few minutes, you'll walk through the old wall (Porta San Miniato) and emerge in the delightful little Oltrarno neighborhood of San Niccolò, with a fun and funky passel of cafés and restaurants (for recommendations, see page 530).

▲▲San Miniato Church

According to legend, the martyred St. Minias—this church's namesake—was beheaded on the banks of the Arno in A.D. 250.

He picked up his head and walked here (this was before the #12 bus), where he died and was buried in what became the first Christian cemetery in Florence. In the 11th century, this church was built to house Minias' remains.

The church's green-and-white marble facade (12th century) is classic Florentine Romanesque, one of the oldest in town. Inside you'll find some wonderful 3-D paintings, a plush ceiling of glazed terra-cotta panels by Luca della Robbia, and an exquisite Renaissance chapel (on the left side of the nave). The highlight for me is the brilliantly preserved art in the sacristy (upstairs to right of altar, in the room on right) showing scenes from the life of St. Benedict (circa 1350, by a follower of Giotto). Drop €2 into the electronic panel in the corner to light the room for five minutes. The evening vesper service with the monks chanting in Latin offers a meditative worship experience—a peaceful way to end your visit.

Cost and Hours: Free, daily 9:30-20:00, mid-Oct-Easter 9:30-13:00 & 15:30-19:00, closed sporadically for special occasions, tel. 055-234-2731, www.sanminiatoalmonte.it.

Getting There: It's about 200 yards above Piazzale Michelangelo. From the station, bus #12 takes you right to the San Miniato al Monte stop (hop off and hike up the grand staircase); bus #13 takes you back down the hill.

Gregorian Chants: To experience this mystical medieval space at its full potential, time your visit to coincide with a prayer service of Gregorian chants. In general, these are held each evening at 17:30 and last 30 minutes—but as the schedule is subject to change, double-check with any TI, the church's website, or call ahead.

Shopping in Florence

Florence may be one of Europe's best shopping towns—it's been known for its sense of style since the Medici days. Many people spend entire days (or lifetimes) shopping here.

Smaller stores are generally open about 9:00-13:00 and 15:30-19:30, usually closed on Sunday, often closed on Monday (or at least Monday morning), and sometimes closed for a couple of weeks around August 15. Bigger stores have similar hours, without the afternoon break. Many stores also have promotional stalls in market squares.

Busy street scenes and markets abound, especially at San Lorenzo Market near Mercato Centrale, near Santa Croce, on Ponte Vecchio, and at Mercato Nuovo (the covered market square three blocks north of Ponte Vecchio, described on page 491). Leather jackets and handbags, perfume and cosmetics, edible goodies, and stationery are popular souvenirs.

You'll find many **art reproductions** of your favorite Florentine pieces on posters, calendars, books, prints, and so on. Major museums—such as the Uffizi and Accademia—have excellent bookstores. The bookstore at the Duomo Museum is well stocked and a bit less crowded than the shops at some of the bigger sights.

Other souvenir ideas include silk ties, scarves, Tuscan ceramics, and wood-carved bowls and spoons. Goofy knickknacks featuring Renaissance masterpieces are popular: Botticelli mouse pads, Raphael lipstick holders, and plaster *David*s.

Prices are soft in markets and even at many midrange leather shops—go ahead and bargain. For authentic, locally produced wares, look for shops displaying the *Esercizi Storici Fiorentini* seal, with a picture of the Palazzo Vecchio's tower. At these city-endorsed "Historical Florentine Ventures," you may pay a premium, but you can be assured of quality (for a list of shops, see www.esercizistorici.it).

For ritzy Italian fashions, the entire area between the Arno River and the cathedral is busy with inviting boutiques. Browse along Via della Vigna Nuova (runs west from Via de' Tornabuoni) and Via degli Strozzi (runs east from Via de' Tornabuoni to Piazza della Repubblica). A tempting string of streets—Borgo Santi Apostoli, Via del Parione, and Borgo Ognissanti—runs parallel to the river one block inland, from near the Uffizi westward.

Across the river in the Oltrarno, known for its artisanal workshops, a short walk past the tourist crowds takes you to some less-discovered zones: near Pitti Palace, and the main street parallel to the river (Borgo San Jacopo to Via di Santo Spirito). For an in-depth look at Oltrarno workshops, pick up the brochure called "A Tour of Artisan Workshops," which you may find at the TI or at participating shops.

Sleeping in Florence

Competition among Florence's hotels is stiff. When things slow down, fancy hotels drop their prices and become a much better value for travelers than the cheap, low-end places. Book your accommodations well in advance if you'll be traveling during peak season or if your trip coincides with a major holiday or festival (see page 1178).

Nearly all of my recommended accommodations are located in the center of Florence, within minutes of the great sights. If arriving by train, you can either walk (usually around 10 minutes) or take a taxi (roughly €6-8) to reach most of my recommended accommodations, as buses don't cover the city center very well.

Florence is notorious for its mosquitoes. If your hotel lacks air-conditioning, request a fan and don't open your windows, especially at night. Many hotels furnish a small plug-in bulb *(zanzariere)*—usually set in the ashtray—that helps keep the bloodsuckers at bay. If not, you can purchase one cheaply at any pharmacy *(farmacia)*.

Museumgoers Take Note: Your hotelier may be able to reserve entry times for you at the Uffizi Gallery and the Accademia

Sleep Code

Hotels are classified based on the average price of a standard double room with breakfast in high season.

$$$$	**Splurge:**	Most rooms over €170
$$$	**Pricier:**	€130-170
$$	**Moderate:**	€90-130
$	**Budget:**	€50-90
¢	**Backpacker:**	Under €50
RS%	Rick Steves discount	

Unless otherwise noted, credit cards are accepted, hotel staff speak basic English, and free Wi-Fi is available. Comparison-shop by checking prices at several hotels (on each hotel's own website, on a booking site, or by email). For the best deal, *book directly with the hotel.* Ask for a discount if paying in cash; if the listing includes **RS%,** request a Rick Steves discount.

(Michelangelo's *David*)—ask about it when you book your room. There may be a fee, but this can be handy if you don't plan to get a Firenze Card and don't want to bother with reserving these sights yourself (for both options, see page 468).

AROUND THE DUOMO

All of these places are within a block of Florence's biggest church and main landmark. While touristy—and expensive—this location puts just about everything in town at your doorstep.

$$$$ Palazzo Niccolini al Duomo, one of five elite Historic Residence Hotels in Florence, is run by the Niccolini di Camugliano family. The lounge (where free chamomile tea is served in the evenings) is palatial, but the six rooms and six suites, while splendid, vary wildly in size. If you have the money and want a Florentine palace to call home, this can be a good bet (RS%, elevator, air-con, pay parking—reserve ahead, Via dei Servi 2, tel. 055-282-412, www.niccolinidomepalace.com, info@niccolinidomepalace.com).

$$$$ Hotel Duomo's 24 rooms are modern and comfortable enough, but you're paying for the location and the views—the Duomo looms like a monster outside the hotel's windows. If staying here, you might as well spring the extra €20 for a "superior" room with a view (RS%, air-con, historic elevator, Piazza del Duomo 1, fourth floor, tel. 055-219-922, www.hotelduomofirenze.it, info@hotelduomofirenze.it; Paolo, Gilvaneide, and Federico).

$$$ Soggiorno Battistero rents seven simple yet pristine rooms, most with great views, overlooking the Baptistery and the Duomo square. Request a view or a quieter room in the back when you book, but keep in mind there's always some noise in the city center. It's a minimalist place with no public spaces or full-time reception, but the location is great (air-con, elevator, Piazza San Giovanni 1, third floor, tel. 055-295-143, www.soggiornobattistero. it, info@soggiornobattistero.it, Francesco).

$$$ Residenza Giotto B&B offers the chance to stay on Florence's upscale shopping drag, Via Roma. Occupying the top floor of a 19th-century building, this place has six bright rooms (three with Duomo views) and a terrace with knockout views of the Duomo's tower. Reception is generally open Mon-Sat 9:00-17:00 and Sun 9:00-13:00; let them know your arrival time in advance (RS%, air-con, elevator, Via Roma 6, tel. 055-214-593, www. residenzagiotto.it, info@residenzagiotto.it, Giorgio).

$$ La Residenza del Proconsolo B&B, run by helpful Mariano, has six older-feeling rooms a minute from the Duomo (three rooms have Duomo views). The place lacks public spaces, but the rooms are quite large and nice—perfect for eating breakfast, which is served in your room (extra cost for slightly larger "deluxe" with view, air-con, no elevator, Via del Proconsolo 18 black, tel. 055-264-5657, mobile 335-657-4840, www.proconsolo.com, info@ proconsolo.com).

NORTH OF THE DUOMO
Near the Accademia
$$$$ Hotel dei Macchiaioli offers 15 fresh and spacious rooms on one high-ceilinged, noble floor in a restored palazzo owned for generations by a well-to-do Florentine family. You'll eat breakfast under original frescoed ceilings while enjoying modern comforts (RS%, air-con, Via Cavour 21, tel. 055-213-154, www. hoteldeimacchiaioli.com, info@hoteldeimacchiaioli.com, helpful Francesca and Paolo).

$$$ Hotel Loggiato dei Serviti, at a prestigious address on the most Renaissance-y square in town, gives you Old World romance with hair dryers. Stone stairways lead you under open-beam ceilings through this 16th-century monastery's monumental public rooms. The 32 well-worn rooms are both rickety and characteristic. The hotel staff is professional yet warm (RS%, family rooms, elevator, pay valet parking, Piazza S.S. Annunziata 3, tel. 055-289-592, www.loggiatodeiservitihotel.it, info@loggiatodeiservitihotel. it; Chiara B., Chiara V., and Alex). Attentive Daniel takes care of breakfast and the bar. When full, they rent five spacious and sophisticated rooms in a 17th-century annex a block away. While they lack the monastic mystique, the annex rooms are bigger, gorgeously refurnished, and cost the same.

$$$ Residenza dei Pucci rents 13 pleasant rooms (each one different) spread over three floors (with no elevator). The decor, a mix of soothing earth tones and aristocratic furniture, makes this place feel upscale for this price range (RS%, family rooms, air-con,

FLORENCE

Florence Hotels

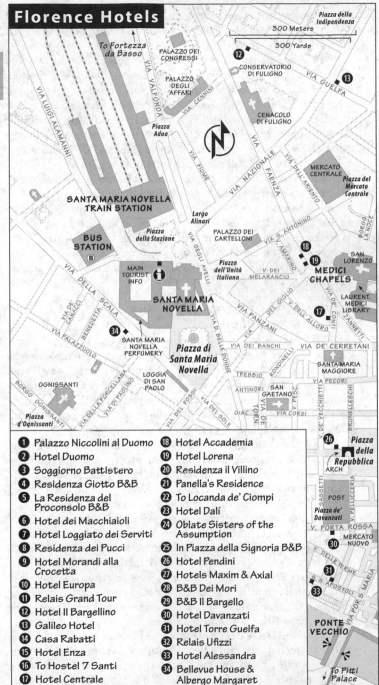

Piazza della Indipendenza

300 Meters

300 Yards

To Fortezza da Basso

PALAZZO DEI CONGRESSI

12

CONSERVATORIO DI FULIGNO

VIA GUELFA

13

PALAZZO DEGLI AFFARI

VIA VALFONDA

VIA GENNINI

CENACOLO DI FULIGNO

VIA LUIGI ALAMANNI

Piazza Adua

VIA FIUME

N

VIA NAZIONALE

VIA DELL'ARIENTO

MERCATO CENTRALE

Piazza del Mercato Centrale

VIA FAENZA

BORGO LA NOCE

SANTA MARIA NOVELLA TRAIN STATION

Largo Alinari

Piazza della Stazione

VIA DEGLI AVELLI

PALAZZO DEI CARTELLONI

VIA S. ANTONINO

V. AMARINO

18

SAN LORENZO

BUS STATION
B

Piazza dell'Unità Italiana

V. DEI MELARANCIO

19

MEDICI CHAPELS

VIA DE LA SCALA

MAIN TOURIST INFO
i

SANTA MARIA NOVELLA

VIA PANZANI

PEL GIGLIO

V. DELL'ALLORO

VIA DE' CONTI

VIA DE' GINORI

LAURENT. MEDICI LIBRARY

VIA DE CANACCI

VIA BENEDETTA

17

VIA DI ZANNETTI

VIA PALAZZUOLO

34

SANTA MARIA NOVELLA PERFUMERY

VIA D. BELLE DONNE

VIA DEI BANCHI

VIA DE' CERRETANI

RONDINELLI

SANTA MARIA MAGGIORE

BORGO OGNISSANTI

OGNISSANTI

VIA DELLA PORCELLANA

VIA DI PAOLINO

LOGGIA DI SAN PAOLO

Piazza di Santa Maria Novella

TREBBIO

VIA PECORI

ANTINORI

SAN GAETANO

VIA DE' VECCHIETTI

BRUNELLESCHI

Piazza d'Ognissanti

VIA DEL FOSSI

VIA DEL SOLE

VIA DE' TORN

GIAC.

V. PESC.

VIA CORSI

26

Piazza della Repubblica

ARCH

SASSETTI

V. DE' PELLICCERIA

POST

Piazza de' Davanzati

V. PORTA ROSSA

30

MERCATO NUOVO

V. DELLE TERME

31

S. S. APOSTOLI

33

PONTE VECCHIO

VIA POR S. MARIA

To Pitti Palace

1 Palazzo Niccolini al Duomo
2 Hotel Duomo
3 Soggiorno Battistero
4 Residenza Giotto B&B
5 La Residenza del Proconsolo B&B
6 Hotel dei Macchiaioli
7 Hotel Loggiato dei Serviti
8 Residenza dei Pucci
9 Hotel Morandi alla Crocetta
10 Hotel Europa
11 Relais Grand Tour
12 Hotel Il Bargellino
13 Galileo Hotel
14 Casa Rabatti
15 Hotel Enza
16 To Hostel 7 Santi
17 Hotel Centrale

18 Hotel Accademia
19 Hotel Lorena
20 Residenza il Villino
21 Panella's Residence
22 To Locanda de' Ciompi
23 Hotel Dalí
24 Oblate Sisters of the Assumption
25 In Piazza della Signoria B&B
26 Hotel Pendini
27 Hotels Maxim & Axial
28 B&B Dei Mori
29 B&B Il Bargello
30 Hotel Davanzati
31 Hotel Torre Guelfa
32 Relais Ufizzi
33 Hotel Alessandra
34 Bellevue House & Albergo Margaret

FLORENCE

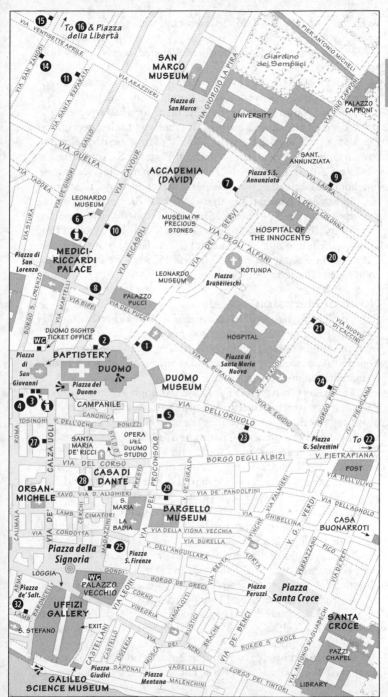

reception open 9:00-20:00, shorter hours off-season—let them know if you'll arrive late, Via dei Pucci 9, tel. 055-281-886, www. residenzadeipucci.com, info@residenzadeipucci.com, friendly Rossella and Marina).

$$$ Hotel Morandi alla Crocetta, a former convent, envelops you in a 16th-century cocoon. Located on a quiet street with 12 rooms, period furnishings, parquet floors, original frescoes, and wood-beamed or painted ceilings, it takes you back a few centuries and up a few social classes (family rooms, air-con, elevator, pay parking—reserve ahead, a block off Piazza S.S. Annunziata at Via Laura 50, tel. 055-234-4747, www.hotelmorandi.it, welcome@hotelmorandi.it, well-run by Maurizio, Rolando, and Cristiano).

$$$ Hotel Europa, family run since 1970, has a welcoming atmosphere fostered by cheery Miriam and Roberto. The breakfast room is spacious, and most of the 12 basic rooms have views of the Duomo, including one with a terrace (RS%, family rooms, air-con, elevator, Via Cavour 14, tel. 055-239-6715, www.webhoteleuropa.com, firenze@webhoteleuropa.com).

North of Mercato Centrale

After dark, this neighborhood can feel a little deserted, but I've never heard of anyone running into harm here. It's a short walk from the train station and an easy stroll to all the sightseeing action. While workaday, it's practical, with plenty of good budget restaurants and markets nearby.

$$ Relais Grand Tour has four charmingly eclectic rooms on a nondescript street between the train station and the Accademia. This cozy B&B will make you feel right at home; it's thoughtfully appointed and the owners, Cristina and Giuseppe, live there. The delightful and spacious suites come with a garden ambience on the ground floor (RS%, cash only, includes breakfast voucher for the corner bar, for cheaper rates ask about skipping breakfast and daily cleaning, air-con, Via Santa Reparata 21, tel. 055-283-955, www. florencegrandtour.com, info@florencegrandtour.com).

$$ Hotel Il Bargellino, run by Bostonian Carmel and her Italian husband Pino, is a good-value place in a residential neighborhood within walking distance of the center. They rent 10 summery rooms decorated with funky antiques and Pino's modern paintings. Guests enjoy relaxing on the big, breezy, momentum-slowing terrace adorned with plants and lemon shrubs (RS%, cheaper rooms with shared bath, no breakfast, air-con extra, north of the train station at Via Guelfa 87, tel. 055-238-2658, www.ilbargellino.com, carmel@ilbargellino.com).

$$ Galileo Hotel, a comfortable business hotel with 31 rooms, is run with familial warmth (RS%, family rooms, quadruple-paned windows shut out street noise, air-con, elevator, Via Nazionale 22a, tel. 055-496-645, www.galileohotel.it, info@galileohotel.it).

$ Casa Rabatti is the ultimate if you always wanted to have a Florentine mama. Its four simple, clean rooms are run with warmth by Marcella. This is a great place to practice your Italian, since Marcella loves to chat and speaks minimal English. Seeing nearly two decades of my family Christmas cards on their walls, I'm reminded of how long she has been keeping budget travelers happy (RS%, cheaper rooms with shared bath, family rooms, cash only but secure reservation with credit card, no breakfast, fans available, 5 blocks from station at Via San Zanobi 48 black, tel. 055-212-393, www.casarabatti.it, casarabatti@inwind.it). In the same building, she also rents three modern and spacious **$$ apartments** that come with kitchenettes and access to a tranquil garden—Ideal for longer stays.

$ Hotel Enza rents 18 basic rooms in a building that feels slightly scruffy. The prices are reasonable for simple hotel comfort (RS%, breakfast extra, air-con, no elevator, Via San Zanobi 45 black, tel. 055-490-990, www.hotelenza.it, info@hotelenza.it).

Hostel: Calling itself a "travelers' haven," **¢ Hostel 7 Santi** fills a former convent, but you'll feel like you're in an old school. Still, it offers some of the best cheap beds in town, is friendly to older travelers, and comes with the services you'd expect in a big, modern hostel, including self-serve laundry. It's in a more residential neighborhood near the Campo di Marte stadium, about a 10-minute bus ride from the center. A far more central hostel is in the Oltrarno, listed later (private rooms available, breakfast and dinner extra, no curfew; Viale dei Mille 11—from train station, take bus #10, #17, or #20, direction: Campo di Marte, to bus stop Chiesa dei Sette Santi; tel. 055-504-8452, www.7santi.com, info@7santi.com).

Near the Medici Chapels

This touristy zone has lots of budget and midrange hotels catering to an international clientele, stacks of basic trattorias, and easy access to major sights (just steps from the Medici Chapels, Basilica of San Lorenzo, and Mercato Centrale, and only a bit farther to the biggies). The mostly pedestrianized Via Faenza is the spine of this neighborhood, with lots of tourist services.

$$$$ Hotel Centrale is indeed central, just a short walk from the Duomo. The 35 spacious but overpriced rooms—with a tasteful mix of old and new decor—are over a businesslike conference center (RS%, air-con, elevator, Via dei Conti 3, check in at big front desk on ground floor, tel. 055-215-761, www.hotelcentralefirenze. it, info@hotelcentralefirenze.it, Margherita and Roberto).

$$$ Hotel Accademia has 21 old-school rooms and a floor plan that defies logic. While the hotel is overpriced and getting a bit long in the tooth, its location is convenient (RS%, air-con, no elevator, Via Faenza 7, tel. 055-293-451, www.hotelaccademiafirenze. com, info@hotelaccademiafirenze.com, Tea).

$ Hotel Lorena, just across from the Medici Chapels, has 19 simple, well-worn rooms (six with shared bathrooms) and a tiny lobby. Though it feels a bit like a youth hostel, it's well located and run with care by the Galli family (breakfast included for Rick Steves readers, air-con, elevator from first floor, Via Faenza 1, tel. 055-282-785, www.hotellorena.com, info@hotellorena.com).

EAST OF THE DUOMO

While convenient to the sights and offering a good value, these places are mostly along nondescript urban streets, lacking the grit, charm, or glitz of some of my other recommended neighborhoods.

$$$ Residenza il Villino has 10 charming rooms and a picturesque, peaceful little courtyard. The owner, Neri, has turned part of the breakfast room into a museum-like tribute to his grandfather, a pioneer of early Italian fashion. As it's in a "little villa" (as the name implies) set back from the street, this is a quiet refuge from the bustle of Florence (RS%, family rooms, air-con, parking available, just north of Via degli Alfani at Via della Pergola 53, tel. 055-200-1116, www.ilvillino.it, info@ilvillino.it).

$$$ Panella's Residence, once a convent and today part of owner Graziella's extensive home, is a classy B&B, with five chic, romantic, and ample rooms, antique furnishings, and historic architectural touches (RS%, air-con, Via della Pergola 42, tel. 055-234-7202, mobile 345-972-1541, www.panellaresidence.com, panella_residence@yahoo.it).

$$ Locanda de' Ciompi, overlooking the inviting Piazza dei Ciompi antique market in a young and lively neighborhood, is just right for travelers who want to feel like a part of the town. Alessio and daughter Lisa have five attractive rooms that are tidy, lovingly maintained, and a good value (RS%, cheaper single with private bath down the hall, includes breakfast at nearby bar, air-con, 8 blocks behind the Duomo at Via Pietrapiana 28—see map on page 502, tel. 055-263-8034, www.bbflorencefirenze.com, info@bbflorencefirenze.com).

$ Hotel Dalí has 10 cheery rooms in a nice location for a great price. Samanta and Marco, who run this guesthouse with a charming passion and idealism, are a delight to know (request one of the quiet and spacious rooms facing the courtyard when you book, cheaper rooms with shared bath available, nearby apartments sleep 2-6 people, no breakfast, fans but no air-con, elevator, free parking, 2 blocks behind the Duomo at Via dell'Oriuolo 17 on the second floor, tel. 055-234-0706, www.hoteldali.com, hoteldali@tin.it).

$ Oblate Sisters of the Assumption run an institutional 30-

room hotel in a Renaissance building with a dreamy garden, great public spaces, appropriately simple rooms, and a quiet, prayerful ambience (family rooms, single beds only, air-con, elevator, Wi-Fi with suggested donation, 23:30 curfew, limited pay parking—request when you book, Borgo Pinti 15, tel. 055-248-0582, www.bb-oblate.com, sroblateborgopinti@virgilio.it, sisters are likely to speak French but not English). As there's no night porter, it's best to time your arrival and departure to occur during typical business hours.

SOUTH OF THE DUOMO
Between the Duomo and Piazza della Signoria

Buried in the narrow, characteristic lanes in the very heart of town, these are the most central of my accommodations recommendations (and therefore a little overpriced). While this location is worth the extra cost for many, nearly every hotel I recommend can be considered central given Florence's walkable, essentially traffic-free core.

$$$$ In Piazza della Signoria B&B, overlooking Piazza della Signoria, is peaceful, refined, and homey at the same time. Fit for a honeymoon, the 10 rooms come with all the special touches and little extras you'd expect in a top-end American B&B, and the service is sharp and friendly. However, the rates are high, and the "partial view" rooms, while slightly larger, require craning your neck to see anything—not worth the extra euros. Guests enjoy socializing at the big, shared breakfast table (RS%, family apartments, lavish bathrooms, air-con, tiny elevator, Via dei Magazzini 2, tel. 055-239-9546, mobile 348-321-0565, www.inpiazzadellasignoria.com, info@inpiazzadellasignoria.com, Sonia and Alessandro).

$$$$ Hotel Pendini, with three stars and 44 plush rooms, fills the top floor of a grand building overlooking Piazza della Repubblica that was built to celebrate Italian unification in the late 19th century. This place just feels classy; as you walk into the lobby, it's as if you're walking back in time (RS%, "deluxe" rooms come with square view and noise, family rooms, air-con, elevator, Via degli Strozzi 2, tel. 055-211-170, www.hotelpendini.it, info@hotelpendini.it).

$$$ Hotel Maxim, run by the Maoli family since 1981, has 26 straightforward rooms in a good location on the main pedestrian drag. Its narrow, painting-lined halls and cozy lounge have old Florentine charm (RS%—use code "RICK," family rooms, air-con, elevator, Via de' Calzaiuoli 11, tel. 055-217-474, www.hotelmaximfirenze.it, reservation@hotelmaximfirenze.it, Chiara).

$$$ Hotel Axial, two floors below its sister Hotel Maxim, has 14 rooms and a more businesslike, modern feel at comparable rates

(RS%—use code "RICK," air-con, elevator, Via de' Calzaiuoli 11, tel. 055-218-984, www.hotelaxial.it, info@hotelaxial.it, Nicola).

$$ B&B Dei Mori, a peaceful haven with a convivial and welcoming living room, rents five colorful rooms ideally located on a quiet pedestrian street near Casa di Dante—within a five-minute walk of the Duomo, the Bargello, or Piazza della Signoria. Accommodating Daniele (Danny) and his staff pride themselves on offering personal service, including lots of tips on dining and sightseeing in Florence (RS%, minimum two-night stay, cheaper rooms with shared bath, pay air-con, no elevator, reception open 8:00-19:00, Via Dante Alighieri 12, tel. 055-211-438, www.facebook.com/DeiMoriFirenze, info@deimori.it).

$$ B&B Il Bargello is a home away from home, run by friendly and helpful Canadian expat Gabriella. Hike up three long flights (no elevator) to reach six smart, relaxing rooms. Gabriella offers a cozy communal living room, kitchen access, and an inviting rooftop terrace with close-up views of Florence's towers (RS%, fully equipped apartment across the hall sleeps up to six in real beds but you'll share one bathroom; air-con, 20 yards off Via Proconsolo at Via de' Pandolfini 33 black, tel. 055-215-330, mobile 339-175-3110, www.firenze-bedandbreakfast.it, info@firenze-bedandbreakfast.it).

Near Ponte Vecchio

This sleepy zone is handy to several sights and some fine shopping streets (from top-end boutiques to more characteristic hole-in-the-wall shops), though it's accordingly pricey and lacks a neighborhood feel of its own.

$$$$ Hotel Davanzati, bright and shiny with artistic touches, has 25 cheerful rooms with all the comforts. The place is a family affair, thoughtfully run by friendly Tommaso and father Fabrizio, who offer drinks and snacks each evening at their candlelit happy hour, plus lots of other extras (RS%, family rooms, free iPads in every room, free on-demand videos—including *Rick Steves' Italy* shows—on your room TV, air-con, 20 steep steps to the elevator, handy room fridges, next to Piazza Davanzati at Via Porta Rossa 5—easy to miss so watch for low-profile sign above the door, tel. 055-286-666, www.hoteldavanzati.it, info@hoteldavanzati.it).

$$$$ Hotel Torre Guelfa has grand public spaces and is topped by a fun medieval tower with a panoramic rooftop terrace (72 stairs take you up—and back 720 years). Its 31 pricey rooms vary wildly in size and furnishings, but most come with the noise of the city center. Room 315, with a private terrace, is worth reserving several months in advance (RS%, family rooms, air-con, elevator, a couple of blocks northwest of Ponte Vecchio, Borgo S.S.

Apostoli 8, tel. 055-239-6338, www.hoteltorreguelfa.com, info@ hoteltorreguelfa.com, Niccolo and Barbara).

$$$$ Relais Uffizi is a peaceful little gem, offering a friendly welcome and 15 classy rooms tucked away down a tiny alley off Piazza della Signoria. The lounge has a huge window overlooking the action in the square below (family rooms, air-con, elevator; official address is Chiasso del Buco 16—from the square, go down tiny Chiasso de Baroncelli lane—right of the loggia—and after 50 yards turn right through the arch and look for entrance on your right; tel. 055-267-6239, www.relaisuffizi.it, info@relaisuffizi.it, charming Alessandro and Elizabetta).

$$$ Hotel Alessandra is a tranquil and sprawling place, occupying part of a 16th-century building with 27 big, old-school rooms and a tiny Arno-view terrace (family rooms, air-con, 30 steps to the elevator, Borgo S.S. Apostoli 17, tel. 055-283-438, www.hotelalessandra.com, info@hotelalessandra.com, Anna and son Andrea).

NEAR SANTA MARIA NOVELLA

These fine, charming little budget options are around the corner from Santa Maria Novella, near the train station.

$$ Bellevue House is a third-floor (no elevator) oasis of tranquility, with six spacious, old-fashioned rooms flanking a long, mellow-yellow lobby. It's a peaceful home away from home, thoughtfully run by the Michel family (RS%, family rooms, no breakfast, air-con, Via della Scala 21, tel. 055-260-8932, www.bellevuehouse. it, info@bellevuehouse.it; Luciano, Susan, and Alessandro). Press the bell at street level, and they'll carry up your bags.

$$ Albergo Margaret, homey yet minimalist, offers seven tidy, simple rooms but no public lounge or breakfast (RS%, some cheaper rooms with shower but toilet down the hall, apartment, air-con in most rooms, Via della Scala 25, tel. 055-210-138, www. hotel-margaret.it, info@hotel-margaret.it; Francesco, Anna, and Graziano).

THE OLTRARNO

Across the river in the Oltrarno area, between the Pitti Palace and Ponte Vecchio, you'll find small, traditional crafts shops, neighborly piazzas, and family eateries. The following places are walkable from Ponte Vecchio. Only the first two are real hotels—the rest are a ragtag gang of budget alternatives.

$$$$ Hotel la Scaletta has 36 pricey, bright rooms hiding in a tortured floor plan. Their fabulous rooftop terrace overlooks the Boboli Gardens (family rooms, breakfast extra, air-con, elevator, Via de' Guicciardini 13, tel. 055-283-028, www.hotellascaletta.it, info@hotellascaletta.it).

FLORENCE

Oltrarno Hotels & Restaurants

1. Hotel la Scaletta
2. To Hotel Silla, Via di San Niccolò Eateries, Zeb Wine Bar; Negroni & Zoe Nightclubs
3. Soggiorno Alessandra
4. Casa Santo Nome di Gesù
5. Istituto Gould
6. Ostello Santa Monaca
7. Signorvino
8. Golden View Open Bar
9. Osteria Ponte Vecchio
10. Gusta Osteria
11. Trattoria Casalinga
12. Gusta Pizza
13. To Burro & Acciughe Fish Restaurant; Trattoria dell'Orto
14. Il Santo Bevitore Ristorante & Enoteca Il Santino Gastronomia
15. Trattoria 4 Leoni
16. To Antico Ristoro Di' Cambi; Trattorias da Sergio & Sabatino
17. Olio & Convivium
18. To Trattoria Al Tranvai
19. Le Volpi e l'Uva Wine Bar
20. Sapori & Dintorni Conad Supermarket

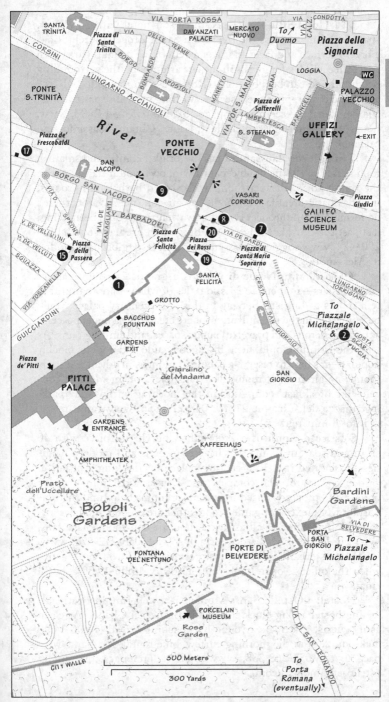

FLORENCE

$$$ Hotel Silla is a classic three-star hotel with 36 cheery, spacious rooms. Across the river from Santa Croce Church, it has a breezy terrace and faces the river, overlooking a small park, with free coffee and tea for guests in the late afternoon. The surrounding neighborhood can be a bit noisy (RS%—use promo code "RICK," air-con, elevator, pricey self-service washing machine, pay parking, Via dei Renai 5—see map on page 502, tel. 055-234-2888, www.hotelsilla.it, hotelsilla@hotelsilla.it; Laura, Chiara, Massimo, and Stefano).

$ Soggiorno Alessandra has five bright, comfy, and smallish rooms. Because of its double-paned windows, you'll hardly notice the traffic noise (cheaper rooms with shared bath, family rooms, includes basic breakfast in room, pay air-con, no elevator; there's no formal reception, so let them know what time you'll be arriving; just past the Carraia Bridge at Via Borgo San Frediano 6, tel. 055-290-424, www.soggiornoalessandra.it, info@soggiornoalessandra.it, Alessandra).

$ Casa Santo Nome di Gesù is a grand, 25-room convent whose sisters—Franciscan Missionaries of Mary—are thankful to rent rooms to tourists. Staying in this 15th-century palace, you'll be immersed in the tranquil atmosphere created by a huge, peaceful garden, generous and prayerful public spaces, and smiling nuns. As with the Istituto Gould, next, it's a good value and understandably popular—it's best to reserve a couple of months in advance (family rooms, no air-con but rooms have fans, elevator, memorable convent-like breakfast room, 1:00 in the morning curfew, pay parking, Piazza del Carmine 21, tel. 055-213-856, www.fmmfirenze.it, info@fmmfirenze.it).

$ Istituto Gould is a Protestant Church-run place with 40 clean and spartan rooms that have twin beds and modern facilities. It's located in a 17th-century palace overlooking a beautiful garden courtyard. The complex also houses kids from troubled homes, and proceeds raised from renting rooms help fund that important work (extra for garden rooms that are quieter and have air-con, family rooms, breakfast extra, non-air-con rooms have fans, Wi-Fi in lobby only, Via dei Serragli 49, tel. 055-212-576, www.firenzeforesteria.it, info@firenzeforesteria.it). If you can't arrive when the office is open (daily 9:00-13:00 & 15:00-19:30), they'll email you a code.

Hostel: ¢ Ostello Santa Monaca is a well-run, institutional-feeling hostel a long block east of the Brancacci Chapel. As clean as its guests, it attracts a young backpacking crowd (10:00-14:00 lock-out, 2:00 in the morning curfew, bike rental, Via Santa Monaca 6, tel. 055-268-338, www.ostellosantamonaca.com, info@ostellosantamonaca.com).

FLORENCE

Eating in Florence

Restaurants in Florence like to serve what's fresh. Seasonal ingredients are most likely featured in the *piatti del giorno* (specials of the day) section on menus. For dessert, it's all about gelato (see sidebar on page 523). Rather than eat it at the restaurant, I'd enjoy a gelato-fueled evening stroll.

Foodies appreciate Elizabeth Minchilli's app, Eat Florence, which has thorough descriptions of all things food-related in the city (www.elizabethminchilliinrome.com).

Budget Eating: To save money and time, you can keep lunches fast and simple by eating at one of the countless sandwich shops and stands, pizzerias, or self-service cafeterias. You'll find a unique range of sandwich options in Florence. In addition to the basic *panino* (usually on a baguette), *crostini* (open-faced, toasted baguette), and *semel* (big, puffy roll), you'll see places advertising *schiaccata* (sandwich made with a "squashed," focaccia-like bread). Florence is home to many carts selling tripe sandwiches—a prized local specialty.

Picnicking is easy. You can picnic your way through Mercato Centrale, near the Basilica of San Lorenzo. You'll also find good *supermercati* throughout the city. I like the classy Sapori & Dintorni markets (run by Conad), which has branches near the Duomo (Borgo San Lorenzo 15 red) and just over Ponte Vecchio in the Oltrarno (Via de' Bardi 45). Despar is another handy grocery chain (there's one around the corner from the Duomo Museum at Via dell'Oriuolo 66).

MERCATO CENTRALE AND NEARBY
In Mercato Centrale
Florence's Industrial Age, steel-and-glass Mercato Centrale (Central Market) is a fun-to-explore food wonderland.

$ Ground Floor: The market zone, with lots of raw ingredients and a few humble food counters, is open only through lunchtime (Mon-Fri 7:00-14:00, Sat 7:00-17:00, closed Sun). Buy a picnic of fresh mozzarella cheese, olives, fruit, and crunchy bread to munch on the steps of the nearby Basilica of San Lorenzo. The fancy deli, **Perini,** is famous for its quality (pricey) products and enticing display. For a simple sit-down meal, head for the venerable **Nerbone in the Market.** Join the shoppers and workers who crowd up to the bar to grab their inexpensive plates, and then find a stool at the cramped shared tables nearby. Of the several cheap market diners, this feels the most authentic (lunch menu served Mon-Sat 12:00-14:00, sandwiches available from 8:00 until the bread runs out, cash only, on the side closest to the Basilica of San

Lorenzo). Its less-famous sisters, nearby, have better seating and fewer crowds.

$$ Upstairs: Under the old glass roof, the upper floor features a dozen upscale food counters open for lunch and dinner (daily 10:00-24:00). Grab what you want—pizza, pasta, fish, meat, *salumi*, *lampredotto*, wine, and so on—and pull up a stool at one of the food-court tables. Before choosing, do a full circuit around the scene to get to know your options.

Near Mercato Centrale

A huge array of eateries is within a couple of blocks of the market. Each has its own distinct vibe, so scout around to find your favorite.

$$ Trattoria Mario's has been serving hearty lunches to market-goers since 1953 (Fabio and Romeo are the latest generation). Their simple formula: no-frills, bustling service, old-fashioned good value, and shared tables. It's *cucina casalinga*—home cooking *con brio*. This place is high-energy and jam-packed, with very tight seating. Their best dishes (*ribollita*, bean soup, *amatriciana*) often sell out first, so go early. If there's a line, put your name on the list (cash only, Mon-Sat 12:00-15:30, closed Sun and Aug, no reservations, Via Rosina 2, tel. 055-218-550).

$ Casa del Vino, Florence's oldest operating wine shop, offers glasses of wine from 25 open bottles. Owner Gianni, whose family has owned the Casa for more than 70 years, is a class act. The sandwiches, crostini, and mixed plates of meat and cheese with fine wine by the glass are perfect. During busy times, it's a mob scene. You'll eat standing outside alongside workers on a quick lunch break. But come early or late, and you can actually connect with Gianni. Ask him for *"uno etto misto €5,"* add two glasses of fine wine, and you've got a memorable and very cheap lunch (Mon-Thu 9:30-15:30, Fri-Sat 9:30-20:30, closed Sun year-round, Sat in summer, and Aug, Via dell'Ariento 16 red, tel. 055-215-609).

$$ Pepò, a colorful and charmingly unpretentious space, is tucked just around the corner from the touristy Trattoria Zà-Zà glitz on Piazza del Mercato Centrale. Pepò handles its neighbor's overflow admirably, with a short menu of simple but well-prepared Florentine classics such as *ribollita* and *pollo alla cacciatora*—chicken cacciatore (daily 12:00-14:30 & 19:00-22:30, Via Rosina 4 red, tel. 055-283-259).

$$ Trattoria Sergio Gozzi is your classic neighborhood lunch-only place, serving hearty, traditional Florentine fare to market-goers since 1915—long before the tourist crush of today. The handwritten menu is limited and changes daily, and the service can be hectic, but it remains a local favorite (Mon-Sat 12:00-15:00, closed Sun, reservations smart, Piazza di San Lorenzo 8, tel. 055-281-941).

$$ Trattoria la Burrasca offers a traditional menu featuring fine beef and good-value seasonal specials of Tuscan home cooking, served by Elio and his staff. It's small, with just 14 tables—and often filled with tourists (Tue-Sun 12:00-15:00 & 19:00-22:30, closed Mon, reservations smart, Via Panicale 6, north corner of Mercato Centrale, tel. 055-215-827).

$ Simbiosi Organic Pizza and Lovely Food is a happy little pizzeria under a medieval vault with a young hip crew, open fire, and healthy energy (open daily, organic and gluten-free, craft beer, Via de' Ginori 56 red, tel. 055-064-0115).

$$$ La Ménagère Bistro and Restaurant is a youthful place serving nicely presented, modern Italian dishes to a smart crowd in a spacious and dressy atmosphere. The more casual bistro in front (which serves salads, sandwiches, and simple plates until 18:00) hides a fancier restaurant in back where you can choose between small tables or bigger shared ones (daily, lunch from 12:00, dinner from 19:30, dinner reservations smart, Via de' Ginori 8 red, tel. 055-075-0600, www.lamenagere.it).

AROUND THE DUOMO

$$ Enoteca Coquinarius feels as welcoming as someone's cool and spacious living room or library. It's an unstressful, hip place with a slow-food ethic and lots of great salads and pastas (daily 12:30-15:30 & 18:30-22:30, a few steps from the Duomo workshop at Via delle Oche 11 red, tel. 055-230-2153).

$$ Miso di Riso Vegetarian Bistro serves nothing with eyeballs. You'll find organic, seasonal, and vegan dishes—especially great salads—served in a homey, artsy atmosphere with an inviting garden courtyard (Wed 12:00-16:00, Thu-Fri 12:00-23:00, Sat-Sun 10:00-23:00, closed Mon-Tue, Borgo degli Albizi 54 red, tel. 055-265-4094).

Fast Meals

$ Self-Service Ristorante Leonardo is an inexpensive, air-conditioned, quick, and handy cafeteria. While it's no-frills and old-school, the food is better than many table-service eateries in this part of town. Stefano and Luciano run the place with enthusiasm and free pitchers of tap water. It's a block from the Duomo, southwest of the Baptistery (lots of veggies, daily 11:45-14:45 & 18:45-21:45, upstairs at Via Pecori 11, tel. 055-284-446).

$$ Paszkowski Café is a venerable place on Piazza della Repubblica. While famously expensive as a restaurant, it serves up inexpensive, quick lunches. At the display case, order a salad or plate of pasta or cooked veggies (or half-and-half), pay the cashier, and find a seat upstairs or at one of the tables reserved for self-serve

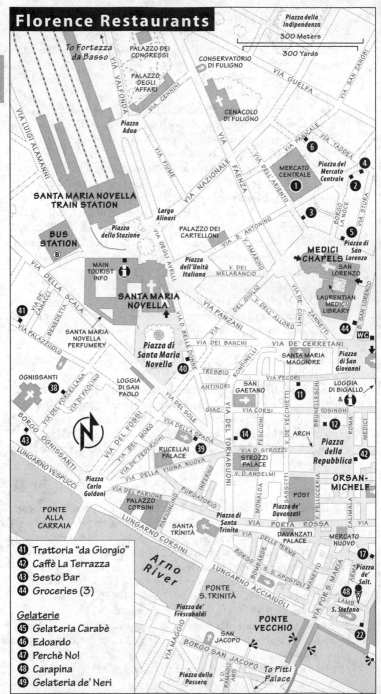

Florence Restaurants

Piazza della Indipendenza

300 Meters

300 Yards

To Fortezza da Basso

PALAZZO DEI CONGRESSI

CONSERVATORIO DI FULIGNO

VIA GUELFA

VIA SAN ZANOBI

PALAZZO DEGLI AFFARI

CENACOLO DI FULIGNO

VIA VALFONDA

VIA CENNINI

Piazza Adua

VIA FIUME

VIA NAZIONALE

VIA FAENZA

VIA DEL ARIENTO

VIA PANICALE

VIA TADDEA

6

MERCATO CENTRALE
1

Piazza del Mercato Centrale
2

4

VIA LUIGI ALAMANNI

SANTA MARIA NOVELLA TRAIN STATION

Largo Alinari

3

BORGO LA NOCE

VIA STURA

5

BUS STATION
B

Piazza della Stazione

PALAZZO DEI CARTELLONI

VIA DEGLI AVELLI

VIA S. ANTONINO

VIA S. AMARINO

Piazza di San Lorenzo

MEDICI CHAPELS

SAN LORENZO

MAIN TOURIST INFO

Piazza dell'Unità Italiana

V. DEI MELARANCIO

VIA DE' ZANNETTI

LAURENTIAN MEDICI LIBRARY

B. SAN LORENZO

44

WC

41

VIA DELLA SCALA

VIA DEL CANACCI

VIA BENEDETTA

SANTA MARIA NOVELLA

VIA DEL GIGLIO

V. DELL'ALLORO

VIA DE' CONTI

VIA PANZANI

VIA DEI BANCHI

VIA DE' CERRETANI

SANTA MARIA MAGGIORE

Piazza di San Giovanni

SANTA MARIA NOVELLA PERFUMERY

Piazza di Santa Maria Novella

40

TREBBIO

RONDINELLI

VIA PECORI

OGNISSANTI

38

LOGGIA DI SAN PAOLO

VIA DEL FOSSI

ANTINORI

SAN GAETANO

VIA CORSI

V. DE' VECCHIETTI

11

BRUNELLESCHI

LOGGIA DI BIGALLO & i

TOSINGHI

12

MEDICI

VIA DEL PAOLINO

VIA DEL FORCELLANA

VIA DEL MORO

VIA DELLA SPADA

GIAC.

VIA DEL TORNABUONI

FESCINI

14

ARCH

Piazza della Repubblica

ROMA

42

BORGO OGNISSANTI

43

LUNGARNO VESPUCCI

RUCELLAI PALACE

39

VIA DE'FEDERIGHI

VIA D. STROZZI

STROZZI PALACE

V. D. ANSELMI

ORSAN-MICHELE

VIA DELLA VIGNA NUOVA

INFERNO

MONALDA

POST

VIA DE' PELLICCERIA

CALIMALA

Piazza Carlo Goldoni

PALAZZO CORSINI

VIA DEL PARIONE

PURGATORIO

PARIONCINO

Piazza de' Davanzati

Piazza di Santa Trinita

VIA PORTA ROSSA

DAVANZATI PALACE

VIA

PONTE ALLA CARRAIA

LUNGARNO CORSINI

SANTA TRINITÀ

VIA DELLE TERME

MERCATO NUOVO

17

Piazza de' Salt.

Arno River

LUNGARNO ACCIAIUOLI

BORGO S. S. APOSTOLI

BOMBARDE

VIA POR S. MARIA

ARMA

48

LAMB.

S. Stefano

PONTE S.TRINITA

Piazza de' Frescobaldi

PONTE VECCHIO

22

VIA MAGGIO

SAN JACOPO

BORGO SAN JACOPO

V. D. RAMAGLI ANTI

To Pitti Palace

Piazza della Passera

41 Trattoria "da Giorgio"
42 Caffè La Terrazza
43 Sesto Bar
44 Groceries (3)

Gelaterie
45 Gelateria Carabè
46 Edoardo
47 Perchè No!
48 Carapina
49 Gelateria de' Neri

1. Mercato Centrale Eateries
2. Trattoria Mario's
3. Casa del Vino
4. Pepò
5. Trattoria Sergio Gozzi
6. Trattoria la Burrasca
7. Simbiosi Organic Pizza & Lovely Food
8. La Ménagère Bistro & Rest.
9. Enoteca Coquinarius
10. Miso di Riso Vegetarian Bistro
11. Self-Service Rist. Leonardo
12. Paszkowski Café
13. EATaly
14. Procacci
15. Turkuaz Döner Kebab
16. To Lovelife Café
17. Rivoire Café
18. Osteria Vini e Vecchi Sapori
19. Frescobaldi Ristorante & Wine Bar
20. Cantinetta dei Verrazzano
21. I Fratellini
22. 'Ino Wine Bar & Sandwiches
23. L'Antico Trippaio, Pizzeria Totò & Supermarket
24. Da' Vinattieri
25. Il Cernacchino
26. Ará è Sicilia
27. Due Sorsi e un Boccone
28. La Mescita Fiaschetteria
29. Pasticceria Robiglio
30. To Antica Trattoria da Tito
31. Ristorante Cafaggi
32. Ristorante del Fagioli
33. Trattoria Anita
34. Trattoria I'cche C'è C'è
35. All'Antico Vinaio
36. Club del Gusto
37. Istanbul Döner Kebap
38. Trattoria Sostanza-Troia
39. Trattoria Marione
40. Trattoria al Trebbio

FLORENCE

Restaurant Price Code

I've assigned each eatery a price category, based on the average cost of a typical main course (pasta or *secondi*). Drinks, desserts, and splurge items (steak and seafood) can raise the price considerably.

$$$$	**Splurge:** Most main courses over €20
$$$	**Pricier:** €15-20
$$	**Moderate:** €10-15
$	**Budget:** Under €10

In Italy, pizza by the slice and other takeaway food is **$**; a basic trattoria or sit-down pizzeria is **$$**; a casual but more upscale restaurant is **$$$**; and a swanky splurge is **$$$$**.

---

diners on the square (lunch served 12:00-15:00, Piazza della Repubblica 35 red—northwest corner, tel. 055-210-236).

$$ EATaly, a slick, modern space a half-block from the Duomo, is an outpost of a chain of foodie mini-malls located in big Italian cities (as well as in Chicago and New York City). Along with a world of gifty edibles, it offers several food options under one roof, including an espresso counter, a soft-serve gelato counter and tempting pastry shop, a grocery store for top-end Italian ingredients and kitchen gadgets, and a bright, modern dining area serving pastas, pizzas, salads, and *secondi*, including daily specials (food shop open daily 10:00-22:30, restaurants open 12:00-15:00 and from 19:00, Via de' Martelli 22 red, tel. 055-015-3601).

$$ Procacci, right on Florence's most genteel boutique-browsing street, is upscale yet still affordable. This wine bar, with a swanky, circa-1885 atmosphere, specializes in pungent truffle-scented ingredients: cheap mini-*panini* and €9-18 sampler plates of *salumi* and cheeses. While the platters are pricey, the sandwiches may be Florence's cheapest way to dine on truffles. Paired with a €5 glass of wine, it makes an elegant light meal (daily 10:00-21:00, Via Tornabuoni 64 red, tel. 055-211-656).

Döner Kebab: A good place to try this cheap Middle Eastern specialty is **$ Turkuaz,** a couple of blocks northeast of the Duomo (Via dei Servi 65 red).

Smoothies and Salads: For green salads, couscous and rice dishes, quiches, and smoothies, try **$ Lovelife** (closed Sun, east of the Duomo at Via dell'Oriuolo 26 red). **$ Il Chiosco** (The Kiosk) is the spot for smoothies and juices (two stands: one facing the southeast corner of the Duomo and another south of Piazza della Repubblica).

NEAR PIAZZA DELLA SIGNORIA

Piazza della Signoria, the scenic square facing the Palazzo Vecchio, is ringed by beautifully situated yet touristy eateries serving overpriced, forgettable food with an unforgettable view. If you're determined to eat on the square, have pizza at the touristy Ristorante il Cavallino, bar food at the adjacent Irish pub, or dine more elegantly at the Gucci Caffè and Restaurant. Piazza della Signoria's saving grace is **$$$ Rivoire** café, famous for its fancy desserts and thick hot chocolate (€7). While obscenely expensive, it has the best view tables on the square. Their delightful bar is perfectly affordable, and drinks often come with fine *aperitivo* munchies (closed Mon, tel. 055-214-412).

Dining near Piazza della Signoria

Two recommended places, one casual, the other fancy, are just off Piazza della Signoria, a half-block north of the Palazzo Vecchio. Facing the bronze equestrian statue in the piazza, go behind the horse's tail and into the corner to the left.

$$ Osteria Vini e Vecchi Sapori is a colorful eatery—tight and tiny, and with attitude. They serve Tuscan food—like *pappardelle* with duck—from a fun, accessible menu of delicious pastas and *secondi* (Mon-Sat 12:30-14:30 & 19:30-22:30, closed Sun, reservations smart, Via dei Magazzini 3 red, tel. 055-293-045, run by Mario while wife Rosanna cooks and son Tommaso serves).

$$$$ Frescobaldi Ristorante and Wine Bar, the showcase of Italy's aristocratic wine family, serves sophisticated dishes by candlelight under high-vaulted ceilings. They offer the same seasonal menu in their cozy interior, tight wine bar, and at a few outside tables. If coming for dinner, make a reservation and dress up (lighter wine-bar and good-value set menus at lunch, daily 12:00-14:30 & 19:00-22:30, air-con, Via dei Magazzini 2 red, tel. 055-284-724, www.deifrescobaldi.it).

Cheap, Simple Eats near Piazza della Signoria

$$ Cantinetta dei Verrazzano, a long-established bakery/café/wine bar, serves delightful sandwich plates in an old-time setting. Their *selezione Verrazzano* is a plate of four little crostini featuring different breads, cheeses, and meats from the Chianti region. The *tagliere di focacce,* a sampler plate of mini-focaccia sandwiches, is also fun (€16 for big plate for two). Add a glass of Chianti to either of these dishes to make a fine, light meal. Office workers pop in for a quick lunch, and it's traditional to share tables. They also have benches and tiny tables for eating at takeout prices. Simply step to the back and point to a hot *focacce* sandwich, order a drink at the bar, and take away your food or sit with Florentines and watch the action while you munch. For dessert, consider their tempting

Florentine and Tuscan Cuisine

In general, Tuscan cuisine is hearty, simple food: grilled meats, high-quality seasonal vegetables, fresh herbs, prized olive oil, and rustic bread. If a dish ends with *"alla toscana"* or *"alla fiorentina,"* it's cooked in the Tuscan or Florentine style—usually a preparation highlighting local products. In addition to specialty dishes, most restaurants also serve pasta and pizza, veal cutlets, and salad (for more on Italian cuisine, see page 1140).

There's nothing wrong with your Tuscan bread—it's supposed to taste like that. *Pane alla toscana* is unsalted and nearly flavorless (from the days when salt's preservative powers made it more valuable than gold). Italians drench it in olive oil and sprinkle it with salt, or use it to scoop up sauce.

Antipasti (Appetizers)
Bruschetta: Toasted bread brushed with olive oil and rubbed with garlic, topped with chopped tomato, mushrooms, or whatever else sounds good.

Crostini: Toasted bread rounds topped with meat or vegetable pastes. *Alla toscana* generally means with chicken liver pâté.

Panzanella: A simple summer salad, made of day-old bread, chopped tomatoes, onion, and basil, tossed in a light vinaigrette.

Pecorino cheese: Fresh *(fresco)* or aged *(stagionato),* from ewe's milk.

Porcini mushrooms: Harvested in fall; used in pasta and soups, as a topping on meats and bruschetta, and sometimes deep-fried.

Salumi: Cold cuts, usually air- or salt-dried pork. Popular kinds include prosciutto (air-cured ham hock), *pancetta* (cured pork belly), *lardo* (cured pork lard), and *finocchiona* (fennel salami). For a list of other *salumi,* see page 1143.

Tagliere: A wooden platter with cold cuts and/or cheeses.

Primo Piatto (First Course)
Carabaccia: Onion soup.

Pappa al pomodoro: Thick stew of tomatoes, olive oil, and bread.

Pappardelle al sugo di lepre: A rich sauce with wild hare over long, broad noodles.

Pici al ragù: A fat, spaghetti-like, hand-rolled pasta served with a meat-tomato sauce.

Ribollita: "Reboiled" soup, traditionally made with leftovers including white beans *(fagioli),* seasonal vegetables, and olive oil, with layers of day-old Tuscan bread.

Zuppa alla volterrana: Volterra-style soup, similar to *ribollita* but with fresh bread.

Secondo Piatto (Second Course)
Arrosto misto: An assortment of roasted meats, sometimes served on a skewer *(spiedino).*

Bistecca alla fiorentina: A thick T-bone steak, generally grilled very rare and lightly seasoned (often sold by weight—per *etto*, or 100 grams). The best—and most expensive—is from the white Chianina breed of cattle you'll see grazing throughout Tuscany.

Cinghiale: Wild boar, served grilled or in soups, stews, and pasta. It is also made into many varieties of sausage and salami.

Fegatelli: Liver meatballs.

Game birds: Squab *(piccione),* pheasant *(fagiano),* and guinea hen *(faraona)* are popular.

Trippa alla fiorentina: Tripe (intestines) and vegetables sautéed in tomato sauce. *Trippa* (and the similar *lampredotto*) are popular in sandwiches; see page 522.

Dolci (Desserts)

Cantucci: Florentines love to end a meal by dipping this crunchy almond cookie in vin santo wine (described below).

Gelato: The Florentines claim they invented Italian-style ice cream. Rather than order dessert in a restaurant, I like to stroll with a gelato. For more on gelato, see page 1144; for tips on enjoying it here, see page 523.

Panforte: Dense, clove-and-cinnamon-spiced cake from Siena.

Local Wines

Many Tuscan wines are made with sangiovese ("blood of Jupiter") grapes. But the characteristics of the soil, temperature, and exposure make each wine unique to its area.

Brunello di Montalcino: One of Italy's best reds, this full-bodied wine comes from the slopes of Montalcino, south of Siena. Smooth and dry, it pairs well with hearty, meaty food.

Chianti: This red hails from the Chianti region (20 miles south of Florence). Varieties range from cheap, acidic basket-bottles of table wine (called *fiaschi*) to the hearty Chianti Classico.

Rosso di Montalcino: This cheaper, younger "baby Brunello," made in Montalcino, lacks Brunello's depth of flavor and complexity—but it's still a great wine at a bargain price.

Super Tuscans: This newer wine blends traditional grapes with locally grown non-Italian grapes (such as cabernet or merlot).

Vernaccia di San Gimignano: This medium-dry white goes well with pasta and salad. Trebbiano and vermentino are two other local white grapes.

Vin Santo: Sweet and syrupy, this "holy" dessert wine is often served with a cookie for dipping.

Vino Nobile di Montepulciano: This high quality, ruby red, dry wine pairs well with meat, especially chicken.

display case of delicious cakes (Mon-Sat 8:00-21:00, Sun 10:00-16:30, no reservations taken, just off Via de' Calzaiuoli, at Via dei Tavolini 18 red, tel. 055-268-590).

$ I Fratellini is a hole-in-the-wall where the "little brothers" have served peasants more than 30 kinds of sandwiches and a fine selection of wine at great prices (see list on wall) since 1875. Join the local crowd to order, then sit on a nearby curb to eat, placing your glass on the wall rack before you leave. Be adventurous with the menu (easy-order by number). Consider *finocchiona e caprino* (#15, a Tuscan salami and soft goat cheese), *lardo di Colonnata* (#22, cured lard aged in Carrara marble), and *cinghiale* (#19, spicy boar salami) sandwiches. It's worth ordering the most expensive wine they're selling by the glass (daily 9:00-19:30 or until the bread runs out, 20 yards in front of Orsanmichele Church on Via dei Cimatori, tel. 055-239-6096).

Sandwich Shop/Wine Bar near Ponte Vecchio: A mod little shop, **$ 'Ino** is filled with gifty edibles. Alessandro and his staff serve creative sandwiches and glasses of wine—you'll munch your meal while perched on a tiny, uncomfortable stool. They can also make a fine €9-12 *piatto misto* of cheeses and meats with bread (daily 11:30-15:30, immediately behind Uffizi Gallery courtyard on Ponte Vecchio side, near the potted olive tree at Via dei Georgofili 7 red, tel. 055-219-208).

Cheap Takeout on Via Dante Alighieri: Three handy places line up on this street, located between Piazza della Signoria and the Duomo. **$ L'Antico Trippaio,** a food cart, is a fixture in the town center. Cheap and authentic as can be, this is where locals come daily for sandwiches *(panini)*, featuring specialties like *trippa* (tripe), *lampredotto,* and a list of more appetizing options, including *bollito.* Lisa, Maurizio, and Roberto offer a free plastic glass of rotgut Chianti with each sandwich for travelers with this book (daily 9:00-21:00, on Via Dante Alighieri, mobile 339-742-5692). **$ Pizzeria Totò,** just next to the tripe stand, has good-and-cheap slices (daily 10:30-22:00, Via Dante Alighieri 28 red, tel. 055-290-406). And a few steps away is a **Carrefour Express supermarket,** with cheap drinks and snacks and a fine *antipasti* case (daily 8:30-21:30, Via Dante Alighieri 24). If you pick up lunch at any of these, the best people-watching place to enjoy your sandwich is on Piazza della Signoria (three blocks south).

More Sandwich Shops: Two well-regarded places to grab a cheap sandwich are **$ Da' Vinattieri,** a literal hole-in-the-wall (*schiacciata* sandwiches plus *trippa* and *lampredotto,* daily 10:00-19:30, next to Casa di Dante at Via Santa Margherita 4 red); and **$ Il Cernacchino** (*panino* sandwiches, Mon-Sat 9:30-19:30, closed Sun, just north of the Palazzo Vecchio at Via della Condotta 38 red, tel. 055-294-119).

Gelato

Italy's best ice cream is in Florence—many think they serve some of the world's best. But beware of scams at touristy joints on busy streets that turn a simple request for a cone into a €10 "tourist special" rip-off. To avoid this, survey the size options and specify what you want—for example, *un cono da tre euro* (a €3 cone). A rule of thumb: Stay away from places with heaping mounds of brightly (artificially) colored gelato. For more gelato tips, see page 1144. All of these places, which are a cut above, are open daily for long hours.

Near the Accademia: A Sicilian choice on a tourist thoroughfare, **Gelateria Carabè** is particularly famous for its pistachio and its luscious *granite*—Italian ices made with fresh fruit. A *cremolata* is a *granila* with a dollop of gelato (almond and pistachio work well together). If you'd like a real Sicilian cannoli, get it here (from the Accademia, it's a block toward the Duomo at Via Ricasoli 60 red—Simone clearly loves his work).

Near the Duomo: A favorite, **Edoardo** features organic ingredients and tasty handmade cones (facing the southwest corner of the Duomo at Piazza del Duomo 45 red).

Near Orsanmichele Church: Perchè No! translates to "Why not!" Which is good advice when it comes to gelato. The shop feels touristy but serves one of the widest range of flavors around, and the quality's top notch (just off the busy main pedestrian drag, Via de' Calzaiuoli, at Via dei Tavolini 19).

Near Ponte Vecchio: Carapina is a modern *gelateria* with some pleasantly atypical flavors, seasonal ingredients, and a loyal following (Via Lambertesca 18 red).

Near the Church of Santa Croce: Florentines flock to **Gelateria de' Neri,** with an enticingly wide array of flavors (Via dei Neri 9 red).

NEAR THE ACCADEMIA

There aren't many appealing sit-down restaurants in the boring streets near the Accademia. But hungry tourists looking for a quick lunch between sightseeing stops find plenty of options. Picnickers can grab a takeout bite at one of these places, then hike around the block and join the bums on the traffic-free **Piazza S.S. Annunziata,** the first Renaissance square in Florence. There's a fountain for washing fruit on the square. Grab a stony seat anywhere you like.

$ Ará è Sicilia, just around the corner from *David*, is tiny, bright, and packed with Italians ordering up chef Carmelo's take on Sicilian street food: *arancini* (filled risotto balls) and *pizzole* (stuffed pizza) in fresh, inventive flavors, chased by homemade sorbet, cannoli, or pistachio biscotti. Order to takeaway or perch on one of the few stools (daily 10:00-22:00, Via degli Alfani 127 red, mobile 333-198-3927).

$ Due Sorsi e un Boccone ("Two Sips and a Bite"), a few steps down the same street, serves just that: cheap glasses of house wine, savory or sweet crêpes, and made-to-order *schiacciate* (sandwiches on flattened, foccacia-like bread). Order your food to go, or squeeze into a spot at the counter. It's run with a fresh, youthful attitude and jammed with local students at lunchtime (Mon-Fri 9:30-17:00, closed Sat-Sun, Via degli Alfani 105 red, mobile 334-264-0931).

$ La Mescita Fiaschetteria is a characteristic hole-in-the-wall, where locals enjoy a simple menu of pastas and *secondi* with tasty, cheap house wine. The place can either be mobbed by students or a peaceful time warp, depending on when you stop by. Mirco and Alessio are gregarious to the point of being a bit pushy... order carefully and check your bill (daily 11:30-15:30, Via degli Alfani 70 red, mobile 338-992-2640).

Supermarket: Carrefour Express, a half-block north of the Accademia, has a sandwich counter and picnic provisions (daily 8:00-20:00, Via Ricasoli 109 red).

Sit-Down Lunch in a Classy Café: A smart little café with friendly service, **$$ Pasticceria Robiglio** has a stately dining area and a few tables on the sidewalk. They have a small menu of salads and daily pasta and *secondi* specials. It's good any time for a coffee and one of their pretty pastries—famous among Florentines (café open daily 7:30-20:00, lunch served 12:00-16:00, a block toward the Duomo off Piazza S.S. Annunziata at Via dei Servi 112 red, tel. 055-212-784).

Memorable Restaurants a Bit Farther from the Accademia

These two places—within a 5- to 10-minute walk of the Accademia—are worth going out of your way for to get a memorable meal.

$$$ Antica Trattoria da Tito, a 10-minute hike from the Accademia along Via San Gallo, can be fun if you want a memorable meal with a local crowd and smart-aleck service. The boss, Bobo, serves quality traditional food and lots of wine. While the food is good, there's no pretense—it's just a playground of Tuscan cuisine. The music is vintage 1980s and can be loud. To gorge on a feast of *antipasti* (cold cuts, cheeses, a few veggies, and bruschetta), consider ordering *fermami* (literally "stop me")—for €18, Bobo brings you food until you say, *"Fermami!"* A couple can get *fermami* for two, desserts, and a nice bottle of wine for around €60 total. Dinner is served in two seatings: 19:30 (more sanity) and 21:30 (less sanity), and reservations are generally necessary (€17 *gran tagliere*—big plate of cheese and meat, travelers with this book get a free after-dinner drink, Mon-Sat 12:30-15:00 & 19:00-23:00, closed Sun, Via San Gallo 112 red, tel. 055-472-475, www.trattoriadatito.it).

$$$ **Ristorante Cafaggi** fills a bright yet low-energy space on a drab street between the Accademia and Mercato Centrale. With a vaguely 1950s vibe, it feels like it's been retro since before it was "retro." The service can be a bit shy; the emphasis here is their generations-old passion for Florentine food. It's been family-run since 1922, with Grandma and Grandpa still puttering around (Mon-Sat 12:30-15:00 & 19:00-22:00, closed Sun and several weeks in Aug, Via Guelfa 35 red, tel. 055-294-989, www.ristorantecafaggi.com).

BETWEEN THE PALAZZO VECCHIO AND SANTA CROCE CHURCH

$$ **Ristorante del Fagioli,** an enthusiastically run eatery where you can sense the heritage, just feels real, from the wood-paneled dining room to the daily specials chalked on a board. The dad, Gigi, commands the kitchen while family members Antonio, Maurizio, and Simone keep the throngs of loyal customers returning. The cuisine: home-style bread soups, hearty steaks, and other Florentine classics. Don't worry—while *fagioli* means "beans," that's the family name, not the extent of the menu (Mon-Fri 12:30-14:30 & 19:30-22:30, closed Sat-Sun, cash only, reserve for dinner, a block north of the Alle Grazie bridge at Corso dei Tintori 47, tel. 055-244-285).

$$ **Trattoria Anita,** midway between the Uffizi and Santa Croce, feels old-school, with wood paneling and rows of wine bottles. Brothers Nicola, Gianni, and Maurizio offer good value—both for their weekday lunch special featuring three hearty Tuscan courses for €11 and their à la carte dinner (Mon-Sat 12:00-14:30 & 19:00-22:15, closed Sun, on the corner of Via Vinegia and Via del Parlagio at 2 red, tel. 055-218-698).

$$ **Trattoria I'cche C'è C'è** is a small, family-run restaurant where Gino, Mara, and their son Jacopo serve basic Florentine dishes. While tired and touristy, it's also cozy and welcoming (Tue-Sun 12:30-14:30 & 19:30-22:30, closed Mon, Via Magalotti 11 red, tel. 055-216-589).

Quick Lunch Places on Via dei Neri: This is *panino* lane, with five high-energy, rustic, and youthful sandwich bars. This street, which runs behind the Palazzo Vecchio and the Uffizi toward Santa Croce, seems to specialize in sightseers seeking lunch between landmarks: $ **All'Antico Vinaio,** a photogenic Florentine favorite, offers two options: stand in the street with a crusty sandwich and pour your own wine, or head across the street to their more comfortable and expensive *osteria* (sandwiches, Mon-Sat 10:30-22:30, Sun 12:00-16:00, Via dei Neri 65 red, tel. 055-238-2723). **$ Club del Gusto,** with friendly owner/chef Paolo, is much quieter. Grab a salad or sandwich to carry away, or enjoy a plate of mixed meats and cheeses, or a made-to-order pasta plate, with their nice house wine at a shared table in back. Enthusiastic about traditional dishes, they provide a good venue for trying *lampredotto*—that's cow stomach (daily 9:00-24:00, Via dei Neri 50 red, tel. 348-090-3142).

$ Döner Kebab: Just south of Santa Croce is **Istanbul Döner Kebap,** a good place for a quick, un-Italian meal (Via dei Benci 18 red).

NEAR THE CHURCH OF SANTA MARIA NOVELLA

$$$ Trattoria Sostanza-Troia, characteristic and well established, is famous for its steaks and its *pollo al burro* (chicken in butter). Whirling ceiling fans and walls strewn with old photos evoke earlier times, while the artichoke pie *(tortino di carciofi)* reminds locals of Grandma's cooking. Crowded, with just eight shared tables, a small menu, and grumpy service, the place feels like a simple bistro. Reservations are essential for their two dinner seatings: 19:30 and 21:00 (cash only, open Mon-Sat, closed Sun year-round and Sat off-season, lunch served 12:30-14:00, Via del Porcellana 25 red, tel. 055-212-691).

$$ Trattoria Marione serves home-cooked-style meals to a mixed group of tourists and Florentines crowding very tight tables beneath hanging ham hocks. The ambience is happy, food-loving, and a bit frantic—no reservations, so arrive early (daily 12:00-17:00 & 19:00-23:00, Via della Spada 27 red, tel. 055-214-756, Fabio).

$$ Trattoria al Trebbio features all the traditional Tuscan classics at average prices in an eclectic, modern setting. Dine inside, surrounded by old movie posters and framed prosciutto legs, or grab one of the few tables outside (daily 12:00-15:00 & 19:00-23:00, half a block off of Piazza Santa Maria Novella at Via delle Belle Donne 47 red, tel. 055-287-089).

$$ Trattoria "da Giorgio" is a rustic family-style diner on a sketchy street serving up simple home cooking to happy locals and tourists alike. Their €14 three-course, fixed-price meal, including a drink, is a great value. This place is completely without pretense—head here for a taste of working-class Florence (Mon-Sat 12:00-14:30 & 18:30-22:00, closed Sun, Via Palazzuolo 100 red, tel. 055-284-302, Silvano).

HIDDEN ROOFTOP CAFÉ TERRACES

If you're willing to pay extra to enjoy a drink surrounded by splendid Florentine views, head to one of these rooftop terraces:

$$ Caffè La Terrazza is on the rooftop of La Rinascente department store overlooking Piazza della Repubblica. While fairly plain, it comes with commanding views of the Duomo, which looms gloriously on the horizon (€6 coffee drinks, daily 9:00-20:30).

$$$$ Sesto is a dressy bar on a partially covered terrace perched on the top floor of the luxurious Westin Hotel. While cocktails here are pricey (€15 and up; €6 coffee drinks), they come with amazing city views. To turn your spendy drink into a light dinner, come by during their *aperitivo* happy hour (19:00-21:00) when, for €18, your drink includes access to a little buffet, giving you something to nibble as you enjoy the sunset (daily 12:00-24:00, Piazza Ognissanti 3, tel. 055-27151, www.sestoonarno.com).

THE OLTRARNO

In general, dining in the Oltrarno, south of the Arno River, offers a more authentic experience. While it's just a few minutes' walk from Ponte Vecchio, this area sees far fewer tourists than the other side of the river. You may even find that Florentines outnumber my readers. For locations, see the map on page 510.

Dining or Drinking with a Ponte Vecchio View

$$ Signorvino is an *enoteca* (wine shop) with a simple restaurant that has a rare terrace literally over the Arno River, with Ponte Vecchio views. It's a fun-loving place with no pretense yet a passion for quality Italian ingredients. They serve regional dishes, and plates of fine meats and cheeses to go with a wonderful array of wines by the glass, allowing you to drink and eat your way merrily across Italy. If you're up for a full bottle, their huge selection is available for the same fair prices at a table as in their wine store (shop open daily 9:30-24:00, food served 11:30-23:00, Via Dei Bardi 46 red, tel. 055-286-258, www.signorvino.com, call to reserve, especially for terrace seating).

$$$ Golden View Open Bar is a modern, noisy, and touristy bistro, good for a salad, pizza, or pasta with fine wine and a fine view of Ponte Vecchio and the Arno River. Its white, minimalist interior is a stark contrast to atmospheric old Florence. Reservations for window tables are essential. They have three seating areas (with the same menu and prices): a riverside pizza place, a classier restaurant, and a jazzy lounge. In the afternoon (12:00-18:00), they offer wine tastings (€9-15) that include three pours and light snacks. Later (18:30 to 21:30), the wine bar serves a buffet of appetizers free with your €10 drink. Mixing their fine wine, river views, and live jazz makes for a wonderful evening (daily 11:30-24:00, café opens at 7:30, jazz usually Mon, Fri, and Sat nights at 21:00, 50 yards east of Ponte Vecchio at Via dei Bardi 58, tel. 055-214-502, www.goldenviewopenbar.com, run by Antonio, Paolo, and Tommaso).

$ Osteria Ponte Vecchio is a tiny place—little more than a bar—serving basic drinks, *panini,* and microwaved snacks with a couple of amazing tables on the river (daily 10:00-23:00, off-season until 20:00 and closed Sun or Mon, a block downstream from Ponte Vecchio at Via Borgo San Jacopo 16 red).

On or near Piazza di Santo Spirito

Piazza di Santo Spirito is a thriving neighborhood square in the heart of the Oltrarno, with a collection of fun eateries and bars. Several bars offer *aperitivo* buffets with their drinks during happy hour. Late in the evening the area becomes a club scene, filled with foreign students and young locals. And every day, when the weather's nice, the tables of Trattoria Borgo Antico and several other characteristic places spill onto the square. After noting the plain facade of the Brunelleschi church facing the square, step inside Caffè Ricchi to see pictures of the many possible ways the church might be finished.

$$ Gusta Osteria, just around the corner from the piazza, serves big salads and predictable Tuscan fare at fun, cozy indoor seating or at outdoor tables (Tue-Sun 12:00-23:00, closed Mon, Via de' Michelozzi 13 red, tel. 055-285-033). For cheaper bites, try its sister restaurant **$ Gusta Panino,** a sandwich bar directly on the square.

$$ Trattoria Casalinga, an inexpensive standby, comes with aproned women bustling around the kitchen. Florentines (who enjoy the tripe and tongue) and tourists (who opt for easier to swallow Tuscan favorites) alike pack the place and leave full and happy, with euros to spare for gelato (Mon-Sat 12:00-14:30 & 19:00-22:00, after 20:00 reserve or wait, closed Sun and Aug, just off Piazza di Santo Spirito, near the church at Via de' Michelozzi 9 red, tel. 055-218-624, www.trattorialacasalinga.it, Andrea and Paolo).

$ Gusta Pizza is your typical jam-packed, cheap, sloppy, and fun neighborhood pizzeria (Tue-Sun 11:30-15:30 & 19:00-23:30, closed Mon, two blocks off Piazza di Santo Spirito at Via Maggio 46 red, tel. 055-285-068).

Beyond Piazza del Carmine, away from Tourists

While Piazza di Santo Spirito is well known by tourists, a short walk beyond it gets you completely away from the tourist scene. These two restaurants (side by side on Via Dell'Orto) are worth the five-minute walk beyond Piazza del Carmine:

$$ Burro & Acciughe Fish Restaurant ("butter and anchovies") is a new, minimalist place packed with locals enjoying enthusiastically presented fresh seafood. With just 35 seats in a long, rustic setting, it's very simple but oozes quality (closed Mon, Via dell'Orto 35 red, tel. 055-045-7286).

$$ Trattoria dell'Orto is a classic Florentine trattoria filled with classic Florentines enjoying steaks, grilled dishes, and quintessential local fare—with no tourists. It has a fun vibe and a nice covered outdoor terrace in back (closed Tue, Via dell'Orto 35a, tel. 055-224-148).

Dining Well in the Oltrarno

Of the many good and colorful restaurants in the Oltrarno, these are my favorites. Reservations are a good idea in the evening.

$$$ Il Santo Bevitore Ristorante, lit like a Rembrandt painting and unusually spacious, serves creative modern Tuscan cuisine at dressy tables. They're enthusiastic about matching quality produce from the area with the right wine. This is a good break from the big, sloppy plates of pasta you'll get at many Florence eateries (good wine list by the glass or bottle, daily 12:30-14:30 & 19:30-23:00, closed Sun or Mon for lunch, reservations smart, three tables on the sidewalk, acoustics can make it noisy inside, Via di Santo Spirito 64 red, tel. 055-211-264, www.ilsantobevitore.com).

$$ Enoteca Il Santino Gastronomia, Il Santo Bevitore's smaller wine bar next door, feels like the perfect after-work hangout for foodies who'd like a glass of wine and a light bite. Tight, cozy, and atmospheric, the place has a prominent bar where you can assemble an €8-12 *tagliere* of local cheeses and *salumi*. They also have a few affordable hot dishes. Both the food and the wine are locally sourced from small producers (daily 12:30-23:00, Via di Santo Spirito 60 red, no reservations, tel. 055-230-2820).

$$$ Trattoria 4 Leoni creates the quintessential Oltrarno dinner scene, and is understandably popular with tourists. The Tuscan-style food is made with an innovative twist and an appreciation for vegetables. You'll enjoy the fun energy and characteristic seating, both outside on the colorful square and inside, where you'll dine in exposed-stone sophistication. While the wines by the glass are pricey, the house wine is good (daily 12:00-24:00, dinner reservations smart; midway between Ponte Vecchio and Piazza di Santo Spirito, on Piazza della Passera; tel. 055-218-562, www.4leoni.com).

$$$ Antico Ristoro Di' Cambi is thick with Tuscan traditions, rustic touches, and T-bone steaks. The bustling scene has a memorable, beer-hall energy. As you walk in, you'll pass a glass case filled with red chunks of Chianina beef that's priced by weight (for the famous *bistecca alla fiorentina* it's €45/kilo—figure a half-kilo per person). Before you OK your investment, they'll show you the cut and tell you the weight. While the steak comes nearly uncooked, it's air-dried for 21 days so it's not really raw, just very tasty and tender—it'll make you happy you're at the top of the food chain. Sit inside the convivial woody interior or outside on a square (Mon-Sat 12:00-14:30 & 18:30-22:30, closed Sun, reserve on weekends and to sit outside, Via Sant'Onofrio 1 red, one block south of Ponte Amerigo Vespucci, see map on page 516, tel. 055-217-134, www.anticoristorodicambi.it, run by Stefano and Fabio, the Cambi cousins).

$$$$ Olio & Convivium is primarily a catering company for top-end events, and this is where they showcase their artful, slow-food cooking (you can buy many of the ingredients on their menu). Their three intimate rooms are surrounded by fine *prosciutti*, cheeses, and wine shelves. It can seem a little formal, but well-dressed foodies will appreciate this place for its clubby atmosphere. Their list of €14-25 *gastronomia* plates offers an array of taste treats and fine wines by the glass. Take full advantage of their passion for olive oil. They also have €35-49 tasting menus and stylish €18 lunches with wine (Tue-Sun 12:00-14:30 & 19:00-22:30, closed Mon, Via di Santo Spirito 4, tel. 055-265-8198, www.oliorestaurant.it, Tommaso is the chef and owner).

Casual Oltrarno Neighborhood Eateries

$$$ Trattoria da Sergio is a tiny eatery about a block before Porta San Frediano, one of Florence's medieval gates. It has a relaxed charm and a strong following, so reservations are a must. The food is on the gourmet side of home cooking—mama's favorites with a modern twist—and therefore is a bit more expensive (Tue-Sat 19:15-22:45, Sun 12:00-14:00, closed Mon, Borgo San Frediano 145 red, see map on page 444, tel. 055-223-449, Sergio and Marco, www.trattoriadasergio.it).

$$ Trattoria Al Tranvai, with tight seating and small dark-wood tables, looks like an old-time tram filled with the neighborhood gang. A 10-minute walk from the river at the edge of the Oltrarno, it feels like a small town's favorite eatery, serving creative dishes for good prices (Mon 19:00-24:00, Tue-Sat 12:30-14:30 & 19:30-22:30, closed Sun; from the Brancacci Chapel, go south on Via del Leone 5 minutes to Piazza Torquato Tasso 14 red, see map on page 444; tel. 055-225-197, www.altranvai.it).

$$ Le Volpi e l'Uva, a wine bar just steps from Ponte Vecchio, has a limited menu of *affettati* (cold cuts), cheese, and *crostone* (hearty bruschetta)—a nice spot for a light lunch (Mon-Sat 11:00-21:00, closed Sun, 65 yards south of Ponte Vecchio—walk through Piazza Santa Felicità to Piazza dei Rossi 1, tel. 055-239-

8132, www.levolpieluva.com, run by wine experts Riccardo, Ciro, and Emilio).

$ Trattoria Sabatino, farthest away of my Oltrarno listings (and not touristy), is a spacious, brightly lit mess hall. You get the feeling it hasn't changed much since it opened—in 1956. It's disturbingly cheap, with family character and a simple menu—a super place to watch locals munch, especially since you'll likely be sharing a table. It's a 15-minute walk from Ponte Vecchio (Mon-Fri 12:00-14:30 & 19:15-22:00, closed Sat-Sun, just outside Porta San Frediano, Via Pisana 2 red, see map on page 444, tel. 055-225-955, little English spoken).

Via di San Niccolò and Nearby

This charming little street (just over Ponte alle Grazie, behind Hotel Silla) is the Oltrarno's "hipster corner" and can be a fun place for young foodies to explore. There's a convivial neighborhood pizzeria, an *enoteca*, a good *gelateria* (**Il Gelato di Filo,** at Via San Miniato 5 red), and a rollicking bar (**Il Baretto del Rifrullo,** at Via San Niccolò 55 red), which serves a generous buffet during happy hour. Street-art lovers enjoy popping into the **Clet gallery,** run by Clet Abraham, the artist who creatively disfigures signs around town. For those looking to dine, two good eateries anchor the square:

$$ Antica Mescita San Niccolò, with traditional decor but a modern approach, feels like the grandkids took over Nonno's trattoria. Technically a wine bar, they also serve up Tuscan standbys (like soups and stews). There's delightful seating outside in good weather; their cellar is less cozy (daily 12:00-24:00, Via San Niccolò 60 red, tel. 055-234-2836).

$$$ Zeb is a tight, mod, minimalist wine-bar/deli with one long counter (just two dozen seats). Although the name stands for *zuppe e bolliti* ("soup and boiled meats"), they dish up all types of well-executed and elegantly presented Florentine food. Portions are large and fun to share, served up by charming Mama Guiseppina and her son Alberto. Dinner reservations are smart (closed Wed, Via San Miniato 2 red, tel. 055-234-2864, www.zebgastronomia.com).

Nightlife: To rub elbows with the locals, head to tiny Piazza Demidoff (cross the bridge east of Ponte Vecchio and turn left, about a 10-minute walk). These places have outdoor seating, chichi interiors, and late hours: **Negroni** (Via dei Renai 17 red, tel. 055-243-647) and **Zoe** (Via dei Renai 13 red, tel. 055-243-111).

Florence Connections

Florence is Tuscany's transportation hub, with fine train, bus, and plane connections to virtually anywhere in Italy. The city has several train stations, a bus station (next to the main train station), and an airport (and Pisa's airport is nearby). Livorno, on the coast west of Florence, is a major cruise-ship port.

BY TRAIN

The departures listed below are operated by Trenitalia; Italo offers additional high-speed connections to major Italian cities (including Milan, Padua, Venice, Rome, and Naples; see page 1157).

From Florence by Train to: Pisa (2-3/hour, 45-75 minutes), **Lucca** (2/hour, 1.5 hours), **Siena** (direct trains hourly, 1.5-2 hours; bus is better because Siena's train station is far from the center), **Camucia-Cortona** (hourly, 1.5 hours), **Livorno** (hourly, 1.5 hours, some change in Pisa), **La Spezia** (for the Cinque Terre, 5/day direct, 2.5 hours, otherwise nearly hourly with change in Pisa), **Milan** (hourly, 2 hours), **Venice** (hourly, 2-3 hours, may transfer in Bologna; often crowded—reserve ahead), **Assisi** (8/day direct, 2-3 hours), **Orvieto** (hourly, 2 hours, some with change in Campo di Marte or Rifredi Station), **Rome** (2-3/hour, 1.5 hours, most require seat reservations), **Naples** (hourly, 3 hours), **Brindisi** (8/day, 8 hours with change in Bologna or Rome), **Interlaken** (2/day, 5.5 hours, 2 changes), **Frankfurt** (6/day, 10-11.5 hours, 2 changes), **Paris** (5/day, 9-10.5 hours, 1-2 changes; 1 night train with change in Milan, 13 hours, important to reserve ahead at www.thello.com), **Vienna** (5/day, 10-11 hours, 1-2 changes).

BY BUS

The BusItalia Station (100 yards west of the train station on Via Santa Caterina da Siena) posts schedules for regional trips, and video monitors show imminent departures. Bus service drops dramatically on Sunday. Generally it's best to buy bus tickets in the station, as you'll pay 30 percent more if you buy tickets onboard. Bus info: tel. 800-373-760 (Mon-Fri 9:00-15:00, closed Sat-Sun), www.fsbusitalia.it.

From Florence by Bus to: San Gimignano (hourly, fewer on Sun, 1.5-2 hours, change in Poggibonsi), **Siena** (roughly 2/hour, 1.5-hour *rapida/via superstrada* buses are faster than the train, avoid the slower *ordinaria* buses, www.sienamobilita.it), **Volterra** (4/day Mon-Sat, 1/day Sun, 2 hours, change in Colle di Val d'Elsa to CTT bus #770, www.pisa.cttnord.it; or train to Pontedera-Casciana Terme and then CTT bus #500 to Volterra, 7/day, fewer on Sun, 1.5 hours, www.pisa.cttnord.it), **Montepulciano** (1-2/day, 2 hours, change in Bettolle, LFI bus, www.lfi.it; or train to Chiusi, then Siena Mobilità bus to Montepulciano, www.sienamobilita.it), **Florence airport** (2/hour, 30 minutes, pay driver and immediately validate ticket, usually departs from platform 1, first bus departs at 5:30).

As some Tuscan towns (including Volterra and Montepulciano) have few connections, day-trippers could instead consider a guided tour such as those offered by Artviva (see page 458).

BY TAXI

For small groups with more money than time, zipping to nearby towns by taxi can be a good value (e.g., €120 from your Florence hotel to your Siena hotel).

A more comfortable alternative is to hire a private car service. Florence-based **Transfer Chauffeur Service** has a fleet of modern vehicles with drivers who can whisk you between cities, to and from the cruise ship port at Livorno, and through the Tuscan countryside for around the same price as a cab (tel. 338-862-3129, www.transfercs.com, marco.masala@transfercs.com, Marco). **Prestige Rent** also has friendly, English-speaking drivers and offers similar services (office near Piazza della Signoria at Via Porta Rossa 6 red, tel. 055-398-6598, mobile 333-842-4047, www.prestigerent.com, usa@prestigerent.com, Saverio).

BY PLANE

For information on Florence's Amerigo Vespucci Airport, see page 450. For Pisa's Galileo Galilei Airport, see page 560.

BY CRUISE SHIP

Cruise ships dock in the coastal town of Livorno (sometimes called "Leghorn" in English), about 60 miles west of Florence. For more details, see my *Rick Steves Mediterranean Cruise Ports* guidebook.

Getting to Florence: To reach Florence by train, ride the cruise line's shuttle bus from the port to downtown Livorno, then walk to Piazza Grande; just beyond the square is the stop for buses for Livorno Centrale Station. From there, trains zip to Florence about hourly (1.5 hours). Other options include day-tripping via a TI-arranged bus (TI tel. 0586-894-236, www.costadeglietruschi.it), sharing a minibus taxi with other travelers (about one hour each way), or joining your cruise line's excursion.

Getting to Pisa and Lucca: To get to Pisa by train, follow the directions above to reach Livorno Centrale Station, then hop on a train to Pisa (2-3/hour, 20 minutes). Alternatives include cheap shuttle buses arranged by the Livorno TI, or the public bus that departs downtown Livorno and drops off near the Pisa train station (1-2/hour, fewer Sat-Sun, 1.25 hours; see page 539 for details on how to reach the Leaning Tower from the Pisa train station).

To also visit the neighboring town of Lucca, take the train there first to avoid the morning cruise-ship crowds in Pisa (trains depart Livorno about hourly, 1-1.5 hours, transfer at Pisa Centrale). A handy bus connects Lucca's Piazzale Giuseppe Verdi to Pisa's Field of Miracles, or take a train from Lucca to Pisa San Rossore Station, near the Field of Miracles (see page 581).

If you value convenience over cost, consider sharing a taxi or taking a cruise-line excursion for your Pisa/Lucca sightseeing.

Local Guide: Karin Kibby, an Oregonian living in Livorno who leads Rick Steves tours, offers a morning "slice of Italian life" walk through Livorno, focusing on local culture (includes its fantastic food market), as well as day trips throughout Tuscany (2-10 people, mobile 333-108-6348, karinkintuscany@yahoo.it).

PISA & LUCCA

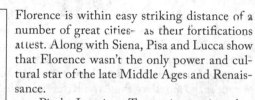

Florence is within easy striking distance of a number of great cities—as their fortifications attest. Along with Siena, Pisa and Lucca show that Florence wasn't the only power and cultural star of the late Middle Ages and Renaissance.

Pisa's Leaning Tower is touristy but worth a visit. Many tourists are surprised to see that the iconic tower is only a small part of a gleaming white architectural complex—featuring a massive cathedral and baptistery—that dominates the grand green square, the Field of Miracles. The rest of the city is virtually tourist-free and merits a wander for its rich history, architecture, and student vibe.

Lucca, contained within its fine Renaissance wall, lacks any blockbuster sights, but has a charm that causes many connoisseurs of Italy to claim it as a favorite stop. The town's garden-topped city wall is perfect for a laid-back bike ride—the single must-do activity in this pleasant getaway.

The two towns are about 25 minutes apart by train and 50 minutes by bus. Each is about 1.5 hours (or less) by train from Florence and well-served by excellent highways.

Using public transportation, you could day-trip from Florence to both cities. But with more time, stay overnight in Lucca. Take the train to Pisa in the morning, do your sightseeing, catch the bus or train to Lucca late in the afternoon, enjoy the evening scene, and stay the night. Sightsee Lucca the next day, then move on to your next destination by train.

Pisa & Lucca Area

Pisa

In A.D. 1200, Pisa's power peaked. For nearly three centuries (1000-1300), Pisa rivaled Venice and Genoa as a sea-trading power, exchanging European goods for luxury items in Muslim lands. As a port near the mouth of the Arno River (six miles from the coast—when the wind blows in a certain direction, you can still smell the sea), the city enjoyed easy access to the Mediterranean, with the added protection of sitting a bit upstream. The Romans made it a naval base, and by medieval times the city was a major player.

The city used its sea-trading wealth to build the grand monuments of the Field of Miracles, including the now-famous Leaning Tower. The Pisans fancied themselves the natural heirs of the Roman Empire, and they peppered Roman engineering—and actual ancient fragments—into their distinct architectural style: Pisan Romanesque. In many of Pisa's buildings and decoration from these glory days, you can see the earliest inklings of the coming Renaissance—centuries before it took hold in earnest in Florence.

Today's Pisa is a thriving midsize city with some fine Renaissance architecture (as well as some gloomy, post-WWII additions). It's still known for two things: its fine university and its remarkable Field of Miracles. That means it's thronged with both students and tourists.

Pisa's important sights—the Duomo, Baptistery, and the Tower—float regally on the best lawn in Italy. The style throughout is the city's very own Pisan Romanesque. Even as the church was being built, Piazza del Duomo was nicknamed the "Campo dei Miracoli," or Field of Miracles, for the grandness of the undertaking.

The Tower recently underwent a decade of restoration and topple-prevention. To ascend, you must get your ticket and book a time at least a few hours in advance.

PLANNING YOUR TIME

For most visitors, Pisa is a touristy quickie—seeing the Tower, visiting the square, and wandering through the Duomo are 90 percent of their Pisan thrills. But it's a shame to skip the rest of the city. Considering Pisa's historic importance and the ambience created by its rich architectural heritage and vibrant student population, the city deserves a half-day visit. For many, the lack of tourists outside the Field of Miracles is both a surprise and a relief.

If you want to climb the Tower, you can buy a ticket and book a time in advance online (no sooner than 20 days but at least one day beforehand) at www.opapisa.it. Otherwise, go straight to the ticket office upon your arrival to snag an appointment—usually for a couple of hours later, especially in summer (for directions to the Field of Miracles, see "Arrival in Pisa," later). If you'll be seeing both the town and the Field of Miracles, plan on a six-hour stop. If just blitzing the Field of Miracles, three hours is the minimum. Spending the night lets you savor a youthful Italian city scene.

If you're connecting Pisa and Lucca, note that a train runs at least hourly between Pisa's San Rossore train station near the Field of Miracles and Lucca (see page 560). This is so quick and easy that if you're just planning on seeing the Field of Miracles sights, Pisa makes a good half-day side-trip from Lucca.

Orientation to Pisa

The city of Pisa is manageable, with just 100,000 people, but its 45,000 students keep it lively, especially at night. The city is framed

on the north by the Field of Miracles (Leaning Tower) and on the south by Pisa Centrale train station. The Arno River flows east to west, bisecting the city. Walking from Pisa Centrale directly to the Tower takes about 30 minutes (but allow an hour if you take my self-guided walk). The two main streets for tourists and shoppers are Via Santa Maria (running south from the Tower) and Corso Italia/Borgo Stretto (running north from the station). A thousand years ago the city was a fortified burg on the north side of the river between those two main streets.

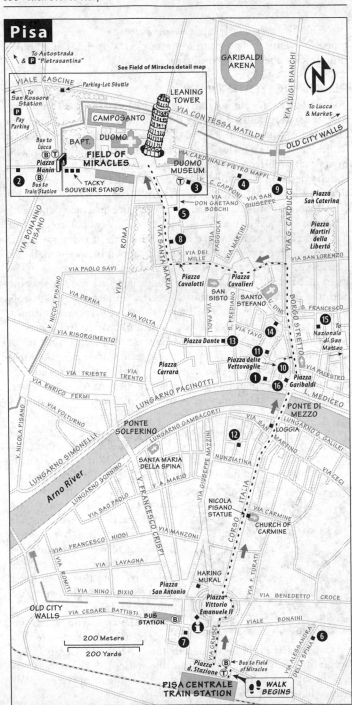

Pisa

To Autostrada
& P "Pietrasantina"

See Field of Miracles detail map

GARIBALDI ARENA

VIALE CASCINE — Parking-Lot Shuttle

To San Rossore Station

P Pay Parking

VIA CONTESSA MATILDE

LEANING TOWER

CAMPOSANTO

DUOMO

BAPT.

FIELD OF MIRACLES

Piazza Manin

Bus to Lucca

Bus to Train Station

TACKY SOUVENIR STANDS

OLD CITY WALLS

To Lucca & Market

VIA LUIGI BIANCHI

VIA CARDINALE PIETRO MAFFI

DUOMO MUSEUM

VIA DON GAETANO BOSCHI

V. C. CAPPONI

VIA SAN GIUSEPPE

Piazza San Caterina

Piazza Martiri della Libertà

VIA G. CARDUCCI

VIA SANTA MARIA

ROMA

VIA DEI MILLE

VIA FAGGIOLA

VIA MARTIRI

VIA SAN LORENZO

VIA PAOLO SAVI

Piazza Cavalotti

Piazza Cavalieri

SAN SISTO

SANTO STEFANO

U. DINI

BORGO STRETTO

S. FRANCESCO

V. NICOLA PISANO

VIA DERNA

VIA VOLTA

VIA U. PIGLIA

S. FREDIANO

V. VIA TAYO

To Nazionale di San Matteo

VIA RISORGIMENTO

Piazza Dante

Piazza delle Vettovaglie

VIA PALESTRO

VIA TRIESTE

VIA TRENTO

Piazza Carrara

Piazza Garibaldi

L. MEDICEO

VIA ENRICO FERMI

LUNGARNO PACINOTTI

PONTE DI MEZZO

VIA VOLTURNO

PONTE SOLFERINO

SANTA MARIA DELLA SPINA

LUNGARNO GAMBACORTI

LUNGARNO G. GALILEI

V. NICOLA PISANO

LUNGARNO SIMONELLI

Arno River

LUNGARNO SONNINO

LUNGARNO SAO PAOLO

V. A. MARIO

VIA GIUSEPPE MAZZINI

NUNZIATINA

LUNGARNO G. GALILEI

VIA CECI

V. FRANCESCO CRISPI

VIA MANZONI

NICOLA PISANO STATUE

CORSO ITALIA

VIA CARMINE

CHURCH OF CARMINE

VIA FRANCESCO NIOSI

VIA LAVAGNA

VIA ROMITI

VIA NINO BIXIO

HARING MURAL

VIA F. TURATI

VIA BENEDETTO CROCE

OLD CITY WALLS

VIA CESARE BATTISTI

Piazza San Antonio

BUS STATION

Piazza Vittorio Emanuele II

VIALE BONAINI

VIA ALESSANDRA DELLA SPINA

200 Meters

200 Yards

VIA GRUSCI

Piazza d. Stazione

Bus to Field of Miracles

PISA CENTRALE TRAIN STATION

WALK BEGINS

Pisa Key

1. Hotel Royal Victoria, Caffè dell'Ussero & De' Coltelli Gelato
2. Hotel Pisa Tower
3. Hotel Villa Kinzica
4. Casa San Tommaso
5. Pensione Helvetia
6. Hotel Alessandro della Spina
7. Hotel Milano
8. Santa Maria Eateries
9. Pizzeria al Bagno di Nerone
10. La Vineria di Piazza & Produce Market
11. Antica Trattoria il Campano
12. Il Vegusto
13. Caffetteria BetsaBea & Pizzeria l'Arancio
14. Il Montino Pizzeria
15. Orzo Bruno Brewpub
16. La Bottega del Gelato

TOURIST INFORMATION

The TI is about 200 yards in front of Pisa Centrale train station. Walk straight out, then turn left under the arcade at Piazza Vittorio Emanuele II to #13 (short and unpredictable hours, generally Mon-Fri 9:30-12:30, Sat-Sun 10:00-13:00, may be open longer in high season, tel. 050-42291, www.pisaunicaterra.it). There's also a TI at the airport, in the arrivals hall.

ARRIVAL IN PISA
By Train

Most trains (and visitors) arrive at Pisa Centrale station, about a mile south of the Tower and Field of Miracles. A few trains, particularly those from Lucca or La Spezia, stop at the smaller Pisa San Rossore station, an easy five-minute walk from the Tower (not all trains stop here, but if yours does, hop off).

Pisa Centrale Station: This station has a baggage-check desk—look for *deposito bagagli* (daily 6:00-21:00). With the tracks to your back, it's to the right at the far end of platform 1, just after the police station.

To get to the Field of Miracles, you can walk (get free map from TI, 30 minutes direct, one hour if you follow my self-guided walk), take a taxi (€10, tel. 050-541-600, taxi stand at station), or go by bus. At all bus stops in Pisa, be cautious of pickpockets, who take advantage of crowds to operate.

Bus **LAM Rossa** ("Red," also marked *L/R*) stops across the street from the train station, in front of the NH Cavalieri Hotel. Buy a €1.20 bus ticket from the tobacco/magazine kiosk in the train station's main hall or at any tobacco shop (€2 on board; bus usually departs every 10 minutes, less frequent off-season, runs until 20:30, 15-minute trip). The bus lets you off at Piazza Manin, in front of the gate to the Field of Miracles (stop: Torre).

To return to the train station from the Tower, catch bus LAM Rossa in front of the BNL bank, across the street from where you got off. You'll also find a taxi stand 30 yards from the Tower (at Bar Duomo).

Pisa San Rossore Station: From this dreary little suburban station, it's just a five-minute walk to the tower. Exit the underpass at platform 2L, and follow the exit signs to *Torre Pendente*. Once out of the station area, turn left and follow brown *Torre Pendente* sights—you'll see the tower soon, straight ahead.

By Car

Driving in the city center is stressful, time-consuming, and risky, as Pisa has several restricted areas that are monitored by camera (you could get a ticket by mail).

For a quick visit, try the **Parcheggio di Piazza dei Miracoli** lot, just northwest of the tower (€2/hour, enter from Via Giovanni Battista Niccolini). From here, the Tower is practically across the street.

For a longer visit—or if the Parcheggio lot is full—it's best to leave your car at the big **Pietrasantina parking lot,** designed for tour buses (which pay to park) and tourists with cars (who park for free). From there, you can walk to the Field of Miracles or hop on a shuttle bus. To reach this parking lot, exit the autostrada at *Pisa Nord* and follow signs to *Pisa* (on the left), then *Bus Parking*. The parking lot has a cafeteria and WC. At the center of the lot is a high-roofed bus stop where you can catch the red-and-orange **shuttle** *(navetta)* to the Field of Miracles (drops you at the Largo Cocco Griffi bus stop—just behind the walls, €1 round-trip, about every 10 minutes in season).

The **walk to the Tower** takes about 15 minutes: From the newspaper/souvenir kiosk at the east end of the lot, turn right onto the curving road. Follow the blue signs indicating a pedestrian path and brown signs pointing to the Leaning Tower. Or, to follow my self-guided walk through Pisa to the Field of Miracles, take bus LAM Rossa (from the glass-covered stop across from *navetta* pick-up) to Pisa Centrale (€1.20 at parking-lot cafeteria, €2 on board; also stops near the Tower at Piazza Manin en route).

By Plane

For details on Pisa's Galileo Galilei Airport, see page 560.

HELPFUL HINTS

Exchange Rate: €1 = about $1.10

Country Calling Code: 39 (see page 1154 for dialing instructions)

Markets: An open-air produce market attracts picnickers to Piazza delle Vettovaglie, one block north of the Arno River near Ponte di Mezzo, and nearby Piazza Sant'Uomobuono (Mon-Sat 8:00-18:00, main section closes at 13:00, closed Sun). A street market—with more practical goods than food—bustles on Wednesday and Saturday mornings between Via del Brennero and Via Paparrelli (8:00-13:00, just outside of wall, about 6 blocks east of the Tower).

Festivals: Noon on March 25 (also the Feast of the Annunciation of the Virgin Mary) is the *Capodanno Pisano*, the end of the year according to the Pisan calendar used in the Middle Ages. In a tradition carried on from medieval times, the city hosts New Year's festivities for several days.

June is a big month in Pisa, when some hotels raise their rates. The first half of June has many events, culminating in a celebration for Pisa's patron saint (June 16-17). The last week in June is the *Gioco del Ponte* ("Game of the Bridge") festival, where burly residents of the city's four districts meet on the bridge for a game of tug-of-war with a big carriage.

Local Guides: Dottore Vincenzo Riolo is a great guide for Pisa and the surrounding area (€145/3 hours, mobile 338-211-2939, www.pisatour.it, info@pisatour.it). **Martina Manfredi** happily guides visitors through the Field of Miracles, but her real passion is helping them discover Pisa's other charms, from hidden gardens and piazzas to cuisine to artisans (€140/3 hours, €250/6 hours, mobile 328-898-2927, www.tuscanyatheart.it, artemarty@libero.it).

Pisa Walk

A leisurely one-hour self-guided stroll from the Centrale train station to the Tower is a great way to get acquainted with the more subtle virtues of this fine city. Because the hordes who descend daily on the Tower rarely bother with the rest of the town, you'll find most of Pisa to be delightfully untouristy—a student-filled, classy, Old World town with an Arno-scape much like its upstream rival, Florence.

• *From Pisa Centrale train station, walk north (under the fascist marble arcade) up Viale Antonio Gramsci to the circular square called...*

Piazza Vittorio Emanuele II

The Allies considered Pisa to be strategically important in World War II, and both the train station and its main bridge were targeted for bombing. Forty percent of this district was destroyed. The piazza has been rebuilt, and now this generous public space with grass and benches is actually a lid for an underground parking lot. The TI is on this piazza, in the arcade to the left. The circular pink building in the middle of the square, on the right, is La Bottega del Parco, a shop that sells Tuscan products.

At the top of the square, on the left (by the Credito Arti-

giano bank), find the little piazza
with a colorful bar/café that faces
a mural, called *Tuttomondo (Whole
Wide World)*, painted by American
artist **Keith Haring** in 1989. Haring (who died of AIDS in 1990)
brought New York City graffiti
into the mainstream. This painting
is a celebration of diversity, chaos,
and the liveliness of our world, vi-
brating with energy.

• *Head back to the big square and walk up the street near the carousel.
This is Pisa's main drag.*

Corso Italia

As you leave Piazza Vittorio Emanuele II, look to the right (on the
wall of the bar on the corner, under the gallery) to see the circa-
1960 wall map of Pisa with a steam train. Then follow the pedestrianized Corso Italia straight north for several blocks, toward the
river. This is Pisa's main shopping street for locals, not tourists. This
is where the midrange department stores are and where students
hang out and stroll—you'll see plenty of youthful fashions.

A few blocks up, in front of the Church of Santa Maria del
Carmine (#88), meet **Nicola Pisano.** He and his son, Giovanni
(who worked in the 13th century) represented the pinnacle of
Gothic art and inspired Michelangelo. Although they were from
the south, their work in their adopted town earned them the name
"Pisano" (from Pisa).

Continuing down Corso Italia, you'll run into a gorgeous **loggia.** Like much of the city, this was built under Medici (Florentine)
rule—and it resembles the markets you'll still find in Florence. But
remember that before Florence ruled Pisa, this city was an independent and strong maritime republic.

• *At the Arno River, cross to the middle of the bridge.*

Ponte di Mezzo

This modern bridge, the site of Pisa's first bridge and therefore its
birthplace, marks the center of Pisa. In the Middle Ages, Ponte di
Mezzo (like Florence's Ponte Vecchio) was lined with shops. It's
been destroyed several times by floods...and in 1943 by British and
American bombers. Enjoy the view from the center of the bridge of
the elegant mansions that line the riverbank, recalling Pisa's days of
trading glory—the cityscape feels a bit like Venice's Grand Canal.
Back when the loggia area was stinky and crowded, nobles preferred to live in stately residences along the river.

• *Cross the bridge to...*

Piazza Garibaldi

This square is named for the charismatic leader of the Risorgimento, the unification movement that led to Italian independence in 1860. Knowing Pisa was strongly nationalist (and gave many of its sons to the national struggle), a wounded Garibaldi came here to be nursed back to health. Study the bronze relief at the base of the statue and see him docking in Pisa and receiving a warm and caring welcome.

For a gelato break, stop by **La Bottega del Gelato,** right on this square and most Pisans' sentimental favorite. Or, for a fresh take on the same old gelato, head about 100 yards downstream (to the left on Lungarno Pacinotti as you come off the bridge) to **De' Coltelli** (at #23), which scoops up organic, artisanal gelato with unusual and vibrant flavors...some of the best I've had. Just beyond that, in the slouching red building (at #28), step into **Caffè dell'Ussero.** This venerable café has long been a hangout of both politicians...and the students bent on overthrowing them. Greet the proprietor and then browse its time-warp interior all the way to its back room—it's lined with portraits and documents from the struggle for Italian independence.

• *Back on Piazza Garibaldi, continue north up the elegantly arcaded street called...*

Borgo Stretto

Welcome to Pisa's other main shopping street—this one higher end. On the right, the Church of St. Michael, with its fine Pisan Romanesque facade, was likely built upon a Roman temple.

From here, look farther up the street and notice how it undulates like a flowing river. In the sixth century B.C., Pisa was born when two parallel rivers were connected by canals. This street echoes the flow of one of those canals. An 11th-century landslide rerouted the second river, destroying ancient Pisa, and the entire city had to regenerate.

• *Just past the church, pause to appreciate the Renaissance arcades (loggias) in every direction. Then detour left onto Via delle Colonne, and walk one block down to...*

Piazza delle Vettovaglie

Pisa's historic market square, Piazza delle Vettovaglie, is lively by day and sketchy by night. Its Renaissance loggia has hosted the fish-and-vegetable market for generations (closed Sun). Stalls are set up in this piazza in the morning and stay open later in the neighboring piazza to the west (Piazza Sant'Uomobuono). You could cobble together a picnic from the sandwich shops and fruit-and-veggie stalls ringing these squares, or enjoy lunch at the recommended

La Vineria di Piazza trattoria (under the arcades of Piazza delle Vettovaglie).

• *Return to Borgo Stretto and continue north another 100 yards, passing an ugly bomb site on the right, with its horrible 1960s reconstruction (Largo Ciro Menotti). You'll pass Pasticceria Salza—while no place for fine food or snappy service, it has been an elegant place for a coffee and a central perch from which to observe the scene since 1898.*

Take the second left on nondescript Via Ulisse Dini (immediately at the arcade's end, just before the pharmacy). This leads to Pisa's historic core, the square called...

Piazza dei Cavalieri (Knights' Square)

With its old clock and colorfully decorated palace, this piazza was once the seat of the independent Republic of Pisa's government.

Around 1500, Florence conquered Pisa and made this square the training place for the knights of its navy. The statue of Cosimo I de' Medici shows the Florentine who ruled Pisa in the 16th century. With a foot on a dolphin, he reminded all who passed that the Florentine navy controlled the sea—at least a little of it. The frescoes on the exterior of the square's buildings, though damaged by salty sea air and years of neglect, reflect Pisa's fading glory under the Medici.

With Napoleon, this complex of grand buildings became part of the University of Pisa. The university is one of Europe's oldest, with roots in a law school that dates back as far as the 11th century. In the mid-16th century, the city was a hotbed of controversy, as spacey professors like Galileo Galilei studied the solar system—with results that challenged the Church's powerful doctrine. Galileo's legacy lives on, as the U of P is most highly regarded for its scientific faculties, especially engineering and medicine.

• *From here, take Via Corsica (to the left of the clock). Follow Via Corsica as it turns into Via dei Mille, then turn right on Via Santa Maria, which leads north, becoming a touristy can-can of eateries, and finally ends at the Field of Miracles and the Tower.*

Sights in Pisa

THE BEST OF THE FIELD OF MIRACLES

Imagine arriving in Pisa as a sailor in the 12th century, when the Arno River came to just outside the walls surrounding this square, the church here was one of the biggest in the world, and this en-

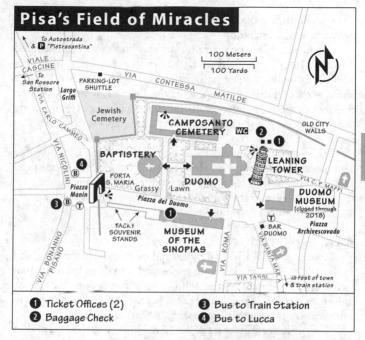

Pisa's Field of Miracles

To Autostrada & **P** "Pietrasantina"

VIALE CASCINE

To San Rossore Station

Largo Griffi

100 Meters
100 Yards

PARKING-LOT SHUTTLE

VIA CONTESSA MATILDE

Jewish Cemetery

CAMPOSANTO CEMETERY WC ② ①

OLD CITY WALLS

BAPTISTERY

④ ⓑ

PORTA S. MARIA

Piazza Manin

Grassy Lawn

DUOMO

Piazza del Duomo

LEANING TOWER

VIA C. P. MAFFI

③ ⓑ ⓣ

TACKY SOUVENIR STANDS

①

MUSEUM OF THE SINOPIAS

VIA ROMA

VIA SANTA MARIA

DUOMO MUSEUM (closed through 2018)

Piazza Archivescovado

BAR DUOMO

ⓣ

VIA CARLO CAMMEO

VIA NICOLINI

VIA BONANNO PISANO

VIA TARSI

To rest of town & train station

● Ticket Offices (2) ❸ Bus to Train Station
❷ Baggage Check ❹ Bus to Lucca

PISA & LUCCA

semble in gleaming white marble was the most impressive space in Christendom. Calling it the Field of Miracles (Campo dei Miracoli) would not have been hyperbole.

Scattered across a golf-course-green lawn are five grand buildings: the cathedral (or Duomo), its bell tower (the Leaning Tower), the Baptis-

tery, the hospital (today's Museum of the Sinopias), and the Camposanto Cemetery. The buildings are constructed from similar materials—bright white marble—and have comparable decoration. Each has a simple ground floor and rows of delicate columns and arches that form open-air arcades, giving the Campo a pleasant visual unity.

The style is called Pisan Romanesque. Unlike traditional Romanesque, with its heavy fortress-like feel—thick walls, barrel arches, few windows—Pisan Romanesque is light and elegant. At ground level, most of the structures have simple half-columns and arches. On the upper levels, you'll see a little of everything—tight rows of thin columns; pointed Gothic gables and prickly spires; Byzantine mosaics and horseshoe arches; and geometric designs (such as diamonds) and striped, colored marbles inspired by mosques in Muslim lands.

Architecturally, the Campo is unique and exotic, so I've rated it ▲▲▲. Lining this field of artistic pearls are dozens of people who have simultaneously had the same bright idea: posing for a photo as though they're propping up the Leaning Tower. Although the smooth green carpet looks like the ideal picnic spot—and many people are doing just that—officially, lounging on this lawn can result in a €25 fine.

If your time is limited, focus on the best of the Campo—the Tower and the Duomo. For a longer visit, also see "The Rest of the Field of Miracles," later in this chapter, for details on the Baptistery, the Museum of the Sinopias, the Camposanto Cemetery, and the Duomo Museum (if open).

▲▲▲Leaning Tower

You've seen it in TV ads, in movies, and on posters, key chains, and souvenir dishes—now it's time to see the actual tower. A 15-foot lean from the vertical makes the Leaning Tower one of Europe's most recognizable images. You can see it for free—it's always viewable—or you can pay to climb nearly 300 stairs to the top.

The off-kilter Tower parallels Pisa's history. It was started in the late 12th century, when Pisa was at its peak: one of the world's richest, most powerful, and most sophisticated cities. Pisans had built their huge cathedral to reflect their city's superpower status, and the cathedral's bell tower—the Leaning Tower—was the perfect complement. But as Pisa's power declined, the Tower reclined, and ever since, both have required a great deal of effort to prop up. However, after a 10-year renovation, the Tower's been stabilized. You can admire it in all its cockeyed glory and even climb up for a commanding view.

Cost and Hours: €18, kids under age 8 not allowed, daily April-Sept 8:00-20:00 (until 22:00 mid-June-Aug), Oct 9:00-19:00, Nov-Feb 10:00-17:00, March 9:00-18:00, ticket office opens 30 minutes early, reservations necessary if you value your time, www.opapisa.it.

Reservations: Entry to the tower is by a timed ticket good for a 30-minute visit. Every 15 minutes, 45 people can clamber up the 294 tilting steps to the top. Children ages 8-12 must be accompanied by—and hold hands at all times with—an adult. Teenagers (under 19) must also be accompanied by an adult.

Reserve your timed entry online or in person at either ticket office. **Online bookings** are accepted no earlier than 20 days and no later than one day in advance. Choose your entry time and buy your ticket at www.opapisa.it. Print out the voucher and bring it to the Tower 15 minutes before your entry time.

Field of Miracles Tickets

Pisa's combo-ticket scheme is designed to get you into its neglected secondary sights: the Baptistery, Camposanto Cemetery, Duomo Museum (closed for renovation), and Museum of the Sinopias (fresco patterns). For €5, you get your choice of one of these sights; for two sights, the cost is €7; for the works, you pay €8 (credit cards accepted). It's free to enter the Duomo, but you either need a voucher with an appointed time, or you can get in anytime with any combo-ticket. With any ticket, you'll pay an additional €18 to climb the Tower.

You can get the Duomo voucher (good for up to 2 people) and any of these tickets from either ticket office on the Field of Miracles: One is behind the Leaning Tower and the other is at the Museum of the Sinopias (near the Baptistery). It's also possible to buy tickets in advance online at www.opapisa.it (no sooner than 20 days but at least one day ahead of your visit; free Duomo voucher not available online).

So, which ticket to buy? This depends on your time and level of interest. The shortest visit doesn't cost a dime: Ogle the Tower and other buildings, and enter the Duomo (with the best interior). With more time, the interiors of the Baptistery and Camposanto Cemetery are well worth paying for and easy to appreciate. The two museums—Duomo Museum and Museum of the Sinopias—are "extra credit" for those fascinated by the artistic details of the other sights; for most travelers, they're skippable.

And what about entering the Tower? Is it worth that hefty price tag—and a likely wait to enter? It's a minor thrill to clomp up those twisty stairs, and the view from the top is enjoyable. But Pisa isn't particularly scenic, and it's a lot of expense and hassle for a view. Unless climbing the Tower is what you came to do, I consider ascending it optional. The real thrill comes from seeing it from the outside.

As you consider your itinerary, remember that until the "cult of the Leaning Tower" was born around 1900, people came to Pisa not to see the tower but to visit the historic Camposanto Cemetery.

To reserve in person, go to the **ticket office,** behind the Tower on the left (in the yellow building), or to the Museum of the Sinopias ticket office. In summer, for same-day entry, you'll likely need to wait two or three hours before going up (see the rest of the monuments and grab lunch while waiting). It's busiest between 12:00 and 15:00; the wait is usually much shorter at the beginning or end of the day.

Planning Your Time: Even though this is technically a guided visit, the "guide" is a museum guard who makes sure you don't stay past your scheduled time. For your 30-minute time slot, figure about a 5-minute presentation at the start, 10 minutes to climb, and 10 to descend. This leaves about five minutes for vertigo at the top.

Baggage Check: You can't take any bags up the Tower, but day-bag-size lockers are available at the ticket office—show your Tower ticket to check your bag. You may check your bag 10 minutes before your reservation time and must pick it up immediately after your Tower visit.

Caution: The railings are skinny, the steps are slanted, and rain makes the marble slippery—all in all, it's more dizzying than you might expect. Anyone with balance issues of any sort should think twice before ascending.

Visiting the Tower

If you're going inside, you may have to wait around for a few minutes at the base of the Tower—the perfect opportunity to read this. If you're not ascending, almost all of this tour is just as interesting from down below.

Yep, There It Is: Rising up alongside the cathedral, the Tower is nearly 200 feet tall and 55 feet wide, weighing 14,000 tons and currently leaning at a five-degree angle (15 feet off the vertical axis). It started to lean almost immediately after construction began (it would take two centuries to finish the structure). Count the eight stories—a simple base, six stories of columns (forming arcades), and a belfry on top. The inner structural core is a hollow cylinder built of limestone bricks, faced with white  marble brought here by barge from San Giuliano, northeast of the city. The thin columns of the open-air arcades make the heavy Tower seem light and graceful.

The Building of the Tower: The Tower was built over two centuries by at least three different architects. You can see how each successive architect tried to correct the leaning problem—once halfway up (after the fourth story), once at the belfry on the top.

The first stones were laid in 1173, probably under the direction of the architect Bonanno Pisano (who also designed the Duomo's bronze back door). Five years later, just as the base and the first arcade were finished, someone said, "Is it just me, or does that look crooked?" The heavy Tower—resting on a very shallow 13-foot foundation—was sinking on the south side into the marshy, multilayered, unstable soil. (Actually, all of the Campo's buildings tilt somewhat.) The builders carried on anyway, until they'd finished four stories (the base, plus three arcade floors). Then, construction suddenly halted—no one knows why—and for a century the Tower sat half-finished and visibly leaning.

Around 1272, the next architect continued, trying to correct the problem by angling the next three stories backward, in the opposite direction of the lean. The project then again sat mysteriously idle for nearly another century. Finally, Tommaso Pisano put the belfry on the top (c. 1350-1372), also kinking it to overcome the leaning.

Man Versus Gravity: After the Tower's completion, several attempts were made to stop its slow-motion fall. The architect/artist/writer Giorgio Vasari reinforced the base in 1550, and it actually worked. But in 1838, well-intentioned engineers pumped out groundwater, destabilizing the Tower and causing it to increase its lean at a rate of a millimeter per year.

It got so bad that in 1990 the Tower was closed for repairs, and $30 million was spent trying to stabilize it. Engineers dried the soil with pipes containing liquid nitrogen, anchored the Tower to the ground with steel cables, and buried 600 tons of lead on the north side as a counterweight (not visible)—all with little success. The breakthrough came when they drilled 15-foot-long holes in the ground on the north side and sucked out 60 tons of soil, allowing the Tower to sink on the north side and straighten out its lean by about six inches.

As well as gravity, erosion threatens the Tower. Since its construction, 135 of the Tower's 180 marble columns have had to be replaced. Stone decay, deposits of lime and calcium phosphate, accumulations of dirt and moss, cracking from the stress of the lean—all of these are factors in its decline.

Thanks to the Tower's lean, there are special trouble spots. The lower south side (which is protected from cleansing rain and wind) is a magnet for dirty airborne particles, while the stone on the upper areas has more decay (from eroding rain and wind).

The Tower, now stabilized, has been cleaned as well. Cracks have been filled, and accumulations removed with carefully formulated atomized water sprays and poultices of various solvents.

All the work to shore up, straighten, and clean the Tower has probably turned the clock back a few centuries. In fact, art historians figure the Tower leans today as much as it did when Galileo reputedly conducted his gravity experiment here 400 years ago.

• *Wait's over? Great. It's time to head inside.*

Climbing the Tower: First, an attendant takes you into the room at the bottom of the tower (known as the *Sala del Pesce* for the Christian fish symbol on the wall) and offers a short explanation of the Tower's construction and history. Gape up through the hollow Tower to the oculus at the top, and marvel at the acoustics. Also check out the heavy metal braces stretching up to the top.

Then you'll wind your way up the outside along a spiraling ramp, climbing 294 stairs. At the top, you'll have fine views over the Duomo and the rest of the Field of Miracles, as well as over the rooftops of Pisa (admittedly, not the most striking city).

▲▲Duomo (Cathedral)

The huge Pisan Romanesque cathedral, with its carved pulpit by Giovanni Pisano, is artistically more important than its more fa-

mous bell tower. Budget some sightseeing time for the church's artistic and historic treasures.

Cost and Hours: Free, pick up a voucher with an entry time—for a maximum of two people—at either ticket office (voucher not available in advance online) or show your combo-ticket (see sidebar on page 547); daily April-Sept 10:00-20:00, Oct 10:00-19:00, Nov-Feb 10:00-13:00 & 14:00-17:00, March 10:00-18:00.

Crowd-Beating Tips: Because the Duomo is the only free interior at the Field of Miracles, it's on every tour itinerary and can be busy. The sights are most crowded between 12:00 and 15:00; ideally, try to see the Duomo before or after that window.

Dress Code: Shorts are OK as long as they're not too short, and shoulders should be covered (although it's not really enforced).

⊙ Self-Guided Tour

The Duomo is the centerpiece of the Field of Miracles' complex of religious buildings. Begun in 1063, it was financed by a galley-load of booty ransacked that year from the Muslim-held capital of Palermo, Sicily. The architect Buschetto created the frilly Pisan Romanesque style that set the tone for the Baptistery and Tower.

In the 1150s, the architect Rainaldo added the impressive main-entrance facade.

The lower half of the church is simple Romanesque, with blind arches. The upper half has four rows of columns that form arcades. Stripes of black-and-white marble, mosaics, stone inlay, and even recycled Roman tombstones complete the decoration.

• *Enter the church at the facade, opposite the Baptistery.*

The 320-foot nave was the longest in Christendom when it was built. It's modeled on a traditional Roman basilica, with 68

Corinthian columns of granite (most shipped from Elba and Corsica in 1063) dividing the space into five aisles. But the striped marble and arches-on-columns give the nave an exotic, almost mosque-like feel.

Hanging from the ceiling of the central nave is **Galileo's lamp.** The bronze incense burner is said to be the one (actually, this is a replacement of the original) that caught the teenage Galileo's attention one day in church. According to legend, someone left a church door open, and a gust of wind set the lamp swinging. Galileo timed the swings and realized that the burner swung back and forth in the same amount of time regardless of how wide the arc. (This pendulum motion was a constant that allowed Galileo to measure our ever-changing universe.)

Galileo Galilei (1564-1642) was born in Pisa, grew up here on Via Giuseppe Giusti, and taught math at the university (1584-1591). Legend says he dropped things off the Tower to time their falls, fascinated by gravity.

• *The upper and front part of the church will be covered by scaffolding through at least 2018. But you can still pick out most of the following details.*

High up in the apse (behind the altar) is the **Apse Mosaic** (c. 1300, partly done by the great artist Cimabue). It shows Christ as the Ruler of All (Pantocrator) between Mary and St. John the Evangelist. The Pantocrator image of Christ is standard fare among Eastern Orthodox Christians—that is, the "Byzantine" people who were Pisa's partners in trade.

Look up into the dome—you'll see the Assumption of Mary. As the heavens open, and rings of saints and angels spiral upward, a hazy God greets Mary (in red). Beneath the dome is an inlaid-marble, Cosmati-style mosaic floor. The modern (and therefore controversial) marble altar and pulpit were carved by a Florentine artist in 2002.

Next to Galileo's lamp, you'll find a 15-foot-tall, octagonal

pulpit by Giovanni Pisano (c. 1240-1319), who left no stone uncarved in his pursuit of beauty. Four hundred intricately sculpted figures smother the pulpit, blurring the architectural outlines. In addition, the relief panels are actually curved, making it look less like an octagon than a circle. The creamy-white Carrara marble has the look and feel of carved French ivories, which the Pisanos loved. At the base, lions roar and crouch over their prey, symbolizing how Christ (the lion) triumphs over Satan (the horse, as in the Four Horsemen of the Apocalypse). Four of the pulpit's support "columns" are statues. The central "column" features three graceful ladies representing Faith, Hope, and Charity, the three pillars of Christianity. Around the top of the pulpit, Christ's life unfolds in a series of panels saturated with carvings.

• *Find the following two sights in the right (south) transept.*

In an ornate, colonnaded, Baroque side-chapel at the end of the transept, you'll see **St. Ranieri's body.** In a glass-lined casket on the altar, Pisa's patron saint lies mummified, encased in silver at his head, with his hair shirt covering his body. The silver, mask-like face dates from the year 2000 and is as realistic as possible—derived from an FBI-style computer scan of Ranieri's skull. Ranieri Scucceri (1117-1161) was the son of a rich sea-trader, who gave up his riches to join, preach, and perform miracles.

Look on the wall to the left to find the **tomb of Holy Roman Emperor Henry VII,** whose untimely death plunged Pisa into its centuries-long decline. Henry lies sleeping, arms folded, his head turned to the side, resting on a soft pillow. This German king (c. 1275-1313) invaded Italy and was welcomed by Pisans as a non-partisan leader who could bring peace to Italy's warring Guelphs and Ghibellines. In 1312, he was crowned emperor by the pope in Rome. He was preparing to polish off the last opposition when he caught a fever and died. No longer enjoying its connection with the Holy Roman Empire, Pisa declined.

• *Exit the church, turn left, and walk around to its back end (facing the Tower).*

Under a canopy you'll find the **bronze doors of St. Ranieri** (Porta San Ranieri). Designed by Bonanno Pisano (c. 1186)—who is thought by some historians to have been the Tower's first architect—the doors have 24 different panels that show Christ's story using the same simple, skinny figures found in Byzantine icons. (The doors are actually copies; the originals are housed—but not always on display—in the Duomo Museum.) Cast using the lost-wax technique, these doors were an inspiration for Lorenzo Ghiberti's bronze doors in Florence.

THE REST OF THE FIELD OF MIRACLES

The Leaning Tower nearly steals the show from the massive cathedral, which muscles out the other sights. But don't neglect the rest of the Field of Miracles: the Baptistery, Camposanto Cemetery, Museum of the Sinopias, and Duomo Museum.

To do all of these sights takes about two hours. Start with the Baptistery, located in front of the Duomo's facade, and then head for Camposanto Cemetery, behind the church on the north side of the Field of Miracles. Next visit the Museum of the Sinopias, across the street from the Baptistery entrance. If it has reopened, end your day at the Duomo Museum, housed behind the Tower.

Cost and Hours: €5 for one sight, €7 for two sights, €8 includes all the sights (see sidebar on page 547 for the rundown on various combo-tickets). All four sights share the same schedule: daily April-Sept 8:00-20:00, Oct 9:00-19:00, Nov-Feb 10:00-17:00, March 9:00-18:00. Note that the Duomo Museum will likely be closed for renovation through 2018.

Baptistery

Pisa's Baptistery is Italy's biggest. It's interesting for its pulpit and interior ambience, and especially great for its acoustics (which are demonstrated twice an hour).

Visiting the Baptistery: The building is 180 feet tall—John the Baptist on top is almost eye-to-eye with the tourists looking out from the nearly 200-foot Leaning Tower. Notice that the Baptistery leans nearly six feet to the north (the Tower leans 15 feet to the south). The building (begun in 1153) is modeled on the circular-domed Church of the Holy Sepulchre in Jerusalem, seen by Pisan Crusaders who occupied Jerusalem in 1099.

Inside, it's simple, spacious, and baptized with light. Tall arches atop thin columns once again echo the Campo's architectural theme of arches above blank spaces. The columns encircle just a few pieces of religious furniture. In the center sits the beautiful marble

octagonal font (1246). A statue of the first Baptist, John the Baptist, stretches out his hand and says, "Welcome to my Baptistery." The font contains plenty of space for baptizing adults by immersion (the medieval custom), plus four wells for dunking babies.

On your left is the **pulpit** created by Niocola Pisano. Is this the world's first Renaissance sculpture? It's the first authenticated

(signed) work by the "Giotto of sculpture," working in what came to be called the Renaissance style. The freestanding sculpture has classical columns, realistic people and animals, and 3-D effects in the carved panels. The speaker's platform stands on columns that rest on the backs of animals, representing Christianity's triumph over paganism. The relief panels, with scenes from the life of Christ, are more readable than the Duomo pulpit. They show bigger, simpler figures in dark marble "frames." Read left to right, starting from the back: Nativity, Adoration of the Magi, Presentation in the Temple, Crucifixion, Last Judgment.

Camposanto Cemetery

Until people started getting excited about the Leaning Tower just a century ago, the big attraction in Pisa was its dreamy and exquisite cemetery, the Camposanto (built from 1278-1465). Lined with faint frescoes, this centuries-old cemetery on the north side of the Campo is famous for its "Holy Land" dirt, reputedly brought here from the Middle East in the 12th century. Highlights are the building's cloistered interior courtyard, some ancient sarcophagi, and the large 14th-century fresco, *The Triumph of Death.*

The delightful open-air courtyard is surrounded by an arcade with intricately carved tracery in the arches. The courtyard's grass grows on special dirt (said to turn a body into bones in a single day) shipped here by returning Crusaders from Jerusalem's Mount Calvary, where Christ was crucified. The arcade floor is paved with the coats of arms of some 600 dearly departed Pisans.

Displayed in the arcade are dozens of ancient Roman sarcophagi. These coffins, which originally held dead Romans, were reused by medieval big shots. In anticipation of death, a wealthy Pisan would shop around, choose a good sarcophagus, and chip his message into it. When he died, his marble box was placed with the others around the exterior of the cathedral. Great sculptors such as Nicola and Giovanni Pisano passed them daily, gaining inspiration.

After decorating these corridors for 600 years, the frescoes of Camposanto Cemetery were badly damaged in World War II; they've been under restoration ever since. Along these walls, you'll see the ones that have been returned to their original position.

The Triumph of Death is a 1,000-square-foot fresco (c. 1340, by a 14th-century master). It captures late-medieval Europe's concern with death—predating but still accurately depicting Pisa's mood in the wake of the bubonic plague (1348), which killed one in three Pisans. Well-dressed ladies and gents (left half of the painting) are riding gaily through the countryside when they come across three coffins with corpses (bottom left). Confronted with death, they each react differently—a woman puts her hand thoughtfully to her chin, a man holds his nose against the stench, and a horse leans in for a better whiff. Above them, a monk scours the Bible for the meaning of death.

In the right half of the painting, young people gather in a garden (bottom right) to play music (symbolizing earthly pleasure), oblivious to the death around them. Winged demons swoop down from above to pluck souls (shown as babies) from a pile of corpses, while winged angels fight them for the souls.

Museum of the Sinopias (Museo delle Sinopie)

Housed in a 13th-century hospital, this museum features the original preliminary sketches (sinopias) for the Camposanto's World War II-damaged frescoes. If you loved *The Triumph of Death* and others in the Camposanto, or if you're interested in fresco technique, this museum is worthwhile. If not, you'll wonder why you're here.

Visiting the Museum: Whether or not you pay to go in, you can watch two free videos in the entry lobby that serve to orient you to the square: a seven-minute, 3-D computer tour of the complex and a 15-minute story of the Tower, its tilt, and its fix. Good students might want to come here first for this orientation.

Once inside the turnstile, the star of this museum are the sinopias: sketches made in red paint directly on the wall, designed to guide the making of the final colored fresco. The master always did the sinopia himself. It was a way for him (and for those who paid for the work) to see exactly how the scene would look in its designated spot. If it wasn't quite right, the master changed a detail here and there. Next, assistants made a "cartoon" by tracing the sinopia onto large sheets of paper *(cartone)*. Then the sinopia was plastered over. To put the drawing back on the wall, assistants perforated the drawing on the cartoon, hung the cartoon over the wall, and dabbed it with a powdered bag of charcoal. This process printed dotted lines onto the newly plastered wall, re-creating the cartoon. While the plaster was still wet, the master and his team quickly filled in the color and details, producing the final frescoes (now on display at the Camposanto). These sinopias—never meant to be seen—were uncovered by the bombing and restoration of the Camposanto and brought here.

Duomo Museum (Museo dell'Opera del Duomo)

Near the Tower is the entrance to the Duomo Museum, which houses many of the original statues and much of the artwork that once adorned the Campo's buildings (where copies stand today), notably the statues by Nicola and Giovanni Pisano. It's big on Pisan art, displaying treasures of the cathedral, paintings, silverware, and sculptures (from the 12th to 14th century), as well as ancient Egyptian, Etruscan, and Roman artifacts. The museum will likely be closed for restoration through sometime in 2018.

Sleeping in Pisa

Pisa is an easy side-trip from Florence or Lucca, either of which is a more all-around pleasant place to stay. But there's more to Pisa than the Tower, and if you want time to experience it, consider a night here. To locate these hotels, see the map on page 538.

NORTH OF THE RIVER, NEAR THE TOWER

$$ Hotel Royal Victoria, a classy place along the Arno River, has been run by the Piegaja family since 1837 (though it was a hotel for more than 400 years before that). With tiled hallways and 38 creaky, historical rooms filled with antiques, it's ideal for romantics who missed out on the Grand Tour. The location—midway between the Tower and Pisa Centrale station—is the most atmospheric of my listings (RS%, family rooms, air-con in most rooms, elevator, pay parking garage, bike rental, lush communal terrace, Lungarno Pacinotti 12, tel. 050-940-111, www.royalvictoria.it, post@royalvictoria.it).

$$ Hotel Pisa Tower provides a yesteryear elegance in a stately mansion with 14 rooms thoughtfully decorated with clean lines and graceful warmth. In good weather, enjoy the garden for breakfast or an *aperitivo*. The annex, with 12 similar rooms, overlooks the tacky-souvenir-stand square just outside the gate to the Field of Miracles, along a busy street. Three more rooms are in a nondescript apartment block across the street from the main building (family rooms, air-con, pay parking; a block west of Piazza Manin at Via Andrea Pisano 3, tel. 050-520-0700, www.hotelpisatower. com, info@hotelpisatower.com).

$$ Hotel Villa Kinzica, a last resort, has 30 tired, worn rooms with high ceilings—and a prime location just steps from the Field of Miracles; ask for a room with a view of the Tower,

> # Sleep Code
>
> Hotels are classified based on the average price of a standard double room with breakfast in high season.
>
> | | |
> |---|---|
> | $$$$ | **Splurge:** Most rooms over €170 |
> | $$$ | **Pricier:** €130-170 |
> | $$ | **Moderate:** €90-130 |
> | $ | **Budget:** €50-90 |
> | ¢ | **Backpacker:** Under €50 |
> | **RS%** | Rick Steves discount |
>
> Unless otherwise noted, credit cards are accepted, hotel staff speak basic English, and free Wi-Fi is available. Comparison-shop by checking prices at several hotels (on each hotel's own website, on a booking site, or by email). For the best deal, *book directly with the hotel*. Ask for a discount if paying in cash; if the listing includes **RS%**, request a Rick Steves discount.

ideally #75 (family rooms, air-con, elevator, Piazza Arcivesco-vado 2, tel. 050-560-419, www.hotelvillakinzica.com, info@hotelvillakinzica.com).

$ Casa San Tommaso has 22 classic-feeling, homey, reverent rooms on a quiet back lane about a five-minute walk from the Tower (air-con, Via San Tommaso 13, tel. 050-830-782, www.casasantommaso.it, santommaso@paimturismo.it).

$ Pensione Helvetia, a no-frills, clean, and quiet inn just 100 yards from the Tower, rents 29 economical rooms over four floors. Ask them to show you the "biggest cactus in Tuscany" in their garden courtyard...it really is (cheaper rooms with shared bath, family rooms, no breakfast, ceiling fans, no elevator, Via Don G. Boschi 31, tel. 050-553-084, www.pensionehelvetiapisa.com, helvetiapisatravel@gmail.com, Micaele and Sandra).

SOUTH OF THE RIVER, NEAR THE TRAIN STATION

This zone is far less atmospheric than the zone near the Tower—with a lot of concrete and congestion. Stay here only if you value the convenience of proximity to the station.

$$$ Hotel Alessandro della Spina, run by Pio and family, has 16 elegant and colorful rooms, each named after a flower (air-con, elevator, pay parking; leaving the station, go right on Viale F. Bonaini, take the third right on Via Alessandro della Spina, then find #5; tel. 050-502-777, www.hoteldellaspina.it, info@hoteldellaspina.it).

$ Hotel Milano has 10 cheap, no-frills rooms in a hum-drum area close to the train station (RS%, cheaper rooms with shared bath, family rooms, no breakfast, air-con, Via Mascagni

14, tel. 050-23-162, www.hotelmilano.pisa.it, hotelmilano.pisa@gmail.com).

Eating in Pisa

A QUICK LUNCH CLOSE TO THE TOWER

The **Via Santa Maria** tourist strip is pedestrianized and lined with touristy eateries. They seem competitive, and you can get a quick sandwich, pizza, or salad at any number of places along this street.

$$ Pizzeria al Bagno di Nerone, a five-minute walk from the Tower, is particularly popular with students. Belly up to the bar and grab a slice to go, or sit in their small dining room for a whole pie. Try the *cecina,* a crepe-like garbanzo-bean cake (Wed-Mon 12:00-14:30 & 17:45-22:30, closed Tue, Largo Carlo Fedeli 26, tel. 050-551-085).

REAL MEALS DEEPER IN THE TOWN CENTER

Make no mistake: Pisa is in Tuscany. And if you want to sample some famously delicious Tuscan cuisine, these restaurants make it easy. All are within about a 10- to 15-minute walk from the Tower, near the river, and several are within a few steps of the old Renaissance-style market loggia, Piazza delle Vettovaglie (described on page 543).

$$ La Vineria di Piazza is a quintessential little Tuscan trattoria tucked under the arcades of Piazza delle Vettovaglie. The chalkboard menu lists today's seasonal choices: a few *antipasti,* a few *primi* (homemade pastas and soups), and a few *secondi.* Ask for a *bis* or even a *tris* to get a tasty sampling of two or three homemade pastas. English-fluent Claudia welcomes you to share dishes family-ly-style, and she and her family make this place feel sophisticated, but without pretense. Sit in the elegantly simple interior or out at long tables facing the market. They typically serve lunch only, as the square can be a bit sketchy after dark (daily 12:30-15:00, Piazza delle Vettovaglie 14, tel. 050-382-0433).

$$ Antica Trattoria il Campano, just off the market square, has a typically Tuscan menu and a candlelit, stay-awhile atmosphere. The ground floor, surrounded by wine bottles, is cozier, while the upstairs—with high wood-beam ceilings—is classier (Thu-Tue 19:30-22:45, closed Wed, may open for lunch Fri-Tue in high season, Via Cavalca 19, tel. 050-580-585, Giovanna).

$$ Il Vegusto is a reasonably priced, quality, vegan restaurant with elegant modern ambience. It sits all by its lonesome on a gloomy square a block off the river (Mon-Fri 12:30-14:30 & 19:30-22:00, Sat 19:30-22:00 only, closed Sun, Piazza dei Facchini 13, tel. 050-520-0667).

Restaurant Price Code

I've assigned each eatery a price category, based on the average cost of a typical main course (pasta or *secondi*). Drinks, desserts, and splurge items (steak and seafood) can raise the price considerably.

$$$$ **Splurge:** Most main courses over €20
$$$ **Pricier:** €15-20
$$ **Moderate:** €10-15
$ **Budget:** Under €10

In Italy, pizza by the slice and other takeout food is **$**; a basic trattoria or sit-down pizzeria is **$$**; a casual but more upscale restaurant is **$$$**; and a swanky splurge is **$$$$**.

MOSTLY-LOCALS OPTIONS IN THE TOWN CENTER

Piazza Dante is a characteristic square popular with university students and fun-loving locals, and graced with several good and economical eateries. I'd survey the five or six options on or near the square before sitting down.

$ Caffetteria BetsaBea is handy for takeaway meals, has good seating on the square, whips up hearty and creative salads—which you design with their interactive menu, and is popular for its *aperitivo* happy hour (Mon-Sat 8:00-24:00, closed Sun, Piazza San Frediano 6).

Just a few steps down Via l'Arancio is **$ Pizzeria l'Arancio,** where Beppe and Papa Filippo have been serving pizza, *antipasti,* focaccia, and the delightful chickpea flatbread known as *cecina* for decades (daily 12:00-15:30 & 19:00-22:00, Via l'Arancio 1, tel. 050-500-729).

$ Il Montino is a favorite for tasty, no-frills pizza. Tucked behind a church in a grubby corner deep in the old center, it has a loyal following—particularly among students. Enjoy full pies in the *nuovo rustico* interior or out on the alley, or get a slice to go (Mon-Sat 11:30-15:00 & 17:30-22:30, closed Sun, Vicolo del Monte 1, tel. 050-598-695).

$$ Orzo Bruno—*il birrifico artigiano* ("the artisan brewpub")—is a lively, rollicking brew hall filled with Pisans of all ages enjoying rock, jazz, and blues, with seven different microbrews (including a rotating tap) and a simple menu of sandwiches and salads (nightly 19:00-late, a block off Borgo Stretto at Via Case Dipinte 6, tel. 050-578-802).

Pisa Connections

Pisa has good connections by train, bus, or car. The busy airport (popular with discount airlines) is practically downtown. Note that the Pisa Centrale station area is a maze of tunnels; leave yourself enough time to find the ticket machines and make it to the platform.

Side-Tripping to Lucca: Pisa and Lucca are well-connected by train and by bus (both options are about €3), making a half-day side-trip from one town to the other particularly easy. The **train** takes about half as long as the bus (about 25 minutes compared with 50 minutes)—but getting to the Centrale train station is more time-consuming. Perhaps the best option: If you're heading to Lucca from the Leaning Tower, you can catch the train at Pisa San Rossore station, about a five-minute walk from the Field of Miracles: From the tacky souvenir zone just outside the gate, cross the busy street and continue straight ahead along Via Andrea Pisano. After two blocks, you'll see the gray gateway to the train station on your right.

A handy **bus** connects the Field of Miracles with Lucca's Piazzale Giuseppe Verdi in about 50 minutes (€3, Mon-Sat hourly, fewer on Sun, buy ticket on bus; in Pisa, wait at the Vaibus signpost, immediately outside the wall behind the Baptistery on the right). You can also catch this bus at Pisa's airport, Pisa Centrale train station, or around the corner from Pisa's TI.

From Pisa Centrale Station by Train to: Florence (2-3/hour, 45-75 minutes), **Livorno** (2-3/hour, 20 minutes), **Rome** (2/hour, many change in Florence, 3-4 hours), **La Spezia** (about hourly, 1 hour), Monterosso (hourly, 1-1.5 hours), **Siena** (2/hour, 2 hours, change at Empoli), **Lucca** (1-2/hour, 30 minutes, also stops at Pisa San Rossore station).

By Car: The drive between Pisa and Florence is that rare case where the regular highway (free, more direct, and at least as fast) is a better deal than the autostrada.

By Plane: Pisa's handy **Galileo Galilei Airport**—just two miles from the train station ("So close you can walk," locals brag)—handles both international and domestic flights (airport code: PSA, tel. 050-849-300, www.pisa-airport.com). The new "Pisa Mover" train, offering an easy connection to Pisa Centrale station (every 10 minutes, 8-minute trip), is planned to start running in late 2016. Until then, a shuttle bus runs the same route. The airport is also on the line for public bus LAM Rossa, which stops first at the station and then continues to the Leaning Tower (usually every 10 minutes, less frequent off-season, €1.20 ticket at kiosk, €2 on board). A taxi into town costs €10.

Pisa's airport is handy for other towns as well: The bus to

Lucca (described earlier) originates at the airport. To reach **Florence**—or other destinations in Italy—take the shuttle bus or Pisa Mover to Pisa Centrale station and connect from there (allow about 1.5 hours total). Two companies also run buses from the airport directly to Florence's Santa Maria Novella train station in about 1.5 hours (about €5 for either one): Terravision (about hourly, www. terravision.eu) and Autostradale (typically coordinated with Ryanair flights, www.autostradale.it).

Lucca

Surrounded by well-preserved ramparts, layered with history, alternately quaint and urbane, Lucca charms its visitors. The city is a paradox. Though it hasn't been involved in a war since 1430, it is Italy's most impressive fortress city, encircled by a perfectly intact wall. Most cities tear down their walls to make way for modern traffic, but Lucca's effectively keeps out both traffic and, it seems, the stress of the modern world. Locals are very protective of their wall, which they enjoy like a community roof garden.

Lucca has no single monumental sight to attract tourists—it's simply a uniquely human and undamaged, never-bombed city.

Romanesque churches seem to be around every corner, as do fun-loving and shady piazzas filled with soccer-playing children. Even its touristic center—the mostly traffic-free old town—feels more local than touristy (aside from a few cruise excursions from nearby Livorno that pass through each day). The city is big enough to have its own heritage and pride, yet small enough that it seems like the Lucchesi (loo-KAY-zee) all went to school together. Simply put, Lucca has elegance and plenty of reason to be so proud.

PLANNING YOUR TIME

Lucca is easy to enjoy. With a day in town, start with my self-guided Lucca Walk and spend the afternoon biking (or strolling) atop the wall, popping in on whatever other sights interest you, and browsing. Music lovers enjoy the Puccini concert in the evening. The busy sightseer can consider visiting Pisa's Field of Miracles (with the Leaning Tower), an easy half-day side-trip away by train (to Pisa San Rossore station in less than 30 minutes) or bus (from downtown Lucca to the Leaning Tower in 50 minutes).

Orientation to Lucca

Lucca (population 87,000, with roughly 10,000 living within the town walls) is big enough to be engaging but small enough to be manageable. Everything of interest to a visitor is within the 2.5-mile-long city wall; it takes just 20 minutes to walk from one end of the old town to the other. The train station sits south of the wall (just beyond the cathedral), and the bus to and from Pisa stops just inside the western tip. My self-guided walk traces the main thoroughfares through town; venturing beyond these streets, you realize Lucca is bigger than it first seems, but its back streets are very sleepy. While the core of the town is based on an old Roman grid street plan, the surrounding areas—especially near the circular footprint of the amphitheater—are more confusing. This, combined with tall houses and a lack of consistent signage, makes Lucca easy to get lost in. Pick up the town map at your hotel and use it.

TOURIST INFORMATION

Lucca's helpful TI is on Piazzale Giuseppe Verdi (daily 9:00-19:00, Oct-March until 17:00, futuristic WC, baggage storage—€1.50/ hour for 2 bags, tel. 0583-583-150, www.luccaitinera.it).

ARRIVAL IN LUCCA

By Train: See "Helpful Hints" for specifics on checking your bags. To reach the city center from the train station, walk toward the walls and head left, to the entry at Porta San Pietro. Or, if you don't mind steps, go straight ahead and follow the path through the moat-like park to go up and over the wall. Taxis may be waiting out front; otherwise, try calling 025-353 (ignore any recorded message—just wait for a live operator); a ride from the station to Piazza dell'Anfiteatro costs about €10.

By Bus: Buses from Pisa, Viareggio, and nearby villages arrive inside the walls at Piazzale Giuseppe Verdi (near the TI).

By Car: Don't try to drive within the walls. Much of the center of Lucca is designated a "ZTL" (limited traffic zone), which could cost you a €90 fine. The old town is ringed by convenient parking lots.

Parking is always free in Piazzale Don Franco, a five-minute walk north of the city walls. If you must park inside the city walls, try just inside Porta Santa Maria, at the northern edge of town (€1.50/hour). Or park outside the gates near the train station or on the boulevard surrounding the city (meter rates vary; about €1/ hour). Overnight parking (20:00-8:00) on city streets and in city lots is usually free. Check with your hotelier to be sure.

HELPFUL HINTS

Shops and Museums Alert: Shops close most of Sunday and Monday mornings. City-run museums are closed Sunday and Monday.

Markets: Lucca's atmospheric markets are worth visiting. On the weekend of the third Sunday of the month, one of the largest **antique markets** in Italy sprawls in the blocks between Piazza Antelminelli and Piazza San Giovanni (8:00-19:00). The last weekend of the month, local artisans sell **arts and crafts** around town, mainly near the cathedral (also 8:00-19:00). At the **general market,** held Wednesdays and Saturdays, you'll find produce and household goods (8:30-13:00, from Porta Elisa to Porta San Jacopo on Via dei Bacchettoni).

Concerts: San Giovanni Church hosts one-hour concerts featuring a pianist and singers performing highlights from hometown composer Giacomo Puccini (€20 at the door, €18 in advance—buy tickets at the venue, the TI, or possibly your hotel; daily April-Oct at 19:00, www.puccinielasualucca.com).

Festivals: On September 13 and 14, the city celebrates Volto Santo ("Holy Face"), with a procession of the treasured local crucifix and a fair in Piazza Antelminelli. Music lovers enjoy the annual Puccini Days festival—get dates at TI.

Baggage Storage: For train travelers, there are two good options for paid baggage storage: **Cicli Primo,** in the train station at track 1 (daily 8:00-20:00, shorter hours off-season, tel. 347-632-4315), and **Tourist Center Lucca,** on the left side of the square as you exit the train station (at #203; daily 9:00-19:00, Nov-March until 18:00). If you're arriving by bus, the TI on **Piazzale Giuseppe Verdi** also stores bags (see earlier).

Laundry: Lavanderia Self-Service Niagara is just off Piazza Santa Maria at Via Rosi 26 (daily 7:00-23:00) and **Easy & Speedy Lavanderia** is at Via San Giorgio 45 (daily 7:00-23:30).

Bike Rental: A one-hour rental (ID required) gives you time for two leisurely loops around the ramparts. Several places with identical prices cluster around Piazza Santa Maria (€3/hour, €15/day, most shops also rent tandem bikes and bike carts, helmets available on request, daily about 9:00-19:00 or sunset). Try these easygoing shops: **Antonio Poli** (Piazza Santa Maria 42, tel. 0583-493-787, enthusiastic Cristiana) and, right next to it, **Cicli Bizzarri** (Piazza Santa Maria 32, tel. 0583-496-682, Australian Dely). At the south end, at Porta San Pietro, you'll find **Chronò** (Corso Garibaldi 93, tel. 0583-490-591, www.chronobikes.com). At the train station, **Cicli Primo** and **Tourist Center Lucca** (both described above under "Baggage Storage") are good.

Local Magazine: For insights into American and British expat life

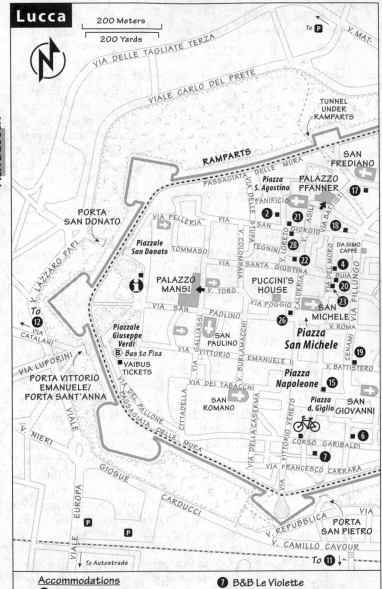

Lucca

200 Meters
200 Yards

N

PISA & LUCCA

VIA DELLE TAGLIATE TERZA

VIALE CARLO DEL PRETE

To P   V. MAT.

TUNNEL UNDER RAMPARTS

RAMPARTS

PASSAGIATA DELLE MURA

SAN FREDIANO

Piazza S. Agostino

PALAZZO PFANNER

17

PORTA SAN DONATO

VIA PELLERIA

VIA DELLA STUFA

PANIFICIO

2

21

28

V. AGILI

V. BATTISTI

18

Piazzale San Donato

TOMMASO

VIA COLOMBAIA

VIA SAN

TEGNINI

SANTA GIUSTINA

VIA LORETO

GIORGIO

DA SIMO CAFFÈ

4

V. DEL MORO

22

BUIA

20

VIA FILLUNGO

PALAZZO MANSI

V. TORO

PUCCINI'S HOUSE

VIA POGGIO

CALDERIA

SAN MICHELE

23

i

VIA SAN

PAOLINO

26

V. ROMA

Piazza San Michele

Piazzale Giuseppe Verdi

B   Bus to Pisa

VAIBUS TICKETS

SAN PAULINO

VIA GALLIASSI

VIA VITTORIO

EMANUELE II

V. BURLAMACCHI

19

V. BATTISTERO

V. CENAMI

To 12

VIA CATALANI

VIA LUPORINI

PORTA VITTORIO EMANUELE/ PORTA SANT'ANNA

VIALE

V. NIERI

PASSAGIATA DELLE MURA

VIA DEL PALLONE

CITTADELLA

VIA DEI TABACCHI

VIA DELLA CASERMA

SAN ROMANO

Piazza Napoleone

15

Piazza d. Giglio

SAN GIOVANNI

VITTORIO VENETO

CORSO GARIBALDI

6

7

VIA FRANCESCO CARRARA

GIOSUE

CARDUCCI

VIALE EUROPA

P

P

PORTA SAN PIETRO

VIA

V. REPUBBLICA

V. CAMILLO CAVOUR

To Autostrada

To 11

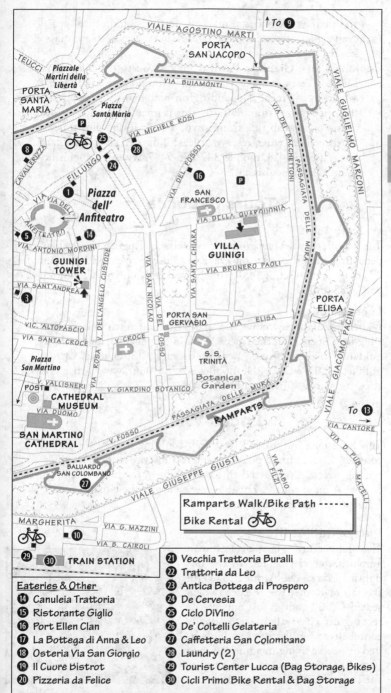

PISA & LUCCA

Ramparts Walk/Bike Path ------
Bike Rental 🚲

Eateries & Other
14 Canuleia Trattoria
15 Ristorante Giglio
16 Port Ellen Clan
17 La Bottega di Anna & Leo
18 Osteria Via San Giorgio
19 Il Cuore Bistrot
20 Pizzeria da Felice
21 Vecchia Trattoria Buralli
22 Trattoria da Leo
23 Antica Bottega di Prospero
24 De Cervesia
25 Ciclo DiVino
26 De' Coltelli Gelateria
27 Caffetteria San Colombano
28 Laundry (2)
29 Tourist Center Lucca (Bag Storage, Bikes)
30 Cicli Primo Bike Rental & Bag Storage

and listings of concerts, markets, festivals, and other special events, pick up a copy of the *Grapevine* (€2), available at news-stands.

Cooking Class: Gianluca Pardini invites you to the hills above Lucca to learn to make Tuscan fare. You prepare and then eat a four-course meal. Depending on how many others attend, the price ranges from €50-70. This is great for groups of four or more (€14 cab ride from town, 3-hour lesson plus time to dine, includes wine, reserve at least 2 days in advance, Via di San Viticchio 414, mobile 347-678-7447, www.italiancuisine. it, info@italiancuisine.it).

Tours in Lucca

Walking Tours

The TI offers two-hour guided city walks in English and Italian, departing from the office on Piazzale Giuseppe Verdi (€10, pay at TI, daily April-Oct at 14:00, likely weekends only in winter, tel. 0583-583-150).

Local Guide

Gabriele Calabrese knows and shares his hometown well. He was a big help in creating the Lucca Walk in this chapter, and with his guidance you'll go even deeper into the city (€130/3 hours, by foot or bike, tel. 0583-342-404, mobile 347-788-0667, www.turislucca. com, turislucca@turislucca.com).

Lucca Walk

This hour-long self-guided walk (not counting time at the sights) connects Lucca's main points of interest by way of its most enter-taining streets. I've started this walk right in the heart of things, at Lucca's main square. For the classic view of the circular square, stand at the east end of the oval at #29.

Piazza dell'Anfiteatro

The architectural ghost of a Roman amphitheater can be felt in the de-lightful Piazza dell'Anfiteatro. With the fall of Rome, the theater (which seated 10,000 and sat just outside the rectangular city walls) was gradually cannibalized for its stones and inhab-ited by people living in a mishmash of huts. The huts were cleared away at the end of the 19th century to better

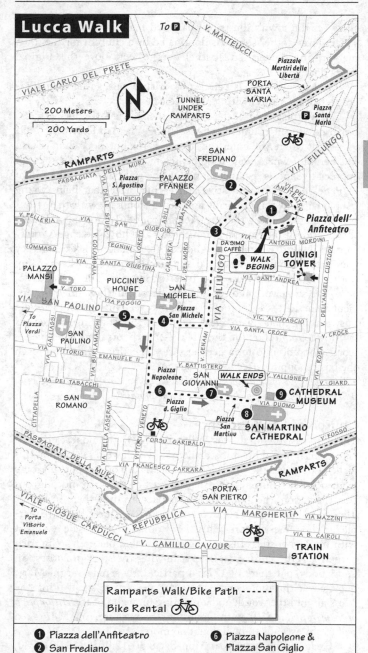

Lucca Walk

To 🅿

V. MATTEUCCI

VIALE CARLO DEL PRETE

Piazzale Martiri della Libertà

PORTA SANTA MARIA

Piazza Santa Maria

🅿

200 Meters

200 Yards

N

TUNNEL UNDER RAMPARTS

RAMPARTS

PASSAGGIATA DELLE MURA

SAN FREDIANO

V. FILLUNGO

VIA PELL'ANFITEAT

②

Piazza S. Agostino

PALAZZO PFANNER

PANIFICIO

VIA ASILI

VIA BATTISTI

V. PELLERIA

VIA

SAN

COLOMBA

GIORGIO

VIA LORETO

V. DEL MORO

CALDERIA

③

DA SIMO CAFFÉ

① Piazza dell' Anfiteatro

VIA ANTONIO MORDINI

VIA DELL'ANGELO CUSTODE

TOMMASO

VIA SANTA GIUSTINA

TEGNINI

VIA SANT'ANDREA

WALK BEGINS

GUINIGI TOWER

PALAZZO MANSI

PUCCINI'S HOUSE

VIA POGGIO

SAN MICHELE

Piazza San Michele

④

VIC. ALTOPASCIO

V. CROCE

V. ROSA

VIA SAN PAOLINO

V. TORO

VIA CENAMI

VIA SANTA CROCE

V. GIARD.

To Piazza Verdi

SAN PAULINO

VIA GALLIASSI

VITTORIO

VIA BURLAMACCHI

EMANUELE II

⑤

V. BATTISTERO

VALLISNERI

VIA DEI TABACCHI

Piazza Napoleone

SAN GIOVANNI

WALK ENDS

⑨ CATHEDRAL MUSEUM

SAN ROMANO

⑥

⑦

Piazza d. Giglio

VIA DUOMO

⑧

Piazza San Martino

SAN MARTINO CATHEDRAL

V. FOSSO

CITTADELLA

VIA DELLA CASERMA

VITTORIO VENETO

CORSO GARIBALDI

PASSAGGIATA DELLA MURA

VIA FRANCESCO CARRARA

RAMPARTS

VIALE GIOSUE CARDUCCI

To Porta Vittorio Emanuele

V. REPUBBLICA

PORTA SAN PIETRO

VIA MARGHERITA

VIA MAZZINI

VIA B. CAIROLI

V. CAMILLO CAVOUR

🚲

TRAIN STATION

Ramparts Walk/Bike Path ------

Bike Rental 🚲

① Piazza dell'Anfiteatro

② San Frediano

③ Via Fillungo

④ Piazza San Michele

⑤ Via San Paolino

⑥ Piazza Napoleone & Piazza San Giglio

⑦ San Giovanni

⑧ San Martino

⑨ Cathedral Museum

show off the town's illustrious past and make one purely secular square (every other square is dominated by a church) for the town market. The modern street level is nine feet above the original arena floor.

Today, the square is a circle of touristy shops, galleries, mediocre restaurants, and inviting al fresco cafés.

Leave the amphitheater through the arch at #42, turn left, and begin circling it counterclockwise along Via Anfiteatro. At #89-95—right where you enter the street—is the butcher's shop (Carni Val Serchio) where Felicino prepares meat and special dishes for appreciative locals. Farther along, on the right at #75, "The Loom of Penelope" is an innovative and caring place that helps young people with mental problems and depression deal with their troubles through weaving therapy. Across from #61, look up and study the exterior of the Roman amphitheater and how scavengers transformed it. Barbarians didn't know how to make bricks. But they could recycle building material and stack stones in order to camp out in Roman ruins. As you circle for the next 100 yards or so, study the stonework and see how medieval buildings filled the ancient arches. At #18 (on the left), you may see Antonio and Fabrizio busy making their gelato. Next you'll pass the tempting Pizzicheria la Grotta *salumi* shop (on the left at #2) with lots of gifty edibles—worth popping into for a peek at local specialties. Then you reach the busy shopping street, Via Fillungo.

• *Turn left and walk a block down Via Fillungo, then go right and cross a little square to the big church with a fine mosaic.*

Church of San Frediano

This impressive church was built in 1112 by the pope to one-up Lucca's bishop and his spiffy cathedral (which we'll see later on this walk). Lucca was the first Mediterranean stop on the pilgrim route from northern Europe, and the pope wanted to remind pilgrims that the action, the glory, and the papacy awaited them in Rome. Therefore, he had the church made "Roman-esque." The pure marble facade frames an early Christian Roman-style mosaic of Christ with his 12 apostles. Inside, there's a notable piece of art in each corner: a 12th-century baptistery showing the story of Moses; St. Zita's body, put there in 1278; a particularly serene Virgin Mary, depicted at the moment she gets the news that she'll bring the Messiah into the world; and a painting on wood of the *Assumption of the Virgin* (c. 1510), with Doubting Thomas receiving Mary's red belt as she ascends so he'll doubt no more.

Cost and Hours: Free, Mon-Sat 8:30-12:00 & 15:00-17:30, Sun 9:00-11:30 & 15:00-17:30, Piazza San Frediano.

• *Leaving the church, head straight back through the little square, and turn right onto...*

Via Fillungo

Lucca's best street to stroll and main pedestrian drag connects the town's two busiest squares: Piazza dell'Anfiteatro (which we just left) and Piazza San Michele. Along the way, you'll get a taste of Lucca's rich past, including several elegant, century-old storefronts.

Head down the street. At #116 (left) is a truffle shop where you can often sample little treats with truffle oil. Just beyond, also on the left, you'll pass Piazza degli Scapellini, with market stalls and another entrance into Piazza dell'Anfiteatro.

Near #104 (on the left) notice the snazzy Old World **shopping gallery,** with glass canopies in the Liberty Style (Italy's version of Art Nouveau, from around 1900).

As you stroll, notice how many of the original storefront paintings, reliefs, and mosaics survive—even if today's shopkeeper sells something entirely different. Observe the warm and convivial small-town vibe on the street. Notice also the powerful heritage of shops named for the families that have run them for many generations, the creative new energy brought by small entrepreneurs, and the aggressive inroads big chain stores are making in this tender urban econo-system.

At #92 (left) is a shop selling an array of beers from nearby microbreweries. Since 2007, vino-centric Italy has enjoyed a trendy and youthful microbrew industry. There are four breweries just in Lucca.

At #97 (right) is the classic old **Carli Jewelry Store.** Signore Carli is the 12th generation of jewelers from his family to work on this spot. (He still has a once-state-of-the-art 17th-century safe in the back.) The Carli storefront has kept its T-shaped arrangement that lets it close up tight as a canned ham. After hours, all you see from the street is a wooden T in the wall, and during opening hours it unfolds with a fine old-time display. This design dates from when the merchant sold his goods in front, did his work in the back, and lived upstairs.

Di Simo Caffè, at #58 (left), has long been the hangout of Lucca's artistic and intellectual elite. Composer and hometown boy Giacomo Puccini tapped his foot while sipping coffee here.

At #67 is a surviving five-story **tower house** (at the corner with Via Buia). At one time, nearly every corner in Lucca sported its own tower. The stubby stones that still stick out once supported wooden staircases (there were no interior connections between floors). So many towers cast shadows over this part of town that this cross-street is called "Dark Street" (Via Buia). Look left down Via Sant'Andrea for a peek at the town's tallest tower, Guinigi, in the distance—capped by its characteristic mini oak-tree forest (see "More Sights in Lucca," later).

The shop at #65 (right) sports a beautiful, Liberty Style *Pro-*

fumaria Venus sign. For over a century, its sexy reliefs (dating from the time of Puccini) have stirred Lucchesi menfolk to buy their woman a fragrant gift. Today the storefront is protected as a historic landmark—and, fittingly, a new perfume shop recently took up residence here.

At #45, you'll see two more good examples of tower houses. On the left is the 14th-century **Clock Tower** (Torre delle Ore), which has a hand-wound Swiss clock that clanged four times an hour since 1754...until it died for good a few years back (€4 to climb the 207 wooden steps to see the view and the nonfunctioning mechanism, €6 combo-ticket includes Guinigi Tower, daily April-Oct 9:30-18:30, Nov-March 9:30-17:30, corner of Via Fillungo and Via del'Arancio).

A bit farther along, on the left, is the striking 13th-century facade of a **Pisan Romanesque church,** now filled with a tacky Leonardo da Vinci exhibition.

The intersection of Via Fillungo and Via Roma/Via Santa Croce marks the center of town, where the two original Roman roads crossed. The big old palace you're facing (on the right)—with the heavy grates on the windows and the benches built into its stony facade—is the **In Mondadori bookstore.** While the interior is worth a peek (for its speckled mosaic floors, columns, and stained-glass skylight), the benches out front are even more interesting: They're the town hangout, where old-timers sit to swap gossip.

• *Turn right down Via Roma, studying the people warming those stone benches along the way. You'll pop out at...*

Piazza San Michele

This square has been the center of town since Roman times, when it was the forum. It's dominated by the **Church of San Michele.**
Circle around to the church's main door. Towering above the fancy Pisan Romanesque facade, the archangel Michael stands ready to flap his wings (which he actually did on special occasions with the help of crude but awe-inspiring-in-its-day mechanical assistance from behind). Perched above many of the columns are the faces of a  dozen or so heroes in the Italian independence and unification movement: Victor Emmanuel II (with a crown, above the short red column on the right, second level up), the Count of Cavour (next to Victor, above the column with black zigzags), and—hey, look—there's Giuseppe Mazzini.

The square is surrounded by an architectural hodgepodge. The circa-1495 loggia (to the right as you face the church) was the first Renaissance building in town. There's a late 19th-century interior in Buccellato Taddeucci, a 130-year-old pastry shop (#34, behind the church, next to its tower). The left section of the BNL bank (#5, facing the church facade) sports an Art Nouveau facade that celebrates both Amerigo Vespucci and Cristoforo Colombo. This was the original facade of the Bertolli shipping company—famed among Italian-Americans as the shipping company their grandfathers sailed with to reach America.

If the church is open, pop in. A fine 12th-century wooden crucifix hangs above the high altar. Immediately to its right is an exquisite painting, *The Four Saints*, by Filippino Lippi (a student of the Florentine master Sandro Botticelli). Look closely at the pillars to see curious little doodles scratched into the marble back in the 12th century.

• *From here, continue out of the square (opposite from where you entered) to take a little detour down...*

Via San Paolino

This bustling street—which eventually goes all the way to Piazzale Guiseppe Verdi (with the TI and bus to Pisa)—is another fine shopping drag. Along here, a wide variety of storefronts cater not just to tourists but also to locals. You'll pass—after just a half-block, on the right—my vote for the best gelato in town (De' Coltelli, Sicilian-style gelato, at #10; described under "Eating in Lucca").

One block down this street, in the little square called **Piazza Citadella** (on the right), a statue of Giacomo Puccini (1858-1924) sits genteelly on a chair, holding court. The great composer of operas was born in the house down the little alley over his left shoulder (now the well-presented Puccini's House museum, worth a visit for music lovers—see "More Sights in Lucca," later). (If you'd like to hear some Puccini while you're in town, soon we'll be passing a church that hosts nightly concerts of his music—see page 563).

• *Feel free to browse your way as far down this street as you like, but eventually return to Piazza San Michele to continue the walk to Lucca's cathedral. Facing the church facade, turn right and go down Via Vittorio Veneto (with the loggia on your left) to the vast, café-lined pair of squares...*

Piazza Napoleone and Piazza del Giglio

The first of these two squares is named for the French despot who was the first outsider to take over Lucca. The dominant building on the right was the seat of government for the independent Republic of Lucca from 1369 to 1799—the year Napoleon came and messed everything up. Caffè Ninci, on the left (with some nice tables for people-watching), has been caffeinating locals since 1925 and serves what's considered the best coffee in town.

Cross diagonally through this square into the smaller **Piazza del Giglio,** dominated by the Giglio Theater. Like a mini-La Scala, this has long been the number one theater (of seven) in the highly cultured city of Puccini.

• *Continue straight, along the big orange building, up Via del Duomo. After a block, you'll see...*

San Giovanni Church

This first cathedral of Lucca is interesting only for its archaeological finds. The entire floor of the 12th-century church has been excavated in recent decades, revealing layers of Roman houses, ancient hot tubs that date back to the time of Christ, early churches, and theological graffiti. Sporadic English translations help you understand what you're looking at. As you climb under the church's present-day floor and wander the lanes of Roman Lucca, remember that the entire city sits on similar ruins. Climb the 190 steps of the church's campanile (bell tower) for a panoramic view (but not quite as good as the one you'll enjoy if you climb the Guinigi Tower).

Cost and Hours: €4, €7 combo-ticket includes cathedral and Cathedral Museum, admission includes tower climb; mid-March-Oct daily 10:00-18:00; Nov-March Mon-Fri 10:00-14:00, Sat-Sun 10:00-18:00; audioguide-€2; see concert info on page 563.

• *Continuing past San Giovanni, you'll be face-to-face with...*

▲San Martino Cathedral

This cathedral—the main church of the Republic of Lucca—begun in the 11th century, is an entertaining mix of architectural and artistic styles. It's also home to the

exquisite 15th-century tomb of Ilaria del Carretto, who married into the wealthy Guinigi family.

The cathedral's elaborate Pisan Romanesque **facade** features Christian teaching scenes, animals, and candy-cane-striped columns. The horseback figure (over the two right arches) is St. Martin, a Roman military officer from Hungary who, by offering his cloak to a beggar, came to more fully understand the beauty of Christian compassion.

The **interior**—bigger than it seems from outside—features brightly frescoed Gothic arches, Renaissance paintings, and stained glass from the 19th century. On the left side of the nave, a small, elaborate, birdcage-like temple contains the wooden crucifix—much revered by locals—called **Volto Santo.** It's said to have been sculpted by Nicodemus in Jerusalem and set afloat in an unmanned boat that landed on the coast of Tuscany, from where wild oxen miraculously carried it to Lucca in 782. On the right side of the nave, the sacristy houses the enchantingly beautiful **memorial tomb of Ilaria del Carretto** by Jacopo della Quercia (1407). This young bride of silk baron Paolo Guinigi is so realistically realized that the statue was nicknamed "Sleeping Beauty." Her nose is partially worn off because of a long-standing tradition of lonely young ladies rubbing it for luck in finding a boyfriend.

Cost and Hours: €3, €7 combo-ticket includes Cathedral Museum and San Giovanni Church; April-Oct Mon-Fri 9:30-18:00, Sat 9:30-18:45, Sun 9:00-10:00 & 12:00-18:00; Nov-March daily 9:30-17:00; Piazza San Martino, www.cattedralelucca.it.

• *There's one more sight to consider, but it's extra credit—worthwhile only if you want to dig deeper into the history of the cathedral. As you face the cathedral facade, on the little square to the left is the entrance to the...*

Cathedral Museum (Museo della Cattedrale)

This beautifully presented museum houses original paintings, sculptures, and vestments from the cathedral and other Lucca churches. Pass through a room with illuminated manuscripts on your way to the ticket desk, then follow the one-way route up and down through the collection. The exhibits in this museum have basic labels and are meaningful only with the slow-talking €2 audioguide—if you're not in the mood to listen, skip the place altogether.

Cost and Hours: €4, €7 combo-ticket includes cathedral and San Giovanni Church; April-Oct daily 10:00-18:00; Nov-March Mon-Fri 10:00-14:00, Sat-Sun until 18:00; left of the cathedral on Piazza Antelminelli.

• *Our walk is finished. From here, it's just a short stroll south to the city wall—and a bike-rental office, if you want to take a spin. Otherwise, simply explore the city...lose yourself in Lucca.*

More Sights in Lucca

▲▲The Lucca Ramparts (and Bike Ride)

Lucca's most remarkable feature, its Renaissance wall, is also its most enjoyable attraction—especially when circled on a rental bike. Stretching for 2.5 miles, this is an ideal place to come for an overview of the city by foot or bike.

Lucca has had a protective wall for 2,000 years. You can read three walls into today's map: the first rectangular Roman wall, the later medieval wall (nearly the size of today's), and the 16th-century Renaissance ramparts that still survive.

With the advent of cannons, thin medieval walls were suddenly vulnerable. A new design—the same one that stands today—was state-of-the-art when it was built (1550-1650). Much of the old medieval wall (look for the old stones) was incorporated into the Renaissance wall (with uniform bricks). The new wall was squat: a 100-foot-wide mound of dirt faced with bricks, engineered to absorb a cannonball pummeling. The townspeople cleared a wide no-man's-land around the town, exposing any attackers from a distance. Eleven heart-shaped bastions (now inviting picnic areas) were designed to minimize exposure to cannonballs and to maximize defense capabilities. The ramparts were armed with 130 cannons.

The town invested a third of its income for more than a century to construct the wall, and—since it kept away the Florentines and nasty Pisans—it was considered a fine investment. In fact, nobody ever bothered to try to attack the wall. Locals say that the only time it actually defended the city was during an 1812 flood of the Serchio River, when the gates were sandbagged and the ramparts kept out the high water.

Today, the ramparts seem made-to-order for a leisurely bike ride (wonderfully smooth 20-30-minute pedal, depending on how fast you go and how crowded the wall-top park is). You can rent bikes cheaply and easily from one of several bike-rental places in town (listed earlier, under "Helpful Hints"). There are also several handy places to get up on the wall. Note that the best people-watching—and slowest pedaling—is during *passeggiata* time, just before dinner, when it seems that all of Lucca is doing slow laps around the wall.

Guinigi Tower (Torre Guinigi)

Many Tuscan towns have towers, but none is quite like the Guinigi family's. Up 227 steps is a small garden with fragrant trees, surrounded by fine views over the city's rooftops. You'll head up wide stone stairs, then huff up twisty metal ones through the hollow brick tower. From the top, orient yourself to the town. Lucca sits in a flat valley ringed by protective hills, so it's easy to see how the town managed

to stay independent through so much of its history, despite its lack of a strategic hilltop position. From up here, pick out landmarks: the circular form of Piazza dell'Anfiteatro to the north, with the mosaic facade of the Church of San Frediano nearby; to the left (east), the open top of the Clock Tower, marking the Roman grid-planned streets of the oldest part of town; and to the south, the big, marble facade of San Martino Cathedral.

Cost and Hours: €4, €6 combo-ticket includes Clock Tower, erratic hours but likely daily April-Sept 9:30-19:30—maybe later in summer, shorter hours off-season, Via Sant'Andrea 41.

Puccini's House

This modern, well-presented museum fills the home where Giacomo Puccini grew up. It's well worth a visit for opera enthusiasts... but mostly lost on anybody else. Buy your ticket at the shop/office on the square, then buzz the door to be let in. You'll tour the composer's birthplace—including the room where he was born—and see lots of artifacts (including the Steinway piano where he did much of his composing, his personal belongings, and pull-out drawers with original compositions and manuscripts). An elaborate costume from one of his works is on display, and if you ask, the attendant can accompany you for a peek in the garret (storage room up above the house), where a stage set from *La Bohème* evokes the composer's greatest work.

Cost and Hours: €7; May-Sept daily 9:30-19:30; April and Oct Wed-Mon 9:30-18:30, closed Tue; Nov-March shorter hours and closed Tue; Corte San Lorenzo 9, tel. 0583-584-028, www.puccinimuseum.it.

Sleeping in Lucca

($$$$ = Splurge, $$$ = Pricier, $$ = Moderate, $ = Budget)
For locations, see the map on page 564.

FANCY LITTLE BOUTIQUE B&Bs WITHIN THE WALLS

$$$ A Palazzo Busdraghi has eight comfortable, pastel-colored rooms with modern baths (some with Jacuzzi-style tubs) in a tastefully converted 13th-century palace tucked inside a creaky old courtyard. Sweet Marta hustles to keep guests happy, and bakes tasty cakes for breakfast. It's conveniently located on busy Via Fillungo, but can be noisy on weekends (family room, air-con, pay parking, Via Fillungo 170, tel. 0583-950-856, www.apalazzobusdraghi.it, info@apalazzobusdraghi.it).

$$$ La Locanda Sant'Agostino has three romantic, bright, and palatial rooms. The oasis-like setting—with a vine-draped terrace, beautiful breakfast spread, and quaint garden views—invites you to relax (family rooms, air-con, Piazza Sant'Agostino 3, tel. 0583-443-100, mobile 346-717-7762, www.locandasantagostino. it, info@locandasantagostino.it, sweet Silvia and gruff Giacomo).

$$ La Romea B&B, in an air-conditioned, restored, 14th-century palazzo near Guinigi Tower, feels like a royal splurge. Its five posh rooms are lavishly decorated in handsome colors and surround a big, plush lounge with stately Venetian-style mosaic-linoleum floors (RS%, family rooms, Vicolo delle Ventaglie 2, tel. 0583-464-175, www.laromea.com, info@laromea.com, Giulio and wife Gaia).

$$ La Bohème B&B has a cozy yet elegant ambience, offering six large rooms, each named for a Puccini opera. Chandeliers, 1920s-vintage tile floors, and tasteful antiques add to the charm (RS%, air-con, Via del Moro 2, tel. 0583-462-404, www.boheme. it, info@boheme.it).

SLEEPING MORE FORGETTABLY WITHIN THE WALLS

$$$ Hotel la Luna, pricey but well-run by the Barbieri family, has 29 rooms in a great location in the heart of the city. Rooms are split between two adjacent buildings just off the main shopping street. Rooms in the main, historical building are larger and classier, with old wood-beam ceilings (and, in some, original frescoes), while the modern building feels newer and has an elevator but less personality (RS%, family rooms, air-con, pay parking, Via Fillungo at Corte Compagni 12, tel. 0583-493-634, www.hotellaluna.it, info@hotellaluna.it).

$$ Albergo San Martino is conveniently located for train travelers, with rooms in three different buildings. The 12 art-adorned rooms in the main hotel—with a nice lounge and curbside breakfast terrace—are cozy, while the six rooms in the **annex** are newer and slightly cheaper. And the nine budget rooms in their sister **$ Hotel Diana** are fresh, minimalist, and retro-style at an affordable price (more hip, but no breakfast; family rooms, air-con, pay parking, reception at Via della Dogana 9, tel. 0583-469-181, www.albergosanmartino.it, info@albergosanmartino.it).

$ At B&B Le Violette, cheerful American Elisabeth will settle you into one of her six homey rooms near the train station inside Porta San Pietro (cheaper rooms with shared bath, air-con in some rooms, communal kitchen, self-service laundry, Via della Polveriera 6, tel. 0583-493-594, mobile 333-588-0982, www. bblevioletteilucca.com, bbleviolette@gmail.com).

¢ Ostello San Frediano, in a central, sprawling ex-convent, comes with huge public spaces and a peaceful garden facing the busy town wall. Its 29 rooms are bright and modern, and some have

PISA & LUCCA

fun lofts (dorms and private rooms, nice two-story family rooms, includes breakfast, no curfew, elevator, restaurant, pay parking, Via della Cavallerizza 12, tel. 0583-348-477, www.ostellolucca.it, info@ostellolucca.it).

OUTSIDE THE WALLS

$$$ Hotel San Marco, a 10-minute walk outside the Porta Santa Maria, is a postmodern place decorated à la Stanley Kubrick. Its 42 rooms are sleek, with all the comforts (air-con, elevator, pool, bike rental, free parking, taxi from station-€13, Via San Marco 368, tel. 0583-495-010, www.hotelsanmarcolucca.com, info@hotelsanmarcolucca.com).

$$ Hotel Rex rents 25 rooms in a practical contemporary building on the train station square. While in the modern world, you're just 200 yards away from the old town and get more space for your money. Ask for a slightly quieter room at the back (family room, children's play area, air-con, elevator, free loaner bikes, free parking, a few steps from the train station at Piazza Ricasoli 19, tel. 0583-955-443, www.hotelrexlucca.com, info@hotelrexlucca.com).

$ Hotel Moderno is indeed modern, with 12 rooms tastefully decorated in shades of white. Although it backs up to the train tracks, the rooms are quiet, and it offers class unusual for this price range (air-con, Via Vincenzo Civitali 38—turn left out of train station and go over stair-heavy bridge across tracks, tel. 0583-55-840, www.albergomodernolucca.com, info@albergomodernolucca.com).

$ La Mimosa B&B has five cozy, if musty, rooms a 10-minute walk west of Porta Sant'Anna. Most practical if you're arriving or leaving Lucca by bus, this funky little house is run by the Zichi cousins, Giuseppe and Stefano, and decorated with modern paintings. It's on a main road, but double-paned windows reduce traffic noise (air-con, free loaner bikes, free street parking nearby, Via Pisana 66; leave Piazzale Giuseppe Verdi through Porta Sant'Anna, swing right, then cross road, walk straight down Via Catalani, and take second road on the left; tel. 0583-583-121, www.bblamimosa.it, info@bblamimosa.it).

$ Sogni d'Oro Guesthouse ("Dreams of Gold"), run by Davide, is a handy budget option for drivers, with five basic rooms and a cheery communal kitchen (grocery store next door). It's a 10-minute walk from the train station and a five-minute walk from the city walls (cheaper rooms with shared bath, free parking, free ride to and from station with advance notice—then call when your train arrives in Lucca; from the station, head straight out to Viale Regina Margherita and turn right, follow the main boulevard as it turns into Viale Giuseppe Giusti, at the curve turn right onto

Via Antonio Cantore to #169; tel. 0583-467-768, mobile 329-582-5062, www.bbsognidoro.com, info@bbsognidoro.com).

Eating in Lucca

($$$$ = Splurge, $$$ = Pricier, $$ = Moderate, $ = Budget)
For locations, see the map on page 564.

FINE AND ROMANTIC DINING

$$ Canuleia Trattoria is run by enthusiastic Matteo (the chef) and Eleonora (head waiter), who make everything fresh in their small kitchen. You can eat tasty Tuscan cuisine in a dressy and romantic little dining room or outside on the garden courtyard. As this place is justifiably popular, reserve for dinner (Tue-Sun 12:00-14:30 & 19:00-22:00, closed Mon, shorter hours in winter, Via Canuleia 14, tel. 0583-467-470, www.canuleiatrattoria.it).

$$$ Ristorante Giglio is a venerable old dining hall where waiters are formal, but not stuffy, and the spirit of Puccini lives on. This is where local families enjoy special occasions under a big chandelier. They also have simple tables outside facing a tranquil square and the old theater. The short but thoughtful menu—with both traditional and creative Tuscan dishes influenced by the mama-and-son who run the place—makes you want to return. It's only slightly pricier than most of my listings, but is a big step up in dining experience (impressive wine list, Wed-Mon 12:15-14:30 & 19:15-22:30, closed Tue, Piazza del Giglio 2, tel. 0583-494-058).

$$ Port Ellen Clan, unusual in traditional Lucca, is a combination restaurant, wine bar, and whisky bar in a trendy modern setting. Though the cuisine is purely Italian with a modern twist, the theme is creative and original, with a Scottish flair (Wed-Fri 12:30-15:00 & 19:30-24:00, Sat-Sun 12:30-15:00 only, closed Mon-Tue, Via del Fosso 120, tel. 0583-493-952, mobile 329-245-2762, www.portellenclan.com).

CHARMING AND RUSTIC DINING

$$ La Bottega di Anna & Leo, run by Claudio and Lidia (and named for their children), is a pastel and lovable little eatery with a simple menu and a passion for quality. They have tight seating inside and a few charming tables facing the side of the Church of San Frediano (Tue-Wed 12:00-14:30, Thu-Sun 12:00-15:00 & 19:30-22:00, closed Mon, reservations smart, Via San Frediano 16, mobile 393-577-9910 or 393-530-2512, www.labottegadiannaeleo.it).

$$ Osteria Via San Giorgio, where Daniela cooks and her brother Piero serves, is a cheery family eatery that satisfies both fish and meat lovers. The seating is tight and convivial (daily 12:00-16:00 & 19:00-23:00, Via San Giorgio 26, tel. 0583-953-233).

Specialties in Lucca

Lucca has some tasty specialties worth seeking out. *Ceci* (CHEH-chee), also called *cecina* (cheh-CHEE-nah), makes an ideal cheap snack any time of day. This garbanzo-bean crêpe is sold in pizza shops and is best accompanied by a nip of red wine. *Farro,* a grain (spelt) dating back to ancient Roman cuisine, shows up In restaurants in soups or as a creamy rice-like dish *(risotto di farro). Tordelli,* the Lucchesi version of *tortelli,* is homemade ravioli. It's traditionally stuffed with meat and served with more meat sauce, but chefs creatively pair cheeses and vegetables, too. *Lardo di Colonnata* is *salumi* made with cured lard and rosemary, sliced thin, and served as an antipasto.

Meat, not fish, is the star at most restaurants, especially steak, which is listed on menus as *filetto di manzo* (filet), *tagliata di manzo* (thin slices of grilled tenderloin), or the king of steaks, *bistecca alla fiorentina.* Order *al sangue* (rare), *medio* (medium rare), *cotto* (medium), or *ben cotto* (well). Anything more than *al sangue* is considered a travesty for steak con-noisseurs. *Ravellino* is a thin cut of beef that's deep-fried, then pan-fried again later to heat it up.

Note that steaks (as well as fish) are often sold by weight, noted on menus as *s.q.* (according to quantity ordered) or *l'etto* (cost per 100 grams—250 grams is about an 8-ounce steak).

For something sweet, bakeries sell *buccellato,* bread dotted with raisins, lightly flavored with anise, and often shaped like a wreath. It's sold only in large quantities, but luckily it stays good for a few days (and it also pairs well with vin santo—fortified Tuscan dessert wine). An old proverb says, "Coming to Lucca without eating the *buccellato* is like not having come at all." *Buon appetito!*

$$ Il Cuore Bistrot is a trendy find for wine tasting or a meal on a piazza. Try the €8 *aperitivo* (available 18:00-20:00), which includes a glass of wine and a plate of cheese, *salumi,* and snacks, or feast on fresh pastas and other high-quality dishes from their lunch and dinner menus (daily 8:00-22:30, shorter hours off-season, closed Jan-Feb, Via del Battistero, tel. 0583-493-196).

$ Pizzeria da Felice is a little mom-and-pop hole-in-the-wall serving *cecina* (garbanzo-bean crêpes) and slices of freshly baked pizza to throngs of snackers. Grab an *etto* of *cecina* and a short glass of wine. From September through April, they're known for their *castagnaccio,* a cake made with roasted chestnuts and ricotta (daily 10:00-20:30 except closed Sun Jan-Aug and closed 2 weeks in Aug, Via Buia 12, tel. 0583-494-986).

Basic Trattorias: For an affordable, fill-the-tank meal in a lively traditional environment, consider these two options, run by relatives. They're a block apart in a quiet part of town, a short walk from the main sights: **$$ Vecchia Trattoria Buralli,** on quiet Piazza Sant'Agostino, has bright-pastel indoor and piazza seating. It's fun to order a *bis* (2 different half-portion pastas) and watch your *tordelli* being handmade at the pasta bar (Thu-Tue 12:00-15:00 & 18:30-22:30, closed Wed, Piazza Sant'Agostino 10, tel. 0583-950-611). **$$ Trattoria da Leo** packs in chatty locals for typical, cheap home cooking in a high-energy, Mel's-diner atmosphere. Sit in the rollicking interior, or out on a tight, atmospheric lane (Mon-Sat 12:00-14:45 & 19:30-22:30, Sun 12:00-14:45, cash only, Via Tegrimi 1, tel. 0583-492-236, www.trattoriadaleo.it).

Fancy Deli: Proudly run by the Marcucci family, **$ Antica Bottega di Prospero** is an artisanal deli shop that feels more like a museum. Peruse their great selection of local meats and cheeses that are perfect for a picnic. You can satisfy your sweet tooth with cookies like *buccellati, cantuccini,* and *befanini,* or pick up dried pasta, spices, and beans for a tasty souvenir (daily 9:00-19:30, a block behind the Church of San Michele at Via Santa Lucia 13).

Après-Bike Drinks: In the little piazza just south of where Piazza Santa Maria (the bike rental hub), meets the end of Via Fillungo, young people gather each evening to socialize and drink. This is a perfect spot to unwind after a late-afternoon cycle on the city wall, before you head to dinner. **De Cervesia** is a craft beer pub, with three microbrews on rotating taps (and one English-style pull) and dozens by the bottle (Tue-Sun 17:00-22:00, closed Mon, Via Michele Rosi 20, tel. 0583-492-620, Matteo). **Ciclo DiVino,** across the street, is a wine bar with a bike-shop theme and enticing snacks (Mon-Fri 10:00-22:00, Sat-Sun 18:00-22:00, Via Michele Rosi 7, tel. 0583-471-869). As this is a fast-emerging scene, scope out the area for other hip new bars before you choose.

Gelato: Just off Piazza San Michele, **De' Coltelli** has some of my favorite gelato in Italy. It's proudly Sicilian-style (with Arab roots) and many of their flavors rotate with the season. The coffee gelato is serious (and not served to children), and their granita takes the slushy to new heights (Sun-Thu 11:00-20:00, Fri-Sat 11:00-21:00, Via San Paolino 10, 0583-050-667).

Refreshments on the Wall: On the city wall, **Caffetteria San Colombano** is a handy pit stop for bikers and walkers. This place is slick with cheap bite-sized snacks and lattes, perfect for a takeaway meal on top of the wall (overpriced at the table). If you're not feeling too wobbly already from biking, try a *caffè corretto* (espresso with your choice of Sambuca, rum, or grappa) or a *Biadina,* a bittersweet liqueur served with pine nuts (daily 9:00-late, near the top of ramp at Baluardo San Colombano, tel. 0583-464-641).

Lucca Connections

Even if you have a car, I'd opt for the much faster and cheaper train or bus to reach the Leaning Tower. For more on day-tripping to Pisa, see page 560.

From Lucca by Train to: Florence (2/hour, 1.5 hours), **Pisa** (roughly 1-2/hour, 30 minutes; if going directly to Leaning Tower, hop off at Pisa San Rossore station), **Livorno** (about hourly, 1-1.5 hours, transfer at Pisa Centrale), **Milan** (2/hour except Sun, 4-5 hours, transfer in Florence), **Rome** (1/hour except Sun, 3-4 hours, change in Florence), **Cinque Terre** (hourly, about 2 hours, transfer in Viareggio and La Spezia).

From Lucca by Bus: Vaibus has handy, direct routes from Lucca's Piazzale Giuseppe Verdi to **Florence** and its **airport** (bus #DD, Mon-Sat nearly hourly, less on Sun, 1.25 hours to airport, 1.5 hours total to downtown Florence), and to **Pisa** and its **airport** (drops you right at the Leaning Tower, Mon-Sat hourly, fewer on Sun, 50 minutes). Before boarding, buy tickets at the bus ticket office on Piazzale Giuseppe Verdi (Mon-Sat 6:00-20:00, Sun 8:00-19:30)—or you can buy them from the driver for a small surcharge.

HILL TOWNS OF CENTRAL ITALY

The sun-soaked hill towns of central Italy offer what to many is the quintessential Italian experience: sun-dried tomatoes, homemade pasta, wispy cypress-lined driveways following desolate ridges to fortified 16th-century farmhouses, atmospheric *enoteche* serving famously tasty wines, and dusty old-timers warming the same bench day after day while soccer balls buzz around them like innocuous flies. Hill towns are best enjoyed by adapting to the pace of the countryside. So, slow...down...and savor the delights that this region offers. Spend the night if you can, as many hill towns are mobbed by day-trippers.

PLANNING YOUR TIME

How in Dante's name does a traveler choose from Italy's hundreds of hill towns? I've listed some of my favorites in the next five chapters. The one(s) you visit will depend on your interests, time, and mode of transportation.

For me, **Volterra**—with its rustic vitality—is a clear winner, and its out-of-the-way location keeps it from being trampled by tourist crowds. Multitowered **San Gimignano** is a classic, but because it's such an easy hill town to visit (about 1.5 hours by bus from Florence), peak-season crowds can overwhelm its charms.

Wine aficionados head for **Montepulciano** (my favorite of the two towns) and **Montalcino**—each a happy gauntlet of wine shops and art galleries. Fans of architecture and urban design appreciate **Pienza**'s well-planned streets and squares. All three towns are covered in the Heart of Tuscany chapter, which also includes driving routes tying together the sights, villages, *agriturismi*, and wineries in the countryside.

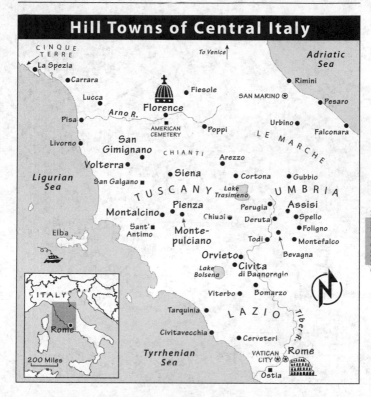

Hill Towns of Central Italy

Assisi, Siena, and Orvieto—while technically hill towns—are in a category by themselves: Bigger and with more major artistic and historic sights, they each get their own chapter. (The Orvieto chapter also includes the stranded-on-a-hilltop Civita di Bagnoregio.)

GETTING AROUND THE HILL TOWNS

While you can reach just about any place with public buses, taxis, and patience, most hill towns are easier and more efficient to visit by car. For more on all of these topics, see the Practicalities chapter.

By Bus or Train

Buses are often the only public-transportation choice to get between small hill towns. While trains link some towns, hill towns—being on hills—don't quite fit the railroad plan. Stations are likely to be in the valley a couple of miles from the town center, con-

Hill Towns: Public Transportation

To Genoa • CINQUE TERRE
To Milan • To Venice • Ravenna
Bologna
Adriatic Sea
La Spezia • Carrara
Rimini
Lucca • Florence • SAN MARINO • Pesaro
Fiesole
Pisa • Empoli • Urbino • Falconara
Livorno • San Gimignano • Arezzo • To Bari & Brindisi
Ligurian Sea • Volterra • Pogg. • Siena • Camucia • Gubbio
Cecina • Colle di Val d'Elsa • Cortona • Terentola
Saline • Perugia • Assisi
Montalcino • Chiusi • Spello • Foligno
Pienza • Monte-pulciano • Todi
Bagnoregio • Orvieto • Spoleto
Civita • Orte
Viterbo
Tarquinia
Civitavecchia • Cerveteri
Rome • To Naples

30 Kilometers
30 Miles

- - - Rail
━━━ High Speed Rail
- - - Bus

HILL TOWNS

nected by a local bus. Buses don't always drive up into the town itself. Fortunately, stations are sometimes connected to the town by escalator or elevator. (For more on traveling by train and bus in Italy, see the appendix.) If you're pinched for time, it makes sense to narrow your focus to one or two hill towns, or rent a car.

By Car

Exploring the hill towns by car can be a great experience. Wait to pick up your car until the last sizable town you visit (or at the nearest airport to avoid big-city traffic), and carry a good, detailed road map in addition to any digital navigation systems. Freeways (such as the toll autostrada and the non-toll *superstrada*) are the fastest way to connect two points, but smaller roads, including the super-scenic S-222, which runs through the heart

Driving in Tuscany

HILL TOWNS

---

of the Chianti region (connecting Florence and Siena), are more rewarding.

Parking can be challenging. Some towns don't allow visitors to park in the city center: Leave your car outside the walls and walk into town. Signs reading *ZTL (Zona Traffico Limitato)*—often above a red circle—indicate no driving or parking is allowed. Parking lots, identified by blue *P* signs, are usually free and plentiful outside city walls (and sometimes linked to the town center by elevators or escalators). If street parking is available, nearby kiosks sell "pay and display" tickets. White lines indicate free parking, blue lines are pay parking, and yellow lines are spaces for local residents. To reduce theft, choose a parking lot instead of street parking if possible. Your hotelier can also recommend parking options.

SLEEPING IN A HILL TOWN

For a relaxing break from big-city Italy, settle down in an *agri-turismo*—a farmhouse that rents out rooms to travelers (usually for a minimum of a week in high season). These rural B&Bs—almost by definition in the middle of nowhere—provide a good home base from which to find the magic of Italy's hill towns. I've listed several good options throughout these chapters. For more information, see *"Agriturismo"* on page 1130.

SIENA

Siena was medieval Florence's archrival. And while Florence ultimately won the battle for political and economic superiority, Siena still competes for the tourists. Sure, Florence has the heavyweight sights. But Siena seems to be every Italy connoisseur's favorite town. In my office, whenever Siena is mentioned, someone exclaims, "Siena? I looove Siena!"

Once upon a time (about 1260-1348), Siena was a major banking and trade center, and a military power in a class with Florence, Venice, and Genoa. With a population of about 50,000, it was even bigger than Paris. Situated on the north-south road to Rome (Via Francigena), Siena traded with all of Europe. Then, in 1348, the Black Death—an epidemic of bubonic plague—swept through Europe, hitting Siena and cutting the population by more than a third. Siena never recovered. In the 1550s, Florence, with the help of Philip II's Spanish army, conquered the flailing city-state, forever rendering Siena a nonthreatening backwater. Siena's loss became our sightseeing gain, as its political and economic irrelevance pickled the city in a purely medieval brine. Today, Siena's population is still at its medieval level of 50,000, although only 18,000 of those live within the walls.

Situated atop three hills, Siena qualifies as Italy's ultimate "hill town." Its thriving historic center, with red-brick lanes cascading every which-way, offers Italy's best medieval city experience. Most people visit Siena, just 35 miles south of Florence, as a day trip, but it's best experienced at twilight. While Florence has the blockbuster museums, Siena has an easy-to-enjoy soul: Courtyards sport flower-decked wells, alleys dead-end at rooftop views, and the sky is a rich blue dome.

For those who dream of a Fiat-free Italy, Siena is a haven. Pedestrians rule in the old center of town, as the only drivers allowed are residents and cabbies. Sit at a café on the main square. Wander narrow streets lined with colorful flags and studded with iron rings to tether horses. Take time to savor the first European city to eliminate automobile traffic from its main square (1966) and then, just to be silly, wonder what would happen if they did it in your hometown.

PLANNING YOUR TIME

On a quick trip, consider spending two nights in Siena (or three nights with a whole-day side-trip into Florence). Whatever you do, be sure to enjoy a sleepy medieval evening in Siena. The next morning, you can see the city's major sights in half a day.

Orientation to Siena

Siena lounges atop a hill, stretching its three legs out from Il Campo. This pedestrianized main square is the historic meeting point of Siena's neighborhoods.

Just about everything mentioned in this chapter is within a 15-minute walk of the square. Navigate by three major landmarks (Il Campo, Duomo, and Church of San Domenico), following the excellent system of street-corner signs. The typical visitor sticks to the Il Campo-San Domenico axis. Make it a point to stray from this main artery. Sienese streets go in anything but a straight line, so it's easy to get lost—but equally easy to get found. Don't be afraid to explore.

Siena itself is one big sight. Its individual attractions come in two little clusters: the square (Civic Museum and City Tower) and the cathedral (Baptistery and Duomo Museum, with its surprise viewpoint), plus the Pinacoteca for art lovers. Check these sights off, and then you're free to wander.

TOURIST INFORMATION

The TI is just across from the cathedral (April-Sept Mon-Fri 10:30-16:30, Sat-Sun until 18:30; shorter hours Oct-March; Piazza del Duomo 1, tel. 0577-280-551, www.terresiena.it). They hand out a few pretty booklets (including the regional *Terre di Siena* guide) and a free map. The bookshop next to the information desk sells more detailed Siena maps.

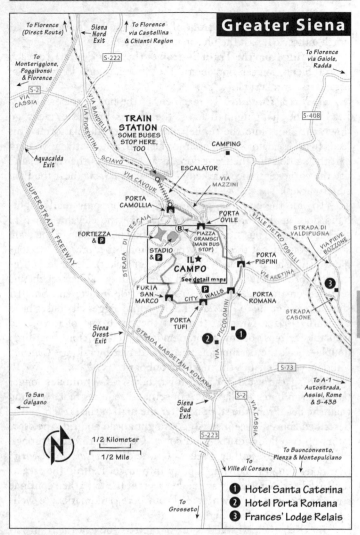

Greater Siena

To Florence (Direct Route)

Siena Nord Exit

↑ To Florence via Castellina & Chianti Region

S-222

To Monteriggione, Poggibonsi & Florence

S-2

VIA CASSIA

VIA BANDELLI

VIA FIORENTINA

To Florence via Gaiole, Radda

S-408

TRAIN STATION
SOME BUSES STOP HERE, TOO

CAMPING

Aquacalda Exit

SCIAVO

VIA CAVOUR

ESCALATOR

VIA MAZZINI

SUPERSTRADA FREEWAY

PORTA CAMOLLIA

PORTA OVILE

VIALE PIETRO TOSELLI

STRADA DI VALDIPUGNA

FORTEZZA & P

STRADA DI PESCAIA

B

PIAZZA GRAMSCI (MAIN BUS STOP)

VIA PIEVE BOZZONE

STADIO & P

IL ★ CAMPO
See detail maps

PORTA PISPINI

VIA ARETINA

❸

FURIA SAN MARCO

CITY WALLS

PORTA ROMANA

STRADA CASONE

Siena Ovest Exit

PORTA TUFI

VIA PICCOLOMINI

STRADA MASSETANA ROMANA

❷

❶

SIENA

S-73

To San Galgano

Siena Sud Exit

S-2

VIA CASSIA

To A-1 Autostrada, Assisi, Rome & S-438

N

1/2 Kilometer

1/2 Mile

S-223

To Ville di Corsano

To Buonconvento, Pienza & Montepulciano

❶ Hotel Santa Caterina
❷ Hotel Porta Romana
❸ Frances' Lodge Relais

To Grosseto

ARRIVAL IN SIENA
By Train

The small train station at the base of the hill, on the edge of town, has a bar/tobacco shop, a bus office (Mon-Fri 7:15-19:30, Sat until 17:45, Sun 7:15-12:00 & 15:15-18:30, opens later in winter), and a newsstand (which sells local bus tickets—buy one now if you're taking the city bus into town), but no baggage check or lockers (stow bags at Piazza Gramsci—see "By Intercity Bus," later). A shopping mall with a Pam supermarket (handy for picnic supplies) is across the plaza right in front of the station. WCs are at the far north on track 1, past the pharmacy to the left.

Getting from the Train Station to the City Center: To reach central Siena, you can hop aboard the city bus, ride a long series of escalators, or take a taxi.

By Bus or Escalator: To reach either the bus or the escalators, head for the shopping mall across the square. From the tracks, go down the stairs into the tunnel that connects the platforms; this leads (with escalators) right up into the mall. Alternatively, you can exit the station out the front door, bear left across the square, and use the corner entrance marked *Galleria Porta Siena* (near the Pam supermarket).

To ride the **city bus,** go through the shopping mall's right-hand door at the corner entrance and take the elevator down to the subterranean bus stop. If you didn't buy bus tickets in the train station, you can get them from the blue machine (press "F" to toggle to English, then select "A" for type of ticket). Buses leave frequently (6/hour, fewer on Sun and after 22:00, €1.20, exact change required on the bus, about a 10-minute ride into town). Smaller shuttle buses go up to Piazza del Sale, while bigger city buses head to nearby Piazza Gramsci (both at the north end of town, and walkable to most of my recommended hotels). Before boarding, double-check the destination with the driver by asking *"Centro?"* Validate your ticket in the machine onboard.

Riding the **escalator** into town takes a few minutes longer (about 15 minutes to Piazza Gramsci) and requires more walking than the bus. From the station, enter the mall at the far-left end as described above. Once inside, go straight ahead and ride the escalators up two floors to the food court. Continue directly through the glass doors to another escalator (marked *Porta Camollia/Centro*) that takes you gradually, up, up, up into town. Exiting the escalator, turn left down the big street, bear left at the fork, then continue straight through the town gate. From here, landmarks are well-signed (go up Via Camollia).

By Taxi: The taxi stand is to your left as you exit the train station, but as the city is chronically short on cabs, getting one here can take a while (about €10 to Il Campo, taxi tel. 0577-49222).

Getting to the Train Station from the City Center: You can ride a smaller shuttle bus directly to the station from Piazza del Sale, or catch an orange or red-and-silver city bus from Piazza Gramsci (which may take a more roundabout route). Multiple bus routes make this trip—look for *Ferrovia* or *Stazione* on schedules and marked on the bus, and confirm with the driver that the bus is going to the *stazione* (staht-see-OH-nay).

By Intercity Bus

Most buses arrive in Siena at Piazza Gramsci, a few blocks north of the city center. (Some buses only go to the train station; others go first to the train station, then continue to Piazza Gramsci—to find out, ask your driver, "pee-aht-sah GRAHM-chee?") The main bus companies are Sena/Baltour and Tiemme/Siena Mobilità. Day-trippers can store baggage in the Sottopassaggio la Lizza passageway underneath Piazza Gramsci at the Tiemme/Siena Mobilità office (daily 7:00-19:00, carry-on-sized luggage no more than 33 pounds, no overnight storage). From Piazza Gramsci, it's an easy walk into the town center—just head in the opposite direction of the tree-filled park. For more on buses, see page 626.

By Car

Siena is not a good place to drive. Plan on parking in a big lot or garage and walking into town.

Drivers coming from the autostrada take the *Siena Ovest* exit and follow signs for *Centro,* then *Stadio* (stadium). The soccer-ball signs take you to the stadium lot (Parcheggio Stadio, €2/hour, pay when you leave) near Piazza Gramsci and the huge, bare-brick Church of San Domenico. The nearby Fortezza lot charges the same amount.

Another good option is the underground Santa Caterina garage (you'll see signs on the way to the stadium lot, same price). From the garage, hike 150 yards uphill through a gate to an escalator on the right, which carries you up into the city. If you're staying in the south end of town, try the Il Campo lot, near Porta Tufi.

On parking spots, blue stripes mean pay and display; white stripes mean free parking. You can park for free in the lot west of the Fortezza; in white-striped spots south of the Fortezza; and overnight in most city lots (20:00-8:00). Signs showing a street cleaner and a day of the week indicate when the street is closed to cars for cleaning.

Driving within Siena's city center is restricted to local cars and is policed by automatic cameras. If you drive or park anywhere marked *Zona Traffico Limitato (ZTL),* you'll likely have a hefty ticket waiting for you in the mail back home. Check with your hotel in advance if you plan to drop off your bags before parking.

HELPFUL HINTS

Exchange Rate: €1 = about $1.10

Country Calling Code: 39 (see page 1154 for dialing instructions)

Combo-Tickets: Siena always seems to be experimenting with different combo-tickets, but in general, only three are worth considering: the €13 Opa Si combo-ticket that includes the Duomo, Duomo Museum, Crypt, and Baptistery (valid 3 days; sold only at ticket office near Duomo Museum entrance); the €13 combo-ticket covering the Civic Museum and Santa Maria della Scala; and the €20 combo-ticket covering the Civic Museum, Santa Maria della Scala, and City Tower (valid 2 days). All of these tickets allow only one entry per sight.

Wednesday Morning Market: The weekly market (clothes, knick-knacks, and food) sprawls between the Fortezza and Piazza Gramsci along Viale Cesare Maccari and the adjacent Viale XXV Aprile.

Useful App: ∩ For a free audio version of my Siena City Walk, get the Rick Steves Audio Europe app (for details, see page 12).

Post Office: It's on Piazza Matteotti (Mon-Fri 8:15-19:00, Sat 8:15-12:30, closed Sun).

Bookstores: For books and magazines in English, try **Libreria Senese** (daily 9:00-20:00, Via di Città 62, tel. 0577-280-845) and the **Feltrinelli** bookstore at Banchi di Sopra 52 (Mon-Sat 9:00-19:45, closed Sun, tel. 0577-271-104).

Laundry: Onda Blu is a modern, self-service launderette just 50 yards from Il Campo (about €6 wash and dry, daily 8:00-21:15, Via del Casato di Sotto 17).

Travel Agency: Carroccio Viaggi sells train, plane, and some bus tickets for a small fee (Mon-Fri 9:00-12:30 & 15:30-19:00, Sat 9:30-12:00, closed Sun, Via Montanini 20, tel. 0577-226-964, www.carroccioviaggi.com, info@carroccioviaggi.com).

Wine Classes: The **Tuscan Wine School** gives two-hour classes on Italian wine and food. The midday class (12:00) focuses on local food culture with tastings at vendors around town. Afternoon classes (16:00) teach Tuscan wines and stay in the classroom (€45/person, 20 percent discount for afternoon class with this book, classes Mon-Sat, closed Sun, Via di Stalloreggi 26, 30 yards from recommended Hotel Duomo, tel. 0577-221-704, mobile 333-722-9716, www.tuscanwineschool.com, tuscanwineschool@gmail.com, Rebecca and Riikka Sofia). They also offer food- and wine-oriented tours into the surrounding countryside, convenient for those without their own wheels (www.siena-wine-tour.com).

Tours in Siena

∩ To sightsee on your own, download my free Siena City Walk audio tour.

Tours by Roberto: Tuscany Minibus Tours

Tours by Roberto, led by Roberto Bechi or one of his guides, offers off-the-beaten-path minibus tours of the surrounding countryside (up to eight passengers, pickup at hotel). Regardless of the size of

Siena at a Glance

▲▲▲Il Campo Best square in Italy. **Hours:** Always open. See page 595.

▲▲▲Duomo Art-packed cathedral with mosaic floors and statues by Michelangelo and Bernini. **Hours:** March-Oct Mon-Sat 10:30-19:00, Sun 13:30-18:00; Nov-Feb closes daily at 17:30. See page 606.

▲▲Civic Museum City museum in City Hall with Sienese frescoes, the *Effects of Good and Bad Government.* **Hours:** Daily 10:00-19:00, Nov-mid-March until 18:00. See page 604.

▲▲Duomo Museum Siena's best museum, displaying cathedral art (including Duccio's *Maestá*) and offering sweeping Tuscan views. **Hours:** Daily March-Oct 10:30-19:00, Nov-Feb until 17:30. See page 610.

▲City Tower Siena's 330 foot tower climb. **Hours:** Daily March-mid-Oct 10:00-19:00, mid-Oct-Feb until 16:00. See page 605.

▲Pinacoteca Fine Sienese paintings. **Hours:** Tue-Sat 8:15-19:15, Sun-Mon 9:00-13:00. See page 605.

▲Baptistery Cave-like building with baptismal font decorated by Ghiberti and Donatello. **Hours:** Daily 10:30-19:00, Nov-Feb until 17:30. See page 612.

▲Santa Maria della Scala Museum with much of the original *Fountain of Joy,* Byzantine reliquaries, and vibrant ceiling and wall frescoes depicting day-to-day life in a medieval hospital. **Hours:** Mid-March-mid-Oct daily 10:30-18:30; closes earlier off-season. See page 613.

Crypt Site of 12th-century church, housing some of Siena's oldest frescoes. **Hours:** Daily 10:30-19:00, Nov-Feb until 17:30. See page 612.

Church of San Domenico Huge brick church with St. Catherine's head and thumb. **Hours:** Daily 9:00-18:00, shorter hours off-season. See page 614.

Sanctuary of St. Catherine Home of St. Catherine. **Hours:** Daily 9:00-18:00, Chapel of the Crucifixion closed 12:30-15:00. See page 614.

your group, they charge per person, so these minibus tours are economical. The first participants to book choose an itinerary—then others can join until the van fills. Roberto and his team share the same passion for Sienese culture, Tuscan history, and local cuisine (tour options explained on website, special Rick Steves discount prices: full-day minibus tours–€90/person, 4-hour off-season tours–€60/person, entry fees extra; booking mobile 320-147-6590, Roberto's mobile 328-425-5648, www.toursbyroberto.com, toursbyroberto@gmail.com). Roberto also offers Siena walks and multiday tours.

Other Local Guides

Federica Olla, who leads walking tours of Siena, is a smart, friendly guide with a knack for creative teaching (€55/hour, mobile 338-133-9525, www.ollaeventi.com, info@ollaeventi.com).

GSO Guides Co-op is a group of 10 young professional guides who offer good tours covering Siena and all of Tuscany and Umbria (€140/half-day, €260/full day, they don't drive but can join you in your car, 10 percent discount for Rick Steves readers, www.guidesienaeoltre.com). Among them, **Stefania Fabrizi** stands out (mobile 338-640-7796, stefaniafabriziguide@gmail.com).

Walking Tours

The **TI** offers walking tours of the old town. Guides usually conduct their walks in both English and Italian (€20—pay guide directly, daily April-Oct at 11:00, 2 hours, no interiors except for the Duomo, depart from TI, Piazza del Duomo 1, tel. 0577-280-551).

Bus Tours

Aggressively utilizing commissions, a company called **My Tour** has a lock on all hotel tour-promotion space. Every hotel has a rack of their brochures, which advertise a variety of five-hour bus tours into the countryside (www.mytours.it, depart from Piazza Gramsci).

Siena City Walk

It's easy to get to know Siena on foot, and this short self-guided walk laces together its most important sights. (🎧 It's also available as a free Rick Steves audio tour.) You can do this walk as a quick orientation, or you can use it to lace together visits to the major sights (breaking the narration to tour City Hall, the Duomo, the Duomo Museum, and Santa Maria della Scala—all described in more detail under "Sights in Siena"). If you do the walk without entering the sights, it works great at night when the city is peaceful.

• *Start in the center of the main square, Il Campo, standing just below the fountain.*

Il Campo

This square is the heart of Siena, both geographically and meta-phorically—and it's worth ▲▲▲. First laid out in the 12th cen-

tury, today Il Campo is the only town square I've seen where people stretch out as if at the beach. At the flat end of its clam-shell shape is City Hall, where you can tour the Civic Museum and climb the City Tower. From there it fans out as if to create an amphitheater. Twice each summer, all eyes are on Il Campo when it hosts the famous

Palio horse races (see sidebar on page 602).

Originally, this area was just a field *(campo)* located outside the city walls (which encircled the cathedral). Bits of those original walls, which curved against today's square, can be seen above the pharmacy (the black-and-white stones, third story up, to the right as you face City Hall). In the 1200s, with the advent of the Sienese republic, the city expanded. Il Campo became its marketplace and the historic junction of Siena's various competing *contrade* (neighborhood districts). The square and its buildings are the color of the soil upon which they stand—a color known to artists and Crayola users as "Burnt Sienna."

City Hall (Palazzo Pubblico), with its looming tower, dominates the square. In medieval Siena, this was the center of the city, and the whole focus of Il Campo still flows down to it.

The **City Tower** was built around 1340. At 330 feet, it's one of Italy's tallest secular towers. Medieval Siena was a proud republic, and this tower stands like an exclamation point—an architectural declaration of independence from papacy and empire. The tower's Italian nickname, Torre del Mangia, comes from a hedonistic bell-ringer who consumed his earnings like a glutton consumes food. (His chewed-up statue is just inside City Hall's courtyard, to the left as you enter.)

The open **chapel** located at the base of the tower was built in 1348 as thanks to God for ending the Black Death (after it killed more than a third of the population). These days, the chapel is used to bless Palio contestants (and to provide an open space for EMTs who stand by during the race).

You can visit the Civic Museum inside City Hall and climb the tower (see page 604).

• *Now turn around and take a closer look at the fountain in the top center of the square.*

SIENA

Fountain of Joy (Fonte Gaia)

This fountain—a copy of an early 15th-century work by Jacopo della Quercia—marks the square's high point. The joy is all about how the Sienese republic blessed its people with water. Find Lady Justice with her scales and sword (right of center), overseeing the free distribution of water to all. The Fountain of Joy still reminds locals that life in Siena is good. Notice the pigeons politely waiting their turn to tightrope gingerly down slippery spouts to slurp a drink from wolves' snouts. The relief panel on the left shows God creating Adam by helping him to his feet. It's said that this

reclining Adam (carved a century before Michelangelo's day) influenced Michelangelo when he painted his Sistine Chapel ceiling. The original fountain is exhibited indoors at Santa Maria della Scala (see page 613).

• *Leave Il Campo uphill on the widest ramp. With your back to the tower, it's at 10:00. After a few steps you reach Via di Città. Turn left and walk 100 yards uphill toward the imposing white palace with brick crenellations on top.*

Halfway there, at the first corner, notice small plaques on the first level of the building facades—these mark the neighborhood, or **contrada**. *If the flags are flying, they reinforce the point. You are stepping from the* contrada *of the Forest* (Selva) *into the* contrada *of the Eagle* (Aquila). *Notice also the once mighty and foreboding medieval* **tower house**. *Towers once soared all around town, but they're now truncated and no longer add to the skyline—look for their bases as you walk the city.*

On the left, you reach the big...

Chigi-Saracini Palace (Palazzo Chigi-Saracini)

This old fortified noble palace is today home to a prestigious music academy, the Accademia Musicale Chigiana. If open, step into the courtyard with its photogenic well (powerful medieval families enjoyed direct connections to the city aqueduct). The walls of the loggia are decorated with the busts of Chigi-Saracini patriarchs, and the vaults are painted in the "grotesque" style popular during the Renaissance. What look like pigeonholes in the other walls are actually for scaffolding, for both construction and ongoing maintenance. The palace hosts a festival each July and August with popular concerts almost nightly, international talent, and affordable tickets (box office just off courtyard; €7 one-hour tours of the palace's library, art, and musical instruments run Mon-Sat at 11:30 plus Thu-Fri at 16:00, closed Sun, call to confirm tour is

being offered in English; Via di Città 89, tel. 0577-22091, www.
chigiana.it).

• *Continue up the hill on Via di Città to the next big intersection. As you
walk, notice how strict rules protect the look of exteriors. Many families
live in each building, but all shutters are the same color. Inside, apartments can be modern, and expensive—some of the priciest in Italy.*

Quattro Cantoni

The intersection known as Quattro Cantoni (the four corners) offers a delightful perch from which to study the city. The modern
column (from 1996) with a Carrara marble she-wolf on top functions as a flag holder for the *contrada*. You are still in the Eagle
district (see the fountain and the corner plaque)—but beware. Just
one block up the street, a ready-to-pounce panther—from the rival
neighboring district—awaits.

Only the very rich could afford stone residences. The fancy
buildings here hide their economical brick construction behind a
stucco veneer. The stone tower on this corner had only one door—
30 feet above street level and reached by ladder, which could be
pulled up as necessary. Within a few doors, you'll find a classy bar,
an elegant grocery store, and a *gelateria*.

Take a little side-trip, venturing up Via di San Pietro. Interesting stops include the window with Palio video clips playing (at
#1), Simon and Paula's art shop with delightful Palio and *contrade*
knickknacks (#5), a weaver's shop (#7), La Vecchia Latteria *gelateria* (#10), an art gallery (#11), and four enticing little osterias. After
a block you'll reach the best art museum in town, the **Pinacoteca**
(for details on its interior, see page 605).

• *Back at the Four Corners, head up Via del Capitano, passing another
massive Chigi family palace (bankers sure know how to get their hands
on people's money) to the cathedral and Piazza del Duomo. Find a shady
seat on the stone bench against the wall of the old hospital opposite the
church.*

Piazza del Duomo and the Duomo

The pair of she-wolves atop columns flanking the cathedral's facade
says it all: The church was built and paid for not by the pope but by
the people and the republic of Siena.

This 13th-century Gothic cathedral, with its striped bell
tower—Siena's ultimate tribute to the Virgin Mary—is heaped
with statues, plastered with frescoes, and paved with art. The current structure dates back to 1215, with the major decoration done
during Siena's heyday (1250-1350). The lower story, by Giovanni
Pisano (who worked from 1284 to 1297), features remnants of the
fading Romanesque style (round arches over the doors), topped
with the pointed arches of the new Gothic style that was seeping

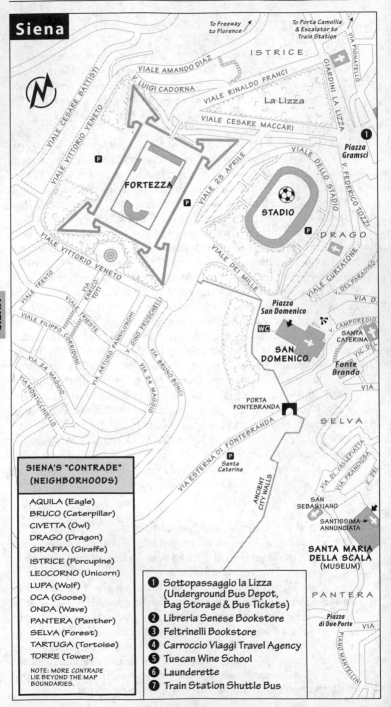

Siena

SIENA

To Freeway to Florence

To Porta Camollia & Escalator to Train Station

ISTRICE

VIALE AMANDO DIAZ

V. LUIGI CADORNA

VIALE RINALDO FRANCI

La Lizza

VIALE CESARE MACCARI

VIA PIGNATELLO

GIARDINI LA LIZZA

Piazza Gramsci

VIALE CESARE BATTISTI

VIALE VITTORIO VENETO

P

FORTEZZA

VIALE 25 APRILE

VIALE DELLO STADIO

V. FEDERICO TOZZI

P

STADIO

P

DRAGO

VIALE VITTORIO VENETO

VIA ENRICO TOTI

VIALE DEI MILLE

VIALE CURTATONE

V. DEL PARADISO

VIA D.

VIALE TRENTO

VIALE TRIESTE

VIALE FILIPPO CORRIDONI

VIA ARTURO PANNILUNGHI

V. GINO PRUSCHELLI

VIA BRUNO BONCI

VIA 24 MAGGIO

VIA MONTICCHIELLO

VIA 24 MAGGIO

Piazza San Domenico

WC

SAN DOMENICO

V. CAMPOREGIO

SANTA CATERINA

VIC. DEL

Fonte Branda

VIA

PORTA FONTEBRANDA

SELVA

VIA ESTERNA DI FONTEBRANDA

Santa Caterina

ANCIENT CITY WALLS

VIA DI ALLEPIATTA

VIA FRANCIOSA

V. DEL

SAN SEBASTIANO

SANTISSIMA ANNUNCIATA

SANTA MARIA DELLA SCALA (MUSEUM)

PANTERA

Piazza di Due Porte

VIA

PIANO MANTELLINI

SIENA'S "CONTRADE" (NEIGHBORHOODS)

AQUILA (Eagle)
BRUCO (Caterpillar)
CIVETTA (Owl)
DRAGO (Dragon)
GIRAFFA (Giraffe)
ISTRICE (Porcupine)
LEOCORNO (Unicorn)
LUPA (Wolf)
OCA (Goose)
ONDA (Wave)
PANTERA (Panther)
SELVA (Forest)
TARTUGA (Tortoise)
TORRE (Tower)

NOTE: MORE *CONTRADE* LIE BEYOND THE MAP BOUNDARIES.

① Sottopassaggio la Lizza (Underground Bus Depot, Bag Storage & Bus Tickets)
② Libreria Senese Bookstore
③ Feltrinelli Bookstore
④ Carroccio Viaggi Travel Agency
⑤ Tuscan Wine School
⑥ Launderette
⑦ Train Station Shuttle Bus

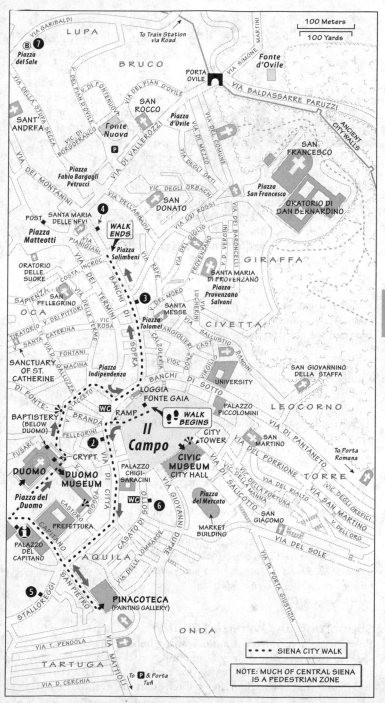

in from France. The upper half, in full-blown frilly Gothic, was designed and built a century later.

The six-story bell tower (c. 1315) looks even taller, thanks to an optical illusion: The white marble stripes get narrower toward the top, making the upper part seem farther away.

The interior is a Renaissance riot of striped columns, remarkably intricate inlaid-marble floors, a Michelangelo statue, evocative Bernini sculptures, and the amazing Piccolomini Library. (If you want to enter now, you'll need a ticket from the booth around to the right; for a self-guided tour of the interior, see page 606.)

Facing the cathedral is Santa Maria della Scala, a huge building that housed pilgrims and, until the 1990s, was used as a hospital. Its labyrinthine 12th-century cellars—carved out of volcanic tuff and finished with brick—go down several floors, and during medieval times were used to store supplies for the hospital upstairs. Today, the exhibit-filled hospital and cellars can be a welcome refuge from the hot streets (for details on visiting its interior, see page 613).

Grand as Siena's cathedral is, it's actually the rump of a failed vision. After rival republic Florence began its magnificent cathedral (1296), proud Siena planned to build an even bigger one, the biggest in all Christendom. Walk around to the right of the church and find the unfinished wall with see-through windows (circa 1330). From here you can envision the audacity of this vision—today's cathedral would have been just a transept. But the vision underestimated the complexity of constructing such a building without enough land. That, coupled with the devastating effects of the 1348 plague, killed the city's ability and will to finish the project. Many Sienese saw the Black Death as a sign from God, punishing them for their pride. They canceled their plans and humbly faded into the background of Tuscan history.

• *Walk to the rear of the church (past the ticket office for the church complex and the Duomo Museum) and pause at the top of the marble stairs leading down. The Duomo Museum (to your right) houses the church's art (see page 610).*

Supporting an Oversized Church

From here, look down the stairs leading behind the church and see the architect's quandary. The church sticks out high above the lower street level. Partway down the stairs is the Crypt, and below that is the Baptistery. Each is an integral part of the foundation for the oversized structure. (Both the Crypt and the Baptistery are worth entering; see page 612.)

• *Descend the stairs, nicknamed "The Steps of St. Catherine," as she would have climbed them each day on her walk from home to the hospital. Below the Baptistery, jog right, then left, and through a tunnel down Via di Diacceto. Pause for a beautiful view of the towering brick Dominican church in the distance on the left. Then continue straight up the lane until you reach the next big square.*

Piazza Indipendenza

This square celebrates the creation of a unified Italy (1860) with a 19th-century loggia sporting busts of the first two Italian kings. Stacking history on history, the neo-Renaissance loggia is backed by a Gothic palace and an older medieval tower.

• *Head right downhill one block (on Via delle Terme), back to the grand Via di Città, and take a few steps to the left to see another, fancier loggia.*

Loggia della Mercanzia

This Gothic-Renaissance loggia was built about 1420 as a kind of headquarters for the union of merchants (it's just above Il Campo). Siena's nobility purchased it, and eventually it became the clubhouse of the local elites. To this day, it's a private, ritzy, and notoriously out-of-step-with-the-times men's club. The "Gli Uniti" above the door is a "let's stick together" declaration.

• *From here, steep steps lead down to Il Campo, but we'll go left and uphill on Via Banchi di Sopra. Pause at the intersection of…*

Via Banchi di Sopra and Via Banchi di Sotto

These main drags are named "upper row of banks" and "lower row of banks." They were once lined with market tables *(banchi),* and vendors paid rent to the city for a table's position along the street. If the owner of a *banco* neglected to pay up, thugs came along and literally broke *(rotto)* his table. It is from this practice—*banco rotto,* broken table—that we get the English word "bankrupt."

In medieval times, these streets were part of the Via Francigena, the main thoroughfare linking Rome with northern Europe. Today, strollers—out each evening for their *passeggiata*—fill Via Banchi di Sopra. Join the crowd, strolling past Siena's finest shops.

A block or so farther up the street, Piazza Tolomei faces the imposing Tolomei family palace (now an imposing bank). This is a center for the Owl *contrada.* The column in the square, topped by

Siena's *Contrade* and the Palio

Siena's 17 historic neighborhoods, or *contrade,* each with a parish church, well or fountain, and square, still play an active role in the life of the city. Each is represented by a mascot (porcupine, unicorn, wolf, etc.) and unique colors worn proudly by residents.

Contrada pride is evident year-round in Siena's parades and colorful banners, lamps, and wall plaques. If you hear the thunder of distant drumming, run to it for some medieval action—there's a good chance it'll feature flag throwers. Buy a scarf in *contrada* colors, and join in the merriment of these lively neighborhood festivals.

Contrade rivalries are most visible twice a year—on July 2 and August 16—during the city's world-famous horse race, the **Palio di Siena.** Ten of the 17 neighborhoods compete (chosen by rotation and lot), hurling themselves with medieval abandon into several days of trial races and traditional revelry. Jockeys—usually from out of town—are considered hired guns, no better than paid mercenaries. Bets are placed on which *contrada* will win...and lose. Despite the shady behind-the-scenes dealing, on the big day the horses are taken into their *contrada*'s church to be blessed. ("Go and return victorious," says the priest.) It's considered a sign of luck if a horse leaves droppings in the church.

On the evening of the race, Il Campo is stuffed to the brim with locals and tourists. Dirt is brought in and packed down to create the track's surface, while mattresses pad the walls of surrounding buildings. The most treacherous spots are the sharp corners, where many a rider has bitten the dust.

Picture the scene: Ten snorting horses and their nervous

the she-wolf, is for *contrada* announcements of births, deaths, parties, festivals, and so on.

• *Continue on Via Banchi di Sopra to Piazza Salimbeni; this gets my vote for Siena's finest stretch of palaces.*

Piazza Salimbeni

The next square, Piazza Salimbeni, is dominated by Monte dei Paschi, the head office of a bank founded in 1472. It's amazing to think this bank has been in business on this square for over 500 years. Originally a kind of community bank for common people, in this generation, Monte dei Paschi's image has sunk to become the poster child for Italian bank scandals. Notice the Fort Knox-style base

riders line up near the pharmacy (on the west side of the square) to await the starting signal. Then they race like crazy while spectators wave the scarves of their neighborhoods.

Every possible vantage point and perch is packed with people straining to see the action. One lap around the course is about a third of a mile (350 meters); three laps make a full circuit. In this no-holds-barred race—which lasts just over a minute—a horse can win even without its rider (jockeys ride precariously without saddles and often fall off the horses' sweaty backs).

When the winner crosses the line, 1/17th of Siena—the prevailing neighborhood—goes berserk. Winners receive a *palio* (banner), typically painted by a local artist and always featuring the Virgin Mary (the race is dedicated to her). But the true prizes are proving that your *contrada* is *numero uno,* and mocking your losing rivals.

All over town, sketches and posters depict the Palio. This is not some folkloric event—it's a real medieval moment. If you're packed onto the square with 60,000 people, all hungry for victory, you may not see much, but you'll feel it. Bleacher and balcony seats are expensive, but it's free to join the masses in the square. Go with an empty bladder as there are no WCs, and be prepared to surrender any sense of personal space.

While the actual Palio packs the city, you can more easily see the horse-race trials—called *prove*—on any of the three days before the main event (usually at 9:00 and after 19:00, free seats in bleachers). For more information, visit www.ilpalio.org.

of the building. The statue in the center honors Sallustio Antonio Bandini. His claim to fame: He invented the concept of collateral.

Directly across from Piazza Salimbeni, the steep little lane called Costa dell'Incrociata leads straight (down and then up) to the Church of San Dominico (it's worth the hike; see page 614). Also nearby (behind the cute green newsstand) is the most elegant grocery store in town, Consorzio Agrario di Siena. It's like a museum of local edibles (for more on this store, see page 625).

• *With this walk under your belt, you've got the lay of the land. The city is ready for further exploration—the sights associated with City Hall and the Duomo are all just a few minutes away. Enjoy delving deeper into Siena.*

Sights in Siena

IL CAMPO AND NEARBY

The gorgeous red-brick square known as Il Campo—worth
▲▲▲—is the best in Italy (for more on the square itself, see page
595). It's also home to City Hall (with the Civic Museum and City
Tower) and other sights.

▲▲Civic Museum (Museo Civico)

Siena's City Hall (Palazzo Pubblico), still the seat of city government, symbolizes a republic independent from the pope and the
Holy Roman Emperor. It also represents a rising secular society,
one that appeared first in Tuscany and then spread throughout Europe in the Renaissance. City Hall also has a fine and manageable
museum that displays a good sampling of Sienese art, including Siena's first fresco (with a groundbreaking down-to-earth depiction
of the Madonna). It's worth strolling through the dramatic halls
to see fascinating frescoes and portraits extolling Siena's greats,
saints, and the city-as-utopia, when this proud town understandably considered itself the vanguard of Western civilization.

Cost and Hours: Museum-€9, €13 combo-ticket with Santa
Maria della Scala, €20 combo-ticket includes City Tower and Santa

Maria della Scala (valid 2 days), ticket
office is straight ahead as you enter
City Hall courtyard, open daily 10:00-
19:00, Nov-mid March until 18:00,
last entry 45 minutes before closing,
videoguide-€5 in bookshop, tel. 0577-
292-614, www.comune.siena.it.

Visiting the Museum: Start in the
Sala del Risorgimento, with dramatic
scenes of the 19th-century unification
of Italy (surrounded by statues that
don't seem to care). Passing through
the chapel, where the city's governors
and bureaucrats prayed, enter the Sala
del Mappamondo. On opposite ends of the room, you'll find two
large frescoes. The beautiful *Maestà* (*Enthroned Virgin*, 1315), by
Siena's great Simone Martini (c. 1280-1344), was the secular counterpart to Duccio's *Maestà* (then in the Duomo, now in the Duomo
Museum). This is a groundbreaking work. It's Siena's first fresco
showing a Madonna not in a faraway, gold-leaf heaven, but under
the blue sky of a real space that we inhabit. Facing the *Maestà* is the
famous *Equestrian Portrait of Guidoriccio da Fogliano* (1330; long attributed to Simone Martini, but more recently art historians have

debated its authorship), which depicts a mercenary commander surveying the imposing castle that his armies have just conquered.

Next is the Sala della Pace—where the Council of Nine, who ruled Siena from 1287 to 1355, met. Looking down on the oligarchy during their meetings was a fascinating fresco series showing the *Effects of Good and Bad Government,* by Ambrogio Lorenzetti (1337-1340). Compare the whistle-while-you-work happiness of the utopian community ruled by the utopian government (in the better-preserved fresco) against the crime, devastation, and societal mayhem of a community ruled by politicians with more typical values. The message: Without justice, there can be no prosperity.

You can cap your visit by climbing up to the loggia for a sweeping view of the city and its surroundings. (For a less impressive version of this view, you could skip the stairs and simply peek behind the curtains in the Sala della Pace.)

Other Sights on or near Il Campo
▲City Tower (Torre del Mangia)

The tower's nearly 400 steps get pretty skinny at the top, but the reward is one of Italy's best views. For more on the tower, see my "Siena City Walk," earlier.

Cost and Hours: €10, €20 combo-ticket with Civic Museum and Santa Maria della Scala, daily March-mid-Oct 10:00-19:00, mid-Oct-Feb until 16:00, last entry 45 minutes before closing, closed in rain, free and mandatory bag check.

Crowd Alert: Admission is limited to 50 people at a time. Wait at the bottom of the stairs for the green *Avanti* light. Try to avoid midday crowds (up to an hour wait at peak times).

▲Pinacoteca

If you're into medieval art, you'll likely find this quiet, uncrowded, colorful museum delightful. The museum walks you through Siena's art chronologically, from the 12th through the 16th century, when a revolution in realism was percolating in Tuscany.

Cost and Hours: €4, Tue-Sat 8:15-19:15, Sun-Mon 9:00-13:00, free and mandatory bag check. From Il Campo, walk out Via di Città and go left on Via San Pietro to #29; tel. 0577-281-161, www.pinacotecanazionale.siena.it.

Visiting the Museum: In general, the collection lets you follow the evolution of painting styles from Byzantine to Gothic, then to International Gothic, and finally to Renaissance.

Long after Florentine art went realistic, the Sienese embraced a timeless, otherworldly style glittering with lots of gold. But Sienese art features more than just paintings. In this city of proud craftsmen, the gilding and carpentry of the frames almost compete with the actual paintings. The exquisite attention to detail gives a glimpse into the wealth of the 13th and 14th centuries, Siena's Golden Age. The woven silk and gold clothing you'll see was worn by the very people who once walked these halls, when this was a private mansion (appreciate the colonnaded courtyard).

The core of the collection is on the second floor, in Rooms 1-19. Works by Duccio di Buoninsegna (the artist of the *Maestà* in the Duomo Museum) feature groundbreaking innovations that are subtle: less gold-leaf background, fewer gold creases in robes, translucent garments, inlaid-marble thrones, and a more human Mary and Jesus. Notice that the Madonna-and-Bambino pose is eerily identical in each version. *St. Augustine of Siena*, by Duccio's assistant, Simone Martini (who did the *Maestà* and possibly the Guidoriccio frescoes in the Civic Museum), sets the saint's life in realistic Sienese streets, buildings, and landscapes. In each panel, the saint pops out at the oddest (difficult to draw) angles to save the day.

Also look for religious works by the hometown Lorenzetti brothers (Ambrogio is best known for the secular masterpiece, the *Effects of Good and Bad Government*, in the Civic Museum). *Città sul Mare (City by the Sea)* and *Castello in Riva al Lago (Castle on the Lakeshore)* feature a strange, medieval landscape Cubism. Notice the weird, melancholy light that captures the sense of the Dark Ages.

Several colorful rooms on the first floor are dedicated to Domenico Beccafumi (1486-1551), who designed many of the Duomo's inlaid pavement panels (including *Slaughter of the Innocents*). With strong bodies, twisting poses, and dramatic gestures, Beccafumi's works epitomize the Mannerist style.

CATHEDRAL AREA
▲▲▲Duomo

Siena's 13th-century cathedral and striped bell tower are one of the most illustrious examples of Romanesque-Gothic style in Italy. This ornate but surprisingly secular shrine to the Virgin Mary is slathered with colorful art inside and out, from inlaid-marble floors to stained-glass windows. The cathedral's interior showcases the work of the greatest sculptors of every era—Pisano, Donatello, Michelangelo, and Bernini—and the Piccolomini Library features a series of 15th-century frescoes chronicling the adventures of Siena's philanderer-turned-pope, Aeneas Piccolomini.

Cost: €4 includes cathedral and Piccolomini Library, buy ticket at Duomo Museum entrance (facing the cathedral entry, the museum is 100 yards to the right, near the south transept). There's talk of moving the ticket office—if it's not here when you visit, check across the square, on the side facing the Duomo facade.

To add the Duomo Museum, Crypt, and Baptistery, consider the €13 Opa Si combo-ticket; to add an escorted visit into the dome and rooftop (described below), pay €20 for the Opa Si Plus combo-ticket.

Hours: March-Oct Mon-Sat 10:30-19:00, Sun 13:30-18:00; Nov-Feb closes daily at 17:30. Tel. 0577-286-300, www.operaduomo.siena.it.

Avoiding Lines: Check the line to get into the Duomo before buying tickets—if there's a long wait, you can pay an extra €1 for a "reservation" that lets you skip the line (available at the "reserved/fast entrance" queue).

Tours: The €8 videoguide covers all of the sights included in the combo-ticket and is informative but dry; I'd stick with the commentary in this chapter.

Going to Church: It's free to enter the cathedral if you are attending Mass; use the entrance to the right of the main one (Mon-Sat at 9:00 and 10:00, Sun at 8:00, 11:00, 12:15, and 18:30).

Dress Code: Modest dress is required, but stylish paper ponchos are provided for the inappropriately clothed.

Cathedral Roof Visit: The Opa Si Plus combo-ticket includes all of the cathedral sights plus a 30-minute Porta del Cielo ("Heaven's Gate") visit to the dome's cupola and roof (timed-entry ticket, escorted visits of 18 people go each half-hour, March-Oct Mon-Sat 10:30-18:00, Sun 13:30-17:00, less frequent off-season, tel. 0577-286-300 for advance reservations).

◑ Self-Guided Tour

Grab a spot on a stone bench opposite the entry to take in this architectural festival of green, white, pink, and gold. The Duomo sits atop Siena's highest point, with one of the most extravagant facades in all of Europe. Like a medieval altarpiece, the facade is divided into sections, each frame filled with patriarchs and prophets, studded with roaring gargoyles, and topped with prickly pinnacles (for more about the facade, see page 597).

• *Step inside, putting yourself in the mindset of a pilgrim as you take in this trove of religious art.*

Nave: The heads of 172 popes—who reigned from the time of St. Peter to the 12th century—peer down from above, looking over the fine inlaid art on the floor. With a forest of striped columns, a coffered dome, a large stained-glass window at the far end (it's a copy—the original is viewable up close in the Duomo Museum), and an art gallery's worth of early Renaissance art, this is one busy interior. If you look closely at the popes, you'll see the same four faces repeated over and over.

For almost two centuries (1373-1547), 40 artists paved the marble floor with scenes from the Old Testament, allegories, and intricate patterns.

The series starts near the entrance with historical allegories; the larger, more elaborate scenes surrounding the altar are mostly stories from the Old Testament. Many of the floor panels are roped off—and occasionally even covered—to prevent further wear and tear. The second pavement panel from the entrance depicts Siena as a **she-wolf.** The proud city of Siena is the center of the Italian universe, orbited by such lesser lights as Roma, Florentia (Florence), and Pisa. The fourth pavement panel from the entrance is the **Fortune Panel,** with Lady Luck (lower right) parachuting down to earth, where she teeters back and forth on a ball and a tipsy boat. The lesson? Fortune is an unstable foundation for life. On the right wall hangs a dim **painting of St. Catherine** (fourth from entrance). Siena's homegrown saint had a vision in which she mystically married Christ.

• *On the opposite wall is a marble altarpiece decorated with statues.*

Piccolomini Altar: This was designed for the tomb of the Sienese-born Pope Pius III (born Francesco Piccolomini), but was

never used. The altar is most interesting for its statues: one by Michelangelo and three by his students. Michelangelo was originally contracted to do 15 statues, but another sculptor had started the marble blocks, and Michelangelo's heart was never in the project. He personally finished only the figure of St. Paul (lower right, clearly more interesting than the bland, bored popes above him).

• *Now grab a seat under the dome.*

Dome and Surrounding Area: The dome sits on a 12-sided base, but its "coffered" ceiling is actually a painted illusion. Get oriented to the array of sights we'll see by thinking of the church floor as a big 12-hour clock. You're the middle, and the altar is high noon: You'll find the *Slaughter of the Innocents* roped off on the floor at 10 o'clock, Pisano's pulpit between two pillars at 11 o'clock, a copy of Duccio's round stained-glass window at 12 o'clock, Bernini's chapel at 3 o'clock, the Piccolomini Altar at 7 o'clock, the Piccolomini Library at 8 o'clock, and a Donatello statue at 9 o'clock.

Pisano's Pulpit: The octagonal Carrara marble pulpit (1268) rests on the backs of lions, symbols of Christianity triumphant.

Like the lions, the Church eats its catch (devouring paganism) and nurses its cubs. The seven relief panels tell the life of Christ in rich detail. The pulpit is the work of Nicola Pisano (c. 1220-1278), the "Giotto of sculpture," whose revival of classical forms (columns, sarcophagus-like relief panels) signaled the coming Renaissance. His son Giovanni (c. 1240-1319) carved many of the panels, mixing his dad's classicism and realism with the decorative detail and curvy lines of French Gothic.

Duccio's Stained-Glass Rose Window: This is a copy of the original window (now in the Duomo Museum). The famous rose window was created in 1288 and dedicated to the Virgin Mary (description on page 611).

Slaughter of the Innocents: This pavement panel shows Herod (left), sitting enthroned amid Renaissance arches, ordering the massacre of all babies to prevent the coming of the promised Messiah. It's a chaotic scene of angry soldiers, grieving mothers, and dead babies, reminding locals that a republic ruled by a tyrant will always experience misery.

• *Step into the chapel just behind you (next to the Piccolomini Library) to see...*

St. John the Baptist Statue: The rugged saint in his famous rags stands in a quiet chapel. Donatello, the aging Florentine sculptor whose style was now considered passé in Florence, came here to build bronze doors for the church (similar to Ghiberti's in Florence). Donatello didn't complete the door project, but he did finish this bronze statue (1457). Notice the cherubs high above in the dome, playfully dangling their feet.

• *Cross the church. Directly opposite find the Chigi Chapel, also known as the...*

Chapel of the *Madonna del Voto*: To understand why Bernini is considered the greatest Baroque sculptor, step into this sumptuous chapel (designed in the early 1660s for Fabio Chigi, a.k.a. Pope Alexander VII). Move up to the altar and look back at the **two Bernini statues:** Mary Magdalene in a state of spiritual ecstasy and St. Jerome playing the crucifix like a violinist lost in beautiful music.

The painting over the altar is the *Madonna del Voto,* a Madonna and Child adorned with a real crown of gold and jewels (painted by a Sienese master in the mid-13th century). In typical medieval fashion, the scene is set in the golden light of heaven. Mary has the almond eyes, long fingers, and golden folds in her robe that are found in orthodox icons of the time. Still, this Mary tilts her head and looks out sympathetically, ready to listen to the prayers of the faithful. This is the Mary to whom the Palio is dedicated, dear to the hearts of the Sienese. In thanks, they give **offerings** of silver hearts and medallions, many of which now hang on the wall just to the left as you exit the chapel

• *Cross back to the other side of the church to find the...*

Piccolomini Library: Brilliantly frescoed, the library captures the exuberant, optimistic spirit of the 1400s, when humanism and the Renaissance were born. The never-restored frescoes look nearly as vivid now as the day they were finished 550 years ago. The painter Pinturicchio (c. 1454-1513) was hired to celebrate the life of one of Siena's hometown boys—a man many call "the first humanist," Aeneas Piccolomini (1405-1464), who became Pope Pius II. Each of the 10 scenes is framed with an arch, as if Pinturicchio were opening a window onto the spacious 3-D world we inhabit.

The library also contains intricately decorated, illuminated music scores and a statue (a Roman copy of a Greek original) of the Three Graces, who almost seem to dance to the beat. The oddly huge sheepskin sheets of music are from the days before individual hymnals—they had to be big so that many singers could read the music from a distance. Appreciate the fine painted decorations on the music—the gold-leaf highlights, the blue tones from expensive ultramarine (made from precious lapis lazuli), and the miniature figures. All of this exquisite detail was lovingly crafted by Benedictine monks for the glory of God.

• *Exit the Duomo and make a U-turn to the left, walking alongside the church to Piazza Jacopo della Quercia.*

Unfinished Church: Had the massive church Siena envisioned been built, the nave would be where the piazza is today. Worship-

pers would have entered the church from the far end of the piazza through the unfinished wall. (Look way up at the highest part of the wall. That viewpoint is accessible from inside the Duomo Museum.) Some of the nave's green-and-white-striped columns were built, but are now filled in with a brick wall. White stones in the pavement mark where a row of pillars would have been. Look through the unfinished entrance facade, note blue sky where the stained-glass windows would have been, and ponder the struggles, triumphs, and failures of the human spirit.

▲▲Duomo Museum
Located in a corner of the Duomo's grand but unfinished extension

(to the right as you face the main facade), Siena's most enjoyable museum (Museo dell'Opera e Panorama) was built to house the cathedral's art. Stand eye-to-eye with the saints and angels who once languished, unknown, in the church's upper reaches (where copies are found today).

Cost and Hours: €7, daily March-Oct 10:30-19:00, Nov-Feb until 17:30, videoguide-€4 (€6/2 people) but you'll do fine with just the commentary in this listing, tel. 0577-286-300, www.operaduomo.siena.it.

Visiting the Museum: Start on the ground floor, which houses the church's original statues, mainly from the facade and exterior. After descending a few steps, turn your back on the hall of statues and a wrought-iron gate. You're now face-to-face with Donatello's *Madonna and Child.* In this round, carved relief, a slender and ten-

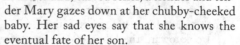

der Mary gazes down at her chubby-cheeked baby. Her sad eyes say that she knows the eventual fate of her son.

On the opposite side of the room is Duccio's stained-glass window. Until recently, this splendid original window was located above and behind the Duomo's altar. Now the church has a copy, and art lovers can enjoy a close-up look at this masterpiece. The **rose window**—20 feet across, made in 1288—is dedicated (like the church and the city itself) to the Virgin Mary.

The work is by Siena's most famous artist, Duccio di Buoninsegna (c. 1255-1319). Duccio combined elements from rigid Byzantine icons (Mary's almond-shaped bubble, called a *mandorla,* and the full-frontal saints that flank her) with a budding sense of 3-D realism (the throne turned at a three-quarter angle to simulate depth, with angels behind).

Upstairs awaits a private audience with Duccio's **Maestà** *(Enthroned Virgin,* 1311). The panels in this room were once part of the Duomo's main altarpiece. Grab a seat and study one of the great pieces of medieval art. Although the former altarpiece was disassembled (and the frame was lost), most of the pieces are displayed here, with the front side (*Maestà,* with Mary and saints; pronounced my-STAH) at one end of the room and the back side (26 Passion panels) at the other.

The painting was revolutionary for the time in its sheer size and opulence, and in Duccio's budding realism, which broke standard conventions. Duccio, at the height of his powers, used every innovative arrow in his quiver. He replaced the standard gold-leaf background (symbolizing heaven) with a gold, intricately patterned curtain draped over the throne. Mary's blue robe opens to reveal her body, and the curve of her knee suggests real anatomy beneath the robe. Baby Jesus wears a delicately transparent garment. Their faces are modeled with light—a patchwork of bright flesh and shadowy valleys, as if lit from the left (a technique he likely learned from Giotto, his contemporary, during a visit to Florence).

The flip side of the altarpiece featured 26 smaller panels—the medieval equivalent of book pages—showing colorful scenes from the **Passion of Christ.**

• *Return to the stairs and continue up. Eventually you'll climb down the steps and then up about 40 claustrophobic spiral stairs to the first view-point. You can continue up another 100 steps of a similar spiral staircase to reach the very top.*

Panorama dal Facciatone: Standing on the wall from this high point in the city, you're rewarded with a stunning view of Siena...and an interesting perspective.

Look toward the Duomo and remember this: To outdo Florence, Siena had planned to enlarge this cathedral by turning it into a transept and constructing an enormous nave. You're standing on top of what would have been the new entrance facade. Had the church been completed, you'd be looking straight down the nave toward the altar.

Other Cathedral-Area Sights
▲Baptistery (Battistero)

This richly adorned and quietly tucked-away cave is worth a look for its cool tranquility and exquisite art, including an ornately painted vaulted ceiling. The highlight is the baptismal font designed by Jacopo della Quercia and adorned with bronze panels and angels by Quercia, Ghiberti, and Donatello. It dates from the 1420s, the start of the Renaissance.

Cost and Hours: €4, daily 10:30-19:00, Nov-Feb until 17:30.

Crypt (Cripta)

The cathedral "crypt" is archaeologically important. The site of a small 12th-century Romanesque church, it was filled in with dirt a century after its creation to provide a foundation for the huge church that sits atop it today. Recently excavated (with modern metal supports from the 1990s), the several rediscovered rooms show off what are likely the oldest frescoes in town (well-described in English).

Cost and Hours: €6, €8 during special exhibitions, daily

10:30-19:00, Nov-Feb until 17:30, entrance near the top of the stairs between the Baptistery and Duomo Museum.

▲Santa Maria della Scala

This museum, opposite the Duomo, operated for centuries as a hospital, foundling home, and pilgrim lodging. Many of those activities are visible in the 15th-century frescoes of its main hall, the Pellegrinaio. Today, the hospital and its cellars are filled with fascinating exhibits (well-described in English).

Cost and Hours: €9, €13 combo-ticket with Civic Museum, €20 combo-ticket includes the Civic Museum and Tower (valid 2 days); mid-March-mid-Oct daily 10:30-18:30; closes earlier off-season; tel. 0577-534-571, www.santamariadellascala.com.

Visiting the Museum: It's easy to get lost in this gigantic complex, so stay focused on the main attractions—the fancily frescoed Pellegrinaio Hall (ground floor), most of the original *Fountain of Joy* and some of the most ancient Byzantine reliquaries in existence (first basement), and the Etruscan collection in the Archaeological Museum (second basement), where the Sienese took refuge during WWII bombing.

From the entrance, go left into the second room to reach the Pellegrinaio—the long room with the colorful frescoes. The sumptuously frescoed walls of **Pellegrinaio Hall**—originally a reception hall for visiting pilgrims, then a hospital—show medieval Siena's innovative health care and social welfare system in action (by Sienese painters, c. 1442, wonderfully described in English). Starting in the 11th century, the hospital nursed the sick and cared for abandoned children, as is vividly portrayed in these frescoes. The good works paid off as bequests and donations poured in, creating the wealth that's evident throughout this building. The video, projected on the left side of the wall, gives interesting insight into medieval life depicted in the scenes. Head down the stairs, then continue straight into the darkened rooms with pieces of Siena's landmark fountain—follow signs to *La Fonte Gaia*.

An engaging exhibit explains Jacopo della Quercia's early 15th-century **Fountain of Joy** (Fonte Gaia)—and displays the disassembled pieces of the original fountain itself. In the 19th century, after serious deterioration, the ornate fountain was dismantled and plaster casts were made. (These casts formed the replica that graces Il Campo today.) Here you'll see the eroded original panels paired with their restored casts, along with the actual statues that once stood on the edges of the fountain.

To visit the reliquaries, retrace your steps and follow the signs for *Il Tesoro*. Many of these **Byzantine reliquaries** are made of gold, silver, and precious stones. Legend has it that some were owned by St. Helen, Constantine's mother. They were "donated"

SIENA

(around 1350) to the hospital shortly after the plague that decimated the city (and the rest of Europe), since the sale of reliquaries was forbidden.

Now, descend into the cavernous second basement. Under the groin vaults of the **Archaeological Museum,** you're alone with piles of ancient Etruscan stuff excavated from tombs dating centuries before Christ (displayed in another labyrinthine exhibit). You'll see terra-cotta funeral urns for ashes (the design was often a standard body with the heads personalized) and piles of domestic artifacts from the 8th to the 5th century B.C.

SAN DOMENICO AREA
Church of San Domenico
This huge brick church is worth a quick look. Spacious and plain (except for the colorful flags of the city's 17 *contrade*), the Gothic interior fits the austere philosophy of the Dominicans and invites meditation on the thoughts and deeds of St. Catherine. Halfway up the church on the right, find a copper bust of St. Catherine (for four centuries it contained her skull), a small case housing her thumb, and a page from her personal devotional book. In the chapel, surrounded with candles, you'll see Catherine's head (a clay mask around her skull with her actual teeth showing through) atop the altar.

Cost and Hours: Free, daily 9:00-18:00, shorter hours off-season, www.basilicacateriniana.com.

Sanctuary of St. Catherine (Santuario di Santa Caterina)
Step into the cool and peaceful site of Catherine's home. Siena remembers its favorite hometown gal, a simple, unschooled, but mystically devout soul who helped convince the pope to return from France to Rome. Pilgrims have visited this place since 1464, and architects and artists have greatly embellished what was probably once a humble home (her family worked as wool dyers). You'll see paintings throughout showing scenes from her life.

Cost and Hours: Free, daily 9:00-18:00, Chapel of the Crucifixion closed from 12:30-15:00 but church stays open, a few downhill blocks toward the center from San Domenico—follow signs to *Santuario di Santa Caterina*—at Costa di Sant'Antonio 6.

Sleep Code

Hotels are classified based on the average price of a standard double room with breakfast in high season.

$$$$	**Splurge:** Most rooms over €170
$$$	**Pricier:** €130-170
$$	**Moderate:** €90-130
$	**Budget:** €50-90
¢	**Backpacker:** Under €50
RS%	Rick Steves discount

Unless otherwise noted, credit cards are accepted, hotel staff speak basic English, and free Wi-Fi is available. Comparison-shop by checking prices at several hotels (on each hotel's own website, on a booking site, or by email). For the best deal, *book directly with the hotel*. Ask for a discount if paying in cash; if the listing includes **RS%,** request a Rick Steves discount.

Sleeping in Siena

Finding a room in Siena is tough during Easter (April 16 in 2017) or the Palio (July 2 and Aug 16). Many hotels won't take reservations until the end of May for the Palio, and even then they might require a four-night stay. While day-tripping tour groups turn the town into a Gothic amusement park in midsummer, Siena is basically yours in the evenings and off-season.

Part of Siena's charm is its lively, festive character—this means that all hotels can be plagued with noise, even (and sometimes especially) the hotels in the pedestrian-only zone. If tranquility is important for your sanity, ask for a room that's off the street, or consider staying at one of the recommended places outside the center. If your hotel doesn't provide breakfast, eat at a bar on Il Campo or near your hotel.

BIGGER HOTELS NEAR IL CAMPO

$$$$ Pensione Palazzo Ravizza is elegant, friendly, and well-run, with 39 rooms and an aristocratic feel—fitting, as it was once the luxurious residence of a noble. Guests enjoy a peaceful garden set on a dramatic bluff, along with a Steinway in the upper lounge (family rooms, rooms in back overlook countryside, air-con, elevator, Via Piano dei Mantellini 34, tel. 0577-280-462, www.palazzoravizza.it, bureau@palazzoravizza.it). As parking here is free and the hotel is easily walkable from the center, this is a particularly good value for drivers.

$$$ Hotel Duomo has 20 spacious but dated rooms (some with Duomo views—request when booking), a picnic-friendly roof terrace, and a bizarre floor plan (family rooms, elevator with some stairs, air-con, expensive pay parking; Via di Stalloreggi 38, tel. 0577-289-088, www.hotelduomo.it, booking@hotelduomo.it, Alessandro). If you arrive by train, take a taxi or ride bus #3 to the Porta Tufi stop, just a few minutes' walk from the hotel.

SIMPLE PLACES NEAR IL CAMPO

Most of these listings are forgettable but well-priced, and just a horse-wreck away from one of Italy's most wonderful civic spaces.

$$ Piccolo Hotel Etruria, with 20 simple, recently redecorated rooms, is well-located, restful, and a fine value (RS%—use code "RSITA," cheaper single room with shared bath, family rooms, breakfast extra, air-con May-Oct only, elevator, at Via delle Donzelle 1, tel. 0577-288-088, www.hoteletruria.com, info@hoteletruria.com, friendly Leopoldo).

$ Albergo Tre Donzelle is a fine budget value with welcoming hosts and 20 homey rooms—these may be the best-value rooms in the center. Il Campo, a block away, is your terrace (cheaper rooms with shared bath, family rooms, breakfast extra, fans, no elevator; with your back to the tower, head away from Il Campo toward 2 o'clock to Via delle Donzelle 5; tel. 0577-270-390, www.tredonzelle.com, info@tredonzelle.com).

$ Hotel Cannon d'Oro, a few blocks up Via Banchi di Sopra, is a labyrinthine slumbermill renting 30 institutional, overpriced rooms (RS%, family rooms, fans, Via dei Montanini 28, tel. 0577-44321, www.cannondoro.com, info@cannondoro.com; Maurizio, Tommaso, Serge, and Rodrigo).

$ Casa Laura has eight clean, charming, well-maintained rooms, some of which have brick-and-beam ceilings (RS%, more expensive rooms with air-con, no elevator, Via Roma 3, about a 10-minute walk from Il Campo toward Porta Romana, tel. 0577-226-061, www.casalaurasiena.com, info@casalaurasiena.com).

B&BS IN THE OLD CENTER

$$ Antica Residenza Cicogna is a seven-room guesthouse with a homey elegance and an ideal location. It's warmly run by the young and charming Elisa and her friend Ilaria, who set out biscotti, vin santo, and tea for their guests in the afternoon. With artfully frescoed walls and ceilings, this is remarkably genteel for the price (air-con, no elevator, Via delle Terme 76, tel. 0577-285-613, mobile 347-007-2888, www.anticaresidenzacicogna.it, info@anticaresidenzacicogna.it).

$$ Palazzo Masi B&B, run by friendly Alizzardo and Daniela, is just below Il Campo. They rent six pleasant, spacious, antique-furnished rooms with shared common areas on the second and third floors of a restored 13th-century building (RS%, cheaper rooms with shared bath, no breakfast, no elevator; from City Hall, walk 50 yards down Via del Casato di Sotto to #29; mobile 349-600-9155, www.palazzomasi.com, info@palazzomasi.it). The place is sometimes unstaffed, so confirm your arrival time in advance.

$$ B&B Alle Due Porte is a charming little establishment renting four big rooms with sweet furniture under big medieval beams. The shared breakfast room is delightful. The manager, Egisto, is a phone call and 10-minute scooter ride away (3 rooms have air-con, Via di Stalloreggi 51, tel. 0577-287-670, mobile 368-352-3530, www.sienatur.it, soldatini@interfree.it).

$ Le Camerine di Silvia, a romantic hideaway perched near a sweeping, grassy olive grove, rents five simple rooms in a converted 16th-century building. A small breakfast terrace with fruit trees and a private hedged garden lends itself to contemplation (cash only, view room on request, no breakfast, fans, free parking nearby, Via Ettore Bastianini 1, just below recommended Pensione Palazzo Ravizza, mobile 338-761-5052 or 339-123-7687, www.lecamerinedisilvia.com, info@lecamerinedisilvia.com, Conti family).

$ B&B Siena in Centro is a clearinghouse managing 15 rooms and five apartments. Their handy office functions as a reception area; stop by here to pick up your key and be escorted. The rooms are generally spacious, quiet, and comfortable. Their website lets you visualize your options (RS%, some with air-con and others with fans, family rooms, reception open 9:00-13:30 & 15:00-22:00, Via di Stalloreggi 16, tel. 0577-48111, mobile 331-281-0136 or 347-465-9753, www.bbsienaincentro.com, info@bbsienaincentro.com, Gioia or Michela).

NEAR SAN DOMENICO CHURCH

$$$ Hotel Chiusarelli, with 48 classy rooms in a beautiful frescoed Neoclassical villa, is just outside the medieval town center on a busy street. Expect traffic noise at night—ask for a quieter room in the back, which can be guaranteed with reservation (RS%, family rooms, air-con, several free parking spots, nearby pay parking, across from San Domenico at Viale Curtatone 15, tel. 0577-280-562, www.chiusarelli.com, info@chiusarelli.com).

$$$ Hotel Villa Elda rents 11 bright and light rooms in a recently renovated villa. It's classy, stately, pricey, and run with a feminine charm (view rooms extra, air-con, no elevator, garden and view terrace, closed Nov-March, Viale Ventiquattro Maggio 10, tel. 0577-247-927, www.villaeldasiena.it, info@villaeldasiena.it).

$$ Albergo Bernini makes you part of a Sienese family in a modest, clean home with 10 traditional rooms. Giovanni, charming wife Daniela, and their daughters welcome you to their spectacular view terrace— a great spot for a glass of wine or a picnic (cheaper rooms with shared bath, family rooms, breakfast extra, fans, on the

SIENA

Siena Hotels & Restaurants

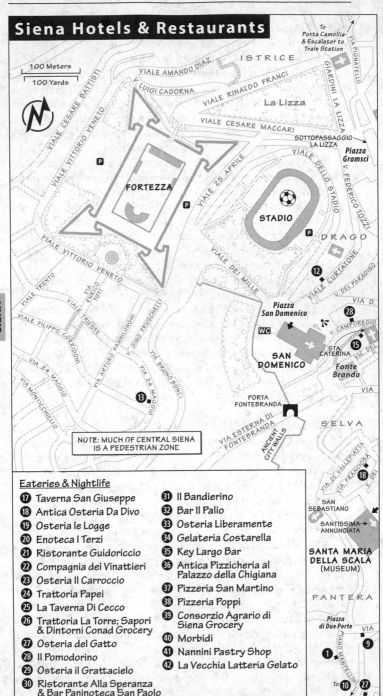

To Porta Camollia & Escalator to Train Station

VIA PIGNATELLO

ISTRICE

VIALE AMANDO DIAZ

V. LUIGI CADORNA

VIALE CESARE BATTISTI

100 Meters

100 Yards

VIALE RINALDO FRANCI

La Lizza

GIARDINI LA LIZZA

VIALE VITTORIO VENETO

VIALE CESARE MACCARI

SOTTOPASSAGGIO LA LIZZA

Piazza Gramsci

V. FEDERICO TOZZI

P

VIALE 25 APRILE

VIALE DELLO STADIO

FORTEZZA

P

STADIO

P

DRAGO

VIALE VITTORIO VENETO

VIALE DEI MILLE

VIALE CURTATONE

VIA D.

VIALE TRENTO

VIA ENRICO TOTI

VIALE TRIESTE

VIA GINO FRUSCHELLI

VIALE FILIPPO CORRIDONI

VIA ARTURO PANNILUNGHI

VIA BRUNO BONCI

12

V. DEL PARADISO

Piazza San Domenico

WC

28

V. CAMPOREGIO

VIA 24 MAGGIO

VIA 24 MAGGIO

SAN DOMENICO

STA. CATERINA

15

VIC. DEL

VIA MONTICCHIELLO

13

Fonte Branda

VIA

PORTA FONTEBRANDA

SELVA

NOTE: MUCH OF CENTRAL SIENA IS A PEDESTRIAN ZONE

VIA ESTERNA DI FONTEBRANDA

ANCIENT CITY WALLS

VIA DI VALLEPIATTA

VIA FRANCIOSA

18

V. DEL

SAN SEBASTIANO

SANTISSIMA ANNUNCIATA

Eateries & Nightlife

- ⑰ Taverna San Giuseppe
- ⑱ Antica Osteria Da Divo
- ⑲ Osteria le Logge
- ⑳ Enoteca I Terzi
- ㉑ Ristorante Guidoriccio
- ㉒ Compagnia dei Vinattieri
- ㉓ Osteria Il Carroccio
- ㉔ Trattoria Papei
- ㉕ La Taverna Di Cecco
- ㉖ Trattoria La Torre; Sapori & Dintorni Conad Grocery
- ㉗ Osteria del Gatto
- ㉘ Il Pomodorino
- ㉙ Osteria il Grattacielo
- ㉚ Ristorante Alla Speranza & Bar Paninoteca San Paolo

- ㉛ Il Bandierino
- ㉜ Bar Il Palio
- ㉝ Osteria Liberamente
- ㉞ Gelateria Costarella
- ㉟ Key Largo Bar
- ㊱ Antica Pizzicheria al Palazzo della Chigiana
- ㊲ Pizzeria San Martino
- ㊳ Pizzeria Poppi
- ㊴ Consorzio Agrario di Siena Grocery
- ㊵ Morbidi
- ㊶ Nannini Pastry Shop
- ㊷ La Vecchia Latteria Gelato

SANTA MARIA DELLA SCALA (MUSEUM)

PANTERA

Piazza di Due Porte

9

PIANO MANFREDI

1

To

10

27

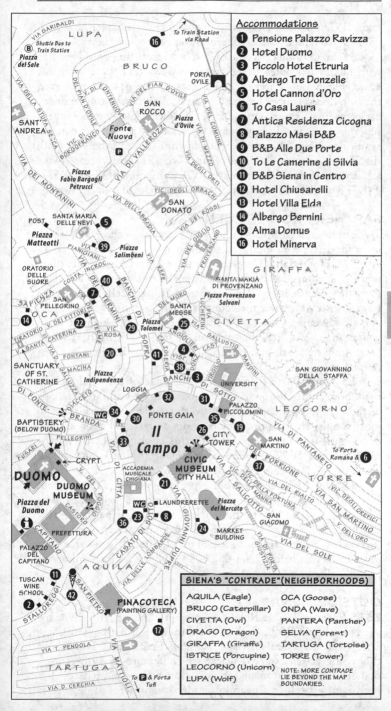

Accommodations

1. Pensione Palazzo Ravizza
2. Hotel Duomo
3. Piccolo Hotel Etruria
4. Albergo Tre Donzelle
5. Hotel Cannon d'Oro
6. To Casa Laura
7. Antica Residenza Cicogna
8. Palazzo Masi B&B
9. B&B Alle Due Porte
10. To Le Camerine di Silvia
11. B&B Siena in Centro
12. Hotel Chiusarelli
13. Hotel Villa Elda
14. Albergo Bernini
15. Alma Domus
16. Hotel Minerva

SIENA'S "CONTRADE" (NEIGHBORHOODS)

AQUILA (Eagle)
BRUCO (Caterpillar)
CIVETTA (Owl)
DRAGO (Dragon)
GIRAFFA (Giraffe)
ISTRICE (Porcupine)
LEOCORNO (Unicorn)
LUPA (Wolf)

OCA (Goose)
ONDA (Wave)
PANTERA (Panther)
SELVA (Forest)
TARTUGA (Tortoise)
TORRE (Tower)

NOTE: MORE CONTRADE
LIE BEYOND THE MAP
BOUNDARIES.

main Il Campo-San Domenico drag at Via della Sapienza 15, tel. 0577-289-047, www.albergobernini.com, hbernin@tin.it).

$ Alma Domus is a church-run hotel featuring 28 tidy rooms with quaint balconies, some fantastic views (ask for a room *con vista*), stately public rooms, and a pleasant atmosphere. However, the thin doors, echoey halls, and nearby church bells can be drawbacks, particularly on upper floors. Consider upgrading to a snazzy superior room for slightly more (RS%, family rooms, air-con, elevator; from San Domenico, walk downhill toward the view with the church on your right, turn left down Via Camporegio, make a U-turn down the brick steps to Via Camporegio 37; tel. 0577-44177, www.hotelalmadomus.it, info@hotelalmadomus.it, Louis).

FARTHER FROM THE CENTER

These options, a 10- to 20-minute walk from the center, are convenient for drivers (for locations, see the map on page 618).

$$$ Hotel Santa Caterina is a three-star, 18th-century place renting 22 comfy rooms. It's professionally run with real attention to quality. While it's on a big city street, it has a delightful garden terrace with views over the countryside (RS%, family rooms, garden side is quieter, air-con, elevator, pay parking—request when you reserve, Via E.S. Piccolomini 7, tel. 0577-221-105, www. hotelsantacaterinasiena.it, info@hotelsantacaterinasiena.it, Lorenza).

$$ Hotel Porta Romana is at the edge of town, off a busy road. Some of its 14 rooms face the open countryside (request one of these), and breakfast is served in the garden (RS%, air-con in most rooms, free parking, inviting sun terrace, outdoor hot tub open April-Oct free to guests with this book, Via E.S. Piccolomini 35, tel. 0577-42299, www.hotelportaromana.com, info@hotelportaromana.com, Marco and Evelia).

$$ Hotel Minerva is your big, professional, plain, efficient option. It has zero personality, but offers predictable comfort in its 56 rooms. It works best for those with cars—its pay parking is reasonable, and it's only a 10-minute walk from the action (view rooms extra, air-con, elevator, just inside Porta Ovile at the north end of town at Via Garibaldi 72, tel. 0577-284-474, www.albergominerva.it, info@albergominerva.it).

OUTSIDE SIENA

$$$$ Frances' Lodge Relais is a tranquil and delightfully managed farmhouse B&B. Each of its six rooms is bursting with character (well-described on their website). Franca and Franco run this rustic-yet-elegant old place, which features a 19th-century orangery that's been made into a "better homes and palaces" living room, as well as a peaceful garden, eight acres of olive trees and vineyards, and great views of Siena and its countryside—even from the swimming pool (RS%, family rooms, air-con, free parking, Strada di Valdipugna 2, tel. 0577-42379, mobile 337-671-608, www.franceslodge.eu). To the center, it's a five-minute walk plus a five-minute bus ride (€1.60), or €10 by taxi. Consider having an al fresco dinner in the gazebo, complete with view (make your own picnic, or have your hosts assemble a very fancy one).

Eating in Siena

Sienese restaurants are reasonably priced by Florentine and Venetian standards. You can enjoy ordering high on the menu here without going broke. For pasta, a good option is *pici* (PEE-chee), a thick Sienese spaghetti that seems to be at the top of every menu.

IN THE OLD TOWN
Fine Dining
These places deliver an upscale ambience, interesting menus, and generally finer food than my less dressy recommendations. Reservations are a good idea at all of them; otherwise arrive early. The first two have no outside seating.

$$$ **Taverna San Giuseppe** offers modern Tuscan cuisine with a chic grotto atmosphere. Under a fine old medieval vault, you'll enjoy beautifully presented dishes from a creative and enticing menu. Attentive Matteo and his wonderful wait staff enjoy showing off their Etruscan wine cellar—be sure to venture down (Mon-Sat 12:00-14:30 & 19:00-22:00, closed Sun, air-con, 7-minute climb up street to the right of City Hall at Via Giovanni Dupre 132, tel. 0577-42286, www.tavernasangiuseppe.it).

$$$$ **Antica Osteria Da Divo** is a great splurge. The kitchen is inventive, the ambience is flowery and candlelit, some of the seating fills old Etruscan tombs, and the food is delicate and top-notch. Chef Pino is fanatical for fresh ingredients and gives traditional dishes a creative spin; he and his wife, Claudia, will make you feel at home (wine by the glass on request, Wed-Mon 12:00-14:30 & 19:00-22:30, closed Tue; facing Baptistery door, take the far right street to Via Franciosa 29; tel. 0577-284-381, www.osteriadadivo.it). Show this book to finish with a complimentary biscotti and vin santo or coffee.

$$$$ **Osteria le Logge** caters to a fancy crowd and offers Tuscan favorites with a gourmet twist, made with seasonal local ingredients. Inside you'll enjoy a gorgeous living-room setting (books, wood, and wine bottles), and outside there's fine seating on a pedestrian street. This is an excellent choice for dining al fresco (Mon-Sat 12:00-15:00 & 19:00-23:00, closed Sun, two

Restaurant Price Code

I've assigned each eatery a price category, based on the average cost of a typical main course (pasta or *secondi*). Drinks, desserts, and splurge items (steak and seafood) can raise the price considerably.

$$$$	**Splurge:** Most main courses over €20
$$$	**Pricier:** €15-20
$$	**Moderate:** €10-15
$	**Budget:** Under €10

In Italy, pizza by the slice and other takeaway food is **$**; a basic trattoria or sit-down pizzeria is **$$**; a casual but more upscale restaurant is **$$$**; and a swanky splurge is **$$$$**.

blocks off Il Campo at Via del Porrione 33, tel. 0577-48013, www.giannibrunelli.it).

$$$ Enoteca I Terzi is dressy and modern under medieval vaults, with a simple yet enticing menu of creative dishes—and one of the most extensive wine selections in town. They have a few tables on a quiet square out front and an elegant main dining area, but avoid the back room (Mon-Sat 12:30-15:00 & 19:30-23:00, closed Sun, Via dei Termini 7, tel. 0577-44329, www.enotecaiterzi.it).

More Dining Options

$$ Ristorante Guidoriccio, just a few steps below Il Campo, feels warm and welcoming. You'll get smiling service from Ercole and Flora—the place has charm—especially if you let gentle Ercole explore the menu with you and follow his suggestions (Mon-Sat 12:30-14:30 & 19:00-22:30, closed Sun, air-con, no outdoor seating, Via Giovanni Dupre 2, tel. 0577-44350).

$$$ Compagnia dei Vinattieri serves modern Tuscan dishes with a creative touch. In this elegant space, you can enjoy a romantic meal under graceful brick arches. The menu is small and accessible. Owners Marco and Gianfranco are happy to take you down to the marvelous wine cellar (beef is big here, leave this book on the table for a complimentary *aperitivo* or *digestivo*, daily 12:30-15:00 & 19:30-23:00, enter at Via dei Pittori 1 or Via delle Terme 79, tel. 0577-236-568).

$$ Osteria Il Carroccio, artsy and convivial, seats guests in a characteristic but tight dining room. They serve traditional "slow food" recipes with innovative flair at affordable prices (€30 tasting *menu*—minimum two people, reservations wise, Thu-Tue 12:30-15:00 & 19:30-22:00, closed Wed, Via del Casato di Sotto 32, tel. 0577-41165).

Traditional and Rustic Places

$$ Trattoria Papei has a casual, rollicking family atmosphere and friendly servers dishing out generous portions of rib-stickin' Tuscan specialties and grilled meats. This big, sprawling place has festive outdoor seating under brown awnings and is often jammed—so call to reserve (daily 12:00-15:00 & 19:00-22:30, on the market square behind City Hall at Piazza del Mercato 6, tel. 0577-280-894, www.anticatrattoriapapei.com; Amedeo and Eduardo speak English).

$$ La Taverna Di Cecco is a simple, comfortable little eatery on an uncrowded back lane where grandma Olga cooks and earnest Luca and Gianni serve. They offer a simple menu of traditional Sienese favorites made with fresh ingredients, along with hearty salads (daily 12:00-16:00 & 19:00-23:00, Via Cecco Angiolieri 19, tel. 0577-288-518).

$$ Trattoria La Torre is an unfussy family-run *casalinga* (home-cooking) place, popular for its homemade pasta, a table of which entices customers as they enter. Its open kitchen and 10 tables are packed under one medieval brick arch. Service is brisk and casual—because the only menu is posted outside, they'll explain your options individually. Still, come here more for the fun atmosphere than the cuisine. Even with its priceless position below the namesake tower, it feels more like a local hangout than a tourist trap (Fri-Wed 12:00-15:00 & 19:00-22:00, closed Thu, just steps below Il Campo at Via di Salicotto 7, tel. 0577-287-548).

$ Osteria del Gatto is another classic little hole-in-the-wall, thriving with townspeople and powered by a passion for good Sienese cuisine. Friendly Marco Coradeschi and his staff cook and serve daily specials with attitude. As it's so small and popular, it can get loud (Mon-Fri 12:30-15:00 & 19:30-22:00, Sat 19:30-22:00 only, closed Sun, reservations recommended, 10-minute walk from Il Campo at Via San Marco 8, look for *La Vecchia Osteria* sign, tel. 0577-287-133).

$ Il Pomodorino is a lively restaurant serving meal-size salads and some of the best pizza in town, and a wide selection of beer—unusual in wine-crazy Tuscany. The intimate modern interior is covered by brick vaulting, but the real appeal is the outdoor terrace with a great view of the Duomo (daily April-Oct 12:00-late, Nov-March 19:00-late, a few steps above the recommended Alma Domus hotel at Via Camporegio 13, tel. 0577-286-811).

$ Osteria il Grattacielo is a funky hole-in-the-wall with a tight and homey interior and three tables under a tunnel-like arch outside, perfect for a cheap, hearty, memorable-yet-no-frills meal. Luca has no menu and just one solid house wine. You'll eat what he's cooking and pay €8-12 for dinner. Lunch is usually a two-course affair with good salads and vegetables (daily 12:00-15:00 &

19:30-21:30, closed for dinner Sun-Mon, Via dei Pontani 8, mobile 334-631-1458).

ON IL CAMPO

If you choose to eat on perhaps the finest town square in Italy, you'll pay a premium, meet waiters who don't need to hustle, and get mediocre food. And yet I highly recommend it. Consider surveying the scene during your sightseeing day and reserving a table of your choice at the place that feels best to you.

Dining and Drinks on the Square

$$$ **Ristorante Alla Speranza** has primo views and is a decent option for dining on the square (daily 9:00-late, Piazza Il Campo 32, tel. 0577-280-190, www.allasperanza.it).

$$$ **Il Bandierino** is another option for drinks or food, with an angled view of City Hall (no cover but a 20 percent service charge, daily 11:00-23:00, Piazza Il Campo 64, tel. 0577-275-894).

$$$ **Bar Il Palio** is the best bar on Il Campo for a before- or after-dinner drink: It has straightforward prices, no cover, and a fantastic perspective out over the square (daily 8:30-late, Piazza Il Campo 47, tel. 0577-282-055).

$$$ **Osteria Liberamente,** a dynamic little bar with a trendy vibe, is popular with young locals. Drinks come with a small plate of snacks, and they also serve light meals (fine wines by the glass and €7 cocktails, daily 9:00-late, Piazza Il Campo 27, tel. 0577-274-733, Pino).

Drinks or Snacks Overlooking Il Campo

$ **Gelateria Costarella,** on the corner of Via di Città and Costarella dei Barbieri, has good drinks, pastries, sandwiches, and light meals (I'd skip their gelato). The real attraction is upstairs—the simple benches perched over Il Campo. To enjoy these, order your drink or snack from the menu rather than the cheaper bar (daily 8:00-late, Via di Città 33).

$ **Bar Paninoteca San Paolo** has a youthful English-pub ambience and a row of stools overlooking the square. They have 50 kinds of sandwiches, big salads, and several beers on tap—it's not traditional Italian, but it's quick and filling (order and pay at the counter, food served daily 12:00-late, under the arch on Vicolo di San Paolo, tel. 0577-226-622).

$ **Key Largo Bar** has a nondescript interior, but two long, upper-story benches in the corner offer a wonderful secret perch. Buy your drink or snack at the bar, climb upstairs, and slide the ancient bar to open the door (no cover and no extra charge to sit on the balcony). Enjoy stretching out, and try to imagine how, during the Palio, three layers of spectators cram into this space—notice the iron railing used to plaster the top row of sardines up against the wall. Suddenly you're picturing Palio ponies zipping wildly around the square's notoriously dangerous corner (Mon-Fri 7:30-late, Sat-Sun 9:00-late, on the corner of Via Rinaldini, tel. 0577-236-339).

EATING CHEAPLY IN THE CENTER

$$ Antica Pizzicheria al Palazzo della Chigiana (a.k.a. *Pizzicheria de Miccoli*) may be the official name, but I bet locals just call it Antonio's. For most of his life, frenzied Antonio has carved salami and cheese for the neighborhood. Locals line up here for their sandwiches—meat and cheese sold by weight—with a good bottle of Chianti (Italian law dictates that he can't sell *vino* by the glass, only bottles, but he's got a number to choose from and will lend you the glasses). Antonio sells an enticing cheese and meat platter (starting at €15 per person)—but be careful...your costs can add up quickly (Mon-Sat 8:00-20:00, Sun 10:00-18:00, standing room only, Via di Città 95, tel. 0577-289-164).

Pizza: Budget eaters look for *pizza al taglio* shops, scattered throughout Siena, selling pizza by the slice. Here are a couple of good bets: **$ San Martino,** a couple of blocks behind Il Campo, is a local-feeling spot with slices and sandwiches to take away or eat in at one of their few tables (Mon-Sat 10:00-21:00, closed Sun, Via del Porrione 64). **$ Pizzeria Poppi,** a block off the Campo, is a simple, old-fashioned shop filled with locals. With very few menu options, the choice is easy. Grab a *ciaccino ripieno* (stuffed "white" pizza—no tomatoes) and use Il Campo as a dining room (Mon-Fri 10:00-15:00 & 16:30-20:30, Sat until 21:00, closed Sun, Via Banchi di Sotto 25—look for white-and-blue *Pizzeria* sign at the corner of Via di Calzoleria).

Gourmet Tuscan Supermarkets/Tavola Calda: Try **Consorzio Agrario di Siena,** a great place to browse, buy edible gifts, or assemble a cheap yet top-quality local meal. Wander through the entire place (salad and smoothie bar at the front, bakery/*rosticcerie*/hot stand-up meals at the back) and enjoy a parade of artisanal Tuscan foods. While office workers pack the eatery in the rear, I create the ultimate salad, choose a smoothie, and enjoy it on the big comfy stone bench across the way on Piazza Salimbeni (Mon-Sat 8:00-20:30, Sun 9:30-20:00, just off Piazza Matteotti, facing Piazza Salimbeni at Via Pianigiani 9).

Morbidi is a modern upscale take on the same artisanal grocery idea, but with more focus on prepared food. It's a good choice for breakfast, a quick lunch, or an *aperitivo*—a before-dinner, light buffet is included with the price of a drink (Mon-Thu 8:00-20:00, Fri-Sat until 22:00, closed Sun, Via Banchi di Sopra 75, tel. 0577-280-268).

Sapori & Dintorni Conad, at the bottom of Il Campo next

to the City Tower, is a classy bakery/supermarket/*rosticceria* serving fresh food to-go or at its bar. This is a good spot to put together a picnic to enjoy on the square (daily 8:30-20:00, Piazza Il Campo 80).

DESSERTS AND TREATS

Siena's claim to caloric fame is its *panforte,* a rich, chewy concoction of nuts, honey, and candied fruits that impresses even fruitcake haters. There are a few varieties: *Margherita,* dusted in powdered sugar, is fruitier, while *panpepato* has a spicy, peppery crust. Locals prefer a chewy, white macaroon-and-almond cookie called *ricciarelli.*

Nannini—ideally located in the center of the evening strolling scene a few blocks off the Campo—is Siena's venerable, top-end pastry shop/café. For a special dessert or a sweet treat any time of day, stop by. The local specialties are around back at the far end of the bar (Mon-Fri 7:30-21:30, Sat-Sun 8:00-23:00, *aperitivo* happy hour 18:00 until closing, Banchi di Sopra 24).

Siena Connections

Siena has sparse train connections but is a great hub for buses to the hill towns, though frequency drops on Sundays and holidays. For most, Florence is the gateway to Siena. Even if you're a rail-pass user, connect these two cities by bus—it's faster than the train, and Siena's bus station is more convenient and central than its train station.

BY TRAIN

Siena's train station is at the edge of town. For details on getting between the town center and the station, see page 589.

From Siena by Train to: Florence (direct trains hourly, 1.5-2 hours; bus is better), **Pisa** (2/hour, 2 hours, change at Empoli), **Assisi** (10/day, about 4 hours, most involve 2 changes, bus is faster), **Rome** (1-2/hour, 3-4 hours, change in Florence or Chiusi), **Orvieto** (12/day, 2.5 hours, change in Chiusi). For more information, visit www.trenitalia.com.

BY BUS

The main bus companies are **Tiemme/Siena Mobilità** (mostly regional destinations, tel. 0577-204-111, www.sienamobilita.it) and **Sena/Baltour** (long-distance connections, tel. 0861-199-1900, www.baltour.it). On schedules, the fastest buses are marked *rapida.* Most buses depart Siena from Piazza Gramsci; others leave from the train station (confirm when you buy your ticket).

Tiemme/Siena Mobilità Buses to: Florence (roughly 2/hour,

1.5-hour *rapida/via superstrada* buses are faster than the train, avoid the 2-hour *ordinaria* buses unless you have time to enjoy the beautiful scenery en route; tickets also available at tobacco shops/*tabacchi;* generally leaves from Piazza Gramsci as well as train station), **San Gimignano** (8/day direct, on Sun must change in Poggibonsi, 1.5 hours, from Piazza Gramsci), **Volterra** (4/day Mon-Sat, no buses on Sun, 2 hours, change in Colle di Val d'Elsa, leaves from Piazza Gramsci), **Montepulciano** (6-8/day, none on Sun, 1.5 hours, from train station), **Pienza** (6/day, none on Sun, 1.5 hours, from train station), **Montalcino** (6/day Mon-Sat, 4/day Sun, 1.5 hours, from train station or Piazza del Sale), **Pisa's Galileo Galilei Airport** (3/day, 2 hours, one direct, two via Poggibonsi), **Rome's Fiumicino Airport** (3/day, 3.5 hours, from Piazza Gramsci).

Sena/Baltour Buses to: Rome (9/day, 3 hours, from Piazza Gramsci, arrives at Rome's Tiburtina station on Metro line B with easy connections to the central Termini train station), **Naples** (2/day, 6.5 hours, one at 17:00 and an overnight bus that departs at 00:20), **Milan** (2/day direct, 4.5 hours, more with change in Bologna, departs from Piazza Gramsci, arrives at Milan's Cadorna Station with Metro access and direct trains to Malpensa Airport), **Assisi** (daily at 17:30, 2 hours, departs from Siena train station, arrives at Assisi Santa Maria degli Angeli; from there it's a 10-minute taxi/bus ride uphill to city center). To reach the town center of **Pisa,** the train is better (described earlier).

Tickets and Information: You can buy tickets in the underground passageway (called Sottopassaggio la Lizza) beneath Piazza Gramsci—look for stairwells in front of NH Excelsior Hotel. The larger office handles Tiemme/Siena Mobilità buses (Mon-Fri 6:30-19:30, Sat-Sun 7:00-19:30). The smaller one is for Sena/Baltour buses (Mon-Fri 7:30-20:00, Sat 7:30-12:30 & 13:45-16:15, Sun 10:15-13:15 & 14:00-18:45; Sena/Baltour office also has a desk selling *Eurolines* tickets for bus connections to other countries). Tiemme/Siena Mobilità is cash-only; Sena/Baltour accepts credit cards. You can also get tickets for both Tiemme/Siena Mobilità buses and Sena/Baltour buses at the train station (look for bus-ticket kiosk just inside main door). If necessary, you can buy tickets from the driver, but it costs €3-5 extra.

Services: Sottopassaggio la Lizza also has luggage storage, posted bus schedules, and pay WCs.

SIENA

VOLTERRA & SAN GIMIGNANO

This fine duo of hill towns—perhaps Italy's most underrated and most overrated, respectively—sits just a half-hour drive apart in the middle of the triangle formed by three major destinations: Florence, Siena, and Pisa. San Gimignano is the region's glamour girl, getting all the fawning attention from passing tour buses. And a quick stroll through its core, in the shadows of its 14 surviving medieval towers, is a delight. But once you've seen it, you've seen it...and that's when you head for Volterra. Volterra isn't as eye-catching as San Gimignano, but it has unmistakable authenticity and surprising depth, richly rewarding travelers adventurous enough to break out of the San Gimignano rut. With its many engaging museums, Volterra offers the best sightseeing of all of Italy's small hill towns.

GETTING THERE

These towns work best for drivers, who can easily reach both in one go. Volterra is farther off the main Florence-Siena road, but it's near the main coastal highway connecting the north (Pisa, Lucca, and Cinque Terre) and south (Montalcino/Montepulciano and Rome).

If you're relying on public transportation, both towns are reachable—to a point. Visiting either one by bus from Florence or Siena requires a longer-than-it-should-be trek, often with a change (in Colle di Val d'Elsa for Volterra, in Poggibonsi for San Gimignano). Volterra can also be reached by a train-and-bus combination from La Spezia, Pisa, or Florence (transfer to a bus in Pontedera). See each town's "Connections" section for details.

San Gimignano is better connected, but Volterra merits the additional effort. Note that while these towns are only about a

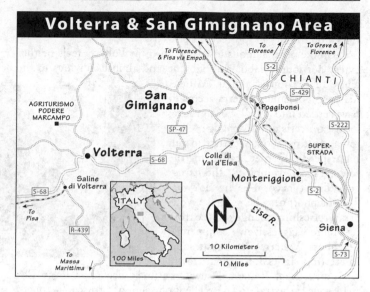

Volterra & San Gimignano Area

30-minute drive apart, they're poorly connected to each other by public transit (requiring an infrequent two-hour connection).

PLANNING YOUR TIME

Volterra and San Gimignano are a handy yin-and-yang duo. Ideally, you'll overnight in one town and visit the other either as a side-trip or en route. Sleeping in Volterra lets you really settle into a charming, real-feeling burg with good restaurants, but it forces you to visit San Gimignano during the day, when it's busiest. Sleeping in San Gimignano lets you enjoy that gorgeous town when it's relatively quiet, but some visitors find it *too* quiet—less interesting to linger in than Volterra. Ultimately I'd aim to sleep in Volterra, and try to visit San Gimignano as early or late in the day as is practical (to avoid crowds).

Volterra

Encircled by impressive walls and topped with a grand fortress, Volterra perches high above the rich farmland surrounding it. More than 2,000 years ago, Volterra was one of the most important Etruscan cities, and much larger than what we see today. Greek-trained Etruscan artists worked here, leaving a significant stash of art, particularly funerary urns. Eventually Volterra was absorbed into the Roman Empire, and for centuries it was an independent city-state. Volterra fought bitterly against the Florentines, but like many Tuscan towns, it lost in the end and was given a Medici fortress atop the city to "protect" its citizens.

Unlike other famous towns in Tuscany, Volterra feels neither cutesy nor touristy...but real, vibrant, and almost oblivious to the allure of the tourist dollar. Millennia past its prime, Volterra seems to have settled into a well-worn groove; locals are resistant to change. At a town meeting about whether to run high-speed Internet cable to the town, a local grumbled, "The Etruscans didn't need it—why do we?" This stubbornness helps make Volterra a refreshing change of pace from its more aggressively commercial neighbors. Volterra also boasts some interesting sights for a small town,

from an ancient Roman theater, to a finely decorated Pisan Romanesque cathedral, to an excellent museum of Etruscan artifacts. And most evenings, charming Annie and Claudia give a delightful, one-hour guided town walk sure to help you appreciate their city (see "Tours in Volterra," later). All in all, Volterra is my favorite small town in Tuscany.

Orientation to Volterra

Compact and walkable, Volterra (pop. 11,000—6,000 inside the old wall) stretches out from the pleasant Piazza dei Priori to the old city gates and beyond. Be ready for lots of steep walking; while the main square and main drag are fairly level, nearly everything else involves a climb.

TOURIST INFORMATION

The helpful TI is on the main square, at Piazza dei Priori 19 (daily 9:30-13:00 & 14:00-18:00, tel. 0588-87257, www.volterratur.it). The TI's excellent €5 audioguide narrates 20 stops (2-for-1 discount with this book). It also produces a free booklet called *Handicraft in Volterra*—useful for understanding the town's traditional artisans. Check the TI website for details on frequent summer festivals and concerts.

ARRIVAL IN VOLTERRA

By Public Transport: Buses stop at Piazza Martiri della Libertà in the town center. Train travelers can reach the town with a short bus ride (see "Volterra Connections," later.)

By Car: Don't drive into the town center; it's prohibited except for locals (and you'll get a huge fine). It's easiest to simply wind to the top where the road ends at Piazza Martiri della Libertà. (Halfway up the hill, there's a confusing hard right—don't take it; keep going straight uphill under the wall.) Immediately before the Piazza Martiri bus roundabout is the entry to an **underground garage** (€2/hour, €15/day, keep ticket and pay as you leave). It's safe, and you pop out within a few blocks of nearly all my recommended hotels and sights.

Parking lots ring the town walls (around €2/hour; try the handy-but-small lot facing the Roman Theater and Porta Fiorentina gate) and a bus parking lot called Stazione (below the road to San Gimignano). Also behind town, a lot named Docciola is free, but it requires a steep climb from the Porta di Docciola gate up into town.

Wherever you park, be sure it's permitted—stick to parking lots and pay street parking (indicated with blue lines). If you're staying in town, check with your hotel about the best parking options.

HELPFUL HINTS

Exchange Rate: €1 = about $1.10

Country Calling Code: 39 (see page 1154 for dialing instructions)

Volterra Card: This €14 card covers all the main sights in town—except for the Palazzo Viti (valid 72 hours, buy at any covered sight). Without the card, the Etruscan Museum and Pinacoteca are €8 each, and the Palazzo Priori and Archeological Park are €5 each. If traveling with kids, ask about the family card, an especially good deal (€22 for 1-2 adults and up to 3 kids under 16).

Market Day: The market is on Saturday morning near the Roman Theater (8:00-13:00, Nov-March it moves to Piazza dei Priori). The TI hands out a list of other market days in the area.

Festivals: Volterra's Medieval Festival takes place on the third and fourth Sundays of August. Fall is a popular time for food festivals.

Wi-Fi: Several cafés offer free Wi-Fi to customers. **Enjoy Café Internet Point,** right by the main bus stop, has public computers and free Wi-Fi with purchase (long hours daily, Piazza dei Martiri 3, tel. 0588-80530).

Laundry: The handy self-service **Lavanderia Azzurra** is just off the main square (€4/wash, €3/dry, change machine, daily 7:00-23:00, Via Roma 7, tel. 0588-80030). Their next-door dry-cleaning shop also provides wash-and-dry services that usually take about 24 hours (€3/kilo, Mon-Fri 8:30-13:00 & 15:30-20:00, Sat 8:30-13:00, closed Sun).

Tours in Volterra

▲▲Guided Volterra Walk

Annie Adair (also listed individually, next) and her colleague Claudia Meucci offer a great one-hour, English-only introductory walking tour of Volterra for €10. The walk touches on Volterra's Etruscan, Roman, and medieval history, as well as the contemporary cultural scene (daily April-Oct, rain or shine—Mon and Wed at 12:30, other days at 18:00; meet in front of alabaster shop on Piazza Martiri della Libertà, no need to reserve, tours run with a minimum of 3 people or €30; www.volterrawalkingtour.com or www.tuscantour.com, info@volterrawalkingtour.com). There's no better way to spend €10 and one hour in this city. I mean it. Don't miss this beautiful experience.

Local Guides

American **Annie Adair** is an excellent guide for private, in-depth tours of Volterra (€60/hour, minimum 2 hours). Her husband **Francesco,** an easy-going sommelier and wine critic, leads a "Wine Tasting 101" crash course in sampling Tuscan wines (€50/hour per group, plus cost of wine). For more in-depth experiences, Annie and Francesco offer excursions to a nearby honey farm, alabaster quarry, and winery, or a more wine-focused trip to Montalcino or the heart of Chianti (about €450/day for 2-3 people), and can even organize Tuscan weddings (mobile 347-143-5004, www.tuscantour.com, info@tuscantour.com).

Sights in Volterra

I've linked these sights with handy walking directions, which provide a useful orientation to the town.
• *Begin at the Etruscan Arch at the bottom of Via Porta all'Arco (about 4 blocks below the main square, Piazza dei Priori).*

▲Etruscan Arch (Porta all'Arco)

Volterra's renowned Etruscan arch was built of massive stones in the fourth century B.C. Volterra's original wall was four miles around—

twice the size of the wall that encircles it today. Imagine: This city had 20,000 people four centuries before Christ. Volterra was a key trading center and one of 12 leading towns in the confederation of *Etruria Propria.* The three seriously eroded heads, dating from the first century B.C., show what happens when you leave something outside for 2,000 years. The newer stones are part of the 13th-century city wall, which incorporated parts of the much older Etruscan wall.

A plaque just outside remembers June 30, 1944. That night, Nazi forces were planning to blow up the arch to slow the Allied advance. To save their treasured landmark, Volterrans ripped up the stones that pave Via Porta all'Arco, plugged up the gate, and managed to convince the Nazi commander that there was no need to blow up the arch. Today, all the paving stones are back in their places, and like silent heroes, they welcome you through the oldest standing gate into Volterra. Locals claim this as the oldest surviving round arch of the Etruscan age; some experts believe this is where the Romans got the idea for using a keystone in their arches.

• *Go through the arch and head up Via Porta all'Arco, which I like to call...*

"Artisan Lane" (Via Porta all'Arco)

This steep and atmospheric lane is lined with interesting shops featuring the work of artisans and producers. Because of its alabaster heritage, Volterra developed a tradition of craftsmanship and artistry, and today you'll find a rich variety of handiwork (shops generally open Mon-Sat 10:00-13:00 & 16:00-19:00, closed Sun).

From the Etruscan Arch, browse your way up the hill, checking out these shops and items (listed from bottom to top): alabaster shops (#57 and #45); book bindery and papery (#26); jewelry (#25); etchings (#23); and bronze work (#6).

• *Reaching the top of Via Porta all'Arco, turn left and walk a few steps into Volterra's main square, Piazza dei Priori. It's dominated by the...*

Palazzo dei Priori

Volterra's City Hall, built about 1200, claims to be the oldest of any Tuscan city-state. It clearly inspired the more famous Palazzo Vecchio in Florence. Town halls like this are emblematic of an era when city-states were powerful. They were architectural exclamation points declaring that, around here, no pope or emperor called the shots. Towns such as Volterra were truly city-states—proudly independent and relatively democratic. They had their own armies, taxes, and even weights and measures. Notice the horizontal "cane" cut into the City Hall wall (10 yards to the right of the door). For a thousand years, this square hosted a market, and the "cane" was the local yardstick. You can pay to see the council chambers, and to climb to the top of the bell tower.

Cost and Hours: €5, includes council chambers and tower climb, covered by Volterra Card, mid-March-Oct daily 10:30-17:30, Nov-mid-March until 16:30.

• *Facing the City Hall, notice the black-and-white-striped wall to the right (set back from the square). The little back door in that wall leads*

VOLTERRA & SAN GIMIGNANO

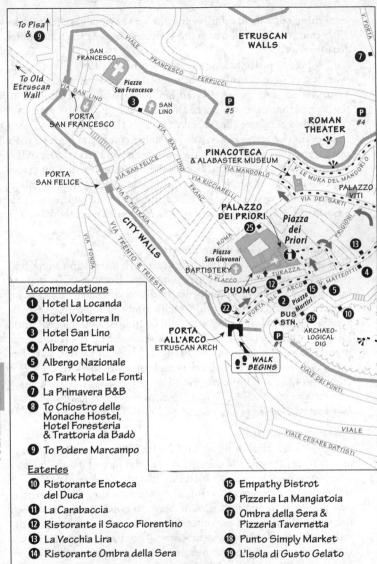

Accommodations

1 Hotel La Locanda
2 Hotel Volterra In
3 Hotel San Lino
4 Albergo Etruria
5 Albergo Nazionale
6 To Park Hotel Le Fonti
7 La Primavera B&B
8 To Chiostro delle Monache Hostel, Hotel Foresteria & Trattoria da Badò
9 To Podere Marcampo

Eateries

10 Ristorante Enoteca del Duca
11 La Carabaccia
12 Ristorante il Sacco Fiorentino
13 La Vecchia Lira
14 Ristorante Ombra della Sera
15 Empathy Bistrot
16 Pizzeria La Mangiatoia
17 Ombra della Sera & Pizzeria Tavernetta
18 Punto Simply Market
19 L'Isola di Gusto Gelato

into Volterra's cathedral. (For a thousand years the bishop has lived next door, conveniently right above the TI.)

Duomo

This church is not as elaborate as its cousin in Pisa, but it is a beautiful example of the Pisan Romanesque style. The simple 13th-century facade conceals a more intricate interior (rebuilt in the late 16th and 19th centuries), with a central nave flanked by mono-

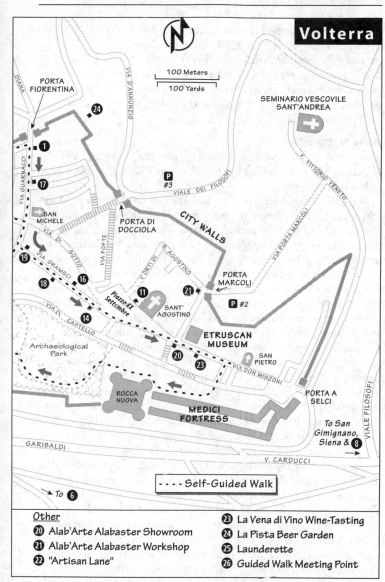

Volterra

SEMINARIO VESCOVILE
SANT'ANDREA

PORTA
FIORENTINA

100 Meters
100 Yards

VIA DIANA

VIA D'ANNUNZIO

❶

⓴

VIA GUARNACCI

❶⓱

P #3

VIALE DEI FILOSOFI

V. VITTORIO VENETO

SAN
MICHELE

VIA DI SOTTO

PORTA DI
DOCCIOLA

CITY WALLS

VIA FORTE

V. ORTI DI S. AGOSTINO

VIA PORTA MARCOLI

⓳

VIA GRAMSCI

⓲ ⓯

Piazza XX
Settembre

⓫

SANT'
AGOSTINO

PORTA
MARCOLI

⓴

P #2

⓮

VIA CASTELLO

Archaeological
Park

⓴

⓳

ETRUSCAN
MUSEUM

SAN
PIETRO

VIA DON MINZONI

ROCCA
NUOVA

MEDICI
FORTRESS

PORTA A
SELCI

GARIBALDI

To San
Gimignano,
Siena & ❽

VIALE FILOSOFI

V. CARDUCCI

- - - - Self-Guided Walk

→ To ❻

VOLTERRA & SAN GIMIGNANO

<u>Other</u>
⓴ Alab'Arte Alabaster Showroom
㉑ Alab'Arte Alabaster Workshop
㉒ "Artisan Lane"

㉓ La Vena di Vino Wine-Tasting
㉔ La Pista Beer Garden
㉕ Launderette
㉖ Guided Walk Meeting Point

lithic stucco columns painted to imitate pink granite, and topped by a gilded, coffered ceiling. Just past the pulpit on the right (at the Rosary Chapel), check out the *Annunciation*, painted in 1497 by Mariotto Albertinelli and Fra Bartolomeo (both were students of Fra Angelico). The two, friends since childhood, delicately give worshippers a way to see Mary "conceived by the Holy Spirit." Note the vibrant colors, exaggerated perspective, and Mary's *contrapposto* pose—all attributes of the Renaissance.

Cost and Hours: Free, daily 8:00-12:30 & 15:00-18:00, Nov-Feb until 17:00, closed Fri 12:30-16:00 for cleaning.

• *Facing the cathedral, circle to the left (passing a 1960 carving of St. Linus, the second pope and friend of St. Peter, who was born here) and go back into the main square, Piazza dei Priori. Face the City Hall, and go down the street to the left; after one short block, you're standing at the head (on the left) of...*

▲Via Matteotti

The town's main drag, named after the popular Socialist leader Giacomo Matteotti (killed by the fascists in 1924), provides a good cultural scavenger hunt.

At #1, on the left, is a typical **Italian bank security door.** (Step in and say, "Beam me up, Scotty.") Back outside, stand at the corner and look up and all around. Find the medieval griffin torch holder—symbol of Volterra, looking down Via Matteotti—and imagine it holding a flaming torch. The pharmacy sports the symbol of its medieval guild. Across the street from the bank, #2 is the base of what was a San Gimignano-style **fortified Tuscan tower.** Look up and imagine heavy beams cantilevered out, supporting extra wooden rooms and balconies crowding out over the street. Throughout Tuscany, today's stark and stony old building fronts once supported a tangle of wooden extensions.

As you head down Via Matteotti, notice how the doors show centuries of refitting work. Doors that once led to these extra rooms are now partially bricked up to make windows. Contemplate urban density in the 14th century, before the plague thinned out the population. Be careful: A **wild boar** (a local delicacy) awaits you at #10.

At #12, on the right, notice the line of doorbells: This typical **palace,** once the home of a single rich family, is now occupied by many middle-class families. After the social revolution in the 18th century and the rise of the middle class, former palaces were condominium-ized. Even so, like in *Dr. Zhivago*, the original family still lives here. Apartment #1 is the home of Count Guidi.

On the right, at #16, pop in to the **alabaster showroom.** Alabaster, mined nearby, has long been a big industry here. Volterra alabaster—softer and more translucent than marble—was sliced thin to serve as windows for Italy's medieval churches.

At #19, the recommended **La Vecchia Lira** is a lively cafeteria and restaurant. The **Bar L'Incontro** across the street is a favorite for breakfast and pastries; in the summer, they sell homemade gelato, while in the winter they make chocolates. In the evening, it's a bustling local spot for a drink.

Across the way, side-trip 10 steps up Vicolo delle Prigioni to the fun **Panificio Rosetti** bakery. They're happy to sell small quantities if you want to try the local *cantuccini* (almond biscotti) or another treat.

Continue on Via Matteotti to the end of the block. At #51, on the left, a bit of **Etruscan wall** is artfully used to display more alabaster art. And #56A is the alabaster **art gallery** of Paolo Sabatini, who specializes in unique, contemporary sculptures.

By the way, you can only buy a package of cigarettes at the machine in the wall just to the right—labeled *"Vietato ai Minori"* (forbidden to minors)—by inserting an Italian national health care card to prove you're over 18.

Locals gather early each evening at **Osteria dei Poeti** (at #57) for some of the best cocktails in town—served with free munchies. The cinema is across the street. Movies in Italy are rarely in *versione originale;* Italians are used to getting their movies dubbed into Italian. To bring some culture to this little town, they also show live broadcasts of operas and concerts (advertised in the window).

On the corner, at #66, another **Tuscan tower** marks the end of the street. This noble house had a ground floor with no interior access to the safe upper floors. Rope ladders were used to get upstairs. The tiny door was wide enough to let in your skinny friends... but definitely not anyone wearing armor and carrying big weapons.

Across the little square stands the ancient **Church of St. Michael.** After long years of barbarian chaos, the Langobards moved in from the north and asserted law and order in places like Volterra. That generally included building a Christian church on the old Roman forum to symbolically claim and tame the center of town. The church standing here today is Romanesque, dating from the 12th century.

Around the right side, find the crude little guy and the smiling octopus under its eaves—they've been making faces at the passing crowds for 800 years.

• *From here you have options. Three more sights—**Palazzo Viti** (fancy old palace), the **Pinacoteca** (Volterra's main painting gallery), and the **Alabaster Museum** (within the Pinacoteca building)—are a short stroll down Via dei Sarti: From the end of Via Matteotti, turn left. If you want to skip straight down to the **Roman Theater,** just head straight from the end of Via Matteotti onto Via Guarnacci, then turn left when you get to the Porta Fiorentina (Florence Gate). To head directly to Volterra's top sight, the **Etruscan Museum,** just turn around, walk a block back up Via Matteotti, turn left on Via Gramsci, and follow it all the way through Piazza XX Settembre up Via Don Minzoni to the museum.*

*Or linger a bit while making your decision over a glass of wine at **Enoteca Scali**, just across the street at Via Guarnacci 3. Friendly Massimo and Patrizia sell a vast selection of wines and local delicacies in an inviting atmosphere.*

▲Palazzo Viti

Palazzo Viti takes you behind the rustic, heavy stone walls of the city to see how the wealthy lived—in this case, rich from the 19th-century alabaster trade. This time warp is popular with Italian movie directors. With 12 rooms on one floor open to the public, Palazzo Viti feels remarkably lived in—because it is. Behind the ropes you'll see intimate family photos. You'll often find Signora Viti herself selling admission tickets. Your visit ends in the cellar with a short wine tasting.

Cost and Hours: €5, April-Oct daily 10:00-13:00 & 14:30-18:30, closed Nov-March, Via dei Sarti 41, tel. 0588-84047, www.palazzoviti.it.

Visiting the Palazzo: The elegant interior is compact and well-described. You'll climb up a stately staircase, buy your ticket, and head into the grand ballroom. From here, you'll tour the blue-hued dining room (with slice-of-life Chinese scenes painted on rice paper); the salon of battles (with warfare paintings on the walls); and the long hall of temporary exhibits. Looping back, you'll see the porcelain hall (decorated with priceless plates) and the inviting library (notice the delicate lamp with a finely carved alabaster lampshade).

The Brachettone Salon is named for the local artist responsible for the small sketch of near-nudes hanging just left of the door into the next room. Brachettone (from *brache*, "pants") is the artistic nickname for Volterra-born Daniele Ricciarelli, who owns the dubious distinction of having painted all those wispy loincloths over the genitalia of Michelangelo's figures in the Sistine Chapel. (In this drawing, notice a similar aversion to showing the full monty... though everything-but is fair game.) On the table, notice the family wedding photo with Pope John Paul II presiding. In the red room, a portrait of Giuseppe Viti (looking like Pavarotti) hangs next to the exit door. He's the man who purchased the place in 1850. Your visit ends with bedrooms and a dressing room, making it easy to imagine how the other half lived...and, from November through March, presumably still does.

Your Palazzo Viti ticket also gets you a fine little cheese, salami, and wine tasting. As you leave the palace, climb down into the cool cellar (used as a disco on some weekends), where you can pop into a Roman cistern, marvel at an Etruscan well, and enjoy a friendly sit-down snack. Take full advantage of this tasty extra.

• *A block past Palazzo Viti, also on Via dei Sarti, is the...*

Pinacoteca and Alabaster Museum

The Pinacoteca fills a 15th-century palace with fine paintings that feel more Florentine than Sienese—a reminder of whose domain this town was in. You'll see a stunning altarpiece by Taddeo di

Bartolo, once displayed in the original residence. You'll also find roomfuls of gilded altarpieces and saintly statues, as well as a trio of striking High Renaissance altar paintings by Signorelli, Fiorentino, and Ghirlandaio.

Cost and Hours: €8, covered by Volterra Card, daily mid-March-Oct 9:00-19:00, Nov-mid-March 10:00-16:30, Via dei Sarti 1, tel. 0588-87580.

• *Exiting the museum, circle right along the side of the museum building into the tunnel-like Passo del Gualduccio passage (which leads to the parking-lot square); turn right and walk along the wall, with fine views of the...*

Roman Theater

Built in the first century A.D., this well-preserved theater has good acoustics. With this fine aerial view from the city wall promenade,

there's no reason to pay to enter (although it is covered by the Volterra Card). The 13th-century wall that you're standing on divided the theater from the town center...so, naturally, the theater became the town dump. Over time, the theater was forgotten—covered in the garbage of Volterra. It was rediscovered in the 1950s and excavated.

The stage wall (immediately in front of the theater seats) was standard Roman design—with three levels from which actors would appear: one level for mortals, one for heroes, and the top one for gods. Parts of two levels still stand. Gods leaped out onto the third level for the last time around the third century A.D., which is when the town began to use the theater stones to build fancy baths instead. You can see the scant remains of the baths behind the theater, including the little round sauna in the far corner with brick supports that raise the heated floor.

From this vantage point, you can trace Volterra's vast Etruscan wall. Find the church in the distance, on the left, and notice the stones just below. They are from the Etruscan wall that followed the ridge into the valley and defined Volterra in the fourth century B.C.

• *From the Roman Theater viewpoint, continue along the wall downhill to the T-intersection (the old gate, Porta Fiorentina, with fine wooden medieval doors, is on your left) and turn right, making your way uphill on Via Guarnacci back to Via Matteotti. A block up Via Matteotti, you can't miss the wide, pedestrianized shopping street called Via Gramsci. Follow this up to Piazza XX Settembre, walk through that leafy square, and continue uphill on Via Don Minzoni. Watch on your left for the...*

▲▲Etruscan Museum (Museo Etrusco Guarnacci)

Filled top to bottom with rare Etruscan artifacts, this museum—even with few English explanations and its dusty, old-school style—makes it easy to appreciate how advanced this pre-Roman culture was.

Cost and Hours: €8, covered by Volterra Card; daily mid-March-Oct 9:00-19:00, Nov-mid-March 10:00-16:30; audioguide-€3, Via Don Minzoni 15, tel. 0588-86347, www.comune.volterra.pi.it/english.

Visiting the Museum: The museum's three floors feel dusty and disorganized. As there are scarcely any English explanations, consider the serious but interesting audioguide; the information below hits the highlights. There's an inviting public garden out back.

The collection starts on the **ground floor** with a small gathering of pre-Etruscan Villanovian artifacts (c. 1500 B.C.), with the oldest items to the left as you enter. To the right are an impressive warrior's hat and a remarkable, richly decorated, double-spouted military flask (for wine and water). Look down to see Etruscan foundations and a road (the discovery of which foiled the museum's attempt to build an elevator here). It's mind-boggling to think that 20,000 people lived within the town's Etruscan walls in 400 B.C.

Filling the rest of the ground floor is a vast collection of Etruscan **funerary urns** (dating from the seventh to the first century B.C.). Designed to contain the ashes of cremated loved ones, each urn is tenderly carved with a unique scene, offering a peek into the still-mysterious Etruscan society. Etruscan urns have two parts: The casket on the bottom (with elaborately carved panels), contained the remains, while the lid was decorated with a sculpture of the departed.

First pay attention to the people on top. While contemporaries of the Greeks, the Etruscans were more libertine. Their religion was less demanding, and their women were a respected part of both the social and public spheres. Women and men alike are depicted lounging on Etruscan urns. While they seem to be just hanging out, the lounging dead were actually offering the gods a banquet—in order to gain the Etruscan equivalent of salvation. Etruscans really did lounge like this in front of a table, but this banquet had eternal consequences. The dearly departed are often depicted holding blank wax tablets (symbolizing blank new lives in the next world). Men hold containers that would generally be used at banquets, including libation cups for offering wine to the gods. The women are finely dressed, sometimes holding a pomegranate (symbolizing fertility) or a mirror. Look at the faces, and imagine the lives they lived and the loved ones they left behind.

Now tune into the reliefs carved into the fronts of the caskets.

The motifs vary widely, from floral patterns to mystical animals (such as a Starbucks-like mermaid) to parades of magistrates. Most show journeys on horseback—appropriate for someone leaving this world and entering the next. Some show the fabled horseback-and-carriage ride to the underworld, where the dead are greeted by Charon, an underworld demon, with his hammer and pointy ears.

While the finer urns are carved of alabaster, most are made of limestone. Originally they were colorfully painted. Many lids are mismatched—casualties of reckless 18th- and 19th-century archaeological digs.

Head upstairs to the **first floor.** You'll enter a room with a circular mosaic in the floor (a Roman original, found in Volterra and transplanted here). Explore more treasures in a series of urn-filled rooms.

Fans of Alberto Giacometti will be amazed at how the tall, skinny figure called *The Evening Shadow* (*L'Ombra della Sera,* third century B.C.) looks just like the modern Swiss sculptor's work—but 2,500 years older. This is an example of the *ex voto* bronze statues that the Etruscans created in thanks to the gods. With his supremely lanky frame, distinctive wavy hairdo, and inscrutable Mona Lisa smirk, this Etruscan lad captures the illusion of a shadow stretching long late in the day. Admire the sheer artistry of the statue; with its right foot shifted slightly forward, it even hints at the *contrapposto* pose that would become common in this same region during the Renaissance, two millennia later.

The museum's other top piece is the **Urn of the Spouses** (*Urna degli Sposi,* first century B.C.). It's unique for various reasons, includ-

ing its material (it's in terra-cotta—a relatively rare material for these funerary urns) and its depiction of two people rather than one. Looking at this elderly couple, it's easy to imagine the long life they spent together and their desire to pass eternity lounging with each other at a banquet for the gods.

Other highlights include alabaster urns with more Greek myths, *ex-voto* water-bearer statues, kraters (vases with handles used for mixing water and wine), bronze hand mirrors, exquisite golden jewelry that would still be fashionable today, a battle helmet ominously dented at the left temple, black glazed pottery, and hundreds of ancient coins.

The **top floor** features a re-created gravesite, with several neatly aligned urns and artifacts that would have been buried with the deceased. Some of these were funeral dowries that the dead would

Under the Etruscan Sun
(c. 900 B.C.-A.D. 1)

Around 550 B.C.—just before the Golden Age of Greece—the Etruscan people of central Italy had their own Golden Age. Though their origins are mysterious, their mix of Greek-style art with Roman-style customs helped lay a civilized foundation for the rise of the Roman Empire. As you travel through Italy—particularly in Tuscany (from "Etruscan")—you'll find traces of this long-lost people. Etruscan tombs and artifacts are still being discovered, often by farmers in the countryside.

The Etruscans first appeared in the ninth century B.C., when a number of cities sprouted up in sparsely populated Tuscany and Umbria, including today's hill towns of Cortona, Chiusi, and Volterra. Possibly immigrants from Turkey, but more likely local farmers who moved to the city, they became sailors, traders, and craftsmen, and welcomed new ideas from Greece.

More technologically advanced than their neighbors, the Etruscans mined metal, exporting it around the Mediterranean, both as crude ingots and as some of the finest-crafted jewelry in the known world. They drained and irrigated large tracts of land, creating the fertile farmland of central Italy's breadbasket. With their disciplined army, warships, merchant vessels, and (from the Greek perspective) pirate galleys, they ruled central Italy and the major ports along the Tyrrhenian Sea. For nearly two centuries (c. 700-500 B.C.), much of Italy lived a Golden Age of peace and prosperity under the Etruscan sun.

Judging from the frescoes and many luxury items that have survived, the Etruscans enjoyed the good life: They look healthy and vibrant as they play flutes, dance with birds, or play party games. Etruscan artists celebrated individual people, showing their wrinkles, crooked noses, silly smiles, and funny haircuts.

Scholars today have deciphered the Etruscans' Greek-style alphabet and some individual words, but they have yet to fully understand their language, which is unlike any other in Europe. Much of what we know of the Etruscans comes from their tombs. The tomb was a home in the hereafter, complete with the deceased's belongings. The funerary urn might have a statue on the lid of the deceased at a banquet—lying across a dining couch, spooning with his wife, smiles on their faces, living the good life for all eternity.

Seven decades of wars with the Greeks (545-474 B.C.) disrupted their trade routes and drained the Etruscan League, just as a new Mediterranean power was emerging: Rome. In 509 B.C., the Romans overthrew their Etruscan king, and Rome expanded, capturing Etruscan cities one by one (the last in 264 B.C.). Etruscan resisters were killed, the survivors intermarried with Romans, and their kids grew up speaking Latin. By Julius Caesar's time, the only remnants of Etruscan culture were its priests, who be-

The Etruscan Empire

Bologna

Ravenna

Adriatic Sea

Appenine Mountains

La Spezia

Ligurian Sea

ITALY

100 Miles

Florence • Fiesole

Arno R.

Pisa

E T R U S C A N

Volterra (M)

Siena •

Cortona (M)

Perugia

Murlo (M)

Chiusi (M)

Lake Trasimeno

Populonia

E M P I R E

Vetulonia ■

Orvieto (M)

Roselle ■

Bolsena

Elba

Lake Bolsena

Tyrrhenian Sea

Vulci

Tiber R.

Tarquinia ■

Veio

Cerveteri ■

Rome (M)

■ Etruscan Cities
• Modern Cities
(M) Etruscan Museum
– – – Border of Tuscany

came Rome's professional soothsayers. Interestingly, the Etruscan prophets had foreseen their own demise, having predicted that Etruscan civilization would last 10 centuries.

But Etruscan culture lived on in Roman religion (pantheon of gods, household gods, and divination rituals), art (realism), lifestyle (the banquet), and in a taste for Greek styles—the mix that became our "Western civilization."

Etruscan Sights

Rome: Traces of original Etruscan engineering projects (e.g., Circus Maximus), Vatican Museum artifacts, and Villa Giulia Museum, with the famous "husband and wife sarcophagus."

Orvieto: Archaeological Museum (coins, dinnerware, and a sarcophagus), necropolis, and underground tunnels and caves.

Volterra: Etruscan gate (Porta all'Arco, from fourth century B.C.) and Etruscan Museum (urns, pottery, and devotional figures).

pack along—including mirrors, coins, hardware for vases, votive statues, pots, pans, and jewelry.

• *After your visit, duck across the street to the alabaster showroom and the wine bar (both described next).*

▲Alabaster Workshop

Across from the Etruscan Museum, Alab'Arte offers a fun peek into the art of alabaster. Their powdery workshop is directly op-

posite the shop, a block down a narrow lane, Via Porta Marcoli (near the wall). Here you can watch Roberto Chiti and Giorgio Finazzo at work. (Everything—including Roberto and Giorgio—is covered in a fine white dust.) Lighting shows off the translucent quality of the stone and the expertise of these artists, who are delighted to share their art with visitors. This is not a touristy guided visit, but something far more special: the chance to see busy artisans practicing their craft. For more such artisans in action, visit "Artisan Lane" (Via Porta all'Arco) described earlier, or ask the TI for their list of the town's many workshops open to the public.

Cost and Hours: Free, showroom—March-Oct daily 9:30-13:00 & 15:00-19:00, closed Nov-Feb, Via Don Minzoni 18; workshop—Mon-Sat 9:30-12:30 & 15:00-19:00, closed Sun, Via Orti Sant'Agostino 28, tel. 340-718-7189, www.alabarte.com.

▲La Vena di Vino (Wine-Tasting with Bruno and Lucio)

La Vena di Vino, also just across from the Etruscan Museum, is a fun *enoteca* where two guys who have devoted themselves to the

wonders of wine share it with a fun-loving passion. Each day Bruno and Lucio open six or eight bottles, serve your choice by the glass, pair it with characteristic munchies, and offer fine music (guitars available for patrons) and an unusual decor (the place is strewn with bras). Hang out here with the local characters. This is your chance to try the Super Tuscan wine—a creative mix of international grapes grown in Tuscany. According to Bruno, the Brunello (€7/glass) is just right with wild boar, and the Super Tuscan (€6-7/glass) is perfect for meditation. Although Volterra is famously quiet late at night, this place is full of action.

Cost and Hours: Pay per glass, open Wed-Mon 11:30-24:00, closed Tue, 3- to 5-glass wine tastings, Via Don Minzoni 30, tel. 0588-81491, www.lavenadivino.com.

• *Volterra's final sight is perched atop the hill just above the wine bar. Climb up one of the lanes nearby, then walk (to the right) along the formidable wall to find the park.*

Medici Fortress and Archaeological Park

The Parco Archeologico marks what was the acropolis of Volterra from 1500 B.C. until A.D. 1472, when Florence conquered the pesky city. The Florentines burned Volterra's political and historic center, turning it into a grassy commons and building the adjacent Medici Fortezza. The old fortress—a symbol of Florentine dominance—now keeps people in rather than out. It's a maximum-security prison housing only about 150 special prisoners.

The park sprawling next to the fortress (toward the town center) is a rare, grassy meadow at the top of a rustic hill town—a favorite place for locals to relax and picnic on a sunny day. Nearby are the scant remains of the acropolis, which can be viewed through the fence for free, or entered for a fee. Of more interest to antiquities enthusiasts is the acropolis' first-century A.D. Roman cistern. You can descend 40 tight spiral steps to stand in a chamber that once held about 250,000 gallons of water, enough to provide for more than a thousand people.

Cost and Hours: Park—free, open until 20:00 in peak of summer, shorter hours off-season; acropolis and cistern—€5, covered by Volterra Card, daily 10:30-17:30, closes at 16:30 off-season.

Evening Scene

La Pista: Volterra is pretty quiet at night. For a little action during summer evenings, you can venture just outside the wall to La Pista, a Tuscan family-friendly neighborhood beer-garden kind of hangout (DJ on weekends, snacks and drinks sold, playground). It's outside the Porta Fiorentina (100 yards to the right in the shadow of the wall).

Passegiata: As they have for generations, Volterrans young and old stroll during the cool of the early evening. The main cruising is along Via Gramsci and Via Matteotti to the main square, Piazza dei Priori.

Aperitivo: Each evening several bars put out little buffet spreads free with a drink to attract a crowd. Bars popular for their *aperitivo* include VolaTerra (Via Turazza 5, next to City Hall), L'Incontro (Via Matteotti 19), and Bar dei Poeti (across from the cinema, Via Matteotti 57). And the gang at La Vena di Vino (described earlier, under "Sights in Volterra") always seems ready for a good time.

Sleeping in Volterra

Volterra has plenty of places offering a good night's sleep at a fair price. Lodgings outside the old town are generally a bit cheaper (and easier for drivers). But keep in mind that these places involve not just walking, but steep walking.

INSIDE VOLTERRA'S OLD TOWN

$$ Hotel La Locanda feels stately and old-fashioned. This well-located place (just inside Porta Fiorentina, near the Roman Theater and parking lot) rents 18 rooms with flowery decor and modern comforts (RS%, family rooms, air-con, elevator, Via Guarnacci 24, tel. 0588-81547, www.hotel-lalocanda.com, staff@hotel-lalocanda.com, Irina).

$$ Hotel Volterra In, opened in 2015, is fresh, tasteful, and in a central-yet-quiet location. Marco rents 10 bright and spacious rooms (RS%, air-con, elevator, Via Porta all'Arco 37, tel. 0588-86820, www.hotelvolterrain.it, info@hotelvolterrain.it).

$$ Hotel San Lino fills a former convent with 42 modern, nondescript rooms at the sleepy lower end of town—close to the Porta San Francesco gate, and about a five-minute uphill walk to the main drag. Although it's within the town walls, it doesn't feel like it: The hotel has a fine swimming pool and view terrace and is the only in-town option that's convenient for drivers, who can pay to park at the on-site garage (pricey "superior" rooms include parking—worthwhile only for drivers, air-con, elevator, Via San Lino 26, tel. 0588-85250, www.hotelsanlino.com, info@hotelsanlino.com).

$ Albergo Etruria is on Volterra's main drag. They offer a warm welcome, a good location, a peaceful rooftop garden, and 18 frilly rooms (RS%, family rooms, fans but no air-con, Via Matteotti 32, tel. 0588-87377, www.albergoetruria.it, info@albergoetruria.it, Paola, Daniele, and Sveva).

$ Albergo Nazionale, with 38 big and aging rooms, is simple, a little musty, popular with school groups, and steps from the bus stop. It's a nicely located last resort if you have your heart set on sleeping in the old town (RS%, family rooms, elevator, Via dei Marchesi 11, tel. 0588-86284, www.hotelnazionale-volterra.it, info@hotelnazionale-volterra.it).

JUST OUTSIDE THE OLD TOWN

These accommodations are within a 5- to 20-minute walk of the city walls.

Sleep Code

Hotels are classified based on the average price of a standard double room with breakfast in high season.

$$$$	**Splurge:** Most rooms over €170
$$$	**Pricier:** €130-170
$$	**Moderate:** €90-130
$	**Budget:** €50-90
¢	**Backpacker:** Under €50
RS%	Rick Steves discount

Unless otherwise noted, credit cards are accepted, hotel staff speak basic English, and free Wi-Fi is available. Comparison-shop by checking prices at several hotels (on each hotel's own website, on a booking site, or by email). For the best deal, *book directly with the hotel*. Ask for a discount if paying in cash; if the listing includes **RS%**, request a Rick Steves discount.

$$$ Park Hotel Le Fonti, a dull and steep 10-minute walk downhill from Porta all'Arco, can't decide whether it's a business hotel or a resort. The spacious, imposing building feels old and stately and has 64 modern, comfortable rooms, many with views. While generally overpriced, it can be a good value if you manage to snag a deal. In addition to the swimming pool, guests can use its small spa (pay more for a view or a balcony, air-con, elevator, on-site restaurant, wine bar, free parking, Via di Fontecorrenti 2, tel. 0588-85219, www.parkhotellefonti.com, info@parkhotellefonti.com).

$ La Primavera B&B feels like a British B&B transplanted to Tuscany. It's a great value just a few minutes' walk outside Porta Fiorentina (near the Roman Theater). Silvia rents five charming, neat-as-a-pin rooms that share a cutesy-country lounge. The house is set back from the road in a pleasant courtyard. With free parking and the shortest walk to the old town among my out-of-town listings, this is a handy option for drivers (fans but no air-con, Via Porta Diana 15, tel. 0588-87295, mobile 328-865-0390, www.affittacamere-laprimavera.com, info@affittacamere-laprimavera.com).

¢ Chiostro delle Monache, Volterra's youth hostel, fills a wing of the restored Convent of San Girolamo with 68 beds in 23 rooms. It's modern, spacious, and very institutional, with lots of services and a tranquil cloister. Unfortunately, it's about a 20-minute hike out of town (private rooms available and include breakfast, family rooms, reception closed 13:00-15:00 and after 20:00, elevator, free parking, kids' playroom; Via dell Teatro 4, look for hospital sign from main Volterra-San Gimignano road; tel. 0588-86613, www.ostellovolterra.it, info@ostellovolterra.it).

$ Hotel Foresteria, near Chiostro delle Monache and run by the same organization, has 35 big, utilitarian, new-feeling rooms with decent prices but the same location woes as the hostel; it's worth considering for a family with a car and a tight budget (family rooms, air-con, elevator, restaurant, free parking, Borgo San Lazzaro, tel. 0588-80050, www.foresteriavolterra.it, info@ foresteriavolterra.it).

NEAR VOLTERRA

$$ Podere Marcampo is a newer *agriturismo* about two miles outside Volterra on the road to Pisa. Run by Genuino (owner of the recommended Ristorante Enoteca del Duca), his wife, Ivana, and their English-speaking daughter, Claudia, this peaceful spot has three well-appointed rooms and three apartments, plus a swimming pool with panoramic views. Genuino produces his Sangiovese and award-winning Merlot on-site and offers €20 wine-tastings with cheese, homemade *salumi*, and grappa. Cooking classes at their restaurant in town are also available (breakfast included for Rick Steves readers, air-con, free self-service laundry, free parking, tel. 0588-85393, Claudia's mobile 328-174-4605, www.agriturismo-marcampo.com, info@agriturismo-marcampo.com).

Eating in Volterra

Menus feature a Volterran take on regional dishes. *Zuppa alla Volterrana* is a fresh vegetable-and-bread soup, similar to *ribollita*. *Torta di ceci*, also known as *cecina*, is a savory pancake-like dish made with garbanzo beans and served at *pizzerie*. Those with more adventurous palates dive into *trippa* (tripe stew, the traditional breakfast of the alabaster carvers). *Fegatelli* are meatballs made with liver.

$$$$ Ristorante Enoteca del Duca, serving well-presented and creative Tuscan cuisine, offers the best elegant meal in town. You can dine under a medieval arch with walls lined with wine bottles, in a sedate, high-ceilinged dining room (with an Etruscan statuette at each table), on a nice little patio out back, or in their little *enoteca* (wine cellar). Chef Genuino, daughter Claudia, and the friendly staff take good care of diners. The fine wine list includes Genuino's own highly regarded Merlot and Sangiovese. The spacious seating, dressy clientele, and calm atmosphere make this a good choice for a romantic splurge. Their €49 food-sampler fixed-price meal comes with a free glass of wine for diners with this book (Wed-Mon 12:30-15:00 & 19:30-22:00, closed Tue, near City Hall at Via di Castello 2, tel. 0588-81510, www.enoteca-delduca-ristorante.it).

$$ La Carabaccia is unique: It feels like a local family invited you over for a dinner of classic Tuscan comfort food that's

Restaurant Price Code

I've assigned each eatery a price category, based on the average cost of a typical main course (pasta or *secondi*). Drinks, desserts, and splurge items (steak and seafood) can raise the price considerably.

$$$$	**Splurge:**	Most main courses over €20
$$$	**Pricier:**	€15-20
$$	**Moderate:**	€10-15
$	**Budget:**	Under €10

In Italy, pizza by the slice and other takeaway food is **$**; a basic trattoria or sit-down pizzeria is **$$**; a casual but more upscale restaurant is **$$$**; and a swanky splurge is **$$$$**.

rarely seen on restaurant menus. They serve only two pastas and two *secondi* on any given day (listed on the chalkboard by the door), in addition to quality cheese-and-cold-cut plates. Committed to tradition, on Fridays they serve only fish. They also have fun, family-friendly outdoor seating on a traffic-free piazza (Tue-Sat 12:30-14:30 & 19:30-22:00, Sun 12:30-14:30, closed Mon, Piazza XX Settembre 4, tel. 0588-86239, Patrizia and her daughters, Sara and Ilaria).

$$ Ristorante il Sacco Fiorentino is a family-run local favorite for traditional cuisine and seasonal specials. While mostly indoors, the restaurant has a few nice tables on a peaceful street (Thu-Tue 12:00-15:00 & 19:00-22:00, closed Wed, Via Giusto Turazza 13, tel. 0588-88537).

$$ Trattoria da Badò, a 10-minute hike out of town (along the main road toward San Gimignano, near the turnoff for the old hospital), is popular for its *tipica cucina Volterrana*. Giacomo and family offer a rustic atmosphere and serve food with no pretense—"the way you wish your mamma cooks." Reserve before you go, as it's often full (Thu-Tue 12:30-14:30 & 19:30-22:00, closed Wed, Borgo San Lazzero 9, tel. 0588-80402).

$$ La Vecchia Lira, bright and cheery, is a classy self-serve eatery that's a hit with locals as a quick and cheap lunch spot by day and a fancier restaurant at night (Fri-Wed 11:30-14:30 & 19:00-22:30, closed Thu, Via Matteotti 19, tel. 0588-86180, Lamberto and Massimo).

$$ Ristorante Ombra della Sera is another good fine-dining option. While they have a dressy interior, I'd eat here to be on the street and part of the *passeggiata* action (Tue-Sun 12:00-15:00 & 19:00-22:00, closed Mon and mid-Nov-mid-March, Via Gramsci 70, tel. 0588-86663, Massimo and Cinzia).

$$ Empathy Bistrot is a good bet for organic and vegetarian dishes. They also make creative cocktails and smoothies and don't close in the afternoon, making this an option at any hour. Choose between charming streetside tables or the modern, stony interior, where the glass floor hovers over an excavated Etruscan archaeological site (Fri-Wed 11:30-21:00, closed Thu, Via Porta All'Arco 11, tel. 0588-81531).

$$ Pizzeria La Mangiatoia is a fun and convivial place with a Tuscan-cowboy interior and picnic tables outside amid a family-friendly street scene. Enjoy pizzas, huge salads, kebabs, and beer (Thu-Tue 12:00-23:00, closed Wed, Via Gramsci 35, tel. 0588-85695).

Side-by-Side Pizzerias: $ Ombra della Sera dishes out what local kids consider the best pizza in town (Tue-Sun 12:00-15:00 & 19:00-22:00, closed Mon and mid-Nov-mid-March, Via Guarnacci 16, tel. 0588-85274). **$ Pizzeria Tavernetta,** next door, has a romantically frescoed dining room upstairs for classier pizza eating (Wed-Mon 12:00-15:00 & 18:30-22:30, closed Tue, Via Guarnacci 14, tel. 0588-88155).

Picnic: You can assemble a picnic at the few *alimentari* around town and eat in the breezy archaeological park. The most convenient supermarket is Punto Simply at Via Gramsci 12 (Mon-Sat 7:30-13:00 & 16:00-20:00, Sun from 8:30).

Gelato: Of the many ice-cream shops in the center, I've found **L'Isola di Gusto** to be reliably high quality, with flavors limited to what's in season (daily 11:00-late, closed Nov-Feb, Via Gramsci 3, cheery Giorgia will make you feel happy).

Volterra Connections

By Bus: In Volterra, buses come and go from Piazza Martiri della Libertà (buy tickets at the tobacco shop right on the piazza or on board for small extra charge). Most connections are with the C.T.T. bus company (www.pisa.cttnord.it) through Colle di Val d'Elsa ("koh-leh" for short), a workaday town in the valley (4/day Mon-Sat, 1/day Sun, 50 minutes; buy ticket from newsstand nearby); for Pisa, you'll change in Pontedera or Saline di Volterra.

From Volterra, you can ride the bus to these destinations: **Florence** (4/day Mon-Sat, 1/day Sun, 2 hours, change in Colle di Val d'Elsa), **Siena** (4/day Mon-Sat, no buses on Sun, 2 hours, change in Colle di Val d'Elsa), **San Gimignano** (4/day Mon-Sat, 1/day Sun, 2 hours, change in Colle di Val d'Elsa, one connection also requires change in Poggibonsi), **Pisa** (9/day, 2 hours, change in Pontedera or Saline di Volterra).

By Train: The nearest train station is in Saline di Volterra, a 15-minute bus ride away (7/day, 2/day Sun); however, trains from Saline run only to the coast, not to the major bus destinations listed here. It's better to take a bus from Volterra to Pontedera (CTT bus #500, 7/day, fewer on Sun, 1.5 hours), where you can catch a train to **Florence, Pisa,** or **La Spezia** (convenient for the Cinque Terre).

San Gimignano

The epitome of a Tuscan hill town, with 14 medieval towers still standing (out of an original 72), San Gimignano (sahn jee-meen-YAH-noh) is a perfectly preserved tourist trap. There are no important interiors to sightsee, and the town feels greedy and packed with crass commercialism. The locals seem spoiled by the easy money of tourism, and most of the rustic is faux. But San Gimignano is so easy to reach and so visually striking that it remains a good stop, especially if you can sidestep some of the hordes. The town is an ideal place to go against the touristic flow—arrive late in the day, enjoy it at twilight, then take off in the morning before the deluge begins. (Or day-trip here from Volterra—a 30-minute drive away—and visit early or late.)

In the 13th century—back in the days of Romeo and Juliet—feuding noble families ran the hill towns. They'd periodically battle things out from the protection of their respective family towers. Pointy skylines, like San Gimignano's, were the norm in medieval Tuscany.

San Gimignano's cuisine is mostly what you might find in Siena—typical Tuscan home cooking. *Cinghiale* (cheeng-GAH-lay, boar) is served in almost every way: stews, soups, cutlets, and, my favorite, salami. The area is well-known for producing some of the best saffron in Italy; you'll find the spice for sale in shops (fairly expensive) and as a flavoring in meals at finer restaurants. Although Tuscany is normally a red-wine region, the most famous Tuscan white wine comes from here: the inexpensive, light, and fruity Vernaccia di San Gimignano.

Orientation to San Gimignano

While the basic ▲▲▲ sight here is the town of San Gimignano itself (pop. 7,000, just 2,000 of whom live within the walls), there are a few worthwhile stops. The wall circles an amazingly preserved stony town, once on the Via Francigena pilgrimage route to Rome. The road, which cut through the middle of San Gimignano, is named for St. Matthew in the north (Via San Matteo) of town and St. John in the south (Via San Giovanni). The town is centered on two delightful squares—Piazza del Duomo and Piazza della Cisterna—where you find the town well, City Hall, and cathedral (along with most of the tourists).

TOURIST INFORMATION

The helpful TI is in the old center on Piazza del Duomo (daily March-Oct 10:00-13:00 & 15:00-19:00, Nov-Feb 10:00-13:00 & 14:00-18:00, bus tickets, tel. 0577-940-008, www.sangimignano. com). They also offer a two-hour minibus tour to a countryside winery (€20, April-Oct Tue and Thu at 17:00, book one day in advance).

ARRIVAL IN SAN GIMIGNANO

The **bus** stops at the main town gate, Porta San Giovanni. There's no baggage storage in town.

You can't **drive** within the walled town; drive past the *ZTL* red circle and you'll get socked with a big fine. Three numbered pay lots are a short walk outside the walls: The handiest is Parcheggio Montemaggio (P2), at the bottom of town near the bus stop, just outside Porta San Giovanni (€2/hour, €20/day). Least expensive is the lot below the roundabout and Coop supermarket, called Parcheggio Giubileo (P1; €1.50/hour, €6/day), a steeper hike into town. And at the north end of town, by Porta San Jacopo, is Parcheggio Bagnaia (P3/P4, €2/hour, €15/day). Note that some lots—including the one directly in front of Coop and the one just outside Porta San Matteo—are designated for locals and have a one-hour limit for tourists.

HELPFUL HINTS

Market Day: Thursday is market day on Piazza del Duomo (8:00-13:00), but for local merchants, every day is a sales frenzy.

Services: A public **WC** is just off Piazza della Cisterna; you'll also find WCs at the Rocca fortress, near San Bartolo church, just outside Porta San Matteo, and at the Parcheggio Bagnaia parking lot.

Shuttle Bus: A little electric shuttle bus does its laps about hourly all day from Porta San Giovanni to Piazza della Cisterna to Porta San Matteo. Route #1 runs back and forth through town; route #2—which runs only in summer—connects the three parking lots to the town center (€0.75 one-way, €1.50 all-day pass, buy ticket in advance at TI or tobacco shop, possible to buy all-day pass on bus). When pedestrian congestion

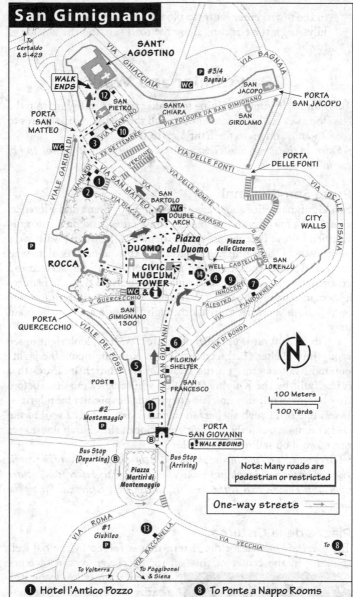

San Gimignano

To Certaldo & S-429

SANT' AGOSTINO

VIA GHIACCIAIA

VIA BAGNAIA

WALK ENDS

P #3/4 Bagnaia

WC

SAN JACOPO

PORTA SAN JACOPO

PORTA SAN MATTEO

San Pietro

SANTA CHIARA

SAN GIROLAMO

VIA FOLGORE DA SAN GIMIGNANO

VIA SAN MARTINO

WC

VIA GARIBALDI

VIALE GARIBALDI

XX SETTEMBRE

VERGINE

VIA DELLE FONTI

PORTA DELLE FONTI

VIA DELLE FONTI

MAINARDI

VIA SAN MATTEO

VIA

VIA DELLE ROMITE

VIA DELLE PISANA

SAN BARTOLO

VIA PIACETO

WC DOUBLE ARCH

CAPASSI

CITY WALLS

Piazza del Duomo

Piazza della Cisterna

DUOMO

ROCCA

P

WELL

CASTELLO

S. STEFANO

SAN LORENZO

CIVIC MUSEUM TOWER &

WC

INNOCENTI

PALESTRO

VIA PIANDORNELLA

SAN GIMIGNANO 1300

PORTA QUERCECCHIO

V. QUERCECCHIO

VIALE DEI FOSSI

VIA DI BONDA

N

PILGRIM SHELTER

100 Meters

100 Yards

POST

SAN FRANCESCO

#2 Montemaggio P

Bus Stop (Departing) B

Piazza Martiri di Montemaggio

Bus Stop (Arriving)

PORTA SAN GIOVANNI

WALK BEGINS

Note: Many roads are pedestrian or restricted

One-way streets

VIA ROMA

#1 Giubileo P

BACCANELLA

VIA VECCHIA

To Voltorra

To Poggibonsi & Siena

To 8

VOLTERRA & SAN GIMIGNANO

1 Hotel l'Antico Pozzo
2 Le Undici Lune
3 Locanda il Pino
4 Hotel la Cisterna
5 Palazzo al Torrione
6 Tobacco Shop (Torrione Keys)
7 Le Vecchie Mura Camere & Ristorante

8 To Ponte a Nappo Rooms
9 Dulcis in Fundo Ristorante
10 Cum Quibus Ristorante
11 Trattoria Chiribiri
12 Locanda di Sant'Agostino
13 Coop Supermarket
14 Gelateria Dondoli

in the town center is greatest (Sat afternoons, all day Sun, and July-Aug), the bus runs along the road skirting the outside of town.

San Gimignano Walk

This quick self-guided walking tour takes you across town, from the bus stop at Porta San Giovanni through the town's main squares to the Duomo, and on to the Sant'Agostino Church.

• *Start at the Porta San Giovanni gate at the bottom (south) end of town.*

Porta San Giovanni

San Gimignano lies about 25 miles from both Siena and Florence, a day's trek for pilgrims en route to those cities, and on a naturally fortified hilltop that encouraged settlement. The town's walls were built in the 13th century, and gates like this helped regulate who came and went. Today, modern posts keep out all but service and emergency vehicles. The small square just outside the gate features a memorial to the town's WWII dead. Follow the pilgrims' route (and flood of modern tourists) through the gate and up the main drag.

About 100 yards up, where the street widens, look right to see a pilgrims' shelter (12th-century, Pisan Romanesque). The eight-pointed Maltese cross on the facade of the church indicates that it was built by the Knights of Malta, whose early mission (before they became a military unit) was to provide hospitality for pilgrims. It was one of 11 such shelters in town. Today, only the wall of the shelter remains, and the surviving interior of the church houses yet one more shop selling gifty edibles.

• *Carry on past all manner of shops, up to the top of Via San Giovanni. Look up at the formidable inner wall, built 200 years before today's outer wall. Just beyond that is the central Piazza della Cisterna. Sit on the steps of the well.*

Piazza della Cisterna

The piazza is named for the cistern that is served by the old well standing in the center of this square. A clever system of pipes  drained rainwater from the nearby rooftops into the underground cistern. This square has been the center of the town since the ninth century. Turn in a slow circle and observe the commotion of rustic-yet-proud facades crowding in a tight huddle around the well. Imagine this square in pilgrimage times, lined by inns and taverns for the town's guests. Now finger the grooves in the lip of the well and imagine generations of maids and children fetching water. Each Thursday morning, the square fills with a market—as it has for more than a thousand years.

• *Notice San Gimignano's famous towers.*

The Towers

Of the original 72 towers, only 14 survive (and one can be climbed—at the City Hall). Some of the original towers were just

empty, chimney-like structures built to boost noble egos, while others were actually the forts of wealthy families.

Before effective city walls were developed, rich people needed to fortify their own homes. These towers provided a handy refuge when ruffians and rival city-states were sacking the town. If under attack, tower owners would set fire to the external wooden staircase, leaving the sole entrance unreachable a story up; inside, fleeing nobles pulled up behind them the ladders that connected each level, leaving invaders no way to reach the stronghold at the tower's top. These towers became a standard part of medieval skylines. Even after town walls were built, the towers continued to rise—now to fortify noble families feuding within a town (Montague and Capulet-style).

In the 14th century, San Gimignano's good times turned very bad. In the year 1300, about 13,000 people lived within the walls. Then, in 1348, a 6 month plague decimated the population, leaving the once-mighty town with barely 4,000 survivors. Once fiercely independent, now crushed and demoralized, San Gimignano came under Florence's control and was forced to tear down most of its towers. (The Banca CR Firenze building occupies the remains of one such toppled tower.) And, to add insult to injury, Florence redirected the vital trade route away from San Gimignano. The town never recovered, and poverty left it in a 14th-century architectural time warp. That well-preserved cityscape, ironically, is responsible for the town's prosperity today.

• *From the well, walk 30 yards uphill to the adjoining square with the cathedral.*

Piazza del Duomo

Stand at the base of the stairs in front of the church. Since before there was gelato, people have lounged on these steps. Take a 360-degree spin clockwise: The cathedral's 12th-century facade is plain-Jane Romanesque—finished even though it doesn't look it. To the right, the two Salvucci Towers (a.k.a. the "Twin Towers") date from the 13th century. Locals like to brag that the architect who designed New York City's Twin Towers was inspired by these. The towers are empty shells, built by the wealthy Salvucci family

simply to show off. At that time, no one was allowed a vanity tower higher than the City Hall's 170 feet. So the Salvuccis built two 130-foot towers—totaling 260 feet of stony ego trip.

The stubby tower next to the Salvucci Towers is the Merchant's Tower. Imagine this in use: ground-floor shop, warehouse upstairs (see the functional shipping door), living quarters, and finally the kitchen on the top (for fire-safety reasons). The holes in the walls held beams that supported wooden balconies and exterior staircases. The tower has heavy stone on the first floor, then cheaper and lighter brick for the upper stories.

Opposite the church stands the first City Hall, with its 170-foot tower, nicknamed "the bad news tower." While the church got to ring its bells in good times, these bells were for wars and fires. The tower's arched public space hosted a textile market back when cloth was the foundation of San Gimignano's booming economy.

Next is the super-sized "new" City Hall, with its 200-foot tower (the only one in town open to the public; for visiting info, see the Civic Museum and Tower listing, later). The climbing lion is the symbol of the city. The coats of arms of the city's leading families have been ripped down or disfigured. In medieval times locals would have blamed witches or ghosts. For the last two centuries, they've blamed Napoleon instead.

Between the City Hall and the cathedral, a statue of St. Gimignano presides over all the hubbub. The fourth-century bishop protected the village from rampaging barbarians—and is now the city's patron saint. (To enter the cathedral, walk under that statue.)

• You'll also see the...

Duomo (Collegiata)

Inside San Gimignano's Romanesque cathedral, Sienese Gothic art (14th century) lines the nave with parallel themes—Old Testament on the left and New Testament on the right. (For example, from back to front: Creation facing the Annunciation, the birth of Adam facing the Nativity, and—farther forward—the suffering of Job opposite the suffering of Jesus.) This is a classic use of art to teach. Study the fine Creation series (along the left side). Many scenes are portrayed with a 14th-century "slice of life" setting to help lay townspeople relate to Jesus—in the same way that many white Christians are more comfortable thinking of Jesus as Caucasian.

To the right of the altar, the St. Fina Chapel honors the devout, 13th-century local girl who brought forth many miracles on her death. Her tomb is beautifully frescoed with scenes from her life by Domenico Ghirlandaio (famed as Michelangelo's teacher). The altar sits atop Fina's skeleton, and its centerpiece is a reliquary that contains her skull (€4, includes dry audioguide; April-Oct Mon-Fri 10:00-19:30, Sat until 17:30, Sun 12:30-19:30; shorter hours off-season; buy ticket and enter from courtyard around left side).

• *From the church, hike uphill (passing the church on your left) following signs to* Rocca e Parco di Montestaffoli. *Keep walking until you enter a peaceful hilltop park and olive grove, set within the shell of a 14th-century fortress the Medici of Florence built to protect this town from Siena.*

Hilltop Views at the Rocca

On the far side, 33 steps take you to the top of a little tower (free) for the best views of San Gimignano's skyline; the far end of town and the Sant'Agostino Church (where this walk ends); and a commanding 360-degree view of the Tuscan countryside. San Gimignano is surrounded by olives, grapes, cypress trees, and—in the Middle Ages—lots of wild dangers. Back then, farmers lived inside the walls and were thankful for the protection.

• *Return to the bottom of Piazza del Duomo, turn left, and continue your walk, cutting under the double arch (from the town's first wall). In around 1200, this defined the end of town. The* **Church of San Bartolo** *stood just outside the wall (on the right). The Maltese cross over the door indicates that it likely served as a hostel for pilgrims. As you continue down Via San Matteo, notice that the crowds have dropped by at least half. Enjoy the breathing room as you pass a fascinating array of stone facades from the 13th and 14th centuries—now a happy cancan of wine shops and galleries. Reaching the gateway at the end of town, follow signs to the right to reach...*

Sant'Agostino Church

This tranquil church, at the far end of town (built by the Augustinians who arrived in 1260), has fewer crowds and more soul. Behind the altar, a lovely fresco cycle by Benozzo Gozzoli (who painted the exquisite Chapel of the Magi in the Medici-Riccardi Palace in Florence) tells of the life of St. Augustine, a North African monk who preached simplicity (pay a few coins for light). The kind, English-speaking friars (from Britain and the US) are happy to tell you about their church and way of life. Pace the peaceful cloister before heading back into the tourist mobs (free, April-Oct daily 10:00-12:00 & 15:00-19:00, shorter hours off-season; Sunday Mass in English at 11:00).

Sights in San Gimignano

▲Civic Museum and Tower (Musei Civici and Torre Grossa)

This small, entertaining museum, consisting of three unfurnished rooms, is inside the City Hall (Palazzo Comunale). The main reason to visit is to scale the tower, which offers sweeping views over San Gimignano and the countryside.

Cost and Hours: €7.50 includes museum and tower; daily April-Sept 9:30-19:00, Oct-March 11:00-17:30, audioguide-€2, Piazza del Duomo, tel. 0577-990-312, www.sangimignanomusei.it.

Visiting the Museum: You'll enter the complex through a delightful stony courtyard (to the left as you face the Duomo). Climb up to the loggia to buy your ticket.

The main room (across from the ticket desk), called the **Sala di Consiglio** (a.k.a. Dante Hall, recalling his visit in 1300), is covered in festive frescoes, including the *Maestà* by Lippo Memmi (from 1317). This virtual copy of Simone Martini's *Maestà* in Siena proves that Memmi didn't have quite the same talent as his famous brother-in-law. The art gives you a peek at how people dressed, lived, worked, and warred back in the 14th century.

Upstairs, the **Pinacoteca** displays a classy little painting collection of mostly altarpieces. The highlight is a 1422 altarpiece by Taddeo di Bartolo honoring St. Gimignano (far end of last room). You can see the saint, with the town—bristling with towers—in his hands, surrounded by events from his life.

Before going back downstairs, be sure to stop by the **Mayor's Room** (Camera del Podestà, across the stairwell from the Pinacoteca). Frescoed in 1310, it offers an intimate and candid peek into the 14th century. As you enter, look right up in the corner to find a young man ready to experience the world. He hits his parents up for a bag of money and is on his way. Suddenly (above the window), he's in trouble,

entrapped by two prostitutes, who lead him into a tent where he loses his money, is turned out, and is beaten. Above the door, from left to right, you see a parade of better choices: marriage, the cradle of love, the bride led to the groom's house, and newlyweds bathing together and retiring happily to their bed.

The highlight for most visitors is a chance to climb the **Tower** (Torre Grossa, entrance halfway down the stairs from the Pinacoteca). The city's tallest tower, 200 feet and 218 steps up, rewards those who climb it with a commanding view. See if you can count the town's 14 towers. It's a sturdy, modern staircase most of the way, but the last stretch is a steep, ladder-like climb.

San Gimignano 1300

Artists and brothers Michelangelo and Raffaello Rubino share an interesting attraction in their workshop: a painstakingly rendered 1:100 scale clay model of San Gimignano at the turn of the 14th century. Step through a shop selling their art to enjoy the model. You can see the 72 original "tower houses," and marvel at how unchanged the street plan remains today. You'll peek into cross-sections of buildings, view scenes of medieval life both within and outside the city walls, and watch a video about the making of the model.

Cost and Hours: Free, daily 10:00-18:00, Dec-April until 17:00, on a quiet street a block over from the main square at Via Costarella 3, mobile 327-439-5165, www.sangimignano1300.com.

Sleeping in San Gimignano

($$$$ = Splurge, $$$ = Pricier, $$ = Moderate, $ = Budget)
Although the town is a zoo during the daytime, locals outnumber tourists when evening comes, and San Gimignano becomes mellow and enjoyable.

NEAR PORTA SAN MATTEO, AT THE QUIET END OF TOWN

If arriving by bus, save yourself a crosstown walk to these accommodations by asking for the Porta San Matteo stop (rather than the main stop near Porta San Giovanni). Drivers can park at the less-crowded Bagnaia lots (P3 and P4), and walk around to Porta San Matteo.

$$$ Hotel l'Antico Pozzo is an elegantly restored, 15th-century townhouse with 18 tranquil, comfortable rooms, a peaceful interior courtyard terrace, and an elite air (air-con, elevator, Via San Matteo 87, tel. 0577-942-014, www.anticopozzo.com, info@anticopozzo.com; Emanuele, Elisabetta, and Mariangela).

$$ Le Undici Lune ("The 11 Moons") is situated in a tight but characteristic circa-1300 townhouse with steep stairs at the tranquil end of town. Its three rooms and one apartment have been tastefully decorated with modern flair by Gabriele (RS%, air-con,

Via Mainardi 9, mobile 389-236-8174, www.leundicilune.com, leundicilune@gmail.com).

$ Locanda il Pino has just seven rooms and a big living room. It's dank but clean and quiet. Run by English-speaking Elena and her family, it sits above their elegant restaurant at the quiet end of town, just inside Porta San Matteo (breakfast extra, fans, Via Cellolese 4, tel. 0577-940-218, www.locandailpino.it, locandailpino@gmail.com).

NEAR THE MAIN SQUARE, AT THE BUSY END OF TOWN

$$ Hotel la Cisterna, right on Piazza della Cisterna, feels old and stately, with 48 aging rooms, some with panoramic view terraces— a scene from the film *Tea with Mussolini* was filmed from one (RS%, air-con, elevator, good restaurant with great view, closed Jan-Feb, Piazza della Cisterna 23, tel. 0577-940-328, www.hotelcisterna.it, info@hotelcisterna.it, Alessio).

$$ Palazzo al Torrione, on an untrampled side street just inside Porta San Giovanni, is quiet and handy, and generally better than most local hotels. Their 10 modern rooms are spacious and tastefully appointed (RS%, family rooms, breakfast extra, air-con, pay parking, inside and left of gate at Via Berignano 76; operated from tobacco shop 2 blocks away, on the main drag at Via San Giovanni 59; tel. 0577-940-480, mobile 338-938-1656, www.palazzoaltorrione.com, palazzoaltorrione@palazzoaltorrione.com, Vanna and Francesco).

$ Le Vecchie Mura Camere offers three good rooms above their recommended restaurant along a rustic lane, clinging just below the main square (no breakfast, air-con, Via Piandornella 15, tel. 0577-940-270, www.vecchiemura.it, info@vecchiemura.it, Bagnai family).

IN THE COUNTRYSIDE, WITH A STUNNING VIEW

$$ Ponte a Nappo, run by enterprising Carla Rossi and her English-speaking sons, Francesco and Andrea, has six basic rooms and two apartments in a kid-friendly farmhouse. Located a mile below town, this place has stunning San Gimignano views. A picnic dinner lounging on their comfy garden furniture next to the big swimming pool as the sun sets is good Tuscan living (RS%—use code "RickSteves," air-con, free parking, tel. 0577-907-282, mobile 349-882-1565, www.accommodation-sangimignano.com, info@rossicarla.it). About 100 yards below the monument square at Porta San Giovanni, find tiny Via Baccanella/Via Vecchia and drive downhill. They also rent a dozen rooms and apartments in town.

Eating in San Gimignano

($$$$ = Splurge, $$$ = Pricier, $$ = Moderate, $ = Budget)
My first two listings cling to quiet, rustic lanes overlooking the
Tuscan hills (yet just a few steps off the main street); the rest are
buried deep in the old center.

$$$ Dulcis in Fundo Ristorante, small and family-run,
proudly serves modest portions of "revisited" Tuscan cuisine (with
a modern twist and gourmet presentation) in a jazzy ambience.
This enlightened place uses top-quality ingredients, many of which
come from their own farm. They also offer vegetarian and gluten-
free options (Thu-Tue 12:30-14:30 & 19:15-21:45, closed Wed and
Nov-Feb, Vicolo degli Innocenti 21, tel. 0577-941-919, Roberto
and Cristina).

$$ Le Vecchie Mura Ristorante has good service, great
prices, tasty if unexceptional home cooking, and the ultimate view.
It's romantic indoors or out. They have a dressy, modern interior
where you can dine with a view of the busy stainless-steel kitchen
under rustic vaults, but the main reason to come is for the incredible, cliff-side garden terrace. Cliff-side tables are worth reserving
in advance by calling or dropping by: Ask for "front view" (open
only for dinner 18:00-22:00, closed Tue, Via Piandornella 15, tel.
0577-940-270, Bagnai family).

$$$ Cum Quibus ("In Company"), tucked away near Porta
San Matteo, has a small dining room with soft music, beamed
ceilings, modern touches, and a sophisticated vibe; it also offers
al fresco tables in its interior patio. Lorenzo and Simona produce
tasty and creative Tuscan cuisine (Wed-Mon 12:30-14:30 & 19:00-
22:00, closed Tue, reservations advised, Via San Martino 17, tel.
0577-943-199).

$ Trattoria Chiribiri, just inside Porta San Giovanni on the
left, serves homemade pastas and desserts at good prices. While
its petite size and tight seating make it hot in the summer, it's a
good budget option—and, as such, it's in all the guidebooks (daily
11:00-23:00, Piazza della Madonna 1, tel. 0577-941-948, Maria
and Maurizio).

$$ Locanda di Sant'Agostino spills out onto the peaceful
square, facing Sant'Agostino Church. It's cheap and cheery, serv-
ing lunch and dinner daily—big portions of basic food in a restful
setting. Dripping with wheat stalks and atmosphere on the inside,
it has shady on-the-square seating outside (daily 11:00-23:00,
closed Wed off-season, closed Jan-Feb, Piazza Sant'Agostino 15,
tel. 0577-943-141, Genziana and sons).

Near Porto San Matteo: Just inside Porta San Matteo are a
variety of handy and inviting good-value restaurants, bars, cafés,

and *gelaterias*. Eateries need to work harder here at the nontouristy end of town.

Picnics: The big, modern **Coop supermarket** sells all you need for a nice spread (Mon-Sat 8:30-20:00, closed Sun, at parking lot below Porta San Giovanni). Or browse the little shops guarded by boar heads within the town walls; they sell pricey boar meat *(cinghiale)*. Pick up 100 grams (about a quarter pound) of boar, cheese, bread, and wine and enjoy a picnic in the garden at the Rocca or the park outside Porta San Giovanni.

Gelato: To cap the evening and sweeten your late-night city stroll, stop by **Gelateria Dondoli** on Piazza della Cisterna (at #4). Gelatomaker Sergio was a member of the Italian team that won the official Gelato World Cup—and his gelato really is a cut above (tel. 0577-942-244, Dondoli family).

San Gimignano Connections

Bus tickets are sold at the bar just inside the town gate or at the TI. Many connections require a change at Poggibonsi (poh-jee-BOHN-see), which is also the nearest train station.

From San Gimignano by Bus to: Florence (hourly, fewer on Sun, 1.5-2 hours, change in Poggibonsi), **Siena** (8/day direct, on Sun must change in Poggibonsi, 1.5 hours), **Volterra** (4/day Mon-Sat; 1/day Sun—in the late afternoon and usually crowded—with no return to San Gimignano; 2 hours, change in Colle di Val d'Elsa, one connection also requires change in Poggibonsi). Note that the bus connection to Volterra is four times as long as the drive; if you're desperate to get there faster, you can pay about €70 for a taxi.

By Car: San Gimignano is an easy 45-minute drive from Florence (take the A-1 exit marked *Firenze Certosa*, then a right past tollbooth following *Siena per 4 corsie* sign; exit the freeway at Poggibonsi). From San Gimignano, it's a scenic and windy half-hour drive to Volterra.

THE HEART OF TUSCANY

Montepulciano • Pienza • Heart of Tuscany Drive •
Montalcino

If your Tuscan dreams feature vibrant neon-green fields rolling to infinity, punctuated by snaking cypress-lined driveways; humble but beautiful (and steep) hill towns; and world-class wines to make a connoisseur weep, set your sights on the heart of this region.

An hour south of Siena, this slice of splendor—which specializes in views and wine—is a highlight, particularly for drivers. With an astonishing diversity of towns, villages, abbeys, wineries, countryside restaurants, and accommodations—all set within jaw-dropping scenery, this subregion of Tuscany is a fine place to abandon your itinerary and just slow down.

Even though the area's towns sometimes seem little more than a rack upon which to hang the vine-draped hills, each one has its own endearing personality. The biggest and most interesting, Montepulciano, boasts a medieval cityscape wearing a Renaissance coat, wine cellars that plunge deep down into the cliffs it sits upon, and a classic town square. Pienza is a sure-of-itself, planned Renaissance town that gave the world a pope. And mellow Montalcino is (even more than most towns around here) all about its wine: the famous Brunello di Montalcino.

PLANNING YOUR TIME

As this compact region is hemmed in by Italy's two main north-south thoroughfares—the A-1 expressway and SR-2 highway—even those with a few hours to spare can get an enticing taste. But ideally, spend two nights and three full days (see my three-day plan, later). Many travelers enjoy home-basing here for up to a week, appreciating not only the area's many attractions, but also its strategic position for day trips to Siena (less than an hour away),

Heart of Tuscany at a Glance

▲▲▲**Montepulciano** Hill town (with grand vistas, wonderful wine cellars, and a medieval soul) that corrals the essence of Tuscany within its walls. See page 670.

▲▲▲**Heart of Tuscany Drive** An unforgettable day lacing together the views, villages, and disparate rural attractions of this region (including both Montepulciano and Pienza). See page 690.

▲▲**Pienza** Unique, pint-sized, planned Renaissance town that's amazingly well-preserved, very touristy, and relatively unhilly. See page 684.

▲▲**Montalcino** Touristy "Brunello-ville" wine capital that still exudes a stony charm; aside from the wine, it feels like a second-rate repeat of Montepulciano. See page 698.

▲▲**Brunello Wineries** My favorite countryside places to sample the famous Brunello di Montalcino, all gorgeously situated among hills and vineyards. **Hours:** Occasionally welcoming to drop-ins, but it's much better to call ahead to schedule a tour and tasting. See page 702.

▲▲**Sleeping at an *Agriturismo* or Countryside B&B** The best way to experience rural Tuscany: rustic, rural accommodations, most run by families who are dedicated to making sure their cows and their guests are both well-fed. See page 667.

▲**La Foce Gardens** Delightful, unique gardens with gorgeous plantings, engaging history, and fine panoramas. **Hours:** Visit by 50-minute tour only; April-Oct Wed at 15:00, 16:00, 17:00, and 18:00; Sat-Sun at 11:30, 15:00, and 16:30; no tours in winter. Reserve in advance. See page 669.

▲**Bagno Vignoni** Quirky little spa town that's simply fun to check out, whether you take a dip or not. See page 696.

Volterra, San Gimignano, Florence, and Orvieto (each about 1.5 hours away).

Choosing a Home Base: Montepulciano is the most all-around engaging town; it's the best choice for those without a car (though connections can still be tricky), and also works well for drivers. With its easy access to the vineyards, Montalcino makes sense for wine pilgrims. And for drivers who'd like to home-base in the countryside, I've listed several *agriturismi* and other rural accommodations later in this section.

The Heart of Tuscany in Three Days

Three days is enough to get a good look at the area's many highlights. Here's a smart plan, assuming you're coming from Siena. (If coming from the south, do it in reverse.)

Day One: On your way south from Siena, visit a winery north of Montalcino before settling into Montepulciano (or your choice of countryside accommodations).

Day Two: Follow my Heart of Tuscany Drive, including a sightseeing-and-gelato stop in Pienza. Have dinner back in Montepulciano, or in the nearby countryside.

Day Three: Your day is free to enjoy and sightsee Montepulciano, or drive to any countryside attractions you've missed so far. You could head to your next destination this afternoon, or spend a third night.

GETTING AROUND THE HEART OF TUSCANY

By Car: This area is ideal by car. Distances are short, and it's easy to mix-and-match sights. Navigate by town names and use a good

map or a mapping app to keep you on track. Google Maps works well (even when it's offline; see page 1170). Be careful to look at the routes it suggests before choosing one and try to stay on main roads that are paved. Some of the sights I've described are on tiny back lanes, marked only with easy-to-miss, low-profile signs from the main roads. I've given distances in kilometers to match up with your rental car's odometer.

In small hill towns, make it a habit to park at the lot just outside town and walk in. White lines indicate free parking; blue lines indicate paid parking (pay at the station, then display the ticket on your windshield); and yellow lines are only for locals. Parking machines typically don't accept bills or give change; have plenty of coins on hand.

By Public Transportation: While you can reach many of this chapter's sights by public buses, connections are slow, infrequent, and often require a transfer. Taxis can help connect the dots more efficiently. Montepulciano is the best home base for those without a car (though it's still not entirely convenient).

TOURS IN TUSCANY

A good local guide can help you take full advantage of everything this area has to offer. One with a car can save you lots of time and stress.

Antonella Piredda, who lives in the village of Montisi (just

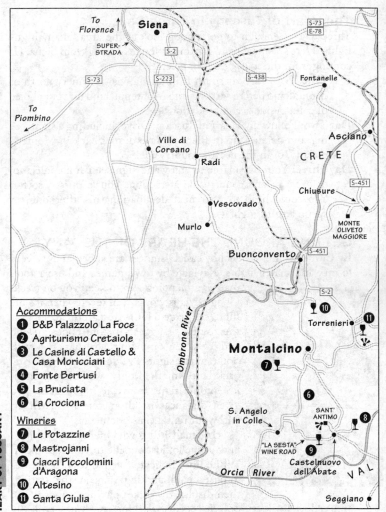

To Florence

Siena

SUPER-STRADA

S-2

S-73

E-78

S-73

S-223

S-438

Fontanelle

To Piombino

Ville di Corsano

Radi

CRETE

Asciano

Chiusure

S-451

Vescovado

Murlo

MONTE OLIVETO MAGGIORE

Buonconvento

S-451

S-2

Ombrone River

Torrenieri

Montalcino

Accommodations
1 B&B Palazzolo La Foce
2 Agriturismo Cretaiole
3 Le Casine di Castello & Casa Moricciani
4 Fonte Bertusi
5 La Bruciata
6 La Crociona

Wineries
7 Le Potazzine
8 Mastrojanni
9 Ciacci Piccolomini d'Aragona
10 Altesino
11 Santa Giulia

S. Angelo in Colle

SANT' ANTIMO

"LA SESTA" WINE ROAD

Orcia River

Castelnuovo dell'Abate

VAL

Seggiano

HEART OF TUSCANY

north of Pienza), is smart, well-organized, and enjoyably opinionated (€60/hour, 3-hour minimum, €350/all day, she can join you in your car or hire a driver for extra, mobile 347-456-5150, anto@antonellapiredda.com, www.antonellapiredda.com).

Roberto Bechi runs all-day minibus tours with a passion for local culture, hands-on experiences, and offbeat sights. The price is reasonable, since he assembles groups of up to eight people to share the experience...and the cost (tour options explained on website, special Rick Steves discount prices: full-day minibus tours-€90/person, booking mobile 320-147-6590, Roberto's mobile 328-425-5648, www.toursbyroberto.com, toursbyroberto@gmail.com). For more on Roberto's tours, see page 592.

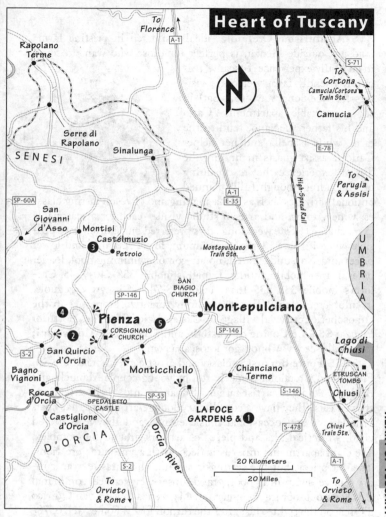

COUNTRYSIDE ACCOMMODATIONS

While I've listed fine accommodations in the towns of Siena, Montepulciano, and Montalcino, a beautiful way to more fully experience this area is to sleep in a farmhouse B&B. For locations, see the map. Some of these are working farms (a prerequisite to be officially called an *agriturismo*) and give a great sense of family life on a farm. Others are just lovely homes in the countryside. The beautiful common denominator is the wonderful people you'll meet as your hosts.

Near Pienza

$$$ Agriturismo Cretaiole, ideally situated in pristine farmland just outside Pienza, is perfect for those who want to settle in and fully experience Tuscany. This family-friendly farm welcomes visitors for weeklong stays (Sat-Sat) in six comfortable apartments. Carlo and his father, Luciano, tend to the farm, while Isabella and her helper Carlotta assist guests in finding the Tuscan experience they're dreaming of—including thoughtfully planned

optional activities such as pasta-making and olive-oil tasting classes, winery tours, and artisan studio visits—each for a reasonable extra charge (RS%, weeklong stays preferred but shorter stays possible when it's slow, 3-night minimum; fewer activities and lower prices mid-Nov-mid-March, no air-con or swimming pool, loaner bikes, loaner mobile phones, Isabella's mobile 338-740-9245, Carlotta's mobile 338-835-1614, tel. 0578-748-083, www.cretaiole. it, info@cretaiole.it). The same family runs two properties in the atmospheric medieval village of Castelmuzio, five miles north of Pienza: **$$$ Le Casine di Castello** and **$$$$ Casa Moricciani;** for details see www.buongiornotoscana.com.

$$$ Fonte Bertusi, a classy and artistic guesthouse between Pienza and Cretaiole, is nicely run by young couple Manuela and Andrea, Andrea's artist-father, Edoardo, and their attention-starved cats. They have a cozy library/lounge/art gallery that hosts installations and occasional music events, and they've scattered vivid, whimsical bits and pieces of artwork around the complex. The eight apartments mix rustic decor with avant-garde creations; it's a bit pricey, but the setting is sublime (breakfast extra, laundry service, swimming pool, grand sunset-view terrace, communal BBQ and outdoor kitchen, just outside Pienza toward San Quirico d'Orcia on the right—just after the turnoff for "Il Fonte," tel. 0578-748-077, Manuela's mobile 339-655-5648, www.fontebertusi.it, info@fontebertusi.it).

$$ La Bruciata is a family-friendly *agriturismo* charmingly tucked in remote-feeling countryside a five-minute drive outside Montepulciano (on the way to Pienza). Can-do Laura and her family produce wine and olive oil and rent seven tasteful, modern rooms split among four apartments (for 2-6 people each) that share a peaceful yard with swimming pool. In the summer (June-Aug), they prefer one-week stays, but shorter visits are possible at other times (air-con for extra charge, farm-fresh meals and cooking classes, Via del Termine 9, tel. 0578-757-704, mobile 339-781-5106, www. agriturismolabruciata.it, info@agriturismolabruciata.it). Leaving

Sleep Code

Hotels are classified based on the average price of a standard double room with breakfast in high season.

$$$$	**Splurge:** Most rooms over €170
$$$	**Pricier:** €130-170
$$	**Moderate:** €90-130
$	**Budget:** €50-90
¢	**Backpacker:** Under €50
RS%	Rick Steves discount

Unless otherwise noted, credit cards are accepted, hotel staff speak basic English, and free Wi-Fi is available. Comparison-shop by checking prices at several hotels (on each hotel's own website, on a booking site, or by email). For the best deal, *book directly with the hotel.* Ask for a discount if paying in cash; if the listing includes **RS%,** request a Rick Steves discount.

Montepulciano toward Pienza, turn off on the left for *Poggiano*, then carefully track red *La Bruciata* signs (using gravel roads).

Near Montalcino

$$ La Crociona, an *agriturismo* farm and working vineyard, rents seven fully equipped apartments with dated furnishings. Fiorella Vannoni and Roberto and Barbara Nannetti offer cooking classes and tastes of the Brunello wine grown and bottled on the premises (reception open 9:00-13:00 & 14:30-19:30, laundry service, covered pool, hot tub, fitness room, La Croce 15, tel. 0577-847-133, www.lacrociona.com, info@lacrociona.com). The farm is about two miles south of Montalcino; don't turn off at the first entrance to the village of La Croce—wait for the second one, following signs to *Tenuta Crocedimezzo e Crociona.* A good restaurant is next door.

At La Foce Gardens, near Montepulciano

$$$ B&B Palazzolo La Foce lets you sleep aristocratically in a small villa just below the La Foce Gardens. Its four colorful rooms share a welcoming kitchen/lounge with a giant fireplace, and an outdoor swimming pool with glorious Tuscan views. All the rooms bask in fine panoramas, and two rooms share a bathroom (no air-con but breezy, Strada della Vittoria 61—but check in at gardens' main entrance to get specific directions to your room, villas also available, tel. 0578-69101, www.lafoce.com, info@lafoce.com).

Montepulciano

Curving its way along a ridge, Montepulciano (mohn-teh-pull-chee-AH-noh) delights visitors with *vino*, views, and—perhaps more than any other large town in this area—a sense of being a real, bustling community rather than just a tourist depot.

Alternately under Sienese and Florentine rule, the city still retains its medieval *contrade* (districts), each with a mascot and flag. The neighborhoods compete the last Sunday of August in the Bravio delle Botti, where teams of men push large wine casks uphill from Piazza Marzocco to Piazza Grande, all hoping to win a banner and bragging rights. The entire last week of August is a festival: Each *contrada* arranges musical entertainment and serves food at outdoor eateries along with generous tastings of the local *vino*.

The city is a collage of architectural styles, but the elegant San Biagio Church, just outside the city walls at the base of the hill, is its best Renaissance building. Most visitors ignore the architecture and focus more on the city's other creative accomplishment, the tasty Vino Nobile di Montepulciano red wine.

Orientation to Montepulciano

Commercial action in Montepulciano centers in the lower town, mostly along Via di Gracciano nel Corso (nicknamed "Corso"). This stretch begins at the town gate called Porta al Prato (near the TI, bus station, and some parking) and winds slowly up, up, up through town—narrated by my self-guided walk. Strolling here, you'll find eateries, gift shops, and tourist traps. The back streets are worth exploring. The main square, at the top of town (up a steep switchback lane from the Corso), is Piazza Grande. Standing proudly above all the touristy sales energy, the square has a noble, Florentine feel.

TOURIST INFORMATION

The helpful TI is just outside the Porta al Prato city gate, directly underneath the small tree-lined parking lot (Mon-Sat 9:30-18:00, Sun until 12:30, daily until 20:00 in July-Aug, books rooms for no fee, public computer, sells bus and train tickets, Piazza Don Minzoni, tel. 0578-757-341, www.prolocomontepulciano.it).

The office on the main square that looks like a TI is actually a privately run "Strada del Vino" (Wine Road) agency. They don't have city info, but they do provide wine-road maps, wine tours in the city, minibus winery tours farther afield, and cooking classes and other culinary experiences (Mon-Fri 10:00-13:00 & 15:00-18:00, Piazza Grande 7, tel. 0578-717-484, www.stradavinonobile. it).

ARRIVAL IN MONTEPULCIANO

By Car: Well-signed pay-and-display parking lots ring the city center (marked with blue lines). Some free spaces are mixed in (marked with white lines)—look around before you park and keep an eye out for time limits.

To start your visit by following my self-guided walk (up the length of the Corso to the main square), park at the north end of town, near the Porta al Prato gate, where you will find the easiest parking options. Around here, the handiest lots are P1 (in front of the TI, with some free spaces) and the unnumbered lot just above, directly in front of the stone gate. If these are full, try lots P2 or P4. Lot P5 is near the bus station (ride up to the gate on the elevator described under "By Bus," later).

To reach the main square quickly, you can ride the twice-hourly shuttle bus up from near the TI (see "Helpful Hints," later). Or you can drive up to parking lots at the top end of town: Approaching Montepulciano, follow signs for *centro storico, duomo,* and *Piazza Grande,* and use the *Fortezza* or *San Donato* lots (flanking the fortress).

Avoid the "ZTL" no-traffic zone (marked with a red circle). If you're sleeping in town, your hotelier can give you a permit to park within the walls; be sure to get very specific instructions before you arrive.

By Bus: Buses leave passengers at the bus station on Piazza Nenni, downhill from the Porta al Prato gate. From the station, cross the street and head inside the modern orange-brick structure burrowed into the hillside, where there's an elevator. Ride to level 1, walk straight down the corridor (following signs for *centro storico*), and ride a second elevator (to a different level 1 and the Poggiofanti Gardens); walk to the end of this park and hook left to find the gate. This is the starting point for my self-guided walk up the Corso to the main square. To get to the top of town in a hurry, you can hop on the shuttle bus either at the bus station itself or near the TI (see "Helpful Hints," next).

HELPFUL HINTS

Exchange Rate: €1 = about $1.10
Country Calling Code: 39 (see page 1154 for dialing instructions)

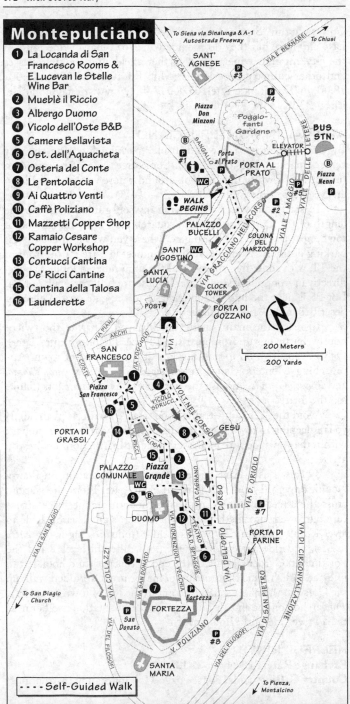

Montepulciano

1 La Locanda di San Francesco Rooms & E Lucevan le Stelle Wine Bar
2 Mueblè il Riccio
3 Albergo Duomo
4 Vicolo dell'Oste B&B
5 Camere Bellavista
6 Ost. dell'Aquacheta
7 Osteria del Conte
8 Le Pentolaccia
9 Ai Quattro Venti
10 Caffè Poliziano
11 Mazzetti Copper Shop
12 Ramaio Cesare Copper Workshop
13 Contucci Cantina
14 De' Ricci Cantine
15 Cantina della Talosa
16 Launderette

- - - - Self-Guided Walk

Market Day: It's on Thursday morning (8:00-13:00), near the bus station.

Services: There's no official **baggage storage** in town, but the TI might let you leave bags with them if they have space. Public **WCs** are located at the TI, to the left of Palazzo Comunale, and at the Sant'Agostino Church.

Shuttle Bus: To avoid the hike up through town to Piazza Grande, you can hop on the orange shuttle bus that departs from near the TI (look for the gray metal canopy over a hotel-booking booth; also stops at the bus station; 2/hour, €1.10, buy tickets at bars, tobacco shops, or the TI).

Laundry: An elegant self-service launderette is at Via del Paolino 2, just around the corner from the recommended Camere Bellavista (daily 8:00-22:00, tel. 0578-717-544).

Taxis: Two taxi drivers operate in Montepulciano. Call 330-732-723 for short trips within town (€10 for rides up or down hill); to reach other towns, call 348-702-4124 (www.strollingintuscany.com).

Montepulciano Walk

This two-part self-guided walk traces the spine of the town from its main entrance up to its hilltop seat of power. Part 1 begins at the big gate at the bottom of town, Porta al Prato (near the TI and several parking lots); Part 2 focuses on the square at the very top of town and the nearby streets. Note that Part 1 is steeply uphill; if you'd rather skip straight to the more level part of town (and Part 2), ride the twice-hourly shuttle bus up, or park at one of the lots near the Fortezza. (When you're done, you can still do Part 1—backward—on the way back down.)

Part 1: Up the Corso

This guided stroll takes you up through Montepulciano's commercial (and touristy) gamut from the bottom of town to the top. While the street is lined mostly with gift shops, you'll pass a few relics of an earlier age.

Begin in front of the imposing Porta al Prato, one of the many stout city gates that once fortified this highly strategic town. Facing the gate, find the sign for the Porta di Bacco *"passaggio segreto"* on the left. While Montepulciano did have secret passages tunneled through the rock beneath it (handy during times of siege), this particular passage—right next to the city's front door—was probably no *segreto*...though it works great for selling salami.

Walk directly through the **Porta al Prato,** looking up to see the slot where the portcullis (heavily fortified gate) could slide down to seal things off. Notice that there are two gates, enabling defenders to trap would-be invaders in a no-man's land where they could be doused with hot tar. Besides having a drop-down portcullis, each gate also had a hinged door—effectively putting four barriers between the town and its enemies.

Pass through the gate and head a block uphill to reach the **Colonna del Marzocco.** This column, topped with a lion holding the Medici shield, is a reminder that Montepulciano existed under the auspices of Florence—but only for part of its history. Originally the column was crowned by a she-wolf suckling human twins, the civic symbol of Siena. At a strategic crossroads of mighty regional powers (Florence, Siena, and the Papal States), Montepulciano often switched allegiances—and this column became a flagpole where the overlords du jour could tout their influence.

The column is also the starting point for Montepulciano's masochistic tradition, the **Bravio delle Botti,** held on the last Sunday of August, in which each local *contrada* (fiercely competitive neighborhood, like Siena's) selects its two stoutest young men to roll a 180-pound barrel up the hill through town. If the vertical climb through town wears you out, be glad you're only toting a camera.

A few steps up, on the right (at #91, with stylized lion heads), is one of the many fine noble palaces that front Montepulciano's main strip. The town is fortunate to be graced with so many bold and noble *palazzi*—Florentine nobility favored Montepulciano as a breezy and relaxed place for a secondary residence. Grand as this palace is, it's small potatoes—the higher you go in Montepulciano, the closer you are to the town center...and the fancier the mansions.

Farther up on the right, at #73 (Palazzo Bucelli), take a moment to examine the **Etruscan and Roman fragments** embedded in the wall, left here by a 19th-century antique dealer. You can quickly distinguish which pieces came from the Romans and those belonging to the earlier Etruscans by their alphabets: The "backwards" Etruscan letters (they read from right to left) resemble Greek. Many of the fragments show a circle flanked by a pair  of inward-facing semicircular designs. This symbol represents the libation cup used for drinking at an Etruscan banquet.

At the top of the block on the right is the **Church of Sant'Agostino.** Its late-Gothic facade features a terra-cotta sculpture group by the architect Michelozzo, a favorite of the Medicis in Florence. Throughout Montepulciano, Florentine touches like this underline that city's influence.

Hike up a few more steps, then take a breather to look back and see the **clock tower** in the middle of the street. The bell ringer at the top takes the form of the character Pulcinella, one of the wild and carefree revelers familiar from Italy's commedia dell'arte theatrical tradition.

Continuing up, at the *alimentari* on the right (at #23), notice the classic old sign advertising milk, butter, margarine, and olive and canola oils. Keep on going (imagine pushing a barrel now), and bear right with the street under another sturdy **gateway**—indicating that this city grew in concentric circles. Passing through the gate and facing the loggia (with the Florentine Medici seal—a shield with balls), turn left and keep on going.

As you huff and puff, notice (on your right, and later on both sides) the steep, narrow, often-covered lanes called *vicolo* ("little street"). You're getting a peek at the higgledy-piggledy medieval Montepulciano. Only when the rationality of Renaissance aesthetics took hold was the main street realigned, becoming symmetrical and pretty. Beneath its fancy suit, though, Montepulciano remains a rugged, Gothic city.

Again, notice the fine and ever bulkier palaces. On the left, a tiny courtyard makes it easier to appreciate the grandiosity of the next palace, now home to **Banca Etruria.** "Etruria"—a name you'll see everywhere around here—is a term for the Etruscan territory of today's Tuscany. By the way, the stone scrolls under the window are a design element called a "kneeling window"—created by Michelangelo and a popular decorative element in High Renaissance and Mannerist architecture. You'll see kneeling windows all over town.

Just after is a fine spot for a coffee break (on the left, at #27): **Caffè Poliziano,** the town's most venerable watering hole (from 1868). Step inside to soak in the genteel atmosphere, with a busy espresso machine, loaner newspapers on long sticks, and a little terrace with spectacular views. It's named for a famous Montepulciano-born 15th-century poet who was a protégé of Lorenzo the Magnificent de Medici and tutored his two sons. So important is he to civic pride that townspeople are nicknamed *poliziani*.

A bit farther up, on the right, notice the precipitous **Vicolo dello Sdrucciolo**—literally "slippery lane." Any *vicolo* on the right can be used as a steep shortcut to the upper part of town, while those on the left generally lead to fine vistas. Many of these side lanes are spanned by brick arches, allowing centuries-old buildings to lean on each other for support rather than toppling over—a fitting metaphor for the tight-knit communities that vitalize Italian small towns.

The next church on the left, the Jesuit **Church of Gesù**, is worth a look. Its interior is elliptical in shape and full of 3-D illusions (don't miss the side chapels and the cupola—all painted on flat surfaces). Soon the street levels out—enjoy this nice, lazy, easy stretch, with interesting shops and artisan workshops (such as the mosaics studio at #14). Across from #64, a lane leads to a charming terrace with a commanding view of the Tuscan countryside.

The **Mazzetti** copper shop (#64) is crammed full of decorative and practical items. Because of copper's unmatched heat conductivity, it's a favored material in premium kitchens. The production of hand-hammered copper vessels like these is a dying art; in this shop, you can see works by Cesare, who makes them in his workshop just up the street. To reach the workshop, go up the tiny covered lane just after the copper shop (Vicolo Benci, on the right). When you emerge, turn right and head uphill steeply; at #4 (on the left), marked *Ramaio,* is Cesare's workshop and museum (for details, see page 679). Continuing steeply uphill will take you to the main square. At the bend just before the square, Cesare's buddy Adamo loves to introduce travelers to Montepulciano's fine wines at the Contucci Cantina (see page 678). Visit Cesare and Adamo now, or head up to the square for Part 2 of this walk.

Either way, Montepulciano's main square is just ahead. You made it!

Part 2: Piazza Grande and Nearby

This pleasant, lively piazza is surrounded by a grab bag of architectural sights. The medieval **Palazzo Comunale,** or town hall, resembles Florence's Palazzo Vecchio—yet another reminder that Florence dominated Montepulciano in the 15th and 16th centuries. The crenellations along the roof were never intended to hide soldiers—they just symbolize power. The big, square central tower makes it clear that the city is keeping an eye out in all directions. It's made of locally quarried travertine stone, the same material ancient Romans used for their great buildings.

Take a moment to survey the square, where the town's four great powers stare each other down. Face the Palazzo Comunale, and keep turning to the right. You'll see the one-time building of the courts, behind the well (Palazzo del Capitano); the noble Palazzo Tarugi, a Renaissance-arcaded confection (with a public loggia at ground level and a private loggia—now enclosed—directly above); and the aristocratic Palazzo Contucci, with its 16th-century Renaissance facade. (The Contucci family still lives in  their palace, producing and selling their own wine.) Continuing your spin, you see the unfinished Duomo looking glumly on, wishing the city hadn't run out of money for its facade.

A cistern system fed by rainwater draining from the roofs of surrounding palaces supplied the fine **well** in the corner. Check out its 19th-century pulleys, the grilles to keep animals from contaminating the water supply, and its decorative top: the Medici coat of arms flanked by lions (representing Florence) dwarfing griffins (representing Montepulciano).

Climbing the town hall's **tower** rewards you with a windblown but commanding panorama from the terrace below the clock. Go into the Palazzo Comunale, head up the stairs to your left, and pay on the second floor. You can pay to go just as far as the terrace, at the base of the tower (€2.50, 71 stairs, or ride the elevator halfway up); or pay more to go all the way to the top, twisting up extremely narrow brick steps past the antiquated bell-ringing mechanism (€5, 76 additional stairs). If you don't mind the claustrophobic climb, it's worth paying extra to reach the very top, from where you can see all the way to Pienza (look just to the right of San Biagio Church; tower open daily May-Oct 10:00-18:00, closed in winter).

The street to the left as you face the tower leads to the **Fortezza** (described later).

To the Church of San Francesco and Views: From the main square, it's a short, mostly level walk to a fine viewpoint. You could head 200 yards straight down the wide street to the right as you face the tower. But for a more interesting look at Montepulciano behind its pretty Renaissance facades, go down the narrow lane between the two palaces in the corner of the square **(Via Talosa).** Pause at the recommended Mueblè il Riccio B&B (with a fine courtyard—peek inside) and look high up across the street to see how centuries of structures have been stitched together, sometimes gracelessly. Across the street is the recommended Cantina della Talosa wine cellar (described later)—imagine the wine caves beneath your feet.

Follow this lane as it bends left, and eventually you'll pop out just below the main square, a few doors from the recommended De' Ricci Cantine wine cellar (described later). Turn right and head down toward the church. Just before #21 (on the left), look for a red-and-gold **shield** over a door with the name *Talosa*. This marks the home of one of Montepulciano's *contrade*, or neighborhoods; birth and death announcements for the *contrada* are posted on the board next to the door.

Across the street and a few steps farther (on the right), you hit a **viewpoint.** From here, it's easy to appreciate Montepulciano's highly strategic position. The ancient town sitting on this high ridge was surrounded by powerful forces—everything you see in this direction was part of the Papal States, ruled from Rome. In the distance is Lake Trasimeno, once a notorious swampland that made it even harder to invade this town.

Continue a few steps downhill, then uphill, into the big parking lot in front of the **Church of San Francesco.** Head out to the overlook for a totally different view: the rolling hills that belonged to Siena. And keep in mind that Montepulciano itself belonged to Florence. For the first half of the 16th century, those three formidable powers—Florence, Siena, and Rome (the papacy)—vied to control this small area. You can also see Montepulciano's most impressive church, San Biagio—well worth a visit for drivers or hikers (described later).

From here, you can head back up to the main square, or drop into one of my recommended cantinas to spelunk their wine cellars.

Sights and Experiences in Montepulciano

For me, Montepulciano's best "experiences" are personal: dropping in on Adamo, the winemaker at Contucci Cantina, and Cesare, the coppersmith at Ramaio Cesare. Both will greet you with a torrent of cheerful Italian; just smile and nod, pick up what you can from gestures, and appreciate this rare opportunity to meet a true local character. If you're visiting one of the wine cellars, study up on the local Vino Nobile di Montepulciano by reading the sidebar on page 702.

▲▲Contucci Cantina

Montepulciano's most popular attraction isn't made of stone—it's the famous wine, Vino Nobile. This robust red can be tasted in any of the cantinas lining Via Ricci and Via di Gracciano nel Corso, but the cantina in the basement of Palazzo Contucci is both historic and fun. Skip the palace's formal wine-tasting showroom facing the square, and instead head down the lane on the right to the actual cellars, where you'll meet lively Adamo (ah-DAH-moh), who has been making wine here since 1961 and welcomes tourists into the cellar. While at the palace, you may meet Andrea or Ginevra Contucci, whose family has lived here since the 11th century. They love to share their family's products with the public. Adamo and the Contuccis usually have a half-dozen bottles open, and at busy times, other members of their staff are likely to speak English.

Cost and Hours: Free drop-in tasting, free cellar tour upon request, daily 9:30-19:00, Piazza Grande 13, tel. 0578-757-006, www.contucci.it.

Visiting the Cantina: After sipping a little wine with Adamo, explore the palace basement, with its 13th-century vaults. Originally part of the town's wall, these chambers have been filled since the 1500s with huge barrels of wine. Dozens of barrels of Croatian and French oak (1,000-2,500 liters each) cradle the wine through a two-year in-the-barrel aging process, while the wine picks up the personality of the wood. After about 35 years, an exhausted barrel has nothing left to offer its wine, so it's retired. Adamo explains that the French oak gives the wine "pure elegance," and the Croatian is more masculine. Each barrel is labeled with the size in liters, the year the wine was barreled, and the percentage of alcohol (determined by how much sun shone in that year). "Nobile"-grade wine needs a minimum of 13 percent alcohol.

▲Ramaio Cesare

Cesare the coppersmith is an institution in Montepulciano, carrying on his father's and grandfather's trade by hammering into existence an immense selection of copper objects in his cavernous workshop. Though his English is limited, Cesare (CHEH-zah-ray) is happy to show you photos of his work—including the copper top of the Duomo in Siena and the piece he designed and personally delivered to Pope Benedict. Peruse his tools: a giant Road Runner-style anvil, wooden hammers, and stencils dating from 1857 that have been passed down from his grandfather and father. Next door, he has assembled a fine museum with items he and his relatives have made, as well as pieces from his personal collection. Cesare is evangelical about copper, and if he's not too busy, he'll create personalized mementoes for visitors—he loves meeting people from around the world who appreciate his handiwork (as his brimming photo album demonstrates). Cesare's justifiable pride in his vocation evokes the hardworking, highly skilled craft guilds that once dominated small-town Italy's commercial and civic life.

Cost and Hours: Demonstration and museum are free, Cesare is generally in his workshop Mon-Sat 8:00-12:30 & 14:30-18:30, closed Sun, 50 yards steeply downhill from the Contucci Cantina at Via del Teatro 4, tel. 0578-758-753, www.rameria.com. Cesare's delightful shop is on the main drag, a block below, at Corso #64—look for *Rameria Mazzetti*, open long hours daily.

Duomo

This church's unfinished facade—rough stonework left waiting for the final marble veneer—is not that unusual. Many Tuscan churches were built just to the point where they had a functional interior, and then, for various practical reasons, the facades were left unfinished. But step inside and you'll be rewarded with some fine art. A beautiful blue-and-white, glazed-terra-cotta *Altar of the Lilies* by Andrea della Robbia is behind the baptismal font (on the left as you enter). The high altar, with a top like a pine forest, features a luminous, late-Gothic Assumption triptych by the Sienese artist Taddeo di Bartolo. Showing Mary in her dreamy eternal sleep as she ascends to be crowned by Jesus, it illustrates how Siena clung to the Gothic aesthetic—elaborate gold leaf and lacy pointed arches—to show heavenly grandeur.

Cost and Hours: Free, daily 8:30-18:30.

▲De' Ricci Cantine

The most impressive wine cellars in Montepulciano sit below the Palazzo Ricci, just a few steps off the main square (toward the Church of San Francesco). Enter through the unassuming door and find your way down, down, down a spiral staircase—with rounded steps designed to go easy on fragile noble feet, and lined with rings held in place by tiny, finely crafted wrought-iron goat heads. You'll wind up in the dramatic cellars, with gigantic barrels under even more gigantic vaults—several stories high. As you go deeper and deeper into the cellars, high up, natural stone seems to take over the brick. At the deepest point, you can peer into the atmospheric Etruscan cave, where a warren of corridors spins off from a filled-in well. Finally you wind up in the shop, where you're welcome to taste a few wines (with some local cheese). Don't miss their delightful dessert wine, vin santo.

Cost and Hours: While tasting is normally €3, it's free for people with this book; €12-20 bottles, affordable shipping, daily 11:00-19:00; enter Palazzo Ricci at Via Ricci 11, look for signs for *Cantine de' Ricci;* tel. 0578-757-166, www.dericci.it, Enrico.

Cantina della Talosa

This historic cellar, which goes down and down to an Etruscan tomb at the bottom, ages a well-respected wine. With a passion and love of their craft, Cristian Pepi and Andrea give enthusiastic tours and tastings. While you can drop by for a free tasting, I'd call ahead to book a tour—€10, including five wines to taste.

Cost and Hours: Free tasting, daily March-Oct 10:00-19:30, shorter hours off-season, a block off Piazza Grande at Via Talosa 8, tel. 0578-757-929, www.talosa.it.

JUST OUTSIDE MONTEPULCIANO
▲San Biagio Church

The church is at the base of Montepulciano's hill, down a picturesque cypress-lined driveway. Often called the "Temple of San Biagio" because of its Greek-cross style, the church—designed by Antonio da Sangallo the Elder and built of locally quarried travertine—feels like perfection (free, generally daily 9:30-17:30). The soaring interior, with a high dome and lantern, creates a quintessential Renaissance space. Stand on the center stone and do a slow 360-degree spin, enjoying the harmony and mathematical perfection in the design. Consider a picnic or snooze on the grass in back, with fine vistas over the Chiana Valley. The restaurant across the street from the church is a local favorite.

Sleeping in Montepulciano

($$$$ = Splurge, $$$ = Pricier, $$ = Moderate, $ = Budget)

$$$$ La Locanda di San Francesco is overpriced but luxurious, with four stylish view rooms over a classy wine bar on a quiet square at Montepulciano's summit (€20 discount for nonrefundable bookings, closed Nov-Easter, air-con, free parking nearby, Piazza San Francesco 5, tel. 0578-758-725, www.locandasanfrancesco.it, info@locandasanfrancesco.it, Cinzia and Luca).

$$ Mueblè il Riccio ("The Hedgehog") is medieval-elegant, with 10 modern and spotless rooms, an awesome roof terrace, and friendly owners. Five are new "superior" rooms with grand views across the Tuscan valleys (family rooms, breakfast extra, air-con, limited free parking—request when you reserve, a block below the main square at Via Talosa 21, tel. 0578-757-713, www.ilriccio.net, info@ilriccio.net, Gió and Ivana speak English). Charming Gió and his son Iacopo give tours of the countryside (€50/hour) in one of their classic Italian cars; for details, see their website. Ivana makes wonderful breakfast tarts.

$$ Albergo Duomo is big, modern, and nondescript, with 13 decent rooms (with small bathrooms) and a comfortable lounge downstairs. With a handy location just a few steps from the main square, it's at the very top of town, with free private parking nearby (family rooms, elevator, air-con in some rooms—extra charge, loaner laptops, Via di San Donato 14, tel. 0578-757-473, www.albergoduomo.it, albergoduomo@libero.it, Elisa and Saverio).

$$ Vicolo dell'Oste B&B, just off the main drag halfway up through town, has five family-friendly modern rooms. Some are like tiny apartments (RS%, includes breakfast at nearby café, on Via dell'Oste 1—an alley leading right off the main drag just after Caffè Poliziano and opposite the *farmacia* at #47, tel. 0578-758-393, www.vicolodelloste.it, info@vicolodelloste.it, Luisa and Giuseppe).

$ Camere Bellavista has 10 tidy rooms. True to its name, each room has a fine view—though some are better than others. Room 6 has a view terrace worth reserving (cash only, no breakfast, lots of stairs with no elevator, reception not always staffed—call before arriving or ring bell, Via Ricci 25, mobile 347-823-2314, www.camerebellavista.it, bellavista@bccmp.com, Gabriella speaks just enough English).

Eating in Montepulciano

These places are all open for lunch (about 12:30-14:30) and again for dinner (about 19:30-22:00). I've noted closed days.

$$$ Osteria dell'Aquacheta is a carnivore's dream come true, beloved among locals for its beef steaks. Its long, narrow room is

jammed with shared tables and tight, family-style seating, with an open fire in back and a big hunk of red beef lying on the counter like a corpse on a gurney. Giulio and his wife, Chiara, run a fun-loving but tight ship—posing with slabs of red meat yet embracing 23 years of trattoria tradition (you'll get one glass to use alternately for wine and water). Steaks are sold by weight (€32/kilo). Typically, two people split a 1.6-kilo steak (that's 3.5 pounds; the smallest they'll cook is 1.2 kilos). They also serve hearty pastas and salads, other meaty plates, and a fine house wine (reservations required, seatings at 12:30, 14:30, 19:30, and 21:30 only, closed Tue, Via del Teatro 22, tel. 0578-717-086, www.acquacheta.eu).

$$ Osteria del Conte, an attractive but humble family-run bistro, offers a €30 *menù del Conte*—a four-course dinner of local specialties including wine—as well as à la carte options and cooking like Mom's. While the interior is very simple, they also have outdoor tables on a stony street at the top of the historic center (closed Wed, Via San Donato 19, tel. 0578-756-062).

$$ Le Pentolaccia is a small, family-run restaurant at the upper, relatively untouristy end of the main drag. With both indoor and outdoor seating, they make tasty traditional Tuscan dishes as well as daily fish specials. Cristiana serves, and husband-and-wife team Jacobo and Alessia stir up a storm in the kitchen (closed Thu, Corso 86, tel. 0578-757-582).

$$ Ai Quattro Venti is right on Piazza Grande, with a simple dining room and outdoor tables on the square. It offers reasonable portions of unfussy Tuscan food in an unpretentious setting. Try their very own organic olive oil and wine (closed Thu, next to City Hall on Piazza Grande, tel. 0578-717-231, Chiara).

Wine Bar/Bistro: With a terrace on a tranquil square in front of the Church of San Francesco, **$ E Lucevan le Stelle** (part of La Locanda di San Francesco), is a fine place to nurse a glass of local wine—€4-9 glasses (also pastas, salads, and soups; daily 12:00-24:00, closed Nov-Easter, Piazza San Francesco 5, tel. 0578-758-725, Luca).

HEART OF TUSCANY

Restaurant Price Code

I've assigned each eatery a price category, based on the average cost of a typical main course (pasta or *secondi*). Drinks, desserts, and splurge items (steak and seafood) can raise the price considerably.

$$$$	**Splurge:** Most main courses over €20
$$$	**Pricier:** €15-20
$$	**Moderate:** €10-15
$	**Budget:** Under €10

In Italy, pizza by the slice and other takeout food is **$**; a basic trattoria or sit-down pizzeria is **$$**; a casual but more upscale restaurant is **$$$**; and a swanky splurge is **$$$$**.

Near Montepulciano, in Monticchiello: If you'd enjoy getting out of town for dinner—but not *too* far—consider the 20-minute drive to the picturesque hill town of Monticchiello, where you can dine at the excellent **Osteria La Porta** with its fine view terrace, or at the modern-feeling **La Cantina della Porta** (both described on page 698). To get there, follow signs to Pienza; then, shortly after passing the road to San Biagio Church (on the right), watch on the left for the Albergo San Biagio. Turn off, take the rough little road that runs up past the left side of this big hotel, and follow it to Monticchiello.

Montepulciano Connections

Get bus schedules at the TI or the bus station on Piazza Pietro Nenni, which seems to double as the town hangout, with a lively bar and locals chatting inside. In fact, there's no real ticket window—buy your tickets at the bar. Check www.sienamobilita.it or www.tiemmespa.it for schedules.

By Bus to: Florence (1-2/day, 2 hours, change in Bettolle, LFI bus, www.lfi.it; or take a bus to Chiusi to catch a train, explained below), **Siena** (6-8/day, none on Sun, 1.5 hours, also possible to change here for Florence express bus), **Pienza** (8/day, 30 minutes), **Montalcino** (3-4/day, none Sun, change in Torrenieri, 1 hour; or consider a taxi—explained below).

By Train: Trains are impractical here; the Montepulciano train station, five miles from town and connected by an infrequent bus, has only milk-run trains (but could be useful for reaching Siena on a Sunday—get details at the TI). More convenient, consider riding the hourly bus 50 minutes to the town of **Chiusi,** which is on the main Florence-Rome rail line.

Taxi Alternatives: As the **Montalcino** bus connection is infrequent and complicated, consider hiring a taxi (about €70; see contact info under "Helpful Hints," earlier).

Pienza

Set on a crest and surrounded by green, rolling hills, the small town of Pienza packs a lot of Renaissance punch. In the 1400s, locally born Pope Pius II of the Piccolomini family decided to remodel his birthplace into a city fit for a pope, in the style that was all the rage: Renaissance. Propelled by papal clout, the town of Corsignano was transformed—in only five years' time—into a jewel of Renaissance architecture. It was renamed Pienza, after Pope Pius. The plan was to remodel the entire town, but work

ended in 1464 when both the pope and his architect, Bernardo Rossellino, died. Their vision—what you see today—was completed a century later.

Pienza's architectural focal point is its main square, Piazza Pio II, surrounded by the Duomo and the pope's family residence, Palazzo Piccolomini. While Piazza Pio II is Pienza's pride and joy, the entire town—a mix of old stonework, potted plants, and grand views—is fun to explore, especially with a camera or sketchpad in hand. You can walk every lane in the tiny town in a few minutes. Pienza is situated on a relatively flat plateau rather than the steep pinnacle of more dramatic towns like Montepulciano and Montalcino. (This is a plus for visitors with limited mobility, who find basically level Pienza easy to explore.)

Tourists flood Pienza on weekends and in peak season, and boutiques selling gifty packages of pecorino cheese and local wine greatly outnumber authentic local shops. Restaurants here tend to be more expensive and less reliable than alternatives in the nearby countryside. For these reasons, Pienza is made to order as a stretch-your-legs break to enjoy the townscape and panoramas, but it's not ideal for lingering overnight (though for some excellent countryside options just outside town, see page 668). For the best experience, visit late in the day, after the day-trippers have dispersed.

Nearly every shop sells the town's specialty: pecorino, a pungent sheep's cheese (you'll smell it before you see it) that's sometimes infused with other ingredients, such as truffles or cayenne pepper. Look on menus for warm pecorino (*al forno* or *alla griglia*), often topped with honey and pine nuts or pears and served with bread. Along with a glass of local wine, this just might lead you to a new understanding of *la dolce vita*.

Orientation to Pienza

Tourist Information: The TI is 10 yards up the street from Piazza Pio II, inside the skippable Diocesan Museum (Wed-Mon 10:30-13:30 & 14:30-18:00, except Sat-Sun 10:00-16:00 in off-season, closed Tue year-round, Corso il Rossellino 30, tel. 0578-749-905). Ignore the *Informaturista* kiosk just outside the gate—it's a private travel agency.

Arrival in Pienza: If **driving,** read signs carefully—some parking spots are reserved for locals, others require the use of a cardboard clock, and others are pay-and-display. Parking is tight, so if you don't see anything quickly, head for the large pay lot at Piazza del Mercato near Largo Roma outside the old town: As you approach town and reach the "ZTL" cul-de-sac (marked with a red circle) in front of the town gate, head up the left side of town and look for the parking turnoff on the left (closed Fri morning during market). **Buses** drop you just a couple of blocks directly in front of the town's main entrance.

Helpful Hints: On Friday mornings, a **market** fills Piazza del Mercato, the main parking lot just outside the town walls. A public **WC,** marked *gabinetti pubblici,* is on the right as you face the town gate from outside on Piazza Dante Alighieri (down the lane next to the faux TI).

Sights in Pienza

I've connected Pienza's main sights with walking directions, which can serve as a handy little orientation to the town. You could do this stroll in 30 minutes, but entering some of the sights could extend your visit to a few hours.

• *Begin in the little park just in front of the town (near the main round-about and bus stop), called Piazza Dante Alighieri. Facing the town, go through the big, ornamental gateway on the right (which was destroyed in World War II, and rebuilt in 1955) and head up the main street...*

Corso il Rossellino

This main drag—named for Bernardo Rossellino (1409-1464), the Renaissance architect who redesigned Pienza according to Pius' orders—is jammed with touristy boutiques. While you won't find great values, these shops are (like Pienza) cute and convenient.

At the end of the second block on the left, at #21, step into the **Marusco e Maria** cheese-and-salami shop. Take a deep whiff and survey the racks of pecorino cheese, made from sheep's milk. For

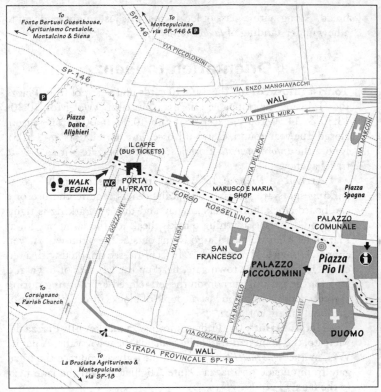

€3 per couple, Fabio or his staff can give you a quick taste of three types of pecorino: *fresco* (young, soft, and mild), *medio* (medium), and *stagionato* (hard, crumbly, and pungent). Consider stocking up at one of these shops for a pricey but memorable picnic. *Finocchiona* is salami with fennel seeds. This was first popularized by wine traders, because fennel seeds make wine taste better. To this day, Italians use the word *infinocchiare* ("fennel-ize") to mean "to trick."

Farther along, watch for the **Church of San Francesco** on the right. It's the only important building in town that dates from before the Pius II extreme makeover. Its humble facade, simple nave, wood-beamed ceiling, bits of 14th-century frescoes, and tranquil adjacent cloister have a charm that's particularly peaceful in the 21st century. But this gloomy medieval style was exactly what Pius wanted to get away from.

• *Continuing one more block, you'll pop out at Pienza's showcase square...*

▲Piazza Pio II

Pienza's small main piazza gets high marks from architecture highbrows for its elegance and artistic unity. The piazza and surround-

Pienza

To Piazza del Mercato Parking

SP-18

100 Meters

100 Yards

Largo Roma

VIA PIA

VIA DOGALI

BUON GIUSTO GELATERIA

"NEW HOUSES"

VIA CASA NUOVE

WALK ENDS

VIA DELL'APPARITA

VIA SANT'ANDREA

SAN CARLO

VIA DELLA VOLPE

LA BANDITA TOWNHOUSE CAFFÈ

VIA SAN CARLO

CORSO

DIOCESAN MUSEUM

ROSSELLINO

VIA FORTUNA

VIA DELL'AMORE

VIA BUIA

VIA CASELLO

TRATTORIA LATTE DI LUNA

PORTA AL CIGLIO

WALL

PORTA AL SANTO

SP-18

P

Note: No cars allowed in town center

- - - - Self-Guided Walk

ing buildings were all designed by Rossellino to form an "outdoor room." Everything is perfectly planned and plotted.

Do a clockwise spin to check out the buildings that face the square, starting with the **Duomo** (which we'll enter soon). High up on the facade is one of many examples you'll spot around town of the Piccolomini family crest: five half-moons, advertising the number of crusades that his family funded. To the right of the Duomo is the **Piccolomini family palace,** now a tourable museum (described later). Notice that the grid lines in the square's pavement continue all the way up the sides of this building, creating a Renaissance cube. Looking farther right, you'll see **City Hall** (Palazzo Comunale), with a Renaissance facade and a fine loggia (to match the square) but a 13th-century bell tower that's shorter than the church's tower. (That's unusual here in civic-minded Tuscany, where municipal towers usually trumpet the importance of town over Church.)

Pope Pius II

Pope Pius II (Enea Silvio Bartolomeo Piccolomini, 1405-1464) was born into one of the most powerful families in Siena. He had an illustrious career as a diplomat, traveled far and wide (fathering two illegitimate children, in Switzerland and Scotland), and gained a reputation for his erotic writings (*The Tale of Two Lovers*). Upon donning the frock, Piccolomini went from ordination to the papacy in just 11 years—a stunning pace spurred, no doubt, by his esteemed lineage. Owing to his educated and worldly upbringing, upon ascending to the papacy Piccolomini chose a name that was not religious, but literary: the ancient poet Virgil first used the term "pious" to describe his hero, Aeneus. One of the most enlightened popes of his time, Pius embraced the burgeoning Renaissance and set out to remake his hometown in pure Renaissance style. Pius was also the first prominent figure known to have suggested the notion of a united Europe, with a common heritage and shared goals (at that time, facing off against the invading Ottomans).

Looking up the lane to the left of City Hall, notice the cantilevered upper floors of the characteristic old houses—a reminder that, while Pienza appears Renaissance on the surface, much of that sheen was added later to fit Pius' vision. Turning right again, see the **Bishop's Palace,** also called the Borgia Palace (now housing the TI and the skippable Diocesan Museum). Pius invited prominent cardinals to occupy the real estate in his custom-built town. The Borgia clan, who built this palace, produced one of the most controversial popes of that age, Alexander VI, who ascended to the papacy a few decades after Pius II. The Borgia were notorious for their shrewd manipulation of power politics. Our word "nepotism"—which comes from the Italian *nipote* (nephew) —dates from this era, when a pope would pull strings to ensure his relatives would succeed him.

Finally, between the Bishop's Palace and the Duomo, a lane leads to the best **view terrace** in town.

• *Now take the time to tour whichever of the square's sights interest you.*

Duomo

The cathedral's classic, symmetrical Renaissance facade (1462) dominates Piazza Pio II. The interior, bathed in light, is an illuminating encapsulation of Pius II's architectural philosophy (free, generally daily 7:00-13:00 & 14:30-19:00). Pius envisioned this church as an antidote to dark, claustrophobic medieval churches, like the Church of San Francesco we saw earlier. Instead, this was to be a "house of glass," representing the cultural enlightenment that came with the Renaissance. The church decoration is also a bit unusual. Rather than Jesus and Mary, the emphasis is on the pope and his family (like the crescent-moon crest of Pius II on the windows). Instead of the colorful frescoes you'd expect, the church has clean, white walls to reflect the light.

▲Palazzo Piccolomini

This palace, the home of Pius II and the Piccolomini family (until 1962), is not quite the interesting slice of 15th-century aristocratic life that it could be (I'd like to know more about the pope's toilet). But this is still the best small-town palace experience I've found in Tuscany. (It famously starred as the Capulets' home in Franco Zeffirelli's 1968 Academy Award-winning *Romeo and Juliet*.) You can peek inside the door for free to check out the well-preserved, painted courtyard. In Renaissance times, most buildings were covered with elaborate paintings like these.

Cost and Hours: €7, audioguide included, Tue-Sun 10:30-12:30 & 14:00-18:00, until 16:30 off-season, closed Mon, live tours also available every half-hour, Piazza Pio II 2, tel. 0578-748-392, www.palazzopiccolominipienza.it.

View Terrace

As you face the church, the upper lane leading left brings you to a panoramic promenade. Views from the terrace include the Tuscan countryside and, in the distance, Monte Amiata, the largest mountain in southern Tuscany. You can exit the viewpoint down the first alley, Via del'Amore—the original Lover's Lane—which leads back to the main drag.

JUST OUTSIDE PIENZA
Corsignano Parish Church (Pieve di Corsignano)

This classic Romanesque parish church *(pieve)*, hugging the slope just below Pienza, is a reminder of a much earlier, rougher, simpler time (before Pope Pius II). This was one of the medieval pilgrimage stops on the Via Francigena. If the church is open, step inside and let your eyes adjust to the very low light. This gloomy, cave-like interior—with just slits for windows—is a far cry from later, brighter architectural styles. Near the entrance on the right, look for the font that was used to baptize the man who would grow up to be Pope Pius II.

Getting There: On foot from Pienza, it's a steep 10-minute downhill walk (as you exit Pienza into the main park, look to your left for *pieve di Corsignano* signs). Similar signs direct drivers to the turnoff just below the old town.

Eating in Pienza

$$$ **La Bandita Townhouse Caffè** offers a break from Tuscan rusticity, focusing instead on tempting modern Italian cuisine (such as spring pea soup or peppered Chianina beef carpaccio). Diners watch the chef work in his open kitchen (lunch served Tue-Sun and dinner nightly, indoor/outdoor seating, Corso il Rossellino 111, easier to enter around the corner on Via Sant'Andrea, tel. 0578-749-005).

$$ **Trattoria Latte di Luna,** with outdoor tables filling a delightful little square, is the more traditional choice. Run by friendly Roberto with Delfina in the kitchen, the dining room features an ancient well and sits on top of Etruscan tunnels (closed Tue, near the end of Corso il Rossellino at Via San Carlo 2, tel. 0578-748-606).

Quick Lunch: For something cheap, characteristic, and fast, just grab a tasty *porchetta* sandwich (€3.50) at the little shop 30 yards off the main square (at Corso il Rossellino 81) to munch under the loggia or at the viewpoint.

Pienza Connections

Bus tickets are sold at the bar/café (marked *Il Caffè*, closed Tue) just outside Pienza's town gate (or pay a little extra and buy tickets from the driver). Buses leave from a few blocks up the street, directly in front of the town entrance. Montepulciano is the nearest transportation hub.

From Pienza by Bus to: Siena (6/day, none on Sun, 1.5 hours), **Montepulciano** (8/day, 30 minutes), **Montalcino** (3-4/day Mon-Sat, none Sun, change in Torrenieri, 45-60 minutes). **Bus info:** www.tiemmespa.it.

Heart of Tuscany Drive

If you have just one day to connect the ultimate Tuscan towns and views, this is the loop I'd stitch together with a driving tour. Most of this journey is through velvety, gentle, rolling hillsides generously draped with vivid-green crops in the springtime, and a parched moonscape in the late summer and fall. This almost otherworldly smoothness constitutes many travelers' notions of Tuscan perfection.

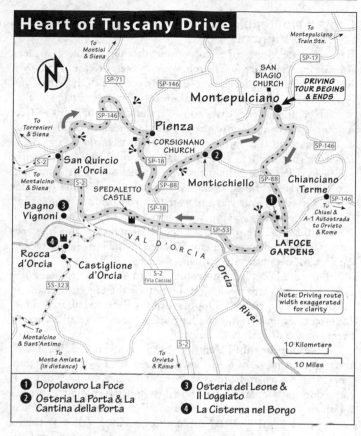

Heart of Tuscany Drive

To Montepulciano Train Stn.

SP-17

DRIVING TOUR BEGINS & ENDS

To Montisi & Siena

SAN BIAGIO CHURCH

SP-71

SP-146

Montepulciano

SP-146

SP-146

Pienza

CORSIGNANO CHURCH

To Torrenieri & Siena

SP-146

SP-18

② **Monticchiello**

SP-88

Chianciano Terme

S-2

San Quircio d'Orcia

SP-88

SP-146

To Montalcino & Siena

S-2

SPEDALETTO CASTLE

SP-18

To Chiusi & A-1 Autostrada to Orvieto & Rome

Bagno Vignoni

③

SP-53

① **LA FOCE GARDENS**

VAL D'ORCIA

④

Rocca d'Orcia

Castiglione d'Orcia

SS-323

S-2 (Via Cassia)

Orcia River

Note: Driving route width exaggerated for clarity

To Montalcino & Sant'Antimo

To Monte Amiata (in distance)

S-2

To Orvieto & Rome

10 Kilometers

10 Miles

① Dopolavoro La Foce
② Osteria La Porta & La Cantina della Porta
③ Osteria del Leone & Il Loggiato
④ La Cisterna nel Borgo

◑ SELF-GUIDED DRIVING TOUR

In addition to larger towns (Montepulciano, Pienza) and smaller ones (Bagno Vignoni, Rocca d'Orcia), this self-guided loop drive, worth ▲▲▲, gives you a good look at the area called the Val d'Orcia (val DOR-chah), boasting some of the best scenery in Italy.

If you're in a rush and don't linger in any of the towns, you could do this drive in a couple of hours. To hit the sights, explore the towns, and linger over a meal or a glass of wine, spread it out over an entire day. (You could even splice in a side-trip to a Brunello winery for a tasting, if you like.) I've started and ended the clockwise loop in Montepulciano, but you could just as easily start and end in Pienza. If gardens are your thing, do this loop when La Foce Gardens are open (Wed, Sat, or Sun afternoons only—for specifics, see page 695).

Leg #1: Montepulciano to La Foce to Bagno Vignoni

Before leaving Montepulciano, consider dropping by the showpiece Renaissance **San Biagio Church,** which sits at the base of the town (watch for its long, level, tree-lined driveway exactly where you leave Montepulciano on the road toward Pienza—see page 680).

To begin our loop, drive south, at first following signs to *Chianciano Terme* and *Chiusi.* Just one kilometer south of Montepulciano, watch on the right for the turnoff to *Castelluccio* and *Monticchiello.* Turn off here and zip along a pastoral back road for five kilometers. Pass the turnoff for Monticchiello on your right, and carry on straight ahead, as the road continues uphill and becomes gravel. Grinding your way up, watch on your right for the jagged Tuscan cliffs called *calanchi.* You'll pop out at the T-intersection in front of the entrance to the **La Foce Gardens** (from this intersection, parking and reception are 50 yards to the left—look for *Loc. La Foce;* for details on the gardens, see page 695).

From La Foce, head downhill toward *Siena* and *Roma.* After a few hundred yards, watch on the left for the big gravel parking lot of the recommended **Dopolavoro La Foce** restaurant (across the street). From this lot, you have a fine view of one of *the* iconic cypress-lined driveways of Tuscany.

Continue downhill along this road for about five kilometers, through pristine farm fields, until you reach a major intersection, where you'll turn right toward *Pienza* and *Siena* (on SP-53). Immersed in spectacular scenery, you'll twist between giant cypresses for about 10 kilometers. This road parallels the region's namesake Orcia River ("Val d'Orcia" means "Orcia River Valley"). Take a moment to simply appreciate your surroundings. The famous Chianti region to the north (right) and the Brunello region to the west (straight ahead) are each a short drive away; in those places, the rocky soil is perfect for grapes. But here, instead of rocks, you're surrounded by clay hills—once the floor of a prehistoric sea—that are ideal for cereal crops. Grains alternate every few years with a crop of fava beans, which help reintroduce nitrogen to the soil. It seems that every grassy hilltop is capped with a family farmhouse. Partway along this road, you'll pass a turnoff (on the right) offering a speedy shortcut to Pienza, just eight stunning kilometers away. But there's so much more to see; I'd rather carry on with our loop.

The tower looming on the hill ahead of you is **Rocca d'Orcia**'s Tentennano Castle (see page 697). Nearing the end of the road, you'll pass (on the left) the front door of an old farmhouse with oddly formidable crenellated towers, like a little castle in the field. This is **Spedaletto Castle,** built during the 12th century as a hospice for pilgrims walking the Via Francigena to Rome. Today it serves a similar purpose, as an *agriturismo* called La Grancia ("The Granary"), housing wayfarers like you.

When you reach a T-intersection with the main S-2 highway, turn left (toward *Roma*), then immediately take the exit for **Bagno Vignoni.** To explore this fascinating medieval spa town—with its main square filled with a thermal-spring-fed pool—see page 696. To see the empty fortress at **Rocca d'Orcia,** stay on the S-2 highway just one kilometer past Bagno Vignoni, then watch for the next turnoff (see page 697).

Leg #2: Bagno Vignoni to Pienza (with Possible Detours to Brunello Wineries and Tuscan Views)

From Bagno Vignoni, head north on SR-2 (toward *San Quiri co d'Orcia* and *Siena*). After just four kilometers, in San Quirico d'Orcia, turn off onto the SP-146 road to Pienza, also marked for *Chiusi, Chianciano Terme,* and *Montepulciano.*

But before heading down that road, consider a few potential detours: First, if you won't have time to delve deeply into Brunello wine country, but would like just a taste, now is a good time to side-trip to your choice of **Brunello wineries;** those I've recommended on page 702 are all within about a 20- to 25-minute drive of San Quirico. Read the descriptions, take your pick, and ideally call ahead to reserve a tour and tasting. Another option is to zip into the town of **Montalcino** itself— an easy and well-signed 15-minute drive from San Quirico—and taste some local vintages at a wine bar there (see page 701).

Back on the SP-146 road from San Quirico to Pienza, you enjoy one of the region's most postcard-worthy stretches—with grand panoramas in both directions, including two quintessential Tuscan scenes: the **Chapel of Madonna di Vitaleta** (after 2 kilometers, on the right); and a classic **farmhouse-with-trees,** just before Pienza (about 9 kilometers after San Quirico, on the left).

Finally you'll pull into **Pienza,** where you can park and tour the town using the information on page 685.

Leg #3: Pienza to Montepulciano (via Monticchiello)

If you're in a hurry or losing sunlight, just hop back on the main SP-146 road for the 12-kilometer straight-shot back to Montepulciano (enjoying some pullouts with fine views of the town on the left). But I prefer this longer, even more dramatic route, via the fortified village of Monticchiello.

From the traffic circle at the entry to Pienza's town center, instead of heading for Montepulciano, follow the road that runs along the left side of town (marked *Amiata* and *Monticchiello*—as you face Pienza, you'll continue straight when the main road bends

The Beauty of Tuscany's Geology (and Vice Versa)

While tourists have romanticized notions of the "Tuscan" land-scape, there's a surprisingly wide variety of land forms in the region. Never having been crushed by a glacier, Tuscany is anything but flat. Its hills and mountains are made up of different substances, each suited to very different types of cultivation.

The Chianti region (between Florence and Siena) is rough and rocky, with an inhospitable soil that challenges grape vines to survive while coaxing them to produce excellent wine grapes.

Farther south, the soil switches from rock to clay, silt, and sand. The region called the Crete Senesi is the perfectly described "Sienese Clay Hills." Looking out from a breezy viewpoint, you can easily visualize how these clay hills were once at the bottom of the sea floor. The soil here is perfect for truffles and for vast fields of wheat, sun-yellow rapeseed (for canola oil), and periodically fava beans (to add nitrogen to the soil). In the spring and summer, the Crete Senesi is blanketed with brightly colorful crops and flowers. But by the fall, after the harvest, it's brown, dusty, and desolate—still picturesque, but in a surface-of-the-moon way. Within the Crete Senesi, you can distinguish two types of hills shaped by erosion: smooth, rounded *biancane* and pointy, jagged *calanchi*.

The area around Montepulciano and Montalcino is more varied, with rocky protuberances that break up the undulating clay hills and provide a suitable  home for wine grapes. Even farther south is the Val d'Orcia. This valley of the Orcia River is similar to the Crete Senesi, but has fewer rocks and jagged *calanchi*. Montepulciano sits in a unique position between the Val d'Orcia and a much flatter valley, the Val di Chiana, through which Italy's main north-south expressway runs.

You'll see many hot springs in this part of Tuscany, as well as town names with the word *Terme* (for "spa" or "hot spring") or *Bagno* ("bath"). These generally occur where clay meets rock: Water moving through the clay encounters a barrier and gets trapped. A byproduct of these mineral springs is the limestone called travertine, explaining the quarries you may see around spa towns.

left). This road loops around behind and below the far end of the village, where you can consider a brief detour to see Pienza's oldest church: Turn off on the right at the brown sign for *Pieve di Corsigiano* and drive a few hundred yards to **Corsignano Parish Church** (described on page 689).

Continuing on the main road past that turnoff, you'll drop steeply down into the valley, feeling as if you're sinking into a lavish painting. Dead ahead is **Monte Amiata,** the tallest mountain in Tuscany. This looming behemoth blocks bad weather, creating a mild microclimate that makes the Val d'Orcia a particularly pleasant place to farm...or to vacation. Meanwhile, don't forget to savor the similarly stellar views of Pienza in your rearview mirror. After five kilometers, watch on the left for the turnoff to *Monticchiello* (brown sign). From here, carry on for four kilometers—watching on the left for fine vistas of Pienza, and for another classic "twisty cypress-lined road"—to the pleasant town of **Monticchiello.** This town, with an excellent recommended restaurant (Osteria La Porta) and a compact, fortified townscape worth exploring, is a good place to stretch your legs (described on page 698).

From Monticchiello, there are two routes back to Montepulciano: For the shorter route (6 kilometers), partly on gravel roads, drive all the way to the base of the Monticchiello old town, then turn right. For the longer route (10 kilometers), which stays on paved roads but circles back the way our loop started, turn off for *Montepulciano* at the main intersection, in the flat part of town that's lower down.

HEART OF TUSCANY SIGHTS

Below are the main sights you'll pass on my Heart of Tuscany driving route. Remember that two of the main stops—the towns of **Montepulciano** and **Pienza**—are covered earlier in this chapter.

▲La Foce Gardens

One of the finest gardens in Tuscany, La Foce (lah FOH-cheh) caps a hill with geometrical Italian gardens and rugged English gardens that flow seamlessly into the

Tuscan countryside. An English-born, Italian-bred aristocrat—Iris Origo—left her mark on this area, and wrote evocatively about her time here. The gardens—which are worth a pilgrimage for garden lovers—can be visited only with a guided tour, and only three days each week (Wed, Sat, Sun) and some holidays.

Cost and Hours: €10; 50-minute tours offered April-Oct

Wed at 15:00, 16:00, 17:00, and 18:00, Sat-Sun and holidays at 11:30, 15:00, and 16:30; private tours available, no tours in winter, confirm tour time and reserve in advance, ticket office opens 15 minutes before tour time, tel. 0578-69101, www.lafoce.com.

Getting There: La Foce sits in the hills above the busy town of Chianciano Terme. To avoid driving through Chianciano (heavy traffic, poor signage), consider a more scenic route through the countryside from Montepulciano (described at the start of my "Heart of Tuscany Drive" on page 691).

Eating and Sleeping near La Foce: Near the gardens, the Origo family runs a remote, restful B&B (described on page 669) and a memorably charming roadside restaurant, **$$ Dopolavoro La Foce** ("After Work"). Once the quitting-time hangout for local farmers, today its interior is country-chic, but with a respect for local tradition. The menu offers basic sandwiches or pasta and meat (featuring elegant hamburgers). The garden terrace out back is a chirpy delight, and the parking lot across the busy road offers one of the best vantage points on that perfect Tuscan road (Tue-Sun 9:00-22:00, closed Mon and Nov-March, Strada della Vittoria 90, tel. 0578-754-025, run with flair by Azia).

▲Bagno Vignoni

Thanks to the unique geology of this part of Tuscany (see sidebar on page 694), several natural hot springs bubble up between the

wineries and hill towns. And the town of Bagno Vignoni (BAHN-yoh veen-YOH-nee)—with a quirky history, a pleasant-to-stroll street plan punctuated with steamy canals, and various places to take a dip—is the most accessible and enjoyable to explore. If you'd like to recuperate from your sightseeing and wine tasting by soaking in the thermal baths, bring your swimsuit.

Getting There: Bagno Vignoni is well-signed, just off the main SR-2 highway linking Siena to Rome (3 miles south of San Quirico d'Orcia). Park in the pay lot (coins only) by the big roundabout and walk into town, taking the left fork (in front of Hotel Le Terme).

Bagno Vignoni Town Walk: Emerging into the main square, walk under the covered loggia and look out over the aptly named **Piazza delle Sorgenti** ("Square of the Sources"), filled with a vast pool. Natural spring water bubbles up at the far end at temperatures around 125 degrees Fahrenheit. Known since Roman times, these hot springs were harnessed for their medicinal properties in the Middle Ages.

You're not allowed to wade or swim in this main pool today, but an easy stroll through town shows you other facets of these healing waters. Facing the pool, turn left, walk to the end of the loggia, then turn left again down Via delle Sorgenti. Listen for the water that gushes under your feet, as it leaves the pool and heads for its big plunge over the cliff. You'll emerge at an open zone with the cliff-capping **ruins** of medieval mills and cisterns that once made full use of Bagno Vignoni's main resource. Here you have a chance to dip your toes or fingers into streams of now-tepid water. At the canals' end, the water plunges down into the gorge carved by the Orcia River.

Taking the Waters: The modern **Piscina Val di Sole** bath complex, inside Hotel Posta Marcucci, is simple but sophisticated—a serene spot to soak (€18, €5 towel rental with €10 deposit, Fri-Wed 9:30-18:00, shorter hours off-season, closed Thu year-round, tel. 0577-887-112, www.piscinavaldisole.it)

Eating in Bagno Vignoni: $$$ Osteria del Leone, on the cheery little *piazzetta* just behind the loggia, is the town's class act, with charming tables out on the square (closed Mon, Via dei Mulini 3, tel. 0577-887-300, www.osteriadelleone.it). For something a bit more affordable and casual, drop by the nearby **$$ Il Loggiato** (closed Thu, Via delle Sorgenti 36, tel. 0577-888-973).

Rocca d'Orcia

The looming fortress overlooking Rocca d'Orcia (ROH-kah DOR-chah) perches high above the main SR-2 highway from Siena to Rome. Likely inhabited and fortified since Etruscan times, this strategic hilltop was a seat of great regional power in the 12th century. During this time, Rocca d'Orcia was one of a chain of forts that watched over pilgrims walking the Via Francigena to Rome.

Today the **Rocca di Tentennano** fortress—an empty shell of a castle with modern steel stairs and a grand 360-degree panorama at its top—looks stark and abandoned. It seems to dare you to pay €3 to take the very steep hike up from the parking lots below (June-Sept daily 10:00-13:00 & 16:00-19:00; Fri-Sun only in May; shorter hours off-season, mobile 333-986-0788).

Eating in Rocca d'Orcia: $$ La Cisterna nel Borgo sits on Rocca's main square, facing the town's namesake cistern. Marta and Fede serve up deliciously executed dishes in a classic setting (Mon-Fri 12:00-14:00 and 19:00-22:00, Sat-Sun dinner only, Borgo Mestro 37, tel. 0577-887-280).

▲Monticchiello

This 200-person fortified village clings to the high ground in the countryside just south of Pienza and Montepulciano. While not quite "undiscovered," Monticchiello is relatively untrampled, and feels like a real place where you can get in touch with authentic Tuscan village life.

Eating in Monticchiello: Just inside the town's gate, **$$$ Osteria La Porta** is where warm and classy Daria pleases diners either indoors or out with traditional Tuscan dishes presented with flair. As this is a destination restaurant, reservations are a must (fixed price lunch *menu,* dinner à la carte, seatings at 12:30, 14:00, 19:30, and 21:30—but they'll seat you at other times if they have room, closed Thu, Via del Piano 1, tel. 0578-755-163, www. osterialaporta.it).

$$ La Cantina della Porta, 50 yards up the hill and to the right, is run by the same family (closed Wed, Via San Luigi 3, tel. 0578-755-170).

Montalcino

On a hill overlooking vineyards and valleys, Montalcino is famous for its delicious and pricey Brunello di Montalcino red wines. It's a pleasant, low-impact town crawling with wine-loving tourists, a smattering of classy shops, but little sight-seeing. Everyone touring this area seems to be relaxed and in an easy groove...as if enjoying a little wine buzz.

In the Middle Ages, Montalcino (mohn-tahl-CHEE-noh) was considered Siena's biggest ally. Originally aligned with Florence, the town switched sides after the Sienese beat up Florence in the Battle of Montaperti in 1260. The Sienese persuaded the Montalcinesi to join their side by forcing them to collect corpses and sleep one night in the bloody, Florentine-strewn battlefield. Later, the Montalcinesi took in Sienese refugees. To this day, in gratitude for their support, the Sienese invite the Montalcinesi to lead the parade that kicks off Siena's Palio celebrations.

Montalcino prospered under Siena, but like its ally, it waned after the Medici family took control of the region. The village became a humble place. Then, in the late 19th century, the Biondi Santi family created a fine, dark red wine, calling it "the brunette" (Brunello). Today's affluence is due to the town's much-sought-after wine. (For more on this wine, see the "Wines in the Region" sidebar on page 702). If you're not a wine lover, you may find Montalcino (a.k.a. Brunello-ville) to be too touristy.

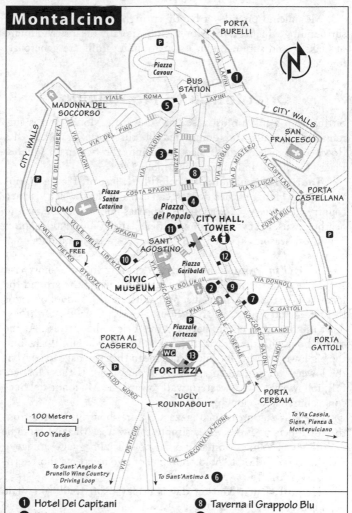

Montalcino

PORTA BURELLI

Piazza Cavour

BUS STATION

VIA LAPINI

VIALE ROMA

LAPINI

CITY WALLS

MADONNA DEL SOCCORSO

SAN FRANCESCO

CITY WALLS

VIA DEL PINO

VIA DELLA LIBERTA

VIA SPAGNI

VIA CIALDINI

VIA MAZZINI

VIA MOGLIO

VIA D. MISTERO

VIA CASTLLANA

PORTA CASTELLANA

Piazza Santa Catarina

COSTA SPAGNI

VIA S. LUCIA

VIA FONTE BUIA

DUOMO

Piazza del Popolo

CITY HALL, TOWER &

VIA SPAGNI

SANT' AGOSTINO

Piazza Garibaldi

CIVIC MUSEUM

VIALE DELLA LIBERTA

VIALE PIETRO STROZZI

FREE

V. BOLGHINI

PAN

VIA RICASOLI

VIA DONNOLI

C. GATTOLI

VIA SOCCORSO SALONI

V. DELLE CASERME

Piazzale Fortezza

PORTA AL CASSERO

WC

FORTEZZA

VIA ALDO MORO

V. LANDI

PORTA GATTOLI

VIA LANDI

"UGLY ROUNDABOUT"

PORTA CERBAIA

100 Meters

100 Yards

VIA OSTICCIO

VIA CIRCONVALLAZIONE

To Via Cassia, Siena, Pienza & Montepulciano

To Sant' Angelo & Brunello Wine Country Driving Loop

To Sant'Antimo & ⑥

① Hotel Dei Capitani

② Palazzina Cesira

③ B&B da Idolina

④ Affittacamere Mariuccia

⑤ Albergo Giardino

⑥ To La Crociona Agriturismo

⑦ Re di Macchia Ristorante

⑧ Taverna il Grappolo Blu

⑨ Ristorante-Pizzeria San Giorgio

⑩ Co-op Supermarket

⑪ Caffè Fiaschetteria Italiana

⑫ Enoteca di Piazza

⑬ Enoteca la Fortezza di Montalcino

Montalcino provides a handy springboard for exploring the surrounding wine region. "Montalcino" literally means "Mountain of Oaks"—and sure enough, its surrounding hills are generously forested.

Orientation to Montalcino

Sitting atop a hill amidst a sea of vineyards, Montalcino is surrounded by walls and dominated by the Fortezza (a.k.a. "La Rocca"). From here, roads lead down into the two main squares: Piazza Garibaldi and Piazza del Popolo.

Tourist Information: The helpful TI, just off Piazza Garibaldi in City Hall, sells bus tickets; can call ahead to book a visit at a countryside winery (€1/person fee); and has information on taxis to nearby towns, abbeys, and monasteries (daily 10:00-19:00, shorter hours off-season, tel. 0577-849-331, www.prolocomontalcino.com).

Arrival in Montalcino: Drivers coming in for a short visit should head to the pay lot in Piazzale Fortezza: Skirt around the fortress, take the first right (just past a little park), and follow signs to *parking* and *Fortezza* (€1.50/hour, free 20:00-8:00). Or, if you don't mind a short climb, park for free below the fortress: At the roundabout with the ugly statue, take the small downhill lane into the big lower parking lot (blue lines mean that you have to pay, but the lower-level unmarked spots are always free). If these lots are full, follow the town's western wall toward the Madonna del Soccorso church and a long pay lot.

The **bus** station is on Piazza Cavour, about 300 yards from the town center. From here, simply follow Via Mazzini straight up into town. While Montalcino has no official baggage storage, a few shops are willing to hold on to one or two bags on a short-term basis; ask at the TI.

Helpful Hints: Market day is Friday (7:00-13:00) on Viale della Libertà, near the Fortezza.

Sights in Montalcino

Fortezza

This 14th-century fort, built under Sienese rule, is now little more than an empty shell. You're welcome to enter the big, open courtyard (with WCs out the far end), or just enjoy a picnic in the park surrounding the fort, but if you want to climb the ramparts for a panoramic view, you'll have to pay (€4, enter though wine bar, daily 9:00-20:00, shorter hours off-season). Most people visit the fortress for its wine bar (see page 708).

Piazza del Popolo

All roads in tiny Montalcino lead to the main square, Piazza del Popolo ("People's Square").

Since 1888, the **Caffè Fiaschetteria Italiana** has been *the* elegant place to enjoy a drink. Its founder, inspired by Caffè Florian in Venice, brought fine coffee to this humble town of woodcutters.

City Hall was the fortified seat of government. It's decorated by the coats of arms of judges who, in the interest of fairness, were from outside of town. Like Siena, Montalcino was a republic in the Middle Ages. When Florentines took Siena in 1555, Siena's ruling class retreated here and held out for four more years. The Medici coat of arms (with the six balls, or pills) dominates the others. This, and the much-reviled statue of Cosimo de' Medici in the loggia, are reminders that Florence finally took Montalcino in 1559.

The one-handed **clock** was the norm until 200 years ago. For five centuries, the arcaded **loggia** hosted the town market. And, of course, it's fun to simply observe the *passeggiata*—these days mostly a parade of tourists here for the wine.

For some wine-centric whimsy, go around the right side of the City Hall and find a series of plaques (each designed by a different artist), which show off the annual rating of the Brunello harvest from two to five stars—important, as wine is the lifeblood of the local economy.

Montalcino Museums (Musei di Montalcino)

While technically three museums in one (archaeology, medieval art, and modern art), and surprisingly big and modern for this little town, Montalcino's lone museum ranks only as a decent bad-weather activity. The cellar is filled with interesting artifacts dating back as far as—gulp—200,000 B.C. The ground, first, and second floors hold the medieval and modern art collections, with an emphasis on Gothic sacred art (with works from Montalcino's heyday, the 13th to 16th century). The ground floor is best, with a large collection of crucifixes and the museum's highlights, a glazed-terra-cotta altarpiece and statue of St. Sebastian, both by Andrea della Robbia.

Cost and Hours: €4.50, Tue-Sun 10:00-13:00 & 14:00-17:50, closed Mon, Via Ricasoli 31, to the right of Sant'Agostino Church, tel. 0577-846-014.

WINERIES NEAR MONTALCINO

The countryside around Montalcino is littered with wineries, some of which offer tastings. As Brunello is the poshest of Italian wines, these wineries feel a bit upscale. While most will accommodate those just dropping by in the afternoon for a quick taste, it's highly recommended and in your interest to reserve ahead. It's a simple process (just call and arrange a time), and they'll delight in show-

Wines in the Region

This region has two well-respected red wines, each centered on a specific town: Montepulciano is known for its Vino Nobile, while Montalcino is famous for its Brunello. In each wine, the predominant grape is a clone of sangiovese (Tuscany's main red wine grape).

Vino Nobile di Montepulciano ("noble wine of Montepulciano") is a high-quality, dry ruby red, made mostly with the Prugnolo Gentile varietal of sangiovese (70 percent), blended with other local varieties (30 percent). Aged two years (or three for a *riserva*)—one year of which must be in oak casks—it's more full-bodied than a typical Chianti and less tannic than a Brunello. It pairs well with meat, especially roasted lamb with rosemary, rabbit or boar ragu over pasta, grilled portobello mushrooms, and local cheeses like pecorino. Several large wineries produce and age their Vino Nobile in the sprawling cellars beneath the town of Montepulciano. Two of these—Contucci Cantina and De' Ricci Cantine—are fun and easy to tour (see "Sights and Experiences in Montepulciano" on page 678). The oldest red wine in Tuscany, Vino Nobile has been produced since the late 1500s. (Don't mistake this wine for lesser-quality wines from the Le Marche or Abruzzo regions that use a grape confusingly named Montepulciano.)

Brunello di Montalcino ("the little brown one of Montalcino"—named for the color of the grapes before harvest) is even more highly regarded and ranks among Italy's finest and most expensive wines. Made from 100 percent Sangiovese Grosso (a.k.a. Brunello) grapes, it's smooth, dry, and aged for a minimum of two years in wood casks, plus an additional four months in the bottle. *Riserva* wines are aged an additional year. Brunello is designed to cellar for 10 years or longer—but who can wait? It pairs well with the local cuisine, but the perfect match is the fine Chianina beef.

First created by the Biondi Santi clan in the late 19th century, this wine quickly achieved a sterling reputation. Today, there are around 240 mostly small producers of Brunello in the Montalcino region; I've recommended just a few, which I find fun and accessible (see listings on the following pages). A simpler option is to sample a few different wines at one of the good wine bars in Montalcino (see page 707).

You'll also see Rosso di Montalcino (a younger version of Brunello), which is aged for one year. This "poor man's Brunello" is very good, at half the price. Note that in lesser-quality harvest years, only Rosso di Montalcino is produced.

Montalcino's climate is drier and warmer than Chianti or Montepulciano. Diverse soils and slopes create many microclimates that affect the wine. Locals explain that, due to overall temperature increases resulting from climate change, wineries on the higher ground reap benefits from slightly cooler temperatures (grapes love hot days and cool nights). Elevation is a bonus for wine-loving tourists, who enjoy stellar views while sampling the best wines.

Touring a winery, you'll see that many winemakers age Brunello in giant oak casks. You'll also notice glass jars (an inven-

tion of Leonardo da Vinci) poking up from the tops of those casks, which allow expansion of the liquid during fermentation, and—by providing a small overflow reservoir—ensure that the wine reaches the very top of the cask. Before placing the wine in casks, modern wineries ferment it in temperature-controlled cement or stainless-steel tanks, which are easier to maintain than wood and preserve a more fruity bouquet.

Strolling through vineyards, you may notice "sentinel" roses at the ends of some of the rows of vines. These aren't just decorative; because disease affects roses before grapes, historically the flowers acted as a kind of canary in a coal mine, giving vintners advance notice if a phylloxera epidemic was imminent. Today the roses can warn of mildew.

But disease isn't the only pest: Locals say that wild boars make the best winemakers—they wait to raid the vineyards until the grapes are perfectly sweet. At that magic moment, it becomes a race between the boars and the human harvesters. But humans have the last laugh (or bite)—boar is found on many Tuscan menus and is considered the perfect accompaniment to the local wines.

HEART OF TUSCANY

ing you around. Tours generally last 45-60 minutes, cost €10-15 per person, and conclude with a tasting of three or four wines. The Montalcino TI can give you a list of more than 150 regional wineries and will call ahead for you. Or check with the vintners' consortium (tel. 0577-848-246, www.consorziobrunellodimontalcino.it). Many wineries are closed on Sunday, so call ahead before heading out.

If you lack a car (or don't want to drive), you can take a tour on the **Brunello Wine Bus,** which laces together visits to four wineries, with a lunch break in the middle, either on your own in Montalcino or at a farmhouse for an extra fee (€90, May-Oct Tue and Thu-Sat, departs at 10:00, returns at 19:00, tours leave from their office, or they will pick you up within 3 miles (5 kilometers) of Montalcino, half-day tours available, Viale della Liberta 12, tel. 0577-846-021, www.winetravelsforyou.com, info@winetravelsforyou.com).

If you're paying for a wine tasting, you aren't obligated to buy. But if a winery is doing a small tasting just for you, they're hoping you'll buy a bottle or two.

SOUTH OF MONTALCINO
Le Potazzine
This endearingly small (38,000 bottles per year), friendly, family-run winery, about a five-minute drive south of Montalcino, is operated by gregarious Gigliola and her assistant, Michele. The name is a type of small bird that also means "Little Girls," in honor of Gigliola's daughters. Call or email ahead to schedule a one-hour tour and tasting (€10-36 bottles, Loc. Le Prata 262, tel. 0577-846-168, www.lepotazzine.it, tenuta@lepotazzine.it). At the south end of Montalcino, head for *Grosetto* and *S. Angelo.* Take the turnoff on the right for *Camigliano* and *Tavernelle* onto SP-103; after a minute, follow the *Castiglion del Bosco* sign; and in another minute, when the road becomes gravel, you'll hit the driveway into Le Potazzine (on the left).

Mastrojanni
Perched high above the Romanesque Sant'Antimo Abbey, overlooking sprawling vineyards, this winery (owned by the Illy coffee company) is big and glitzy—yet doesn't feel as corporate or soulless as some of the bigger players (€17-36 bottles, Podere Loreto e San Pio, tel. 0577-835-681, www.mastrojanni.com, Andrea). To reach it, head up into the town of Castelnuovo dell'Abate (just above Sant'Antimo Abbey), bear left at the Bassomondo restaurant, and continue up along the gravel road (enjoying vineyard and abbey views).

Ciacci Piccolomini d'Aragona

This well-respected, family-run vineyard has a classy tasting room/ *enoteca* and an outdoor view terrace. If you're just dropping in, belly up to the wine bar for two or three free tastes. Or reserve ahead for a more formal tasting of top-quality wines for €10-25, which includes a tour of the cellar (open Mon-Fri 9:00-19:00, Sat 10:30-18:30, closed Sun; head toward Castelnuovo dell'Abate but go right before entering that town, following signs toward Sant'Angelo in Colle, tel. 0577-835-616, www.ciaccipiccolomini.com, visite@ ciaccipiccolomini.com).

Castello Banfi-Poggio alle Mura

Much bigger and glossier than the other recommended wineries, Banfi is one of the largest producers in the area. Despite its size, the estate is charming, set in a castle located in a picturesque corner southwest of Sant'Antimo. This is a great option for Sundays, when other places are closed, or for a spontaneous drop-in tasting at the winery's *enoteca* (tastings start at €12, daily 10:00-19:30, closes at 18:00 Nov-March, tours available on request, tel. 055-877-500, www.castellobanfiilborgo.com, enoteca@banfi.it). You'll find Banfi about 20 minutes south of Montalcino; follow SP-14 to Borgo Santa Rita and cut back north, following signs to *Poggio alle Mura*.

NORTH OF MONTALCINO

Altesino

Elegant and stately, Altesino owns perhaps the most stunning location of all, just off the back road connecting Montalcino north to Buonconvento. You'll twist up on cypress-lined gravel lanes to this perch, which looks out over an expanse of vineyards with Montalcino hovering on the horizon (€15 for tour and basic tasting, daily, Loc. Altesino 54, tel. 0577-806-208, www.altesino.it, info@ altesino.it). You'll find the turnoff for Altesino along the back road (SP-45) between Montalcino and Buonconvento.

Santa Giulia

On the outskirts of Torrenieri, this may be the quintessential family-run winery, with an emphasis on quality over quantity (only 10,000 bottles a year). They also produce excellent olive oil, prosciutto, and salami. Flatter, a bit less picturesque, and much more rustic (with a working-farm feel rather than a swanky tasting room) than the others listed here, a tour here is a Back Door experience. The son, Gianluca, and his wife, Kae, enjoy showing off the entire farm—ham hocks, cheese, and winery—before giving you a chance to taste their produce. Call to find a time that fits their schedule; around lunchtime, you can arrange a "Zero Kilometer" meal, with everything farm-made (€15 for tasting and tour,

2-person minimum, €12-27 bottles, Loc. San Giulia 48, closed Sun, tel. 0577-834-270, www.santagiuliamontalcino.it, info@santagiuliamontalcino.it). From Torrenieri's main intersection, follow the brown *Via Francigena* signs. After crossing the train tracks and a bridge, watch on the left to follow signs for *Sasso di Sole*, then *Sta. Giulia;* you'll take gravel roads through farm fields to the winery.

Sleeping in Montalcino

($$$$ = Splurge, $$$ = Pricier, $$ = Moderate, $ = Budget)
$$$ Hotel Dei Capitani, at the end of town near the bus station, has plush public spaces, an inviting pool, and a cliffside terrace offering plenty of reasons for lounging. About half the 29 rooms come with vast Tuscan views for the same price (request a view room when you reserve), the nonview rooms are bigger, and everyone has access to the terrace (RS%, air-con, elevator, limited free parking—first come, first served, Via Lapini 6, tel. 0577-847-227, www.deicapitani.it, info@deicapitani.it).

$$ Palazzina Cesira, right in the heart of the old town, is a gem, renting five spacious and tastefully decorated rooms in a fine 13th-century residence with a palatial lounge and a pleasant garden. You'll enjoy a refined and tranquil ambience, a nice breakfast (with eggs), and the chance to get to know Lucilla and her American husband, Roberto, who are generous with local advice (2-night minimum, 3-night minimum on holiday weekends, air-con, free off-street parking, Via Soccorso Saloni 2, tel. 0577-846-055, www.montalcinoitaly.com, info@montalcinoitaly.com).

$$ B&B da Idolina has four good, midrange rooms above a wine shop on the main street (includes basic breakfast in shared kitchen, check-in 14:00-20:00—call if arriving later, parking available, Via Mazzini 65, mobile 342-852-2080, www.bebidolina.com, info@bebidolina.com, Fulvia).

$ Affittacamere Mariuccia has three small, colorful, good-value, Ikea-chic rooms on the main drag over a heaven-scented bakery (air-con, check in across the street at Enoteca Pierangioli before 20:00 or let them know arrival time, Piazza del Popolo 16, rooms at #28, tel. 0577-849-113, mobile 347-365-5364, www.affittacameremariuccia.it, enotecapierangioli@hotmail.com, Alessandro and Stefania).

$ Albergo Giardino, a great value, has nine big rooms done in a modern-minimalist style, no public spaces, and a convenient location near the bus station (RS%, no breakfast, Piazza Cavour 4, tel. 0577-848-257, mobile 320-404-4655, www.albergoilgiardino.it, info@albergoilgiardino.it, Roberto and dad Mario).

Eating in Montalcino

RESTAURANTS

$$$ Re di Macchia is an invitingly intimate restaurant where Antonio serves up the Tuscan fare Roberta cooks. Look for their seasonal menu and a fine Montalcino wine list. Consider the €25 fixed-price meal. For €17 more, it's paired with local wines carefully selected to accompany each dish (Fri-Wed 12:00-14:00 & 19:00-21:00, closed Thu, reservations strongly recommended, Via Soccorso Saloni 21, tel. 0577-846-116).

$$ Taverna del Grappolo Blu is bright and fresh; it's a place that's unpretentious, friendly, and serious about its wine, game, homemade pasta, and vegetarian options (Sat-Thu 12:00-15:00 & 19:00-22:00, closed Fri, reservations smart, a few steps off Via Mazzini at Scale di Via Moglio 1, tel. 0577-847-150, Luciano, www.grappoloblu.it).

$$ Ristorante-Pizzeria San Giorgio is a homey trattoria/pizzeria with traditional decor and reasonable prices. It's great for families and a reliable choice for a simple meal (daily 12:00-15:00 & 19:00-22:30, closed Tue off-season, Via Soccorso Saloni 10, tel. 0577-848-507, Mara).

Picnic: Gather ingredients at the **Co-op supermarket** on Via Sant'Agostino (Mon-Sat 8:30-13:00 & 16:00-20:00, closed Sun, just off Via Ricasoli in front of Sant'Agostino Church), then enjoy your feast up at the Madonna del Soccorso Church, with vast territorial views.

WINE BARS

These places also serve light food.

Caffè Fiaschetteria Italiana, a classic café/wine bar, was founded by Ferruccio Biondi Santi, the creator of the famous Brunello wine. The wine library in the back of the café boasts many local choices. A meeting place since 1888, this grand café also serves light lunches and espresso to tourists and locals alike (€6-13 Brunellos by the glass, light snacks and plates; same prices inside, outside, or in back room; daily 7:30-23:00, Piazza del Popolo 6, tel. 0577-849-043). And if it's coffee you need, this place—with its classic 1961 espresso machine—is considered the best in town.

Enoteca di Piazza is one of a chain of wine shops with a system of mechanical dispensers. A "drink card" (like a debit card) keeps track of the samples you take, for which you'll pay from €1 to €9 for each 60-milliliter taste of 100 different wines, including some whites—rare in this town. They hope you'll buy a bottle of the samples you like, and are happy to educate you in English. (Rule of thumb: A bottle costs about 10 times the price of the sample. If you buy a bottle, the sample of that wine is free.) While the place feels a little formulaic, it can be fun—the wine is great, and the staff is casual and helpful. Their small restaurant lets you enjoy your drink card with local dishes (daily 9:00-20:00, near Piazza del Popolo at Via Matteotti 43, tel. 0577-848-104, www.enotecadipiazza.com).

Enoteca la Fortezza di Montalcino offers a chance to taste top-end wines by the glass, each with an English explanation. While the prices are a bit higher than other *enoteche* in town, the medieval setting inside Montalcino's fort is a hit for most visitors. Spoil yourself with Brunello in the cozy *enoteca* or at an outdoor table in the fortress courtyard (tastings start at €13 for 3 wines and go up from there; sampler plates of cheeses, *salumi,* honeys, and olive oil; daily 9:00-20:00, closes at 18:00 Nov-March, inside the Fortezza, tel. 0577-849-211).

Montalcino Connections

Montalcino is well-connected to Siena; other bus connections are inconvenient but generally workable. Montalcino's bus station is on Piazza Cavour, within the town walls. Bus tickets are sold at the bar on Piazza Cavour, at the TI, and at some tobacco shops, but not on board. Check schedules at the TI, at the bus station, or online (at www.sienamobilita.it or www.tiemmespa.it). The nearest train station is a 30-minute bus ride away, in Buonconvento.

From Montalcino by Bus: The handiest direct bus is to **Siena** (6/day Mon-Sat, 4/day Sun, 1.5 hours). To reach **Pienza** or **Montepulciano,** ride bus #114 to Torrenieri (3-4/day Mon-Sat, none on Sun, 20 minutes), where you'll switch to line #112 for the rest of the way (from Torrenieri: 25 minutes to Pienza, 45 minutes to Montepulciano). Since the Montepulciano bus connection is sporadic, consider hiring a taxi (about €70 one-way). Anyone going to **Florence** by bus changes in Siena; since the bus arrives at Siena's train station, it's handier to go the rest of the way to Florence by train.

ASSISI

Assisi is famous for its hometown boy, St. Francis, who made very, very good. While Francis the saint is interesting, Francesco Bernardone the man is even more so, and mementos of his days in Assisi are everywhere—where he was baptized, a shirt he wore, a hill he prayed on, and a church where a vision changed his life.

About the year 1200, this simple friar from Assisi countered the decadence of Church government and society in general with a powerful message of nonmaterialism and a "slow down and smell God's roses" lifestyle. Like Jesus, Francis taught by example, living without worldly goods and aiming to love all creation. A huge monastic order grew out of his teachings, which were gradually embraced (some would say co-opted) by the Church. Christianity's most popular saint and its purest example of simplicity is now glorified in beautiful churches, along with his female counterpart, St. Clare. In 1939, Italy made Francis one of its patron saints; in 2013, the newly elected pope took his name.

Francis' message of love, simplicity, and sensitivity to the environment has a broad and timeless appeal. But every pilgrimage site inevitably gets commercialized, and Francis' legacy is now Assisi's basic industry. In summer, this Umbrian town bursts with flash-in-the-pan Francis fans and Franciscan knickknacks. Those able to see past the glow-in-the-dark rosaries and bobblehead friars can actually have a "travel on purpose" experience. Even a block or two off the congested main drag, you'll find pockets of serenity that, it's easy to imagine, must have made Francis feel at peace.

PLANNING YOUR TIME

Assisi is worth a day and a night. Its walled old town has a half-day of sightseeing and another half-day of wonder. The essential sight is the Basilica of St. Francis. For a good visit, take my self-guided Assisi Walk, going from the top of town to the basilica at the bottom, and my Basilica of St. Francis Tour. With more time, be sure to wander the back streets and linger on the main square, Piazza del Comune.

Most visitors are day-trippers. While the town's a zoo by day, it's a delight at night. Assisi after dark is closer to a place Francis could call home.

Orientation to Assisi

Crowned by a ruined castle, Assisi spills downhill to its famous Basilica of St. Francis. The town is beautifully preserved and rich in history. A 5.5-magnitude earthquake in 1997 did more damage to the tourist industry than to the town's buildings. Fortunately, tourists—whether art lovers, pilgrims, or both—have returned, drawn by Assisi's special allure.

The city stretches across a ridge that rises from a flat plain. The Basilica of St. Francis sits at the low end of town; Piazza Matteotti (bus stop and parking lot) is at the high end; and the main square, Piazza del Comune, lies in between. The main drag (called Via San Francesco for most of its course) runs from Piazza del Comune to the basilica. Capping the hill above the town is the ruined castle, called the  Rocca Maggiore, and rising above that is Mount Subasio. The town is smaller than its fame might lead you to think: Walking uphill from the basilica to Piazza Matteotti takes 30 minutes, while the downhill journey takes about 15 minutes. Some Francis sights lie outside the city walls, in the valley beneath the ridge (the modern part of town, called Santa Maria degli Angeli) and in the hills above.

TOURIST INFORMATION

The TI is in the center of the old town on Piazza del Comune (Mon-Fri 8:00-14:00 & 15:00-18:30, Sat-Sun 9:30-17:00—until 18:00 April-Oct, tel. 075-813-8680, www.visit-assisi.it). From April to October, there's also a branch down in the valley in Santa Maria degli Angeli, across the street from the big piazza in front of the Basilica of St. Mary of the Angels.

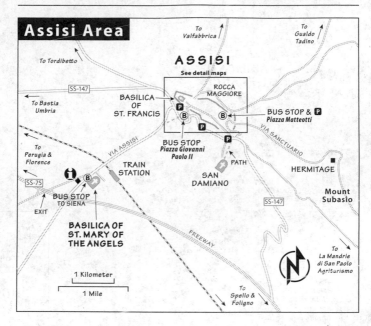

Assisi Area

To Valfabbrica

To Gualdo Tadino

To Tordibetto

SS-147

ASSISI
See detail maps

ROCCA MAGGIORE

BASILICA OF ST. FRANCIS

To Bastia Umbria

BUS STOP & Piazza Matteotti

VIA SANCTUARIO

VIA ASSISI

To Perugia & Florence

BUS STOP Piazza Giovanni Paolo II

PATH

HERMITAGE

TRAIN STATION

SAN DAMIANO

SS-75

BUS STOP TO SIENA

EXIT

Mount Subasio

SS-147

BASILICA OF ST. MARY OF THE ANGELS

FREEWAY

To La Mandrie di San Paolo Agriturismo

N

1 Kilometer

1 Mile

To Spello & Foligno

ARRIVAL IN ASSISI

By Train: The train station is about two miles below Assisi, in Santa Maria degli Angeli. You can check bags in the station at the newsstand (daily 6:45-12:30 & 13:00-19:30). There's no baggage storage in the old town.

Orange city **buses** (line #C) connect the station with the hilltop old town, stopping just outside the wall at three convenient places: at Piazza Giovanni Paolo II, near the Basilica of St. Francis; Largo Properzio, just outside the Porta Nuova city gate; and at Piazza Matteotti, at the top of the old town.

Buses usually leave at :16 and :46 past the hour from the bus stop immediately to your left as you exit the station (daily 5:30-23:00, 15 minutes; buy tickets at the newsstand inside the train station for €1.30, or on board the bus for €2—exact change only, validate in yellow box as you board, valid 1.5 hours after being stamped, also good for any bus within the old town). The bus may actually be awaiting the arrival of your train. If so, don't dawdle or you may just miss it.

Returning from the old town to the train station, the orange buses reverse the route, starting at the top at Piazza Matteotti (usually at :10 and :40 past the hour), stopping in the middle next (outside Porta Nuova at Largo Properzio), and then at the bottom (Piazza Giovanni Paolo II), before zipping down to the station.

All buses are marked either *SM degli Angeli/Stazione* or *Matteotti/S. Francesco*. While you may find yourself looping into

ASSISI

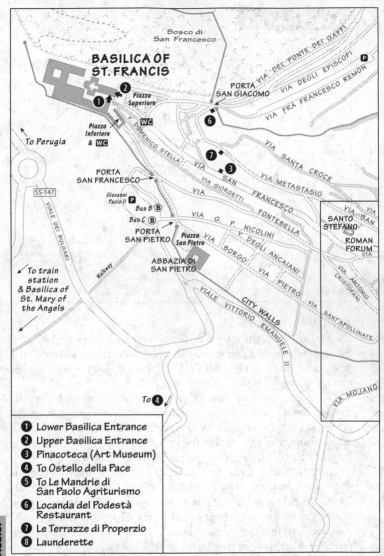

Bosco di San Francesco

BASILICA OF ST. FRANCIS

① **②** Piazza Superiore

① Piazza Inferiore & WC

To Perugia

PORTA SAN FRANCESCO

SS-147

Giovanni Paolo II P
Bus B Ⓑ
Bus C Ⓑ
PORTA SAN PIETRO

ABBAZIA DI SAN PIETRO

Piazza San Pietro

PORTA SAN GIACOMO

VIA DEL PONTE DEI GALLI

VIA DEGLI EPISCOPI

VIA FRA FRANCESCO REMON

⑥

WC

V. DOMENICO STELLA

⑦

③

VIA SAN FRANCESCO

VIA SANTA CROCE

VIA METASTASIO

VIA GIORGETTI

VIA FONTEBELLA

VIA G. P. NICOLINI

V. DEGLI ANCAIANI

VIA BORGO

VIA PIETRO

VIA SANT'APOLLINATE

SANTO STEFANO

ROMAN FORUM

VIA SAN

VIA ANTONIO CRISTOFANI

VIALE DEI BULGARI

← To train station & Basilica of St. Mary of the Angels

Walkway

VIALE VITTORIO EMANUELE II

CITY WALLS

VIA MOJANO

To **④**

① Lower Basilica Entrance
② Upper Basilica Entrance
③ Pinacoteca (Art Museum)
④ To Ostello della Pace
⑤ To Le Mandrie di San Paolo Agriturismo
⑥ Locanda del Podestà Restaurant
⑦ Le Terrazze di Properzio
⑧ Launderette

ASSISI

the hinterland, most of these buses also go to the Basilica of St. Mary of the Angels (Santa Maria degli Angeli, one stop beyond the station, confirm with driver). The middle Assisi stop (Porta Nuova) is best for hotels in the center, leaving you a long but level walk to the main square.

Taxis from the train station to the old town cost about €15. There are extra charges for luggage, night service, additional people (four is customary)...and sometimes just for being a tourist. When departing the old town, you'll find taxi stands at Piazza Giovanni

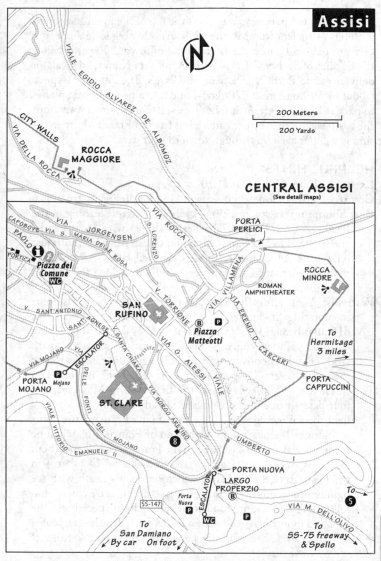

Paolo II, the Basilica of St. Francis, the Basilica of St. Clare, and Piazza del Comune (or have your hotel call for you, tel. 075-812-600). Expect to pay a minimum of €10 for any ride.

By Bus: Buses from Siena may arrive at the stop next to the Basilica of St. Mary of the Angels (Santa Maria degli Angeli), near the train station (see above for directions from the station into town). Most other intercity buses arrive at the base of the old town.

By Car: Drivers coming in for the day can follow the signs to several handy parking lots *(parcheggi)*. Piazza Matteotti's wonderful underground parking garage is at the top of the town and comes with bits of ancient Rome in the walls. Another big lot, Parcheggio Giovanni Paolo II, is at the bottom end of town, 200 yards below the Basilica of St. Francis. At Parcheggio Porta Nuova, an escalator delivers you to Porta Nuova near St. Clare's. The lots vary in price (about €1.50/hour, most €20/day). For day-trippers, the best plan is to park at Piazza Matteotti, follow my self-guided town walk, tour the basilica, and then either catch a bus back to Piazza Matteotti or simply wander back up through town to your car.

HELPFUL HINTS

Exchange Rate: €1 = about $1.10

Country Calling Code: 39 (see page 1154 for dialing instructions)

Best Shopping: Tacky knickknacks line the streets leading to the Basilica of St. Francis. For better shops (with local handicrafts), head to Via San Rufino and Corso Mazzini (both just off Piazza del Comune, shops described later). A Saturday-morning market fills Via Borgo San Pietro (along the bottom edge of town).

Festivals: Assisi annually hosts several interesting festivals commemorating St. Francis and life in the Middle Ages. **Festa di Calendimaggio** is a springtime medieval festival featuring costume parades, concerts, and competitions among Assisi's rival neighborhoods (www.calendimaggiodiassisi.it). Rustic medieval "taverns" pop up around the center offering *porchetta* (roasted pig) and *vino* (starts the first Wed in May and lasts four days; if one of these days is already a public holiday, it's held the following week). The **Settimana Francescana** commemorates the beginning of the end of Francis' life, when he made his way for the last time to the Porziuncola Chapel (Sept 28). This week-long celebration culminates on October 4 in the **Festa di San Francesco,** which marks his death with religious processions, special services, and an arts, crafts, and folklore fair, including food stalls selling local specialties. The TI has a monthly *Assisi Informa* leaflet with details on upcoming festivals and celebrations; see also the event listings at www.visit-assisi.it.

Laundry: 3 Elle Blu' Lavanderia can do a load of laundry for you at a reasonable price on the same day, if they're not too busy (Mon-Fri 9:00-18:00, Sat until 13:00, closed Sun, Via Borgo Aretino 6a—see map on page 712, tel. 075-816-084).

Travel Agencies: You can purchase train, bus, and plane tickets at **Agenzia Viaggi Stoppini,** centrally located between Piazza del Comune and the Basilica of St. Clare. Manager Fabrizio is patient with tourists' needs (Mon-Fri 9:00-12:30 & 15:30-19:00, Sat 9:00-12:30, closed Sun, also offers day trips to nearby towns, Corso Mazzini 31—see map on page 744, tel. 075-812-597, www.viaggistoppiniassisi.it).

Local Guides: Giuseppe Karabotis is a good licensed guide (€130/3 hours, €260/6 hours, mobile 328-867-0567, iokarabot@libero.it). **Daniela Moretti** is a hardworking young guide from Perugia who knows both Assisi and all of Umbria (€120/half-day, €240/day, mobile 335-829-9984, www.danyguide.com, danyguide@hotmail.com). If they're busy, they can recommend other guides.

GETTING AROUND ASSISI

Most visitors need only their feet to get everywhere in Assisi, except to the train station and nearby Basilica of St. Mary of the Angels (via bus #C—see directions in "Arrival in Assisi").

Within the old town, pale yellow minibuses #A and #B run every 20-40 minutes, linking the lower end (near the Basilica of St. Francis) with the middle (Piazza del Comune) and the top (Piazza Matteotti). While it's only a 15-minute stroll from the upper end to the lower, the climb back up can have you looking for a lift. Hop on a bus marked *Piazza Matteotti* if you're exhausted after your basilica visit and need a sweat-free five-minute return to the top of the old town (near many of my recommended hotels). Before boarding, confirm the destination (catch the bus below the Basilica of St. Francis, just outside the Porta San Francesco).

You can buy a bus ticket (good on any city bus) at a newsstand or tobacco shop for €1.30, or get a ticket from the driver for €2 (exact change only). After you've stamped your ticket on board the bus, it's valid for 90 minutes.

Assisi Walk

There's much more to Assisi than just St. Francis and what the blitz tour groups see. This self-guided walk, worth ▲▲, covers the town from top to bottom. To get to Piazza Matteotti, ride the bus from the train station (or from Piazza Giovanni Paolo II) to the last stop; drive up (and park in the underground lot); or hike five minutes uphill from Piazza del Comune.

♫ Download my free Assisi Town Walk audio tour.

• *Start 50 yards beyond Piazza Matteotti (down the small lane between two stone houses, away from city center—see map on page 718).*

❶ Roman Amphitheater (Anfiteatro Romano)

A lane named Via Anfiteatro Romano skirts the cozy neighborhood built around the site of a long-gone Roman amphitheater—a reminder that Assisi was once an important Roman town. Circle to the right along the curved lane that marks the amphitheater's foot-

ASSISI

print. Imagine how colorful the town laundry basin (on the right) must have been in previous generations, when the women of Assisi gathered here to do their wash. Just beyond, above another small rectangular basin, are the coats of arms of Assisi's leading families. A few steps farther, leave the amphitheater, hiking up the stairs on the right to the top of the hill, for an overhead view of the ancient oval. The Roman stones have long been absorbed into the medieval architecture. It was Roman tradition to locate the amphitheater outside of town, which this used to be. While the amphitheater dates from the first century A.D., the buildings filling it today were built in the 13th and 14th centuries. Notice the town's carefully maintained complexion: When redoing a roof, locals will mix old and new tiles.

• *Continue on, enjoying the grand view of the fortress in the distance. The lane leads down to a city gate on the right and an...*

❷ Umbrian View

Step outside of Assisi at the Porta Perlici for a commanding view. Umbria, called the "green heart of Italy," is the country's geographical center and only landlocked region. Enjoy the various shades of green: silver green on the valley floor (olives), emerald green (grapevines), and deep green on the hillsides (evergreen oak trees). The valleys are dotted by small family farms, many of which rent rooms as *agriturismos*. Also notice Rocca Maggiore ("big fortress"), which provided townsfolk a refuge in times of attack, and, behind you atop the nearer hill, Rocca Minore ("little fortress"), which gives the town's young lovers a little privacy. The quarry (under the Rocca Maggiore) was a handy source for Assisi's characteristic pink limestone.

• *Go back through the gate and follow Via Porta Perlici—it's immediately on your right—downhill into town (toward Hotel La Rocca).*

*Enjoy the higgledy-piggledy archi-
tecture (this neighborhood has some
of the most photogenic back lanes
in town). Fifty yards down, to the
left of the arched gate, find the wall
containing an* **aqueduct** *that dates
back to Roman times. It still brings
water from a mountain spring
into the city (push the brass tap for
a taste). After another 50 yards,
turn left through a medieval town
gate (with Hotel La Rocca on your*

right). Just after the hotel, you'll pass a second gate dating from Roman times. Follow Via Porta Perlici downhill until you hit a fine square facing a big church.

❸ Cathedral of San Rufino (Cattedrale San Rufino)

Trick question: Who's Assisi's patron saint? While Francis is one of Italy's patron saints, Rufino (the town's first bishop, martyred and buried here in the third century) is Assisi's. This cathedral (seat of the local bishop) is 11th-century Romanesque with a Neo-classical interior, and dedicated to Rufino. Although it has what is considered to be one of the best and purest Romanesque facades in all of Umbria, the big triangular top (just a decorative wall) was added in Gothic times.

Cost and Hours: Cathedral—free, daily 7:30-19:00, Nov-mid-March closed Mon-Fri 12:30-14:30, tel. 075-812-712; museum—€3.50, Thu-Tue 10:00-13:00 & 15:00-18:00, closed Wed, shorter hours off-season and Sun, www.assisimuseodiocesano.com.

Visiting the Church: Before going in, study the facade—a jungle of beasts emphasizing how the church was a refuge and sanctuary in a scary world. Notice the lions at the base of the facade, flanking each door. One is eating a Christian martyr, reminding worshippers of the courage of early Christians. Here, as in other medieval Assisi churches, worshippers absorbed pre-Christian themes and symbols into their world.

Enter the church. While the front of the church is an unremarkable mix of 17th- and 18th-century Baroque and Neoclassical, the rear (near where you enter) has several points of interest. Notice first the two fine statues: *St. Francis* and *St. Clare* (by Giovanni Dupré, 1888). To your right is an old baptismal font (in the corner with the semicircular black iron grate). In about 1181, a baby boy was baptized in this font. His parents were upwardly mobile Francophiles who called him Francesco ("Frenchy"). In 1194, a nobleman baptized his daughter Clare here. Eighteen years later, their paths crossed in this same church, when Clare attended a class and became mesmerized by the teacher—Francis. Traditionally, the children of Assisi are still baptized here.

The striking glass panels in the floor reveal foundations preserved from the ninth-century church that once stood here. You're walking on history. After the 1997 earthquake, structural inspectors checked the church from ceiling to floor. When they looked under the paving stones, they discovered graves (until Napoleon decreed otherwise, it was common practice to bury people in churches). Underneath that level, they found Roman foundations

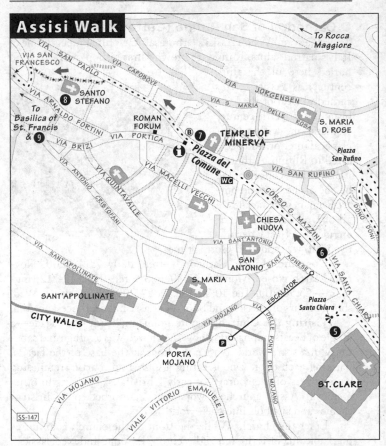

and some animal bones (suggesting the possibility of animal sacrifice). There might have been a Roman temple here; churches were often built upon temple ruins. Stand at the back of the church facing the altar, and look left to the Roman cistern that collected rainwater (just beyond the great stone archway, next to where you entered). Take the three steps down (to trigger the light) and marvel at the fine stonework and Roman engineering. In the Middle Ages, this was the town's emergency water source when under attack.

Diocesan Museum: Underneath the church, incorporated into the Roman ruins and columns, are the foundations of an earlier Church of San Rufino, now the crypt and a fine little museum. When it's open, you can go below to see the saint's sarcophagus (third century) and the cathedral's art from centuries past (down the stairs, near the baptismal font, well-described in English).

• *Leaving the church, take a sharp left (at the pizza-by-the-slice joint, on Via Dono Doni). After 20 yards, take a right and go all the way down the stairway to see some...*

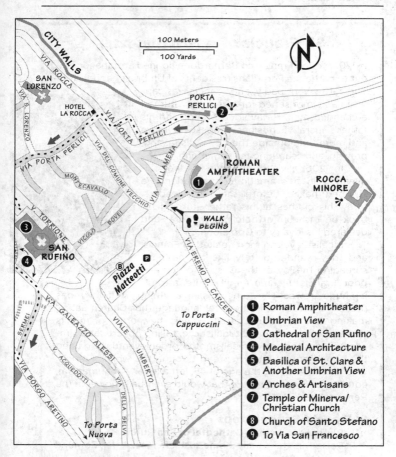

100 Meters
100 Yards

CITY WALLS

SAN LORENZO

HOTEL LA ROCCA

VIA S. LORENZO

VIA ROCCA

VIA PORTA PERLICI

VIA PORTA PERLICI

PORTA PERLICI

VIA DEL COMUNE VECCHIO

MONTECAVALLO

VIA VILLAMENA

ROMAN AMPHITHEATER

ROCCA MINORE

V. TORRIONE

VICOLO BOVEI

WALK BEGINS

③

SAN RUFINO

④

Piazza Matteotti

P

B

VERMEI

VIA GALEAZZO ALESSI

V. ACQUEDOTTI

VIA EREMO D. CARCERI

VIALE UMBERTO I

VIA DELLA SELVA

To Porta Cappuccini

VIA BORGO ARETINO

To Porta Nuova

❶ Roman Amphitheater
❷ Umbrian View
❸ Cathedral of San Rufino
❹ Medieval Architecture
❺ Basilica of St. Clare & Another Umbrian View
❻ Arches & Artisans
❼ Temple of Minerva/ Christian Church
❽ Church of Santo Stefano
❾ To Via San Francesco

❹ Medieval Architecture

At the bottom of the stairs, notice the pink limestone pavement, part of the surviving medieval town. The arches built over door-ways indicate that the buildings date from the 12th through the 14th century, when Assisi was booming. Italian cities such as Assisi—thriving on the north-south trade between northern Europe and Rome—were in the process of inventing free-market capital-ism, dabbling in democratic self-rule, and creating the modern urban lifestyle. The vaults you see that turn lanes into tunnels are reminders of medieval urban expansion—creating more living space (mostly 15th century). While the population grew, people wanted to live within the town's protective walls. Medieval Assisi had several times the population density of modern Assisi.

Notice the blooming balconies; Assisi holds a flower competi-tion each June.

• *From the bottom of the stairs, head to the left and continue downhill.*

St. Francis of Assisi (1181-1226)

In 1202, young Francesco Bernardone donned armor and rode out to battle the Perugians (residents of Umbria's capital city). The battle went badly, and Francis was captured and imprisoned for a year. He returned a changed man. He avoided friends and his father's lucrative business and spent more and more time outside the city walls fasting, praying, and searching for something.

In 1206, a vision changed his life, culminating in a dramatic confrontation. He stripped naked before the town leaders, threw his clothes at his father—turning his back on the comfortable material life—and declared his loyalty to God alone.

Idealistic young men flocked to Francis, and they wandered Italy like troubadours, spreading the joy of the Gospel to rich and poor. Francis became a cult figure, attracting huge crowds. They'd never seen anything like it—sermons preached outdoors, in the local language (not Church Latin), making God accessible to all. Francis' new order of monks was also extremely unmaterialistic, extolling poverty and simplicity. Despite their radicalism, the order eventually gained the pope's approval and spread through the world. Francis, who died in Assisi at the age of 45, left a legacy of humanism, equality, and love of nature that would eventually flower in the Renaissance.

In Francis' Sandal Steps

1. Baptized in Assisi's **Cathedral of San Rufino.**
2. Raised in the family home just off Piazza del Comune (now the **Chiesa Nuova**).
3. Heard call to "rebuild church" in **San Damiano.** (The crucifix of the church is now in the **Basilica of St. Clare.**)
4. Settled and established his order of monks at the **Porziuncola Chapel** (inside today's St. Mary of the Angels Basilica).
5. Met Clare. (Her tomb and possessions are at the **Basilica of St. Clare.**)
6. Received the pope's blessing for his order (1223 document in the reliquary chapel at the **Basilica of St. Francis**).
7. Had many visions and was associated with miracles during his life (depicted in **Giotto's frescoes** in the Basilica of St. Francis' upper level).
8. Died at the **Porziuncola,** his body later interred beneath the **Basilica of St. Francis.**

When you arrive at a street, turn left, going slightly uphill for a long block, then take the low road (right) at the Y, and head down Via Sermei. Continue down to the big church. Walk right, under the three massive buttresses, to Piazza Santa Chiara and the front of the church.

❺ Basilica of St. Clare (Basilica di Santa Chiara)

Dedicated to the founder of the Order of the Poor Clares, this Umbrian Gothic church is simple, in keeping with the nuns' dedication to a life of contemplation. In Clare's lifetime, the order was located in the humble Church of San Damiano, in the valley below, but after Clare's death, they needed a bigger and more glorious building. The church was built in 1265, and the huge buttresses were added in the next century.

Cost and Hours: Free, daily 6:30-12:00 & 14:00-19:00, until 18:00 in winter, tel. 075-812-282.

Visiting the Basilica: The interior's fine frescoes were white-washed in Baroque times. The battered remains of one on the left show how the fresco surface was hacked up so whitewash would stick. Imagine all the pristine frescoes hiding behind the whitewash (here and all over Europe).

The Chapel of the Crucifix of San Damiano, on the right, has the simple wooden crucifix that changed Francis' life. In 1206, an emaciated, soul-searching, stark-raving Francis knelt before this crucifix of a living Christ (then located in the Church of San Damiano) and asked for guidance. According to legend, the crucifix spoke: "Go and rebuild my Church, which you can see has fallen into ruin." Francis followed the call.

Stairs lead from the nave down to the tomb of St. Clare. Her tomb—discovered in about 1850—is at the far right end of the richly ornamented neo-Gothic crypt (the image is fiberglass; her actual bones lie underneath). As you circulate with the crowd of pilgrims, notice the paintings on the walls depicting spiritual lessons from Clare's life and death. At the opposite end of the crypt (back between the stairs, in a large glassed-in area, well-described on the wall) are important relics: the saint's robes, hair (in a silver box), and an enormous tunic she made—along with relics of St. Francis (including a blood-stained stocking he wore after receiving the stigmata). The attached cloistered community of the Poor Clares has flourished for 700 years.

• *Leave the church and belly up to the viewpoint at the edge of the square for...*

St. Clare
(1194-1253)

The 18-year-old rich girl of Assisi fell in love with Francis' message, and made secret arrangements to meet him. The night of Palm Sunday, 1212, she slipped out of her father's mansion in town and escaped to the valley below. A procession of friars with torches met her and took her to (what is today) St. Mary of the Angels Basilica. There, Francis cut her hair, clothed her in a simple brown tunic, and welcomed her into a life of voluntary poverty. Clare's father begged, ordered, and physically threatened her to return, but she would not budge.

Clare was joined by other women who banded together as the Poor Clares. She spent the next 40 years of her life within the confines of the convent of San Damiano: barefoot, vegetarian, and largely silent. Her regimen of prayer, meditation, and simple manual labor—especially knitting—impressed commoners and popes, leading to her canonization almost immediately after her death. St. Clare is often depicted carrying a monstrance (a little temple holding the Eucharist wafer).

Another Umbrian View: On the left is the convent of St. Clare (global headquarters of all the Poor Clares). Below you lies the olive grove of the Poor Clares, which has been there since the 13th century. In the distance is a grand Umbrian view. Assisi overlooks the richest and biggest valley in otherwise hilly and mountainous Umbria. Across the valley to the far right (and over the Tiber River), the rival town Perugia, where Francis was imprisoned, sits on its own hill.

The lower town, called Santa Maria degli Angeli, grew up with the coming of the railway in the 19th century. In the haze, the church with the grayish-blue dome is St. Mary of the Angels (described later), the cradle of the Franciscan order. A popular pilgrimage site today, it marks the place where St. Francis lived, worked, and died.

By the way, many Spanish-speaking Franciscans settled in California. Three of their missions grew into major cities: Los Angeles (named after this church), San Francisco (named after St. Francis), and Santa Clara (named after St. Clare).

• *From the church square, step out into Via Santa Chiara.*

❻ Arches and Artisans

Notice the three medieval town gates (two behind the church, and one uphill toward the town center). The gate over the road behind the church dates from 1265. (Farther on, you can just see the crenellations of the 1316 Porta Nuova, which marks the final medieval expansion of Assisi.) Toward the city center (on Via Santa Chiara, the high road), an arch marks the site of the Roman wall. These three gates represent the town's three walls, illustrating how much the city has grown since ancient times.

Walk uphill along Via Santa Chiara (which becomes Corso Mazzini) to the city's main square. As you pass under the arch you enter what was Roman Assisi—the city that Francis knew. The street is lined with interesting shops selling traditional embroidery, religious souvenirs, and gifty local edibles. The shops on Corso Mazzini, on the stretch between the gate and Piazza del Comune, show off many local crafts. As you browse, watch for the following shops: Galleria d'Arte Perna (on the left, #20b) sells the medieval fantasy townscapes of Paolo Grimaldi, a local painter who runs this shop with his brother, Alessandro. A helpful travel agency is across the street and a few steps up (at #31, Agenzia Viaggi Stoppini; see "Helpful Hints," earlier).

Next, the aptly named Assisi Olive Wood (on the left at #14E) sells olive-wood carvings, as does d'Olivo, across the street at #23. It's said that St. Francis made the first Nativity scene to help humanize and, therefore, teach the Christmas message. That's why you'll see so many crèches in Assisi. (Even today, nearby villages are enthusiastic about their "living" manger scenes, and Italians everywhere enjoy setting up elaborate crèches in churches for Christmas.) At #14A is a bakery, Bar Sensi, selling the traditional raisin-and-apple strudel called *rocciata* (roh-CHAH-tah, splittable and served warm). Farther along on the left (on the corner at #2b) is Antichita Il Duomo, selling religious art, manger scenes, Christmas ornaments, and crucifixion figurines. Across the street is Galleria del Corso, selling finely embroidered linens and baby clothes. And on the square (at #34, opposite City Hall), the recommended La Bottega dei Sapori is worth a visit for edible and drinkable souvenirs.

You've walked up what was, in ancient times, the main drag into town. Ahead of you, the six fluted Corinthian columns of the Temple of Minerva marked the forum (today's Piazza del Comune). Sit at the fountain on the piazza for a few minutes of people-watching—don't you just love Italy? Within a few hundred yards of this square, on either side, were the medieval walls. Imagine the commotion of 5,000 people confined within these walls. No wonder St. Francis needed an escape for some peace and quiet.

Today, while the municipality of Assisi has a population of

ASSISI

25,000, only 3,500 people live in the old town: Many who left damaged homes after the 1997 earthquake decided to stay in the modern city below. This is one reason for the old town's plethora of tourist shops (and few services for residents like supermarkets or hardware stores).

• *Now, head over to the temple on the square.*

❼ Temple of Minerva/Christian Church

Assisi has always been a spiritual center. The Romans went to great lengths to make this first-century B.C. Temple of Minerva a cen-

terpiece of their city. Notice the columns that cut into the stairway. It was a tight fit here on the hilltop. In ancient times, the stairs went down—about twice as far as they do now—to the main drag, which has gradually been filled in over time. The Church of Santa Maria sopra ("over") Minerva was added in the 9th century. The bell tower is from the 13th century.

Pop inside the temple/church. Today's interior is 17th-century Baroque. Walk to the front. Flanking the altar to the back are the original Roman temple floor stones. You can even see the drains for the bloody sacrifices that took place here. Behind the statues of Peter and Paul, the original Roman embankment peeks through.

As you exit the church, look to the right, next to the door of the bell tower. The shapes set into the wall are the medieval city standards for the market that used to take place here. The large shapes are building materials, bricks, and roof tiles. The metal bars were the official measuring sticks for goods sold by length, a measurement that could change from city to city.

Cost and Hours: Free, daily 7:15-19:30, in winter closes at sunset and midday.

• *Across the square next to #11, step into the 16th-century frescoed vaults of the...*

Loggia of the Palazzo del Comune: Notice the Italian flair for fine design. Even this little loggia features decorative art (in the Grotesque style—named for the fanciful paintings of bizarre creatures found on unfinished lower-level walls at Nero's Golden House in Rome). This scene was indisputably painted after 1492. How do they know? Because it features turkeys—first seen in Europe after Columbus returned from the Americas with his ship full of exotic souvenirs. The turkeys painted here may have been that bird's European debut.

• *From the main square, hike left past the temple up the high road, Via*

San Paolo. After 200 yards (across from #24), a sign directs you down a stepped lane to the...

❽ Church of Santo Stefano
(Chiesa di Santo Stefano)

Surrounded by cypress, fig, and walnut trees, Santo Stefano—which used to be outside the town walls in the days of St. Francis—is a delightful bit of offbeat Assisi (free, daily 8:30-20:00, shorter hours off-season). Legend has it that Santo Stefano's bells miraculously rang on October 3, 1226, the day St. Francis died. Step inside. This is the typical rural Italian Romanesque church—no architect, just built by simple stonemasons who put together the most basic design. Hundreds of years later, it still stands.

• *The lane zigzags down to Via San Francesco. Turn right and walk under the arch toward the Basilica of St. Francis.*

❾ Via San Francesco

This main drag leads from the town to the basilica holding the body of St. Francis. Francis was a big deal even in his own day. He was made a saint in 1228—the same year that the basilica's foundations were laid—and his body was moved here by 1230. Assisi was a big-time pilgrimage center, and this street was its booming hub. The arch marks the end of what was Assisi in St. Francis' day. Notice the fine medieval balcony immediately past the arch (on the left). About 30 yards farther down (on the left), find the fountain where medieval pilgrims might have cooled themselves. The hospice next door was built in 1237 to house pilgrims. Notice the three surviving faces of its fresco: Jesus, Francis, and Clare. Farther down on the left, across from #12A, is the Oratorio dei Pellegrini, dating from the 1450s. A brotherhood ran a hostel here for travelers passing through to pay homage to St. Francis. The chapel offers a richly frescoed 14th-century space designed to inspire pilgrims—perfect for any traveler to pause and contemplate the saint's message.

• *Continuing on, you'll eventually reach Assisi's main sight, the Basilica of St. Francis. For the start of my self-guided tour, walk downhill to the basilica's lower courtyard.*

Basilica of St. Francis Tour

The Basilica of St. Francis (Basilica di San Francesco), worth ▲▲▲, is one of the artistic and religious highlights of Europe. It rises where, in 1226, St. Francis was buried (with the outcasts he had stood by) outside of his town on the "Hill of the Damned"—now called the "Hill of Paradise." The basilica is frescoed from top to bottom with scenes by the leading artists of the day: Cimabue, Giotto, Simone Martini, and Pietro Lorenzetti. A 13th-century

historian wrote, "No more exquisite monument to the Lord has been built."

From a distance, you see the huge arcades "supporting" the basilica. These were 15th-century quarters for the monks. The arcades that line the square and lead to the church housed medieval pilgrims.

ORIENTATION

Cost and Hours: Free entry; lower basilica and tomb—daily 6:00-18:45, Nov-March until 17:45; reliquary chapel in lower basilica—generally open Mon-Fri 9:00-18:00, often closed Sat-Sun and occasionally at other times for religious services; upper basilica—daily 8:30-18:45, Nov-March until 18:00.

Dress Code: Modest dress is required to enter the church—no above-the-knee skirts or shorts and no sleeveless tops for men, women, or children.

Information: An office at the courtyard entrance of the lower basilica is often staffed by native English-speaking friars (Mon-Sat 9:15-17:30, closed Sun year-round, tel. 075-819-001, www.sanfrancescoassisi.org). Call or check the website to find out about upcoming events at the basilica.

Tours: Videoguides loaded with a 60-minute tour are available at the kiosk located outside the entrance of the lower basilica (€6, €10 for 2 people) or download the €2 "Basilica San Francesco Assisi" app to your own device.

🎧 Download my free Basilica of St. Francis audio tour.

Bookstore: The church bookshop is in the inner courtyard behind the upper and lower basilica. It sells an excellent guidebook, *The Basilica of Saint Francis: A Spiritual Pilgrimage* (€3, by Goulet, McInally, and Wood; I used this book, and a tour with Brother Michael, as sources for this self-guided tour).

Services: Go before you enter, as there aren't any WCs inside. There are two different pay WCs within a half-block of the lower entrance: With your back to the lower entrance, you'll find a WC up the road to the left in a squat building, and a larger WC halfway down the arcaded piazza directly in front of you (on the left).

Attending Mass: To worship in the basilica, consider joining the Franciscan brothers for Mass in *Italiano* (Sun at 7:30, 9:00, 10:30, 12:00, 17:00, and 18:30; Nov-March at 7:15, 11:00, and 17:00), or experience a Mass sung by the basilica choir many Sundays at 10:30. On Sundays in summer (Easter-Oct), there's an English Mass in the upper basilica at 9:00. Additional English and sung Masses don't follow a set schedule. Call the basilica to find out when English-speaking pilgrimage groups or choirs have reserved Masses, and attend with them (tel. 075-819-001).

OVERVIEW

The Basilica of St. Francis, a theological work of genius, can be difficult for the 21st-century tourist/pilgrim to appreciate.

Since the basilica is the reason that most people visit Assisi, and the message of St. Francis has even the least devout sightseers blessing the town Vespas, I've designed this self-guided tour with an emphasis on the place's theology (rather than art history).

A disclaimer before we start: Just as Francis used many biblical legends to help teach the Christian message, legends from the life of Francis were told in later ages to teach the same message. Are they true? In general, probably not. Are they in keeping with Francis' message? Yes. Do I share legends here as if they are historic? Sure.

The church has three parts: the upper basilica, the lower basilica, and the saint's tomb (below the lower basilica). To get oriented, stand at the lower entrance in the courtyard. While empty today, centuries ago this main piazza was cluttered with pilgrim services and the medieval equivalent of souvenir shops. Opposite the entry to the lower basilica on the right is the information center.

◑ SELF-GUIDED TOUR

Enter through the grand doorway of the lower basilica. Just inside, decorating the top of the first arch, look up and see St. Francis, who greets you with a Latin inscription. Sounding a bit like John Wayne, he says the equivalent of, "Slow down and be joyful, pilgrim. You've reached the Hill of Paradise. And, if you're observant and thoughtful, this church will knock your spiritual socks off."

• *Start with the tomb. To get there, turn left into the nave. Midway down, follow the signs and go right, to the tomb downstairs.*

The Tomb

The saint's remains are above the altar in the stone box with the iron ties. In medieval times, pilgrims came to Assisi because St.

The Franciscan Message

Francis' message caused a stir. Not only did he follow Christ's teachings, he followed Christ's lifestyle, living as a poor, wandering preacher. He traded a life of power and riches for one of obedience, poverty, and chastity. He was never ordained as a priest, but his influence on Christianity was monumental.

The Franciscan realm (Brother Sun, Sister Moon, and so on) is a space where God, man, and the natural world frolic harmoniously. Francis treated every creature—animal, peasant, pope—with equal respect. He and his "brothers" (*fratelli*, or friars) slept in fields, begged for food, and exuded the joy of nonmaterialism. Franciscan friars were known as the "Jugglers of God," modeling themselves on French troubadours who roved the countryside singing, telling stories, and cracking jokes.

In an Italy torn by conflict between towns and families, Francis promoted peace and the restoration of order. (He set an example by reconstructing the crumbled San Damiano chapel.) While the Church was waging bloody Crusades, Francis pushed ecumenism and understanding. And the Franciscan message had an impact. In 1288, just 62 years after Francis died, a Franciscan became pope (Nicholas IV). Francis' message also led to Church reforms that many believe delayed the Protestant Reformation by a century.

Francis was buried here. Holy relics were the "ruby slippers" of medieval Europe. Relics gave you power—they answered your prayers and won your wars—and ultimately helped you get back to your eternal Kansas. Assisi made no bones about promoting the saint's relics, but hid his tomb for obvious reasons of security. His body was buried secretly while the basilica was under construction, and over the next 600 years, the exact location was forgotten. When the tomb was to be opened to the public in 1818, it took more than a month to find his actual remains.

Francis' four closest friends and first followers are memorialized in the corners of the room. Opposite the altar, up four steps between the entrance and exit, notice the small copper box behind the metal grill. This contains the remains of Francis' rich Roman patron, Jacopa dei Settesoli. She traveled to see him on his deathbed but was turned away because she was female. Francis waived the rule and welcomed "Brother Jacopa" to his side. These five tombs—in the Franciscan spirit of being with your friends—were added in the 19th century.

ASSISI

The richly decorated Assisi basilica seems to contradict the teachings of the poor monk it honors, but it was built as an act of religious and civic pride to remember the hometown saint. It was also designed—and still functions—as a pilgrimage center and a splendid classroom. Though monks in robes may not give off an "easy-to-approach" vibe, the Franciscans of today are still God's jugglers (and many of them speak English).

Here is Francis' message, in his own words:

The Canticle of the Sun

Good Lord, all your creations bring praise to you!

Praise for Brother Sun, who brings the day. His radiance reminds us of you!

Praise for Sister Moon and the stars, precious and beautiful.

Praise for Brother Wind, and for clouds and storms and rain that sustain us.

Praise for Sister Water. She is useful and humble, precious and pure.

Praise for Brother Fire who cheers us at night.

Praise for our sister, Mother Earth, who feeds us and rules us.

Praise for all those who forgive because you have forgiven them.

Praise for our sister, Bodily Death, from whose embrace none can escape.

Praise and bless the Lord, and give thanks, and, with humility, serve him.

The candles you see are the only real candles in the church (others are electric). Pilgrims pay a coin, pick up a candle, and place it in the small box on the side. The friars will light it later.

• *Climb back up to the lower nave.*

Lower Basilica

Appropriately Franciscan—subdued and Romanesque—this nave is frescoed with parallel scenes from the lives of Christ (right) and Francis (left), connected by a ceiling of stars. The Passion of Christ and the Compassion of Francis lead to the altar built over Francis' tomb. After the church was built and decorated, side chapels were erected to provide mausoleums for the rich families that patronized the work of the order. Unfortunately, in the process, huge arches were cut out of some frescoed scenes, but others survive. In the fresco directly above the entry to the tomb, Christ is being taken down from the cross (just the bottom half of his body can be seen, on the left), and it looks like the story is over. Defeat. But in the opposite fresco (above the tomb's exit), we see Francis preaching to

ASSISI

the birds, reminding the faithful that the message of the Gospel survives.

These stories directed the attention of the medieval pilgrim to the altar, where he could meet God through the sacraments. The church was thought of as a community of believers sailing toward God. The prayers coming out of the nave (*navis*, or ship) fill the triangular sections of the ceiling—called *vele*, or sails—with spiritual wind. With a priest for a navigator and the altar for a helm, faith propels the ship.

Walk around the altar, stand behind it (toes to the bottom step, facing the entrance), and look up. The three scenes above you represent the creed of the Franciscans: Directly above the tomb of St. Francis, to the right, **Obedience** (Francis appears twice, wearing a rope harness and kneeling in front of Lady Obedience); to the left, **Chastity** (in her tower of purity held up by two angels); and straight ahead, **Poverty**. Here Jesus blesses the marriage as Francis slips a ring on Lady Poverty. In the foreground, two "self-sufficient" yet pint-size merchants (the new rich of a thriving northern Italy) are throwing sticks and stones at the bride. But Poverty, in her patched wedding dress, is fertile and strong, and even bare brambles blossom into a rosebush crown.

St. Francis called money the "devil's dung." The jeweled belt of a rich person was all about material wealth. A bag of coins hung from it, as did a weapon to protect that person's wealth. The simple rope Franciscan monks use to tie their tunics has three knots that symbolize—and serve as constant reminders of—their vows of obedience, chastity, and poverty.

Now turn around and put your heels to the altar and—bending back like a drum major—look up for a peek at the reward for a life of obedience, chastity, and poverty: **Francis on a heavenly throne** in a rich, golden robe. He traded a life of earthly simplicity for glory in heaven.

• *Turn to the right and march to the corner, where steps lead down into the...*

Reliquary Chapel

This chapel is filled with fascinating relics (which a €0.50 flier explains in detailed English; often closed Sat-Sun). Step in and circle the room clockwise. You'll see the silver chalice and plate that Francis used for the bread and wine of the Eucharist (in a small, dark, windowed case set into the wall, marked *Calice e Patena*). Francis believed that his personal possessions should be simple, but the items used for worship should be made of the finest materials. Next, the Veli di Lino is a cloth Jacopa wiped her friend's brow with on his deathbed. In the corner display case is a small section of the itchy haircloth *(cilizio)*—not sheep's wool, but cloth made

Basilica of St. Francis—Lower Level

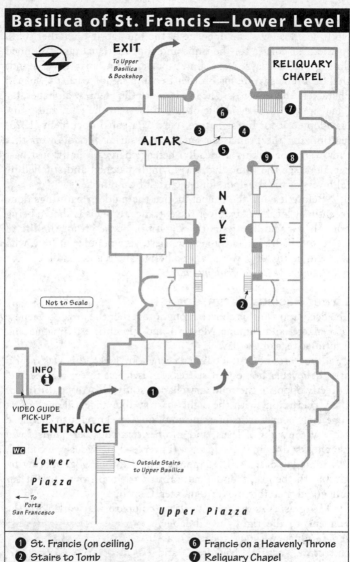

EXIT
*To Upper
Basilica
& Bookshop*

RELIQUARY
CHAPEL

⑦

⑥
③ ④
ALTAR
⑤

⑨ ⑧

N
A
V
E

Not to Scale

❷

INFO ℹ

VIDEO GUIDE
PICK-UP

❶

↱

ENTRANCE

WC
Lower

Piazza

Outside Stairs
to Upper Basilica

← To
Porta
San Francesco

Upper Piazza

ASSISI

❶ St. Francis (on ceiling)
❷ Stairs to Tomb
❸ Obedience (on ceiling)
❹ Chastity (on ceiling)
❺ Poverty (on ceiling)

❻ Francis on a Heavenly Throne
❼ Reliquary Chapel
❽ GIOTTO – Crucifixion
❾ CIMABUE – St. Francis

from scratchy horse or goat hair—worn by Francis as penance (the cloth he chose was the opposite of the fine fabric his father sold). In the next corner are the tunic and slippers that Francis donned during his last days. Next, find a prayer (in a fancy silver stand) that St. Francis wrote for Brother Leo and signed with a T-shaped character—his tau cross. The last letter in the Hebrew alphabet, tav ("tau" in Greek) is symbolic of faithfulness to the end, and Francis adopted it for his signature. Next is a papal document (1223) legitimizing the Franciscan order and assuring his followers that they were not risking a (deadly) heresy charge. Finally, just past the altar, see the tunic that was lovingly patched and stitched by followers of the five-foot, four-inch-tall St. Francis.

Before leaving the chapel, notice the modern paintings done recently by local artists. Over the entrance, Francis is shown being born in a stable like Jesus (by Capitini). Scenes from the life of Clare and Padre Pio (a Capuchin priest, very popular in Italy, who was sainted in 2002) were painted by Stefanelli and Antonio.

• *Return up the stairs, stepping into the...*

Lower Basilica's Transept

The decoration of this church brought together the greatest Sienese (Lorenzetti and Simone Martini) and Florentine (Cimabue and Giotto) artists of the day.

Look around at the painted scenes. In 1300, this was radical art—believable homespun scenes, landscapes, trees, real people. Directly opposite the reliquary chapel, study **Giotto's painting of the Crucifixion,** with the eight sparrow-like angels. For the first time, holy people are expressing emotion: One angel turns her head sadly at the sight of Jesus, and another scratches her hands down her cheeks, drawing blood. Mary (lower left), previously in control, has fainted in despair. The Franciscans, with their goal of bringing God to the people, found a natural partner in Europe's first naturalist (and therefore modern) painter, Giotto.

To grasp Giotto's artistic leap, compare his work with the painting to the right, by Cimabue. It's Gothic, without the 3-D architecture, natural backdrop, and slice-of-life reality of Giotto's work. **Cimabue's St. Francis** (far right) shows the saint with the stigmata—Christ's marks of the Crucifixion. Contemporaries described Francis as being short, with a graceful build, dark hair, and sparse beard. (This is considered the most accurate portrait of Francis—done according to

the description of one who knew him.) The sunroof haircut (tonsure) was standard for monks of the day. According to legend, the brown robe and rope belt were inventions of necessity. When Francis stripped naked and ran away from Assisi, he grabbed the first clothes he could, a rough wool peasant's tunic and a piece of rope, which became the uniform of the Franciscan order. To the left, at eye level under the sparrow-like angels, are paintings of saints and their exquisite halos (by Simone Martini or his school). To the right of the door at the same level, see five of Francis' closest followers—clearly just simple folk.

Francis' friend, "Sister Bodily Death," was really not all that terrible. In fact, Francis would like to introduce you to her now (above and to the right of the door leading into the reliquary chapel). Go ahead, block the light from the door with this book and meet her. Before his death, Francis added a line to *The Canticle of the Sun:* "Praise for our sister, Bodily Death, from whose embrace none can escape."

• *Now, cross the transept to the other side of the altar (enjoying some of the oldest surviving bits of the inlaid local-limestone flooring—c. 13th century) and find the staircase going up. Immediately above the stairs is* **Lorenzetti's** *(Francis is considered the first person ever to earn the marks of the cross through his great faith and love of the Church). Make your way up the stairs to the...* **Francis Receiving the Stigmata.** *(Francis is considered the first person ever to earn the marks of the cross through his great faith and love of the Church.) Make your way up the stairs to the...*

Courtyard

The courtyard overlooks the 15th-century cloister, the heart of this monastic complex. Pope Sixtus IV (of Sistine Chapel fame) had it built as a secure retreat for himself. Balanced and peaceful by design, the courtyard also functioned as a cistern to collect rainwater, supplying enough for 200 monks (today, there are about 40). The Franciscan order emphasizes teaching. This place functioned as a kind of theological center of higher learning, which rotated monks in for a six-month stint, then sent them back home more prepared and better inspired to preach effectively. That explains the complex narrative of the frescoes wallpapering the walls and halls here.

The **treasury** *(Museo del Tesoro)* to the left of the bookstore features ornately decorated chalices, reliquaries, vestments, and altarpieces (free but donation requested, daily 10:00-17:30).

• *From the courtyard, climb the stairs (next to the bookshop) to the...*

Upper Basilica

Built later than its counterpart below, the brighter upper basilica is considered the first Gothic church in Italy (started in 1228). You've followed the intended pilgrims' route, entering the lower

church and finishing here. Notice how the pulpit (embedded in the corner pillar) can be seen and heard from every spot in the packed church. The spirit of the order was to fill the church and preach. See also the design in the round window in the west end (high above the entry). The tiny centerpiece reads "IHS" (the first three letters of Jesus'
name in Greek). And, as you can see, this trippy kaleidoscope seems to declare that all light radiates from Jesus.

The windows here are treasures from the 13th and 14th centuries. Those behind the apse are among the oldest and most precious in Italy. Imagine illiterate medieval peasants entranced by these windows, so full of meaning that they were nicknamed "Bibles of the Poor." But for art lovers, the basilica's draw is that Giotto and his assistants practically wallpapered it circa 1297-1300. Or perhaps the job was subcontracted to other artists—scholars debate it (for more on Giotto, see page 132). Whatever the case, the anatomy, architectural depth, and drama of these frescoes helped to kick off the Renaissance. The gallery of frescoes shows 28 scenes from the life of St. Francis. The events are a mix of documented history and folk legend.

• *Working clockwise, start on the north wall (to the left, if you just climbed the stairs from the bookstore) and follow along with the help of the numbered map key. The subtitles in the faded black strip below the frescoes describe each scene in clear Latin—and affirm my interpretation.*

❶ **A common man spreads his cape before Francis** in front of the Temple of Minerva on Piazza del Comune. Before his conversion, young Francis was the model of Assisian manhood—handsome, intelligent, and well-dressed, befitting the son of a wealthy cloth dealer. Above all, he was liked by everyone, a natural charmer who led his fellow teens in nights of wine, women, and song. Medieval pilgrims understood the deeper meaning of this scene: The "eye" of God (symbolized by the rose window in the Temple of Minerva) looks over the young Francis, a dandy "imprisoned" in his own selfishness (the Temple—with barred windows—was once a prison).

❷ **Francis offers his cape to a needy stranger.** Francis was always generous of spirit. He became more so after being captured in battle and held for a year as a prisoner of war, then suffering from illness. Charity was a Franciscan forte.

❸ **Francis is visited by the Lord in a dream.** Still unsure of his calling, Francis rode off to the Crusades. One night, he dreams

Basilica of St. Francis—Upper Level

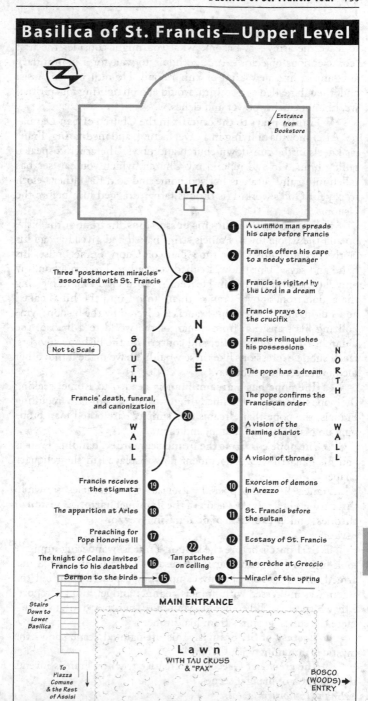

ALTAR

NAVE

SOUTH WALL

NORTH WALL

Not to Scale

Three "postmortem miracles" associated with St. Francis ⑳ 21

Francis' death, funeral, and canonization ⑳ 20

Francis receives the stigmata ⑲ 19

The apparition at Arles ⑱ 18

Preaching for Pope Honorius III ⑰ 17

The knight of Celano invites Francis to his deathbed ⑯ 16

Sermon to the birds → ⑮ 15

Stairs Down to Lower Basilica

① 1 A common man spreads his cape before Francis

② 2 Francis offers his cape to a needy stranger

③ 3 Francis is visited by the Lord in a dream

④ 4 Francis prays to the crucifix

⑤ 5 Francis relinquishes his possessions

⑥ 6 The pope has a dream

⑦ 7 The pope confirms the Franciscan order

⑧ 8 A vision of the flaming chariot

⑨ 9 A vision of thrones

⑩ 10 Exorcism of demons in Arezzo

⑪ 11 St. Francis before the sultan

⑫ 12 Ecstasy of St. Francis

⑬ 13 The crèche at Greccio

⑭ 14 ← Miracle of the spring

㉒ 22 Tan patches on ceiling

MAIN ENTRANCE ↑

ASSISI

Entrance from Bookstore

L a w n
WITH TAU CROSS
& "PAX"

To
Piazza
Comune
& the Rest
of Assisi
↓

BOSCO
(WOODS)
ENTRY →

of a palace filled with armor marked with crosses. Christ tells him to leave the army—to become what you might consider the first "conscientious objector"—and go home to wait for a nonmilitary assignment in a new kind of knighthood. He returned to Assisi and, though reviled as a coward, would end up fighting for spiritual wealth, not earthly power and riches.

❹ **Francis prays to the crucifix** in the Church of San Damiano. After months of living in a cave, fasting, and meditating, Francis kneels in the run-down church and prays. The crucifix speaks, telling him: "Go and rebuild my Church, which you can see has fallen into ruin." Francis hurried home and sold his father's cloth to pay for God's work. His furious father dragged him before the bishop.

❺ **Francis relinquishes his possessions.** In front of the bishop and the whole town, Francis strips naked and gives his dad his clothes, credit cards, and a time-share on Capri. Francis raises his hand and says, "Until now, I called you father. From now on, my only father is my Father in Heaven." Notice God's hand blessing the action from above. Francis then ran off into the hills, naked and singing. In this version, Francis is covered by the bishop, symbolizing his transition from a man of the world to a man of the Church. Notice the disbelief and concern on the bishop's advisors' faces; subtle expressions like these wouldn't have made it into other medieval frescoes of the day.

❻ **The pope has a dream.** Francis headed to Rome, seeking the pope's blessing on his fledgling movement. Initially rebuffing Francis, the pope then dreams of a simple, barefooted man propping up his teetering Church, and then...

❼ **The pope confirms the Franciscan order,** handing Francis and his gang the 1223 document now displayed in the reliquary chapel.

Francis' life was peppered with visions and miracles, shown in three panels in a row: ❽ **vision of the flaming chariot,** ❾ **vision of thrones,** and ❿ **exorcism of demons in Arezzo.**

• *Next see...*

⓫ **St. Francis before the sultan.** Francis' wandering ministry took him to Egypt during the Crusades (1219). He walked unarmed into the Muslim army camp. They captured him, but the sultan was impressed with Francis' manner and let him go, reportedly whispering, "I'd convert to your faith, but they'd kill us both." Here the sultan gestures from his throne.

⓬ **Ecstasy of St. Francis.** This oft-painted scene shows the mystic communing with Christ.

⓭ **The crèche at Greccio.** A creative teacher, Francis invents the tradition of manger scenes.

• *Around the corner, see the...*

❹ **Miracle of the spring.** Shown here getting water out of a rock to quench a stranger's thirst, Francis felt closest to God when in the hills around Assisi, seeing the Creator in the creation.

• *Cross over to the far side of the entrance door.*

❺ **Sermon to the birds.** In his best-known miracle, Francis is surrounded by birds as they listen to him teach. Francis embraces all levels of creation. One interpretation of this scene is that the birds, which are of different species, represent the diverse flock of humanity and nature, all created and beloved by God and worthy of one another's love.

This image of well-fed birds is an appropriate one to take with you. It's designed to remind pilgrims that, like the birds, God gave us life, plenty of food, feathers, wings, and a world to fly around in. Francis, patron saint of the environment and animals, taught his followers to see God in nature and to count their blessings. A monk here reminded me that even a student backpacker today eats as well as the wealthiest nobleman in the days of Francis.

• *Continue to the south wall for the rest of the panels.*

Despite the hierarchical society of his day, Francis was welcomed by all classes, shown in these three panels: ❻ **the knight of Celano invites Francis to his deathbed;** ❼ **preaching for Pope Honorius III,** who listens intently; and ❽ **the apparition at Arles,** which illustrates how Francis could be in two places at once (something only Jesus and saints can pull off). The proponents of Francis, who believed he was destined for sainthood, show him performing the necessary miracles.

❾ **Francis receives the stigmata.** It's September 17, 1224, and Francis is fasting and praying on nearby Mount Alverna when a six-winged angel (called a seraph) appears with holy laser-like powers to burn in the marks of the Crucifixion, the stigmata. For the strength of his faith, Francis is given the marks of his master, the "battle scars of love." These five wounds suffered by Christ (nails in palms and feet, lance in side) marked Francis' body for the rest of his life.

The next panels deal with ❿ **Francis' death, funeral, and canonization.** The last panels show ⓫ **miracles** associated with the saint after his death, proving that he's in heaven and bolstering his eligibility for sainthood.

Francis died thanking God and singing his *Canticle of the Sun,* in which he refers to the sun as his brother and the moon as his sister. Francis also called his body "Brother Ass" (because of the heavy burdens he asked it to carry)—and conceded on his deathbed that he'd been a bit tough on Brother Ass. Ravaged by an asceticism extreme enough to earn him the stigmata, Francis died in 1226.

Before leaving through the front entrance, look up at the ceiling and the walls near the rose window to see ⓬ **large tan patches.**

ASSISI

In 1997, when a 5.5-magnitude quake hit Assisi, it shattered the upper basilica's frescoes into 300,000 fragments. An aftershock then shook the ceiling frescoes down, killing two monks and two art scholars who were standing here. Later, the fragments were meticulously picked up and pieced back together.

Outside, on the lawn, the Latin word *pax* (peace) and the Franciscan tau cross are sculpted from shrubbery. For a drink or snack, the Bar San Francesco (facing the upper basilica) is handy. For *pax,* take the high lane back to town, up to the castle, or into the countryside.

More Sights in Assisi

▲▲Basilica of St. Mary of the Angels (Basilica di Santa Maria degli Angeli)

This huge basilica, towering above the buildings of Santa Maria degli Angeli—the modern part of Assisi in the flat valley below the hill town—marks the spot where Francis lived, worked, and died. It's a grandiose church built around a humble chapel—reflecting the monumental impact of this simple saint on his town and the world.

Cost and Hours: Free, Mon-Sat 6:15-12:50 & 14:30-19:30, Sun from 6:45, tel. 075-805-11. A little TI kiosk is across the street from the souvenir stands (generally daily 10:00-13:00 & 15:00-18:30 but hours a bit erratic, tel. 075-804 4354). As you face the church, the best WC is behind the bushes on your right.

Dress Code: Modest dress is required (no shorts or tank tops).

Getting There: Whether you're traveling by car or by train, it's most practical to visit this sight on the way into or out of town. From Assisi's train station—which has baggage storage—it's a five-minute walk to the basilica (exit station left, after 50 yards take the underground pedestrian walkway—*sottopassaggio*—on your left, then walk straight ahead, passing several handy eateries). There's ample well-marked parking next to the train station.

If you're coming from the old town, you can reach the basilica on the same orange bus (line #C) that runs down to the train station (stay on one more stop to reach the basilica; confirm with driver). In the opposite direction, buses from the basilica up to the old town run twice hourly, usually at :14 and :44 after the hour.

Leaving the church, the stop is on your right, by the side of the building. For tickets, see "Getting Around Assisi," earlier.

Visiting the Basilica: This grand church was built in the 16th century around the tiny but historic **Porziuncola Chapel** (now di-

rectly under the dome) after the chapel became too small to accommodate the many pilgrims wanting to pay homage to St. Francis. Some local monks had given Francis this *porziuncola*, or "small portion," after his conversion—a little land with a fixer-upper chapel. Francis lived here after he founded the Franciscan order, and this was where he consecrated St. Clare as a Bride of Christ. What would humble Francis think of the huge church—Christianity's 10th largest—built over his tiny chapel?

Behind the Porziuncola Chapel on the right, find the **Cappella del Transito,** which marks the site of Francis' death on October 3, 1226. Francis died as he'd lived—simply, in a small hut located here. On his last night on earth, he invited some friars to join him in a Last Supper-style breaking of bread. Then he undressed, lay down on the bare ground, and began to recite Psalm 141: "Lord, I cry unto thee." He spoke the last line, "Let the wicked fall into their own traps, while I escape"...and he passed on.

From the right transept, follow *Roseto* signs to the rose garden. You'll walk down a passage with gardens on either side (viewable through the windows)—on the left, a tranquil park with a statue of Francis petting a sheep, and on the right, the **rose garden.** Francis, fighting a temptation that he never named, once threw himself onto the roses. As the story goes, the thorns immediately dropped off. Thornless roses have grown here ever since.

Exiting the passage, turn right to find the **Rose Chapel** (Cappella delle Rose), built over the place where Francis lived.

The displays in the next hallway change with the seasons. In the autumn, a room displays a giant animated Nativity scene (a reminder to pilgrims that Francis first established the tradition of manger scenes as a teaching aid). The bookshop has some works in English and an "old pharmacy" selling herbal cures.

Continuing on, you'll pass the **Porziuncola Museum,** featuring early depictions of St. Francis by 13th-century artists, a model of Assisi during Francis' lifetime, and religious art and objects from the basilica. On the museum's upper floor are some monks' cells, which provide intriguing insight into the spartan lifestyles of the pious and tonsured (€3, ask for English brochure, Tue-Sun 9:30-12:30 & 15:30-19:00, Nov-March until 18:30, tel. 075-805-1419, www.porziuncola.org).

▲Roman Forum (Foro Romano)

For a look at Assisi's Roman roots, check out the Roman Forum, beneath Piazza del Comune. During your visit, you'll see a small part of the excavation and a few surviving odd bits and obscure pieces. You'll also walk on an ancient Roman road and view some video recreations.

Cost and Hours: €4, €8 combo-ticket includes the next two sights, daily June-Aug 10:00-13:00 & 14:30-19:00, shorter hours off-season; from Piazza del Comune, go a half-block to Via Portica 2—it's on your right; tel. 075-815-5077.

Pinacoteca

This small, unexciting museum attractively displays its 13th- to 17th-century art (mainly frescoes), with general English information in nearly every room. There's a damaged Giotto Madonna and a rare secular fresco (to the right of the Giotto art), but it's mainly a peaceful walk through a pastel world—best for art lovers.

Cost and Hours: €3, €8 combo-ticket includes Forum and Rocca Maggiore, same hours as Roman Forum, on main drag between Piazza del Comune and Basilica of St. Francis at Via San Francesco 12—look for banner above entryway, tel. 075-815-5234.

▲Rocca Maggiore

The "big castle" offers a few restored medieval rooms, a good look at a 14th-century fortification, and a fine view of Assisi and the Umbrian countryside. If you're pinching your euros, skip it—the view is just as good from outside the castle.

Cost and Hours: €5.50, €8 combo-ticket includes Forum and Pinacoteca, daily 10:00 until an hour before sunset—about 19:15 in summer, Via della Rocca, tel. 075-815-5077.

ON THE OUTSKIRTS

Church of San Damiano (Chiesa di San Damiano)

Located on the slope steeply below the Basilica of St. Clare, this modest church and convent was where Francis received his call and where Clare spent her days as mother superior of the Poor Clares. As you enter, signs point you through a series of simple rooms—including the dining hall where Clare ate with her flock and the room where she died—to a peaceful, flowery courtyard. Drivers can zip right there (watch for the turnoff on the road up to Piazza Matteotti), while walkers descend pleasantly from Assisi for 15 minutes through an olive grove.

In 1206, Francis was inside when he heard the wooden crucifix order him to rebuild the church. (The crucifix in San Damiano is a copy; the original is now displayed in the Basilica of St. Clare.) Francis initially interpreted these miraculous words as a call to rebuild crumbling San Damiano. He sold his father's cloth for money to fix the church. (The church we see today, however, was rebuilt later by others.) Eventually, Francis realized his charge was to revitalize the Christian Church at large.

As he approached the end of his life, Francis came to San Damiano to visit his old friend Clare. She set him up in a simple reed hut in the olive grove, where he was inspired to write his poem *The Canticle of the Sun* (see page 729).

Cost and Hours: Free, daily, convent open 10:00-12:00 & 14:00-18:00, closes at 16:30 in winter, church opens at 6:15; start walking from the Porta Nuova parking lot at the south end of Assisi and follow the signs; tel. 075-812-273, www.assisiofm.it.

Commune with Nature

For a picnic with the same birdsong and views that inspired St. Francis, leave the tourists behind and **hike to the Rocca Minore** (small private castle, not tourable) above Piazza Matteotti.

For a more organized nature experience, try the 160-acre **San Francesco Woods** (Bosco di San Francesco), where you can follow three routes through forest, monastery ruins, and a land-art installation (€4 suggested donation, picnic area; April-Sept Tue-Sun 10:00-19:00, Oct-March until 16:00, closed Mon; entry is off the piazza in front of the upper basilica, tel. 075-813-157).

Hermitage (Eremo delle Carceri)

If you want to follow further in St. Francis' footsteps, take a trip up the rugged slopes of nearby Mount Subasio to the humble, peaceful hermitage where Francis and his followers retreated for solitude. Today the spot is marked by a 14th-century friary that's still occupied by Franciscan monks. A self-guided tour twists you through the head-thumping doorframes and steep stairways of the medieval structure, the highlight of which is the tiny, dank cave where Francis would retire for private prayer. Outside, you'll see the ancient tree (held together with braces) that's said to be where Francis preached to the birds. Rustic paths lead to open-air "chapels" in the surrounding forest.

Cost and Hours: Free, daily 8:30-18:30, until 17:30 in winter, tel. 075-812-301.

Getting There: Drive, take a taxi, or hike—there is no public transportation. Drivers can follow signs out of Assisi toward Mount Subasio, then park on the switchback just above the entrance, along the left side of the road. For hikers starting from Assisi's Porta Cappuccino gate, it's a stiff 3-mile, 1.5-hour hike with an elevation gain of about 1,000 feet. You'll walk along a narrow, paved road

ASSISI

Sleep Code

Hotels are classified based on the average price of a standard double room with breakfast in high season.

$$$$	**Splurge:** Most rooms over €170
$$$	**Pricier:** €130-170
$$	**Moderate:** €90-130
$	**Budget:** €50-90
¢	**Backpacker:** Under €50
RS%	Rick Steves discount

Unless otherwise noted, credit cards are accepted, hotel staff speak basic English, and free Wi-Fi is available. Comparison-shop by checking prices at several hotels (on each hotel's own website, on a booking site, or by email). For the best deal, *book directly with the hotel*. Ask for a discount if paying in cash; if the listing includes **RS%,** request a Rick Steves discount.

(with no shoulders) enjoying brisk air and sporadic views. A souvenir kiosk at the entrance sells drinks and sandwiches.

Sleeping in Assisi

Assisi accommodates large numbers of pilgrims on religious holidays (see list on page 1178). Finding a room at any other time should be easy. I've listed prices for spring (April-mid-June) and fall (mid-Aug-Oct). At most places, expect slightly lower rates in midsummer and winter.

Few hotels are air-conditioned. Locals suggest that you keep your windows closed through the middle of the day so that your room will be as cool as possible in the evening.

HOTELS AND ROOMS

$$$ Hotel Ideale, on a ridge overlooking the valley, offers 13 bright and airy remodeled rooms with new furnishings (all with views and balconies), a tranquil garden setting, and free (but tight) private parking (RS%, two apartments with fully equipped kitchens available, air-con, Piazza Matteotti 1, tel. 075-813-570, www. hotelideale.it, info@hotelideale.it, friendly sisters Lara and Ilaria). The hotel is off the main road into town and is the best pick for timid drivers. It's across the street from the parking lot at Piazza Matteotti, at the top end of town.

$$ Hotel Umbra, a quiet villa in the middle of town, has 24 spacious but overpriced rooms with great view terraces. While well-worn, it's friendly and beautifully located. Stepping into the breakfast room is like entering a time warp (RS%, family rooms, air-con, elevator, peaceful garden, and view sun terrace, most rooms have views, closed Dec-March, just off Piazza del Comune under the arch at Via degli Archi 6, tel. 075-812-240, www.hotelumbra. it, info@hotelumbra.it, family Laudenzi).

$ Hotel Belvedere, a great value, is a modern building with 12 spacious, classic-feeling rooms; eight come with sweeping views (breakfast extra, elevator, large communal view terrace, 2 blocks past Basilica of St. Clare at Via Borgo Aretino 13, tel. 075-812-460, www.assisihotelbelvedere.com, hotelbelvedereassisi@yahoo. it, thoughtful Enrico speaks fluent New Jerseyan). Coming by bus from the train station, get off at Porta Nuova; the hotel is steps away.

$ Hotel Pallotta offers seven fresh, bright, small rooms and a shared top-floor lounge with view. Friendly and helpful, the owners provide guests with loads of extra niceties including a loaner Assisi guidebook, free use of washer and drying rack, and free hot drinks and cake at teatime (RS%, a block off Piazza del Comune at Via San Rufino 6; tel. 075-812-307, www.pallottaassisi.it, pallotta@ pallottaassisi.it; Stefano, Serena, and family).

$ Hotel San Rufino offers a great locale, solid stone quality, and 11 comfortable rooms (breakfast extra, elevator, air-con, family rooms; from Cathedral of San Rufino, follow sign to Via Porta Perlici 7; tel. 075-812-803, www.hotelsanrufino.it, info@ hotelsanrufino.it).

$ Albergo Il Duomo, Hotel San Rufino's nine-room annex a block away, is tidy and *tranquillo*. Located on a stair-stepped lane, it's more atmospheric and has nicer bathrooms than its parent hotel, but more steps and no elevator (breakfast extra, Vicolo San Lorenzo 2 but check in at Hotel San Rufino—see earlier, tel. 075-812-742, www.hotelsanrufino.it, info@hotelsanrufino.it).

$ Hotel La Rocca, on the peaceful top end of town, has 32 solid and modern, business-like rooms in a medieval shell (breakfast extra, air-con, elevator, pay parking, sunny rooftop terrace, decent restaurant upstairs, 3-minute walk from Piazza Matteotti at Via Porta Perlici 27, tel. 075-812-284, www.hotelarocca.it, info@ hotelarocca.it, Carlo).

$ Hotel Sole, renting 38 rooms in a 15th-century building, is low-energy, well-worn, and forgettable, but the location is central. Half of its rooms are in a newer annex across the street (RS%, air-con, elevator in annex only, public parking nearby, 100 yards before Basilica of St. Clare at Corso Mazzini 35, tel. 075-812-373, www. assisihotelsole.com, info@assisihotelsole.com).

¢ Camere Carli has six spacious rooms with bizarre floor plans in a solid, minimalist place above an art gallery. The loft rooms are a great value for families (RS%, no breakfast, family rooms, lots of stairs and no elevator, free parking 150 yards away, just off Piazza San Rufino at Via Porta Perlici 1, tel. 075-812-490, mobile 339-

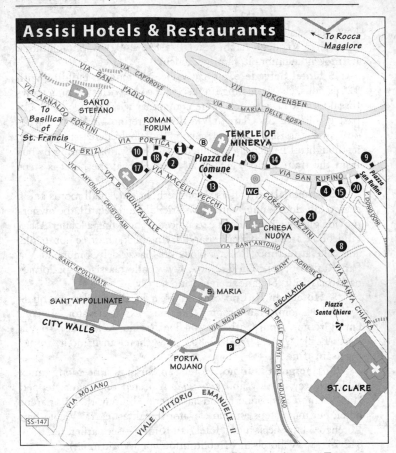

Assisi Hotels & Restaurants

531-1366, www.camerecarli.it, carliarte@live.it, pleasant Franco, who runs the pottery shop below and speaks limited English).

¢ **Camere Annalisa Martini** is a cheery home amid vines and roses in the town's medieval core. This is a good budget choice—Annalisa enthusiastically accommodates her guests with a picnic garden, pay washing machine, communal refrigerator, and six homey rooms with cheerful peeling wallpaper and flea market furniture (cash only, 3 rooms share 2 bathrooms, no breakfast; one block from Piazza del Comune—go downhill toward basilica, turn left on Via San Gregorio to #6; tel. 075-813-536, www.cameremartiniassisi.it, cameremartini@libero.it, Mamma Rosignoli doesn't speak English, but Annalisa does).

Hostel: Francis probably would have bunked with the peasants in Assisi's 65-bed ¢ **Ostello della Pace** (private rooms available, dinner extra, laundry service, free parking, lockout 10:00-16:00, midnight curfew, closed Nov-Feb; take orange shuttle bus from station to Piazza Giovanni Paolo II, then walk 15 minutes

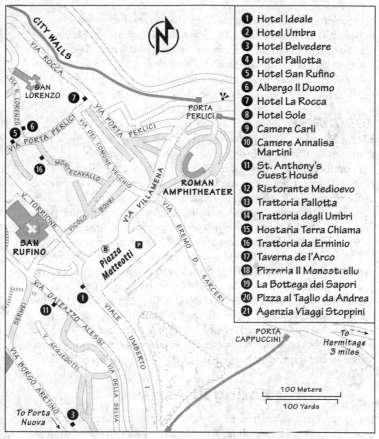

CITY WALLS

VIA ROCCA

SAN LORENZO

VIA S. LORENZO

VIA PORTA PERLICI

MONTECAVALLO

VIA DEL COMUNE VECCHIO

VIA PORTA PERLICI

PORTA PERLICI

VIA VILLAMENA

ROMAN AMPHITHEATER

VICOLO BOVEI

V. TORRIONE

SAN RUFINO

Piazza Matteotti

VIA EREMO D. CARCERI

VIA GALEAZZO ALESSI

SERMEI

V. ACQUEDOTTI

VIA DELLA SELVA

VIALE UMBERTO

PORTA CAPPUCCINI

To Hermitage 3 miles

VIA BORGO ARETINO

To Porta Nuova

100 Meters
100 Yards

1 Hotel Ideale
2 Hotel Umbra
3 Hotel Belvedere
4 Hotel Pallotta
5 Hotel San Rufino
6 Albergo Il Duomo
7 Hotel La Rocca
8 Hotel Sole
9 Camere Carli
10 Camere Annalisa Martini
11 St. Anthony's Guest House
12 Ristorante Medioevo
13 Trattoria Pallotta
14 Trattoria degli Umbri
15 Hostaria Terra Chiama
16 Trattoria da Erminio
17 Taverna de l'Arco
18 Pizzeria Il Monastello
19 La Bottega dei Sapori
20 Pizza al Taglio da Andrea
21 Agenzia Viaggi Stoppini

downhill on Via Marconi, then left at bend on Via di Valecchie to #4—see map on page 712; tel. 075-816-767, www.assisihostel.com, info@assisihostel.com).

SWEET DREAMS IN A CONVENT

Assisi is filled with convents, most of which rent rooms to pilgrims and travelers. While you don't need to be a pilgrim or even a Christian to be welcome, it's just common sense to stay in a convent *only* if you're approaching Assisi with a contemplative mindset. Convents feel institutional, house many groups, and are not particularly cheap—but they come with all the facilities you might need to enjoy a spirit-filled visit to Assisi.

$ St. Anthony's Guest House is where the Franciscan Sisters of the Atonement offer a very warm and tranquil welcome. Their oasis of peace is just above the Basilica of St. Clare. They have 35 beds in 19 sparkling-clean rooms, some with great views—request when you reserve (family rooms available, cash only for short stays,

ASSISI

no problem if couples want to share a bed, elevator, no air-con but fans, 23:00 curfew, closed mid-Nov-Feb, library, views, picnic garden, parking by donation; from the parking cashier in Piazza Matteotti, take the stairs down to the *"tunnel romano,"* then continue down on the elevator—it's just to the left at Via Galeazzo Alessi 10; tel. 075-812-542, atoneassisi@tiscali.it).

AGRITURISMO NEAR ASSISI

$$ Le Mandrie di San Paolo ("The Herd of St. Paul") is a meticulously restored 1,000-year-old stone house renting 13 rustic but comfortable rooms on a hillside high above the valley. Soulful Alex, his wife, Elena, and the Damiani family are justifiably proud of their passion for hospitality and connection to the land. They have an olive grove, lots of animals, a beautiful swimming pool, sauna, fine restaurant, and spectacular views over Assisi and the valleys of Umbria (apartments and family rooms, mobile 349-821-7867, tel. 075-806-4070, www.agriturismomandriesanpaolo.it, mandrie10@gmail.com). Their **$$$$** restaurant is a great choice: They produce their own olive oil, cheese, salami, and flour, and fire their bread ovens with their own wood (daily 19:30-22:00, in winter on request, reservations preferred). It's about a 10-minute drive from Assisi, above the village of Viole (a.k.a. San Vitale). Just head southeast of Assisi following signs for *Viole;* when you enter town, before you reach the arch, turn left and follow signs up the hill.

Eating in Assisi

I've listed decent, central, good-value restaurants. Assisi's food is heavy and rustic. Locals brag about their sausage and love to grate truffles on pasta.

To bump up any meal, consider a glass or bottle of the favorite homegrown red wine, Sagrantino de Montefalco. Sagrantino is Umbria's answer to Brunello (although many wine lovers around here would say that it's vice versa). Before or after dinner, enjoy a drink on the main square facing the Roman temple...or hang out with the local teens with a takeaway beer under the temple's columns.

FINE DINING

$$$ Ristorante Medioevo is my vote for your best splurge. With heavy but spacious cellar vaults, William Ventura's restaurant is an elegant, accessible playground of gastronomy. He features traditional cuisine with a modern twist, dictated by what's in season. While his first passion is cooking, his second is music—mellow jazz and bossa nova give a twinkle to the medieval atmosphere. Dishes are well-presented; beef and game dishes are the specialties,

Restaurant Price Code

I've assigned each eatery a price category, based on the average cost of a typical main course (pasta or *secondi*). Drinks, desserts, and splurge items (steak and seafood) can raise the price considerably.

$$$$	**Splurge:** Most main courses over €20
$$$	**Pricier:** €15-20
$$	**Moderate:** €10-15
$	**Budget:** Under €10

In Italy, pizza by the slice and other takeout food is **$**; a basic trattoria or sit-down pizzeria is **$$**; a casual but more upscale restaurant is **$$$**; and a swanky splurge is **$$$$**.

and the wonderful Sagrantino wine is served by the glass. To better understand the Italian fascination with "a good marriage" between food and wine, readers of this book will get a small slice of strong pecorino cheese to go with any glass of Sagrantino ordered—just request it (good €16 fixed-price lunch or €40 tasting menu with matching wines, Tue-Sun 12:15-15:00 & 19:00-22:00, closed Mon, in winter open weekends only; from the fountain on Piazza del Comune, hike downhill two blocks to Via Arco dei Priori 4; tel. 075-813-068, www.ristorantemedioevoassisi.it).

$$$ Trattoria Pallotta is a local favorite with white table-cloths and a living-room ambience. It's run by a friendly and hardworking family—with Margarita in charge of the kitchen—and offers delicious, well-presented regional specialties, such as *piccione* (squab, a.k.a. pigeon) and *coniglio* (rabbit). And they enjoy serving split courses *(bis)* featuring the two local pastas. Reservations are smart (always a vegetarian menu, €28 fixed-price meal showcases local specialties; Wed-Mon 12:15-14:30 & 19:15-23:00, closed Tue, a few steps off Piazza del Comune across from temple/church at Vicolo della Volta Pinta 2, tel. 075-812-649, www.pallottaassisi.it).

Countryside Farm-to-Table Dinner: $$$$ Le Mandrie di San Paolo, in a 1,000-year-old farmhouse (described earlier), makes many of their own ingredients and serves an exquisite dinner to guests and nonguests alike (€25-30 four-course meal, daily 19:30-22:00, in winter on request, reservations preferred, a 10-minute drive from Assisi—see "Sleeping in Assisi" for details, www.agriturismomandriesanpaolo.it).

CASUAL EATERIES

$$ Trattoria degli Umbri is your best bet for a meal overlooking Assisi's main square, with a few nice tables just above the fountain.

ASSISI

They serve delightful Umbrian dishes and top-notch wines by the glass (closed Thu, Piazza del Comune 40, tel. 075-812-455).

$$ Hostaria Terra Chiama is a bright, modern little eight-table place run by Diego and his family, who serve traditional Umbrian dishes with seasonal specials (daily, lunch from 12:30, dinner from 19:00, Via San Rufino 16, tel. 075-819-9051).

$$ Locanda del Podestà is where chef Stelvio cooks up tasty grilled Umbrian sausages, *gnocchi della locanda,* and all manner of truffles, while Romina graciously serves happy diners who know a good value. Try the tasty *scottadito* ("scorch your fingers") lamb chops (Thu-Tue 12:00-14:45 & 19:00-21:30, closed Wed and Feb, 5-minute walk uphill along Via Cardinale Merry del Val from basilica, Via San Giacomo 6C—see map on page 712, tel. 075-816-553).

$$ Le Terrazze di Properzio, just up the street from Podestà, offers seasonal specials, a traditional menu, and Assisi's best view terrace for dining (Thu-Wed 12:00-14:30 & 19:00-21:30, closed Tue, terrace closed in bad weather, Via Metastasio 9, tel. 075-816-868).

$$ Trattoria da Erminio has peaceful tables on a tiny square, and indoor seating under a big, medieval (but air-conditioned) brick vault. Run by Federico and his family for three generations, it specializes in local meat cooked on an open-fire grill. They have good Umbrian wines—before you order, ask Federico or Giuliana for a taste of the Petranera wine (Fri-Wed 12:00-14:30 & 19:00-21:00, closed Thu; from Piazza San Rufino, go a block up Via Porta Perlici and turn right to Via Montecavallo 19; tel. 075-812-506).

$$ Taverna de l'Arco is one of the oldest restaurants in Assisi, but its new, young owners are bringing a fresh energy to the place. The spacious vaulted dining room, reasonably priced menu, and homemade pastas and gnocchi make it worth considering (Thu-Tue 12:00-14:30 & 19:00-22:00, closed Wed, one block from Piazza del Comune at Via San Gregorio 8, tel. 075-816-689).

$ Pizzeria Il Menestrello serves huge, inexpensive Umbrian-style pizzas (wood-fired, thin, and crisp) in an elegant medieval vaulted setting that makes your beer and pizza feel like something King Arthur would eat for dinner (daily 12:00-14:30 & 19:00-22:30, Via San Gregorio 1/A, tel. 075-812-746).

PICNIC ON THE MAIN SQUARE

There are many little grocery stores *(alimentari)* near Piazza del Comune (one is a block uphill from the main square, at Via San Rufino 19), plus bakeries selling pizza by the slice.

La Bottega dei Sapori is handy for assembling a picnic of Umbrian treats: good *porchetta* sandwiches and specialty items, including truffle paste and olive oil. Sandwich chefs Saverio and Katia make a nice *taglieri misti* (meat and cheese plate) for €7. It can get pricey here (especially if you eat in), so be sure you understand the cost before ordering anything (local wines to go, daily 9:30-21:00, Piazza del Comune 34, tel. 075-812-294, Fabrizio). You can eat your sandwich on any of the benches surrounding the piazza.

Pizza al Taglio da Andrea, facing the Church of San Rufino on Piazza San Rufino, has perhaps the best pizza by the slice in town. Locals also like their *torta al testo,* the Umbrian flatbread sandwich (daily, Via San Rufino 26, tel. 075-815-325).

Assisi Connections

The train station's ticket office is often open only Mon-Fri 12:30-20:00, closed Sat-Sun; when the office is closed, use the ticket machine (newsstand sells only regional tickets). Up in Assisi's old town, you can get train information and tickets from Agenzia Viaggi Stoppini (see "Helpful Hints" on page 714).

From Assisi by Train to: Rome (nearly hourly, 2-3.5 hours, 5 direct, most others change in Foligno), **Florence** (8/day direct, 2-3 hours), **Orvieto** (roughly hourly, 2-3 hours, with transfer in Terontola or Orte), **Siena** (10/day, about 4 hours, most involve 2 changes; bus is faster). Italian train timetables change frequently—double-check details at www.trenitalia.com.

By Bus: Service to **Rome** is operated by the Sulga bus company (2/day, 3 hours, pay driver, departs from Piazza San Pietro, arrives at Rome's Tiburtina station, where you can connect with the regional train to Fiumicino airport, tel. 800-099-661, www.sulga.it). A bus for **Siena** (daily at 10:20, 2 hours, www.baltour.it, search "Santa Maria degli Angeli" for timetable) departs from the stop next to the Basilica of St. Mary of the Angels, near the train station; you usually can't buy Siena tickets from the driver—buy them at Assisi's Agenzia Viaggi Stoppini (see "Helpful Hints" on page 714). Don't take the bus to **Florence;** the train is better.

By Plane: Perugia/Assisi Airport, about 10 miles from Assisi, has daily connections to London, Brussels, Barcelona, and a few Mediterranean destinations (airport code: PEG, tel. 075-592-141, www.airport.umbria.it). Bus service between Assisi and the airport is so sporadic (just a few times a day—see www.umbriamobilita.it) that you should plan on taking a taxi (about €30).

ASSISI

ORVIETO & CIVITA

While Tuscany is justifiably famous for its many fine hill towns, Umbria, just to the south, has some stellar offerings of its own. Assisi (covered in its own chapter) is a must for nature lovers and Franciscan pilgrims. But if you're after views, wine, and charming villages, you'll find Umbria's best in Orvieto and in Civita di Bagnoregio (which is technically just across the border in Lazio, the same region as Rome). About a 30-minute drive apart, these hill towns—one big, one small—perch high above scenic plains. Pleasant Orvieto is best known for its colorful-inside-and-out cathedral and its fine Orvieto Classico wine. Tiny Civita di Bagnoregio, once my favorite hill town, is now a "dead city": It's effectively a museum with a couple of places in which to eat and sleep, perched precariously on a hill pinnacle that you pay to enter. Taken together, Orvieto and Civita make a perfect duet for experiencing what all the hill-town fuss is about.

PLANNING YOUR TIME

Orvieto and Civita deserve at least an overnight, although even a few hours in each is enough to sample what they have to offer. Both are also great places to slow down and relax. Stay in one and side-trip to the other (Orvieto has more restaurants and other amenities and is easier to reach, while Civita really lets you get away from it all). The two are connected by a 30-minute drive or a 60-minute bus ride, and Orvieto is conveniently close to Rome (about an hour away by train or expressway).

Orvieto

Just off the freeway and the main train line, Umbria's grand hill town entices those heading to and from Rome. While no secret, it's well worth a visit. The town sits majestically on its *tufo* throne a thousand feet above the valley floor (for more on volcanic tuff, see the sidebar on page 765).

A few centuries before Christ, Orvieto—then called Velzna—was one of a dozen major Etruscan cities. Some historians believe it may have been a religious center—a kind of Etruscan Mecca (locals are looking for archaeological proof—the town and surrounding countryside are dotted with Etruscan ruins).

Imagine the history: From 900 B.C. to 264 B.C., the town was Etruscan Velzna. After a two year Roman siege, it was destroyed and the ruins left abandoned for six centuries. Rome fell in A.D. 476, and in the chaos of that power vacuum, with invaders from the north terrorizing the peninsula, people in the valley headed back into the hills in search of safety. They rebuilt over the old Etrusan foundations, and named the settlement Urbs Vetus, meaning "old town" in Latin. Over time, Urbs Vetus became Orvieto.

Orvieto flourished as a Middle Ages regional power. During Orvieto's glory days—from the 11th to 13th centuries—it was a city-state of about 30,000 people, like Perugia, Assisi, and Siena, and an occasional home to the pope. Today it's again a small town, with only 5,000 people living in under a square mile atop its hill, and only half of its 50 churches still active.

Orvieto has three claims to fame: cathedral, Classico wine, and ceramics. Drinking a shot of the local white wine in a ceramic cup as you gaze up at the cathedral lets you experience Orvieto's three C's all at once. (Is the cathedral best in the afternoon, when the facade basks in golden light, or early in the morning, when it rises above the hilltop mist? You decide.) Though loaded with tourists by day, Orvieto is quiet by night, and a visit here comes with a wonderful bonus: close proximity to the unforgettable Civita di Bagnoregio (covered later in this chapter).

Orientation to Orvieto

Orvieto has two distinct parts: the old-town hilltop and the dreary new town below (called Orvieto Scalo). Whether coming by train or car, you first arrive in the nondescript, modern lower part of town. From there you can drive or take the funicular, elevator, or escalator up to the medieval upper town, an atmospheric labyrinth of streets and squares where all the sightseeing action is.

Orvieto

200 Meters
200 Yards

To Train
Station

STR. DEL KIOKSO

STRADA DELLA STAZIONE

STRADA DELLA STAZIONE

VIALE CARDUCCI

ETRUSCAN
NECROPOLIS

LA RUPE PATH

Park

30

Piazza
Corsica

C l i f f s

P

VIA CORSICA

VIA D.

6

SANT'
AGOSTINO

SAN
GIOVENALE

Piazza
S. Giovenale

9

24

VIA DEL POPOLO

PALAZZO
DEL POPOLO

STRADA DELLE CONC.

31

PALAZZO
FILIPPESCHI

V. CACCIA

MALABRANCA

VIA DELLA CAVA

V. MAGALOTTI

FILIPPESCHI

Piazza
Vittozzi

2

Piazza
del Popolo

16

14

30

VIA PECORELLI

12

Piazza
Repubblica

23

TORRE
DEL MORO

22

VIA DEL DUOMO

27

PORTA
MAGGIORE

WELL
OF THE
CAVE

V. RANIERI

18

CITY
HALL

SANT'
ANDREA

V. MICHELANGELI

21

17

20

4

To Bolsena
& Viterbo

SAN GIOVANNI
EVANGELISTA

V. GARIBALDI

11

7

26

15

IL MAGO
DI OZ

Campo
della Fiera

P

31

STRADA DI

VIA RIPA MEDICI

V. COZZA

5

V. ANGELICO

13

30

PORTA
ROMANA

VIC. VOLSINIA

ELEVATOR &
ESCALATOR

VIA DELLA SEGHERIA

VIA DEGLI ALBERICI

V. CLEMENTINI

LIPICINI

VIA MAITANI

10

PORTA
ROMANA

Piazza
Febei

- - - - LA RUPE VIEW WALK
· · · · · RAMPARTS WALK

C l i f f s

1 Hotel Duomo
2 Grand Hotel Italia
3 Hotel Corso
4 La Magnolia B&B
5 B&B Michelangeli
6 Affittacamere Valentina
7 Hotel Posta
8 Villa Mercede

9 Istituto S.S. Salvatore
10 Casa Sèlita B&B
11 Trattoria La Palomba
12 L'Antica Trattoria dell'Orso
13 Trattoria La Pergola
14 Trattoria del Moro Aronne
15 Trattoria la Grotta &
   Sigma Supermarket

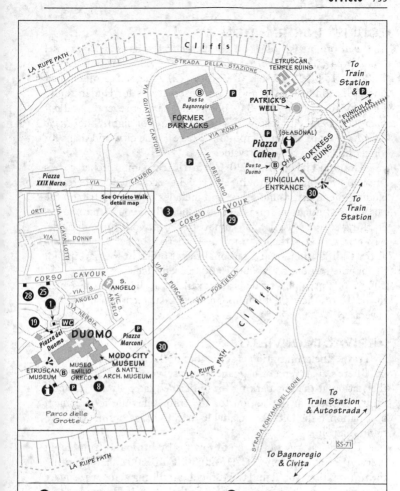

16 Trattoria da Carlo

17 Trattoria Antico Bucchero

18 Pizzeria & Rist. Charlie

19 Enoteca al Duomo & Pasqualetti Gelateria

20 L'Oste del Re

21 Caffè ClanDestino

22 Café Barrique

23 Caffè Montanucci

24 Bar Palace

25 Café del Teatro

26 Bar Duomo

27 Mille300 Music&Drinks

28 Metà Supermarket

29 Tobacco Shop (Bus Tickets)

30 Rupe Hike Access (5)

31 Romantic Rampart Stroll (2)

TOURIST INFORMATION

The well-organized TI is on the cathedral square at Piazza del Duomo 24 (Mon-Fri 8:15-13:50 & 16:00-19:00, Sat-Sun 10:00-13:00 & 15:00-18:00, tel. 0763-341-772). The ticket office next door sells combo-tickets and books reservations for Underground Orvieto Tours (tel. 0763-340-688). The TI has several excellent maps: a general city map with current hours for sights, the *Anello della Rupe* map for a hike around the base of the city, and maps for longer hikes into the countryside.

Combo-Ticket: The €20 **Carta Unica** combo-ticket covers Orvieto's top sights (virtually every sight recommended here, including the underground tours) and includes one round-trip on the bus and/or funicular. This is a good value only if you plan to do everything covered. To use the combo-ticket for your funicular ride, buy it on arrival in the lower town—either at the bar or newsstand at the train station, or at a seasonal ticket office in the parking lot (below the station, daily 9:00-16:00, closed Oct-Easter, tel. 0763-302-378). The combo-ticket is also available at the ticket office next to the TI on Piazza del Duomo, as well as at most of the sights it covers.

ARRIVAL IN ORVIETO

By Train: The train station is at the foot of the hill the old town sits on. There's a convenient baggage check service below and behind the station at the bus parking lot (described later, under "Helpful Hints"). Check at the station for the train schedule to your next destination (schedule also available at the TI or online at www.trenitalia.com).

The easiest way to the top of town is by **funicular** (runs about every 10 minutes Mon-Sat 7:15-20:30, Sun 8:00-20:30). Exiting the train station, you'll find the funicular building across the square to the left under the *Funicolare* sign. Tickets (€1.30, good for 90 minutes, sold inside funicular station) include the minibus from Piazza Cahen at the top of the funicular to Piazza del Duomo. Or buy a Carta Unica combo-ticket (described earlier), which includes the funicular ride.

As you exit the funicular at the top, you're in Piazza Cahen, located at the east end of the upper town. To your left is a ruined fortress with a garden and a commanding view. Beyond that is a war memorial with more fine views. To your right, down a steep path, is St. Patrick's Well. Farther to the right is a park with the ruins of an Etruscan temple and another sweeping view.

Just in front of you is the small **shuttle bus** (usually white or orange), waiting to take you to Piazza del Duomo (included in your funicular ticket; 3-6/hour). The bus fills up fast, but the views from the ruined fortress are worth pausing for—if you miss the bus, you can wait for the next one, or just walk to the cathedral (head uphill on Corso Cavour; after about 10 minutes, take a left at the clock tower onto Via del Duomo). The bus drops you in Piazza del Duomo, just steps from the TI and within easy walking distance of most of my recommended sights and hotels.

If you arrive outside the funicular's operating hours, you can reach the upper part of town by **taxi** (see later) or **bus** to Piazza della Repubblica (buses run roughly 2/hour until midnight, buy €1.30 ticket at bar inside station).

By Car: The huge free parking lot below the train station is by far your best bet for short- and long-term parking (5 minutes off the autostrada; turn right immediately after the autostrada underpass and follow *Tour Bus Parking* signs). From the parking lot, walk through the station and ride the funicular up the hill (see "By Train," above).

There are several pay options for short-term parking in the center of the hilltop old town (about €1/hour): blue-lined spots on Piazza Cahen; a parking lot on Via Roma northwest of Piazza Cahen; and the Campo della Fiera lot just below the west end of town (from the lot's top level, walk up into town or ride the escalator—7:00-21:00—or elevator—7:00-24:00; both are free). The private, tree-lined lot with an attendant just beyond Piazza Marconi, next to the cathedral, is best for overnight stays (€12/day). While white lines generally indicate free parking, much of it is marked for residents only. Blue lines require you to buy a "pay and display" slip from a nearby machine.

While you can drive up Via Postierla and Via Roma to reach central parking lots, Corso Cavour and other streets in the old center are closed to traffic and monitored by cameras (look for red lights, and avoid streets marked by a red circle).

By Taxi: Taxis line up in front of the train station and charge about €15 for a ride to the cathedral (a ridiculous price considering the ease and pleasure of the €1.30 funicular/shuttle-bus ride; tel. 0763-301-903).

HELPFUL HINTS

Exchange Rate: €1 = about $1.10

Country Calling Code: 39 (see page 1154 for dialing instructions)

Info Point Bike Rental and Bag Check: The bright and helpful Info Point, run by Valerio, welcomes visitors just below and behind the train station at the tour bus depot/big free parking lot. They offer free Wi-Fi and some tourist information, rent electronic bikes (€10/half-day, €15/day), and have a secure bag check—the only one in town (9:00-18:00 daily).

Market Days and Festivals: On Thursday and Saturday mornings, Piazza del Popolo becomes a busy farmers' market. The city's biggest event is Corpus Domini (June 18 in 2017), a medieval procession and festival celebrating a miraculous relic (described in the Duomo tour on page 761). Corpus Domini events include flag tossing, concerts, and a giant chess game with costumed people as pieces. Orvieto is also busy during the Umbria Jazz festival (late each December, www.umbriajazz.com).

Wi-Fi: Many of Orvieto's cafés have Wi-Fi for customers, including all the popular spots along the Corso. The recommended **Caffè Montanucci** has the best atmosphere for lingering over coffee and email.

Bookstore: Mondadori Libreria dei Sette has a small selection of English-language books (daily 9:30-13:00 & 16:00-20:00, next to Torre del Moro at Corso Cavour 85, tel. 0763-344-436).

Laundry: There's a coin launderette in the lower town, a 10-minute walk from the train station. It's a long haul from central hotels, and instructions are in Italian only, but workable if desperate (daily 7:00-22:00, Piazza del Comercio, off via Monte Nibbio, mobile 393-758-6120).

Taxi Excursions: Giuliotaxi, run by English-speaking Giulio and his sister, Maria Serena, offers two Civita excursions from Orvieto for Rick Steves readers: to and from Civita with a one-hour wait (€90/car for up to 4 people, €120/minibus for up to 8), or a two-hour visit to Civita and Lake Bolsena (5 hours total, €160/car, €200/minibus, mobile 349-690-6547, giuliotaxi@libero.it). **Taxis** hang around the Orvieto train station ready to negotiate a little excursion to Civita, likely for a better price than Giuliotaxi.

Car Rental: Hertz has an office 100 yards to the left of the lower funicular station (Via Sette Martiri 32f, tel. 0763-301-303).

Local Guide: Manuela del Turco is good (€120/2.5-hour tour, mobile 333-221-9879, manueladel@virgilio.it). **David Tordi** organizes custom tours focused on food and culture (€250/half-day, €350/day, tel. 0763-340-688, www.orvietoviva.com).

Guided Tours: David Tordi and his colleagues offer walking tours of the Duomo and the city center (€10 each; March-Oct Mon, Tue, Fri, and Sat; Duomo tour at 13:00, city center tour at 14:15; buy ticket in advance or just show up, meet at Underground Orvieto ticket office at Piazza Duomo 23, contact information above). For €20, you get both tours back-to-back... why not?

After Dark: In the evening, there's little going on other than strolling and eating. The big *passeggiata* scene is down Via del Duomo and Corso Cavour. See page 757 for good places to enjoy the show. **Bar Duomo** on Largo Barzini off of Via del Duomo is lively late. For chic nightlife, try **Mille300 Music&Drinks,** a stylish hangout with fancy cocktails and occasional live music. Their mod interior is fitted into an old church (Via dei Gualtieri 2, tel. 0763-340-439).

Orvieto Walk

This quickie L-shaped self-guided walk takes you from the Duomo through Orvieto's historic center to the ramparts above the original Etruscan part of town, with vast Umbrian views. Each evening, this route is the scene of the local *passeggiata*.

❶ **Piazza del Duomo:** Start at the cathedral and admire its attention-grabbing facade (see the "Duomo" listing under "Sights in Orvieto" for a full explanation). Imagine how, as World War II raged around Orvieto, the fine reliefs gracing the front of the cathedral were encased in protective *tufa* walls. (Orvieto and its cathedral were spared destruction, perhaps thanks to a "safe cities" designation by a Nazi general who appreciated the town—or one of its women). As you face the cathedral, the papal palace (now hosting various museums) is to your right, and the TI and shuttle bus to the funicular are over your right shoulder. A nice gelato shop is around the church to the left.

• *Head left a few steps to the...*

❷ **Clock Tower** and **Via del Duomo:** Also known as the Maurizio Tower, this was built in the 14th century and equipped with an early mechanized clock, originally used to keep track of workers' time while building the cathedral. Step into the lobby to see a video and check whether the tower is open to climb.

The tower marks the start of Via del Duomo, lined with shops selling ceramics. The tradition of fine ceramics in Orvieto goes way back—the clay from the banks of the nearby Tiber is ideal for pottery. During the Renaissance, the town's pottery was brightly painted and highly prized.

• *Stroll down Via del Duomo.*

At the second left, The Wizard of Oz (Il Mago di Oz) awaits a few steps down Via dei Magoni (at #3). The shop is a wondrous toy land created by eccentric Giuseppe Rosella. Have Giuseppe push a few buttons, and you're far from Kansas.

Back on Via del Duomo, about 30 yards before the next tower is Emilio's meat-and-cheese shop (at #11). Pop in for a fragrant reminder that wild boar is an Umbrian specialty—and they love their other meats and cheeses too.

• *Follow Via del Duomo to Orvieto's main intersection, where it meets Corso Cavour. Here you'll find the tall, stark, 11th-century...*

❸ **Tower of the Moor** (Torre del Moro): Eighty such towers, each the pride and security of a powerful noble family, once decorated the town's skyline. Today only a few survive. This tower marks the center of town, serves as a handy orientation tool, and is decorated by the coats of arms of past governors. An elevator leaves you with 173 steps still to go to earn a commanding view (€3, daily March-Oct 10:00-19:00, May-Aug until 20:00, shorter hours off-season).

This crossroads divides the town into four quarters (notice the *Quartiere* signs on the corners). In the past, residents of the four districts competed in a lively equestrian competition, parading all over town during the annual Corpus Domini celebration. Historically, the four streets led from here to four landmarks: Piazza del Popolo with its market and fine palazzo, St. Patrick's Well, the Duomo, and the City Hall.

• *Before heading left down Corso Cavour, side-trip a block farther ahead, behind the tower, for a look at the striking...*

❹ **Palazzo del Popolo:** Built of local *tufo,* this is a textbook example of a fortified medieval public palace: a fortress designed to house the city's leadership and military (built atop an Etruscan temple), with a market at its base, fancy meeting rooms upstairs, and aristocratic living quarters on the top level. A lively market still bustles here every Thursday and Saturday mornings, selling food, clothes, and household goods.

• *Return to the tower, turn right, and head down Corso Cavour past classic storefronts to...*

❺ **Piazza della Repubblica** and **Church of Sant'Andrea:** The original vision—though it never came to fruition—was for the City Hall to have five arches flanking the central arch (marked by the flags today). The Church of Sant'Andrea (left of City Hall) sits atop an Etruscan temple that was likely the birthplace of Orvieto centuries before Christ. Inside is an interesting architectural progression: 11th-century Romanesque (with few frescoes surviving), Gothic (the pointy vaults over the altar), and a Renaissance barrel vault in the apse (behind the altar)—all dimly lit by alabaster windows.

On this spot, visitors can track a layer cake of history: Under the Christian church lie the remains of the Etruscan city, destroyed by the Romans. The ruins, currently accessible only with a tour, give you a sense of the history stacked beneath your feet throughout Orvieto (€5/person, call archaeologist Francesco Pascelli to book, tel. 328-191-1316).

• *From Piazza Repubblica, continue straight downhill for 100 yards on Via Filippeschi until you reach a fork. Check out the friendly, traditional* **bakery** *on the right (at Via Malabranca 6; we'll return to this intersection after a short detour). Walk downhill along Via della Cava about 50 yards to a restaurant with a green sign to find the...*

❻ **Well of the Quarry** (Pozzo della Cava): While renovating their trattoria here in the oldest part of town, an Orvieto family discovered a vast underground network of Etruscan-era caves, wells, and tunnels. The excavation started in 1984 and continues to this day. A visit to the well makes for a fun subterranean wander (see page 771 for details), keeping in mind that the whole city sits on top of a honeycomb of tunnels like these.

Outside, Via della Cava, meaning "Quarry Street," was a main source for building material for Orvieto's predecessor, Etruscan Velzna. The street kept getting lower and lower as more and more stones were cut out of it. Downhill is the site of the town's original gate.

• *Climb back up to the fork (with the bakery), then take a hard left up Via Malabranca. After about 80 yards, at #22, you'll reach...*

❼ **Palazzo Filippeschi** and **Viewpoint:** The friendly, noble Filippeschi family leaves their big, green door open so visitors can peek into their classic medieval courtyard, with black travertine columns scavenged from nearby ancient Roman villas. Enjoy a moment of exquisite medieval tranquility.

Immediately across from the palazzo, belly up to the viewpoint overlooking a commotion of red-tile roofs. This tradition goes back to Etruscan times, when such tiles were molded on a seated tile-maker's thigh—wide to narrow. They nest so that water flows without leaking—handy for both rooftops and plumbing. Originally scavenged from Etruscan ruins and reused as watertight roofing, this tradition survives.

• *Continue on, downhill now, as the street crests.*

Over the next 200 yards notice faded frescoes on stucco walls, arches from previous iterations of buildings (left for structural and nostalgic reasons), built-in letterboxes, and the three local building stones—basalt white, black travertine, and brown tufa. You'll pass an innovative-in-1991 green defibrillator station (one of 15 in town, the first such project in Europe) before reaching a square with the Church of Sant'Agostino, which hosts a museum (part of the MoDo City Museum, described on page 769). Then you'll pass the Church of San Giovenale, the oldest in town, with 11th-century frescoes, finally reach a commanding...

❽ **Rampart View:** You're at the end of Orvieto. The fertility of the land (with its olives, vines, and fruit orchards) is clear. The manicured little forest of cypress trees straight ahead marks the

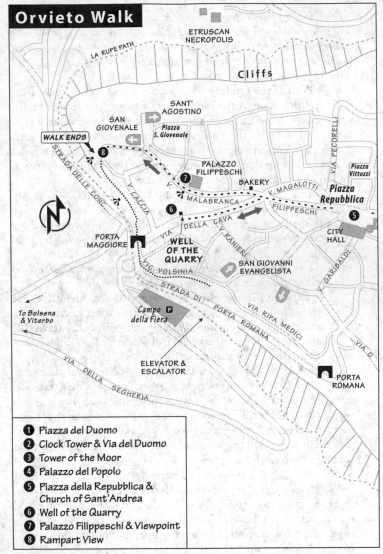

Orvieto Walk

- **1** Piazza del Duomo
- **2** Clock Tower & Via del Duomo
- **3** Tower of the Moor
- **4** Palazzo del Popolo
- **5** Piazza della Repubblica & Church of Sant'Andrea
- **6** Well of the Quarry
- **7** Palazzo Filippeschi & Viewpoint
- **8** Rampart View

Orvieto cemetery. In the distance to the right is Mount Cetona, guarding the south end of Tuscany.

Go 50 yards along the rampart to the left for the best view of the natural fortification that made this town the choice of Etruscans before the rise of ancient Rome, of stability-starved peasants after the fall of Rome, and of several popes in the high Middle Ages. From this perch you can understand why the city was never taken by force.

• *The walk is over. From here, you can retrace your steps or follow the*

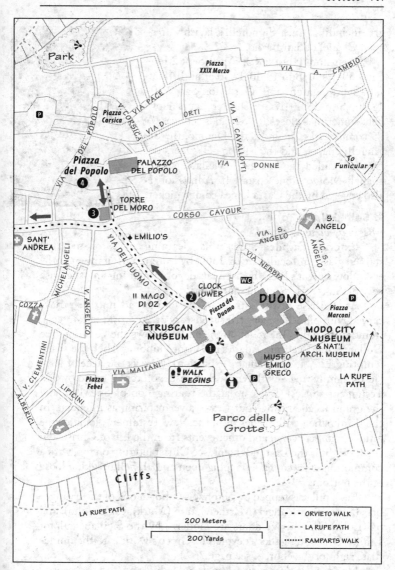

rampart farther left, down and up, over the original Etruscan town gate and circle back to the center from there.

Sights in Orvieto

▲▲▲Duomo

Orvieto's cathedral has Italy's liveliest facade. This colorful, prickly Gothic facade, divided by four pillars, has been compared to a medieval altarpiece. The optical-illusion interior features some fine

ORVIETO & CIVITA

art, including Luca Signorelli's lavishly frescoed Chapel of San Brizio.

Cost and Hours: €3; April-Sept Mon-Sat 9:30-19:00, Sun 13:00-17:30 or until 18:30 July-Sept; March and Oct Mon-Sat 9:30-18:00, Sun 13:00-17:30; shorter hours Nov-Feb; sometimes closes for religious services. A €5 combo-ticket includes the Duomo, the Signorelli chapel, and the Museo dell'Opera del Duomo, called the "MoDo" (available at the chapel; MoDo alone costs €4). Admission is also covered by the Carta Unica combo-ticket.

❷ Self-Guided Tour

• *Begin by viewing the...*

Exterior Facade: Study this gleaming mass of mosaics, stained glass, and sculpture (c. 1300, by Lorenzo Maitani and others). Note how it's literally just a facade, ornamenting an otherwise very plain, mostly Romanesque exterior.

At the base of the cathedral, the four broad **marble pillars** carved with biblical scenes tell the history of the world in four acts, from left to right. The relief on the far left shows the Creation (see God creating Eve from Adam's rib, Cane clubbing Abel, the snake tempting Eve, and a dramatic expulsion). Next is the Tree of Jesse (Jesus' family tree—with Mary, then Jesus, on top) flanked by Old Testament stories). Look up at the roaring lion of St. Mark and the grand facade filling your view—awe-inspiring as intended. In the third panel, with scenes from the New Testament, look for the unique manger scene, and other events from the life of Christ. On the far right is the Last Judgment; see Christ judging on top, with a commotion of sarcophagi popping open and all hell breaking loose at the bottom.

Each pillar is topped by a bronze symbol of one of the Evangelists (left to right): angel (Matthew), lion (Mark), eagle (John), and ox (Luke). The bronze doors are modern, by the Sicilian sculptor Emilio Greco. (A gallery devoted to Greco's work is to the immediate right of the church; see page 769.)

Stand back and survey the facade, looking for the central theme—it's clear the church is dedicated to the ascension of Mary. In the mosaic below the rose window, Mary is transported to heaven. In the uppermost mosaic, Mary is crowned.

• *Now step inside.*

Nave: The nave feels spacious and less cluttered than most Italian churches. Until 1877, it was much busier, with statues of the apostles at each column and fancy chapels. Then the people decided they wanted to "un-Baroque" their church. (The original stat-

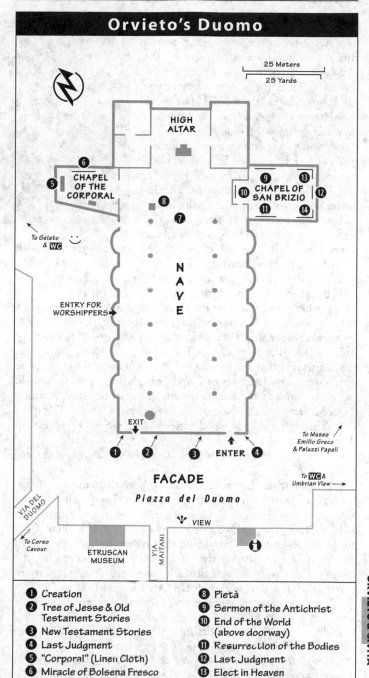

Orvieto's Duomo

25 Meters
25 Yards

HIGH ALTAR

⑥ CHAPEL OF THE CORPORAL
⑤

⑨ ⑬ CHAPEL OF SAN BRIZIO
⑩ ⑫
⑪ ⑭

To Gelato & WC

⑧
⑦

N A V E

ENTRY FOR WORSHIPPERS →

EXIT
① ② ③ ENTER ④

To Museo Emilio Greco & Palazzi Papali

FACADE

Piazza del Duomo

To WC & Umbrian View →

VIEW

VIA DEL DUOMO

To Corso Cavour

ETRUSCAN MUSEUM

VIA MAITANI

ℹ

① Creation
② Tree of Jesse & Old Testament Stories
③ New Testament Stories
④ Last Judgment
⑤ "Corporal" (Linen Cloth)
⑥ Miracle of Bolsena Fresco
⑦ Marble Floor Patch
⑧ Pietà
⑨ Sermon of the Antichrist
⑩ End of the World (above doorway)
⑪ Resurrection of the Bodies
⑫ Last Judgment
⑬ Elect in Heaven
⑭ Damned in Hell

ORVIETO & CIVITA

ues are now on display in the Church of Sant'Agostino, at the west end of town.) Bits of medieval fresco survive in the niches—once covered by altars and confessionals. From the back of the nave you can appreciate the fine stained glass above the altar—it's original from the 14th century and some of the oldest in Italy. The stripes of the church are purely decorative, made of locally quarried basalt and black travertine.

The interior is warmly lit by **alabaster windows,** highlighting the black-and-white striped stonework. Why such a big and impressive church in such a little town? First of all, it's not as big as it looks. By lining the nave with striped columns and opening up the side aisles with arcaded chapels, the architect made the space seem longer and bigger than it is. Still, it's a big and rich cathedral—the seat of a bishop.

The cathedral's historic importance and wealth is thanks to a miracle that happened nearby in 1263. According to the story, a skeptical priest named Peter of Prague passed through the town of Bolsena (12 miles from Orvieto) while on a pilgrimage to Rome. He had doubts that the bread used in communion could really be transformed into the body of Christ. But during Mass, as he held the host aloft and blessed it, the bread began to bleed, running down his arms and dripping onto a linen cloth (a "corporal") on the altar. That miraculously blood-stained cloth is now kept here, in the Chapel of the Corporal.

• *We'll tour the church's interior. First, find the chapel in the north transept, left of the altar.*

Chapel of the Corporal: The bloody cloth from the miracle is displayed in the turquoise frame atop the chapel's altar. It was brought from Bolsena to Orvieto, where Pope Urban IV happened to be visiting. The amazed pope proclaimed a new holiday, Corpus Domini (Body of Christ), and the Orvieto cathedral was built (begun in 1290) to display the miraculous relic. For centuries, the precious linen was paraded through the streets of Orvieto in an ornate reliquary (now in the MoDo City Museum).

The room was frescoed in the 14th century with scenes attesting to Christ's presence in the communion wafer and offering a vivid peek at life here at that time. The miracle of Bolsena (here set in 13th-century Orvieto) is depicted on the chapel's right wall.

• *Now walk to the middle front of the church, where you'll see a decorative area in the floor the size of a Turkish carpet.*

Marble Floor Patch: This patch in the marble floor marks

Italy Is Made of Tuff Stuff

Tuff (*tufo* in Italian) is a light-colored volcanic rock that is common in Italy. A part of Tuscany is even called the "Tuff Area."

The seven hills of Rome are made of tuff, and quarried blocks of this stone can be seen in the Colosseum, Pantheon, and Castel Sant'Angelo. Just outside of Rome, the catacombs were carved from tuff. Sorrento rises above the sea on a tuff outcrop. Orvieto, Civita di Bagnoregio (pictured), and many other hill towns perch on bluffs of tuff.

Italy's early inhabitants, including the Etruscans and Romans, carved caves, tunnels, burial niches, and even roads out of tuff. Blocks of this rock were quarried to make houses and walls. Tuff is soft and easy to carve when it's first exposed to air, but hardens later, which makes it a good building stone.

Italy's tuff-producing volcanoes resulted from a lot of tectonic-plate bumping and grinding. This violent geologic history is reflected in Italy's volcanoes, like Vesuvius and Etna, and earthquakes such as the 2009 quake in the L'Aquila area northeast of Rome.

Tuff is actually just a big hardened pile of old volcanic ash. When volcanoes hold magma that contains a lot of water, they erupt explosively (think heat + water = steam = POW!). The exploded rock material gets blasted out as hot volcanic ash, which settles on the surrounding landscape, piles up, and over time welds together into the rock called tuff.

So when you're visiting an area in Italy of ancient caves or catacombs built out of this material, you'll know that at least once (and maybe more) upon a time, it was a site of a lot of volcanic activity.

where the altar stood before the Counter-Reformation. It's a reminder that as the Roman Catholic Church countered the Reformation, it made reforms of its own. For instance, altars were moved back so that the congregation could sit closer to the spectacular frescoes and stained glass. (These decorations were designed to impress commoners by illustrating the glory of heaven—and the Catholic Church needed that propaganda more than ever during the Counter-Reformation.)

Enjoy the richness that surrounds you. This cathedral put Orvieto on the map, and with lots of pilgrims came lots of wealth. The town—perched on its easy-to-defend hilltop—was used off and on for a couple centuries as a papal refuge, whenever the current pope's enemies forced him to flee Rome. The brilliant stained glass is the painstakingly restored original, from the 14th century. The fine organ, high on the left, has more than 5,000 pipes. Look high up in the right transept at the alabaster rose window. Then turn and face down the nave, the way you came in. Note how the architect's trick—making the church look bigger from the rear—works in reverse from here. From this angle, the church appears stubbier than it actually is.

• *A few steps to your left as you face the altar, near the first pillar, is a beautiful white-marble statue.*

Pietà: The marble *pietà* (statue of Mary holding Jesus' just-crucified body) was carved in 1579 by local artist Ippolito Scalza. Clearly inspired by Michelangelo's *Pietà*, this exceptional work, with four figures, was sculpted from one piece of marble. Walk around it to notice the texture that Scalza achieved, and how the light plays on the sculpture from every angle.

• *Now face the main altar. To the right is Orvieto's one must-see artistic sight, the...*

Chapel of San Brizio: This chapel features Luca Signorelli's brilliantly lit frescoes of the Day of Judgment and Life after Death (painted 1499-1504). Step into the chapel and you're surrounded by vivid scenes crammed with figures. Although the frescoes refer to themes of resurrection and salvation, they also reflect the turbulent political and religious atmosphere of late 15th-century Italy.

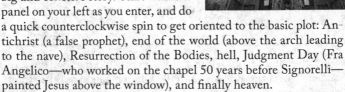

The chapel is decorated in one big and cohesive story. Start with the panel on your left as you enter, and do a quick counterclockwise spin to get oriented to the basic plot: Antichrist (a false prophet), end of the world (above the arch leading to the nave), Resurrection of the Bodies, hell, Judgment Day (Fra Angelico—who worked on the chapel 50 years before Signorelli—painted Jesus above the window), and finally heaven.

Now do a slower turn to take in the full story: In the **Sermon of the Antichrist** (left wall), a crowd gathers around a man preaching from a pedestal. It's the Antichrist, who comes posing as Jesus to mislead the faithful. This befuddled Antichrist forgets his lines midspeech, but the Devil is on hand to whisper what to say next. Notice how the arm in front of the Antichrist is attached to both figures, suggesting they are joined as one. His words sow wickedness through the world, including executions (upper right). The worried woman in red and white (foreground, left of pedestal) gets money from a man for something she's not proud of (perhaps receiving funds from a Jewish moneylender—notice the Stars of David on his purse). Many of the faces in the crowd are probably actual portraits.

Most likely, the Antichrist himself is a veiled reference to Savonarola (1452-1498), the charismatic Florentine monk who defied the pope, drove the Medici family from power, and riled the populace with apocalyptic sermons. Many Italians—including the painter Signorelli—viewed Savonarola as a tyrant and heretic, the Antichrist who was ushering in the Last Days.

In the upper left, notice the hardworking angel. He looks as if he's at batting practice, hitting followers of the Antichrist back to earth as they try to get through the pearly gates. In the bottom left is a self portrait of the artist, **Luca Signorelli** (c. 1450-1523), well-dressed in black with long golden hair. Signorelli, from nearby Cortona, was at the peak of his powers, and this chapel was his masterpiece. He looks out proudly as if to say, "I did all this in just three years, on time and on budget," confirming his reputation as a speedy, businesslike painter. Next to him (also in black) is the artist Fra Angelico, who started the chapel decoration five decades earlier but completed only a small part of it: the Last Judgment over the window and the angels around it.

Compare the style of painting between these two masters—Angelico's angels stacked like little wooden dolls next to Signorelli's intertwined naked bodies. You can clearly see the huge effect the Renaissance had on painting in just a few decades.

Around the arch, opposite the windows, are signs of the **end of the world:** eclipse, tsunami, falling stars, earthquakes, violence in the streets, and a laser-wielding gray angel.

On the right wall (opposite the Antichrist) is the **Resurrection of the Bodies.** Trumpeting angels blow a wake-up call, and the dead climb dreamily out of the earth to be clothed with new bodies, some of the randy skeletons finding time for flirting. On the same wall (below the action, at eye level) is a gripping *pietà*. Also by Signorelli, this *pietà* gives insight into the artist's genius and personality. Look at the emotion in the faces of the two Marys

and consider that Signorelli's son had just died. The small black-and-white Deposition scene (behind Jesus' leg) seems inspired by ancient Greek scenes of a pre-Christian hero's death. In the confident spirit of the Renaissance, the artist incorporates a pagan scene to support a Christian story. This 3-D realism in a 2-D sketch shows the work of a talented master.

The altar wall (with the windows) features the **Last Judgment.** To the left of the altar (and continuing around the corner, filling half the left wall) are the **Elect in Heaven.** They spend eternity posing like bodybuilders while listening to celestial Muzak. To the right (and continuing around the corner on the right wall) are the **Damned in Hell,** in the scariest mosh pit ever. Devils torment sinners in graphic detail, while winged demons control the airspace overhead. In the center, one lusty demon turns to tell the frightened woman on his back exactly what he's got planned for their date. (According to legend, this was Signorelli's lover, who betrayed him...and ended up here.) Signorelli's ability to tell a story through human actions and gestures, rather than symbols, inspired his younger contemporary, Michelangelo, who meticulously studied the elder artist's nudes.

In this chapel, Christian theology sits physically and figuratively upon a foundation of classical logic. Below everything are Greek and Latin philosophers, plus Dante, struggling to reconcile Classical truth with Church doctrine. You can see the intellectual challenge on their faces as they ponder the puzzle of theology that survives the test of reason.

The figures are immersed in fanciful Grotesque (i.e., grottoesque) decor. Dating from 1499, this is one of the first uses of the frilly, nubile, and even sexy "wallpaper pattern" so popular in the Renaissance. (It was inspired by the decorations found in Nero's Golden House in Rome, which had been discovered under street level just a few years earlier and was mistaken for an underground grotto.)

During the Renaissance, nakedness symbolized purity. When attitudes changed during the Counter-Reformation, the male figures in Signorelli's frescoes were given penis-covering sashes. In a 1982 restoration, most—but not all—of the sashes were removed. A little of that prudishness survives to this day, as those in heaven were left with their sashes modestly in place.

• *Our tour is finished. Leaving the church, turn left (passing a small parking lot and WC) to reach a park that affords a fine Umbrian view. Turn left twice, and you'll circle behind the church to reach the cathedral's art collections (part of MoDo, described next). Or take a right out of the church for a gelato break at the recommended Pasqualetti.*

MUSEUMS NEAR THE DUOMO
▲▲MoDo City Museum (Museo dell'Opera del Duomo)

This museum is an ensemble of three different sights scattered around town: the cathedral art collection behind the cathedral; the Emilio Greco collection (next to the cathedral, in Palazzo Soliano); and, at the far end of town, the Church of Sant'Agostino, which has statues of the 12 apostles that were added to the Duomo in the Baroque Age (c. 1700) and removed in the late 1800s.

Cost and Hours: €4 MoDo ticket covers all MoDo sights (or get the €5 combo-ticket that includes the Duomo); April-Sept daily 9:30-19:00; March and Oct Wed-Mon 10:00-17:00, closed Tue; midday closure Nov-Feb; Piazza Duomo, tel. 0763-343-592, www.opsm.it.

Cathedral Art Collections: Behind the Duomo, a complex of medieval palaces called Palazzi Papali shows off the city's best devotional art. It comes in two parts: the skippable collection of frescoes on the ground floor, and a delightful collection up the metal staircase. The highlight is just inside the upstairs entrance: a marble Mary and Child who sit beneath a bronze canopy, attended by exquisite angels. This proto-Renaissance ensemble, dating from around 1300, once filled the niche in the center of the cathedral's facade (where a replica sits today). In several art-filled rooms on this floor, you'll find Baroque paintings from the late 1500s that decorated the side chapels with a harsh Counter-Reformation message; a *Madonna and Child* from 1322 by the Sienese great Simone Martini, who worked in Orvieto; saintly wooden statues and fine inlaid woodwork from the original choir; a carved 14th-century Crucifixion that shows the dead Christ in gripping detail; Luca Signorelli's *Mary Magdalene* (1504); and more church art surrounded by *sinopias* (preliminary drawings for the frescoes decorating the cathedral's Chapel of the Corporal, with a roughed-up surface so the wet plaster would stick).

Museo Emilio Greco: This fresh little collection shows off the work of Emilio Greco (1913-1995), a Sicilian artist who designed the modern doors of Orvieto's cathedral. His sketches and about 30 of his bronze statues are on display here, showing his absorption with gently twisting and turning nudes. Greco's sketchy outlines of women are simply beautiful. The artful installation of his work in this palazzo, with walkways and a spiral staircase up to the ceiling, is designed to let you view his sculptures from different angles.

National Archaeological Museum of Orvieto (Museo Archeologico Nazionale di Orvieto)

This small five-room collection, immediately behind the cathedral in the ground floor of Palazzi Papali (under MoDo), beautifully shows off a trove of well-preserved Etruscan bronzes, terra-cotta objects, and ceramics—many from the necropolis at the base of Orvieto, and some with painted colors surviving from 500 B.C. To see the treasure of this museum, ask an attendant for the Golini tombs (named after the man who discovered them in 1836). She'll escort you to the reconstructed, fourth-century B.C. tombs, frescoed with scenes from an Etruscan banquet in the afterlife.

Cost and Hours: €3, €5 combi-ticket with Etruscan Necropolis, daily 8:30-19:30, tel. 0763-341-039, www.archeopg.arti. beniculturali.it. For background on the Etruscans, see page 642.

▲Etruscan Museum (Museo Claudio Faina e Museo Civico)

This 19th-century, Neoclassical nobleman's palace stands on the main square facing the cathedral. Its elegantly frescoed rooms hold an impressive Etruscan collection. The ground floor features the "Museo Civico," with fragments of Etruscan sculpture. On the first floor is the "Collezione Conti Faina," with Etruscan jewelry and an extensive array of Roman coins (push the brass buttons and the coins rotate so you can see both sides). The top floor features the best of the Etruscan and proto-Etruscan (from the ninth century B.C.) vases and bronzes, lots of votives found buried in nearby tombs, and fine views of the Duomo.

Cost and Hours: €4.50; April-Sept daily 9:30-18:00; Oct-March Tue-Sun 10:00-17:00, closed Mon; tel. 0763-341-511, www.museofaina.it.

Teatro Mancinelli

Teatro Mancinelli is a fine 19th-century Italian theater (from 1866) with 500 seats, elegant boxes, and frilly Romantic ceiling paintings—all well-described in English. Visitors are welcome to climb upstairs to the foyer for a chance to peek into a private box. The theater hosts the Café del Teatro—buy a drink and you can wander the theater without paying the €2 entry fee (see café listing on page 781).

UNDERGROUND ORVIETO
▲▲St. Patrick's Well (Pozzo di San Patrizio)

Modern engineers are impressed by this deep well—175 feet deep and 45 feet wide—designed in the 16th century with a double-helix pattern. The two spiral stairways allow an efficient one-way traffic flow: intriguing now, but critical then. Imagine if donkeys and people, balancing jugs of water, had to go up and down the same stairway. At the bottom is a bridge that people could walk on to scoop up water.

The well was built because a pope got nervous. After Rome was sacked in 1527 by renegade troops of the Holy Roman Empire, the pope fled to Orvieto. He feared that even this little town (with no water source on top) would be besieged. He commissioned a well, which was started in 1527 and finished 10 years later. It was a huge project. (As it turns out, the town was never besieged, but supporters believe that the well was worth the cost and labor because of its deterrence value—attackers would think twice about besieging a town with a reliable water source.) Even today, when a local is faced with a difficult task, people say, "It's like digging St Patrick's Well." It's a total of 496 steps up and down—lots of exercise and not much to see other than some amazing 16th-century engineering.

Cost and Hours: €5, interesting €1 audioguide, daily May-Aug 9:00-19:00, shorter hours off-season, to your right as you exit the funicular, Viale Sangallo, tel. 0763-343-768. Bring a sweater if you plan to descend to the chilly depths, and allow at least 20 minutes to go down and up.

▲Well of the Quarry (Pozzo della Cava)

This complex of Etruscan-era caves, wells, and tunnels leads down to a fat, cylindrical, beautifully carved 2,500-year-old well. Go ahead, spit (or drop a coin 100 feet down—coins are collected each Christmas for a local charity). Your visit is capped with a review of local pottery-making (€3, €2 with this book, Tue-Sun 9:00-20:00, closed Mon, Via della Cava 28).

Orvieto Underground Tours (Parco delle Grotte)

Guides weave archaeological history into a good look at about 100 yards of Etruscan and medieval caves. You'll see the remains of an old olive press, an impressive 130-foot-deep Etruscan well shaft, what's left of a primitive cement quarry, and an extensive dovecote (pigeon coop) where the birds were reared for roasting (pigeon dishes are still featured on many Orvieto menus; look for—or avoid—*piccione*).

Cost and Hours: €6; one-hour English tours depart at 11:00, 12:15, 16:00, and 17:15; more often with demand, walk-up reservations OK but better to book in advance for English guide, book tour and depart from ticket office at Piazza Duomo 23 (next to TI); confirm times at TI or by calling 0763-340-688, www.orvietounderground.it.

Etruscan Necropolis
(Necropoli Etrusca di Crocifisso del Tufo)

Below town, at the base of the cliff, is a remarkable "city of the dead" that dates back to the sixth to third century B.C. The tombs, which are laid out in a kind of street grid, are empty, and there's precious little to see here other than the basic stony construction. But it is both eerie and fascinating to wander the streets of an Etruscan cemetery.

Cost and Hours: €3, €5 combi-ticket with National Archaeological Museum, daily 10:00-19:00, Oct-March until 18:00; drivers will find it on the ring road below town, hikers can reach it via the Rupe path (see next); tel. 0763-343-611, www.archeopg.arti.beniculturali.it.

VIEW WALKS
▲Hike Around the City on the Rupe

Orvieto's Rupe is a peaceful path that completely circles the town at the base of the cliff upon which it sits. With the help of the TI's *Anello della Rupe* map, you'll see there are five access points from the town for the three-mile walk, which includes a series of sightseeing stops along the way (allow about two hours round-trip). From the access points, you'll walk or take stairs down, down, down to the trail that hugs the cliff. The easy-to-follow path is wide and partially paved, though it has some steep, gravelly descents—wear good shoes and be prepared for a climb. On one side you have the cliff, with the town high above. On the other side you have Umbrian views stretching into the distance. The path is peaceful, with few other people and only the sound of the wind and birds to accompany you. It makes for a delightful evening walk (not lit after dark).

I'd leave Orvieto at Piazza Marconi and walk left (counterclockwise) three-quarters of the way around the town (there's a fine view down onto the Etruscan Necropolis midway), and ride the escalator and elevator back up to the town from the big Campo della Fiera parking lot. If you're ever confused about the path, follow signs for *Anello della Rupe*.

▲**Shorter Romantic Rampart Stroll**

Thanks to its dramatic hilltop setting, several fine little walks wind around the edges of Orvieto. My favorite after dark, when it's lamp-lit and romantic, is along the ramparts at the far west end of town. Start at the Church of Sant'Agostino (near the end of my self-guided Orvieto Walk). With your back to the church, go a block to the right to the end of town. Then head left along the ramparts, with cypress-dotted Umbria to your right, and follow Vicolo Volsinia to the Church of San Giovanni Evangelista, where you can reenter the old town center near several recommended restaurants.

NEAR ORVIETO
Wine Tasting

Orvieto Classico wine is justly famous. Two inviting wineries sit just outside Orvieto on the scenic Canale route to Bagnoregio; if you're side-tripping to Civita, it's easy to stop at either or both for a tasting (call ahead for a reservation). Two more wineries lie to the north where the soil changes from *tufo* to clay, which changes the character of the wines.

Between Orvieto and Bagnoregio: For a short tour of a historic winery with Etruscan cellars, make an appointment to visit **Tenuta Le Velette,** where English-speaking Corrado and Cecilia (cheh-CHEEL-yah) Bottai offer a warm welcome. Their wines are considered to be some of the best in the region (€8-24 for tour and tasting, price varies depending on wines, number of people, and if food is requested, Mon-Fri 8:30-12:00 & 14:00-17:00, Sat 8:30-12:00, closed Sun, also has accommodations—see listing on page 777, tel. 0763-29090, mobile 348-300-2002, www.levelette. it). From their sign (5-minute drive past Orvieto at top of switchbacks just before Canale, on road to Bagnoregio), cruise down a long tree-lined drive, then park at the striped gate (must call ahead; no drop-ins).

Custodi is another respected family-run winery that produces Orvieto Classico, grappa, and olive oil on a modern 140-acre estate. Helpful Chiara and Laura Custodi speak English. Reserve ahead for a tour of their cantina, an explanation of the winemaking process, and a tasting of four wines. An assortment of *salumi* and local cheeses to go with your wine-tasting is available on request (€10/person for wines only, €20/person with light lunch, daily 8:30-12:30 & 15:30-18:30 except closed Sun afternoon, Viale Venere S.N.C. Loc. Canale; on the road from Orvieto to Civita, a half-mile after Le Velette, it's the first building before Canale; tel. 0763-29053, mobile 338-316-0405, www.cantinacustodi.com).

To the North: Neri lies just to the north, in rolling hills. The estate grounds are postcard-pretty, with an ancient manor house and grand views of Orvieto and the countryside. Their wines are simple and traditional (tour and tastings from €10, reservations preferred, daily 9:30-17:00; just down the road from recommended Agriturismo Cioccoleta at Località Bardano 28—head north from Orvieto following signs to *Sferracavallo* and *Bardano;* tel. 0763-316-196, mobile 393-331-3844, www.neri-vini.it, visite@neri-vini.it, Enrico).

Argillae is farther out in the clay hills north of Orvieto. Their modern cantina is surrounded by dramatic hills and valleys, and if you ask, they will take you out in a truck to see the vineyard up close (tastings from €10, by reservation only, Vocabolo Pomarro in Allerona, 20 minutes north of Orvieto, tel. 0763-624-604, www.argillae.com).

Sleeping in Orvieto

Orvieto's high season (with higher hotel prices) is roughly May to early July, September, and October. You'll save a little money off-season.

IN THE TOWN CENTER

$$$ Hotel Duomo is centrally located and modern, with splashy art in 17 rooms and a friendly welcome. Double-paned windows keep the sound of the church bells well-muffled (RS%, family rooms, air-con, elevator, private pay parking, sunny terrace, a block from the Duomo at Vicolo di Maurizio 7, tel. 0763-341-887, www.orvietohotelduomo.com, info@orvietohotelduomo.com, Gianni and Maura Massaccesi don't speak English, daughter Elisa and son-in-law Diego do). They also own a three-room B&B 50 yards from the hotel (lower prices, breakfast at the main hotel).

$$$ Grand Hotel Italia is impersonal and businesslike, bringing predictable modern amenities to this small town. The 46 rooms are well-located in the heart of Orvieto, near the market square (RS%, air-con, elevator, stay-awhile lobby and terrace, pay parking—reserve ahead, Via di Piazza del Popolo 13, tel. 0763-342-065, www.grandhotelitalia.it, hotelita@libero.it).

$$ Hotel Corso is friendly, with 18 frilly and flowery rooms—a few with balconies and views. Their sunlit little terrace is enjoyable, but the location—halfway between the center of town and the funicular—is less convenient than others (RS%, family rooms, ask for quieter room off street, air-con, elevator, reserved pay parking, Corso Cavour 339, tel. 0763-342-020, www.hotelcorso.net, info@hotelcorso.net, Carla).

$ La Magnolia B&B has lots of fancy terra-cotta tiles, a couple of rooms with frescoed ceilings, terraces, and other welcoming touches. Its seven unique rooms, some like mini-apartments with

Sleep Code

Hotels are classified based on the average price of a standard double room with breakfast in high season.

$$$$	**Splurge:** Most rooms over €170
$$$	**Pricier:** €130-170
$$	**Moderate:** €90-130
$	**Budget:** €50-90
¢	**Backpacker:** Under €50
RS%	Rick Steves discount

Unless otherwise noted, credit cards are accepted, hotel staff speak basic English, and free Wi-Fi is available. Comparison-shop by checking prices at several hotels (on each hotel's own website, on a booking site, or by email). For the best deal, *book directly with the hotel.* Ask for a discount if paying in cash; if the listing includes **RS%,** request a Rick Steves discount.

kitchens, are cheerfully decorated and on the town's main drag. The three units facing the busy street are air-conditioned and have double-paned windows (RS%, family rooms, no elevator, washing machine; Via Duomo 29, tel. 0763-342-808, mobile 349-462-0733, www.bblamagnolia.it, info@bblamagnolia.it, Serena and Loredana).

$ B&B Michelangeli offers two comfortable and well-appointed apartments hiding along a residential lane a few blocks from the tourist scene. It's run by eager-to-please Francesca, who speaks limited English but provides homey touches and free tea, coffee, and breakfast supplies. From the Corso, follow Via Michelangeli, a street full of wood sculptures made by her famous artistic family (family rooms, fully equipped kitchen, washing machine, private pay parking, Via dei Saracinelli 20—ring bell labeled *M. Michelangeli,* tel. 0763-393-862, mobile 347-089-0349, www.bbmichelangeli.com).

$$ Affittacamere Valentina rents six clean, airy, well-appointed rooms, all with big beds and antique furniture. Her place is located in the heart of Orvieto, on a quiet street behind the palace on Piazza del Popolo (RS%, family rooms, pay parking, Via Vivaria 7, tel. 0763-341-607, mobile 393-970-5868, www.bandbvalentina.com, camerevalentina@gmail.com). Welcoming Valentina also rents three lower-priced rooms across the square (shared bath and kitchen, no air-con) and three offsite apartments.

$ Hotel Posta is a centrally located, long-ago-elegant palazzo renting 20 quirky, clean rooms with chipped plaster and vintage furniture. It feels a little institutional, but the rooms without private bath are among the cheapest in town (breakfast extra, elevator,

Via Luca Signorelli 18, tel. 0763-341-909, www.orvietohotels.it, hotelposta@orvietohotels.it, Alessia).

$ Villa Mercede, a good value and excellent location, is owned by a religious institution and offers 23 cheap, simple, mostly twin-bedded rooms, each with a big modern bathroom and many with glorious Umbrian views (elevator, free parking, a half-block from Duomo at Via Soliana 2, reception upstairs, tel. 0763-341-766, www.villamercede.it, info@villamercede.it).

$ Istituto S.S. Salvatore rents nine spotless twin rooms and five singles in their convent, which comes with a peaceful terrace and garden, great views, and a 23:00 curfew. Though the nuns don't speak English, they have mastered Google Translate, and will happily use it to answer your questions (cash only, no break-fast, elevator, Wi-Fi in common areas only, free parking, just off Piazza del Popolo at Via del Popolo 1, tel. 0763-342-910, www.istitutosansalvatore.it, istitutosansalvatore@tiscali.it).

Just Outside the Town Center: **$ Casa Sèlita B&B,** a peaceful country house, offers easy access to Orvieto (best for drivers, but workable for adventurous train travelers who want an *agriturismo*-style experience). It's nestled in an orchard just below the town cliffs; to get to town, you'll climb an uphill path through their olive orchard (with a view terrace along the way) to reach the Campo della Fiera parking lot, with its handy escalator taking you the rest of the way up into Orvieto. Its five rooms with terraces are airy and fresh, with dark hardwood floors, fluffy down comfort-ers, and modern baths. Enjoy the views from the relaxing garden. Conscientious Sèlita, her husband, Ennio, and daughter Elena are gracious hosts (RS%, cash preferred, extra fee for air-con or heat, free parking, closed Nov-Easter, Strada di Porta Romana 8, ask for directions—GPS or Google will send you to the wrong loca-tion, mobile 339-225-4000 or 328-611-2052, www.casaselita.com, info@casaselita.com).

NEAR ORVIETO

All of these (except the last one) are within a 20-minute drive of Orvieto, in different directions, and require a car—see the map on page 782.

$$$ Alta Rocca Wine Resort, run by Emiliano and Sabrina, is a fancy "country resort" and spa, located 15 minutes north of Or-vieto. They produce their own olive oil and wine, and rent 30 mod-ern and air-conditioned rooms and a few apartments. Popular on weekends as a wedding location, this place has *luna di miele* (hon-eymoon) written all over it (2 pools, panoramic view restaurant, wellness center with Jacuzzi and steam room, massages and spa treatments available, visit to winery and wine tasting upon request, gym, mountain bikes, bocce court, hiking paths to private lake, tel.

0763-344-210 or 0763-393-437, www.altaroccawineresort.com, info@altaroccawineresort.com).

$$$ Agriturismo Locanda Rosati, where you'll be greeted by friendly host Giampiero Rosati, rents 10 tastefully decorated rooms in a pleasant, homey atmosphere. The peaceful, flower-lined grounds are perfect for a retreat (RS%, family rooms, full traditional dinners for €40 on request, air-con, swimming pool, 5 miles from Orvieto on the road to Viterbo, tel. 0763-217-314, www. locandarosati.it, info@locandarosati.it).

$$ Agriturismo Poggio della Volara, located between Todi and Orvieto (12 miles from either), has seven apartments (sleeping from two to five people) and five rooms in two buildings overlooking a swimming pool. Along with keeping rabbits, geese, dogs, and ducks, Marco produces wine, olive oil, and salami made from wild boar that he hunts. If you're looking for a real farmhouse experience far out in the countryside, this is it (air-con, €30-35 dinners on request, mobile 347-335-2523, www.poggiodellavolara.it, info@ poggiodellavolara.it).

$$ Tenuta le Velette is a sprawling, historic, family-run estate and winery. Cecilia and Corrado Bottai rent six fully furnished apartments and villas scattered over their family's expansive and scenic grounds. Rooms range wildly in size—accommodating from 2 to 14 people—but they all nestle in perfect Umbrian rural peace and tranquility (see website for details on various villas (2-night minimum, discount for weekly stay, pool, bocce court, 10 minutes from Orvieto—drive toward Bagnoregio-Canale and follow *Tenuta le Velette* signs, tel. 0763-29090, mobile 348-300-2002, www. levelette.it, cecilialevelette@libero.it). They also offer wine tastings (see page 773).

$$ Agriturismo Cioccoleta ("Little Stone") has eight rooms with cozy country decor, each named after one of the grapes grown in the agriturismo's vineyards. It's family-run and offers sweeping views of Orvieto and the pastoral countryside (RS%, fans, 3 miles north of Orvieto at Località Bardano 34 in Bardano, tel. 0763-316-011, mobile 349-860-9780, www.cioccoleta.it, info@cioccoleta.it, Angela Zucconi).

Farther Out, Northwest of Todi: **$$$$ Agriturismo Fattoria di Vibio** produces olive oil and honey, sells organic products, and offers classes and spa services. In August, its 14 rooms rent at peak prices and have a minimum stay requirement. The rest of the year, no minimum stay is required, although rates drop dramatically for longer visits. Its two cottages sleep from four to six people and rent only by the week (panoramic pool, expensive restaurant, farthest cottage is 20 miles northeast of Orvieto, tel. 075-874-9607, www. fattoriadivibio.com, info@fattoriadivibio.com).

Eating in Orvieto

TRATTORIAS IN THE CENTER

$$$ Trattoria La Palomba features excellent game and truffle specialties in a wood-paneled dining room. Giampiero, Enrica, and the Cinti family enthusiastically take care of their diners, offering a fine value, high quality, and classy conviviality. Truffles are shaved right at your table—try the *umbricelli al tartufo* (homemade pasta with truffles) or *spaghetti dell'Ascaro* (with truffles). Their *filetto alla cardinale* and mixed-cheese plates are popular. As slow-foodies, they use organic and locally sourced ingredients (Thu-Tue 12:30-14:15 & 19:30-22:00, closed Wed and July, reservations smart, off Piazza della Repubblica at Via Cipriano Manente 16, tel. 0763-343-395).

$$$ L'Antica Trattoria dell'Orso offers well-prepared Umbrian cuisine paired with fine wines in a homey, bohemian-chic, peaceful atmosphere. Owner Stefano and chef Hania offer an good deal for my readers: €30 for two people, including their house wine and water—my vote for the best dining value in town (Wed-Mon 12:00-14:30 & 19:30-22:00, closed Tue and Feb, just off Piazza della Repubblica at Via della Misericordia 18, tel. 0763-341-642).

$$$ Trattoria La Pergola, run by chef Enrico and family, with a serious kitchen in back next to a covered patio, offers a small, accessible menu of seasonal Umbrian specialties. Closer to the center, this spot is pretty touristy, but the food is tasty and lovingly presented (reservations smart, air-con, closed Wed, Via dei Magoni 9, tel. 0763-343-065).

$$ Trattoria del Moro Aronne is a long-established family bistro run by Cristian and his mother, Rolanda, who lovingly prepare homemade pasta and market-fresh Umbrian specialties. Consider their *nidi*—folds of fresh pasta enveloping warm, gooey pecorino cheese sweetened with honey. Three small and separate dining areas make the interior feel intimate. While touristy and not particularly atmospheric, this place is known locally as an excellent value (Wed-Mon 12:30-14:30 & 19:30-22:00, closed Tue, Via San Leonardo 7, tel. 0763-342-763).

$$$ Trattoria la Grotta prides itself on serving only the freshest food and finest wine. The decor is Signorelli-mod, and the ambience is quiet, with courteous service. Owner-chef Franco has been at it for 52 years, and promises diners a free coffee, grappa, *limoncello*, or *vin santo* with this book (Wed-Mon opens at 12:00 for lunch and at 19:00 for dinner, closed Tue, Via Luca Signorelli 5, tel. 0763-341-348).

$$ Trattoria da Carlo, hiding on its own little *piazzetta* between Via Corso Cavour and Piazza del Popolo, is a cozy spot with a bright, white-tiled interior and inviting tables outside. Ani-

> ## Restaurant Price Code
>
> I've assigned each eatery a price category, based on the average cost of a typical main course (pasta or *secondi*). Drinks, desserts, and splurge items (steak and seafood) can raise the price considerably.
>
> **$$$$** **Splurge:** Most main courses over €20
> **$$$** **Pricier:** €15-20
> **$$** **Moderate:** €10-15
> **$** **Budget:** Under €10
>
> In Italy, pizza by the slice and other takeout food is **$**; a basic trattoria or sit-down pizzeria is **$$**; a casual but more upscale restaurant is **$$$**; and a swanky splurge is **$$$$**.

mated and opinionated Carlo—a young, likeable loudmouth—holds court, chatting up his diners as much as he cooks, while his mama scuttles about taking orders, bussing dishes, and lovingly rolling her eyes at her son's big personality. His slogan is "simple food for simple people." He puts an unpretentious modern twist on traditional dishes such as pasta with *guanciale* (pork cheeks—like bacon), fennel fronds, and pecorino cheese (daily 12:00-15:00 & 19:00-24:00, Vicolo del Popolo 1, tel. 0763-343-916).

$$$ Trattoria Antico Bucchero, elegant under a big, white vault, makes for a nice memory with its candlelit ambience and delicious food—especially game and wild boar (daily 12:00-15:00 & 19:00-23:00 except closed Wed Nov-March, seating indoors and on a peaceful square in summer, air-con, a half-block south of Corso Cavour, between Torre del Moro and Piazza della Repubblica at Via de Cartari 4, tel. 0763-341-725; Piero and Silvana, plus sons Fabio and Pericle).

$$ Pizzeria & Ristorante Charlie is a local favorite. Its noisy dining room and stony courtyard are reminiscent of a beer hall, and popular with families and students for casual dinners of wood-fired gourmet pizzas. They also have a small menu of big salads, homemade pastas, and *secondi*. In a quiet courtyard guarded by a medieval tower, it's a block southwest of Piazza della Repubblica (Wed-Mon 12:30-14:30 & 19:00-23:00, no midday closure in summer, closed Tue year-round, Via Loggia dei Mercanti 14, tel. 0763-344-766).

$$ Enoteca al Duomo is to the left of the Duomo and has pleasant outdoor seating with a cathedral view. They serve a small variety of rustic *panini* (cheaper to go), wines by the glass and a vast selection of Italian wines by the bottle, and a full menu of local dishes in a wine-bar atmosphere (daily 10:00-24:00, closed Feb, Piazza del Duomo 13, tel. 0763-344-607).

FAST AND CHEAP EATS

$ L'Oste del Re is a simple *osteria* on Corso Cavour, where Maria Grazia and Claudio offer pasta, bruschetta, enticing meat-and-cheese plates, and hearty, made-to-order sandwiches to eat in or take out (good gluten-free options, daily 11:00-15:30 & 19:00-22:00, Corso Cavour 58, tel. 0763-343-846).

$ Caffè Montanucci, the dominant hangout on the main street—for good reasons—lays out an appetizing display of pastas and main courses behind the counter. Choose one (or two—called a *bis*), find a seat in the modern interior or sunny courtyard, and they'll bring it out on a tray. You'll eat among newspaper-reading locals on lunch break. They also serve dinner with regular table service, as well as good *caffè*, simple sandwiches, and tasty sweets all day (good Wi-Fi, daily 7:00-24:00, Corso Cavour 21, tel. 0763-341-261).

Panini and a Picnic: Scattered around town you'll find many *alimentari* (grocers) selling cured meats, cheese, and other staples. If you're feeling gamey, order prosciutto or salami made from *cinghiale* (cheen-gee-AH-lay; wild boar), a surprisingly mild-tasting local favorite. They're usually willing to make you a simple sandwich of bread, cold cuts, and/or cheese for a few euros.

Elsewhere along the Corso Cavour, you'll find places selling fruit, vegetables, and other picnic items. The fortress/garden, to the right as you face the funicular, is a great spot to enjoy it.

Groceries: While a small *alimentari* might have what you need for a picnic, two slightly larger markets are tucked away two minutes from the Duomo: **Metà** (daily 8:30-20:00, Corso Cavour 100, opposite Piazza Cesare Fracassini) and **Sigma** (Mon-Sat 8:30-20:00, Sun 9:00-13:00, just past recommended Trattoria la Grotta at Via Luca Signorelli 23).

Gelato: For dessert, *gelateria* **Pasqualetti,** next to the cathedral, is a favorite (daily 12:00-21:00, stays open later June-Aug, closed Dec-Feb, next to left transept of church, Piazza del Duomo 14; another branch is at Via Duomo 10, both close earlier in winter or in cold weather).

CORSO CAVOUR CAFÉ SCENE

Orvieto has a charming, traffic-free, pedestrian-friendly vibe. To enjoy it, be sure to spend a little time savoring *la dolce far niente* while sitting at a café. There are inviting places all over town. The first three listed below are along Corso Cavour, the main strolling drag, and offer the very best people-watching.

Caffè ClanDestino is the town hot spot, with a youthful energy. It's well-located, with plenty of streetside seating and endless little bites served with your drink (Corso Cavour 40). **Café Barrique** is less crowded, less trendy, and quieter, with nice outdoor tables and good free snacks with your drink (Corso Cavour 111). **Caffè Montanucci** is the town's venerable place for a coffee and pastry, but has no on-street seating (Corso Cavour 21, described earlier). **Bar Palace,** on Piazza del Popolo, is a sunny, relaxed perch facing a big square that's generally quiet (except on market day), with free Wi-Fi and quality coffee and pastries.

Café del Teatro, at Teatro Mancinelli (see page 770), can be a fun experience. While entry to the historic theater is normally €2, if you buy a drink, you're free to wander around on your own. Drink streetside, at the bar, or in the theater lobby (daily 8:00-21:00, happy hour from 18:00 means free nibbles with your drink, Corso Cavour 122, tel. 0763-531-502).

Cafés Facing the Cathedral: Several cafés on Piazza del Duomo invite you to linger over a drink with a view of Orvieto's amazing cathedral.

Orvieto Connections

From Orvieto by Train to: Rome (roughly hourly, 1-1.5 hours), **Florence** (6/day, 2.5 hours, use Firenze S.M.N. train station), **Siena** (12/day, 2.5 hours, change in Chiusi, all Florence-bound trains stop in Chiusi), **Assisi** (roughly hourly, 2-3 hours, 1 or 2 transfers), **Milan** (2/day direct, 5.5 hours; otherwise about hourly with a transfer in Florence, Bologna, or Rome, 4.5-5 hours). The train station's Buffet della Stazione is surprisingly good if you need a quick focaccia sandwich or pizza picnic for the train ride.

Tip for Drivers: If you're thinking of driving to Rome, consider stashing your car in Orvieto instead. You can easily park the car, safe and free, in the big lot below the Orvieto train station (for up to a week or more), and zip effortlessly into Rome by train (roughly hourly, 1-1.5 hours).

Civita di Bagnoregio

Perched on a pinnacle in a grand canyon, the 2,500-year-old, traffic-free village of Civita di Bagnoregio is Italy's ultimate hill town. Civita's only connection to town of Bagnoregio—and the world—is a long pedestrian bridge. In the last decade, the old, self-sufficient Civita (chee-VEE-tah) has died—the last of its lifelong residents have passed on, and the only employment here is in serving gawking sightseers. But Civita remains an amazing place to visit. (It's even become popular as a backdrop for movies, soap operas, and advertising campaigns.)

Civita's history goes back to Etruscan and ancient Roman

Orvieto & Civita Area

1. Alta Rocca Wine Resort
2. Agriturismo Locanda Rosati
3. Agriturismo Poggio della Volara
4. Tenuta Le Velette Winery & Accommodations
5. Agriturismo Cioccoleta & Neri Winery
6. Agriturismo Fattoria di Vibio
7. Custodi Winery

times. In the early Middle Ages, Bagnoregio was a suburb of Civita, which had a population of about 4,000. Later, Bagnoregio surpassed Civita in size—especially following a 1695 earthquake, after which many residents fled Civita to live in Bagnoregio, fearing their houses would be shaken off the edge into the valley below. Bagnoregio is dominated by Renaissance-style buildings while, architecturally, Civita remains stuck in the Middle Ages.

Civita can be very crowded, especially on the weekends and at lunchtime. The best way to enjoy Civita is early or late in the day, when you have the village to yourself. While Bagnoregio lacks the pinnacle-town romance of Civita, it's actually a healthy, vibrant community (unlike Civita, now nicknamed "the dead city"). In Bagnoregio, get a haircut, sip a coffee on the square, and walk down to the old laundry (ask, *"Dov'è la lavanderia vecchia?"*).

GETTING THERE

To reach Civita from Orvieto, you'll first head for the adjacent town of Bagnoregio. From there, it's a 30-minute walk or 5-minute drive to the base of Civita's pedestrian bridge, followed by a fairly steep 10-minute walk up to the town's main square.

By Bus to Bagnoregio: The trip from Orvieto to Bagnoregio takes about 45 minutes (€2.20 one-way if bought in advance at a bar or tobacco shop, €7 one-way if purchased from driver—this includes a fine for not buying your ticket in advance).

Here are likely departure times (confirm at the TI) from Orvieto, Monday to Saturday only (no buses on Sundays or holidays): 6:20, 7:25, 7:50, 12:45, 13:55, 14:00, 15:45, 17:40, and 18:20. It's nice to get up early, take the 7:50 bus, and see Civita in the cool morning calm. If you take the 12:45 bus, you can make the last (17:20) bus back, but your time in Civita may feel a little rushed.

From the upper town, buy your ticket from Silvia at the tobacco shop at Corso Cavour 306, a block up from the funicular (daily 7:00-13:00 & 16:00-20:00)—otherwise you'll pay the premium ticket price on board the bus. If you'll be returning to Orvieto by bus, it's simpler to get a return ticket now rather than in Bagnoregio.

The blue Cotral bus to Bagnoregio departs from a courtyard within the former military barracks, marked *Ex Caserma Piave* on maps. With your back to the funicular, walk to the right. At the end of Piazza Cahen, you'll see a large building across the street on the left. Follow *Parking* signs to find the buses waiting between yellow lines in the parking lot at the center of the building—look for the *A.co.tra.l. Capolinea* sign. The bus you want says *Bagnoregio* in the window. (Lots of buses marked *Umbria Mobilità* stop in front of the funicular; but Civita is served by a different bus company—Cotral.)

Buses departing the barracks stop five minutes later at Orvieto's train station—to catch the bus there, wait to the left of the funicular station (as you're facing it); schedule and tickets are available in the tobacco shop/bar in the train station.

For information on buses returning to Orvieto see "Bagnoregio Connections," later.

Getting from Bagnoregio Bus Stop to Civita: The simplest way to get from the Bagnoregio bus stop in Piazzale Battaglini to the base of Civita's pedestrian bridge is to **walk** (20-30 minutes, slightly uphill at first, but downhill overall). The walk through Bagnoregio also offers a delightful look at a workaday Italian town. Take the road going uphill, Via Garibaldi (overlooking the big parking lot). Once on the road, take the first right, and then an immediate left, to cut over onto the main drag, Via Roma. Follow this straight out to the belvedere for a superb viewpoint. From there, backtrack a few steps (staircase at end of viewpoint is a dead end) and take the stairs down to the road leading to the bridge.

A **shuttle bus** runs to the belvedere from a stop just 20 yards from the Piazzale Battaglini bus stop. Look for white minibuses labeled *EPF Tours*. Skip the shuttle bus unless it's pouring rain, but take it on the uphill return; it will drop you at the Orvieto-bound bus stop. Note the return times on the schedule posted by the belvedere or ask at the recommended Trattoria Antico Forno in Civita (usually 1-2/hour, 5 minutes, 7:30-18:15 but few buses 13:15-15:30 or on Sun Oct-March, €0.70 one-way, €1 round-trip, pay driver).

By Taxi or Shared Taxi to Civita: If you can share cost, a 30-minute taxi ride from Orvieto to Civita is a good deal (basic rate: €50 one-way, €75 round-trip with an hour wait). Giuliotaxi can take groups by car or minibus (see page 756 for details).

By Car to Bagnoregio and Civita: Driving from Orvieto to Civita takes about 30 minutes. Orvieto overlooks the autostrada (and has its own exit). From the Orvieto exit, the shortest way to Civita is to turn left (below Orvieto), and then simply follow the signs to *Lubriano* and *Bagnoregio*.

A more winding and scenic route takes about 10-15 minutes longer: From the Orvieto exit on the autostrada, go right (toward *Orvieto*), then at the first big roundabout, follow signs to *Bolsena* (passing under hill-capping Orvieto on your right). Take the first left (direction: Bagnoregio), winding up past great Orvieto views and the recommended Tenuta Le Velette and Custodi wineries (reservations required) en route to Canale, and through farms and fields of giant shredded wheat to Bagnoregio.

Whichever route you take, for a breahaking view of Civita, just before Bagnoregio, follow signs left to *Lubriano*, head into that village, turn right as you enter town, and pull into the first little square by the yellow church (on the left). You'll find an even better view farther into the town, from the tiny square at the next church (San Giovanni Battista). Then return to the Bagnoregio road.

Drive through the town of Bagnoregio (following yellow *civita* signs), park in the pay-and-display lot just before the belvedere, and take the stairs down to the bridge. If that small lot is full, there are often spots along the road leading up to it.

Orientation to Civita

Civita charges an €1.50 **admission fee** to enter the old town (waived for overnight guests). The revenue helps with its extensive maintenance expenses. Buy your ticket from the brown kiosk, just before the bridge, on the left. On summer weekends, tours may be offered from here—ask.

HELPFUL HINTS

Market Day: A lively market fills the Bagnoregio bus-station parking lot each Monday.

Baggage Storage: While there's no official baggage-check service in Bagnoregio, I've arranged with Mauro Laurenti, who runs the **Bar/Enoteca/Caffè Gianfu** and **Cinema Alberto Sordi,** to let you leave bags for a small fee (Thu-Tue 6:00-13:00 & 13:30-24:00, closed Wed, tel. 0761-792-580). As you get off the bus, backtrack about 50 yards in the direction that the Orvieto bus just came from, and go right around corner.

Food near Bagnoregio Bus Stop: Across the street from Mauro's bar/cinema and baggage storage is **L'Arte del Pane,** with fresh pastries (Via Matteotti 5). Thirty yards down the road, Mauro runs a small eatery, **Il Ripi&Go** (Via Giacomo Matteotti 35). On the other side of the old-town gate (Porta Albana), in the roundabout, is a small grocery store.

Orvieto Bus Tickets: To save money on bus fare back to Orvieto, buy a ticket before boarding from the newsstand (named Edicola 76), across from the gas station near the Bagnoregio bus stop—look for the white awning at #47 (Sat-Thu 7:00-13:00 & 17:00-20:00, closed Fri, €2.20 one-way in advance; €7 from driver).

Civita Walk

Civita was once connected to Bagnoregio, before the saddle between the separate towns eroded away. Photographs around town show the old donkey path, the original bridge. It was bombed in

World War II and replaced in 1966 with the new footbridge that you're climbing today.

• *Entering the town, you'll pass through Porta Santa Maria, a 12th-century Romanesque arch. This stone passageway was cut by the Etruscans 2,500 years ago, when this town was a stop on an ancient trading route. Inside the archway, you enter a gar-*

Civita di Bagnoregio

Note: Map not to scale; a walk across Civita takes approx. 5 minutes—but don't rush it!

den of stones. Stand in the little square—the town's antechamber—facing the Bar La Piazzetta. To your right are the remains of a...

Renaissance Palace

The wooden door and windows (above the door) lead only to thin air. They were part of the facade of one of five palaces that once graced Civita. Much of the palace fell into the valley, riding a chunk of the ever-eroding rock pinnacle. Today, the door leads to a remaining section of the palace—complete with Civita's first hot tub. It was once owned by the "Marchesa," a countess who married into Italy's biggest industrialist family.

• *A few steps uphill, farther into town (on your left, beyond the Bottega souvenir store), notice the two shed-like buildings.*

Old WC and Laundry

In the nearer building (covered with ivy), you'll see the town's old laundry, which dates from just after World War II, when water was finally piped into the town. Until a few years ago, this was a lively village gossip center. Now, locals park their mopeds here. Just behind that is another stone shed, which houses a poorly marked and less-than-pristine WC.

• *The main square is just a few steps farther along, but we'll take the scenic circular route to get there, detouring around to the right. Belly up to the...*

Canyon Viewpoint

Lean over the banister and listen to the sounds of the birds and the bees. Survey old family farms, noticing how evenly they're spaced. Historically, each one owned just enough land to stay in business. Turn left along the belvedere and walk a few steps to the site of the long-gone home of Civita's one famous son, St. Bonaventure, known as the "second founder of the Franciscans" (look for the small plaque on the wall).

• *From here, a lane leads past delightful old homes and gardens, and then to...*

Civita's Main Square

The town church faces Civita's main piazza. Grab a stone seat along the biggest building fronting the square (or a drink at Peppone's

bar) and observe the scene. They say that in a big city you can see a lot, but in a small town like this you can feel a lot. The generous bench is built into the long side of the square, reminding me of how, when I first discovered Civita back in the 1970s and 1980s, the town's old folks would gather here every night.

The piazza has been integral to Italian culture since ancient Roman times. While Civita is humble today, imagine the town's former wealth, when mansions of the leading families faced this square, along with the former City Hall (opposite the church, to your left). The town's history includes a devastating earthquake in 1695. Notice how stone walls were reinforced with thick bases, and how old stones and marble slabs were recycled and built into walls.

Here in the town square, you'll find Bar Da Peppone (open daily, local wines and microbrews, inviting fire in the winter) and two restaurants. There are wild donkey races on the first Sunday of June and the second Sunday of September. At Christmastime, a living Nativity scene is enacted in this square, and if you're visiting at the end of July or beginning of August, you might catch a play here. The pillars that stand like giants' bar stools are ancient Etruscan. The church, with its *campanile* (bell tower), marks the spot where an Etruscan temple, and then a Roman temple, once stood. Across from Peppone's, on the side of the former City Hall, is a small, square stone counter. Old-timers remember when this was a meat shop, and how one day a week the counter was stacked with fish for sale.

The humble **Geological Museum,** next to Peppone's, tells the story of how erosion is constantly shaping the surrounding "Bad Lands" valley, how landslides have shaped (and continue to threaten) Civita, and how the town plans to stabilize things (€3,

June-Sept Tue-Sun 9:30-13:30 & 14:00-18:30, closed Mon, Fri-Sun only off-season, www.museogeologicoedellefrane.it, mobile 328-665-7205).

• *Now step inside...*

Civita's Church

A cathedral until 1699, the church houses records of about 60 bishops that date back to the seventh century (church open daily 10:00-13:00 & 15:00-17:00, often closed Feb). Inside you'll see Romanesque columns and arches with faint Renaissance frescoes peeking through Baroque-era whitewash. The central altar is built upon the relics of the Roman martyr St. Victoria, who once was the patron saint of the town. St. Marlonbrando served as a bishop here in the ninth century; an altar dedicated to him is on the right. The fine crucifix over this altar, carved out of pear wood in the 15th century, is from the school of Donatello. It's remarkably expressive and greatly venerated by locals. Jesus' gaze is almost haunting. Some say his appearance changes based on what angle you view him from: looking alive from the front, in agony from the left, and dead from the right. Regardless, his eyes follow you from side to side. On Good Friday, this crucifix goes out and is the focus of the midnight procession.

On the left side, midway up the nave above an altar, is an intimate fresco of the *Madonna of the Earthquake,* given this name because—in the great shake of 1695—the whitewash fell off and revealed this tender fresco of Mary and her child. (During the Baroque era, a white-and-bright interior was in vogue, and churches such as these—which were covered with precious and historic frescoes—were simply whitewashed over. Look around to see examples.) On the same wall—just toward the front from the *Madonna*—find the faded portrait of Santa Apollonia, the patron saint of your teeth; notice the scary-looking pincers.

• *From the square, you can follow...*

The Main Street

A short walk takes you from the church to the end of the town. Along the way, you'll pass a couple of little eateries (described later, under "Eating in Civita"), olive presses, gardens, a rustic town museum, and valley views. The rock below Civita is honeycombed with ancient tunnels, caverns (housing olive presses), cellars (for keeping wine at a constant temperature all year), and cisterns (for collecting rainwater, since there was no well in town). Many date from Etruscan times.

Wherever you choose to eat (or just grab a bruschetta snack), be sure to take advantage of the opportunity to poke around—every place has a historic cellar. At the trendy **Alma Civita,** notice

the damaged house facing the main street—broken since the 1695 earthquake and scarred to this day. Just beyond, the rustic **Antico Frantoio Bruschetteria** serves bruschetta in an amazing old space. Whether or not you buy food, venture into their back room to see an interesting collection of old olive presses (if you're not eating here, a €1 donation is requested). The huge olive press in the entry is about 1,500 years old. Until the 1960s, blindfolded donkeys trudged in the circle here, crushing olives and creating paste that filled the circular filters and was put into a second press. Notice the 2,500-year-old sarcophagus niche. The hole in the floor (with the glass top) was a garbage hole. In ancient times, residents would toss their jewels down when under attack; excavations uncovered a windfall of treasures.

In front is the well head of an ancient cistern—designed to collect rainwater from neighboring rooftops—carved out of *tufo* and covered with clay to be waterproof.

• *Across the street and down a tiny lane, find...*

Antica Civita

This is the closest thing the town has to a history museum. The humble collection is the brainchild of Felice, the old farmer who's hung black-and-white photos, farm tools, olive presses, and local artifacts in a series of old caves. Climb down to the "warm blood machine" (another donkey-powered grinding wheel) and a viewpoint. You'll see rooms where a mill worker lived until the 1930s. Felice wants to give visitors a feeling for life in Civita when its traditional economy was strong (€1, daily 10:00-19:00, until 17:00 in winter, some English explanations, tel. 320-110-4279).

• *Another few steps along the main street take you to...*

The End of Civita

Here the road is literally cut out of the stone, with a dramatic view of the Bad Lands opening up. Pop into the cute "Garden of Poets" (immediately on the left just outside town, with the tiny local crafts shop) to savor the view. Then, look back up at the end of town and ponder the precarious future of Civita. There's a certain stillness here, far from the modern world and high above the valley.

Continue along the path a few steps toward the valley below the town, and you come to some shallow caves used as stables until a few years ago. The third cave, cut deeper into the rock, with a barred door, is the **Chapel of the Incarcerated** (Cappella del Car-cere). In Etruscan times, the chapel—with a painted tile depicting the Madonna and child—may have been a tomb, and in medieval times, it was used as a jail (which collapsed in 1695).

Although it's closed to the public now, an Etruscan tunnel just beyond the Chapel of the Incarcerated cuts completely through the hill. Tall enough for a woman with a jug on her head to pass through, it may have served as a shortcut to the river below. It was widened in the 1930s so that farmers could get between their scattered fields more easily. Later, it served as a refuge for frightened villagers who huddled here during WWII bombing raids.

• *Hike back into town. Make a point to take some time to explore the peaceful back lanes before returning to the modern world.*

Sleeping in Civita or Bagnoregio

($$$$ = Splurge, $$$ = Pricier, $$ = Moderate, $ = Budget)
Civita has nine B&B rooms up for grabs. Bagnoregio has larger lodgings, and there are plenty of *agriturismi* nearby; otherwise, there's always Orvieto. Off-season, when Civita and Bagnoregio are deadly quiet—and cold—I'd side-trip in from Orvieto rather than spend the night here.

IN CIVITA

$$$ Alma Civita is a classic old stone house that was recently renovated by a sister-and-brother team, Alessandra and Maurizio (hence the name: Al-Ma). These are Civita's two most comfortable, modern, and warmly run rooms (Wi-Fi in restaurant, tel. 0761-792-415, mobile 347-449-8892, www.almacivita.com, prenotazione@almacivita.com).

$$ Locanda della Buona Ventura rents four overpriced rooms with tiny bathrooms, up narrow stairs, decorated in medieval rustic-chic, and overlooking Civita's piazza. You're not likely to see the owner—the La Cisterna Etrusca shop across the square functions as the reception (skimpy breakfast, no Wi-Fi, tel. 0761-792-025, mobile 347-627-5628, www.locandabuonaventura.it, info@locandabuonaventura.it).

$$ Civita B&B, run by gregarious Franco Sala, has three little rooms above Trattoria Antico Forno, each overlooking Civita's main square. Two are doubles with private bath. The third is a triple (with one double and one kid-size bed), which has its own bathroom across the hall (RS%, family rooms, continental breakfast, Piazza del Duomo Vecchio, tel. 076-176-0016, mobile 347-611-5426, www.civitadibagnoregio.it, fsala@pelagus.it). Franco also rents two apartments, one in Civita and one in Bagnoregio.

IN BAGNOREGIO

$ Romantica Pucci B&B is a haven for city-weary travelers. Its five spacious rooms are indeed romantic, with canopied beds and flowing veils (air-con, free parking, Piazza Cavour 1, tel. 0761-792-121, www.hotelromanticapucci.it, info@hotelromanticapucci.it). It's just above the public parking lot you see when you arrive in Bagnoregio: From the bus stop, take Via Garibaldi uphill above the parking lot, and then turn right, before the *Forno,* sign onto Via Roma. The B&B is just to the left.

$ Hotel Divino Amore has 23 bright, modern rooms, four with perfect views of a miniature Civita. These view rooms, and the seven rooms with air-conditioning, don't cost extra—but they book up first (closed Jan-March, Via Fidanza 25-27, tel. 076-178 0882, mobile 329-344-8950, www.hoteldivinoamore.com, info@hoteldivinoamore.com, Silvia). From the bus stop, passing the *Forno* sign where the street becomes Via Fidanza, follow Via Garibaldi uphill above the parking lot for 200 yards.

Eating in Civita or Bagnoregio

IN CIVITA

$$ Osteria Al Forno di Agnese is a delightful spot where Manuela and her friends serve visitors simple yet delicious meals, including good salads, on a covered patio just off Civita's main square or in a little dining room in gloomy weather (gluten-free options, good selection of local wines, opens daily at 12:00 for lunch, June-Sept also at 19:00 for dinner, closed sometimes in bad weather, tel. 0761-792-571, mobile 340-1259-721).

$$ Trattoria Antico Forno serves up rustic dishes, homemade pasta, and salads at affordable prices. Try their homemade pasta with truffles (daily for lunch 12:30-15:30 and dinner 19:00-22:00, on main square, also rents rooms—see Civita B&B listing earlier, tel. 076-176-0016, Franco, daughter Elisabetta, and assistant Nina).

$$ Trattoria La Cantina de Arianna is a family affair, with a busy open fire specializing in grilled meat and wonderful bruschetta. It's run by Arianna, her sister, Antonella, and their parents, Rossana and Antonio. After eating, wander down to their cellar, where you'll see traditional winemaking gear and provisions for rolling huge kegs up the stairs. Tap on the kegs in the bottom level to see which are full (daily 11:00-16:30, tel. 0761-793-270).

$$ Alma Civita feels like a fresh, new take on old Civita. It's owned by two of its longtime residents: Alessandra (an architect) and her brother, Maurizio (who runs the restaurant). Choose from one of three seating areas: outside on a stony lane, in the modern and trendy-feeling main-floor dining room, or in the equally modern but atmospheric cellar. Even deeper is an old Etruscan tomb that's now a wine cellar (May-Oct lunch Wed-Mon 12:00-16:00, dinner Fri-Sat only 19:00-21:30, closed Tue; Nov-April Fri-Sun only for lunch, tel. 0761-792-415).

$ Antico Frantoio Bruschetteria, the last place in town, is a rustic, super-atmospheric spot for a bite to eat. The specialty here: delicious bruschetta toasted over hot coals. Peruse the menu, choose your toppings (chopped tomato is super), and get a glass of wine for a fun, affordable snack or meal (roughly 10:00-18:00, mobile 328-689-9375, Fabrizio).

AT THE FOOT OF THE BRIDGE

$$$ Hostaria del Ponte—recently closed due to erosion problems but hoping to reopen—is a more serious restaurant than anything in Civita itself. It offers creative and traditional cuisine with a great view terrace at the parking lot at the base of the bridge to Civita. Big space heaters make it comfortable to enjoy the wonderful view as you dine from their rooftop terrace, even in spring and fall (tel. 076-179-3565, www.hostariadelponte.it, Lorena).

IN BAGNOREGIO

The recommended **$$ Romantica Pucci B&B** offers a small restaurant with tables in its private garden (closed Mon, see contact details earlier).

Bagnoregio Connections

From Bagnoregio to Orvieto: Cotral buses (45 minutes, €2.20 one-way if purchased in advance, €7 one-way from driver) connect Bagnoregio to Orvieto. Departures from Bagnoregio—Monday to Saturday only (no buses on Sunday or holidays)—are likely to be at the following times (confirm locally): 5:30, 6:35, 6:50, 9:55, 10:10, 13:00, 13:35, 14:40, and 17:25. For information, call 06-7205-7205 or 800-174-471 (press 7 for English), or see www.cotralspa.it (click "Orari," then fill in "Bagnoregio" and "Orvieto" in the trip planner—Italian only). For info on coming from Orvieto, see "Getting There" on page 783).

If you're side-tripping from Orvieto, buy two tickets in Orvieto so you already have one when you're ready to come back.

From Bagnoregio to Points South: Cotral buses also run to **Viterbo,** which has a good train connection to Rome (buses go weekdays at 5:10, 6:30, 7:15, 8:10, 7:40, 10:00, 13:00, 13:45, and 14:55; less frequent Sat-Sun, 35 minutes).

ROME

Roma

Rome is magnificent and brutal at the same time. It's a showcase of Western civilization, with astonishingly ancient sights and a modern vibrancy. But if you're careless, you'll be run down or pickpocketed. And with the wrong attitude, you'll be frustrated by the kind of chaos that only an Italian can understand. On my last visit, a cabbie struggling with the traffic said, _"Roma chaos."_ I responded, _"Bella chaos."_ He agreed.

Rome is a magnificent tangled urban forest. If your hotel provides a comfortable refuge; if you pace yourself; if you accept—and even partake in—the siesta plan; if you're well-organized for sightseeing; and if you protect yourself and your valuables with extra caution and discretion, you'll love it. (And Rome is much easier to live with if you can avoid the midsummer heat.)

Over two thousand years ago the word "Rome" meant civilization itself. Everything was either civilized (part of the Roman Empire, Latin- or Greek-speaking) or barbarian. Today, Rome is Italy's political capital, the capital of Catholicism, and the center of its ancient empire, littered with evocative remains. As you peel through its fascinating and jumbled layers, you'll find Rome's buildings, cats, laundry, traffic, and 2.7 million people endlessly entertaining. And then, of course, there are its stupendous sights.

Visit St. Peter's, the greatest church on earth, and scale Michelangelo's 448-foot-tall dome. Learn something about eternity by touring the huge Vatican Museums. You'll find the story of creation—bright as the day it was painted—in the restored Sistine Chapel. Do the "Caesar Shuffle" through ancient Rome's Forum and Colosseum. Savor Europe's most sumptuous building, the Borghese Gallery, and take an early evening "Dolce Vita Stroll" down Via del Corso with Rome's beautiful people. Dine well at least once. And enjoy an after-dark walk from Campo de' Fiori to the Spanish Steps, lacing together Rome's Baroque and bubbly nightspots.

PLANNING YOUR TIME

Rome is wonderful, but it's huge and exhausting. On a first-time visit, many travelers find that Rome is best done quickly—Italy is more charming elsewhere. But whether you're here for a day or a week, you won't be able to see all of these sights, so don't try— you'll keep coming back to Rome. After several dozen visits, I still have a healthy list of excuses to return.

Rome in a Day: Some people actually "do" Rome in a day. Crazy as that sounds, if all you have is a day, it's one of the most exciting days Europe has to offer. Start at 8:30 at the Colosseum. Then explore the Forum, hike over Capitoline Hill, and cap your "Caesar Shuffle" with a visit to the Pantheon. After a quick lunch, taxi to the Vatican Museums (lines usually die down midafternoon, or you can reserve a visit online in advance). See the Vatican Museums, then St. Peter's Basilica (open until 19:00 April-Sept). Taxi back to Campo de' Fiori to find dinner. Finish your day lacing together all the famous floodlit spots (follow my self-guided Heart of Rome Walk). Note: This busy plan is possible only if you ace the line-avoidance tricks mentioned in this chapter.

Rome in Two to Three Days: On the first day, do the "Caesar Shuffle" from the Colosseum to the Forum, then over Capitoline Hill to the Pantheon. After a siesta, join the locals strolling from Piazza del Popolo to the Spanish Steps (follow my self-guided "Dolce Vita Stroll"). On the second day, see Vatican City (St. Peter's, climb the dome, tour the Vatican Museums). Have dinner near the atmospheric Campo de' Fiori, and then walk to the Trevi Fountain and Spanish Steps (following my Heart of Rome Walk). With a third day, add the Borghese Gallery (reservations required) and the Capitoline Museums.

Orientation to Rome

Sprawling Rome actually feels manageable once you get to know it. The old core, with most of the tourist sights, sits inside a diamond formed by Termini train station (in the east), the Vatican (west), Villa Borghese Gardens (north), and the Colosseum (south). The Tiber River snakes through the diamond from north to south. At the center of the diamond is Piazza Venezia, a busy square and traffic hub. It takes about an hour to walk from Termini station to the Vatican.

Rome's Neighborhoods

VATICAN
MUSEUMS

**VATICAN
CITY**

ST.
PETER'S

NORTH ROME

PIAZZA
DEL POPOLO

VILLA
BORGHESE

BORGHESE
GALLERY

"SHOPPING
TRIANGLE"

SPANISH
STEPS

TERMINI
TRAIN STATION

NATIONAL
MUSEUM

**PANTHEON
NEIGHBORHOOD**

PIAZZA
VENEZIA

Tiber River

CAPITOLINE
HILL

**ANCIENT
ROME**

FORUM

COLOSSEUM

EAST ROME

PILGRIM'S
ROME

SAN GIOVANNI
IN LATERANO

SANTA
MARIA

TRASTEVERE

TESTACCIO

SOUTH ROME

SOUTH OF
TESTACCIO

E.U.R.

APPIAN
WAY

Not to Scale

ROME: A VERBAL MAP

Think of Rome as a collection of neighborhoods, huddling around major landmarks.

Ancient Rome: In ancient times, this was home to the grandest buildings of a city of a million people. Today, the best of the classical sights stand in a line from the Colosseum to the Forum to the Pantheon. Just north of this area, between Via Nazionale and Via Cavour, is the atmospheric and trendy Monti district.

Pantheon Neighborhood: The Pantheon anchors the neighborhood I like to call the "Heart of Rome." It stretches eastward from the Tiber River through Campo de' Fiori and Piazza Navona, past the Pantheon to the Trevi Fountain. Between the river and the Pantheon area is the former Jewish ghetto.

Vatican City: Located west of the Tiber, it's a compact world of its own, with two great, huge sights: St. Peter's Basilica and the Vatican Museums.

North Rome: With the Spanish Steps, Villa Borghese Gardens, and trendy shopping streets (Via Veneto and the "shopping triangle"—the area along Via del Corso and between the Spanish Steps, Piazza Venezia, and Piazza del Popolo), this is a more modern, classy area.

East Rome: This includes the area around Termini Station and Piazza della Repubblica, with many recommended hotels and public-transportation connections.

Trastevere: South of Vatican City and just west of the Pantheon neighborhood is Trastevere, the colorful, wrong-side-of-the-river neighborhood with a village feel. It's the city at its crustiest—and perhaps most "Roman."

South Rome: Farther south are the postindustrial Testaccio neighborhood, the 1930s suburb of E.U.R., and the Appian Way.

Within each of these neighborhoods, you'll find elements from the many layers of Rome's 2,500-year story: the marble ruins of ancient times; tangled streets of the medieval world; early Christian churches; grand Renaissance buildings and statues; Baroque fountains and church facades; 19th-century apartments; and 21st-century boulevards choked with traffic.

Since no one is allowed to build taller than St. Peter's dome, and virtually no buildings have been constructed in the city center since Mussolini got distracted in 1938, central Rome has no modern skyline. The Tiber River is basically ignored—after Italy unified (1870) and Rome became the capital, the banks were built up very high to guard against the frequent floods, and Rome turned its back on its naughty river.

TOURIST INFORMATION

Rome has about a dozen small city-run tourist information offices scattered around town that sell city maps and Roma Passes (explained on page 804). The largest TIs are at Fiumicino Airport (Terminal 3, daily 9:00-17:30, longer in summer) and Termini train station (daily 8:00-18:45, exit by track 24 and walk 100 yards down along Via Giovanni Giolitti). Little kiosks (most open daily 9:30-19:00) are on Via Nazionale (at Palazzo delle Esposizioni), between the Trevi Fountain and Pantheon (at the corner of Via del Corso and Via Minghetti), near Piazza Navona (at Piazza delle Cinque Lune), and in Trastevere (at Piazza Sidney Sonnino). A larger information center is directly across from the Forum entrance, on Via dei Fori Imperiali (see page 854). There are also offices at Tiburtina train station and Ciampino Airport.

The TI's website is www.turismoroma.it, but a better site for practical information is www.060608.it. That's also the number for Rome's **call center**—the best source of up-to-date tourist information, with English speakers on staff (answered daily 9:00-21:00, just dial 06-0608, and press 2 for English).

At any TI, ask for a free city map (or pay for a better one). Your hotel will have a freebie map and may also have a booklet with up-to-date listings of the city's sights and hours. To find the city's many small streets and alleys, map apps work better than paper maps. If you do want a paper map, you'll find better quality ones at bookstores than at newsstands. See page 806 for recommended public transport maps.

ARRIVAL IN ROME
By Train at Termini Station

Termini, Rome's main train station (www.romatermini.com), is a buffet of tourist services. At the head of the tracks are two atriums. The inner atrium, open at both ends, houses shops and eateries. The outer atrium, with glass walls, houses ticket windows and ticket machines plus a good-sized bookstore. Outside the station is a large square where city buses depart. A basement shopping area extends beneath both atriums. Various services (outlined below) are located in halls along the sides of the tracks.

For security, entry to the train platforms themselves is restricted to ticketholders. Entrances are from the inner atrium and from the halls to the sides of the tracks. On my last visit, I needed to show my ticket, but there were no metal detectors and lines were short.

Services: The customer service and ticket windows (in the outer, glassed-in atrium) can be jammed with travelers—find the small red kiosk, take a number, and wait. Whenever possible, use the ticket machines. Though most trains departing from Termini are operated by Italy's state rail company, Trenitalia (www.trenitalia.com), some are run by a private company, Italo (www.italotreno.it), with its own ticket machines and windows in the outer atrium.

In the hall along Via Giovanni Giolitti, on the southwest side of the station (near track 24), you'll find the **TI** (daily 8:00-18:45), a **hotel booking** office, and **car rental** desks. The **baggage storage** *(deposito bagagli)* is in the basement (use the elevator, daily 6:00-23:00). The **Leonardo Express train** to Fiumicino Airport runs from track 23 or 24 on this side of the station (see page 936).

In general, the best places in the station to sit are in its eateries. A snack bar and a good self-service **cafeteria** (Ciao) are perched one floor above the ticket windows in the outer atrium, accessible from the side closest to track 24 (daily 11:00-22:30). For good-quality **sandwiches** to go, try VyTA in the inner atrium across from track 1.

In the hall along Via Marsala, on the northeast side of the station (near track 1), you'll find a **pharmacy** and an often-cramped **waiting room.** On the basement shopping level, below the inner atrium (go down the escalators on the Via Marsala side), is the large Sapori & Dintori **supermarket** (daily 7:00-24:00). Pay **WCs** are also down the escalators from the inner atrium.

The station has some sleazy sharks with official-looking business cards; avoid anybody selling anything unless they're in a legitimate shop at the station. Other shady characters linger around the ticket machines—offers to help usually come with the expectation of a "tip." There are no official porters; if someone wants to carry your bags or help you find your platform, they are simply angling for some cash.

Getting Between Termini and Rome Hotels: From Termini, many of my recommended hotels are easily accessible by foot or by Metro (for those in the Colosseum and Vatican neighborhoods). The Termini Metro station, where Metro lines A and B intersect, is beneath the station. City buses leave from the square directly in front of the outer atrium. Buses to the airport leave from the streets on both sides of the station. Taxis queue in front and outside exits on both the north and south sides; if there's a long taxi line in front, try a side exit instead. Avoid con men hawking "express taxi" services in unmarked cars (only use official white taxis with the maroon *Roma Capitale* logo).

By Train or Bus at Tiburtina Station

Tiburtina, Rome's second-largest train station (www.stazioneromatiburtina.it), is next to the Tiburtina Metro station in the city's northeast corner, and across the road from Rome's bus station. It's a pass-through station: Fast trains along the Milan-Naples line stop here and continue on quickly. A few of these fast trains now stop only at Tiburtina, but most stop at both Tiburtina and Termini. Use the station that's most convenient for you.

Getting Between Tiburtina and Downtown Rome: Tiburtina is on Metro line B, four stops from Termini. Note that when going to Tiburtina, Metro line B splits—you want a train signed *Rebibbia*, not *Jonio*. Bus #492 runs conveniently between Tiburtina, several city-center stops (including Piazza Barberini, Piazza Venezia, and Piazza Navona), and the Vatican neighborhood (as you emerge from the train station's front door, the city bus stop is just to the left).

By Car

Your car is a worthless headache in Rome. Avoid a pile of stress and save money by parking at the huge, easy, free, and relatively safe lot behind the train station in the hill town of Orvieto (follow *P* signs from the autostrada) and catching an €8 *regionale* train to Rome (every 1-2 hours, 1.5 hours).

Or, if Rome is the first stop of your trip and you plan to rent a car for the rest of Italy, you could sightsee Rome, then take the

ROME

train to Orvieto and rent a car there (Hertz has an office facing the base of the funicular). If you absolutely must drive and park a car in Rome, there's a large underground garage at the Villa Borghese Gardens near the Spagna Metro station, just outside the restricted downtown zone (€18/day, Viale del Galoppatoio 33, www.sabait.it).

By Plane or Cruise Ship

For information on Rome's airports and Civitavecchia's cruise ship terminal, see the end of this chapter.

HELPFUL HINTS

Exchange Rate: €1 = about $1.10

Country Calling Code: 39 (see page 1154 for dialing instructions).

Sightseeing Tips: Those planning at least a couple days of sightseeing can save money by buying the Roma Pass (see the "Rome Sightseeing Tips" sidebar on page 804), available at TIs and participating sights—buy one before visiting the Colosseum or Forum, and you can shorten your wait in line. Another way to speed your entry to the Colosseum and Forum is to buy tickets online in advance (see page 831). If you want to see the Borghese Gallery, remember to reserve ahead (see page 881). To sidestep the long Vatican Museums line, reserve an entry time online (see page 869 for details).

Closed Days: If you're in Rome on a Sunday, note that the Vatican Museums are closed (except for last Sun of the month, when it's free and even more crowded). The Borghese Gallery is closed on Tuesdays, and St. Peter's Basilica may close on Wednesday mornings for a papal audience.

Wi-Fi: All the hotels in this book have Wi-Fi, but if yours doesn't, your hotelier can point you to a café that does.

Useful App: 🎧 For free audio versions of walks through the "Heart of Rome," Jewish Ghetto, and Trastevere, and my tours of the Pantheon, Colosseum, Roman Forum, St. Peter's Basilica, Vatican Museums, and Sistine Chapel, get the **Rick Steves Audio Europe** app (for details, see page 12).

Bookstores: It's easy to find stores selling English-language books (all below are open daily except Open Door, closed Sun). There are two large chains: **Borri Books** is at Termini station, while **Feltrinelli International,** with a large English section, is just off Piazza della Repubblica at Via Vittorio Emanuele Orlando 86 (see map on page 886, tel. 06-487-0171). A few small, independent bookstores have a more personal touch: The **Anglo-American Bookshop** has great art and history sections (closed all day Sun and Mon morning, a few blocks south of Spanish Steps at Via della Vite 102—see map on page 818, tel. 06-679-

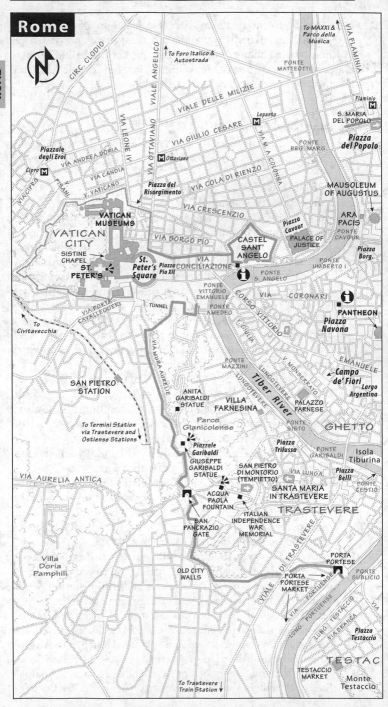

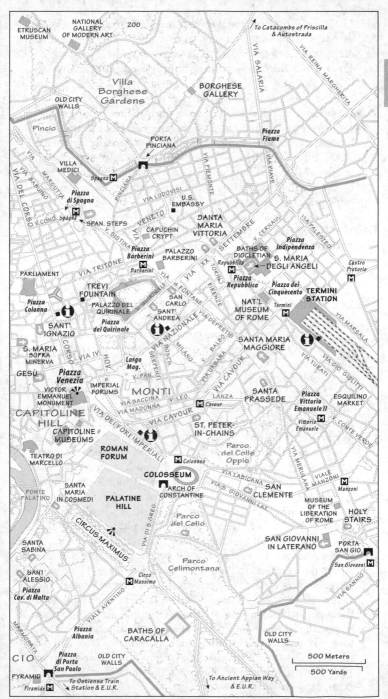

ROME

5222). In Trastevere, the **Almost Corner Bookshop** stocks an extensive Italian-interest section (Via del Moro 45—see map on page 907, tel. 06-583-6942, Dermot from Ireland), and the **Open Door Bookshop** carries the only used books in English in town (closed Sun, Via della Lungaretta 23—see map on page 907, tel. 06-589-6478).

Laundry: Coin launderettes are common in Rome; your hotelier can direct you to the closest one. The **Ondablu** chain has a branch near Termini station (about €8/load, usually open daily 8:00-21:00, Via Principe Amedeo 70b—see map on page 887, tel. 06-474-4647). The Funny Palace Hostel's **Splashnet,** two blocks from Termini, offers full-serve laundry for about the same price (see details on page 900).

DEALING WITH (AND AVOIDING) PROBLEMS

Theft Alert: While violent crime is rare in the city center, petty theft is rampant. Always use your money belt. If you must carry a backpack, never leave it unattended, and try to keep it attached to your body in some way (such as when you're seated for a meal). Be particularly on guard in crowds and wear back-packs in front, especially when boarding and leaving buses and subways. You'll find less crowding and commotion—and less risk—waiting for the end cars of a subway rather than the middle cars. Thieves are particularly thick on the Metro and the crowded and made-for-tourists buses #40 and #64.

Thieves strike when you're distracted. Don't trust kind strangers or be deceived by appearance: Sneaky thieves may pose as businessmen or tourists, or may be moms with babies or gangs of children.

Scams abound: Always be clear about what paper money you're giving someone, demand clear and itemized bills, and count your change. Don't give your wallet to self-proclaimed "police" who stop you on the street, warn you about counterfeit (or drug) money, and ask to see your cash. If a bank machine eats your ATM card, see if there's a thin plastic insert with a tongue hanging out that thieves use to extract it.

Reporting Losses: To report lost or stolen items, file a police report (at Termini Station, with *polizia* at track 11 or with Carabinieri at track 20; offices are also at Piazza Venezia and at the corner of Via Nazionale and Via Genova). You'll need the report to file an insurance claim for lost gear, and it can help with replacing your passport—first file the police report, then call your embassy to make an appointment (US embassy: tel. 06-46741, http://italy.usembassy.gov, Via Vittorio Veneto 121). For information on how to report lost or stolen credit cards, see page 1117.

ROME

Emergency Numbers: Police—tel. 113. Ambulance—tel. 118.

Pedestrian Safety: Your main safety concern in Rome is crossing streets. Use extreme caution. Some streets have pedestrian-crossing signals (red means stop—or jaywalk carefully; green means go...also carefully; and yellow means go...extremely carefully, as cars may be whipping around the corner). But just as often, multilane streets have crosswalks with no signals at all. And even when there are traffic lights, they are provisional: Scooters don't need to stop at red lights, and even cars exercise what drivers call the "logical option" of not stopping if they see no oncoming traffic. Each year, as noisy gasoline-powered scooters are replaced by electric ones, the streets get quieter (hooray) but more dangerous for pedestrians.

Follow locals like a shadow when you cross a street (or spend a good part of your visit stranded on curbs). When you do cross alone, don't be a deer in the headlights. Find a gap in the traffic and walk with confidence while making eye contact with approaching drivers—they won't hit you if they can tell where you intend to go.

Staying/Getting Healthy: The siesta is a key to survival in summertime Rome. Lie down and contemplate the extraordinary power of gravity in the Eternal City. I drink lots of cold, refreshing water from Rome's many drinking fountains (the Forum has three).

Every neighborhood has a **pharmacy** (marked by a green cross). The 24-hour Farmacia Piram is several blocks down from Piazza della Repubblica at Via Nazionale 228 (tel. 06-488-4437). Pharmacies stay open late in Termini Station (daily 7:30-22:00, along northeast side of station, enter from Via Marsala), at Piazza dei Cinquecento 51 (Mon-Fri 7:00-23:30, Sat-Sun 8:00-23:00, next to Termini Station on the corner of Via Cavour—see map on page 886, tel. 06-488-0019), and in the Pantheon neighborhood (Farmacia Senato, between Piazza Navona and the Pantheon, Mon-Fri 7:30-24:30, Sat 8:30-24:30, Sun 12:00-23:00, Corso del Rinascimento 50—see map on page 822).

Embassies and hotels can recommend English-speaking doctors. Consider MEDline, a 24-hour private home-medical service; doctors speak English and make calls at hotels for about €150 (tel. 06-808-0995, www.soccorso-medico.com). Another private clinic is International Medical Services, Via Firenze 47, tel. 06-488-2371, www.imc84.com. Anyone is entitled to free emergency treatment at public hospitals. The hospital closest to Termini Station is Policlinico Umberto 1 (entrance for emergency treatment on Via Lancisi, translators available, Metro: Policlinico).

ROME

Rome Sightseeing Tips

These tips will help you use your time and money efficiently, making the Eternal City seem less eternal and more entertaining. For general advice on sightseeing, see page 1119.

The Roma Pass

The full **three-day Roma Pass** (www.romapass.it) costs €36, includes free admission to your first two sights, a discount on subsequent sights, and unlimited use of public transit (buses, trams, and Metro, plus the suburban train to Ostia, but not the airport train). Using the pass at the Colosseum/ Roman Forum/Palatine Hill (considered a single sight) lets you stand in the line for people who already have tickets (which in theory gets you in faster). Other sights include Borghese Gallery (reservations required), Capitoline Museums, Ara Pacis, and Trajan's Market. The pass also covers the four branches of the National Museum of Rome (considered a single sight). The pass does not cover the Vatican Museums (which contain the Sistine Chapel).

The Roma Pass saves most visitors a little money and a lot of ticket-buying stress. To get the most out of your pass, visit the two most expensive sights first—for example, the Colosseum/ Roman Forum/Palatine Hill (€12) and the National Museum of Rome (€10). A three-day transit pass normally costs €18, so you can quickly get €40 of value from the pass, plus any discounts on subsequent sights.

The pass is sold at participating sights, TIs, and many tobacco shops and newsstands all over town (look for a *Roma Pass* sign; all should charge the same price). Don't wait to buy it at a crowded sight like the Colosseum. There's no advantage in ordering a pass online—you still have to pick it up in Rome.

Validate your Roma Pass by writing your name and validation date on the card. Then insert it directly into the turnstile at your first two (free) sights. At other sights, show it at the ticket office and you'll get the same reduction as local students (usually about 30 percent).

To use the included transit pass, write your name and birthdate on the pass and validate it on your first bus or Metro ride by passing it over a sensor at a turnstile or validation machine (look for a yellow circle). Now you can take unlimited rides within Rome's city limits (until midnight of the third day). Once the pass is validated you can hop on any bus without showing it, but you'll need to swipe it to get through Metro turnstiles.

The **48-hour Roma Pass** costs €28 and includes free entry

to one sight, the same discounts on additional ones, and unlimited use of public transit (for 48 hours after validation—a €12.50 value). It saves money only if you visit at least one or two sights beyond your free one, but it can save time if you're visiting the Colosseum/Roman Forum/Palatine Hill and don't have a reservation.

For families, only adults will need a Roma Pass. Children under age 18 get into national museums and sights for free, and kids under 6 get into city museums, including Museo dell'Ara Pacis, for free; they can skip the lines alongside their pass-holding parents. Note that passports may be required as proof of age (driver's licenses may not be accepted). Kids 10 and over need their own transit tickets or passes; those 9 and under ride free.

Top Tips

Museum Reservations: The marvelous Borghese Gallery requires reservations in advance (for specifics, see page 880). You can reserve online to avoid long lines at the Vatican Museums (see page 869).

Opening Hours: Rome's sights have notoriously variable hours from season to season. It's smart to check each sight's website in advance. On holidays, expect shorter hours or closures.

Forum/Palatine Hill: These two sights share a single admission ticket. If you want to visit Palatine Hill after seeing the Forum, go to the Arch of Titus and climb Palatine Hill from there. (You can't exit the Forum and reenter at Palatine Hill.)

Churches: Many churches, which have divine art and free entry, open early (around 7:00-7:30), close for lunch (roughly 12:00-15:30), and close late (about 19:00). Kamikaze tourists maximize their sightseeing hours by visiting churches before 9:00 or late in the day; during the siesta, they see major sights that stay open all day (St. Peter's, Colosseum, Forum, Capitoline Museums, Pantheon, and National Museum of Rome). Dress modestly for church visits.

Picnic Discreetly: Public drinking and eating is not allowed at major sights, though the ban has proven difficult to enforce To avoid the risk of being fined, choose an empty piazza for your picnic, or keep a low profile.

Miscellaneous Tips: I carry a water bottle and refill it at Rome's many public drinking spouts. Because public restrooms are scarce, use toilets at museums, restaurants, and bars.

GETTING AROUND ROME

Sightsee on foot, by city bus, by Metro, or by taxi. I've grouped your sightseeing into walkable neighborhoods. Make it a point to visit sights in a logical order. Needless backtracking wastes precious time.

Public Transportation

Rome's public transportation system is cheap and efficient, but also confusing and crowded. Consider it part of your Roman experience, and if you get a seat, think of it as a bonus. The three Metro lines are relatively sane and straightforward, but serve a limited area. Buses are more chaotic—there are no posted timetables or maps, and stop names are announced only in the newest vehicles. But they run frequently and go everywhere. If you're in town for more than a day or two, mastering a couple key bus routes serving your neighborhood is worth the effort and will make you feel like a Rome pro.

The websites www.muovi.roma.it (with a very clean, quick interface), www.agenziamobilita.roma.it, and www.atac.roma.it all have **journey planners** in English that will help you sort through the thicket of routes. The ATAC website has downloadable network maps. If you have a smartphone and an international data plan, consider downloading the free apps "Roma Bus" (by Movenda) or "Muoversi a Roma." There's no official paper map of the system, but Edizioni Lozzi produces a frequently updated "Roma Metro Bus" map for €6 (at bookstores), which includes a booklet with details on all bus routes. For information by phone, call ATAC at 06-57003.

Buying Tickets

All public transportation uses the same ticket. It costs €1.50 and is valid for one Metro ride—including transfers underground—plus unlimited city buses and trams during a 100-minute period. Passes good on buses and the Metro are sold in increments of 24 hours (€7), 48 hours (€12.50), 72 hours (€18), one week (€24, about the cost of three taxi rides), and one month (€35, plus €3 for the rechargeable card, valid for a calendar month).

You can purchase tickets and passes from machines at Metro stations and a few major bus stops (cash only), and from some newsstands and tobacco shops (*tabacchi*, marked by a black-and-white *T* sign). Tickets are not sold on board. It's smart to stock up on tickets early, or to buy a pass or a Roma Pass (which includes public transportation—see page 804). That way, you don't have to run around searching for an open tobacco shop when you spot your bus approaching.

Validate your ticket by sticking it in the Metro turnstile (magnetic-strip-side up, arrow-side first) or in the machine when you board the bus (magnetic-strip-side down, arrow-side first)—watch others and imitate. It'll return your ticket with your expiration time printed. To get through a Metro turnstile with a transit pass or Roma Pass, use it just like a ticket; on buses and trams, however, you need to validate your pass only if that's your first time using it.

If you need help from a real person, ATAC runs a small ticket office at Termini Station. Follow signs for *Metro Linea B,* then *ATAC ticket office* (Mon-Sat 7:00-20:00, Sun 8:00-20:00).

By Metro

The Roman subway system (Metropolitana, or "Metro") is simple, clean, cheap, and fast. The two lines you need to know—A and B—intersect at Termini Station. The Metro runs from 5:30 to 23:30 (Fri-Sat until 1:30 in the morning). The subway's first and last compartments are generally the least crowded, and the least likely to harbor pickpockets.

By Bus

The Metro is handy, but it won't get you everywhere—you often have to take the bus (or tram). Bus routes are listed at each stop. Route and system maps aren't posted, but with some knowledge of major stops, you can wing it without one. (The ATAC website has a PDF bus map that you can download, bookstores sell paper transport maps, and the various journey planners are helpful.)

Buses—especially the touristy #40 and #64—are havens for thieves and pickpockets. These two lines in particular can be nose-to-armpit crowded during peak times...and while you're sniffing that guy's pit, his other hand could be busily rifling through your pockets. Assume any commotion is a thief-created distraction. If one bus is packed, there's likely a second one on its tail with far fewer crowds and thieves. Or read the
signs posted at stops to see if a different, less crowded bus route can get you to or near your destination.

ROME

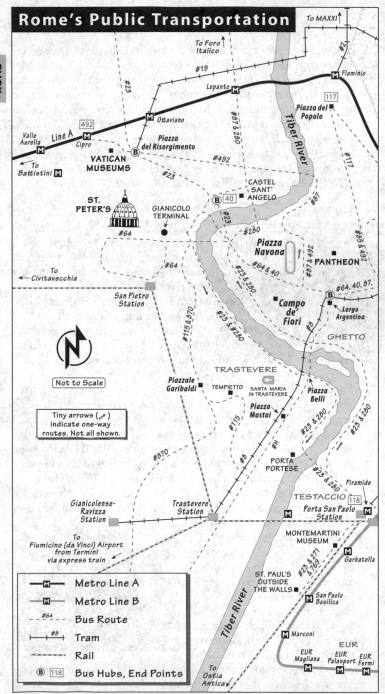

Rome's Public Transportation

To MAXXI↑

To Foro Italico↑

#19

#2

Flaminio

Lepanto

#23

Ottaviano

#87 & 280

Piazza del Popolo

117

To Battistini

Valle Aurelia

Line A

492

Cipro

Piazza del Risorgimento

VATICAN MUSEUMS

#492

#117

Tiber River

#87

ST. PETER'S

GIANICOLO TERMINAL

#64

#23

CASTEL SANT' ANGELO

40

#25

#280

#87 & 492

Piazza Navona

#95 & 492

PANTHEON

#87 & 492

#64 & 40

#64, 40, 87

To Civitavecchia

#64

San Pietro Station

#23 & 280

Campo de' Fiori

Largo Argentina

GHETTO

#115 & 870

#23 & 280

#8

N

Not to Scale

Tiny arrows (⬎) indicate one-way routes. Not all shown.

TRASTEVERE

Piazzale Garibaldi

TEMPIETTO

SANTA MARIA IN TRASTEVERE

Piazza Belli

#23 & 280

Piazza Mastai

#115

#23 & 280

#8

#H

PORTA PORTESE

#870

Gianicolense-Ravizza Station

Trastevere Station

Piramide

TESTACCIO

118

Porta San Paolo Station

To Fiumicino (da Vinci) Airport from Termini via express train

MONTEMARTINI MUSEUM

#23 & 271 & 769

Garbatella

ST. PAUL'S OUTSIDE THE WALLS

San Paolo Basilica

Tiber River

Marconi

EUR

EUR Magliana

EUR Palasport

EUR Fermi

To Ostia Antica↓

Ⓜ	Metro Line A
Ⓜ	Metro Line B
#64	Bus Route
#8	Tram
	Rail
Ⓑ 118	Bus Hubs, End Points

ROME

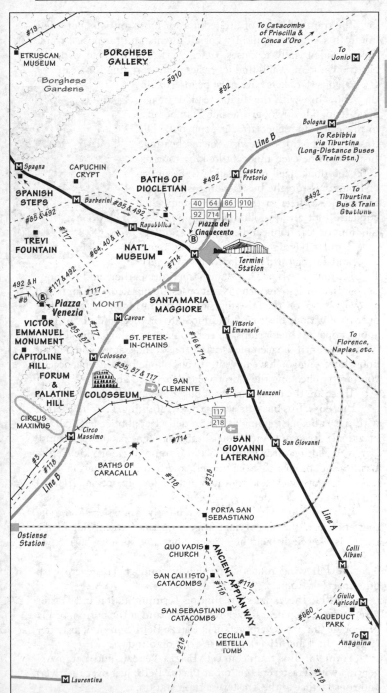

The tram lines are of limited use for most tourists, but a few lines can save some walking. For all intents and purposes, trams function identically to buses. Once you're comfortable with the bus/tram system, you'll find it's easier than searching for a cab.

On buses, tickets have must be inserted in the yellow box with the digital readout (magnetic-strip-side down, arrow-side first; be sure to retrieve your ticket after it's spit out). Do this as you board, otherwise you're cheating. Inspectors fine even innocent-looking tourists €50. You don't need to validate a transit pass or Roma Pass on the bus, as long as it's been stamped elsewhere in the transit system. Bus etiquette (not always followed) is to board at the front or rear doors and exit at the middle.

Regular bus lines start running at about 5:30, and during the day major routes run every 10-15 minutes. After 23:30 (and sometimes earlier) and on Sundays, buses are less frequent. Night buses are marked with an *N* and an owl symbol on the bus-stop signs. Frustratingly, the exact frequency of various bus routes is difficult to predict (and not printed at bus stops). At major stops, an electronic board shows the number of minutes until the next buses arrive, but at most stops you'll never know how long you have to wait. If your phone has Internet access, you can try checking the journey planners listed above.

These are the most important bus routes for tourists:

Bus #64: This bus cuts across the city, linking Termini Station with the Vatican, stopping at Piazza della Repubblica (sights), Via Nazionale (recommended hotels), Piazza Venezia (near Forum), Largo Argentina (near Pantheon and Campo de' Fiori), St. Peter's Basilica (get off just past the tunnel), and San Pietro Station. Ride it for a city overview and to watch pickpockets in action. The #64 can get horribly crowded.

Bus #40: This express bus, which mostly follows the #64 route (but ends near the Castel Sant'Angelo on the Vatican side of the river), is especially helpful—fewer stops and (somewhat) fewer crowds.

The following routes conveniently connect Trastevere with other parts of Rome:

Bus #H: This express bus, linking Termini Station and Trastevere, makes a stop near Piazza Repubblica and at the bottom of Via Nazionale (for Trastevere, get off at Piazza Belli/Sonnino, just after crossing the Tiber River). It doesn't run on Sundays.

Tram #8: This tram connects Piazza Venezia and Largo Argentina with Trastevere (get off at Piazza Belli, just over the river) and runs farther to the Trastevere train station.

Buses #23 and #280: These link the Vatican with Trastevere and Testaccio, stopping at the Vatican Museums (nearest stop is Via Leone IV), Castel Sant'Angelo, Trastevere (Piazza Belli), Porta Portese (Sunday flea market), and Piramide (Metro and gateway to Testaccio).

Other useful routes include:

Bus #49: Piazza Cavour/Castel Sant'Angelo, Piazza Risorgimento (Vatican), and Vatican Museums.

Bus #62: Tiburtina, Piazza Barberini, Piazza Venezia, Piazza Pia (near Castel Sant'Angelo).

Bus #81: San Giovanni in Laterano, Largo Argentina, and Piazza Risorgimento (Vatican).

Buses #85 and #87: Piazza Navona (#87 only), Pantheon, Via del Corso (#85 only), Piazza Venezia, Forum, Colosseum, San Clemente, and San Giovanni in Laterano.

Bus #492: Travels east-west across the city, connecting Tiburtina (train and bus stations), Largo Santa Susanna (near Piazza della Repubblica), Piazza Barberini, Piazza Venezia, Largo Argentina (near Pantheon and Campo de' Fiori), Piazza Cavour (Castel Sant'Angelo), and Piazza Risorgimento (St. Peter's Basilica and Vatican).

Tram #3: Zips from the Colosseum to the Etruscan Museum in one direction, and to Trastevere in the other.

Tram #19: Connects Piazza del Risorgimento and the Ottaviano Metro stop (by the Vatican Museums) to the Villa Borghese.

***Elettrico* Minibuses:** Cute *elettrico* minibuses that wind through the narrow streets of old and interesting neighborhoods are great for transport or simple joyriding (although they're so small it can be hard to find a seat). *Elettrico* #117 connects San Giovanni in Laterano, Colosseo, Via dei Serpenti, Trevi Fountain, Piazza di Spagna, and Piazza del Popolo—and vice versa. Where Via del Corso hits Piazza del Popolo, a #117 is usually parked and ready to go. Riding it from here to the end of the line, San Giovanni in Laterano, makes for a fine joyride that leaves you, conveniently, at a great sight.

By Taxi

I use taxis in Rome more often than in other cities. They're reasonable and useful for efficient sightseeing in this big, hot metropolis. Taxis start at €3, then charge about €1.50 per kilometer (surcharges: €1.50 on Sun, €3.50 for nighttime hours of

22:00-6:00, one regular suitcase or bag rides free, tip by rounding up—€1 or so). Sample fares: Termini area to Vatican-€15; Termini area to Colosseum-€7; Termini area to the Borghese Gallery-€9; Colosseum to Trastevere-€12 (or look up your route at www.worldtaximeter.com). Three or four companions with more money than time should taxi almost everywhere.

Romans don't hail taxis. Find the nearest taxi stand (many are marked on this book's maps) or ask a passerby or a clerk in a shop, *"Dov'è una fermata dei taxi?"* (doh-VEH OO-nah fehr-MAH-tah DEH-ee TAHK-see). Easiest of all, have your hotel or restaurant call a taxi for you. (It's routine for Romans to ask the restaurant to call a taxi when they're ready to go.) The meter starts when the call is received. To call a cab on your own, dial 06-3570, 06-4994, or 06-6645, or use the official city taxi line, 06-0609; they'll likely ask you for an Italian phone number (give them your mobile number or your hotel's).

Beware of corrupt taxis. First, only use official Rome taxis. They're white, with a taxi sign on the roof and a maroon logo on the door that reads *Roma Capitale*. When you get in, make sure the meter *(tassametro)* is turned on (you'll see the meter either on the dashboard or up by the rearview mirror). If the meter isn't on, get out and find another cab. Check that the meter is reset to the basic drop charge (should be around €3, or around €5 if you phoned for the taxi). Some meters show both the fare and the time elapsed during the ride, and some tourists—mistaking the time for the fare—end up paying more than the fair meter rate. Also, keep an eye on the fare on the meter as you near your destination; some cabbies turn the meter off instantly when they stop and tell you a higher price.

By law, every cab must display a multilingual official price chart—usually on the back of the seat in front of you. If the fare doesn't seem right, point to the chart and ask the cabbie to explain it. When you pay the cabbie, have your wits about you. A common cabbie scam is to take your €20 note, drop it, and pick up a €5 note (similar color), claiming that's what you gave him. To avoid this scam, pay in small bills; if you only have a large bill, show it to the cabbie as you state its face value.

At the train station or airport, avoid hustlers conning naive visitors into unmarked, rip-off "express taxis" (for tips on taking a taxi from the airport, including how not to get scammed, see page 937). If you encounter any problems with a taxi, making a show of writing down the taxi number (to file a complaint) can motivate a driver to quickly settle the matter.

Tours in Rome

On Foot

Local guides are good but pricey. Tour companies are cheaper, but quality and organization are unreliable. If you do hire a private Italian guide and it feels tough on your budget, consider inviting others from your hotel to join you and split the cost (around €180 for a three-hour tour). This ends up costing about the same per person as going on a scheduled tour from one of the walking-tour companies listed below—and you'll likely get a better guide.

🎧 To sightsee on your own, download my free audio tours that illuminate some of Rome's top sights and neighborhoods, including walks through the "Heart of Rome," Jewish Ghetto, and Trastevere, and tours of the Pantheon, Colosseum, Roman Forum, St. Peter's Basilica, Vatican Museums, and Sistine Chapel (see sidebar on page 12 for details).

Local Guides

I've worked with and enjoyed each of these licensed independent local guides. They're native Italians, speak excellent English, and enjoy tailoring tours to your interests. Their prices (roughly €60/hour) flex with the day, season, and demand. Arrange your date and price by email. **Carla Zaia** (carlaromeguide@gmail.com); **Cristina Giannicchi** (mobile 338-111-4573, www.crisromanguide.com, crisgiannicchi@gmail.com); **Sara Magister** (a.magister@iol.it); **Giovanna Terzulli** (gioterzulli@gmail.com); **Alessandra Mazzoccoli** (www.romeandabout.com, alemazzoccoli@gmail.com); and **Massimiliano Canneto** (a Catholic guide with a Vatican forte, but does all of Rome, massicanneto@gmail.com).

Francesca Caruso, who works almost full time with my tours when in Rome, has contributed generously to this chapter (www.francescacaruso.com, francescainroma@gmail.com). Popular with my readers, Francesca understandably books up quickly; if she's busy, she'll recommend one of her colleagues. At her website you can listen to the many interviews I've enjoyed with Francesca on my public radio program.

Walking-Tour Companies

Rome has many highly competitive tour companies, each offering a series of themed walks through various slices of Rome. Three-hour guided walks generally cost €25-30 per person. Guides are usually native English speakers, often American expats. Tours are limited to small groups, geared to American tourists, and given in English only. Before your trip, spend some time on these companies' websites to get to know your options, as each company has a particular teaching and guiding personality. Some are highbrow and more expensive. Others are less scholarly. It's sometimes required, and

Rome at a Glance

▲▲▲**Colosseum** Huge stadium where gladiators fought. **Hours:** Daily 8:30 until one hour before sunset: April-Aug until 19:15, Sept until 19:00, Oct until 18:30, off-season closes as early as 16:30. See page 831.

▲▲▲**Roman Forum** Ancient Rome's main square, with ruins and grand arches. **Hours:** Same as Colosseum. See page 836.

▲▲▲**Capitoline Museums** Ancient statues, mosaics, and expansive view of Forum. **Hours:** Daily 9:30-19:30. See page 849.

▲▲▲**Pantheon** The defining domed temple. **Hours:** Mon-Sat 8:30-19:30, Sun 9:00-18:00, holidays 9:00-13:00. See page 856.

▲▲▲**St. Peter's Basilica** Most impressive church on earth, with Michelangelo's *Pietà* and dome. **Hours:** Church—daily April-Sept 7:00-19:00, Oct-March until 18:00, often closed Wed mornings; dome—daily April-Sept 8:00-18:00, Oct-March until 17:00. See page 859.

▲▲▲**Vatican Museums** Four miles of the finest art of Western civilization, culminating in Michelangelo's glorious Sistine Chapel. **Hours:** Mon-Sat 9:00-18:00. Closed on religious holidays and Sun, except last Sun of the month (open 9:00-14:00). May be open some Fri nights by online reservation only. Hours are subject to change. See page 869.

▲▲▲**Borghese Gallery** Bernini sculptures and paintings by Caravaggio, Raphael, and Titian in a Baroque palazzo. Reservations mandatory. **Hours:** Tue-Sun 9:00-19:00, closed Mon. See page 879.

▲▲▲**National Museum of Rome** Greatest collection of Roman sculpture anywhere. **Hours:** Tue-Sun 9:00-19:45, closed Mon. See page 884.

▲▲**Palatine Hill** Ruins of emperors' palaces, Circus Maximus view, and museum. **Hours:** Same as Colosseum. See page 846.

▲▲**Trajan's Column, Market, and Forum** Tall column with narrative relief, forum ruins, and museum with entry to Trajan's Market. **Hours:** Forum and column always viewable; museum open daily 9:30-19:30. See page 851.

▲▲**Museo dell'Ara Pacis** Shrine marking the beginning of Rome's Golden Age. **Hours:** Daily 9:30-19:30. See page 819.

▲▲**Dolce Vita Stroll** Evening *passeggiata*, where Romans strut their stuff. **Hours:** Roughly Mon-Sat 17:00-19:00 and Sun afternoons. See page 817.

▲▲**Catacombs of Priscilla** Underground tomb just outside city walls. **Hours:** Tue-Sun 9:00-12:00 & 14:00-17:00, closed Mon, closed one random month a year. See page 883.

▲**Arch of Constantine** Honors the emperor who legalized Christianity. **Hours:** Always viewable. See page 835.

▲**St. Peter-in-Chains** Church with Michelangelo's *Moses*. **Hours:** Daily 8:00-12:20 & 15:00-19:00, off-season until 18:00. See page 854.

▲**Piazza del Campidoglio** Square atop Capitoline Hill, designed by Michelangelo, with a museum, grand stairway, and Forum overlooks. **Hours:** Always open. See page 847.

▲**Victor Emmanuel Monument** Gigantic edifice celebrating Italian unity, with "Rome from the Sky" elevator ride up to 360-degree city view. **Hours:** Monument open daily 9:30-18:30; elevator open Mon-Thu 9:30-18:30, Fri-Sun until 19:30. See page 850.

▲**Trevi Fountain** Baroque hot spot into which tourists throw coins to ensure a return trip to Rome. **Hours:** Always flowing. See page 858.

▲**Baths of Diocletian/Basilica S. Maria degli Angeli** Once ancient Rome's immense public baths, now a Michelangelo church. **Hours:** Mon-Sat 7:00-18:30, Sun 7:00-19:30. See page 885.

always smart, to book a spot in advance (easy online). Readers report that advertising can be misleading, and scheduling mishaps are common. Make sure you know what you are booking and when.

These companies are each well-established, creative, and competitive with their various tours explained on their websites. Each offers a 10 percent discount with online bookings for Rick Steves travelers:

Enjoy Rome (tel. 06-445-1843, www.enjoyrome.com, info@enjoyrome.com).

Rome Walks (mobile 347-795-5175, www.romewalks.com, info@romewalks.com, Annie).

Europe Odyssey (tel. 06-8854-2416, mobile 328-912-3720, www.europeodyssey.com, Rahul).

Through Eternity (for discount look for "Group Tours Rome" and enter "RICKSTEVES," tel. 06-700-9336, www.througheternity.com, office@througheternity.com, Rob).

Walks of Italy (for discount enter "10ricksteves," US tel. 888/683-8670, tel. 06-9480-4888, www.walksofitaly.com).

The Roman Guy (enter "ricksteves" for discount, ask about electric-assist bike tours, www.theromanguy.com, Sean Finelli).

Miles & Miles Private Tours, described under "Car & Minibus Tours," below, also offers walking tours (www.milesandmiles.net).

Context Rome's walking tours are more intellectual than most, designed for travelers with longer-than-average attention spans. They are more expensive than others (no discounts) and are led by "docents" rather than guides (tel. 06-9672-7371, US tel. 800-691-6036, www.contexttravel.com).

Sketching Rome Tours, offered by American expat Kelly Medford, draw on your creative side with fun, three-hour sketching tours geared to (aspiring) artists of any skill level ($125, www.sketchingrometours.com).

On Wheels
Hop-On, Hop-Off Bus Tours
Several different agencies run hop-on, hop-off tours around Rome. These tours are constantly evolving and offer varying combinations of sights. You can grab one (and pay as you board; usually around €20) at any stop; Termini Station and Piazza Venezia are handy hubs. Although the city is perfectly walkable and traffic jams can

make the bus dreadfully slow, these open-top bus tours remain popular.

Car and Minibus Tours

Miles & Miles Private Tours, a family-run company, offers a number of tours, all with good English-speaking Italian driver/guides (descriptions and pricing on their website, mention Rick Steves when booking directly, then show the book on the day of service to get a discount). They also provide walking tours, shore excursions (from Civitavecchia, Livorno, Naples, Venice, and other ports), and unguided long-distance transportation; if traveling with a small group or a family from Rome to Florence, the Amalfi Coast, or elsewhere, consider paying extra to turn the trip into a memorable day tour with door-to-door service (mobile 331-166-4900, www.milesandmiles.net, info@milesandmiles.net).

Tour Packages for Students

Andy Steves (Rick's son) runs Weekend Student Adventures (WSA Europe), offering 3- and 10-day budget travel packages across Europe including accommodations, skip-the-line sightseeing, and unique local experiences. Locally guided and DIY unguided options are available for student and budget travelers in 12 of Europe's most popular cities, including Rome (guided trips from €199, see www.wsaeurope.com for details).

Walks in Rome

These self-guided walks give you a moving picture of Rome, an ancient yet modern city. You'll take a refreshing early evening walk (Dolce Vita Stroll) and enjoy the thriving local scene, best at night (Heart of Rome Walk).

DOLCE VITA STROLL

This is Romans' favorite place for a chic evening stroll, worth ▲▲ (and a Mediterranean institution; see the sidebar on page 891). You'll walk from Piazza del Popolo (Metro: Flaminio) down a wonderfully traffic-free section of Via del Corso, and up Via Condotti to the Spanish Steps. Although busy at any hour, this area really attracts crowds from around 17:00 to 19:00 each evening (Fri and Sat are best), except on Sunday, when it occurs earlier in the afternoon. Leave before 18:00 if you plan to visit the Ara Pacis (Altar of Peace), which closes at 19:30.

As you stroll, you'll see shoppers, people watchers, and flirts on the prowl filling this neighborhood of some of Rome's most fashionable stores (some open after siesta, roughly 16:00-19:30). The most elegance survives in the grid of streets between Via

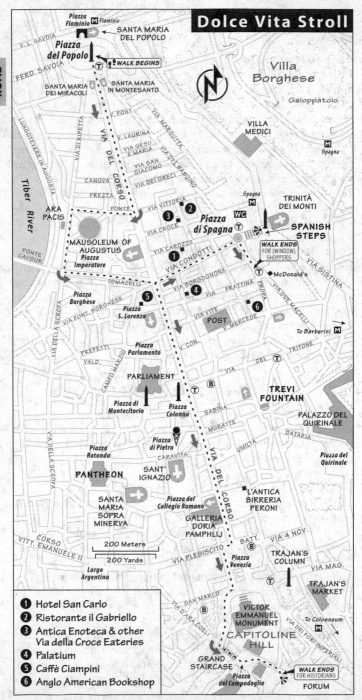

Dolce Vita Stroll

ROME

1 Hotel San Carlo
2 Ristorante il Gabriello
3 Antica Enoteca & other Via della Croce Eateries
4 Palatium
5 Caffè Ciampini
6 Anglo American Bookshop

del Corso and the Spanish Steps. If you get hungry during your stroll, see page 925 for listings of neighborhood wine bars and restaurants.

To reach **Piazza del Popolo,** where the stroll starts, take Metro line A to Flaminio and walk south to the square. Delightfully car-free, Piazza del Popolo is marked by an obelisk that was brought to Rome by Augustus after he conquered Egypt. (It used to stand in the Circus Maximus.) In medieval times, this area was just inside Rome's main entry (for more background on the square, see page 701).

If starting your stroll early enough, the Baroque church of **Santa Maria del Popolo** is worth popping into (Mon-Sat until 19:00, Sun until 19:30, next to gate in old wall on north side of square). Inside, look for Raphael's Chigi Chapel (second on left as you face the main altar) and two paintings by Caravaggio (in the Cerasi Chapel, left of altar).

From Piazza del Popolo, shop your way down **Via del Corso.** Though many Italians shop online or at the mall these days, this remains a fine place to feel the pulse of Rome at twilight.

History buffs can side-trip right down Via Pontefici past the fascist architecture to see the massive, round-brick **Mausoleum of Augustus,** topped with overgrown cypress trees. This long-neglected sight, honoring Rome's first emperor, is slated for restoration and redevelopment. Beyond it, next to the river, is the **Ara Pacis,** consecrated by Augustus in 9 B.C. and today enclosed within a protective glass-walled museum worth ▲▲ (€10.50, or look in through huge windows for free, daily 9:30-19:30). From the mausoleum, walk down Via Tomacelli to return to Via del Corso and the 21st century.

From Via del Corso, window shoppers should take a left down **Via Condotti** to join the parade to the **Spanish Steps** (described in more detail later, under the Heart of Rome Walk), passing big-name boutiques. The streets that parallel Via Condotti to the south (Borgognona and Frattina) are also elegant and filled with high-end shops. A few streets to the north hides the narrow Via Margutta. This is where Gregory Peck's *Roman Holiday* character lived (at #51); today it has a leafy tranquility and is filled with pricey artisan and antique shops.

Historians: Another option is to ignore Via Condotti and forget the Spanish Steps. Stay on Via del Corso, which has been straight since Roman times, and walk a half-mile down to the Victor Emmanuel Monument. Climb Michelangelo's stairway to his glorious (especially when floodlit) square atop Capitoline Hill. Stand on the balcony (just past the mayor's palace on the right), which overlooks the Forum. As the horizon reddens and cats prowl the unclaimed rubble of ancient Rome, it's one of the finest views in the city.

HEART OF ROME WALK

Rome's most colorful neighborhood features narrow lanes, intimate piazzas, fanciful fountains, and some of Europe's best people-watching. During the day, this walk—worth ▲▲▲—shows off the colorful Campo de' Fiori market and trendy fashion boutiques as it meanders past major monuments such as the Pantheon and the Spanish Steps.

But the sunset brings unexpected magic. A stroll in the cool of the evening is made memorable by the romance of the Eternal City at its best. Sit so close to a bubbling fountain that traffic noise evaporates. Jostle with kids to see the gelato flavors. Watch lovers straddling more than the bench. Jaywalk past *polizia* in flak-proof vests. And marvel at the ramshackle elegance that softens this brutal city for those who were born here and can't imagine living anywhere else. These are the flavors of Rome, best enjoyed after dark.

This walk is equally pleasant in reverse order. You could ride the Metro to the Spanish Steps and finish at Campo de' Fiori, near many recommended restaurants.

Length of This Walk: Allow anywhere from one to three hours for this mile-long walk, depending on whether you linger and tour the Pantheon. To lengthen this walk, you could continue on from the Spanish Steps to Piazza del Popolo.

Tours: 🎧 Download my free Heart of Rome Walk audio tour.

❷ Self-Guided Walk

• *Start this walk at Campo de' Fiori, my favorite outdoor dining room (especially after dark—see "Eating in Rome" on page 909). It's a few blocks west of Largo Argentina, a major transportation hub. Buses #40, #64, and #492, and tram #8, stop at Largo Argentina and/or along Corso Vittorio Emanuele II (a long block northwest of Campo de' Fiori). A taxi from Termini station costs about €10.*

❶ **Campo de' Fiori:** Kick off this walk in one of Rome's most colorful spots, Campo de' Fiori. This bohemian piazza hosts a fruit and vegetable **market** in the morning, cafés in the evening, and crowds of drunks late at night. In ancient times, the "Field of Flowers" was an open meadow. Later, Christian pilgrims passed through on their way to the Vatican, and a thriving market developed.

Lording over the center of the square is a statue of **Giordano Bruno,** an intellectual heretic who was burned on this spot in 1600. The pedestal shows scenes from Bruno's trial and execution, and reads, "And the flames rose up." The statue honoring the heretic faces a Vatican administration building and was erected in 1889, a time when the new state of Italy and the Vatican were feuding. The Vatican protested, but they were overruled by angry neighborhood locals. This district is still known for its free spirit and antiauthoritarian demonstrations.

Campo de' Fiori is the product of centuries of unplanned urban development. At the east end of the square (behind Bruno), ramshackle apartments are built right into the old outer wall of ancient Rome's mammoth Theater of Pompey (you can actually see two white columns and bits of the ancient wall high above street level). This entertainment complex covered several city blocks, stretching from here to Largo Argentina. Julius Caesar was assassinated in the Theater of Pompey, where the Senate was meeting while its main Forum building was being repaired after a fire.

The square is surrounded by fun eateries, and is great for people-watching. Bruno faces the bustling **Forno** (in the left corner of the square), where takeout *pizza bianca* is sold hot out of the oven. On weekend nights, when the Campo is packed with beer-drinking kids, the medieval square is transformed into one vast Roman street party.

• *If Bruno did a hop, step, and jump forward, then turned left, in a block he'd reach...*

❷ **Piazza Farnese:** While the higgledy-piggledy Campo de' Fiori feels free and easy, the 16th-century Renaissance Piazza Farnese, named for the family whose palace dominates it, seems to stress order. The Farnese family was nouveau riche and needed to make a statement. They hired Michelangelo to design the top part of their palace's facade—which today houses the French embassy, hence the French flag and the security. The twin Roman tubs in the fountains decorating the square date from the third century and are from the Baths of Caracalla. They ended up here because Pope Paul III, who was a Farnese, ordered the excavation of the baths, and the family had first dibs on the choicest finds.

• *Walk back to Campo de' Fiori, cross the square, and continue a couple of blocks down...*

❸ **Via dei Baullari and Corso Vittorio Emanuele II:** As you slalom through the crowds, notice the crush of cheap cafés, bars, and restaurants—the center of medieval Rome is morphing into a playground for tourists, students, and locals visiting from the suburbs. High rents are driving families out and changing the character of this district. That's why the Campo de' Fiori market

ROME

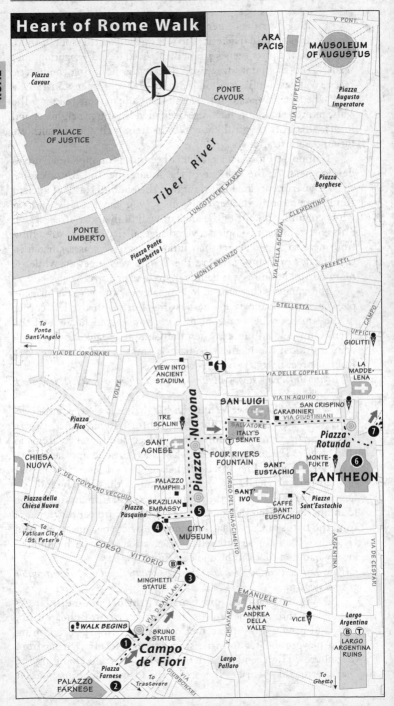

Heart of Rome Walk

ARA PACIS

MAUSOLEUM OF AUGUSTUS

Piazza Cavour

V. PONT.

PALACE OF JUSTICE

PONTE CAVOUR

V. DI RIPETTA

Piazza Augusto Imperatore

Tiber River

LUNGOTEVERE MARZIO

Piazza Borghese

PONTE UMBERTO

VIA DELLA SCROFA

CLEMENTINO

To Ponte Sant'Angelo

Piazza Ponte Umberto I

MONTE BRIANZO

VIA DELLA SCROFA

PREFETTI

STELLETTA

CAMPO

VIA DEI CORONARI

VIEW INTO ANCIENT STADIUM

VIA DELLE COPPELLE

UFFICI GIOLITTI

LA MADDE-LENA

VOLPE

Piazza Fico

TRE SCALINI

Piazza Navona

SAN LUIGI

VIA IN AQUIRO

SAN CRISPINO

CARABINIERI
VIA GIUSTINIANI

SALVATORE
ITALY'S SENATE

SANT' AGNESE

FOUR RIVERS FOUNTAIN

Piazza Rotunda

CHIESA NUOVA

V. DEL GOVERNO VECCHIO

SANT' EUSTACHIO

MONTE-FURKE

PANTHEON

Piazza della Chiesa Nuova

PALAZZO PAMPHILJ

SANT' IVO

CAFFÈ SANT' EUSTACHIO

CORSO DEL RINASCIMENTO

To Vatican City & St. Peter's

BRAZILIAN EMBASSY

Piazza Pasquino

CITY MUSEUM

Piazza Sant'Eustachio

ARGENTINA

VIA DE CESTARI

CORSO VITTORIO

MINGHETTI STATUE

VIA D. BAULLARI

EMANUELE II

SANT' ANDREA DELLA VALLE

VICE

Largo Argentina

WALK BEGINS

BRUNO STATUE

Campo de' Fiori

Y. CHIAVARI

LARGO ARGENTINA RUINS

Piazza Farnese

VIA GIUBBONARI

Largo Pallaro

To Ghetto

PALAZZO FARNESE

To Trastevere

ROME

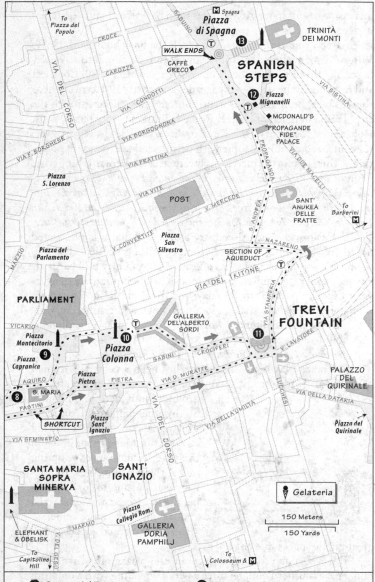

To
Piazza
del
Popolo

CROCE

VIA DEL CORSO

CAROZZE

BABUINO

M Spagna
*Piazza
di Spagna*

WALK ENDS Ⓣ

CAFFÈ
GRECO

Ⓑ

TRINITÀ
DEI MONTI

**SPANISH
STEPS**

VIA SISTINA

VIA CONDOTTI

VIA BORGOGNONA

VIA FRATTINA

Ⓒ *Piazza
Mignanelli*
Ⓣ

◆ MCDONALD'S

"PROPAGANDE
FIDE"
PALACE

PROPAGANDA

VIA DUE MACELLI

VIA F. BORGHESE

*Piazza
S. Lorenzo*

VIA VITE

POST

V. MERCEDE

S. ANDREA

SANT'
ANDREA
DELLE
FRATTE

To
Barberini
M

MARZIO

*Piazza del
Parlamento*

V. CONVERTITE

*Piazza
San
Silvestro*

SECTION OF
AQUEDUCT

NAZARENO

Ⓣ

VIA DEL TRITONE

PARLIAMENT

VICARIO

*Piazza
Montecitorio*

Ⓘ

*Piazza
Capranica*

AQUIRO

Ⓗ

S. MARIA

PASTINI

SHORTCUT

VIA SEMINARIO

Ⓣ

*Piazza
Colonna*
Ⓙ

GABINI

*Piazza
Pietra*

PIETRA

GALLERIA
DELL'ALBERTO
SORDI

CROCIFERI

VIA D. MURATTE

VIA STAMPERIA

**TREVI
FOUNTAIN**

Ⓚ

V. LAVATORE

LUCCHESI

**PALAZZO
DEL
QUIRINALE**

VIA DELLA DATARIA

*Piazza
Sant'
Ignazio*

VIA DEL CORSO

VIA DELL'UMILTÀ

*Piazza del
Quirinale*

**SANTA MARIA
SOPRA
MINERVA**

**SANT'
IGNAZIO**

V. DEL GESU

MARMO

*Piazza
Collegio Rom.*

**ELEPHANT
& OBELISK**

To
Capitoline
Hill

**GALLERIA
DORIA
PAMPHILJ**

To
Colosseum & **M**

🍦 Gelateria

150 Meters

150 Yards

Ⓐ Campo de' Fiori
Ⓑ Piazza Farnese
Ⓒ Via dei Baullari &
   Corso Vittorio Emanuele II
Ⓓ Pasquino Statue
Ⓔ Piazza Navona
Ⓕ Pantheon
Ⓖ Caffè Tazza d'Oro

Ⓗ Piazza Capranica
Ⓘ Piazza di Montecitorio
Ⓙ Piazza Colonna & Via del Corso
Ⓚ Trevi Fountain
Ⓛ Column of the Immaculate
   Conception
Ⓜ Spanish Steps

increasingly sells more gifty edibles than basic fruits and vegetables with each passing year.

After a couple of blocks, you reach the busy boulevard, Corso Vittorio Emanuele II. In Rome, any road big enough to have city buses like this is post-unification: constructed after 1870. Look left and right down the street—the facades are mostly 19th century neo-Renaissance, built after this main thoroughfare sliced through the city. Traffic in much of central Rome is limited to city buses, taxis, motorbikes, "dark cars" (limos and town cars of VIPs), delivery vans, residents, and disabled people with permits (a.k.a., friends of politicians). This is one of the increasingly rare streets where anything goes.

• *Cross Corso Vittorio Emanuele II, and enter a square with a statue of Marco Minghetti, an early Italian prime minister. Angle left at the statue, walking along the left side of the Museum of Rome, down Via di San Pantaleo. A block down, at the corner, you'll find a beat-up old statue.*

❹ **Pasquino:** A third-century B.C. statue that was discovered near here, Pasquino, is one of Rome's "talking statues." For 500 years, this statue has served as a kind of community billboard, allowing people to complain anonymously when it might be dangerous to speak up. And, to this day, you'll see old Pasquino strewn with political posters, strike announcements, and grumbling graffiti. The statue looks literally worn down by centuries of complaining about bad government.

• *Wrap around Pasquino and head up Via di Pasquino to...*

❺ **Piazza Navona:** This square has been a center of Roman life since ancient times. It retains the oblong shape of the athletic

grounds built here around A.D. 80 by the emperor Domitian. Today's square, while following its ancient foundation, is from the late Renaissance. Coming out of the Middle Ages, the papacy was putting major scandals behind it. Rome was energized and laying out more efficient street plans, grand palaces, and great public spaces like this.

Three Baroque fountains decorate the piazza. The first fountain, at the southern end, features a Moor wrestling with a dolphin. In 17th-century Rome, Moors (Africans) represented all that was exotic and mysterious. In the fountain at the northern end, Neptune slays a giant octopus.

The most famous fountain, though, is in the center: the **Four Rivers Fountain** by Gian Lorenzo Bernini, the man who remade Rome in the Baroque style. As the water of the world gushes everywhere, four burly river gods (representing the four quarters of the

world) support an Egyptian-style obelisk that was made in Rome. (The obelisk was popular with Roman emperors because Egyptian society saw its rulers as divine—an idea Rome liked to promote.) Bernini enlivens the fountain with horses plunging through rocks and the exotic flora and fauna of faraway lands.

Stroll around the fountain counterclockwise and admire the gods: The good-looking figure represents the Danube (for Europe). Next comes the Ganges (for Asia), holding an oar. After an exotic palm tree, you find the Nile (for Africa) with his head covered, since its headwaters were unknown back then. Uruguay's Rio de la Plata, representing the Americas, tumbles backward in shock, wondering how he ever made the top four. The spilled coins represent the easy-to-harvest wealth of the New World.

Piazza Navona is Rome's most interesting night scene, with street music, artists, fire-eaters, local Casanovas, ice cream, and outdoor cafés that are worthy of a splurge if you've got time to sit and enjoy Italy's human river.

• *Leave Piazza Navona directly across from* **Tre Scalini** *(famous for its* tartufo, *a rich, chocolate gelato concoction), and go east down Corsia Agonale, past rose peddlers and palm readers. Ahead of you (across the busy street) stands the stately Palazzo Madama, where the Italian Senate meets. (Hence, security is high.) Jog left around this building, and follow the brown sign to the Pantheon, straight down Via del Salvatore.*

After a block, you'll pass (on your left) the **Church of San Luigi dei Francesi,** *with its* très *French decor and precious Caravaggio paintings. If it's open, pop in. Otherwise, continue along, following the crowd, as everyone seems to be heading to the...*

❻ **Pantheon:** Sit for a while under the portico of the Pantheon, perhaps the most magnificent building surviving from ancient Rome.

The 40-foot, single-piece granite columns of the Pantheon's entrance (romantically floodlit and moonlit at night) show the scale the ancient Romans built on. The columns support a triangular Greek-style roof with an inscription that says "M. Agrippa" built it. In fact, it was built *(fecit)* by Emperor Hadrian (A.D. 120), who gave credit to the builder of an earlier structure. This impressive entranceway gives no clue

that the greatest wonder of the building is inside—a domed room that inspired later domes, including Michelangelo's St. Peter's and Brunelleschi's Duomo in Florence.

If the Pantheon is open, go in and take a look around (free to enter; for details on the interior, see page 856). Also consider detouring to several interesting churches near the Pantheon before continuing on the walk (**Santa Maria sopra Minerva,** with its purely Gothic interior, and **Sant'Ignazio,** with its 3-D Baroque illusions, are just a few steps away). For details on these other churches, see page 858.

• *With your back to the Pantheon, veer to the right, uphill toward the yellow sign on Via Orfani that reads* Casa del Caffè—*you've reached the...*

❼ **Caffè Tazza d'Oro:** This is one of Rome's top coffee shops, dating back to the days when this area was licensed to roast coffee beans. Locals come here for a shot of espresso or, when it's hot, a refreshing *granita di caffè con panna* (coffee and crushed ice with whipped cream).

Circle through the interior and absorb the aroma and energy of a classic Italian café scene. Coffee to-go is simply wrong here in Rome. Locals pay at the cashier, bring their receipt to the barista, and enjoy an elegant little break.

• *From here, our walk continues past some interesting landmarks to the Trevi Fountain. If you'd like to get there a bit more directly, you can take a* **shortcut** *by bearing right at the coffee shop onto Via de' Pastini, which leads through Piazza di Pietra (with some surviving chunks of the Temple of Hadrian), then across busy Via del Corso, where it becomes the touristy, pedestrianized Via delle Muratte and heads straight for the fountain.*

To stick with me for the slightly longer version, bear left at the coffee shop and continue up Via degli Orfani to the next square...

❽ **Piazza Capranica:** This square is home to the big, plain Florentine-Renaissance-style Palazzo Capranica (directly opposite as you enter the square). Its stubby tower was once much taller, but when a stronger government arrived, the nobles were all ordered to shorten their towers. The six-story building to the left was once an apartment building for 17th-century Rome's middle class. Like so many of Rome's churches, Santa Maria in Aquiro, the church on the square, is older than the facade it was given during the Baroque period. Notice the circular little shrine on the street corner (between the palace and the apartment building). For centuries, worshipful spots like this have made pilgrims (and, today, tourists) feel welcome.

• *Leave the piazza to the right of the palace, heading down Via in Aquiro. The street jogs to the left and into a square that's home to Italy's Parliament.*

❾ Piazza di Montecitorio: The square is marked by a sixth-century B.C. **Egyptian obelisk** taken as a trophy by Augustus after his victory in Egypt over Mark Antony and Cleopatra. The obelisk—the only one in Rome still capped with a pre-Christian ornament—was originally set up as a sundial. Follow the zodiac markings to the well-guarded front door of Italy's **parliament building.** This is where the lower house meets; you may see politicians, political demonstrations, and TV cameras.

• *One block to your right is Piazza Colonna, where we're heading next—unless you like gelato: A one-block detour to the left (past Albergo Nazionale) brings you to Rome's most famous gelateria. Giolitti is reasonable for takeout or elegant and splurge-worthy for a sit among classy locals (open daily until past midnight, Via Uffici del Vicario 40); get your gelato in a cone (cono) or cup (coppetta).*

❿ Piazza Colonna and Via del Corso: The centerpiece of **Piazza Colonna** is a huge column that's stood on this spot since the second century. The decorative relief wrapped like a scroll around its length (called a "continuous narration") comes with a propaganda message. It depicts the victories of Emperor Marcus Aurelius over the barbarians. When Marcus died in A.D. 180, the barbarians began to get the upper hand, beginning Rome's long three-century fall. Marcus Aurelius once capped the column, but he was replaced by Paul, one of Rome's patron saints. (Peter, the city's other patron saint, stands atop Trajan's Column nearby.)

Beyond Piazza Colonna runs noisy **Via del Corso,** Rome's main north-south boulevard. It's named for the Berber horse races—without riders—that took place here during Carnevale. This wild tradition continued until the late 1800s, when a series of fatal accidents (including, reportedly, one in front of Queen Margherita) led to its cancellation. Historically the street was filled with meat shops. When Via del Corso became one of Rome's first gas-lit streets, in 1854, the butcher shops were banned and replaced by classier boutiques, jewelers, and antique dealers. Nowadays the northern part of Via del Corso is closed to traffic, and for a few hours every evening it becomes a wonderful parade of Romans out for a stroll (see the "Dolce Vita Stroll," earlier). Before crossing the street, look left (to the obelisk marking Piazza del Popolo—the ancient north gate of the city) and right (to the Victor Emmanuel Monument).

• *Cross Via del Corso to enter a big palatial building with columns, the **Galleria Alberto Sordi** shopping mall. To the left are convenient toilets and ahead is Feltrinelli, the biggest Italian bookstore chain.*

Go to the right and exit out the back (if you're here after 21:00, when the mall is closed, circle around the right side of the Galleria on Via dei Sabini). Once out the back, the tourist kitsch builds as you head up Via de Crociferi to the roar of the water, lights, and people at the...

⓫ Trevi Fountain: This fountain shows how Rome took full advantage of the abundance of water brought into the city by its great aqueducts. It was built to celebrate the reopening of several of ancient Rome's aqueducts in the Renaissance and Baroque eras. After a thousand years of surviving on poor-quality well water, Romans could once again enjoy pure water brought from the distant hills east of the city.

This watery Baroque avalanche by Nicola Salvi was completed in 1762. Salvi used the entire Neoclassical facade of the palace

behind the fountain as a theatrical backdrop for the figure of Neptune, who represents water in every form. The statue surfs in his shell-shaped chariot through his wet kingdom—with water gushing from 24 spouts and tumbling over 30 different kinds of plants—while Triton—Neptune's trumpeter—blows his conch shell.

The magic of the square is enhanced by the fact that no vehicular streets directly approach it. You can hear the excitement as you draw near, and then—*bam!*—you're there. The scene is always lively, with lucky Romeos clutching dates while unlucky ones clutch beers. Romantics toss coins over their shoulders, thinking it will give them a wish and assure their return to Rome. That may sound silly, but every year I go through this tourist ritual...and it actually seems to work.

Take some time to people-watch (whisper a few breathy *bellos* or *bellas*) before leaving. There's a peaceful zone at water level on the far right.

• *Facing the Trevi Fountain, walk along its right side up Via della Stamperia. Cross busy Via del Tritone. Continue 100 yards up Via del Nazareno (passing an exposed bit of the ancient aqueduct that for 2,000 years has brought water into Rome). At the T-intersection ahead, veer right on Via Sant'Andrea delle Fratte. The security is protecting the headquarters of Italy's Democratic Party (on the right).*

The street becomes Via di Propaganda, and at the far end (on the right), it's dominated by a palace that, back in the 17th century, housed the Propaganda Fide—the university where missionaries learned how to evangelize. This was just one arm of the Catholic Church's Counter-Reformation "propaganda" movement—a priority after the Protestants began stealing converts.

Here the street opens up into a long piazza. You're approaching the Spanish Steps. But first, pause at the...

⑫ Column of the Immaculate Conception: An ancient column, topped with a statue of Mary, is dedicated to the Immaculate Conception of Mary. In Christian belief, everyone is born with the stain of original sin. But for Mary to be a worthy and super-pure vessel for Jesus, the Catholic Church decided she needed to be "immaculately conceived"—born without sin. Pope Pius IX and the Vatican finally settled the long theological debate in 1854 by formally establishing the dogma of Mary's Immaculate Conception. Three years later, officials erected this column honoring Mary, complete with venerable Church prophets—all in total agreement—at its base. Every year on December 8, the feast day of the Immaculate Conception, this spot is the scene of a special celebration. The pope attends, the fire department places flowers on Mary's statue (see remains of the festooning), and the Christmas season is kicked off.

To Mary's immediate left stands the Spanish embassy to the Vatican. Rome has double the embassies of a normal capital because here countries need two: one to Italy and one to the Vatican. And because of this embassy, the square and its famous steps are called "Spanish."

• *Just 100 yards past Mary, you reach the...*

⑬ Spanish Steps: Piazza di Spagna, with the very popular Spanish Steps, is named for the Spanish embassy to the Vatican,

which has been here for 300 years. It's been the hangout of many Romantics over the years (Keats, Wagner, Openshaw, Goethe, and others). In the 1700s, British aristocrats on the Grand Tour of Europe came here to ponder Rome's decay. The British poet John Keats pondered his mortality, then died of tuberculosis at age 25 in the orange building on the right side of the steps. Fellow Romantic Lord Byron lived across the square at #66. Nearby, Caffè Greco opened in 1760 and was a favored haunt of artists and writers (just down Via dei Condotti at #86, with a historic interior; www.anticocaffegreco.eu).

The wide, curving staircase of the Spanish Steps is one of Rome's iconic sights. Its 138 steps lead sharply up from Piazza di Spagna, forming a butterfly shape as they fan out around a central terrace. The design culminates at the top in an obelisk framed between two Baroque church towers.

The **Sinking Boat Fountain** at the foot of the steps, built by Bernini or his father, Pietro, is powered by an aqueduct. Actually, all of Rome's fountains are aqueduct-powered; their spurts are determined by the water pressure provided by the various aqueducts. This one, for instance, is much weaker than the Trevi's gush.

The piazza is a thriving scene at night. From here you can window-shop along Via Condotti, which stretches away from the steps. This is where Gucci and other big names cater to well-heeled jetsetters. It's clear that the main sight around here is not the famous steps, but the people who sit on them.

• *Our walk is finished. If you'd like to reach the top of the steps sweat-free, take the free elevator just inside the Spagna Metro stop (to the left, as you face the steps; elevator closes at 21:00). A pay WC is underground in the piazza near the Metro entrance, by the middle palm tree (10:00-19:30). The nearby McDonald's (as you face the Spanish Steps, go right one block) is big and lavish, with a salad bar and WC. When you're ready to leave, you can zip home on the Metro (usually open until 23:30, later on Fri-Sat) or grab a taxi at either the north or south side of the piazza.*

Sights in Rome

I've clustered Rome's sights into walkable neighborhoods, some quite close together (see map on page 795). Save transit time by grouping your sightseeing according to location. For example, in one great day you can start at the Colosseum, then go to the Forum, then Capitoline Hill, and from there either to the Pantheon or back to the Colosseum (by way of additional ruins along Via dei Fori Imperiali).

When you see a 𝛀 in a listing, it means the sight is also covered in a free audio tour (via my Rick Steves Audio Europe app—see page 12).

For general tips on sightseeing, see page 1119. Rome's good city-run information website, www.060608.it, lists current opening hours.

ANCIENT ROME

The core of ancient Rome, where the grandest monuments were built, is between the Colosseum and Capitoline Hill. Among the ancient forums, a few modern sights have popped up. I've listed these sights from south to north, starting with the biggies—the Colosseum and Forum—and continuing up to Capitoline Hill and Piazza Venezia. Then, as a pleasant conclusion to your busy day, consider my relaxing self-guided walk back south along the broad, parklike main drag—Via dei Fori Imperiali—with some enticing detours to nearby sights (described in Imperial Forums listing, later).

Ancient Core
▲▲▲Colosseum (Colosseo)

This 2,000-year-old building is the classic example of Roman en-

gineering. Used as a venue for entertaining the masses, this colossal, functional stadium is one of
Europe's most recognizable landmarks. Whether you're playing
gladiator or simply marveling at
the remarkable ancient design and
construction, the Colosseum gets a
unanimous thumbs-up.

Cost and Hours: €12 combo-ticket includes Roman Forum
and Palatine Hill, free and very crowded first Sun of the month,
open daily 8:30 until one hour before sunset (see page 816 for
times), last entry one hour before closing, audioguide-€5.50,
Metro: Colosseo.

Avoiding Lines: Smart travelers buy a ticket in advance, and
visit when fewer people are trying to get in. The Colosseum allows a maximum of 3,000 visitors inside at any one time, so you
may have to wait in a long line even with an advance ticket. (Only
groups get timed-entry tickets that allow them to waltz straight in.)
Generally, crowds are thinner (and lines shorter) in the afternoon
(especially after 15:00 in summer); this is also true at the Forum.
There's usually a huge line at 8:30 when the Colosseum opens.

Ticket-Buying Strategies: You can avoid slow ticket-buyer
lines by buying your combo-ticket in advance online, buying the
Roma Pass, buying a ticket at a less-crowded ticket office, booking
a guided tour, or renting an audioguide or videoguide. Here are
the options:

1. Buy and print a combo-ticket online at www.coopculture.
it (€2 booking fee). Make sure to print the ticket, not the voucher.
The "free tickets" you'll see listed are valid only for EU citizens
with ID.

2. Buy a Roma Pass (see page 804), which you can use to cover
your Colosseum and Forum admissions. The pass is sold at TIs,
many tobacco shops and newsstands, at the green kiosk in front of
the Colosseo Metro station, and at the Roman Forum information
center on Via dei Fori Imperiali (see page 796). It should cost the
same no matter where you buy it.

3. Buy a combo-ticket at a less-crowded place than the Colosseum. First check the Forum/Palatine Hill entrance facing the
Colosseum. If that's also crowded, try the Forum/Palatine Hill entrance 150 yards away, on Via di San Gregorio (facing the Forum,
with Colosseum at your back, go left down the street).

ROME

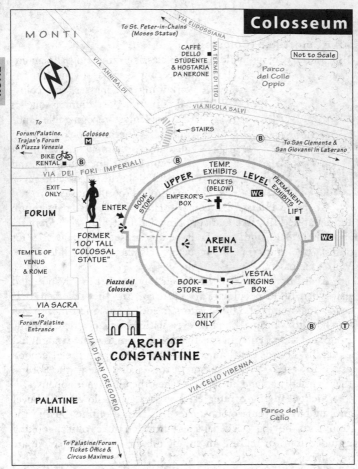

4. Pay to join an official guided tour, or rent an audioguide or videoguide (see "Tours," later). If the guard asks, say that you want to sign up for a tour, and they'll let you march right up to the Colosseum's guided visits *(Visite didattiche)* desk. Even if you don't actually do the tour, the extra cost might be worth it just to skip the ticket line.

5. Hire a private walking-tour guide. Guides of varying quality linger outside the Colosseum, offering tours that may allow you to enter more quickly. Be aware that these private guides may try to mislead you into thinking the Colosseum lines are longer than they really are. Also, the Colosseum administration frowns on these guides and warns visitors against hiring them. For more on this option, see "Tours," later.

Warning: Beware of the crude, modern-day gladiators, hoping to intimidate easy-to-swindle tourists into paying (too much) for a photo op. Also, look out for pickpockets and con artists in this prime tourist spot.

Getting There: The Colosseo Metro stop on line B is just across the street from the monument. Except on Sundays, buses #51, #85, #87, #118, #186, and #810 stop along Via dei Fori Imperiali near the Colosseum entrance, one of the Forum/Palatine Hill entrances, and Piazza Venezia. Tram #3 stops behind the Colosseum.

Getting In: The entrance is divided into two queues: those who need to buy a ticket (the slowest line), and those who are already ticket holders (combo-ticket, online ticket, Roma Pass, or signing up for a tour). There's also a separate entrance for groups, so be sure you follow the signs to get in the right line.

Information: Call center for assistance with tickets and tours: Tel. 06-3996-7700 (Mon-Fri 9:00-13:00 & 14:00-17:00, Sat 9:00-14:00, closed Sun); or www.coopculture.it. General info: www.archeoroma.beniculturali.it/en.

Tours: A fact-filled audioguide is available just past the turnstiles (€5.50/2 hours). A handheld videoguide senses where you are in the site and plays related clips (€6).

🎧 Download my free Colosseum audio tour.

Official guided tours in English depart roughly hourly between 10:15 and 17:15, and last 45-60 minutes (€5 plus Colosseum ticket, purchase inside the Colosseum near the ticket booth marked *Visite didattiche*).

A longer, 1.5-hour tour takes you through areas that are off-limits to regular visitors, including the top floor and underground passageways. While interesting, this tour certainly isn't essential to appreciating the Colosseum. Although it's possible to sign up for this tour at the Colosseum's guided-tours window, advance reservations are strongly advised, either by phone or online (no same-day reservations, see "Information," earlier). After dialing, wait for English instructions on how to reach a live operator.

Private guides stand outside the Colosseum looking for business (€25-30/2-hour tour of the Colosseum, Forum, and Palatine Hill). If booking a private guide, make sure that your tour will start right away and that the ticket you receive covers all three sights: the Colosseum, Forum, and Palatine Hill.

Services: A WC (often crowded) is inside the Colosseum, and there's also a water fountain.

Background: Built when the Roman Empire was at its peak, in A.D. 80, the Colosseum represents Rome at its grandest. The Flavian Amphitheater (the Colosseum's real name) was an arena for gladiator contests and public spectacles. When killing became a spectator sport, the Romans wanted to share the fun with as many people as possible, so they stuck two semicircular theaters together

ROME

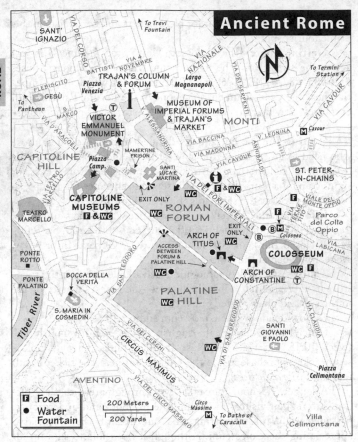

Ancient Rome

To Trevi Fountain

SANT'
IGNAZIO

VIA DEL CORSO

VIA BATTISTI

VIA 4 NOVEMBRE

VIA NAZIONALE

VIA DEI SERPENTI

To Termini
Station

PLEBISCITO

GESÙ

To Pantheon

VIA D'ARACOELI

S. MARCO

Piazza
Venezia

TRAJAN'S COLUMN
& FORUM

Largo
Magnanapoli

MUSEUM OF
IMPERIAL FORUMS
& TRAJAN'S
MARKET

VIA CAVOUR

VICTOR
EMMANUEL
MONUMENT

T

VIA ALESSANDRINA

MONTI

VIA BACCINA

VIA MADONNA

ANNIBALDI

M Cavour

V. LEONINA

Piazza
Camp.

MAMERTINE
PRISON

VIA CAVOUR

ST. PETER-
IN-CHAINS

CAPITOLINE
HILL

VIA TEATRO MARCELLO

CAPITOLINE
MUSEUMS

F & WC

SANTI
LUCA E
MARTINA

EXIT ONLY

i

F & WC

ROMAN
FORUM

WC

VIA DEI FORI IMPERIALI

F

VIALE DEL
MONTE OPPIO

F

VIA TERME TITO

M

Parco
del Colle
Oppio

TEATRO
MARCELLO

B M
Colosseo

VIA LABICANA

PONTE
ROTTO

BOCCA DELLA
VERITÀ

ACCESS
BETWEEN
FORUM &
PALATINE HILL

WC

ARCH OF
TITUS

EXIT
ONLY

WC

COLOSSEUM

PONTE
PALATINO

VIA SAN TEODORO

WC

ARCH OF
CONSTANTINE

WC F

T

S. MARIA IN
COSMEDIN

Tiber River

PALATINE
WC HILL

VIA CLAUDIA

VIA DEI CERCHI

VIA DI SAN GREGORIO

SANTI
GIOVANNI
E PAOLO

CIRCUS MAXIMUS

WC

Piazza
Celimontana

AVENTINO

VIA DEL CIRCO MASSIMO

Circo
Massimo

M

To Baths of
Caracalla

Villa
Celimontana

F Food
● Water
Fountain

200 Meters

200 Yards

to create a freestanding amphitheater. The outside (where slender cypress trees stand today) was decorated with a 100-foot-tall bronze statue of Nero that gleamed in the sunlight. In a later age, the colossal structure was nicknamed a "coloss-eum," the wonder of its age. Towering 150 feet high, it could accommodate 50,000 roaring fans (100,000 thumbs).

Visiting the Colosseum: The exterior says a lot about the Romans. They were great engineers, not artists, and the building is more functional than beautiful. (If ancient Romans visited the US today as tourists, they might send home postcards of our greatest works of "art"—freeways.) While the essential structure of the Colosseum is Roman, the four-story facade is decorated with mostly Greek columns—Doric-like Tuscan columns on the ground level, Ionic on the second story, Corinthian on the next level, and at the top, half-columns with a mix of all three. Originally, copies of

Greek statues stood in the arches of the middle two stories, giving a veneer of sophistication to this arena of death.

Only a third of the original Colosseum remains. Earthquakes destroyed some of it, but most was carted off as easy precut stones for other buildings during the Middle Ages and Renaissance.

The games took place in this oval-shaped arena, 280 feet long by 165 feet wide. When you look down into the arena, you're seeing the underground passages beneath the playing surface (which can only be visited on a private tour). The arena was originally covered with a wooden floor, then sprinkled with sand (*arena* in Latin). The bit of reconstructed floor gives you an accurate sense of the original arena level and the subterranean warren where animals and prisoners were held. As in modern stadiums, the spectators ringed the playing area in bleacher seats that slanted up from the arena floor. Around you are the big brick masses that supported the tiers of seats.

The games began with a few warm-up acts—dogs bloodying themselves attacking porcupines, female gladiators fighting each other, or a one-legged man battling a dwarf. Then came the main event—the gladiators.

"Hail, Caesar! *(Ave, Caesar!)* We who are about to die salute you!" The gladiators would enter the arena from the west end, parade around to the sound of trumpets, acknowledge the Vestal Virgins (on the south side), then stop at the emperor's box (supposedly marked today by the cross that stands at the "50-yard line" on the north side—although no one knows for sure where it was). They would then raise their weapons, shout, and salute—and begin fighting. The fights pitted men against men, men against beasts, and beasts against beasts. Picture 50,000 screaming people around you (did gladiators get stage fright?), and imagine that they want to see you die.

Consider the value of these games in placating and controlling the huge Roman populace. Imagine never having seen an actual lion, and suddenly one jumps out to chase a prisoner in the arena. Seeing the king of beasts slain by a gladiator reminded the masses of man's triumph over nature.

▲Arch of Constantine

This well-preserved arch, which stands between the Colosseum and the Forum, commemorates a military coup and, more importantly, the acceptance of Christianity by the Roman Empire. When the ambitious Emperor Constantine (who had a vision that he'd win under the sign of the cross) defeated his rival Maxentius in A.D. 312, Constantine became sole emperor of the Roman Empire and legalized Christianity. The arch is free to see—always open and viewable.

Roman Forum and Palatine Hill

Though I've covered them separately, the Forum and Palatine Hill are organized as a single sight with one admission (ticket also includes Colosseum). The passage between the Forum and Palatine Hill is near the Arch of Titus. Don't exit the Forum through the turnstiles, hoping to walk down the street to the Palatine and re-enter; you won't be allowed in.

Cost and Hours: €12 combo-ticket includes Roman Forum, Palatine Hill, and Colosseum—see page 831, free and very crowded first Sun of the month, open same hours as Colosseum, audioguide-€5, Metro: Colosseo, tel. 06-3996-7700, www.archeo-roma.beniculturali.it/en.

▲▲▲Roman Forum (Foro Romano)

This is ancient Rome's birthplace and civic center, and the common ground between Rome's famous seven hills. As just about anything important that happened in ancient Rome happened here, it's arguably the most important piece of real estate in Western civilization. While only a few fragments of that glorious past remain, history seekers find plenty to ignite their imaginations amid the half-broken columns and arches.

Avoiding Lines: See tips on page 831.

Getting There: The closest Metro stop is Colosseo. Except on Sundays, buses #51, #85, #87, #118, #186, and #810 stop along Via dei Fori Imperiali near the Colosseum, the Forum, and Piazza Venezia.

Getting In: The Forum and Palatine Hill share three entrances. The handiest (but often most crowded) is directly across from the **Colosseum.** This entrance puts you right by the Arch of Titus, where our tour begins. The **Palatine Hill** entrance (on Via di San Gregorio) is often less crowded. After buying your ticket, reach the Arch of Titus by taking the path to the right; the path to the left goes uphill to the Palatine Hill ruins. A third entrance is along **Via dei Fori Imperiali,** about halfway between the Colosseum and Piazza Venezia, near the intersection with Via Cavour (and through a low-profile building set well back from the street). To reach the Arch of Titus from here, walk down the ramp and turn left.

Tours: An unexciting yet informative audioguide helps decipher the rubble (€5/2 hours, €7 version includes Palatine Hill and lasts 3 hours, must leave ID), but you have to return it to where you rented it—meaning you may not be able to exit directly to Capitoline Hill or the Colosseum, for example.

🎧 Download my free Roman Forum audio tour.

Services: WCs are at the Palatine Hill and Via dei Fori Imperiali ticket entrances. Within the Forum itself, there's one near the Arch of Titus (in the "Soprintendenza" office), and another in the middle, near #6 on the map. Others are atop Palatine Hill.

➍ Self-Guided Tour: As you begin this Forum tour, here's a tip for seeing things with "period eyes." We imagine the structures

in ancient Rome as mostly white, but ornate buildings and monuments like the Arch of Titus were originally more colorful. Through the ages, builders scavenged stone from the Forum, and the finest stone—the colored marble—was cannibalized first. If any was left, it was generally the white stone. Statues that filled the niches were vividly painted, but the organic paint rotted away as statues lay buried for centuries. Lettering was inset bronze and eyes were inset ivory. Even seemingly intact structures, like the Arch of Titus, have been reassembled. Notice the columns are half smooth and half fluted. The fluted halves are original; the smooth parts are reconstructions—intentionally not trying to fake the original.

• *Start at the Arch of Titus, which rises above the rubble on the Colosseum end of the Forum.*

❶ Arch of Titus (Arco di Tito): The Arch of Titus commemorated the Roman victory over the province of Judaea (Israel) in A.D. 70. The Romans had a reputation as benevolent conquerors who tolerated local customs and rulers. All they required was allegiance to the empire, shown by worshipping the emperor as a god. No problem for most conquered people, who already had half a dozen gods on their prayer lists anyway. But Israelites believed in only one god, and it wasn't the emperor. Israel revolted. After a short but bitter war, the Romans defeated the rebels, took Jerusalem, destroyed their temple (leaving only a fragment of one wall's foundation—today's revered "Wailing Wall"), and brought home 50,000 Jewish slaves...who were forced to build this arch (and the Colosseum).

• *Walk down Via Sacra into the Forum. Imagine Roman sandals on these original basalt stones—the oldest street you'll ever walk. Many of*

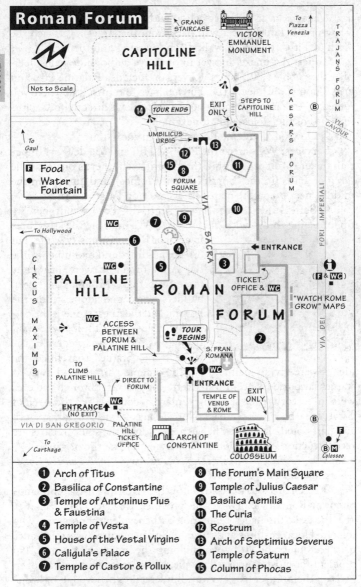

Roman Forum

CAPITOLINE HILL

Not to Scale

GRAND STAIRCASE

VICTOR EMMANUEL MONUMENT

To Piazza Venezia

TRAJAN'S FORUM

VIA CAVOUR

To Gaul

F Food
● Water Fountain

EXIT ONLY

STEPS TO CAPITOLINE HILL

CAESARS FORUM

14 TOUR ENDS

UMBILICUS URBIS

13

12

15

8

FORUM SQUARE

11

10

VIA SACRA

To Hollywood

WC

7

9

6

4

3

← ENTRANCE

5

TICKET OFFICE & **WC**

WC

CIRCUS MAXIMUS

PALATINE HILL

WC

R O M A N

F O R U M

2

FORI IMPERIALI

i **F** & **WC**

"WATCH ROME GROW" MAPS

VIA DEI

ACCESS BETWEEN FORUM & PALATINE HILL

WC

TOUR BEGINS

S. FRAN. ROMANA

1 **WC**

ENTRANCE

TO CLIMB PALATINE HILL

DIRECT TO FORUM

ENTRANCE (NO EXIT)

WC

EXIT ONLY

TEMPLE OF VENUS & ROME

B

F

PALATINE HILL TICKET OFFICE

VIA DI SAN GREGORIO

To Carthage

ARCH OF CONSTANTINE

COLOSSEUM

B **M** Colosseo

1 Arch of Titus	**8** The Forum's Main Square
2 Basilica of Constantine	**9** Temple of Julius Caesar
3 Temple of Antoninus Pius & Faustina	**10** Basilica Aemilia
4 Temple of Vesta	**11** The Curia
5 House of the Vestal Virgins	**12** Rostrum
6 Caligula's Palace	**13** Arch of Septimius Severus
7 Temple of Castor & Pollux	**14** Temple of Saturn
	15 Column of Phocas

the stones under your feet were walked on by Caesar Augustus 2,000 years ago. After about 50 yards, turn right and follow a path uphill to the three huge arches of the...

2 Basilica of Constantine (Basilica Maxentius): Yes, these are big arches. But they represent only one-third of the original Basilica of Constantine, a mammoth hall of justice. The arches were matched by a similar set along the Via Sacra side (only a few squat brick piers remain). Between them ran the central hall, which was spanned by a roof 130 feet high—about 55 feet higher than the side arches you see. (The stub of brick you see sticking up began an arch that once spanned the central hall.) The hall itself was as long as a football field, lavishly furnished with colorful inlaid marble, a gilded bronze ceiling, and statues, and filled with strolling Romans. At the far (west) end was an enormous marble statue of Emperor Constantine on a throne. (Pieces of this statue, including a hand the size of a man, are on display in Rome's Capitoline Museums.)

The basilica was begun by the emperor Maxentius, but after he was trounced in battle, the victor Constantine completed the massive building. No doubt about it, the Romans built monuments on a more epic scale than any previous Europeans, wowing their "barbarian" neighbors.

For the next few years, you'll see construction in and around the basilica for Rome's new Metro line, currently scheduled to reach here in 2021.

• *Now stroll deeper into the Forum, downhill along Via Sacra, through the trees. Pass by the only original bronze door still swinging on its ancient hinges (the green door at the Tempio di Romolo, the round building on the right—if it happens to be open, peek in). Just past that, 10 columns stand in front of a much newer-looking church. The colonnade was part of the...*

❸ **Temple of Antoninus Pius and Faustina:** The Senate built this temple to honor Emperor Antoninus Pius (A.D. 138-161) and his deified wife, Faustina. (The lintel's inscription calls them "*divo*" and "*divae.*") The 50-foot-tall Corinthian (leafy) columns must have been awe-inspiring to out-of-towners who grew up in thatched huts. Although the temple has been inhabited by a church, you can still see the basic layout—a staircase led to a shaded porch (the columns), which admitted you to the main building (now a church), where the statue of the god sat. Originally, these columns supported a triangular pediment decorated with sculptures.

Picture these columns, with gilded capitals, supporting brightly painted statues in the pediment, and the whole building capped with a gleaming bronze roof. The stately gray rubble of today's Forum is a faded black-and-white photograph of a 3-D Technicolor era.

The building is a microcosm of many changes that occurred after Rome fell. In medieval times, the temple was pillaged. Note the diagonal cuts high on the marble columns—a failed attempt by scavengers to cut through the pillars to pull them down for their precious stone. (They used vinegar and rope to cut the marble... but because vinegar also eats through rope, they abandoned the attempt.) In 1550, a church was housed inside the ancient temple.

Rome: Republic and Empire (500 B.C.-A.D. 500)

Ancient Rome lasted for a thousand years, from about 500 B.C. to A.D. 500. During that time, Rome expanded from a small tribe of barbarians to a vast empire, then dwindled slowly to city size again. For the first 500 years, when Rome's armies made her ruler of the Italian peninsula and beyond, Rome was a republic governed by elected senators. Over the next 500 years, a time of world conquest and eventual decline, Rome was an empire ruled by a military-backed dictator.

Julius Caesar bridged the gap between republic and empire. This ambitious general and politician, popular with the people because of his military victories and charisma, suspended the Roman constitution and assumed dictatorial powers in about 50 B.C. A few years later, he was assassinated by a conspiracy of senators. His adopted son, Augustus, succeeded him, and soon "Caesar" was not just a name but a title.

Emperor Augustus ushered in the Pax Romana, or Roman peace (A.D. 1-200), a time when Rome reached her peak and controlled an empire that stretched even beyond Eurail—from England to Egypt, Turkey to Morocco.

The green door shows the street level at the time of Michelangelo. The long staircase was underground until excavated in the 1800s.

• *With your back to the colonnade, walk straight ahead—jogging a bit to the right to stay on the path—and head for the three short columns, all that's left of the...*

❹ **Temple of Vesta:** This is perhaps Rome's most sacred spot. Rome considered itself one big family, and this temple represented a circular hut, like the kind that Rome's first families lived in. Inside, a fire burned, just as in a Roman home. And back in the days before lighters and butane, you never wanted your fire to go out. As long as the sacred flame burned, Rome would stand. The flame was tended by priestesses known as Vestal Virgins.

• *Just to the left and up the stairs is a big, enclosed field with two rectangular brick pools (just below the hill). This was the courtyard of the...*

❺ **House of the Vestal Virgins:** The Vestal Virgins lived in a two-story building surrounding a long central courtyard with two pools at one end. Rows of statues depicting leading Vestal Virgins flanked the courtyard. This place was the model—both architecturally and sexually—for medieval convents and monasteries.

Chosen from noble families before they reached the age of 10, the 6 Vestal Virgins served a 30-year term. Honored and revered by the Romans, the Vestals even had their own box opposite the emperor in the Colosseum. The statues that line the courtyard honor dutiful Vestals.

As the name implies, a Vestal took a vow of chastity. If she served her term faithfully—abstaining for 30 years—she was given a huge dowry and allowed to marry. But if they found any Virgin who wasn't, she was strapped to a funeral car, paraded through the streets of the Forum, taken to a crypt, given a loaf of bread and a lamp...and buried alive. Many women suffered the latter fate.

• *Looming just beyond this field is Palatine Hill—the corner of which may have been...*

❻ **Caligula's Palace (Palace of Tiberius):** Emperor Caligula (ruled A.D. 37-41) had a huge palace on Palatine Hill overlooking the Forum. It actually sprawled down the hill into the Forum (some supporting arches remain in the hillside).

Caligula was not a nice person. He tortured enemies, stole senators' wives, and parked his chariot in handicap spaces. But Rome's luxury-loving emperors only added to the glory of the Forum, each one trying to make his mark on history.

• *Continue downhill, passing the three short columns of the Temple of Vesta, and head for the three taller columns just beyond it.*

❼ **Temple of Castor and Pollux:** These three columns—all that remain of a once-prestigious temple—have become the most photographed sight in the Forum. The temple was one of the city's oldest, built in the fifth century B.C. It commemorated the Roman victory over the Tarquin, the notorious Etruscan king who once oppressed them. After the battle, the legendary twin brothers Castor and Pollux watered their horses here, at the Sacred Spring of Juturna (which has been recently excavated nearby).

As a symbol of Rome's self-governing republic, the temple was often used as a meeting place of senators, and its front steps served as a podium for free speech. The three columns are Corinthian style, featuring leafy capitals and fluting. They date from a later incarnation of the temple (first century).

• *You're now standing at the corner of a flat, grassy area.*

❽ **The Forum's Main Square:** The original Forum, or main square, was this flat patch about the size of a football field, stretching to the foot of Capitoline Hill. Surrounding it were temples, law courts, government buildings, and triumphal arches.

Rome was born right here. According to legend, twin brothers Romulus (Rome) and Remus were orphaned in infancy and raised by a she-wolf on top of Palatine Hill. Growing up, they found it hard to get dates. So they and their cohorts attacked the nearby Sabine tribe and kidnapped their women. After they made peace, this marshy valley became the meeting place and then the trading center for the scattered tribes on the surrounding hillsides.

The square was the busiest and most crowded—and often the seediest—section of town. Besides the senators, politicians, and currency exchangers, there were even sleazier types—souvenir hawkers, pickpockets, fortune-tellers, gamblers, slave marketers, drunks, hookers, lawyers, and tour guides.

Ancient Rome's population exceeded one million, more than any city until London and Paris in the 19th century. All those Roman masses lived in tiny apartments as we would live in tents at a campsite, basically just to sleep. The public space—their Forum, today's piazza—is where they did their living. Consider how, to this day, the piazza is still such an important part of any Italian town. Since Roman times, the piazza has reflected and accommodated the gregarious and outgoing nature of the Italian people.

The Forum is now rubble, but imagine it in its prime: blindingly brilliant marble buildings with 40-foot-high columns and shining metal roofs; rows of statues painted in realistic colors; processional chariots rattling down Via Sacra. Mentally replace tourists in T-shirts with tribunes in togas. Imagine the buildings towering and the people buzzing around you while an orator gives a rabble-rousing speech from the Rostrum. If things still look like just a pile of rocks, at least tell yourself, "But Julius Caesar once leaned against these rocks."

• At the near (east) end of the main square (the Colosseum is to the east) are the foundations of a temple now capped with a peaked wood-and-metal roof.

❾ **Temple of Julius Caesar (Tempio del Divo Giulio, or Ara di Cesare):** On March 15, in 44 B.C., Julius Caesar was stabbed 23 times by political conspirators. After his assassination, Caesar's body was cremated on this spot (under the metal roof). Afterward, this temple was built to honor him. Peek behind the wall into the small apse area, where a mound of dirt usually has fresh flowers—given to remember the man who, more than any other, personified the greatness of Rome.

Caesar (100-44 B.C.) changed Rome—and the Forum—dramatically. He cleared out many of the wooden market stalls and began to ring the square with even grander buildings. Caesar's house was located behind the temple, near that clump of trees. He walked right by here on the day he was assassinated ("Beware the Ides of March!" warned a street-corner Etruscan preacher).

Though he was popular with the masses, not everyone liked Caesar's urban design or his politics. When he assumed dictatorial powers, he was ambushed and stabbed to death by a conspiracy of senators, including his adopted son, Brutus *("Et tu, Brute?")*.

The funeral was held here, facing the main square. The citizens gathered, and speeches were made. Mark Antony stood up to say (in Shakespeare's words), "Friends, Romans, countrymen, lend me your ears. I come to bury Caesar, not to praise him." When Caesar's body was burned, his adoring fans threw anything at hand on the fire, requiring the fire department to come put it out. Later, Emperor Augustus dedicated this temple in his name, making Caesar the first Roman to become a god.

• *Continue past the Temple of Julius Caesar, to the open area between the columns of the Temple of Antoninus Pius and Faustina (which we passed earlier) and the boxy brick building (the Curia). You can view these ruins of the Basilica Aemilia from a ramp next to the Temple of Antoninus Pius and Faustina, or find the entrance near the Curia (if it's not closed for archaeological work).*

⓾ Basilica Aemilia: The word "basilica" originally meant a covered public forum, often serving as a Roman hall of justice. In a society that was as legal-minded as America is today, you needed a lot of lawyers—and a big place to put them. Citizens came here to work out matters such as inheritances and building permits or to sue somebody.

Notice the layout. It was a long, rectangular building. The stubby columns all in a row form one long, central hall flanked by two side aisles. Medieval Christians required a larger meeting hall for their worship services than Roman temples provided, so they used the spacious Roman basilica as the model for their churches. Cathedrals from France to Spain to England, from Romanesque to Gothic to Renaissance, all have the same basic floor plan as a Roman basilica.

• *Now head for the big, well-preserved brick building (just beyond the basilica ruins) with the triangular roof—the Curia. (Ongoing archaeological work may restrict access to the Curia, as well as the Arch of Septimius Severus—described later—and the exit to Capitoline Hill.)*

⓫ The Curia (Senate House): The Curia was the most important political building in the Forum. While the present building dates from A.D. 283, this was the site of Rome's official center of government since the birth of the republic. Three hundred senators, elected by the citizens of Rome, met here to debate and create the laws of the land. Their wooden seats once circled the building in three tiers; the Senate president's podium sat at the far end. The marble floor is from ancient times. Listen to the echoes in this vast room—the acoustics are great.

Rome prided itself on being a republic. Early in the city's history, its people threw out the king and established rule by elected representatives. Each Roman citizen was free to speak his mind and have a say in public policy. Even when emperors became the supreme authority, the Senate was a power to be reckoned with. The Curia building is well preserved, having been used as a church since early Christian times. In the 1930s, it was restored and opened to the public as a historic site. (Note: Although Julius Caesar was assassinated in "the Senate," it wasn't here—the Senate was temporarily meeting across town.)

A statue and two reliefs inside the Curia help build our mental image of the Forum. The statue, made of porphyry marble in about A.D. 100 (with its head, arms, and feet now missing), was a tribute to an emperor, probably Hadrian or Trajan. The two relief panels may have decorated the Rostrum. Those on the left show people (with big stone tablets) standing in line to burn their debt records following a government amnesty. The other shows the distribution of grain (Rome's welfare system), some buildings in the background, and the latest fashion in togas.

• *Go back down the Senate steps and find the 10-foot-high wall just to the left of the big arch, marked...*

❷ **Rostrum:** Nowhere was Roman freedom more apparent than at this "Speaker's Corner." The Rostrum was a raised platform, 10 feet high and 80 feet long, decorated with statues, columns, and the prows of ships.

On a stage like this, Rome's orators, great and small, tried to draw a crowd and sway public opinion. Mark Antony rose to offer Caesar the laurel-leaf crown of kingship, which Caesar publicly (and hypocritically) refused while privately becoming a dictator. Men such as Cicero railed against the corruption and decadence that came with the city's newfound wealth. In later years, daring citizens even spoke out against the emperors, reminding them that Rome was once free. Picture the backdrop these speakers would have had—a mountain of marble buildings piling up on Capitoline Hill.

In front of the Rostrum are trees bearing fruits that were sacred to the ancient Romans: olives (provided food, light, and preservatives), figs (tasty), and wine grapes (made a popular export product).

• *The big arch to the right of the Rostrum is the...*

❸ **Arch of Septimius Severus:** In imperial times, the Rostrum's voices of democracy would have been dwarfed by images of the empire, such as the huge six-story-high Arch of Septimius Severus (A.D. 203). The reliefs commemorate the African-born emperor's battles in Mesopotamia. Near ground level, see soldiers marching captured barbarians back to Rome for the victory parade. Despite Severus' efficient rule, Rome's empire was crumbling under the weight of its own corruption, disease, decaying infrastructure, and the constant attacks by foreign "barbarians."

• *Pass beneath the Arch of Septimius Severus and turn left. If the path is blocked, backtrack toward the Temple of Julius Caesar and around the square. On the slope of Capitoline Hill are the eight remaining columns of the...*

❹ **Temple of Saturn:** These columns framed the entrance to the Forum's oldest temple (497 B.C.). Inside was a humble, very old wooden statue of the god Saturn. But the statue's pedestal held the

Rome Falls

Remember that Rome lasted 1,000 years—500 years of growth, 200 years of peak power, and 300 years of gradual decay.

The fall had many causes, among them the barbarians who pecked away at Rome's borders. Christians blamed the fall on moral decay. Pagans blamed it on Christians. Socialists blamed it on a shallow economy based on the spoils of war. (Republicans blamed it on Democrats.) Whatever the reasons, the far-flung empire could no longer keep its grip on conquered lands, and it pulled back. Barbarian tribes from Germany and Asia attacked the Italian peninsula and even looted Rome itself in A.D. 410, leveling many of the buildings in the Forum. In 476, when the last emperor checked out and switched off the lights, Europe plunged into centuries of ignorance, poverty, and weak government—the Dark Ages.

But Rome lived on in the Catholic Church. Christianity was the state religion of Rome's last generations. Emperors became popes (both called themselves "Pontifex Maximus"), senators became bishops, orators became priests, and basilicas became churches. The glory of Rome remains eternal.

gold bars, coins, and jewels of Rome's state treasury, the booty collected by conquering generals.

Even older than the Temple of Saturn is the Umbilicus Urbis, which stands nearby (next to the Arch of Septimius Severus). A humble brick ruin marks this historic "Navel of the City." The spot was considered the center of the cosmos, and all distances in the empire were measured from here.

• *Standing at the Temple of Saturn, one of the Forum's first buildings, look east at the lone, tall...*

⓯ Column of Phocas: This is the Forum's last monument (A.D. 608), a gift from the powerful Byzantine Empire to a fallen empire—Rome. Given to commemorate the pagan Pantheon's becoming a Christian church, it's like a symbolic last nail in ancient Rome's coffin. After Rome's 1,000-year reign, the city was looted by Vandals, the population of a million-plus shrank to about 10,000, and the once-grand city center—the Forum—was abandoned, slowly covered up by centuries of silt and dirt. In the 1700s, an English historian named Edward Gibbon overlooked this spot from Capitoline Hill. Hearing Christian monks singing at these pagan ruins, he looked out at the few columns poking up from the ground, pondered the decline and fall of the Roman Empire, and thought, "Hmm, that's a catchy title..."

• *Your tour is over. From the Forum, you have several options:*

1. Your closest exit is right by the Arch of Septimius Severus. From here, you can walk out to Via dei Fori Imperiali, near Trajan's Column and the Imperial Forums (described on page 851). Or you can climb 50 steps up to Capitoline Hill (described on page 847).

2. To exit near the Colosseum, return to the Arch of Titus and look for the *uscita/exit* signs. You'll pop out facing the Colosseum, near where you entered.

3. The Forum's Via dei Fori Imperiali entrance spills you back out onto Via dei Fori Imperiali near Via Cavour.

• *If you want to see Palatine Hill, don't leave the complex; you won't be allowed back in without a new ticket. Return to the Arch of Titus, from where you can climb Palatine Hill.*

▲▲Palatine Hill (Monte Palatino)

The hill overlooking the Forum is jam-packed with history—"the huts of Romulus," the huge Imperial Palace, a view of the Circus Maximus—but only the barest skeleton of rubble is left to tell the story.

We get our word "palace" from this hill, where the emperors chose to live. It was once so filled with palaces that later emperors had to build out. (Looking up at it from the Forum, you see the substructure that supported these long-gone palaces.) The Palatine Museum contains statues and frescoes that help you imagine the luxury of the imperial Palatine. From the pleasant garden, you'll get an overview of the Forum. On the far side, unless excavations are blocking the viewpoint, look down into an emperor's private stadium and then beyond at the grassy Circus Maximus, once a chariot course. Imagine the cheers, jeers, and furious betting.

While many tourists consider Palatine Hill just extra credit after the Forum, it offers insight into the greatness of Rome that's well worth the effort. (And, if you're visiting the Colosseum or Forum, you've got a ticket whether you like it or not.)

Cost and Hours: Covered by same ticket and open same hours as Colosseum and Roman Forum, listed above.

Getting In: To enter Palatine Hill directly, use the entrance on Via di San Gregorio, 150 yards from the Colosseum. You can also enter through the Forum entrances (usually more crowded), see the Forum first if you wish, and then take the path from the Forum over to Palatine Hill and climb to the top.

Services: WCs at the ticket office when you enter, at the museum in the center of the site, and hiding among the orange trees in the Farnese Gardens.

Capitoline Hill

Of Rome's famous seven hills, this is the smallest, tallest, and most famous—home of the ancient Temple of Jupiter and the center of city government for 2,500 years. There are several ways to get to the top of Capitoline Hill. If you're coming from the north (from Piazza Venezia), take Michelangelo's impressive stairway to the right of the big, white Victor Emmanuel Monument. Coming from the southeast (the Forum), take the steep staircase near the Arch of Septimius Severus. From near Trajan's Forum along Via dei Fori Imperiali, take the winding road. All three converge at the top, in the square called Campidoglio (kahm-pee-DOHL-yoh).

▲Piazza del Campidoglio

This square atop the hill, once the religious and political center of ancient Rome, is still the home of the city's government. In the 1530s, the pope called on Michelangelo to reestablish this square as a grand center. Michelangelo placed the ancient equestrian stat-

ue of Marcus Aurelius as its focal point—very effective. (The original statue is now in the adjacent museum.) The twin buildings on either side are the Capitoline Museums. Behind the replica of the statue is the mayoral palace (Palazzo Senatorio).

Michelangelo intended that people approach the square from his grand stairway off Piazza Venezia. From the top of the stairway, you see the new Renaissance face of Rome, with its back to the Forum. Michelangelo gave the buildings the "giant order"—huge pilasters make the existing two-story buildings feel one-storied and more harmonious with the

ROME

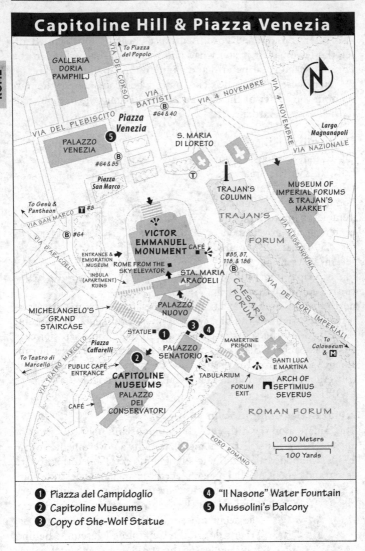

Capitoline Hill & Piazza Venezia

GALLERIA
DORIA
PAMPHILJ

To Piazza
del Popolo

VIA DEL CORSO

VIA
BATTISTI

VIA 4 NOVEMBRE

VIA 4 NOVEMBRE

Ⓑ
#64 & 40

VIA DEL PLEBISCITO

*Piazza
Venezia*

Largo
Magnanapoli

PALAZZO
VENEZIA

❺

S. MARIA
DI LORETO

VIA NAZIONALE

Ⓑ
#64 & 85

Ⓣ

*Piazza
San Marco*

To Gesù &
Pantheon

Ⓣ #8

VIA SAN MARCO

TRAJAN'S
COLUMN

MUSEUM OF
IMPERIAL FORUMS
& TRAJAN'S
MARKET

Ⓑ #64

VIA D'ARACOELI

VICTOR
EMMANUEL
MONUMENT

CAFÉ

TRAJAN'S

FORUM

VIA ALESSANDRINA

#85, 87,
118, & 186
Ⓑ

ENTRANCE &
EMIGRATION MUSEUM

ROME FROM THE
SKY ELEVATOR

STA. MARIA
ARACOELI

CAESAR'S

VIA DEI FORI IMPERIALI

INSULA
(APARTMENT)
RUINS

FORUM

MICHELANGELO'S
GRAND
STAIRCASE

PALAZZO
NUOVO

VIA TEATRO MARCELLO

STATUE ▪ ❶

*Piazza
Caffarelli*

❸ ❹

To Teatro di
Marcella

PUBLIC CAFÉ
ENTRANCE

❷

PALAZZO
SENATORIO

MAMERTINE
PRISON

To
Colosseum
& Ⓜ

CAPITOLINE
MUSEUMS

SANTI LUCA
E MARTINA

CAFÉ ➤

PALAZZO
DEI
CONSERVATORI

TABULARIUM

FORUM
EXIT

ARCH OF
SEPTIMIUS
SEVERUS

ROMAN FORUM

FORO ROMANO

100 Meters

100 Yards

❶ Piazza del Campidoglio
❷ Capitoline Museums
❸ Copy of She-Wolf Statue

❹ "Il Nasone" Water Fountain
❺ Mussolini's Balcony

new square. Notice how the statues atop these buildings welcome
you and then draw you in.

The terraces just downhill (past either side of the mayor's palace) offer grand views of the Forum. To the left of the mayor's palace is a copy of the famous she-wolf statue on a column. Farther
down is *il nasone* ("the big nose"), a refreshing water fountain (see
photo on previous page). Block the spout with your fingers, and
water spurts up for drinking. Romans joke that a cheap Roman boy
takes his date out for a drink at *il nasone*.

▲▲▲Capitoline Museums (Musei Capitolini)

Some of ancient Rome's most famous statues and art are housed in the two palaces (Palazzo dei Conservatori and Palazzo Nuovo) that flank the equestrian statue in the Campidoglio. They're connected by an underground passage that leads to the Tabularium, an ancient building with panoramic views of the Roman Forum.

Cost and Hours: €15, €11.50 if no special exhibitions, daily 9:30-19:30, last entry one hour before closing, audioguide-€5, tel. 06-0608, www.museicapitolini.org.

Visiting the Museums: Enter at the Palazzo dei Conservatori (on your right as you face the equestrian statue), cross underneath the square (beneath the Palazzo Senatorio, the mayoral palace, not open to public), and exit from the Palazzo Nuovo (on your left).

With lavish rooms and several great statues, the worthwhile **Palazzo dei Conservatori** claims to be one of the world's oldest, founded in 1471 when a pope gave ancient statues to the citizens of Rome. Many of the museum's statues have gone on to become instantly recognizable cultural icons, including the 13th-century *Capitoline She-Wolf* (the little statues of Romulus and Remus were added in the Renaissance). Don't miss the *Boy Extracting a Thorn* and the enchanting *Commodus as Hercules*. Behind Commodus is a statue of his dad, Marcus Aurelius, on a horse. The greatest surviving equestrian statue of antiquity, this was the original centerpiece of the square (where a copy stands today). Christians in the Dark Ages thought that the statue's hand was raised in blessing, which probably led to their misidentifying him as Constantine, the first Christian emperor. While most pagan statues were destroyed by Christians, "Constantine" was spared.

The museum's second-floor café, **Caffè Capitolino,** has a splendid patio offering city views. It's lovely at sunset (public entrance for those without a museum ticket off Piazzale Caffarelli and through door #4).

The **Tabularium,** built in the first century B.C., once held the archives of ancient Rome. (The word "Tabularium" comes from "tablet," on which Romans wrote their laws.) You won't see any tablets, but you will see a stunning head-on view of the Forum from the windows.

The **Palazzo Nuovo** houses mostly portrait busts of forgotten emperors. But it also has two must-see statues: the Dying Gaul and the Capitoline Venus (both on the first floor up).

Piazza Venezia

This vast square, dominated by the big, white Victor Emmanuel Monument, is a major transportation hub and the focal point of modern Rome. With your back to the monument (you'll get the best views from the terrace by the guards and eternal flame), look down Via del Corso, the city's axis, surrounded by Rome's classi-est shopping district. In the 1930s, Benito Mussolini whipped up Italy's nationalistic fervor from a balcony above the square (it's the less-grand building on the left). Fascist masses filled the square screaming, "Four more years!"—or something like that. Mussolini created the boulevard Via dei Fori Imperiali (to your right, capped by Trajan's Column) to open up views of the Colosseum in the distance. Mussolini lied to his people, mixing fear and patriotism to push his country to the right and embroil the Italians in expensive and regrettable wars. In 1945, they shot Mussolini and hung him from a meat hook in Milan.

With your back still to the monument, circle around the left side. At the back end of the monument, look down into the ditch on your left to see the ruins of an ancient apartment building from the first century A.D.; part of it was transformed into a tiny church (faded frescoes and bell tower). Rome was built in layers—almost everywhere you go, there's an earlier version beneath your feet.

Continuing on, you reach two staircases leading up Capitoline Hill. One is Michelangelo's grand staircase up to the Campidoglio. The steeper of the two leads to **Santa Maria in Aracoeli,** a good example of the earliest style of Christian church. The contrast between this climb-on-your-knees ramp to God's house and Michelangelo's elegant stairs illustrates the changes Renaissance humanism brought civilization.

From the bottom of Michelangelo's stairs, look right several blocks down the street to see a condominium actually built upon the surviving ancient pillars and arches of Teatro di Marcello.

▲Victor Emmanuel Monument

This oversize monument to Italy's first king, built to celebrate the 50th anniversary of the country's unification in 1861, was part of

Italy's push to overcome the new country's strong regionalism and create a national identity. Today, the "Vittoriano" houses museums (including an excellent **museum of Italian emigration**), a café with a great view, and an elevator to an even better view. See the map on page 834.

The scale of the monument is over-the-top: 200 feet high, 500 feet wide. The 43-foot-long statue of the king on his high horse is one of the biggest equestrian statues in the world. The king's moustache forms an arc five feet long, and a person could sit within the horse's hoof. At the base of this statue, Italy's Tomb of the

Unknown Soldier (flanked by Italian flags and armed guards) is watched over by the goddess Roma (with the gold mosaic background).

With its gleaming white sheen (from a recent scrubbing) and enormous scale, the monument provides a vivid sense of what Ancient Rome looked like at its peak—imagine the Forum filled with shiny, grandiose buildings like this one.

Cost and Hours: Monument and museum of Italian emigration—free, daily 9:30-18:30, a few WCs scattered throughout, tel. 06-6920-2049; Rome from the Sky Elevator—€7, Mon-Thu 9:30-18:30, Fri-Sun 9:30-19:30, ticket office closes 45 minutes earlier, WC at entrance, tel. 06-679-3598; follow *ascensori panoramici* signs inside the Victor Emmanuel Monument (no elevator access from street level).

The Imperial Forums

Though the original Roman Forum is the main attraction for today's tourists, there are several more ancient forums nearby. These forums stretch in a line along Via dei Fori Imperiali, from Piazza Venezia to the Colosseum. Today, the once-noisy boulevard is a pleasant walk, since it now is closed to private vehicles—and, on Sundays and holidays, to all traffic.

The ruins are out in the open, never crowded, and free to view any time, any day.

◑ Self-Guided Walk: For an overview of the archaeological area, take this walk from Piazza Venezia down Via dei Fori Imperiali to the end of the Imperial Forums.

• *Start at Trajan's Column, the colossal pillar that stands alongside Piazza Venezia.*

Trajan's Column: The world's grandest column from antiquity (rated ▲▲) anchors the first of the forums we'll see—Trajan's Forum. The 140-foot column is decorated with a spiral relief of 2,500 figures trumpeting the emperor's exploits. It has stood for centuries as a symbol of a truly cosmopolitan civilization. At one point, the ashes of Trajan and his wife were held in the base, and the sun glinted off a polished bronze statue of Trajan at the top. (Since the 1500s, St. Peter has been on top.) Built as a stack of 17 marble doughnuts, the column is hollow (note the small window slots) with a spiral staircase inside, leading up to the balcony.

The **relief** unfolds like a scroll, telling the story of Rome's last and greatest foreign conquest, Trajan's defeat of Dacia (modern-day Romania). Originally, the entire story was painted in bright colors. If you were to unwind the scroll, it would stretch over two football fields—it's far longer than the frieze around the Parthenon in Athens.

• *Now, start heading toward the Colosseum, walking along the left side of Via dei Fori Imperiali. You're walking alongside...*

Trajan's Forum: The dozen-plus gray columns mark one of the grandest structures in Trajan's Forum, the Basilica Ulpia, the largest law court of its day. Nearby stood two libraries that contained the world's knowledge in Greek and Latin.

Rome peaked under Emperor Trajan (ruled A.D. 98-117), when the empire stretched from England to the Sahara, from Spain to the Fertile Crescent. A triumphant Trajan returned to Rome with his booty and shook it all over the city. Most was spent on this forum, complete with temples, law courts, and the monumental column trumpeting his exploits. To build his forum, Trajan literally moved mountains. He cut away a ridge that once connected the Quirinal and Capitoline hills, creating this valley. This was the largest forum ever, and its opulence astounded even jaded Romans.

• *But most astounding of all was Trajan's Market. That's the big, semi-circular brick structure nestled into the cutaway curve of Quirinal Hill. If you want a closer look, there's a pedestrian pathway that leads you up to it.*

Trajan's Market: This structure was part shopping mall, part warehouse, and part administration building and/or government offices. For now the convention-al wisdom holds that at ground level, the 13 tall (shallow) arches housed shops selling fresh fruit, vegetables, and flowers to people who passed by on the street. The 26 arched windows (above) lit a covered walkway lined with shops that sold wine and olive oil. On the roof (now lined with a metal railing) ran a street that likely held still more shops, making about 150 in all. Shoppers could browse through goods from every corner of Rome's vast empire—exotic fruits from Africa, spices from Asia, and fish-and-chips from Londinium.

Above the semicircle, the upper floors of the complex housed bureaucrats in charge of a crucial element of city life: doling out free grain to unemployed citizens, who lived off the wealth plundered from distant lands. Better to pacify them than risk a riot. Above the offices, at the very top, rises a tower added in the Middle Ages.

If you'd like to walk around the market complex and see some excavated statues, visit the **Museum of the Imperial Forums,** which features discoveries from the forums built by the different emperors (enter just uphill from Trajan's Column; €11.50 when no special exhibitions, daily 9:30-19:30, last entry one hour before closing).

• *Return to the main street, and continue toward the Colosseum for about 100 more yards.*

You're still walking alongside Trajan's Forum, but the ruins you see in this section are actually from the medieval era. These are the foundations of the old neighborhood that was built atop the ancient city. In modern times, that neighborhood was cleared out to build the new boulevard.

You'll soon reach a bronze **statue of Trajan** himself. Though the likeness is ancient, this bronze statue is not. It was erected by the dictator Benito Mussolini when he had the modern boulevard built. Notice the date on the pedestal—Anno XI. That would be "the 11th year of the Fascist Renovation of Italy"—i.e., 1933. Across the street is a similar statue of **Julius Caesar.** That marks the first of these imperial forums, built by Julius in 46 b.c., as an extension of the Roman Forum. Near him stand the three remaining columns of his forum's Temple of Venus—the patron goddess of the Julian family.

• *Continue along (down the left side). As Trajan's Forum narrows to an end, you reach a statue of Emperor Augustus that indicates...*

The Forums of Augustus and Nerva: The statue captures **Emperor Augustus** in his famous hailing-a-cab pose (a copy of the original, which you can see at the Vatican Museums). This is actually his "commander talking to his people" pose. Behind him was the Forum of Augustus. Find the four white, fluted, Corinthian columns that were part of the forum's centerpiece, the Temple of Mars. The ugly gray stone wall that borders the forum's back end was built for security. It separated fancy "downtown Rome" from the workaday world beyond (today's characteristic and trendy Monti neighborhood) and protected Augustus' temple from city fires.

Farther along is a statue of **Emperor Nerva,** trying but failing to have the commanding presence of Augustus. Behind Nerva, you can get a closer look at his forum. Gaze down at an original marble inlaid floor that was once under a grand roof, surrounded by offices and shops within a semicircular mall. As with Augustus' Forum, the big stone wall (composed of volcanic tuff) on the far side was built to protect the "important" part of town from the fire-plagued working-class zone beyond.

Continuing a little farther (toward the Colosseum), find some fine marble reliefs from Nerva's Forum showing women in pleated robes parading in religious rituals.

• *You've reached the end of the Imperial Forums at the intersection of Via dei Fori Imperiali and busy Via Cavour.*

Nearby is the colorful neighborhood of Monti, home to a slew of fun little eateries (see page 927). Two blocks up Via Cavour is the Cavour Metro stop. From there, you could turn right to find St. Peter-in-Chains Church. Across Via dei Fori Imperiali is an entrance to the Roman Forum (see page 836); 100 yards farther down Via dei Fori Imperiali (on the left) is a tourist information center with a handy café, info desk, and WC.

North of Via dei Fori Imperiali
Several worthwhile sights sit across Via dei Fori Imperiali from the Roman Forum—and offer a break from the crowds.

▲St. Peter-in-Chains Church (San Pietro in Vincoli)
Built in the fifth century to house the chains that held St. Peter, this church is most famous for its Michelangelo statue of Moses, intended for the tomb of Pope Julius II (which was never built). Check out the much-venerated chains under the high altar, then focus on mighty Moses. (Note that this isn't the famous St. Peter's Basilica, which is in Vatican City.)

Pope Julius II commissioned Michelangelo to build a massive tomb, with 48 huge statues, topped with a grand statue of this ego-maniacal pope. The pope had planned to have his tomb placed in the center of St. Peter's Basilica. When Julius died, the work had barely been started, and no one had the money or necessary commitment to Julius to finish the project.

In 1542, some of the remnants of the tomb project were brought to St. Peter-in-Chains and pieced together by Michelangelo's assistants. Some of the best statues ended up elsewhere, such as the *Prisoners* in Florence and the *Slaves* in the Louvre. *Moses* and the Louvre's *Slaves* are the only statues Michelangelo personally completed for the project. Flanking *Moses* are the Old Testament sister-wives of Jacob, Leah (to our right) and Rachel, both begun by Michelangelo but probably finished by pupils.

The powerful statue of Moses—mature Michelangelo—is worth studying. Moses has received the Ten Commandments. As he holds the stone tablets, his eyes show a man determined to stop his tribe from worshipping the golden calf and idols...a man determined to win salvation for the people of Israel. Why the horns? Centuries ago, the Hebrew word for "rays" was mistranslated as "horns."

Cost and Hours: Free, daily April-Sept 8:00-12:20 & 15:00-

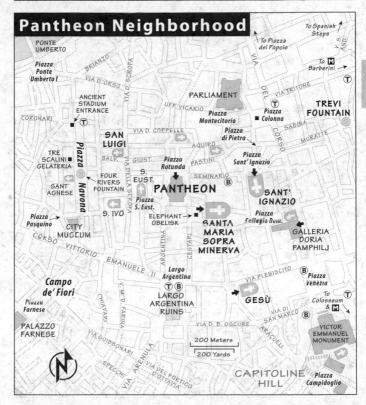

Pantheon Neighborhood

PONTE UMBERTO

Piazza Ponte Umberto I

ANCIENT STADIUM ENTRANCE

CORONARI

BRIANZO

VIA D'ORSO

VIA DELLA SCROFA

PARLIAMENT

UFF. VICARIO

VIA D. COPPELLE

To Piazza del Popolo

To Spanish Steps

To M Barberini

VIA DEL CORSO

VIA TRITONE

TREVI FOUNTAIN

SABINA

MURATTE

Piazza Montecitorio

Piazza di Pietra

Piazza Colonna

SAN LUIGI

TRE SCALINI GELATERIA

SANT' AGNESE

Piazza Navona

SALV.

GIUST.

S. EUST.

Piazza Rotunda

PANTHEON

FOUR RIVERS FOUNTAIN

Piazza S. Eust.

S. IVO

Piazza Pasquino

CITY MUSEUM

CORSO

VITTORIO

EMANUELE II

ELEPHANT OBELISK

SANTA MARIA SOPRA MINERVA

VIA DELLA SCROFA

PASTINI

SEMINARIO

AQUIRO

Piazza Sant' Ignazio

SANT' IGNAZIO

Piazza Collegio Rom.

GALLERIA DORIA PAMPHILJ

ARGENTINA

CESTARI

Largo Argentina

LARGO ARGENTINA RUINS

VIA PLEBISCITO

GESÙ

Piazza Venezia

To Colosseum & M

Campo de' Fiori

Piazza Farnese

PALAZZO FARNESE

V. M. D. FARINA

CHIAVARI

VIA GIUBBONARI

SPECCHI

ARENULA

VIA DEL PORTICO D'OTTAVIA

VIA D. B. OSCURE

ARACOELI

VIA DI SAN MARCO

VICTOR EMMANUEL MONUMENT

CAPITOLINE HILL

Piazza Campidoglio

200 Meters
200 Yards

ROME

19:00, Oct-March until 18:00, modest dress required; the church is a 10-minute uphill walk from the Colosseum, or a shorter, simpler walk (but with more steps) from the Cavour Metro stop; tel. 06-9784-4950.

PANTHEON NEIGHBORHOOD

Besides being home to ancient sites and historic churches, the area around the Pantheon is another part of Rome with an urban-village feel. Wander narrow streets, sample the many shops and eateries, and gather with the locals in squares marked by bubbling fountains. Just south of the Pantheon is the Jewish quarter, with remnants of Rome's Jewish history and culture. Exploring this area is especially nice in the evening, when restaurants bustle and streets are jammed with foot traffic. For a self-guided walk in this neighborhood, from Campo de' Fiori to the Trevi Fountain (and ending at the Spanish Steps), see my Heart of Rome Walk on page 820.

Getting There: Many buses (including #40, #64, #H, #492, #85, #87, and tram #8) stop on the major boulevards near the Pantheon (Via del Corso, Corso Rinascimento, and Corso Vittorio

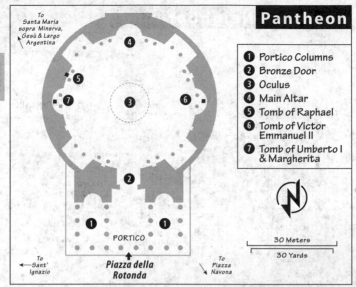

To Santa Maria sopra Minerva, Gesù & Largo Argentina

Pantheon

1 Portico Columns
2 Bronze Door
3 Oculus
4 Main Altar
5 Tomb of Raphael
6 Tomb of Victor Emmanuel II
7 Tomb of Umberto I & Margherita

PORTICO

30 Meters
30 Yards

To Sant' Ignazio

Piazza della Rotonda

To Piazza Navona

Emanuele); from any of these it's about a three-block walk. You can also walk from the Spagna or Barberini Metro stops in about 15 minutes.

▲▲▲Pantheon

For the greatest look at the splendor of Rome, antiquity's best-preserved interior is a must. Built two millennia ago, this influential domed temple served as the model for Michelangelo's dome of St. Peter's and many others.

Cost and Hours: Free, Mon-Sat 8:30-19:30, Sun 9:00-18:00, holidays 9:00-13:00, audioguide–€5, tel. 06-6830-0230.

When to Go: Don't go midday, when the Pantheon is packed. Visit before 9:00, and you'll have it all to yourself.

Dress Code: No skimpy shorts or bare shoulders allowed.

Tours: Audioguides cost €5 and last 25 minutes (€8/2 people). ∩ Download my free Pantheon audio tour.

Services: The nearest WCs are at bars and cafés on the Pantheon's square.

Visiting the Pantheon: The Pantheon was a Roman temple dedicated to all *(pan)* of the gods *(theos)*. The original temple was built in 27 B.C. by Emperor Augustus' son-in-law, Marcus Agrippa. In fact, the inscription below the triangular **pediment** proclaims in Latin, "Marcus Agrippa, son of Lucio, three times consul made this." But after a couple of fires, the structure we see today was completely rebuilt by Emperor Hadrian around A.D. 120. After the fall of Rome, the Pantheon became a Christian church (from "all the gods" to "all the martyrs"), which saved it from architectural cannibalism and ensured its upkeep through the Dark Ages.

The Pantheon looks like a pretty typical temple from the outside, but this is perhaps the most influential building in art history. Its dome was the model for the Florence cathedral dome, which launched the Renaissance, and for Michelangelo's dome of St. Peter's, which capped it all off. Even the US Capitol in Washington, DC, was inspired by this dome.

The **portico** is Greek in style, which is logical, because Hadrian was a Grecophile. This fine porch is a visual reminder of the great debt Roman culture owed to the Greeks. Fittingly, you cross this Greek space to enter a purely Roman space, the rotunda. The columns are huge and unadorned, made from 40-foot-high single pieces of red-gray granite rather than the standard stacks of cylindrical pieces. They were quarried in Egypt, then shipped down the Nile and across the Mediterranean to Rome.

The **dome,** which was the largest made until the Renaissance, is set on a circular base. The mathematical perfection of this dome on-a-base design is a testament to Roman engineering. The dome is as high as it is wide—142 feet from floor to rooftop and from side to side. To picture it, imagine a basketball wedged inside a wastebasket so that it just touches bottom. It is made from concrete (a Roman invention) that gets lighter and thinner as it reaches the top. The base of the dome is 23 feet thick and made from heavy concrete mixed with travertine, while near the top, it's less than five feet thick and made with a lighter volcanic rock (pumice) mixed in. Note the square indentations in the surface of the dome. This **coffered ceiling** reduces the weight of the dome without compromising strength. The walls are strengthened by brick relieving arches ("blind" arches)—visible in the exposed brickwork in a few of the interior niches and easy to see from outside.

Both Brunelleschi and Michelangelo studied this dome before building their own (in Florence and the Vatican, respectively). Remember, the grandiose vision for St. Peter's Basilica was to place the dome of the Pantheon atop the Forum's Basilica of Constantine.

At the top, the oculus, or eye-in-the-sky, is the building's only light source. It's completely open and almost 30 feet across. The 1,800-year-old floor—with 80 percent of its original stones surviving—has holes in it and slants toward the edges to let the rainwater drain. Though some of the floor's marble has been replaced, the design—alternating circles and squares—is original.

While its ancient statuary is long gone, the interior holds decorative statues and the tombs of famous people from more recent centuries. The artist **Raphael** lies to the left of the main altar in a lighted glass niche. Facing each other across the base of the dome are the tombs of modern Italy's first two kings.

▲▲Churches near the Pantheon

The following churches are free to visit; modest dress is recommended.

The **Church of San Luigi dei Francesi** has a magnificent chapel painted by Caravaggio (daily 9:30-12:30 & 14:30-18:30 except opens Sun at 10:30, between the Pantheon and the north end of Piazza Navona). The only Gothic church in Rome is the **Church of Santa Maria sopra Minerva,** with a little-known Michelangelo statue, *Christ Bearing the Cross* (Mon-Fri 7:30-19:00, Sat-Sun 8:00-12:30 & 15:30-19:00, on a little square behind the Pantheon, to the east). The **Church of Sant'Ignazio,** several blocks east of the Pantheon, is a riot of Baroque illusions with a false dome (Mon-Sat 7:30-19:00, Sun 9:00-19:00). A few blocks away, across Corso Vittorio Emanuele, is the rich and Baroque **Gesù Church,** headquarters of the Jesuits in Rome (daily 7:00-12:30 & 16:00-19:45, interesting daily ceremony at 17:30).

▲Trevi Fountain

The bubbly Baroque fountain, worth ▲▲ by night, is a minor sight to art scholars...but a major nighttime gathering spot for teens on the make and tourists tossing coins. Those coins are collected daily to feed Rome's poor. For more on the fountain, see page 828.

Jewish Quarter

From the 16th through the 19th century, Rome's Jewish population was forced to live in a cramped ghetto at an often-flooded bend of the Tiber River. While the medieval Jewish ghetto is long gone, this area—between Campo de' Fiori and Capitoline Hill—is still home to fragments of Rome's Jewish heritage and its modern **synagogue** (€11 ticket includes museum, audioguide, and guided synagogue tour, closed Sat, modest dress required, on Lungotevere dei Cenci, tel. 06-6840-0661, www.museoebraico.roma.it).

∩ Download my free Jewish Ghetto Walk audio tour.

VATICAN CITY

Vatican City, the world's smallest country, contains St. Peter's Basilica (with Michelangelo's exquisite *Pietà*) and the Vatican Museums (with Michelangelo's Sistine Chapel). The entrances to St. Peter's and the Vatican Museums are a 15-minute walk apart (follow the outside of the Vatican wall, which links the two sights). The nearest Metro stop—Ottaviano—still involves a 10-minute walk to either sight.

Dress Code: Modest dress is required of men, women, and children throughout Vatican City, even outdoors. Cover your shoulders; bring a light jacket or cover-up if you're wearing a tank top. Wear long pants instead of shorts. Skirts or dresses should extend below your knee.

St. Peter's Square

St. Peter's Square, with its ring of columns, symbolizes the arms of the church welcoming everyone—believers and nonbelievers—

with its motherly embrace. It was designed a century after Michelangelo by the Baroque architect Gian Lorenzo Bernini, who did much of the work that we'll see inside. Numbers first: 284 columns, 56 feet high, in stern Doric style. Topping them are Bernini's 140 favorite saints, each 10 feet tall. The "square" itself is actually elliptical, 660 by 500 feet (roughly the same dimensions as the Colosseum). Though large, it's designed like a saucer, a little higher around the edges, so that even when full of crowds (as it often is), it allows those on the periphery to see above the throngs.

The **obelisk** in the center is 90 feet of solid granite weighing more than 300 tons. It once stood about 100 yards from its current location, in the center of the circus course (to the left of where St. Peter's is today). Think for a second about how much history this monument has seen. Originally erected in Egypt more than 2,000 years ago, it witnessed the fall of the pharaohs to the Greeks and then to the Romans. Then the emperor Caligula moved it to imperial Rome, where it stood impassively watching the slaughter of Christians at the racecourse and the torture of Protestants by the Inquisition (in the yellow-and-rust building just outside the square, to the left of the church). Today, it watches over the church, a reminder that each civilization builds on the previous ones. The puny cross on top reminds us that Christian culture has cast but a thin veneer over our pagan origins.

▲▲▲St. Peter's Basilica (Basilica San Pietro)

There is no doubt: This is the richest and grandest church on earth. To call it vast is like calling Einstein smart. Plaques on the floor show you where other, smaller churches would end if they were placed inside. The ornamental cherubs would dwarf a large man. Birds roost inside, and thousands of people wander about, heads

ROME

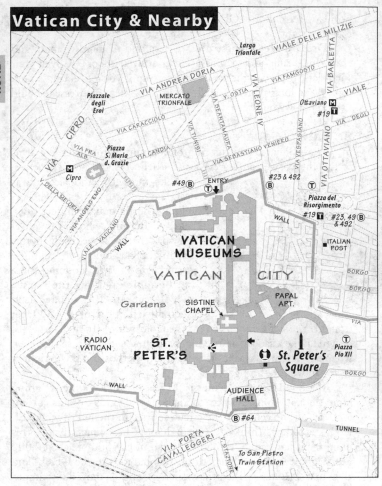

Vatican City & Nearby

craned heavenward, hardly noticing each other. Don't miss Michelangelo's *Pietà* (behind bulletproof glass) to the right of the entrance. Bernini's altarwork and twisting, towering canopy are brilliant.

Cost: Free entry to basilica and crypt. Dome climb-€5 if you take the stairs all the way up, or €7 to ride an elevator partway (to the roof), then climb to the top of the dome (cash only; for details, see "Dome Climb" on page 865). Treasury Museum-€7 (€3 audioguide).

Hours: The **church** is open daily April-Sept 7:00-19:00, Oct-March 7:00-18:00. It closes on Wednesday mornings during papal audiences (until roughly 13:00). The **dome** *(cupola)* is open to climbers daily from 8:00; to climb the stairs all the way up, the last entry time is 17:00 (16:00 Oct-March); to ride the elevator, you can enter until 18:00 (17:00 Oct-March). The **Treasury Museum** is

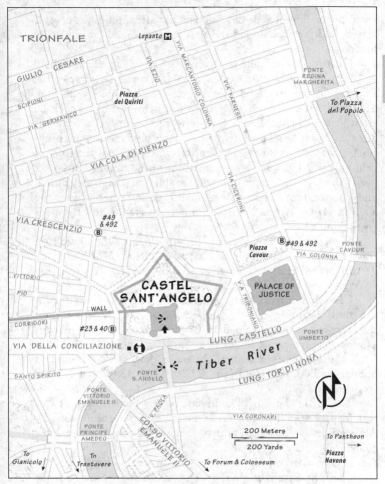

TRIONFALE

Lepanto Ⓜ

GIULIO CESARE

SCIPIONI

VIA GERMANICO

VIA EZIO

Piazza
dei Quiriti

VIA MARCANTONIO COLONNA

VIA FARNESE

PONTE
REGINA
MARGHERITA

To Piazza
del Popolo

VIA COLA DI RIENZO

VIA CICERONE

VIA CRESCENZIO

#49
& 492

Ⓑ #49 & 492

Piazza
Cavour

VITTORIO

PIO

CASTEL
SANT'ANGELO

PONTE
CAVOUR

VIA COLONNA

PALACE OF
JUSTICE

VIA TRIBONIANO

CORRIDORI

WALL

#23 & 40 Ⓑ

VIA DELLA CONCILIAZIONE

LUNG. CASTELLO

PONTE
UMBERTO

SANTO SPIRITO

PONTE
S.ANGELO

Tiber River

LUNG. TOR DI NONA

PONTE
VITTORIO
EMANUELE II

VIA PAOLA

VIA CORONARI

To Pantheon

PONTE
PRINCIPE
AMEDEO

CORSO VITTORIO
EMANUELE II

200 Meters

200 Yards

Piazza
Navona

To
Gianicolo

To
Trastevere

To Forum & Colosseum

ROME

open daily 8:00-18:50, Oct-March until 17:50. The **crypt** *(grotte)* is
open daily 9:00-16:00.

Avoiding Lines: There's often a bottleneck at the security
check. The checkpoint is typically on the north side of the square,
but is sometimes closer to the church or tucked under the south
colonnade.

If you're also visiting the Vatican Museums (and going through
security there), a shortcut usually—but not always—lets you exit
from the Sistine Chapel directly into St. Peter's. This is a great
time-saving trick, but unfortunately not a reliable one (for details,
see page 879).

Visiting before 10:00 is one way to avoid the worst crowds.
Crowds also thin after 16:00, when sunbeams work their magic on
the altar, and the 17:00 Mass (Mon-Sat) in the apse fills the place

with spiritual music. The downside is that after 16:00, the crypt is closed, and the area around the altar is often roped off to prepare for Mass.

Getting There: Take the Metro to Ottaviano, then walk 10 minutes south on Via Ottaviano. The #40 express bus drops off at Piazza Pio, next to Castel Sant'Angelo—a 10-minute walk from St. Peter's. The more crowded bus #64, beloved by pickpockets, stops just outside St. Peter's Square to the south (get off the bus after it crosses the Tiber, at the first stop past the tunnel; backtrack toward the tunnel and turn left when you see the rows of columns; the return bus stop is adjacent to the tunnel). Bus #492 heads through the center of town, stopping at Largo Argentina, and gets you near Piazza Risorgimento (get off when you see the Vatican walls). A taxi from Termini train station to St. Peter's costs about €15.

Information: The Vatican TI, up close to the church on the left (south) side of the square, is excellent (Mon-Sat 8:30-18:15, closed Sun, tel. 06-6988-1662). For the Vatican, see www.vaticanstate.va.

Church Services: Mass, generally in Italian, is said either in the south (left) transept, the Blessed Sacrament Chapel (on right side of nave), or at the main altar. Confirm times on the signboard as you enter. Typical schedule: Mon-Sat at 8:30, 9:00, 10:00, 11:00, 12:00, 16:30, and (in Latin, at the main altar) at 17:00; Sun and holidays at 9:00, 10:30 (in Latin), 11:30, 12:15, 13:00, 16:00, 16:45 (vespers), and 17:30.

Tours: The Vatican TI conducts free 1.5-hour tours of St. Peter's (depart from TI Mon-Fri at 14:15, confirm schedule at TI). Audioguides can be rented near the baggage check (€5 plus ID, for church only, daily 9:00-17:00).

⌒ Download my free St. Peter's Basilica audio tour.

To see St. Peter's original grave, you can take a *Scavi* (excavations) tour into the Necropolis under the basilica (€13, 1.5 hours, ages 15 and older only, no photos). Book at least two months in advance by email (scavi@fsp.va) or fax (06-6987-3017), following the detailed instructions at www.vatican.va (search for "Excavations Office"); no response means they're booked.

Dome Climb: You can take the elevator (€7) or stairs (€5) to the roof (231 steps), then climb another 323 steps to the top of the dome. The entry to the elevator is just outside the north side of the basilica—look for signs to the *cupola*.

Length of This Tour: Allow one hour, plus another hour if you climb the dome (or a half-hour to the roof). With as little as 15 minutes, you could stroll the nave, glance up at the dome, down at St. Peter's resting place, and adore the *Pietà* on your way out.

Baggage Check: The free bag check (mandatory for bags larger than a purse or daypack) is inside security, but outside the basilica (to the right as you face the entrance). Pocketknives are not allowed inside the basilica.

Vatican Museums Tickets: The Vatican TI at St. Peter's often has museum tickets on sale for €20. There may also be a table selling museum tickets in the narthex (portico) of St. Peter's (€16 entry plus €9 service fee). You skip the ticket-buying line at the Vatican Museums and get an entry time, generally for the same day (see page 869 for other Vatican Museums ticketing options).

Services: WCs are on both sides of St. Peter's Square (by the TI and just outside security), near the baggage check down the steps by the church entrance, and on the roof.

⊘ Self-Guided Tour

To sample the basilica's highlights, follow these points:

❶ The narthex (portico) is itself bigger than most churches. The huge white columns on the portico date from the first church (fourth century). Five famous bronze doors lead into the church. Made from the melted-down bronze of the original door of Old St. Peter's, the central door was the first Renaissance work in Rome (c. 1450). It's only opened on special occasions.

The far-right entrance is the **Holy Door,** opened only during Holy Years (and special "Jubilee" years designated by the pope). On Christmas Eve every 25 years, the pope knocks three times with a silver hammer and the door opens, welcoming pilgrims to pass through.

• *Enter the church.*

Looking down the nave, we get a sense of the splendor of ancient Rome that was carried on by the Catholic Church. The

floor plan, with a central aisle (nave) flanked by two side aisles, is based on that of ancient Roman basilicas—large halls built to accommodate business and legal meetings. In fact, many of the stones used to build St. Peter's were scavenged from the ruined law courts of ancient Rome.

• *Head to the round maroon pavement stone on the floor near the central doorway.*

❷ This is the spot where, on Christmas night in A.D. 800, the king of the Franks **Charlemagne was crowned** Holy Roman Em-

ROME

St. Peter's Basilica

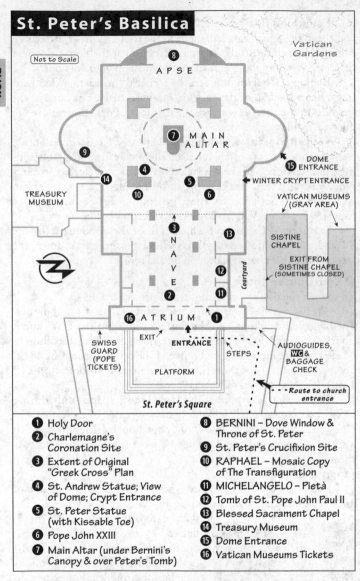

1 Holy Door

2 Charlemagne's Coronation Site

3 Extent of Original "Greek Cross" Plan

4 St. Andrew Statue; View of Dome; Crypt Entrance

5 St. Peter Statue (with Kissable Toe)

6 Pope John XXIII

7 Main Altar (under Bernini's Canopy & over Peter's Tomb)

8 BERNINI – Dove Window & Throne of St. Peter

9 St. Peter's Crucifixion Site

10 RAPHAEL – Mosaic Copy of The Transfiguration

11 MICHELANGELO – Pietà

12 Tomb of St. Pope John Paul II

13 Blessed Sacrament Chapel

14 Treasury Museum

15 Dome Entrance

16 Vatican Museums Tickets

peror. Look down the main hall—this church is huge. The golden window at the far end is two football fields away. The dove in the golden window has the wingspan of a 747 (OK, maybe not quite, but it is big). The church covers six acres. The babies at the base of the pillars along the main hall (the nave) are adult-size. The lettering in the gold band along the top of the pillars is seven feet high.

Really. The church has a capacity of 60,000 standing worshippers (or 1,200 tour groups).

• *Now, walk straight up the center of the nave toward the altar.*

❸ Michelangelo was 71 years old when the pope persuaded him to take over the church project and cap it with a dome. He agreed, intending to put the dome over Donato Bramante's original **Greek-Cross floor plan,** with four equal arms. In optimistic Renaissance times, this symmetrical arrangement symbolized perfection—the orderliness of the created world and the goodness of man (who was created in God's image). But the Church, struggling against Protestants and its own corruption, opted for a plan designed to impress the world with its grandeur—the Latin cross of the Crucifixion, with its nave extended to accommodate the grand religious spectacles of the Baroque period.

❹ Park yourself in front of the statue of **St. Andrew** to the left of the altar, the guy holding an X-shaped cross. (Note that the **crypt** entrance, described later, is usually here.) Like Andrew, gaze up into the dome, and also like him, gasp.

The **dome** soars higher than a football field on end, 448 feet from the floor of the cathedral to the top of the lantern. It glows with light from its windows, the blue and gold mosaics creating a cool, solemn atmosphere. In this majestic vision of heaven (not painted by Michelangelo), we see (above the windows) Jesus, Mary, and a ring of saints, rings of more angels above them, and, way up in the ozone, God the Father (a blur of blue and red, unless you have binoculars).

❺ Back in the nave sits a bronze **statue of Peter** under a canopy. This is one of a handful of pieces of art that were in the earlier church. In one hand he holds keys, the symbol of the authority given him by Christ, while with the other hand he blesses us. His big right toe has been worn smooth by the lips of pilgrims and foot fetishists. Stand in line to kiss it, or, to avoid foot-and-mouth disease, touch your hand to your lips, then rub the toe. This is simply an act of reverence with no legend attached, though you can make one up if you like.

• *Circle to the right around the statue of Peter to find the lighted glass niche.*

❻ The red-robed body is **Pope John XXIII,** whose papacy lasted from 1958 to 1963. Nicknamed "the good pope," he is best known for initiating the landmark Vatican II Council (1962-1965) that instituted major reforms, bringing the Church into the modern age. In 2000, during the beatification process (a stop on the way to sainthood), Church authorities checked his body, and it was surprisingly fresh. So they moved it upstairs, put it behind glass, and now old Catholics who remember him fondly enjoy another stop on their St. Peter's visit. Pope John was canonized in 2014.

❼ Sitting over St. Peter's tomb, the **main altar** (the white marble slab with cross and candlesticks) beneath the dome and canopy is used only when the pope himself says Mass. He sometimes conducts the Sunday morning service when he's in town, a sight worth seeing.

The tiny altar would be lost in this enormous church if it weren't for Gian Lorenzo Bernini's seven-story **bronze canopy** (God's "four-poster bed"), which "extends" the altar upward and reduces the perceived distance between floor and ceiling. The corkscrew columns echo the marble ones that surrounded the altar/tomb in Old St. Peter's.

❽ Bernini (1598-1680), the Michelangelo of the Baroque era, is the man most responsible for the interior decoration of the church.

His **dove window** shines above the smaller front altar used for everyday services. The Holy Spirit, in the form of a six-foot-high dove, pours sunlight onto the faithful through the alabaster windows, turning into artificial rays of gold and reflecting off swirling gold clouds, angels, and winged babies. During a service, real sunlight passes through real clouds of incense, mingling with Bernini's sculpture. Beneath the dove is the centerpiece of this structure, the so-called **Throne of St. Peter,** an oak chair built

in medieval times for a king. Subsequently, it was encrusted with tradition and encased in bronze by Bernini as a symbol of papal authority.

In the apse, Mass is said daily for pilgrims, tourists, and Roman citizens alike (for Mass times, see "Church Services," earlier).

• *To the left of the main altar is the **south transept**. It may be roped off for worship, but anyone can step past the guard if you say you're there "for prayer." At the far end, left side, find the dark "painting" of St. Peter crucified upside down.*

❾ This marks the exact spot (according to tradition) of **Peter's crucifixion site.** Peter had come to the world's greatest city to preach Jesus' message of love to the pagan, often-hostile Romans. During the reign of Emperor Nero, he was arrested and brought to Nero's Circus so all of Rome could witness his execution. When

ROME

the authorities told Peter he was to be crucified just like his Lord, Peter said, essentially, "I'm not worthy" and insisted they nail him on the cross upside down.

❿ Around the corner on the right (heading back toward the central nave), pause at the mosaic copy of Raphael's epic painting of *The Transfiguration.* The original is now beautifully displayed in the Pinacoteca of the Vatican Museums. This and all the other "paintings" in the church are actually mosaic copies made from thousands of colored chips the size of your little fingernail. (Because smoke and humidity would damage real paintings, church officials since about 1600 have replaced the paintings with mosaics (a.k.a. the "art of eternity") produced by the Vatican Mosaic Studio.)

• *Back near the entrance of the church, in the far corner, behind bulletproof glass, is the sculpture everyone has come to see, the* pietà.

⓫ Michelangelo was 24 years old when he completed his *pietà*—a representation of Mary with the body of Christ taken from the cross. It was his first major commission, done for Holy Year 1500. Michelangelo, with his total mastery of the real world, captures the sadness of the moment. Mary cradles her crucified son in her lap. Christ's lifeless right arm drooping down lets us know how heavy this corpse is. Mary looks at her dead son with sad tenderness. Her left hand turns upward, asking, "How could they do this to you?"

• *In the chapel to the left is the tomb of Pope John Paul II.*

⓬ John Paul II (1920-2005) was one of the most beloved popes of recent times. During his papacy (1978-2005), he was the highly visible face of the Catholic Church as it labored to stay relevant in an increasingly secular world. The first non-Italian pope in four centuries, he oversaw the fall of communism in his native Poland. He survived an assassination attempt, and he publicly endured his slow decline from Parkinson's disease with great stoicism.

When John Paul II died in 2005, hundreds of thousands lined up outside the church, waiting up to 24 hours to pay their respects. He was sainted in April 2014, just nine years after his death...light speed by Vatican standards. St. John Paul

II lies beneath a painting of the steadfast St. Sebastian, his favorite saint.

You're welcome to step through the metalwork gates into the **⓭ Blessed Sacrament Chapel,** an oasis of peace reserved for prayer and meditation on the right-hand side of the church, about midway to the altar. Mass is sometimes said here.

The **⓮ Treasury Museum,** located on the left side of the nave near the altar, contains the room-size tomb of Sixtus IV by Antonio Pollaiuolo, a big pair of Roman pincers used to torture Christians, an original corkscrew column from Old St. Peter's, and assorted jewels, papal robes, and golden reliquaries—a marked contrast to the poverty of early Christians.

Other Sights at the Church

When you're finished viewing the church's interior, you can go down to the foundations of Old St. Peter's, to the **crypt** (*grotte* or *tombe*) containing tombs of popes and memorial chapels. (I've saved the crypt for last because it exits outside the basilica.) In summer, the crypt entrance is usually beside the statue of St. Andrew, to the left of the main altar; in winter, it's by the cupola entrance. Stairs lead you down to the floor level of the previous church, where you'll pass the sepulcher of Peter. This lighted niche with an icon is not Peter's actual tomb, but part of a shrine that stands atop Peter's tomb. Next are the tombs of past popes, including the traditionalist Paul VI (1897-1978) and a few column fragments from Old St. Peter's (a.k.a. "Basilica Costantiniana"). Continue your one-way visit until it spills you out, usually near the checkroom.

For one of the best views of Rome, go up to the **dome.** The entrance is along the right (north) side of the church, but the line begins to form out front, at the church's right door (as you face the church). Look for *cupola* signs.

There are two levels: the rooftop of the church and the very top of the dome. Climb or take an elevator to the first level, on the church roof just above the facade. From the roof, you can also go inside the gallery ringing the interior of the dome and look down inside the church. To go all the way up to the top of the dome, you'll take a staircase that actually winds between the outer shell and the inner one. It's a sweaty, crowded, claustrophobic 15-minute, 323-step climb, but the view from the summit is great, the fresh air even better. Admire the arms of Bernini's colonnade encircling St. Peter's Square. Find the big, white Victor

Emmanuel Monument and the Pantheon, with its light, shallow dome. The large rectangular building to the left of the obelisk is the Vatican Museums complex, stuffed with art. And down in the square are tiny pilgrims buzzing like electrons around the nucleus of Catholicism.

▲▲▲Vatican Museums (Musei Vaticani)

The four miles of displays in this immense museum complex—from ancient statues to Christian frescoes to modern paintings—culminate in the Raphael Rooms and Michelangelo's glorious Sistine Chapel. This is one of Europe's top three or four houses of art. It can be exhausting, so plan your visit carefully, focusing on a few themes. Allow two hours for a quick visit, three or four hours for enough time to enjoy it.

Cost and Hours: €16, €4 online reservation fee, Mon-Sat 9:00-18:00, last entry at 16:00 (though the official closing time is 18:00, the staff starts ushering you out at 17:30), closed on religious holidays and Sun except last Sun of the month (when it's free, more crowded, and open 9:00-14:00, last entry at 12:30); may be open Fri nights May-July and Sept-Oct 19:00-23:00 (last entry at 21:30) by online reservation only—check the website. Hours are subject to frequent change and holidays; look online for current times.

The museum is closed on many holidays (mainly religious ones), including, for 2017: Jan 1 (New Year's), Jan 6 (Epiphany), Feb 11 (Vatican City established), March 19 (St. Joseph's Day), April 16 and 17 (Easter Sunday/Monday), May 1 (Labor Day), June 29 (Sts. Peter and Paul), Aug 15 (Assumption of the Virgin), Nov 1 (All Saints' Day), Dec 8 (Immaculate Conception), and Dec 25 and 26 (Christmas). Because changes in hours and other holiday closures may occur, always check the current hours and calendar at http://mv.vatican.va.

Individual rooms may close at odd hours, especially in the afternoon. The rooms described here are usually open.

Reservations: The Vatican Museums can be extremely crowded, with waits of up to two hours to buy tickets. Bypass the long ticket lines by reserving an entry time at http://mv.vatican.va for €20 (€16 ticket plus €4 booking fee). It's easy. Just choose your day and time, then check your email for your confirmation and print

ROME

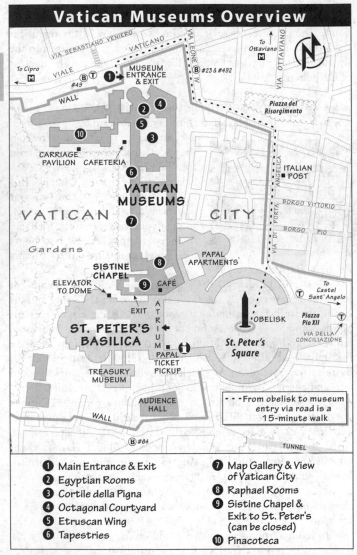

Vatican Museums Overview

1 Main Entrance & Exit
2 Egyptian Rooms
3 Cortile della Pigna
4 Octagonal Courtyard
5 Etruscan Wing
6 Tapestries

7 Map Gallery & View of Vatican City
8 Raphael Rooms
9 Sistine Chapel & Exit to St. Peter's (can be closed)
10 Pinacoteca

out the voucher. At the Vatican Museums, bypass the ticket-buying line and queue up at the "Visitor Entrance with Online Reservations" line (to the right). Show your voucher to the guard and go in. Once inside the museum, present your voucher at a ticket window *(cassa),* either in the lobby or upstairs, and they'll issue your ticket.

When to Go: Except in winter, the museum is generally hot and crowded, with long ticket lines and shoulder-to-shoulder sightseeing through much of it. The worst days are Saturdays, the last

Sunday of the month (when it's free), Mondays, rainy days, and any day before or after a holiday closure. Mornings are most crowded. The best (or least-worst) time to visit is a weekday after 14:00—the later the better. Another good time is during the papal audience on Wednesday morning, when many tourists are at St. Peter's Square (the only drawback is that St. Peter's Basilica is closed until roughly 13:00, as is the exit to it from the Sistine Chapel—described later, under "Museum Strategies").

More Line-Beating Tips: Booking a **guided tour** gets you right in—just show the guard your voucher. You can often buy **same-day tickets** without a ticket-buying line at the Vatican TI in St. Peter's Square (€20; to the left, as you face the basilica). If you're going to St. Peter's Basilica first, you can normally buy Vatican Museums tickets in the narthex (€25). The Opera Romana Pellegrinaggi (a.k.a. Roma Cristiana), a private pilgrimage tour company, also sells same-day tickets (€27.50, entrances almost hourly, office in front of St. Peter's Square, Piazza Pio XII 9, tel. 06-6980-6380, www.operaromanapellegrinaggi.org). Hawkers peddling skip-the-line access swarm the Vatican area, offering tours with guides of varying quality—museum staff advise against accepting their offers.

Getting There: The Ottaviano Metro stop is a 10-minute walk from the entrance. Bus #49 from Piazza Cavour/Castel Sant'Angelo stops at Piazza Risorgimento and continues right to the entrance. Bus #23 from Trastevere hugs the west bank of the Tiber and stops on Via Leone IV, just downhill from the entrance. Bus #492 heads from the city center past Piazza Risorgimento and the Vatican walls, and also stops on Via Leone IV. Bus #64 stops on the other side of St. Peter's Square, a 15- to 20-minute walk (facing the church from the obelisk, take a right through the colonnade and follow the Vatican Wall). Or take a taxi from the city center—they are reasonable (hop in and say, "moo-ZAY-ee vah-tee-KAH-nee").

Getting In: Make sure you get in the right entry line. Generally, individuals without tickets line up against the Vatican City wall (to the left of the entrance as you face it), and reservation holders (both individuals and groups) enter on the right. All visitors must pass through a metal detector (no pocketknives allowed).

Tours: A €7 audioguide is available at the top of the spiral ramp/escalator, and can be prepaid when you book tickets online. No ID is required to rent an audioguide, and you can drop it off either where you rented it or after leaving the Sistine Chapel if taking the shortcut to St. Peter's (described later, under "Museum Strategies"). Confirm the drop-off location when renting.

∩ Download my free Vatican Museums and Sistine Chapel audio tours.

Vatican City

The tiny independent country of Vatican City is contained entirely within Rome. (Its 100 acres could fit eight times over in New York's Central Park.) The Vatican has its own postal system, euro coin (with a portrait of the pope), armed guards, beautiful gardens, a helipad, mini train station, and radio station (KPOP). It also has two huge sights: St. Peter's Basilica and the Vatican Museums. Politically powerful, the Vatican is the religious capital of 1.2 billion Roman Catholics. If you're not a Catholic, become one for your visit.

The pope is both the religious and secular leader of Vatican City. For centuries, the Vatican was the capital of the Papal States, and locals referred to the pontiff as "King Pope." Because of the Vatican's territorial ambitions, it didn't always have good relations with Italy. Even though modern Italy was created in 1870, the Holy See didn't recognize it as a country until 1929.

Vatican Gardens: To walk through the manicured Vatican Gardens (with views over Rome and a good look at St. Peter's dome), you must book a guided tour several days in advance at http://biglietteriamusei.vatican.va (€32, 2 hours, daily except Wed and Sun, includes entry to Vatican Museums; tours usually start at 9:30 or 11:00 at Vatican Museums tour desk). On rare occasions, same-day tickets are available at the Vatican TI. A 45-minute open-bus tour through the gardens is offered in good weather (€36 includes audioguide and admission to Vatican Museums).

General Audience Tickets: For the Wednesday audience, you need a (free) ticket to get close to the papal action and get a seat. Reserve tickets (available about a month or two in advance) by sending a request by mail or fax (access the form at www.vatican.va, under "Prefecture of the Papal Household"). You'll then pick up the tickets at St. Peter's Square before the audience

The Vatican offers guided tours in English that are easy to book on their website (€32, includes admission). As with individual ticket reservations, present your confirmation voucher to a guard to the right of the entrance; then, once inside, go to the Guided Tours desk (in the lobby, up a few stairs).

For private tour companies and guides, see page 813.

Length of This Tour: Until you expire, the museum closes, or 2.5 hours pass, whichever comes first. If you're short on time, see the octagonal courtyard (*Laocoön*), then follow the crowd flow directly to the Sistine Chapel, sightseeing along the way. From the Sistine Chapel, head straight to St. Peter's via the shortcut, if open (see "Museum Strategies," below).

Services: The museum's "checkroom" (to the right after security) takes only bigger bags, not day bags. The post office, with (available Tue 15:00-19:00 and Wed 7:00-9:00; usually under Bernini's colonnade, to the left of the church).

You can also book tickets online through the American Catholic Church in Rome (details at www.santasusanna.org; free, but donations appreciated). Pick up your reserved tickets or check for last-minute availability at the church office the Tuesday before the audience between 16:30 and 18:15 (Via XX Settembre 15, Metro: Repubblica, tel. 06-4201-4554—charming Rosanna speaks English).

Finally, starting the Monday before the audience, Swiss Guards hand out tickets from their station near the basilica exit (see map on page 864). There's no need to go through security—just march up, ask nicely, and say *"danke."* While this is perhaps the easiest way, I'd reserve in advance to guarantee a ticket.

General Audience Tips: On Wednesday morning, you'll need to be dressed appropriately (shoulders and knees covered) and clear security (no big bags; lines tend to move more quickly on the side of the square farthest from the Metro stop). To get a seat (much less a good one), it's smart to be there a couple of hours early—there are far fewer seats than ticketholders. If you just want to see the pope, get a good photo, and don't mind standing, you can show up later (though still at least 30 minutes early) and take your place in the standing-room section in the back half of the square. The service gets underway around 9:30, when the names of attending pilgrim groups are announced. Shortly thereafter, the Popemobile appears, winding through the adoring crowd (the best places—seated or standing—are near the cloth-covered wooden fences that line the Popemobile route). Around 10:00, the Pope's multilingual message begins and lasts for about an hour (you can leave at any time).

stamps that make collectors drool, is upstairs. WCs are mainly at the entrance/exit, plus a few scattered within the collection.

Museum Strategies: The museum has two exits. The **main exit** is near the entrance. Use this one if you're asked to return an audioguide there or if you plan on following this self-guided tour exactly as laid out, visiting the Pinacoteca at the end.

The other exit is a handy (but sometimes closed) **shortcut** that leads from the Sistine Chapel directly to St. Peter's Basilica (spilling out alongside the church; see map on page 864). The shortcut saves you a 30-minute walk backtracking to the basilica's main entrance and lets you avoid the often-long security line there. Officially, this exit is for Vatican guides and their groups only. However, it's often open to anyone (depending on how crowded the chapel is and how the guards feel). It's worth a shot (try blending in with

ROME

a group that's leaving), but be prepared for the possibility that you won't get through.

Photography: No photos allowed in the Sistine Chapel, but photos without flash are permitted elsewhere.

◉ Self-Guided Tour

Start, as civilization did, in **Egypt and Mesopotamia.** Decorating the museum's courtyard are some of the best **Greek and Roman statues** in captivity. The *Apollo Belvedere* is a Roman copy (4th century B.C.) of a Hellenistic original that followed the style of the great Greek sculptor Praxiteles. It fully captures the beauty of the human form. The anatomy is perfect, his pose is natural. Instead of standing at attention, face-forward with his arms at his sides (Egyptian-style), Apollo is on the move, coming to rest with his weight on one leg.

Laocoön was sculpted some four centuries after the Golden Age (5th-4th century B.C.), after the scales of "balance" had been tipped. Whereas *Apollo* is a balance between stillness and motion, this is unbridled motion. *Apollo* is serene, graceful, and godlike, while *Laocoön* is powerful, emotional, and gritty. The figures (carved from four blocks of marble pieced together seamlessly) are powerful, not light and graceful. The poses are as twisted as possible, accentuating every rippling muscle and bulging vein.

The centerpiece of the next hall is the *Belvedere Torso* (just a 2,000-year-old torso, but one that had a great impact on the art of Michelangelo). Finishing off the classical statuary are two fine fourth-century porphyry sarcophagi. These royal purple tombs were made (though not used) for the Roman emperor Constantine's mother (Helena, on left) and daughter (Constanza, on right).

After long halls of tapestries, old maps, broken penises, and fig leaves, you'll come to what most people are looking for: the Raphael Rooms and Michelangelo's Sistine Chapel.

Raphael Rooms: The highlight of the Raphael Rooms, frescoed by Raphael and his assistants, is the restored *School of Athens*. It is remarkable for its blatant pre-Christian classical orientation, especially considering it originally wallpapered the apartments of Pope Julius II. Raphael honors the great pre-Christian thinkers—Aristotle, Plato, and company—who are portrayed as the leading artists of Raphael's  day. There's Leonardo da Vinci, whom Raphael worshipped, in the role of Plato. Michelangelo broods in the foreground, added later. When Raphael snuck a peek at the Sistine Chapel, he decided that his arch-competitor was so good that he had to put their personal differences aside and include him in this tribute to the artists of his generation. Today's St. Peter's was under construction as Raphael was working. In the *School of Athens*, he gives us a sneak preview of the unfinished church.

Sistine Chapel: Next is the brilliantly restored Sistine Chapel. This is the pope's personal chapel and also the place where, upon the death of the ruling pope, a new pope is elected.

The Sistine Chapel is famous for Michelangelo's pictorial culmination of the Renaissance, showing the story of creation, with a powerful God weaving in and out of each scene through that busy first week. This is an optimistic and positive expression of the High Renaissance and a stirring example of the artistic and theological maturity of the 33-year-old Michelangelo, who spent four years on this work.

The ceiling shows the history of the world before the birth of Jesus. We see God creating the world, creating man and woman, destroying the earth by flood, and so on. God himself, in his purple robe, actually appears in the first five scenes. Along the sides (where the ceiling starts to curve), we see the Old Testament prophets and pagan Greek prophetesses who foretold the coming of Christ. Dividing these scenes and figures are fake niches (a painted 3-D illusion) decorated with nude statue-like figures with symbolic meaning.

In the central panel of the *Creation of Adam*, God and man take center stage in this Renaissance version of creation. Adam, newly formed in the image of God, lounges dreamily in perfect naked innocence. God, with his entourage, swoops in with a swirl of activity (which—with a little imagination— looks like a cross-section of a human brain...quite  a strong humanist statement). Their reaching hands are the center of this work. Adam's is limp and passive; God's is strong and forceful, his finger twitching upward with energy. Here is the very moment of creation, as God passes the spark of life to man, the crowning work of his creation.

This is the spirit of the Renaissance. God is not a terrifying giant reaching down to puny and helpless man from way on high. Here they are on an equal plane, divided only by the diagonal bit of sky. God's billowing robe and the patch of green upon which Adam is lying balance each other. They are like two pieces of a jigsaw puzzle, or two long-separated continents, or like the yin and

The Sistine Ceiling

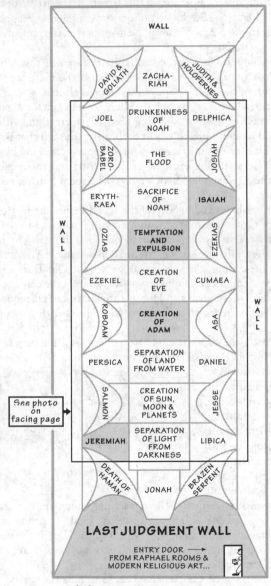

WALL

DAVID & GOLIATH

JUDITH & HOLOFERNES

ZACHA-RIAH

JOEL

DRUNKENNESS OF NOAH

DELPHICA

ZORO-BABEL

THE FLOOD

JOSIAH

ERYTH-RAEA

SACRIFICE OF NOAH

ISAIAH

OZIAS

TEMPTATION AND EXPULSION

EZEKIAS

EZEKIEL

CREATION OF EVE

CUMAEA

ROBOAM

CREATION OF ADAM

ASA

PERSICA

SEPARATION OF LAND FROM WATER

DANIEL

SALMON

CREATION OF SUN, MOON & PLANETS

JESSE

JEREMIAH

SEPARATION OF LIGHT FROM DARKNESS

LIBICA

WALL

WALL

See photo on facing page →

DEATH OF HAMAN

JONAH

BRAZEN SERPENT

LAST JUDGMENT WALL

ENTRY DOOR →
FROM RAPHAEL ROOMS &
MODERN RELIGIOUS ART...

☆ TO USE THIS DIAGRAM:
FACE THE LAST JUDGMENT &
HOLD THE BOOK UP TO THE CEILING.

yang symbols finally coming together—uniting, complementing each other, creating wholeness. God and man work together in the divine process of creation.

When the ceiling was finished and revealed to the public, it simply blew 'em away. It both caps the Renaissance and turns it in a new direction. In perfect Renaissance spirit, it mixes Old Testament prophets with classical figures. But the style is more dramatic, shocking, and emotional than the balanced Renaissance works before it. This is a very personal work—the Gospel according to Michelangelo—but its themes and subject matter are universal. Many art scholars contend that the Sistine ceiling is the single greatest work of art by any one human being.

Later, after the Reformation wars had begun and after the Catholic army of Spain had sacked the Vatican, the reeling Church began to fight back. As part of its Counter-Reformation, a much older Michelangelo was commissioned to paint the *Last Judgment* (behind the altar).

It's Judgment Day, and Christ—the powerful figure in the center, raising his arm to spank the wicked—has come to find out who's naughty and who's nice. Beneath him, a band of angels blows its trumpets Dizzy Gillespie-style, giving a wake-up call to the sleeping dead. The dead at lower left leave their graves and prepare to be judged. The righteous, on Christ's right hand (the left side of the picture), are carried up to the glories of heaven. The wicked on the other side are hurled down to hell, where demons wait to torture them. Charon, from the underworld of Greek mythology, waits below to ferry the souls of the damned to hell.

When *The Last Judgment* was unveiled to the public in 1541, it caused a sensation. The pope is said to have dropped to his knees and cried, "Lord, charge me not with my sins when thou shalt come on the Day of Judgment."

And it changed the course of art. The complex composition, with more than 300 figures swirling around the figure of Christ, went far beyond traditional Renaissance balance. The twisted figures shown from every imaginable angle challenged other painters to try and top this master of 3-D illusion. And the sheer terror and drama of the scene was a striking contrast to the placid optimism of, say, Raphael's *School of Athens*. Michelangelo had Baroque-en all the rules of the Renaissance, signaling a new era of art.

ROME

Exiting the Vatican Museums: To go **directly to St. Peter's Basilica** (see "Museum Strategies," earlier), take the shortcut exit at the far-right corner of the chapel (with your back to the altar—once through this door, you've left the Vatican Museums). Though this corner door is likely labeled "Exit for authorized guides and tour groups only," you can probably slide through with the crowds (or protest that your group has left you behind). If this exit is closed (which can happen without notice), hang out in the Sistine Chapel for a few more minutes—it'll likely reopen shortly.

If you skip the shortcut and take the long march back, you'll find, along with the Pinacoteca, a cafeteria (long lines, uninspired food), the underrated early-Christian art section, and the exit through the souvenir shop.

NORTH ROME
Borghese Gardens
▲Villa Borghese Gardens

Rome's semi scruffy three-square-mile "Central Park" is great for its quiet shaded paths and for people-watching plenty of modern-day Romeos and Juliets. The best entrance is at the head of Via Veneto (Metro: Barberini, then 10-minute walk up Via Veneto and through the old Roman wall at Porta Pinciana, or catch a cab to Via Veneto—Porta Pinciana). There you'll find a cluster of buildings with a café, a kiddie arcade, and bike rental (€4/hour). Rent a bike or, for romantics, a pedaled rickshaw (*risciò*, €12/hour).

Bikes come with locks to allow you to make sightseeing stops. Follow signs to discover the park's cafés, fountains, statues, lake, and prime picnic spots. Some sights require paid admission, including the Borghese Gallery, Rome's zoo, and the National Gallery of Modern Art (which holds 19th-century art).

You can also enter the gardens from the top of the Spanish Steps (facing the church, turn left and walk down the road 200 yards beyond Villa Medici, then angle right on the small pathway into the gardens), and from Piazza del Popolo (in the northeast corner of the piazza, stairs lead to the gardens via a terrace with grand views out to St. Peter's Basilica—bikes and Segways can be rented nearby).

▲▲▲Borghese Gallery (Galleria Borghese)

This plush museum, filling a cardinal's mansion in the park, offers one of Europe's most sumptuous art experiences. You'll enjoy

ROME

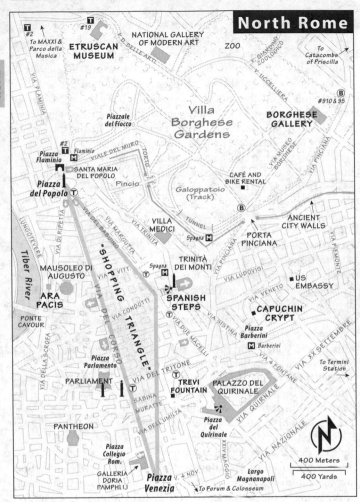

North Rome

To MAXXI & Parco della Musica · #2 · #19 · NATIONAL GALLERY OF MODERN ART · ZOO · ETRUSCAN MUSEUM · V. D. BELLE ARTI · To Catacombs of Priscilla · V. GIACOMO ZOOLOGICO · V. UCCELLIERA · VIA FLAMINIA · #910 & 95 · B · Piazzale del Fiocco · Villa Borghese Gardens · BORGHESE GALLERY · VIA MUSEO BORGHESE · VIA PINCIANA · #2 · Flaminio · VIALE DEL MURO · Piazza Flaminio · M · SANTA MARIA DEL POPOLO · TORTO · CAFÉ AND BIKE RENTAL · Pincio · Galoppatoio (Track) · Piazza del Popolo · T · VIA DI RIPETTA · VIA DEL BABUINO · VIA MARGUTTA · VIA TRINITA · VILLA MEDICI · TUNNEL · B · Spagna · M · ANCIENT CITY WALLS · PORTA PINCIANA · VIA PIEMONTE · Tiber River · LUNGOTEVERE · MAUSOLEO DI AUGUSTO · VIA VITT. · Spagna · T · M · TRINITÀ DEI MONTI · VIA PINCIANA · VIA LUDOVISI · US EMBASSY · "SHOPPING TRIANGLE" · VIA DEL CORSO · VIA CONDOTTI · SPANISH STEPS · VIA DUE MACELLI · VIA SISTINA · VIA VENETO · CAPUCHIN CRYPT · ARA PACIS · VIA DELLA SCROFA · PONTE CAVOUR · Piazza Parlamento · PARLIAMENT · Piazza Barberini · Barberini · M · VIA XX SETTEMBRE · To Termini Station · VIA DEL TRITONE · SABINA · MURATTE · TREVI FOUNTAIN · T · PALAZZO DEL QUIRINALE · VIA 4 FONTANE · VIA QUIRINALE · PANTHEON · VIA DELL'UMILTÀ · Piazza del Quirinale · Piazza Collegio Rom. · XXIV MAGGIO · VIA NAZIONALE · GALLERIA DORIA PAMPHILIJ · Piazza Venezia · V. 4 NOV · Largo Magnanapoli · To Forum & Colosseum · 400 Meters · 400 Yards

a collection of world-class Baroque sculpture, including Bernini's *David* and his excited statue of Apollo chasing Daphne, as well as paintings by Caravaggio, Raphael, Titian, and Rubens. The museum's mandatory reservation system keeps crowds to a manageable size.

Cost and Hours: €11, free and very crowded first Sun of the month, Tue-Sun 9:00-19:00, closed Mon. The 1.5-hour audioguide (€5) is excellent.

Reservations: Reservations are required and simple to get.

Entry times are 9:00, 11:00, 13:00, 15:00, and 17:00 (and you'll get exactly two hours for your visit). The sooner you reserve, the better—at least several days in advance for a weekday visit, and at least a week ahead for weekends. (In winter, you may be able to get tickets on shorter notice.) It's easiest to book online at www.tosc. it, though it costs an additional €4 (€15 total). When the site asks what "Dispatch Type" you want, choose "Pick-up at the venue box office." You can also reserve by telephone (with a real person) for no extra fee (tel. 06-32810, press 2 for English, phones answered Mon-Fri 9:00-18:00, Sat 9:00-13:00, closed Sat in Aug and Sun year-round). After you reserve a day and time, you'll get a claim number. The museum recommends that you arrive at the gallery 30 minutes before your appointed time to pick up your ticket in the lobby on the lower level. Don't cut it close—arriving late can mean forfeiting your reservation. You can use a Roma Pass for free or discounted entry, but you're still required to make a reservation (by phone only—not online; specify that you have the Roma Pass).

Getting There: The museum is set idyllically but inconveniently in the vast Villa Borghese Gardens. The most foolproof approach by public transportation is on bus #910, which goes from Termini train station (and Piazza della Repubblica) to the Via Pinciana stop, 100 yards from the museum. Bus #53 runs to the same stop from the Barberini Metro station.

You can also go by foot (20 minutes) from the Barberini Metro stop: walk 10 minutes up Via Veneto, enter the park, and turn right, following signs another 10 minutes to the Borghese Gallery.

Tours: Guided English tours are offered in the 9:00 and 11:00 time slots (€6.50). You can't book a tour when you make your museum reservation—sign up when you arrive. Or consider the excellent 1.5-hour audioguide tour (€5).

Length of This Tour: Two hours is all you get...and you'll want every minute. Budget most of your time for the more interesting ground floor, but set aside 30 minutes for the paintings of the Pinacoteca upstairs (highlights are marked by the audioguide icons).

Services: Baggage check is free, mandatory, and strictly enforced.

Photography: Allowed without flash.

Visiting the Museum: It's hard to believe that a family of cardinals and popes would display so many works with secular and sensual—even erotic—themes. But the Borgheses felt that all forms of human expression, including pagan myths and physical passion, glorified God.

The essence of the collection is the connection of the Renaissance with the classical world. As you enter, notice the second-century Roman reliefs with Michelangelo-designed panels above

ROME

Borghese Gallery—Ground Floor

Stairs up
to Pinacoteca

ROOM VI ROOM V ROOM IV **9** ROOM III

6 **4** CHAPEL **3**

5

ROOM VII MAIN ENTRY HALL ROOM II **2**

7

ROOM VIII START ROOM I **1**

8 PORTICO

Not to Scale

To Basement
(Tickets, Info, Shop, WC)

1 CANOVA – Pauline Borghese as Venus
2 BERNINI – David
3 BERNINI – Apollo and Daphne
4 BERNINI – The Rape of Proserpina

5 UNKNOWN – Diana the Hunter; other marbles
6 BERNINI – Aeneas, Anchises, and Ascanius
7 "Theater of the Universe"
8 CARAVAGGIO – Various
9 Stairs up to Pinacoteca

either end of the portico. The villa was built in the early 17th century by the great art collector Cardinal Scipione Borghese, who wanted to prove that the glories of ancient Rome were matched by the Renaissance.

In the main entry hall, high up on the wall, is a thrilling first-century Greek sculpture of a horse falling. The Renaissance-era rider was added by Pietro Bernini, father of the famous Gian Lorenzo Bernini.

Each room seems to feature a Baroque masterpiece. In Room I is *Pauline Borghese as Venus,* for which Napoleon's sister went

the full monty for the sculptor Canova, scandalizing Europe. ("How could you have done such a thing?!" she was asked. She replied, "The room wasn't cold.") With the famous nose of her conqueror brother, she strikes the pose of Venus as conqueror of men's hearts. Her

relaxed afterglow and slight smirk say she's already had her man. The light dent she puts in the mattress makes this goddess human.

Notice the contrasting textures that Canova (1757-1822) gets out of the pure white marble: the rumpled sheet versus her smooth skin, the satiny-smooth pillows and mattress versus the creases in them, her porcelain skin versus the hint of a love handle. Canova polished and waxed the marble until it looked as soft and pliable as cloth.

The mythological pose, the Roman couch, the ancient hairdo, and the calm harmony make Pauline the epitome of the Neoclassical style.

In Room II, Gian Lorenzo Bernini's **David** twists around to put a big rock in his sling. He purses his lips, knits his brow, and winds his body like a spring as his eyes lock onto the target: Goliath, who's somewhere behind us, putting us right in the line of fire. Compared with Michelangelo's *David*, this is unvarnished realism—an unbalanced pose, bulging veins, unflattering face, and armpit hair. Michelangelo's *David* thinks, whereas Bernini's acts. Bernini slays the pretty-boy *David*s of the Renaissance and prepares to invent Baroque.

The best one of all is in Room III: Bernini's **Apollo and Daphne.** It's the perfect Baroque subject—capturing a thrilling, action-filled moment. In the mythological story, Apollo—made stupid by Cupid's arrow of love—chases after Daphne, who has been turned off by the "arrow of disgust." Just as he's about to catch her, she calls to her father to save her. Magically, her fingers begin to sprout leaves, her toes become roots, her skin turns to bark, and she transforms into a tree. Frustrated Apollo will end up with a handful of leaves. Walk slowly around the statue. It's more air than stone.

But don't stop here. In Room IV, admire Bernini's **The Rape of Proserpina,** proof that even at the age of 24 the sculptor was the master of marble. Over in Room VI, Bernini's first major work for Cardinal Borghese—**Aeneas, Anchises, and Ascanius**—reveals the then-20-year-old sculptor's astonishing aptitude for portraying human flesh, though the statue lacks the Baroque energy of his more mature work. And in Room VIII is a fabulous collection of paintings by **Caravaggio,** who brought Christian saints down to earth with gritty realism.

Upstairs, in the Pinacoteca (Painting Gallery), are busts and paintings by Bernini, as well as paintings by Raphael, Titian, Correggio, and Domenichino.

▲▲Catacombs of Priscilla (Catacombe di Priscilla)

While most tourists head to the Appian Way to see the famous catacombs of San Sebastiano and San Callisto (7.5 miles south of downtown, easiest by taxi), the Catacombs of Priscilla are less commercialized and less crowded—they just feel more intimate, as catacombs should. Explore the result of 250 years of tunneling that occurred from the second to the fifth century. Visits are by 30-minute guided tour only (English-language tours generally every 20 minutes). You'll see a few thousand carved burial niches and some beautiful frescoes, including what is considered the first depiction of Mary nursing the Baby Jesus.

Cost and Hours: €8, Tue-Sun 9:00-12:00 & 14:00-17:00, closed Mon, closed one random month a year—check website or call first, Via Salaria 430, tel. 06-8620-6272, www.catacombepriscilla.com.

Getting There: The catacombs are on the northeast edge of the city but well-served by direct buses (30 minutes from Termini or 40 minutes from Piazza Venezia) or a €15 taxi ride. From Termini, take bus #92 or #310 from Piazza Cinquecento. From Piazza Venezia, along Via del Corso or Via Barberini, take bus #63 or #83. Tell the driver "Piazza Crati" and "kah-tah-KOHM-bay" and he'll let you off near Piazza Crati (at the Nemorense/Crati stop). From there, walk through the little market in Piazza Crati, then down Via di Priscilla (about 5 minutes). The entrance is in the orange building on the left at the top of the hill.

EAST ROME
Near Termini Train Station

Most of these sights are within a 10-minute walk of the train station.

▲▲▲National Museum of Rome (Museo Nazionale Romano Palazzo Massimo alle Terme)

The National Museum's main branch, at Palazzo Massimo, houses the greatest collection of ancient Roman art anywhere, including busts of emperors and a Roman copy of the Greek *Discus Thrower*.

Cost and Hours: €10 combo-ticket covers three other branches—all skippable, free and very crowded first Sun of the month, Tue-Sun 9:00-19:45, closed Mon, last entry one hour before closing, audioguide-€5, about 100 yards from train station, Metro: Repubblica or Termini, tel. 06-3996-7700, www.archeoroma.beniculturali.it/en.

Getting There: The museum is between Piazza della Repubblica and Termini Station, a few minutes' walk from either the Repubblica or Termini Metro stop. As you leave Termini, it's the sandstone-brick building on your left. Enter at the far (west) end, at Largo di Villa Peretti.

Visiting the Museum: The museum is rectangular, with rooms and hallways built around a central courtyard. The ground-floor sculptures follow Rome's history as the city changes from a republic to a dictatorial empire. The first-floor exhibits take Rome from its peak through its slow decline. The second floor houses rare frescoes and fine mosaics, and the basement presents coins and everyday objects. As you tour this museum, note that in Italian, "room" is *sala* and "hall" is *galleria*.

On the first floor, along with statues and busts showing such emperors as Trajan and Hadrian, you'll see the best-preserved Roman copy of the Greek *Discus Thrower*. Statues of athletes like this commonly stood in the baths, where Romans cultivated healthy bodies, minds, and social skills, hoping to lead well-rounded lives. Other statues on this floor originally stood in the pleasure gardens of the Roman rich—surrounded by greenery with the splashing sound of fountains, all painted in bright, lifelike colors. Though created by Romans, the themes are mostly Greek, with godlike humans and human-looking gods.

The second floor contains frescoes and mosaics that once decorated the walls and floors of Roman villas. They're remarkably realistic and unstuffy, featuring everyday people, animals, flowery patterns, and geometrical designs. The Villa Farnesina frescoes—in black, red, yellow, and blue—are mostly architectural designs, with fake columns, friezes, and garlands. The Villa di Livia frescoes, owned by the wily wife of Augustus, immerse you in a leafy green garden full of birds and fruit trees, symbolizing the gods.

Finally, descend into the basement to see fine gold jewelry, the mummified body of an eight-year-old girl, and vault doors leading into the best coin collection in Europe, with fancy magnifying glasses maneuvering you through cases of coins from ancient Rome to modern times.

▲Baths of Diocletian/Church of Santa Maria degli Angeli (Terme di Diocleziano/Basilica S. Maria degli Angeli)

Of all the marvelous structures built by the Romans, their public baths were arguably the grandest, and the Baths of Diocletian were

the granddaddy of them all. Built by Emperor Diocletian around A.D. 300 and sprawling over 30 acres—roughly five times the size of the Colosseum—these baths could cleanse 3,000 Romans at once. They functioned until A.D. 537, when barbarians attacked and the city's aqueducts fell into disuse, plunging Rome into a thousand years of poverty, darkness, and BO. Today, tourists can visit one grand section of the baths, the former main hall. This impressive remnant of the ancient complex was later transformed

ROME

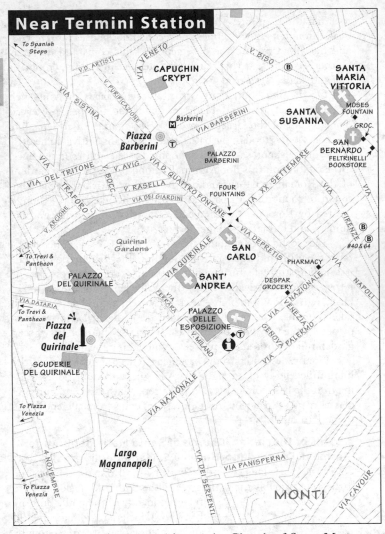

Near Termini Station

To Spanish Steps

V. D. ARTISTI

VIA VENETO

V. BISO

CAPUCHIN CRYPT

B

SANTA MARIA VITTORIA

VIA SISTINA

V. PURIFICAZIONE

Barberini

MOSES FOUNTAIN

GROC.

M

VIA BARBERINI

SANTA SUSANNA

Piazza Barberini

T

SAN BERNARDO

VIA DEL TRITONE

V. AVIG.

PALAZZO BARBERINI

FELTRINELLI BOOKSTORE

V. BOCC.

VIA D. QUATTRO FONTANE

VIA TRAFORO

V. RASELLA

FOUR FOUNTAINS

VIA XX. SETTEMBRE

VIA DEI GIARDINI

VIA FIRENZE

V. ARGONE.

VIA DEPRETIS

B

B

#40 & 64

V. LAV.

Quirinal Gardens

VIA QUIRINALE

SAN CARLO

PHARMACY

To Trevi & Pantheon

PALAZZO DEL QUIRINALE

SANT' ANDREA

DESPAR GROCERY

VIA NAPOLI

VIA DATARIA

VIA FERRARA

VIA NAZIONALE

GENOVA

PALERMO

To Trevi & Pantheon

Piazza del Quirinale

PALAZZO DELLE ESPOSIZIONE

V. MILANO

VIA VENEZIA

i

T

SCUDERIE DEL QUIRINALE

To Piazza Venezia

VIA NAZIONALE

To Piazza Venezia

4 NOVEMBRE

Largo Magnanapoli

VIA PANISPERNA

VIA DEI SERPENTI

MONTI

VIA CAVOUR

(with help from Michelangelo) into the Church of Santa Maria degli Angeli.

Cost and Hours: Free, Mon-Sat 7:00-18:30, Sun until 19:30, entrance on Piazza della Repubblica (Metro: Repubblica), www. santamariadegliangeliroma.it. Note that the Museum of the Bath, attached to the back (north side) of the complex and entered separately, is not part of the church but rather a branch of the National Museum of Rome that houses an exhibit of ancient inscriptions.

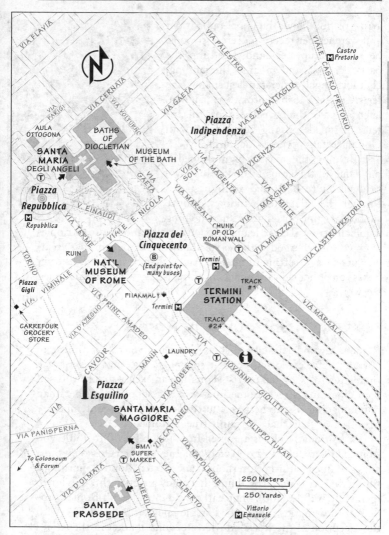

▲Church of Santa Maria della Vittoria

This church, originally a poor Carmelite church, was slathered with Baroque richness in the 17th century. It houses Bernini's best-known statue, the swooning *St. Teresa in Ecstasy*.

Cost and Hours: Free (anyone collecting money at the door is not affiliated with the church), pay €0.50 for light, Mon-Sat 8:30-12:00 & 15:30-18:00, Sun 15:30-18:00, about 5 blocks northwest of Termini train station at Via XX Settembre 17, Metro: Repubblica.

Visiting the Church: Inside the church, you'll find St. Teresa to the left of the altar. Teresa has just been stabbed with God's

arrow of fire. Now, the angel pulls it out and watches her reaction. Teresa swoons, her eyes roll up, her hand goes limp, she parts her lips...and moans. The smiling, cherubic angel understands just how she feels. Teresa, a 16th-century Spanish nun, later talked of the "sweetness" of "this intense pain," describing her oneness with God in ecstatic, even erotic, terms.

Bernini, the master of multimedia, pulls out all the stops to make this mystical vision real. Actual sunlight pours through the alabaster windows, bronze sunbeams shine on a marble angel holding a golden arrow. Teresa leans back on a cloud and her robe ripples from within, charged with her spiritual arousal. Bernini has created a little stage-setting of heaven. And watching from the "theater boxes" on either side are members of the family who commissioned the work.

Shopping in Rome

Rome is a wonderful city to shop in. Even if you're not aiming to buy anything, exploring popular shopping areas provides a break from stressful, clogged tourist sights and an excuse to lose yourself on a charming street. Sometimes window-shopping, rather than museumgoing, is the best way to connect with the contemporary life of a city. And that's certainly true in Rome.

Traditionally, shops are open from roughly 9:00 to 13:00 and from 15:30 or 16:00 to 19:00 or 19:30. They're often closed on Sundays, summer Saturday afternoons, and winter Monday mornings. But in the city center, you'll find that many are open through lunch (generally 10:00-19:00). Shop early if you intend to hit Rome's produce or flea markets (described at the end of this section)—with the exception of the weekend MercatoMonti market in the Monti neighborhood, they typically close by 13:30.

Department Stores

The shopping complex under Termini train station is a convenient place to peruse clothes, bags, shoes, and perfume at several major Italian chain stores (most open daily 8:00-22:00).

Large department stores offer relatively painless one-stop shopping. A good upscale department store is **La Rinascente** (like Nordstrom or Macy's). Its main branch is on Piazza Fiume (east of Borghese Gallery near the old city walls), and a smaller store is on Via del Corso in the **Galleria Alberto Sordi,** an elegant 19th-century "mall" (across from Piazza Colonna). **UPIM** is a popular midrange department store (many branches, including inside Termini train station, Via Nazionale 111, and Piazza Santa Maria Maggiore). **Oviesse/OVS,** a cheap clothing outlet, is near the Vatican Museums (on the corner of Via Candia and Via Mocenigo, Metro: Cipro) and also near Piazza Barberini (Via del Tritone 172, Metro: Barberini).

Affordable Shopping

The shopping area all along **Via del Corso** features moderately priced goods, with prices increasing as you head toward Piazza di Spagna (by the Spanish Steps). **Via Nazionale** also features a range of reasonably priced shops, especially for clothes and shoes. Near the bottom of Via Nazionale, in the **Monti** neighborhood near the Roman Forum, Via del Boschetto and Via dei Serpenti are more unique, with a mix of clothing shops and designer bric-a-brac. **Via Cola di Rienzo,** near the Vatican, is good for midrange clothes. Cheapskates scrounge through the junky but dirt-cheap shops in the gritty area around **Piazza Vittorio.**

Boutique Shopping: Rome's "Shopping Triangle"

The triangular-shaped area between the Spanish Steps, Piazza Venezia, and Piazza del Popolo (along Via del Corso, see map on page 800) contains Rome's highest concentration of upscale boutiques and fashion stores. For top fashion, stroll the streets around the Spanish Steps, including **Via Condotti, Via Borgognona** (for the big-name shops), and **Via del Babuino** (more big names and a few galleries). For antiques and vintage items, wander **Via dei Coronari** (between Piazza Navona and the bend in the river), **Via Giulia** (between Campo de' Fiori and the river), **Via dei Banchi Vecchi** (parallel to Via Giulia), and the super-chic **Via Margutta,** with art galleries too (hidden parallel to Via del Babuino and running from the Spanish Steps to Piazza del Popolo). For dozens of stores selling affordable apparel aimed mainly at a younger crowd, try **Via Giubbonari** near Campo de' Fiori.

Flea Markets

For antiques and fleas, the granddaddy of markets is the **Porta Portese** *mercato delle pulci* (flea market). This Sunday-morning

market is long and spindly, running between the actual Porta Portese (a gate in the old town wall) and the Trastevere train station. While the shopping gets old (and the vendor food shouldn't be consumed), the people-watching is endlessly entertaining (6:30-13:00 Sun only, on Via

Portuense and Via Ippolito Nievo; to get to the market, catch bus #75 from Termini train station or tram #8 from Piazza Venezia, get off the bus or tram on Viale di Trastevere, and walk toward the river—and the noise).

At the **Via Sannio** market, you'll find new and used clothing and leather goods, some handicrafts, and random items that were probably stolen. You won't find antiques (Mon-Sat 9:00-13:30, closed Sun, behind Coin department store, just outside the walls of San Giovanni in Laterano, Metro: San Giovanni).

For something a bit hipper, don't miss the weekend **Mercato-Monti**. This Monti district flea market has an emphasis on vintage clothes and housewares and up-and-coming designers (Sat-Sun 10:00-20:00, closed July-Aug, Hotel Palatino, Via Leonina 46, Metro: Cavour).

Open-Air Produce Markets

Rome's outdoor markets provide a fun and colorful dimension of the city that even the most avid museumgoer should not miss. Wander through the easygoing neighborhood produce markets that clog certain streets and squares every morning (7:00-13:30) except Sunday. Consider the huge **Mercato Trionfale** (three blocks north of Vatican Museums at Via Andrea Doria). Another great food market is the **Mercato Esquilino** (Via Filippo Turati, Metro: Vittorio Emanuele). The covered **Mercato di Testaccio** sells produce and housewares and is a hit with photographers and people-watchers (Metro: Piramide). Smaller but equally charming slices of everyday Roman life are at markets on these streets and squares: **Piazza delle Coppelle** (near the Pantheon), **Via Balbo** (near Termini train station), and **Via della Pace** (near Piazza Navona). And **Campo de' Fiori,** despite having become quite touristy, is still a fun scene.

Nightlife in Rome

Romans get dressed up and eat out in casual surroundings for their evening entertainment. For most visitors, the best after-dark activity is simply to grab a gelato and stroll the medieval lanes that connect the romantic, floodlit squares and fountains. Head for Piazza Navona, the Pantheon, Campo de' Fiori, Trevi Fountain, the Spanish Steps, Via del Corso, Trastevere (around the Santa Maria in Trastevere Church), or Monte Testaccio.

Evening Sightseeing: Some museums have later opening hours (especially on Sat in summer), offering a good chance to see art in a cooler, less-crowded environment. See the "Rome at a Glance" sidebar on page 814, and ask the TI if any museums are currently open late.

The *Passeggiata*

Throughout Italy, early evening is time to stroll. While else-where in Italy this is called the *passeggiata,* in Rome it's a cruder, big-city version called the *struscio* (meaning "to rub").

Unemployment among Italy's youth is very high; many stay with their parents even into their 30s. They spend a lot of time being trendy and hanging out. Like American kids gathering at the mall, working-class suburban youth *(coatto)* converge on the old center, as there's little to keep them oc-cupied in Rome's dreary outskirts (which lack public spaces). The hot *vroom-vroom* motor scooter is their symbol; haircuts and fashion are follow-the-leader.

In a more genteel small town, the *passeggiata* comes with sweet whispers of *"bella"* and *"bello"* ("pretty" and "hand-some"). In Rome, the admiration is stronger, oriented toward consumption—they say *"buona"* and *"buono"*—meaning, roughly, "tasty." But despite how lusty this all sounds, you'll see just as many chunky, middle-aged Italians out and about as hormone-charged youth.

Performances and Film: Check out the current listings of concerts, operas, dance, and films. Posters around town also ad-vertise upcoming events. For the most up-to-date events calendar, check these English-language websites: www.inromenow.com, www.wantedinrome.com, and www.rome.angloinfo.com.

Music: Music lovers will seek out the mega-music complex of the **Rome Auditorium** (Auditorium Parco della Musica), de-signed by contemporary architect Renzo Piano (€20-60 tickets, check availability in advance—concerts often sell out, Viale Pietro de Coubertin 30, take Metro to Flaminio and then catch tram #2 to Apollodoro, from there it's a 5-minute walk east, just beyond the elevated road, tram/Metro runs until 23:30, box office toll tel. 892-101, www.auditorium.com). Also called the "Park of Music," it's a place where many Romans go just for the scene—music store, res-taurants, cafés, and fresh modern architecture with three state-of-the-art auditoriums (known as "the beetles" for their appearance).

Classical Music and Opera: The **Teatro dell'Opera** has an active schedule of opera and classical concerts. In the summer, the productions move to the Baths of Caracalla, where ancient ruins make an evocative backdrop. You'll see locals in all their finery, so pull your fanciest outfit from your backpack (tickets from €25, online reservations encouraged, box office takes phone reserva-tions beginning 5 days prior at tel. 06-4816-0255; Via Firenze 72, a block off Via Nazionale, Metro: Repubblica; www.operaroma.it).

More tourist-oriented musical events take place at the Epis-copal **Church of St. Paul's Within the Walls.** The music ranges

from orchestral concerts (usually Tue and Fri at 20:30) to full operatic performances (usually Sat at 20:30). Some Sunday evenings at
18:30, the church hosts hour-long candlelit "Luminaria" concerts.
Check the church website (under "Music") to see what's on (€10-
30, same-day tickets usually available, arrive 30-45 minutes early
for best seat, Via Napoli 58 at corner of Via Nazionale, Metro: Repubblica, tel. 06-482-6296, www.stpaulsrome.it).

Jazz: Rome has a small but vibrant jazz scene. **Alexander-
platz** is the venerable club in town, with performances most
evenings (Sun-Thu concerts at 21:45, Fri-Sat at 22:30, closed in
summer, Via Ostia 9, Metro: Ottaviano, tel. 06-3972-1867, www.
alexanderplatzjazzclub.it).

Il Pentagrappolo is an *enoteca* that hosts live music (usually
jazz) many Thursday, Friday, and Saturday evenings starting at
22:00 from September to June—check under "Eventi musicali" on
their website to confirm (Tue-Sun 18:00-24:00, best to reserve on
weekends, three blocks east of the Colosseum at Via Celimontana
21—see map on page 900, www.ilpentagrappolo.com, tel. 06-709-
6301).

Bars and Nightspots

These fun neighborhoods are worth exploring after dark, along
with a few bars and *enoteche* (wine bars) in each. Most of these
places are recommended in the "Eating in Rome" section, where
you'll find more details.

Heart of Rome, near the Pantheon: The scene here is touristy but delightful. The monuments—especially the Pantheon and
Trevi Fountain—are magically floodlit at night. Not far from the
Trevi Fountain, **L'Antica Birreria Peroni** is a big, boisterous beer
hall. Farther south, Campo de' Fiori and the surrounding streets
become one big, rude street party around 22:00. One good place to
sample the youthful energy, as well as some craft beers, is the rollicking **Open Baladin** pub.

North Rome, near the Spanish Steps and Via del Corso:
A babel of international tourists, this glitzy zone is bustling after
dark. For many, just hanging out on and around the Spanish Steps
is enough to fill an evening.

Near the Colosseum and Forum, in Monti: The best plan in
this lively village Rome zone is to pop the top off a brew and hang
out at the fountain on Piazza della Madonna dei Monti. To join the
after-dark scene, buy a drink at the shop on the uphill side of the
square (cheap bottles of wine with plastic glasses, beer, fruit, and
munchies) and be part of what becomes the hottest bar in the area.
There are plenty of makeshift benches around the fountain. For
something a bit less casual, try **Enoteca Cavour 313** or **Fafiuché**.
For more details, see the page 927.

Sleeping in Rome

Choosing the right neighborhood in Rome is as important as choosing the right hotel. All of my recommended accommodations are in safe areas convenient to sightseeing. The Termini train station neighborhood is handy for public transit and services, though not particularly charming. Hotels near ancient Rome are close to the Colosseum and Roman Forum. The most romantic ambience is in neighborhoods near the Pantheon, which encompass the Campo de' Fiori and the Jewish Ghetto. Equally pleasant, if a bit rougher, is Trastevere. Finally, hotels near Vatican City put St. Peter's and the Vatican Museums at your doorstep.

Rome also has many convents that rent out rooms. At convents, the beds are twins and English is often in short supply, but the price is right. I've listed four nun-run places in this chapter: the expensive but divine Casa di Santa Brigida (near Campo de' Fiori), Suore di Santa Elisabetta (near Termini Station), Casa Il Rosario (near Piazza Venezia), and Casa per Ferie Santa Maria alle Fornaci (near the Vatican). For a longer list of convents, see the Church of Santa Susanna's website (www.santasusanna.org, select "Resources" and then "Convent Accommodations").

Book your accommodations well in advance if you'll be traveling during peak season (April-June and Sept-early Nov) or if your trip coincides with a major holiday or festival (see page 1178).

NEAR TERMINI STATION

While this neighborhood is not as atmospheric as other areas of Rome, the hotels near Termini train station are less expensive, and the Metro and buses link you easily to the rest of the city. All the listings below are within a 10-minute walk of the station (some are actually closer to the Repubblica Metro stop).

West of the Station

Most of these hotels are on or near Via Firenze, a safe, handy, central, and relatively quiet street that's a 10-minute walk from Termini and the airport train, and two blocks beyond Piazza della Repubblica. The Defense Ministry is nearby, so you've got heavily armed guards watching over you all night.

The neighborhood is served by two Metro stops: Repubblica (line A), and Termini (intersection of lines A and B). Virtually all the city buses that rumble down Via Nazionale (#60, #64, #70, and the #40 express) take you to Piazza Venezia (near the Forum). From Piazza Venezia, bus #64 (jammed with people and thieves) and the #40 express bus continue to Largo Argentina (for the Pantheon and Campo de' Fiori) and the Vatican area. Or, at Piazza Venezia, you can transfer to tram #8 to Trastevere (get off at first

---

Sleep Code

Hotels are classified based on the average price of a standard double room with breakfast in high season.

$$$$	**Splurge:** Most rooms over €170
$$$	**Pricier:** €130-170
$$	**Moderate:** €90-130
$	**Budget:** €50-90
¢	**Backpacker:** Under €50
RS%	**Rick Steves discount**

Unless otherwise noted, credit cards are accepted, hotel staff speak basic English, and free Wi-Fi is available. Comparison-shop by checking prices at several hotels (on each hotel's own website, on a booking site, or by email). For the best deal, *book directly with the hotel.* Ask for a discount if paying in cash; if the listing includes **RS%,** request a Rick Steves discount.

---

stop after crossing the river). Bus #H also runs direct to Trastevere, leaving from Piazza della Repubblica (on the northeast side of the square, near the entrance to Baths of Diocletian; none on Sun). If you're staying near the Santa Susanna and Santa Maria della Vittoria churches, buses from nearby Largo Santa Susanna (#62, #85, and #492) wind through the city center (leaving from the Bissolati stop; returning, the stop name is Largo S. Susanna). It's actually a pleasant downhill walk from these hotels to the Pantheon (about 25 minutes along Via Rasella and past the Trevi Fountain); you can save the bus for the uphill return journey.

Neighborhood **supermarkets** include **Despar** at Via Nazionale 213 (daily 7:30-20:30, at the corner of Via Venezia); **Sma** behind Santa Maria Maggiore Church (Piazza Santa Maria Maggiore 5B, in the basement, daily 8:00-21:00); and **Sapori & Dintori,** downstairs from the inner atrium at Termini Station (daily 7:00-24:00). There are many smaller grocery stores as well.

$$$$ Residenza Cellini feels like the guest wing of a gorgeous Neoclassical palace. It offers 11 rooms, "ortho/anti-allergy beds," four-star comforts and service, and a small, breezy terrace (RS%, air-con, elevator, Via Modena 5, third floor, tel. 06-4782-5204, www.residenzacellini.it, info@residenzacellini.it, Barbara, Gaetano, and Donato).

$$$$ Hotel Modigliani, a delightful 23-room place, is energetically run in a clean, bright, minimalist yet in-love-with-life style that its artist namesake would appreciate. It has a vast and plush lounge, a garden, and a newsletter introducing you to each of the staff (RS%, air-con, elevator; northwest of Via Firenze—from Tritone Fountain on Piazza Barberini, go 2 blocks up Via della Purificazione to #42; tel. 06-4281-5226, www.hotelmodigliani.com, info@hotelmodigliani.com, Giulia and Marco).

$$$$ IQ Hotel, in a modern blue building facing the Opera House, feels almost Scandinavian in its efficiency, without a hint of the Old World. It lacks charm, but more than compensates with modern amenities. Its 88 rooms are fresh and spacious, the roof garden comes with a play area and foosball, and vending machines dispense bottles of wine (family rooms, breakfast extra, air-con, elevator, cheap self-service laundry, gym, Via Firenze 8, tel. 06-488-0465, www.iqhotelroma.it, info@iqhotelroma.it, manager Diego).

$$$ Hotel Oceania is a peaceful slice of air-conditioned heaven. The 24 rooms are spacious, quiet, and tastefully decorated, and the elegant sitting room has a manor-house feel. Stefano runs a fine staff, serves wonderful coffee, provides lots of thoughtful extra touches, and works hard to maintain a caring family atmosphere (RS%—use code "RICKSTEVES," family rooms, elevator, videos in TV lounge, Via Firenze 38, third floor, tel. 06-482-4696, www.hoteloceania.it, info@hoteloceania.it; Anna, Kira, and Roberto round out the staff).

$$$ Hotel Aberdeen, which combines quality and friendliness, is warmly run by Annamaria, with support from sister Laura and cousin Cinzia, and staff members Mariano, Costel, and Matteo. The 37 comfy rooms, on the ground floor and one floor up, are a fine value (RS%—use "Rick Steves reader reservations" link, family rooms, air-con, Via Firenze 48, tel. 06-482-3920, www.hotelaberdeen.it, info@hotelaberdeen.it).

$$$ Hotel Opera Roma, with contemporary furnishings and marble accents, boasts 15 spacious, modern, and thoughtfully appointed rooms. It's quiet and just a stone's throw from the Opera House (RS%, air-con, elevator, Via Firenze 11, tel. 06-487-1787, www.hoteloperaroma.com, info@hoteloperaroma.com, Reza, Litu, and Federica).

$$$ Hotel Selene Roma spreads its 40 stylish rooms out on a few floors of a big palazzo. With elegant furnishings and room to breathe, it's a good value (RS%, family rooms, air-con, elevator, Via del Viminale 8, tel. 06-474-4781, www.hotelseleneroma.it, reception@hotelseleneroma.it).

$$$ Hotel Sonya offers 40 well-equipped if small rooms, a hearty breakfast, and decent prices (RS%, family rooms, air-con, elevator, faces the Opera House at Via Viminale 58, Metro: Repubblica or Termini, tel. 06-481-9911, www.hotelsonya.it, info@hotelsonya.it, Francesca and Ivan).

$$$ Target Inn is a sleek, practical six-room place next to Residenza Cellini (listed earlier). It's owned by the same people who run the recommended Target Restaurant nearby (RS%, air-

ROME

Hotels near Termini Station

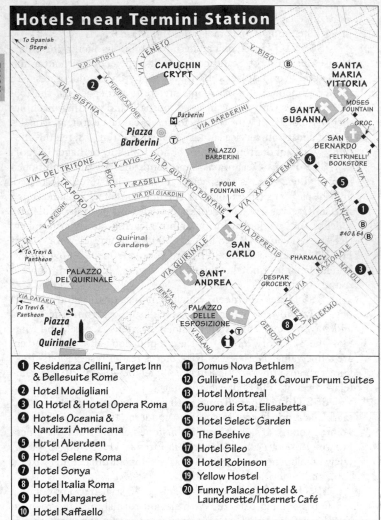

① Residenza Cellini, Target Inn & Bellesuite Rome
② Hotel Modigliani
③ IQ Hotel & Hotel Opera Roma
④ Hotels Oceania & Nardizzi Americana
⑤ Hotel Aberdeen
⑥ Hotel Selene Roma
⑦ Hotel Sonya
⑧ Hotel Italia Roma
⑨ Hotel Margaret
⑩ Hotel Raffaello
⑪ Domus Nova Bethlem
⑫ Gulliver's Lodge & Cavour Forum Suites
⑬ Hotel Montreal
⑭ Suore di Sta. Elisabetta
⑮ Hotel Select Garden
⑯ The Beehive
⑰ Hotel Sileo
⑱ Hotel Robinson
⑲ Yellow Hostel
⑳ Funny Palace Hostel & Launderette/Internet Café

con, elevator, Via Modena 5, third floor, tel. 06-474-5399, www. targetinn.com, info@targetinn.com).

$$$ Bellesuite Rome offers six small but nice rooms that are worth considering for the location—in the same fine building as Residenza Cellini and Target Inn (RS%, family rooms, air-con, elevator, Via Modena 5, third floor, tel. 06-9521-3049, www. bellesuiterome.com, mail@bellesuiterome.com, Martina).

$$ Hotel Nardizzi Americana, with a small rooftop terrace, 40 standard rooms, and a laidback atmosphere, is another decent value (RS%—use "Rick Steves readers reservations" link, family rooms, air-con, elevator, Via Firenze 38, reception on fourth floor,

ROME

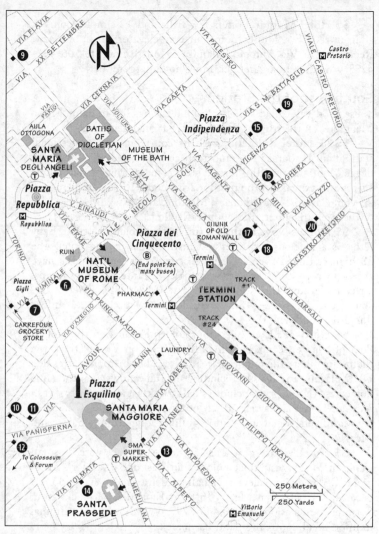

tel. 06-488-0035, www.hotelnardizzi.it, info@hotelnardizzi.it; friendly Stefano, Fabrizio, Mario, and Giancarlo).

$$ Hotel Italia Roma, in a busy and handy locale, is located safely on a quiet street next to the Ministry of the Interior. Thoughtfully run by Andrea, Sabrina, Abdul, and Gabriel, it has 35 modest but comfortable rooms plus four newer, more expensive "residenza" rooms on the third floor (RS%, family rooms, air-con, elevator, Via Venezia 18, just off Via Nazionale, tel. 06-482-8355, www.hotelitaliaroma.it, info@hotelitaliaroma.it). They offer eight similar annex rooms across the street for the same price as the main hotel.

$$ Hotel Margaret offers few frills and 12 simple rooms at a fair price (RS%, family rooms, air-con, elevator, north of Piazza Repubblica at Via Antonio Salandra 6, fourth floor, tel. 06-482-4285, www.hotelmargaret.net, info@hotelmargaret.net).

Southwest of the Station

These good-value places cluster around the basilica of Santa Maria Maggiore, on the edge of Rome's international district.

$$$$ Hotel Raffaello, with its courteous and professional staff, offers 41 rooms in a grand 19th-century building on the edge of the Monti district. This formal hotel comes with generous public spaces and a breakfast room fit for aristocrats (RS%, family rooms, air-con, elevator, Via Urbana 3, Metro: Cavour, tel. 06-488-4342, www.hotelraffaello.it, info@hotelraffaello.it).

$$ Domus Nova Bethlem, run by the Oblate Sisters of Baby Jesus, is a spacious, pristine, and institutional-feeling hotel. The 38 high-ceilinged rooms are modest yet classy, and guests have access to a peaceful and leafy courtyard garden (family rooms, air-con, elevator, 1:00 a.m. curfew, Via Cavour 85A, Metro: Cavour, tel. 06-4782-4414, www.domusnovabethlem.it, info@domusnovabethlem.it).

$$ Gulliver's Lodge has four colorful rooms on the ground floor of a large, secure building. Though it's on a busy street, the rooms are quiet. The public spaces are few, but in-room extras like DVD players (and DVDs, including my Italy shows) make it a fine home base (RS%, price includes small breakfast at nearby bar, cash only, air-con, Via Cavour 101, Metro: Cavour, tel. 06-9727-3787, www.gulliverslodge.com, info@gulliverslodge.com, Sara and Mary).

$$ Hotel Montreal is a basic, three-star place with 27 small rooms on a big, noisy street a block southeast of Santa Maria Maggiore (RS%, air-con, elevator, small garden terrace, Via Carlo Alberto 4, 1 block from Metro: Vittorio Emanuele, 3 blocks from Termini train station, tel. 06-445-7797, www.hotelmontrealroma.it, info@hotelmontrealroma.it, Pasquale).

$ Suore di Santa Elisabetta is a heavenly Polish-run convent with a serene garden, roof terrace with grand views, and 37 rooms. All doubles have twin beds. Often booked long in advance, with such tranquility it's a super value (family rooms, cheaper rooms with shared bath, fans but no air-con, elevator for top floors, guest kitchen, Wi-Fi in lounge only, 23:00 curfew, a block southwest of Santa Maria Maggiore at Via dell'Olmata 9, Metro: Termini or Vittorio Emanuele, tel. 06-488-8271, www.csse-roma.com, select "Casa per ferie" for English, ist.it.s.elisabetta@libero.it).

Sleeping Cheaply, Northeast of the Station

The cheapest beds in town are beyond Termini train station, to the northeast: Standing so that the tracks dead-end into your back, this neighborhood is to your right (Metro: Termini). The streets quiet down a block or so away from the station, and these hotels feel plenty safe. The **Splashnet** launderette/Internet café is handy (€8 full-serve wash and dry, €2/day luggage storage, daily 8:30-23:00, just off Via Milazzo at Via Varese 33, tel. 06-4470-3523).

$$ Hotel Select Garden, a modern and comfortable 21-room hotel run by the cheery Picca family, boasts lively modern art adorning the walls and a beautiful lemon-tree garden. It's a safe, tranquil, and welcoming refuge just a couple of blocks from the train station (RS%, air-con, Via V. Bachelet 6, tel. 06-445-6383, www.hotelselectgarden.com, info@hotelselectgarden.com, Cristina and Maurizia).

$ The Beehive gives vagabonds—old and young—a cheap, clean, and comfy home in Rome. Thoughtfully and creatively run by friendly Americans Steve and Linda and their hardworking staff, the place offers six great-value artsy-mod double rooms with shared baths and an eight-bed dorm in the main building (no air-con, only fans). Their nearby annexes have similar style and several rooms with private baths (breakfast extra, air-con extra, private garden terrace, dinner sometimes available, 2 blocks from Termini train station at Via Marghera 8, tel. 06-4470-4553, www.the-beehive.com, info@the-beehive.com). They're also a good resource for apartments across the city (www.cross-pollinate.com).

$ Hotel Sileo, with shiny chandeliers in dim rooms, is a homey little place renting 10 basic rooms. It's worn, but run with warmth by friendly Alessandro and Maria Savioli (who don't speak English) and their daughter Anna (who does); their other daughter, Stefania, painted the wall murals (RS%, air-con, elevator, Via Magenta 39, fourth floor, tel. 06-445-0246, www.hotelsileo.com, info@hotelsileo.com).

$ Hotel Robinson is just a few steps from the station, but tucked away from the commotion. Set on an interior courtyard, it has 20 small and simple good-value rooms, handsomely decorated with dark-wood accents (RS%, breakfast extra, air-con extra, Via Milazzo 3, tel. 06-491-423, www.hotelrobinsonrome.com, info@hotelrobinsonrome.com).

¢ Yellow Hostel rents 220 beds to 18-45-year-olds only (I'd skip their 16 private rooms, which are basic and overpriced). Hip yet sane, it's well-run with fine facilities, including a café/late-night bar (reserve online—no telephone reservations accepted, breakfast extra, elevator, no curfew, 6 blocks from station, just past Via Vicenza at Via Palestro 44, tel. 06-4938-2682, www.yellowhostel.com, questions@the-yellow.com).

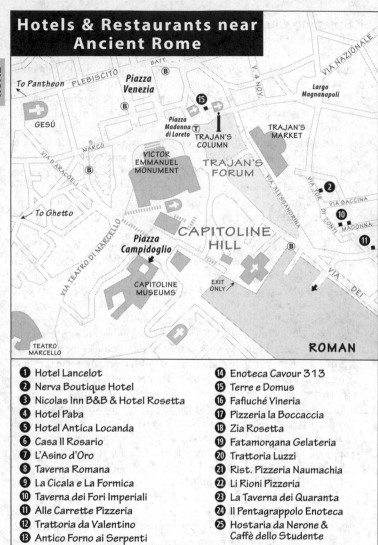

Hotels & Restaurants near Ancient Rome

To Pantheon — PLEBISCITO — BATT.

Piazza Venezia

V. 4 NOV.

VIA NAZIONALE

GESÙ

Largo Magnanapoli

S. MARCO

Piazza Madonna di Loreto

TRAJAN'S COLUMN

TRAJAN'S MARKET

VIA D'ARACOELI

VICTOR EMMANUEL MONUMENT

TRAJAN'S FORUM

To Ghetto

VIA ALESSANDRINA

VIA TOR DE' CONTI

VIA BACCINA

MADONNA

VIA TEATRO DI MARCELLO

Piazza Campidoglio

CAPITOLINE HILL

CAPITOLINE MUSEUMS

EXIT ONLY

VIA DEI

TEATRO MARCELLO

ROMAN

1 Hotel Lancelot
2 Nerva Boutique Hotel
3 Nicolas Inn B&B & Hotel Rosetta
4 Hotel Paba
5 Hotel Antica Locanda
6 Casa Il Rosario
7 L'Asino d'Oro
8 Taverna Romana
9 La Cicala e La Formica
10 Taverna dei Fori Imperiali
11 Alle Carrette Pizzeria
12 Trattoria da Valentino
13 Antico Forno ai Serpenti

14 Enoteca Cavour 313
15 Terre e Domus
16 Fafiuché Vineria
17 Pizzeria la Boccaccia
18 Zia Rosetta
19 Fatamorgana Gelateria
20 Trattoria Luzzi
21 Rist. Pizzeria Naumachia
22 Li Rioni Pizzeria
23 La Taverna dei Quaranta
24 Il Pentagrappolo Enoteca
25 Hostaria da Nerone & Caffè dello Studente

¢ **Funny Palace Hostel,** adjacent to Splashnet and run by the same entrepreneurial owner, Mabri, rents dorm beds in quiet four-person rooms and 18 stark-but-clean private rooms. It's far less convivial than Yellow Hostel, but suitable for introverts (cash only, includes breakfast in café, elevator, guest kitchen, reception in the launderette—described earlier, Via Varese 33, tel. 06-4470-3523, www.hostelfunny.com, info@hostelfunny.com).

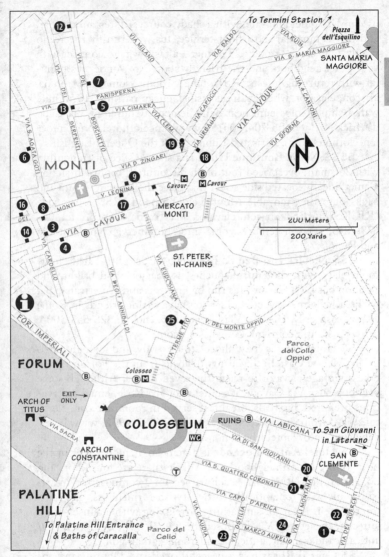

NEAR ANCIENT ROME

This area is central, so you'll find these hotels are a short walk from the Colosseum and Roman Forum, as well as restaurants and shopping in the Monti district (see pages 926 and 890). All except Hotel Lancelot are within a 10-minute walk of the Cavour Metro stop.

$$$$ Hotel Lancelot is a comfortable refuge—a 60-room hotel with an elegant feel at a fair price. Located in a pleasant, low-key residential neighborhood a 10-minute stroll from the Colosseum, it's quiet and safe, with a shady courtyard, restaurant, bar, and tiny communal sixth-floor terrace. It's well-run by the Khan family, who serve a good €25 dinner—a tasty way to connect with your hotel neighbors and the friendly staff. No wonder it's popular with returning guests (RS%, family rooms, some view rooms, air-con, elevator, wheelchair-accessible, cheap parking, 10-minute walk behind Colosseum near San Clemente Church at Via Capo d'Africa 47, tel. 06-7045-0615, www.lancelothotel.com, info@lancelothotel.com). Faris and Lubna speak the Queen's English.

$$$$ Nerva Boutique Hotel is a snazzy slice of tranquility with 20 small, overpriced (but often discounted) rooms. It sits on a quiet, ideally located side street that faces the Roman Forum and backs onto the enjoyable Monti neighborhood (RS%—use code "RICKSTEVES," air-con, elevator, Via Tor de' Conti 3, tel. 06-678-1835, www.hotelnerva.com, info@hotelnerva.com, Antonio and Paolo).

$$$ Nicolas Inn Bed & Breakfast, a delightful little four-room place with thoughtful touches, is spacious and bright, and right on busy Via Cavour. It's run by François and American expat Melissa, who make you feel like you have caring friends in Rome (RS%, cash only, air-con, Via Cavour 295, mobile 328-555-3004, www.nicolasinn.com, info@nicolasinn.com).

$$ Hotel Paba is cozy, chocolate-box-tidy, and lovingly cared for by Alberta Castelli. It's just two blocks from the Forum. You'll take a vintage elevator to reach the seven rooms. Although some overlook busy Via Cavour, it's quiet enough (RS%, email reservations preferred, big beds, breakfast served in room, air-con, elevator, Via Cavour 266, second floor, tel. 06-4782-4902, www.hotelpaba.com, info@hotelpaba.com).

$$ Hotel Antica Locanda is a gem on a small street in the heart of the Monti neighborhood. While there are four floors and no elevator, the 10 rooms—each named for a composer or an artist—come with romantically rustic, stylish furnishings. The rooftop terrace is great for sunbathing or relaxing with a sunset drink (air-con, no elevator, Via del Boschetto 84, tel. 06-487-1164, http://anticalocandaroma.it, anticalocandaroma@gmail.com).

$$ Casa Il Rosario is a peaceful, well-run Dominican convent renting 40 rooms with monastic simplicity to both pilgrims and tourists in a steep but pleasant corner of the Monti neighborhood. Doubles have two single beds that can be pushed together (cheaper single rooms with shared bath, reserve several months in advance, some rooms with air-con and others with fans, elevator, small garden and rooftop terrace, 23:00 curfew, near bottom of Via Nazionale at Via Sant'Agata dei Goti 10, bus #40 or #170 from Termini, tel. 06-679-2346, www.casailrosarioroma.it, irodopre@tin.it).

$ Hotel Rosetta, a homey and family-run *pensione* in the same building as Nicolas Inn, rents 15 simple rooms. It's pretty minimal, with no lounge and no breakfast, but its great location makes it a fine budget option (air-con, up one flight of stairs, Via Cavour 295, tel. 06-4782-3069, www.rosettahotel.com, info@rosettahotel.com, Antonietta and Francesca).

PANTHEON NEIGHBORHOOD

Winding, narrow lanes filled with foot traffic and lined with small shops and tiny trattorias...this part of Rome still feels like a village. As in a real village, buses and taxis are the only practical way to connect with other destinations. The atmosphere doesn't come cheap, but this is a great place to be—especially at night, when Romans and tourists gather in the floodlit piazzas.

This neighborhood has two main transportation hubs: Piazza delle Cinque Lune (just north of Piazza Navona) has a TI, a taxi stand, and (just around the corner) handy buses #81 and #87. Largo Argentina has buses to almost everywhere, a taxi stand, and the tram to Trastevere (#8). Peruse my recommended buses on page 807, and you'll likely find a few (#81, #87, #492, and others) that stop near your hotel.

Neighborhood **supermarkets** include **Despar,** half a block from the Pantheon toward Piazza Navona (daily 8:30-22:00, Via Giustiniani 18). A larger supermarket with a good bakery and sandwich section is the **Co-op,** three blocks away (Mon-Sat 8:00-21:00, Sun from 9:00, Corso Vittorio Emanuele II 42).

Near Largo Argentina and Campo de' Fiori

Each of these places is romantically set deep in the tangled back streets near the idyllic Campo de' Fiori and, for many, worth the extra money. This area is connected to Termini Station by bus along Via Nazionale (#40 or #64). From the airport, consider taking the regional train to Trastevere Station and then the #8 tram to Largo Argentina.

$$$$ Casa di Santa Brigida overlooks the elegant Piazza Farnese. With soft-spoken sisters gliding down polished hallways and pearly gates instead of doors, this lavish 20-room convent makes exhaust-stained Roman tourists feel like they've died and gone to heaven. If you don't need a double bed or a TV in your room, it's worth the splurge—especially if you luxuriate in its ample public spaces or on its lovely roof terrace (book well in advance, air-con, elevator, tasty €25 dinners, roof garden, plush library, Via di Monserrato 54, tel. 06-6889-2596, www.brigidine.org, piazzafarnese@brigidine.org, many of the sisters are from India and speak English—pray you get to work with wonderful sister Gertrude).

$$$$ Relais Teatro Argentina, a six-room gem, is steeped in

ROME

Hotels in the Pantheon Neighborhood

1 Casa di Santa Brigida
2 Relais Teatro Argentina
3 Hotel Smeraldo
4 Hotel Arenula
5 Hotel Nazionale
6 Albergo Santa Chiara
7 Hotel Portoghesi
8 Hotel Due Torri

tasteful old-Rome elegance, but has all the modern comforts. It's cozy and quiet like a B&B and couldn't be more centrally located (air-con, 3 flights of stairs, breakfast in room, Via del Sudario 35, tel. 06-9893-1617, mobile 331-198-4708, www.relaisteatroargentina.com, info@relaisteatroargentina.com, Carlotta).

$$$ Hotel Smeraldo, with 66 rooms, is clean and a reasonable deal in a good location. Sixteen of the rooms are in an annex across the street, but everyone has breakfast in the main building (RS%—use code "ricksteves," air-con, elevator, flowery roof terrace, midway between Campo de' Fiori and Largo Argentina at Via dei Chiavari 20, tel. 06-687-5929, www.smeraldoroma.com, info@smeraldoroma.com; Massimo and Walter).

$$ Hotel Arenula, with 50 decent rooms, is the only hotel in Rome's old Jewish ghetto. Though it has the ambience of a gym and attracts lots of students, it is in the thick of old Rome (RS%, family rooms, air-con, no elevator, down side street from the fountain in the park on Via Arenula, Via Santa Maria de' Calderari 47, tel. 06-687-9454, www.hotelarenula.com, info@hotelarenula.com).

Close to the Pantheon

These places are buried in the pedestrian-friendly heart of ancient Rome, each within about a five-minute walk of the Pantheon. They're an easy walk from many sights, but are a bit distant from the major public transportation arteries (though buses do run nearby). To get close, arrive and depart by taxi.

$$$$ Hotel Nazionale, a four-star landmark, is a 16th-century palace that shares a well-policed square with the Italian Parliament building. Its 101 rooms are accentuated by lush public spaces, fancy bars, a uniformed staff, and a marble-floored restaurant. It's a big, stuffy hotel, but it's a worthy splurge if you want security, comfort, and the heart of Rome at your doorstep (air-con, elevator, Piazza Montecitorio 131, tel. 06-695-001, www.hotel-nazionale.it, info@hotelnazionale.it).

$$$$ Albergo Santa Chiara, in the old center, is big, solid, and hotelesque. Flavia, Silvio, and their fine staff offer marbled elegance (but basic furniture) and all the hotel services. Its ample public lounges are dressy and professional, and its 97 rooms are quiet and spacious (RS%, elevator, air-con, behind the Pantheon at Via di Santa Chiara 21, tel. 06-687-2979, www.albergosanta-chiara.com, info@albergosantachiara.com).

$$$$ Hotel Portoghesi is a classic hotel with 27 colorful rooms in the medieval heart of Rome. It's peaceful, quiet, and calmly run, and comes with a delightful roof terrace—though you pay for the location (family rooms, breakfast on roof, air-con, elevator, Via dei Portoghesi 1, tel. 06-686-4231, www.hotelportoghesi-roma.it, info@hotelportoghesiroma.it).

$$$$ Hotel Due Torri, hiding out on a tiny quiet street, is beautifully located. It feels professional yet homey, with an accommodating staff, generous public spaces, and 26 rooms (the ones on upper floors are smaller but have views). While the location and lounge are great, the rooms are overpriced unless you score a discount (family rooms, air-con, elevator, a block off Via della Scrofa at Vicolo del Leonetto 23, tel. 06-6880-6956, www.hotelduetor-riroma.com, info@hotelduetorriroma.com, Cinzia).

Near the Spanish Steps

$$$$ Hotel San Carlo is buried in the thick of Rome's bustling pedestrian-friendly "shopping triangle" and conveniently close

ROME

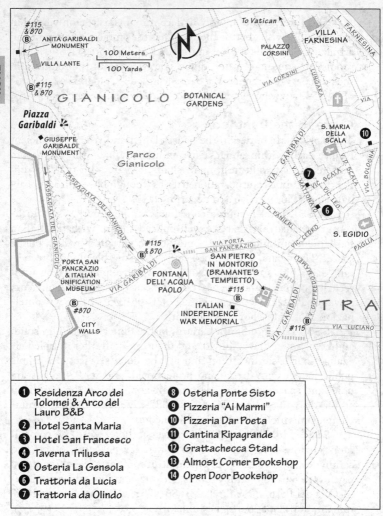

To Vatican

VILLA FARNESINA

PALAZZO CORSINI

#115 & 870
ANITA GARIBALDI MONUMENT

VILLA LANTE

100 Meters
100 Yards

#115 & 870

GIANICOLO

BOTANICAL GARDENS

VIA CORSINI

LUNGARA

VIA

S. MARIA DELLA SCALA

⑩

Piazza Garibaldi

GIUSEPPE GARIBALDI MONUMENT

Parco Gianicolo

VIA GARIBALDI

⑦

VIC. SCALA

V. D. NATIONALE

VIC. LEO

V. D. PANIERI

⑥

VIC. CEDRO

S. EGIDIO

PAGLIA

PASSAGGIATA DEL GIANICOLO

#115 & 870

VIA PORTA SAN PANCRAZIO

PORTA SAN PANCRAZIO & ITALIAN UNIFICATION MUSEUM

VIA GARIBALDI

FONTANA DELL' ACQUA PAOLO

SAN PIETRO IN MONTORIO (BRAMANTE'S TEMPIETTO)
#115

TRA

#870

CITY WALLS

ITALIAN INDEPENDENCE WAR MEMORIAL

V. DI GOFFREDO MAMELI

VIA GARIBALDI

#115

VIA LUCIANO

① Residenza Arco dei Tolomei & Arco del Lauro B&B
② Hotel Santa Maria
③ Hotel San Francesco
④ Taverna Trilussa
⑤ Osteria La Gensola
⑥ Trattoria da Lucia
⑦ Trattoria da Olindo

⑧ Osteria Ponte Sisto
⑨ Pizzeria "Ai Marmi"
⑩ Pizzeria Dar Poeta
⑪ Cantina Ripagrande
⑫ Grattachecca Stand
⑬ Almost Corner Bookshop
⑭ Open Door Bookshop

to the Spagna Metro stop. Thoughtfully run by Alberto and his staff, its 47 rooms, connected by a treehouse floor plan, provide a tranquil haven (RS%—use code "ricksteves," air-con, elevator, Via delle Carrozze 92—see map on page 818, tel. 06-678-4548, www. hotelsancarloroma.com, info@hotelsancarloroma.com).

TRASTEVERE

Colorful and genuine, with uneven cobbles and remnants of its tumbledown past, Trastevere is a treat for travelers looking for a more residential, bohemian atmosphere. (Ω Download my free Trastevere Walk audio tour to explore the neighborhood.) The heart of Rome and its ancient ruins are just across the river, and

ROME

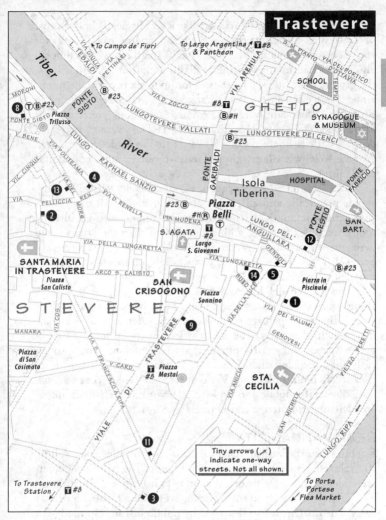

tram #8 makes getting there and back a snap. Convenient buses #23 and #280 run to the Vatican area and the Piramide Metro stop, and bus #H runs direct to Termini (none on Sun). From the airport, you can reach these listings by taking the regional train to Trastevere train station, and the #8 tram downhill from there.

$$$$ Residenza Arco dei Tolomei is your most poetic Trastevere experience imaginable, with six small, unique, antique-filled rooms, some boasting fragrant balconies. In this quiet and elegant setting, you can pretend you're visiting aristocratic relatives (reserve well in advance, from Piazza Piscinula a block up Via dell'Arco de' Tolomei at #27, tel. 06-5832-0819, www.bbarcodeitolomei.com, info@bbarcodeitolomei.com; Marco and Gianna Paola).

$$$$ Hotel Santa Maria sits like a lazy hacienda in the midst of Trastevere. Surrounded by a medieval skyline, you'll feel as if you're on some romantic stage set. Its 20 small but well-equipped, air-conditioned rooms—former cells in a cloister—are mostly on the ground floor, as are a few suites for up to six people. The rooms circle a gravelly courtyard of orange trees and stay-awhile patio furniture (RS%, family rooms, email reservations preferred, free loaner bikes, face church on Piazza Maria Trastevere and go right down Via della Fonte d'Olio 50 yards to Vicolo del Piede 2, tel. 06-589-4626, www.hotelsantamariatrastevere.it, info@hotelsanta-maria.info).

$$$$ Hotel San Francesco, big and blocky yet welcoming, stands practically and efficiently at the far end of all the Traste-vere action. It rents 24 trim rooms and comes with an inviting roof terrace. It's fine, but a bit more distant than the others listed here (email reservations preferred, air-con, elevator, Via Jacopa de' Settesoli 7, tel. 06-5830-0051, www.hotelsanfrancesco.net, hotel-sanfrancesco@gmail.com).

$$$ Arco del Lauro B&B rents six tight, whitewashed, straightforward rooms around a dim, quiet back courtyard. Con-sider it the less expensive version of the Residenza Arco dei Tolo-mei, which is upstairs. The lower prices make up for the lack of public spaces and mostly offsite management (one family room, cash only, includes small breakfast at nearby café, air-con, from Piazza Piscinula a block up Via dell'Arco de' Tolomei at #29, tel. 06-9784-0350, mobile 346-244-3212, www.arcodellauro.it, info@arcodellauro.it, Lorenza and Daniela).

NEAR VATICAN CITY

Sleeping near the Vatican costs a little more, but some enjoy calling this relaxed, residential neighborhood home. The tree-lined streets are wider than in the historical center, so it feels less claustropho-bic. Though it's handy to the Vatican, everything else is a long way away. Fortunately, it's well-served by public transit, especially the Metro (line A).

$$$$ Hotel Alimandi Vaticano, facing the Vatican Muse-ums, is beautifully designed. Run by the Alimandi family (Enrico, Irene, and Germano), it features four stars, 24 spacious rooms, and all the modern comforts you can imagine (air-con, elevator, Viale Vaticano 99, tel. 06-3974-5562, www.alimandi.com, alimandivati-cano@alimandi.com).

$$$$ Family-run **Hotel dei Consoli,** with 28 rooms, is a lesser value pleasantly located on a side street. In warm months, breakfast is served on its leafy rooftop terrace, with a view to St. Peter's—a nice way to start the day (air-con, elevator, Via Varrone

2D, tel. 06-6889-2972, www.hoteldeiconsoli.com, info@hoteldei-consoli.com, friendly Laura and mom Amalia).

$$$ Hotel Gerber, set in a quiet residential area, is family-run with 27 thoughtfully decorated rooms—some chic and modern, others polished and businesslike (RS%, family rooms, air-con, elevator, small leafy terrace; from Lepanto Metro station, go one block down Via M. Colonna and turn right to Via degli Scipioni 241; tel. 06-321-6485, www.hotelgerber.it, info@hotelgerber.it, Piero and Simonetta).

$$$ Hotel Museum is located steps from the Vatican Museums and run by another branch of the entrepreneurial Alimandi family—Paolo, Luigi, Marta, and Barbara. It has 27 modest but comfortable rooms and large public spaces, including a piano lounge, pool table, and rooftop terrace where the grand buffet breakfast is served (elevator, air-con, down the stairs directly in front of Vatican Museums, Via Tunisi 8, Metro: Ottaviano, tel. 06-3972-3941, www.hotelmuseum.com, info@hotelmuseum.com).

$$$ Hearth Hotel, a block from the Vatican wall, has 22 small, modern, efficient, and characterless rooms (RS%—use code "rick steves," air-con, elevator, Via Santamaura 2, tel. 06-3903-8383, www.hearthhotel.com, info@hearthhotel.com).

$$ Casa Valdese is a well-managed, Protestant church-run hotel that's a good value and feels a bit institutional. Its 33 recently renovated—but basic—rooms come with the bonus of two breezy, communal roof terraces with incredible views (RS%, family rooms, air-con, elevator; Via Alessandro Farnese 18, tel. 06-321-5362, www.casavaldeseroma.it, reception@casavaldeseroma.it, Matteo).

$$ Casa per Ferie Santa Maria alle Fornaci is simple and efficient, housing pilgrims and secular tourists just a five-minute walk south of the Vatican in a dull, high-rise residential zone. Its 54 utilitarian rooms are mostly twin-bedded. Reserve at least three months in advance (air-con, elevator; take bus #64 from Termini train station to San Pietro train station, then walk 100 yards north along Via della Stazione di San Pietro to Piazza Santa Maria alle Fornaci 27; or from the airport, take the train to Trastevere Station, then transfer to San Pietro Station; tel. 06-3936-7632, www.santamariafornaci.com, Carmine).

Eating in Rome

Romans take great pleasure in dining well. Embrace this passion over a multicourse meal at an outdoor table, watching a parade of passersby while you sip wine with loved ones.

Simple, fresh, seasonal ingredients dominate the dishes. The *cucina* is robust, strongly flavored, and unpretentious—much like the people who've created it over the centuries. It is said that Roman

ROME

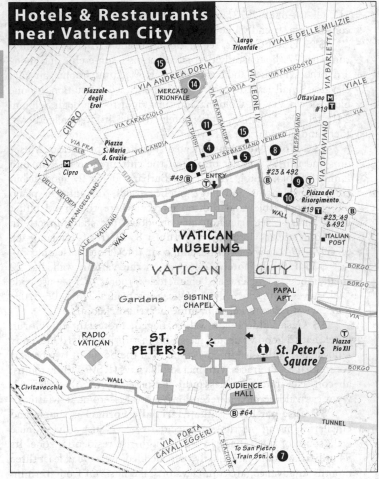

Hotels & Restaurants near Vatican City

cooking didn't come out of emperors' or popes' kitchens, but from the *cucina povera*—the home cooking of the common people. This may explain the Romans' fondness for meats known as the *quinto quarto* ("fifth quarter"), such as tripe, tail, brain, and pigs' feet, as well as their interest in natural preservatives like chili peppers and garlic.

Rome belongs to the warm, southern region of Lazio, which produces a rich variety of flavorful vegetables and fruit that are the envy of American supermarkets. Rome's proximity to the Mediterranean also allows for a great variety of seafood (especially on Fridays), which can be pricey if you're dining out.

ROME

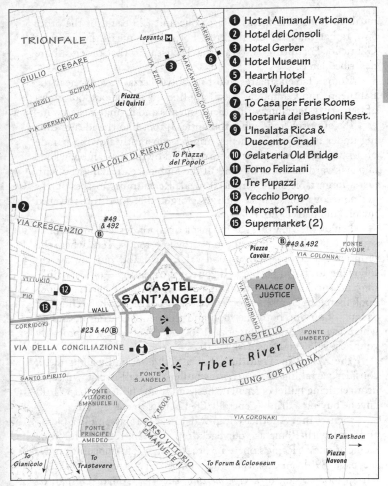

1. Hotel Alimandi Vaticano
2. Hotel dei Consoli
3. Hotel Gerber
4. Hotel Museum
5. Hearth Hotel
6. Casa Valdese
7. To Casa per Ferie Rooms
8. Hostaria dei Bastioni Rest.
9. L'Insalata Ricca & Duecento Gradi
10. Gelateria Old Bridge
11. Forno Feliziani
12. Tre Pupazzi
13. Vecchio Borgo
14. Mercato Trionfale
15. Supermarket (2)

EATING TIPS

Kitchens close at most restaurants between lunch and dinner; if it's a quality restaurant, it won't reopen before 19:00. If a smaller restaurant is booked up later in the evening (from 20:30 or so), they may accommodate walk-ins if you're willing to eat quickly (no lingering).

Choosing Restaurants: I've listed restaurants that I enjoy. Many are in quaint and therefore pricey and touristy areas such as Trastevere, Piazza Navona, and Campo de' Fiori. Others are tucked away from the tourist crush.

I'm impressed by how small the price difference can be between a mediocre Roman restaurant and a fine one. You can pay about 20 percent more for double the quality. If I had $100 for three meals in Rome, I'd spend $50 for one and $25 each for the other two, rather than $33 on all three. For splurge meals, I'd consider Gabriello, Fortunato, and Taverna Trilussa (in that order; all are described later).

Rome's fabled squares (most notably Piazza Navona, near the Pantheon, and Campo de' Fiori) are lined with the outdoor tables of touristy restaurants with enticing menus and formal-vested waiters. The atmosphere is super romantic. I, too, like the idea of dining under floodlit monuments, amid a constantly flowing parade of people. But you'll likely be surrounded by tourists and hawkers, and awkward interactions can kill the ambience...leaving you with just a forgettable and overpriced meal. Restaurants in these areas are notorious for surprise charges, forgettable food, microwaved ravioli, and bad service.

I enjoy the view by savoring just a drink or dessert on a famous square, but I dine with locals on nearby low-rent streets, where the proprietor needs to serve a good-value meal and nurture a local following to stay in business. If you're set on eating—or just drinking and snacking—on a famous piazza, you don't need a guidebook listing to choose a spot; enjoy the ritual of slowly circling the square, observing both the food and the people eating it, and sit where the view and menu appeal to you. (And pizza is probably your best value and least risky bet.)

The *Aperitivo* Tradition: For a budget-friendly light meal, consider partaking in an *aperitivo* buffet. Bars all over town serve up an enticing buffet of small dishes, and from about 18:00 to 21:00 anyone buying a drink (generally €8-12) gets to eat "for free."

Picnicking: Another cheap way to eat is to assemble a picnic and dine with Rome as your backdrop. Buy ingredients for your picnic at one of Rome's open-air produce markets (mornings only; see page 890); an *alimentari* (corner grocery store); a *rosticcerie* (cheap food to go); or a *supermercato,* such as Conad, Despar, or Co-op. You'll find handy late-night supermarkets near the Pantheon (Via Giustiniani), Spanish Steps (Via Vittoria), Trevi Fountain (Via del Bufalo), and Campo de' Fiori (Via di Monte della Farina). Note that Rome discourages people from picnicking or drinking at historic monuments (such as on the Spanish Steps) in the old center. Technically violators can be fined, though it rarely happens. You'll be fine if you eat *with* a view rather than *on* the view.

TRASTEVERE

Restaurants line the streets of colorful Trastevere. It's a favorite dining neighborhood for both Romans and tourists—more rustic than the downtown zone, but just a short walk across the river. (🎧 Download my free Trastevere Walk audio tour to combine sightseeing with dinner.) Go beyond the central square, Piazza di Santa

> ## Restaurant Price Code
>
> I've assigned each eatery a price category, based on the aver-
> age cost of a typical main course (pasta or *secondi*). Drinks,
> desserts, and splurge items (steak and seafood) can raise the
> price considerably.
>
> **$$$$** **Splurge:** Most main courses over €20
> **$$$** **Pricier:** €15-20
> **$$** **Moderate:** €10-15
> **$** **Budget:** Under €10
>
> In Italy, pizza by the slice and other takeaway food is **$**; a basic
> trattoria or sit-down pizzeria is **$$**; a casual but more upscale
> restaurant is **$$$**; and a swanky splurge is **$$$$**.

Maria in Trastevere, into the back streets, and you'll find places
that serve with the most sincerity and charm. For locations, see the
map on page 906.

$$$$ Taverna Trilussa is your best bet for dining well in
Trastevere. Brothers Massimo and Maurizio offer quality without
pretense. With a proud 100-year-old tradition, this place has the
right mix of style and informality. The service is fun-loving (they're
happy to let you split plates into smaller portions to enjoy a family-
style meal), yet professional. The menu celebrates local classics and
seasonal specials—as well as their award-winning *pasta amatriciana*—and comes with a big wine selection. The spacious dining
hall is strewn with eclectic Roman souvenirs. Outdoors, Trilussa
has an actual hedged-in terrace rather than just tables jumbled together on the sidewalk (dinner only—Mon-Sat from 19:30, closed
Sun, reservations smart, Via del Politeama 23, tel. 06-581-8918,
www.tavernatrilussa.it).

$$$ Osteria La Gensola, a seafood restaurant, is a good place
to indulge (they also have Roman classics on the menu). The inte-
rior (no outside seating), which feels like a rustic yet sophisticated
living room, is pleasantly homey (daily 13:00-15:00 & 19:30-23:00,
Piazza della Gensola 15, tel. 06-581-6312, www.osterialagensola.
it).

$$ Trattoria da Lucia is your basic old-school, Trastevere
dining experience, and has been family-run since before World
War II. The specialty is *spaghetti alla Gricia*, with *pancetta* (Tue-
Sun 12:30-15:00 & 19:30-23:00, closed Mon and much of Aug,
cash only, evocative outdoor or comfy indoor seating—but avoid
back room, just off Via del Mattonato at Vicolo del Mattonato 2,
tel. 06-580-3601)

$$ Trattoria da Olindo takes homey to extremes. You really
feel like you dropped in on a family that cooks for the neighbor-
hood. The menu is short, with a choice of about five €8 pastas and

Roman Cuisine

Here are some of the specialties you may find on the menu. For more on Italian food, including *salumi,* cheeses, pizza, and pasta, see page 1140.

Antipasti (Appetizers)

Antipasto misto: A plate of marinated or grilled vegetables (eggplant, artichokes, peppers, mushrooms), cured meats, cheeses, or seafood (anchovies, octopus).

Bruschetta: Toasted bread brushed with olive oil and garlic, topped with chopped tomatoes, mushrooms, or other tidbits.

Fritti: Fried snacks that have been either battered or breaded—often olives stuffed with meat, potato croquettes, and mozzarella cheese. Other classic *fritti* are *supplí* (rice balls with tomato sauce and mozzarella) and *fiori di zucca* (squash blossoms filled with mozzarella and anchovies).

Prosciutto e melone: Cantaloupe wrapped in thin-sliced ham.

Primo Piatto (First Course)

Bucatini all'amatriciana: Thin pasta tubes with a sauce of tomatoes, onion, pancetta, and pecorino cheese.

Gnocchi alla romana: Small, flattened dumplings made from semolina (not potatoes) and baked with butter and cheese.

Penne all'arrabbiata: Spicy tomato sauce with chili peppers (*pepperoncini*) and garlic over penne.

Rigatoni con la pajata: Pasta topped with a stew of calf intestines.

Spaghetti alla carbonara: Eggs, pancetta or *guanciale* (cured pork cheek), cheese (*pecorino romano* or *parmigiano reggiano*), and black pepper over pasta.

Spaghetti alle vongole veraci: Pasta served with small clams in the shell sautéed with white wine and herbs.

Stracciatella alla romana: Meat broth with whipped eggs, topped with parmesan.

Secondo Piatto (Second Course)

Abbacchio alla scottadito: Baby lamb chops grilled and eaten as finger food.

Anguillette in umido: Stewed baby eels from Lake Bracciano.

Coda alla vaccinara: Oxtail braised with garlic, wine, tomato, and celery.

Filetti di baccalà: Fried salt cod (like fish-and-chips minus the chips).

Involtini di vitello al sugo: Veal cutlets rolled with prosciutto, celery, and cheese in a tomato sauce.

Saltimbocca alla romana: "Jump-in-the-mouth"—thinly sliced veal layered with prosciutto and sage, then lightly fried.

Trippa alla romana: Tripe braised with onions, carrots, and mint.

Contorni (Side Dishes)

You may want to order a side dish if your second course is not served with a vegetable. Note that if you order a salad, olive oil and wine vinegar are the only dressings.

Carciofi: Artichokes served either *alla romana* (simmered with garlic and mint) or *alla giudia* (flattened and fried).

Fave al guanciale: Fava beans simmered with cured pork cheek and onion.

Misticanza: Mixed green salad of arugula *(rucola)* and curly endive *(puntarelle)* with anchovies.

Dolci (Desserts)

Dessert can be a seasonal fruit, such as *fragole* (strawberries) or *pesche* (peaches), or even cheese, such as *pecorino romano* (made from ewe's milk) or *caciotta romana* (combination of ewe's and cow's milk).

Bignè: Cream puff-like pastries filled with *zabaione* (egg yolks, sugar, and Marsala wine).

Crostata di ricotta: A cheesecake-like dessert with ricotta, sweet Marsala wine, cinnamon, and bits of chocolate.

Grattachecca: Sweetened shaved ice. Vendors at little booths scrape shavings off ice blocks, then flavor them with syrups, such as *limoncocco* (lemon and coconut with fresh chunks of coconut).

Tartufo: Rich dark-chocolate gelato ball with a cherry inside, sometimes served *con panna* (with whipped cream).

Roman Pizza

Roman-style pizza is made with a very thin and crispy dough called *scrocchiarella* (thinner and less chewy than Neapolitan-style pizza). In Rome, *pizza bianco* (white pizza) can mean a pizza

made without tomato sauce, but can also simply mean a chunk of flat, crispy bread, or a sandwich made with that bread (similar to what's called a *panino* in other parts of Italy).

Local Wines

Rome is located in the region of Lazio, which produces several pleasant white wines and a few reds. Frascati, probably the best-known wine of the region, is an inexpensive dry white made from trebbiano (from the hills just south of Rome) and malvasia grapes. Castelli Romani, light and fairly dry, is made from trebbiano grapes and is similar to Marino, Colli Albani, and Velletri wines. Torre Ercolana is a dense, balanced, medium-bodied red made from the regional cesanese grape, as well as cabernet and merlot (known as Lazio's best-quality red, aged at least five years).

five €10 *secondi* (Mon-Sat 19:30-22:30, closed Sun, cash only, indoor and funky outdoor seating, Vicolo della Scala 8 at the corner of Via del Mattonato, tel. 06-581-8835).

$$ Osteria Ponte Sisto, by the river, has a more touristy, old-school feel with nice place settings, white tablecloths, and traditional Roman and Neapolitan cuisine (Thu-Tue 12:30-15:00 & 19:00-23:30, closed Wed, reservations smart, 100 yards in front of the bridge at Via di Ponte Sisto 80, tel. 06-588-3411, www.osteria-pontesisto.com, Oliviero).

$$ Pizzeria "Ai Marmi" is a noisy festival of pizza. Tight marble-slab tables (hence the nickname "the Morgue") fill the seating area in front of the oven and pizza-assembly line. It's a classic Roman scene, whether you enjoy the chaos inside, sit at a sidewalk table, or take the famously good, thin, and crispy €8-9 pizza home. They also serve fried cod, rice balls with mozzarella, and bean dishes. Expect brusque service and a long line between 20:00 and 22:00 (Thu-Tue 18:30 until late, closed Wed, cash only, tram #8 from Piazza Venezia to first stop over bridge, just beyond Piazza Sonnino at Viale di Trastevere 53, tel. 06-580-0919).

$$ Pizzeria Dar Poeta, tucked in a back alley and a hit with local students, cranks out €9 wood-fired pizzas and €8 calzones. These pizzas are easily splittable and, if you're extra hungry, pay an extra euro for *pizza alta* (thicker crust). Choose between their sloppy, cramped interior or the lively tables outside on the cobblestones (daily 12:00-24:00, call to reserve or expect a wait, 50 yards directly in front of Santa Maria della Scala Church at Vicolo del Bologna 45, tel. 06-588-0516).

$$ Cantina Ripagrande, a block over Viale di Trastevere from the touristy action, has a funky romantic charm and a small but creative menu for lunch (13:00-15:30) and dinner (19:30-22:30). Drinks are served the rest of the day and during happy hour from 18:00 to 20:30, when a €7 drink comes with a well-made little buffet that can turn into a cheap, light dinner (daily 11:30-late, Via San Francesco a Ripa 73, tel. 06-4547-6237).

PANTHEON NEIGHBORHOOD

I've listed the restaurants in this central area based on which landmark they're closest to: Campo de' Fiori, Piazza Navona, the Trevi Fountain, or the Pantheon itself.

On and near Campo de' Fiori

By day, Campo de' Fiori hosts a colorful fruit-and-veggies market (with an increasing number of tourist knickknacks; Mon-Sat closes around 13:30, closed Sun). Combined with a sandwich and a sweet from the **Forno** (bakery) in the west corner of the square (behind the fountain), you can assemble a nice picnic.

In the evening, Campo de' Fiori offers a characteristic setting—once romantic, but now overrun with students and tourists out drinking. The square is lined with popular and interesting bars, pizzerias, and small restaurants—all great for people-watching over a glass of wine. Later at night any charm is smothered by a younger clubbing crowd, but romance lives on the nearby streets.

$$ Enoteca L'Angolo Divino is an inviting little wine bar run by Massimo Crippa, a sommelier who beautifully describes a fine array of wines along with the best accompanying meats, cheeses, and pastas. With tiny tables, a tiny menu, intriguing walls of wine bottles, smart advice, and more locals than tourists, this place can leave you with a lifelong memory (lots of wines by the glass, daily 11:00-15:00 & 17:00-24:00, no afternoon closure Sun-Mon, a block off Campo de' Fiori at Via dei Balestrari 12, tel. 06-686-4413).

$$$ Salumeria e Vineria Roscioli is an elegant *enoteca* that's a hit with local foodies, so reservations are a must. While it's just a salami toss away from touristy Campo de' Fiori, you'll dine with classy locals, and feel like you're sitting in a romantic (and expensive) deli after hours. While a bit pretentious, they have a good selection of fine cheeses, meats, local dishes, and top-end wines by the glass (Mon-Sat 12:30-16:00 & 19:00-24:00, closed Sun, 3 blocks east of Campo de' Fiori at Via dei Giubbonari 21, tel. 06-687-5287, www.salumeriaroscioli.com).

$ Forno Roscioli, their attractive upscale bakery just down the street, will sell you a quick slice of pizza or pastry to go (Mon-Sat 6:00-20:00, closed Sun, Via dei Chiavari 34).

$$$ Trattoria der Pallaro, an eccentric and well-worn eatery that has no menu, has a slogan: "Here, you'll eat what we want to feed you." Paola Fazi—with a towel wrapped around her head turban-style—and her gang dish up a five-course meal of homey Roman food. You have three menu choices: €25 for the works; €20 for appetizers, *secondi,* and dessert; or €16 for appetizers and pasta. Any option is filling and includes wine. While the service can be odd and the food is, let's say...rustic, the experience is fun (daily 12:00-16:00 & 19:00-24:00, reserve if dining after 20:00, cash only, indoor/outdoor seating on quiet square, a block south of Corso Vittorio Emanuele, down Largo del Chiavari to Largo del Pallaro 15, tel. 06-6880-1488).

$$ Filetti di Baccalà is a cheap and basic Roman classic, where nostalgic regulars cram in at wooden tables and savor €5 fried cod finger-food fillets and raw, slightly bitter *puntarelle* greens (slathered with anchovy sauce, available in spring and winter). Study what others are eating, and order from your grease-stained server by pointing at what you want. Sit in the fluorescent-lit interior or try to grab a seat out on the little square, a quiet haven a

ROME

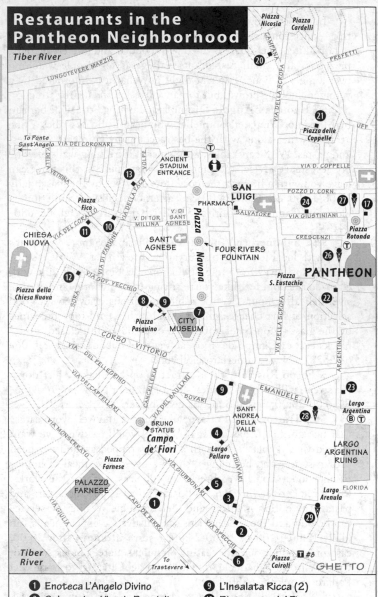

Restaurants in the Pantheon Neighborhood

Tiber River

Piazza Nicosia

Piazza Cardelli

20

LUNGOTEVERE MARZIO

VIA DELLA SCROFA

CAMPANA

PREFETTI

UFF

To Ponte
Sant'Angelo

VIA DEI CORONARI

21

Piazza delle
Coppelle

VOLPE

ANCIENT
STADIUM
ENTRANCE

T

i

VIA D. COPPELLE

13

Piazza
Fico

VIA DELLA PACE

V. DI TOR
MILLINA

V. DI
SANT'AGNESE

Piazza
Navona

**SAN
LUIGI**

PHARMACY

SALVATORE

POZZO D. CORN.

24

VIA GIUSTINIANI

27

17

Piazza
Rotonda

CHIESA
NUOVA

VIA DEL CORALLO

11

10

VIA DI PARIONE

SANT'
AGNESE

FOUR RIVERS
FOUNTAIN

CRESCENZI

26

T

VIA DELLA VETRINA

VIA DEL CORALLO

SORA

12

VIA GOV. VECCHIO

Piazza della
Chiesa Nuova

8

9

Piazza
Pasquino

7

CITY
MUSEUM

Piazza
S. Eustachio

PANTHEON

VIA DELLA SCROFA

22

CORSO   VITTORIO

VIA DEL PELLEGRINO

VIA DEL CAPPELLARI

CANCELLERIA

VIA DEL BAULLARI

B. VARI

9

EMANUELE   II

SANT'
ANDREA
DELLA VALLE

23

Largo
Argentina

B

T

28

ARGENTINA

VIA MONSERRATO

BRUNO
STATUE

Campo
de' Fiori

Largo
Pallaro

4

VIA GIUBBONARI

CHIAVARI

LARGO
ARGENTINA
RUINS

FLORIDA

Piazza
Farnese

**PALAZZO
FARNESE**

CAPO DE FERRO

1

5

3

Largo
Arenula

VIA GIULIA

VIA SPECCHI

2

29

Tiber
River

6

Piazza
Cairoli

T #8

GHETTO

To
Trastevere

1 Enoteca L'Angelo Divino	**9** L'Insalata Ricca (2)
2 Salumeria e Vineria Roscioli	**10** Ristorante del Fico
3 Forno Roscioli	**11** Rist. Pizzeria "da Francesco"
4 Trattoria der Pallaro	**12** Pizzeria da Baffetto
5 Filetti di Baccalà	**13** Chiostro del Bramante
6 Open Baladin Pub	**14** To Hostaria Romana
7 Vivi Bistrot	**15** L'Antica Birreria Peroni
8 Cul de Sac	**16** Rist. Pizzeria Sacro e Profano

ROME

Gelateria

17 Ristorante da Fortunato
18 Enoteca Corsi
19 Trattoria dal Cavalier Gino
20 Ristorante la Campana
21 Osteria delle Coppelle &
   Osteria da Mario
22 Miscellanea
23 Frullati Pascucci

24 Supermarkets (2)
25 Gelateria Giolitti
26 Crèmeria Monteforte
27 San Crispino Gelateria
28 Gelateria Vice
29 Gelateria Artigianale Corona

block east of Campo de' Fiori (Mon-Sat 17:00-23:00, closed Sun, cash only, Largo dei Librari 88, tel. 06-686-4018). If you're not into greasy spoons, avoid this place.

$$ Open Baladin is a busy, modern brewpub featuring a few dozen Italian craft beers on tap and menu of burgers, salads, and freshly cooked potato chips. As burger bars are trendy in Italy, prices are somewhat high. It's a nice break if you're parched and ready for pub grub (daily 12:00-very late, Via degli Specchi 5, tel. 06-683-8989).

Near Piazza Navona

Piazza Navona and the streets just to the west are jammed with an amazing array of restaurants. The places lining the piazza itself are traditional and touristy. Instead, survey the scene on the two streets heading west from the square. Here are my favorites in that zone:

$$ Vivi Bistrot, in the Museum of Rome building, is a good value at the south end of Piazza Navona, with two delightful window tables overlooking the square. This smart little restaurant serves salads, pastas, and burger plates all day and a €10 drink-and-antipasto-plate deal nightly from 19:00 to 22:00 (Tue-Sun 10:00-24:00, closed Mon, Piazza Navona 2, tel. 06-683-3779, www.vivibistrot.com).

$$ Cul de Sac, a corridor-wide trattoria lined with wine bottles, is packed with an enthusiastic crowd enjoying a wide-ranging menu, from pasta to homemade pâté. They have fun sampler plates of *salumi* and cheese, good wines by the glass, and fine outdoor seating. It's small, and they don't take reservations—come early to avoid a wait (daily 12:00-24:00, a block off Piazza Navona on Piazza Pasquino 73, tel. 06-6880-1094).

$ L'Insalata Ricca, a popular local chain, specializes in filling salads and also serves pasta and €10-12 meal deals (available all day) that include a drink. A small branch is at Piazza Pasquino 72 (tel. 06-6830-7881) and a more spacious and enjoyable location is a couple of blocks toward Largo Argentina, just across busy Corso Vittorio Emanuele (Largo dei Chiavari 85, tel. 06-6880-3656). Both are open daily 12:00-24:00.

$$ Ristorante del Fico is a sprawling, rustic-chic place that feels like a huge Italian saloon filled with young in-the-know locals. It has both a fun energy and an easy-to-enjoy, traditional Italian menu (nightly from 19:30, 3 blocks west of Piazza Navona at Via della Pace 34, tel. 06-688-91373).

$$ Ristorante Pizzeria "da Francesco," bustling and authentic, has a 50-year-old tradition, a hardworking young waitstaff, great indoor seating, and a few tables on the quiet street. Their blackboard explains the daily specials (daily 12:00-15:30 & 19:00-24:00, Piazza del Fico 29, tel. 06-686-4009).

$$ Pizzeria da Baffetto is famous among visiting Italians and therefore generally comes with a ridiculous line—get there very early or late. The pizzas are great, the service is surly, and the tables are tightly arranged amid the mishmash of sketches littering the walls. The pizza-assembly kitchen keeps things energetic, and the pizza oven keeps the main room warm. Take out or eat in: Street-side tables are less congested and sweaty, but also less memorable (daily 12:00-15:30 & 18:30 until late, cash only; order "P," "M," or "D"—small, medium, or large; Via del Governo Vecchio 114, tel. 06-686-1617).

$$ Chiostro del Bramante is a museum café serving light lunches of sandwiches, salads, and pastas in a unique setting—overlooking the tranquil open-air *chiostro* (cloister) of the San Bramante church. Find the stairs just to the left of the church entrance and tell the ticket-window staff that you're just going to the café. Though portions are small, the setting is memorable, peaceful, and relaxing—this is the place to sit and get some writing done (café open daily 10:00-20:00, meals served 12:00-15:00, Arco della Pace 5, tel. 06-6880-9035).

Near the Trevi Fountain
The streets surrounding the Trevi Fountain are littered with mediocre restaurants catering exclusively to tourists. Skip them and walk a few blocks away to one of these.

$$ Hostaria Romana is a busy bistro with a hustling and fun-loving gang of waiters. The upstairs is a tight, tidy, glassed-in terrace, while the cellar has noisy walls graffitied by happy eaters. As its menu specializes in traditional Roman dishes, it's a good place to try *saltimbocca alla romana* or *bucatini all'amatriciana*. Their €12 *antipasti della casa* plate, with a variety of vegetables and cheeses, makes a hearty start to your meal (Mon-Sat 12:30-15:00 & 19:15-23:00, closed Sun and Aug, reservations smart, Via del Boccaccio 1—see map on page 918, walk along Via Rasella to reach restaurant, tel. 06-474-5284, www.hostariaromana.it).

$ L'Antica Birreria Peroni is Rome's answer to a German beer hall. Serving hearty mugs of the local Peroni beer and lots of just-plain-fun beer-hall food and Italian classics, the place is a hit with Romans for a cheap night out (Mon-Sat 12:00-24:00, closed Sun, midway between Trevi Fountain and Capitoline Hill, a block off Via del Corso at Via di San Marcello 19, tel. 06-679-5310).

$$ Ristorante Pizzeria Sacro e Profano, filling an old church, serves spicy southern Italian (Calabrian) cuisine just far enough away from the Trevi mobs. Their pizza oven is wood-fired, and their hearty €15 *golosità calabresi* appetizer plate is a filling

Resources for Foodies

For those looking to take their Roman culinary endeavors seriously, there's no shortage of in-depth advice. Books and blogs on Roman cuisine abound, and several local companies run food- and wine-themed tours. Here is a sampling:

Katieparla.com, food author Katie Parla's website, has all the latest on the Roman food scene. She also offers private food-oriented tours and tastings.

Katie Parla's Rome, Parla's app, transfers her highly selective, top-notch recommendations into an easy-to-use, searchable format (and once on your device, it doesn't require an Internet connection).

Eat Italy, an excellent iPhone-only app covering many cities—including Rome—by food writer Elizabeth Minchilli, lists a wider range of good eateries and food-oriented shops (works off-line). Her website also features recipes and private food tours (www.elizabethminchilliinrome.com).

Eating Italy Food Tours leads fun and insightful walks almost daily through Rome's colorful Testaccio and Trastevere neighborhoods, interspersing history, tradition, and local food culture while giving you a glimpse into daily life in less-seen parts of the city. Each group of about a dozen people makes about 10 tasty stops. The Testaccio tour is better (€75-88, 4 hours, several morning and evening departures Mon-Sat, www.eatingitalyfoodtours.com). They also offer cooking classes. Rick Steves readers get a 10 percent discount (use promo code "ricksteves").

Vino Roma is a small wine "school" run by several sommeliers who offer evening tasting classes (€50/person), designed to help you understand and enjoy Italian wine. They also offer several neighborhood walks (www.vinoroma.com).

Buon appetito, e salute!

montage of Calabrian taste treats (Tue-Sun 12:00-15:00 & 18:00-23:00, closed Mon, a block off Via del Tritone and Via della Panetteria at Via dei Maroniti 29, tel. 06-679-1836).

Close to the Pantheon

Eating on the square facing the Pantheon is a temptation, and I'd consider it just to relax and enjoy the Roman scene. But if you walk a block or two away, you'll get less view and better value. Here are some suggestions.

$$$$ Ristorante da Fortunato is an Italian classic, with fresh flowers on the tables and white-coated, black-tie career waiters politely serving good meat and fish to politicians, foreign dignitaries, and well-heeled tourists with good taste. Peruse the photos of their famous visitors—everyone from Muammar Gaddafi and Prince

Charles to Bill Clinton are pictured with Signore Fortunato, who started this restaurant in 1975 and was a master of simple edible elegance. (His son Jason now runs the show.) The outdoor seating is fine for people-watching, but the elegance is inside. For a dressy night out, this is a reliable and surprisingly reasonable choice—reserve ahead (figure €50/person, daily 12:30-23:30, a block in front of the Pantheon at Via del Pantheon 55, tel. 06-679-2788, www.ristorantefortunato.it).

$$ Enoteca Corsi, a wine shop that grew into a thriving restaurant, is a charming local scene with the family table in back, where the kids do their homework. The Paiella family serves straightforward, traditional cuisine to an appreciative crowd of office workers. The board lists daily specials (gnocchi on Thursday, fish on Friday, and so on). Friendly Manuela and her staff welcome eaters with €9 pastas, €13 main dishes, and fine wine at a third of the price you'd pay in normal restaurants—buy from their shop and pay a corking fee; this can be a good value. Show this book for a free glass of homemade *limoncello* for dessert (Mon-Sat 12:00-15:30, Thu-Fri also 19:00-22:30, closed Sun, no reservations, a block toward the Pantheon from the Gesù Church at Via del Gesù 87, tel. 06-679-0821).

$$ Trattoria dal Cavalier Gino, tucked away on a tiny street behind the Parliament, has been a favorite since 1963. Photos on the wall recall the days when it was the haunt of big-time politicians. English-speaking siblings Carla and Fabrizio serve up traditional Roman favorites. Reserve ahead, even for lunch, as you'll be packed in with savvy locals (cash only, Mon-Sat 13:00-14:45 & 20:00-22:30, closed Sun, behind Piazza del Parlamento and just off Via di Campo Marzio at Vicolo Rosini 4, tel. 06-687-3434).

$$ Ristorante la Campana is a classic—an authentic slice of old Rome appreciated by well-dressed locals. Claiming a history dating to 1518, this place feels unchanged over the years. It serves typical Roman dishes and €10 daily specials, plus it has a good self-service *antipasti* buffet (Tue-Sun 12:30-15:00 & 19:30-23:00, closed Mon, inside seating only, reserve for dinner, just off Via della Scrofa and Piazza Nicosia at Vicolo della Campana 18, tel. 06-687-5273, www.ristorantelacampana.com).

$$ Osteria delle Coppelle, a slapdash trendy place, serves traditional dishes to a local crowd. It has a rustic interior and jumbled exterior seating, and a fun selection of €3 *cicchetti* that lets you enjoy a variety of Roman dishes as tapas (daily 12:30-16:00 & 19:00 until late, Piazza delle Coppelle 54, tel. 06-4550-2826). On the same charming square, the more old-school **Osteria da Mario** is also worth considering.

$$ Miscellanea is run by much-loved Mikki, who's on a mission to keep foreign students well-fed. He offers hearty €4 sandwiches, pizza-like bruschetta, and a long list of €7-8 salads, along with pasta and other staples—it's a good value for a cheap and hearty dinner in a convenient location. Mikki (and his son Romeo) often tosses in a fun little extra (like their "sexy wine") if you have this book on the table (daily 9:00-24:00, indoor/outdoor seating, facing the rear of the Pantheon at Via della Palombella 34, tel. 06-6813-5318).

Picnicking Close to the Pantheon

It's fun to picnic with a view of the Pantheon. (Remember to be discreet.) Here are some options.

$ Frullati Pascucci, a hole-in-the-wall convenient for takeaway, has been making refreshing €3-4 fruit *frullati* and frappés (like smoothies and shakes), plus fruit salads, for more than 75 years. Add a €4 sandwich to make a healthy light meal (Mon-Sat 6:00-23:00, closed Sun, north of Largo Argentina at Via di Torre Argentina 20, tel. 06-686-4816).

Supermarkets: For picnic goodies, try **Despar,** half a block from the Pantheon (daily 8:30-22:00, Via Giustiniani 18) or **Co-op,** three blocks away (Mon-Sat 8:00-21:00, Sun 9:00-21:00, Corso Vittorio Emanuele II 42).

Gelato Close to the Pantheon

Several fine *gelaterie* are within three or four blocks of the Pantheon.

Giolitti is Rome's most famous and venerable ice-cream joint (although few would say it has the best gelato). Takeaway prices are reasonable, and it has elegant Old World seating (just off Piazza Colonna and Piazza Montecitorio at Via Uffici del Vicario 40).

Crèmeria Monteforte is known for its traditional gelato and super-creamy sorbets *(cremolati)*. The fruit flavors are especially refreshing—think gourmet slushies (closed Mon, faces the west side of the Pantheon at Via della Rotonda 22).

San Crispino serves small portions of tasty gourmet gelato. Because of their commitment to natural ingredients, the colors are muted; ice-cream purists know that bright colors are artificial and used to attract children (a block in front of the Pantheon at Piazza della Maddalena 3).

Gelateria Vice might be the best of all. They use top-quality ingredients in innovative ways, and the flavors change with the seasons (around the northwest corner of Largo Argentina at Corso Vittorio Emanuele II 96).

Gelateria Artigianale Corona feels like a time warp and is nothing fancy, but it's got some of the finest homemade gelato in town, with an array of creative flavors (just south of Largo Argentina at Largo Arenula 27).

NEAR THE SPANISH STEPS AND ARA PACIS

To locate these restaurants, see the "Dolce Vita Stroll" map on page 818.

$$$ Ristorante il Gabriello is inviting and small—modern under medieval arches—and provides a peaceful and local-feeling respite from all the top-end fashion shops in the area. Claudio serves with charisma, while his brother, Gabriello, cooks creative Roman cuisine using fresh, organic products from his wife's farm. Italians normally just trust their waiter and say, "Bring it on." Tourists are understandably more cautious, but you can be trusting here. Invest €45—not including wine—in "Claudio's Extravaganza," created especially for my readers (not on the menu). Specify whether you'd prefer fish, meat, or both. (Romans think raw shellfish is the ultimate in fine dining. If you differ, make that clear.) When finished, I stand up, hold my belly, and say, *"Ahhh, la vita è bella."* While you're likely to dine surrounded by my readers here (especially if eating before 21:00), the atmosphere is fun and convivial (dinner only, Mon-Sat 19:00-23:00, closed Sun, reservations smart, air-con, dress respectfully—no shorts, 3 blocks from Spanish Steps at Via Vittoria 51, tel. 06-6994-0810, www.ilgabriello.it).

$$ Antica Enoteca, an upbeat, atmospheric 200-plus-year-old *enoteca,* has around 60 Italian-only wines by the glass. For a light and memorable lunch, enjoy a glass of their best wine at the bar (listed on a big blackboard) and split a €14 *antipasti* plate of veggies, *salumi,* and cheese. There's a full menu of eating options, including daily *piatto unico* specials, and the food comes with wonderful ambience both inside and out (daily 12:00-24:00, best to reserve for outdoor seating, Via della Croce 76B, tel. 06-679-0896).

$$ Palatium is a crisp, modern restaurant funded by the government of Lazio (the region around Rome) to show off its finest agricultural fare. Surrounded by locals, you'll enjoy generous, €12-14 shareable plates of cheeses and *salumi,* a limited menu of pasta and meat, and a huge selection of local wine (daily 9:00-22:30, closed three weeks in Aug, 5 blocks in front of the Spanish Steps at Via Frattina 94, tel. 06-6920-2132).

$$$ Caffè Ciampini is delightfully set on a fine traffic-free square. The food is quite pricey and won't win any awards—and you pay for the location—so I'd only stop here for a drink or dessert. Sit outside and people-watch amidst a professional Roman crowd. The cocktails come with a little tray of finger sandwiches and nuts; for some it's a light and inexpensive meal (€20-35 fixed-price dinners; daily 7:30-20:30, later in summer, Piazza San Lorenzo in Lucina 29, tel. 06-687-6606, www.ciampini.com).

Stand-Up Food Crawl down Via della Croce: Two blocks north of the Spanish Steps, Via della Croce is a fun street to shop for a light meal or snack. As you walk down this street from Via del Corso, you'll first pass several takeout shops for pizza and sandwiches, including the pretty but overpriced **$ Grano Frutta e Farina** (#49A). Next, the **Co-op** minisupermarket at #48 fits the bill for budget picnickers, or you can try a sandwich-on-request from the **Foccaci** deli (at #43) with a long, enticing counter of meats and cheeses. Farther down is the more formal, sit-down **Antica Enoteca** (#76b, described earlier). Then comes another classic *alimentari* (corner grocery/deli), **Salsamenteria F.lli Fabbi** at #28. They'll make a sandwich to your specs and price it by weight. **Venchi** (#25-26) has chocolate in every form. **Pompi** (#82), the self-proclaimed "kingdom of tiramisu," features several flavors (classic, strawberry, pistachio) in €4 portions. And finally, **$ Pastificio** (#8) serves up two fresh €4 pasta dishes each day; a cup of water or wine is included if you eat at the stools along the wall (daily 13:00-21:30).

ANCIENT ROME

Within a block of the Colosseum and Forum, you'll find convenient eateries catering to weary sightseers, most offering neither memorable food nor good value. To get your money's worth, stick with one of my recommendations, even if it means a 10-15 minute walk from the ruins. For locations, see the map on page 900.

Monti

Tucked behind Trajan's Forum, in the tight and cobbled lanes between Via Nazionale and Via Cavour, is the characteristic Monti neighborhood. It's just a few steps farther from the ancient sites than the battery of forgettable touristy restaurants, but that extra effort opens up a world of inexpensive and characteristic dining experiences. From the Forum, head up Via Cavour and then left on Via dei Serpenti; the action centers on Piazza della Madonna dei Monti and nearby lanes.

$$$ L'Asino d'Oro ("The Golden Donkey") is a top choice for foodies in this neighborhood (so reserve ahead). Chef Lucio Sforza serves Umbrian cuisine with a creative twist—and mingles savory and sweet flavors to create a memorable meal. The service is crisp, the pasta is homemade, and the simple, modern space is filled with savvy diners (Tue-Sat 19:30-23:00, closed Sun-Mon, Via del Boschetto 73, tel. 06-4891-3832).

$$ Taverna Romana is small, simple, and a bit chaotic—with an open kitchen and hams and garlic hanging from the ceiling. This family-run eatery's *cacio e pepe* (cheese and pepper pasta) is a favorite. Arrive early or call to reserve (Mon-Sat 12:30-15:00 & 19:00-23:00, closed Sun, Via della Madonna dei Monti 79, tel. 06-474-5325).

$$ La Cicala e La Formica ("The Cicada and the Ant") has its own little nook on Via Leonina. The terrace dining is good for people-watching, while the homey interior is livelier. The cuisine is Mediterranean and Italian, and their weekday lunch specials are good values (daily 12:00-15:30 & 18:30-23:00, Via Leonina 17, tel. 06-481-7490).

$$ Taverna dei Fori Imperiali serves typical, slightly higher-priced Roman cuisine in a snug interior that bustles with energy (Wed-Mon 12:30-15:00 & 19:30-22:30, closed Tue, Via della Madonna dei Monti 9, reserve for dinner, tel. 06-679-8643, www.latavernadeiforiimperiali.com).

$$ Alle Carrette Pizzeria, simple and rustic, serves great wood-fired pizza just 200 yards from the Forum's side entrance, hidden off a tiny square (daily 12:00-15:30 & 19:00-24:00, Vicolo delle Carrette 14, tel. 06-679-2770).

$ Trattoria da Valentino is a classic time warp hiding under its historic (and therefore protected) Birra Peroni sign. They specialize in €9 *scamorza* (grilled cheese with various toppings), list the day's pastas on a chalkboard, and serve a variety of meat dishes (Mon-Sat 13:00-15:00 & 19:00-23:00, closed Sun, Via del Boschetto 37, tel. 06-488-0643).

$ Antico Forno ai Serpenti, a hip bakery, puts out a small buffet of pastas and vegetables at lunch and dinner for €10, which includes a drink—a fine value. They also bake good bread and pastries and do breakfasts. With only a few tables, it can fill up (Mon-Sat 8:00-23:00, Sun 9:00-22:00, Via dei Serpenti 122, tel. 06-4542-7920).

$$ Enoteca Cavour 313, a wine bar with a slightly unconventional menu ranging from couscous and salads to high-quality *affettati* (cold cuts) and cheese, makes a nice alternative to the usual pasta/pizza choices. You'll be served with a mellow ambience under lofts of wine bottles (daily 12:30-14:45 & 18:30-24:00, 100 yards off Via dei Fori Imperiali at Via Cavour 313, tel. 06-678-5496).

At Trajan's Column: **$$ Terre e Domus** is one of the few options around the otherwise unwelcoming Piazza Venezia. Immediately below Trajan's Column, it's a modern little place with a cool, peaceful, and well-lit dining room. Run by the city of Rome, its mission is to showcase local ingredients and cuisine, and to help out-of-work residents return to the job market (daily 9:00-23:30, Foro Traiano 82, tel. 06-6994-0273).

The Monti Four-Course Food Crawl

The streets of Monti are crowded with fun and creative places offering inexpensive quality snacks and light meals to eat on tiny informal tables or to take away. For a fun, four-course movable feast, essentially on one street cutting right through the heart of Monti, drop into each of these places for a little bite. Be open to whatever appeals along the way. Here's your mobile menu:

Course 1, Wine with *Aperitivo* (dinner only): $$ Fafiuché is an intimate yet vibrant family-run wine bar with a fun-loving vibe and no pretense. They serve a broad selection of wines and beers inside or at tables on the cobblestones outside. Each evening from 18:30 to 21:00 Andrea and Maria offer a popular *aperitivo* special: €8 covers a glass of wine and one trip to the buffet—making it a cheap, light meal. Or, for more money, you can order serious regional specialties from Apulia and Piedmont (Mon-Sat 17:30 until late, closed Sun, Via della Madonna dei Monti 28).

Course 2, Pizza by the Slice on the Square: $ Pizzeria la Boccaccia, a hole-in-the-wall, is good for a takeaway pizza slice. Point at what you like and mime how big of a rectangle you want (daily 9:00-24:00, Via Leonina 73). Take it a block away to eat while making the scene at the neighborhood gathering point, Piazza Santa Maria del Monti, where you can buy a to-go bottle of beer at the top of the square.

Course 3, Gourmet Sandwich and Veggie Juice: $ Zia Rosetta specializes in gourmet *rosette*, sandwiches on rose-shaped buns. At €2-3 for the tiny ones or €5-6 for the standard size, they're perfect for a light bite—either to take away or eat in. Their fun, healthy, and creative menu includes salads and €4 *centrifughe*—fresh-squeezed, vitamin-bomb fruit and veggie juices (Tue-Sun 11:00-22:00, closed Mon, Via Urbana 54).

Course 4, Gelato: Fatamorgana, hiding on the welcoming little square just above Zia Rosetta, features some of the most creative gelato flavor combinations I've seen in Italy—along with more conventional ones. Portions are small but good quality—everything is organic and gluten-free (Piazza degli Zingari 5).

Behind the Colosseum

A pleasant little residential zone just up the street from the back of the Colosseum (the opposite direction from the Forum) features a real neighborhood feel and a variety of restaurants that capably serve tired and hungry sightseers.

$ Trattoria Luzzi is a well-worn, no-frills eatery serving simple food in a high-energy—sometimes chaotic—environment (as they've done since 1945). With good prices, big portions, and proximity to the Colosseum, it draws a crowd—reserve or expect a short wait at lunch and after 19:30 (Thu-Tue 12:00-24:00, closed Wed, Via San Giovanni in Laterano 88, tel. 06-709-6332).

$$ Ristorante Pizzeria Naumachia is a good second bet if Trattoria Luzzi next door is jammed up. It's a bit more upscale and serves good-quality pizza and pastas at decent prices (Via Celimontana 7, tel. 06-700-2764).

$$ Li Rioni, a pizzeria, is open only for dinner, when its over-the-rooftops interior and terrace out front are jammed with Romans watching the busy chef plunge dough into its wood-fired oven, then pull out crispy-crust Roman-style pizzas (Wed-Mon 19:30-24:00, closed Tue, Via dei S.S. Quattro 24, tel. 06-7045-0605).

$$ La Taverna dei Quaranta, a casual neighborhood favorite, has a humble, red-checkered tablecloth ambience. They fire up the wood oven for pizza, to go along with a basic menu of Roman classics and seasonal specialties. As the place caters mostly to locals, service can be a bit slow and straightforward (daily 12:00-16:00 & 18:00-23:30, Via Claudia 24, tel. 06-700-0550).

$$ Il Pentagrappolo is an intimate *enoteca*, serving light meals (proudly, no pasta) to go with their selection of quality wines, many organic. Their €10 lunches include water and are convenient to the Forum and Colosseum (food served Mon-Fri 12:00-15:00, Tue-Sun 18:00-24:00, best to reserve on weekends, three blocks east of the Colosseum at Via Celimontana 21, www.ilpentagrappolo.com, tel. 06-709-6301).

Between the Colosseum and St. Peter-in-Chains Church

You'll find these places across the street and up the hill from the Colosseum. They're more convenient than high cuisine, though they work fine in a pinch.

$$ Hostaria da Nerone is a traditional place serving hearty classics, including tasty homemade pasta dishes. Their *antipasti* plate—with a variety of veggies, fish, and meat—is a good value for a quick lunch. While the *antipasti* menu indicates specifics, you can have a plate of whatever's out—just direct the waiter to assemble the €10 *antipasti* plate of your lunchtime dreams (Mon-Sat 12:00-15:00 & 19:00-23:00, closed Sun, indoor/outdoor seating, Via delle Terme di Tito 96, tel. 06-481-7952).

$ Caffè dello Studente, a normal neighborhood bar popular with tourists and students attending the nearby University, is run by Pina, her perky daughter, Simona, and son-in-law, Emiliano. I'd skip the microwaved pasta and stick to toasted sandwiches and salad. If it's not busy, show this book when you order at the bar and sit at a table without paying extra (daily 7:30-20:00, closed Sun Nov-March, Via delle Terme di Tito 95, mobile 320-854-0333).

NEAR TERMINI STATION

These restaurants work well for those staying at my recommended hotels around Via Nazionale, Via Firenze, and Termini Station. The station itself has a lot of eateries, and there are many Asian restaurants along nearby streets.

ROME

Restaurants near Termini Station

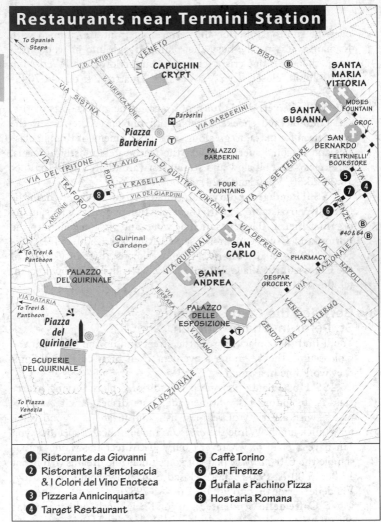

1 Ristorante da Giovanni
2 Ristorante la Pentolaccia & I Colori del Vino Enoteca
3 Pizzeria Annicinquanta
4 Target Restaurant
5 Caffè Torino
6 Bar Firenze
7 Bufala e Pachino Pizza
8 Hostaria Romana

Around Via Flavia

Though a few minutes out of the way, these places are in a quieter neighborhood with less traffic.

$$ Ristorante da Giovanni is an old-fashioned, basement-level neighborhood restaurant where hardworking cooks and waiters serve standard dishes at great prices to a committed clientele (daily specials, Mon-Sat 12:00-15:00 & 19:00-22:00, closed Sun and Aug, corner of Via XX Settembre at Via Antonio Salandra 1, tel. 06-485-950).

$$$ Ristorante la Pentolaccia, more upscale and romantic

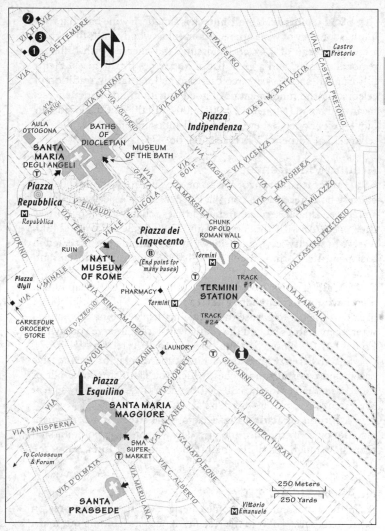

than the nearby Da Giovanni, is a dressy but still tourist-friendly place with tight seating and traditional Roman cooking—consider their daily specials. This is a local hangout, and reservations are smart (daily 12:00-15:00 & 17:30-23:00, a block off Via XX Settembre at Via Flavia 38, tel. 06-483-477, www.lapentolaccia. eu). To start things off with a free bruschetta, leave this book on the table.

$$ Pizzeria Annicinquanta, big and modern, serves Neapolitan-style pizzas in a calm ambience with outdoor seating (daily 12:30-15:30 & 19:30-24:00 except no lunch on Sat, Via Flavia 3, tel. 06-4201-0460).

\$\$\$ I Colori del Vino Enoteca is a modern wine bar that feels like a laboratory of wine appreciation. It has woody walls of bottles, a creative menu of *affettati* (cold cuts) and cheeses with different regional themes, and a great list of fine wines by the glass. Helpful, English-speaking Marco carries on a long family tradition of celebrating the fundamentals of good nutrition: fine wine, cheese, meat, and bread (Mon-Fri 12:00-15:00 & 19:00-23:00, closed Sat-Sun—except open Sat evenings April-June and Sept-Nov, Via Aureliana 15 at corner of Via Flavia, tel. 06-474-1745).

Around Via Firenze
\$\$\$ Target Restaurant seems to be the favorite recommendation of every hotel receptionist on Via Firenze. It has a sleek and dressy ambience, capable service, and food that's reliably good, but pricey (free *aperitivo* with this book, daily 12:00-15:30 & 19:00-24:00, reserve to specify seating outside or inside—avoid getting seated in basement, Via Torino 33, tel. 06-474-0066, www.targetrestaurant. it).

\$ Caffè Torino is a workers' favorite for a quick, cheap lunch. They have good, fresh, hot dishes ready to go for a good price. Head back past the bar to peruse their enticing display, point at what you want, then grab a seat and the young waitstaff will serve you (Mon-Fri 6:00-17:00, closed Sat-Sun, Via Torino 40A, tel. 06-474-2767).

\$ Bar Firenze puts out a lunchtime display of inexpensive pastas and colorful sandwiches, which you can get to take out or eat at casual tables (daily 6:30-24:00, under the "Snack Bar" sign at Via Firenze 33, tel. 06-488-3862).

\$ Bufala e Pachino Pizza, across the street, is a convenient place for pizza by the slice and priced by weight—just point and tell them how much you'd like (daily 8:00-23:00, Via Firenze 54, tel. 06-474-3668).

NEAR VATICAN CITY
As in the Colosseum area, some eateries near the Vatican prey on exhausted tourists. Avoid the restaurant pushers handing out fliers: They're usually hawking places with bad food and expensive menu tricks. Instead, tide yourself over with a slice of pizza or at any of these eateries (see map on page 910), and save your euros for a better meal elsewhere.

Handy Lunch Places near Piazza Risorgimento
These listings are a stone's throw from the Vatican wall. They're mostly fast and cheap, with a good *gelateria* nearby.

\$\$ Hostaria dei Bastioni, run by Antonio while Emilio cooks, has noisy streetside seating and a quiet interior (Mon-Sat

12:00-15:00 & 18:00-23:00, closed Sun, at corner of Vatican wall at Via Leone IV 29, tel. 06-3972-3034).

$ L'Insalata Ricca is another branch of the popular chain that serves hearty salads and pastas (daily 12:00-23:30, across from Vatican walls at Piazza Risorgimento 5, tel. 06-3973-0387, www. insalataricca.it).

$ Duecento Gradi is a good bet for fresh and creative sandwiches—though at €5-8 they're expensive by Roman standards. Munch your lunch sitting down (€1 extra) or take it away (daily 10:30-24:00, Piazza Risorgimento 3, tel. 06-3975-4239).

Gelato: **Gelateria Old Bridge** scoops up hearty portions of fresh gelato for tourists and nuns alike—join the line (just off Piazza Risorgimento across from Vatican walls at Viale dei Bastioni di Michelangelo 3).

Other Options in the Vatican Area

Most of these listings are near the Vatican Museums and Cipro Metro stop. The Borgo Pio eateries are near St. Peter's Basilica.

Viale Giulio Cesare and *Via Candia:* These streets are lined with cheap *pizza rustica* shops and self-serve places. **$ Forno Feliziani** (closed Sun, Via Candia 61) is a fancy version with nicely presented pizza by the slice and simple cafeteria-style dishes that you can eat in or take out.

Covered Market: Turn your nose loose in the wonderful **Mercato Trionfale,** one of the city's best market halls. It's more of a sight than a place to eat. Almost completely untouristy (with lots of vendors, but no real prepared-food stands aside from a bakery and a sandwich counter), it's located just three blocks north of the Vatican Museums (Mon-Sat roughly 7:00-14:00, Tue and Fri some stalls stay open until 19:00, closed Sun, corner of Via Tunisi and Via Andrea Doria). If the market is closed, the **Co-op** supermarket to the northwest has a big bakery section with tables where you can eat pizza by the slice (Mon-Sat 8:00-20:30, Sun 9:00-20:00, Via Andrea Doria 46). Closer to the Vatican is a smaller grocery store, **Carrefour Express** (daily 8:00-20:30, Via Sebastiano Veniero 16).

Eating Close to St. Peter's: The pedestrians-only Borgo Pio—a block from Piazza San Pietro—has restaurants worth a look, such as the traditional **$$ Tre Pupazzi** (Mon-Sat 12:00-15:00 & 19:00-23:00, closed Sun, at corner of Via Tre Pupazzi and Borgo Pio, tel. 06-6880-3220). At **$ Vecchio Borgo,** across the street, you can get pasta, pizza by weight, and veggies to go or to eat at simple tables (daily 9:30-22:30, Borgo Pio 27a).

Rome Connections

Rome is well-connected with the rest of the planet: by train, plane, bus, car, and cruise ship. This section explains the various options for your arrival and departure from the city.

BY TRAIN

Rome's primary train station, centrally located **Termini,** has high-speed connections to other Italian cities and fast trains to the airport. Rome's other major station is called **Tiburtina.** The most convenient connections for travelers nearly all depart from Termini. But it's always smart to confirm whether your train departs from Termini or Tiburtina (or one of Rome's even smaller stations). For in-depth descriptions of Termini and Tiburtina stations, see page 936.

Minimize your time in a station by using the banks of user-friendly ticket machines. Machines for the state-run Trenitalia (marked *Trenitalia/Biglietti*) are handy but cover Italian destinations only. They take euros and credit cards, display schedules, issue tickets, and even make reservations for rail pass holders (found under the "Global Pass" ticket type). If you're not near a station—or for international tickets—it's quickest to get tickets and train info online, or from travel agencies in town. For general information on train travel in Italy—including ticket-buying options—see page 1157.

Smaller stations include **Ostiense** (regional rail service) and its neighbor, **Porta San Paolo** (connections to Ostia Antica). If you're staying near the Vatican and taking a regional train, it saves time to get off at the **San Pietro** train station rather than at Termini; from this station, bus #64 connects you to the Vatican area and to other major landmarks around Rome. Cruise-ship passengers coming from Civitavecchia on a day trip usually use Ostiense or San Pietro.

From Rome's Termini Station by Train: Note that unless otherwise specified, the following connections are for Trenitalia. **Fiumicino Airport** (Leonardo Express; 2/hour, 32 minutes—see details under "By Plane," later), **Venice** (Trenitalia: hourly, 4 hours, 1 direct night train, 7 hours; Italo: 4/day, 3-3.5 hours), **Florence** (Trenitalia: 2-3/hour, 1.5 hours; Italo: 2/hour, 1.5 hours), **Siena** (1-2/hour, 1 change, 3-4 hours), **Orvieto** (11/day, 1-1.5 hours; regional trains are half the price and only slightly slower than Intercity trains), **Assisi** (4/day direct, 2 hours; more with change in Foligno), **Pisa** (1-2/hour, 3 hours, some change in Florence), **La Spezia** (7/day direct, 3-4 hours), **Milan** (Trenitalia: 1-3/hour, 3-3.5 hours; Italo: 11/day nonstop, 3 hours, more with stops), **Naples** (Trenitalia: 1-4/hour, 1 hour on Frecciarossa, 2 hours on Intercity, 2.5 hours and much cheaper on regional trains; Italo: hourly, 70 minutes), **Civitavecchia** cruise-ship port (regional trains roughly hourly, 80 minutes; faster but pricier trains every 2 hours, 40-50 minutes), **Brindisi** (3/day, 5 hours), **Bern** (3/day, 6.5 hours, change in Milan), **Munich** (4/day, 10 hours, change in Verona or Padua; 1 direct night train, 11.5 hours), **Nice** (2/day, 8-9 hours, change in Milan), **Paris** (2/day, 11.5 hours, change in Turin; 1 night train, 14.5 hours, change in Milan), **Vienna** (3/day, 12 hours, 1-2 changes; 1 direct night train, 15 hours).

BY BUS

Long-distance buses use Autostazione Tiburtina, 200 yards from the Tiburtina train and Metro station. Buses are slower than trains, but fares are cheap (as little as €5 to Naples or Florence). Buses are also handy for destinations poorly served by rail. To reach the bus station from either Tiburtina station, don't follow the *Bus* signs, which lead to the city bus stop. Instead, exit the station, cross the street under the elevated freeway, and look for the fenced-in area with bus platforms. The station is chaotic and crowded, with nowhere to sit. Ticket window lines can be slow, so buy your ticket online in advance if possible. If your bus departure platform isn't listed on the digital board, ask one of the drivers for help.

From Rome by Bus to: **Siena** (9/day, 2.5-3 hours, www.baltour.it), **Sorrento** (1-2/day, 4 hours; this is a cheap and easy way to go straight to Sorrento, buy tickets at www.marozzivt.it—in Italian only, at the Tiburtina ticket office, travel agencies, or on board for a €3.50 surcharge; tel. 080-579-0111), **Naples** (every 1-2 hours, 3 hours, www.baltour.it or www.megabus.com), **Florence** (every 1-2 hours, 4 hours, www.baltour.it or www.megabus.com), **Assisi** (2/day, 3 hours, www.sulga.it—the train makes much more sense).

BY PLANE

Rome's two airports—**Fiumicino** (a.k.a. Leonardo da Vinci, airport code: FCO) and the small **Ciampino** (airport code: CIA)—share the same website (www.adr.it).

Fiumicino Airport

Rome's major airport is manageable. Terminals T1, T2, and T3 are all under one roof—walkable end to end in 20 minutes. T5 is a separate building requiring a short shuttle trip. (T4 is still being built.) The T1-2-3 complex has ground transport, a TI (in T3, daily 9:00-17:30, longer in summer), ATMs, banks, luggage storage, shops, and bars. For airport information, call 06-65951.

Getting Between Fiumicino Airport and Downtown Rome

In either direction, give yourself lots of time to allow for traffic delays, travel between your hotel and the train/bus station, finding your train or bus, and walking to the terminal.

By Train: Trenitalia's slick, direct, first-class-only Leonardo Express train connects the airport train station (called Fiumicino Aeroporto) and Rome's central Termini Station in 32 minutes for €14. Trains run at least twice hourly in both directions from roughly 6:00 to 23:00 (leaving the airport usually at :23 and :53).

From the airport's arrival gate, follow signs to the train icon or *Stazione/Railway Station*. Buy your ticket from a Trenitalia machine, the ticket office *(biglietteria)*, or a newsstand near the platform; then validate it in a green machine near the track. Machines sell open tickets that can be used on any train. (You know you're in Italy when the machine makes you choose a departure time—even though you're allowed to take any train.) Make sure the train you board is going to the central "Roma Termini" station, as trains from the airport serve other destinations too.

Returning from Termini train station to the airport, trains depart at about :05 and :35 past each hour, usually from track 23 or 24. Check the departure boards for "Fiumicino Aeroporto" and confirm with an official or a local on the platform that the train is indeed going to the airport (€14, buy ticket from Trenitalia machines or any train station tobacco shop or newsstand). Read your ticket: If it requires validation, stamp it in the green machines near the platform before boarding.

You can access most of the airport's terminals from the airport train station. If your flight leaves from terminal T5 (where most American air carriers flying directly to the US depart), catch the T5 shuttle bus *(navetta)* on the sidewalk in front of T3—it's too far to walk with luggage.

Cheaper (€8) local trains also run from the airport to some of Rome's smaller train stations (including Trastevere, Ostiense, and Tiburtina). If you're staying in Trastevere or the Pantheon area, it can be simpler and cheaper to take the local train to Trastevere station, then walk out to the street and take the #8 tram downhill to your hotel. The train to Tiburtina is useful if you have a long-distance bus to catch.

Only a couple of long-distance trains per day serve the airport. To connect to other Italian cities, you'll usually have to change at Termini or Tiburtina.

By Bus: Four bus companies—Terravision (www.terravision. eu), SIT (www.sitbusshuttle.com), T.A.M. (www.tambus.it), and Schiaffini (www.romeairportbus.com)—connect Fiumicino and Termini train station. The SIT bus also stops near the Vatican. I'd just hop on whichever one is departing first (every 10-15 minutes at peak times). While much cheaper than the train (about €5 one-way), buses take twice as long (about an hour, depending on traffic) and can potentially fill up (allow plenty of extra time). At the airport, the bus station is at the far end of terminal T3. At Termini, T.A.M. and Schiaffini depart from the south side of the station; Terravision and SIT from the north side.

By Airport Shuttle: Shared shuttle van services run to and from the airport and can be economical for one or two people. Consider Rome Airport Shuttle (€25/1 person, extra people–€6 each, by reservation only, tel. 06-4201-4507 or 06-4201-3469, www.airportshuttle.it).

By Taxi: A taxi between Fiumicino and downtown Rome takes 45 minutes in normal traffic (for tips on taxis, see page 811) and costs exactly €48. (You could add a tip for good service.) From the airport, be sure to catch an official taxi (white, with maroon *Roma Capitale* logo on the door) at the taxi stand. Avoid unmarked, unmetered taxis; these guys will try to tempt you away from the taxi stand lineup by offering an immediate (rip-off) ride. By law, taxi drivers can only charge €48 for the ride to anywhere in the historic center (within the old city walls, where all of my recommended hotels are located). The fare covers up to four people with normal-size bags (to save money, try teaming up with any tourist also just arriving—most are heading for hotels near yours in the center). An official taxi will have that €48 fare clearly posted on its door.

Less frequent cabs based in Fiumicino (the town near the airport) are allowed to charge €60 for the ride. Signs stating the Rome and Fiumicino price caps are posted next to the taxi stand. It's best to use the Rome city cabs and establish the price before you get in. If your driver tries to point to the price for Fiumicino-based cabs or otherwise charge you more than €48 from the airport into town, say, *"Quarant'otto euro—è la legge"* (kwah-RAHNTOH-toe AY-oo-roh—ay lah LEJ-jay, which means, "Forty-eight euros—it's the law"), and they should back off.

When departing Rome, your hotel can arrange a taxi to the airport at any hour. Alternatively, they sometimes work with comparably priced private car services, which are usually just fine (if not nicer than a regular cab).

Ciampino Airport

Rome's smaller airport (tel. 06-6595-9515) handles charter flights and some budget airlines (including most Ryanair flights).

Getting Between Ciampino Airport and Downtown Rome: Various **bus** companies—including Cotral, Terravision, Schiaffini, and SIT—will take you to Rome's Termini train station (about €5 and 2/hour, 45 minutes). Cotral also runs a quicker route (25 minutes) to the Anagnina Metro stop, where you can connect by Metro to the stop nearest your hotel (departs every 40 minutes).

The fixed price for any official **taxi** (with the maroon *Roma Capitale* logo on the door) is €30 to downtown (within the old city walls, including most of my recommended hotels).

Rome Airport Shuttle also offers shared van rides to and from Ciampino (€25/1 person, listed earlier).

BY CRUISE SHIP

Hundreds of cruise ships dock each year at the small, manageable port city of Civitavecchia (chee-vee-tah-VEH-kyah), about 45 miles northwest of Rome. For more details, see my *Rick Steves Mediterranean Cruise Ports* guidebook.

Getting to Rome: As road traffic between Civitavecchia and Rome is terrible, generally the fastest (and most economical) way to day-trip into Rome is to take the **train.** Trains connect Civitavecchia with several stations in Rome, including Ostiense (two Metro stops from the Colosseum), San Pietro (a short walk from Vatican City), or Termini (the main transit hub, but farther from key sights). Trains depart frequently for Rome and take 40-80 minutes. You can buy train tickets at Civitavecchia's station, or the Agenzie 365/Freccia Viaggi travel agency, just outside the station, which also sells transportation tickets of all types, including expensive but time-saving "skip the line" tickets for the Vatican and Colosseum. To reach Civitavecchia's train station, take a free shuttle bus from your ship to the main port gate and then walk (about 25 minutes) or ride an orange city bus (€2, 3/hour, often no buses 12:00-14:30, catch from main port gate). I'd avoid the expensive taxi ride from the cruise port to the station.

Other options for getting into Rome include a cruise-ship excursion package, a taxi, or organized tours run by private tour companies. A **taxi** into Rome takes about 1.5 hours and costs around €110-150 one-way, though many cabbies will inflate their prices (avoid the unlicensed taxis offering a huge price break; you can be fined for taking one). **Organized tours** into Rome are offered by Can't Be Missed Tours (mobile 329-129-8182, www.cantbemissedtours.com, ask about Rick Steves discount) and Miles & Miles Private Tours (see page 817).

NAPLES

Napoli

If you like Italy as far south as Rome, go farther south—it gets better. If Italy is getting on your nerves, stop at Rome. Italy intensifies as you plunge deeper. Naples is Italy in the extreme—its best (birthplace of pizza and Sophia Loren) and its worst (home of the Camorra, Naples' "family" of organized crime).

Neapolis ("new city") was a thriving Greek commercial center 2,500 years ago. Today, it remains southern Italy's leading city. Naples impresses visitors with one of Europe's top archaeological museums (showcasing the artistic treasures of Pompeii), fascinating churches that convey the city's unique personality and powerful devotion, an underground warren of Greek and Roman ruins, fine works of art (including pieces by Caravaggio, who lived here for a time), and evocative Nativity scenes (called *presepi*). Of course, Neapolitans make great pizza and tasty pastries (try the crispy, ricotta-stuffed *sfogliatella*). But more than anything, Naples has a brash and vibrant street life—"Italy in your face" in ways both good and bad. Walking through its colorful old town is one of my favorite experiences anywhere in Europe. For a grand overlook, head

to the hilltop viewpoint (San Martino) for sweeping views of the city and its bay.

Naples is Italy's third-largest city and Europe's most densely populated, with more than one million people and few open spaces or parks. Watching the police try to enforce traffic sanity is almost comical in this gritty, crowded, and crime-ridden metropolis. Yet Naples surprises the observant traveler with its impressive knack for living, eating, and raising children with good humor and decency. Overcome your fear of being run down or ripped off long enough to talk with people. Enjoy a few smiles and jokes with the man running the neighborhood tripe shop, or the woman taking her daycare class on a walk through the traffic.

The pulse of Italy throbs in Naples. Like Cairo or Mumbai, it's appalling and captivating at the same time, the closest thing to "reality travel" that you'll find in Western Europe. But this tangled mess still somehow manages to breathe, laugh, and sing—with a joyful Italian accent. Thanks to its reputation as a dangerous place, Naples doesn't get nearly as many tourists as it deserves. While the city has its problems, it has improved a lot in recent years. And even though it's a bit edgy, I feel comfortable here. Naples richly rewards those who venture in.

Naples is also the springboard to an array of nearby of sightseeing treats (covered in the next three chapters): Just beyond Naples are the remarkable ruins of Pompeii and Herculaneum, and the brooding volcano that did them both in, Mount Vesuvius. A few more miles down the road is the pleasant resort town of Sorrento and the offshore escape isle of Capri. Next comes the dramatic scenery of the Amalfi Coast. And plunging even farther south, you'll reach the Greek temples of Paestum.

PLANNING YOUR TIME

Naples makes an ideal day trip either from Rome or from the comfortable home base of Sorrento, each just over an hour away. Or you can stow your bag at the station and see Naples in a few hours while you change trains here on the way between Rome and Sorrento. A little Naples goes a long way; if you're not comfortable in chaotic and congested cities, think twice before spending the night here. But those who are intrigued by the city's sights and street life enjoy overnighting in Naples.

On a quick visit, start with the Archaeological Museum (closed Tue), follow my self-guided Naples walk, and celebrate your survival with pizza. With more time, dip into more churches, go underground to see Greek and Roman ruins, trek to Capodimonte to see art treasures, or consider ascending San Martino for the view. Of course, Naples is huge. But even with limited time, if you stick to the prescribed route and grab a cab when you're lost or tired, it's fun. Treat yourself well in Naples; the city is cheap by Italian standards. Splurging on a sane and comfortable hotel is a worthwhile investment.

For a blitz tour from Rome, you could have breakfast on an early Rome-Naples express train (usually daily 7:35-8:45), do Naples and Pompeii in a day, and be back in Rome in time for bed. That's exhausting, but more memorable than a fourth day in Rome.

On summer afternoons, Naples' street life slows and many churches, museums, and shops close as the temperature soars. The city comes back to life in the early evening.

Orientation to Naples

Naples is set deep inside the large, curving Bay of Naples, with Mount Vesuvius looming just five miles away. Although Naples is a sprawling city, its fairly compact core contains the most interesting sights. The tourist's Naples is a triangle, with its points at the Centrale train station in the east, the Archaeological Museum to the west, and Piazza del Plebiscito (with the Royal Palace) and the port to the south. Steep hills rise above this historic core, including San Martino, capped with a mighty fortress.

TOURIST INFORMATION

Central Naples has multiple small TIs, none of them particularly helpful—just grab a map and browse the brochures. The handiest one is in **Centrale train station** (daily 9:00-18:00, near track 23, tel. 081-268-779). Two others are by the entrance to the **Galleria Umberto I** shopping mall, across from Teatro di San Carlo (Mon-Sat 9:00-17:00, Sun 9:00-13:00, tel. 081-402-394); and on Spaccanapoli, across from the **Church of Gesù Nuovo** (Mon-Sat 9:00-17:00, Sun 9:00-13:00, tel. 081-551-2701). For information online, the best overall website is www.inaples.it.

ARRIVAL IN NAPLES
By Train

There are several Naples train stations, but all trains coming into town stop at either Napoli Centrale or Garibaldi—which are essentially the same place, with Centrale on top of Garibaldi. Stretching in front of this station complex is the vast Piazza Garibaldi, with a new underground shopping mall and Metro entrance.

Centrale Station, on the ground floor, is the slick, modern main station. It has a small TI (near track 23), an ATM (at Banco di Napoli near track 24), a bookstore (La Feltrinelli, near track 24—beyond the pharmacy), and baggage check (*deposito bagagli*, near track 5). Pay WCs are down the stairs across from track 13. Shops and eateries are concentrated in the underground level. A good supermarket (Sapori & Dintorni) is out the front door and to the left.

Garibaldi Station, on the lower level of the complex, is used exclusively by the narrow-gauge Circumvesuviana commuter train (which you'll most likely use to connect to Sorrento or Pompeii).

Planning Your Time in the Region

On a quick trip, give the entire area—including Sorrento and Naples—a minimum of three days. If you use Sorrento as your sunny springboard (see Sorrento chapter), you can spend a day in Naples, a day exploring the Amalfi Coast, and a day split between Pompeii and the town of Sorrento. While Paestum (Greek temples), Mount Vesuvius, Herculaneum (an ancient Roman site like Pompeii), and the island of Capri are fine destinations, they are worthwhile only if you have more time. For a map, see page 987.

The **Campania ArteCard** regional pass may save you a few euros if you're here for two or three days, using public transportation, and plan to visit multiple major sights (including Pompeii, Herculaneum, Paestum, Naples' Archaeological Museum, and several other museums in Naples). There are three versions of the card: The **three-day,** €32 Tutta la Regione version is good if you'll be visiting both Naples and Sorrento; it includes free entry to two sights (plus a 50 percent discount off others) and transportation within Naples, on the Circumvesuviana train, and on Amalfi Coast buses. A **seven-day,** €34 Tutta la Regione option covers five sights (and discounts on the others) but no transportation. If you're focusing on Naples, the **three-day,** €21 **Napoli-only** version covers transportation within Naples and three city sights, plus discounts on the others (but it doesn't cover the outlying ancient sites). You can buy the card at some Naples TIs and at participating sights (cards activate on first use, expire 3 days later at midnight, www.campaniartecard.it).

For more on the Circumvesuviana, see the "Getting Around the Region" sidebar on page 986. Note that this is not the terminus for the Circumvesuviana; that's one stop farther downtown, at the station called Porta Nolana.

Getting Downtown from the Station: Arriving at either station, the best bet for reaching most sights and hotels is either the Metro or a taxi. In the lower-level corridor (below the main Centrale hall), look for signs to **Metro** lines 1 and 2. Line 1 is handy for city-center stops, including the cruise port (Municipio), the main shopping drag (Toledo and Dante), and the Archaeological Museum (Museo). Line 2 is slightly quicker for reaching the Archaeological Museum (ride it to the Cavour stop and walk 5 minutes). For tips on navigating the Metro, see "Getting Around Naples," later.

A long row of white **taxis** line up out front. Ask the driver to charge you the fixed rate *(tariffa predeterminata),* which varies from €7 for the old center to €13 for the most distant hotel I list. The TI in the station can tell you the going rate.

By Ferry or Cruise Ship

Naples is a ferry hub with great boat connections to Sorrento, Capri, and other nearby destinations. Cruise ships use the giant Stazione Marittima cruise terminal, hydrofoils and faster ferries use the Molo Beverello dock (to the west of the terminal), and slower car ferries leave from Calata Porta di Massa, east of the terminal. The port area is at the southeast edge of downtown Naples, near Castel Nuovo.

Whether arriving by ferry or cruise ship, you can get to the city center by taxi, tram, Metro, or on foot; the Alibus shuttle bus runs to the airport (see "By Plane," below).

The **taxi** stand is in front of the port area. There's a fixed €11 rate to the train station or to the Archaeological Museum.

If you're taking public transportation, a €1 single ticket covers either the tram or the Metro. You can buy tickets at any tobacco shop: There's one (Caffè Moreno) under the canopy between the two buildings of the cruise terminal, and another (Caffè Beverello) along the busy street. Remember to validate your ticket as you board the tram or enter the Metro station.

Tram #1 stops at the busy road directly in front of the cruise terminal and heads to Piazza Garibaldi and the train station, where you can connect to trains to sights outside of town (6/hour, 15 minutes). If you're taking the Circumvesuviana commuter line to Pompeii or Sorrento, hop off this tram a bit earlier, at Porta Nolana, where you can catch the train at its starting point.

Straight ahead across the road from the cruise terminal (on the right side of the big fortress) is Piazza Municipio, with the handy Municipio **Metro** stop. From here, Line 1 zips you right to the Archaeological Museum (Museo stop) or, in the opposite direction, to the train station (Garibaldi stop). Piazza Municipio may be torn up due to the excavation of ancient ruins found while digging the Metro station.

On foot, it's a seven-minute **walk**—past the gigantic Castel Nuovo—to Piazza del Plebiscito and the old city center. From Piazza del Plebiscito, you could do a truncated version of my self-guided walk (begin near the end of "Part 2," do that stretch backward up the hill, then launch right into "Part 3").

By Plane

Naples International Airport (a.k.a. Capodichino, code: NAP) is close to town (tel. 081-789-6767, handy info desk just outside baggage claim, www.gesac.it). Alibus shuttle buses zip you in 15 minutes from the airport to Piazza Garibaldi, by Naples' Centrale train station, and then head to the port/Piazza Municipio for boats to Capri and Sorrento (buses run daily 6:00-24:00, 3/hour, 30 minutes to the port, €3 ticket from a tobacco shop or €4 on board, stops at train station and port only). The shuttle bus leaves and departs from the bus platforms at the northwest corner of Piazza Garibaldi—the far right corner when exiting the train station. If you take a taxi to or from the airport, ask the driver for the fixed price (€16 to the train station, €19 to the port, €23 to the Chiaia district near the waterfront).

To reach **Sorrento** from Naples Airport, take the direct Curreri bus (see page 1035). A taxi to Sorrento costs about €100.

HELPFUL HINTS

Exchange Rate: €1 = about $1.10

Country Calling Code: 39 (see page 1154 for dialing instructions)

Theft Alert: While most travelers visit Naples completely safely, err on the side of caution. Don't venture into neighborhoods that make you uncomfortable. While the train station has been nicely spruced up, its glow only extends for a block or so. The areas a little farther away are especially seedy and frequented by some of Italy's most downtrodden people. Walk with confidence, as if you know where you're going and what you're doing. Touristy Spaccanapoli and the posh Via Toledo shopping boulevard are more upscale, but you'll still see rowdy kids and panhandlers. Assume able-bodied beggars are thieves.

Stick to busy streets and beware of gangs of hoodlums. A third of the city is unemployed, and past local governments have set an example that the Mafia would be proud of. Assume con artists are more clever than you. Any jostle or commotion is probably a thief-team smokescreen. To keep bags safe, it's probably best to leave them at your hotel or at the left-luggage office in Centrale Station.

Always walk on the sidewalk (even if the locals don't) and carry your bag on the side away from the street—thieves on scooters have been known to snatch bags as they swoop by. The less you have dangling from you (including cameras and necklaces), the better. Keep valuables buttoned up.

Perhaps your biggest risk of theft is while catching or riding the Circumvesuviana commuter train. At the train station, carry your own bags—there are no official porters. If you're connecting from a long-distance express, you'll be going from a relatively secure compartment into an often crowded and dingy train, where disoriented tourists with luggage delicately mix with the residents of Naples' most down-and-out districts. It's prime hunting ground for thieves. While I ride the Circumvesuviana comfortably and safely, each year I hear of many travelers who get ripped off on this ride. You won't be mugged—but you may be conned or pickpocketed. Be ready for this very common trick: A team of thieves blocks the door at a stop, pretending it's stuck. While everyone rushes to try to open it, an accomplice picks their pockets. Especially late at night, the Circumvesuviana train is plagued by intimidating ruffians. For maximum safety and peace of mind, sit in the front car, where the driver will double as your protector, and avoid riding it after dark.

Traffic Safety: In Naples, red lights are discretionary, and pedestrians need to be wary, particularly of motor scooters. Even on "pedestrian" streets, stay alert to avoid being sideswiped by scooters that nudge their way through the crowds. Keep children close. Smart tourists jaywalk in the shadow of bold locals, who generally ignore crosswalks. Wait for a break in traffic, cross with confidence, and make eye contact with approaching drivers. The traffic will stop.

Bookstore: La Feltrinelli, conveniently located in Centrale Station, carries a small selection of English-language books (daily 7:00-21:00, near track 24).

Laundry: Lavasciuga, a block from the Università Metro stop, is convenient but has just three washers (Mon-Sat 9:00-19:00, closed Sun, Via Sedile di Porto 54, mobile 327-754-6639).

GETTING AROUND NAPLES

Naples' entire public transportation system—Metro, buses, funicular railways, and the single tram line—uses the same tickets, which must be stamped as you enter (in the yellow machines). A €1 single ticket *(corsa singola)* covers any ride on most modes of transportation (bus, tram, funicular, or Metro line 1), with no transfers; for Metro line 2 you need the €1.20 version (it's considered a "suburban" line). If you need to transfer, buy the €1.50 *90 minuti* ticket. Tickets are sold at *tabacchi* stores, some newsstands, clunky machines at Metro stations (coins and small bills only), and occasionally at station windows. A *giornaliero* day pass costs €3.50 (or €4.50 including Metro line 2), and pays for itself quickly, but can be hard to find; many *tabacchi* stores don't sell them. A weekly ticket (Monday to Sunday) costs €12, or €15.80 including Metro line 2. Several versions of the Campania ArteCard (see sidebar on page 942) include free public transport in Naples. For general information, maps, and fares in English, visit www.unicocampania. it. The TI hands out a good free map showing bus, Metro, and funicular routes. For schedules, your only option is the Italian-only site www.anm.it. For journey planning, use maps.google.com.

By Metro: Naples' subway, the *Metropolitana,* has three main lines *(linea).* Station entrances and signs to the Metro are marked by a red square with a white *M.*

Line 1 is very useful for tourists. Starting from the train station (stop name: Garibaldi), it heads to Università (the university),

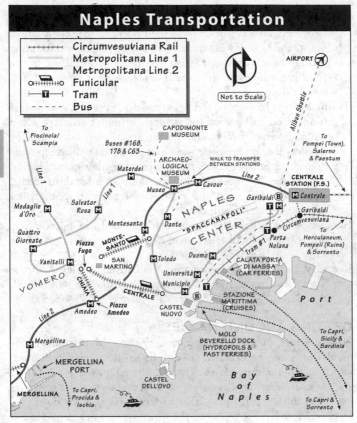

Naples Transportation

Circumvesuviana Rail	
Metropolitana Line 1	
Metropolitana Line 2	
Funicular	
Tram	
Bus	

Not to Scale

AIRPORT

To Piscinola/ Scampia

Line 1

CAPODIMONTE MUSEUM

Buses #168, 178 & C63

ARCHAEO-LOGICAL MUSEUM

WALK TO TRANSFER BETWEEN STATIONS

Line 2

To Pompei (Town), Salerno & Paestum

Materdei

Museo

Cavour

Line 1

CENTRALE STATION (F.S.)

Medaglie d'Oro

Salvator Rosa

Dante

NAPLES

Garibaldi

Centrale

Garibaldi

Montesanto

CENTER

"SPACCANAPOLI"

Circumvesuviana

Quattro Giornate

Piazza Fuga

MONTE-SANTO

To Herculaneum, Pompeii (Ruins) & Sorrento

Vanitelli

SAN MARTINO

Toledo

Duomo

Porta Nolana

Tram #1

Università Municipio

CALATA PORTA DI MASSA (CAR FERRIES)

VOMERO

CHIAIA

CENTRALE

Amedeo

Piazza Amedeo

CASTEL NUOVO

STAZIONE MARITTIMA (CRUISES)

Port

Line 2

Mergellina

MOLO BEVERELLO DOCK (HYDROFOILS & FAST FERRIES)

MERGELLINA PORT

CASTEL DELL'OVO

Bay of Naples

MERGELLINA

To Capri, Procida & Ischia

To Capri, Sicily & Sardinia

To Capri & Sorrento

Municipio (at Piazza Municipio, just above the harbor and cruise terminal), Toledo (south end of Via Toledo, near Piazza del Plebiscito), Dante (Piazza Dante), and Museo (Archaeological Museum). Four stops beyond Museo is the Vanvitelli stop, near the hilltop San Martino sights. Many of line 1's new stations are huge and elaborate, designed by prominent artists and architects; Naples is proud of them, and locals are excited to tell you about their favorite.

Line 2 (part of the Italian national rail system) is most useful for getting quickly from the train station to Piazza Cavour (a 5-minute walk from the Archaeological Museum) or Montesanto (the top of the Spanish Quarter and Spaccanapoli street, and base of one funicular up to San Martino).

The new **line 6** may not yet be completed by the time of your visit; it will begin at Municipio and head west—unlikely to be of much use to tourists.

By Funicular: Central Naples' three funiculars *(funicolare)* carry commuters and sightseers into the hilly San Martino neighborhood just west of downtown. All three converge near Piazza Fuga, a short walk from the hilltop fortress and monastery/museum. The Centrale line runs from the Spanish Quarter, just near Piazza del Plebiscito and the Toledo Metro stop; the Montesanto line from the Montesanto Metro stop and Via Pignasecca market zone; and the Chiaia line from near the Piazza Amadeo Metro stop.

By Bus: Buses can be handy for certain trips, such as getting to Capodimonte. But buses are crowded and poorly signed, and aren't a user-friendly option for uninitiated newcomers.

By Tram: Tram line #1 runs along Corso Garibaldi (at the other end of the big square from Centrale Station) and down to the waterfront, terminating by the ferry and cruise terminals (direction: *Stazione Marittima*). It's useful if you're connecting from boat to train, or returning to the port after finishing my self-guided walk.

By Taxi: A short ride in town should cost €10-12. Ask for the *tariffa predeterminata* (a fixed rate). Your hotel or a TI can tell you the going rate for a given ride. You can also ask the driver to use the meter—for metered rides there are some legitimate extra charges (baggage fees, €2.50 supplement after 22:00 or all day Sun and holidays). Radio Taxi 8888 is one reputable company (tel. 081-8888).

Tours in Naples

Local Guides
Pina Esposito has a Ph.D. in ancient archaeology and art and does fine private walking and driving tours of Naples and the region (Pompeii, Capri, the Amalfi Coast, etc.), including Naples' Archaeological Museum (€60/hour, 2-hour minimum, 10 percent off with this book, mobile 338-763-4224, annamariaesposito1@virgilio.it).

The team at **Mondo Guide** offers private tours of the Archaeological Museum (€120/2 hours) and city (€240/4 hours), and can provide guides or drivers throughout the region (tel. 081-751-3290, www.mondoguide.com, info@mondoguide.com).

Walking Tours
Mondo Guide offers my readers special shared tours of Naples and of Pompeii, as well as other trips in the region. For details, see the sidebar on the next page.

Hop-On, Hop-Off Bus Tours
CitySightseeing Napoli tour buses make three different hop-on, hop-off loops through the city. Only one of these—the red line, which loops around the historical center and stops at the Archaeological Museum and Capodimonte—is particularly helpful. The bus route will give you a sense of greater Naples that this chapter

Mondo Guide's Tours of Pompeii, Naples, the Amalfi Coast, and Capri for My Readers

Mondo Guide, a big Naples-based company, offers "shared tours" for Rick Steves readers. These allow you the luxury of a private, professional guide at a fraction of the usual cost, because you'll be sharing the expense with other travelers using this book. Their tours, which run from April through October, include **Pompeii,** a walking tour of **Naples,** and two longer-distance trips from Sorrento: an **Amalfi Coast** van tour and a private boat to the **isle of Capri.** The Pompeii and Naples tours are designed to work together—they are timed so you can do both on the same day. Mondo also offers shore excursions for cruise passengers arriving in Naples or Salerno. I don't receive a cut from the tours; I set this up with Mondo Guide to help my readers have the most economical experience in this region.

Reservations are required. For specifics and to sign up, see their website, www.mondoguide.com, and select the "Shared Tours for Rick Steves" tab (Mondo tel. 081-751-3290, mobile 340-460-5254, info@mondoguide.com). On the website, use your credit-card number to reserve a spot. You'll then pay cash for the tour. If you must cancel, email them more than three days in advance or you'll be billed.

Each tour requires a minimum of six participants. You'll be sent an email confirmation as soon as they're sure your tour will run. If there's not enough demand to justify the trip, they'll notify you three days before the departure date (giving you time to come up with an alternative plan). Confirmed departures are continually updated on the website.

Here's a brief description of the tours:

Pompeii Tour: This two-hour guided walk brings to life the ruins of the excavated city (€15, doesn't include €12 Pompeii entry, but your guide will collect money and buy tickets, daily at 11:00; meet at Hotel/Ristorante Suisse, a 5-minute walk from the train station—exiting the station, turn right, pass the Porta Marina entrance, and continue down the hill to the restaurant, on the right).

Historic Naples Walk: Naples is a challenge to enjoy and un-

largely ignores (€22, ticket valid 24 hours, infrequent departures, buy from driver or from kiosk at Piazza Municipio in front of Castel Nuovo near the port, scant recorded narration; for details, see the brochure at hotels and TI, tel. 081-551-7279, www.napoli.citysightseeing.it). The same company offers a shorter, more frequent route around the old center in an open-top minibus (€7, €25 combo-ticket with the main route, 40-minute loop, departs in front of the Church of Gesù Nuovo).

NAPLES

derstand; on this three-hour walk, a local Neapolitan guide helps you uncover the true character of the city (€25; daily at 15:00; meet at the steps of the Archaeological Museum—you can do the museum on your own before joining your guide).

Full-Day Amalfi Coast Minibus Tour from Sorrento: The Amalfi Coast can be complicated and time-consuming to visit on your own, making a shared eight-seat van the simplest and most affordable way to enjoy the sights. This nine-hour trip will save time and money and maximize your experience. It begins in Sorrento and heads south for the breathtaking (and lightly narrated) drive, several photo stops, and an hour or two on your own in each of the three main towns—Positano, Amalfi, and Ravello—before returning to Sorrento. Lunch isn't included; to save time for exploring, just grab a quick lunch in one of the towns (€50, daily at 9:00; meet in front of Hotel Antiche Mura, at Via Fuorimura 7, a block inland from Piazza Tasso).

Full-Day Capri Boat Trip from Sorrento: To sidestep the hassles of taking public boats from Sorrento for a Capri side-trip, Mondo offers a trip to the island on a small private boat (10 people maximum), which includes an early visit to the Blue Grotto sea cave when conditions allow (€13, optional) and about four hours of free time to explore the island on your own. After your time on land, the boat takes you on a lightly narrated trip around the island with drinks, snacks, and a chance to swim if the weather cooperates (€80, daily at 8:00, pickup at hotel, may be cancelled in case of bad weather).

Shore Excursions from Naples or Salerno: If you're arriving on a cruise ship at the port of Naples or the port of Salerno, Mondo Guide offers an all-day itinerary that combines three big sights in the region and the scenic Amalfi Coast. From Naples, a guided visit to Pompeii with an hour of free time each in Sorrento and Positano; from Salerno, a guided visit to Pompeii with an hour of free time each in Sorrento and Amalfi town (€65/person, departing daily at 8:00-8:30 from the main exit of the Naples cruise terminal building or from your ship in Salerno).

Cruise-Ship Excursions
Mondo Guide offers shared shore excursions for my readers. For details, see the sidebar.

Convenient for cruise-ship passengers, the **Can't Be Missed** tour company takes you from the port of Naples on an all-day, big-bus trip along the Amalfi Coast that also includes a stop in Sorrento and a guided tour of Pompeii (€65, meet at 8:00 in front of port, bus leaves at 8:30, returns at 17:15, Pompeii ticket extra, mobile 329-129-8182, www.cantbemissedtours.com, 10 percent discount with this book—use promo code "RICKSTEVES" on their website).

Archaeological Museum Tour

Naples' Archaeological Museum (Museo Archeologico), worth ▲▲▲, offers the best possible peek at the art and decorations of Pompeii and Herculaneum, the two ancient burgs that were buried in ash by the eruption of Mount Vesuvius in A.D. 79. For lovers of antiquity, this museum alone makes Naples a worthwhile stop. When Pompeii was excavated in the late 1700s, Naples' Bourbon king bellowed, "Bring me the best of what you find!" The finest art and artifacts ended up here, and today, the ancient sites themselves are impressive but barren. (Both sites are an easy train ride from Naples—see the next chapter.)

ORIENTATION

Cost and Hours: €8, sometimes more for temporary exhibits, free first Sun of the month, Wed-Mon 9:00-19:30, closed Tue. Early and temporary closures are noted on a board near the ticket office: Expect some rooms to be closed in July and August.

Getting There: To take the **Metro** *(Metropolitana)* from Centrale Station, first buy a single €1.20 transit ticket at a newsstand or tobacco shop (unless you're getting a pass). Then follow the signs for *Metro Linea 2* (down the stairs in front of track 13). Validate your ticket in the small yellow boxes near the escalator going down to the tracks. You're looking for line 2 trains heading in the direction of Pozzuoli (they generally depart from track 4). Ride one stop to Piazza Cavour, and take the underground passage following the *Museo* signs. Or exit and walk five minutes uphill through the park along the busy street. Look for a grand old red building located up a flight of stairs at the top of the block.

You can also take the Metro's cheaper line 1 five stops from Centrale Station to Museo—it's only a little slower.

Figure on €11 for a **taxi** from the train station to the museum.

Information: The shop sells a worthwhile *National Archaeological Museum of Naples* guidebook for €12. Tel. 081-442-2149.

Tours: My self-guided tour (below) covers all the basics. For more detail, the decent audioguide costs €5 (at ticket desk). For a guided tour, book Pina Esposito (see "Tours in Naples," earlier).

Baggage Check: Bag check is obligatory and free.

Photography: Photos are allowed without a flash.

Eating: The museum has no café, but vending machines sell drinks and snacks. There are several good places to grab a meal within a few blocks; see page 985.

OVERVIEW

Entering the museum, stand at the base of the grand staircase. To your right, on the ground floor, are the larger-than-life statues of the Farnese Collection, starring the *Toro Farnese* and the *Farnese Hercules*. Up the stairs on the mezzanine level are mosaics and frescoes from Pompeii, including the Secret Room of erotic art. On the top floor are more frescoes, a scale model of Pompeii, and bronze statues from Herculaneum. WCs are behind the staircase.

• *From the base of the grand staircase, turn right through the door marked* Collezione Farnese *and wind to the far end—walking through a rich collection of idealistic and realistic ancient portrait busts. Stop in the farthest room (Sala XIII).*

⊘ SELF-GUIDED TOUR
Ground Floor: The Farnese Collection

The museum's ground floor alone has enough Greek and Roman art to put it on the map. This floor has nothing from Pompeii; its highlight is the Farnese Collection, a grand hall of huge, bright, and wonderfully restored statues excavated from Rome's Baths of Caracalla. Peruse the larger-than-life statues filling the hall. They were dug up in the 1540s at the behest of Alessandro Farnese (by then Pope Paul III) while he was building the family palace on the Campo de' Fiori in Rome. His main purpose in excavating the baths was to scavenge quality building stone. The sculptures were a nice extra and helped the palace come in under budget on decorations. In the 1700s, the collection ended up in the hands of Charles, the Bourbon king of Naples (whose mother was a Farnese). His son, the next king, had it brought to Naples.

• *Quick—look down to the left end of the hall. There's a woman being tied to a snorting bull.*

The tangled **Toro Farnese** tells a thrilling Greek myth. At 13 feet, it's the tallest ancient marble group ever found, and the largest intact statue from antiquity. A third-century A.D. copy of a lost bronze Hellenistic original, it was carved out of one piece of marble. Michelangelo and others "restored" it at the pope's request—meaning that they integrated surviving bits into a new work. Panels on the wall show which pieces were actually carved by Michelangelo (in blue on the chart): the head of the woman in back, the torso of the aunt under the bull, and the dog. (Imagine how the statue would stand out if it were thoughtfully lit and not surrounded by white walls.)

Here's the tragic story behind the statue: Once upon an ancient Greek time, King Lycus was bewitched by Dirce. He abandoned his pregnant wife, Antiope (standing regally in the background). The single mom gave birth to twin boys. When they grew up, they killed their deadbeat dad and tied Dirce to the horns of a bull to be bashed against a mountain. Captured in marble, the action is thrilling: cape flailing, dog snarling, hooves in the air. You can almost hear the bull snorting. And in the back, Antiope oversees this harsh ancient justice with satisfaction.

At the opposite end of the hall stands the *Farnese Hercules.* The great Greek hero is exhausted. He leans wearily on his club (draped with his lion skin) and bows his head. He's just finished the daunting Eleventh Labor, having traveled the world, fought men and gods, freed Prometheus from his rock, and carried Atlas' weight of the world on his shoulders. Now he's returned with the prize: the golden apples of the gods, which he cups behind his back. But, after all that, he's just been told he has to return the apples and do one final labor: descend into hell itself. Oh, man.

The 10-foot colossus is a third-century A.D. Roman marble copy (signed by "Glykon") of a fourth-century B.C. Greek bronze original (probably by Lysippos). The statue was enormously famous in its day. Dozens of copies—some marble, some bronze—have been found in Roman villas and baths. This version was unearthed in Rome's Baths of Caracalla in 1546, along with the *Toro Farnese.*

The *Farnese Hercules* was equally famous in the 16th-18th centuries. Tourists flocked to Rome to admire it, art students studied it from afar in prints, Louis XIV made a copy for Versailles, and petty nobles everywhere put small-scale knock-offs in their gardens. This curly-haired version of Hercules became the modern world's image of the Greek hero.

• *Backtrack to the main entry hall, then head up to the mezzanine level (turn left at the lion and go under the* Mosaici *sign).*

Mezzanine: Pompeiian Mosaics and the Secret Room

Most of these mosaics—of animals, musicians, and geometric designs— were taken from Pompeii's House of the Faun (see page 1003). Walk into the third room and look for the 20-inch-high statue in a freestanding glass case: the house's delightful centerpiece, the *Dancing Faun*. This rare surviving Greek bronze statue (from the fourth century B.C.) is surrounded by some of the best mosaics of that age.

A museum highlight, just beyond the statue, is the grand *Battle of Alexander,* a second-century B.C. copy of the original Greek fresco, done a century earlier. It decorated a floor in the House of the Faun and was found intact; the damage you see occurred as this treasure was moved from Pompeii to the king's collection here. Alexander (left side of the scene, with curly hair and sideburns) is about to defeat the Persians under Darius

(central figure, in chariot with turban and beard). This pivotal victory allowed Alexander to quickly overrun much of Asia (331 B.C.). Alexander is the only one without a helmet...a confident master of the battlefield while everyone else is fighting for their lives, eyes bulging with fear. Notice how the horses, already in retreat, add to the scene's propaganda value. Notice also the shading and perspective, which Renaissance artists would later work so hard to accomplish. (A modern reproduction of the mosaic is now back in Pompeii, at the House of the Faun.)

Farther on, the **Secret Room (Gabinetto Segreto)** contains a sizable assortment of erotic frescoes, well-hung pottery, and perky statues that once decorated bedrooms, meeting rooms, brothels, and even shops at Pompeii and Herculaneum. These bawdy statues and frescoes—many of them once displayed in Pompeii's grandest houses—were entertainment for guests. (By the time they made it to this museum, in 1819, the frescoes could be viewed only with permission from the king—see the letters in the glass case just outside the door.) The Roman nobles commissioned the wildest scenes imaginable. Think of them as ancient dirty jokes.

At the entrance, you're enthusiastically greeted by big stone penises that once projected over Pompeii's doorways. A massive phallus was not necessarily a sexual symbol, but a magical amulet used against the "evil eye." It symbolized fertility, happiness, good luck, riches, straight A's, and general wellbeing.

Circulating counterclockwise through this section, look for the following: a faun playfully pulling the sheet off a beautiful woman, only to be grossed out by a hermaphrodite's plumbing (perhaps the original *"Mamma mia!"*; #12); horny pygmies from Africa in action (#27); a toga with an embarrassing bulge (#34); a particularly high-quality statue of a goat and a satyr engaging in a lewd act (#36); and, watching over it all with remarkable aplomb, Venus, the patron goddess of Pompeii (#39).

The back room is furnished and decorated the way an ancient brothel might have been. The 10 frescoes on the wall functioned as both a menu of services offered and as a kind of *Kama Sutra* of sex positions. The glass cases contain more phallic art.

• *So, now that your travel buddy is finally showing a little interest in art...finish up your visit by climbing the stairs to the top floor.*

Top Floor: Frescoes, Statues, Artifacts, and a Model of Pompeii

At the top of the stairs, go through the center door to enter a grand, empty hall. (If the doors are locked, circle around through the side wing.) This was the **great hall** of the university (17th and 18th centuries) until the building became the royal museum, in 1777. Walk to the center. The sundial (from 1791) still works. Look up to the far-right corner of the hall and find the tiny pinhole. At noon (13:00 in summer), a ray of sun enters the hall and strikes the sundial, showing the time of the year...if you know your zodiac.

To your left, you'll see a door marked *affreschi*. This leads to eight rooms showing off the museum's impressive and well-described collection of (nonerotic) **frescoes** taken from the walls of Pompeii villas. Pompeiians loved to decorate their homes with scenes from mythology (Hercules' labors, Venus and Mars in love), landscapes, everyday market scenes, and faux architecture. Continue around this wing counterclockwise (with the courtyard on your left) through rooms of artifacts found at Pompeii. Look for the famous portrait of baker Terentius Neo and his wife in Room LXXVIII. At the far end is a scale model of Pompeii as excavated in 1879 *(plastic di Pompeii)*. Another model (on the wall) shows the site in 2004, after more excavations.

• *Eventually you'll end up back in the great hall.*

Step out to the top landing of the staircase you climbed earlier. Turn left and go down, then up, 16 steps and into the wing labeled *La Villa dei Papiri*. This exhibition shows off artifacts (particularly bronze statues) from the Herculaneum holiday home of

Julius Caesar's father-in-law. In the second room (numbered CXVI), look into the lifelike blue eyes of the intense *Corridore* (athletes), bent on doing their best. The *Five Dancers*, with

their inlaid-ivory eyes and graceful poses, decorated a portico. The next room (CXVII) has more fine works: *Resting Hermes* (with his tired little heel wings) is taking a break. Nearby, the *Drunken Faun* (singing and snapping his fingers to the beat, a wineskin at his side) is clearly living for today—true to the *carpe diem* preaching of the Epicurean philosophy. Caesar's father-in-law was a fan of Epicurean philosophy, and his library—containing 2,000 papyrus scrolls—supported his outlook. Back by the entrance, check out the plans of the villa, and in the side room, see how the half-burned scrolls were unrolled and (with luck) read after excavation in the 1750s.

• *Return to the ground floor. The exit hall (right) leads around the museum courtyard and to the gift shop.*

Doriforo

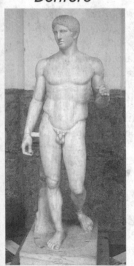

For extra credit on your way out, find **Doriforo.** He was last spotted on the right as you walk down the exit hall. (If he's been moved, ask a guard, *"Dov'è il Doriforo?"*) This seven-foot-tall "spear-carrier" (the literal translation of *doriforo*) just stands there, as if holding a spear. What's the big deal about this statue, which looks like so many others? It's a marble replica made by the Romans of one of the most-copied statues of antiquity, a fifth-century B.C. bronze Greek original by Polyclitus. This copy once stood in a Pompeii gym, where it inspired ancient athletes by showing the ideal proportions of Greek beauty. So full of motion, and so realistic in its *contrapposto* pose (weight on one foot), the *Doriforo* would later inspire Donatello and Michelangelo, helping to trigger the Renaissance. And so the glories of ancient Pompeii, once buried and forgotten, live on today.

Naples Walk

▲▲▲A SLICE OF NEAPOLITAN LIFE

This self-guided walk takes you from the Archaeological Museum through the heart of town and back to Centrale Station. Allow at least three hours, plus time for pizza and sightseeing stops. If you're in a rush, do it in half the time by walking briskly and skipping Part 2.

Naples, a living medieval city, is its own best sight. Couples artfully make love on Vespas surrounded by more fights and smiles per cobblestone than anywhere else in Italy. Rather than seeing Naples as a list of sights, visit its one great museum and then capture its essence by taking this walk through the core of the city.

Part 1: From the Archaeological Museum to Piazza Bellini and Piazza Dante

The first two parts of this walk are a mostly straight one-mile ramble down a fine boulevard (with a few colorful detours) to the waterfront at Piazza del Plebiscito. Your starting point is the Archaeological Museum (at the top of Piazza Cavour, Metro: Cavour or Museo; for a self-guided tour of the museum, see earlier). As you stroll, remember that here in Naples, red traffic lights are considered "decorations." When crossing a street, try to draft behind a native.

• *From the door of the Archaeological Museum, cross the street, veer right, and enter the fancy mall. (If the mall is closed for renovation, simply loop around the block to its back door.)*

Galleria Principe di Napoli: This was named for the first male child of the royal Savoy family, the Prince of Naples. Walk

directly through it, enjoying this fine shopping gallery from the late 19th century, similar to those popular in Paris and London. In the US, we call this style Art Nouveau; in Italy it's "Liberty Style," named for a British department store that was in vogue at a time when Naples was nicknamed the "Paris of the South." Parisian artist Edgar Degas left Paris to adopt Naples—which he actually considered more cosmopolitan and sophisticated—as his hometown.

• *Leaving the gallery through the opposite end, walk one block downhill. At Via Conte di Ruvo, head left, passing the fine Bellini Theater (also in*

NAPLES

the Liberty Style). After one block, turn right on Via Costantinopoli, continuing directly downhill to Piazza Bellini. As you walk, look up to enjoy architecture built in the late 19th century, when Naples was the last stop on Romantic Age travelers' Grand Tour of Europe. (From a tourism perspective, Sorrento only rose with the cultural and economic fall of Naples in the decades following Italian independence, around the early 20th century.)

Soon you'll run into the ragtag urban park called...

Piazza Bellini: Walking between columns of two grand churches, suddenly you're in neighborhood Napoli. A statue of Sicilian opera composer Vincenzo Bellini, who worked in Naples in the early 1800s, marks the center of the park. Survey the many balconies—and the people who use them as a "backyard" in this densely packed city. The apartment blocks were originally the palaces of noble families, as indicated by the stately family crests above grand doorways. At the downhill end of the square, peer down into the sunken area to see the ruined Greek walls: tuff blocks without mortar. This was the wall, and you're standing on land that was outside of the town. You can see the street level from the fifth century B.C., when Neapolis—literally, "the new city"—was founded. For 2,500 years, laundry has blown in the breeze right here.

• *Walk 30 yards downhill. Stop at the horseshoe-shaped Port'Alba gate (on the right). Spin slowly 360 degrees and take in the scene. The proud tile across the street (upstairs, between the two balconies) shows Piazza Bellini circa 1890. Learn to ignore graffiti (as the locals do). Pass through the gate, and stroll past the book stalls down Via Port'Alba to the next big square...*

Piazza Dante: This square is marked by a statue of Dante, the medieval poet. Fittingly, half the square is devoted to bookstores. Old Dante looks out over an urban area that was once grand, then chaotic, and is now slowly becoming grand again.

While this square feels perfectly Italian to me, for many Neapolitans it represents the repression of the central Italian state. When Napoleon was defeated, Naples briefly became its own independent kingdom. But within a few decades of Italian unification, in 1861, Naples went from being a thriving cultural and political capital to a provincial  town, its money used to help establish the industrial strength of the north, its dialect considered backward, and its bureaucrats transferred to Rome.

NAPLES

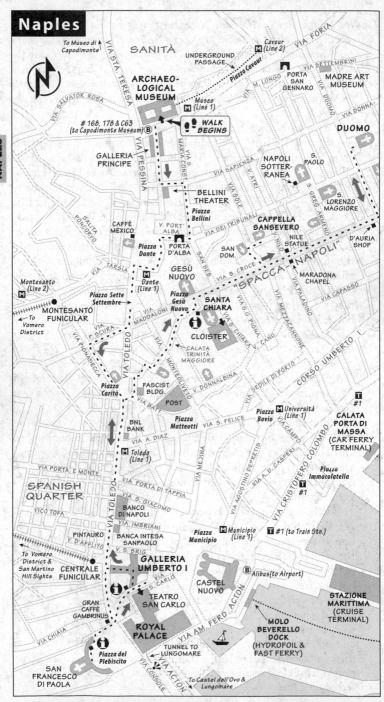

Naples

To Museo di Capodimonte

SANITÀ

VIA STA. TERESA

VIA SALVATOR ROSA

UNDERGROUND PASSAGE

Cavour (Line 2)

VIA FORIA

Piazza Cavour

VIA SETTEMBRINI

VIA M. LONGO

PORTA SAN GENNARO

MADRE ART MUSEUM

ARCHAEO-LOGICAL MUSEUM

Museo (Line 1)

WALK BEGINS

VIA DUOMO

VIA DONNA

DUOMO

#168, 178 & C63 (to Capodimonte Museum)

VIA PESSINA

VIA S. MARIA COST.

VIA SAPIENZA

NAPOLI SOTTER-RANEA

S. PAOLO

GALLERIA PRINCIPE

VIA ATRI

VIA SOLE

S. GREG. ARMENO

S. LORENZO MAGGIORE

SALITA PONGROYO

CAFFÈ MEXICO

BELLINI THEATER

Piazza Bellini

VIA DEI TRIBUNALI

CAPPELLA SANSEVERO

D'AURIA SHOP

Piazza Dante

V. PORT' ALBA

PORTA D'ALBA

NILE STATUE

SAN DOM.

VIA B. CROCE

"SPACCA-NAPOLI"

VIA TARSIA

Dante (Line 1)

GESÙ NUOVO

VIA SEB.

MARADONA CHAPEL

VIA MEZZACANNONE

VIA PALADINO

VIA CAPASSO

Montesanto (Line 2)

Piazza Sette Settembre

MONTESANTO FUNICULAR

To Vomero District

VIA P. SCURA

VIA PIGNASECCA

Piazza Gesù Nuovo

SANTA CHIARA

CLOISTER

VIA S. G. PIGNA.

VIA MADDALONI

CALATA TRINITÀ MAGGIORE

VIA S. CHIARA

V. CAND.

CORSO UMBERTO I

Piazza Carità

VIA TOLEDO

VIA MONTEOLIVETO

VIA DONNALBINA

V. SEDILE DI PORTO

FASCIST BLDG.

POST

VIA BATT.

Piazza Matteotti

V. DONNALBINA

BNL BANK

VIA A. DIAZ

Piazza Bovio

VIA S. FELICE

Università (Line 1)

VIA G. CAMPO

CALATA PORTA DI MASSA (CAR FERRY TERMINAL)

Toledo (Line 1)

VIA PORTA E MONTE

SPANISH QUARTER

VICO TOFA

VIA TOLEDO

VIA MEZINA

VIA PORTA DI TAPPIA

VIA S. GIACOMO

BANCO DI NAPOLI

VIA IMBRIANI

BANCA INTESA SANPAOLO

V. S. BRIG.

VIA A. D'ASPERI

VIA AGOSTINO DEPRETIS

VIA A.D. GASPERI

Piazza Immacolatella

#1

VIA CRISTOFERO COLOMBO

Piazza Municipio

Municipio (Line 1)

#1 (to Train Stn.)

PINTAURO V. D'AFFLITO

To Vomero District & San Martino Hill Sights

CENTRALE FUNICULAR

GRAN CAFFÈ GAMBRINUS

GALLERIA UMBERTO I

TEATRO SAN CARLO

CASTEL NUOVO

Alibus (to Airport)

VIA AM. FERD. ACTON

MOLO BEVERELLO DOCK (HYDROFOIL & FAST FERRY)

STAZIONE MARITTIMA (CRUISE TERMINAL)

ROYAL PALACE

VIA CHIAIA

SAN FRANCESCO DI PAOLA

Piazza del Plebiscito

TUNNEL TO LUNGOMARE

VIA ACTON

VIA CONSOLE

To Castel dell'Ovo & Lungomare

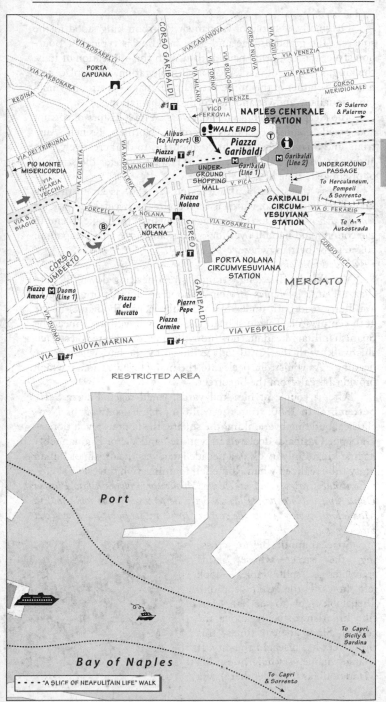

NAPLES

Map labels:
VIA ROSARELLI
CORSO GARIBALDI
VIA CASANOVA
CORSO NUOVA
VIA AQUILA
VIA VENEZIA
PORTA CAPUANA
VIA CARBONARA
VIA MILANO
VIA TORINO
VIA BOLOGNA
VIA FIRENZE
VIA PALERMO
CORSO MERIDIONALE
REGINA
#1 T
VICO FERROVIA
NAPLES CENTRALE STATION
To Salerno & Palermo
VIA DEI TRIBUNALI
Alibus (to Airport) B
WALK ENDS
Piazza Garibaldi
T
PIO MONTE MISERICORDIA
Piazza Mancini
#1 T
VIA MANCINI
Garibaldi (Line 1)
Garibaldi (Line 2)
T
UNDERGROUND PASSAGE
VIA S. VICARIA VECCHIA
VIA COLLETTA
VIA MADDALENA
UNDER-GROUND SHOPPING MALL
V. PICA
To Herculaneum, Pompeii & Sorrento
FORCELLA
V. NOLANA
Piazza Nolana
GARIBALDI CIRCUM-VESUVIANA STATION
VIA G. FERARIS
VIA S. BIAGIO
B
PORTA NOLANA
VIA ROSARELLI
To A-3 Autostrada
CORSO UMBERTO I
CORSO GARIBALDI
#1 T
PORTA NOLANA CIRCUMVESUVIANA STATION
CORSO LUCCI
Piazza Amore
Duomo (Line 1)
VIA DUOMO
Piazza del Mercato
Piazza Pepe
MERCATO
Piazza Carmine
VIA VESPUCCI
NUOVA MARINA
T #1
VIA
T #1
RESTRICTED AREA
Port
Bay of Naples
To Capri, Sicily & Sardina
To Capri & Sorrento

- - - - "A SLICE OF NEAPOLITAN LIFE" WALK

Originally, a statue of a Spanish Bourbon king stood in the square. (The grand orange-and-gray building is typical of Bourbon structures from that period.) But with the unification of Italy, the king, symbolic of Naples' colonial subjugation, was replaced by Dante, the father of the unified Italian language—a strong symbol of nationalism (and yet another form of subjugation).

The Neapolitan people are survivors. A long history of corrupt and greedy colonial overlords (German, Norman, French, Austrian, and Spanish) has taught Neapolitans to deal creatively with authority. Many credit this aspect of Naples' past for the strength of organized crime here.

Across the street, **Caffè Mexico** (at #86) is an institution known for its espresso, which is served already sweetened—ask for *senza zucchero* if you don't want sugar (pay first, then take receipt to the counter and hand it over). Most Italians agree that Neapolitan coffee is the best anywhere.

• *Walk downhill on...*

Via Toledo: The long, straight street heading downhill from Piazza Dante is Naples' principal shopping drag. It originated as a military road built under Spanish rule (hence the name) in the 16th century. Via Toledo skirted the old town wall to connect the Spanish military headquarters (now the museum where you started this walk) with the Royal Palace (down by the bay, where you're heading). As you stroll, peek into the many lovely atriums, which provide a break from the big street.

After a couple of hundred yards, you'll reach **Piazza Sette Settembre.** In 1860, from the white marble balcony of the Neoclassical building overlooking the square, the famous revolutionary Giuseppe Garibaldi declared Italy united and Victor Emmanuel II its first king. Only in 1870, a decade later, was the dream of Italian unity fully realized when Rome fell to unification forces.

• *Continue straight on Via Toledo. About three blocks below Piazza Dante and a block past Piazza Sette Settembre, you'll come to Via Maddaloni, which marks the start of the long, straight, narrow street nicknamed...*

Spaccanapoli: Before crossing the street—whose name translates as "split Naples"—look left (toward the train station). Then look right (to see San Martino hill rising steeply above the center). Since ancient times, this thin street has bisected the city. It changes names several times: Via Maddaloni (as it's called here), Via

B. Croce, Via S. Biagio dei Librai, and Via Vicaria Vecchia. We'll return to this intersection later.

• *If you want to abbreviate this walk, turn left here and skip ahead to Part 3. Part 2, described next, is a bit of a detour, and requires backtracking uphill (or a short taxi ride) later. But if you have time, it's worth the effort.*

Part 2: Monumental Naples (Via Toledo, the Spanish Quarter, and Piazza del Plebiscito)

• *We'll detour off of Via Toledo for just a couple of blocks (rejoining it later). At the Spaccanapoli intersection, go right (toward the church facade on the hill, up Via Pasquale Scura). After about 100 yards, you hit a busy intersection. Stop. You're on one of Naples' most colorful open-air market streets...*

Via Pignasecca Market: Snoop around from here if you are so inclined. Then, turn left down Via Pignasecca and stroll this colorful strip. You'll pass meat and fish stalls, produce stands, streetfood vendors, and much more. This is a taste of Naples' famous Spanish Quarter, which we'll experience more of later in this walk.

• *Via Pignasecca meets back up with Via Toledo at the square called...*

Piazza Carità: This square, built for an official visit by Hitler to Mussolini in 1938, is full of stern, straight, obedient lines.

The big building belonged to an insurance company. (For the best example of fascist architecture in town, take a slight detour from here: With your back to Via Toledo, leave Piazza Carità downhill on the right-hand corner and walk a block to the Poste e Telegrafi building. There you'll see several government buildings with stirring reliefs singing the praises of lobotomized workers and a totalitarian society.)

In Naples—long a poor and rough city—rather than being heroic, people learn from the cradle the art of survival. The modern memorial statue in the center of the square celebrates **Salvo d'Acquisto,** a rare hometown hero. In 1943, he was executed after falsely confessing to sabotage...in order to save 22 fellow Italian soldiers from a Nazi revenge massacre.

• *From Piazza Carità, continue south down Via Toledo for a few blocks, looking to your left for more...*

Fascist Architecture (Banks): You can't miss the two big, blocky bank buildings. First comes the chalky-white BNL Bank. A bit farther down, past the Metro, imagine trying to rob the even more imposing Banco di Napoli (Via Toledo 178). Step across the street and check out its architecture: typical fascist arches and

reliefs, built to celebrate the bank's 400th anniversary (est. 1539—how old is *your* bank?).

The street here was pedestrianized after the Toledo Metro stop opened in 2012. Now the street is even more popular for strolling, property values have risen, and international brands have moved in.

• *On the next block (at #184) is the...*

Banca Intesa Sanpaolo: This fills an older palace—take a free peek at the opulent atrium. In the entry hall, you can buy a ticket for the **Galleria d'Italia Palazzo Zevallos Stigliano,** a small collection located in the upper two floors. The gallery's only piece worth seeing—on the second floor—is a great late Caravaggio painting. *The Martyrdom of Saint Ursula* shows a terrible scene: His marriage proposal rejected, the king of the Huns shoots an arrow into Ursula's chest. Blood spurts, Ursula is stunned but accepts her destiny sweetly, and Caravaggio himself—far right, his last self-portrait—screams to symbolize the rejection of evil. The rest of the second floor holds opulent chandeliered apartments, a few Neapolitan landscapes, and little else. The first floor has temporary exhibits (€5, more for special exhibits, Tue-Sun 10:00-18:00, closed Mon; entry includes audioguide, a look at old Naples paintings, and a fine WC; Via Toledo 185, tel. 800-454-229, www.palazzozevallos.com).

• *Feeling bold? From here, side-trip uphill a couple of blocks into the...*

Spanish Quarter: This is a classic world of *basso* (low) living. The streets—which were laid out in the 16th century for the Span-

ish military barracks outside the city walls—are unbelievably narrow (and cool in summer), and the buildings rise five stories high. In such tight quarters, life—flirting, fighting, playing, and loving—happens in the road. This is *the* cliché of life in Naples, as shown in so many movies. The Spanish Quarter is Naples at its most characteristic. The shopkeepers are friendly, and the mopeds are bold (watch out). Concerned locals will tug on their lower eyelids, warning you to be wary. Hungry? Pop into a grocery shop and ask the clerk to make you his best prosciutto-and-mozzarella sandwich (the price should be about €4).

• *Return to Via Toledo and work your way down. Near the bottom of the street, on the right at #275, is **Pintauro**, a takeaway bakery famous for* *its* sfogliatelle. *These classic, ricotta-filled Neapolitan pastries are often served warm from the oven and make a tasty €2 treat.*

Just beyond, on the right, notice the station for the **Centrale funicular.** *If you have extra time and enjoy city views, this can take you sweat-free up to the top of San Martino, the hill with a fortress and a monastery/museum looming over town (see page 974 for details). Across the street is the impressive Galleria Umberto I—but don't go in now, as you'll see it in a minute from the other side.*

For now, just keep heading down the main drag and through the smaller Piazza Trieste e Trento to the immense...

Piazza del Plebiscito: This square celebrates the 1861 vote (*plebiscito,* plebiscite) in which Naples chose to join Italy. Dominating the top of the square is the Church of San Francesco di Paola, with its Pantheon-inspired dome and broad, arcing colonnades. If it's open, step inside to ogle the vast interior—a Neoclassi-

cal re-creation of one of ancient Rome's finest buildings (free, daily 8:30-12:00 & 16:00-19:00).

• *Opposite is the...*

Royal Palace *(Palazzo Reale):* Having housed Spanish, French, and even Italian royalty, this building displays statues of

all those who stayed here. Look for eight kings in the niches, each from a different dynasty (left to right): Norman, German, French, Spanish, Spanish, Spanish, French (Napoleon's brother-in-law), and, finally, Italian—Victor Emmanuel II, King of Savoy. The statues were done at the request of V. E. II's son, so his dad is the most dashing of the group. While you could consider touring the interior, it's relatively unimpressive (described under "Sights in Naples," later).

• *Continue 50 yards past the Royal Palace (toward the trees) to enjoy a...*

Fine Harbor View: While boats busily serve Capri and Sorrento, Mount Vesuvius smolders ominously in the distance. Look back to see the vast

"Bourbon red" palace—its color inspired by Pompeii. The hilltop above Piazza del Plebiscito is San Martino, with its Carthusian monastery-turned-museum and Castle of St. Elmo (remember, the Centrale funicular to the top is just across the square and up Via Toledo). The promenade you're on continues to Naples' romantic harborfront—the fishermen's quarter (Borgo Marinaro)—a fortified island connected to the mainland by a stout causeway, with its fanciful, ancient Castel dell'Ovo (Egg Castle) and trendy harborside restaurants. Farther along the harborfront stretches the Lungomare promenade and Santa Lucia district. (The long harborfront promenade, Via Francesco Caracciolo, is a delightful people-watching scene on balmy nights.)

• *Head back through the piazza and pop into...*

Gran Caffè Gambrinus: This coffee house, facing the piazza, takes you back to the elegance of 1860. It's a classic place to sample a crispy *sfogliatella* pastry, or perhaps the mushroom-shaped, rum-soaked bread-like cakes called *babà*, which come in a huge variety. Stand at the bar *(banco)*, pay double to sit *(tavola)*, or just wander around as you imagine the café buzzing with the ritzy intellectuals, journalists, and artsy bohemian types who munched on *babà* here during Naples' 19th-century heyday (daily 7:00-24:00, Piazza del Plebiscito 1, tel. 081-417-582).

• *A block away, tucked behind the palace, you can peek inside the Neoclassical...*

Teatro di San Carlo: Built in 1737, 41 years before Milan's La Scala, this is Europe's oldest opera house and Italy's second-most-respected (after La Scala). The theater burned down in 1816, and was rebuilt within the year. Guided 35-minute visits in English basically just show you the fine auditorium with its 184 boxes—each with a big mirror to reflect the candlelight (€6; tours Mon-Sat at 10:30, 11:30, 12:30, 14:30, 15:30, and 16:30; Sun at 10:30, 11:30, and 12:30; tel. 081-797-2468, www.teatrosancarlo.it).

Beyond Teatro di San Carlo and the Royal Palace is the huge, harborfront **Castel Nuovo,** which houses government bureaucrats and the **Civic Museum.** It feels like a mostly empty shell, with a couple of dusty halls of Neapolitan art, but the views over the bay from the upper terraces are impressive (€6, Mon-Sat 8:30-19:00, closed Sun, last entry one hour before closing, tel. 081-795-7722, www.comune.napoli.it).

Cross the street from Teatro di San Carlo and go through the tall yellow arch into the Victorian iron and glass of

the 100-year-old shopping mall, **Galleria Umberto I.** It was built in 1892 to reinvigorate the district after a devastating cholera epidemic occurred here. Gawk up, then walk left to bring you back out on Via Toledo.

• *For Part 3 of this walk, double back up Via Toledo to Piazza Carità, veering right (just above the first big fascist-style building we saw earlier) on Via Morgantini through Piazza Monteoliveto. Cross the busy street, then angle up Calata Trinità Maggiore to the fancy column at the top of the hill. (To avoid the backtracking and uphill walk, catch a €10 taxi to the Church of Gesù Nuovo—JAY-zoo noo-OH-voh.)*

Part 3: Spaccanapoli Back to the Station

You're back at the straight-as-a-Greek-arrow Spaccanapoli, formerly the main thoroughfare of the Greek city of Neapolis.

• *Stop at...*

Piazza Gesù Nuovo: This square is marked by a towering 18th-century Baroque monument to the Counter-Reformation.

Although the Jesuit order was powerful in Naples because of its Spanish heritage, locals never attacked Protestants here with the full fury of the Spanish Inquisition.

If you'd like, you can visit two bulky old churches, starting with the dark, fortress-like, 17th-century **Church of Gesù Nuovo,** followed by the simpler **Church of Santa Chiara** (in the courtyard across the street). Both are described in more detail later, under "Sights in Naples."

• *After touring the churches, continue along the main drag. Since this is a university district, you'll see lots of students and bookstores. This neighborhood is also famously superstitious. Look for incense-burning women with carts full of good-luck charms for sale.*

Farther down Spaccanapoli—passing Palazzo Venezia, the embassy of Venice to Naples when both were independent powers—you'll see the next square...

Piazza San Domenico Maggiore: This square is marked by an ornate 17th-century monument built to thank God for ending the plague. From this square, detour left along the right side of the castle-like church, then follow yellow signs, taking the first right and walking one block to the remarkable **Cappella Sansevero.** This Baroque chapel is well worth visiting (described later, under "Sights in Naples").

• *After touring the chapel, return to Via B. Croce (a.k.a. Spaccanapoli), turn left, and continue your cultural scavenger hunt. At the intersection of Via Nilo, find the...*

Statue of the Nile (on the left): A reminder of the multiethnic makeup of Greek Neapolis, this statue is in what was the Egyptian quarter. Locals like to call this statue *The Body of Naples,* with the overflowing cornucopia symbolizing the abundance of their fine city. (I once asked a Neapolitan man to describe the local women, who are famous for their beauty, in one word. He replied, simply, "Abundant.") This intersection is considered the center of old Naples.

• *Directly opposite the statue, inside of Bar Nilo, is the...*

"Chapel of Maradona": The small "chapel" on the right wall is dedicated to Diego Maradona, a soccer star who played for Naples in the 1980s. Locals consider soccer almost a religion, and this guy was practically a deity. You can even see a "hair of Diego" and a teardrop from the city when he went to another team for more money. Unfortunately, his reputation has since been sullied by problems he's had with organized crime, drugs, and police. Perhaps inspired by Maradona's example, the coffee bar has posted a quadrilingual sign (though, strangely, not in English) threatening that those who take a picture without buying a cup of coffee may find their camera damaged...*Capisce?*

• *As you continue, you'll begin to see shops selling...*

Presepi **(Nativity Scenes)** and *Corno:* Just as many Americans keep an eye out year-round for Christmas-tree ornaments, Italians

regularly add pieces to the family *presepe,* the centerpiece of their holiday decorations. Stop after a few blocks at the tiny square, where Via San Gregorio Armeno leads left into a colorful district with the highest concentration of shops selling fantastic *presepi* and their tiny components, including figurines caricaturing local politicians and celebrities. Some even move around.

Another popular Naples souvenir that you'll see sold here—and all over the city—is the *corno,* a skinny, twisted, red horn that resembles a chili pepper. The *corno* comes with a double symbolism for fertility: It's a horn of plenty, and it's also a phallic symbol turned upside-down. Neapolitans explain that fertility isn't sexual; it provides the greatest gift a person can give—life—and it ensures that one's soul will live on through the next generation. Interestingly, in today's Naples, just as in yesterday's Pompeii (where bulging erections greeted visitors at the entrance to a home), fertility is equated with good luck.

By the way, a bit farther up Via San Gregorio Armeno, you'll find the underground **Napoli Sotterranea archaeological site,** along Via dei Tribunali, which also has some of the city's best **pizzerias** (both are described later).

Back on Spaccanapoli and a bit farther along, on the right at #87, the **D'Auria** shop sells some of the best-quality *presepi* in town, many of them the classy *campane* version, under a glass bell.

• *As Via B. Croce becomes Via S. Biagio dei Librai, notice the...*

Gold and Silver Shops: Some say stolen jewelry ends up here, is melted down immediately, and gets resold in some other form as soon as it cools. Look for *compro oro* ("I buy gold") signs (for example, in the window of the shop at #95)—a sign of Italy's economic tough times.

• *Cross busy Via Duomo. If you have time and aren't already churched out, consider detouring five minutes north (left) up Via Duomo to visit Naples'* **Duomo;** *just around the corner is the* **Pio Monte della Misericordia Church,** *with a fine Caravaggio painting (both described later, under "Sights in Naples"). Afterward, continue straight along Via Vicaria Vecchia. As you stroll, ponder Naples' vibrant...*

Street Life, Past and Present: Here along Via Vicaria Vecchia, the street and side-street scenes intensify. The area is said to be a center of the Camorra (organized crime), but as a tourist, you won't notice. Paint a picture with these thoughts: Naples has the most intact street plan of any surviving ancient Greek or Roman city. Imagine this city during those times (and retain these images as you visit Pompeii), with streetside shop fronts that close up after dark, and private homes on upper floors. What you see today is just one more page in a 2,000-year-old story of a city: all kinds of meetings, beatings, and cheatings; kisses, near misses, and little-boy pisses.

You name it, it occurs right on the streets today, as it has since ancient times. People ooze from crusty corners. Black-and-white

death announcements add to the clutter on the walls. Widows sell cigarettes from buckets. For a peek behind the scenes in the shade of wet laundry, venture down a few side streets. Buy two carrots as a gift for the woman on the fifth floor, if she'll lower her bucket to pick them up. The neighborhood action seems best at about 18:00.

A few blocks on, at the tiny fenced-in triangle of greenery, hang out for a few minutes to just observe the crazy motorbike action and teen scene.

• *From here, veer right onto Via Forcella (which leads to the busy boulevard that takes you to Centrale Station). A block down, a tiny, fenced-in traffic island protects a chunk of the ancient Greek wall of Neapolis. Turn right here on Via Pietro Colletta, walk 40 yards, and step into the North Pole, at the...*

Polo Nord Gelateria: The oldest *gelateria* in Naples has had four generations of family working here since 1931. Before you order, sample a few flavors, including their *bacio*, or "kiss," flavor (chocolate and hazelnut)—all are made fresh daily (Via Pietro Colletta 41). Via Pietro Colletta leads past two of Napoli's most competitive **pizzerias** (see "Eating in Naples," later) to Corso Umberto I.

• *Turn left on the grand boulevard-like Corso Umberto I. From here to Centrale Station, it's at least a 10-minute walk (if you're tired, hop on a bus; they all go to the station). To finish the walk, continue on Corso Umberto I—past a gauntlet of purse/CD/sunglasses salesmen and shady characters hawking stolen mobile phones—to the vast Piazza Garibaldi, with a shiny new modern canopy in the middle. On the far side is the station. You made it.*

Sights in Naples

Naples' best sights are the Archaeological Museum and my self-guided Naples walk, both covered earlier.

CHURCHES ON OR NEAR SPACCANAPOLI

These churches are linked—in this order—on Part 3 of my self-guided walk, earlier.

▲Church of Gesù Nuovo

This church's unique pyramid-grill facade survives from a fortified 15th-century noble palace. Step inside for a brilliant Neapolitan Baroque interior. The second chapel on the right features a much-adored **statue of St. Giuseppe Moscati** (1880-1927), a Christian doctor famous for helping the poor. In 1987, Moscati became the first modern doctor to be canonized. Sit and watch a steady stream of Neapolitans taking turns to kiss and touch the altar, then hold the good doctor's highly polished hand.

Continue on to the third chapel and

enter the **Sale Moscati.** Look high on the walls of this long room to see hundreds of ex-votos—tiny red-and-silver plaques of thanksgiving for prayers answered with the help of St. Moscati (each has a symbol of the ailment cured). Naples' practice of using ex-votos, while incorporated into its Catholic rituals, goes back to its pagan Greek roots. Rooms from Moscati's nearby apartment are on display, and a glass case shows possessions and photos of the great doctor. As you leave the Sale Moscati, notice the big bomb casing that hangs high in the left corner. It fell through the church's dome in 1943, but caused almost no damage...yet another miracle.

Cost and Hours: Free, daily 6:45-13:00 & 16:00-19:30, Piazza del Gesù Nuovo, www.gesunuovo.it.

Church of Santa Chiara

Dating from the 14th century, this church is from a period of French royal rule under the Angevin dynasty. Consider the stark contrast between this church (Gothic) and the Gesù Nuovo (Baroque), across the street. Inside, look for the faded Trinity on the back wall (on the right as you face the door, under the stone canopy), which shows a dove representing the Holy Spirit between the heads of God the Father and Christ (c. 1414). This is an example of the fine frescoes that once covered the walls. Most were stuccoed over during Baroque times or destroyed in 1943 by Allied bombs. Continuing down the main aisle, you'll step over a huge inlaid-marble Angevin coat of arms on the floor. The altar is adorned with four finely carved Gothic tombs of Angevin kings. A chapel stacked with Bourbon royalty is just to the right.

Cost and Hours: Free, daily 7:30-13:00 & 16:30-20:00, Piazza del Gesù Nuovo, www.monasterodisantachiara.com. Its tranquil cloistered courtyard, around back, is not worth its €6 entry fee.

▲▲Cappella Sansevero

This small chapel is a Baroque explosion mourning the body of Christ, who lies on a soft pillow under an incredibly realistic veil. It's also the personal chapel of Raimondo de Sangro, an eccentric Freemason, containing his tomb and the tombs of his family. Like other 18th-century Enlightenment figures, Raimondo was a wealthy man of letters, scientist and inventor, and patron of the arts—and he was also a grand master of the Freemasons of the Kingdom of Naples. His chapel—filled with Masonic symbolism—is a complex ensemble, with statues representing virtues such as self-control, religious zeal, and the Masonic philosophy of freedom through enlightenment. Though it's a pricey private enterprise, the chapel is worth a visit.

Cost and Hours: €7, buy tickets at office at the corner, Wed-Mon 9:30-18:30, closed Tue, no photos, Via de Sanctis 19, tel.

NAPLES

081-551-8470, www.museosansevero.it. Pick up the free floor plan, which identifies each of the statues lining the nave.

Visiting the Chapel: Study the incredible *Veiled Christ* in the center. Carved out of marble, it's like no other statue I've seen (by Giuseppe "Howdeedoodat" Sammartino, 1753). The Christian message (Jesus died for our salvation) is accompanied by a Masonic message (the veil represents how the body and ego are obstacles to real spiritual freedom). As you walk from Christ's feet to his head, notice how the expression on Jesus' face goes from suffering to peace.

Raimondo's mom and dad are buried on either side of the **main altar.** To the right of the altar, marking his father's tomb, a statue representing *Despair* or *Disillusion* struggles with a marble rope net (carved out of a single piece of stone), symbolic of a troubled mind. The flames on the head of the winged boy represent human intellect—more Masonic symbolism, showing how knowledge frees the human mind. To the left of the main altar is a statue of *Modesty,* marking the tomb of Raimondo's mother (who died after his birth, and was only 20). The veiled woman fingers a broken tablet, symbolizing an interrupted life.

Raimondo de Sangro himself lies buried in a side altar (on the right). Among his inventions was the deep-green pigment used on the ceiling fresco. The inlaid M. C. Escher-esque maze on the floor around de Sangro's tomb is another Masonic reminder of how the quest for knowledge gets you out of the maze of life. This tilework once covered the floor of the entire chapel.

Your Sansevero finale is downstairs: two mysterious...**skeletons.** Perhaps another of the mad inventor's fancies: Inject a corpse with a fluid to fossilize the veins so that they'll survive the body's decomposition. While that's the legend, investigations have shown that the veins were artificial, and the models were created to illustrate how the circulatory system works.

▲Duomo

Naples' historic cathedral, built by imported French Anjou kings in the 14th century, boasts a breathtaking Neo-Gothic facade. Step into the vast interior to see the mix of styles along the side chapels—from pointy Gothic arches to rounded Renaissance ones to gilded Baroque decor.

Cost and Hours: Free, Mon-Sat 8:30-13:30 & 14:30-20:00, Sun 8:30-13:30 & 16:30-19:30, Via Duomo.

Visiting the Church: Explore the two largest side-chapels (flanking the nave, about halfway to the transept). Each is practically a church in its own right. On the left, the **Chapel of St. Restituta** stands on the site of the original, early-Christian church that predated the cathedral (at the far end, you can pay a small fee to see its sixth-century baptismal font under mosaics and go downstairs to see its even earlier foundations; shorter hours than cathedral). On the right is the **Chapel of San Gennaro**—dedicated to the beloved patron saint of Naples—decorated with silver busts of centuries of bishops, and seven paintings done on bronze.

The cathedral's **main altar** at the front is ringed by carved wooden seats, filled three times a year by clergy to witness the Miracle of the Blood. Thousands of Neapolitans cram into this church for a peek at two tiny vials with the dried blood of St. Gennaro. As the clergy roots—or even jeers—for the miracle to occur, the blood temporarily liquefies. Neapolitans take this ritual with deadly seriousness, and believe that if the blood remains solid, it's terrible luck for the city. Sure enough, on the rare occasion that the miracle fails, locals can point to a terrible event soon after—such as an earthquake, an eruption of Mount Vesuvius, or an especially disappointing soccer loss.

The stairs beneath the altar take you to a **crypt** with the relics of St. Gennaro and (across the room) a statue of the bishop who rescued the relics from a rival town and returned them to Naples.

Pio Monte della Misericordia

This small church (near the Duomo, and run by a charitable foundation) displays one of the best works by Caravaggio, *The Seven Works of Mercy*. Upstairs is a ho-hum art gallery. The price is steep, but it may be worth it for Caravaggio fans.

Cost and Hours: €7, includes audioguide, Thu-Tue 9:00-14:30, closed Wed, Via dei Tribunali 253, tel. 081-446-944, www.piomontedellamisericordia.it.

Visiting the Church: Caravaggio's *The Seven Works of Mercy* hangs over the main altar in a humble gray chapel. It's well lit, allowing Caravaggio's characteristically dark canvas to really pop. In one crowded canvas, the great early-Baroque artist illustrates seven virtues: burying the dead (the man carrying a corpse by the ankles); visiting the imprisoned and feeding the hungry (Pero breastfeeding her starving father—a scene from a famous Roman story); sheltering the homeless (a pilgrim on the Camino de Santiago, with his floppy hat, negotiates with an innkeeper); caring for the sick and clothing the naked (St. Martin offers part of his cloak to the injured man in the foreground); and giving drink to the thirsty (Samson chugs from a jawbone in the background)—all of them set in a dark Neapolitan alley and watched over by Mary, Jesus, and a pair of angels. Caravaggio painted this work in Naples in 1607, while in exile from Rome, where he had been sentenced to death for killing a man in a duel. Your ticket also lets you in to the foundation's sprawling but dull upper-floor museum, with some minor Neapolitan paintings.

IN THE CITY CENTER
Royal Palace (Palazzo Reale)
Facing Piazza del Plebiscito, this huge, lavish palace welcomes the public. The palace's grand Neoclassical staircase leads up to a floor with 30 plush rooms. You'll follow a one-way route (with some English descriptions) featuring the palace theater, paintings by "the Caravaggio Imitators," Neapolitan tapestries, fine inlaid-stone tabletops, chandeliers, gilded woodwork, and more. The rooms do feel quite grand, but they lack the personality and sense of importance of Europe's better palaces. Don't miss the huge, tapestry-laden Hercules Hall. On the way out, step into the chapel, with a fantastic Nativity scene—a commotion of 18th-century ceramic figurines.

Cost and Hours: €4, includes painfully dry audioguide, free first Sun of the month, Thu-Tue 9:00-20:00, closed Wed, last entry one hour before closing, tel. 848-082-408, www. palazzorealenapoli.it.

▲Napoli Sotterranea
This archaeological site, a manmade underground maze of passageways and ruins from Greek and Roman times, can only be toured with a guide. You'll descend 121 steps under the modern city to explore two different underground areas. One is the old Greek tuff quarry used to build the city of Neapolis, which was later converted into an immense cistern by the Romans. The other is an excavated portion of the Greco-Roman theater that once seated 6,000 people. It's clear that this space has been encroached upon by modern development—some current residents' windows literally look down into the theater ruins. The tour involves a lot of stairs, as well as a long, narrow 20-inch-wide walkway—lit only by candlelight—that uses an ancient water channel (a heavyset person could not comfortably fit through this, and claustrophobes will be miserable). Although there's not much to actually see, the experience is fascinating and includes a little history from World War II—when

the quarry/cistern was turned into a shelter to protect locals from American bombs.

Cost and Hours: €10; includes 1.5-hour tour. Tours in English are offered daily every two hours from 10:00 to 18:00. Bring a light sweater. Tel. 081-296-944, www.napolisotterranea.org.

Getting There: The site is at Piazza San Gaetano 68, along Via dei Tribunali. It's a 15-minute walk from the Archaeological Museum, and just a couple of blocks uphill from Spaccanapoli's statue of the Nile. The entrance is immediately to the left of the Church of San Paolo Maggiore (look for the *Sotterranea* signs).

NAPLES

Porta Nolana Open-Air Fish Market

Naples' fish market squirts and stinks as it has for centuries under the Porta Nolana (gate in the city wall), immediately in front of the

Napoli Porta Nolana Circumvesuviana station and four long blocks from Centrale Station. Of the town's many boisterous outdoor markets, this will net you the most photos and memories. From Piazza Nolana, wander under the medieval gate and take your first left down Vico Sopramuro, enjoying this wild and entirely edible cultural scavenger hunt (Tue-Sun 8:00-14:00, closed Mon).

Two other markets with more clothing and fewer fish are at Piazza Capuana (several blocks northwest of Centrale Station and tumbling down Via Sant'Antonio Abate, Mon-Sat 8:00-18:00, Sun 9:00-13:00) and a similar cobbled shopping zone along Via Pignasecca (just off Via Toledo, west of Piazza Carità, described on page 961).

Lungomare *Passeggiata*

Each evening, relaxed and romantic Neapolitans in the mood for a scenic harborside stroll do their *vasche* (laps) along the inviting Lungomare promenade. To join in this elegant people-watching scene (best after 19:00), stroll about 15 minutes from Piazza del Plebiscito along Via Nazario Sauro.

Detour out along the fortified causeway to poke around Borgo Marinaro ("fishermen's quarter"), with its striking Castel dell'Ovo and a trendy restaurant scene, where you can dine amidst yachts with a view of Vesuvius. This is known as the Santa Lucia district because this is where the song "Santa Lucia" was first performed. (The song is probably so famous in America because immigrants from Naples sang it to remember the old country.) Beyond that stretches the Lungomare, along Via Francesco Caracciolo. Taxi home or retrace your steps back to the old center.

MADRE

MADRE, a museum of contemporary art, displays works by Jeff Koons, Anish Kapoor, Francesco Clemente, and other big names in the art world. Aficionados of modern art consider it one of the better collections in the country. Some descriptions are in English—you'll need them.

Cost and Hours: €7, free on Mon; Wed-Mon 10:00-19:30, closed Tue, last entry one hour before closing; Via Settembrini 79, tel. 081-1931-3016, www.madrenapoli.it.

ON SAN MARTINO

The ultimate view overlooking Naples, its bay, and the volcano is from the hill called San Martino, just above (and west of) the city center. Up top you'll find a mighty

fortress (which charges for entry but offers the best views from its ramparts) and the adjacent monastery-turned-museum. While neither of these sights is exciting in its own right, the views are. And the surrounding neighborhood (especially Piazza Fuga) has a classy "uptown" vibe compared to the gritty city-center streets below. Cheapskates can enjoy the views for free from the benches on the square in front of the monastery.

Getting There: From Via Toledo, the Spanish Quarter gradually climbs up San Martino's lower slopes, before steep paths take you up the rest of the way. But the easiest way to ascend San Martino is by funicular. Three different funicular lines lead from lower Naples to the hilltop: the Centrale line from near the bottom of Via Toledo; the Montesanto line from the Metro stop of the same name (near the top end of Via Toledo); and the Chiaia line from farther out, near Piazza Amadeo (all three are covered by any regular local transit ticket). Ride any of these three up to the end of the line. All three lines converge within a few blocks at the top of the hill—Centrale and Chiaia wind up at opposite ends of the charming Piazza Fuga, while Montesanto terminates a bit closer to the fortress and museum.

Leaving any of the funiculars, head uphill, carefully tracking the brown signs for *Castel S. Elmo* and *Museo di San Martino* (strategically placed escalators make the climb easier). Regardless of where you come up, you'll pass the Montesanto funicular station—angle right (as you face the station) down Via Pirro Ligorio, and then continue following the signs. You'll reach the castle first, and then the monastery/museum (both about 10 minutes' walk from Piazza Fuga).

Another convenient—if less scenic—approach is via the Metro's line 1 to the Vanvitelli stop, which is near the upper funicular terminals.

Castel Sant'Elmo

While it's little more than an empty husk with a decent modern art museum, this 16th-century, Spanish-built, star-shaped fortress boasts commanding views over the city and the entire Bay of Naples. Buy your ticket at the booth, then ride the elevator up to the upper courtyard and climb up to the ramparts for a slow circle to enjoy the 360-degree views. In the middle of the yard is the likeable little Museo del Novecento, a gallery of works by 20th-century Neapolitan artists (covered by same ticket); the castle also hosts temporary exhibits.

Cost and Hours: €5, open Wed-Mon 9:00-19:00, closed Tue, last entry one hour before closing, Via Tito Angelini 22, tel. 081-229-4401, www.polomusealocampania.beniculturali.it.

▲San Martino Carthusian Monastery and Museum (Certosa e Museo di San Martino)

The monastery, founded in 1325 and dissolved in the early 1800s, is now a sprawling museum with several parts. The square out front has city views nearly as good as the ones you'll pay to see from inside, and a few cafés angling for your business.

Cost and Hours: €6, Thu-Tue 8:30-19:30, closed Wed, last entry one hour before closing, audioguide-€5, Largo San Martino 8, tel. 081-229-4502.

Visiting the Monastery and Museum: If you want to tour the place, buy your ticket and head into the complex. Step into the church, a Baroque explosion with beautifully decorated chapels. Around the humble cloister are a variety of museum exhibits. The Naval Museum has nautical paintings, model boats, and giant ceremonial gondolas. In an adjacent hall is an excellent collection of *presepi* (Nativity scenes), both life-size and miniature, including a spectacular one by Michele Cucinello—the best I've seen in this *presepi*-crazy city. Beyond that is the larger garden cloister, ringed with a painting gallery (with lots of antique maps and artifacts of old Naples), and an entrance to a pretty view terrace.

ON CAPODIMONTE
▲Capodimonte Museum (Museo di Capodimonte)

Another hilltop, about a mile due north from the Archaeological Museum, is home to Naples' top art museum. Worth ▲▲ to art lovers, this pleasantly uncrowded collection has lesser-known (but still masterful) works by Michelangelo, Raphael, Titian, Caravaggio, and other huge names. It fills the Bourbons' cavernous summer palace, set in the midst of a sprawling hilltop park overlooking Naples, and part of the museum showcases the palace's history and furnishings. While most visitors to Naples prefer to focus on the city's vibrant street life, characteristic churches, and ancient artifacts, art lovers and royalty buffs enjoy a visit to Capodimonte.

Cost and Hours: €7.50, free first Sun of the month, Thu-Tue 8:30-19:30, closed Wed, last entry one hour before closing, audioguide-€5, café, Via Miano 2, tel. 081-749-9111, www.museocapodimonte.beniculturali.it.

Getting There: This museum is a bit harder to reach than the other sights in this chapter, but the trip is manageable. It's easiest by taxi (figure €10-12 from the town center). You can also catch the bus from Piazza Dante or from the stop directly in front of the Archaeological Museum (#168 or #178 to the Miano stop, or #C63 to the Capodimonte stop; buy €1 ticket at a newsstand or tobacco shop before you board).

Visiting the Museum: The collection fills a gargantuan palace—pace yourself. After buying your ticket, pick up the free map and head up several flights of stairs to the "first" floor and the Galleria Farnese. At the far end of the first big hall (Room 2) is Titian's portrait of Alessandro Farnese, the local bigwig whose family married into Bourbon royalty; later, as Pope Paul III, he was responsible for bringing great art to Naples. (To the right, you'll see Raphael's portrait of the same pope as a much younger cardinal.) In the next, smaller Room 3, the section of an altarpiece (1426) by the early Renaissance pioneer Masaccio shows a primitive attempt at 3-D: Masaccio has left out Jesus' neck to create the illusion that he's looking down on us. Don't miss the adjoining Room 4 (lights go on as you enter), with large charcoal drawings by Raphael (Moses shields his eyes from the burning bush, 1514) and Michelangelo (a group of soldiers, 1546; and *Venus and Love*, 1534).

Continuing into the Borgia Collection (Room 8), look for works by Mantegna (including the *Portrait of Francesco Gonzaga*, c. 1461, a very small but finely executed profile portrait) and Giovanni Bellini's *Transfiguration*. In Room 10 is one of many versions of Titian's *Danaë*, where—as told in the Greek myth—the central character looks up at a cloud containing the essence of Zeus, about to impregnate her. Nearby, Titian's poignant portrait of a penitent Mary Magdalene has finely detailed tears running down her cheeks (1565).

Parmigianino's *Antea* (1531-35), in Room 12, another of the collection's highlights, addresses us with an unblinking, dilated gaze. As we visually follow the mink around her neck, we see—in a surreal spin—that the critter's disgusting little teeth are biting into her gloved hand. In the small, dim, adjoining Room 14 is the *Farnese Box* (*Cassetta Farnese*, 1563), a masterwork of gold decoration.

Down the main hall in Room 17 are two works by Pieter Bruegel the Elder: *The Parable of the Blind* (*Parabola dei Ciechi*, 1568) is a literal and darkly comic illustration of "the blind leading the blind." *The Misanthrope* (1568) suggests the pointlessness of giving up on life and becoming a hermit; cut off from the world and lost in thought, the title figure doesn't even notice that he's about to step on a thorn, or that his wallet is being stolen by a wild-eyed young man. (Hey! I saw that guy on the Circumvesuviana!)

In Room 20, Annibale Carracci's *Hercules at the Crossroads* (1596) presents the hero with a choice: virtue (on the left, nature and letters) or vice (on the right, scantily clad women, music, theater masks). While his foot points one way, he looks the other...his mind not yet made up.

From here on out, you'll pass through some of the opulent apartments of this building, decorated with stunning period details and furniture. One room is slathered with red frescoes, as the houses at Pompeii once were. Another, with astonishing porcelain decor, is a masterwork of *chinoiserie*—a style reflecting Europe's fascination with Chinese culture. In Room 54, get face-to-face with Napoleon.

Circling back to where you started, head up four flights of stairs to the second floor. You'll see a cycle of tapestries, then halls of Gothic altarpieces. In Room 67, find Colantonio's painting *San Girolamo nello Studio* (c. 1445), in which the astonishing level of detail—from the words on the page of the open book, to the balled-up pages tucked away at the bottom of the frame—drives home the message: Only through complete devotion and meticulous dedication can you hope to accomplish great things...like pulling a thorn out of a lion's paw.

Farther along on this floor, in Room 78, you'll reach another of the museum's top pieces, Caravaggio's *The Flagellation*. Typical of his *chiaroscuro* (light/dark) style, Caravaggio uses a ribbon of light to show us only what he wants us to see: A broken Christ about to be whipped, and the manic fury of the man (on his left) who will do the whipping. This scene could be set in a Naples alley. Compare this with most of the paintings we've seen so far—of popes, saints, and aristocrats. Caravaggio was revolutionary in showing real life

rather than idealized scenes—helping common people to better relate to these stories. Next, Room 79 is filled with Caravaggio imitators, including Artemisia Gentileschi, one of his female followers
who adapted his style for her own use (in this case, the gruesome
murder of a man by a woman).

Nearby: Capodimonte is separated from Naples' town center by the gritty **Sanità** district. One of Naples' most historic and
colorful zones, Sanità is sometimes called "the living *presepe*" for
the way people live stacked on top of each other in rustic conditions like an elaborate manger scene. Sanità has several important
churches, including some with catacombs that you can tour (because this district was just outside the city walls, the dead were buried here; for details, see www.catacombedinapoli.it). The main road
from the Archaeological Museum to Capodimonte passes above
this district on a Napoleon-built bridge. But if you have time and
curiosity, consider walking back to the town center through this
vivid neighborhood.

Sleeping in Naples

As an alternative to intense Naples, most travelers prefer to sleep
in mellow Sorrento, just over an hour away (see Sorrento chapter).
But, if needed, here are a few good options. High season in Naples
is spring and late fall. Prices are soft during the hot, slow summer
months (July-Sept) and plunge during the pleasantly cool winters.

ON AND AROUND VIA TOLEDO

To see the city's best face, stay in the area that stretches between
the Archaeological Museum and the port.

$$$ Decumani Hotel de Charme is a classy oasis tucked
away on a residential lane in the very heart of the city, just off Spac-
canapoli. While the street is Naples-dingy, the hotel is an inviting
retreat, filling an elegant 17th-century palace with 39 rooms and
a gorgeous breakfast room (air-con, elevator, Via San Giovanni
Maggiore Pignatelli 15, Metro: Università; if coming from Spac-
canapoli, this lane is one street toward the train station from Via
Santa Chiara, tel. 081-551-8188, www.decumani.com, info@
decumani.com).

$$$ Hotel Piazza Bellini is an artistically decorated hotel
with 48 stripped-down, minimalist but comfy rooms surrounding
a quiet courtyard. Two blocks below the Archaeological Museum
and just off the lively Piazza Bellini, it offers modern sanity in the
city center (air-con, elevator, Via Santa Maria di Constantinopoli
101, Metro: Dante, tel. 081-451-732, www.hotelpiazzabellini.com,
info@hotelpiazzabellini.com).

$$$ Chiaja Hotel de Charme, with the same owner as the

Sleep Code

Hotels are classified based on the average price of a standard double room with breakfast in high season.

$$$$	**Splurge:** Most rooms over €170
$$$	**Pricier:** €130-170
$$	**Moderate:** €90-130
$	**Budget:** €50-90
¢	**Backpacker:** Under €50
RS%	**Rick Steves discount**

Unless otherwise noted, credit cards are accepted, hotel staff speak basic English, and free Wi-Fi is available. Comparison-shop by checking prices at several hotels (on each hotel's own website, on a booking site, or by email). For the best deal, *book directly with the hotel.* Ask for a discount if paying in cash; if the listing includes **RS%,** request a Rick Steves discount.

Decumani (listed earlier), rents 33 rooms on the Via Chiaia pedestrian shopping drag near Piazza del Plebiscito. The building has a fascinating history. Part of it was the residence of a marquis, and the rest was one of Naples' most famous brothels (some view rooms, air-con, elevator, Via Chiaia 216, first floor, Metro: Toledo, tel. 081-415-555, www.hotelchiaia.it, info@hotelchiaia.it, Pietro Fusella).

$$$ Art Resort Galleria Umberto has 15 rooms in two different buildings inside the Umberto I shopping gallery at the bottom of Via Toledo, just off Piazza del Plebiscito. This genteel-feeling place gilds the lily, with an aristocratic setting and decor but older bathrooms. Consider paying €20 extra for a room overlooking the gallery (air-con, elevator, Galleria Umberto 83, fourth floor—ask at booth for coin to operate elevator if needed, Metro: Toledo, tel. 081-497-6224, www.artresortgalleriaumberto.it, info@artresortgalleriaumberto.it).

$$$ Hotel Il Convento, with 14 small but comfortable rooms with balconies, is a good choice for those who want to sleep in the gnarly, tight tangle of lanes called the Spanish Quarter—quintessential Naples. While the neighborhood can feel off-putting after dark, it's not especially unsafe. You're only a couple of short blocks off the main Via Toledo drag, and heavy-duty windows help block out some—but not all—of the scooter noise and church bells. A rare haven in this characteristic corner of town, it's in all the guidebooks (family rooms, air-con, elevator; Via Speranzella 137A, Metro: Toledo—from just below Banco di Napoli entrance, walk two blocks up Via Tre Re a Toledo; tel. 081-403-977, www. hotelilconvento.com, info@hotelilconvento.com).

AT THE TRAIN STATION

These hotels are less convenient for sightseeing and dining, and the neighborhood gets dodgy as you move away from the station. But they're handy for train travelers, practical for a quick stay, and less expensive.

$$ Hotel Stelle has 38 sterile, identical, newly remodeled rooms with modern furnishings. It feels very secure, and a back entrance leads directly into the train station (air-con, elevator, Corso Meridionale 60, exit station near track 5, tel. 081-1889-3090, www.stellehotel.com, info@stellehotel.com).

$ Grand Hotel Europa, across the seedy street right next to the station, has 89 decent rooms whimsically decorated with not-quite-right reproductions of famous paintings. Though a bit worn, the hotel is a decent value, and its 1970s-era tackiness (including the Kool-Aid and canned fruit at breakfast) is good for a laugh (RS%, family rooms, air-con, elevator, restaurant, Corso Meridionale 14, across street from station's north exit near track 5, tel. 081-267-511, www.grandhoteleuropa.com, info@grandhoteleuropa.com).

$$ Ibis Styles Napoli Garibaldi, with 88 rooms, offers chain predictability and a bright, youthful color scheme a three-minute walk from the station (breakfast optional, air-con, elevator, pay parking; Via Giuseppe Ricciardi 33, exit station onto Piazza Garibaldi, then take second left onto Via G. Ricciardi; tel. 081-690-8111, www.ibis.com, h3243@accor.com).

Eating in Naples

CHEAP AND FAMOUS PIZZA

Naples is the birthplace of pizza. Its pizzerias bake just the right combination of fresh dough (soft and chewy, as opposed to Roman-

style, which is thin and crispy), mozzarella, and tomatoes in traditional wood-burning ovens. You can head for the famous, venerable places (I've listed five below), but these can have long lines stretching out the door, and half-hour waits for a table. If you want to skip the hassle, just ask your hotel for directions to the neighborhood pizzeria. An average one-person pie (usually the only size available) costs €4-8; most places offer both take-out and eat-in, and pizza is often the only thing on the menu.

Near the Station

These two pizzerias—the most famous—are both a few long blocks

---

Restaurant Price Code

I've assigned each eatery a price category, based on the average cost of a typical main course (pasta or *secondi*). Drinks, desserts, and splurge items (steak and seafood) can raise the price considerably.

$$$$ **Splurge:** Most main courses over €20
$$$ **Pricier:** €15-20
$$ **Moderate:** €10-15
$ **Budget:** Under €10

In Italy, pizza by the slice and other takeout food is **$**; a basic trattoria or sit-down pizzeria is **$$**; a casual but more upscale restaurant is **$$$**; and a swanky splurge is **$$$$**.

---

from the train station, and at the end of my self-guided Naples walk.

$ Antica Pizzeria da Michele is for pizza purists. Filled with locals (and tourists), it serves just two varieties: *margherita* (tomato sauce and mozzarella) and *marinara* (tomato sauce, oregano, and garlic, no cheese). Come early to sit and watch the pizza artists in action. A pizza with beer costs around €7. As this place is often jammed with a long line, arrive early or late to get a seat. If there's a mob, head inside to get a number. If it's just too crowded to wait, the less-exceptional Pizzeria Trianon (described next) generally has room (Mon-Sat 10:30-24:00, closed Sun; look for the vertical red *Antica Pizzeria* sign at the intersection of Via Pietro Colletta and Via Cesare Sersale at #1; tel. 081-553-9204).

$ Pizzeria Trianon, across the street and left a few doors, has been da Michele's archrival since 1923. It offers more choices, higher prices (€5-8, plus a 15 percent service charge), air-conditioning, and a cozier atmosphere. For less chaos, head upstairs. While waiting for your meal, you can survey the transformation of a humble wad of dough into a smoldering, bubbly feast in their entryway pizza kitchen (daily 11:00-15:30 & 19:00-23:00, Via Pietro Colletta 42, tel. 081-553-9426).

On Via dei Tribunali

This street, which runs a couple of blocks north of Spaccanapoli, is home to several pizzerias that are more convenient to sightseeing. Three in particular are on all the "best pizza in Naples" lists...as you'll learn the hard way if you show up at peak mealtimes, when huge mobs of locals crowd outside the front door waiting for a table.

$$ Gino Sorbillo is a local favorite (Mon-Sat 12:00-15:30 & 19:00-24:00, closed Sun, Via dei Tribunali 32—don't confuse this with his relatives' similarly named places at #35 and #37 on the same street, tel. 081-446-643).

NAPLES

Naples Hotels & Restaurants

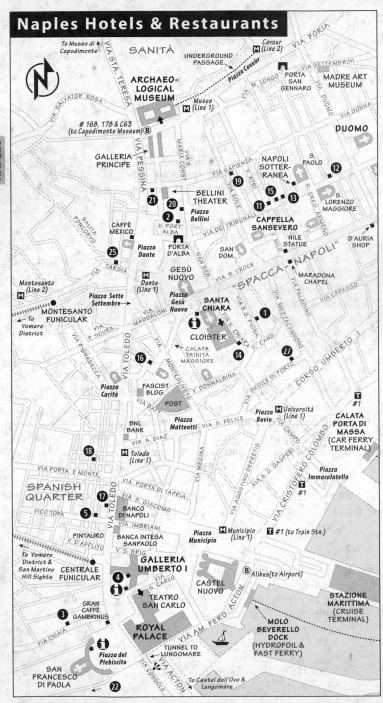

To Museo di
Capodimonte

SANITÀ

Cavour
(Line 2)

VIA FORIA

UNDERGROUND
PASSAGE

Piazza Cavour

VIA M. LONGO

Porta
San
Gennaro

VIA SETTEMBRINI

MADRE ART
MUSEUM

VIA STA. TERESA

VIA SALVATOR ROSA

ARCHAEO-
LOGICAL
MUSEUM

Museo
(Line 1)

VIA DUOMO

VIA DONNA

DUOMO

#16B, 17B & C63
(to Capodimonte Museum)

GALLERIA
PRINCIPE

VIA PESSINA

VIA S. MARIA CONST.

VIA SAPIENZA

Napoli
Sotter-
ranea

S.
PAOLO

S.
GREG.
ARMENO

S.
LORENZO
MAGGIORE

D'AURIA
SHOP

SALITA PONCORVO

Caffè
Mexico

BELLINI
THEATER

Piazza
Bellini

V. PORT'
ALBA

Porta
D'Alba

VIA DEI TRIBUNALI

CAPPELLA
SANSEVERO

NILE
STATUE

Piazza
Dante

Dante
(Line 1)

VIA TARSIA

Montesanto
(Line 2)

MONTESANTO
FUNICULAR

To
Vomero
District

Piazza Sette
Settembre

Gesù
Nuovo

Piazza
Gesù
Nuovo

VIA MADDALONI

VIA P. SCURA

VIA TOLEDO

VIA MONTEOLIVETO

SAN
DOM.

VIA B. CROCE

"SPACCA-NAPOLI"

MARADONA
CHAPEL

VIA PALADINO

VIA CAPASSO

SANTA
CHIARA

CLOISTER

VIA S. CHIARA

VIA S. PIGNA

CALATA
TRINITÀ
MAGGIORE

V. DONNALBINA

VIA SEDILE DI PORTO

CORSO UMBERTO I

Piazza
Carità

FASCIST
BLDG.

POST

VIA BATT.

Piazza
Matteotti

BNL
BANK

VIA A. DIAZ

Toledo
(Line 1)

VIA S. FELICE

VIA MEDINA

Piazza
Bovio

Università
(Line 1)

VIA CAMPO

CALATA
PORTA DI
MASSA
(CAR FERRY
TERMINAL)

Piazza
Immacolatella

#1

VIA PORTA E MONTE

SPANISH
QUARTER

VICO TOFA

VIA PORTA DI TAPPIA

VIA S. GIACOMO

Banco
DI NAPOLI

VIA IMBRIANI

Banca Intesa
Sanpaolo

V. S. BRIG.

PINTAURO

V. D'AFFLITO

CENTRALE
FUNICULAR

To Vomero
District &
San Martino
Hill Sights

VIA TOLEDO

VIA AGOSTINO DEPRETIS

VIA A. D. GASPERI

VIA CRISTOFORO COLOMBO

#1

Piazza
Municipio

Municipio
(Line 1)

#1 (to Train Stn.)

GALLERIA
UMBERTO I

V. S. CARLO

TEATRO
SAN CARLO

CASTEL
NUOVO

Alibus (to Airport)

VIA AM. FERD. ACTON

STAZIONE
MARITTIMA
(CRUISE
TERMINAL)

GRAN
CAFFÈ
GAMBRINUS

VIA CHIAIA

ROYAL
PALACE

Piazza del
Plebiscito

SAN
FRANCESCO
DI PAOLA

TUNNEL TO
LUNGOMARE

VIA ACTON

VIA CONSOLE

MOLO
BEVERELLO
DOCK
(HYDROFOIL &
FAST FERRY)

To Castel dell'Ovo &
Lungomare

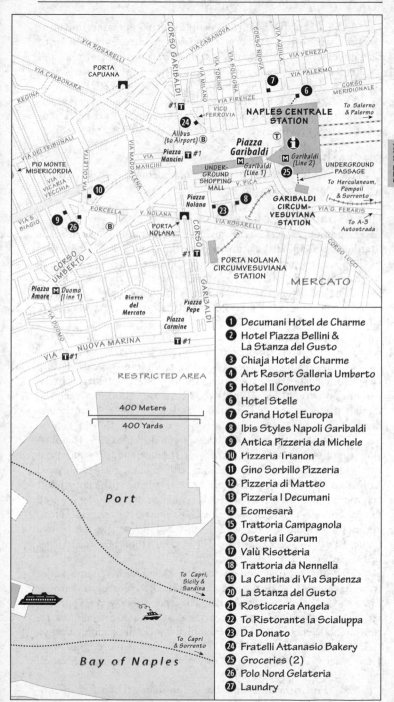

1 Decumani Hotel de Charme

2 Hotel Piazza Bellini & La Stanza del Gusto

3 Chiaja Hotel de Charme

4 Art Resort Galleria Umberto

5 Hotel Il Convento

6 Hotel Stelle

7 Grand Hotel Europa

8 Ibis Styles Napoli Garibaldi

9 Antica Pizzeria da Michele

10 Pizzeria Trianon

11 Gino Sorbillo Pizzeria

12 Pizzeria di Matteo

13 Pizzeria I Decumani

14 Ecomesarà

15 Trattoria Campagnola

16 Osteria il Garum

17 Valù Risotteria

18 Trattoria da Nennella

19 La Cantina di Via Sapienza

20 La Stanza del Gusto

21 Rosticceria Angela

22 To Ristorante la Scialuppa

23 Da Donato

24 Fratelli Attanasio Bakery

25 Groceries (2)

26 Polo Nord Gelateria

27 Laundry

At **$$ Pizzeria di Matteo,** people waiting out front line up at the little window to snack on deep-fried goodies—*arancini* (with rice, gooey cheese, peas, and sausage), *frittatine* (balls of mac and cheese plus sausage), and *crocché* (croquettes)—for €1 apiece (sometimes closed Sun, Via dei Tribunali 94, tel. 081-455-262).

$$ Pizzeria I Decumani has a bit nicer seating and is perhaps less chaotic (closed Mon, on Piazza San Gaetano at Via dei Tribunali 61, takeout window at #58, tel. 081-557-1309).

RESTAURANTS

If you want a full meal rather than a pizza, consider these options, which I've organized by neighborhood.

Near Spaccanapoli and Via Toledo

$$$ Ecomesarà serves up quality Neapolitan and *meridionale* (southern Italian) dishes, abiding by the Slow Food ethic, in a modern setting just below the Santa Chiara cloister, a long block south of Spaccanapoli. The atmosphere is mellow, modern, and international. Cristiano and his staff are happy to explain the menu (Tue-Sun 13:00-15:00 & 20:00-23:30, closed Mon, Via Santa Chiara 49, tel. 081-1925-9353).

$ Trattoria Campagnola is a classic family place with a daily home-cooking-style chalkboard menu on the back wall, mama busy cooking in the back, and wine on tap. Here you can venture away from pastas, be experimental with a series of local dishes, and not go wrong (daily 12:00-16:00 & 19:00-23:00, between the famous pizzerias at Via Tribunali 47, tel. 081-459-034 but no reservations).

$$ Osteria il Garum is great if you'd like to eat on a classic Neapolitan square. It's named for the ancient fish sauce that was widely used in Roman cooking. These days, mild-mannered Luigi and his staff inject their pricey local cuisine with centuries of tradition, served in a cozy split-level cellar or outside on a covered terrace facing a neighborhood church. It's just between Via Toledo and Spaccanapoli, a short walk from the Church of Gesù Nuovo (daily 12:00-15:30 & 19:00-23:30, Piazza Monteoliveto 2A, tel. 081-542-3228).

$$ Valù, with a modern red-and-black color scheme and a wine-bar vibe, sits sane and romantic in the colorful and rowdy Spanish Quarter just a block off Via Toledo. This *risotteria* specializes in risotto (which is not a local dish), serving 20 different variations. Choose between the interior or a few outdoor tables along a tight alley (Mon-Sat 12:30-16:00 & 19:00-24:00, closed Sun, Vico Lungo del Gelso 80, up alley directly opposite Banco di Napoli entrance, tel. 081-038-1139).

$$ Trattoria da Nennella is fun-loving chaos, with red-shirted waiters barking orders, a small festival anytime someone puts a tip in the bucket, and the fruit course served in plastic bidets. There's one price—€12 per person—and you choose three courses plus a fruit. House wine and water is served in tiny plastic cups, the crowd is ready for fun, and the food's good. It's buried in the Spanish Quarter. You can sit indoors or on a cobbled terrace under a trellis (Mon-Sat 12:00-15:00 & 19:15-23:15, closed Sun, leave Via Toledo a block down from the BNL bank and walk up Vico del Teatro Nuovo three blocks to the corner, Vico Lungo Teatro Nuovo 103, tel. 081-414-338 but no reservations).

$ La Cantina di Via Sapienza is a lunch-only hole-in-the-wall, serving up traditional Neapolitan fare in an interior that feels like a neighborhood joint (but has also been discovered by tourists). It's a block north of the congested, pizzeria-packed Via dei Tribunali, and a good alternative if those places are just too crowded and your heart isn't set on pizza (Mon-Sat for lunch only, closed Sun, Via Sapienza 40, tel. 081-459-078).

Near the Archaeological Museum

$$ La Stanza del Gusto, two blocks downhill from the museum, tackles food creatively and injects crusty Naples with a little modern color and irreverence. The downstairs is casual, trendy, and playful, while the upstairs is more refined yet still polka-dotted (weekday lunch specials, Tue-Sat 12:00-15:30 & 19:30-23:30, closed Sun-Mon, Via Santa Maria di Constantinopoli 100, tel. 081-401-578).

$ Rosticceria Angela is a *tavola calda* with hot ready-to-eat dishes (€3-5) and a coffee bar, run by a team of older gentlemen. Pricing is honest and there's simple, peaceful, air-conditioned indoor seating. Next door (same name, different management) is a tiny meat, cheese, and bread shop with all you need for a cheap meal to go (*rosticceria* open Mon-Sat 7:00-21:00, closed Sun, 3 blocks below museum at Via Conte di Ruvo 21, between Via Pessina and Via Bellini, tel. 081-033-2928).

A Romantic Splurge on the Harbor

$$$ Ristorante la Scialuppa ("The Rowboat") is a great bet for a fine local meal on the harbor. Located in the romantic Santa Lucia district, you'll walk across the causeway to the Castel dell'Ovo in the fisherman's quarter (the castle on the island) just off Via Partenope. They boast fine indoor and outdoor seating, attentive waitstaff, a wonderful assortment of *antipasti*, great seafood, and predictably high prices. Reservations are smart (Tue-Sun 12:30-15:00 & 19:30-24:00, closed Mon, Piazzetta Marinari 5, tel. 081-764-5333, www.ristorantelascialuppa.net).

Getting Around the Region

To connect Naples, Sorrento, and the Amalfi Coast, you can travel on land by train, bus, and taxi. Whenever possible, consider taking a boat—it's faster, cooler, and more scenic, and you can take coastline photos that you can't get from land. For specifics, check the "Connections" sections of each chapter. Confirm times and prices locally.

By Circumvesuviana Train: This useful narrow-gauge commuter train—popular with locals, tourists, and pickpockets—links Naples, Herculaneum, Pompeii, and Sorrento. The most important Circumvesuviana station in Naples (called "Garibaldi") is underneath Naples' Centrale Station. To find it, follow the *Circumvesuviana* signs downstairs and down the corridor to the Circumvesuviana ticket windows and turnstiles (no self-service ticket machines—line up). Insert your ticket at the turnstiles and head down another level to the platforms.

The Circumvesuviana is covered by the Campania ArteCard (see page 942), but not by rail passes. If you're heading to **Pompeii** or **Herculaneum,** take any Circumvesuviana train marked *Sorrento*—they all stop at both places (usually depart from platform 3). Sorrento-bound trains depart twice hourly, and take about 20 minutes to reach Ercolano Scavi (for the Herculaneum ruins, €2 one-way), 40 minutes to reach Pompei Scavi-Villa dei Misteri (for the Pompeii ruins, €2.60 one-way), and 70 minutes to reach **Sorrento,** the end of the line (€3.60 one-way). Express trains to Sorrento marked *DD* (6/day) reach Sorrento 15 minutes sooner (and also stop at Herculaneum and Pompeii). For schedules, see www.eavsrl.it.

On the platform, double-check with a local that the train goes to Sorrento, as the Circumvesuviana has several lines that branch out to other destinations. When returning to Naples on the Circumvesuviana, get off at the next-to-the-last station, Garibaldi (Centrale Station is just up the escalator).

You may save a few pennies with a "TIC" ticket, which covers the Circumvesuviana plus public transport to and from the train station in Naples (for example, Pompeii to Napoli Centrale, then by Metro to your hotel).

By Regular Train: The national rail network is useful only if you need to get to Salerno (for boats and buses to Amalfi) or Paestum—direct trains run to both from Naples.

By Bus: Crowded SITA buses are most useful for traversing the popular Amalfi Coast; see "Getting Around the Amalfi Coast—By Bus" on page 1053.

By Taxi: For €100, you can take a 30-mile taxi ride from Naples directly to your Sorrento hotel (ask the drive for the non-metered *tariffa predeterminata*). You can hire a cab on Capri for

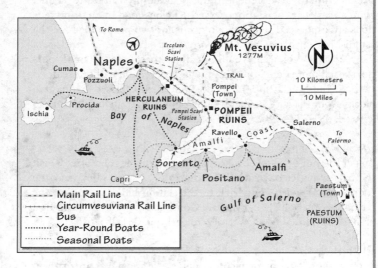

Main Rail Line
Circumvesuviana Rail Line
Bus
Year-Round Boats
Seasonal Boats

about €70/hour. Taxis on the Amalfi Coast are generally expensive, and more than willing to overcharge you, but they can be convenient, especially with a larger group. See "Getting Around the Amalfi Coast—By Taxi" on page 1054.

By Boat: Major companies include Caremar (www.caremar.it), SNAV (www.snav.it), Gescab (a.k.a. NLG Jet, www.gescab.it), Navigazione Libera del Golfo (www.navlib.it), Alilauro (www.alilauro.it), Travelmar (www.travelmar.it), and Alicost (www.alicost.it). Each company has different destinations and prices; some compete for the same trips. Some lines (like Sorrento-Capri) run all year; others (on the Amalfi Coast, for example) only in summer. Trips can be cancelled in bad weather. Faster watercraft cost a little more than slow car ferries. A hydrofoil, sometimes called a "jet boat," skims between Naples and Sorrento—it's swifter, safer from pickpockets, more scenic, and more expensive than the train.

For schedules, check online (the best collection is at www.capritourism.com; click "Shipping Timetable"), or ask at any TI, or at Naples' Molo Beverello boat dock. Most boats charge €2 or so for luggage. If you plan to arrive at and leave a destination by boat, note the return times—the last boat usually leaves before 19:00.

The preset price for a taxi from Naples' Centrale train station to its port (Molo Beverello) is €11, or you can just hop on tram #1 from the far end of the big square in front of the station.

Near the Station

$$ Da Donato, an excellent, traditional, family-run trattoria on a glum street near the station, serves delicious food in an unpretentious atmosphere. The best approach is for two people to share the astonishing antipasti sampler—*degustazione "fantasia" della Casa Terra e Mare*—for €25. You'll get more than a dozen small portions, each more delicious than the last. A version without seafood is €15 (Tue-Sun 12:30-14:30 & 19:30-22:00, closed Mon, two blocks from Piazza Garibaldi—turn down Via Silvio Spaventa to #39, tel. 081-287-828).

PASTRY

To get the full overview of Neapolitan pastries at good prices, visit the bakery outlet of **Fratelli Attanasio** on a small alley near the train station—with your back to the station building, it's off the far right corner of the big square. Come early if possible (Tue-Sun 6:30-19:30, closed Mon, Vico Ferrovia 1, tel. 081-285-675).

PICNICS

A good supermarket for picnic supplies is **Sapori & Dintorni,** in the train station complex (Mon-Sat 8:00-20:30, Sun 8:00-15:00, enter from outside, by bookstore). By Piazza Dante is a small **Superò** that's convenient to Via Toledo hotel listings (corner of Via Tarsia and Vico San Domenico Soriano, Mon-Sat 8:30-20:30, Sun 8:30-14:00).

Naples Connections

From Naples by Boat to: Sorrento (6/day, more in summer, departs roughly every 2 hours starting at 9:00, few or no boats on winter weekends, leaves from Molo Beverello, 35 minutes), **Capri** (roughly hourly, more in summer, hydrofoil: 45 minutes from Molo Beverello; ferries: 50-80 minutes from Calata Porta di Massa). Sometimes there are also seasonal boats to **Positano** and **Amalfi,** on the Amalfi Coast—ask. For a map showing boat connections, see page 1014. For timetables, visit www.capritourism.com and click "Shipping Timetable."

By Train to: Rome (at least 2/hour, 70 minutes on Frecciarossa express trains; 2 hours on cheaper Intercity trains), **Civitavecchia** (at least hourly, 3 hours, most change in Rome), **Florence** (1-2/hour, 3 hours), **Salerno** (at least hourly, 35-45 minutes, change in Salerno for bus or boat to Amalfi; best to take "regionale" trains—Intercity and Freccia express trains are much more expensive but no faster; also avoid slower "Metropolitana" trains that leave from the same platforms as Metro's line 2), **Paestum** (10/day, 1.5 hours, direction: Sapri), **Brindisi** (4/day, 5-6 hours, change in Caserta;

from Brindisi, ferries sail to Greece), **Milan** (2/hour, 4-5 hours), **Venice** (almost hourly, 5.5 hours, some change in Bologna or Rome), **Palermo** (2/day direct, 9.5 hours, also an overnight train). Any train listed on the schedule as leaving Napoli PG or Napoli-Garibaldi departs not from Napoli Centrale, but from the adjacent Garibaldi Station.

Note that the departures listed above are Trenitalia connections; Italo offers additional high-speed options to **Rome, Salerno, Florence, Milan,** and **Venice** (www.italotreno.it).

By Circumvesuviana Train: See the "Getting Around the Region" sidebar for information on getting to Herculaneum, Pompeii, and Sorrento.

To Pompeii: To visit the ancient site of Pompeii, don't use national train connections to the city of Pompei (which is far from the site). Instead, ride the Circumvesuviana train, which takes you to the Pompei Scavi-Villa dei Misteri stop near the actual site.

POMPEII & NEARBY

Pompeii • Herculaneum • Vesuvius

Stopped in their tracks by the eruption of Mount Vesuvius in A.D. 79, Pompeii and Herculaneum offer the best look anywhere at what life in Rome must have been like around 2,000 years ago. These two cities of well-preserved ruins are yours to explore. Of the two sites, Pompeii is grander, while Herculaneum is smaller, more intimate, and more intact; both are easily reached from Naples on the Circumvesuviana commuter train (for details, see "Getting Around the Region" on page 986). Vesuvius, still smoldering ominously, rises up on the horizon. It last erupted in 1944, and is still an active volcano. Buses from the train stations at Herculaneum or Pompeii drop you a half-hour hike below the crater rim.

Pompeii

A once-thriving commercial port of 20,000, Pompeii (worth ▲▲▲) grew from Greek and Etruscan roots to become an important Roman city. Then, on August 24, A.D. 79, everything changed. Vesuvius erupted and began to bury the city under 30 feet of hot volcanic ash. For the archaeologists who excavated it centuries later, this was a shake-and-bake windfall, teaching them

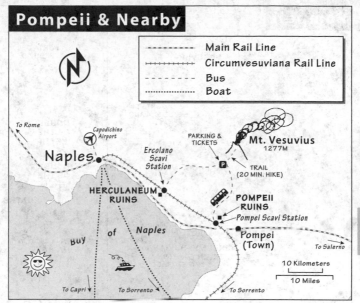

Pompeii & Nearby

Main Rail Line
Circumvesuviana Rail Line
Bus
Boat

To Rome
Capodichino Airport
Naples
Ercolano Scavi Station
PARKING & TICKETS
Mt. Vesuvius 1277M
TRAIL (20 MIN. HIKE)
HERCULANEUM RUINS
POMPEII RUINS
Pompei Scavi Station
Bay of Naples
Pompei (Town)
To Salerno
To Capri
To Sorrento
To Sorrento
10 Kilometers
10 Miles

volumes about daily Roman life. Pompeii was accidentally redis-covered in 1599; excavations began in 1748.

GETTING TO POMPEII

By Train: Pompeii is roughly midway between Naples and Sor-rento on the Circumvesuviana train line (2/hour, 40 minutes from Naples, 30 minutes from Sorrento, either trip costs about €2.60 one-way, not covered by rail passes). Get off at the Pompei Scavi-Villa dei Misteri stop; from Naples, it's the stop after Torre Annun-ziata. The DD express trains (6/day) bypass several stations but do stop at Pompei Scavi, shaving 10 minutes off the trip from Naples. From the Pompei Scavi train station, it's just a two-minute walk to the Porta Marina entrance: Turn right and walk down the road about a block to the entrance (on your left).

Pompei vs. Pompei Scavi: Make sure you're taking the Cir-cumvesuviana commuter train to Pompei Scavi (*scavi* means "ex-cavations"), the station right next to the ancient site. Pompei is the name of a separate train station on the main national rail line that's a long, dull walk from the ruins. It serves the ugly modern city of Pompei (always with one "i"). Even when coming from Rome, it's better to transfer at Naples' Centrale Station to the Circumvesuvi-ana for Pompei Scavi than to take the train straight to the Pompei city station and walk from there.

By Car: Parking is available at Camping Zeus, next to the Pompei Scavi train station (€2.50/hour, €10/12 hours, 10 percent

POMPEII & NEARBY

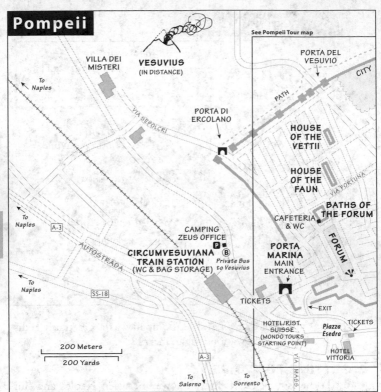

Pompeii

See Pompeii Tour map

VESUVIUS (IN DISTANCE)

VILLA DEI MISTERI

PORTA DEL VESUVIO

CITY

To Naples

PATH

VIA SEPOLCRI

PORTA DI ERCOLANO

HOUSE OF THE VETTII

HOUSE OF THE FAUN

VIA FORTUNA

To Naples

A-3

BATHS OF THE FORUM

CAFETERIA & WC

AUTOSTRADA

CAMPING ZEUS OFFICE

CIRCUMVESUVIANA TRAIN STATION (WC & BAG STORAGE)

Private Bus to Vesuvius

PORTA MARINA MAIN ENTRANCE

FORUM

To Naples

SS-18

TICKETS

EXIT

To Naples

200 Meters
200 Yards

HOTEL/RIST. SUISSE (MONDO TOURS STARTING POINT)

Piazza Esedra

TICKETS

A-3

VIA MASS.

HOTEL VITTORIA

To Salerno

To Sorrento

discount with this book); several other campgrounds/parking lots are nearby.

ORIENTATION TO POMPEII

Cost: €12, possibly more during special exhibits, free first Sun of each month, €21 combo-ticket includes Herculaneum (valid 3 consecutive days). If you plan to eat or sightsee outside of the archaeological site, ask for an entrance/exit bracelet that allows you reenter the site up to three times on the same day. Also consider the Campania ArteCard (see page 942) if visiting other sights in the region.

Hours: Daily April-Oct 9:00-19:30, Nov-March 8:30-17:00, last entry 1.5 hours before closing.

Closures: Some buildings and streets are bound to be closed for restoration when you visit. Pompeii's best-preserved home—the House of the Vettii—has been completely blocked off for years; unfortunately, it's unlikely to reopen in time for your visit. If you get totally derailed, just use the map and numbers to find your way.

Crowd-Beating Tip: Up to 15,000 visitors are allowed on the first

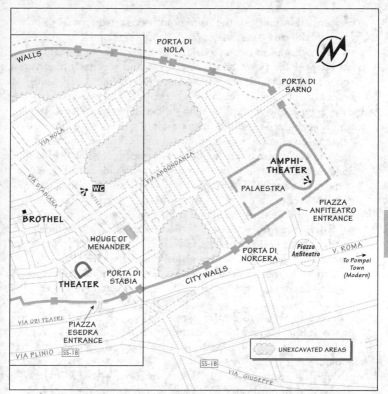

Sun of the month when it's free—and packed. I'd make a point to avoid Pompeii on that day.

Information: Ignore the "info point" kiosk at the station, which is a private agency selling tours. Once at the site, pick up the free, helpful map and booklet at the entrance (ask for it when you buy your ticket, or check at the info window to the left of the WCs—the maps aren't available within the walls of Pompeii). Tel. 081-857-5347, www.pompeiisites.org.

The bookshop sells a couple of books with plastic overlays that allow you to re-create Pompeii from the ruins (€16; if you buy from a street vendor, pay no more than that).

Tours: My **self-guided tour** in this chapter covers the basics and provides a good framework for exploring the site on your own, as does my ∩ free Pompeii audio tour.

For a guided tour, your best bet is to join the Mondo Guide tours for Rick Steves readers (€15, doesn't include €12 Pompeii entry, daily at 11:00, reservations required; meet at Hotel/Ristorante Suisse, just down the hill from the Porta Marina entrance; see page 948). Stepping off the train, you'll be accosted by touts for the "info point" kiosk, which sells €12 tours that depart whenever enough people sign up.

Private guides (around €110/2 hours) of varying quality cluster near the ticket booth at the site and may try to herd you into a group with other travelers, which is fine as long as it makes the price more reasonable for you. For a better experience, reserve one of the following guides in advance and mention this book: **Antonio Somma** mainly specializes in Pompeii and gives good, straightforward tours (€120/2 hours for up to 6 people, also offers regional transport, mobile 393-406-3824, tel. 081-850-1992, www.tourspompeiiguide.com, info@pompeitour.com). **Gaetano Manfredi** is pricey but brings energy and theatricality to his tours (€170/2 hours for up to 4 people, www.pompeiitourguide.com, gaetanoguide@hotmail.it). **Silvia Braggio** (mobile 347-643-2307, www.silviaguide.it, silvia@silviaguide.it) and the Naples-based guides recommended on page 947 can also guide you at Pompeii. Parents, note that the ancient brothel and its sexually explicit frescoes are included on tours; let your guide know if you'd rather skip that stop.

Audioguides are available from a kiosk near the ticket booth at the Porta Marina entrance (€6.50, €10 for 2, ID required), but they offer basically the same info as your free booklet.

Length of This Tour: Allow two hours, or three if you visit the theater and amphitheater. With less time, focus on the Forum, Baths of the Forum, House of the Faun, and brothel.

Baggage Check: Use the free baggage check near the turnstiles at the site entrance (just yards from the station). The train station also offers pay luggage storage (downstairs, by the WC).

Services: There's a pay WC at the train station. The Pompeii site has three WCs—one near the entrance, one in the cafeteria, and another near the end of this tour, uphill from the theaters.

Eating: The **$ Ciao cafeteria** within the site serves good sandwiches, pizza, and pasta. **$ Bar Sgambati,** the café/restaurant in the train station, has air-conditioning, Wi-Fi, and reasonably priced pastas and pizzas (tel. 081-861-0966). Your cheapest bet may be to bring your own food for a discreet picnic.

Starring: Roofless (collapsed) but otherwise intact Roman buildings, plaster casts of hapless victims, a few erotic frescoes, and the dawning realization that these ancient people were not that different from us.

BACKGROUND

Pompeii, founded in 600 B.C., eventually became a booming Roman trading city. Not rich, not poor, it was middle class—a

perfect example of typical Roman life. Most streets would have been lined with stalls and jammed with customers from sunup to sundown. Chariots vied with shoppers for street space. Two thousand years ago, Rome controlled the entire Mediterranean—making it a kind of free-trade zone—and Pompeii was a central and bustling port.

There were no posh neighborhoods in Pompeii. Rich and poor mixed it up as elegant houses existed side by side with simple homes. While nearby Herculaneum would have been a classier place to live (traffic-free streets, fancier houses, far better drainage), Pompeii was the place for action and shopping. It served an estimated 20,000 residents with more than 40 bakeries, 30 brothels, and 130 bars, restaurants, and hotels. With most of its buildings covered by brilliant white ground-marble stucco, Pompeii in A.D. 79 was an impressive town.

As you tour Pompeii, remember that its best art is in the Archaeological Museum in Naples (described in the previous chapter).

◎ SELF-GUIDED TOUR
• *Just past the ticket-taker, start your approach up to the...*

❶ Porta Marina

The city of Pompeii was born on the hill ahead of you. This was the original town gate. Before Vesuvius blew and filled in the harbor, the sea came nearly to here. Notice the two openings in the gate (ahead, up the ramp). Both were left open by day to admit major traffic. At night, the larger one was closed for better security.

• *Pass through the Porta Marina and continue up to the top of the street, pausing at the three large stepping-stones in the middle.*

❷ Pompeii's Streets
Every day, Pompeiians flooded the streets with gushing water to clean them. These stepping-stones let pedestrians cross without getting their sandals wet. Chariots traveling in either direction could straddle the stones (all had standard-size axles). A single stepping-stone in a road means it was a one-way street, a pair indi-

cates an ordinary two-way, and three (like this) signifies a major thoroughfare. The basalt stones are the original Roman pavement. The sidewalks (elevated to hide the plumbing) were paved with bits of broken pots (an ancient form of recycling) and studded with reflective bits of white marble. These "cats' eyes" helped people get around after dark, either by moonlight or with the help of lamps.

• *Continue straight ahead, don your mental toga, and enter the city as the Romans once did. The road opens up into the spacious main square: the Forum. Stand at the right end of this rectangular space and look toward Mount Vesuvius.*

❸ The Forum (Foro)

Pompeii's commercial, religious, and political center stands at the intersection of the city's two main streets. While it's the most ruined part of Pompeii, it's grand nonetheless. Picture the piazza surrounded by two-story buildings on all sides. The pedestals that line the square once held statues (now safely displayed in the museum in Naples). In Pompeii's heyday, its citizens gathered here in the main square to shop, talk politics, and socialize. Business took place in the important buildings that lined the piazza.

The Forum was dominated by the **Temple of Jupiter,** at the far end (marked by a half-dozen ruined columns atop a stair-step base). Jupiter was the supreme god of the Roman pantheon—you might be able to make out his little white marble head at the center-rear of the temple. To the left of the temple is a fenced-off area, the **Forum granary,** where many artifacts from Pompeii are stored.

At the near end of the Forum (behind where you're standing) is the **curia,** or city hall. Like many Roman buildings, it was built with brick and mortar, then covered with marble walls and floors. To your left (as you face Vesuvius and the Temple of Jupiter) is the **basilica,** or courthouse.

Since Pompeii was a pretty typical Roman town, it has the same layout and components that you'll find in any Roman city—main square, curia, basilica, temples, axis of roads, and so on. All power converged at the Forum: religious (the temple), political (the curia), judicial (the basilica), and commercial (this piazza was the

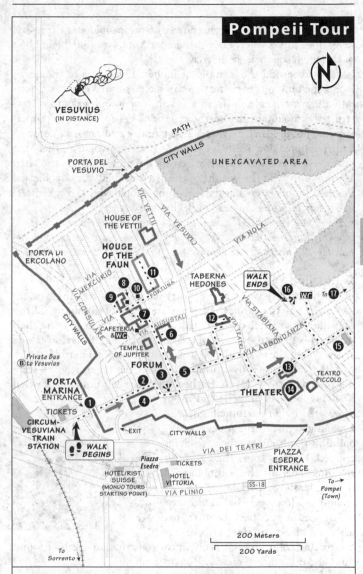

Pompeii Tour

1. Porta Marina
2. Pompeii's Streets
3. Forum
4. Basilica
5. Via Abbondanza
6. Fish & Produce Market; Plaster Casts of Victims
7. Baths of the Forum
8. Fast-Food Joint
9. House of the Tragic Poet
10. Aqueduct Arch
11. House of the Faun
12. Brothel
13. Temple of Isis
14. Theater
15. House of Menander
16. Viewpoint
17. To Amphitheater

main marketplace). Even the power of the people was expressed here, since this is where they gathered to vote. Imagine the hubbub of this town square in its heyday.

Look beyond the Temple of Jupiter. Five miles to the north looms the ominous backstory to this site: **Mount Vesuvius.** Mentally draw a triangle up from the two remaining peaks to reconstruct the mountain before the eruption. When it blew, Pompeiians had no idea that they were living under a volcano, as Vesuvius hadn't erupted for 1,200 years. Imagine the wonder—then the horror—as a column of pulverized rock roared upward, and then ash began to fall. The weight of the ash and small rocks collapsed Pompeii's roofs later that day, crushing people who had taken refuge inside buildings instead of fleeing the city.

• *As you face Vesuvius, the basilica is to your left, lined with stumps of columns. Backtrack to the three stepping stones we saw earlier to go inside. (If it's fenced off, peer through the gate.)*

❹ Basilica

Pompeii's basilica was a first-century palace of justice. This ancient law court has the same floor plan later adopted by many Christian churches (which are also called basilicas). The big central hall (or nave) is flanked by rows of columns marking off narrower side aisles. Along the side walls are traces of the original marble.

The columns—now stumps all about the same height—were not ruined by the volcano. Rather, they were left unfinished when Vesuvius blew. Pompeii had been devastated by an earthquake in A.D. 62, and was just in the process of rebuilding the basilica when Vesuvius erupted, 17 years later. The half-built columns show off the technology of the day. Uniform bricks were stacked around a cylindrical core. Once finished, they would have been coated with marble dust stucco to simulate marble columns—an economical construction method found throughout Pompeii (and the Roman Empire).

Besides the earthquake and the eruption, Pompeii's buildings have suffered other ravages over the years, including Spanish plunderers (c. 1800), 19th-century souvenir hunters, WWII bombs, wild vegetation, another earthquake in 1980, and modern neglect. The fact that the entire city was covered by the eruption of A.D. 79 actually helped preserve it, saving it from the sixth-century barbarians who plundered many other towns into oblivion.

• *Exit the basilica and cross the short side of the square, to where the city's main street hits the Forum. Stop at the three white stones that stick up from the cobbles.*

❺ Via Abbondanza

Glance down Via Abbondanza, Pompeii's main street. Lined with shops, bars, and restaurants, it was a lively, pedestrian-only zone.

The three "beaver-teeth" stones are traffic barriers that kept chariots out. On the corner at the start of the street (just to the left), take a close look at the dark travertine column standing next to the white one. Notice that the marble drums of the white column are not chiseled entirely round —another construction project left unfinished when Vesuvius erupted.

• *Head toward Vesuvius, walking along the right side of the Forum. Immediately across from the Temple of Jupiter is a building with four round arches. Go in the door just to the right.*

❻ Fish and Produce Market, with Plaster Casts of Victims

As the frescoes on the wall (just inside on the left) indicate, this is where Pompeiians came to buy their food—fish, bread, chickens, and so on. These fine examples of Roman art—with their glimpses of everyday life and their mastery of depth and illusion—would not be matched until the Renaissance, a thousand years after the fall of Rome.

The glass cases here hold casts of Pompeiians, eerily captured in their last moments. They were quickly suffocated by a superheat-ed avalanche of gas and ash, and their bodies were encased in volcanic debris. While exca-vating, modern archaeologists detected hollow spaces under-foot, created when the victims' bodies decomposed. By gently filling the holes with plaster,

the archaeologists were able to create molds of the Pompeiians who were caught in the disaster.

• *Exit the market, turn right, and go under the arch. On the pillar to the right, look for the pedestrian-only road sign (two guys carrying an amphora, or ancient jug; it's above the REG VII INS IV sign). In the road are more "beaver-teeth" traffic blocks. The modern cafeteria is the only eatery inside the archaeological site (with a coffee bar and WC upstairs).*

The Eruption of Vesuvius

At about 1:00 in the afternoon on August 24, A.D. 79, Mount Vesuvius erupted, sending a mushroom cloud of ash, dust, and rocks 12 miles into the air. It spewed for 18 hours straight, as winds blew the cloud southward. The white-gray ash settled like a heavy snow on Pompeii, its weight eventually collapsing roofs and floors, but leaving the walls intact. And though most of Pompeii's 20,000 residents fled that day, about 2,000 stayed behind.

Although the city of Herculaneum was closer to the volcano—about four miles away—at first it largely escaped the rain of ash, due to the direction of the wind. However, 12 hours after Vesuvius awoke, the type of eruption suddenly changed. The mountain let loose a superheated avalanche of ash, pumice, and gas. This red-hot "pyroclastic flow" sped down the side of the mountain at nearly 100 miles per hour, engulfing Herculaneum and cooking its residents alive. Several more flows over the next few hours further entombed Herculaneum, burying it in nearly 60 feet of hot material that later cooled into rock, freezing the city in time. Then, at around 7:30 in the morning, another pyroclastic flow headed south and struck Pompeii, dealing a fatal blow to those who'd remained behind.

Twenty yards past the cafeteria, on the left-hand side at #24, is the entrance to the...

❼ Baths of the Forum (Terme del Foro)

Pompeii had six public baths, each with a men's and a women's section. You're in the men's zone. The leafy courtyard at the entrance was the gymnasium. After working out, clients could relax with a hot bath *(caldarium)*, warm bath *(tepidarium)*, or cold plunge *(frigidarium)*.

The first big, plain room you enter served as the **dressing room.** Holes on the walls were for pegs to hang clothing. High up, the window (with a faded Neptune underneath) was originally covered with a less-translucent Roman glass. Walk over the nonslip mosaics into the next room.

The ***tepidarium*** is ringed by mini statues or *telamones* (male caryatids, figures used as supporting pillars), which divided the lockers. Clients would undress and warm up here, perhaps stretching out on one of the bronze benches near the bronze heater for a massage. Look at the ceiling—half crushed by the eruption and half intact, with its fine blue-and-white stucco work.

Next, admire the engineering in the steam-bath room, or ***caldarium.*** The double floor was heated from below—so nice with bare feet (look into the grate across from where you entered to

see the brick support towers). The double walls with brown terra-cotta tiles held the heat. Romans soaked in the big tub, which was filled with hot water. Opposite the big tub is a fountain, which spouted water onto the hot floor, creating steam. The lettering on the fountain reminded those enjoying the room which two politicians paid for it...and how much it cost them (5,250 *sestertii*). To keep condensation from dripping annoyingly from the ceiling, fluting (ribbing) was added to carry water down the walls.

• *Today's visitors exit the baths through the original entry (at the far end of the dressing room). Hungry? Immediately across the street is an ancient...*

❽ Fast-Food Joint

After a bath, it was only natural to want a little snack. So, just across the street is a fast-food joint, marked by a series of rect-angular marble counters. Most ancient Romans didn't cook for themselves in their tiny apartments, so to-go places like this were commonplace. The holes in the counters held the pots for food. Each container was like a thermos, with a wooden lid to keep the soup hot, the wine cool, and so on. Notice the groove in the front doorstep and the holes out on the curb. The holes likely accommodated cords for stretching awnings over the sidewalk to shield the clientele from the hot sun, while the grooves were for the shop's folding accordion doors. Look at the wheel grooves in the pavement, worn down through centuries of use. Nearby are more stepping-stones for pedestrians to cross the flooded streets.

• *Just a few steps uphill from the fast-food joint, at #5 (with a locked gate), is the...*

❾ House of the Tragic Poet (Casa del Poeta Tragico)

This house is typical Roman style. The entry is flanked by two family-owned shops (each with a track for a collapsing accordion door). The home is like a train running straight away from the street: atrium (with skylight and pool to catch the rain), den (where deals were made by the shopkeeper), and garden (with rooms facing it and a shrine to remember both the gods and family ancestors). In the entryway is the famous "Beware of Dog" *(Cave Canem)* mosaic.

Today's visitors enter the home by the back door (circle around to the left). On your way there, look for the modern exposed pipe on the left side of the lane; this is the same as ones used in the ancient plumbing system, hidden beneath the raised sidewalk. Inside the house, the grooves on the marble well-head in the entry hall (possibly closed) were formed by generations of inhabitants dragging the bucket up by rope. The richly frescoed dining room is off the garden. Diners lounged on their couches (the Roman custom) and enjoyed frescoes with fake "windows," giving the illusion of a bigger and airier room. Next to the dining room is a humble BBQ-style kitchen with a little closet for the toilet (the kitchen and bathroom shared the same plumbing).

• *Return to the fast-food place and continue about 10 yards downhill to the big intersection. From the center of the intersection, look left to see a giant arch, framing a nice view of Mount Vesuvius.*

⑩ Aqueduct Arch—Running Water

Water was critical for this city of 20,000 people, and this arch was part of Pompeii's water-delivery system. A 100-mile-long aqueduct

carried fresh water down from the hillsides to a big reservoir perched at the highest point of the city wall. Since overall water pressure was disappointing, Pompeiians built arches like the brick one you see here (originally covered in marble) with hidden water tanks at the top. Located just below the altitude of the main tank, these smaller tanks were filled by gravity and provided each neighborhood with reliable pressure. Look closely at the arch and you'll see 2,000-year-old pipes (made of lead imported from Britannia) embedded in the brick.

If there was a water shortage, democratic priorities prevailed: First the baths were cut off, then the private homes. The last to go were the public fountains, where all citizens could get drinking and cooking water.

• *If you're thirsty, fill your water bottle from the modern fountain. Then continue straight downhill one block (50 yards) to #2 on the left.*

⓫ House of the Faun (Casa del Fauno)

Stand across the street and marvel at the grand entry with *"HAVE"* (hail to you) as a welcome mat. Go in. Notice the two shrines above

the entryway—one dedicated to the gods, the other to this wealthy family's ancestors. (Contemporary Neapolitans still carry on this practice; you'll notice little shrines embedded in walls all over Naples.)

You are standing in Pompeii's largest home, where you're greeted by the delightful small bronze statue of the *Dancing Faun*, famed for its realistic movement and fine proportion. (The original, described on page 953, is in Naples' Archaeological Museum.) With 40 rooms and 27,000 square feet, the House of the Faun covers an entire city block. The next floor mosaic, with an intricate diamond-like design, decorates the homeowner's office. Beyond that, at the far end of the first garden, is the famous floor mosaic of the *Battle of Alex-*

ander. (The original is also at the museum in Naples.) In 333 B.C., Alexander the Great beat Darius and the Persians. Romans had great respect for Alexander, the first great emperor before Rome's. While most of Pompeii's nouveau riche had notoriously bad taste and stuffed their palaces with over-the-top, mismatched decor, this guy had class. Both the faun (an ancient copy of a famous Greek statue) and the Alexander mosaic show an appreciation for history.

The house's back courtyard is lined with pillars rebuilt after the A.D. 62 earthquake. Take a close look at the brick, mortar, and fake marble stucco veneer.

• *Now retrace your steps to the Forum. At the Forum's far end, find Via Abbondanza (where you saw the three "beaver-teeth" stones a few minutes ago). Follow this, passing the water fountain on the left with the cornucopia (horn of plenty) that gives the street its name. Turn left up the street after the second fountain (marked* REG VII INS I, *with a small* Vicolo del Lupanare *sign). This leads to the entrance of the...*

⓬ Brothel (Lupanare)

You'll find the biggest crowds in Pompeii at a place that was likely popular 2,000 ago, too—the brothel. Prostitutes were nicknamed *lupe* (she-wolves), alluding to the call they made when trying to attract business. The brothel was a simple place, with beds and pillows made of stone and then covered with mattresses. The ancient graffiti includes tallies and exotic names of the women, indicating the prostitutes came from all corners of the Mediterranean (it also served as feedback from satisfied customers). The faded frescoes above the cells may have been a kind of menu for services offered. Note the idealized women (white, which was considered beautiful; one wears an early bra) and the rougher men (dark, considered horny). The bed legs came with little disk-like barriers to keep critters from crawling up.

• *Leaving the brothel, go right, then take the first left, and continue going downhill two blocks to return to Via Abbondanza. The Forum—and exit—are now to the right, but you should go left.*

Continue for 60 yards, then turn right just beyond the fountain, and walk down Via dei Teatri (labeled REG VIII INS IV*). Turn left before the columns, and head downhill another 60 yards to #28, which marks the...*

⓭ Temple of Isis

This temple served Pompeii's Egyptian community. The little white stucco shrine with the modern plastic roof housed holy water from the Nile. Isis, from Egyptian myth, was one of many foreign gods adopted by the eclectic Romans. Pompeii must have had a synagogue, too, but it has yet to be excavated.

• *Now your goal is the large theater just behind the temple. Try getting there this way: Exit the temple where you entered, and go left, then left again (following the* Foro Triangolare *sign) along the columns, and then left into the theater's upper stands. (If this is closed off, try circling around the other way). There's also a similar but smaller-sized theater next to the large one.*

⓮ Theater

Originally a Greek theater (Greeks built theirs with the help of a hillside), this was the birthplace of the Greek port here in 470 B.C. During Roman times, the theater sat 5,000 people in three sets of seats, all with different prices: the five marble terraces up close (filled with romantic wooden seats for two), the main section, and the cheap nosebleed section (surviving only on the high end, near the trees). The square stones above the cheap seats once supported a canvas rooftop. Take note of the high-profile boxes, flanking the stage, for guests of honor. From this perch, you can see the gladiator barracks—the colonnaded courtyard beyond the theater. They lived in tiny rooms, trained in the courtyard, and fought in the nearby amphitheater.

• *From the theater, return to the street where you entered the Temple of Isis, and turn right (away from the Forum). In a block and a half, on the right, you'll see the...*

⑮ House of Menander (Casa di Menandro)

Once owned by a wealthy Pompeiian, this house takes its current name from a fresco of the Greek playwright Menander on one of the walls. Admire the grand atrium (with an altar to the family gods in the corner), the wall frescoes, and the mosaics. The cloister-like back courtyard leads to a room with skeletons (not plaster casts) of eruption victims from this house. Farther back, a passage leads to the servants' quarters.

• *When you're ready to leave, backtrack to the main road and find the sign for the (modern) toilets. Climb up the stairs and find the viewpoint over the ruins.*

⑯ Viewpoint

You're at ground level—post-eruption. To the right (inland), the farmland shows how locals lived on top of the ruins for centuries without knowing what was underneath. To the left, you can see the entire city of Pompeii spread out in front of you and appreciate the magnitude of the excavations.

• *To leave the site, head back down the stairs, turn right on Via Abbondanza, and go uphill to the Forum, where you'll find the main exit. For a shortcut back to the entrance area (with the bookstore, luggage storage, and quickest access to the train station), when you are halfway down the exit ramp, take the eight steps on the right and follow the signs. Otherwise, you'll end up on the main road—where you'll head right and loop around.*

However, there's much more to see—three-quarters of Pompeii's 164 acres have been excavated, but this tour has covered only a third of the site. If you still have energy to see more, continue along Via Abbondanza toward the eastern part of the site, where the crowds thin out. Go

straight for about 10 minutes, likely jogging right after a bit (just follow the posted maps). You'll wind up passing through a pretty, forested area. At the far end is the...

⑰ Amphitheater

If you can, climb to the upper level of the amphitheater (though the stairs are often blocked). With Vesuvius looming in the background, mentally replace the tourists below with gladiators and wild animals locked in combat. Walk along the top of the amphitheater and look down into the grassy rectangular area surrounded by columns. This is the **Palaestra,** an area once used for athletic training. (If you can't get to the top of the amphitheater, you can see the Palaestra from outside—in fact, you can't miss it, as it's right next door.) Facing the other way, look for the bell tower that tops the roofline of the modern city of Pompei, where locals go about their daily lives in the shadow of the volcano, just as their ancestors did 2,000 years ago.

• *If it's too crowded to bear hiking back along uneven lanes to the entrance, you can slip out the site's "back door," which is next to the amphitheater. Exiting, turn right and follow the site's wall all the way back to the entrance.*

Herculaneum

Smaller, less crowded, and not as ruined as its famous big sister, Herculaneum (worth ▲▲, Ercolano in Italian) offers a closer, more intimate peek into ancient Roman life but lacks the grandeur of Pompeii (there's barely a colonnade).

GETTING TO HERCULANENUM
Ercolano Scavi, the nearest train station to Herculaneum, is about 20 minutes from Naples and 50 minutes from Sorrento on the same Circumvesuviana train that goes to Pompeii (for details on the Circumvesuviana, see page 986). Walking from the Ercolano Scavi train station to the ruins takes 10 minutes: Leave the station and turn right, then left down the main drag; continue straight, eight blocks gradually downhill, to the end of the road, where you'll run right into the grand arch that marks the entrance to the ruins. (Skip Museo MAV.) Pass through the arch and continue 200 yards down the path—taking in the bird's-eye first impression of the site to your right—to the ticket office in the modern building.

ORIENTATION TO HERCULANEUM
Cost: €11, free first Sun of each month, €21 combo-ticket includes Pompeii and three lesser sites (valid 3 consecutive days); also covered by the Campania ArteCard (see page 942).

Hours: Daily April-Oct 8:30-19:30, Nov-March until 17:00, ticket office closes 1.5 hours earlier.

Closures: Like Pompeii, various sections of Herculaneum can be closed unexpectedly.

Use this book's map (or the one available on site) to navigate around any closures.

Information: Pick up a free, detailed map and excellent booklet at the info desk next to the ticket window. The booklet gives you a quick explanation of each building. There's a bookstore inside the site, next to the audioguide stand. Tel. 081-777-7008, www.pompeiisites.org.

Tours: The informative and interesting audioguide sheds light on the ruins and life in Herculaneum in the first century A.D. (€6.50, €10 for 2, ID required, rent at kiosk near site entry).

Length of This Tour: Allow one hour.

Baggage Storage: Herculaneum is harder than Pompeii for those with luggage, but not impossible. Herculaneum's train station has lots of stairs and no baggage storage, but you can roll wheeled luggage down to the ruins and store it for free in a locked area in the ticket office building (pick up bags at least 30 minutes prior to site closing). To get back to the station, consider splurging on a €5 taxi (ask the staff to call one for you).

Services: There's a free WC in the ticket office building, and another near the site entry.

Eating: Vending machines and café tables are near the entry to the site. There are also several eateries on the way from the train station.

◎ SELF-GUIDED TOUR

Caked and baked by the same A.D. 79 eruption that pummeled Pompeii (see sidebar on page 1000), Herculaneum is a small community of intact buildings with plenty of surviving detail. While Pompeii was initially smothered in ash, Herculaneum was spared at first—due to the direction of the wind—but got slammed about 12 hours after the eruption started by a superheated avalanche of ash and hot gases roaring off the volcano. The city was eventually buried under nearly 60 feet of ash, which hardened into tuff, perfectly preserving the city until excavations began in 1748.

After leaving the ticket building, go through the turnstiles and walk the path below the site to the entrance. Look seaward and note where the shoreline is today; before the eruption, it was where you are standing, a quarter-mile inland. This gives you a sense of how much volcanic material piled up. The present-day city of Ercolano looms just above the ruins. The modern buildings don't look much different from their ancient counterparts.

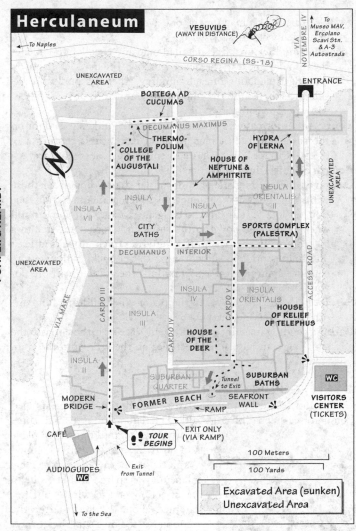

Herculaneum

VESUVIUS
(AWAY IN DISTANCE)

To
Museo MAV,
Ercolano
Scavi Stn.
& A-3
Autostrada

VIA NOVEMBRE IV

← To Naples

CORSO REGINA (SS-18)

ENTRANCE

UNEXCAVATED
AREA

BOTTEGA AD
CUCUMAS

DECUMANUS MAXIMUS

THERMO-
POLIUM

COLLEGE
OF THE
AUGUSTALI

HYDRA
OF LERNA

HOUSE
OF
NEPTUNE &
AMPHITRITE

INSULA
ORIENTALIS
II

INSULA
VI

INSULA
V

INSULA
VII

CITY
BATHS

SPORTS COMPLEX
(PALESTRA)

UNEXCAVATED
AREA

DECUMANUS   INTERIOR

UNEXCAVATED
AREA

CARDO III

INSULA
IV

INSULA
ORIENTALIS

HOUSE
OF RELIEF
OF TELEPHUS

ACCESS ROAD

INSULA
III

CARDO IV

CARDO V

INSULA
II

HOUSE
OF THE
DEER

VIA MARE

SUBURBAN
QUARTER

Tunnel
to Exit

SUBURBAN
BATHS

WC

MODERN
BRIDGE

FORMER BEACH

SEAFRONT
WALL

VISITORS
CENTER
(TICKETS)

RAMP

CAFÉ

TOUR
BEGINS

EXIT ONLY
(VIA RAMP)

AUDIOGUIDES
WC

Exit
from Tunnel

100 Meters

100 Yards

↓ To the Sea

Excavated Area (sunken)
Unexcavated Area

As you cross the modern bridge into the excavation site, look down into the moat-like **ditch.** On one side, you see Herculaneum's seafront wall. On the other, the wall that you've just been walking on is the solidified ash layer from the volcano and shows how deeply the town was buried.

After crossing the bridge, stroll straight to the end of the street and find the **College of the Augustali** (Sede degli Augustali, #24). Decorated with frescoes of Hercules (for whom this city was named), it belonged to an association of freed slaves working together to climb their way up the ladder of Roman society. Here and farther on, look around doorways and ceilings to spot ancient wood charred by the pyroclastic flows. Most buildings were made of stone, with wooden floors and beams (which were preserved here by the ash but rarely survive at ancient sites).

Leave the building through the back and go to the right, down the lane. The adjacent *thermopolium* (#19) was the Roman equivalent of a lunch counter or fast-food joint, with giant jars for wine, oil, and snacks. Most of the buildings along here were shops, with apartments above.

A few steps on, the **Bottega ad Cucumas** wine shop (#14, on the right) still has charred remains of beams, and its drink list remains frescoed on the outside wall (under glass).

Take the next right, go halfway down the street, and on the left find the **House of Neptune and Amphitrite** (Casa di Nettuno e Anfitrite, #7). Outside, notice the intact upper floor and imagine it going even higher. Inside, you'll see colorful mosaics and a unique "frame" made of shells.

Back outside, continue downhill to the intersection, then head left for a block and proceed straight across the street into the don't-miss-it **sports complex** (*palestra*; #4). First you'll see a row of "marble" columns, which (look closer) are actually made of rounded bricks covered with a thick layer of plaster, shaped to look like carved marble. While important buildings in Rome had solid marble columns, these fakes are typical of ordinary buildings.

Continuing deeper into the complex, look for the hole in the hillside and walk through one of the triangular-shaped entrances to find the highlight: the Hydra of Lerna, a sculpted bronze fountain that features the seven-headed monster defeated by Hercules as one of his 12 labors. If this cavernous space is unlit, go to the second doorway on the left wall and press the light switch.

Return through the sports complex and turn downhill to the **House of the Deer** (Casa dei Cervi, #21). It's named for the statues of deer being attacked by dogs in the garden courtyard (these are copies; the originals are in the Archaeological Museum in Naples). As you wander through the rooms, notice the colorfully frescoed walls. Ancient Herculaneum, like all Roman cities of that age, was filled with color, rather than the stark white we often imagine (even the statues were painted).

You can see more of these colors, this time bright orange, across the street in the **House of Relief of Telephus** (Casa del Rivielo del Telefo, #2).

Continue downhill through the archway. The **Suburban Baths** illustrate the city's devastation (Terme Suburbane, #3; enter near the side of the statue on the terrace, sometimes closed). After you descend into the baths, look back at the steps. You'll see the original wood charred in the disaster, protected by the wooden planks you just walked on. At the bottom of the stairs, in the waiting room to the right, notice where the floor collapsed under the sheer weight of the volcanic debris. (The sunken pavement reveals the baths' heating system: hot air generated by wood-burning furnaces and circulated between the different levels of the floor.) A doorway in front of the stairs is still filled with solidified ash. Despite the damage, elements of refinement remain intact, such as the delicate stuccoes in the *caldarium* (hot bath).

Back outside, make your way down the steps to the sunken area just below. As you descend, you're walking across what was formerly Herculaneum's beach. Looking back, you'll see **arches** that were part of boat storage areas. Archaeologists used to wonder why so few victims were found in Herculaneum. But during excavations in 1981, hundreds of skeletons were discovered here, between the wall of volcanic stone behind you and the city in front of you. Some of Herculaneum's 4,000 citizens tried to escape by sea, but were overtaken by the pyroclastic flows.

Thankfully, your escape is easier. Either follow the sound of water and continue through the tunnel (you'll climb up and pop out near the site entry), or, more scenically, backtrack and exit the same way you entered.

Vesuvius

The 4,000-foot-high Vesuvius, mainland Europe's only active volcano, has been sleeping restlessly since 1944. While Europe has other dangerous volcanoes, only Vesuvius sits in the middle of a three-million-person metropolitan area that would be impossible to evacuate quickly.

Many tourists don't know that you can easily visit the summit. Up top, it's desolate and lunar-like, and the rocks are newly born. Walk the entire accessible part of the crater lip for the most interesting views; the far end overlooks Pompeii. Be still. Listen to the wind and the occasional cascades of rocks tumbling into the crater. Any steam? Vesuvius could blow again. (Don't worry—there'd likely be at least a few hours or days of warning.)

GETTING TO VESUVIUS

By Car or Taxi: Drivers take the exit *Torre del Greco* and follow the signs to *Vesuvio*. Just drive to the end of the road and pay €6 to park. A taxi costs €90 round-trip from Naples, including a 2-hour wait; it's about €70 from Pompeii.

By Private Bus from Pompeii: From the Pompei Scavi train station on the Circumvesuviana line (just outside the main entrance to the Pompeii ruins), you have two bus services to choose from, each taking about three hours (40 minutes up, 40 minutes down, and about 1.5 hours at the summit).

The old-fashioned **Vesuvius Trolley Tram** (Tramvia del Vesuvio) uses the main road up (€12 round-trip plus €10 summit admission, 6/day, tickets sold at and departs from Camping Zeus next to Pompei Scavi train station, tel. 081-861-5320, www.campingzeus. it).

Busvia del Vesuvio winds you up a bumpy back road to the crater rim (Via Boscotrecase) in a cross between a shuttle bus and a monster truck. The walk up to the rim at the end is about the same, but you approach it from the other direction. It's a fun, more scenic way to go, but not for the easily queasy (€22 includes summit admission, hourly April-Oct Mon-Sat 9:00-15:00, until later June-Aug, rarely Sun or Nov-March, buy tickets at "info point" at Pompei Scavi train station, mobile 340-935-2616, www. busviadelvesuvio.com).

By Private Bus from Herculaneum: The quickest trip up is on the **Vesuvio Express.** These small buses leave from the Ercolano Scavi train station (on the Circumvesuviana line, where you get off for the Herculaneum ruins; €10 round-trip plus €10 summit admission, daily from 9:30, runs every 45 minutes based on demand, 20 minutes each way—about 2.5 hours total, office on square in front of train station, tel. 081-739-3666, www.vesuvioexpress.it).

ORIENTATION TO VESUVIUS

Cost and Hours: €10 covers national park entry and the park guide's orientation; ticket office open daily July-Aug 9:00-18:00, April-June and Sept until 17:00, closes earlier off-season; these are last entry times— you can stay in the park one hour later. Bad weather can occasionally close the trail.

Information: The ticket office is 200 yards downhill from the parking lot. Tel. 081-865-3911 or 081-239-5653, www.vesuviopark. it (official site) or www.guidevesuvio.it (more helpful site run by guides).

When to Go: Early-morning visitors enjoy the freshest air and snare the best parking spots. The mountain is open all year, but spring and fall are the most comfortable times to visit. Yellow broom flowers blossom in May and June.

VISITING VESUVIUS

Bring sunscreen, water, a light jacket in summer, and a hat and warm coat in winter. By bus, taxi, or private car, you'll reach the volcano crater up a good but windy road from Torre del Greco (between Herculaneum and Pompeii). As you drive up, you'll pass the remnants of the pre-A.D. 79 mountain (on your left, now called Monte Somma) and lava flows from the most recent 1944 eruption. No matter how you travel up, you'll land at the parking lot.

Backtrack 200 yards downhill to buy your ticket at the office. Use the pay WC, as there's none at the summit. From the parking lot, it's a moderately steep half-mile, 20-minute hike (with a 600-foot elevation gain) up a dirt access road to the top. Say "no thank you" to the gentleman passing out walking sticks in return for a tip—you don't need one.

At the rim, a sweeping view of the Bay of Naples is on your right; on your left, fenced off, there's a fearsome drop into the crater. Mountain guides orient you and then set you free. There are souvenir stands at the rim, but no WC.

SORRENTO & CAPRI

Just an hour south of Naples, and without a hint of big-city chaos, serene Sorrento makes an ideal home base for exploring this fascinating region, from Naples to the Amalfi Coast to Paestum. And the jet-setting island of Capri is just a short cruise from Sorrento, offering more charm and fun than its glitzy reputation would lead you to believe (at least, outside the crowded months of July and August).

Sorrento

Wedged on a ledge under the mountains and over the Mediterranean, spritzed by lemon and olive groves, Sorrento is an attractive resort of 20,000 residents and, in summer, just as many tourists. It's as well-located for regional sightseeing as it is a fine place to stay and stroll. The Sorrentines have gone out of their way to create a completely safe and relaxed place for tourists to come and spend money. As 90 percent of the town's economy is tourism, everyone seems to speak fluent English and work for the Chamber of Commerce. This gateway to the Amalfi Coast has an unspoiled old quarter, a lively shopping street, and a spectacular cliffside setting. Residents are proud of the many world-class romantics who've vacationed here, such as famed tenor Enrico Caruso, who chose Sorrento as the place to spend his last weeks in 1921.

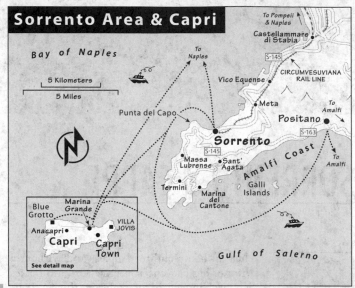

Sorrento Area & Capri

Bay of Naples

To Pompeii & Naples

Castellammare di Stabia

S-145

To Naples

5 Kilometers

5 Miles

Vico Equense

CIRCUMVESUVIANA RAIL LINE

Punta del Capo

Meta

To Amalfi

Positano

S-163

Sorrento

S-145

Amalfi Coast

To Amalfi

Massa Lubrense

Sant' Agata

Termini

Marina del Cantone

Galli Islands

Blue Grotto

Marina Grande

VILLA JOVIS

Anacapri

Capri

Capri Town

See detail map

Gulf of Salerno

PLANNING YOUR TIME

Sorrento itself has no world-class sights, but it can easily give you a few pleasant hours. More importantly, Sorrento is a fine base for visiting Naples (by boat or train); Pompeii, Herculaneum, and Mount Vesuvius (by train, plus a bus for Vesuvius); the Amalfi Coast (by bus or boat); and the island of Capri (by boat). All of these destinations are within an hour or so of Sorrento. Of the region's attractions, only Paestum's Greek temples are a little hard to reach from Sorrento, and even they can be seen in a long day.

Sorrento hibernates in winter. Many places close down in November—others after the New Year—and stay closed until the town reawakens sometime in March.

Orientation to Sorrento

Downtown Sorrento is long and narrow. Piazza Tasso marks the town's center. The congested main drag, Corso Italia, runs paral-

lel to the sea, passing 50 yards below the train station, through Piazza Tasso, and then out toward the cape, where the road's name becomes Via Capo. Nearly everything mentioned here (except Meta beach and the hotels on Via Capo) is within a 10-minute walk of the station.

The town is perched on a cliff (some hotels have elevators down to sundecks on the water); the best real beaches are a couple of miles away.

Sorrento has two separate port areas: Marina Piccola, below Piazza Tasso, is a functional harbor with boats to Naples and Capri, as well as cruise-ship tenders. (While the big cruise ships dock in Naples, smaller ships drop anchor at Sorrento.) Marina Grande, below the other end of downtown, is a little fishing village, with recommended restaurants and more charm.

TOURIST INFORMATION

The helpful regional TI (labeled *Azienda di Soggiorno*)—located inside the **Foreigners' Club**—hands out a great city map and schedules for boats and buses (June-Oct Mon-Sat 9:00-19:00, Sun 9:00-18:00 except closed Sun April-May; Nov-March Mon-Fri 8:30-16:00, closed Sat-Sun; Via Luigi de Maio 35, tel. 081-807-4033, www.sorrentotourism.com; Nino and Fabiola). If you arrive after the TI closes, look for their useful handouts in the lobby of the Foreigners' Club (open until midnight, closed in winter).

You may see small "Info Points" conveniently located around town, where you can get answers to basic questions (open in warm months only). Find them just outside the **train station** in the green caboose; near **Piazza Tasso** at the corner of Via Correale (under the yellow church); at **Marina Piccola,** where cruise-ship tenders and boats from Naples arrive; and at the Achille Lauro **parking garage.**

ARRIVAL IN SORRENTO

By Train or Bus: Sorrento is the last stop on the Circumvesuviana train line from Naples. In front of the train station is the town's main bus stop, as well as taxis waiting to overcharge you (€15 minimum). All recommended hotels—except those on Via Capo—are within a 10-minute walk. For details on taking the bus to hotels on Via Capo, see page 1030.

By Boat: Passenger boats and cruise-ship tenders dock at Marina Piccola. As you walk toward town from the marina, go up the big staircase where the pier bends. Standing on the promenade and facing town, you'll see the bus stop directly ahead; a TI kiosk and ticket windows for boats to Capri and Naples in the lower area to your left; and the elevator up to town to the right, about a five-minute walk along the base of the cliff (follow *lift/acensore* signs).

The elevator (€1) is a bit faster, cheaper, and more predictable than a bus. It takes you to the Villa Comunale city park. From there, exit through the park's gate and bear left; Piazza Tasso is about four blocks away. Buses take you directly to Piazza Tasso (city bus #B or #C, buy €1.20 ticket at newsstand or *tabbachi* store;

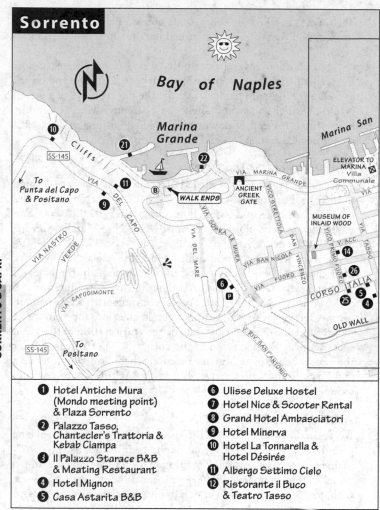

Sorrento

Bay of Naples

Marina Grande

Marina San

Cliffs

SS-145

To Punta del Capo & Positano

VIA DEL CAPO

VIA NASTRO VERDE

VIA CAPODIMONTE

SS-145

To Positano

VIA SOPRA LE MURA

VIA DEL MARE

VIA MARINA GRANDE

ANCIENT GREEK GATE

VIA STREKTOLA

SAN VINCENZO

VIA SAN NICOLA

VIA FUORO

Y. RIV SANT'ANTONIO

ELEVATOR TO MARINA
Villa Communale

MUSEUM OF INLAID WOOD

VICO PRIMO FUORO

V. ACC.

CORSO ITALIA

OLD WALL

VIA TASSO

WALK ENDS

1	Hotel Antiche Mura (Mondo meeting point) & Plaza Sorrento	6	Ulisse Deluxe Hostel
2	Palazzo Tasso, Chantecler's Trattoria & Kebab Ciampa	7	Hotel Nice & Scooter Rental
		8	Grand Hotel Ambasciatori
		9	Hotel Minerva
3	Il Palazzo Starace B&B & Meating Restaurant	10	Hotel La Tonnarella & Hotel Désirée
4	Hotel Mignon	11	Albergo Settimo Cielo
5	Casa Astarita B&B	12	Ristorante il Buco & Teatro Tasso

private buses cost the same, pay driver); for more on both buses, see "Getting Around Sorrento," later.

By Car: The Achille Lauro underground parking garage is centrally located, just a couple of blocks in front of the train station (€2/hour, €24/24 hours, on Via Correale).

HELPFUL HINTS

Exchange Rate: €1 = about $1.10

Country Calling Code: 39 (see page 1154 for dialing instructions)

Church Services: The **cathedral** hosts an English-language Anglican service at 17:00 most Sundays from April to October (but not in August). At **Santa Maria delle Grazie** (perhaps

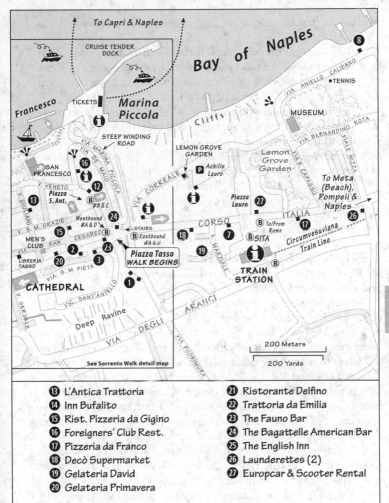

13 L'Antica Trattoria	**21** Ristorante Delfino
14 Inn Bufalito	**22** Trattoria da Emilia
15 Rist. Pizzeria da Gigino	**23** The Fauno Bar
16 Foreigners' Club Rest.	**24** The Bagattelle American Bar
17 Pizzeria da Franco	**25** The English Inn
18 Decò Supermarket	**26** Launderettes (2)
19 Gelateria David	**27** Europcar & Scooter Rental
20 Gelateria Primavera	

SORRENTO & CAPRI

the most beautiful Baroque church in town), cloistered nuns sing from above and out of sight during a Mass each morning at 7:30 (on Via delle Grazie).

Bookstore: Libreria Tasso has a decent selection of books in English, including this one (daily 9:30-23:00, closed in winter, Via San Cesareo 96, one block north of cathedral, near Sorrento Men's Club, tel. 081-807-1639).

Laundry: Sorrento has two handy self-service launderettes (both open daily 7:00-24:00, shorter hours off-season). One is in the old center, just down the alley next to Corso Italia 30 (Vico I Fuoro 3, mobile 338-506-0942). The other is a couple of long blocks past the station, at the corner of Corso Italia and Via degli Aranci.

Guided Tours of Pompeii, Naples, the Amalfi Coast, and Capri: Naples-based **Mondo Guide** offers affordable tours of these destinations, including an Amalfi Coast drive that starts from Sorrento (meet in front of the Hotel Antiche Mura). You'll sign up in advance and team up with fellow Rick Steves readers to split the cost. For details, see page 948.

Local Guides: Giovanna Donadio is a good tour guide for Sorrento, Amalfi, and Capri (€100/half-day, €160/day, same price for any size group, mobile 338-466-0114, giovanna_dona@ hotmail.com). **Giovanni Visetti** is a nature lover, mapmaker, and orienteer who organizes hikes and has a fine website describing local trails (mobile 339-694-2911, www.giovis.com, giovis@giovis.com).

GETTING AROUND SORRENTO

By Bus: City buses all stop near the main square, Piazza Tasso, and run until at least 20:00 (for info, see www.eavsrl.it). Bus #A (2-3/hour) takes a long route parallel to the coast, heading east to Meta beach or west to the hotels on Via Capo before continuing to Massa Lubrense; buses #B and #C make a loop up and down, connecting the port (Marina Piccola) to the town center; and bus #D heads to the fishing village (Marina Grande). The trip between Piazza Tasso and Marina Piccola costs just €1.20; for other trips, tickets cost €1.60 and are good for up to one hour (purchase at tobacco shops and newsstands). Stamp your ticket upon entering the bus. The €8, 24-hour Costiera SITA Sud pass, good for the entire Amalfi Coast, also covers local buses in Sorrento.

Bus stops can be tricky to find. Buses #A and #D stop where Corso Italia passes through Piazza Tasso. If you're heading west (to Via Capo or Marina Grande), find the stop at the west end of the piazza, across from the statue of Torquato Tasso. If you're heading east (to Meta), catch the bus in front of the yellow church at the east end of the piazza. Buses #B and #C stop at the corner of Piazza Sant'Antonino, just down the hill toward the water.

A different bus (operated by a private company, www. cooperativatasso.com) runs only between the port and Piazza Tasso (3/hour in season, €1.20, buy ticket from driver, not covered by 24-hour pass).

By Scooter: Several places near the station rent motor scooters for about €35 per day, including **Europcar** (Corso Italia 210p, tel. 081-878-1386, www.sorrento.it) and **Autoservizi De Martino,** in Hotel Nice (Corso Italia 259, tel. 081-878-2801, www.admitaly. com). Don't rent a vehicle in summer unless you enjoy traffic jams.

By Taxi: Taxis are expensive, charging an outrageous €15 for the short ride from the station to most hotels (more for Via Capo). Because of heavy traffic and the complex one-way road system, you can often walk faster than you can ride. If you do use a taxi, even if you agree to a set price, be sure it has a meter (all official taxis have one). I think taxis here are a huge rip-off, since city officials don't have the nerve to regulate them, and hotels are afraid to alienate them. Walk or take the bus instead.

By Bus Tour: To see more of the Sorrentine Peninsula, consider **CitySightseeing Sorrento**'s hop-on, hop-off bus tours, with headphone commentary about the two bays flanking this scenic spit of land (€12, buy tickets on board, daily 4/day April-Oct, full loop is seven stops in 1.75 hours, departs from front of train station, www.sorrento.city-sightseeing.it). The same company's Amalfi Coast bus is a good alternative for linking to Amalfi or Positano if the public buses are too crowded (see "Getting Around the Amalfi Coast" on page 1051). Skip the pointless **tourist train** you'll see departing from Piazza Tasso, which loops only through the town itself.

Sorrento Walk

Get to know Sorrento with this lazy self-guided town stroll that ends down by the waterside at the small-boat harbor, Marina Grande.

• *Begin on the main square. Stand under the flags with your back to the sea, and face...*

❶ **Piazza Tasso:** As in any southern Italian town, this "piazza" is Sorrento's living room. It may be noisy and congested, but locals

want to be where the action is...and be part of the scene. The most expensive apartments and top cafés are on or near this square. City buses stop at or close to the square on their way to Marina Piccola and Via Capo. The train station is a five-minute walk to the left. A statue of St. Anthony, patron of Sorrento, faces north as if greeting those coming from Naples (on festival days, he's equipped with an armload of fresh lemons and oranges).

This square bridges a gorge that divides downtown Sorrento. The newer section (to your left) was farm country just two centuries ago. The older part is to your right, with an ancient Greek gridded street plan (like much of southern Italy, Sorrento was Greek-speaking for centuries before it was Romanized).

For a glimpse at the city's gorge-gouged landscape, consider this quick detour: With the water to your back, cross (carefully)

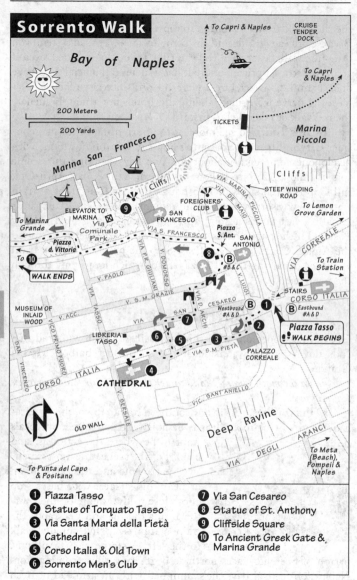

Sorrento Walk

Bay of Naples

To Capri & Naples

CRUISE TENDER DOCK

To Capri & Naples

200 Meters

200 Yards

TICKETS

Marina Piccola

Marina San Francesco

Cliffs

Cliffs

VIA MARINA PICCOLA

STEEP WINDING ROAD

To Lemon Grove Garden

ELEVATOR TO MARINA

Via Comunale Park

FOREIGNERS' CLUB

SAN FRANCESCO

VIA DE MAIO

To Marina Grande

VIA S. FRANCESCO

Piazza S. Ant.

SAN ANTONIO

VIA CORREALE

Piazza d. Vittoria

To

10

WALK ENDS

V. PAOLO

V.F.K. GIULIANI

VIA DOMORSO

8

B

#B & C

To Train Station

STAIRS

CORSO ITALIA

B Eastbound #A & D

MUSEUM OF INLAID WOOD

V. ACC.

VIA TASSO

V.S. M. GRAZIE

SAN

VIA D. ACCHI

CESAREO

7

Westbound #A & D

B

1

Piazza Tasso

WALK BEGINS

LIBRERIA TASSO

VIA

6

5

3

VIA S.M. PIETA

2

PALAZZO CORREALE

SAN VINCENZO

VICO PRIMO FUORO

CORSO ITALIA

4

V. SERSALE

CATHEDRAL

VIC. SANT'ANIELLO

N

OLD WALL

Deep Ravine

VIA DEGLI

ARANCI

To Punta del Capo & Positano

VIA

To Meta (Beach), Pompeii & Naples

1 Piazza Tasso
2 Statue of Torquato Tasso
3 Via Santa Maria della Pietà
4 Cathedral
5 Corso Italia & Old Town
6 Sorrento Men's Club

7 Via San Cesareo
8 Statue of St. Anthony
9 Cliffside Square
10 To Ancient Greek Gate & Marina Grande

through the square and walk straight ahead a block inland, under a canopy of trees and past a long taxi queue. Belly up to the green railing in front of Hotel Antiche Mure and look down to see steps that were carved in the fifth century B.C. The combination of the gorge and the seaside cliffs made Sorrento easy to defend. A small section of wall closed the landward gap in the city's defenses (you can still see fragments today a few blocks away, near Hotel Mignon).

Sorrento's name may come from the Greek word for "siren," the legendary half-bird, half-woman who sang an intoxicating lullaby. According to Homer, the sirens lived on an island near here. No one had ever sailed by the sirens without succumbing to their incredible musical charms...and to death. But Homer's hero Ulysses was determined to hear the song. He put wax in his oarsmen's ears and had himself lashed to the mast of his ship. Oh, it was nice. The sirens, thinking they had lost their powers, threw themselves into the sea, and the place became safe to inhabit. Ulysses' odyssey was all about the westward expansion of Greek culture, and to the ancient Greeks, places like Sorrento were the wild, wild west.

• *Back at Piazza Tasso, face the sea and head to the far-left corner of the square. You'll find a...*

❷ **Statue of Torquato Tasso:** The square's namesake, a Sorrento native, was a lively Renaissance poet—but today he seems only to wonder which restaurant to choose for dinner. Directly behind the statue, pop into the **Fattoria Terranova** shop, one of the zillions of fun, touristy boutiques in Sorrento that sells regional goodies and offers free biscuits and tastes of liqueurs. This one makes all of its own entirely organic products on its *agriturismo* farm outside the city.

Just to the right of the shop, peek into the big courtyard of **Palazzo Correale** (#18) to get a feel for an 18th-century aristocratic palace's courtyard, its walls lined with characteristic tiles.

• *As you're leaving the courtyard, on your immediate left you'll see the narrow...*

❸ **Via Santa Maria della Pietà:** Here, just a few yards off the noisy main drag, is a street that goes back centuries before Christ. About 100 yards down the lane, at #24 (on the left), find a 13th-century palace (no balconies back then...for security reasons), now an elementary school. A few steps farther on, you'll see a tiny shrine across the street. Typical of southern Italy, it's where the faithful pray to their saint, who contacts Mary, who contacts Jesus, who contacts God. This shrine is a bit more direct—it starts right with Mary.

• *Continue down the lane, which ends at the delightful...*

❹ **Cathedral:** Walk alongside this long church until you reach the doors facing the street, halfway down. Step inside the outer door (free, daily 8:00-12:30 & 16:30-20:30, no visits during Mass, www.cattedralesorrento.it) and examine the impressive *intarsio* (inlaid-wood) interior doors. They're inlaid on both sides and show scenes of the town and its industry, as well as an old-town map. These were made to celebrate the pope's visit in 1992. Story, continue into the church for a cool stroll around the am¹ checking out the intricate inlaid Stations of the Cross. Work your way toward the back door. Before exiting, on the right find the fine *presepe* (manger scene). This one takes Bethlehem on that first Christmas and sets it in Naples—with pasta, mozzarella, salami, and even Mount Vesuvius in the background. Exiting through the back door, notice that these doors are also finely inlaid wood.

• *Backtrack 10 yards down Via Santa Maria della Pietà, turn left at the passage under the covered arcade, and cross busy Corso Italia.*

❺ **Corso Italia and the Old Town:** In the summer, this stretch of road is closed to traffic each evening, when it hosts the best of the *passeggiata*. Look back at the bell tower, with the scavenged ancient Roman columns at its base. Now go straight down Via P. Reginaldo Giuliani, following the old Greek street plan. Locals claim the ancient Greeks laid out the streets east-west for the most sunlight and north-south for the prevailing and cooling breeze. Pause at the poster board on your right to see who's died lately.

• *One block ahead, on your right, the 14th-century loggia (called Sedil Dominova) is home to the...*

❻ **Sorrento Men's Club:** Once the meeting place of the town's nobles, for generations now the Sedil Dominova has been a retreat for retired working-class men. Strictly no women—and no phones.

Italian men venerate their mothers. (Italians joke that Jesus must have been a southern Italian because his mother believed her son was God, he believed his mom was a virgin, and he lived at home with her until he was 30.) But Italian men have also built into their culture ways to be on their own. Here, men play cards and gossip under an historic emblem of

the city and a finely frescoed 16th-century dome, with its marvelous 3-D scenes.

• *Turn right for a better view of the Men's Club and a historical marker describing the building. Then continue along...*

❼ **Via San Cesareo:** This touristy pedestrian-only shopping street leads back to Piazza Tasso. It's lined with competitive little shops where you can peruse (and sample) lemon products. Notice the huge ancient doorways with their tiny doors—to let the right people in, carefully, during a more dangerous age.

• *After a block, take a left onto Via degli Archi, go under the arch, and then hang a right (under another arch) to the square with the...*

❽ **Statue of St. Anthony** (Antonino): Sorrento's town saint looms among the palms, facing the basilica where the reliquary containing a few of his bones lies (free, downstairs in the

crypt beneath the altar, surrounded by lots of votives).

• *Exit the square at the bottom-left (following the* Lift to the Port *signs; don't go down the street with the line of trees and the* Porto *signs). Watch on the left for* **The Corner Shop**, *where Giovanni sells a wide variety of wines, limoncello, pastas, and other foods, specializing in high-quality products from the Campania region. Soon after, on the right you'll see the trees in front of the Imperial Hotel Tramontano, and to their right a path leading to a...*

❾ **Cliffside Square:** This fine public square, the Villa Comunale, overlooks the harbor. Belly up to the banister to enjoy the

view of Marina Piccola and the Bay of Naples. From here, steps zigzag down to the harbor, where lounge chairs, filled by vacationers working on tans, line the sundecks (there's also the elevator to the harbor). The Franciscan church fronting this square faces a fine modern statue of Francis across the street. Next to the church is a dreamy little cloister. Pop inside to see Sicilian Gothic—a 13th-century mix of Norman, Gothic, and Arabic styles, all around the old pepper tree. This is an understandably popular spot for weddings and concerts.

• *From here, you can quit the walk and stay in the town center or continue another few minutes downhill to the waterfront at Marina Grande (if it's before 20:00, you'll be able to catch a bus back; otherwise, you'll have to walk back uphill).*

❿ *To continue on to Marina Grande, return to the road and keep going downhill. At the next square (Piazza della Vittoria), which offers*

another grand view, cut over to the road closest to the water. After winding steeply down for a few minutes, it turns into a wide stairway, then makes a sharp and steep switchback (take the right fork to continue downhill). Farther down, just before reaching the waterfront, you pass under an...

Ancient Greek Gate: This gate marks the boundary between Sorrento and Marina Grande, technically a separate town with its own proud residents—it's said that even their cats look different. Because Marina Grande dwellers lived outside the wall and were more susceptible to rape, pillage, and plunder, Sorrentines believe that they come from Saracen (Turkish pirate) stock. Sorrentines still scare their children by saying, "Behave—or the Turks will take you away."

• *Now go all the way down the steps into Marina Grande, Sorrento's "big" small-boat harbor.*

Marina Grande: Until recently, this little community was famously traditional, with its economy based on its fishing fleet.

Locals recall when women wore black when a relative died (1 year for an uncle, aunt, or sibling; 2-3 years for a husband or parent). Men got off easy, just wearing a black memorial button.

There are two recommended restaurants on the harbor. **Trattoria da Emilia** has an old newspaper clipping, tacked near the door, about Sophia Loren filming here. On the far side of the harbor, **Ristorante Delfino** boasts a sundeck for a lazy drink before or after lunch.

• *From here, buses return to the center at Piazza Tasso every hour. Or you can walk back up.*

Sights in Sorrento

▲▲Strolling

Take time to explore the surprisingly pleasant old city between Corso Italia and the sea. The views from Villa Comunale, the

public park next to Imperial Hotel Tramontano, are worth the detour. Each night in summer (May-Oct at 19:30; Nov-April weekends only), the police close off Corso Italia to traffic, and Sorrento's main drag becomes a thriving people scene. The *passeggiata* peaks at about 22:00.

Lemon Products Galore

Via San Cesareo is lined with hardworking rival shops selling a mind-boggling array of lemon products and offering samples of lots of sour goodies. You'll find *limoncello,* lemon biscuits, lemon pasta, lemon drops, lemon chocolate, lemon perfume, lemon soap, and on and on. Poke around for a pungent experience (and read the "Lemons" sidebar, later). A few produce stands are also mixed in.

▲Lemon Grove Garden (Agruminato)

This lemon-and-orange grove, lined with shady, welcoming paths, was rescued from development by the city of Sorrento and turned into a park. The family that manages it have seasoned green thumbs and are descended from the family that started working here decades ago, when the grove was still in private hands. The garden is dotted with benches, tables, and an inviting little tasting (and buying) stand. You'll get a chance to sniff and taste the varieties of lemons and enjoy free samples of chilled *limoncello* along with other homemade liqueurs made from basil, mandarins, or fennel. Check out how they've grafted orange-tree branches onto a lemon tree so that both fruits grow on the same tree.

Cost and Hours: Free, daily 10:00-sunset, closed in rainy weather, tel. 081-878-1888, www.igiardinidicataldo.it. Enter the garden on Corso Italia (100 yards north of the train station— where painted tiles show lemon fantasies) or at the intersection of Via Capasso and Via Rota (next to Hotel La Meridiana Sorrento).

Nearby: The family's small "factory"—where you can see how they use the lemons and buy a tasty gelato, *granita,* or lemonade— is just past the parking garage along the road below the garden (Via Correale 27). They also have a small shop across from the Corso Italia entrance (at #267).

Museum of Inlaid Wood
(Museobottega della Tarsialignea)

Sorrento doesn't have much in the way of museums, but if you want to get out of the heat and crowds, this is a good place to do it. It's not only a collection of inlaid wood, but also a painting gallery featuring scenes of 19th-century Sorrento, antique maps, and portraits, as well as a fine decorative arts collection. The basement displays modern examples of inlaid wood. While pricey, it's serious, thoughtfully presented, and bursting with local pride.

Cost and Hours: €8, daily 10:00-18:30, Nov-March until 17:30, Via San Nicola 28, tel. 081-877-1942, www.museomuta.it.

▲Swimming near Sorrento

If you require immediate tanning, you can rent a chair on a pier by the port. There are no great beaches in Sorrento—the gravelly, jam-packed private beaches of **Marina Piccola** are more for partying than pampering, and there's just a tiny spot for public use. The elevator in Villa Comunale city park (next to the Church of San Francesco) gets you down for €1. At **Marina Grande,** Restaurant Delfino has a pier lined with rentable lounge chairs for sunbathing (free for those with this book who buy lunch).

There's a classic, sandy Italian beach two miles away at **Meta,** although it's generally overrun by teenagers from Naples. While the Meta Circumvesuviana stop is a very long walk from

Lemons

Around here, *limoni* are ubiquitous: screaming yellow painted on ceramics, dainty bottles of *limoncello*, and lemons the size of softballs at the fruit stand.

The Amalfi Coast and Sorrento area produce several different kinds of lemons. The gigantic, bumpy "lemons" are actually citrons, called *cedri*, and are more for show—they're pulpier than they are juicy, and make a good marmalade. The juicy *sfusato sorrentino*, grown only in Sorrento, is shaped like an American football, while the *sfusato amalfitano*, with knobby points on both ends, is less juicy but equally aromatic. These two kinds of luscious lemons are used in sweets such as *granita* (shaved ice doused in lemonade), *limoncello* (a candy-like liqueur with a big kick, called *limoncino* on the Cinque Terre), *delizia* (a dome of fluffy cake filled and slathered with a thick whipped lemon cream), *spremuta di limone* (fresh-squeezed lemon juice), and, of course, gelato or *sorbetto alla limone*.

the beach (or a €25 cab ride), bus #A goes directly from Piazza Tasso to Meta beach (last stop, schedule posted for hourly returns). At Meta, you'll find pizzerias, snack bars, and a little free section of beach, but the place is mostly dominated by several sprawling private-beach complexes—if you go, pay for a spot in one of these. Lido Metamare seems best (May-Sept; lockable changing cabins, lounge chairs, and more available for an extra fee; tel. 081-532-2505). It's a very Italian scene—locals complain that it's "too local" (i.e., inundated with riffraff)—with light lunches, a playground, a manicured beach, loud pop music...and no international tourists.

Tarzan might take Jane to the wild and stony beach at **Punta del Capo,** a 15-minute bus ride from Piazza Tasso (the same bus #A explained above, but in the opposite direction from Meta; 2/hour, get off at stop in front of the American Bar, then walk 10 minutes past ruined Roman Villa di Pollio).

Another good choice is **Marina di Puolo,** a tiny fishing town popular in the summer for its sandy beach, surfside restaurants, and beachfront disco (to get here, stay on bus #A a bit farther—ask driver to let you off at Marina di Puolo—then follow signs and hike down about 15 minutes).

More Activities

The Sorrento Sport Snack Bar has two **tennis courts** open to the public (long hours daily, pay to use the court and rent equipment, call to reserve, across from recommended Grand Hotel Ambasciatori at Via Califano 5, tel. 081-807-1616).

To escape the shops, go **snorkeling** or **scuba diving** in the Mediterranean. Contact Futuro Mare for details on the one-hour boat ride out to the protected marine zone that lies between Sorrento and Capri (options for snorkelers, beginners, and experienced certified divers; about 3 hours round-trip, call 1-2 days in advance to reserve, mobile 349-653-6323, www.sorrentodiving.it, info@futuromare.it).

You can **rent motorboats** big enough for four people (with your back to the ferry-ticket offices, it's to the left around the corner at Via Marina Piccola 43; tel. 081-807-2283, www.nauticasicsic. com).

Nightlife in Sorrento

PUBS AND CLUBS

Sorrento is a fun place to enjoy a drink or some dancing after dinner. The crowd is older, and the many local English expats seem to have paved the way for you.

The Fauno Bar, which dominates Piazza Tasso with tables spilling onto the square, is a fine place to make the scene over a drink any time of day.

The Bagattelle American Bar, run by DJ Daniele, who tailors music to the audience (including karaoke, if you ask nicely), is the oldest club in town. The scene, while sloppy, is generally comfortable for the 30- to 60-year-old crowd. If you're alone, there's a pole you can dance with (no cover charge, try their signature cocktail, "Come Back to Sorrento," a mojito made with *limoncello*—no food, nightly from 21:30, down the steps from the flags at Piazza Tasso 10).

The English Inn offers both a streetside pub and a more refined-feeling garden out back—at least until the evening, when the music starts blaring. English vacationers come to Sorrento in droves (many have holidayed here annually for decades). The menu includes fish-and-chips, all-day English breakfast, baked beans on toast, and draft beer (daily, Corso Italia 55, tel. 081-878-2570).

The Foreigners' Club offers live Neapolitan songs, Sinatra-style classics, and jazzy elevator music nightly at 20:00 throughout the summer. It's just right for old-timers feeling frisky (in the center).

THEATER SHOW

At **Teatro Tasso,** a hardworking troupe puts on *The Sorrento Musical,* a folk-music show that treats visitors to a schmaltzy dose of Neapolitan Tarantella music and dance—complete with "Funiculì Funiculà" and "Santa Loo-chee-yee-yah." The 75-minute Italian-language extravaganza features a cast of 14 playing guitar, mandolin, saxophone, and tambourines, and singing operatically from Neapolitan balconies...complete with Vesuvius erupting in the background. Your €25 ticket (€50 with 4-course dinner) includes a drink before and after the show. Maurizio promises my readers a €5 discount if you buy directly from the box office and show this book (2 tickets/book, 3-5 nights/week mid-April-Oct at 21:30, bar opens 30 minutes before show, dinner starts at 20:00 and must be reserved in advance—in person or by email, box office open virtually all day long, theater seats 500, facing Piazza Sant'Antonino in the old town, tel. 081-807-5525, www.teatrotasso.com, info@teatrotasso.com).

Sleeping in Sorrento

Given the location, hotels here often have beautiful views, and many offer balconies. At hotels that offer sea views, ask for a room *"con balcone, con vista sul mare"* (with a balcony, with a sea view). *"Tranquillo"* is taken as a request for a quieter room off the street.

Hotels listed are either near the train station and city center (where balconies overlook city streets) or on cliffside Via Capo (with sea-view balconies). Via Capo is a 20-minute walk—or short bus ride—from the station (for locations, see the map on page 1016).

You should have no trouble finding a room any time except in August, when the town is jammed with Italians and prices often rise above the regular high-season rates.

Note: The spindly, more exotic, and more tranquil Amalfi Coast town of Positano (see next chapter) is also a good place to spend the night.

IN THE TOWN CENTER

$$$$ Hotel Antiche Mura, with 50 rooms and four stars, is sophisticated, elegant, and plush. It offers all the amenities you could need, including an impressive breakfast buffet. Surrounded by lemon trees, the pool and sundeck offer a peaceful oasis. Just a block off the main square, it's quieter than some central hotels because it's perched on the ledge of a dramatic ravine (RS%, some rooms with balconies, family rooms, air-con, elevator, pay parking, closed in winter, a block inland from Piazza Tasso at Via Fuorimura 7, tel. 081-807-3523, www.hotelantichemura.com, info@

Sleep Code

Hotels are classified based on the average price of a standard double room with breakfast in high season.

$$$$	**Splurge:** Most rooms over €170
$$$	**Pricier:** €130-170
$$	**Moderate:** €90-130
$	**Budget:** €50-90
¢	**Backpacker:** Under €50
RS%	**Rick Steves discount**

Unless otherwise noted, credit cards are accepted, hotel staff speak basic English, and free Wi-Fi is available. Comparison-shop by checking prices at several hotels (on each hotel's own website, on a booking site, or by email). For the best deal, *book directly with the hotel*. Ask for a discount if paying in cash; if the listing includes **RS%,** request a Rick Steves discount.

---

hotelantichemura.com, Michele). Meet in front of the hotel for the Mondo Guide full-day Amalfi Coast Minibus tour (see page 948).

$$$$ Palazzo Tasso, nicely located near the center, has 11 small, sleek, fashionably designed modern rooms; there's no public space except for the breakfast room (some rooms with balconies, air-con, elevator, Via Santa Maria della Pietà 33, tel. 081-878-3579, www.palazzotasso.com, info@palazzotasso.com).

$$$$ Plaza Sorrento is a contemporary-feeling, upscale refuge in the very center of town (next door to Antiche Mura but not as elegant). Its 65 rooms mix mod decor with wood grain, and the rooftop swimming pool is inviting (RS%, some rooms with balconies, air-con, elevator, closed in winter, Via Fuorimura 3, tel. 081-878-2831, www.plazasorrento.com, info@plazasorrento.com).

$$ Il Palazzo Starace B&B, conscientiously run by Massimo, offers seven tidy, modern rooms in a little alley off Corso Italia, one block from Piazza Tasso (RS%, some rooms with balconies, family room, air-con, lots of stairs, no elevator but a luggage dumbwaiter, closed in winter, ring bell around corner from Via Santa Maria della Pietà 9, tel. 081-807-2633, mobile 366-950-5377, www.palazzostarace.com, info@palazzostarace.com).

$$ Hotel Mignon rents 22 soothing blue rooms with beautiful, tiled public spaces, a rooftop sundeck, and a small garden surrounded by a lemon grove (RS%, most rooms have balconies but no views, air-con, closed in winter; from the cathedral, walk a block farther up Corso Italia and look for the hotel up a small gated lane to your left; Via Sersale 9, tel. 081-807-3824, www.sorrentohotelmignon.com, info@sorrentohotelmignon.com, Paolo).

$$ Casa Astarita B&B, hiding upstairs in a big building facing the busy main street, has a crazy-quilt-tiled entryway and six bright, tranquil, creatively decorated, air-conditioned rooms (three with little balconies). Thin doors, echoey tile, and a buzzing location can result in noise...bring earplugs (air-con, open all year, 50 yards past the cathedral on Corso Italia at #67, tel. 081-877-4906, www.casastarita.com, info@casastarita.com, Annamaria and Alfonso). If there's no one at reception, ask at Hotel Mignon (described above)—the same family runs both hotels.

$ Ulisse Deluxe Hostel is the best budget deal in town. This "hostel" is actually a hotel, with 56 well-equipped, marble-tiled rooms and elegant public areas, but it also has two single-sex dorm rooms with bunks (RS%, family rooms, breakfast buffet extra, air-con, elevator, spa and pool use extra, pay parking, closed Jan-mid-Feb, Via del Mare 22, tel. 081-877-4753, www.ulissedeluxe.com, info@ulissedeluxe.com, Chiara). It's a five-minute walk from the old-town action: From Corso Italia, walk down the stairs just beyond the hospital *(ospedale)* to Via del Mare. Go downhill along the right side of the big parking lot to find the entrance.

$ Hotel Nice rents 29 simple, cramped, cheap rooms with high ceilings 100 yards in front of the train station on the noisy main drag. This last resort is worth considering only for its very handy-to-the-train-station location. Alfonso promises that you can have a quiet room—critical given the thin windows and busy location—if you request it with your booking email (RS%, air-con, elevator, rooftop terrace, closed Nov-March, Corso Italia 257, tel. 081-878-1650, www.hotelnice.it, info@hotelnice.it).

AT THE EAST END OF TOWN

$$$$ Grand Hotel Ambasciatori is a sumptuous four-star hotel with 100 rooms, a cliffside setting, a sprawling garden, and a pool. This is Humphrey Bogart land, with plush public spaces, a relaxing stay-awhile ambience, and a free elevator to its "private beach"— actually a sundeck built out over the water (RS%, some view rooms, balconies in most rooms, air-con in summer, elevator, pay parking, closed Nov-March, Via Califano 18, tel. 081-878-2025, www.ambasciatorisorrento.com, ambasciatori@manniellohotels.com). It's a short walk from the town center (10-15 minutes from the train station or Piazza Tasso).

WITH A VIEW, ON VIA CAPO

These cliffside hotels are outside of town, toward the cape of the peninsula (from the train station, go straight out Corso Italia, which turns into Via Capo). Once you're set up, commuting into town by bus or on foot is easy. Hotel Minerva is my favorite Sorrento splurge, while Hotel Désirée is a super budget bet with comparable views. If you're in Sorrento to stay put and luxuriate, especially with a car, these accommodations are perfect (although I'd rather luxuriate in Positano—see next chapter).

Getting to Via Capo: From the city center, it's a gradually uphill 15-minute walk (20 minutes from train station, last part is a bit steeper), a €20 taxi ride, or a cheap bus ride. If you're arriving with luggage, you can wait at the train station for one of the long-distance SITA buses that stop on Via Capo on their way to Massa Lubrense (about every 40 minutes; some buses heading for Positano/Amalfi also work—check with the driver). Frequent Sorrento city buses leave from Piazza Tasso in the city center, a five-minute walk from the station (go down a block and turn left on Corso Italia; from far side of the piazza, look for bus #A, about 2-3/hour). Tickets for either bus are sold at the station newsstand and tobacco shops (€1.60). Get off at the Hotel Belair stop for the hotels listed here.

Getting from Via Capo into Town: Buses work great once you get the hang of them (and it's particularly gratifying to avoid the taxi racket). To reach downtown Sorrento from Via Capo, catch any bus heading downhill from Hotel Belair (2-3/hour, buses run all day and evening).

$$$ Hotel Minerva is like a sun-worshipper's temple. The road-level entrance (on a busy street) leads to an elevator that takes you to the fifth-floor reception. Getting off, you'll step onto a spectacular terrace with outrageous Mediterranean views. Bright common areas, a small rooftop swimming pool, and a cold-water Jacuzzi complement 60 large, tiled, colorful rooms with views, some with balconies (RS%, some rooms with balconies, 3-night peak season minimum, air-con, pay parking, closed Nov-March, Via Capo 30, tel. 081-878-1011, www.minervasorrento.com, info@minervasorrento.com).

$$$ Hotel La Tonnarella is an old-time Sorrentine villa turned boutique hotel, with several terraces, stylish tiles, and indifferent service. Eighteen of its 24 rooms have views of the sea, and you can pay extra for a terrace (air-con, pay parking, small beach with private elevator access, closed Nov-March, Via Capo 31, tel. 081-878-1153, www.latonnarella.it, info@latonnarella.it).

$$$ Albergo Settimo Cielo ("Seventh Heaven") is an old-fashioned, family-run cliffhanger sitting 300 steps above Marina Grande. The reception is just off the waterfront side of the road, and the elevator passes down through four floors with 50 clean but spartan rooms—all with grand views, and many with balconies. The rooms feel dated for the price—you're paying for the views (RS%, family rooms, air-con in summer, parking, inviting pool, sun terrace, closed Nov-March, Via Capo 27, tel. 081-878-1012, www.hotelsettimocielo.com, info@hotelsettimocielo.com; Giuseppe, sons Stefano and Massimo, and daughter Serena).

$ Hotel Désirée is a modest affair, with reasonable rates, humbler vistas, and no traffic noise. The 22 basic rooms have high, ravine-facing or partial-sea views, and half come with balconies (all the same price). There's a fine rooftop sunning terrace and a lovable cat, Tia. Owner Corinna (a committed environmentalist), daughter Cassandra, and receptionist Antonio serve an organic breakfast and are hugely helpful with tips on exploring the peninsula (family rooms, most rooms have fans, lots of stairs with no elevator, laundry services, free parking, shares driveway and beach elevator with La Tonnarella, closed early-Nov-Feb except open at Christmas—rare for this area, Via Capo 31, tel. 081-878-1563, www.desireehotelsorrento.com, info@desireehotelsorrento.com).

Eating in Sorrento

GOURMET SPLURGES DOWNTOWN

In a town proud to have no McDonald's, consider eating well for a few extra bucks. Both of these places are worthwhile splurges run by a hands-on boss with a passion for good food and exacting service. The first is gourmet and playful. The second is classic. Both are romantic. Be prepared to relax and stay awhile.

$$$$ Ristorante il Buco, once the cellar of an old monastery, is now a small, dressy restaurant that serves delightfully presented, playful, and creative modern Mediterranean dishes under a grand, rustic arch. Peppe holds a Michelin star, and he and his staff love to explain exactly what's on the plate—often sophisticated dishes with an emphasis on seafood. Reserve ahead (extravagant-tasting €75-100 *menu*s, 10 percent discount when you show this book, good vegetarian selection, Thu-Tue 12:30-14:30 & 19:30-22:30, closed Wed and Jan; just off Piazza Sant'Antonino—facing the basilica, go under the grand arch on the left and immediately enter the restaurant at II Rampa Marina Piccola 5; tel. 081-878-2354, www.ilbucoristorante.it).

$$$$ L'Antica Trattoria enjoys a sedate, *romantico,* candlelit ambience, tucked away in its own little world. The cuisine is traditional but with modern flair, and the inviting menu is fun to peruse (though pricey). Run by the same family since 1930, the restaurant has a trellised garden outside and intimate nooks inside. Aldo and sons will take care of you while Vincenzo—the Joe Cocker-esque resident mandolin player—entertains. Readers who show this book can choose a 10 percent discount on a fixed-price meal or a free *limoncello* if ordering à la carte. Reservations are smart (good vegetarian options, daily 12:00-23:30, closed Mon Nov-Dec, closed Jan-Feb, air-con, Via Padre R. Giuliani 33, tel. 081-807-1082, www.lanticatrattoria.it).

Restaurant Price Code

I've assigned each eatery a price category, based on the average cost of a typical main course (pasta or *secondi*). Drinks, desserts, and splurge items (steak and seafood) can raise the price considerably.

$$$$	**Splurge:** Most main courses over €20
$$$	**Pricier:** €15-20
$$	**Moderate:** €10-15
$	**Budget:** Under €10

In Italy, pizza by the slice and other takeout food is **$**; a basic trattoria or sit-down pizzeria is **$$**; a casual but more upscale restaurant is **$$$**; and a swanky splurge is **$$$$**.

MIDPRICED RESTAURANTS DOWNTOWN

$$$ Inn Bufalito specializes in all things buffalo: *mozzarella di bufala* (and other buffalo milk cheeses), steak, sausage, salami, carpaccio, and buffalo-meat pasta sauce. The smartly designed space has a modern, borderline-trendy, casual atmosphere and a fun indoor-outdoor vibe (don't miss the seasonal specialties on the blackboard, daily 12:00-23:00, closed Nov-March, Vico I Fuoro 21, tel. 081-365-6975).

$$ Ristorante Pizzeria da Gigino, lively and congested with a sprawling interior and tables spilling onto the street, makes huge, tasty Neapolitan-style pizzas in their wood-burning oven (good gnocchi, daily 12:00-24:00, closed Jan-Feb, just off Piazza Sant'Antonino at Via degli Archi 15, tel. 081-878-1927, Antonino).

$$ Meating, as its name implies, focuses on top-quality meats, from homemade sausages to giant steaks on a charcoal grill. They also have vegetarian options and a short, thoughtfully selected list of pastas (Wed-Mon 12:00-15:00 & 18:00-24:00, closed Tue, Via Santa Maria della Pietà 20, tel. 081-878-2891).

$$ Chantecler's Trattoria is a hole-in-the-wall, family-run place with big-screen TVs going; it's on the narrow lane that leads to the cathedral. Their lunch menu is very affordable: €4 *primi* and €5 *secondi*. At dinner, prices are slightly higher but still easy on the budget (good vegetarian dishes, take out or eat in, Tue-Sun 12:00-15:00 & 18:30-23:00, closed Mon, Via Santa Maria della Pietà 38, tel. 081-807-5868; Luigi, Francesco, and family).

With a Sea View: **$$$** The **Foreigners' Club Restaurant** has some of the best sea views in town (with a sprawling terrace under breezy palms), live music nightly at 20:00 (May-mid-Oct), and affordable—if uninspired—meals. It's a good spot for dessert or an after-dinner *limoncello* ("snack" menu with light meals, daily, bar opens at 9:30, meals served 11:00-23:00, Via Luigi de Maio 35, tel.

081-877-3263). If you'd enjoy eating along the water (rather than just with a water view), see "Harborside in Marina Grande," later.

CHEAP EATS DOWNTOWN

Pizza: $ Pizzeria da Franco seems to be Sorrento's favorite place for basic, casual pizza in a fun, untouristy atmosphere. There's nothing fancy about this place—just locals on benches eating hot sandwiches and great pizzas served on waxed paper in a square tin. It's packed to the rafters with a youthful crowd that doesn't mind the plastic cups (takeout possible, daily 8:00-late, just across from Lemon Grove Garden on busy Corso Italia at #265, tel. 081-877-2066).

Kebabs: $ Kebab Ciampa, a little hole-in-the-wall, has a passionate following among eaters who appreciate Andrea's fresh bread, homemade sauces, and ethic of buying meat fresh each day (and closing when the supply is gone). This is your best non-Italian €6 meal in town. Choose beef or chicken—locals don't go for pork—and garnish with fries and/or salad (nightly from 17:00, before the cathedral off Via Santa Maria della Pietà, at Vico il Traversa Pietà 23, tel. 081-807-4595).

Picnics: Get groceries at the **Decò** supermarket (Mon-Sat 8:30-19:55, Sun 9:30-13:00 & 16:30-19:55, Corso Italia 223) or at the **Carrefour** supermarket underneath Hotel Mignon (similar hours).

Gelato: Near the train station, **Gelateria David** has many repeat customers (so many flavors, so little time; they make 145 different flavors, but have about 30 at any one time). In 1957, Augusto Davide opened a *gelateria* in Sorrento, and his grandson Mario proudly carries on the tradition today, still making the gelato on-site. Before choosing a flavor, sample *Profumi di Sorrento* (an explosive sorbet of mixed fruits), "Sorrento moon" (white almond with lemon zest), or lemon crème (daily 9:00-24:00, shorter hours off-season, closed Dec-Feb, a block below the train station at Via Marziale 19, tel. 081-807-3649). Mario also offers gelato-making classes (€12/person, 5-person minimum, 1 hour, call or email ahead to reserve, www.gelateriadavidsorrento.it, gelateriadavid@yahoo.it). Don't mistake this place for the similarly named Gelateria Davide, in the town center.

At **Gelateria Primavera,** Antonio and Alberta whip up 70 exotic flavors...and still have time to make pastries for the pope and other celebrities—check out the photos. Famous and a bit overrated, it's a Sorrento institution (daily 9:00-24:00, just west of Piazza Tasso at Corso Italia 142, tel. 081-807-3252).

HARBORSIDE IN MARINA GRANDE

For a decent dinner *con vista,* head down to either of these restaurants by Sorrento's small-boat harbor, Marina Grande. To get to Marina Grande, follow the directions from the cliffside square on my self-guided Sorrento walk, earlier. For a less scenic route, walk down Via del Mare, past the recommended Ulisse Deluxe Hostel, to the harbor. Either way, it's about a 15-minute stroll from downtown. You can also take bus #D from Piazza Tasso. Be prepared to walk back (last bus leaves at 20:00) or spring for a pricey taxi.

$$$ **Ristorante Delfino** serves fish in big portions to hungry locals in a quiet and bright, Seattle-style pier restaurant. The cooking, service, and setting are all top-notch. The restaurant is lovingly run by Luisa, her brothers, Andrea and Roberto, and her husband, Antonio. Show this book for a free glass of *limoncello* to cap the meal. If you're here for lunch, take advantage of the sundeck—show this book to get an hour of relaxation and digestion on the lounge chairs (daily 12:00-14:30 & 18:30-21:30, closed Nov-March, reservations recommended; at Marina Grande, facing the water, go all the way to the left and follow signs; tel. 081-878-2038).

$$ **Trattoria da Emilia**, at the opposite end of the tranquil Marina Grande waterfront, is considerably more rustic, less expensive, and good for straightforward, typical Sorrentine home-cooking, including fresh fish, lots of fried seafood, and *gnocchi di mamma*—potato dumplings with meat sauce, basil, and mozzarella (daily 12:15-15:00 & 19:00-22:30 except closed Tue Sept-Oct, closed Nov-Feb, no reservations taken, indoor and outdoor seating, tel. 081-807-2720).

Sorrento Connections

It's impressively fast to zip by boat from Sorrento to many coastal towns and islands during the summer—in fact, it's quicker and easier for residents to get around by fast boat than by car or train (see "By Boat," later, and the map on page 1059).

BY TRAIN AND BUS

From Sorrento to Naples, Pompeii, and Herculaneum by Circumvesuviana Train: This commuter train runs twice hourly between Naples and Sorrento (www.eavcampania.it). The schedule is available at the TI. From Sorrento, it's about 30 minutes to Pompeii (€2.20), 50 minutes to Herculaneum (€2.70), and 70 minutes to Naples (€3.60). If there's a line at the train station, you can also buy tickets at the snack bar (across from the main ticket office) or downstairs at the newsstand. For more information on the Circumvesuviana, see "Getting Around the Region" on page 986 of the Naples chapter. Note that the risk of theft on this train is mostly limited to suburban Naples. Going between Sorrento and Pompeii or Herculaneum is generally safer.

From Sorrento to Naples Airport: Six Curreri buses run daily to and from the airport (€10, pay driver, daily at 6:30, 8:30, 10:30, 12:00, 14:00, and 16:30, likely 2 additional departures in summer, 1.5 hours, departs from in front of train station, tel. 081-801-5420, www.curreriviaggi.it).

From Sorrento to the Amalfi Coast: See page 1051.

From Sorrento to Rome: Most people ride the Circumvesuviana 70 minutes to Naples, then catch the Frecciarossa or Italo express train to Rome. Another option is the Sorrento-Rome bus: It's direct, comfortable, cheaper, and all on one ticket—although the departure times can be inconvenient (Mon-Sat at 6:00 and 17:00, Sun at 17:00; off-season Mon-Sat at 6:00, Fri-Sun at 17:00; 4 hours; departs Sorrento from Corso Italia 259B, by Bar Kontatto, a block from the train station, and runs to Tiburtina bus station in Rome; buy tickets at www.marozzivt.it—in Italian only, at some travel agencies, or on board for a surcharge; tel. 080-579-0111).

BY BOAT

The number of boats that run per day varies: The frequency indicated here is for roughly mid-May through mid-October, with more boats per day in the peak of summer and fewer off-season. The specific companies operating each route also tend to change from season to season. Check all schedules locally with the TI, your hotel, or online (use the individual boat company websites—see below—or visit www.capritourism.com, select English, and click "Shipping timetable"). Some ferry-company websites sell tickets online. You can always buy tickets at the port (especially if you're watching the weather); next-day tickets typically go on sale starting the evening before. All boats take several hundred people each—and frequently fill up.

From Sorrento to Capri: Boats run at least hourly. Your options are a fast **ferry** (*traghetto* or *nave veloce*, takes cars, 4/day, 30 minutes, Caremar, tel. 081-807-3077, www.caremar.it) or a slightly faster and pricier **hydrofoil** (*aliscafi*, up to 20/day, 20 minutes, Gescab, tel. 081-807-1812, www.gescab.it). To visit Capri when it's least crowded, it's best to buy your ticket at 8:00 and take the 8:30 hydrofoil (try to depart by 9:45 at the very latest). These early boats can be jammed, but it's worth it once you reach the island.

From Sorrento to Other Points: Naples (6/day, more in summer, departs roughly every 2 hours starting at 7:20, few or no boats on winter weekends, arrives at Molo Beverello, 35 minutes), **Positano** (mid-April-mid-Oct only, 2-4/day, 35 minutes), **Amalfi** (mid-April-mid-Oct only, 2-4/day, 1 hour).

Getting to Sorrento's Port (Marina Piccola): To walk, either hike steeply down directly from Piazza Tasso (find the stairs under the flags), or walk to the Villa Comunale public park (see my self-guided Sorrento Walk, earlier), where you can pay €1 to ride the elevator down (from the bottom, it's a 5-minute walk to the port). Otherwise, catch bus #B or #C from Piazza Sant'Antonino (buy ticket at tobacco shop and specify that you're going to the *porto*), or hop on the little private bus that leaves from under the flags in Piazza Tasso (pay driver; both buses cost €1.20 and run 3/hour).

Capri

Capri was made famous as the vacation hideaway of Roman emperors Augustus and Tiberius. In the 19th century, it was the haunt

of Romantic Age aristocrats on their Grand Tour of Europe. Later it was briefly a refuge for Europe's artsy gay community: Oscar Wilde, D. H. Lawrence, and company hung out here back when being gay could land you in jail...or worse. And these days, the island is a world-class tourist trap, packed with gawky, nametag-wearing visitors searching

for the rich and famous—and finding only their prices.

The "Island of Dreams" is a zoo in July and August—overrun with tacky, low-grade group tourism at its worst. At other times of year, though still crowded, it can provide a relaxing and scenic break from the cultural gauntlet of Italy. Pack your patience, be ready to wait around a bit (for buses, boats, etc.), and try to enjoy being on vacation. What gets lost in all of the fame and glitz is simply how gorgeous a place it is: Chalky white limestone cliffs rocket boldly from the shimmering blue and green surf. Strategically positioned gardens, villas, and other viewpoints provide stunning vistas of the Sorrento Peninsula, Amalfi Coast, Vesuvius, and Capri itself.

PLANNING YOUR TIME

This is the best see-everything-in-a-day plan from Naples or Sorrento: Take an early hydrofoil to Capri (from Sorrento, buy ticket at 8:00, boat leaves around 8:30 and arrives around 8:50—smart). Go directly by boat to the Blue Grotto. Instead of taking the boat back, catch a bus from the grotto to Anacapri, which has two or three hours' worth of sightseeing. In Anacapri, see the town, ride the chairlift to Monte Solaro and back (or hike down), stroll out

SORRENTO & CAPRI

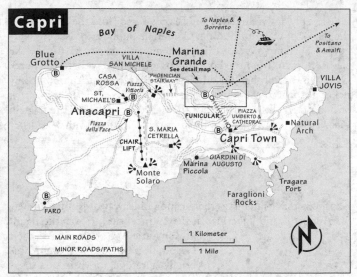

Capri

Bay of Naples

To Naples & Sorrento

Blue Grotto

VILLA SAN MICHELE

Marina Grande
See detail map

To Positano & Amalfi

CASA ROSSA

"PHOENICIAN STAIRWAY"

ST. MICHAEL'S

Piazza Vittoria

VILLA JOVIS

Anacapri

FUNICULAR

PIAZZA UMBERTO & CATHEDRAL

Piazza della Pace

S. MARIA CETRELLA

Natural Arch

CHAIR LIFT

Capri Town

Marina Piccola

GIARDINI DI AUGUSTO

Monte Solaro

Tragara Port

Faraglioni Rocks

FARO

---- MAIN ROADS
---- MINOR ROADS/PATHS

1 Kilometer

1 Mile

N

from the base of the chairlift to Villa San Michele for the view, and eat lunch. Afterward, catch a bus to Capri town, which is worth at least a half-hour. Finally, ride the funicular from Capri town down to the harbor and laze on the free beach or wander the yacht harbor while waiting for your boat back to Sorrento.

If you're heading to Capri specifically to see the Blue Grotto, be sure to check the weather and sea conditions. If the tide is too high or the water too rough, the grotto can be closed. Ask the TI or your hotelier before going. If the Blue Grotto is closed or you're just not keen on seeing it, you can enjoy a leisurely day on the island seeing the sights in Anacapri and Capri town.

Efficient travelers can see Capri on the way between destinations: Sail from Sorrento, check your bag at the harbor, see Capri, and take a boat directly from there to Naples or to the Amalfi Coast (or vice versa).

If you buy a one-way ticket to Capri (there's no round-trip discount), you'll have maximum schedule flexibility and can take any convenient hydrofoil or ferry back. (Check times for the last return crossing upon arrival with any TI on Capri, or at www.capritourism.com; the last return trips usually leave between 18:30 and 19:30.) During July and August, however, it's wise to get a round-trip boat ticket with a late return time (ensuring you a spot on a boat at the time they're most crowded)—you can always use the ticket to return earlier if you like. On busy days, be 20 minutes early for the boat, or you can be bumped.

Starting your day as early as is reasonably possible is key to an enjoyable trip to Capri. Day-trippers come down from as far as Rome, creating a daily rush hour in each direction (arriving between 10:00-11:00, leaving around 17:00). If you arrive before them, the entire trip to and into the Blue Grotto might take just a half-hour; arrive later and you might face a two-hour delay.

GETTING TO CAPRI

For instructions on getting to Capri by **scheduled ferry,** check the "Connections" sections of the Sorrento and Naples chapters and the "Getting Around the Amalfi Coast" section of the Amalfi Coast chapter.

Another option is to visit Capri by **tour boat. Mondo Guide** offers my readers a great-value, no-stress, all-day itinerary for €80: You'll be picked up at your Sorrento hotel around 8:00 and driven to the port, where you'll board a small boat (maximum 10 people, shared with other Rick Steves readers) and be taken across to Capri to visit the Blue Grotto (optional entry fee to hop in one of the little rowboats to go in). Then you'll continue to Marina Grande for about four hours of free time on the island—just enough to head to Anacapri for sightseeing and the Monte Solaro chairlift (island transportation and admissions on your own). Finally you'll reboard the boat for a lightly narrated circle around the island and pass through the iconic Faraglioni Rocks (includes drinks, a snack, and—conditions permitting—a chance to swim from the boat). Considering the expense and hassle of doing all this on your own, the tour is a good value—you're basically paying about €20-30 extra for a less stressful, more personal experience. The trip only goes if enough people sign up, and reservations are required—book online at www.mondoguide.com. For details on Mondo and their tours, see page 948. If Mondo's tour isn't running on a day that you want to go, **Tempio Travel**—based at the Sorrento train station—offers a similar trip at a similar price (tel. 081-878-2103, www.tempiotravel.com, or drop by their office).

Orientation to Capri

First thing—pronounce it right: Italians say KAH-pree, not kah-PREE like the song or the pants. The island is small—just four miles by two miles—and is separated from the Sorrentine Peninsula by a narrow strait. Home to 13,000 people, Capri has only two towns to speak of: Capri and Anacapri. The island also has some scant Roman ruins and a few interesting churches and villas. But its chief attraction is its famous Blue Grotto, and its best activity is the chairlift from Anacapri up the island's Monte Solaro.

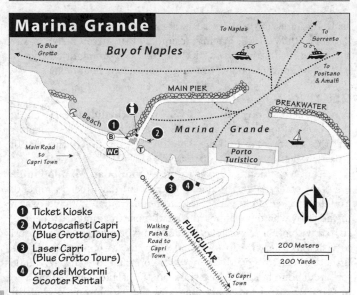

1. Ticket Kiosks
2. Motoscafisti Capri (Blue Grotto Tours)
3. Laser Capri (Blue Grotto Tours)
4. Ciro dei Motorini Scooter Rental

TOURIST INFORMATION

Capri's efficient English-speaking TI has branches in Marina Grande, Capri town, and Anacapri. Their well-organized website has schedules and practical information in English (www. capritourism.com). At any TI, pick up the free map or pay for a better one if you'll be venturing to the outskirts of Capri town or Anacapri.

The **Marina Grande TI** is by the Motoscafisti Capri tour boat dock (May-Sept Mon-Sat 9:00-13:30 & 15:30-18:00, Sun 9:00-13:00, shorter hours off-season, tel. 081-837-0634).

The **Capri town TI** fills a closet under the bell tower on Piazza Umberto I and is less crowded than its sister at the port (same hours as Marina Grande TI, WC and baggage storage downstairs behind TI, tel. 081-837-0686).

The tiny **Anacapri TI** is on the main pedestrian/shopping street, Via Orlandi, at #59 (Mon-Sat 9:00-15:00, closed Sun, shorter hours Nov-Easter, tel. 081-837-1524).

ARRIVAL IN CAPRI

Get oriented on the boat before you dock, as you near the harbor with the island spread out before you. The port is a small community of its own, called **Marina Grande,** connected by a funicular and buses to the rest of the island. **Capri town** fills the ridge high above the harbor. The ruins of Emperor Tiberius' palace, **Villa Jovis,** cap the peak on the left. To the right, the dramatic *"Mamma mia!"* road arcs around the highest mountain on the island (**Monte Solaro),** leading up to **Anacapri** (the island's second town, just out of sight). Notice the old zigzag steps below that road. Until 1874, this was the only connection between Capri and Anacapri. (Though it's quite old, it's nowhere near as old as implied by its nickname, "The Phoenician Stairway.") The white house on the ridge above the zigzags is **Villa San Michele** (where you can go later for a grand view of boats like the one you're on now).

Arrival at Marina Grande: Upon arrival, get your bearings. Find the base of the **funicular railway** (signed *funicolare*) that runs up to Capri town, and stand facing it, with your back to the water.

The fourth little clothing-and-souvenir shop to the right of the funicular provides **baggage storage** (look inside for *left luggage* sign on far back wall, daily 9:00-18:00, tel. 081-837-4575, shorter hours or closed in winter). If it's closed, your best option is at the upper funicular station in Capri town (bag storage near public WCs, daily 7:00-20:00; be aware that you may have to pay extra to take big bags up the funicular).

To your right are ticket windows with counters for **funicular and bus tickets** and for **boat tickets** to Naples and Sorrento. Just beyond these is the **stop for buses** to the rest of the island. (Notice how long the line is for your destination, and how small the buses are—and line up accordingly.) Across the street is a pay **WC**, and a little farther on is Marina Grande's pebbly public beach.

Two companies offer **boat trips** around the island and to the Blue Grotto: Laser Capri and Motoscafisti Capri. Motoscafisti Capri's ticket shed is along the pier; Laser Capri's office is halfway down the waterfront to the left at Via Cristoforo Colombo 69. Both offer similar services (see "Getting Around Capri," later).

The **TI** is along the pier, facing the Motoscafisti Capri dock.

From the port, you can take a boat to the Blue Grotto (my recommended plan) or around the island, the funicular to Capri town, or a bus to various destinations on Capri. If you have energy to burn, you can follow the steep paved footpath that connects the port area with Capri town. It starts a block inland from the ferry dock (follow the signs to *Capri centro;* allow 30 minutes).

HELPFUL HINTS

Cheap Tricks: A cheap day trip to Capri is tough. Hydrofoils from Sorrento cost €17 each way, and a Blue Grotto ticket (including boat transportation) comes to €28—so you've already broken €60 per person before factoring in bus tickets and admissions elsewhere on the island. You can save a few euros by taking the slightly slower (but less frequent) Caremar ferry to Capri instead of the hydrofoil, and another few euros by using the bus to the Blue Grotto instead of the boat.

Best Real Hike: Serious hikers love the peaceful and scenic three-hour Fortress Hike, which takes you entirely away from the tourists. You'll walk under ruined forts along the rugged coast, from the Blue Grotto to the *faro* (lighthouse). From there, you can take a bus back to Anacapri (3/hour). The TI has a fine map/brochure.

Free Beach: Marina Grande has a free pebbly beach (you can pay for a shower at the bar).

Local Guides: Friendly **Anna Bilardi Leva** lives on Capri and is licensed to guide both on the island and elsewhere around the region (€150/half-day, €220/day, 10 percent discount if you show this book, mobile 339-712-7416, www.capritourinformation.com, annaleva@hotmail.it).

GETTING AROUND CAPRI

By Bus and Funicular: Tickets for the island's buses and funicular cost €1.80 per ride and are available at newsstands, tobacco shops, official ticket offices, or from the driver. Validate your ticket when you board. The €8.60 all-day pass (available only at official ticket offices) doesn't pay for itself unless you ride around like mad.

Schedules are clearly posted at all bus stations. Public buses are orange, while the gray and blue buses are for private tour groups. Public buses from the port to Capri town, and from Capri town to Anacapri, are frequent (4/hour, 10 minutes). The direct bus between the port and Anacapri runs less often (2/hour, 25 minutes). From Anacapri, branch bus lines run to the parking lot above the Blue Grotto and to the lighthouse (3/hour each). Buses are teeny (because of the island's narrow roads) and often packed. At most stops, you'll see ranks for passengers to line up in. When the driver changes the bus's display to read *completo* (full), you just have to wait for the next one.

By Taxi: Taxis have fixed rates, listed at www.capritourism.com (Marina Grande to Capri town-€17; Marina Grande to Anacapri-€23). You can hire a taxi for about €70 per hour—negotiate.

By Scooter: If you are an experienced scooter rider, this is the perfect way to have the run of the island. (For novice riders, Capri's steep and narrow roads aren't a good place to start.) **Ciro dei Motorini** proudly rents bright-yellow scooters with 50cc engines—strong enough to haul couples. Rental includes a map and instructions with parking tips and other helpful information (€15/hour, €55/day, 10 percent discount with this book for 2 hours or more; includes helmet, gas, and insurance; daily April-Oct 9:30-19:00, may open in good weather off-season, look for Ferrari logo at Via Don Giobbe Ruocco 55, Marina Grande, mobile 338-360-6918, www.capriscooter.com).

Boat Trips Around the Island: Both **Laser Capri** and **Moto-scafisti Capri** run quick one-hour trips that circle the island, passing stunning cliffs, caves, and views that most miss when they go only to the Blue Grotto (€18; see contact info under "Blue Grotto," later). With both companies, you can combine the boat trip with a stop at the Blue Grotto at no extra charge (this adds about an hour; check schedules to find out which tours include the optional Blue Grotto stop). As the trip just to the grotto already costs €15, the island circle is well worth the extra few euros (boats leave daily from 9:00 until 13:00 or possibly later—whenever Blue Grotto rowboats stop running).

Sights in Capri

CAPRI TOWN AND NEARBY

This is a cute but extremely clogged and touristy shopping town. It's worth a brief visit, including the Giardini di Augusto, before moving on to more interesting parts of the island.

The funicular drops you just around the corner from Piazza Umberto, the town's main square. With your back to the funicular, the bus stop is 50 yards straight ahead down Via Roma. You'll find the **TI** under the bell tower on Piazza Umberto (see "Tourist Information," earlier). The footpath to the port starts just behind the TI, near the baggage storage (follow signs to *Il Porto,* 15-minute walk).

Capri town's multidomed Baroque **cathedral,** which faces the square, is worth a quick look. Its multicolored marble floor at the

altar was scavenged from Emperor Tiberius' villa in the 19th century.

To the left of City Hall (Municipio, lowest corner), a narrow, atmospheric lane leads into the medieval part of town, which has plenty of eateries and is the starting point for the walk to Villa Jovis.

The lane to the left of the cathedral (past Bar Tiberio, under the wide arch) is a fashionable shopping strip that's justifiably been dubbed **"Rodeo Drive"** by residents. Walk a few minutes down Rodeo Drive (past Gelateria Buonocore at #35, with its tempting fresh waffle cones) to Quisisana Hotel, the island's top old-time hotel. From there, head left for fancy shops and villas, and right for gardens and views.

Downhill and to the right, a five-minute walk leads to a lovely public garden, **Giardini di Augusto** (€1, April-Oct daily 9:00-19:30, Nov-March until 17:30, free to enter off-season, no picnicking). While the garden itself is modest, it boasts great views over the famous Faraglioni Rocks—handy if you don't have the time, money, or interest to access the higher vantage points near Anaca-pri (Monte Solaro, Villa San Michele).

Villa Jovis and the Emperor's Capri

Even before becoming emperor, Augustus loved Capri so much that he traded the family-owned Isle of Ischia to the (then-inde-pendent) Neapolitans in exchange for making Capri his personal property. Emperor Tiberius spent a decade here, A.D. 26-37. (Some figure he did so in order to escape being assassinated in Rome.)

Emperor Tiberius' ruined villa, Villa Jovis, is a scenic 45-min-ute hike from Capri town. You won't find any statues or mosaics here—just an evocative, ruined complex of terraces clinging to a rocky perch over a sheer drop to the sea...and a lovely view. You can make out a large water reservoir for baths, the foundations of servants' quarters, and Tiberius' private apartments (fragments of marble flooring still survive). The ruined lighthouse dates from the Middle Ages.

Cost and Hours: €2, Wed-Mon 10:00-18:00, closed Tue, shorter hours and possibly closed off-season—check at Capri TI.

▲▲ BLUE GROTTO

Three thousand tourists a day spend a couple of hours visiting Ca-pri's Blue Grotto (Grotta Azzurra). I did—early (when the light is best), without the frustration of crowds, and with choppy waves nearly making entrance impos-sible...and it was great.

The actual cave experience isn't much: a five-minute dinghy ride through a three-foot-high entry hole to reach a 60-yard-long cave, where the sun reflects brilliantly blue on its limestone bottom. But the experience—getting there, getting in, and getting back—is a scenic hoot. You get a fast ride and scant narration on a 30-foot boat partway around the gorgeous island; along the way, you see bird life and dramatic limestone cliffs. You'll understand why Roman emperors appre-ciated the invulnerability of the island—it's surrounded by cliffs, with only one good access point, and therefore easy to defend.

Just outside the grotto, your boat idles as you pile into eight-foot dinghies that hold up to four passengers each. Next, you'll be taken to a floating ticket counter and asked to pass the €13 grotto entry fee over the side. From there, your ruffian rower will elbow his way to the tiny hole, then pull fast and hard on the cable at the low point of the swells to squeeze you into the grotto (keep your head down and hands in the boat). Then your man rows you around, spouting off a few descriptive lines and singing "O Sole Mio." Depending upon the strength of the sunshine that day, the blue light inside can be brilliant.

The grotto was actually an ancient Roman *nymphaeum*—a retreat for romantic hanky-panky. Many believe that, in its day, a tunnel led here directly from the palace, and that the grotto experience was enlivened by statues of Poseidon and company, placed half-underwater as if emerging from the sea. It was ancient Romans who smoothed out the entry hole that's still used to this day.

When dropping you off, your boatman will fish for a tip—it's optional, and €1 is enough (you've already paid plenty). If you don't want to return by boat, ask to be let off at the little dock, where stairs lead up to a café and the Blue Grotto bus stop.

Cost: The €13 entry fee (separate from the €15 ride from Marina Grande and back) includes €9 for the rowboat service plus €4 for admission to the grotto itself. Though some people swim in for free from the little dock after the boats stop running, it's illegal and can be dangerous.

Timing: When waves or high tide make entering dangerous, the boats don't go in—the grotto can close without notice, sending tourists (flush with anticipation) home without a chance to squeeze through the little hole. (If this happens to you, consider the one-hour boat ride around the island instead.)

If you're coming from Capri's port (Marina Grande), allow 1-3 hours for the entire visit, depending on the chaos at the caves. Going with the first trip will get you there at the same time as the boatmen in their dinghies—who hitch a ride behind your boat—resulting in less chaos and a shorter wait at the entry point.

If you arrive on the island later in the morning—when the Blue Grotto is already jammed—you could try waiting to visit until about 15:00, when most of the tour groups have vacated. But this may only work by bus (not boat). Confirm that day's closing time with a TI before making the trip.

Getting There: You can take the boat directly from Marina Grande, as most people do, or save money by taking the bus via Anacapri.

By Boat from Marina Grande: Two companies make the boat trip from different parts of Marina Grande—Laser Capri and Motoscafisti Capri (€15 round-trip with either company, no one-way discount; Motoscafisti Capri—tel. 081-837-7714, www.motoscafisticapri.com; Laser Capri—tel. 081-837-5208, www.lasercapri.com). The first boats depart Marina Grande at 9:00, and continue at least until 13:00—or later, depending on when the rowboats stop running (likely 17:00 in summer).

By Bus via Anacapri: If you're on a budget, you can take the

SORRENTO & CAPRI

bus from Anacapri to the grotto (rather than a boat from Marina Grande). You'll save almost €8, lose time, and see a beautiful, calmer side of the island.

Anacapri-Blue Grotto buses (roughly 3/hour, 10 minutes) depart only from the Anacapri bus station at Piazza della Pace (not from the bus stop at Piazza Vittoria 200 yards away, which is more popular with tourists). If you're coming from Marina Grande or Capri town and want to transfer to the Blue Grotto buses, don't get off when the driver announces "Anacapri." Instead, ride one more stop to Piazza della Pace. If in doubt, ask the driver or a local. At the Piazza della Pace bus station, notice the two lines: Grotta Azzurra for the Blue Grotto, and Faro for the lighthouse.

Getting Back from the Blue Grotto: You can take the boat back or ask your boatman to drop you off on the small dock next to the grotto entrance, from where you climb up the stairs to the stop for the bus to Anacapri (if you came by boat, you'll still have to pay the full round-trip boat fare).

ANACAPRI TOWN AND NEARBY

Capri's second town has two or three hours' worth of interesting sights. Though Anacapri sits higher up on the island ("ana" means "upper" in Greek), there are no sea views at street level in the town center.

When visiting Anacapri by bus, note that there are two stops: Piazza Vittoria, in the center of town near the base of the Monte Solaro chairlift; and 200 yards farther along at Piazza della Pace (pronounced "PAH-chay"), a larger bus station near the cemetery. Piazza Vittoria gets you a bit closer to the main sights (chairlift and Villa San Michele), while Piazza della Pace is where you transfer to the Blue Grotto bus. When leaving Anacapri for Capri town or Marina Grande, buses can be packed. Your best chance of getting a seat is to catch the bus from Piazza della Pace.

Regardless of where you get off, make your way to **Via Orlandi,** Anacapri's pedestrianized main street. From Piazza Vittoria, the street is right there—just go down the lane to the right of the Anacapri statue. From Piazza della Pace, reach it via the crosswalk and then the small lane called Via Filietto. Anacapri's **TI** is at Via Orlandi 59, near Piazza Vittoria.

To see the town, stroll along Via Orlandi for 10 minutes or so. Signs suggest a quick circuit that links the Casa Rossa, St. Michael's Church, and peaceful side streets. You'll also find shops and eateries, including good choices for quick, inexpensive pizza, *panini,* and other goodies (both open daily in peak season): **$ Sciué Sciué** (same price for informal seating or takeaway, near the TI at #73, tel. 081-837-2068) and **$ Pizza e Pasta** (takeaway only, just before the church at #157, tel. 328-623-8460).

Of the sights below, the first two are in the heart of town (on or near Via Orlandi), while the next two are a short walk away.

Casa Rossa (Red House)

This "Pompeiian-red," eccentric home, a hodgepodge of architectural styles, is the former residence of John Clay MacKowen, a Louisiana doctor and ex-Confederate officer who moved to Capri in the 1870s and married a local girl. (MacKowen and the Villa San Michele's Axel Munthe—see later—loathed each other, and even tried to challenge each other to a duel.) Its small collection of 19th-century paintings of scenes from around the island recalls a time before mass tourism. Don't miss the second floor, with more paintings and four ancient, sea-worn statues, which were recovered from the depths of the Blue Grotto in the 1960s and 1970s.

Cost and Hours: €3.50; discounted to €1 with ticket stub from Blue Grotto, Villa San Michele, or Monte Solaro chairlift; June-Sept Tue-Sun 10:00-13:30 & 17:30-20:00; shorter hours April-May and Oct; closed Nov-March and Mon year-round, Via Orlandi 78, tel. 081-838-2193.

▲Church of San Michele

This Baroque church in the village center has a remarkable majolica floor showing paradise on earth in a classic 18th-century Neapoli-

tan style. The entire floor is ornately tiled, featuring an angel (with flaming sword) driving Adam and Eve from paradise. The devil is wrapped around the trunk of a beautiful tree. The animals—happily ignoring this momentous event—all have human expressions. For the best view, climb the spiral stairs from the postcard desk. Services are held only during the first two weeks of Advent, when the church is closed to visitors.

Cost and Hours: €2, daily April-Oct 9:00-18:30, Nov and mid-Dec-March usually 10:00-14:00, closed late Nov-mid Dec, in town center just off Via Orlandi—look for *San Michele* signs, tel. 081-837-2396, www.chiesa-san-michele.com.

▲Villa San Michele

This is the 19th-century mansion of Axel Munthe, Capri's grand personality, an idealistic Swedish doctor who lived here until 1943 and whose services to the Swedish royal family brought him into contact with high society. At the very least, walk the path from Piazza Victoria past the villa to a superb, free view-point over Capri town, Marina Grande, and—in the distance—Mount Vesuvius and Sorrento. Paying to enter the villa lets you see a few rooms with period furnishings; a well-done but ho-hum exhibit on Munthe; and one of this region's most delightful gardens, with a chapel, the Olivetum (a tiny museum of native birds and bugs), and a view that's slightly better than the free one outside. Throughout the gardens and the house, you'll see a smattering of original ancient objects unearthed here—and lots and lots of copies. A café (also with a view) serves affordable sandwiches.

Cost and Hours: €7, daily 9:00-18:00, closes earlier Oct-April, tel. 081-837-1401, www.villasanmichele.eu.

Getting There: From Piazza Vittoria, walk up the grand staircase and turn left onto Via Capodimonte. At the start of the shopping street, on your right, pass the deluxe Capri Palace Hotel—venture in if you can get past the treacherously eye-catching swimming pool windows (behind the pillars). After lots of over-priced shops, just before the villa, notice the Swedish consulate. In honor of Munthe, Swedes get into the villa for free.

▲▲Chairlift up to Monte Solaro

From Anacapri, you can ride the chairlift *(seggiovia)* to the 1,900-foot summit of Monte Solaro for a commanding view of the Bay of

Naples. Work on your tan as you float over hazelnut, walnut, chestnut, apricot, peach, kiwi, and fig trees, past a montage of tourists (mostly from cruise ships; when the grotto is closed—as it often is—they bring passengers here instead). Prospective smoochers should know that the lift seats are all single. As you ascend, consider how Capri's real estate has been priced out of the locals' reach. The ride takes 13 minutes each way, and you'll want at least 30 minutes on top, where there are picnic benches and a café with WCs.

Cost and Hours: €8 one-way, €11 round-trip, daily 9:30-17:00, last run down at 17:30; March-April until 16:00, Nov-Feb until 15:30, tel. 081-837-1438, www.capriseggiovia.it.

Getting There: From the Piazza Vittoria bus stop, just climb the steps and look right.

At the Summit: You'll enjoy the best panorama possible: lush cliffs busy with seagulls enjoying the ideal nesting spot. Find the

Faraglioni Rocks—with tour boats squeezing through every few minutes—which are an icon of the island. The pink building nearest the rocks was an American R&R base during World War II. Eisenhower and Churchill met here. On the peak closest to Cape Sorrento, you can see the distant ruins of Emperor Tiberius' palace, Villa Jovis. Pipes from the Sorrento Peninsula bring water to Capri (demand for fresh water here long ago exceeded the supply provided by the island's three natural springs). The Galli Islands mark the Amalfi Coast in the distance. Cross the bar terrace for views of Mount Vesuvius and Naples.

Hiking Down: A highlight for hardy walkers (provided you have strong knees and good shoes) is the 40-minute down-

hill hike from the top of Monte Solaro, through lush vegetation and ever-changing views, past the 14th-century Chapel of Santa Maria Cetrella (at the trail's only intersection, it's a 10-minute detour to the right), and back into Anacapri. The trail starts downstairs, past the WCs (last chance).

Down two more flights of stairs, look for the sign to *Anacapri e Cetrella*—you're on your way. While the trail is well established, you'll encounter plenty of uneven steps, loose rocks, and few signs.

Lighthouse near Anacapri

The lighthouse *(faro)*, at the rocky, arid, and desolate southwestern corner of the island, is a favorite place to enjoy the sunset. This area has a private beach, pool, small restaurants, and a few fishermen. Reach it by bus from Anacapri (3/hour, departs from Piazza della Pace stop).

Capri Connections

From Capri's Marina Grande by Boat to: Sorrento (ferry: 4/day, 30 minutes, www.caremar.it; hydrofoil: up to 20/day, 20 minutes, www.gescab.it), **Naples** (roughly hourly, more in summer, hydrofoil: 45 minutes, arrives at Molo Beverello; ferries: 50-80 minutes, arrive at Calata Porta di Massa), **Positano** (mid-April-mid-Oct, 2-4/day, 30-60 minutes), **Amalfi** (mid-April-mid-Oct, 1/day, 1.5 hours). Confirm the schedule carefully at TIs or www.capritourism.com—the last boats back to the mainland usually leave around 19:00-20:00.

AMALFI COAST & PAESTUM

With its stunning scenery, hill- and harbor-hugging towns, and historic ruins, Amalfi is Italy's coast with the most. The breathtaking trip from Sorrento to Salerno is one of the world's great bus rides. It will leave your mouth open and your camera's memory card full. You'll gain respect for the 19th-century Italian engineers who built the roads—and even more for the 21st-century drivers who squeeze past each other here daily. Cantilevered garages, hotels, and villas cling to the vertical terrain, and beautiful but out-of-reach coves tease from far below. As you hyperventilate, notice how the Mediterranean, a sheer 500-foot drop below, really twinkles. All this beautiful scenery apparently inspires local Romeos and Juliets, with the latex evidence of late-night romantic encounters littering the roadside turnouts. Over the centuries, the spectacular scenery and climate have been a siren call for the rich and famous, luring Roman Emperor Tiberius, Richard Wagner, Sophia Loren, Gore Vidal, and others to the Amalfi Coast's special brand of *la dolce vita*.

The two main Amalfi Coast towns (Positano and Amalfi) are pretty, but they're also touristy, congested, and overpriced. (Many visitors prefer side-tripping in from Sorrento.) Most beaches here are private, pebbly, and expensive. Check and understand your bills in this greedy region.

At Paestum, farther south, you can see one of the world's best collections of ruined Greek temples, a worthwhile museum with artifacts from the site, and the remains of a Roman town.

Amalfi Coast

The Amalfi Coast is one of those places with a "must see" reputation. Staggeringly picturesque and maddeningly touristy, it can be both rewarding and frustrating. As if an antidote to intense Naples, it is the perfect place for a romantic break, if done right and if you can afford it. These towns are the big three sights of the Amalfi Coast: Positano is like a living Gucci ad; Amalfi evokes a day when small towns with big fleets were powerhouses on the Mediterranean; and Ravello is fun for that tramp-in-a-palace feeling.

PLANNING YOUR TIME

On a quick visit, use Sorrento (see previous chapter) as your home base and do the Amalfi Coast as a day trip (skipping Paestum). But for a small-town vacation from your vacation, spend a few more days on the coast, sleeping in Positano or Amalfi town.

Trying to decide between staying in Sorrento, Positano, or Amalfi? Sorrento is the largest of the three, with useful services and the best transportation connections and accommodations. Tiny Positano is the most chic and picturesque, with a decent beach, but it's perhaps the most touristy. The town of Amalfi feels like a real, workaday city—with the most actual sights and good hiking opportunities—but it lacks the romantic charm of the others.

Naples or Paestum can also work as a base for an Amalfi Coast day trip, if you get an early start and the timetables align. From Naples, you have two options by public transport: train to Salerno, then bus (or boat) to Amalfi town; or, Circumvesuviana train to Sorrento, then bus to Positano and/or Amalfi. (You can go out one way and return the other.) From Paestum, you can take the train to Salerno, then the bus (or boat) to Amalfi.

GETTING AROUND THE AMALFI COAST

The real thrill here is the scenic drive between Sorrento and Salerno. The stretch from Positano to Amalfi is the best. This is treacherous stuff—even if you have a car, you may want to take the bus or hire a driver. Brave souls enjoy seeing the coast by scooter or motorbike (rent in Sorrento).

Below, I've outlined your options by bus, boat, and taxi. Many travelers do the Amalfi Coast as a round-trip by bus, but a good strategy is to go one way by bus and return by boat. For

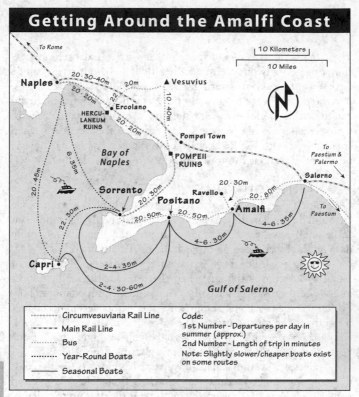

Getting Around the Amalfi Coast

To Rome

Naples 20·30-40m 20m ▲ Vesuvius

20·20m

Ercolano 10·40m

HERCU-
LANEUM
RUINS 20·20m

Pompei Town

6·35m Bay of Naples POMPEII RUINS To Paestum & Palermo

20·45m Sorrento 20·30m Ravello 20·30m Salerno

22·30m 20·50m Positano 20·50m Amalfi 20·30m To Paestum

Capri 2-4·35m 4-6·30m

2-4·30-60m Gulf of Salerno

10 Kilometers
10 Miles

N

Code:
1st Number - Departures per day in summer (approx.)
2nd Number - Length of trip in minutes
Note: Slightly slower/cheaper boats exist on some routes

··········· Circumvesuviana Rail Line
– – – – – Main Rail Line
············· Bus
--------- Year-Round Boats
———— Seasonal Boats

AMALFI COAST

example, instead of bussing from Sorrento to Salerno (end of the line) and back again, consider taking the bus along the coast to Positano and/or Amalfi, then catching the ferry back. Ferries run less often in spring and fall, and some don't run at all off-season (mid-Oct-mid-April). Boats don't run in stormy weather at any time of year. If boats aren't running between Amalfi and Sorrento, change boats in Capri.

Looking for exercise? Consider an Amalfi Coast hike (see "Hikes" on page 1076). Numerous trails connect the main coastal towns with villages on the hills. Get a good map before you venture out.

Moving on from the Amalfi Coast: It can be easier to continue around the coast to Salerno, a major transportation hub, than retrace your steps to Sorrento. For example, if you're overnighting in Positano or Amalfi and headed to Naples or Rome in the morning, you can catch a boat or bus to Salerno and take advantage of faster trains from there.

By Bus

SITA buses from Sorrento to Amalfi, via Positano, are the most common, inexpensive way to see the coast (for schedules, see www.sitabus.it or—easier to read—www.positano.com). In Sorrento, buses depart from in front of the train station beginning at 6:30; from 8:30 they run roughly every half hour until 16:00, then hourly until 22:00 in summer, until 19:00 in winter (50-minute trip to Positano; another 50 minutes to Amalfi). To reach Ravello (the hill town beyond Amalfi) or Salerno (at the far end of the coast), transfer in Amalfi.

Individual tickets are inexpensive (€2-4). All rides are covered by the 24-hour Costiera SITA Sud pass (€8), which may not save you money but does save time buying tickets. Tickets are sold at tobacco shops and newsstands, not by drivers; in Sorrento, buy them at an outdoor stand by the bus stop or in train station shops.

Line up under the *Bus Stop SITA* sign across from the train station (10 steps down). A schedule is posted on the wall: Carefully note the lettered codes that differentiate daily buses from weekend-only buses. *Giornaliero (G)* means daily; *Feriale (F)* denotes Monday-Saturday departures; and *Festivo (H)* is for Sundays and holidays.

Leaving Sorrento, grab a seat on the right for the best views. If you return by bus, it's fun to sit directly behind the driver for a box seat with a view over the twisting hairpin action. Sitting toward the front will also help minimize carsickness.

Avoiding Crowded Buses: Amalfi Coast public buses are routinely unable to handle demand during summer months and holidays (perhaps because the fares are so cheap). Generally, if you don't get on one bus, you're well positioned to catch the next one. From Sorrento, aim to leave on the 8:30 bus at the latest, and earlier if possible. Departures between 9:00 and 11:00 are crowded and frustrating.

Note that an eight-seater minibus and driver costs about €300 for the day: If you can organize a small group, €40 per person is a very good deal. (For options, see "By Taxi," later.)

When to Stop in Positano: Summer congestion can be so bad—particularly in July and August—that Amalfi-Sorrento buses don't even stop in Positano (because they fill up in Amalfi). Those trying to get back from Positano to Sorrento are stuck taking an extortionist taxi or hopping a boat...if one's running. When day-tripping from Sorrento to Amalfi, it's safest to make your Positano stop on the outbound leg, then come straight home from Amalfi, where the bus originates.

Alternative Private Bus: From April through October, **City Sightseeing Sorrento**'s bright red buses travel between Sorrento and Amalfi via Positano, offering commentary along the way.

They're more expensive than the public bus, but they're definitely worth considering if the public buses are full (Sorrento-Amalfi-€10, round-trip discount; buy tickets onboard, departs hourly from Sorrento's train station starting at 8:45, www.sorrento.citysightseeing.it).

By Boat

A few passenger boats a day link Positano and Amalfi with Sorrento, Capri, and Salerno; they generally run from April through October (no service off-season). The last daily departure can be as early as midafternoon and is never much later than 18:00. Check schedules carefully: Frequency varies from month to month, and boats may be suspended without notice in bad weather (especially at Positano, where there's no real pier). The specific companies operating each route change frequently, compete for passengers, and usually claim to know nothing about their rivals' services. The best sources for timetables are www.capritourism.com (under "Shipping Timetable") and www.positano.com (under "Ferry Schedules"). You can also check ferry company websites (such as www.travelmar.it, www.alicost.it, and www.gescab.it). It's smartest to confirm locally: The region's TIs hand out flyers with current schedules. Buy tickets on the dock. For a summary of sample routes, frequencies, and travel times, see the map on page 1052.

If you're going to Capri from Positano or Amalfi, check whether there's a boat that goes directly to the Blue Grotto (rather than dropping you in the port to catch another boat from there). Here's another useful trick: If no boats are going directly between Sorrento and Positano/Amalfi, you can usually still connect the two sides of the peninsula via Capri.

By Taxi

Given the hairy driving, impossible parking, congested buses, and potential fun, you might consider splurging to hire your own car and driver for the Amalfi day. (Don't bother for Pompeii, as the Circumvesuviana train serves it conveniently and only licensed guides can take you into the site.)

The Monetti family car-and-driver service—Raffaele, brother-in-law Tony, and cousin Lorenzo—have taken excellent care of my readers' transit needs for decades. Sample trips and rates: all-day Amalfi Coast (Positano, Amalfi, Ravello), 8 hours, €280; Amalfi Coast and Paestum, 10 hours, €400; transfer to Naples airport or train station to Sorrento,

€110. These prices are for up to four people; you'll pay more for a larger eight-seater van. Though based in Sorrento, they also do trips from Naples. Payment is by cash only (as with most of the car services listed). Their reservation system is simple and reliable (Raffaele's mobile 335-602-9158 or 338-946-2860, "office" run by his English-speaking Finnish wife, Susanna, www.monettitaxi17. it, monettitaxi17@libero.it). Don't just hop into any taxi claiming to be a Monetti—call first. If you get into any kind of serious jam in the area, you can call Raffaele for help.

Francesco del Pizzo is another smooth and honest Sorrento-based driver. A classy young man who speaks English well, Francesco enjoys explaining things as he drives (9 hours or so in a car with up to 4 passengers, €280; up to 8 passengers in a minibus, €320; mobile 333-238-4144, francescodelpizzo@yahoo.it).

Benvenuto Tours (based in Praiano, near Positano) is a larger company offering transport, narrated tours, and shore excursions throughout the Amalfi Coast, as well as in other parts of Italy. They're more upmarket and formal, with steeper rates explained on their website (tel. 081-007-2114, mobile 346-684-0226, US tel. 310-424-5640, www.benvenutolimos.com, info@benvenutolimos. com).

Sorrento Silver Star is another reliable company with professional, English-speaking drivers. Prices are generally between the Monettis' and Benvenuto (tel. 081-877-1224, mobile 339-388-8143, www.sorrentosilverstar.com, luisa@sorrentosilverstar.com, Luisa).

Anthony Buonocore, based in Amalfi, specializes in cruise shore excursions, as well as transfers anywhere in the region in his eight-person Mercedes van (rates vary, tel. 349-441-0336, www. amalfitransfer.com, buonocoreanthony@yahoo.it).

Rides Only: If you're hiring a cabbie off the street for a ride and not a tour, here are sample fares from Sorrento to Positano: up to four people one-way for about €80 in a car, or up to six people for €90 in a minibus. Figure on paying 50 percent more to Amalfi. While taxis must use a meter within a city, a fixed rate is OK otherwise. Negotiate—ask about a round-trip.

By Tour

While hiring your own driver is convenient, it's also expensive. To bring the cost down, split the trip—and the bill—with other travelers using this book. Naples-based **Mondo Guide** offers a nine-hour minibus trip that departs from Sorrento and heads down the Amalfi Coast, with brief stops in Positano, Amalfi, and Ravello, before returning to Sorrento (€50/person). They also offer Rick Steves readers shared tours in Pompeii and in Naples. For details, see page 948.

Amalfi Coast Bus Tour

The bus trip from Sorrento to Salerno is one of the all-time great white-knuckle rides. Gasp from the right side of the bus as you go out and from the left as you return to Sorrento. (Those on the wrong side really miss out.) Traffic is so heavy that private tour buses are only allowed to go in one direction (southbound from Sorrento). Summer traffic is infuriating. Fluorescent-vested policemen are posted at tough bends during peak hours to help fold in side-view mirrors and keep things moving. Here's a loose, self-guided tour of what you're seeing as you travel from west to east.

⊙ **Self-Guided Tour:** Leaving **Sorrento,** the road winds up into the hills past lemon groves and hidden houses. The gray-green trees are olives. (Notice the green nets slung around the trunks; these are unfurled in October and November, when the ripe olives drop naturally, for an easy self-harvest.) Dark, green-leafed trees planted in dense groves are the source of the region's lemons (many destined to become *limoncello* liqueur) and big, fat citrons (*cedri,* mostly used for marmalade). The black nets over the orange and lemon groves create a greenhouse effect, trapping warmth and humidity for maximum tastiness, while offering protection from extreme weather (preserving the peels used for *limoncello*).

Atop the ridge outside Sorrento, look to your right: The two small islands are the **Li Galli Islands,** where some say the sirens in Homer's *Odyessy* lived (see page 1021 for the ancient connection). The largest of these islands was once owned by the famed ballet dancer Rudolf Nureyev; it's now a luxury residence, rented to wealthy visitors for upward of $100,000 per week (bring your own yacht or arrive by helicopter).

When Nureyev bought the island, the only building standing was the stony watchtower—the first of many you'll see all along the coast. These were strategically placed within sight of one another so that a relay of rooftop bonfires could quickly spread word of a Saracen (Turkish pirate) attack.

The limestone cliffs that plunge into the sea were traversed by a hand-carved trail that became a modern road in the mid-19th century. Fruit stands sell produce from farms and orchards just over the hill. Limestone absorbs the heat and rainwater, making this south-facing coastline a fertile suntrap, with temperatures as much as 10 degrees higher than in nearby Sorrento. The chalky, reflective limestone, which extends below the surface, accounts for the uniquely colorful blues and greens of the water. Bougainvillea, geraniums, oleander, and wisteria grow like weeds here in the summer. Notice the nets pulled tight against the cliffs—they're designed to catch rocks that often tumble loose after absorbing heavy rains.

The dramatic, exotic-looking town of **Positano** is the main stop along the coast. Notice that the town is built on a series of man-made terraces, which were carefully carved out of the steep rock, then filled with fertile soil carried here from Sorrento on the backs of donkeys. You can read the history of the region in Positano's rooftops—a mix of Roman-style red terracotta tiles and white domes inspired by the Saracens.

If you're getting off here, stay on through the first stop by the round-domed yellow church (Chiesa Nova), which is a very long walk above town. Instead, get off at the second stop, Sponda, then head downhill toward the start of my self-guided Positano Walk (see page 1063). Sponda is also the best place to catch the onward bus to Amalfi. If you're coming on a smaller minibus, you'll twist all the way down—seemingly going in circles—to the start of the walk.

Just south of Positano, **St. Peter's Hotel** (Il San Pietro di Positano, camouflaged below the tiny St. Peter's church) is just about the most posh stop on the coast. In the adjacent gorge, notice the hotel's terraced gardens (where they grow produce for their restaurant) above an elevator-accessible beach and dock.

Just around the bend, **Praiano** comes into view. Less ritzy or charming than Positano or Amalfi, it's notable for its huge Cathedral of San Gennaro, with a characteristic majolica-tiled roof and dome—a reminder of this region's respected ceramics industry. In spindly Praiano, most of the homes are accessible only by tiny footpaths and staircases. Near the end of town, just before the big tunnel, watch on the left for the big *presepe* (manger scene) embedded into the cliff face. This Praiano-in-miniature was carved by one local man over several decades. At Christmastime, each house is filled with little figures and twinkle lights.

Just past the tunnel, look below and on the right to see another Saracen watchtower. (Yet another caps the little point on the horizon.)

A bit farther along, look down to see the fishing hamlet of **Marina di Praia** tucked into the gorge (*furore*) between two tunnels. If you're driving—or being driven—consider a detour down here for a coffee break or meal. This serene, tidy nook has its

AMALFI COAST

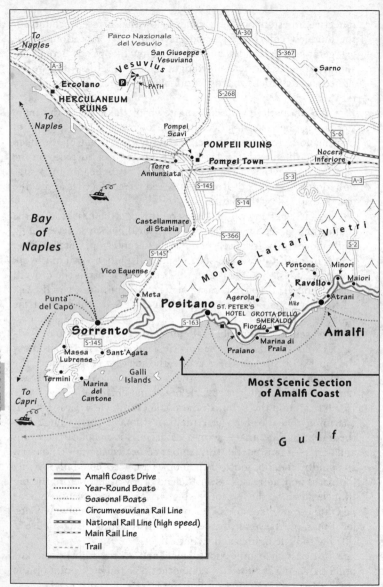

own little pebbly beach with great views of the stout bluffs and watchtower that hem it in. A seafront walkway curls around the bluff all the way to the tower.

Just after going through the next tunnel, watch for a jagged rock formation on its own little pedestal. Locals see the face of the Virgin Mary in this natural feature and say that she's holding a flower (the tree growing out to the right). Also notice several

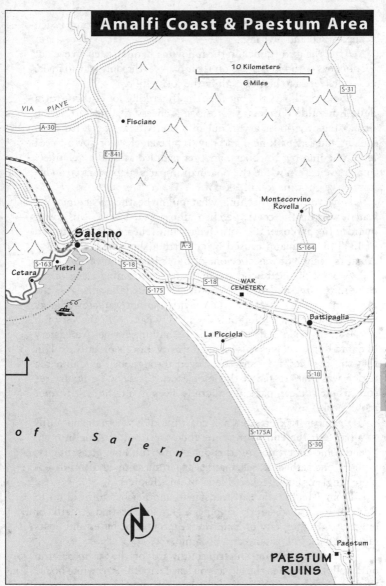

Amalfi Coast & Paestum Area

10 Kilometers

6 Miles

VIA PIAVE

A-30

• Fisciano

E-841

Montecorvino
Rovella •

Salerno

S-163 Vietri

Cetara

S-18

A-3

S-164

S-175

S-18

WAR
CEMETERY

Battipaglia

La Picciola
•

S-18

o f   S a l e r n o

S-175A

S-30

AMALFI COAST

Paestum •

**PAESTUM
RUINS**

S-31

caged, cantilevered parking pads sticking out from the road. This stretch of coastline is popular for long-term villa rentals—Italians who want to really settle in to Amalfi life.

Look down and left for the blink-or-you'll-miss-it fishing village that's aptly named **Fiordo** ("fjord"), filling yet another gorge. You'll see humble homes burrowed into the cliff face, tucked so far into the gorge that they're entirely in shadow for much of the year.

Today these are rented out to vacationers; the postage-stamp beach is uncrowded and inviting.

After the next tunnel, in the following hamlet, keep an eye out for donkeys with big baskets on their backs—the only way to make heavy deliveries to homes high in the rocky hills.

Soon you'll pass the big-for-Amalfi parking lot of the **Grotta dello Smeraldo** ("Emerald Grotto"), a cheesy roadside attraction that wrings the most it can out of a pretty, seawater-filled cave. Passing tourists park here and pay to take an elevator down to sea level, pile into big rowboats, and get paddled around a genuinely impressive cavern while the boatman imparts sparse factoids. Unless you've got time to kill, skip it.

Now you're approaching what might be the most dramatic watchtower on the coast, perched atop a near-island. This tower guarded the harbor of the Amalfi navy until the fleet was destroyed in 1343 by a tsunami caused by an earthquake, which also led to Amalfi's decline (it was once one of Italy's leading powers).

Around the next bend you're treated to stunning views of the coastline's namesake town—**Amalfi.** The white villa sitting on the low point between here and there (with another watchtower at its tip) once belonged to Sophia Loren. Now pan up to the very top of the steep, steep cliffs overhead. The hulking former Monastery of Santa Rosa occupies this prime territory. Locals proudly explain that the *sfogliatella* dessert so beloved throughout the Campania region was first created at this monastery. (Today it's a luxury resort, where you can pay a premium to sleep in a tight little former monk's cell.)

The most striking stretch of coastline ends where the bus pulls to a halt—at the end of the line, the waterfront of Amalfi town. Spend some time enjoying this once-powerful, now-pleasant city, with its fine cathedral, fascinating paper museum, and fun-to-explore tangle of lanes (covered later in this chapter).

From Amalfi, you can transfer to another bus to head up to **Ravello** (described later), capping a cliff just beyond Amalfi, or onward to the big city of **Salerno.** Alternatively, buses and boats take you back to Positano and Sorrento.

If you're continuing the trip southward (on the bus to Salerno or Ravello), look up to the left as you leave Amalfi—the white house that clings to a cliff (Villa Rondinaia) was home for many years to writer Gore Vidal. Soon you'll pass through the low-impact, pleasantly untouristy town of **Atrani** (described on page 1077). From here, you'll enjoy fine (though slightly less thrilling) scenery all the way to Salerno.

Positano

According to legend, the Greek god Poseidon created Positano for Pasitea, a nymph he lusted after. History says the town was

 founded when ancient Greeks at Paestum decided to move out of the swamp (to escape the malaria carried by its mosquitoes). Specializing in scenery and sand, Positano hangs halfway between Sorrento and Amalfi town on the most spectacular stretch of the coast.

In antiquity, Positano was famed for its bold sailors and hearty fleet. But after a big 1343 tsunami and the pirate raids of the Middle Ages, its wealth and power declined. It flourished again as a favorite under the Bourbon royal family in the 1700s, when many of its fine mansions were built. Until the late 1800s, the only access was by donkey path or by sea. In the 20th century, Positano became a haven for artists and writers escaping Communist Russia or Nazi Germany. In 1953, American writer John Steinbeck's essay on the town popularized Positano among tourists, and soon after it became a trendy Riviera stop. That was when the town gave the world "Moda Positano"— a leisurely *dolce vita* lifestyle of walking barefoot; wearing bright, happy, colorful clothes; and sporting skimpy bikinis.

Today, the village, a breathtaking sight from a distance, is a pleasant gathering of cafés and expensive stores draped over an almost comically steep hillside. Terraced gardens and historic houses cascade downhill to a stately cathedral and a broad, pebbly beach. Positano is famous for its fashions—and 90 percent of its shops are women's clothing boutiques (linen is a particularly popular item).

The "skyline" looks like it did a century ago. Notice the town's characteristic Saracen-inspired rooftop domes. Filled with sand, these provide low-tech insulation—to help buildings in the days before air-conditioning stay cool in summer and warm in winter. Traditionally, they were painted white in summer and black in winter.

It's been practically impossible to get a building permit in Positano for over 25 years now, and landowners who want to renovate can't make external changes. Endless staircases are a way of life for the 4,000 hardy locals. Only one street in Positano allows motorized traffic; the rest are narrow pedestrian lanes. Because hotels don't take large groups (bus access is too difficult), this town—unlike Sorrento—has been spared the ravages of big-bus tourism.

Consider seeing Positano as a day trip from Sorrento: Take

the bus out and the afternoon ferry home, but be sure to check the boat schedules when you arrive—the last ferry often leaves before 18:00 and doesn't always run in spring and fall. Or spend the night to enjoy the magic of Positano. The town has a local flavor at night, when the grown-ups stroll and the kids play soccer on the church porch.

Orientation to Positano

Squished into a ravine, with narrow alleys that cascade down to the harbor, Positano requires you to stroll, whether you're going up or heading down. The center of town has no main square (unless you count the beach). There's little to do here but eat, window shop, and enjoy the beach and views...hence the town's popularity.

TOURIST INFORMATION

The TI is a block from the beach, in the red building a half-block beyond the bottom of the church steps (Mon-Sat 9:00-18:00 or later, Sun 9:00-14:00, shorter hours off-season, Via Regina Giovanna 13, tel. 089-875-067, www.aziendaturismopositano.it).

Local Guide: Lucia Ferrara (a.k.a. "Zia Lucy") is a Positano native who brings substance to this glitzy town. During the day, she leads guided hiking tours, including the "Path of the Gods" above Amalfi town (about 4 miles, 4 hours, €45-55/person); in the afternoons and evenings, she leads town walking tours (3 hours, €30/person; ask about possible food tours of Positano, contact for specific rates and schedules, mobile 339-272-0971, www.zialucy. com).

ARRIVAL IN POSITANO

The main coastal highway winds above the town. Regional SITA buses stop at two scheduled bus stops located at either end of town: Chiesa Nuova (at Bar Internazionale, near the Sorrento end of town; use this one only if you're staying at Brikette Hostel) and Sponda (nearer Amalfi town). Although both stops are near roads leading downhill through the town to the beach, Sponda is closer and less steep; from this stop, it's a scenic 20-minute downhill stroll/shop/munch to the beach (and TI).

Neither bus stop has easy **baggage storage,** which makes it hard to visit Positano on the way (for example, between overnights in Sorrento and Amalfi). Positano does have porter services: A porter can meet you at the Sponda bus stop and watch your bags for €5 apiece—but you have to call them in advance (try Blu Porter, tel. 089-811-496). Another option is to get off at Chiesa Nuova and head for the Brikette Hostel, which offers day privileges for €10, including luggage storage, Wi-Fi, and showers. A last resort is to get off at the Sponda stop and roll your bags all the way down to Piazza dei Mulini, where the porters tend to hang out.

If you're catching the SITA bus from Positano, be aware that it may leave from the Sponda stop up to five minutes before the printed departure time. There's simply no room for the bus to wait, so in case the driver is early, you should be, too. Buy tickets at the tobacco shop in the town center (on Piazza dei Mulini) or just below the Sponda bus stop at the Li Galli Bar or Total gas station (across from Hotel Marincanto).

If the walk up to the stop is too tough, take the dizzy little local red-and-white shuttle bus (marked *Interno Positano*), which constantly loops through Positano, connecting the lower town with the highway's two bus stops (2/hour, €1.30 at tobacco shop on Piazza dei Mulini, €1.70 on board, catch it at convenient stop at the corner of Via Colombo and Via dei Mulini, heads up to Sponda). Collina Bakery, located off Piazza dei Mulini (as close as cars, taxis, and the shuttle bus can get to the beach), is just across from the shuttle bus stop, with a fine, breezy terrace to enjoy while you wait.

Drivers must go with the one-way flow, entering the town only at the Chiesa Nuova bus stop (closest to Sorrento) and exiting at Sponda. Driving is a headache here. Parking is even worse.

Positano Walk

While there's no real sightseeing in Positano, this short, self-guided stroll downhill will help you get your bearings from top to bottom.
• *Start at...*

Piazza dei Mulini: This is the upper-town meeting point—as close to the beach as vehicles can get—and the lower stop for the little red-and-white shuttle bus. Collina Bakery is a local hangout (in this small town, gossiping is a big pastime)—older people tend to gather inside, while the younger crowd congregates on the wisteria-draped terrace across the street. The terrace also shades the best *granita* (lemon slush) stand in town, where the family has been following the same secret recipe for generations.

Dip into the little yellow Church of the Holy Rosary (by the road), with a serene 12th-century interior. Up front, to the right of the main altar, find the delicately carved fragment of a Roman sarcophagus (first century B.C.). Positano sits upon the site of a sprawling Roman villa, and we'll see a scant few reminders of that age as we walk.

Now continue downhill into town, passing a variety of shops—many selling linen and ceramics. These industries boomed when tourists discovered Positano in the 1970s. The beach-inspired Moda Positano fashion label was born as a break from the rigid dress code of the '50s. For tips on shopping for linen (and other

things), see "Shopping," later. Positano also considers itself an artists' colony, so you'll see many galleries featuring the work of area artists.

• *Wander downhill to the "fork" in the road (stairs to the left, road to the right). You've reached...*

Midtown: At Enoteca Cuomo (#3), butchers Pasquale and Rosario stock fine local red wines and are happy to explain their virtues. They also make homemade sausages, salami, and *panini*—good for a quick lunch. The smaller set of stairs leads to the recommended Delicatessen grocery store, where Emilia can fix you a good picnic (see "Eating in Positano," later).

La Zagara (across the lane from the steps, at #10) is a pricey pastry shop by day and a piano bar by night. Tempting pastries such as the rum-drenched *babà* (a southern Italian favorite) fill the window display. After hours, it's filled with traditional Neapolitan music and dancing. A bit farther downhill, Brunella (on the right, at #24) is respected for traditional, quality, and locally made linens.

Across the street, Hotel Palazzo Murat fills what was once a grand Benedictine monastery. Napoleon, fearing the power of the Church, had many such monasteries closed during his rule here. This one became a private palace, named for his brother-in-law, who was briefly the King of Naples. Step into the plush courtyard

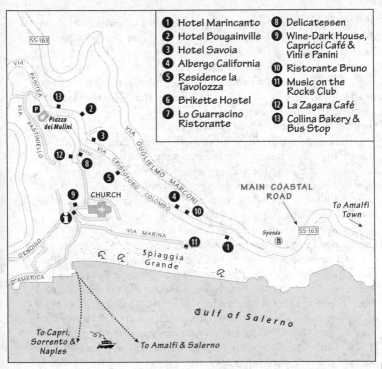

❶ Hotel Marincanto	❽ Delicatessen
❷ Hotel Bougainville	❾ Wine-Dark House, Capricci Café & Vini e Panini
❸ Hotel Savoia	
❹ Albergo California	❿ Ristorante Bruno
❺ Residence la Tavolozza	⓫ Music on the Rocks Club
❻ Brikette Hostel	⓬ La Zagara Café
❼ Lo Guarracino Ristorante	⓭ Collina Bakery & Bus Stop

to enjoy the scene, with great views of the cathedral's majolica-slathered dome. Continuing on, under a fragrant wisteria trellis, you'll pass "street merchants' gulch," where artisans display their goodies.

• *Continue straight down. You'll run into a fork at the big church. For now, turn right and go downstairs to Piazza Flavio Gioia, facing the big...*

Church of Santa Maria Assunta: This church, which sits upon Roman ruins, was once the abbey of Positano's 12th-century Benedictine monastery. Originally Romanesque, it was eventually abandoned (along with the entire lower town) out of fear of pirate attacks. When the coast was clear in the 18th century, the church was given an extreme Baroque makeover.

Step **inside.** Renovation may be under way when you visit; try to find these items: In the first chapel on the left is a fine manger scene *(presepe)*. Its original 18th-century figurines give you an idea of the folk costumes of the age. Above the main altar is the Black Madonna, an icon-like Byzantine painting, which was likely brought here in the 12th century by Benedictine monks. But locals prefer the romantic legend: Saracen pirates had it on their ship as plunder. A violent storm hit—sure to sink the evil ship. The painting of Mary spoke, saying, *"Posa, posa"* (lay me down), and the ship glided safely to this harbor. The pirates were so stricken they became Christians. Locals kept the painting, and the town became known as *Posa-tano* (recalling Mary's command). To the right of the altar, a small freestanding display case holds a silver and copper bust of St. Vitus—the town patron, who brought Christianity here in about A.D. 300. In the adjacent niche (on the right) is a rare 1599 painting by Fabrizio Santafede of Baby Jesus being circumcised, considered the finest historic painting in town.

Back outside, you'll see the **bell tower,** dating from 1707. Above the door, it sports a Romanesque relief scavenged from the original church. The scene—a wolf mermaid with seven little fish—was a reminder to worshippers of how integral the sea was to their livelihood. Notice the characteristic shallow, white "insulation domes" on rooftops in front of the church.

• *Backtrack up the steps, circling around the church. You'll likely see a construction zone, and possibly a new museum.*

The entire town center of today's Positano—from this cathedral all the way up to the Piazza dei Mulini, where we started this walk—sits upon the site of a huge **Roman villa complex,** buried when Mount Vesuvius erupted in A.D. 79. Positano recently began excavating one small part of the villa, and a small museum planned here will provide views of a surviving fragment of a large Roman fresco. You may also be able to take the stairs down to two glass doors that offer a peek into the church's crypt—originally the early church's altar. According to local legend, the Benedictines sat their dead brothers on the stone choir chairs here to decompose and remind all of their mortality.

• *Continue climbing down the steps arcing to the right (following* beach/spiaggia *signs). You'll eventually come to the little square, with concrete benches, facing the beach.*

Piazzetta: This is the town gathering point in the evening, as local boys hustle tourist girls into the nearby nightclub. Residents traded their historic baptistery font with Amalfi town for the two iron lions you see facing the beach. Around the staircase, you'll also see some original Roman columns, scavenged from the buried villa. Look up and admire the colorful majolica tiles so typical of church domes in this region.

The Positano **beach,** called Spiaggia Grande, is half public (straight ahead) and half private (to the left, behind the little fence). It's atmospherically littered with resting fishing boats. The big kiosk on the beach straight ahead sells excursions to Capri and elsewhere.

Looking out over the beach, from this point you can see three of the **watchtowers** built centuries ago to protect the Amalfi Coast from Saracen pirates: one on the far-left horizon, just below Praiano; a small one on the Li Galli Islands, straight ahead; and the rectangular one far to the right, marking the end of Fornillo Beach. (The round tower in the foreground is modern.) Defenders used these towers—strategically situated within sight of each other—to relay smoke signals. In more recent times, the tower on the right (near Fornillo Beach) was a hangout for artists, who holed up inside for inspiration. (The people of Positano pride themselves on being artists rather than snazzy jet-setters like those in Capri.)

As you face out to sea, on the far-left side of the beach (below Rada Restaurant) is **Music on the Rocks,** a chic club that's the only remaining piece of the 1970s scene, when Positano really rocked. While it's dead until about 23:00, if you just want to stop for a drink, the cool troglo-disco interior opens at 21:00.

• *Now turn right and wander across the beach. Behind the kiosks that sell boat tickets, find the steps up to the path that climbs up and over, past a 13th-century lookout fort from Saracen pirate days, to the next beach. It's a worthwhile little five-minute walk to...*

Fornillo Beach: This is where locals go for better swimming and to escape some of the tourist crowds. The walk over offers a welcome change of scene, as the path winds through a shady ravine.

• *Our walk is over. Time to relax.*

Sights in Positano

Beaches

Positano's pebbly and sandy primary beach, **Spiaggia Grande,** is colorful with umbrellas as it stretches wide around the cove. It's mostly private (pay to enter, includes lounge chair and umbrella), with a free section near the middle, close to where the boats take off. Look for the pay showers. The nearest WC is beneath the steps to the right (as you face the water).

Fornillo Beach, a less-crowded option just around the bend (to the west) of Spiaggia Grande, is favored by residents, with more affordable chair/umbrella rentals. It has a mellow Robinson Crusoe vibe, with a sturdy Saracen tower keeping watch overhead. This beach has a few humble snack bars and lunch eateries. Note that its position, tucked back in the rocks, means it gets shade earlier in the day than the main beach.

Boat Trips

Boats serving Positano pull up to the dock at the west end of Spiaggia Grande (to the right as you face the sea; booths sell tickets). Also consider renting a rowboat, or see whether they can talk you into taking a boat tour. Passenger boats run to Amalfi, Capri, Salerno, and Sorrento; see page 1054.

Shopping

Linen: Garments made of **linen** (especially women's dresses) are popular items in Positano. To find a good-quality piece that will last, look for "Made in Positano" (or at least "Made in Italy") on the label, and check the percentage of linen; 60 percent or more is excellent quality. Two companies with top reputations and multiple outlets are **Brunella** and **Pepito's** (each has shops on Via Colombo, near the top of town; along Via Pasitea, the main drag; and along claustrophobic Saraceno lane, near the bottom of town, parallel to the beach).

Ceramics: Ceramica Assunta, one of the oldest ceramics stores in Positano, carries colorful Solimene dinnerware and more at two locations (Via Colombo 97 and Via Colombo 137).

Custom Sandals: Positano has a tradition of handmade sandals, crafted to your specifications while you wait (prices start at about €50). One good shop, La Botteguccia, faces the tranquil little square just up from the TI; around the corner, in front of the Capricci restaurant, you'll see Carmine Todisco, who loves to explain how his grandfather shod Jackie O.

Nightlife

The big-time action in the old town center is the impressive club **Music on the Rocks,** literally carved into the rocks on the beach (opens at 21:00 mid-April-Oct but party starts about 23:30, €10-20 cover charge in summer includes a drink, go to dance or just check out the scene, closed off-season, Via Grotte Dell'Incanto 51, tel. 089-875-874, www.musicontherocks.it). For a more low-key atmosphere, café/pastry shop **La Zagara** hosts music nightly in summer (starts around 21:00, Via dei Mulini 10, tel. 089-875-964, www.lazagara.com).

Sleeping in Positano

These hotels—with the exception of the hostel—are all on or near Via Cristoforo Colombo, which leads from the Sponda bus stop down into the village (ideal for arrival by bus). Outside high season (May-Sept), prices go soft. Most places close in the winter (Dec-Feb or longer). Expect to pay more than €20 a day to park, except at Albergo California.

$$$$ Hotel Marincanto is a recently restored, somewhat impersonal four-star hotel with 32 beautiful rooms and a bright breakfast terrace practically teetering on a cliff. Suites seem to be designed for a *luna di miele*—honeymoon (air-con, elevator, pool, stairs down to a private beach, pay parking, closed Nov-March, 50 yards below Sponda bus stop at Via Cristoforo Colombo 50, recep-

---

Sleep Code

Hotels are classified based on the average price of a standard double room with breakfast in high season.

$$$$	**Splurge:** Most rooms over €170
$$$	**Expensive:** €130-170
$$	**Moderate:** €90-130
$	**Budget:** €50-90
¢	**Hostel/Backpacker:** Under €50
RS%	**Rick Steves discount**

Unless otherwise noted, credit cards are accepted, hotel staff speak basic English, and free Wi-Fi is available. Comparison-shop by checking prices at several hotels (on each hotel's own website, on a booking site, or by email). For the best deal, *book directly with the hotel*. Ask for a discount if paying in cash; if the listing includes **RS%,** request a Rick Steves discount.

---

tion on bottom floor, tel. 089-875-130, www.marincanto.it, info@ marincanto.it).

$$$$ Hotel Bougainville rents 16 comfortable rooms, half with balconies. Everything's bright, modern, and tasteful (RS%, rooms without views are cheaper, air-con, small elevator, closed Nov-March, Via Cristoforo Colombo 25, tel. 089-875-047, www. bougainville.it, info@bougainville.it, friendly Marella).

$$$ Hotel Savoia, run by the friendly D'Aiello family, has 39 sizeable, breezy, bright, simple, tiled rooms (RS%, some cheaper nonview rooms, some rooms with balcony or terrace, air-con, elevator, closed Nov-March, Via Cristoforo Colombo 73, tel. 089-875-003, www.savoiapositano.it, info@savoiapositano.it).

$$$ Albergo California has 15 spacious rooms (all with lofty views), a grand terrace draped with vines, and full breakfasts. The Cinque family—including Maria, Bronx-born son John, and grandchildren Giuseppe and Maria—will welcome you (RS%, air-con, free parking, closed Nov-Easter, Via Cristoforo Colombo 141, tel. 089-875-382, www.hotelcaliforniapositano.it, info@ hotelcaliforniapositano.it).

$$ Residence la Tavolozza is an attractive six-room hotel, warmly run by Celeste (cheh-LEHS-tay) and daughters Francesca (who speaks English) and Paola. Each cheerily tiled room comes with a view, a terrace, and silence (RS%, lavish à la carte breakfast extra, families can ask for sprawling "Royal Apartment," air-con, confirm by phone if arriving late, closed Dec-Feb, Via Cristoforo Colombo 10, tel. 089-875-040, www.latavolozzapositano.it, info@ latavolozzapositano.it).

$ Brikette Hostel offers your best budget option in this otherwise ritzy town. Its 35 dorm beds are pricey by hostel standards, but you're in Positano. It has a great sun and breakfast terrace and a youthful ambience (private and family rooms available, breakfast extra, cheap dinners, air-con; day privileges for day-trippers, including luggage storage-€10; closed Nov-March but a few apartments without breakfast are available all year long; leave bus at Chiesa Nuova/Bar Internazionale stop and backtrack uphill 500 feet to Via G. Marconi 358, www.hostel-positano.com, hostelpositano@gmail.com, Cristiana). The hostel isn't reachable by phone; email instead.

Eating in Positano

On the Beach: At the waterfront, several interchangeable restaurants with view terraces leave people fat and happy, albeit with

skinnier wallets (figure €15-20 pastas and *secondi*, plus pricey drinks and sides, and a cover charge). Little distinguishes one place from the next; all are scenic, convenient, and overpriced.

Near the Beach: $$ Lo Guarracino, hidden on the path to Fornillo Beach, is a local favorite for its great views and good food at prices similar to the beachfront places (daily 12:00-15:30 & 19:00-23:00, closed Nov-Easter, follow path behind the boat-ticket kiosks 5 minutes to Via Positanesi d'America 12, tel. 089-875-794). **$$ Wine-Dark House,** tucked around the corner from the beach (and the TI), fills a cute little piazzetta at the start of Via del Saraceno. They serve good pastas and *secondi,* have a respect for wine (several local wines), and are popular with Positano's youngsters for their long list of sandwiches (closed Tue, Via del Saraceno 6/8, tel. 089-811-925). Next door, **$$ Capricci** is budget-priced (for downtown Positano). This informal café and *tavola calda* serves up €8 pizzas and main courses that you can eat on the spot (at a long counter overlooking the beach) or take away. If you sit down at their white-tablecloth restaurant across the street, you get the same food but the prices go up (daily 9:00-23:00, Via Regina Giovanna 12, delivery available, tel. 089-812-145, www.capriccipositano.it).

Picnics: If a picnic dinner on your balcony or the beach sounds good, sunny Emilia at the **Delicatessen** grocery store can supply the ingredients: *antipasto misto,* pastas, home-cooked dishes, and sandwiches made to order. She'll heat it up for you and throw in the picnic ware. Come early for the best selection (all sold by weight, daily 7:00-22:00, shorter hours off-season, just below car park at

Restaurant Price Code

I've assigned each eatery a price category, based on the average cost of a typical main course (pasta or *secondi*). Drinks, desserts, and splurge items (steak and seafood) can raise the price considerably.

$$$$ **Splurge:** Most main courses over €20
$$$ **Pricier:** €15-20
$$ **Moderate:** €10-15
$ **Budget:** Under €10

In Italy, pizza by the slice and other takeout food is **$**; a basic trattoria or sit-down pizzeria is **$$**; a casual but more upscale restaurant is **$$$**; and a swanky splurge is **$$$$**.

Via del Mulini 5, tel. 089-875-489). **Vini e Panini,** another small grocery, is a block from the beach a few steps above the TI. Daniela, the fifth-generation owner, speaks English and happily makes sandwiches to order. Choose from the "Caprese" (mozzarella and tomato), the "Positano" (mozzarella, tomato, and prosciutto), or create your own. They also have a nice selection of well-priced regional wines (daily 8:00-20:00, until 22:00 in summer, closed mid-Nov-mid-March, just off church steps, tel. 089-875-175).

"Uptown": The unassuming, family-run **$$$ Ristorante Bruno** is handy to my listed hotels. While expensive, it has nice views and is worth considering if you want a meal without hiking down into the town center (daily 12:30-23:00, closed Nov-Easter, near the top of Via Cristoforo Colombo at #157, tel. 089-875-179).

Amalfi Town

After Rome fell, the town of Amalfi was one of the first to trade goods—coffee, carpets, and paper—between Europe and points

east. Its heyday was the 10th and 11th centuries, when it was a powerful maritime republic—a trading power with a fleet that controlled this region and rivaled Pisa, Genoa, and Venice. The Republic of Amalfi founded a hospital in Jerusalem and claims to have founded the Knights of Malta order—even giving them the Amalfi cross, which became the famous Maltese cross. Amalfi minted its own coins and established "rules of the sea"—the basics of which survive today.

In 1343, this little powerhouse was suddenly destroyed by a

tsunami caused by an undersea earthquake. That disaster, compounded by devastating plagues, left Amalfi a humble backwater. Much of the culture of this entire region was driven by this town—but because it fell from power, Amalfi doesn't always get the credit it deserves. Today its 5,000 residents live off tourism. The coast's namesake is not as picturesque as Positano or as well-connected as Sorrento, but it has a real-life feel and a vivacious bustle.

Amalfi's one main street runs up from the waterfront through a deep valley, with stairways to courtyards and houses on either side. It's worth walking uphill to the workaday upper end of town. Super-atmospheric, narrow, stepped side lanes branch off, squeezing between hulking old buildings. If you hear water under a grate in the main street, it's the creek that runs through the ravine—a reminder that the town originally straddled the stream but later paved over it to create a main drag. As you return downhill, be sure to explore up the winding and narrow lanes and arcaded passages on either side of the main street.

Though less touristy than Positano, Amalfi is still packed during the day with big-bus tours (whose drivers pay €50 an hour to park while their groups shop for *limoncello* and ceramics). Amalfi's charms reveal themselves early and late in the day, when the crowds dissipate.

Orientation to Amalfi Town

Amalfi's waterfront is the coast's biggest transport hub. Right next to each other are the bus station, ferry docks, and a parking lot (€5/hour; if the lot is full, park in the huge Lunarossa garage, burrowed into the hillside just past town, before Atrani). They are overlooked by a statue of local boy Flavio Gioia, the purported inventor of the magnetic compass. Amalfi's TI is just up the main road, right before the post office and overlooking the beach.

Before you enter the town, notice the colorful tile above the Porta della Marina gateway, showing off the trading domain of the maritime Republic of Amalfi. Just to the left, along the busy road, a series of arches marks the long, narrow, vaulted halls of Amalfi's arsenal—where ships were built in the 11th century. One of these is now the fine little Arsenal Museum.

Venture into town, and you'll quickly come to Piazza Duomo, the main square, with the cathedral—the town's most important sight—and a spring water-spewing statue of St. Andrew.

As you get farther away from the water, Amalfi becomes less glitzy and more traditional. The Paper Museum is a 10-minute walk up Via Lorenzo d'Amalfi, the main drag. From here, the road narrows and you can turn off onto a path leading to the shaded Valle dei Mulini; it's full of paper-mill

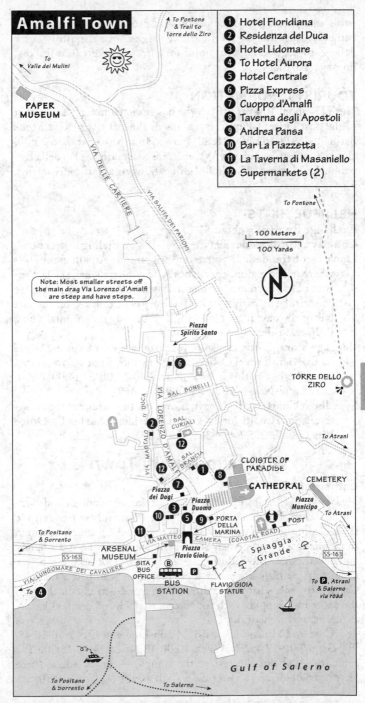

Amalfi Town

↑ To Pontone
& Trail to
Torre dello Ziro

To
Valle dei Mulini

PAPER MUSEUM

1. Hotel Floridiana
2. Residenza del Duca
3. Hotel Lidomare
4. To Hotel Aurora
5. Hotel Centrale
6. Pizza Express
7. Cuoppo d'Amalfi
8. Taverna degli Apostoli
9. Andrea Pansa
10. Bar La Piazzetta
11. La Taverna di Masaniello
12. Supermarkets (2)

VIA DELLE CARTIERE

VIA SALITA DEI PARONI

To Pontone

100 Meters

100 Yards

N

Note: Most smaller streets off
the main drag Via Lorenzo d'Amalfi
are steep and have steps.

Piazza Spirito Santo

SAL. BONELLI

VIA LORENZO D'AMALFI

VIA MASTALO II DUCA

6

2

SAL. CURIALI

12

SAL. D'ANCIA

TORRE DELLO ZIRO

To Atrani

CLOISTER OF PARADISE

CATHEDRAL

CEMETERY

1

8

12

7

Piazza dei Dogi

Piazza Duomo

Piazza Municipo

To Atrani

POST

10

3

9

PORTA DELLA MARINA

11

5

VIA MATTEO CAMERA (COASTAL ROAD)

To Positano
& Sorrento

ARSENAL MUSEUM

Piazza Flavio Gioia

SS-163

Spiaggia Grande

SS-163

VIA LUNGOMARE DEI CAVALIERE

SITA
BUS OFFICE

B

P

BUS STATION

FLAVIO GIOIA STATUE

To 4

To P, Atrani
& Salerno
via road

Gulf of Salerno

To Positano
& Sorrento

To Salerno

AMALFI COAST

ruins that recall this once proud and prosperous industry. The ruined castle clinging to the rocky ridge above Amalfi is Torre dello Ziro, a good lookout point for intrepid hikers (see "Hikes" on page 1076).

TOURIST INFORMATION

The TI is about 100 yards from the bus station and ferry dock, next to the post office; facing the sea, it's to the left (April-Oct Mon-Sat 8:30-13:00 & 14:00-18:00, Nov-March Mon-Sat 8:30-13:00, closed Sun year-round, pay WC in same courtyard, Corso della Repubbliche Marinare 27, tel. 089-871-107, www.amalfitouristoffice.it).

HELPFUL HINTS

Exchange Rate: €1 = about $1.10

Country Calling Code: 39 (see page 1154 for dialing instructions)

Don't Get Stranded: If you're day-tripping to Amalfi from elsewhere in the region, check locally to confirm when the last return bus to Sorrento or Salerno leaves in the evening (in winter this can be as early as 19:00). Don't plan to leave on the last bus of the day; if that bus is full, your only option might be a €100 taxi ride.

Baggage Storage: You can store your bag safely for €5 at the **Divina Costiera Travel Office** facing the waterfront square, across from the bus parking area (daily 8:00-13:00 & 14:00-19:00, closed mid-Nov-March, tel. 089-872-467).

Speedboat Charters: To hire your own boat for a tour of the coastline from Amalfi (or to Capri), consider **Charter La Dolce Vita** (mobile 335-549-9365, www.amalficoastyacht.it).

Sights in Amalfi Town

Cathedral

This church is "Amalfi Romanesque" (a mix of Moorish and Byzantine flavors, built c. 1000-1300), with a fanciful Neo-Byzantine facade from the 19th century. Climb the imposing stairway, which functions as a mini Spanish Steps-style hangout zone and a handy outdoor theater. The 1,000-year-old bronze door at the top was given to Amalfi by a wealthy local merchant who had it made in Constantinople. Visitors are directed on a one-way circuit through the cathedral complex with four stops: the cloister, original basilica, crypt, and cathedral.

Cost and Hours: €3, daily March-June and Oct 9:00-18:45, July-Sept 9:00-19:45, Nov-Feb 10:00-13:00 & 14:30-16:30. The cathedral—but not the rest of the complex—can be entered free for prayer or discreet visits daily 7:30-10:00 & 17:00-19:30; it's

closed 10:00-17:00 except as part of the paid visit; tel. 089-871-324, www.parrocchiaamalfi.com. There's a fine, free WC at the top of the steps (through unmarked green door, just a few steps before ticket booth, ask for key at desk).

Visiting the Cathedral: You'll follow a self-guided, one-way tour of the complex, beginning in a courtyard of 120 graceful columns—the **"Cloister of Paradise."** This was the cemetery for nobles in the 13th century (note their stone sarcophagi). Don't miss the fine view of the bell tower and its majolica tiles.

The original ninth-century church, known as the **Basilica of the Crucifix,** boasts a fine 13th-century wooden crucifix. Today the basilica is a museum filled with the cathedral's art treasures. The Angevin Mitre (Mitra Angioina), with a "pavement of tiny pearls" setting off its gold and gems, has been worn by bishops since the 14th century. Also on display (waist-high, facing the altar) is a carved wooden decoration from a Saracen pirate ship that wrecked just outside of town in 1544 during a freak storm. The church is dedicated to St. Andrew, whom believers credit with causing the storm and saving the town from certain Turkish pillage and plunder.

Down the stairs to the right of the basilica's altar is the **Crypt of St. Andrew.** Just as Venice needed St. Mark to get on the pilgrimage map, Amalfi needed St. Andrew—one of the apostles who, along with his brother Peter, left their fishing nets to become the original "fishers of men." Under the huge bronze statue, you'll see a reliquary holding what are believed to be Andrew's remains. These were brought here from Constantinople in 1206 during the Crusades—an indication of the wealth and importance of Amalfi back then.

Climb the stairs up into the **cathedral** itself. Behind the main altar is a painting of St. Andrew martyred on an X-shaped cross flanked by two Egyptian granite columns supporting a triumphal arch. Before leaving, check out the delicate mother-of-pearl crucifix (right of door in back).

▲Paper Museum

This excellent little museum—worth ▲▲▲ for engineers—makes for a good excuse to break free from the crowds and walk up the main drag to a quieter, more local part of town. Paper has been an important industry here since Amalfi's glory days in the Middle Ages. Millworkers would pound rags into pulp in a big vat, pull it up using a screen, and air-dry each sheet (the same technique used to make artisan paper today—look for it at shops in town). At this cavernous, cool 13th-century paper mill-turned-museum, a multi-lingual guide collects groups at the entrance (no particular times) for a 25-minute tour. The guide recounts the history and process of papermaking and turns on the museum's vintage machinery. You'll see how the Amalfi River (which you can still hear rumbling underfoot) powered this important industry, and learn the origins of the term "watermark." Kids can dip a screen into the rag pool and make a sheet of paper. It's amazing to think this factory produced paper through 1969 (when it was replaced by a modern facility up the valley).

Cost and Hours: €4; March-Oct daily 10:00-18:30; Nov-Feb Tue-Wed and Fri-Sun 10:00-15:30, closed Mon and Thu; a 10-minute walk up the main street from the cathedral, look for signs to *Museo della Carta;* tel. 089-830-4561, www.museodellacarta.it. On the way up to the museum, don't miss the huge, outdoor *presepi* (Nativity scenes) on your left.

Arsenal Museum

This small, underground museum just across the road from the bus station tells the history of Amalfi's maritime glory years. Stepping into the single long room under the dramatic vaulted stone ceiling, you can just tell that 1,000 years ago, they made ships here. The collection is small, but there are plenty of historic artifacts from Amalfi's city-state days of independence (839-1135). You'll learn about the early compass "invented" here in 1302, which ultimately opened up exploration of the New World. In 1080, it was written, "This city appears opulent and popular; no other city is as rich in silver, garments, and gold. Here dwells navigators very expert at pointing out the ways of the sea and the sphere of the heavens."

Cost and Hours: €2, Tue-Sun 10:00-13:00 & 16:00-19:00, closed Mon and Feb, Piazza Flavio Gioia, mobile 334-917-7814.

Performances: Half of the arsenal space is a venue for performances of *Amalfi Musical,* a 1.5-hour musical bonanza loosely based on local history (English subtitles, 2/week in summer, www.amalfimusical.it).

HIKES

Amalfi is the starting point for several fine hikes, two of which I've described here. The TI hands out photocopies of Giovanni Visetti's trail maps (or download them from his engaging website, www.giovis.com). The best book on local hikes is Julian Tippett's *Sorrento Amalfi Capri Car Tours and Walks* (2015), with useful color-coded maps and info on public transportation to the trailheads. Lucia Ferrara, a great guide based in Positano, leads hikes around Amalfi (see page 1062).

Hike #1: Pontone

This loop trail leads up the valley past paper-mill ruins, ending in the tiny town of Pontone; you can get lunch there, and head back down to the town of Amalfi (allow 3 hours total). Bring a good map, since it's easy to veer off the main route. Start your hike by following the main road (Via Lorenzo d'Amalfi) away from the sea.

After the Paper Museum, jog right, then left to join the trail, which runs through the shaded woods along a babbling stream. Heed the signs that warn people to stay away from the ruins of paper mills (no matter how tempting they look), since many are ready to collapse on unwary hikers. Continue up to Pontone, where Trattoria l'Antico Borgo offers wonderful cuisine and a great view (Via Noce 4, tel. 089-871-469). After lunch, return to Amalfi via a steep stairway.

If you're feeling ambitious, before you head back to Amalfi, add a one-hour detour (30 minutes each way) to visit the ridge-hugging **Torre dello Ziro** (ask a local how to find the trail to this tower). You'll be rewarded with a spectacular view.

Hike #2: Atrani

For an easier stroll, head to the nearby town of Atrani. This village, just a 15-minute stroll beyond Amalfi town, is a world apart; its 1,500 residents consider themselves definitely *not* from Amalfi. Leave Amalfi via the main road and stay on the water side until the promenade ends. Cross the street, continue a few more yards, then go up the whitewashed staircase just past the pizzeria. From here, twist up through old lanes to a paved route that takes you over the hill and drops you into Atrani in about 15 minutes.

With relatively few tourists, a delightful town square, and a free, sandy beach (if you drive here, pay for parking at harbor), Atrani has none of Amalfi's trendy resort feel. Piazza Umberto is the core of town, with cafés, restaurants, and little grocery stores that can make sandwiches. A whitewashed staircase leads up to the serene and beautiful town church (under the clock face).

To save time and sweat on the return walk, follow the promenade just above water level toward Amalfi. Then walk up through the restaurant terrace and find the big, long tunnel next to the parking garage—this will deposit you in the middle of Amalfi.

From Atrani, you could theoretically continue up to **Ravello** (described later in this chapter). But unless you're part mountain goat, you'll probably prefer catching the bus to Ravello from Amalfi town instead.

Sleeping in Amalfi Town

($$$$ = Splurge, $$$ = Pricier, $$ = Moderate, $ = Budget)
Accommodations are much better in Positano (nicer views) or Sorrento (lower prices), but if you're marooned in Amalfi, here are some options. The rankings given are based on prices in high season (roughly April-Oct); prices can spike in August and drop in spring and fall. Hotels are tricky to find in this town's labyrinthine street plan; from Piazza Duomo, look carefully for big hotel signs to get started in the right direction. Rooms without views are generally cheaper.

$$ Hotel Floridiana, just off the main drag and five minutes by foot from the harbor, is only three short flights of steps up from the street. Though lacking views, the 13 rooms are neat and clean. The well-run hotel has a gorgeous, frescoed breakfast room and comes with free garage parking—very unusual here (air-con, elevator, closed Nov-March; pass the Duomo, take the next right through tiny arch—Salita Brancia—and go up 30 steps to Via Brancia 1; tel. 089-873-6373, www.hotelfloridiana.it, info@hotelfloridiana.it, Agnese).

$$ Residenza del Duca is a little seven-room B&B with ornate furnishings, up many flights of stairs in the heart of this touristy enclave (RS%, no views but glimpses of ocean through the rooftops, air-con; 25 yards uphill from Piazza Duomo, take the first left, go up stairs and follow signs, then go up more stairs—over 70 total—to Via Mastalo II Duca 3; luggage service available April-Oct 8:00-20:00—call ahead, tel. 089-873-6365, www.residencedelduca.it, info@residencedelduca.it, Andrea).

$$ Hotel Lidomare's 18 rooms are decorated in traditional majolica tiles and rich antique furnishings just a few steps from the Duomo. While a bit long in the tooth, it's central and conscientiously run by the aptly named Camera ("Room") family (air-con, open year-round, faces its own little square just up the stairs across from the Duomo stairs—veer left to Largo Piccolomini 9, tel. 089-871-332, www.lidomare.it, info@lidomare.it, Santolo and his sister Maria).

$$ Hotel Aurora is a tranquil, bright, and cheery respite from Amalfi crowds. With 28 rooms, it's at the base of the biggest pier, overlooking the harbor and pedestrian promenade—a scenic 10-minute waterfront stroll from the town center (family apartments available, air-con, elevator, pay parking, closed late Oct-early April, Piazzale dei Protonini, tel. 089-871-209, www.aurora-hotel.it, info@aurora-hotel.it).

$$ Hotel Centrale—with 17 rooms in a, yes, central location—is faded and overpriced. It's a last resort that's worth considering only if you can score one of the eight rooms that have a stunning view of the cathedral. These cost the same but come with some noise (air-con, lots of stairs, open year-round, Largo Piccolomini 1, tel. 089-872-608, www.amalfihotelcentrale.it, amalfihotelcentrale@msn.com).

Eating in Amalfi Town

Grabbing a Quick Bite: Walk five minutes up the main drag; on the right, past the first archway, is **$ Pizza Express,** with honest pies, calzones, and heated sandwiches to go (Mon-Sat 9:00-21:00, closed Sun, Via Capuano 46, mobile 339-581-2336). The **Cuoppo d'Amalfi** fried-fish stand at Piazza dei Dogi (described below) is another good option.

Supermarkets: There's a small supermarket facing Piazza dei Dogi, and another one (Decò) just off the main drag (up an alley to the right near #34, at Via Dei Curiali 6). Both close for a midafternoon break and all day Sunday.

On the Main Square, Piazza Duomo: Several pricey places face the cathedral steps. The best of the bunch is tucked just around the left side of the grand staircase, up a smaller flight of stairs: **$$ Taverna degli Apostoli,** with colorful outdoor tables and cozy upstairs dining room in what was once an art gallery. The menu is brief but thoughtful, going beyond the old standbys, and everything is well executed (daily 12:00-16:00 & 19:00-24:00, Supportico San Andrea 6, tel. 089-872-991). For dessert, the **Andrea Pansa** pastry shop and café, to the right as you face the cathedral steps, is the most venerable place in town—a good spot to try *sfogliatella* (the delicate pastry invented at a nearby monastery) and other desserts popular in southern Italy.

Near the Main Square, on Piazza dei Dogi: If you walk straight ahead from the cathedral stairs, go up the little covered lane, and hook right at the fork, you'll pop out in atmospheric little Piazza dei Dogi. Slightly less trampled and more neighborhood-feeling than Piazza Duomo, this has several decent (if forgettable) restaurants aimed squarely at pleasing tourists. The **$ Cuoppo d'Amalfi** fried-fish shop, on the right as you enter the square, fills cardboard cones with all manner of deep-fried sea life. **$$ Bar La Piazzetta** has good prices at its tables right in the middle of the square. And tucked at the corner of the square leading to the port, **$$ La Taverna di Masaniello** is a bit pricier, with good food.

Ravello

The Amalfi Coast's version of a hill town, Ravello (a 30-minute bus ride from Amalfi town) sits atop a lofty perch 1,000 feet above the sea. It boasts an interesting church, two villas with stunning gardens, and breathtaking views that have attracted celebrities for generations. Gore Vidal, Richard Wagner, D. H. Lawrence, M. C. Escher, Henry Wadsworth Longfellow, and Greta Garbo all have succumbed to Ravello's charms and called it home.

The town is like a lush and peaceful garden floating above it all. It seems to be made entirely of cafés, stonework, old villas-turned-luxury hotels, tourists, and grand views. It feels like a place to convalesce.

Ravello can make for a half-day outing from Amalfi, or a full day from Positano with a stop in Amalfi. The views from the bus ride up and back are every bit as stunning as those along the coastal route.

Sights in Ravello

To see the sights listed here, start at the bus stop and walk through the tunnel to the main square, where you'll find the Villa Rufolo on the left, the church on the right, and the **TI** down the street past the church (TI open daily May-Oct 10:00-18:00, closes earlier off-season, 100 yards from the square—follow signs to Via Roma 18, tel. 089-857-096, www.ravellotime.it). Villa Cimbrone is a 10-minute walk from the square (follow the signs).

If you have time for only one villa, consider this: Villa Rufolo is easier to reach (facing the main square) and has a stunning terrace garden. Villa Cimbrone requires an up-and-down hike, but it's bigger and more rugged and offers even grander views in both directions along the coast.

Piazza Duomo

The town's entry tunnel deposits you on the main square. Though Ravello is perfectly peaceful today, the watchtower of Villa Rufolo—which once kept an eye out for fires and invasions—is a reminder that it wasn't always postcards and *limoncello*. The facade of the cathedral is plain because the earlier, fancy west portal was destroyed in a 1364 earthquake. The front door is locked; to enter, go through the museum on Viale Wagner, around the left side. The fine umbrella pines on the square provide a shady meeting place for strollers ending up here on the piazza. Opposite the church is a fine view of the terraced hillside and the community of Scala (which means "steps"—historically a way of life there). The terraces—supporting grapevines and lemon trees—mostly date from the 16th century. Viale Wagner climbs to the top of town for sea views and ruined villas that are now luxury hotels. The town is essentially traffic-free.

Duomo

Ravello's cathedral, overlooking the main square, feels stripped-down and Romanesque, with tastefully restrained decoration and a floor that slopes upward. The key features of this church are its 12th-century bronze doors (from Constantinople), with 54 Biblical scenes; the carved marble pulpit supported by six lions; and the chance to get a close-up look at the relic of holy blood (left of main altar). The geometric designs show Arabic influence. The humble cathedral museum, through which you'll enter, is two rooms of well-described carved marble that evoke the historical importance of the town.

Cost and Hours: €3 for the museum—which also gets you into the church, daily May-Oct 9:00-19:00, Nov-April until 18:00, enter through museum (around left side of cathedral).

Villa Rufolo

The villa, built in the 13th-century ruins of a noble family's palace, presents wistful gardens among stony walls, with oh-my-God views. The Arabic/Norman gardens seem designed to frame commanding coastline vistas (you can enjoy the same view, without the entry fee, from the bus parking lot just below the villa). It's also one of the venues for Ravello's annual arts festival (July-Sept, www.ravellofestival.com) and music society performances (April-June and Sept-Oct, www.ravelloarts.org). Musicians perch on a bandstand on the edge of the cliff for a combination of wonderful music and dizzying views. Wagner visited here and was impressed enough to set the second act of his opera *Parsifal* in the villa's magical gardens. By all accounts, the concert on the cliff is a sublime experience.

Cost and Hours: €5, daily May-Sept 9:00-20:00, Oct-April 9:00 until sunset, may close earlier for concerts, tel. 089-857-621, www.villarufolo.it.

Visiting the Villa: From Piazza Duomo, you'll enter through the stout watchtower to buy your ticket, then walk through part of the sprawling villa ruins. Finally you'll pop out at a viewpoint overlooking the neatly geometrical garden terrace, which you're welcome to climb down and explore.

AMALFI COAST

▲Villa Cimbrone

This villa offers another romantic garden, this one built upon the ruins of an old convent. Located at the opposite end of Ravello, it was created in the 20th century by Englishman William Beckett. His mansion is now a five-star hotel. It's a longish walk to the end of town, where you explore a bluff dreamily landscaped around the villa. At the far end, above a sublime café on the lawn, "the Terrace of Infinity" dangles high above the sea.

Cost and Hours: €7, daily 9:00-sunset, tel. 089-857-459, www.villacimbrone.com.

Getting There: Facing the cathedral on Piazza Duomo, exit the square to the right and follow signs. You'll climb up and down (and up and down) some stair-step lanes, enjoying a quieter side of Ravello, before reaching the villa at the point.

Visiting the Villa: Buy your ticket and pick up the free map/guide of the gardens. Across from the ticket booth, duck into the old monastery. Then pass the rose-garden terrace and head up the "main boulevard," which leads straight to the stunning Terrace of Infinity, with 360-degree views up and down the coast. If you have the interest and energy, loop back along the more rugged downhill slope (facing the adjacent town of Scala). Tiny lizards scurry underfoot, while mythological statues (Mercury's Seat, Temple of Bacchus, Eve's Grotto) strike their poses before a stunning and serene backdrop.

▲Hike to Amalfi Town from Villa Cimbrone

To walk downhill from Ravello's Villa Cimbrone to the town of Amalfi (a path for hardy hikers only—follow the TI's map), retrace your steps back toward town. Take the first left, which turns into a stepped path winding its way below the cliff. Pause here to look back up at the rock with a big white mansion—Villa La Rondinaia, where Gore Vidal lived for many years. Continue down the fairly steep path about 40 minutes to the town of Atrani, where several bars on the main square offer well-deserved refreshments. From here, it's about a 15-minute walk back to Amalfi (see "Hike #2" on page 1077).

Eating in Ravello

Several no-brainer, interchangeable restaurants face Piazza Duomo and line the surrounding streets. To enjoy this fine setting, just take your pick. You can also grab a takeaway lunch at one of the little groceries and sandwich shops that line Via Roma (between Piazza Duomo and the TI). Enjoy your meal at the panoramic benches at the far end of Piazza Duomo (facing the cathedral), or facing even better views just outside of town, near the bus stop and Ristorante Da Salvatore. (Picnicking isn't allowed inside the two villas.)

$$$ Ristorante Da Salvatore, near the Ravello bus stop (at the other end of the little tunnel from the Duomo), serves a serious sit-down lunch with great views. Pino, the English-speaking owner of this formal restaurant, serves nicely presented, traditional Amalfi cuisine from a fun, if pricey, menu. Be adventurous when ordering and share dishes. Pato, the parakeet, is learning English (Tue-Sun 12:30-15:00 & 19:30-22:00, closed Mon, Via della Repubblica 2, tel. 089-857-227, reservations smart, www. salvatoreravello.com).

Ravello Connections

Ravello and the town of **Amalfi** are connected by bus along a very windy road. Coming from Amalfi town, buy your bus ticket at the bar on the waterfront, and ask where the stop for Ravello is (normally by the statue on the waterfront, just to the statue's left as you face the water). When returning from Ravello, line up early, since the buses are often crowded (at least every 40 minutes, 30-minute trip, €1.20, buy ticket in tobacco shop; catch bus 100 yards off main square, at other end of tunnel). Coming from Positano or Sorrento, you'll change buses in Amalfi. From Naples or Paestum, you have to change twice (in Salerno and Amalfi), making for a long day.

Paestum

The ruins at Paestum (PASTE-oom) include one of the best collections of Greek temples anywhere—and certainly the most accessible to Western Europe. Serenely situated, Paestum is surrounded by fields and wildflowers. It also has a functional zone with a bus stop, train station, church, and a straggle of houses and cafés that you could barely call a village.

This town was founded as Poseidonia by Greeks in the sixth century B.C. and became a key stop on an important trade route. In the fifth century B.C., the Lucanians, a barbarous inland tribe, conquered Poseidonia and tried to adopt the cultured ways of the Greeks. By the time of the Romans, who took over in the third century B.C., the name Poseidonia had been

Salerno Connections

(map labels:)

To Naples

To Old Town

Piazza XXIV Maggio

CORSO VITTORIO EMANUELE II

VIA F. PRINCIPATI
VIA F. P. VOLPE
VIA GUARANTA
VIA CILENTO
VIA GEN. AMANDO ZITO
VIA F. MANZO
VIA BALZICO
VIA SANTI
MARTIRI SALERNITANI
VIA LUIGI CACCIATORE

CORSO GIUSEPPE GARIBALDI
LUNGOMARE
VIA FELICE
TRIESTE

GELATI
(MAIN PEDESTRIAN STREET)
BAR CIOFFI
ROST.
Piazza Veneto
Piazza Mazzini
TABACCHI
PIZZA
BUSES TO AMALFI COAST

TRAIN STATION

To Paestum & Palermo

BUSES TO PAESTUM
Piazza della Concordia
P

Porto Turistico

BOATS TO AMALFI & POSITANO
HYDROFOIL TERMINAL

Fiume Irno

To Paestum

200 Meters
200 Yards

Gulf of Salerno

simplified to Paestum. The final conquerors of Paestum, malaria-carrying mosquitoes, kept the site wonderfully deserted for nearly a thousand years. The temples were never buried—just ignored. Rediscovered in the 18th century, Paestum today offers the only well-preserved Greek ruins north of Sicily.

While most visitors do Paestum as a day trip (it's 1.5 hours south of Naples by convenient direct train), it's not a bad place to overnight. Accommodations offer great value, and though it's a bit far, you could use Paestum as a base for day trips to Naples or the Amalfi Coast. There's a beach nearby, and hotels can help arrange visits to local buffalo-milk dairies.

Tourist Information: There's a small TI window at the train station (daily 8:30-18:30) and a bigger one next to the Paestum Archaeological Museum (daily 9:00-13:00 & 15:00-17:00, tel. 0828-811-016, www.infopaestum.it).

GETTING THERE

Direct trains to Paestum run from Naples and Salerno; from elsewhere, you'll need to transfer at one of those two points. For those transferring in Salerno, see the map on the facing page, which shows train, bus, and boat stops as well as a few handy takeaway places if you need to grab a bite.

From Naples: Direct **trains** run from Naples' Centrale Station to Paestum for €6 (10/day, 1.5 hours, direction: Sapri). Buy tickets from the ticket windows or machines at the station (stamp before boarding). For a day trip from Naples, it's wise to get an early start—especially in warm weather. Most recently, trains left at 6:50, 7:25, 7:55, and 8:55, then not until 12:07 (confirm schedule at station or www.trenitalia.it).

From Amalfi Town: First take a 75-minute bus ride (or possibly a boat) to Salerno, where you can catch the **train** on its way from Naples (30-40 minutes from Salerno to Paestum). You'll need to leave Amalfi early—8:00 at the latest—to make the last morning train. In Salerno, buy your train ticket at the ticket machines, ticket office, or the newsstand in the train station (stamp before boarding). Buses from Amalfi terminate at the Salerno train station, but if you arrive in Salerno from the Amalfi Coast by boat, you'll walk from the boat dock a few short blocks up to the train station (about 10 minutes, mostly level; see map).

If you're in a pinch—for example, you've arrived in Salerno during the midday lull in the train schedule—you could take **local CSTP bus #34** from Salerno to Paestum (about hourly, less on Sun, 1-hour trip). It seems convenient to the port (it departs from Piazza della Concordia—look for bus shelter between the big parking lot and the main road, no posted schedule), but you can't buy tickets nearby—the closest sales point is the tobacco shop a block in front of the train station. In Paestum, this bus drops you only slightly closer to the ruins than does the train.

From Positano: The extra 50 minutes by road to Amalfi, plus time spent changing buses there, makes a day trip from Positano to Paestum more difficult than from Amalfi town. It's possible, though (take a crack-of-dawn bus to Amalfi or the first ferry of the day to Salerno), especially in summer, when return buses from Amalfi run until late in the evening.

From Sorrento: The smart (if dull) approach is to go by Circumvesuviana train to Naples (70 minutes), catch the direct Naples-Paestum train, and return the same way. While it's technically possible to do one leg of the trip via an Amalfi Coast bus, this makes for a very long day marred by worry about making connections back. Other options are to rent a car or hire a taxi for the day. From Sorrento, Paestum is 60 miles and at least 3 hours (depending on traffic) via the Amalfi Coast road, but a smooth 2 hours by autostrada. To reach Paestum from Sorrento via the autostrada, drive toward Naples, catch the autostrada (direction: Salerno), skirt

AMALFI COAST

Salerno (direction: Reggio), exit at Battipaglia, and drive straight through the roundabout.

If you drive to Paestum, you'll see signs for *mozzarella di bufala*, cheese made from the milk of water buffalo. Try it here—it couldn't be any fresher.

Arrival at Paestum: If you arrive by train, cross under the tracks, exit the tiny station, and walk through the ancient city gate; the ruins are a 10-minute walk straight ahead, up a dusty road. When you hit the street with hotels and shops, turn right to find the museum and site entrance. Buses from Salerno stop near a corner of the ruins (at a little bar/café). There's no official baggage storage at the train station or museum. If you're desperate, you can try nicely asking one of the bars along the main road (they may want a small payment).

ORIENTATION TO PAESTUM

Cost: €7, €10 with special exhibits, includes site and museum. The site alone is €6 on days when the museum is closed; the museum alone is €4 after dark on winter evenings, when the site is closed.

Hours: Museum open daily 8:30-19:30 (last ticket sold at 18:50), except closed the first and third Mon of each month. Site open daily 8:30 to one hour before sunset (as late as 19:30 June-July, as early as 16:00 in late Nov-Dec, last site ticket sold 40 minutes before closing).

Getting In: The site and museum have separate entrances. The museum, just outside the ruins, is in a cluster with the TI and a small early-Christian basilica. Most visitors buy tickets at the museum and use the entrance across the street, but another ticket office and entrance are near the recommended Ristorante Nettuno (at the south end of the site). On days when the museum is closed, you have to buy tickets at the site entrances.

Information: Although there are only scant descriptions at the site, my self-guided tours provide all the information you need for both the site and the museum. Skip the museum bookshop's mediocre guidebooks and dull audioguide. Info tel. 0828-811-023, www.museopaestum.beniculturali.it.

Local Guide: Silvia Braggio is a good guide who specializes in Paestum and gives a fine two-hour walk of the site and museum (special rate with this book-€100, arrange in advance, mobile 347-643-2307, www.silviaguide.it, silvia@silviaguide.it). She also offers walking tours of Pompeii and Herculaneum.

Eating: Several cafés and bars cluster around the museum (all open long hours daily in summer). **$ La Basilica Café,** facing a pretty little garden between the parking lot and TI, is the most straightforward and reasonable option, with good pizzas and other lunch fare (Via Magna Grecia 881, tel. 0828-811-301). **Ristorante Nettuno,** with quality food and good temple views, is at the south entrance to the site. They have a fine little glassed-in **$$** café facing the ruins (affordable light food, including a fixed-price lunch) and a dressier, more expensive **$$$** restaurant across the path (Via Nettuno 2, tel. 0828-811-028).

Length of This Tour: Allow two hours to see the ruins and the museum. Which one you see first depends on your interest and the heat: You'll enjoy the coolest temperatures in the morning, but the best light and smallest crowds late in the day.

BACKGROUND

While Paestum is famous for its marvelous Greek temples, most of the structures you see are Roman. Five elements of Greek Paestum survive: three misnamed temples, a memorial tomb, and a circular meeting place (the Ekklesiasterion). The rest, including the wall that defines the site, is Roman.

Paestum was once a seaport (the ocean is now about a mile away—the wall in the distance, which stretches about three miles, is about halfway to today's coastline). Only about a fifth of the site has been excavated. The Greek city, which archaeologists figure had a population of about 13,000, was first conquered by Lucanians (distant relatives of the Romans, who spoke a language related to Latin), and then by the Romans (who completely made it over and built the wall you see today).

The remaining Greek structures survive because the Romans were superstitious—they respected sacred areas and didn't mess with temples and tombs. While most old Christian churches are built upon Roman temples (it tends to be what people do when they conquer another culture), no Roman temple is built upon a Greek temple. Romans appreciated how religion could function as the opiate of the masses. As long as people paid their taxes and obeyed the emperor's dictates, the practical Romans had no problem with any religion. The three Greek temples that you'll see here today have stood for about 2,500 years.

❂ SELF-GUIDED TOUR
Paestum Archaeological Site

This part of the tour starts at the entrance by the museum, visits the Temple of Ceres, goes through the center of the Roman town past the Greek Memorial Tomb, circles around the other two Greek temples, and then leaves the site to walk down the modern road to the Ekklesiasterion (which faces the museum).

• *Buy your ticket at the museum, then head to the right to find the site's north entrance. Once inside, stand in front of the...*

Temple of Ceres: All three Paestum temples have inaccurate names, coined by 19th-century archaeologists who based their "discoveries" on wishful thinking. (While the Romans made things easy by leaving lots of inscriptions, the Greeks did not.) Those 1800s archaeologists

wanted this temple to be devoted to Ceres, the goddess of agriculture. However, all the little votive statues found later, when modern archaeologists dug here, instead depicted a woman with a big helmet: Athena, goddess of wisdom and war. (The Greeks' female war goddess was also the goddess of wisdom—thinking...strategy... female. The Romans' masculine war god was Mars—just fighting.) Each temple is part of a sanctuary—an open, sacred space around the temple. Because regular people couldn't go into the temple, the altar logically stood outside.

The Temple of Ceres dates from 500 B.C. It's made of locally quarried limestone blocks. Good roads and shipping didn't come along until the Romans, so the Greeks' buildings were limited to local materials. The wooden roof is long gone. Like the other two temples, this one was once painted white, black, and red, and has an east-west orientation—facing the rising sun. This temple's *cella* (interior room) is gone, cleared out when it was used as a Christian church in the sixth century. In medieval times, Normans scavenged stones from here; chunks of these temples can be found in Amalfi's cathedral.

Walk around to the back side of the Temple of Ceres. The capitals broke in a modern earthquake, so a steel bar provides necessary support. Each of the Paestum temples is Doric style—with three stairs, columns without a base, and shafts that narrow at the top to a simple capital of a round, then a square, block. While there were no carved reliefs, colorful frescoes once decorated the pediments.

As you walk away, look back at the temple. Traditionally, Greeks would build a sanctuary of Athena on a city's highest spot (like the Parthenon in Athens, on the Acropolis). Paestum had no hill, so the Greeks created a mound. The hill was more impressive in its time because the level of the Greek city was substantially lower than the Roman pavement stones you'll walk on today.

• *Continue all the way past the temple, follow the path down, and turn left to walk on the paving stones of Via Sacra toward the other Greek temples. After about 100 yards, to the left of the road, you'll see a little half-buried house with a tiled roof.*

Greek Memorial Tomb (Heroon): This tomb (from 500 B.C.)

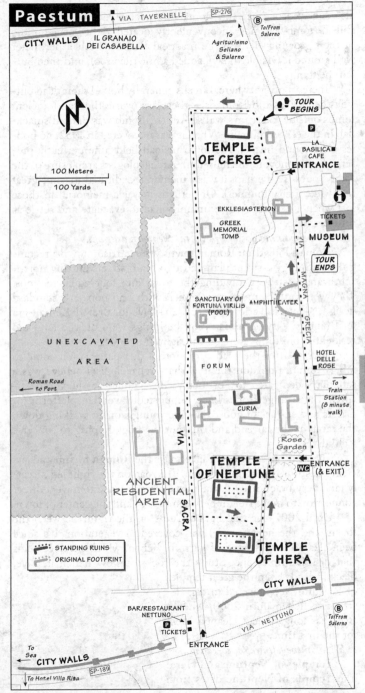

also survived because the Romans respected religious buildings. But the tomb was most inconveniently located, right in the middle of their growing city. So the practical Romans built a perimeter wall around it (visible today), added a fine tiled roof, and then buried the tomb.

There's a mystery here. Greeks generally buried their dead outside the city (as did Romans)—there are over a thousand ancient tombs outside Paestum's walls—yet this tomb was parked smack-dab in the center of town. When it was uncovered in 1952, no bodies were found inside. The tomb instead held nine perfectly preserved vases (now in the museum). Archaeologists aren't sure of the tomb's purpose. Perhaps it was a memorial dedicated to some great hero (like a city founder). Or perhaps it was a memorial to those lost when a neighboring community had to evacuate and settle as refugees here.

• *Continue walking down Via Sacra, the main drag of...*

Roman Paestum: Roman towns were garrison towns: rectangular with a grid street plan and two main streets cutting north-south and east-west, dividing the town into four equal sections. They were built by military engineers with a no-nonsense standard design. New excavations (on the left) have uncovered Roman-era lead piping. City administration buildings were on the left, and residential buildings were on the right.

Shortly after the road turns into a dirt path, you'll come to a big **Roman pool** (on the left) that archaeologists believe was a sanctuary dedicated to Fortuna Virilis, goddess of luck and fertility. The strange stones likely supported a wooden platform for priests and statues of gods. Imagine young women walking down the ramp at the far end and through the pool, hoping to conceive a child.

The next big square on the left was the **Roman forum** and ancient Paestum's main intersection. The road on the right led directly (and very practically) to the port. It made sense to have a direct connection to move freight between the sea and the center of town.

Until 2007, the vast field of ruins on the right (between the forum and the next temple) was covered in vegetation. It's since been cleared and cleaned of harmful lichen, which produce acids that dissolve limestone. Study the rocks: Yellow lichen is alive, black is dead. Even the great temples of Paestum were covered in this destructive lichen until 2000, when a two-year-long project cleaned them for the first time.

• *Ahead on the left are the so-called...*

Temples of Neptune and Hera: The **Temple of Neptune** dates from

450 B.C. and employs the Greek architectural trick where the base line is curved up just a tad to overcome the illusion of sagging caused by a straight base. The Athenians built their Parthenon (with a similar bowed-up base line) just 30 years after this. Many think this temple could have been their inspiration.

The adjacent **Temple of Hera,** dating from 550 B.C., is the oldest of Paestum's three temples and one of the oldest Greek temples still standing anywhere. Notice the change 100 years makes in the architectural styles: Archaic Doric in 550 B.C. versus Classic Doric in 450 B.C.

Archaeologists now believe the "Temple of Neptune" was actually devoted to a different god. Votive statues uncovered here suggest that Hera was the focus (perhaps this was a new-and-improved version of the adjacent, simpler, and older Temple of Hera). Or perhaps it was a temple to Zeus, Hera's husband, to honor the couple together.

Together, the two temples formed a single huge sanctuary with altars on the far (east) side. Walk between the temples, then hook right to get a good look at the front of the Temple of Hera. Notice how overbuilt this temple appears. Its columns and capitals are closer together than necessary, as if the builders lacked confidence in their ability to span the distance between supports. Square pillars mark the corners of the *cella* inside. Temples with an odd number of columns (here, nine) had a single colonnade crossing in the center inside to support the wooden roof. More modern temples (such as the Temple of Neptune) had six columns, with two colonnades passing through the *cella*. This left a line of vision open through the middle so that worshippers could see the big statue of the god.

By the way, in 1943, Allied paratroopers dropped in near here during the famous "Landing of Salerno," when the Allies (who had already taken Sicily) invaded mainland Italy. Paestum was part of their first beachhead. The Temple of Hera served as an Allied military tent hospital. From here, the Allies pushed back the Nazis, marching to Naples, Cassino, and finally to Rome.

• *Leave the site (using the exit straight ahead from the Temple of Neptune and a bit to the left) and turn left on the modern road...*

Via Magna Grecia: The king of Naples had this Naples-to-Paestum road built in 1829 to inspire his people with ancient temples. While he was modern in his appreciation of antiquity, his road project destroyed a swath of the ancient city, as you'll see as you pass by half of the small amphitheater.

AMALFI COAST

• *Just past the amphitheater, you'll find the...*

Ekklesiasterion: Immediately across the street from the museum is what looks like a sunken circular theater. This rare bit of ancient Greek ruins was the Ekklesiasterion, a meeting place where the Greeks would get together to discuss things and vote. Archaeologists believe that the agora (market) would also have been located here.

• *Across the street is the...*

Paestum Archaeological Museum

Paestum's museum offers the rare opportunity to see artifacts—dating from prehistoric to Greek to Roman times—at the site where they were discovered. These beautifully crafted works (with good English descriptions throughout) help bring Paestum to life. Not everything you see here is from Paestum, though, as the museum also collects artifacts from other nearby sites.

Before stepping into the museum, notice the proud fascist architecture. Though the building dates from 1954, it was designed in 1938. It seems to command that you *will* enjoy this history lesson.

The exhibit is on several levels. You'll find mostly Greek pieces on the ground floor (artifacts from the Temple of Hera in front, frescoes from tombs in the back), Paleolithic to Iron Age artifacts on the mezzanine level, and Roman art on the top floor (statues, busts, and inscriptions dating from the time of the Roman occupation). While Roman art is not unique to Paestum, the Greek collection is—so that's what you should focus on. Here are the highlights:

Temple Reliefs: The museum's first room is designed like a Greek temple, with an inner *cella* that is used for temporary exhibitions. The large carvings overhead that wrap around this inner sanctum once adorned a sanctuary of the goddess Hera (wife of Zeus) five miles away. This sanctuary, called Heraion del Sele, was discovered and excavated in 1934. Some of the carvings show scenes from the life of Hercules.

• *Along the back wall of this room, find the glass case holding nine perfectly preserved...*

Vases: One ceramic and eight bronze, with artistic handles, these vases were found in Paestum's Greek Memorial Tomb (if these vases are off-view for restoration, look for the similar bronze vases upstairs, at the end of this tour). Greek bronzes are rare because Romans often melted them down to make armor. These were discovered in 1952, filled with still-liquid honey and sealed with beeswax. The honey (as you can see in the display cases below) has since crystallized. Honey was a standard part of a funeral because, to ancient Greeks, honey symbolized immortality...it lasts forever.

• *Enter the room at the far end of the main hall, filled with ancient Greek...*

Votive Offerings: These were dug up at Heraion del Sele (not at Paestum). Such offerings are a huge help to modern archaeologists, since the figures that worshippers brought to a temple are clues as to which god the temple honored. These votives depict a woman with a crown on a throne—clearly Hera. The clay votives were simple, affordable, and accessible to regular people.

• *Now enter the large room (broken up by pillars and interior walls) that holds...*

Relics from the Temples at Paestum: This room displays smaller pieces. Displays (mostly in Italian) tell in which temple each relic was found. The Temple of Ceres is often referred to as the Temple of Athena or as the northern *(settentrionale)* sanctuary. The Temples of Neptune and Hera are spoken of as the southern *(meridionale)* sanctuaries. Before exploring the collection, notice the display case near the entrance with the **huge book** turned to a page with a fine drawing by the Italian artist Giovanni Piranesi, showing his visit to Paestum in 1777.

Across the room, look for the short fragment of a frieze with lion heads. Paestum's three temples were once adorned with decorations, such as these ornamental spouts that spurted rainwater out of lions' mouths. Notice the bits of the surviving black, red, and white paint. Reconstructions on the adjacent wall show archaeologists' best guesses as to how the original decorations might have looked.

Farther into the room, you can't miss the display case of a statue's **torso** emblazoned with swastikas—a reminder that this symbol (carrying completely different meanings) predated Hitler by millennia.

In a glass case nearby, find the seated statue of **Zeus**. This painted clay Zeus dates from 520 B.C. The king of the gods was so lusty with his antics, he's still smirking.

• *Look out the museum's back window for a good, if distant...*

View of Paestum's Walls: The walls of ancient Paestum reach halfway to the mountain—a reminder that most of the site is still private property and yet to be excavated. The town up on the mountainside is Capaccio, established in the eighth century when inhabitants of the original city of Paestum were driven out by malaria and the city was abandoned.

• *Walk along the corridor at the back of the museum, which shows...*

Objects from Tombs: More than 1,000 tombs have been identified outside the ancient city's wall. About 100 were found decorated with frescoes or containing objects such as these.

• *At the far end of the corridor, turn left to see...*

AMALFI COAST

The Tomb of the Diver: This is the museum's treasure and the most precious Paestum find. Dating from 480 B.C., it's not only the sole ancient Greek tomb fresco in the museum—it's the only one ever found in southern Italy. Discovered in 1968, it has five frescoed slabs

(four sides and a lid; the bottom wasn't decorated). The Greeks saw death as a passage: diving from mortality into immortality...into an unknown world. Archaeologists believe that the pillars shown on the fresco represent the Pillars of Hercules at Gibraltar, which in ancient times defined the known world. The ocean beyond the Mediterranean was the great unknown...like the afterlife. The Greek banquet makes it clear that this was an aristocratic man.

• *After the Tomb of the Diver, the next room displays...*

Lucanian Tomb Frescoes: The many other painted slabs in the museum date from a later time, around 350 B.C., when Paestum fell under Lucanian rule. These frescoes are cruder than their earlier Greek counterpart. The people who conquered the Greeks tried to appropriate their art and style, but they lacked the Greeks' distinctive light touch. Still, these offer fascinating glimpses into ancient life here at Paestum.

• *Beyond this room, you'll find yourself back at the entrance. Before you leave, go up the stairs by the bookshop for a glimpse at the mezzanine level, which focuses on prehistoric archaeology. The exhibit here has much better English translations than the ground floor. At the very least, near the end of the first hall, check out the...*

Film Footage from WWII: A 10-minute continuous film loop, subtitled in English, tells the story of Allied soldiers' encounters with the ruins in 1943. You'll see footage of soldiers hanging up their laundry and shaving in the temples, which they actually safeguarded well. Part of the film focuses on excavations directed by a British archaeologist who was attached to the invading forces.

• *The back wall of the mezzanine displays **bronze vases**, mostly from Gaudo, a half-mile from Paestum. If the vases downstairs are missing, here's your chance to see some rare surviving examples of this common Greek vessel.*

SLEEPING IN PAESTUM

($$$$ = Splurge, $$$ = Pricier, $$ = Moderate, $ = Budget)

Paestum at night, with views of the floodlit ruins, is magic. Accommodations here offer great value. You can sleep in a mansion for the same price you'd pay for a closet in Positano. All listings have free parking.

$ Il Granaio dei Casabella, a converted old granary with 14 attractive, reasonably priced rooms, is a 10-minute walk from the ruins. It has a beautiful garden and pretty common areas, and four rooms have temple views (RS%, family rooms, air-con, closed Dec-Feb, just west of the bus stop closest to Salerno at Via Tavernelle 84, tel. 0828-721-014, www.ilgranaiodeicasabella.com, info@ilgranaiodeicasabella.com, hospitable Celardo family).

$ Hotel Villa Rita is a tidy, quiet country hotel set on two acres within walking distance of the beach and the temples. It has 22 rooms, a kid-friendly swimming pool, and attractive grounds with grassy lawns and a little soccer field (RS%, extra bed possible, lunch or dinner-€22, air-con, closed Nov-mid-March, Via Nettuno 9, tel. 0828-811-081, www.hotelvillarita.it, info@hotelvillarita.it, Luigi). The hotel is a 10-minute walk west of the Hera entrance and public bus stop, and a 20-minute walk from the train station (they can usually pick you up, if you're arriving with luggage).

$ Hotel delle Rose, with 10 small, basic rooms with minuscule bathrooms, is near the Neptune entrance on the street bordering the ruins. It's an acceptable choice for those on a budget and is also the option closest to the ruins and the train station (RS%, family rooms, air-con, Via Magna Grecia 943, tel. 0828-199-0692, www.hotelristorantedellerose.com, info@hotelristorantedellerose.com, Luigi).

Outside of Town: $$ Agriturismo Seliano is a great option for drivers, with plush public spaces, a pool, and 14 grand, spacious rooms on a peaceful, once-elegant farm estate that's been in the same family for 300 years (air-con, closed Nov-March; one mile north of ruins on main road—Via Magna Grecia—a small *Azienda Agrituristica Seliano* sign directs you down long dirt driveway; Via Seliano, tel. 0828-723-634, www.agriturismoseliano.it, seliano@agriturismoseliano.it). They serve a fine lunch or dinner for guests and nonguests—made with produce fresh from the garden—and can also organize cooking classes. The place is run by Cecilia—an English-speaking baroness—and her family, including about a dozen dogs.

PAESTUM CONNECTIONS

By Train: Ten slow, milk-run trains a day head to Salerno (30-40 minutes) and Naples (1.5 hours). In Salerno, you can change for the bus to Amalfi or walk down to the harbor to catch an Amalfi- or Positano-bound boat. You can buy train tickets at machines in the (unstaffed) Paestum station.

By Bus to Salerno: Buses depart from Paestum to Salerno roughly every hour (less on Sun; one-hour trip). Buy a ticket from one of the bars in Paestum, then go to either of the intersections that flank the ruins (see map on page 1084), flag down any northbound bus, and ask, "Salerno?" From Salerno, you can continue on to Amalfi or Positano by boat or walk up to the train station to catch an Amalfi-bound SITA bus or a train.

ITALIAN HISTORY

Italy has a lot of history, so let's get started.

ORIGINS OF ROME (c. 753 B.C.-450 B.C.)

A she-wolf breastfed two human babies, Romulus and Remus, who grew to build the city of Rome in 753 B.C.—you buy that? Closer to fact, farmers and shepherds of the Latin tribe settled near the mouth of the Tiber River, a convenient trading location. The crude settlement was sandwiched between two sophisticated civilizations—Greek colonists to the south (Magna Grecia, or greater Greece), and the Etruscans of Tuscany, whose origins and language are largely still a mystery to historians (for more on the Etruscans, see page 642). Baby Rome was both dominated and nourished by these societies.

When an Etruscan king raped a Roman woman (509 B.C.), her husband led a revolt, driving out the Etruscan kings and replacing them with elected Roman senators and (eventually) a code of law (Laws of the Twelve Tables, 450 B.C.). The Roman Republic was born.

THE ROMAN REPUBLIC EXPANDS
(c. 509 B.C.-A.D. 1)

Located in the center of the peninsula, Rome was perfectly situated for trading salt and wine. Roman businessmen, backed by a disciplined army, expanded through the Italian peninsula, establishing a Roman infrastructure as they went. Rome soon swallowed up its northern Etruscan neighbors, conquering them by force and absorbing their culture.

Next came Magna Grecia, with Rome's legions defeating the Greek general Pyrrhus after several costly "Pyrrhic" victories (c. 275 B.C.). Rome now ruled a united federation stretching from Tuscany to the tip of the Italian peninsula, with a standard currency, a system of roads (including the Via Appia), and a standing army of a half-million soldiers ready for the next challenge: Carthage.

Carthage (modern-day Tunisia) and Rome fought the three bitter Punic Wars for control of the Mediterranean (264-201 B.C. and 146 B.C.). The balance of power hung precariously in the Second Punic War (218-201 B.C.), when Hannibal of Carthage crossed the sea to Spain with a huge army of men and elephants. He marched 1,200 miles overland, crossed the Alps, and forcefully penetrated Italy from the rear. Almost at the gates of the city of Rome, he was finally turned back. The Romans prevailed, and, in the mismatched Third Punic War, they burned the city of Carthage to the ground (146 B.C.).

The well-tuned Roman legions easily subdued sophisticated Greece in three Macedonian Wars (215-146 B.C.). Though Rome conquered Greece, Greek culture dominated the Romans. From hairstyles to statues to temples to the evening's entertainment, Rome was forever "Hellenized," becoming the curators of Greek culture, passing it down to future generations.

By the first century B.C., Rome was master of the Mediterranean. Booty, cheap grain, and thousands of captured slaves poured in, transforming the economic model from small farmers to unemployed city dwellers living off tribute from conquered lands. The Republic had changed.

CIVIL WARS AND THE TRANSITION TO EMPIRE (First Century B.C.)

With easy money streaming in and traditional roles obsolete, Romans bickered among themselves over their slice of the pie. Wealthy landowners (patricians, the ruling Senate) wrangled with the middle and working classes (plebeians) and with the growing population of slaves, who demanded greater say-so in government. In 73 B.C., Spartacus—a Greek-born soldier-turned-Roman slave who'd been forced to fight as a gladiator—escaped to the slopes of Mount Vesuvius, where he amassed an army of 70,000 angry slaves. After two years of fierce fighting across Italy, the Roman legions crushed the revolt and crucified 6,000 rebels along the Via Appia as a warning.

Amid the chaos of class war and civil war, charismatic generals who could provide wealth and security became dictators—men such as Sulla, Crassus, Pompey...and Caesar. Julius Caesar (100-44 B.C.) was a cunning politician, riveting speaker, conqueror of Gaul, author of *The Gallic Wars,* and lover of Cleopatra, Queen of Egypt. In his four-year reign, he reformed and centralized the government around himself. Disgruntled Republicans feared that he would make himself king. At his peak of power, they surrounded

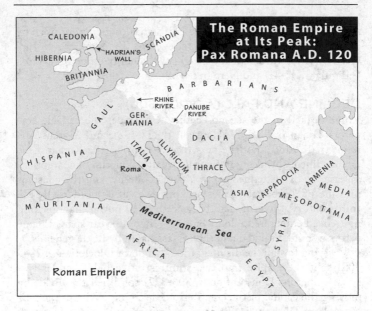

The Roman Empire at Its Peak: Pax Romana A.D. 120

Caesar in the Senate on the "Ides of March" (March 15, 44 B.C.) and stabbed him to death.

Julius Caesar died, but the concept of one-man rule lived on in his adopted son. Named Octavian at birth, he defeated rival Mark Antony (another lover of Cleopatra, 31 B.C.) and was proclaimed Emperor Augustus (27 B.C.). Augustus outwardly followed the traditions of the Republic, while in practice he acted as a dictator with the backing of Rome's legions and the rubber-stamp approval of the Senate. He established his family to succeed him (making the family name "Caesar" a title) and set the pattern of rule by emperors for the next 500 years.

THE ROMAN EMPIRE (c. A.D. 1-500)

In his 40-year reign, Augustus ended Rome's civil wars and ushered in the Pax Romana: 200 years of prosperity and relative peace. Rome ruled an empire of 54 million people, stretching from Scotland to northern Africa, from Spain to the Euphrates River. Conquered peoples were welcomed into the fold of prosperity, linked by roads, common laws, common gods, education, and the Latin language. The city of Rome, with more than a million inhabitants, was decorated with Greek-style statues and monumental structures faced with marble. It was the marvel of the known world.

The empire prospered on a (false) economy of booty, slaves, and cheap imports. On the Italian peninsula, traditional small farms were swallowed up by large farming and herding estates. In this "global economy," the Italian peninsula became just one province among many in a worldwide Latin-speaking empire, ruled by an emperor who was likely born elsewhere. The empire even survived the often turbulent and naughty behavior of emperors such as Caligula (r. 37-41) and Nero (r. 54-68).

DECLINE AND FALL (A.D. 200-500)

Rome peaked in the second century A.D. under the capable emperors Trajan (r. 98-117), Hadrian (r. 117-138), and Marcus Aurelius (r. 161-180). For the next three centuries, the Roman Empire declined, shrinking in size and wealth, a victim of corruption, disease, an overextended army, a false economy, and the constant pressure of "barbarian" tribes pecking away at its borders. By the third century, the army had become the real power, handpicking figurehead emperors to do its bidding—in a 40-year span, 15 emperors were first saluted and then assassinated by fickle generals.

Trying to stall the disintegration, Emperor Diocletian (r. 284-305) split the empire into two administrative halves under two equal emperors. Constantine (r. 306-337) solidified the divide by moving the capital of the empire from decaying Rome to the new city of Constantinople (330, present-day Istanbul). Almost instantly, the once-great city of Rome became a minor player in imperial affairs. (The eastern "Byzantine" half of the empire would thrive and live on for another thousand years.) Constantine also legalized Christianity (313), and the once-persecuted cult soon became virtually the state religion, the backbone of Rome's fading hierarchy.

By 410, "Rome" had shrunk to just the city itself, surrounded by a protective wall. Barbarian tribes from the north and east poured in to loot and plunder. The city was sacked by Visigoths (410) and vandalized by Vandals (455), and the pope had to plead with Attila the Hun for mercy (451). The peninsula's population fell to six million, trade and agriculture were disrupted, schools closed, and the infrastructure collapsed. Peasants huddled near powerful lords for protection from bandits, planting the seeds of medieval feudalism.

In 476, the last emperor sold his title for a comfy pension, and Rome fell like a huge column, kicking up dust that would plunge Europe into a thousand years of darkness. For the next 13 centuries, there would be no "Italy," just a patchwork of rural dukedoms and towns, victimized by foreign powers. Italy lay in shambles, helpless.

INVASIONS (A.D. 500-1000)

In 500 years, Italy suffered through a full paragraph of invasions: Lombards (568) and Byzantines (under Justinian, 536) occupied the north. In the south, Muslim Saracens (827) and Christian Normans (1061) established thriving kingdoms. Charlemagne, king of the Germanic Franks, defeated the Lombards, and on Christmas Day, A.D. 800, he knelt before the pope in St. Peter's in Rome to be crowned Holy Roman Emperor, an empty title meant to resurrect the glory of ancient Rome united with medieval Christianity. For the next thousand years, Italians would pledge nominal allegiance to weak, distant German kings as their Holy Roman Emperor.

Through all the invasions and chaos, the glory of ancient Rome was preserved in the pomp, knowledge, hierarchy, and wealth of the Christian Church. Strong popes (Leo I, 440-461, and Gregory the Great, 590-604) ruled like small-time emperors, governing territories in central Italy called the Papal States.

PROSPERITY AND POLITICS (A.D. 1000-1300)

Italy survived Y1K, and the economy picked up. Sea-trading cities like Venice, Genoa, Pisa, Naples, and Amalfi grew wealthy as middlemen between Europe and the Orient. During the Crusades (e.g., First Crusade 1097-1130), Italian ships ferried Europe's Christian soldiers eastward, then returned laden with spices and highly marked-up luxury goods from the Orient. Trade spawned banking, and Italians became capitalists, loaning money at interest to Europe's royalty. Italy pioneered a new phenomenon in Europe—cities (comuni) that were self-governing commercial centers. The medieval prosperity of the cities laid the foundation of the future Renaissance.

Politically, the Italian peninsula was dominated by two rulers—the pope in Rome and the German Holy Roman Emperor (with holdings in the north). Italy split into two warring political parties: supporters of the popes (called Guelphs, centered in urban areas) and supporters of the emperors (Ghibellines, popular with the rural nobility).

THE UNLUCKY 1300s

In 1309, the pope—enticed by France, Europe's fast-rising power—moved from Rome to Avignon, France. At one point, two rival popes reigned, one in Avignon and the other in Rome, and they excommunicated each other. The papacy eventually returned to Rome (1377), but the schism created a breakdown in central authority that was exacerbated by an outbreak of bubonic plague (Black Death, 1347-1348), which killed a third of the Italian population.

In the power vacuum, new players emerged in the independent cities. Venice, Florence, Milan, and Naples were under the protection and leadership of local noble families (signoria) such as the Medici in Florence. Florence thrived in the wool and dyeing trade, which led to dominance in international banking, with branches in all of Europe's capitals. A positive side effect of the terrible Black

Church Architecture

History comes to life when you visit a centuries-old church. Even if you wouldn't know your apse from a hole in the ground, learning a few simple terms will enrich your experience. Note that not every church has every feature, and that a "cathedral" isn't a type of church architecture, but rather a designation for a church that's a governing center for a local bishop.

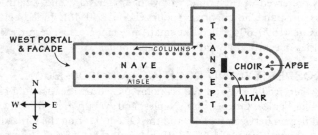

Aisles: The long, generally low-ceilinged arcades that flank the nave.

Altar: The raised area with a ceremonial table (often adorned with candles or a crucifix), where the priest prepares and serves the bread and wine for Communion.

Apse: The space beyond the altar, generally bordered with small chapels.

Barrel Vault: A continuous round-arched ceiling that resembles an extended upside-down U.

Choir: A cozy area, often screened off, located within the church nave and near the high altar, where services are sung in a more intimate setting.

Cloister: Covered hallways bordering a square or rectangular open-air courtyard, traditionally where monks and nuns got fresh air.

Facade: The exterior surface of the church's main (west) entrance, viewable from outside and generally highly decorated.

Groin Vault: An arched ceiling formed where two equal barrel vaults meet at right angles. Less common usage: term for a medieval jock strap.

Narthex: The area (portico or foyer) between the main entry and the nave.

Nave: The long, central section of the church (running west to east, from the entrance to the altar) where, in medieval times, the congregation sits or stands through the service.

Transept: In a traditional cross-shaped floor plan, the transept is one of the two parts forming the "arms" of the cross. The transepts run north-south, perpendicularly crossing the east-west nave.

West Portal: The main entry to the church (on the west end, opposite the main altar).

Death was that the now-smaller population got a bigger share of the land, jobs, and infrastructure. By century's end, Italy was poised to enter its most glorious era since antiquity.

THE RENAISSANCE (1400s-1600s)

The Renaissance (Rinascimento)—the "rebirth" of ancient Greek and Roman art styles, knowledge, and humanism—began in Italy (c. 1400) and spread through Europe over the next two centuries. Many of Europe's most famous painters, sculptors, and thinkers— Michelangelo, Leonardo, Raphael, etc.—were Italian.

It was a cultural boom that changed people's thinking about every aspect of life. In politics, it meant an eventual rebirth of Greek ideas of democracy. In religion, it meant a move away from Church dominance and toward the assertion of man (humanism) and a more personal faith. Science and secular learning were revived after centuries of superstition and ignorance. In architecture, it was a return to the balanced columns and domes of Greece and Rome. In painting, the Renaissance meant 3-D realism.

Italians dotted their cities with publicly financed art—Greek gods, Roman-style domed buildings. They preached Greek-style democracy and explored the natural world. The cultural boom was financed by thriving trade and lucrative banking. During the Renaissance, the peninsula once again became the trendsetting cultural center of Europe.

FOREIGN INVASIONS (1500s)

In May 1498, Vasco da Gama of Portugal landed in India, having found a sea route around Africa. Italy's monopoly on trade with the East was broken. Portugal, France, Spain, England, and Holland—nation-states under strong central rule—began to overtake decentralized Italy. Italy's once-great maritime cities now traded in an economic backwater, just as Italy's bankers (such as the Medici in Florence) were going bankrupt. While the Italian Renaissance was all the rage throughout Europe, it declined in its birthplace. Italy—culturally sophisticated but weak and decentralized—was ripe for the picking by Europe's rising powers.

Several kings of France invaded (1494, 1495, and 1515)— initially invited by Italian lords to attack their rivals—and began divvying up territory for their noble families. Italy also became a battleground in religious conflicts between Catholics and the new Protestant movement. In the chaos, the city of Rome was brutally sacked by foreign mercenaries (1527).

FOREIGN RULE (1600-1800)

For the next two centuries, most of Italy's states were ruled by foreign nobles, serving as prizes for the winners of Europe's dynastic

Top 10 Italians

Romulus: Breastfed on wolf milk, this legendary orphan grew to found the city of Rome (traditionally in 753 B.C.). Over the next seven centuries, his descendants dominated the Italian peninsula, ruling from Rome as a Republic.

Julius Caesar (100-44 B.C.): After conquering Gaul (France), subduing Egypt, and winning Cleopatra's heart, Caesar ruled Rome with king-like powers. In an attempt to preserve the Republic, senators stabbed him to death, but the concept of one-man rule lived on.

Augustus (born Octavian, 63 B.C.-A.D. 14): Julius' adopted son became the first of the Caesars that ruled Rome during its 500 years as a Europe-wide power. He set the tone for emperors both good (Trajan, Hadrian, Marcus Aurelius) and bad (Caligula, Nero, and dozens of others).

Constantine (c. 280-337 A.D.): Raised in a Christian home, this emperor legalized Christianity, almost instantly turning a persecuted sect into a Europe-wide religion. With the Fall of Rome, the Church was directed by strong popes and so guided Italians through the next thousand years of invasions, plagues, political decentralization, and darkness.

Lorenzo the Magnificent (1449-1492): Soldier, poet, lover, and ruler of Florence in the 1400s, this Renaissance Man embodied the "rebirth" of ancient enlightenment. Lorenzo's wealthy Medici family funded Florentine artists who pioneered a realistic 3-D style.

Michelangelo Buonarroti (1475-1564): His statue of David—slaying an ignorant brute—stands as a monumental symbol of Italian enlightenment. Along with fellow geniuses Leonardo da Vinci and

HISTORY

wars. Italy ceased to be a major player in Europe, politically or economically. Italian intellectual life was often cropped short by a conservative Catholic Church trying to fight Protestantism. Galileo, for example, was forced by the Inquisition to renounce his belief that the earth orbited the sun (1633). But Italy did export Baroque art (Giovanni Lorenzo Bernini) and the budding new medium of opera.

The War of the Spanish Succession (1713)—a war in which Italy did not participate—gave much of northern Italy to Austria's ruling family, the Habsburgs (who now wore the crown of Holy Roman Emperor). In the south, Spain's Bourbon family ruled the Kingdom of Naples (known after 1816 as the Kingdom of the Two Sicilies), making it a culturally sophisticated but economically backward area, preserving a medieval, feudal caste system.

In 1720, a minor war (the War of Austrian Succession) created

Raphael, Michelangelo spread the Italian Renaissance (painting, sculpture, architecture, literature, and ideas) to a worldwide audience.

Giovanni Lorenzo Bernini (1598-1680): The "Michelangelo of Baroque" kept Italy a major exporter of sophisticated trends. Bernini's ornate statues and architecture decorated palaces of the rising power in France, even as Italy was reverting to an economically stagnant patchwork of foreign-ruled states.

Victor Emmanuel II (1820-1878): As the only Italian-born ruler on the peninsula, this King of Sardinia became the rallying point for Italian unification. Aided by the general Garibaldi, writer Mazzini, and politician Cavour (with a soundtrack by Verdi), he became the first ruler of a united, democratic Italy, in September 1870. (The preceding proper nouns have since come to adorn streets and piazzas throughout Italy.)

Benito Mussolini (1883-1945): An inspiration for Hitler, he derailed Italy's fledgling democracy, becoming dictator of a fascist state, leading the country into defeat in World War II. No public places honor Mussolini, but many streets and piazzas throughout Italy bear the name of Giacomo Matteotti (1885-1924), a politician whose outspoken opposition to Mussolini got him killed by Fascists.

Federico Fellini (1920-1993): Fellini's films (*La Strada, La Dolce Vita, 8½*) chronicle Italy's postwar years in gritty black and white—the poverty, destruction, and disillusionment of the war followed by the optimism, decadence, and materialism of the economic boom. He captured the surreal chaos of Italy's abrupt social change from traditional Catholic to a secular, urban world presided over by Mafia bosses and weak government.

a new state at the foot of the Alps, called the Kingdom of Sardinia (a.k.a. the Kingdom of Piedmont, or Savoy). Ruled by the Savoy family, this was the only major state on the peninsula that was actually ruled by Italians. It proved to be a toehold to the future.

ITALY UNITES—THE RISORGIMENTO (1800s)

In 1796, Napoleon Bonaparte swept through Italy and changed everything. He ousted Austrian and Spanish dukes, confiscated Church lands, united scattered states, and crowned himself "King of Italy" (1805). After his defeat (1815), Italy's old ruling order (namely, Austria and Spain) was restored. But Napoleon had planted a seed: What if Italians could unite and rule themselves like Europe's other modern nations?

For the next 50 years, a movement to unite Italy slowly grew. Called the Risorgimento—a word that means "rising again"—the

Italian Unification

NOTE: Dates indicate the year of annexation to the Kingdom of Sardinia. After 1861, this became the Kingdom of Italy.

SWITZERLAND

AUSTRIA

FRANCE

VENETIA (1866)

Venice

LOMBARDY (1859)

PIEDMONT

PARMA

MODENA

Florence

KINGDOM OF SARDINIA

TUSCANY (1860)

STATES OF THE CHURCH (1870)

Adriatic Sea

Rome

Naples

SARDINIA

KINGDOM OF THE TWO SICILIES (1860)

Mediterranean Sea

SICILY

100 Kilometers

100 Miles

movement promised a revival of Italy's glory. It started as a revolutionary, liberal movement—taking part in it was punishable by death. Members of a secret society called the Carbonari (led by a professional revolutionary named Giuseppe Mazzini) exchanged secret handshakes, printed fliers, planted bombs, and assassinated conservative rulers. Their small revolutions (1820-1821, 1831, 1848) were easily and brutally slapped down, but the cause wouldn't die.

Gradually, Italians of all stripes warmed to the idea of unification. Whether it was a united dictatorship, a united papal state, a united kingdom, or a united democracy, most Italians could agree that it was time for Spain, Austria, and France to leave.

The movement coalesced around the Italian-ruled Kingdom of Sardinia and its king, Victor Emmanuel II. In 1859, Sardinia's prime minister, Camillo Cavour, cleverly persuaded France to drive Austria out of northern Italy, leaving the region in Italian hands. A plebiscite (vote) was held, and several central Italian states (including some of the pope's) rejected their feudal lords and chose to join the growing Kingdom of Sardinia.

After victory in the north, Italy's most renowned Carbonari general, Giuseppe Garibaldi (1807-1882), steamed south with a thousand of his best soldiers *(I Mille)* and marched on the Spanish-ruled city of Naples (1860). The old order simply collapsed. In two short months, Garibaldi had achieved a seemingly impossible victory against a far superior army. Garibaldi sent a one-word telegram to the king of Sardinia: *"Obbedisco"* (I obey). The following year, an assembly of deputies from throughout Italy met in Turin and crowned Victor Emmanuel II "King of Italy." Only the pope in Rome held out, protected by French troops. When the city finally fell—easily—to the unification forces on September 20, 1870, the Risorgimento was complete. Italy went ape.

The Risorgimento was largely the work of four men: Garibaldi (the sword), Mazzini (the spark), Cavour (the diplomat), and Victor Emmanuel II (the rallying point). Today, street signs throughout Italy honor them and the dates of their great victories.

MUSSOLINI AND WAR (1900-1950)

Italy —now an actual nation-state, not just a linguistic region—entered the 20th century with a progressive government (a constitutional monarchy), a collection of colonies, and a flourishing northern half of the country. In the economically backward south (the Mezzogiorno), millions of poor peasants emigrated to the Americas. World War I (1915-1918) left 650,000 Italians dead, but being on the winning Allied side, survivors were granted possession of the alpine regions. In the postwar cynicism and anarchy, many radical political parties rose up—Communist, Socialist, Popular, and Fascist.

Benito Mussolini (1883-1945), a popular writer for socialist and labor-union newspapers, led the Fascists. ("Fascism" comes from Latin *fasci,* the bundles of rods that symbolized unity in ancient Rome.) Though only a minority (6 percent of the parliament in 1921), they intimidated the disorganized majority with organized violence by black-shirted Fascist gangs. In 1922, Mussolini seized the government (see "The March on Rome" sidebar) and began his rule as dictator for the next two decades.

Mussolini solidified his reign among Catholics by striking an agreement with the pope (Concordato, 1929), giving Vatican City to the papacy, while Mussolini ruled Italy with the implied blessing of the Catholic Church. Italy responded to the great worldwide Depression (1930s) with big public works projects (including Rome's subway), government investment in industry, and an expanded army.

Mussolini allied his country with Hitler's Nazi regime, draw-

The March on Rome

In October 1922, Benito Mussolini, head of the newly formed Fascist Party, boldly proposed a coup d'état, saying: "Either the government will be given to us, or we will take it by marching on Rome." Throughout Italy, black-shirted Fascists occupied government buildings in their hometowns. Others grabbed guns, farming hoes, and kitchen knives and set off to converge on the outskirts of Rome. (Estimates of the size of the Fascist band range from 300 to the 300,000 of Fascist legend.) Mussolini sent the government an ultimatum to surrender. Though the Fascists were easily outmanned and outgunned by government forces, the show of force intimidated the king, Victor Emmanuel III, into avoiding a nasty confrontation. He invited Mussolini to Rome. Mussolini arrived the next day (by first-class train), was made prime minister, then marched his black-shirted troops triumphantly through the streets of Rome.

ing an unprepared Italy into World War II (1940). Italy's lame army was never a factor in the war, and when Allied forces landed in Sicily (1943), Italians welcomed them as liberators. The Italians toppled Mussolini's government and surrendered to the Allies, but Nazi Germany sent troops to rescue Mussolini. The war raged on as Allied troops inched their way north against German resistance. Italians were reduced to dire poverty. In the last days of the war (April 1945), Mussolini was captured by the Italian resistance. They shot him and his girlfriend and hung their bodies upside down in a public square in Milan.

POSTWAR ITALY

At war's end, Italy was physically ruined and extremely poor. The nation rebuilt in the 1950s and 1960s (the "economic miracle") with Marshall Plan aid from the United States. Many Italian men moved to northern Europe to find work; many others left farms and flocked to the cities. Italy regained its standing among nations, joining the United Nations, NATO, and what would later become the European Union.

However, the government remained weak, changing on average once a year, shifting from right to left to centrist coalitions (it's had 63 governments since World War II). Afraid of another Mussolini, the authors of the postwar constitution created a feeble executive branch; without majorities in both houses of parliament nothing could get done. All Italians acknowledged that the real power lay in the hands of backroom politicians and organized crime—a phenomenon called *Tangentopoli*, or "Bribe City." The country remained strongly divided between the rich, industrial north and the poor, rural south.

Italian society changed greatly in the 1960s and 1970s, spurred by the liberal reforms of the Catholic Church at the Vatican II conference (1962-1965). The once-conservative Catholic country legalized divorce and contraception, and the birth rate plummeted. In the 1970s, the economy slowed thanks to inflation, strikes, and the worldwide energy crisis. Italy suffered a wave of violence from left- and right-wing domestic terrorists and organized crime, punctuated by the assassination of former Prime Minister Aldo Moro (1978). A series of coalition governments in the 1980s brought some stability to the economy.

ITALY TODAY

In the early 1990s, the judiciary launched a campaign to rid politics of corruption and Mafia ties. Though still ongoing, the investigation sent a message that Italy would no longer tolerate evils that were considered necessary just a generation earlier. As home to the Vatican, Italy keeps a close watch on the Catholic Church's ongoing scandal of pedophile priests.

Over the last decade, the Great Recession hit the Italian economy hard and led to the downfall of Prime Minister Silvio Berlusconi—the controversial owner of many of Italy's media outlets and the country's richest person. Like other European nations, Italy had run up big deficits by providing comfy social benefits without sufficient tax revenue, forcing the Italian government to tighten its belt. By the end of 2011, Italy's debt load was the second worst in the euro zone, behind only Greece. To calm the markets, Berlusconi resigned.

A caretaker government imposed severe austerity measures, leading to 12 percent unemployment in 2013—with youth unemployment around 40 percent. Italy wanted change, and got it when 39-year-old Matteo Renzi took over as prime minister in early 2014—the youngest prime minister in modern Italian history. Renzi's nickname is Il Rottamatore ("The Scrapper")—and he says he wants to "scrap" most of Italy's political establishment, starting with one of the houses of the Italian parliament. He forced the resignation of the CEOs of Italy's biggest state-owned companies and appointed women to replace several of them. To stimulate the moribund economy, he's pushed for tax cuts and investments in job growth.

For a time, the dynamic Renzi was immensely popular. More recently, though, he's been dogged by a persistently sluggish economy, repeated corruption scandals, and an immigration crisis brought on by the influx of people streaming from across the Mediterranean seeking a better life in Europe.

HISTORY

As you travel through Italy today, you'll encounter a fascinating country with a rich history and a per-capita income that comes close to its neighbors to the north. Despite its ups and downs, Italy remains committed to Europe...yet it's as wonderfully Italian as ever.

If you want to learn more about Italian history, consider *Europe 101: History and Art for the Traveler,* written by Rick Steves and Gene Openshaw (available at www.ricksteves.com).

HISTORY

PRACTICALITIES

This chapter covers the practical skills of European travel: how to get tourist information, pay for things, sightsee efficiently, find good-value accommodations, eat affordably but well, use technology wisely, and get between destinations smoothly. To study ahead and round out your knowledge and skills, check out "Resources from Rick Steves."

Tourist Information

Before your trip, scan the website of the Italian national tourist office (www.italia.it) for a wealth of travel information. If you have a specific question, try contacting one of their US offices (New York: Tel. 212/245-5618, newyork@enit.it; Chicago: Tel. 312/644-0996, chicago@enit.it; Los Angeles: Tel. 310/820-1898, losangeles@enit.it).

In Italy, a good first stop in every town is generally the tourist information office (abbreviated **TI** in this book). Be aware that TIs are in business to help you enjoy spending money in their town. (Once upon a time, they were actually information services, but today some have become ad agencies masquerading as TIs.) While this corrupts much of their advice—and you can get plenty of information online—I still make a point to swing by the local TI to confirm sightseeing plans, pick up a city map, and get information on public transit (including bus and train schedules), walking tours, special events, and nightlife. Prepare a list of questions and a proposed plan to double-check. While Italian TIs are about half as helpful as those in other countries, their information is twice as important.

Some TIs have information on the entire country or at least the region, so try to pick up maps and printed information for destinations you'll be visiting later in your trip.

Be wary of travel agencies or special information services that masquerade as TIs but serve fancy hotels and tour companies. They're in the business of selling things you don't need.

Travel Tips

Emergency and Medical Help: In Italy, dial 112 for English-speaking police help. To summon an ambulance, call 118. If you get sick, do as the locals do and go to a pharmacist for advice. Or ask at your hotel for help—they'll know the nearest medical and emergency services.

Theft or Loss: To replace a passport, you'll need to go in person to an embassy (see page 1178). If your credit and debit cards disappear, cancel and replace them (see "Damage Control for Lost Cards" on page 1117). File a police report, either on the spot or within a day or two; you'll need it to submit an insurance claim for lost or stolen rail passes or travel gear, and it can help with replacing your passport or credit and debit cards. For more information, see www.ricksteves.com/help.

Avoiding Theft and Scams: Although violent crime is rare in Italy, petty theft is rampant in large cities. With sweet-talking con artists meeting you at the station, well-dressed pickpockets on buses, and thieving gangs of children roving ancient sites, tourists face a gauntlet of rip-offs. Although it's not as bad as it was a few years ago, and pickpockets don't want to hurt you—they usually just want your money and gadgets—green or sloppy tourists will be scammed.

Thieves strike when you're distracted. Don't trust kind strangers. Keep nothing important in your pockets. Be on guard while boarding and leaving buses and subways. Thieves jam up the door, then stop and turn while others crowd and push from behind. You'll find less crowding and commotion—and less risk—on the end cars of a subway rather than the middle cars. The sneakiest thieves pretend to be well-dressed businessmen or tourists wearing fanny packs and toting cameras and even Rick Steves guidebooks.

Scams abound. When paying for something, be aware of how much cash you're handing over, demand clear and itemized bills, and count your change. Don't give your wallet to self-proclaimed "police" who stop you on the street, warn you about counterfeit (or drug) money, and ask to see your cash. If a bank machine eats your ATM card, check for a thin plastic insert with a tongue hanging out (thieves use these devices to extract cards).

Watch out for fast-fingered moms with babies and groups of children picking the pockets and handbags of naive tourists. Pickpockets troll tourist crowds around major sights and at train and Metro stations. Watch them target tourists who are overloaded with bags or distracted with their smartphones. Kids look like beggars and hold up newspapers or cardboard signs to confuse their victims. They scram like stray cats if you're on to them.

This all sounds intimidating, and perhaps I'm overstating the dangers. Don't be scared—just be aware and be smart, and you'll be fine.

Time Zones: Italy, like most of continental Europe, is generally six/nine hours ahead of the East/West Coasts of the US. The exceptions are the beginning and end of Daylight Saving Time: Europe "springs forward" the last Sunday in March (two weeks after most of North America), and "falls back" the last Sunday in October (one week before North America). For a handy online time converter, see www.timeanddate.com/worldclock.

Business Hours: Traditionally, Italy has used the siesta plan, with people generally working from about 9:00 to 13:00 and from 15:30 or 16:00 to 19:00 or 19:30, Monday through Saturday (though in tourist areas, larger shops may be open through lunch). Expect small towns and villages to be more or less shut tight during the midafternoon. Stores are usually closed on Sunday, and often on Monday. Many shops close for a couple of weeks around August 15. Banking hours are generally Monday through Friday 8:30 to 13:30 and 15:30 to 16:30, but can vary wildly.

Saturdays are virtually weekdays, with earlier closing hours. Sundays have the same pros and cons as they do for travelers in the US: Sightseeing attractions are generally open, while banks and many shops are closed, public transportation options are fewer (for example, no bus service to or from the smaller towns), and there's no rush hour. Friday and Saturday evenings are lively; Sunday evenings are quiet.

Watt's Up? Europe's electrical system is 220 volts, instead of North America's 110 volts. Most newer electronics (such as laptops, battery chargers, and hair dryers) convert automatically, so you won't need a converter, but you will need an adapter plug with

PRACTICALITIES

two round prongs, sold inexpensively at travel stores in the US. However, sockets in Italy (and Switzerland) only accept plugs with slimmer prongs, so don't buy an adapter with the thicker ("Schuko" style) prongs—it won't work. Avoid bringing older appliances that don't automatically convert voltage; instead, buy a cheap replacement in Europe.

Discounts: Discounts for sights are generally not listed in this book. However, many sights offer discounts or free admission for youths (up to age 18), students (with proper identification cards, www.isic.org), families, seniors (loosely defined as retirees or those willing to call themselves a senior), and groups of 10 or more. Always ask. Italy's national museums generally offer free admission to children under 18, but some discounts are available only for citizens of the European Union (EU).

Tobacco Shops: Known as *tabacchi* (often indicated with a big *T* sign), these shops are ubiquitous across Italy as handy places to pay for street parking and to buy postage or tickets for city buses and subways.

Online Translation Tips: Google's Chrome browser instantly translates websites. You can also paste text or the URL of a foreign website into the translation window at http://translate.google. com. The Google Translate app converts spoken English into most European languages (and vice versa) and can also translate text it "reads" with your mobile device's camera.

Money

This section offers advice on how to pay for purchases on your trip (including getting cash from ATMs and paying with plastic), dealing with lost or stolen cards, VAT (sales tax) refunds, and tipping.

WHAT TO BRING

Bring both a credit card and a debit card. You'll use the debit card at cash machines (ATMs) to withdraw local cash for most purchases, and the credit card to pay for larger items. Some travelers carry a third card, in case one gets demagnetized or eaten by a temperamental machine.

For an emergency stash, bring $100-200 in hard cash. Although banks in some countries don't exchange dollars, in a pinch you can always find exchange desks at major train stations or airports—convenient but with crummy rates.

CASH

Although credit cards are widely accepted in Europe, day-to-day spending is generally more cash-based. I find cash is the easiest—and sometimes only—way to pay for cheap food, bus fare, taxis,

---

Exchange Rate

1 euro (€) = about $1.10

To convert prices in euros to dollars, add about 10 percent: €20 = about $22, €50 = about $55. (Check www.oanda.com for the latest exchange rates.) Just like the dollar, one euro is broken down into 100 cents. Coins range from €0.01 to €2, and bills from €5 to €200 (bills over €50 are rarely used; €500 bills are being phased out).

---

and local guides. Some vendors will charge you extra for using a credit card, some won't accept foreign credit cards, and some won't take credit cards at all. Having cash on hand can help you avoid a stressful predicament if you find yourself in a place that won't accept your card.

Throughout Europe, ATMs are the easiest and smartest way for travelers to get cash. They work just like they do at home. To withdraw money from an ATM (known as a *bancomat* in Italy), you'll need a debit card (ideally with a Visa or MasterCard logo), plus a PIN code (numeric and four digits). For increased security, shield the keypad when entering your PIN code, and don't use an ATM if anything on the front of the machine looks loose or damaged (a sign that someone may have attached a "skimming" device to capture account information). Try to withdraw large sums of money to reduce the number of per-transaction bank fees you'll pay.

When possible, use ATMs located outside banks—a thief is less likely to target a cash machine near surveillance cameras, and if your card is munched by a machine during banking hours, you can go inside for help. Stay away from "independent" ATMs such as Travelex, Euronet, YourCash, Cardpoint, and Cashzone, which charge huge commissions, have terrible exchange rates, and may try to trick users with "dynamic currency conversion" (described later). Although you can use a credit card to withdraw cash at an ATM, this comes with high bank fees and only makes sense in an emergency.

While traveling, if you want to access your accounts online, be sure to use a secure connection (see page 1153).

Pickpockets target tourists. To safeguard your cash, wear a money belt—a pouch with a strap that you buckle around your waist like a belt and tuck under your clothes. Keep your cash, credit cards, and passport secure in your money belt, and carry only a day's spending money in your front pocket or wallet.

PRACTICALITIES

CREDIT AND DEBIT CARDS

For purchases, Visa and MasterCard are more commonly accepted than American Express. Just like at home, credit or debit cards work easily at larger hotels, restaurants, and shops. I typically use my debit card to withdraw cash to pay for most purchases. I use my credit card sparingly: to book hotel reservations, to buy advance tickets for events or sights, to cover major expenses (such as car rentals or plane tickets), and to pay for things online or near the end of my trip (to avoid another visit to the ATM). While you could instead use a debit card for these purchases, a credit card offers a greater degree of fraud protection.

Ask Your Credit- or Debit-Card Company: Before your trip, contact the company that issued your debit or credit cards.

Confirm your **card will work overseas,** and alert them that you'll be using it in Europe; otherwise, they may deny transactions if they perceive unusual spending patterns.

Ask for the specifics on transaction **fees.** When you use your credit or debit card—either for purchases or ATM withdrawals—you'll typically be charged additional "international transaction" fees of up to 3 percent (1 percent is normal). If your card's fees seem high, consider getting a card just for your trip: Capital One (www.capitalone.com) and most credit unions have low-to-no international fees.

Verify your daily ATM **withdrawal limit,** and if necessary, ask your bank to adjust it. I prefer a high limit that allows me to take out more cash at each ATM stop and save on bank fees; some travelers prefer to set a lower limit in case their card is stolen. Note that foreign banks also set maximum withdrawal amounts for their ATMs.

Get your bank's **emergency phone number** in the US (but not its 800 number, which isn't accessible from overseas) to call collect if you have a problem.

Ask for your credit card's **PIN** in case you need to make an emergency cash withdrawal or encounter payment machines using the chip-and-PIN system; the bank won't tell you your PIN over the phone, so allow time for it to be mailed to you.

Chip and PIN: While much of Europe is shifting to a chip-and-PIN security system for credit cards, Italy still uses the old magnetic-stripe technology. (European chip-and-PIN cards are embedded with an electronic security chip and require a four-digit PIN to make a purchase.) If you happen to encounter chip and PIN, it will probably be at payment machines, such as those at toll roads or unattended gas pumps. On the outside chance that a machine won't take your card, find a cashier who can make your card work (they can print a receipt for you to sign), or find a machine that takes cash. Most American travelers don't run into problems.

Still, it pays to carry euros; remember, you can always use an ATM to withdraw cash with your magnetic-stripe debit card.

If you're concerned, ask if your bank offers a chip-and-PIN card. Andrews Federal Credit Union (www.andrewsfcu.org) and the State Department Federal Credit Union (www.sdfcu.org) offer these cards and are open to all US residents.

Dynamic Currency Conversion: If merchants or hoteliers offer to convert your purchase price into dollars (called dynamic currency conversion, or DCC), refuse this "service." You'll pay extra for the expensive convenience of seeing your charge in dollars. Some ATMs and retailers try to confuse customers by presenting DCC in misleading terms. If an ATM offers to "lock in" or "guarantee" your conversion rate, choose "proceed without conversion." Other prompts might state, "You can be charged in dollars: Press YES for dollars, NO for euros." Always choose the local currency.

Damage Control for Lost Cards

If you lose your credit or debit card, you can stop people from using your card by reporting the loss immediately to the respective global customer-assistance centers. Call these 24-hour US numbers collect: Visa (tel. 303/967-1096), MasterCard (tel. 636/722-7111), and American Express (tel. 336/393-1111). In Italy, to make a collect call to the US, dial 800-172-444. Press zero or stay on the line for an English-speaking operator. European toll-free numbers (listed by country) can also be found at the websites for Visa and MasterCard.

If you are the secondary cardholder, you'll need to provide the primary cardholder's identification-verification details (such as birth date, mother's maiden name, or Social Security number). You can generally receive a temporary card within two or three business days in Europe (see www.ricksteves.com/help for more).

If you report your loss within two days, you typically won't be responsible for any unauthorized transactions on your account, although many banks charge a liability fee of $50.

TIPPING

Tipping in Italy isn't as automatic and generous as it is in the US. For special service, tips are appreciated, but not expected. As in the US, the proper amount depends on your resources, tipping philosophy, and the circumstances, but some general guidelines apply.

Restaurants: In Italy, a service charge (*servizio*) is usually built into your bill, so the total you pay already includes a basic tip. It's up to you whether to tip beyond this. For more details on restaurant tipping, see page 1133.

Taxis: To tip the cabbie, round up your fare a bit (for instance, if the fare is €4.50, pay €5). If the cabbie hauls your bags and zips you to the airport to help you catch your flight, you might want to toss in a little more. But if you feel like you're being driven in circles or otherwise ripped off, skip the tip.

Services: In general, if someone in the tourism or service industry does a super job for you, a small tip of a euro or two is appropriate...but not required. If you're not sure whether (or how much) to tip, ask a local for advice.

GETTING A VAT REFUND

Wrapped into the purchase price of your Italian souvenirs is a Value-Added Tax (VAT) of about 22 percent. You're entitled to get most of that tax back if you purchase more than €155 (about $170) worth of goods at a store that participates in the VAT-refund scheme. Typically, you must ring up the minimum at a single retailer—you can't add up your purchases from various shops to reach the required amount.

Getting your refund is usually straightforward and, if you buy a substantial amount of souvenirs, well worth the hassle. If you're lucky, the merchant will subtract the tax when you make your purchase. (This is more likely to occur if the store ships the goods to your home.) Otherwise, you'll need to:

Get the paperwork. Have the merchant completely fill out the necessary refund document. You'll have to present your passport. Get the paperwork done before you leave the store to ensure you'll have everything you need (including your original sales receipt).

Get your stamp at the border or airport. Process your VAT document at your last stop in the European Union (such as at the airport) with the customs agent who deals with VAT refunds. Arrive an additional hour early before you need to check in for your flight to allow time to find the local customs office—and to stand in line. It's best to keep your purchases in your carry-on. If they're too large or dangerous to carry on (such as knives), pack them in your checked bags and alert the check-in agent. You'll be sent (with your tagged bag) to a customs desk outside security; someone will examine your bag, stamp your paperwork, and put your bag on the belt. You're not supposed to use your purchased goods before you leave. If you show up at customs wearing your new Italian leather shoes, officials might look the other way—or deny you a refund.

Collect your refund. You'll need to return your stamped document to the retailer or its representative. Many merchants work with services—such as Global Blue or Premier Tax Free—that have offices at major airports, ports, or border crossings (either before or after security, probably strategically located near a duty-free shop). These services, which extract a 4 percent fee, can refund your money immediately in cash or credit your card (within two billing cycles). Other refund services may require you to mail the documents from home or, more quickly, from your point of departure (using an envelope you've prepared in advance or one that's been provided by the merchant). You'll then have to wait—it can take months.

CUSTOMS FOR AMERICAN SHOPPERS

You are allowed to take home $800 worth of items per person duty-free, once every 31 days. As for food, you can take home many processed and packaged foods: vacuum-packed cheeses, dried herbs, jams, baked goods, candy, chocolate, oil, vinegar, mustard, and honey. Fresh fruits and vegetables and most meats are not allowed, with exceptions for some canned items. As for alcohol, you can bring in one liter duty-free (it can be packed securely in your checked luggage, along with any other liquid-containing items).

To bring alcohol (or liquid-packed foods) in your carry-on bag on your flight home, buy it at a duty-free shop at the airport. You'll increase your odds of getting it onto a connecting flight if it's packaged in a "STEB"—a secure, tamper-evident bag. But stay away from liquids in opaque, ceramic, or metallic containers, which usually cannot be successfully screened (STEB or no STEB).

For details on allowable goods, customs rules, and duty rates, visit http://help.cbp.gov.

Sightseeing

Sightseeing can be hard work. Use these tips to make your visits to Italy's finest sights meaningful, fun, efficient, and painless.

MAPS AND NAVIGATION TOOLS

A good map is essential for efficient navigation while sightseeing. The black-and-white maps in this book are concise and simple, designed to help you locate recommended destinations, sights, and local TIs, where you can pick up more in-depth maps. Maps with even more detail are sold at newsstands and bookstores.

You can also use a mapping app on your mobile device. Be aware that pulling up maps or looking up turn-by-turn walking directions on the fly usually requires an Internet connection: To use this feature, it's smart to get an international data plan (see page 1151) or only connect using Wi-Fi. With Google Maps or Apple Maps, it's possible to download a map while online, then go offline and navigate without incurring data-roaming charges, though you can't search for an address or get real-time walking directions. A handful of other apps—including City Maps 2Go, OffMaps, and Navfree—also allow you to use maps offline.

PLAN AHEAD

Set up an itinerary that allows you to fit in all your must-see sights. For a one-stop look at opening hours, see the "At a Glance" sidebars for each major city (Venice, Milan, Florence, Siena, and Rome). Most sights keep stable hours, but you can easily confirm the latest by checking with the TI or visiting museum websites. Or call sights in the morning and ask: "Are you open today?" (*"Aperto oggi?"*; ah-PER-toh OH-jee) and "What time do you close?" (*"A che ora chiuso?"*; ah kay OH-rah kee-OO-zoh).

Use the suggestions in this book to avoid waiting in line to buy tickets or enter sights. Sometimes you can make reservations for an entry time (for example, at Florence's Uffizi Gallery or Rome's Vatican Museums). Some cities offer museum passes for admission to several museums (e.g., Roma Pass and Firenze Card) that let you skip ticket-buying lines. At some popular places (such as Rome's Colosseum or Venice's Doge's Palace), you can get in more quickly by buying your ticket or pass at a less-crowded sight (Rome's Palatine Hill or Venice's Correr Museum). Booking a guided tour can help you avoid lines at many popular sights. Admission is free at state museums on the first Sunday of the month—expect crowds.

Don't put off visiting a must-see sight—you never know when a place will close unexpectedly for a holiday, strike, or restoration. Many museums are closed or have reduced hours at least a few days a year, especially on holidays such as Labor Day (May 1), Christmas, and New Year's. A list of holidays is on page 1178; check online for possible museum closures during your trip. In summer, some sights may stay open late. Off-season, many museums have shorter hours.

Going at the right time helps avoid crowds. This book offers tips on specific sights. Try visiting popular sights very early or very late. Evening visits are usually peaceful, with fewer crowds.

Study up. To get the most out of the self-guided tours and sight descriptions in this book, read them before you visit.

AT SIGHTS

Here's what you can typically expect:

Entering: Be warned that you may not be allowed to enter if you arrive less than 30 to 60 minutes before closing time. And guards start ushering people out well before the actual closing time, so don't save the best for last.

Some important sights have a security check, where you must open your bag or send it through a metal detector. Some sights require you to check daypacks and coats. (If you'd rather not check your daypack, try carrying it tucked under your arm like a purse as you enter.)

Photography: If the museum's photo policy isn't clearly posted, ask a guard. Generally, taking photos without a flash or tripod is allowed. Some sights ban photos altogether; others ban selfie sticks.

Temporary Exhibits: Museums may show special exhibits in addition to their permanent collection. Some exhibits are included in the entry price, while others come at an extra cost (which you may have to pay even if you don't want to see the exhibit).

Expect Changes: Artwork can be on tour, on loan, out sick, or shifted at the whim of the curator. Pick up a floor plan as you enter, and ask the museum staff if you can't find a particular item. Say the title or artist's name, or point to the photograph in this book and ask, *"Dov'è?"* (doh-VEH, meaning "Where is?").

Audioguides and Apps: Many sights rent audioguides, which generally offer excellent recorded descriptions in English. If you bring your own earbuds, you can enjoy better sound and avoid holding the device to your ear. To save money, bring a Y-jack and share one audioguide with your travel partner. Museums and sights often offer free apps that you can download to your mobile device (check their websites). And, I've produced free, downloadable audio tours for some of Italy's major sights; look for the 🎧 in this book. For more on my audio tours, see page 12.

Dates for Artwork: It helps to know the terms. Art historians and Italians refer to the great Florentine centuries by dropping a thousand years. The Trecento (300s), Quattrocento (400s), and Cinquecento (500s) were the 1300s, 1400s, and 1500s. The Novecento (900s) means modern art (the 1900s). In Italian museums, art is dated with *sec* for *secolo* (century, often indicated with Roman numerals), A.C. (*avanti Cristo*, or B.C.), and D.C. (*dopo Cristo*, or A.D.). OK?

Visitor Services: Important sights may have an on-site café or cafeteria (usually a handy place to rejuvenate during a long visit). The WCs at sights are free and generally clean.

Before Leaving: At the gift shop, scan the postcard rack or thumb through a guidebook to be sure you haven't overlooked something that you'd like to see.

Every sight or museum offers more than what is covered in this book. Use the information in this book as an introduction—not the final word.

FIND RELIGION

Churches offer some amazing art (usually free), a cool respite from heat, and a welcome seat.

A modest dress code—no bare shoulders or shorts for anyone, even kids—is enforced at larger churches, such as Venice's St. Mark's Basilica and the Vatican's St. Peter's, but is often overlooked elsewhere. If you're caught by surprise, you can improvise, using maps to cover your shoulders and a jacket for your knees. A few major churches let you borrow or buy disposable ponchos to cover up in a pinch. (I wear a super-lightweight pair of long pants rather than shorts for my hot and muggy big-city Italian sightseeing.)

Some churches have coin-operated audioboxes that describe the art and history; just set the dial on English, put in your coins, and listen. Coin boxes near a piece of art illuminate the art (and present a better photo opportunity). I pop in a coin whenever I can. It improves my experience, is a favor to other visitors trying to appreciate a great piece of art in the dark, and is a little contribution to that church and its work. Whenever possible, let there be light.

Sleeping

I favor hotels and restaurants that are handy to your sightseeing activities. Rather than list hotels scattered throughout a city, I choose hotels in my favorite neighborhoods. My recommendations run the gamut, from dorm beds to fancy rooms with all of the comforts. To stay in the countryside, try *agriturismo* farmhouses—I've listed several.

Extensive and opinionated listings of good-value rooms are a major feature of this book's Sleeping sections. I like places that are clean, central, relatively quiet at night, reasonably priced, friendly, small enough to have a hands-on owner and stable staff, and run with a respect for Italian traditions. I'm more impressed by a convenient location and a fun-loving philosophy than flat-screen TVs and a fancy gym. Most places I recommend fall short of perfection. But if I can find a place with most of these features, it's a keeper.

Book your accommodations well in advance, especially if you want to stay at one of my top listings or if you'll be traveling during busy times. See page 1178 for a list of major holidays and festivals in Italy; for tips on making reservations, see page 1128.

Some people make reservations as they travel, calling hotels a few days to a week before their arrival. If you anticipate crowds (weekends are worst) on the day you want to check in, call hotels at about 9:00 or 10:00, when the receptionist knows who'll be checking out and which rooms will be available. Some apps—such as HotelTonight.com—specialize in last-minute rooms, often at business-class hotels in big cities. If you encounter a language barrier, ask the fluent receptionist at your current hotel to call for you.

RATES AND DEALS

I've categorized my recommended accommodations based on price, indicated with a dollar-sign rating (see sidebar). The price ranges suggest an estimated cost for a one-night stay in a standard double room with a private toilet and shower in high season, include

Sleep Code

Hotels are classified based on the average price of a standard double room with breakfast in high season.

$$$$	**Splurge:** Most rooms over €170
$$$	**Pricier:** €130-170
$$	**Moderate:** €90-130
$	**Budget:** €50-90
¢	**Backpacker:** Under €50
RS%	Rick Steves discount

Unless otherwise noted, credit cards are accepted, hotel staff speak basic English, and free Wi-Fi is available. Comparison-shop by checking prices at several hotels (on each hotel's own website, on a booking site, or by email). For the best deal, *book directly with the hotel.* Ask for a discount if paying in cash; if the listing includes **RS%,** request a Rick Steves discount.

breakfast, and assume you're booking directly with the hotel (not through a booking site, which extracts a commission and logically closes the door on special deals). Room prices can fluctuate significantly with demand and amenities (size, views, room class, and so on), but these relative price categories remain constant. While most taxes are included in the price, a variable city tax of €1.50-5/person per night is often added to hotel bills (and is not included in the prices in this book). Some hoteliers will ask to collect the city tax in cash to make their bookkeeping and accounting simpler.

Room rates are especially volatile at larger hotels that use "dynamic pricing" to predict demand. Rates can skyrocket during festivals and conventions, while business hotels can have deep discounts on weekends when demand plummets. For this reason, of the many hotels I recommend, it's difficult to say which will be the best value on a given day—until you do your homework.

Once your dates are set, check the specific price for your preferred stay at several hotels. You can do this either by comparing prices online on the hotels' own websites, or by emailing several hotels directly and asking for their best rate. Even if you start your search on a booking site such as TripAdvisor or Booking.com, you'll usually find the lowest rates through a hotel's website.

Many hotels offer a discount to those who pay cash or stay longer than three nights. To cut costs further, try asking for a cheaper room (for example, with a shared bathroom or no window) or offer to skip breakfast.

Additionally, some accommodations offer a special discount for Rick Steves readers, indicated in this guidebook by the abbreviation "RS%." Discounts vary: Ask for details when you book. Generally, to qualify you must book directly (that is, not through a booking site), mention this book when you reserve, show the book upon arrival, and sometimes pay cash or stay a certain number of nights. In some cases, you may need to enter a discount code (which I've provided in the listing) in the booking form on the hotel's website. Rick Steves discounts apply to readers with ebooks as well as printed books. Understandably, discounts do not apply to promotional rates.

Haggle if you arrive late in the day during off-season (roughly mid-July through August and November through mid-March). It's common for hotels in Rome to lower their prices 10-50 percent in the off-season, although prices at hostels and cheaper hotels won't fluctuate much. Room rates are lowest in sweltering August.

TYPES OF ACCOMMODATIONS
Hotels

The Italian word for "hotel" is *hotel*, and in smaller, nontouristy towns, *albergo*. A few places have kept the old titles *locanda* or *pensione*, indicating that they offer budget beds.

Double rooms listed in this book range from about €50 (very simple, toilet and shower down the hall) to €450 (maximum plumbing and more), with most clustered around €140 (with private bathrooms). Prices are higher in big cities and heavily touristed cities, and lower off the beaten path. Traveling alone can be expensive: A *camera singola* is often only 25 percent less than a *camera doppia*.

Double beds are called *matrimoniale*, even though hotels aren't interested in your marital status. Twins are *due letti singoli*. Convents offer cheap accommodation but have more *letti singoli* than *matrimoniali*.

Some hotels can add an extra bed (for a small charge) to turn a double into a triple; some offer larger rooms for four or more people (I call these "family rooms" in the listings). If there's space for an extra cot, they'll cram it in for you. In general, a triple room is cheaper than the cost of a double and a single. Three or four people can economize by requesting one big room.

Arrival and Check-In: Hotels and B&Bs are sometimes located on the higher floors of a multipurpose building with a secured door. In that case, look for your hotel's name on the buttons by the main entrance. When you ring the bell, you'll be buzzed in. (The hotelier doesn't control the building's common areas, so try not to let a slightly dingy entryway color your opinion of the hotel.)

Hotel elevators are becoming more common, though some older buildings still lack them. You may have to climb a flight of stairs to reach the elevator (if so, you can ask the front desk for help carrying your bags up). Elevators are typically very small—pack light, or you may need to send your bags up one at a time.

When you check in, the receptionist will normally ask for your

The Good and Bad of Online Reviews

User-generated review sites and apps such as Yelp, Booking. com, and TripAdvisor are changing the travel industry. These sites can give you a consensus of opinions about everything from hotels and restaurants to sights and nightlife. If you scan reviews of a hotel and see several complaints about noise or a rotten location, it tells you something important that you'd never learn from the hotel's own website.

But review sites are only as good as the judgment of their reviewers. And while these sites work hard to weed out bogus users, my hunch is that a significant percentage of user reviews are posted by friends or enemies of the business being reviewed.

As a guidebook writer, my sense is that there is a big difference between this uncurated information and a guidebook. A user-generated review is based on the experience of one person, who likely stayed at one hotel and ate at a few restaurants, and doesn't have much of a basis for comparison. A guidebook is the work of a trained researcher who visited many alternatives to assess their relative value. I recently checked out some top-rated user-reviewed hotel and restaurant listings in various towns; when stacked up against their competitors, some were gems, while just as many were duds.

Both types of information have their place, and in many ways, they're complementary. If something is well-reviewed in a guidebook, and also gets good ratings on one of these sites, it's likely a winner.

passport and keep it for anywhere from a couple of minutes to a couple of hours. The EU requires that hotels collect your name, nationality, and ID number. Relax. Americans are notorious for making this chore more difficult than it needs to be.

If you're arriving in the morning, your room probably won't be ready. Check your bag safely at the hotel and dive right into sightseeing.

In Your Room: More pillows and blankets are usually in the closet or available on request. Towels and linens aren't always replaced every day. Hang your towel up to dry. Some hotels use lightweight "waffle," or very thin, tablecloth-type towels; these take less water and electricity to launder and are preferred by many Italians.

Nearly all places offer private bathrooms, which have a bath or shower, a toilet, and a bidet (which Italians use for quick sponge baths). The cord over the tub or shower is not a clothesline. You pull it when you've fallen and can't get up.

Most hotel rooms have a TV, telephone, and free Wi-Fi (although in old buildings with thick walls, the Wi-Fi signal doesn't always make it to the rooms; sometimes it's only available in the lobby). There's often a guest computer with Internet access in the lobby. Simpler places rarely have a room phone, but often have free Wi-Fi. Pricier hotels usually come with a small fridge stocked with beverages called a *frigo bar* (FREE-goh bar; pay for what you use).

Breakfast and Meals: Italian hotels typically include breakfast in their room prices. If breakfast is optional, you may want to skip it. While convenient, it's usually pricey for what you get: a simple continental buffet with (at its most generous) bread, ham, cheese, yogurt, and unlimited *caffè latte*. A picnic in your room followed by a coffee at the corner café can be lots cheaper.

Hotels in resort areas will often charge you for half-pension, called *mezza pensione,* during peak season (about May-mid-Oct for resorts). Half-pension means that you pay for one meal per day per person (lunch or dinner, though usually dinner), whether you want to or not. Wine is rarely included. If half-pension is required, you can't opt out and pay less. If it's offered as an option, it can be worth considering, especially if they charge less per meal than you've been paying for an average restaurant meal (and provided the chef is good).

Checking Out: While it's customary to pay for your room upon departure, it can be a good idea to settle your bill the day before, when you're not in a hurry and while the manager's in. That way you'll have time to discuss and address any points of contention.

Hotelier Help: Hoteliers can be a great help and source of advice. Most know their city well, and can assist you with everything from public transit and airport connections to finding a good restaurant, the nearest launderette, or a late-night pharmacy. English works in all but the cheapest places.

Hotel Hassles: Even at the best places, mechanical breakdowns occur: Sinks leak, hot water turns cold, toilets may gurgle or smell, the Wi-Fi goes out, or the air-conditioning dies when you need it most. Report your concerns clearly and calmly at the front desk. For more complicated problems, don't expect instant results. If you find that night noise is a problem (if, for instance, your room is over a nightclub), ask for a quieter room in the back or on an upper floor. To guard against theft in your room, keep valuables out of sight. Some rooms come with a safe, and other hotels have safes at the front desk. I've never bothered using one.

Above all, keep a positive attitude. Remember, you're on vacation. If your hotel is a disappointment, spend more time out enjoying the place you came to see.

Short-Term Rentals

A short-term rental—whether an apartment, house, or room in a local's home—is an increasingly popular alternative to a B&B

Keep Cool

If you're visiting Italy in the summer, the extra expense of an air-conditioned room can be money well spent, particularly in the south. Most hotel rooms with air-conditioners come with a control stick (like a TV remote; the hotel may require a deposit) that generally has similar symbols and features: fan icon (click to toggle through wind power, from light to gale); louver icon (choose steady airflow or waves); snowflake and sunshine icons (cold air or heat); clock ("O" setting: run X hours before turning off; "I" setting: wait X hours to start); and the temperature control (20 degrees Celsius is comfortable; also see the thermometer diagram on page 1188). When you leave your room for the day, turning off the air-conditioning is good form.

or hotel, especially if you plan to settle in one location for several nights. For stays longer than a few days, you can usually find a rental that's comparable to—or even cheaper than—a hotel room with similar amenities. Plus, you'll get a behind-the-scenes peek into how locals live.

The rental route isn't for everyone. Many places require a minimum night stay, and compared to hotels, rentals usually have less-flexible cancellation policies. Also you're generally on your own: There's no hotel reception desk, breakfast, or daily cleaning service.

Finding Accommodations: Websites such as www.airbnb. com, www.roomorama.com, and www.vrbo.com let you browse properties and correspond directly with European property owners or managers. For more guidance, consider using a rental agency such as www.interhomeusa.com or www.rentavilla.com. Agency-represented apartments may cost more, but this route often offers more help and safeguards than booking directly. Or try Steve and Linda of Cross-Pollinate, a booking service for private rooms and apartments in the old centers of Rome, Florence, and Venice; rates start at €30 per person (www.cross-pollinate.com).

Before you commit to a rental, be clear on the details, location, and amenities. I like to virtually "explore" the neighborhood using the Street View feature on Google Maps. Also consider the proximity to public transportation, and how well-connected it is with the rest of the city. Ask about amenities that are important to you (elevator, laundry, coffee maker, Wi-Fi, parking, etc.). Reading reviews from previous guests can help identify trouble spots that are glossed over in the official description.

Apartments and Rental Houses: If you're staying somewhere for four nights or longer, it's worth considering an apartment or rental house (anything less than that isn't worth the extra effort involved, such as arranging key pickup, buying groceries, etc.).

PRACTICALITIES

Making Hotel Reservations

Reserve your rooms several weeks or even months in advance—or as soon as you've pinned down your travel dates. Note that some national holidays merit your making reservations far in advance (see page 1178).

Requesting a Reservation: It's easiest to book your room through the hotel's website. (For the best rates, use the hotel's official site and not a booking agency's site.) If there's no reservation form, or for complicated requests, send an email. Most recommended hotels take reservations in English.

The hotelier wants to know:

- the size of your party and type of rooms you need
- your arrival and departure dates, written European-style—day followed by month and year (for example, 18/06/17 or 18 June 2017); include the total number of nights
- special requests (such as en suite bathroom vs. down the hall, cheapest room, twin beds vs. double bed, quiet room)
- applicable discounts (such as a Rick Steves reader discount, cash discount, or promotional rate)

Confirming a Reservation: Most places will request a credit-card number to hold your room. If they don't have a secure online reservation form—look for the *https*—you can email it (I do), but it's safer to share that confidential info via a phone call or fax.

Canceling a Reservation: If you must cancel, it's courteous—and smart—to do so with as much notice as possible, especially for smaller family-run places. Cancellation policies can be strict; read the fine print or ask about these before you book. Many discount deals require prepayment, with no cancellation refunds.

Reconfirming a Reservation: Always call or email to reconfirm your room reservation a few days in advance. For B&Bs or very small hotels, I call again on my day of arrival to tell my host what time I expect to get there (especially important if arriving late—after 17:00).

Phoning: For tips on calling hotels overseas, see page 1154.

From: rick@ricksteves.com
Sent: Today
To: info@hotelcentral.com
Subject: Reservation request for 19-22 July

Dear Hotel Central,

I would like to reserve a room for 2 people for 3 nights, arriving 19 July and departing 22 July. If possible, I would like a quiet room with a double bed and a bathroom inside the room.

Please let me know if you have a room available and the price.

Thank you!
Rick Steves

Apartment and house rentals can be especially cost-effective for groups and families. European apartments, like hotel rooms, tend to be small by US standards. But they often come with laundry machines and small, equipped kitchens *(cucinetta)*, making it easier and cheaper to dine in. If you make good use of the kitchen (and Europe's great produce markets), you'll save on your meal budget.

Private and Shared Rooms: In small towns, there are often few hotels or apartments to choose from, but an abundance of *affittacamere*, or rental rooms. This can be anything from a set of keys and a basic bed to a cozy B&B with your own Tuscan grandmother. Renting a room in someone's home is a good option for those traveling alone, as you're more likely to find true single rooms—with just one single bed, and a price to match. Beds range from air-mattress-in-living-room basic to plush-B&B-suite posh. Some places allow you to book for a single night; if staying for several nights, you can buy groceries just as you would in a rental house. While you can't expect your host to also be your tour guide—or even to provide you with much info—some may be interested in getting to know the travelers who come through their home.

In Italy, even luxury B&Bs can suffer from absentee management—the proprietors often live off site (or even in another town) and may be around only when they are expecting guests, so clearly communicate your arrival time. After checking in, be sure you have your host's telephone number in case you need to reach them.

Local TIs can give you a list of possibilities (or try the free Ciao Italia Bed & Breakfast, which books B&Bs and hostels in Rome, Florence, and Venice; www.ciaoitalia-bb.com). These rooms are usually a good budget option, but since they vary in quality, shop around to find the best value. It's always OK to ask to see the room before you commit.

Other Options: Swapping homes with a local works for people with an appealing place to offer, and who can live with the idea of having strangers in their home (don't assume where you live is not interesting to Europeans). A good place to start is HomeExchange (www.homeexchange.com).

To sleep for free, Couchsurfing.com is a vagabond's alternative to Airbnb. It lists millions of outgoing members who host fellow "surfers" in their homes.

Hostels

A hostel provides cheap beds in dorms where you sleep alongside strangers for about €20-30 per night. Travelers of any age are welcome if they don't mind dorm-style accommodations and meeting other travelers. Most hostels offer kitchen facilities, guest computers, Wi-Fi, and a self-service laundry. Hostels almost always pro vide bedding, but the towel's up to you (though you can usually rent one for a small fee). Family and private rooms are often available.

Independent hostels tend to be easygoing, colorful, and informal (no membership required; www.hostelworld.com). You may pay slightly less by booking directly with the hostel. **Official hostels** are part of Hostelling International (HI) and share a booking site (www.hihostels.com). HI hostels typically require that you be a member or pay extra per night.

Agriturismo

Agriturismo—working farms that double as countryside B&Bs—began cropping up in the 1980s to allow small family farms to survive (as in the US, many have been squeezed out by giant agribusinesses). By renting rooms to travelers, farmers receive generous tax breaks that allow them to remain on their land and continue to grow food crops. These B&Bs make a peaceful home base for those exploring rural Italy, and are ideal for those traveling by car—especially families.

It's wise to book several months in advance for high season (late April-mid-Oct). July and August are jammed with Italians and other European vacationers; in spring and fall, it's mostly Americans. Weeklong stays (typically Saturday to Saturday) are preferred at busy times, but shorter stays are possible off-season. To sleep cheaper, avoid peak season. In the winter, you might be charged extra for heat, so confirm the price ahead of time. Payment policies vary, but generally a deposit is required (about 25 percent; lost if you cancel), and the balance is due one month before arrival.

As the name implies, *agriturismi* are in the countryside, although some are located on the outskirts of a large town or city. Most are family-run. *Agriturismi* vary dramatically in quality—some properties are rustic, while others are downright luxurious, offering amenities such as swimming pools and riding stables. The rooms are usually clean and comfortable. Breakfast is often included, and *mezza pensione* (half-pension, which in this case means a home-cooked dinner) might be built into the price whether you want it or not. Most places serve tasty homegrown food; some are vegetarian or organic, others are gourmet. Kitchenettes are often available to cook up your own feast.

To qualify officially as an *agriturismo*, the farm must still generate more money from its farm activities, thereby ensuring that the land is worked and preserved. Some farmhouse B&Bs aren't working farms, but are still fine places to stay. Travelers who are enticed by romanticized dreams of *agriturismi* may be turned off when they arrive to actual farm smells and sounds. These folks would be more comfortable with a countryside B&B or villa that offers a bit more upscale comfort. In this book, I've listed both types of rural accommodations; if you want the real thing, make sure the owners call their place an *agriturismo*.

In addition to my listings, local TIs can give you a list of places in their area. For a sampling, visit www.agriturismoitaly.it or search online for *agriturismo*. One booking agency among many is Farm Holidays in Tuscany (closed Sat-Sun, tel. 0564-417-418, www.byfarmholidays.com, info@byfarmholidays.com).

Eating

The Italians are masters of the art of fine living. That means eating long and well. Lengthy, multicourse meals and endless hours sitting in outdoor cafés are the norm. Americans eat on their way to an evening event and complain if the check is slow in coming. For Italians, the meal is an end in itself, and only rude waiters rush you.

A highlight of your Italian adventure will be this country's cafés, cuisine, and wines. Trust me: This is sightseeing for your palate. Even if you liked dorm food and are sleeping in cheap hotels, your taste buds will relish an occasional first-class splurge. You can eat well without going broke. But be careful: You're just as likely to blow a small fortune on a disappointing meal as you are to dine wonderfully for €25. Rely on my recommendations in the various Eating sections throughout this book.

In general, Italians eat meals a bit later than we do. At 7:00 or 8:00, they have a light breakfast (coffee—usually cappuccino or espresso—and a pastry, often standing up at a café). Lunch (between 13:00 and 15:00) is traditionally the largest meal of the day. Then they eat a late, light dinner (around 20:00-21:30, or maybe earlier in winter). To bridge the gap, people drop into a bar in the late afternoon for a *spuntino* (snack) and aperitif.

RESTAURANT PRICING

I've categorized my recommended eateries based on price, indicated with a dollar-sign rating (see sidebar). The price ranges suggest the average price of a typical main course—but not necessarily a complete meal. Sticking to pastas will save you plenty over ordering meat-and-fish *secondi*. Obviously, expensive items (steak, seafood, truffles), fine wine, appetizers, and dessert can significantly increase your final bill.

The dollar-sign categories also indicate the overall personality and "feel" of a place:

Restaurant Price Code

I've assigned each eatery a price category, based on the average cost of a typical main course (pasta or *secondi*). Drinks, desserts, and splurge items (steak and seafood) can raise the price considerably.

$$$$ **Splurge:** Most main courses over €20
$$$ **Pricier:** €15-20
$$ **Moderate:** €10-15
$ **Budget:** Under €10

In Italy, pizza by the slice and other takeaway food is **$**; a basic trattoria or sit-down pizzeria is **$$**; a casual but more upscale restaurant is **$$$**; and a swanky splurge is **$$$$**.

$ Budget eateries include street food, takeaway, order-at-the-counter shops, basic cafeterias, and bakeries selling sandwiches.

$$ Moderate eateries are typically nice (but not fancy) sit-down restaurants, ideal for a straightforward, fill-the-tank meal. Most of my listings fall in this category—great for getting a good taste of the local cuisine on a budget.

$$$ Pricier eateries are a notch up, with more attention paid to the setting, service, and cuisine. These are ideal for a memorable meal that's relatively casual and doesn't break the bank. This category often includes affordable "destination" or "foodie" restaurants.

$$$$ Splurge eateries are dress-up-for-a-special-occasion-swanky—Michelin star-type restaurants, typically with an elegant setting, polished service, pricey and intricate cuisine, and an expansive (and expensive) wine list.

To assign price ranges for restaurants in Italy, these price points were my rule of thumb: **$$$$**—most pastas over €13, *secondi* over €20; **$$$**—most pizzas/pastas €11-12, *secondi* €15-20; **$$**—most pizzas/pastas under €11, *secondi* under €15; **$**—meals under €10. I haven't categorized places where you might snack, graze, or assemble a picnic: supermarkets, delis, ice-cream stands, cafés or bars specializing in drinks, chocolate shops, and so on.

BREAKFAST

Italian breakfasts, like Italian bath towels, are small: The basic, traditional version is coffee and a roll with butter and marmalade. These days, many places also have yogurt and juice (the delicious red orange juice—*spremuta d'arancia rossa*—is made from Sicilian blood oranges), and possibly also cereal, cold cuts and sliced cheese, and eggs (typically hard-boiled; scrambled or fried eggs are rare). Small budget hotels may leave a basic breakfast in your room (stale croissant, roll, jam, yogurt, coffee).

If you want to skip your hotel breakfast, consider browsing

for a morning picnic at a local open-air market. Or do as the Italians do: Stop into a bar or café to drink a cappuccino and munch a *cornetto* (croissant) while standing at the bar. While the *cornetto* is the most common pastry, you'll find a range of *pasticcini* (pastries, sometimes called *dolci*—sweets). Look for *otto* (an 8-shaped pastry, often filled with custard, jam, or chocolate), *sfoglia* (can be fruit-filled, like a turnover), or *ciambella* (doughnut filled with custard or chocolate)—or ask about local specialties.

ITALIAN RESTAURANTS

While *ristorante* is self-explanatory, you'll also see other types of Italian eateries. A *trattoria* and an *osteria* (which can be more casual) are both generally family-owned places serving home-cooked meals, often at moderate prices. A *locanda* is an inn, a *cantina* is a wine cellar, and a *birreria* is a brewpub. *Pizzerie, rosticcerie* (delis), *tavola calda* bars (cafeterias), *enoteche* (wine bars), and other alternatives are explained later.

When restaurant-hunting, choose a spot filled with locals, not the place with the big neon signs boasting, "We speak English and accept credit cards." Restaurants parked on famous squares generally serve bad food at high prices to tourists. Venturing even a block or two off the main drag leads to higher-quality food for less than half the price of the tourist-oriented places. Locals eat better at lower-rent locales. Family-run places operate without hired help and can offer cheaper meals.

Most restaurant kitchens close between their lunch and dinner service. Good restaurants don't reopen for dinner before 19:00. Small restaurants with a full slate of reservations for 20:30 or 21:00 often will accommodate walk-in diners willing to eat a quick, early meal, but you aren't expected to linger.

When you want the bill, mime-scribble on your raised palm or request it: *"Il conto, per favore."* You may have to ask for it more than once. If you're in a hurry, request the check when you receive the last item you order.

Cover and Tipping

Before you sit down, look at a menu to see what extra charges a restaurant tacks on. Two different items are routinely factored into your bill: the *coperto* and the *servizio*.

The **coperto** (cover charge), sometimes called *pane e coperto* (bread and cover), is the fee for your table setting (including the typical basket of bread). It's not negotiable, even if you don't eat the bread. Think of it as covering the cost of using the table for as long as you like. (Italians like to linger.) Most restaurants add the *coperto* onto your bill as a flat fee (€1-3 per person; the amount should be clearly noted on the menu). Technically, cover charges are forbidden by law in Rome, although you may occasionally still see them.

The *servizio* (service charge) of about 10 percent is similar to the mandatory gratuity that American restaurants often add for groups of six or more. Most eateries don't have a tacked-on service charge, but instead include it in the menu prices. The words *servizio incluso* on the menu and/or the receipt indicate that you're not required to pay anything beyond the listed prices (the *servizio* is built in). You can add an additional tip, if you choose, by including €1-2 for each person in your party. While Italians don't think about tips in terms of percentages—and some don't tip at all—this extra amount usually comes out to about 5 percent (10 percent is excessive for all but the very best service).

Some touristy or trendy restaurants don't include the service in the menu prices—instead they tack a *servizio* charge onto your bill. In these cases you'll see something like *"servizio 10%"* on the menu, and the fee will be added onto your bill (so you don't need to calculate it yourself and pay it separately). Rarely, you'll see the words *servizio non incluso* on the menu or bill; here you are expected to add a tip of about 10 percent.

Most Italian restaurants have a cover charge and include service in the menu prices. A few have just a service charge (especially in Rome, where cover charges are banned). Places with *both* a cover and a tacked-on service charge are best avoided—that's a clue that a restaurant is counting on a nonlocal clientele who can't gauge value. Self-service restaurants never have a cover or service charge, and in recent years some (especially less formal) cafés and restaurants with table service have stopped charging these fees as well.

Courses: *Antipasto, Primo,* and *Secondo*

For a list of Italian cuisine staples, including some of the most common dishes, see page 1140. A full Italian meal consists of several courses:

Antipasto: An appetizer such as bruschetta, grilled veggies, deep-fried tasties, thin-sliced meat (such as prosciutto or carpaccio), or a plate of olives, cold cuts, and cheeses. To get a sampler plate of cold cuts and cheeses in a restaurant, ask for *affettato misto* (mixed cold cuts), *antipasto misto* (cold cuts, cheeses, and marinated vegetables), or—in Tuscany—*tagliere* (a sampler "board"). This could make a light meal in itself.

Primo piatto: A "first dish" generally consisting of pasta, rice, or soup. If you think of pasta when you think of Italy, you can dine well here without ever going beyond the *primo*.

Secondo piatto: A "second dish," equivalent to our main course, of meat or fish/seafood. Italians freely admit the *secondo* is the least interesting part of their cuisine. A vegetable side dish *(contorno)* may come with the *secondo* but more often must be ordered separately.

For most travelers, a meal with all three courses (plus *contorni*, dessert, and wine) is simply too much food—and euros can add up in a hurry. To avoid overeating (and to stretch your budget), share dishes. A good rule of thumb is for each person to order any two courses. For example, a couple can order and share one antipasto, one *primo*, one *secondo*, and one dessert; or two *antipasti* and two *primi;* or whatever combination appeals.

Another good option is sharing an array of *antipasti*—either by ordering several specific dishes or, at restaurants that offer self-serve buffets, by choosing a variety of cold and cooked appetizers from an *antipasti* buffet spread out like a salad bar. At buffets, you pay per plate; a typical serving costs about €8 (generally Italians don't treat buffets as all-you-can-eat, but take a one-time moderate serving; watch others and imitate).

To maximize the experience and flavors, small groups can mix *antipasti* and *primi* family-style (skipping *secondi*). If you do this right, you can eat well in better places for less than the cost of a tourist *menù* in a cheap place.

A few restaurants serve a *piatto unico*, with smaller portions of each course on one dish (for instance, a meat, starch, and vegetable).

Ordering Tips

Seafood and steak may be sold by weight (priced by the kilo—1,000 grams, or just over two pounds; or by the *etto*—100 grams). The abbreviation *s.q. (secondo quantità)* means an item is priced "according to quantity." Unless the menu indicates a fillet *(filetto)*, fish is usually served whole with the head and tail. However, you can always ask your waiter to select a small fish for you. Sometimes, especially for steak, restaurants require a minimum order of four or five *etti* (which diners can share). Make sure you're clear on the price before ordering.

Some special dishes come in larger quantities meant to be shared by two people. The shorthand way of showing this on a menu is "X2" (for two), but the price listed generally indicates the cost per person.

In a traditional restaurant, if you order a pasta dish and a side salad—but no main course—the waiter will bring the salad after the pasta (Italians prefer it this way, believing that it enhances digestion). If you want the salad with your pasta, specify *insieme* (een-see-YEH-meh; together). At eateries more accustomed to tourists, you may be asked when you want the salad.

Because pasta and bread are both starches, Italians consider them redundant. If you order only a pasta dish, bread may not come with it; you can request it, but you may be charged extra. On the other hand, if you order a vegetable antipasto or a meat *secondo*, bread is often provided to balance the ingredients.

At places with counter service—such as at a bar or a freeway rest-stop diner—you'll order and pay at the *cassa* (cashier). Take your receipt to the counter to claim your food.

Fixed-Price Meals and Ordering à la Carte

You can save by getting a fixed-priced meal, which is frequently exempt from cover and service charges. Avoid the cheapest ones (often called a *menù turistico*), which tend to be bland and heavy, pairing a very basic pasta with reheated schnitzel and roast meats. Look instead for a genuine *menù del giorno* (menu of the day), which offers diners a choice of appetizer, main course, and dessert. It's worth paying a little more for an inventive fixed-price meal that shows off the chef's creativity.

MENU € 19,00
TURISTICO

ANTIPASTO di MARE

PRIMI PIATTI
RISOTTO alla PESCATORA
SPAGHETTI alla MARINARA
SPAGHETTI allo SCOGLIO
TRENETTE al PESTO

SECONDI PIATTI
PESCE ai FERRI
FRITTO MISTO
GRIGLIATA di CARNE

CONTORNI
PATATE FRITTE o INSALATA

While fixed-price meals can be easy and convenient, galloping gourmets prefer to order à la carte with the help of a menu translator (see "Italian Cuisine Staples," later). When going to an especially good restaurant with an approachable staff, I like to find out what they're eager to serve. Sometimes I'll simply say, *"Mi faccia felice"* (Make me happy) and set a price limit.

BUDGET EATING

Italy offers many budget options for hungry travelers, but beware of cheap eateries that sport big color photos of pizza and piles of different pastas. They often have no kitchens and simply microwave disgusting prepackaged food.

Self-service cafeterias offer the basics without add-on charges. Travelers on a hard-core budget equip their room with a pantry stocked at the market (fruits and veggies are remarkably cheap), or pick up a sandwich or *döner kebab*, then dine in at picnic prices. Bars and cafés are also good places to grab a meal on the go.

PRACTICALITIES

Pizzerias

Pizza is cheap and readily available. Stop by a pizza shop for stand-up or takeout (*pizza al taglio* means "by the slice"). Supermarkets

usually have a pizza counter too. Some shops sell individual slices of round, Naples-style pizza, while others feature *pizza rustica*—thick pizza baked in a large rectangular pan and sold by weight. If you simply ask for a piece, you may wind up with a gigantic slab and be charged top euro. Instead, clearly indicate how much you want: 100 grams, or *un etto*, is a hot and cheap snack; 200 grams, or *due etti*, makes a light meal. Or show the size with your hands—*tanto così* (TAHN-toh koh-ZEE; this much). They'll often helpfully cut it up into smaller pieces. If you want your pizza warm, say *"si"* when they ask if you want it heated up (*scaldare;* skahl-DAH-ray). For a rundown of common types of pizza, see page 1140.

Bars/Cafés

Italian "bars" are not taverns, but inexpensive cafés. These neighborhood hangouts serve coffee, minipizzas, sandwiches, and drinks from the cooler. Many dish up plates of fried cheese and vegetables from under the glass counter, ready to reheat. This budget choice is the Italian equivalent of English pub grub.

Many bars are small—if you can't find a table, you'll need to stand or find a ledge to sit on outside. Most charge extra for table service. To get food to go, say, *"da portar via"* (for the road). All bars have a WC *(toilette, bagno)* in the back, and customers—and the discreet public—can use it.

Food: For quick meals, bars usually have trays of cheap, pre-made sandwiches (*panini*, on a baguette; *piadini*, on flatbread; or *tramezzini*, on crustless white bread)—some are delightful grilled. (Others have too much mayo.) To save time for sightseeing and room for dinner, stop by a bar for a light lunch, such as a ham-and-cheese sandwich (called *toast*); have it grilled twice if you want it really hot.

Prices and Paying: You'll notice a two- or three-tiered pricing system. Drinking a cup of coffee while standing at the bar is cheaper than drinking it at an indoor table (you'll pay still more at an outdoor table). Many places have a *lista dei prezzi* (price list) with two columns—*al bar* and *al tavolo* (table)—posted somewhere by the bar or cash register. If you're on a budget, don't sit down without first checking out the financial consequences. Ask, "Same price if I sit or stand?" by saying, *"Costa uguale al tavolo o al banco?"* (KOH-stah oo-GWAH-lay ahl TAH-voh-loh oh ahl BAHN-koh). Throughout Italy, you can get cheap coffee at the bar of any establishment, no matter how fancy, and pay the same low, government-regulated price (generally less than a euro if you stand).

If the bar isn't busy, you can probably just order and pay when you leave. Otherwise: 1) Decide what you want; 2) find out the price by checking the price list on the wall, the prices posted near the food, or by asking the barista; 3) pay the cashier; and 4) give the receipt to the barista (whose clean fingers handle no dirty euros) and tell him or her what you want.

For more on drinking, see "Beverages" on page 1145.

Ethnic Food

A good bet for a cheap, hot meal is a *döner kebab* (Middle Eastern-style rotisserie meat wrapped in pita bread). Look for little hole-in-the-wall kebab shops, where you can get a hearty takeaway dinner wrapped in pita bread for €3.50. Pay an extra euro to supersize it, and it'll feed two. Asian restaurants, although not as common as in northern Europe, usually serve only Chinese dishes and can also be a good value.

Tavola Calda Bars and *Rosticcerie*

For a fast and cheap lunch, find an Italian variation on the corner deli: a *rosticceria* (specializing in roasted meats and accompanying *antipasti*) or a *tavola calda* bar (a "hot table" point-and-shoot cafeteria with a buffet spread of meat and vegetables; sometimes called *tavola fredda*, or "cold table," in the north). For a healthy, light meal, ask for a mixed plate of vegetables with a hunk of mozzarella (*piatto misto di verdure con mozzarella;* pee-AH-toh MEE-stoh dee vehr-DOO-ray). Don't be limited by what's displayed. If you'd like a salad with a slice of cantaloupe and a hunk of cheese, they'll whip that up for you in a snap. Belly up to the bar; with a pointing finger, you can assemble a fine meal. If something's a mystery, ask for *un assaggio* (oon ah-SAH-joh) to get a little taste. To have your choices warmed up, ask for them to be heated (*scaldare;* skahl-DAH-ray).

Wine Bars

Wine bars *(enoteche)* are a popular, fast, and inexpensive option for lunch. Surrounded by the office crowd, you can get a salad, a plate of meats (cold cuts) and cheeses, and a glass of good wine (see blackboards for the day's selection and price per glass). A good *enoteca* aims to impress visitors with its wine, and will generally feature excellent-quality ingredients for the simple dishes it offers with the wine (though the prices add up—be careful with your ordering to keep this a budget choice). For more on Italian cocktails and wines, see page 1147.

Aperitivo Buffets

The Italian term *aperitivo* means a predinner drink, but it's also used to describe their version of what we might call happy hour: a light buffet that many bars serve to customers during the predinner hours (typically around 18:00 or 19:00 until 21:00). The drink itself may not be cheap (typically around €8-12), but bars lay out an enticing array of meats, cheeses, grilled vegetables, and other *antipasti*-type dishes, and you're welcome to nibble to your heart's content while you nurse your drink. While it's intended as an appetizer course before heading out for a full dinner, light eaters could discreetly turn this into a small meal. Drop by a few bars around this time to scope out their buffets before choosing.

Groceries and Delis

Another budget option is to visit a supermarket, *alimentari* (neighborhood grocery), or *salumeria* (delicatessen) to pick up some cold cuts, cheeses, and other supplies for a picnic. Some *salumerie*, and any *paninoteca* or *focacceria* (sandwich shop), can make a sandwich to order. Just point to what you want, and they'll stuff it into a *panino;* if you want it heated, remember the word *scaldare* (skahl-DAH-ray). If ordering an assortment of cold cuts and cheeses, some unscrupulous shops may try to pad the bill by pushing their most expensive ingredients. Be clear on what you want: *"antipasto misto da __ euro, per favore."* For more on *salumi* and cheeses, see page 1143.

Picnics

Picnicking saves lots of euros and is a great way to sample regional specialties. A typical picnic for two might be fresh rolls, 100 grams—or about a quarter pound—of cheese (*un etto,* EH-toh, plural *etti,* EH-tee), and 100 grams of meat, sometimes ordered by the slice *(fetta)* or piece *(pezzi).* For two people, I might get *cinque pezzi* (five pieces) of prosciutto. Add two tomatoes, three carrots, two apples, yogurt, and a liter box of juice. Total cost: about €10.

In the process of assembling your meal, you get to deal with Italians in the market scene. For a colorful experience, gather your ingredients in the morning at a produce market; you'll probably need to hit several market stalls to put together a complete meal (note that many stalls close in the early afternoon).

While it's fun to visit small specialty shops, an *alimentari* is your one-stop corner grocery store (most will slice and stuff your sandwich for you if you buy the ingredients there). A rare *supermercato* (look for the Conad, Despar, and Co-op chains) gives you more efficiency with less color for less cost. At busier supermarkets, you'll need to take a number for deli service. And *rosticcerie* sell cheap food to go—you'll find options such as lasagna, rotisserie chicken, and sides like roasted potatoes and spinach.

Picnics can be an adventure in high cuisine. Be daring. Try the fresh mozzarella, *presto* pesto, shriveled olives, and any regional specialties the locals are excited about. If ordering *antipasti* (such as grilled or marinated veggies) at a deli counter, you can ask for *una porzione* in a takeaway container *(contenitore)*. Use gestures to show exactly how much you want. The word *basta* (BAH-stah; enough) works as a question or as a statement.

Shopkeepers are happy to sell small quantities of produce, but it's customary to let the merchant choose for you. Say *"per oggi"* (pehr OH-jee; for today) and he or she will grab you something ready to eat. To avoid being overcharged, know the cost per kilo, study the weighing procedure, and do the arithmetic.

ITALIAN CUISINE STAPLES

Much of your Italian eating experience will likely involve the big five: pizza, pasta, *salumi*, cheese, and gelato. Here's a rundown on what you might find on menus and in stores. I've included specifics on regional cuisine throughout this book. For more food help, try a menu translator, such as the *Rick Steves Italian Phrase Book & Dictionary*, which has a menu decoder and plenty of useful phrases for navigating the culinary scene.

Pizza

Here are some of the pizzas you might see at restaurants or at a pizzeria. Note that if you ask for pepperoni on your pizza, you'll get *peperoni* (green or red peppers, not sausage); request *diavola*, *salsiccia piccante*, or *salame piccante* instead (the closest thing in Italy to American pepperoni).

Bianca: White pizza with no tomatoes (also called *ciaccina*).

Capricciosa: Prosciutto, mushrooms, olives, and artichokes—literally the chef's "caprice."

Funghi: Mushrooms.

Margherita: Tomato sauce, mozzarella, and basil—the red, white, and green of the Italian flag.

Marinara: Tomato sauce, oregano, garlic, no cheese.

Napoletana: Mozzarella, anchovies, and tomato sauce.

Eating with the Seasons

Italian cooks love to serve you fresh produce and seafood at its tastiest. If you must have porcini mushrooms outside of fall, they'll be dried. Each region in Italy has its specialties, which

you'll see displayed in open-air markets. To get a plate of the freshest veggies at a fine restaurant, request *"Un piatto di verdure della stagione, per favore"* (A plate of seasonal vegetables, please). Italians take fresh, seasonal ingredients so seriously that a restaurant cooking with frozen ingredients must note it on the menu—

look for *congelato*.

Here are a few examples of what's fresh when:

April-May: Calamari (Venice), romanesco (similar to cauliflower) and fava beans (Rome), green beans, and artichokes

April-May and Sept-Oct: Black truffles

April-June: Asparagus, zucchini flowers, and zucchini

May-June: Mussels, cantaloupe, loquats, and strawberries

May-Aug: Eggplant, clams

July-Sept: Figs

Oct-Nov: Mushrooms, white truffles, persimmons, and chestnuts

Nov-Feb: Radicchio (Venice), cardoon (wild artichoke), puntarelle (chicory shoots; Rome)

Fresh year-round: Meats and cheese

Ortolana: "Greengrocer-style," with vegetables (also called *vegetariana).*

Quattro formaggi: Four different cheeses.

Quattro stagioni: Different toppings on each of the four quarters.

Pasta

While we think of pasta as a main dish, in Italy it's considered a *primo piatto*—first course. There are more than 600 varieties of Italian pasta, and each is specifically used to highlight a certain sauce, meat, or regional ingredient. Italian pasta falls into two broad categories: *pasta lunga* (long pasta) and *pasta corta* (short pasta).

Pasta lunga can be round, such as *capellini* (thin "little hairs"), *vermicelli* (slightly thicker "little worms"), and *bucatini* (long and hollow), or it can be flat, such as *linguine* (narrow "little tongues"), *fettuccine* (wider "small ribbons"), *tagliatelle* (even wider), and *pappardelle* (very wide, best with meat sauces).

The most common *pasta corta* are tubes, such as *penne, rigatoni, ziti, manicotti,* and *cannelloni;* they come either *lisce* (smooth) or *rigate* (grooved—better to catch and cling to sauce). Many short pastas are named for their shapes, such as *conchiglie* (shells), *farfalle* (butterflies), *cavatappi* (corkscrews), *ditali* (thimbles), *gomiti* ("elbow" macaroni), *lumache* (snails), *marziani* (spirals resembling "Martian" antennae), and even *strozzapreti* (priest stranglers). Some are filled *(ripieni),* including *tortelli* (C-shaped, stuffed ravioli) and *angolotti* or *mezzelune* (shaped like "priest's hats" or "half-moons").

Most types of pasta come in slightly different variations: If it's a bit thicker, *-one* is added to the end; if it's a bit thinner, *-ine, -ette,* or *-elle* is added. For example, *tortellini* are smaller *tortelli,* while *tortelloni* are bigger. And there are regional pasta variations too. Look for *pici* (thick, hand-formed noodles) in Tuscany, especially Siena, *umbricelli* (thick, chewy, rolled pasta) in Umbria, and *trenette* (long, flat, and with one ruffled edge) in the Riviera. Most pastas in Italy are made fresh.

Here's a list of common pasta toppings and sauces. On a menu, these terms are usually preceded by *alla* (in the style of) or *in* (in):

Aglio e olio: Garlic and olive oil.

Alfredo: Butter, cream, and parmesan.

Amatriciana: Pork cheek, *pecorino* cheese, and tomato.

Arrabbiata: "Angry," spicy tomato sauce with chili peppers.

Bolognese: Meat and tomato sauce.

Boscaiola: Mushrooms and sausage.

Burro e salvia: Butter and sage.

Cacio e pepe: *Parmigiano* cheese and ground pepper.

Carbonara: Bacon, egg, cheese, and pepper.

Carrettiera: Spicy and garlicky, with olive oil and little tomatoes.

Diavola: "Devil-style," spicy hot.

Frutti di mare: Seafood.

Genovese: Basil ground with *parmigiano* cheese, garlic, pine nuts, and olive oil; a.k.a. pesto.

Gricia: Cured pork and *pecorino romano* cheese.

Marinara: Usually tomato, often with garlic and onions, but can also be a seafood sauce ("sailor's style").

Norma: Tomato, eggplant, and ricotta cheese.

Pajata: Calf intestines (also called *pagliata*).

Pescatora: Seafood ("fisherman style").

Pomodoro: Tomato only.

Puttanesca: "Harlot-style" tomato sauce with anchovies, olives, and capers.

Ragù: Meaty tomato sauce.

Scoglio: Mussels, clams, and tomatoes.

Sorrentina: "Sorrento-style," with tomatoes, basil, and mozzarella (usually over gnocchi).

Sugo di lepre: Rich sauce made of wild hare.

Tartufi: Truffles (also called *tartufate*).
Umbria: Sauce of anchovies, garlic, tomatoes, and truffles.
Vongole: Clams and spices.

Salumi

Salumi ("salted" meats), also called *affettati* ("cut" meats), are an Italian staple. While most American cold cuts are cooked, in Italy they're far more commonly cured by air-drying, salting, and smoking. (Don't worry; these so-called "raw" meats are safe to eat, and you can really taste the difference.)

The two most familiar types of *salumi* are *salame* and *prosciutto*. *Salame* is an air-dried, sometimes spicy sausage that comes in many varieties. When Italians say *"prosciutto,"* they usually mean *prosciutto crudo*—the raw ham that air-cures on the hock and is then thinly sliced. Produced mainly in the north of Italy, *prosciutto* can be either *dolce* (sweet) or *salato* (salty). Purists say the best is *prosciutto di Parma*.

Other *salumi* may be less familiar:
Bresaola: Air-cured beef.
Capocollo: Peppery pork shoulder (also called *coppa*).
Culatello: Prosciutto made with only the finest cuts of meat.
Finocchiona: *Salame* with fennel seeds.
Lonzino: Cured pork loin.
Mortadella: A finely ground pork loaf, similar to our bologna.
Pancetta: Salt-cured, peppery pork belly meat, similar to bacon; can be eaten raw or added to cooked dishes.
Quanciale: Tender pork cheek.
Salame di Sant'Olcese: What we'd call "Genoa salami."
Salame piccante: Spicy hot, similar to pepperoni.
Speck: Smoked pork shoulder.

If you've got a weak stomach, avoid *testa in cassetta* (headcheese—organs in aspic), *lampredotto* (cow stomach), and *sopressata* (in other parts of Italy, this is a spicy *salame*—but in Tuscany, it's often headcheese).

Cheese

When it comes to cheese *(formaggio),* you're probably already familiar with most of these Italian favorites:
Asiago: Hard cow cheese that comes either *mezzano* (young, firm, and creamy) or *stravecchio* (aged, pungent, and granular).
Burrata: A creamy mozzarella.
Fontina: Semihard, nutty, Gruyère-style mountain cheese.
Gorgonzola: Pungent, blue-veined cheese, either *dolce* (creamy) or *stagionato* (aged and hard).
Mascarpone: Sweet, buttery, spreadable dessert cheese.
Mozzarella di bufala: Made from the milk of water buffaloes.

Parmigiano-reggiano: Hard, crumbly, sharp, aged cow cheese with more nuanced flavor than American parmesan; *grana padano* is a less expensive variation.

Pecorino: Either *fresco* (fresh, soft, and mild) or *stagionato* (aged and sharp, sometimes called *pecorino romano*).

Provolone: Rich, firm, aged cow cheese.

Ricotta: Soft, airy cheese made by "recooking" leftover whey.

Scamorza: Similar to mozzarella, but often smoked.

Gelato

While American ice cream is made with cream and has a high butterfat content, Italian gelato is made with milk. It's also churned more slowly, making it denser. Connoisseurs believe that because gelato has less air and less fat (which coats the mouth and blocks the taste buds), it's more flavorful than American-style ice cream.

A key to gelato appreciation is sampling liberally and choosing flavors that go well together. At a *gelateria,* ask, as Italians do, for a taste: *"Un assaggio, per favore?"* (oon ah-SAH-joh pehr fah-VOH-ray). You can also ask what flavors go well together: *"Quali gusti stanno bene insieme?"* (KWAH-lee GOO-stee STAH-noh BEH-nay een-see-EH-may).

Most *gelaterie* clearly display prices and sizes. But in the textbook *gelateria* scam, the tourist orders two or three flavors—and the clerk selects a fancy, expensive chocolate-coated waffle cone, piles it high with huge scoops, and cheerfully charges the tourist €10. To avoid rip-offs, point to the price or say what you want—for instance, a €3 cup: *"Una coppetta da tre euro"* (OO-nah koh-PEH-tah dah tray eh-OO-roh).

The best *gelaterie* display signs reading *artiginale, nostra produzione,* or *produzione propia,* indicating that the gelato is made on the premises. Seasonal flavors are also a good sign, as are mellow hues (avoid colors that don't appear in nature). Gelato stored in covered metal tins (rather than white plastic) is more likely to be homemade. Gourmet gelato shops are popping up all over Italy, selling exotic flavors. Avoid a chain called Grom—it's the Starbucks of gelato in Italy. Classic gelato flavors include:

After Eight: Chocolate and mint.

Bacio: Chocolate hazelnut, named for Italy's popular "kiss" candies.

Cassata: With dried fruits.

Cioccolato: Chocolate.

Crema: Vanilla.

Croccantino: "Crunchy," with toasted peanut bits.

Fior di latte: Sweet milk.

Fragola: Strawberry.

Macedonia: Mixed fruits.

Malaga: Similar to rum raisin.

Riso: With actual bits of rice mixed in.
Stracciatella: Vanilla with chocolate shreds.
Tartufo: Super chocolate.
Zabaione: Named for the egg yolk and Marsala wine dessert.
Zuppa inglese: Sponge cake, custard, chocolate, and cream.

Gelato variations or alternatives include *sorbetto* (sorbet—made with fruit, but no milk or eggs); *granita* or *grattachecca* (a cup of slushy ice with flavored syrup); and *cremolata* (a gelato-*granita* float).

BEVERAGES

Italian bars serve great drinks—hot, cold, sweet, caffeinated, or alcoholic.

Water, Juice, and Cold Drinks

Italians are notorious water snobs. At restaurants, your server just can't understand why you wouldn't want good water to go with your good food. It's customary and never expensive to order a *litro* or *mezzo litro* (half-liter) of bottled water. *Acqua leggermente effervescente* (lightly carbonated water) is a mealtime favorite. Or simply ask for *con gas* if you want fizzy water and *senza gas* if you prefer still water. You can ask for *acqua del rubinetto* (tap water) in restaurants, but your server may give you a funny look. Chilled bottled water—still *(naturale)* or carbonated *(frizzante)*—is sold cheap in stores. Half-liter mineral-water bottles are available everywhere for about €1. (I refill my water bottle with tap water.)

Juice is *succo,* and *spremuta* means freshly squeezed. Order *una spremuta* (don't confuse it with *spumante,* sparkling wine)—it's usually orange juice *(arancia),* and from February through April it's almost always made from blood oranges *(arance rosse).*

In grocery stores, you can get a liter of O.J. for the price of a Coke or coffee. Look for *100% succo* or *senza zucchero* (without sugar) on the label—or be surprised by something diluted and sugary sweet. Hang on to your water bottles. Buy juice in cheap liter boxes, then drink some and store the extra in your water bottle.

Tè freddo (iced tea) is usually from a can—sweetened and flavored with lemon or peach. Lemonade is *limonata.*

Coffee and Other Hot Drinks

The espresso-based style of coffee so popular in the US was born in Italy. If you ask for *"un caffè,"* you'll get a shot of espresso in a little cup—the closest thing to American-style drip coffee is a *caffè americano.* Most Italian coffee drinks begin with espresso, to which they add varying amounts of hot water and/or steamed or foamed milk. Milky drinks, like cappuccino or *caffè latte,* are served to locals before noon and to tourists any time of day (to an Italian,

Ordering Wine

To order a glass of red or white wine, say, *"Un bicchiere di vino rosso/bianco."* House wine comes in a carafe; choose from a quarter-liter pitcher (8.5 oz, *un quarto*), half-liter pitcher (17 oz, *un mezzo*), or one-liter pitcher (34 oz, *un litro*). When ordering, have some fun, gesture like a local, and you'll have no problems speaking the language of the *enoteca*. *Salute!*

English	Italian
wine	*vino* (VEE-noh)
house wine	*vino della casa* (VEE-noh DEH-lah KAH-zah)
glass	*bicchiere* (bee-kee-EH-ree)
bottle	*bottiglia* (boh-TEEL-yah)
carafe	*caraffa* (kah-RAH-fah)
red	*rosso* (ROH-soh)
white	*bianco* (bee-AHN-koh)
rosé	*rosato* (roh-ZAH-toh)
sparkling	*spumante/frizzante* (spoo-MAHN-tay/freed-ZAHN-tay)
dry	*secco* (SEH-koh)
earthy	*terroso* (teh-ROH-zoh)
elegant	*elegante* (eh-leh-GAHN-tay)
fruity	*fruttato* (froo-TAH-toh)
full-bodied	*corposo/pieno* (kor-POH-zoh/pee-EH-noh)
mature	*maturo* (mah-TOO-roh)
sweet	*dolce* (DOHL-chay)
tannic	*tannico* (TAH-nee-koh)
young	*giovane* (JOH-vah-nay)

cappuccino is a morning drink; they believe having milk after a big meal or anything with tomato sauce impairs digestion). If they add any milk after lunch, it's just a splash, in a *caffè macchiato*. Italians like their coffee only warm—to get it very hot, request *"Molto caldo, per favore"* (MOHL-toh KAHL-doh pehr fah-VOH-ray). Any coffee drink is available decaffeinated—ask for it *decaffeinato* (deh-kah-feh-NAH-toh). *Cioccolato* is hot chocolate. *Tè* is hot tea.

Experiment with a few of the options:

Cappuccino: Espresso with foamed milk on top (*cappuccino freddo* is iced cappuccino).

Caffè latte: Espresso mixed with hot milk, no foam, in a tall glass (ordering just a "latte" gets you only milk).

Caffè macchiato: Espresso "marked" with a splash of milk, in a small cup.

Latte macchiato: Layers of hot milk and foam, "marked" by an espresso shot, in a tall glass. Note that if you order simply a "*macchiato*," you'll probably get a *caffè macchiato*.

Caffè corto/lungo: Concentrated espresso diluted with a tiny bit of hot water, in a small cup.

Caffè americano: Espresso diluted with even more hot water, in a larger cup.

Caffè corretto: Espresso "corrected" with a shot of liqueur (normally *grappa, amaro,* or *sambuca*).

Marocchino: "Moroccan" coffee with espresso, foamed milk, and cocoa powder; the similar *mocaccino* has chocolate instead of cocoa.

Caffè freddo: Sweet and iced espresso.

Caffè hag: Instant decaf.

Alcoholic Beverages

Beer: While Italy is traditionally considered wine country, in recent years there's been a huge and passionate growth in the production of craft beer *(birra artigianale)*. Even in small towns, you'll see microbreweries slinging their own brews. You'll also find local brews (Peroni and Moretti), as well as imports such as Heineken. Italians drink mainly lager beers. Beer on tap is *alla spina*. Get it *piccola* (33 cl, 11 oz), *media* (50 cl, about a pint), or *grande* (a liter). A *lattina* (lah-TEE-nah) is a can and a *bottiglia* (boh-TEEL-yah) is a bottle.

Cocktails and Spirits: Italians appreciate both *aperitivi* (palate-stimulating cocktails) and *digestivi* (after-dinner drinks designed to aid digestion). Popular *aperitivo* options include Campari (dark-colored bitters with herbs and orange peel), Americano (vermouth with bitters, brandy, and lemon peel), Cynar (bitters flavored with artichoke), and Punt e Mes (sweet red vermouth and red wine). Widely used vermouth brands include Cinzano and Martini.

Digestivo choices are usually either strong herbal bitters or something sweet. Many restaurants have their own secret recipe for a bittersweet herbal brew called *amaro*; popular commercial brands are Fernet Branca and Montenegro. If your tastes run sweeter, try *amaretto* (almond-flavored liqueur), Frangelico (hazelnut liqueur), *limoncello* (lemon liqueur), *nocino* (dark, sweet, walnut liqueur), and *sambuca* (syrupy, anise-flavored liqueur; *con moscha* adds "flies"— three coffee beans). *Grappa* is a brandy distilled from grape skins and stems; *stravecchio* is an aged, mellower variation.

Wine: The ancient Greeks who colonized Italy more than 2,000 years ago called it Oenotria—land of the grape. Centuries later, Galileo wrote, "Wine is light held together by water." Wine *(vino)* is certainly a part of the Italian culinary trinity—grape, olive, and wheat. (I'd add gelato.) Ideal conditions for grapes (warm climate, well-draining soil, and an abundance of hillsides) make

PRACTICALITIES

Regional Wines

In almost every part of Italy, you'll find wine varieties designed to go with the regional cuisine.

Tuscany (Florence, Siena, and Nearby): Many Tuscan wines are made with sangiovese ("blood of Jupiter") grapes, including the well-known Chiantis, which range from cheap, acidic basket-bottles of table wine (called *fiaschi*) to the hearty Chianti Classico. Vino Nobile di Montepulciano is a high-quality dry ruby red that pairs well with meat, especially chicken. One of Italy's top reds is Brunello di Montalcino (smooth, dry, aged at least four years in wood); a cheaper, younger "baby Brunello" is Rosso di Montalcino. Pricey Super Tuscans blend traditional grapes with locally grown non-Italian grapes (such as cabernet or merlot). A decent white choice is Vernaccia di San Gimignano (medium-dry, pairs well with pasta and salad). Trebbiano and vermentino are two other local white grapes. Vin santo is a sweet, syrupy, "holy" dessert wine, often served with a cookie for dipping.

Veneto (near Venice): Valpolicella grapes are used to make a light, fruity, dry, red table wine as well as Amarone (full-bodied red made from partially dried—*passito*—grapes, then aged for at least four years in oak) and Recioto (sweet dessert wine made with high-sugar grapes that are dried and aged). Bardolino is a light, fruity, Beaujolais-like picnic wine. Whites include Soave (crisp, dry white that goes well with seafood; the best is Soave Classico), Pinot Grigio, and Bianco di Custoza. If you like bubbles, try Fragolino (sweet, slightly fizzy dessert wine made from a strawberry-flavored grape) or prosecco (connoisseurs say the best hails from Valdobbiadene).

Umbria (Assisi, Orvieto, and Nearby): Trebbiano is this region's main white grape. Look for Orvieto Classico (a golden, dry white). For reds, consider Sagrantino de Montefalco (dark, tannic) or Torgiano Rosso Riserva (elegant, smooth). Wines from the quality producer Lungarotti are worth trying.

Liguria (Italian Riviera, including Cinque Terre): This coastal region produces light, delicate whites (using mostly bosco grapes) that go well with seafood. Dolceacqua is a medium-bodied red.

the Italian peninsula a paradise for grape growers, winemakers, and wine drinkers.

Even if you're clueless about wine, the information on an Italian wine label can help you choose something decent. Terms you may see on the bottle include *classico* (from a defined, select area), *annata* (year of harvest), *vendemmia*

After dinner, try Sciacchetrà (a silky sweet, potent, amber-colored wine made with raisins).

Lazio (Rome and Nearby): Wines to try here include Frascati (inexpensive dry white); Castelli Romani, Marino, Colli Albani, and Velletri (all light and fairly dry); and Torre Ercolana (balanced, medium-bodied, best-quality red).

Dolomites: While beer is king here, look for reds like St. Magdalaner (light, dry, made from schiava grapes); Lagrein Scuro (full-bodied, dry and fruity, similar to a cabernet sauvignon or merlot); or whites like Pinot Grigio, Gewürztraminer, and Pinot Blanc. Nosiola is an aromatic local grape used for dessert and sparkling wine.

Piedmont (near Milan and the Lakes): This region specializes in bold, dry reds that go with the rich, local cuisine. Nebbiolo is the main red grape. Wine lovers drool over Barolo (big, tannic, aged three years or more) or its "little brother," Barbaresco (elegant, aged two years). For lighter, less tannic reds, try Barbera or Dolcetto (soft, fruity). Whites include Gavi (light, fruity) and Arneis (flowery, medium-bodied). For bubbly wines, try Brachetto (crimson, sweet, berry notes, excellent aperitif), Moscato d'Asti (semi-sweet, slightly fizzy), and Asti Spumante (dry).

Campania (Naples, Sorrento, and Nearby): Plentiful sun and Mt. Vesuvius' volcanic soils provide great wine-growing conditions. Taurasi is an excellent ruby-colored, tannic, aged, full-bodied red from the aglianico grape. Lacryma Christi ("tears of Christ") comes in both red (medium body) and white (dry and fruity, great with seafood). Other whites are Greco di Tufo (dry, pale yellow) and Fiano di Avellino (soft, flavorful, dry).

Sicily: The main red is Nero d'Avola (jammy, full-bodied, tannic). Corvo, Regaleali, and Planeta are some established producers. White wines use indigenous grapes like grillo, inzolio, and catarrato. Try Bianca d'Alcamo (dry, fresh, fruity) and Etna Bianco (dry, lemon flavors, pairs well with shellfish). Marsala is a (usually) sweet fortified dessert wine.

(harvest), and *imbottigliato dal produttore all'origine* (bottled by producers). To figure out what you like—and what suits your pocketbook—visit an *enoteca* (wine bar) and sample wines side by side. For tips on ordering wine, see the sidebar.

In general, Italy designates its wines by one of four official categories:

Vino da Tavola (VDT) is table wine, the lowest grade, made from grapes grown anywhere in Italy. It's often inexpensive, but Italy's wines are so good that, for many people, a basic *vino da tavola* is just fine with a meal. Many restaurants, even modest ones, take pride in their house wine *(vino della casa)*, bottling their own or working with wineries.

Denominazione di Origine Controllata (DOC) meets national standards for high-quality wine. Made from grapes grown in a defined area, it's usually quite affordable and can be surprisingly good. Hundreds of wines have earned the DOC designation. In Tuscany, for example, many such wines come from the Chianti region, located between Florence and Siena.

Denominazione di Origine Controllata e Guarantita (DOCG), the highest grade, meets national standards for the highest-quality wine (made with grapes from a defined area whose quality is "guaranteed"). These wines can be identified by the pink or green label on the neck...and the scary price tag on the shelf. Only a limited number of wines in Italy can be called DOCG. They're generally a good bet if you want a quality wine, but you don't know anything else about the winemaker. (*Riserva* indicates a DOC or DOCG wine matured for a longer, more specific time.)

Indicazione Geographica Tipica (IGT) is a broad group of wines that range from basic to some of Italy's best. These wines don't follow the strict "recipe" required for DOC or DOCG status, but give local vintners creative license. This category includes the Super Tuscans—wines made from a mix of international grapes (such as cabernet sauvignon) grown in Tuscany and aged in small oak barrels for only two years. The result is a lively full-bodied wine that dances all over your head...and is worth the steep price for aficionados.

Staying Connected

One of the most common questions I hear from travelers is, "How can I stay connected in Europe?" The short answer is: more easily and cheaply than you might think.

The simplest solution is to bring your own device—mobile phone, tablet, or laptop—and use it just as you would at home (following the tips below, such as connecting to free Wi-Fi whenever possible). Another option is to buy a European SIM card for your mobile phone—either your US phone or one you buy in Europe. Or you can travel without a mobile device and use European landlines and computers to connect. Each of these options is described below, and you'll find even more details at www.ricksteves.com/phoning. For a very practical one-hour lecture covering tech issues for travelers, see www.ricksteves.com/travel-talks.

USING YOUR OWN MOBILE DEVICE IN EUROPE

Without an international plan, typical rates from major service providers (AT&T, Verizon, etc.) for using your device abroad are

Hurdling the Language Barrier

Many Italians—especially those in the tourist trade and in big cities—speak English. Still, you'll get better treatment if you learn and use Italian pleasantries. In smaller, nontouristy towns, Italian is the norm. Italians have an endearing habit of talking to you even if they know you don't speak their language—and yet, thanks to gestures and thoughtfully simplified words, it somehow works. Don't stop them to tell them you don't understand every word—just go along for the ride. For a list of survival phrases, see page 1191.

Note that Italian is pronounced much like English, with a few exceptions, such as: c followed by e or i is pronounced ch (to ask, "Per centro?"—To the center?—you say, pehr CHEHN-troh). In Italian, ch is pronounced like the hard c in Chianti (chiesa—church—is pronounced kee-AY-zah). Adding a vowel to the English word often gets you close to the Italian one. Give it your best shot. Italians appreciate your efforts.

about $1.70/minute for voice calls, 50 cents to send text messages, 5 cents to receive them, and $10 to download one megabyte of data. At these rates, costs can add up quickly. Here are some budget tips and options.

Use free Wi-Fi whenever possible. Unless you have an unlimited-data plan, you're best off saving most of your online tasks for Wi-Fi. You can access the Internet, send texts, and make voice calls over Wi-Fi.

Many cafés (including McDonald's) have free hotspots for customers; look for signs offering it and ask for the Wi-Fi password when you buy something. You'll also often find Wi-Fi at TIs, city squares, major museums, public-transit hubs, airports, highway rest stops (Autogrills), and aboard trains and buses.

Sign up for an international plan. Most providers offer a global calling plan that cuts the per-minute cost of phone calls and texts, and a flat-fee data plan. Your normal plan may already include international coverage (T-Mobile's does).

Before your trip, call your provider or check online to confirm that your phone will work in Europe, and research your provider's international rates. Activate the plan a day or two before you leave, then remember to cancel it when your trip's over.

Minimize the use of your cellular network. When you can't find Wi-Fi, you can use your cellular network to connect to the Internet, text, or make voice calls. When you're done, avoid further charges by manually switching off "data roaming" or "cellular data" (in your device's Settings menu; for help, ask your service provider or Google it). Another way to make sure you're not accidentally using data roaming is to put your device in "airplane" or "flight" mode (which also disables phone calls and texts), and then turn on Wi-Fi as needed.

Don't use your cellular network for bandwidth-gobbling tasks, such as Skyping, downloading apps, and watching YouTube: Save these for when you're on Wi-Fi. Using a navigation app such as Google Maps over a cellular network can take lots of data, so do this sparingly or use it offline.

Limit automatic updates. By default, your device constantly checks for a data connection and updates apps. It's smart to disable these features so your apps will only update when you're on Wi-Fi, and to change your device's email settings from "auto-retrieve" to "manual" (or from "push" to "fetch").

It's also a good idea to keep track of your data usage. On your device's menu, look for "cellular data usage" or "mobile data" and reset the counter at the start of your trip.

Use Skype or other calling/messaging apps for cheaper calls and texts. Certain apps let you make voice or video calls or send texts over the Internet for free or cheap. If you're bringing a tablet or laptop, you can also use it for voice calls and texts. All you have to do is log on to a Wi-Fi network, then contact any of your friends or family members who are also online and signed into the same service.

You can make voice and video calls using Skype, Viber, FaceTime, and Google+ Hangouts. If the connection is bad, try making an audio-only call. You can also make voice calls from your device to telephones worldwide for just a few cents per minute using Skype, Viber, or Hangouts if you buy credit first.

To text for free over Wi-Fi, try apps like Google+ Hangouts, WhatsApp, Viber, Facebook Messenger, and iMessage. Make sure you're on Wi-Fi to avoid data charges.

USING A EUROPEAN SIM CARD IN A MOBILE PHONE

This option works well for those who want to make a lot of voice calls at cheap local rates, and those who need faster connection speeds than their US carrier provides. Either buy a basic cell phone in Europe (as little as $40 from mobile-phone shops anywhere), or bring an "unlocked" US phone (check with your carrier about unlocking it). With an unlocked phone, you can replace the original SIM card (the microchip that stores info about the phone) with one that will work with a European provider.

In Europe, buy a SIM card. Inserted into your phone, this card gives you a European phone number—and European rates. SIM cards are sold at mobile-phone shops, department-store electronics counters, newsstands, and vending machines. Costing about $5-10, they usually include about that much prepaid calling credit,

Tips on Internet Security

Using the Internet while traveling brings added security risks, whether you're getting online with your own device or at a public terminal using a shared network. Here are some tips for securing your data:

First, make sure that your device is running the latest version of its operating system and security software, and that your apps are up to date. Next, ensure that your device is password- or passcode-protected so thieves can't access it if your device is stolen. For extra security, set passwords on apps that access key info (such as email or Facebook).

On the road, use only legitimate Wi-Fi hotspots. Ask the hotel or café staff for the specific name of their Wi-Fi network, and make sure you log on to that exact one. Hackers sometimes create a bogus hotspot with a similar or vague name (such as "Hotel Europa Free Wi-Fi"). The best Wi-Fi networks require a password. If you're not actively using a hotspot, turn off your device's Wi-Fi connection so it's not visible to others.

Be especially cautious when accessing financial information online. Experts say it's best to use a banking app rather than sign in to your bank's website via a browser (the app is less likely to get hacked). Refrain from logging in to any personal finance sites on a public computer. Even if you're using your own mobile device at a password-protected hotspot, there's a remote chance that a hacker who's logged on to the same network could see what you're doing.

Never share your credit-card number (or any other sensitive information) online unless you know that the site is secure. A secure site displays a little padlock icon, and the URL begins with *https* (instead of the usual *http*).

with no contract and no commitment. A SIM card that also includes data costs (including roaming) will cost $20-40 more for one month of data within the country in which it was purchased. This can be faster than data roaming through your home provider. To get the best rates, buy a new SIM card whenever you arrive in a new country.

I like to buy SIM cards at a mobile-phone shop where there's a clerk to help explain the options and brands. In Italy, the major mobile phone providers are Wind, TIM, Vodafone, and 3 ("Tre"). Certain SIM-card brands—including Lebara and Lycamobile, both of which operate in multiple European countries—are reliable and economical. Ask the clerk to help you insert your SIM card, set it up, and show you how to use it. In some countries—including Italy—you'll be required to register the SIM card with your passport as an antiterrorism measure (which may mean you can't use the phone for the first hour or two).

Find out how to check your credit balance. When you run out

How to Dial

International Calls

Whether phoning from a US landline or mobile phone, or from a number in another European country, here's how to make an international call. I've used one of my recommended Florence hotels as an example (tel. 055-213-154).

Initial Zero: Drop the initial zero from international phone numbers—except when calling Italy.

Mobile Tip: If using a mobile phone, the "+" sign can replace the international access code (for a "+" sign, press and hold "0").

US/Canada to Europe

Dial 011 (US/Canada international access code), country code (39 for Italy), and phone number.

▶ To call the Florence hotel from home, dial 011-39-055-213-154.

Country to Country Within Europe

Dial 00 (Europe international access code), country code, and phone number.

▶ To call the Florence hotel from Germany, dial 00-39-055-213-154.

Europe to the US/Canada

Dial 00, country code (1 for US/Canada), and phone number.

▶ To call from Europe to my office in Edmonds, Washington, dial 00-1-425-771-8303.

Domestic Calls

To call within Italy (from one Italian landline or mobile phone to another), simply dial the phone number, including the initial 0 if there is one.

▶ To call the Florence hotel from Rome, dial 055-213-154.

More Dialing Tips

Italian Phone Numbers: Italian phone numbers vary in length; a hotel can have, say, an eight-digit phone number

of credit, you can top it up at newsstands, tobacco shops, mobile-phone stores, many other businesses (look for your SIM card's logo in the window), or online.

UNTETHERED TRAVEL:
PUBLIC PHONES AND COMPUTERS

It's possible to travel in Europe without a mobile device. You can check email or browse websites using public computers and Internet cafés, and make calls from your hotel room and/or public phones.

and a nine-digit fax number. Italy's landlines start with 0; mobile lines start with 3 and cost substantially more to dial.

Toll and Toll-Free Calls: Italy's toll-free lines, called *numero verde* (green number), begin with 800 or 803. They can be dialed free from Italian phones without using a phone card but don't work from the US. Any Italian phone number that starts with 8 but isn't followed by a 0 is a toll call (generally costing €0.10-0.50/minute). International rates apply to US toll-free numbers dialed from Italy—they're not free.

More Phoning Help: See www.howtocallabroad.com.

European Country Codes			
Austria	43	Italy	39
Belgium	32	Latvia	371
Bosnia-Herzegovina	387	Montenegro	382
Croatia	385	Morocco	212
Czech Republic	420	Netherlands	31
Denmark	45	Norway	47
Estonia	372	Poland	48
Finland	358	Portugal	351
France	33	Russia	7
Germany	49	Slovakia	421
Gibraltar	350	Slovenia	386
Great Britain	44	Spain	34
Greece	30	Sweden	46
Hungary	36	Switzerland	41
Ireland & N. Ireland	353 / 44	Turkey	90

PRACTICALITIES

Phones in your **hotel room** generally have a fee for placing local and "toll-free" calls, as well as long-distance or international calls—ask for the rates before you dial. Since you're never charged for receiving calls, it's better to have someone from the US call you in your room.

If these fees are low, hotel phones can be used inexpensively for calls made with cheap international phone cards (*carta telefonica prepagata internazionale,* KAR-tah teh-leh-FOHN-ee-kah pray-pah-GAH-tah in-ter-naht-zee oh-NAH-lay—sold at many post offices, newsstands, street kiosks, tobacco shops, and train stations). You'll either get a prepaid card with a toll-free number and a scratch-to-reveal PIN code, or a code printed on a receipt.

Although they're becoming rare, you'll see **public pay phones** in a few post offices and train stations. The phones generally come with multilingual instructions, and most work with insertable Telecom Italia phone cards (sold at post offices, newsstands, etc.). With the exception of Great Britain, each European country has its own insertable phone card—so your Spanish card won't work in an Italian phone.

Public computers are easy to find. Many hotels have one in their lobby for guests to use; otherwise you can find them at Internet cafés and public libraries (ask your hotelier or the TI for the nearest location). If typing on a European keyboard, use the "Alt Gr" key to the right of the space bar to insert the extra symbol that appears on some keys. Italian keyboards are a little different from ours; to type an @ symbol, press the "Alt Gr" key and the key that shows the @ symbol. If you can't locate a special character, simply copy it from a Web page and paste it into your email message.

MAIL

You can mail one package per day to yourself worth up to $200 duty-free from Europe to the US (mark it "personal purchases"). If you're sending a gift to someone, mark it "unsolicited gift." For details, visit www.cbp.gov, select "Travel," and search for "Know Before You Go."

The Italian postal service works fine, but for quick transatlantic delivery (in either direction), consider services such as DHL (www.dhl.com).

Transportation

When deciding how to get between destinations in Europe, consider these factors: Cars are best for three or more traveling together (especially families with small kids), those packing heavy, and those delving into the countryside. Trains and buses are best for solo travelers, blitz tourists, city-to-city travelers, and those who don't want to drive in Europe. Intra-European flights are an increasingly inexpensive option. While a car gives you more freedom, trains and buses zip you effortlessly and scenically from city to city, usually dropping you in the center, often near a TI.

Considering how handy and affordable Italy's trains and buses are (and that you're likely to go both broke and crazy driving in Italian cities), I'd do most of Italy by public transportation. If you want to drive, consider doing the big, intense stuff (Rome, Naples area, Milan, Florence, and Venice) by train or bus and renting a car for the hill towns of central Italy and for the Dolomites. A car is a worthless headache on the Riviera and in the Lake Como area.

If your itinerary mixes cities and countryside, arrange your car rental strategically: Wait to pick up your car until the last big city you visit, then use it for lacing together the hill towns and exploring the countryside. For more detailed information on transportation throughout Europe, including trains, buses, flying, renting a car, and driving, see www.ricksteves.com/transportation.

TRAINS

To travel by train affordably in Italy, you can simply buy tickets as you go. For travelers ready to lock in dates and times weeks or months in advance, buying nonrefundable tickets online can cut costs in half. Note that the Italy rail pass is generally not a good value; but if your travel extends beyond Italy, there are various multicountry rail passes that might be worth checking into. For advice on figuring out the smartest train-ticket or rail-pass options for your trip, visit the Trains & Rail Passes section of my website at www.ricksteves.com/rail.

Types of Trains

Most trains in Italy are operated by the state-run **Trenitalia** company (www.trenitalia.com, a.k.a. Ferrovie dello Stato Italiane, ab-

breviated FS or FSI). Since ticket prices depend on the speed of the train, it helps to know the different types of trains: pokey R or REG *(regionali);* medium-speed RV *(regionali veloce)*, IR (InterRegio), D *(diretto)*, and E *(espresso);* fast IC (InterCity) and EC (EuroCity); and super-fast Frecce trains: Frecciabianca ("White Arrow"), faster Frecciargento ("Silver Arrow"), Frecciarossa ("Red Arrow"), and the newest Frecciarossa 1000 or Freccemille (up to 225 mph). You may also see the Frecce trains marked on schedules as ES, AV, or EAV. If you're traveling with a rail pass, note that reservations are required for IC, EC, and international trains (€5) and for Frecce trains (€10). You can't make reservations for regional trains, such as most Pisa-Cinque Terre connections.

A private train company called **Italo** runs fast trains on major routes in Italy. Italo is focused on two corridors: Venice-Padua-Bologna-Florence-Rome and Turin-Milan-Bologna-Florence-Rome-Naples. Their high-speed trains have fewer departures than Trenitalia, but they do offer discounts for tickets booked well in advance. In some cities, such as Milan, their trains use secondary stations—if taking an Italo train, pay attention to which station you need.

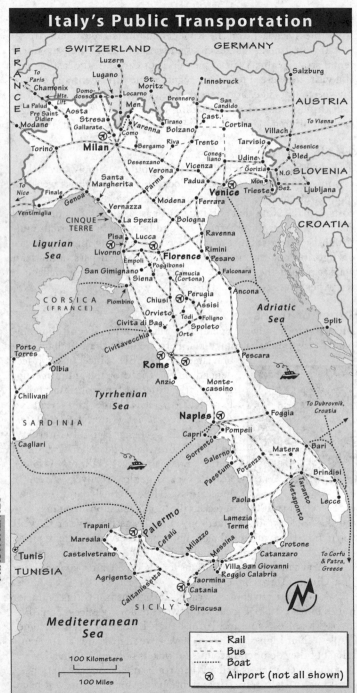

Italy's Public Transportation

Legend:
- Rail
- - - Bus
- ...... Boat
- ✈ Airport (not all shown)

100 Kilometers

100 Miles

Italo does not accept rail passes, but they're a worthy alternative for point-to-point tickets. You can book in person (look for Italo ticket offices or their red machines), by phone (tel. 06-0708), or on their user-friendly website (www.italotreno.it).

Schedules

At the train station, the easiest way to check schedules is at a handy ticket machine (described later, under "Buying Tickets"). Enter the desired date, time, and destination to see all your options. Printed schedules are also posted at the station (departure—*partenzi*—posters are always yellow).

Newsstands sell up-to-date regional and all-Italy timetables (€5, ask for the *orario ferroviaro*). You can also check www.trenitalia.it and www.italotreno.it (domestic journeys only); for international trips, use www.bahn.com (Germany's excellent all-Europe schedule website). Trenitalia offers a single all-Italy telephone number for train information (24 hours daily, toll tel. 892-021, in Italian only, consider having your hotelier call for you). For Italo trains, call tel. 06-0708.

Be aware that Trenitalia and Italo don't cooperate at all. If you buy a ticket for one train line, it's not valid on the other. Even if you're just looking for schedule information, the company you ask will most likely ignore the other's options.

Point-to-Point Tickets

Train tickets are a good value in Italy. Fares are shown on the map on page 1165, though fares can vary for the same journey, mainly depending on the time of day, the speed of the train, and advance discounts. **First-class** tickets cost up to 50 percent more than **second-class.**

Frecce and Italo trains offer several classes of service where all seats are reserved: Standard, Premium, Business, or Executive on Frecciarossa; Smart, Prima, or Club on Italo; and standard first and second class on other trains. Buying up gives you a little more elbow room, or perhaps a better chance at seating a group together, if you're buying on short notice. Ticket price levels for both companies are Base (full fare, easily changeable or partly refundable before scheduled departure), Economy (one schedule change allowed before departure, for a fee), and Super Economy or Low Cost (sells out quickly, no refund or exchange). Discounted fares typically sell out several days before departure. Fares labeled *servizi abbonati* are available only for locals with monthly passes—not tourists.

Speed vs. Savings: For point-to-point tickets, you'll pay more the faster you go. Spending a modest amount of extra time in transit can save money. On longer, mainline routes, fast trains save more time and provide most of the service. For example, super-

PRACTICALITIES

Deciphering Italian Train Schedules

At the station, look for the big yellow posters labeled *Partenze—Departures* (white posters show arrivals). Departures are listed chronologically, hour by hour, showing the trains leaving the station throughout the day.

Reading from the left, the schedule lists the time of departure *(ora)*, the type of train *(treni)*, and service classes offered *(classi servizi)*—first- and second-class cars, dining car, *cuccetta* berths, and, more important, whether you need reservations (usually denoted by an R in a box). All Frecce trains, many EuroCity (EC) and InterCity (IC) trains, and most international trains require reservations.

The next column lists the train's destination *(principali fermate destinazioni)*, often showing intermediate stops (with arrival times in parentheses). Note that your destination may be listed in fine print as an intermediate stop. For example, if you're going from Milan to Florence, scan the schedule and you'll notice that virtually all trains that terminate in Rome stop in Florence en route. Travelers who read the fine print end up with a far greater choice of trains.

You may also see pertinent notes about the train, such as "also stops in..." *(ferma anche a...)*, "doesn't stop in..." *(non ferma a...)*, "stops in every station" *(ferma in tutte le stazioni)*, "delayed..." *(ritardo...)*, and so on.

The last column gives the track *(binario)* the train departs from. Confirm the *binario* with a ticket seller or railway official, the electronic board that lists immediate departures, or monitors on the platform.

For any odd symbols on the poster, look at the key at the end. Some phrasing can be deciphered easily, such as *servizio periodico* (periodic service—doesn't always run). For the trickier ones, ask a local or railway official, or try your *Rick Steves' Italian Phrase Book & Dictionary*.

You can also check schedules for trains anywhere in Italy at ticket machines. Enter the date and time of your desired departure (to or from any Italian station), and you can view all your options.

fast Rome-Venice trains run hourly, cost €76 in second class, and make the trip in 4 hours, while infrequent InterCity trains (only 1-2/day) cost €50 and take 6 hours. Speedy Florence-Rome trains run hourly, cost €45 in second class, and make the trip in 1.5 hours, while infrequent InterCity trains (only 1-2/day) cost €35 and take 3 hours. On routes like Verona-Padua-Venice, regional trains cost considerably less than IC and ES express trains, and are only a little slower.

Discounts: Families with young children can get price breaks—kids ages 3 and under travel free; ages 4-11 at half-price. Ask for the "Offerta Familia" deal when buying tickets at a counter (or, at a ticket machine, choose "Yes" at the "Do you want ticket issue?" prompt, then choose "Familia"). With the discount, families of 3 to 5 people with at least 1 kid (under 12) get 50 percent off the child fare and 20 percent off the adult fare. The deal doesn't apply to all trains at all times, but it's worth checking out.

Discounts for youths and seniors require purchase of a separate card (Carta Verde for ages 12-26 costs €40; Carta Argento for ages 60 and over is €30), but the discount on tickets is so minor (10-15 percent, respectively, for domestic travel), it's not worth it for most.

Buying Tickets: Avoid train station ticket lines whenever possible by using the ticket machines in station halls. Pay all ticket costs in the station before you board, or you'll pay a penalty on the train. You'll be able to easily purchase tickets for travel within Italy (not international trains), make seat reservations, and even book a *cuccetta* (koo-CHEH-tah; overnight berth). If you do use the ticket windows, be sure you're in the correct line. Key terms: *biglietti* (general tickets), *prenotazioni* (reservations), *nazionali* (domestic), and *internazionali*.

Trenitalia's ticket machines (either green-and-white or red; marked *Trenitalia/Biglietti*) are user-friendly and found in all but the tiniest stations in Italy. You can pay by cash (they give change) or by debit or credit card (even for small amounts, but you may need to enter your PIN). Select English, then your destination. If you don't immediately see the city you're traveling to, keep keying in the spelling until it's listed. You can choose from first- and second-class seats, request tickets for more than one traveler, and (on the high-speed Frecce trains) choose an aisle or window seat. Don't select a discount rate without being sure that you meet the criteria (for example, Americans are not eligible for certain EU or resident discounts). Rail-pass holders can use the machines to make seat reservations. If you need to validate your ticket, you can do it in the same machine if you're boarding your train right away.

For longer-haul runs, it can be cheaper to buy Trenitalia tickets in advance, either at the station or on their website. Because most Italian trains run frequently and there's no deadline to buy tickets,

Open or Non-Reserved Ticket—Need to Validate

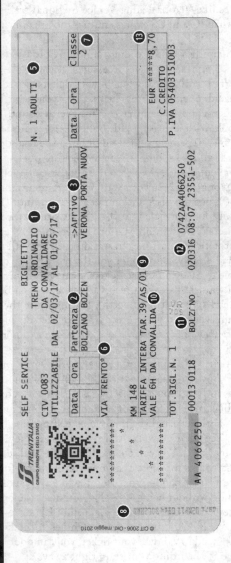

1 Open ticket for non-express train, must be validated
2 Point of departure
3 Destination
4 Period in which ticket is valid
5 Number of passengers
6 Route
7 Class of travel (1st or 2nd)
8 Validation stamp
9 Full fare for non-express train
10 Ticket good for 1 trip within 6 hours after validation
11 Location of ticket sale
12 Date of ticket purchase
13 Ticket cost

Reserved Ticket (Fast Train)—Need Not Validate

1. Departure date & time
2. Point of departure
3. Destination
4. "Ticket with reservation"
5. Number of passengers
6. Arrival date & time
7. Class of travel (1st or 2nd)
8. "Present to official if changing trains"
9. Train, car & seat numbers (finestrino = window seat)
10. Fast-train fare
11. Location of ticket sale
12. Date of ticket purchase
13. Booking ID
14. Ticket cost
15. Amount of CO_2 usage reduced by this train trip

you can keep your travel plans flexible by purchasing tickets as you go. (You can buy tickets for several trips at one station when you are ready to commit.) For busy weekend or holiday travel, however, it can be a good idea to buy tickets in advance, whether online or at a station. Reserved, domestic train tickets purchased online offer a "ticketless" option that means you only need the booking code.

To buy tickets for **Italo** trains, look for a dedicated service counter (in most major rail stations) or a red ticket machine labeled *Italo*. You can also book Italo tickets by phone (tel. 06-0708) or online (www.italotreno.it).

You can't buy most international tickets from machines; for this and anything else that requires a real person, you must go to a ticket window at the station. A good alternative, though, is to drop by a local travel agency. Agencies sell domestic and international tickets and make reservations. They charge a small fee, but the language barrier (and the lines) can be smaller than at the station's ticket windows. For German-run trains in northern Italy, you can also buy tickets at www.bahn.com.

Validating Tickets: If your ticket includes a seat reservation on a specific train *(biglietto con prenotazione)*, you're all set and can just get on board. An open ticket with no seat reservation (generally for a *regionali* train) must always be validated. Before you board, stamp your ticket (it may say *da convalidare* or *convalida*) in the machine near the platform (usually marked *convalida biglietti* or *vidimazione*). Once you validate a ticket, you must complete your trip within the timeframe shown on the ticket. If you forget to validate your ticket, go right away to the train conductor—before he comes to you—or you'll pay a fine. Note that you don't need to validate a rail pass each time you board (just make sure you've validated it before its first use).

Rail Passes

The **Italy Pass** for the Italian state railway may save you money if you're taking three long train rides or prefer first-class travel, but don't count on it for hop-on convenience on every train. Use the price map on the next page to add up your ticket costs (prices on the map are for the fastest trains on a given route, many of which have reservation costs built in). Remember that rail passes are not valid on Italo-brand trains.

Rail pass travelers must make separate seat reservations (€5-10 each) for the fastest trains between major Italian cities, but can just hop on regional trains (no reservations possible). Reservations for berths on overnight trains cost extra, aren't covered by rail passes, and aren't reflected on the ticket-cost map.

A **Global Pass** can work well throughout most of Europe, but it's a bad value for travel exclusively in Italy. A cheaper version, the

Rail Passes

Prices listed are for 2016 and are subject to change. For the latest prices, details, and train schedules (and easy online ordering), see www.ricksteves.com/rail.

"Saver" prices are per person for two or more people traveling together. "Youth" means under age 26. Up to two kids age 4-11 travel free with each adult on any Eurail-brand pass. Additional kids pay the youth rate. Kids under age 4 travel free.

Map key: Approximate point-to-point one-way second-class rail fares in US dollars. First class costs 50 percent more.

Before purchasing a rail pass, add up the approximate ticket costs for your itinerary. If you'll be making short, inexpensive trips each day, you'll probably find it's cheaper to buy tickets as you go in Italy.

ITALY PASS

	1st Class Adult	1st Class Saver	1st Class Youth	2nd Class Adult	2nd Class Saver	2nd Class Youth
3 days in 1 month	$226	$193	$182	$182	$155	$149
4 days in 1 month	271	231	218	218	186	178
5 days in 1 month	312	266	251	251	214	205
8 days in 1 month	421	359	338	338	288	275

Select Pass prices vary depending on which countries they cover. Two-country pass options allow you to combine Italy with Spain, France, Austria, or Greece, but not Switzerland. Spain-Italy pass does not cover travel through France. Passes do not cover private trains operated by Italo or Thello (which includes the night trains to/from Paris). See website www.ricksteves.com for 4-country option and more details.

EURAIL SELECT PASS—UPPER PRICE RANGE

3 Countries	1st Class Indiv.	1st Class Saver	1st Class Youth	2nd Class Youth
5 days in 2 months	$440	$375	$354	$289
6 days in 2 months	485	413	389	318
8 days in 2 months	567	483	455	372
10 days in 2 months	638	543	512	417

2 Countries	1st Class Indiv.	1st Class Saver	1st Class Youth	2nd Class Indiv.	2nd Class Saver	2nd Class Youth
4 days in 2 months	$362	$308	$291	$291	$248	$238
5 days in 2 months	408	348	328	328	280	268
6 days in 2 months	451	384	362	362	309	296
8 days in 2 months	525	447	421	421	359	344
10 days in 2 months	591	504	474	474	404	387

Select Pass, allows you to tailor a pass to your trip, provided you're traveling in two to four adjacent countries directly connected by rail or ferry. For instance, with a four-country pass allowing 10 days of train travel within a two-month period (about $700 for a single adult in 2016), you could choose France-Switzerland-Italy-Greece or Benelux-Germany-Austria-Italy. A two-country version could cover France and Italy or Austria and Italy, but there isn't one for Switzerland and Italy. Note that none of these passes covers overnight trains between Italy and Paris—they require a separate ticket. Before you buy a Select Pass, consider how many travel days you'll really need. Use the pass only for travel days that involve long hauls or several trips. Pay out of pocket for tickets on days you're taking only short, cheap rides.

Train Tips

Seat Reservations: Trains can fill up, even in first class. If you're on a tight schedule, you'll want to reserve a few days ahead for fast trains (see "Types of Trains," earlier). Purchasing tickets or pass-holder reservations onboard a train comes with a nasty penalty. Buying them at the station can be a time waster unless you use the ticket machines.

If you don't need a reservation, and if your train originates at your departure point (e.g., you're catching the Florence-Pisa train in Florence), arriving at least 15 minutes before the departure time will help you snare a seat.

On the platforms of some major stations, posters showing the train composition *(composizione principali treni)* indicate where first- and second-class cars will line up when the trains arrive (letters on the poster are supposed to correspond to letters posted over the platform—but they don't always). Other stations may post the order of the cars on video screens along the track shortly before the train arrives. Since most trains now allow you to make reservations up to the time of departure, conductors post a list of the reservable and nonreservable seat rows (sometimes in English) in each train car's vestibule. This means that if you board a crowded train and get one of the last seats, you may be ousted when the reservation holder comes along.

Baggage Storage: Many Italian stations have *deposito bagagli* where you can safely leave your bag for a standardized but rather steep price (€6/5 hours, €12/12 hours, €17/24 hours, payable when you pick up the bag, double-check closing hours; they may ask to photocopy your passport). Because of security concerns, no Italian stations have lockers.

Theft Concerns: In big cities, exercise caution and prudence at train stations to avoid thieves and con artists. Homeless and marginalized people lurk around the station trying to skim tips (or worse) from unsuspecting tourists. If someone helps you to find your train or carry your bags, be aware that they are not an official porter; they are simply hoping for some cash. And if someone other than a uniformed railway employee tries to help you use the ticket machines, politely refuse.

Italian trains are famous for their thieves. Never leave a bag unattended. Police do ride the trains, cutting down on theft. Still, for an overnight trip, I'd feel safe only in a *cuccetta* (a bunk in a special sleeping car with an attendant who keeps track of who comes and goes while you sleep—approximately €20 in a six-bed compartment, €25 in a less-cramped four-bed compartment, €50 in a more private, double compartment).

Strikes: Strikes, which are common, generally last a day (often a Friday). Train employees will simply explain, *"Sciopero"* (strike). But in actuality, a minimum amount of "essential" mainline service is maintained (by law) during strikes. When a strike is pending, travel agencies (and hoteliers) can check to see when the strike goes into effect and which trains will continue to run. Revised schedules may be posted in Italian at stations, and station personnel still working can often tell you what trains are expected to run. If I need to get somewhere and know a strike is imminent, I leave early (before the strike, which often begins at 9:00), or I just go to the station with extra patience in tow and hop on anything rolling in the direction I want to go.

BUSES

You can usually get anywhere you want to in Italy by bus, as long as you're not in a hurry and plan ahead using bus schedules (pick up at local TIs). For reaching small towns, buses are sometimes the only option if you don't have a car. In many hill towns, trains leave you at a station in the valley far below, while buses more likely drop you right into the thick of things. (If the bus stop or station is below town, sometimes an escalator or elevator helps get you up into town.)

Long-distance buses are catching on in Italy as an alternative to the train. They are usually cheaper, modern, and often (unlike trains) have free Wi-Fi. They're especially useful on routes poorly served by train. Some of the operators you'll see are Eurolines/Baltour (www.baltour.it), Megabus (www.megabus.com), Flixbus (www.flixbus.com), and Marozzi (www.marozzivt.it). In general, orange buses are local city buses, and blue buses are for long distances.

Larger towns have a (usually chaotic) long-distance bus station *(stazione degli autobus),* with ticket windows and several stalls (usually labeled *corsia, stallo,* or *binario*)—but to save time, buy your ticket at a travel agent or online, and print it out. Smaller towns—

where buses are more useful—often have a central bus stop *(fermata),* likely along the main road or on the main square, and maybe several more scattered around town. In small towns, buy bus tickets at newsstands or tobacco shops (with the big *T* signs). When buying your ticket, confirm the departure point *("Dov'è la fermata?").*

Before boarding, confirm the destination with the driver. You are expected to stow big backpacks underneath the bus (open the luggage compartment yourself if it's closed). Upon arrival, double-check that the posted schedule lists your next destination and departure time.

Sundays and holidays are problematic; even from large cities, schedules are sparse, departing buses are jam-packed, and ticket offices are often closed. Plan ahead and buy your ticket in advance. Most travel agencies book bus (and train) tickets for a small fee.

RENTING A CAR

If you're renting a car in Italy, bring your driver's license. You're also technically required to have an International Driving Permit—an official translation of your driver's license (sold at your local AAA office for $20 plus the cost of two passport-type photos; see www.aaa.com). While that's the letter of the law, I generally rent cars without having this permit. How this is enforced varies from country to country: Get advice from your car-rental company.

Rental companies require you to be at least 21 years old and to have held your license for one year. Drivers under age 25 may incur a young-driver surcharge, and some rental companies do not rent to anyone 75 or older. If you're considered too young or old, look into leasing (covered later), which has less stringent age restrictions.

Research car rentals before you go. It's cheaper to arrange most car rentals from the US. Consider several companies to compare rates.

Most of the major US rental agencies (including Avis, Budget, Enterprise, Hertz, and Thrifty) have offices throughout Europe. Also consider the two major Europe-based agencies, Europcar and Sixt. It can be cheaper to use a consolidator, such as Auto Europe/Kemwel (www.autoeurope.com—or the often cheaper www.autoeurope.eu) or Europe by Car (www.europebycar.com), which compares rates at several companies to get you the best deal—but because you're working with a middleman, it's especially important to ask in advance about add-on fees and restrictions.

Always read the fine print carefully for add-on charges—such as one-way drop-off fees, airport surcharges, or mandatory insurance policies—that aren't included in the "total price." You may need to query rental agents pointedly to find out your actual cost.

For the best deal, rent by the week with unlimited mileage. To save money on fuel, you can request a diesel car. I normally rent the smallest, least-expensive model with a stick shift (generally cheaper than an automatic). Almost all rentals are manual by default, so if you need an automatic, request one in advance; be aware that these cars are usually larger models (not as maneuverable when dealing with tight parking spaces and narrow, winding roads). You'll do yourself a favor by renting the smallest car that meets your needs.

Figure on paying roughly $230 for a one-week rental. Allow extra for supplemental insurance, fuel, tolls, and parking.

Picking Up Your Car: Big companies have offices in most cities; ask whether they can pick you up at your hotel. Small local rental companies can be cheaper but aren't as flexible.

Compare pickup costs (downtown can be less expensive than the airport) and explore drop-off options. Always check the hours of the location you choose: Many rental offices close from midday Saturday until Monday morning and, in smaller towns, at lunchtime.

When selecting a location, don't trust the agency's description of "downtown" or "city center." In some cases, a "downtown" branch can be on the outskirts of the city—a long, costly taxi ride from the center. Before choosing, plug the addresses into a mapping website. You may find that the "train station" location is handier. But returning a car at a big-city train station or downtown agency can be tricky; get precise details on the car drop-off location and hours, and allow ample time to find it. And be aware that most Italian cities have a "ZTL" (limited traffic zone) that's carefully monitored by cameras. If your drop-off point is near this zone, get clear directions on how to get there without crossing the line and getting a big fine.

When you pick up the rental car, check it thoroughly and make sure any damage is noted on your rental agreement. Rental agencies in Europe are very strict when it comes to charging for even minor damage, so be sure to mark everything. Before driving off, find out how your car's gearshift, lights, turn signals, wipers, radio, and fuel cap function, and know what kind of fuel the car takes (diesel vs. unleaded). When you return the car, make sure the agent verifies its condition with you. Some drivers take pictures of the returned vehicle as proof of its condition.

Car Insurance Options

Accidents can happen anywhere, but when you're on vacation, the last thing you need is stress over car insurance. When you rent a car, you're liable for a very high deductible, sometimes equal to the entire value of the car. Limit your financial risk in case of an accident by choosing one of these two options: Buy Collision Damage Waiver (CDW) coverage from the car-rental company (figure roughly 30 percent extra), or get coverage through your credit card (free, but more complicated).

In Italy, most car-rental companies' rates automatically include CDW coverage. Even if you try to decline CDW when you reserve your Italian car, you may find when you show up at the counter that you must buy it after all.

While each rental company has its own variation, basic CDW costs $10–30 a day and reduces your liability, but does not eliminate it. When you pick up the car, you'll be offered the chance to "buy down" the deductible to zero (for an additional $10-30/day; this is sometimes called "super CDW" or "zero-deductible coverage").

If you opt for credit-card coverage, there's a catch. You'll technically have to decline all coverage offered by the car-rental company, which means they can place a hold on your card for up to the full value of the car. In case of damage, it can be time-consuming to resolve the charges with your credit-card company. Before you decide on this option, quiz your credit-card company about how it works.

For more on car-rental insurance, see www.ricksteves.com/cdw.

Theft Insurance: Note that theft insurance (separate from CDW insurance) is mandatory in Italy. The insurance usually costs about $15-20 a day, payable when you pick up the car.

Leasing

For trips of three weeks or more, consider leasing (which automatically includes zero-deductible collision and theft insurance). By technically buying and then selling back the car, you save lots of money on tax and insurance. Leasing provides you a brand-new car with unlimited mileage and a 24-hour emergency assistance program. You can lease for as little as 21 days to as long as five and a half months. Car leases must be arranged from the US. One of many companies offering affordable lease packages is Europe by Car (www.europebycar.com/lease).

Navigation Options

If you'll be navigating using your phone or a GPS unit from home, remember to bring a car charger and device mount.

Your Mobile Device: The mapping app on your mobile phone works fine for navigation in Europe, but for real-time turn-by-turn directions and traffic updates, you'll generally need access to a cellular network. A helpful exception is Google Maps, which provides turn-by-turn driving directions and recalibrates even when it's offline.

To use Google Maps offline, you must have a Google account and download your map while you have a data connection. Later—

even when offline—you can call up that map, enter your destination, and get directions. View maps in standard view (not satellite view) to limit data demands.

GPS Devices: If you prefer the convenience of a dedicated GPS unit, consider renting one with your car ($10-30/day). These units offer real-time turn-by-turn directions and traffic without the data requirements of an app. Note that the unit may only come loaded with maps for its home country; if you need additional maps, ask. Also make sure your device's language is set to English before you drive off.

A less expensive option is to bring a GPS device from home. Be aware that you'll need to buy and download European maps before your trip.

Maps and Atlases: Even when navigating primarily with a mobile app or GPS, I always make it a point to have a paper map. The free maps you get from your car-rental company usually don't have enough detail. It's smart to buy a better map before you go, or pick one up at European gas stations, bookshops, newsstands, and tourist shops.

DRIVING

Driving in Italy can be scary—a video game for keeps, and you only get one quarter. Italian drivers can be aggressive. They drive fast and tailgate as if it were required. They pass where Americans are taught not to—on blind corners and just before tunnels. Roads have narrow shoulders or none at all. Driving in the countryside is less stressful than driving through urban areas or on busy highways, but stay alert. On one-lane roads, larger vehicles have the right-of-way. If you're on a truckers' route, stifle your Good Samaritan impulse when you see provocatively dressed women standing by camper-vans at the side of the road; they're not having car trouble.

Road Rules: Stay out of restricted traffic zones or you'll risk huge fines. Car traffic is restricted in many city centers. Don't

drive or park in any area that has a sign reading *Zona Traffico Limitato* (ZTL, often shown above a red circle—see image). If you do, your license plate will likely be photographed and a hefty (€100-plus) ticket mailed to your home without your ever having met a cop. Bumbling in and out of these zones can net you multiple fines. If your hotel is within a restricted area, it's best to ask your hotelier to direct you to parking outside the zone. (Although your hotelier can register your car as an authorized vehicle permitted to enter the zone, this usually isn't worth the hassle.) If you get a ticket, it could take months to

Driving in Italy

AUSTRIA

SWITZERLAND

Brenner Pass

Dolomites (Bolzano) Villach

70m·2h

260m·5h

Mt. Blanc Tunnel

Lake Como (Varenna)

100m·1.5h

160m·4.5h (Via Cortina)

155m·2.5h

SLOVENIA

Trieste

145m·2.5h

110m·2.5h

30m·.75h

Verona

95m·1.75h

200m·4h

Milan

100m·1.75h

80m·1.5h

Venice

185m·3.25h

225m·4h

85m·2.5h

135m·2.5h

175m·2.75h

155m·3h

Ravenna

CROATIA

160m·2.75h

155m·2.5h

115m·2h

90m·1.75h

Florence

Cinque Terre (La Spezia)

50m·1h

100m·2h

Ventimiglia

Pisa

70m·1.5h

45m· 1h

100m

125m· 2.25h

Siena

80m· 2h

Assisi

75m·1.5h

55m· 1.5h

115m·2.25h

210m·4h

Orvieto

75m·1.5h

Note: Your times may vary based on traffic, construction, and road conditions.

Rome

155m·2.5h

35m·1h

m = miles
h = hours

Naples

Salerno

30m·.75h

30m· 1h

Sorrento

30m·1.5h

Paestum

show up (for specifics relating to Tuscany, see www.bella-toscana.com/traffic_violations_italy.htm).

Be aware of typical European road rules; for example, many countries require headlights to be turned on at all times, and nearly all forbid talking on a mobile phone without a hands-free headset. Seatbelts are mandatory, and children under age 12 must ride in child-safety or booster seats. In Europe, you're not allowed to turn right on a red light, unless there is a sign or signal specifically authorizing it, and on expressways it's illegal to pass drivers on the right. Ask your car-rental company about these rules, or check the US State Department website (www.travel.state.gov, search for your country in the "Learn about your destination" box, then click on "Travel and Transportation").

Drive carefully: Italians are aggressive drivers. Even worse, motor scooters are very popular, and scooter drivers often see themselves as exempt from rules that apply to automobiles.

Tolls: Italy's freeway system, the autostrada, is as good as our interstate system, but you'll pay a toll (for costs, use the trip-planning tool at www.autostrade.it or search "European Tolls" on www.theaa.com). When approaching a tollbooth, skip lanes marked *Telepass;* for an attended booth, choose a lane with a sign that shows a hand.

While I favor the freeways because I feel they're safer and less nerve-racking than smaller roads, savvy local drivers know which toll-free *superstradas* are actually faster and more direct than the autostrada (e.g., Florence to Pisa). In some cases, if you have some time to spare, scenic smaller roads can be worth the extra hassle—for example, the super-scenic S-222, which runs through the heart of the Chianti region (connecting Florence and Siena); or the SR2-south from Siena into the heart of Tuscany (en route to Montepulciano, Orvieto, and Rome).

Fuel: Fuel is expensive—often about $8 per gallon. Diesel cars are more common in Europe than back home, so be sure you know what type of fuel your car takes before you fill up. Diesel costs less, about $7.50 per gallon. Gas pumps are color-coded: green for unleaded *(senza piombo),* black for diesel *(gasolio).* Autostrada rest stops are self-service stations open daily without a siesta break. Many 24-hour-a-day stations are entirely automated. Small-town stations are usually cheaper and offer full service but shorter hours.

STOP AND LEARN THESE ROAD SIGNS

Speed Limit (km/hr) — Yield — No Passing — End of No Passing Zone — One Way — Intersection — Main Road — Expressway — Roundabout Ahead — Danger — No Entry — All Vehicles Prohibited — No Through Road — Restrictions No Longer Apply — Yield to Oncoming Traffic — No Stopping — Parking — No Parking — Customs or Toll Road — Peace

Maps and Signage: A big, detailed regional road map (buy one at a newsstand, gas station, or bookstore) and a semiskilled navigator are essential. Learn the universal road signs (see illustration). Although roads are numbered on maps, actual road signs give just a city name (for example, if you were heading west out of Venice, the map would be marked "route s-11"—but you'd follow signs to *Padua,* the next town along this road). The signs are inconsistent: They may direct you to the nearest big city or simply the next town along the route.

Theft: Cars are routinely vandalized and stolen. Thieves easily recognize rental cars and assume they are filled with a tourist's gear. Be sure all of your valuables are out of sight and locked in the trunk, or even better, with you or in your room.

Parking: White lines generally mean parking is free. Yellow lines mean that parking is reserved for residents only (who have permits). Blue lines mean you'll have to pay—usually around €1.50 per hour (use machine, leave time-stamped receipt on dashboard). You'll usually pay at a centrally located pay-and-display machine, then put the receipt in your windshield. Study the signs. Often the free zones have a 30- or 60-minute time limit. Signs showing a street cleaner and a day of the week indicate which day the street is cleaned; there's a €100 tow-fee incentive to learn the days of the week in Italian.

Zona disco has nothing to do with dancing. Italian cars come equipped with a time disc (a cardboard clock), which you can use in a *zona disco*—set the clock to your arrival time and leave it on the dashboard. (If your rental car doesn't come with a *disco*, pick one up at a tobacco shop or just write your arrival time on a piece of paper and place it on the dashboard.)

Garages are safe, save time, and help you avoid the stress of parking tickets. Take the parking voucher with you to pay the cashier before you leave.

FLIGHTS

The best comparison search engine for both international and intra-European flights is www.kayak.com. For inexpensive flights within Europe, try www.skyscanner.com.

Flying to Europe: Start looking for international flights at least four to six months before your trip, especially for peak-season travel. Off-season tickets can usually be purchased a month or so in advance. Depending on your itinerary, it can be efficient to fly into one city and out of another. If your flight requires a connection in Europe, see my hints on navigating Europe's top hub airports at www.ricksteves.com/hub-airports.

Flying Within Europe: If you're considering a train ride that's more than five hours long, a flight may save you both time and money. When comparing your options, factor in the time it takes to get to the airport and how early you'll need to arrive to check in.

Well-known cheapo airlines include easyJet (www.easyjet. com) and Ryanair (www.ryanair.com). Be aware of the potential drawbacks of flying with a discount airline: nonrefundable and nonchangeable tickets, minimal or nonexistent customer service, pricey and time-consuming treks to secondary airports, and stingy baggage allowances with steep overage fees. If you're traveling with lots of luggage, a cheap flight can quickly become a bad deal. To avoid unpleasant surprises, read the small print before you book.

These days you can also fly within Europe on major airlines affordably—and without all the aggressive restrictions—for around $100 a flight.

Flying to the US and Canada: Because security is extra tight for flights to the US, be sure to give yourself plenty of time at the airport. It's also important to charge your electronic devices before you board because security checks may require you to turn them on (see www.tsa.gov for the latest rules).

Resources from Rick Steves

Begin your trip at www.ricksteves.com: My mobile-friendly **website** is *the* place to explore Europe. You'll find thousands of fun articles, videos, photos, and radio interviews organized by country; a wealth of money-saving tips for planning your dream trip; monthly travel news dispatches; a collection of over 30 hours of practical travel talks; my travel blog; my latest guidebook updates (www.ricksteves.com/update); and my free Rick Steves Audio Europe app. You can also find links to follow me on Facebook and Twitter.

Our **Travel Forum** is an immense, yet well-groomed collection of message boards, where our travel-savvy community answers questions and shares their personal travel experiences—and our well-traveled staff chimes in when they can be helpful (www.ricksteves.com/forums).

Our **online Travel Store** offers travel bags and accessories that I've designed specifically to help you travel smarter and lighter. These include my popular bags (rolling carry-on and backpack versions, which I helped design...and live out of four months a year), money belts, totes, toiletries kits, adapters, other accessories, and a wide selection of guidebooks and planning maps.

Choosing the right **rail pass** for your trip—amid hundreds of options—can drive you nutty. Our website will help you find the perfect fit for your itinerary and your budget: We offer easy, one-stop shopping for rail passes, seat reservations, and point-to-point tickets.

Tours: Want to travel with greater efficiency and less stress? We organize **tours** with more than three dozen itineraries and more than 900 departures reaching the best destinations in this book...and beyond. Our Italy tours include "the best of" in 17 days, Village Italy in 14 days, South Italy in 13 days, Sicily in 11 days, Venice Florence-Rome in 10 days, the Heart of Italy in 9 days, a My Way: Italy "unguided" tour in 13 days, and a week-long Rome tour. You'll enjoy great guides, a fun bunch of travel partners (with small groups of 24 to 28 travelers), and plenty of room to spread out in a big, comfy bus when touring between towns. You'll find European adventures to fit every vacation length. For all the details,

PRACTICALITIES

and to get our Tour Catalog, visit www.ricksteves.com/tour or call us at 425/608-4217.

Books: *Rick Steves Italy 2017* is one of many books in my series on European travel, which includes country guidebooks; city guidebooks (Rome, Florence, Venice, Paris, London, etc.); Snapshot guidebooks (excerpted chapters from my country guides); Pocket guidebooks (full-color little books on big cities); "Best Of" guidebooks (condensed country guides in a full-color, easy-to-scan format, including Italy); and my budget-travel skills handbook, *Rick Steves Europe Through the Back Door.* Most of my titles are available as ebooks.

My phrase books—for Italian, French, German, Spanish, and Portuguese—are practical and budget-oriented. My other books include *Europe 101* (a crash course on art and history designed for travelers); *Mediterranean Cruise Ports* and *Northern European Cruise Ports* (how to make the most of your time in port); and *Travel as a Political Act* (a travelogue sprinkled with tips for bringing home a global perspective). A more complete list of my titles appears near the end of this book.

TV Shows: My public television series, *Rick Steves' Europe,* covers Europe from top to bottom with over 100 half-hour episodes. To watch full episodes online for free, visit www.ricksteves.com/tv.

Travel Talks on Video: You can raise your travel I.Q. with video versions of our popular classes (including talks on travel skills, packing smart, cruising, tech for travelers, European art for travelers, travel as a political act, and individual talks covering most European countries). See www.ricksteves.com/travel-talks.

Audio: My weekly public radio show, *Travel with Rick Steves,* features interviews with travel experts from around the world. A complete archive of 10 years of programs (over 400 in all) is

available at www.ricksteves.com/radio. I've also produced free, self-guided audio tours of the top sights in Rome. Most of this audio content is available for free through my **Rick Steves Audio Europe app,** an extensive online library organized by destination. For more on my app, see page 12.

APPENDIX

Useful Contacts

Emergency Needs
Police, Fire, and Ambulance (Europe-wide): 112
Italian State Police: 113
Ambulance: 118
Road Service: 116

Embassies and Consulates
US Embassy in Rome: 24-hour emergency line—tel. 06-46741, nonemergency—tel. 06-4674-2420 (by appointment only, Via Vittorio Veneto 121, http://italy.usembassy.gov)

US Consulates: Milan—tel. 02-290-351 (Via Principe Amedeo 2/10, http://milan.usconsulate.gov), **Florence**—tel. 055-266-951 (Lungarno Vespucci 38, http://florence.usconsulate.gov), **Naples**—tel. 081-583-8111 (Piazza della Repubblica, http://naples.usconsulate.gov)

Canadian Embassy in Rome: Tel. 06-854-442-911 (Via Zara 30, www.italy.gc.ca)

Canadian Consulate in Milan: Tel. 02-626-94238 (Piazza Cavour 3, www.italy.gc.ca)

Holidays and Festivals

In Italy, holidays seem to strike without warning. Every town has a festival honoring its patron saint. And the Vatican Museums in Rome close for many lesser-known Catholic holidays—confirm their schedule at http://mv.vatican.va.

This list includes selected festivals in major cities in 2017, plus national holidays observed throughout Italy. Many sights and banks close down on national holidays—keep this in mind when planning your itinerary. Before planning a trip around a festival, verify its dates by checking the festival's website or TI sites (www.italia.it).

In Italy, hotels get booked up on Easter weekend (from Good Friday through Easter Monday), April 25 (Liberation Day), May 1 (Labor Day), November 1 (All Saints' Day), and on Fridays and Saturdays year-round. Some hotels require you to book the full three-day weekend around a holiday.

For festivals and events in the Cinque Terre, see page 320.

Jan 1	New Year's Day
Jan 6	Epiphany
Jan	Fashion convention, Florence
Feb 11-28	Carnevale, Venice (Mardi Gras, www.carnevale.venezia.it)
Feb- early March	Carnevale Celebrations/Mardi Gras, Florence (costumed parades, street water fights, jousting competitions)
March 26-29	Vinitaly, Verona (wine festival)
April 16	Easter Sunday (and Scoppio del Carro fireworks in Florence)
April 17	Easter Monday
April 25	Italian Liberation Day
April/May	Italy's Cultural Heritage Week (www.beniculturali.it)
May 1	Labor Day
May 25	Feast of the Ascension Day
Late May	Cricket Festival, Florence (music, food, pet crickets for sale)
Late May- early June	Fashion convention, Florence
Late May- early June	Vogalonga Regatta, Venice

June 1-30	Annual Flower Display, Florence (carpet of flowers on the main square, Piazza della Signoria)
June 2	Anniversary of the Republic
June 16-17	Festival of St. Ranieri, Pisa
June 24	St. John the Baptist Day, Rome; Festival of St. John the Baptist, Florence (parades, dances, boat races); and Calcio Fiorentino, Florence (costumed soccer game on Piazza Santa Croce)
June 29	Sts. Peter and Paul's Day, most fervently celebrated in Rome
June-Aug	Verona Opera season
Late June- early Sept	Florence's annual outdoor cinema season (contemporary films)
July 2	Palio horse race, Siena
July 15-16	Feast and Regatta of the Redeemer, Venice (third weekend of month)
July-Aug	Musical Weeks, Lake Maggiore
Aug 10	St. Lawrence Day, Rome
Aug 15	Feast of the Assumption (Ferragosto)
Aug 16	Palio horse race, Siena
Sept 3	Historical Regatta, Venice
Sept 7	Festa della Rificolona, Florence (children's procession with lanterns, street performers, parade)
Sept 13-14	Volto Santo, Lucca (procession and fair)
Sept-Oct	Chestnut Festivals, most towns, mainly north of Rome (festivals, chestnut roasts)
Late Sept or early Oct	Musica dei Popoli Festival, Florence (ethnic and folk music and dances)
Oct 13-15	Castelrotto Music Festival (Kastelruther Spatzenfest), Dolomites
Nov 1	All Saints' Day
Nov 21	Feast of Our Lady of Good Health, Venice
Dec	Christmas Market, Rome, Piazza Navona; and crèches in churches throughout Italy
Dec 8	Feast of the Immaculate Conception
Dec 25	Christmas
Dec 26	St. Stephen's Day

APPENDIX

Recommended Books and Films

To learn more about Italy past and present, check out a few of these books and films.

Nonfiction

Absolute Monarchs (John Julius Norwich, 2011). This warts-and-all illustrated guide to the most significant popes in history is a readable best seller.

Ancient Rome: The Rise and Fall of an Empire (Simon Baker, 2007). Baker chronicles the rise and demise of the great Roman Empire and its powerful leaders.

The Architecture of the Italian Renaissance (Peter Murray, 1969). Heavily illustrated, this classic presents the architectural life of Italy from the 13th through the 16th century.

La Bella Figura: A Field Guide to the Italian Mind (Beppe Severgnini, 2005). Severgnini strips down the idealized vision of Italy to reveal its more authentic self—at its best and its worst.

Christ Stopped at Eboli: The Story of a Year (Carlo Levi, 1945). Levi recounts the harsh yet beautiful existence he found in exile to a remote region of southern Italy during Mussolini's reign.

City: A Story of Roman Planning and Construction (David Macaulay, 1974). Macaulay's illustrated book about the Eternal City will please both kids and adults.

A Concise History of Italy (Christopher Duggan, 1994). Duggan's history starts with the fall of Rome but zooms in on the political difficulties of unified Italy over the last two centuries.

Delizia!: The Epic History of the Italians and Their Food (John Dickie, 2007). History buffs and foodies alike will enjoy this vibrant exploration of Italy's famed cuisine.

Desiring Italy (Susan Cahill, 1997). In this anthology, 28 women writers offer a mix of fiction, memoirs, and essays about the complexity and allure of Italy.

Eat, Pray, Love (Elizabeth Gilbert, 2006). Gilbert undertakes a stirring journey of self-discovery through Italy, India, and Indonesia (also a 2010 movie with Julia Roberts).

Excellent Cadavers: The Mafia and the Death of the First Italian Republic (Alexander Stille, 1995). This true account of Sicilian Mafia assassinations in the 1990s is as much thriller as it is history.

A History of Venice (John Julius Norwich, 1977). English Lord Norwich's engaging account spans more than a century, from Venice's fifth-century origins to the arrival of Napoleon.

The House of Medici (Christopher Hibbert, 1974). Florence's first family of the Renaissance included power-hungry bankers, merchants, popes, art patrons—and two queens of France.

Italian Days (Barbara Grizzuti Harrison, 1989). Harrison's appealing travel essays about Italy's varied regions cover everything from architecture to food to history.

Italian Neighbors (Tim Parks, 1992). Parks describes an Englishman's humorous and sometimes difficult attempt to live as a local in a small Italian town.

Italian Renaissance Art (Laurie Schneider Adams, 2001). In one of the definitive works on this pivotal period, Adams focuses on the most important and innovative artists and their best works.

The Italians (John Hooper, 2015). A veteran English correspondent in Italy probes the fascinating paradoxes of contemporary Italian life.

Italy for the Gourmet Traveler (Fred Plotkin, 1996). Plotkin, who's been described as an expert on everything Italian, shares his knowledge of Italy's culinary world in this food/travel guide.

The Lives of the Artists (Giorgio Vasari, 1550). The man who invented the term "Renaissance" offers anecdote-filled biographies of his era's greatest artists, some of whom he knew personally.

Michelangelo and the Pope's Ceiling (Ross King, 2003). The story behind the Sistine Chapel includes Michelangelo's technical difficulties, personality conflicts, and money troubles.

Midnight in Sicily (Peter Robb, 1996). Robb offers a good general history of Sicily, covering its decadent pleasures and its literature, politics, art, and crimes.

The Prince (Niccolò Machiavelli, 1532). The original "how-to" for gaining and maintaining political power, still chillingly relevant after 500 years.

Saints & Sinners (Eamon Duffy, 1997). Everything you always wanted to know about the popes, but were afraid to ask.

The Secrets of Rome: Love and Death in the Eternal City (Corrado Augias, 2005). Augias takes readers back through 27 centuries of Roman history, secrets, and conspiracies.

A Small Place in Italy (Eric Newby, 1994). A young American couple tries to renovate a Tuscan farmhouse in the late 1960s.

The Stones of Florence (Mary McCarthy, 1956). McCarthy applies wit and keen observation to produce a quirky, impressionistic investigation of Florence and its history.

Travelers' Tales Italy (Anne Calcagno, 2001). Calcagno's guide is an excellent compilation of travel writing, including pieces by Tim Parks, Patricia Hampl, Mary Taylor Simeti, and many others.

Under the Tuscan Sun (Frances Mayes, 1996). Mayes's best seller describes living *la dolce vita* in the Tuscan countryside (and is better than the movie of the same name).

Venice Observed (Mary McCarthy, 1963). This snappy and engaging memoir details the Venetian ethos through the eyes of a sharply critical writer.

The Venetian Empire: A Sea Voyage (Jan Morris, 1990). Morris brings a maritime empire to life in this book that illustrates the city's place on a larger historical canvas.

Fiction

The Agony and the Ecstasy (Irving Stone, 1958). Stone fictionalizes Michelangelo's struggle to paint the Sistine Chapel (also a 1965 movie starring Charlton Heston).

The Aspern Papers and Other Stories (Henry James, 1894). An American editor travels to Venice in search of letters written to his mistress. Other James works about Italy include *Italian Hours* and *Daisy Miller.*

Beautiful Ruins (Jess Walter, 2012). This comedic romance, which follows an Italian innkeeper's search for lost love over 50 years, is the perfect beach read for the Cinque Terre.

A Bell for Adano (John Hersey, 1944). Hersey's novel about an American major overseeing a town in WWII Sicily won him the Pulitzer Prize in 1945.

Birth of Venus (Sarah Dunant, 2003). Dunant follows the life of a Florentine girl who develops feelings for the boy hired to paint the walls of the family's chapel.

The Day of the Owl (Leonardo Sciascia, 1961). This classic murder mystery set in a mid-20th century Sicilian village is a fascinating window into the Mafia.

Death at La Fenice (Donna Leon, 1992). This chilling Venetian mystery and the others in Leon's Commissario Brunetti series reveal more about "real" Italy than many memoirs do.

Death in the Mountains: The True Story of a Tuscan Murder (Lisa Clifford, 2008). This fictionalized account of an unsolved murder reveals the hardship of early-20th-century Tuscan farming life.

Death in Venice and Other Tales (Thomas Mann, 1912). The centerpiece of this collection is an eloquent classic that explores obsession, beauty, and death in plague-ridden Venice (also a 1971 film).

The Decameron (Giovanni Boccaccio, 1348). Boccaccio's collection of 100 hilarious, often bawdy tales is a masterpiece of Italian literature and inspired Chaucer, Keats, and Shakespeare.

Divine Comedy (Dante Alighieri, 1321). Dante's epic poem—a journey through hell, purgatory, and paradise—is one of the world's greatest works of literature.

The First Man in Rome (Colleen McCullough, 1990). The author of *The Thorn Birds* describes the early days of the Roman Republic, in the first of a best-selling series of historical fiction.

Galileo's Daughter (Dava Sobel, 1999). Sobel's historical memoir centers on Galileo's correspondence with his oldest daughter and confidante.

I, Claudius (Robert Graves, 1934). This brilliant history of ancient Rome is told by Claudius, the family's laughingstock who becomes emperor himself. The sequel is *Claudius the God* (1935).

I'm Not Scared (Niccolò Ammaniti, 2001). A boy stumbles on a terrible secret in an abandoned farmhouse in this thriller set in the 1970s Italian South.

Invisible Cities (Italo Calvino, 1972). Marco Polo tells of the fantastical cities he's seen...or is he just describing the many facets of his beloved Venice?

Italian Journey (Johann Wolfgang von Goethe, 1786). In his 18th-century collection of writings, Goethe describes his travels to Rome, Sicily, and Naples.

The Leopard (Giuseppe Tomasi di Lampedusa, 1957). Sicilian aristocrats see their world slipping away during the turmoil of the Risorgimento (also a 1963 movie starring Burt Lancaster).

The Light in the Piazza (Elizabeth Spencer, 1960). A mother and daughter are intoxicated by the beauty of 1950s Florence (also a 1962 movie and an award-winning Broadway musical).

Lucrezia Borgia (Maria Bellonci, 1939). In this historically based tale of court intrigue, a daughter of Pope Alexander VI navigates passions, plots, and controversy in Renaissance Rome.

The Merchant of Venice (William Shakespeare, 1598). In addition to *Merchant*, other Shakespearean plays set in Italy include *Romeo and Juliet* (Verona), *Much Ado About Nothing* (Sicily), *The Two Gentlemen of Verona*, and *The Taming of the Shrew* (Padua).

The Neapolitan Novels (Elena Ferrante, 2012-2015). This popular four-novel series traces two girls' coming of age in mid-20th-century Naples.

The Passion of Artemisia (Susan Vreeland, 2001). This novel is based on the life of Artemisia Gentileschi, one of the rare female post-Renaissance artists who gained fame in her own time.

Pompeii (Robert Harris, 2003). The engineer responsible for Pompeii's aqueducts has a bad feeling about Mount Vesuvius in this historical novel.

A Room with a View (E. M. Forster, 1908). A young Englishwoman visiting Florence finds a socially unsuitable replacement for her snobby fiancé (also a 1985 movie starring Helena Bonham Carter).

The Sixteen Pleasures (Robert Hellenga, 1994). Set during the 1966 floods in Florence, a young student discovers an erotic manuscript banned by the pope and lost for centuries.

A Soldier of the Great War (Mark Helprin, 1991). A young Roman lawyer falls in love with an art student, but World War I rips them apart.

That Awful Mess on the Via Merulana (Carlo Emilio Gadda, 1957). This detective story about a murder and a burglary in an apartment building in central Rome shines a harsh light on fascist Italy.

A Thread of Grace (Mary Doria Russell, 2004). This historical novel fictionalizes the story of how more than 43,000 Jews were saved by Italian citizens during World War II.

Film and TV

1900 (1976). Bernardo Bertolucci's epic tale of early-20th-century Italy follows the relationship between two young men—one rich (Robert De Niro), one poor (Gérard Depardieu).

Ben-Hur (1959). At the height of the Roman Empire, a Jewish prince is enslaved by a friend, and later seeks revenge in a stunning chariot race (the film won a record 11 Oscars).

The Best of Youth (2003). Beginning in the turbulent 1960s, this award-winning miniseries follows the dramatic ups and downs in the lives of two brothers over four decades.

Bicycle Thieves (1948). A poor man looks for his stolen bicycle in busy Rome in this inspirational classic of Italian Neorealism.

Caterina in the Big City (2003). A teenager whose family moves to Rome from a small town is the focus of this bitter comedy about the crisis of contemporary Italian society.

Cinema Paradiso (1988). This Oscar-winning drama about a friendship between a film projectionist and a little boy is a compelling portrayal of post-WWII Sicily and a tribute to movies everywhere.

La Dolce Vita (1960). Director Federico Fellini tells a series of stories that capture the hedonistic days of early 1960s Rome.

Enchanted April (1991). Filmed in Portofino, this languid film follows an all-star British cast as they fall in love, discuss relationships, eat well, and take naps in the sun.

The First Beautiful Thing (2010). A man returns to his hometown in Tuscany to aid his dying mother, a woman determined to live life to the fullest while being a good parent to her children.

Gladiator (2000). An enslaved Roman general (Russell Crowe) fights his way back to freedom in Ridley Scott's Oscar winner.

The Godfather (1969). Francis Ford Coppola's famous film and its two sequels portray the multigenerational saga of a Sicilian family at the center of organized crime in New York.

Golden Door (2006). Poor Sicilian immigrants give up everything for a passage to America, but find a less-than-enthusiastic welcome at Ellis Island.

Gomorrah (2008). This mob drama, which reveals details about the Camorra (Neapolitan mafia), is not for the faint of heart.

The Great Beauty (2013). This thoughtful movie, named Best Foreign Film at the 2014 Academy Awards, showcases Rome in all of its decadence and splendor.

The Italian Job (1969). This classic English film features a crew of thieves attempting a high-stakes gold heist in Turin under the nose of the Mafia.

Life Is Beautiful (1997). In this tragicomic winner of three Oscars, a Jewish man from Tuscany finds imaginative ways to protect his son from the truth after they arrive at a Nazi concentration camp.

Il Postino (1994). Poet Pablo Neruda befriends his Italian postman, who uses a newfound love for Italian poetry to woo a local beauty.

Marriage Italian Style (1964). A young Neapolitan prostitute (Sophia Loren) begins a lifelong on-again, off-again relationship with a cynical businessman in this Academy Award-nominated comedy.

Mid-August Lunch (2008). A broke Roman bachelor gets more than he bargained for when he agrees to take care of an elderly lady during a summer holiday to pay off a debt.

Quo Vadis (1951). A Roman general falls in love with a Christian hostage in this epic that includes the burning of Rome, the crucifixion of St. Peter, and the madness of Nero.

Rome (2005-2007). This BBC/HBO miniseries focusing on Julius Caesar and Augustus intertwines the perspectives of aristocratic and ordinary Romans during the transition from republic to empire.

Roman Holiday (1953). Audrey Hepburn plays a princess who escapes her royal minders, falls for an American newspaperman (Gregory Peck), and discovers Rome on the back of his scooter.

Spartacus (1960). In this epic directed by Stanley Kubrick, a gladiator (Kirk Douglas) leads a slave revolt in the last days of the Roman Republic.

A Special Day (1977). On the day of Hitler's visit to Rome, the wife of a militant fascist (Sophia Loren) has a fateful meeting with a persecuted journalist (Marcello Mastroianni).

Tea with Mussolini (1999). Franco Zeffirelli's look at pre-war Florence involves proper English ladies, a rich American Jew, and the son of a local businessman—all caught in the rise of fascism.

The Wings of the Dove (1997). Based on the Henry James novel, this romantic drama is a tale of desire that takes full advantage of its Venetian locale.

Conversions and Climate

NUMBERS AND STUMBLERS

- Europeans write a few of their numbers differently than we do. 1 = 1, 4 = 4, 7 = 7.
- In Europe, dates appear as day/month/year, so Christmas 2017 is 25/12/17.
- Commas are decimal points and decimals commas. A dollar and a half is $1,50, one thousand is 1.000, and there are 5.280 feet in a mile.
- When counting with fingers, start with your thumb. If you hold up your first finger to request one item, you'll probably get two.
- What Americans call the second floor of a building is the first floor in Europe.
- On escalators and moving sidewalks, Europeans keep the left "lane" open for passing. Keep to the right.

METRIC CONVERSIONS

A kilogram is 2.2 pounds, and 1 liter is about a quart, or almost 4 to a gallon. A kilometer is six-tenths of a mile. I figure kilometers to miles by cutting them in half and adding back 10 percent of the original (120 km: 60 + 12 = 72 miles, 300 km: 150 + 30 = 180 miles).

1 foot = 0.3 meter	1 square yard = 0.8 square meter
1 yard = 0.9 meter	1 square mile = 2.6 square kilometers
1 mile = 1.6 kilometers	1 ounce = 28 grams
1 centimeter = 0.4 inch	1 quart = 0.95 liter
1 meter = 39.4 inches	1 kilogram = 2.2 pounds
1 kilometer = 0.62 mile	32°F = 0°C

ROMAN NUMERALS

In the US, we still use ancient Roman numerals for copyright dates, on clocks, and at the Super Bowl. In Italy, you're likely to see these numbers chiseled on statues and buildings. In Roman numerals, the highest numbers (thousands, hundreds) come first, followed by smaller numbers. Many numbers are made by combining numerals into sets: V = 5, so VIII = 8 (5 plus 3). Roman numerals follow a subtraction principle for multiples of fours (4, 40, 400, etc.) and nines (9, 90, 900, etc.); the number four, for example, is written as IV (1 subtracted from 5), rather than IIII. The number nine is IX (1 subtracted from 10).

Rick Steves Italy 2017—written in Italian with Roman numerals—would translate as *Rick Steves Italia MMXVII*. Big numbers such as dates can look daunting at first. The easiest way to handle them is to break them down into discrete chunks. For example,

Michelangelo was born in MCDLXXV: M (1,000) + CD (100 subtracted from 500, or 400) + LXX (50 + 10 + 10, or 70) + V (5) = 1475. It was a very good year.

M	= 1000	XC	= 90	IX	= 9
CM	= 900	L	= 50	V	= 5
D	= 500	XL	= 40	IV	= 4
CD	= 400	X	= 10	I	= duh
C	= 100				

CLOTHING SIZES

When shopping for clothing, use these US-to-European comparisons as general guidelines (but note that no conversion is perfect).

Women: For clothing or shoe sizes, add 30 (US shirt size 10 = European size 40; US shoe size 8 = European size 38-39).

Men: For shirts, multiply by 2 and add about 8 (US size 15 = European size 38). For jackets and suits, add 10. For shoes, add 32-34.

Children: For clothing, subtract 1-2 sizes for small children and subtract 4 for juniors. For shoes up to size 13, add 16-18, and for sizes 1 and up, add 30-32.

ITALY'S CLIMATE

First line, average daily high; second line, average daily low; third line, average days without rain. For more detailed weather statistics for destinations in this book (as well as the rest of the world), check www.wunderground.com.

J	F	M	A	M	J	J	A	S	O	N	D
Rome											
52°	55°	59°	66°	74°	82°	87°	86°	79°	71°	61°	55°
40°	42°	45°	50°	56°	63°	67°	67°	62°	55°	49°	44°
13	19	23	24	26	26	30	29	25	23	19	21
Milan and Florence											
40°	46°	56°	65°	74°	80°	84°	82°	75°	63°	51°	43°
32°	35°	43°	49°	57°	63°	67°	66°	61°	52°	43°	35°
25	21	24	22	23	21	25	24	25	23	20	24
Venice											
42°	46°	53°	62°	70°	76°	81°	80°	75°	65°	53°	46°
33°	35°	41°	49°	56°	63°	66°	65°	61°	53°	44°	37°
25	21	24	21	23	22	24	24	25	24	21	23

Fahrenheit and Celsius Conversion

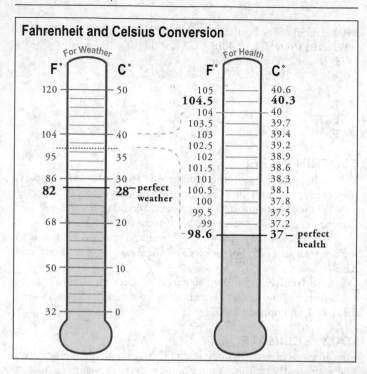

Europe takes its temperature using the Celsius scale, while we opt for Fahrenheit. For a rough conversion from Celsius to Fahrenheit, double the number and add 30. For weather, remember that 28°C is 82°F— perfect. For health, 37°C is just right. At a launderette, 30°C is cold, 40°C is warm (usually the default setting), 60°C is hot, and 95°C is boiling. Your air conditioner should be set at about 20°C.

Packing Checklist

Whether you're traveling for five days or five weeks, you won't need more than this. Pack light to enjoy the sweet freedom of true mobility.

Clothing

- ❑ 5 shirts: long- & short-sleeve
- ❑ 2 pairs pants (or skirts/capris)
- ❑ 1 pair shorts
- ❑ 5 pairs underwear & socks
- ❑ 1 pair walking shoes
- ❑ Sweater or warm layer
- ❑ Rainproof jacket with hood
- ❑ Tie, scarf, belt, and/or hat
- ❑ Swimsuit
- ❑ Sleepwear/loungewear

Money

- ❑ Debit card(s)
- ❑ Credit card(s)
- ❑ Hard cash ($100-200 in US dollars)
- ❑ Money belt

Documents

- ❑ Passport
- ❑ Tickets & confirmations: flights, hotels, trains, rail pass, car rental, sight entries
- ❑ Driver's license
- ❑ Student ID, hostel card, etc.
- ❑ Photocopies of important documents
- ❑ Insurance details
- ❑ Guidebooks & maps
- ❑ Notepad & pen
- ❑ Journal

Toiletries Kit

- ❑ Basics: soap, shampoo, toothbrush, toothpaste, floss, deodorant, sunscreen, brush/comb, etc.
- ❑ Medicines & vitamins
- ❑ First-aid kit
- ❑ Glasses/contacts/sunglasses
- ❑ Sewing kit
- ❑ Packet of tissues (for WC)
- ❑ Earplugs

Electronics

- ❑ Mobile phone
- ❑ Camera & related gear
- ❑ Tablet/ebook reader/media player
- ❑ Laptop & flash drive
- ❑ Headphones
- ❑ Chargers & batteries
- ❑ Smartphone car charger & mount (or GPS device)
- ❑ Plug adapters

Miscellaneous

- ❑ Daypack
- ❑ Sealable plastic baggies
- ❑ Laundry supplies: soap, laundry bag, clothesline, spot remover
- ❑ Small umbrella
- ❑ Travel alarm/watch

Optional Extras

- ❑ Second pair of shoes (flip-flops, sandals, tennis shoes, boots)
- ❑ Travel hairdryer
- ❑ Picnic supplies
- ❑ Water bottle
- ❑ Fold-up tote bag
- ❑ Small flashlight
- ❑ Mini binoculars
- ❑ Small towel or washcloth
- ❑ Inflatable pillow/neck rest
- ❑ Tiny lock
- ❑ Address list (to mail postcards)
- ❑ Extra passport photos

Italian Survival Phrases

English	Italian	Pronunciation
Good day.	Buon giorno.	bwohn **jor**-noh
Do you speak English?	Parla inglese?	**par**-lah een-**gleh**-zay
Yes. / No.	Sì. / No.	see / noh
I (don't) understand.	(Non) capisco.	(nohn) kah-**pees**-koh
Please.	Per favore.	pehr fah-**voh**-ray
Thank you.	Grazie.	**graht**-see-ay
You're welcome.	Prego.	**preh**-go
I'm sorry.	Mi dispiace.	mee dee-spee-**ah**-chay
Excuse me.	Mi scusi.	mee **skoo**-zee
(No) problem.	(Non) c'è un problema.	(nohn) cheh oon proh-**bleh**-mah
Good.	Va bene.	vah **beh**-nay
Goodbye.	Arrivederci.	ah-ree-veh-**dehr**-chee
one / two	uno / due	**oo**-noh / **doo**-ay
three / four	tre / quattro	tray / **kwah**-troh
five / six	cinque / sei	**cheeng**-kway / **seh**-ee
seven / eight	sette / otto	**seh**-tay / **oh**-toh
nine / ten	nove / dieci	**noh**-vay / dee-**ay**-chee
How much is it?	Quanto costa?	**kwahn**-toh **koh**-stah
Write it?	Me lo scrive?	may loh **skree**-vay
Is it free?	È gratis?	eh **grah**-tees
Is it included?	È incluso?	eh een-**kloo**-zoh
Where can I buy / find...?	Dove posso comprare / trovare...?	**doh**-vay poh-soh kohm-**prah**-ray / troh-**vah**-ray
I'd like / We'd like...	Vorrei / Vorremmo...	voh-**reh**-ee / voh-**reh**-moh
...a room.	...una camera.	**oo**-nah **kah**-meh-rah
...a ticket to ____.	...un biglietto per ____.	oon beel-**yeh**-toh pehr ____
Is it possible?	È possibile?	eh poh-**see**-bee-lay
Where is...?	Dov'è...?	doh-**veh**
...the train station	...la stazione	lah staht-see-**oh**-nay
...the bus station	...la stazione degli autobus	lah staht-see-**oh**-nay **dehl**-yee ow-toh-boos
...tourist information	...informazioni per turisti	een-for-maht-see-**oh**-nee pehr too-**ree**-stee
...the toilet	...la toilette	lah twah-**leh**-tay
men	uomini / signori	**woh**-mee-nee / seen-**yoh**-ree
women	donne / signore	**doh**-nay / seen-**yoh**-ray
left / right	sinistra / destra	see-**nee**-strah / **deh**-strah
straight	sempre dritto	**sehm**-pray **dree**-toh
What time does this open / close?	A che ora apre / chiude?	ah kay **oh**-rah ah-**pray** / kee-**oo**-day
At what time?	A che ora?	ah kay **oh**-rah
Just a moment.	Un momento.	oon moh-**mehn**-toh
now / soon / later	adesso / presto / tardi	ah-**deh**-soh / **preh**-stoh / **tar**-dee
today / tomorrow	oggi / domani	**oh**-jee / doh-**mah**-nee

In an Italian Restaurant

English	Italian	Pronunciation
I'd like...	Vorrei...	voh-**reh**-ee
We'd like...	Vorremmo...	vor-**reh**-moh
...to reserve...	...prenotare...	preh-noh-**tah**-ray
...a table for one / two.	...un tavolo per uno / due.	oon **tah**-voh-loh pehr **oo**-noh / **doo**-ay
Is this seat free?	È libero questo posto?	eh **lee**-beh-roh **kweh**-stoh **poh**-stoh
The menu (in English), please.	Il menù (in inglese), per favore.	eel meh-**noo** (een een-**gleh**-zay) pehr fah-**voh**-ray
service (not) included	servizio (non) incluso	sehr-**veet**-see-oh (nohn) een-**kloo**-zoh
cover charge	pane e coperto	**pah**-nay ay koh-**pehr**-toh
to go	da portar via	dah **por**-tar vee-ah
with / without	con / senza	kohn / **sehnt**-sah
and / or	e / o	ay / oh
menu (of the day)	menù (del giorno)	meh-**noo** (dehl **jor**-noh)
specialty of the house	specialità della casa	speh-chah-lee-**tah** **deh**-lah **kah**-zah
first course (pasta, soup)	primo piatto	**pree**-moh pee-**ah**-toh
main course (meat, fish)	secondo piatto	seh-**kohn**-doh pee-**ah**-toh
side dishes	contorni	kohn-**tor**-nee
bread	pane	**pah**-nay
cheese	formaggio	for-**mah**-joh
sandwich	panino	pah-**nee**-noh
soup	zuppa	**tsoo**-pah
salad	insalata	een-sah-**lah**-tah
meat	carne	**kar**-nay
chicken	pollo	**poh**-loh
fish	pesce	**peh**-shay
seafood	frutti di mare	**froo**-tee dee **mah**-ray
fruit / vegetables	frutta / legumi	**froo**-tah / lay-**goo**-mee
dessert	dolce	**dohl**-chay
tap water	acqua del rubinetto	**ah**-kwah dehl roo-bee-**neh**-toh
mineral water	acqua minerale	**ah**-kwah mee-neh-**rah**-lay
milk	latte	**lah**-tay
(orange) juice	succo (d'arancia)	**soo**-koh (dah-**rahn**-chah)
coffee / tea	caffè / tè	kah-**feh** / teh
wine	vino	**vee**-noh
red / white	rosso / bianco	**roh**-soh / bee-**ahn**-koh
glass / bottle	bicchiere / bottiglia	bee-kee-**eh**-ray / boh-**teel**-yah
beer	birra	**bee**-rah
Cheers!	Cin cin!	cheen cheen
More. / Another.	Di più. / Un altro.	dee pew / oon **ahl**-troh
The same.	Lo stesso.	loh **steh**-soh
The bill, please.	Il conto, per favore.	eel **kohn**-toh pehr fah-**voh**-ray
Do you accept credit cards?	Accettate carte di credito?	ah-cheh-**tah**-tay **kar**-tay dee **kreh**-dee-toh
tip	mancia	**mahn**-chah
Delicious!	Delizioso!	day-leet-see-**oh**-zoh

For more user-friendly Italian phrases, check out *Rick Steves' Italian Phrase Book & Dictionary* or *Rick Steves' French, Italian, and German Phrase Book*.

INDEX

INDEX

INDEX

INDEX

MAP INDEX

MAP INDEX

Explore Europe

At ricksteves.com you can browse through thousands of articles, videos, photos and radio interviews, plus find a wealth of money-saving travel tips for planning your dream trip. And with our mobile-friendly website, you can easily access all this great travel information anywhere you go.

TV Shows

Preview the places you'll visit by watching entire half-hour episodes of Rick Steves' Europe (choose from all 100 shows) on-demand, for free.

ricksteves.com

your travel dreams into affordable reality

Radio Interviews

Enjoy ready access to Rick's vast library of radio interviews covering travel

tips and cultural insights that relate specifically to your Europe travel plans.

Travel Forums

Learn, ask, share! Our online community of savvy travelers is a great resource for first-time travelers to Europe, as well as seasoned pros. You'll find forums on each country, plus travel tips and restaurant/hotel reviews. You can even ask one of our well-traveled staff to chime in with an opinion.

Travel News

Subscribe to our free Travel News e-newsletter, and get monthly updates from Rick on what's happening in Europe.

Audio Europe™

Rick's Free Travel App

Get your FREE **Rick Steves Audio Europe**™ app to enjoy…

- Dozens of self-guided tours of Europe's top museums, sights and historic walks

- Hundreds of tracks filled with cultural insights and sightseeing tips from Rick's radio interviews

- All organized into handy geographic playlists

- For iPhone, iPad, iPod Touch, Android

With Rick whispering in your ear, Europe gets even better.

Find out more at ricksteves.com

Pack Light and Right

Gear up for your next adventure at ricksteves.com

Light Luggage

Pack light and right with Rick Steves' affordable, custom-designed rolling carry-on bags, backpacks, day packs and shoulder bags.

Accessories

From packing cubes to moneybelts and beyond, Rick has personally selected the travel goodies that will help your trip go smoother.

Rick Steves has

Save time and energy

This guidebook is your independent-travel toolkit. But for all it delivers, it's still up to you to devote the time and energy it takes to manage the preparation and logistics that are essential for a happy trip. If that's a hassle, there's a solution.

Rick Steves Tours

A Rick Steves tour takes you to Europe's most interesting places with great

great tours, too!

with minimum stress

guides and small groups of 28 or less. We follow Rick's favorite itineraries, ride in comfy buses, stay in family-run hotels, and bring you intimately close to the Europe you've traveled so far to see. Most importantly, we take away the logistical headaches so you can focus on the fun.

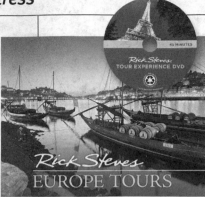

customers—along with us on 40 different itineraries, from Ireland to Italy to Istanbul. Is a Rick Steves tour the right fit for your travel dreams? Find out at ricksteves.com, where you can also get Rick's latest tour catalog and free Tour Experience DVD.

Join the fun

This year we'll take 18,000 free-spirited travelers— nearly half of them repeat

Europe is best experienced with happy travel partners. We hope you can join us.

Rick Steves®

Nearly all Rick Steves guides are available as ebooks. Check with your favorite bookseller.

Rick Steves guidebooks are published by Avalon Travel, an imprint of Perseus Books, a Hachette Book Group company.

Maximize your travel skills with a good guidebook.

RickSteves.com @RickSteves

Rick Steves books are available at bookstores
and through online booksellers.

Credits

RESEARCHERS

To update his books on Italy, Rick relied on the help of...

Ben Cameron

Ben experienced his first taste of European travel when he was a little guy, exploring medieval castles with his parents. Returning after graduation, he was hooked and has spent much of his time since exploring Europe independently and leading tours for Rick Steves' Europe. When not living out of his backpack, Ben splits his time between Rome and the great Pacific Northwest.

Trish Feaster

As a high-school Spanish teacher in San Diego, Trish frequently took her students on summer trips to Europe, sharing her passion for language, history, culture, and cuisine. She later earned a degree in French and now uses her language and teaching skills—along with her love of travel—as a Rick Steves' Europe tour guide and guidebook researcher, and as a travel blogger at thetravelphile.com. Trish enjoys traveling, binge-watching favorite shows, and playing *pétanque* with her partner in their hometown of Edmonds, Washington.

Cameron Hewitt

Born in Denver and raised in central Ohio, Cameron settled in Seattle in 2000. Ever since, he has spent three months each year in Europe, contributing to guidebooks, tours, radio and television shows, and other media for Rick Steves' Europe, where he serves as content manager. Cameron married his high-school sweetheart (and favorite travel partner), Shawna, and enjoys taking pictures, trying new restaurants, and planning his next trip.

Sarah Murdoch

Sarah trained as an architect, then abandoned her drafting board in 2000 to lead tours and research guidebooks for Rick Steves' Europe. She blogs about her crazy life on adventureswithsarah.net and often writes about her passion for the perfectly packed bag. She lives in Seattle with her husband, Patrick, and sons, Lucca and Nicola.

Ian Watson

Ian has worked with Rick's guidebooks since 1993, after starting out with *Let's Go* and Frommer's guides. Originally from upstate New York, Ian speaks several European languages, including Italian, and lives with his family in Germany.

Amanda Zurita

Amanda Zurita caught the travel bug early—she's been flying since before she could walk. When she's not hovering over a bowl of *cacio e pepe* in Rome, checking out vintage shops in Florence, or riding bikes around Lucca, she lives in Seattle with her beloved Labrador, Hadrian.

CONTRIBUTOR

Gene Openshaw

Gene has co-authored a dozen *Rick Steves* books, specializing in writing walks and tours of Europe's cities, museums, and cultural sights. He also contributes to Rick's public television series, produces tours for Rick Steves Audio Europe, and is a regular guest on Rick's public radio show. Outside of the travel world, Gene has co-authored *The Seattle Joke Book.* As a composer, Gene has written a full-length opera called *Matter* (soundtrack available on Amazon), a violin sonata, and dozens of songs. He lives near Seattle with his daughter, enjoys giving presentations on art and history, and roots for the Mariners in good times and bad.

Avalon Travel
An imprint of Perseus Books
A Hachette Book Group company
1700 Fourth Street
Berkeley, CA 94710

Text © 2016 by Rick Steves' Europe, Inc. All rights reserved.
Maps © 2016 by Rick Steves' Europe, Inc. All rights reserved.

Printed in Canada by Friesens
First printing January 2017

ISBN 978-1-63121-443-1
ISSN 1084-4422

For the latest on Rick's lectures, guidebooks, tours, public radio show, and public television series, contact Rick Steves' Europe, Inc., 130 Fourth Avenue North, Edmonds, WA 98020, tel. 425/771-8303, www.ricksteves.com, rick@ricksteves.com.

Rick Steves' Europe

Managing Editor: Jennifer Madison Davis
Special Publications Manager: Risa Laib
Editors: Glenn Eriksen, Tom Griffin, Katherine Gustafson, Suzanne Kotz, Cathy Lu, John Pierce, Carrie Shepherd
Editorial & Production Assistant: Jessica Shaw
Editorial Intern: Lester Tobias
Researchers: Ben Cameron, Trish Feaster, Cameron Hewitt, Sarah Murdoch, Ian Watson, Amanda Zurita
Contributor: Gene Openshaw
Graphic Content Director: Sandra Hundacker
Maps & Graphics: David C. Hoerlein, Lauren Mills, Mary Rostad

Avalon Travel

Senior Editor and Series Manager: Madhu Prasher
Editor: Jamie Andrade
Associate Editor: Sierra Machado
Copy Editor: Maggie Ryan
Proofreaders: Jenny Malnick and Patty Mon
Indexer: Stephen Callahan
Production and Typesetting: Rue Flaherty, Sarah Wildfang
Cover Design: Kimberly Glyder Design
Maps & Graphics: Kat Bennett, Mike Morgenfeld

Photo Credits

Front Cover: Varenna, Lake Como © Cameron Hewitt
Title Page: Piazza dei Signori, Padua © Dominic Arizona Bonuccelli
Front Matter: p. xiv Venice © Michael Potter; p. xxiv, Venice © Laura VanDeventer
Additional Photography: Sistine Chapel, p. 877 © Erich Lessing/Art Resources, NY; Dominic Arizona Bonuccelli, Ben Cameron, Julie Coen, Jennifer Hauseman, Cameron Hewitt, David C. Hoerlein, Gene Openshaw, Michael Potter, Robyn Stencil, Rick Steves, Bruce VanDeventer, Laura VanDeventer, Les Wahlstrom, Tom Wallace, Ian Watson, Wikimedia Commons (PD-Art/PD-US), Deanna Woodruff (photos are used by permission and are the property of the original copyright owners).

Want More Italy?
Maximize the experience with Rick Steves as your guide

Guidebooks
Venice, Florence, and Rome guides make side-trips smooth and affordable

Phrase Books
Rely on Rick's Italian Phrase Book & Dictionary

Rick's TV Shows
Preview where you're going with 18 shows on Italy

Free! Rick's Audio Europe™ App
Free audio tours for Italy's top sights

Small Group Tours
Rick offers several great itineraries through Italy

For all the details, visit ricksteves.com